D1320228

# THE AMERICAN COLONIES

## IN THE

## EIGHTEENTH CENTURY

# THE AMERICAN COLONIES

## IN THE

# EIGHTEENTH CENTURY

BY

HERBERT L. OSGOOD, Ph.D., LL.D.

PROFESSOR OF HISTORY IN COLUMBIA UNIVERSITY

VOLUME III

Gloucester, Mass.

## PETER SMITH

1958

973
Os3
V. 3

Copyright, 1924, 1958
By COLUMBIA UNIVERSITY PRESS

———

Reprinted, 1958, by Permission of
Columbia University Press

# CONTENTS

## VOLUME III

### PART TWO — *Continued*

#### CHAPTER VIII

MARYLAND UNDER THE RESTORED PROPRIETARY GOVERNMENT, 1715–1742

## CONTENTS

## CHAPTER IX

### GEORGIA AS A PROPRIETARY PROVINCE, 1732–1752

CHAPTER X

The English Church and the Dissenters under the Early
Hanoverians

I.

## CHAPTER XI

### THE ENGLISH CHURCH AND THE DISSENTERS UNDER THE EARLY HANOVERIANS

### II

## CHAPTER XII

### INTERNAL CONFLICTS IN MASSACHUSETTS UNDER SHUTE AND BURNET. QUESTION OF THE GOVERNOR'S SALARY

## CHAPTER XIII

### The Outlying Colonies of New England: New Hampshire

## CHAPTER XIV

### THE OUTLYING COLONIES OF NEW ENGLAND: RHODE ISLAND

## CHAPTER XV

### THE OUTLYING COLONIES OF NEW ENGLAND: CONNECTICUT

## CHAPTER XVI

MASSACHUSETTS AND NEW HAMPSHIRE UNDER BELCHER, 1730–1740.
END OF THE CONFLICT OVER GOVERNOR'S SALARY.
RISE OF THE STRUGGLE OVER THE LAND BANK

## CHAPTER XVII

### INDIAN RELATIONS DURING THE SECOND QUARTER OF THE EIGHTEENTH CENTURY

# PART III

### THE GROWTH OF THE SPIRIT OF INDEPENDENCE DURING THE PERIOD OF THE THIRD AND FOURTH INTERCOLONIAL WARS, 1740–1763

## CHAPTER I

### THE GREAT AWAKENING

## CHAPTER II

### Ecclesiastical Relations at the Middle of the Century

## CHAPTER III

### REOPENING OF THE STRUGGLE WITH THE BOURBON ALLIANCE. THE THIRD INTERCOLONIAL WAR, 1739–1748

## CHAPTER IV

MASSACHUSETTS UNDER SHIRLEY. MID-CENTURY PROBLEMS OF COLONIAL
ADMINISTRATION, 1740–1754

# PART TWO

*(Continued)*

## THE COLONIES DURING THE INTERVAL OF PEACE BETWEEN THE SECOND AND THIRD INTERCOLONIAL WARS
## 1714–1740

# CHAPTER VIII

On August 24, 1715, John Hart, the governor, informed the executive council at Annapolis that he had received a letter from Lord Guilford informing him that Benedict Leonard Calvert had just died, leaving Charles, Lord Baltimore, as his heir and the proprietor. As Charles was a minor, Lord Guilford had been appointed his guardian, and he now informed Hart that, with the approval of the king, he would be continued in the governorship and would receive a commission and instructions accordingly. The commission, dated May 30, had in fact arrived and was now read by Hart to the board. But he added that he had received not the least information from the crown that the government had been restored to Lord Baltimore. In explanation of this almost incredible neglect, it should be remembered that the new Hanoverian government was just then entering upon its struggle with the Pretender and was beset with difficulties at home and abroad. As the Maryland council was filled with Anglicans who were interested in the continuance of royal government unless, with the full restoration of the proprietorship, they could be assured that the Catholics would not return to power, they were perplexed by the new turn in affairs. When they were asked by Hart to give their opinions severally upon the question, whether or not he should accept the office tendered by the commission without due legal notice from the crown that it had restored the government to the proprietor, they expressed themselves unanimously in the negative. They said that he ought not to resign his position as royal governor until his majesty's pleasure was signified to him for so doing.[1]

Nothing further occurred in this connection until Decem-

[1] Maryland Archives, XXV, 314, 315.

ber. In the meantime Lord Guilford and the young proprietor had been informed of the scruples of Hart and the council, and the governor had now received from them the king's instructions, under his manual and privy seal, for the enforcement of the act of trade in Maryland and the continuance of its executive in office. In view of this evidence the council now advised Hart to surrender the government of the province to the proprietor and execute his commission. The following day the proprietor's commission was published at the court house and a proclamation was issued dissolving the assembly.[1] The first proprietary assembly did not meet until the following April, the members of the council having meantime received commissions from the new proprietor. After organizing and listening to such general information about the change of government as the governor was able to give them, the assembly was prorogued until July. By these steps, so few and imperceptible that the people in general could hardly have perceived a change, the proprietary régime was restored and the charter of 1632 again put into force. The style of enactment was changed by substituting the title " Lord Proprietary " for that of king, and, as the laws had been revised since the accession of George I, it was concluded that very few of them needed change or reenactment.[2]

If the government in England at this crisis had not been both weak and indifferent, this would not have occurred. The fact that the head of the proprietary family had accepted Anglicanism was not sufficient of itself to justify the measure. In the light of the objects toward which the British government, in its imperial relations, had been striving for half a century, the restoration of proprietary government in any province must be regarded as a backward step. It meant loose and inefficient government, even when measured by the low standards of that time. Proprietors had neither means nor desire to make it anything essentially different. The instructions which they gave their governors were few and meagre,[3] and with the withdrawal of royal instructions — except those relating to trade — and of the continuous pres-

[1] Md. Arch., XXV, 323–326, 327, 337.

[2] Md. Arch., XXX, 393, 394; Steiner, in Report of Am. Hist. Assoc. 1899, I, 263.

[3] Md. Arch., XXV, 353, 538; XXVIII, 67, 142.

sure which came from correspondence with the administrative officials and boards in England, the province to a large extent ceased to feel the impulse toward wider views and broader policies which come through these channels. The home government also lost the right to inspect the legislative and executive journals and to a large extent also its control over the legislation of the province. The avenues through which appeals might be sent to England were also neglected or wholly closed. The province, in a word, tended to lapse into seventeenth-century isolation. But it could not wholly do this, because of the extent to which the governors were bound to enforce the acts of trade, of the presence of certain imperial officials within its borders, of the expansion of the problem of defence, of the gradual extension of settlement and the improvement of means of communication with other colonies. Royal government, too, could not exist for twenty-five years in a colony without leaving some permanent effects. Its traditions were not lost in Maryland. Though, for example, little had been done during the royal period to change the principles on which the land office and territorial revenue were administered, the assembly now assumed an attitude of opposition to the proprietor on several questions, which it maintained in a way quite equal to what was occurring in the royal provinces.

The fact that the proprietary family came back as Protestants was of decided importance. The Anglicans did not relax their hold and Catholics were never again to enjoy the ascendancy which in certain ways they had held in the earlier proprietary period. The principle of toleration, as it was first set forth in Maryland, was not reaffirmed, but the legislation of the royal period on this subject, supported by that of England, continued in force.[1]

And yet the Calverts were very recent converts to Protestantism, and the motives which had led to their change were at least in part political. It might be inferred by Catholics in Maryland that their attitude toward the old faith would still be friendly. They might yield to its adherents in certain points or at least fail to support a Protestant governor as the crown might have done. At the time also the hopes

---

[1] Md. Arch., **XXIII**, 289; Mereness, *op. cit.*, 489.

of Catholic enthusiasts were raised high by the effort of the Pretender in Great Britain. His health was drunk in Maryland and reports that he was successful or likely to be so were circulated. Certain suspicious letters, written by a priest, were brought to light. To check these stirrings the sheriffs and justices were warned to tender to Catholics the oaths which they were required to take by English law. One night in June, 1716, while Governor Hart was absent in Cecil county, two cannon were fired on the court house hill in celebration of the Pretender's birth. By this time Hart's keen suspicions as a Protestant were aroused and he offered a reward for the discovery of the offenders. Two were discovered, tried and imprisoned. Two others were convicted of drinking the Pretender's health and speaking contemptuously of the king, and were fined. One of the last mentioned pair was a nephew of Charles Carroll, then the leading Catholic layman in the province, a lawyer and man of wealth, long connected with the Calverts while they were still Catholics. Thomas MacNemara, another relative of Carroll, appeared as counsel for the accused in one or both of these trials. MacNemara was by nature a bully, loud and insolent in speech, and given to tactics which were intended to overawe judges and jurors. He had already practised law in Philadelphia and had been reproved by the grand jury for insolent behavior in court. In Maryland he now repeated his tactics, among other things challenging the authority of the court before which his Catholic clients were being tried. Though on this occasion he was defeated, MacNemara was destined for years to make trouble for the governor and the Anglicans, reminding one in some ways of the career of John Coode.[1]

It was in connection with the trial of his nephew that Charles Carroll produced a commission from the proprietor which gave him surprisingly large powers.[2] By it the proprietor appointed him his agent, escheater, naval officer and receiver general, with the widest authority over land and finance which his titles implied. All other powers and commissions touching the premises were annulled and whatever

[1] Md. Arch., XXV, 334 *et seq*; XXX, 373.
[2] Md. Arch., XXX, 375.

Carroll had lawfully done under a previous letter from Benedict Calvert was confirmed. Carroll now proposed to pay the fines of the two who had been convicted of firing the cannon and thus procure their release from prison on his own order to the sheriff. The court of oyer and terminer now interposed and ordered the accused remanded to prison until they had fully complied with the terms of their sentence.

When Carroll's commission was first read in council Governor Hart called attention to the fact that it contravened several of the acts of trade by conferring upon its recipient powers which could be legally performed only by officials of the governor's appointment. Other objections he also made, but his general attitude toward it was shown by the statement that his power had been so lessened by it that, especially as it had been granted to a Catholic, he desired to be recalled unless the full authority which he had held under the crown was restored. When one reads in the commission that control of indefinite extent was given to Carroll not only over the territorial revenue but over that which accrued under acts of the legislature, and that whatever Carroll should legally do was confirmed in advance, notwithstanding any defects in the words of the grant, it is clear that Hart drew the natural inference when he concluded that the young proprietor and his guardian had been deceived into granting what they had no right to concede. This view was confirmed by the demand of Carroll that the governor should account to him for the 3s. per hogshead which had been appropriated for the purchase of arms and ammunition for the defence of the province. The appointment of rangers, an office to which the governor by statute had the right to fill, was now transferred to Carroll. He hastened to require Carroll to take the oaths which by law were provided for all who would execute such an office. These Carroll refused to take. Hart then referred the case to the upper house and they voted not only that he had deceived the proprietor when the grant was procured but that now he was incapable of executing it, so far as any public affairs or interest of the province were concerned. Hart now insisted that Carroll should execute his commission only so far as the private estate of the proprietor was concerned, and refused to admit appointees of his to office, until they had taken the required oaths.[1]

Carroll was now called before the upper house and asked whether he had acquainted the proprietor and his guardian with the statutes which were likely to affect the issue of his commission; also, whether, when he presented his patent for the naval office to the commissioners of the customs in order to get their approval of his security for executing it, he had informed them that he was a Catholic; finally, how he had come to take upon himself all these offices when he did not intend to take the oath of abjuration which was required by statute of all who held office in Maryland.  Carroll's answers were to the effect that in England he did not make the statements referred to because he did not think there was any provision in the acts of trade which would hinder the proprietor from appointing him, while it would have been an impertinence for him to have made a profession of his faith before the customs board.  During the later years of royal government he had held all the offices in the proprietor's grant and, as he believed the oath of abjuration had been repealed in 1715, he thought he could hold the additional offices without offence.[2]  As the surveyors for whom commissions had been sent over could not receive them, because of the action of the council, Carroll declared the land office closed.  The upper house, on Carroll again refusing to take the oath, resolved that he was not capable of performing the duties of naval officer.

Both parties now sought redress in England,[3] Hart insisting that he must retire from office unless the offensive commissions were recalled and the Catholics seeking to procure his removal as a chief obstacle to their return to office.  From the first Carroll had insisted that his co-religionists had a right to hold office in Maryland, and for a partial justification of their claim they fell back upon the practices of the earlier proprietary period.  Hart, in his contention, had the earnest support of both houses of the assembly.  Joint addresses were presented by them to the governor and to the proprietor.  In

---

[1] Md. Arch. XXX, 375 et seq.; XXXIII, 568–574.
[2] Ibid., XXX, 403; Steiner, op. cit., 266.
[3] Md. Arch. XXXIII, 120, 571.

the former they congratulated the governor on the energy which he had shown against the Catholics and deplored the fact that some of his powers had been transferred to a papist, and still more they feared the outward results which might follow his resignation. To the proprietor they declared that those who had advised him thus to transfer authority to a Catholic who refused to take the required oaths had more in view their own private interest than the honor and safety of his lordship's government.[1]

The assembly also, as a double precaution for the future against such efforts as Carroll had been making, passed a stringent act, including not only the oath of allegiance and the abjuration of the law of 1715, but the declaration against transsubstantiation and the oath of abjuration of the damnable doctrine that the pope might depose heretic princes, thus reviving the words, if not the spirit, of the sixteenth and seventeenth centuries. The penalty for holding office without taking those oaths before a court of record was that the offender's commission should be declared void *ab initio* and he should be liable to a fine of £250. The same penalties, with total exclusion from office, should be inflicted if, at any time after the oaths had been taken, the official in question should attend any Catholic assembly or join in the mass. The incumbent also might be required at any time to take the oath anew. After some opposition in the lower house, a clause was inserted exempting those who were concerned only in the management of Lord Baltimore's private affairs from the provisions of this ironclad law.

In due time a reply was received from the proprietor which indicated the trouble was due to the zeal and craft of Carroll and that the issue of his commission was an act of inadvertence on the part of Lord Guilford and his ward. Early in 1717 Hart was able to read before the executive council a letter from Lord Guilford [2] fully confirming his inferences as to the way in which Carroll's commission had been obtained and expressing confidence that all grievances would be redressed and that he would continue cheerfully to perform the

[1] Md. Arch., XXXIII, 514. Carroll warned Hart against assenting to such acts as this without a saving clause, and even undertook in a way to specify the amount of the governor's salary, to the added disgust of Hart.    *Ibid.*,599.

[2] *Ibid.*, XXV, 344–346.

duties of governor. It was after the full restoration of the proprietor's authority that Carroll had surprised them into adding the naval office to his grant, while as to the surveyors they desired the governor to appoint them and to exercise the powers of surveyor general. This gave the governor the custody of the proprietor's seal and enabled him to claim fees to which Carroll had hitherto considered himself fully entitled.

When the assembly met in May of this year, Hart laid before it a statement from the proprietors [1] that they had approved all the acts of the assembly of 1715 except one laying an increased duty upon the importation of servants (including Protestants) from Ireland and one for ascertaining the ton of tobacco hogsheads. As to the zeal shown for the Protestant succession, they highly approved of it and also of the act of 1716 for the better security of the province, showing thereby that the young Lord Baltimore was not " a Papist in Masquerade, but a true Protestant of the Church of England, in which faith he is Resolved to live and die." The promise, which accompanied this, that no one who failed to qualify himself according to law should be promoted to office, made an end of the commission to Carroll and removed all reason for the resignation of Hart. Baltimore's desires in reference to the bills concerning the guage of tobacco hogsheads and the importation of Irish servants were met at this session, all restrictions in particular upon the importation of Protestants from Ireland being removed.[2]

But though the controversy between the governor and Carroll was coming to an end, MacNemara, who now was naval officer, became so noisy and insolent before the courts and elsewhere that Hart, while sitting in chancery, suspended him from practice, except for finding cases involving crown revenue, until he made due submission. The lawyer took an appeal to the proprietors, but from them he received no support. The lower house and the judges of the provincial court became involved and they unqualifiedly supported the governor, the judges threatening to resign if so turbulent and insolent a person was longer allowed to practice before them.[3]

[1] Md. Arch., XXXIII, 4.
[2] *Ibid.*, 112.
[3] *Ibid.*, 125–139, 169–172, 181.

A bill passed the two houses and was approved by the governor disabling MacNemara from practicing before the courts of the province, but it was disallowed by the proprietors for the reason that it was directed against a particular person, to whom a hearing — the right of every subject — had not been granted.[1]  Another act with a similar title and purpose was passed in the session of 1719,[2] but before action could be taken under it MacNemara died.  Previous to his death, however, he had made acceptable submission to the proprietor and by him the suspension from the right to practice had been removed.[3]  As his own dignity and that of the courts had not received the support which it was generally felt that they merited, Hart was dissatisfied with the way in which this affair ended, but since the close of his administration was near nothing further was done.

In the spring session of 1718 the last of the anti-Catholic laws of Hart's administration was passed.[4]  By this they were excluded from the suffrage unless they took the oaths required by the act for the better security of the government and Protestant interest in the province.  At the same time the act of 1704 for preventing the growth of popery within the province was repealed, on the ground that the objects sought by that law could be well accomplished by the 11 and 12 William III, since it extended to the dominions as well as the realm.  In view of the stringent test acts which had now been placed upon the Maryland statute book it is not strange that the Catholics complained of persecution.  Their complaints to this effect both in the province and in England made it necessary for Hart to defend his policy, which he did in his letters and in vigorous speeches to his last assemblies.  He stated that his object had been to prevent them from holding office or having any influence, either publicly or privately, on the administration of government.[5]  He looked upon this as his indispensable duty, for the discharge of which he always stood ready to give account to his superiors.

---

[1] Md. Arch., 197, 298, 303, 305–307.
[2] Ibid., 361.
[3] Ibid., 491–493.
[4] Ibid., 288, 289.  See also the addresses of the following session (1719) for strong Protestant sentiments.
[5] Ibid., 299 et seq.

In those sentiments he was fully sustained by both legislative houses, who never tired of approving to the letter this feature of the governor's policy. Certainly in no other colony did circumstances, so late as this, call for such action or the expression of such opinions, and whether events would have gone so far had royal government continued is open to question. Under later governors feeling abated and the Catholic question sank into the background.

Though the Anglicans felt somewhat less secure under proprietary rule than they would have under the crown, there was probably little reason for their apprehensions. It is true that they were not so favorably situated as they had been under governors so strongly partisan as Nicholson and Hart and with a spirit behind them like that which prevailed in the reign of Anne. But it is hardly possible that they would have received more considerate treatment from any of the early Hanoverian governments than was accorded them by the proprietor. The Anglican clergy met the chief crisis of this period in 1728 and it was in part the result of the persistently low price of tobacco, coupled with the inferiority of the Maryland product to that which was raised in Virginia. The governor and council at a later period described the cause of the difficulty very well in these words: [1] " Our unhappy situation arises from this, that our people are under no kind of restraint, and the generality of them are unwilling to be under any which may have the least appearance of lessening the quantity of tobacco they make; under which general denomination all manner of trash is included and so intermixt with what is really merchantable as to render the whole of little value." By judicious regulation Virginia had kept the quality of her product at a higher level and it therefore controlled the market.

In 1726 the governor and council of Maryland corresponded with those of Virginia in reference to joint regulation of the tobacco industry. Virginia was then legislating on the subject in her own interest. The year following Maryland passed an act to prevent the fraudulent packing of poor tobacco.[2] In 1728, after much controversy, a law was passed limiting

[1] Md. Arch., XXVIII, 308.
[2] Ibid., XXV, 454, 456, 458; Ms. Laws of Md.

the planting of tobacco to 7000 plants for every taxable person and overseer within the province, and 3500 plants for all laborers of either sex who were between twelve and sixteen years of age.[1] The act contained other specifications, besides many administrative provisions necessitating the action of the parish authorities in enforcement.

The chief interest of the act in this connection arises not from its bearing on the tobacco industry, but from its effect on the remuneration of all those who were paid fees or wages in tobacco. The discussion of the measure when it was on its passage was carried on in close connection with the controversy over fees which was then in progress. The intention of its supporters was to check the fall or actually raise the price of tobacco by limiting the supply. Under the law of 1702 for the establishment of the church forty pounds of tobacco per poll were levied for the support of the clergy. Opposition to this feature of the law was caused not only by the inferior character of many of the clergy but by the fact that it was a perpetual law which carried a revenue provision. The bill of 1728 reduced their remuneration by one-fourth.[2] A possible alternative payment in money offered no more favorable prospect to the parsons, while they feared lest the time of payment would be so postponed as to leave them with an unmarketable commodity or embarrass them in other ways. For these reasons the clergy claimed that the conditions upon which they had come to the colony were broken and made united opposition to the measure in England. Jacob Henderson, the able and energetic commissary, went thither as their agent, with addresses to the Venerable Society, the bishop of London and the king, as well as to the proprietor. As the proprietor was at the time absent on the continent, Henderson had a good opportunity to bring his cause before the crown officials. It was referred to the committee of the privy council on plantation affairs and its action was probably prevented only by the return of Baltimore and his hearing the parties to the case and vetoing of the act.[3]

[1] Hawks, Eccl. Contributions, II, 197; U. H. J. and L. H. J., Oct., 1728 The Act is printed in Hist. Colls. of Am. Colonial Church, IV, 270.

[2] Ibid., 263, 265, 279. In justice to the authors of the bill it should be said that it applied to all who owed debts in tobacco.

[3] Acts of P. C. Col. 1720–1745, p. 252; Ms. Calvert Papers, No. 275, 1–2.

In 1730 the legislature passed another very similar act for the limitation of the tobacco crop, but included in it a provision that one-fourth of the forty pounds per poll might be paid to the clergy in other products than tobacco — in wheat, barley, Indian corn and oats — but at such rates and under such conditions that the parties affected claimed they would be as badly off as under the previous measure.[1]  The clergy complained that they were being deprived of their property without their consent and that payments would probably be made in the least valuable of the products of which a choice was offered, and as for marketing the surplus which the clergymen did not need, it would be a practical impossibility.  Both parties ‘again sent addresses to England, though Henderson had now returned to Maryland and the clergy were not able to employ an agent in his place.  In Maryland itself the contest was bitter, Dulany and Henderson being pitted against each other in the pamphlet war which followed.  When Henderson attempted to discipline certain of the profligate clergy his enemies denied his authority on the ground that he could not produce a commission which had been issued since the accession of George II.  The proprietor finally assented to this act and a precedent unfavorable to the claims of the clergy was thus established which many years later was followed with great popular acclaim in the famous parson's cause in Virginia.

Toward the close of his administration and in his capacity as chancellor, Hart became involved in the complaints against Maurice Birchfield, a surveyor general of his majesty's customs in America.  In May, 1718, the committee of grievances of the lower house reported that many of the inhabitants of the province had been summoned before the court of chancery on complaint of Birchfield, who charged that they were indebted to merchants in London.  It was alleged that though the sums involved were so small that they were not properly cognizable before the chancery, the alleged debtors were forced to defend themselves at great cost and trouble and also without proper notifications.  In April, 1720, nearly two years later, the customs board in England, having

[1] Hist. Colls. of Am. Col. Church, IV, 284; U. H. J. and L. H. J., June 1730; Ms. Laws; Hawks, op. cit., 209.

examined into Birchfield's conduct, exonerated him, and in a letter to the proprietor charged Hart, in his capacity as chancellor, with having obstructed the surveyor general on several occasions.[1]  Hart laid this letter before the assembly with a complaint that he had been misrepresented.  In connection with the MacNemara affair he had already resigned the chancellorship and now he declared that the suggestions concerning him were false and that his conduct in that office had always been above reproach; he had always furthered the interests of the crown.  Both houses supported the governor in these statements and several messages were exchanged on the subject, it being proposed that after Hart's return to England either he or Blakiston, the agent, should prosecute this case.[2]  Hart expressed the belief that this charge was connected with those which the Catholics were making against him, and together they made him restive in his government and contributed to his recall in 1720.

For more than a decade to come members of the Calvert family held the office of governor, as had been their practice in the seventeenth century, and as was soon to be the custom in the proprietary family of Pennsylvania.  The two incumbents during this period were Charles Calvert (1720–1727), a cousin of the proprietor, and Benedict Leonard Calvert (1727–1731), the proprietor's brother.  The proprietor himself had now reached majority and was no longer under guardianship.  During this, as well as the earlier, period the Calverts kept a certain centralized control and escaped the unfortunate litigation and joint rule which so weakened the Penn family for purposes of administration.  This is far from implying that the rule of the two Calverts we are considering was strong or marked by any special distinction.  It was not so.  There is nothing to indicate that they were able men, either physically or mentally; but they maintained the quiet routine of proprietary government in a time of peace in America and of indifference in England in such a way as not to provoke attacks upon the institution as such and demands for a restoration of government by the crown.  In their time there were, as we shall see, controversies over a

---

[1] Md. Arch., *loc. cit.*, 249, 290–1.
[2] *Ibid.*, XXV, 358, XXXIII, 514 *et passim* to 635.  See Index.

number of questions, political and economic, but none of these imperilled fundamental proprietary rights or seriously affected relations with the crown. Therefore the institution lived on and in a province like Maryland, whose coast and frontier alike were relatively protected, it survived till the close of colonial existence.

The usual controversies occurred over the relative positions of the two houses of the legislature. In 1725 the lower house declared that " we are the people's representatives, for whom all laws are made and become government established." To this the upper house replied that they were " an intermediate between the prerogative and the liberties of the people." These assertions were made in the course of a long controversy [1] over the question, which house should have the custody of engrossed bills between the time of their final passage and their acceptance by the governor at the close of the session. The lower house claimed this in accordance, as it insisted, with general practice in Maryland before 1715; the upper house claimed in accordance with practice since that date and also for the convenience of the governor who no longer presided at its sessions and therefore needed to have the engrossed bills in order to examine them before he gave them his assent. The upper house finally had its way.

In 1722 a curious departure from British custom, but an anticipation of later American practice, appeared in the form of a resolve of the lower house that the acceptance of an office under the government should disqualify a person for a seat in that house.[2] In 1734 it began expelling members for accepting office, and at that time the governor reproved them for this conduct and dissolved the assembly.[3] In 1740, however, the practice was continued by a resolve that a member had disqualified himself even by accepting one of the lower county offices. The governor again administered a sharp reproof, followed not by a dissolution, though he thought they deserved it, but by a prorogation. His thought in this address was that the house was by its mere resolve creating a qualification for membership which was unknown either to Maryland

---

[1] U. H. J. and L. H. J., October, 1725.

[2] L. H. J., Oct. 29, 1722.

[3] Md. Arch., XXVIII. 65.

or British law, was doing what it willed with its own members. This he considered to be in violation of precedent and of the principle of English liberty, an ignoring of such checks as ought to be observed by every legislative body.[1]

Relations between the lower house in particular and the executive were early illustrated by a prolonged discussion over granting an allowance to the council. Statutory provision was made for the wages of the assemblymen, but no express enactment provided for those of the council. Out of the export duty on tobacco since 1671 an allowance had been paid to the councillors, so that they might attend to public affairs and the administration of justice without prejudice to their private interests. After 1694 every councillor was allowed 150 lbs. of tobacco per day while on service. This fact was brought to the attention of the lower house as the result of an inquiry which it specially ordered in 1717. But it was also stated that this was paid only for service while the assembly was in session.[2] Nothing further appears until 1723, when, during the controversy over English statutes, the lower house withheld the usual allowance. A long debate then followed between the two houses. The lower house insisted that the laws which had provided for the grant had now expired and if the support was to be continued, because of the position of the council in the government, the proprietor should furnish it. The council defended its own utility as an intermediary between the proprietor and the people and as largely responsible for the regular discharge of the functions of government. A conference was held, but it was not possible to reach an agreement. For a time the council held up the journal of accounts, but at last sent it down with its approval but with a reservation of its claim in the premises. In 1724 this claim was renewed and several messages passed on the subject.[3] The following year the proprietor in a letter to the assembly said that in the seventeenth century the council had been supported by the country and when the act of 1671 was passed it was not so much as surmised that its support would come from the proprietor. The governor added to this state-

[1] L. H. J., July 24 and 29, 1740.
[2] L. H. J., May 29 and 31, 1717, June 6, 1717; Mereness, *op. cit.*, 181.
[3] L. H. J. and U. H. J. for Oct. 1723 and Oct. 1724.

ment an assurance that the services of the council fully entitled them to the grant. After another interchange of
messages, in which each house accused the other of being
obstinate, the lower house asked the proprietor that some
support be provided for them in their executive capacity.[1]
The proprietor again urged the matter, but without success,
and at intervals until 1736 the subject was discussed, but
without change in the attitude of the lower house. In 1739
and 1740 the lower house even omitted from the journal of
accounts the allowance for the clerk of the council.[2]

Encroachments which during the royal period were made
on the right of the executive to appoint to office were checked
after the resumption of proprietary rule. This was conspicuously true in the case of the treasurers. Though in the
royal period they had been designated by the lower house
and its right to do this had been conceded by the council,
in 1736 it was denied and, supported by an opinion from the
attorney general in England, the appointment was made by
the governor.[3] On the passage of a currency act in 1732 the
lower house, especially as it was a money bill, claimed the
sole right of naming the commissioners who were to execute it.
But to this the upper house objected, citing precedents both
from England and from the earlier practice of the colony for
the exercise of this right by the executive. After some discussion a compromise seems to have been reached according
to which the legislature as a whole should name the commissioners, but that when it should appear to the governor or
other executive that they were unfit or had misbehaved they
should be removed.[4]

Though at the beginning of the royal period the precedent
had been established that money bills should originate only
in the lower house, it was not until the expedition to the West
Indies was fitted out in 1740 that the upper house was denied
the right to amend such bills. In agreement with usage up
to that time, the upper house had suggested several amendments to the bill to raise and issue money for maintaining the
force to be levied in Maryland and transporting it to the

[1] L. H. V. and U. H. J. for Nov. 1725.
[2] U. H. J. and L. H. J. for 1726, 1728, 1736, 1739, 1740.
[3] Md. Arch., XXVIII, 109, 119.
[4] U. H. J. and L. H. J., Aug. 7 and 8, 1732, Mar. 30, 1733.

place of rendezvous in the West Indies. The lower house replied that the granting of money and the raising of funds for repaying it were its peculiar privileges and rights, and no sufficient reason had been offered to induce them to change it. They even declined to go into a conference on the subject and with this the upper house ceased to urge its claim.[1] About two years before this, when the discussion over appropriations for this expedition was beginning, the differences between the constitution of the two houses were gone into at considerable length. The lower house then commented on the fitness of the council to be a legislative body as follows: "Suppose the Peers in Great Britain held their seats there at the pleasure of the Prince and that he could place and displace them as he thought fit; suppose them also possessed of all the great offices of the Government upon the same precarious terms; Could that be called a free and independent branch of the Legislature, which should keep a balance between the Prince on the one side and the people on the other, or could it with any color of reason be said that a house so composed or so endowed enjoyed all freedom of action and was at all times clear from any restraint?" This clearly shows the reason why in all the provinces the representative lower houses, especially in time of war, steadily encroached upon the hybrid bodies with which they were associated in legislation.

The name of Sir Thomas Lawrence was again mentioned when, in 1716, the proprietor revived the practice of the seventeenth century by proposing that the fines for licenses to keep ordinaries be granted to his secretaries. When it was asked to pass an act to this effect, the lower house expressed doubt as to the right of the proprietor to this sum and insisted that the subject be postponed until the next session.[2] The matter was brought up again the next year, and then the house proposed that this money be given to free schools. But this the upper house opposed and the assembly yielded. The act desired by the proprietor was passed. Such laws were passed at intervals thereafter, though occasionally the lower house continued to make objections.[3]

[1] U. H. J. and L. H. J., July 15 and 16, 1740.
[2] Md. Arch., XXX, 434, 439, 444, 448, 567, 569.
[3] U. H. J., May 28, June 3 and 6, 1717; L. H. J., June 8, 1717, Apr., 1720.

With the death of Charles, the second proprietor, in 1715 the act of 1671 for the payment of 12d. per hogshead on the export of tobacco in lieu of quit rents and alienation fines expired. It was immediately renewed for one year. But at the same time, because of the inferior quality of the Maryland product, it became necessary to enlarge the size of tobacco hogsheads and this in turn necessitated a change in the terms of the impost when it came in 1716 to be re-enacted for a period of four years.[1] An offer was then made to the new proprietor of a duty of 18d. per hogshead on condition that he would continue to accept payment for his quit rents and alienation fines in tobacco at 2d. per pound.[2] Fifteen pence per hogshead was also to be levied for the support of the government and the purchase of arms and ammunition, raising the total export duty on tobacco from 2s. to 2s. 8d. per hogshead. While this change was under consideration, Henry Darnall produced a lease from the proprietor of his rents for the term of six years at £300 st. and 67,000 pounds of tobacco per annum. But this was rejected by the assembly and instead the act of 1716, as just described, was passed.[3] This was accepted by the proprietor, a discount being made for the cost of collecting, and was continued in force by successive reenactments until 1733. But occasionally complaints were expressed on both sides, the assembly claiming that the proprietor was getting the better of the bargain and the proprietor that his rent roll really yielded much more than would be due to him under the agreement. The vote in the lower house against renewing the act was carried by the members from the four western counties and the city of Annapolis, giving a majority of five.

After the act had been allowed to expire the proprietor instructed the governor — then Samuel Ogle — to have his rents and alienation fines collected in accordance with the terms of the grants.[4] This involved the payment of money, and in amounts presumably in excess of the value which had been due under the former law. At any rate, complaints were soon

---

[1] Md. Arch., XXX, 316, 348.

[2] Ibid., 364; Mereness, op. cit., 79.

[3] Md. Arch., XXV, 604–607; XXX, 364, 384, 388, 397, 398, 399, 502, 627; Bacon, Laws of Maryland: U. H. J. July 14, 1726.

[4] Md. Arch., XXVIII, 67.

made by the people of lack of money with which to pay their
rents, and in April, 1735, these were reflected in a series of messages between the houses, a conference and an interchange
of views with the proprietor.[1]  To the proprietor the houses
admitted that they had made a mistake and asked that he
would accept a lump sum in lieu of his rents and fines.  To
this the proprietor expressed himself ready to agree if one
estimate could be reached of what would be a fair equivalent.
The lower house suggested £4000 per year; the council at
first objected that this was not enough,[2] but later joined in
submitting it to the proprietor.  He rejected the offer.  The
issue was not raised again, at least to prominence, for eight
years.  By that time, owing to the extension of settlement,
the value of the proprietor's revenue had become so large that
it was probably impossible for the assembly to offer a sum
which would have been a fair equivalent.[3]

The collection of that part of the export duty on tobacco
which went for the support of the government, and which had
been transferred to the crown by the acts of 1692 and 1704,
was continued after the full restoration of proprietary authority in 1715.  Though in subsequent laws notice was taken
of the existence of this part of the levy, no express reenactment of the grant or transfer of it from the crown back to
the proprietor was made.  It continued thus as a permanent
grant without question until 1739.  In May of that year,
while engaged in a controversy over fees, the lower house,
probably as a means of bringing stronger pressure to bear
on the executive, sent up a bill for an annual appropriation
for the support of government and declared that since 1732
the impost of 12d. per hogshead had been levied without lawful authority.  The upper house denied this statement and also
in particular criticised the new bill as an instance of the
dangerous preference for temporary laws which was abroad
in the colonies.  In its reply the delegates said, " Whatever
Your Honors may think of raising money on a people by
perpetual laws, we imagine it a doctrine that would sound
harsh in the ears of our mother country, and what we in

---

[1] L. H. J. and U. H. J. for Apr. 1735.
[2] L. H. J. and U. H. J., Apr. and May 1736.
[3] Mereness, 82–84.

justice to ourselves and our posterity are resolved as much as [lies] in our power to avoid." To the governor they said that the officers had informed them that they were collecting the duty under authority of the act of 1704, but that revenue which had been voted to the crown could be transferred to the proprietor without express enactment they denied. Ogle stated in reply that the act in question had always been regarded by all parties as in force and expressly so in 1733, when the whole subject was last under consideration. He advised them to renew the law of 1704, but desired the upper house to join with them in appropriating money for sending an agent to present this and a number of other grievances to the crown. When it refused to do this, the lower house drew up an address of its own to the king.[1] But, as the crown was far from favoring temporary acts for the support of government, there would have been slight prospect of success if the appeal had ever been earnestly made. And it was not the intention of the proprietor to allow this course of action to persist. Two bills were sent to the upper house providing for the continuance of the existing rate of duty for three years, granting £1000 to the governor, retaining the rest for arms and ammunition.[2] These did not become law and therefore the collection of the impost continued under authority of the act of 1704 until the Revolution.

Discussion of the ever present subject of officers' fees went on during nearly the whole of the period we are now considering. In 1719 an act limiting fees and reducing them in the case of some officials was passed.[3] This was done under the protest of the proprietor and to a certain extent of the council. It did not dispute the right of the legislature to act in this matter, but it thought the reductions in some cases were too great and thus were an evidence of ingratitude to the proprietor. But the lower house insisted that with the growth of settlement and of business the fees, in gross amounts if not in rates, tended steadily upward. The rates finally enacted were

---

[1] U. H. J. and L. H. J., May and June 1739; Md. Arch., XXVIII, 167–171; Mereness, 355 et seq.

[2] This is shown by instructions of the proprietor to have been the salary of both Charles Calvert and Benedict Leonard Calvert as governors. Ms. Calvert Papers, No. 278.

[3] Md. Arch., XXXIII, 458; Mereness, 375 et seq.

decided upon in a conference between the houses.  So far as changes were made they were downward, affecting the fees of the secretary, commissary general, surveyor general and his deputies, the clerk of the council and the clerks of the county courts.  The duration of the bill was limited to three years. The proprietors thought it was not to their honor nor to the people's interest in the dispatch of business that officials should be deprived of the allowance which by law they had enjoyed and which ought to be large enough to encourage men of ability and integrity to hold office.  But they did not veto the bill.[1]  The debate, however, went on at intervals between the two houses and with the proprietors during the next two years.  To the contention that fees were lower in Virginia than in Maryland the reply was made that that was probably accounted for by the superior quality of Virginia tobacco. The members of the upper house, who as office holders were interested, suggested that the rates prior to 1719 be restored, but the delegates preferred to await the further pleasure of the proprietor.  He finally said that he would not veto the act, but trusted that the assembly itself would one day alter it.[2] In 1723 and again in 1724 the act of 1719 was revived for one year, but at the same time the lower house thought that fees ought to be reduced one half, an opinion which the upper house pronounced totally unreasonable and unbecoming.

In 1725 an act was passed reducing the rate of fees by about one quarter, the delegates arguing that such legislation was in line with the proprietor's own interest, for such payments, as well as the doubling of the price of land since the Revolution, were as great obstacles to the settling of the back country.[3]  The upper house did not obstruct the passage of this bill, being reasonably sure that the proprietor would veto it, which proved true, though the veto occasioned considerable complaint in the province.  In 1727 the governor informed the assembly of the proprietor's desire that an act be passed reestablishing the rates of 1719.  The house declined to take action, though the council regarded it as certain that many disputes and probably law suits would follow from

[1] L. H. J. and U. H. J., June 1719 and Apr. and Oct. 1720.
[2] L. H. J., Oct. 1720, and July and Aug. 1721; U. H. J., Aug. 1721, Oct. 1722.
[3] L. H. J., Nov. 3, 1725.

the unregulated condition of things.¹  In the following year a fee bill was discussed in connection with a bill to limit the production of tobacco.²  This proposal was at once made an excuse for a demand that fees be further reduced to correspond with a possible contraction of the tobacco crop; but the upper house insisted on waiting until it could be known whether a rise in the price of tobacco would follow.  A fee bill passed, but from it the governor withheld his assent.  He wrote to the proprietor, " The officers are without an execution for their fees, which makes them very ill paid, to the no small loss of the officers, but really to a disruption and disregard of their offices; since every insolent follow thinks himself free to refuse payment and browbeat, as it were, the officers." ³  He submitted several queries to the proprietor, the purpose of which was to ascertain whether he had any power to regulate fees and how it could be exerted, or, if not, what remedy officials could use for the recovery of their fees or support when there was no law on the subject.  " We can do no more than insist on your instructions but that will not get us the fees unless we can be put into some method to exact them without the help of an act of assembly, which cannot easily be obtained."

In 1730 a bill newly regulating the fees of attorneys was passed, but this, upon an opinion of the law officers, Yorke and Talbot, in England, the proprietor disallowed.⁴  In 1733, after another unsuccessful attempt by the legislature to pass a fee bill, the proprietor issued a proclamation fixing their amount at nearly the same as was provided in the act of 1719.⁵  This, of course, was not satisfactory to the lower house, and in every succeeding year it introduced a fee bill, that of 1736 having as one of its objects to secure the assent of the proprietor to their payment in currency.  This they thought would give a needed spur to its circulation, but the proprietor declined to accede.⁶  In May, 1738, the fees, as then being taken, were denounced by the committee of the house

---

¹ U. H. J., Oct. 28, 1727.
² U. H. J., and L. H. J. Oct. 1728.
³ Md. Arch., XXV, 607.
⁴ Journals, May 26, 1730 and July 30, 1731.
⁵ Md. Arch., XXXIII, 31.
⁶ Journals, March and April, 1736.

in a strong report as a grievance.[1]  The fact that fees were
being collected at rates fixed by the executive, and often, it
was implied, at the arbitrary will of the official, was an
invasion of rights of property and of the constitution of the
province.  Many poor tradesmen and others were being ruined
or driven out of the province by such extortionate fees,
whether payable in currency or tobacco.  The following year
a committee, of which Dulany and Carroll were members,
was appointed by the lower house to prepare a bill, regard
being had to the fees which existed in Virginia and Pennsylvania.[2]  By this time the practice in courts and offices had
become general of taking judgment bonds for fees before they
became due, and of requiring bonds for the payment of fees
before the business of an applicant would be done.  This
shows the confusion which prevailed and the wrong which
was being done to all parties.  The lower house denounced the
practice as extortion and insisted that there was no way of
selling fees except by statute.  They said they were aroused
by complaints which came in from all parts of the province.
The council was indifferent to these, thinking they were
exaggerated or came from turbulent persons.  While admitting
fully the right now being exercised by the proprietor, the
upper house conferred repeatedly with the lower over a
bill, but the two failed utterly to agree on its duration.  The
upper house desired a perpetual law and the other only a
temporary, and so for nearly a decade longer the question
was left unsettled.

The various controversies whose history we have been outlining, when viewed collectively, indicate not only the dual-
ism of executive and lower house, but a jealousy of proprietary
government as such.  This jealousy in Maryland was scarcely
articulate as yet and it never became definitely so, as was
the case in South Carolina and Pennsylvania.  A result of
that kind was obviated by the change of religion on the part
of the proprietors and by their orderly and respectable administration after they had been restored to power.  The homo-
geneousness of the population of Maryland also was not
seriously impaired by immigration and the formation of dis-

---

[1] Mereness, *op. cit.*, 382 *et seq.*
[2] Journals, May and June, 1739.

tinct groups within its limits.  Its westward extension was not
such as to permit a development of this kind on any large
scale.  On the other hand, the growth of Anglicanism and the
period of royal government would have easily prepared the
way for a second overthrow of proprietary rule, had there
been serious cause for dissatisfaction.  The underlying current of feeling is best indicated by the controversy over the
binding force of English statutes in the colony.  Such a discussion as this could scarcely have arisen in a royal province
and in fact did not develop in any colony except Maryland.
But during the decade following 1720 it occupied a very
prominent place in the minds of legislators at Annapolis.

This was primarily a question of the extent to which
judges should be permitted to follow their discretion in administering civil and criminal justice.  It had been mooted in the
seventeenth century.[1]  As in the other colonies, the tendency
then was strong toward a system of law and forms of procedure which were essentially colonial, leaving the judges
with unlimited discretion in all cases for which express provision was not made in the laws of the province.  Law and
practice reflected English usage in general, but with little
definite borrowing from the statutes of the mother country.
English statute books were so few and acquaintance with their
contents so slight among the colonists that a different result
at the time was hardly possible.  Laws of the province, so
far as they had such, were founded of course upon those of
England, but in a free and general way.  The procedure in
cases where there was no statute of the colony was well
stated in an act of 1642, that in civil cases justice should be
administered according to equity and good conscience, " not
neglecting the rules by which right and justice used and ought
to be determined in England in the same or like cases."

The subjects of controversy to which reference has thus
far been made were common, in one form or another, to the
colonies in general.  But in no colony except Maryland was
the subject of the extension to itself of English statutes as
a whole the occasion of such prolonged and earnest debate as
it was in this province.  From an early date the lower house
had shown itself both sensitive and persistent on this point.

[1] Mereness, *op. cit.*, 257 *et seq.*

Before the middle of the seventeenth century the question had been raised.[1]  But just after the Restoration, during the administration of Charles Calvert, an act was passed which provided that where the laws of the province were silent justice should be administered according to the laws of England if they were pleaded and produced.  Previous to this time, when the laws of the province were silent, it had been the custom to rely upon the discretion of the judges.  But now it was thought by the lower house that that had been carried too far.  The upper house, however, called attention to the obvious fact that many English laws were not applicable to the colonies, that there were many inconsistencies in them, and that judges of the county courts, for instance, could not well know when a law of England was pleaded.  In 1674, after this law had been in force for more than a decade, the upper house desired that a list might be prepared of such English laws as were considered necessary for the guidance of the judges of the provincial courts in criminal cases.  The lower house voted that such a list was unnecessary, because they believed that the laws of England as a whole were or should be in force in Maryland.  It was always their contention that this was necessary to the proper securing of the liberties of subjects and they were deaf to all arguments as to the difficulties and absurdities involved in such a course of procedure.  The proprietor, also, was opposed to the contention of the lower house, and in 1684 told them that it was not safe to have justice administered according to the laws of England, where the laws of the province were silent, without due regard to the consistency of such laws with the constitution and present condition of the assembly itself, for it would tie their hands in legislation in such ways as were by no means contemplated in the charter — it would be injurious and might be ruinous.  He refused to assent to a bill on this subject unless discretion was given to the governor or justices of his court to act in accordance with English laws only if they found them consistent with the condition of the province.

During the royal period this subject remained somewhat in abeyance, though occasionally it came to the surface, as in the sweeping clause which occasioned the disallowance of

[1] Mereness, *op. cit.*, 257 *et seq.*

the act of 1696 for the establishment of the English Church
in Maryland, and in repeated attempts beginning with 1706
to have a list of English statutes prepared and declared to be
in force in Maryland. After a considerable period of quiet,
though no reference was made to this subject, the young
proprietor, in 1722, disallowed a bill for the limitation of
actions of trespass and ejectment, stating that by implication
it seemed to introduce English statutes, though it had been
always held that they did not extend to the plantations except
by express words of enactment. The governor was instructed
to permit no doubts on this subject to be entertained, no
attempts to be made to introduce statutes in the lump.[1]
This stirred the lower house to action. Its committee of
grievances was made also a committee on courts of justice,
with the duty of reporting any changes in the commissions
and oaths of the judges which might weaken their obligation
to administer justice according to the laws of England.[2]
The house also entered as permanent resolves on its journal
statements to the effect that Maryland was not a conquered
country but an English colony and whoever advanced the
idea that they had forfeited any part of English liberty were
its ill wishers and failed to understand its happy constitution;
that it had always had the common law and such general
statutes of England as were not restrained by words of local
limitation which, with the laws of the province, furnished
the rules of action, and any who should advise the proprietors
to govern by other rules would infringe on English liberties
and in great measure frustrate the purpose of the original
grant. These views were also laid before the proprietor.

In 1724 the controversy was extended to the form of the
judge's oath, so far as this affected the question of English
statutes.[3] At that time the oath mentioned only the customs
and precedents of the province and acts of assembly as the
guiding principles to be added to the cunning, skill and knowledge of the judge. This was not sufficiently explicit to suit
the lower house and therefore it tried to have the form of
oath determined by act of assembly. At its request, Daniel

[1] U. H. J., Mar. 19, 1722.
[2] Ibid., Oct. 25, 1722.
[3] Journals of the two houses, Oct. 1724.

Dulany, the attorney general, drew up a form of oath which included a reference to the laws of England as well as to the acts and usage of Maryland.  This was not wholly satisfactory to the upper house and it proposed that it be not adopted until the proprietor was consulted.  The lower house insisted that it was quite in harmony with the commissions of the judges and that its adoption should be strongly urged upon the proprietor.  With a few verbal changes the oath drawn by Dulany was accepted by the upper house, but was rejected by both the governor and the proprietor.  In letters to the assembly the proprietor referred to the opinions of the best lawyers of England as being opposed to its contention and cited the *habeas corpus* act as often adjudged not to extend either to Ireland or the plantations, and other acts, as that of 5th Eliz. relating to servants and the statute of usury and of frauds, the extension of which to the colonies would be ruinous.  He also referred to a recent law of Jamaica which was disallowed in England lest its effect might be to introduce the whole body of English laws, which would do great mischief to all parties concerned.  As he afterward instructed the governor, Calvert was unalterably opposed to the introduction of English laws in gross.[1]

During the years which followed feeling on this subject became more intense, while the fact that uniformity in the oaths actually taken by the judges ceased led some to fear that justice and government in the province would be seriously weakened.[2]  After further discussion and a conference the two houses agreed upon another bill, in which recognition was given both to acts of assembly and to reasonable laws and customs of England which were agreeable to the constitution of the province.  This, without apparent reason, the proprietor disallowed and sent over a form of oath the meaning of which it would be very difficult to distinguish from that agreed upon by the two houses.  This action aroused stronger feeling than before in the province, and it was at this juncture that Daniel Dulany began to take a leading part as a defender of the views of the lower house, of which he was a member.  He was perhaps the ablest lawyer of the time in

---

[1] Md. Arch., XXV, 538.

[2] Mereness, *op. cit.*, 272 *et seq.*; L. H. J., Oct. 14, 1727.

Maryland and, as chairman of the committee on laws, made a report on the form of the judge's oath, in the fall of 1728.[1] In the same year he also published his pamphlet on " The Right of the Inhabitants of Maryland to the Benefit of the English Laws." The view which he maintained in both these was that the right to the entire body of English law was necessary to the liberties of the colonists and he who should consent to lessen this would be guilty of treachery to their highest interests. In his pamphlet he labored through much of the undigested material of the time with the purpose of showing that Maryland was not a conquered territory, but had been settled by British subjects who had always lived under the mutual obligations of allegiance and protection and therefore were entitled to the enjoyment of liberty and property under the laws of England. In this he contended that there was no difference between inhabitants of the dominions and those of the realm and therefore the former had a right to all the laws by which the latter were governed. Dulany, of course, must have admitted that he was desirous of securing the benefit only of such English laws as told in favor of the liberty of the subject. There were also many of the opposite character and to these the colonists never even tacitly offered to submit. In view of this simple fact the exaggeration of the choice, as then made by Dulany and the members of the Maryland assembly, becomes sufficiently clear. The position held by the upper house, the proprietor and all English lawyers and officials on the subject was correct and amply provided for the liberties of the colonists. The opposite contention would have made them a privileged class. It is hard to account for the persistence with which the agitation was kept up unless it was meant as a covert attack on the authority of the proprietor. That this, however, was its intent there is no express proof.

In 1730 the proprietor for the fourth time disallowed an oath bill, though he was urged by a joint address of the houses to accept it.[2] A still later bill failed to gain the approval of Governor Ogle, in the first year of his administration. But in the following year, 1732, a newly elected assem-

[1] L. H. J., Oct. 15, 1728.
[2] L. H. J., July, 1731.

bly affected an agreement upon the terms of a bill with both the upper house and the governor, and this measure was signed by the proprietor. The oath,[1] as provided in this act, differed in no essential particular from the form to which all parties had signified their willingness to agree four years before. It required a proper regard for the laws of both the province and the parent state and was continued in force without further dispute until the close of the colonial period.

About the beginning of the third intercolonial war a prolonged struggle developed between the two houses over the appropriation and expenditure of the 3d. per hogshead for arms and ammunition. Provision had been expressly made by law for the expenditure in 1716,[2] and it was continued in force until 1733, though the revenue thus arising was not always used for the purpose indicated. During the long period of peace, accompanied with an almost total indifference to the militia or arms and their improvement, it was natural that this revenue should be used, as it often was, for the repair of the council room. During two years the appropriation was in abeyance. Then, in 1735, a bill for the purpose was passed to continue in force for three years and until the end of the next session of assembly after its expiration.[3] Control over the expenditure was intrusted to the governor and council. The lower house presently began to call for accounts of the use of this money, and, stirred up by disputes over fees and other subjects, in 1739 a controversy over this duty began to develop. War with Spain was now becoming inevitable and, as it came and developed into a general European war, the subject of this appropriation became more pressing.

In 1739 the lower house declined to make the appropriation again on the plea that the money had not been used for the purpose for which it had been raised.[4] They stated that more than £2500 sterling was not accounted for, and nearly as much had been allowed to accumulate unexpended. In view of this it seemed to them that the governor and upper house considered arms useless or that they had a sufficient

[1] Mereness, 276.
[2] Md. Arch., XXX, 628.
[3] Mereness, *op. cit.*, 291 *et seq.*
[4] L. H. J. and U. H. J., May and June 1739.

stock already. Until the money was accounted for or expended they thought a further appropriation unnecessary. The upper house challenged the assembly to furnish proof of its charge that the appropriation had been misapplied and the governor expressed great surprise that the grant was refused on the eve of war. For months thereafter this charge was bandied back and forth between the houses, but without effort on the part of either to test its truth. The governor, of course, was touched by it and charged the lower house with making unwarrantable complaints, and the unwise course which he took so broadened the scope of the conflict and increased its intensity as to defeat his immediate purposes. On the advice of the executive council the governor secured the continuance of the existing law and the collection of the duty under it by refusing to assent to any bills and thus preventing a session. He was enabled to do this because of the technical requirement that without the passage of at least one law a meeting of the assembly could not be called a session. This was sharp practice and it cost the province and those who indulged in it somewhat heavily, as was revealed in the sequel.

The next year the lower house passed a bill for continuing the duty until September, 1741, but with the condition that its expenditure should be strictly accounted for and what money remained in the hands of the treasurers at the end should be disposed of as the two houses should direct.[1] The upper house rejected this bill and then it was that the province was plunged into a controversy, extending through several years and many sessions, over frequent assemblies and definite or short-time appropriations. A long series of messages passed between the houses, in which appear not a few forcible and telling passages on the character and position of the upper house as bearing especially on the passage of money bills, on English precedents relating to the peerage and to annual appropriations, and on the extent to which liberty in Maryland was bound up with frequent sessions, appropriations for short periods and the supremacy of the lower house in all that related to money. It was essentially

---

[1] U. H. J. and L. H. J., May, 1740; Mereness, Md. as a Proprietary Prov., 346 et seq.

the old story, repeated in all the colonies, and now discussed at great length because in Maryland the executive and upper house still retained considerable discretion in these matters. The controversy over fees was still in progress and had its influence on this question. So, of course, did the war and the weak militia and inadequate militia law. The need of defence determined, as it always did, the views of the executive, while the peril to liberty, which they thought they saw in the power of the proprietor to take money under the color of a perpetual law and to settle fees by ordinance, fixed the attention of the lower house.

The necessity of passing a general supply bill for the support of the war caused the meeting of the assembly in May, 1740, to become technically a session, and by virtue of this the law of 1734 relating to arms and ammunition expired. Several other important laws also terminated with this session. It thus became necessary to call the assembly together again in July. The policy then adopted by the upper house was to withhold the bills recently expired which the lower house wished to have enacted, as a means of extorting from the latter the desired appropriations. After two weeks the lower house asked the governor to prorogue the assembly. This induced the upper house to send down some bills, but it still retained one for circuit courts and one on officers' fees. This drew from the lower house a long address to the governor, in which they complained that their power was being reduced to a shadow, they being deprived of that share in legislation to which by charter and birthright they were entitled. They closed with the plain declaration that they would proceed no further with any money bill, except what related exclusively to the king's service, until all their useful and necessary bills were sent down and the regular method of business with the other branch of the legislature was restored. But as the upper house sent down the two remaining bills not passed, no agreement was reached.

In 1741 the favorite bills which had expired were passed by the upper house and in return the lower house passed one for military stores.

# CHAPTER IX

In the founding of Georgia appears an odd mingling of the crude and primitive and of the later and developed features of colonial policy. The incorporation of a board of proprietors under the name of trustees and the bestowment upon them of a charter which conveyed a tract of land in perpetuity, powers of government for twenty one years and all rights connected therewith that were necessary for the establishment of a colony, involved a return to a method of procedure which had been used whenever colonies were settled. A half-century had passed since Pennsylvania, the last of the "newly settled" provinces, had been founded, and during most of this interval a policy hostile to chartered colonies had been followed and several important restrictions had been laid upon them. But now that a new settlement was to be made, one of the original forms of government for it was selected. This was natural and perhaps unavoidable, though it is worthy of note that it was done under the early Hanoverians, when signs appeared of a return in matters of colonial government to the indifference of earlier times. But on the other hand, it was a new proprietary province and not a corporate colony which was created, with the proprietors resident in England. They were incorporated and, like the Virginia Company, no limit was set to the increase of membership. They were also subjected to various requirements now in vogue, that those whom they appointed governors should receive the approval of the king, take the oath and give security to enforce the acts of trade and obey instructions issued in pursuance thereof. The crown also reserved the right to appoint the officers who should collect the king's revenue in the province, while an annual accounting to the home government for all the receipts and expenditures of the province was required of the trustees.

It is true that the trustees were fully incorporated, the forms under which they should do business were prescribed and they were empowered in the usual way to govern their province. Georgia was declared to be a province distinct from all others, being carved out of the territory of Carolina between the Savannah and Altamaha rivers and extending westward to the south sea. Within these bounds the trustees could found settlements, develop a land system, govern the settlers through officials of their own appointment, establishing courts for the purpose and making use of the customary forms of executive order and legislation. But the very limited degree of independence which was given to the trustees and their province is shown by the requirements that from time to time accounts of the progress of the colony should be given to the secretaries of state and the board of trade, that the above mentioned financial accounting should be enforced, that the laws which were drafted for the province should receive the approval of the crown before they were put into force, that no provision was made for an assembly in the province, and that the entire grant of powers to the trustees was to terminate in twenty-one years.

Under these conditions local institutions and self-government could not fully develop in proprietary Georgia. The creation of the proprietorship was only temporary, to facilitate the establishment of the colony, after which it would be taken over by the crown. The enterprise took its start with the individuals in England who secured the charter, and it was their intention, as well as that of the British government, that the colony should be kept under strict control. Two motives gave rise to the experiment, both of which appear in the preamble of the charter and in the negotiations preliminary to its issue which went on between the petitioners and the committee of council, board of trade and other officials who were concerned in making the grant.[1] One motive was the desire, on the part of benevolent persons like James Oglethorpe and others, to provide a refuge for the indigent who were crowding the debtors' prisons and burdening the poor rates of the large English cities, and yet who themselves were

[1] Ga. Col. Recs., I, 11; C. O., 5/656, f. 322; Acts P. C. Col., 1720–1745, p. 299 *et seq.*

not so unworthy but that under the stimulus of a new country they might be expected to become self-supporting. From
the time of Captain John Smith down, relief of this kind
always had been sought from emigration, but it appears more
prominently in the Georgia enterprise than in any other. The
other object which was sought was military and defensive in
character. It was to create a border colony that should
secure for the British the territory in southern Carolina which
was in dispute between them and the Spanish and to provide
a barrier against attacks from the south and west. As Great
Britain at the time was at peace with both France and Spain,
it was defence against the Indians which was emphasized in
the charter, but it was from their supposed alliance with
hostile European powers that the natives derived much of
their significance. In view of these motives, the founding
of Georgia, unlike the settlement of New England and of
such provinces as Maryland and Pennsylvania, was not the
result of religious schism in England and therefore was not
intended to furnish a means of escape from control or to be
a step toward independence. It was rather an imperialistic
move and falls in line with the policy which had been slowly
maturing for the past fifty years. Therefore it was not the
creation of a chartered colony in the old sense of the word,
but a temporary utilizing of that institution for the purpose
of extending the British frontier on the south.

The original petition for a charter called for the formation
of a charitable society which should use colonization as a
means for the exercise of its powers. Through its activity
the poor were to be relieved outside the realm instead of
within it. This feature of the scheme gave rise to the provision that no member of the corporation should receive a
grant of land in Georgia, nor should any be made directly
or indirectly for his benefit. This requirement alone, so
peculiar was it, made a radical difference between Georgia
and all other proprietary provinces. Another important restriction limited grants to five hundred acres each, and though
this was not entirely adhered to, it prevented the development
of large estates which were so important an element in the
other provinces. The peculiar philanthropic objects of the
enterprise were also revealed in the provisions of the charter

which forbade members of the corporation holding offices of profit under it. If such an office was accepted, that of itself would terminate the membership of the appointee in the trust. Whatever service was performed for the colony by the proprietors must be disinterested and without a view to profit — a condition precisely the opposite of that which lay at the basis of all other proprietorships.

The effort toward social betterment which was involved in the settlement of Georgia awakened an unusual interest in the plan in Great Britain. Its significance from the standpoint of defence was also highly appreciated by all in official and military circles. The reputation of Oglethorpe as a soldier, a prison reformer and a member of parliament was of the greatest value in advertising the plan of the trustees when it became known that he was a prime mover among them. By 1730 the newspaper and periodical press was well developed in England and its influence was enlisted on behalf of Georgia to an extent which was never dreamed of in the case of any other colony. A long time had passed since any new settlement in America had been attempted and this province was acclaimed as the great achievement of British enterprise and good will under Whig leadership and in the Georgian era. Meetings of the trustees were chronicled in the press. Oglethorpe after his successive returns from America, bringing first a band of Indian chiefs and later crowned with added military laurels, was welcomed with odes and ascriptions not only from the pens of Pope and Thomson, but in terms of most extravagant eulogy from many an anonymous writer in the public prints.[1] Heroes were not common in that age, at least in the British Isles, but Oglethorpe seemed to fulfil the requirements sufficiently for the talk of the time. Every colony, in the imagination of its historians, must have a " founder," and at the time and ever since Oglethorpe has received the credit of this achievement, but none of the earlier founders became a social lion or connected his name with a tradition of unusual heroism. In respect of the reputation of its so-called founder and of the general favor with which it was regarded by the merchants and gentry of England, Georgia may be called a colony *de luxe*. It and, some years later,

[1] See the volumes of Gentleman's Mag. from 1732 to 1742.

Nova Scotia, at the other extremity of the frontier, attracted unusual attention because of their value from the military and naval standpoints, and as the struggle with the French in North America approached its culmination they helped greatly to emphasize the importance of seaboard colonies.

The charter members of the board of trustees of Georgia were twenty in number and they were somewhat increased by election at later times. To aid in the discharge of their executive functions provision was made in the charter for a common council of fifteen members, to act under oath as a standing committee with a quorum of eight. As no quorum was designated for the trustees, their business was often transacted by as few as three members. A president was chairman of the trustees, while the title of chairman was applied to the presiding officer of the common council. Both offices were held in rotation by all the members, each serving for only one meeting. As funds had to be collected in Great Britain for the support of the colony as a charitable enterprise, the trustees had charge of these matters. They also were the general law-making body of the corporation, were the grantees of the land of the colony, issued and enforced general executive orders, established courts and provided for the defence of the province.

In general the common council performed the detailed work of administration. It issued all grants of land and specified their terms. It appointed all officials of the colony, civil and military, and designated the titles. It expended all moneys, made contracts, fixed salaries, appointed secretaries, treasurers and other officials who were necessary for the administration of affairs in England. Such officers it could remove. And yet the correspondence of officials was carried on with the trustees and the latter had the right to do much which was actually performed by the common council. On an average for the entire period of the proprietorship, the trustees met fortnightly and the common council met much less often; this being due to the requirement as to a quorum in the case of the latter. Sometimes a meeting of the trustees was changed into one of the common council or vice versa. Committees were appointed in large numbers by both these bodies, while the corporation had as permanent officials a secretary, Benjamin Martyn, and an accountant, Harmon Verelst. Among the committees that of the trustees on correspondence, which existed throughout the proprietary period, was one of the most important. It inspected all incoming letters and prepared drafts of those which were sent in reply. Among the committees of the common council, those which were concerned with financial business and accounts were the most important. When administrative orders and instructions to magistrates had to be prepared, special committees for these purposes were created. When the period for which the trust was formed was approaching its close, committees were appointed to wind up its affairs. With the exception of a few years at the beginning of the trust, the attendance of members was small. A considerable proportion of its enrolled members never took an active interest in the enterprise and others lost interest after the first decade had passed. Attendance, especially at meetings of the trustees, fell off. As is natural in all human relations, the control of affairs from the first was in the hands of a few and as time passed the number of these diminished. The tendency therefore was toward a virtual committee organization for the transaction of all the business of the trust

A careful study of the lists of those who were in attendance at meetings of the trustees, common council and committees during the entire continuance of the trust shows that the business of the corporation was really transacted by ten men, that they counted for more by far than all the rest of the members combined. Among these ten the first place was held by James Vernon. He attended more meetings than any other and, according to all available evidence, was the most persistent and effective administrator among the trustees. He was the son of James Vernon, who was secretary of state and associate of Shrewsbury and Somers under William III, and brother of Edward Vernon, the admiral. He was therefore widely connected among the Whigs, and his cooperation in the work of Dr. Thomas Bray, as well as in that of Oglethorpe, proves that he had philanthropic ideals. His fidelity to the trustees and their province continued to the last, and among the interests to which he specially devoted himself were those of sending over German emigrants, particularly the Salzburgers, and procuring missionaries for the colony from the Society for the Propagation of the Gospel. Next in record of attendance to Vernon, but superior to him in the social influence which he possessed was John, Viscount Perceval, soon to be first earl of Egmont. Of his connection with the trustees, of whom he was the first president, a detailed account has been left in his published journal. He was a man of ability and reputation and the father of a still more famous son. Though Egmont was a Whig, he was not a blind admirer of Walpole, was suspicious of his attitude toward Georgia, and in the person of the son this developed into pronounced opposition to the prime minister and to his successors, the Pelhams, which carried him over to the party of the prince of Wales and thence to a position among the king's friends at the beginning of the reign of George III The services of the first earl among the trustees were specially valuable at the outset in securing contributions and giving prestige to the enterprise.

Egmont and Oglethorpe, the one in England and the other chiefly in America, were the only persons who in the eye of the general public gave character to the Georgia plan. It was doubtless to these two men and to Vernon that one is chiefly to attribute the peculiar policies which were applied in founding that province. Owing to undue sensitiveness under criticism and distrust of the government, Egmont capriciously resigned from the common council in 1742. This diminished his activity, and his death, in 1748, removed him from the scene some years before the termination of the trust. As Oglethorpe spent much of the first decade of the existence of the trust in Georgia and after his final return to England, in 1743, failed to agree with his colleagues and was an object of their criticism, he became irregular in his attendance on their meetings and seems never to have appeared at one of them after March, 1749. So far, then, as permanence of connection with the work of the governing body in England was concerned, the record of Vernon stands highest. But both Egmont and Oglethorpe wielded a kind of influence which, so far as we know, was superior to that of Vernon. In negotiations with parliament and with the government we may suppose that for a time the services of Egmont were more valuable than those of any one else. Through his close connection with the colony itself, and especially with its defence, Oglethorpe, as is clearly proven by his correspondence, for more than a decade performed a work which was unique and of great value in connection with the founding of Georgia. Others who worked more silently also did their part and the result of the joint activity of all who were concerned was the effective settlement of this territory, which otherwise would probably have fallen into the hands of Spain.

Notwithstanding the fact that Georgia was a chartered colony, its relations with the British government were particularly close. This, as has been noted, was due to the fact that it was not founded until the system of imperial administration was fully developed. The regular and successful appeals which the trustees made to parliament for aid also established an unusually close connection with that body. But at the same time the trustees endeavored to maintain a certain independence in the exercise of the powers bestowed by their charter and, in doing so, they felt that they incurred the dislike of the board of trade and that they experienced the evil results of this especially in their relations with South Carolina. At the outset, in order to avoid the control which the crown exercised over governors, the trustees resolved to appoint no governor, but instead sent Oglethorpe out simply as their attorney. Later, Stephens was appointed president, and so proprietary Georgia never had a governor. Though the evidence that the board of trade resented this is vague, Egmont's journal shows that when the question of the relations of Georgia and South Carolina to the Indian trade came up, the trustees felt that the board assumed an unfair attitude toward them and appealed to the privy council on the subject.[1] But though their feeling may have been justified, the general attitude of the board on this subject may be explained on other grounds. Some of the trustees also took it hard that their act concerning Indian trade was in part dispensed with through instructions issued by the crown for the adjustment of this dispute. When, in 1740, the board reported on a pilot act which had been drafted by the trustees, Egmont

[1] Ga. Col. Recs., I, 301; V, 840, 46, 54–55; Acts of P. C. Col., 284, 1720–1745, p. 511 *et seq.*

considered that it showed " great animosity against us; but
we were not much surprised at it, that Board being constantly
our Enemies." [1]

When, a few months later, Vernon was discussing a form
of executive in the province to take the place of the rule of
Oglethorpe, he proposed two presidents instead of one, since
the appointment of one, said he, " would be in a manner to
surrender our Charter, for when Once we had established
a Governor whose choice must be approved of by the king,
we could not again remove him at our pleasure, and by our
Charter such Governor would be obliged to obey not only
the Trustees Orders, but Orders also of the Board of Trade.
Our Enemies, who would become our Masters, and without
regarding the Trustees, . . . would send over such orders as
they pleased, which in a multitude of cases might clash with
Orders sent by the Trustees; so that no Gentleman would
continue in the Trust to be revil'd, disputed with, and become subservient to the board of Trade, who know as little
of the Colony as they do of trade." [2] This anticipation of
the later criticism of Burke was certainly the result largely
of irritation on the part of the defenders of special privilege
at the application to them of the general principles of policy
in reference to the colonies which long experience justified.
It reappeared whenever the crown found it necessary to comment or act adversely on any of the peculiar practices of
the trustees or their colony, as in the case of the high rate
of quit rents which they maintained, and particularly in
reference to the restrictions which they imposed upon traffic
in rum.[3] That the trustees were not always well informed
concerning the law on these matters is shown by their insistence, in opposition to the customs board, upon their right to
appoint a naval officer, and in opposition to the admiralty
board on something very much like the right of assent to the
appointment of a judge of admiralty in Georgia.[4] Their attitude on the latter question was taken as late as 1748. In
not a few respects the condition and progress of Georgia were
not such as to warrant enthusiastic approval. And yet, on
the whole, and under the limitations of time set in the

---

[1] Ga. Col. Recs., V, 390.     [3] Ibid., I, 406, 453, 465.
[2] Ibid., 415.     [4] Ibid., 518, V, 228.

charter, the board of trade favored the colony, and the relations between it and the trustees never developed into a controversy or reached a point where a break was imminent.

It was their financial relations and need of funds which brought the colony and its proprietors into close relations with parliament, closer even than was the case with any other province. The Bank of England was made the financial agent of the trustees and they were required annually to submit their accounts to the lord chancellor and lord chief justice.[1] At regular intervals also the trustees petitioned the house of commons for appropriations in aid of their enterprise, stating more or less briefly on every occasion the reasons for their demands. Their first petition, May 10, 1733, set forth their plan for settling the province and transporting thither numbers of German and English colonists and stated that the generous benefactions which they had received were not sufficient to enable them to do this without the aid of the government. An appropriation of £10,000 out of the proceeds of the sale of lands in St. Christopher was made in response to this plea. Annually thereafter, until subsequently to the beginning of the war with Spain, grants varying from £2500 to £26,000 were obtained, apparently without opposition.[2] These were intended chiefly for the defence of the province, and when Oglethorpe's regiment was sent over the entire cost of this service was assumed by the British government. Thereafter such special appropriations as were made must be for civil affairs alone, and as it was more difficult to secure them for this purpose, it was desired by the trustees that they be put into the yearly estimates, thus removing the need for annual petitions.[3] At first Walpole seemed to assent to this, but failed to give permission because in the estimates provision was made only for the army and navy, and the custom of petitioning had to be continued.

The negotiating of the convention with Spain in 1738 and the struggle in parliament which was occasioned thereby closely affected the fortunes of Georgia. It had been preceded

[1] Ga. Col. Recs., I, 129, 134; II, 4; III, 25 et seq.

[2] Journals of H. of C., XVII and XVIII, under dates of May 10, 1733, Feb. 28, 1733–4, Mar. 10, 1734–5, etc. Ga. Col. Recs., I, 132, 188, 215, 253 et seq.

[3] Egmont Journal, Ga. Recs., V, 34, 88.

by a statement, through the Spanish minister, of the claim of that country to Georgia and Walpole considered this claim a subject of negotiation.  He even went so far as to ask the trustees to prepare to surrender all or a part of it, if by this means the acceptance of the convention might be assured. This caused much anxiety to the friends of Georgia and, lest they might weaken their case by preparing a statement of their claim, they decided to rest it upon their charter and to leave the drafting of any further statements to the more skilful hands of the law officers and the board of trade.[1]  The needs of the colony were now so great that the trustees were forced to raise their demand for 1739 from £8000 to £20,000. They desired to keep Georgia and their interests there out of politics, but it was difficult to do so.  They did not trust Walpole and he considered them not friendly toward him. When the trustees thought of enlisting the anti-ministerial party in their cause, it insisted that they should join in the general attacks on the prime minister and his policy.  For this the trustees were not ready, while Walpole stated that he had no intention of surrendering Georgia.  He succeeded, however, in postponing their grant until after the convention had been carried and among the reduced majority of thirty-two by which that was passed were the votes of the trustees.[2] Their appropriation was then secured and Keene at Madrid was instructed to insist that the St. John's river should be the boundary.  This was not the result of a bargain, but it was the order in which events occurred.

Walpole was given to understand by some of his friends among the trustees that no grant was needed for 1740, and therefore these members insisted that an application should not be made, giving as a reason that it was sure to be denied. But Egmont and the majority were sure that further aid was needed and resolved, as a means of escaping from such complete dependence upon the minister and of answering attacks which had been made upon them, to lay their condition and needs directly before the house.  They courted an inquiry but Walpole avoided this by consenting to a grant of £4000.  But a brief debate occurred and as an incident of this

[1] Egmont Journal 97, 98, 100–101, 107–109.
[2] *Ibid.*, 120–154.

some information concerning the condition of the colony was brought to the attention of the house.[1] In 1741 an " Account of the Progress of the Colony of Georgia in America from its first Establishment " was prepared and circulated among the members of the Commons.[2] This pamphlet was used as a reply to the attacks of Thomas Stephens and it helped to procure an additional grant of £10,000.[3]

In tracing the history of these successive grants it should be borne in mind that they and the relations which gave rise to them were exceptional in the history of the colonies. Never before had the British government undertaken the financial support of a colony, and in the case of Georgia the thing was done without an actual change of policy. The conduct of the government in this special case was doubtless due to the importance which was attributed to Georgia as a barrier colony against the Spanish and to the influence of the trustees and others in impressing this fact on the government. At the same time, the inadequacy for such purposes of the funds which could be provided by a corporation or raised by subscription was well understood. The limited population and resources of the colony, taken in connection with certain peculiar lines of policy which the trustees had adopted, proved the need of attention and help. These features also occasioned complaints and attacks, the nature of which will be explained when we come to speak of the province itself. In 1742 these took the form of a violent attack upon the trustees in England by Thomas Stephens, the son of the president of the colony. Walpole had then been driven from office and the minority which had succeeded under the nominal control of Lord Wilmington appeared to be less friendly to the trustees than the great Whig leader had been. To the astonishment of the trustees a motion to refer their application for a grant to the committee of supply was lost by a small majority.[4] Attempts were made to secure the money in the committee of supply itself, but these also failed. Meantime Stephens' complaints had been laid before the administration boards and thence came to the knowledge of the

[1] Ga. Recs. V, 272, 280, 288, 293–302, 309–311, 316.
[2] *Ibid.*, III, 369–411.
[3] *Ibid.*, V, 433–445, 455, 459, 471, 484, 489–491.
[4] *Ibid.*, V, 607.

commons. The trustees, in order to avoid smothering their case in a committee, now insisted upon a hearing before the whole house. Their plea was granted and both parties were heard by counsel and with the submission of evidence. The result was that the house in six resolutions expressed the opinion that Georgia was of such value from its location, its harbors and the fertility of its soil that it should receive the support of the nation.[1] The petition of Stephens against the trustees was then declared to be scandalous and malicious and he was compelled to kneel in the presence of the house and receive the reprimand of the speaker. This result was decisive, and during the remaining years of its existence as a proprietary province, Georgia received from parliament without serious opposition such sums as the expenditures of the war and the general condition of the budget made possible.[2] During three years of that period — 1746 to 1749 — the trustees did not apply for a grant, but thereafter small sums were received at intervals and accounts were duly rendered of their expenditure. Grants were even continued after Georgia became a royal province, and that for the support of her civil establishment.[3] When the trustees surrendered the province to the crown, they had expended upon it about £154,000, of which approximately £130,000 had been granted by parliament. Nearly all of the remainder had been raised by subscription, principally during the few years which immediately followed the granting of the charter. Most of the private contributions were for general purposes, the whole enterprise being considered a worthy philanthropy, but a few were specific, such as for the improvement of botany and agriculture; for the assistance of persecuted foreign Protestants, especially the Salzburgers; for the maintenance of a missionary at Savannah and of a minister among the Scotch at Darien.[4]

Turning now to the province itself, in the management of their land, the trustees at the beginning resolved that they

[1] Ga. Recs., V, 612–621, 635, 639; Jour. of Commons, XXIV, Apr., May and June, 1742.

[2] Ibid., 681, 682; I, 469, 481, 497; II, 524; Jour. of H. of Commons, XXV and XXVI.

[3] Jour. of Commons, XXVII, XXVIII, XXIX, Jan. 28, 1755/6, Feb. 10, 1758, Jan. 26, 1763, Mar. 15, 1764.

[4] Ga. Recs., I, 123, 181, 331, 371, 385.

would seek no profit from the sales or leases, that grants should be small and that they should be entailed.  As in the Carolinas, provision had to be made for Carteret's undivided share and right to a certain quit rent, for it was assigned to him.[1]  A system of quit rents was instituted by the charter to go into effect ten years after the date of the grants.  The rent was first fixed at the rate of 4s. sterling per hundred acres and was payable to the king and Carteret in proclamation money.  But in 1733 the rent, for those who went at their own expense, was raised to the very high rate of 20s. per hundred acres and remained at that figure until the close of the proprietary period.[2]  Prompt occupation and settlement was required and estates could not be transferred without license from the common council.  The expectation of developing silk culture led to the requirement that the grantees should plant a certain number of white mulberry trees.  The most peculiar feature of the land system and the one which provoked most criticism was the revival of the antiquated rule of descent by tail male, it being justified, as in the middle age, by the argument that, as Georgia was a border province, every grant should be a sort of military fief and should always have a man as its defender.  The great majority of the settlers the trustees transported free across the ocean, supported them for a year after their arrival in the colony and provided them with tools, arms and other necessities.  As a class also they had not been successful in England and therefore could not be expected thriftily to manage property in the colony.  It was for settlers of this type that the small grants of fifty acres were intended to be held in tail male and with strict limitations on their alienability.  It was found, if grants were made in fee simple with the right of free alienation, that inequality would soon be introduced, large estates would be accumulated in a few hands and undesirable colonists would come in.  The limit to the size of estates which was fixed in the charter was five hundred acres, and grants of this size were offered to gentlemen adventurers who would bring over ten servants, cultivate at least one-tenth

[1] Ga. Recs., V, 675.

[2] McCain, Georgia as a Proprietary Province; The Execution of a Trust, p. 249 *et seq.;* Ga. Recs., III. 412.

of the estate, remain in the province at least three years unless licensed to depart, and conform to the general regulations which applied to all estates, large and small. Had these regulations been strictly adhered to, a system of equality in landholding, with relatively small estates, but kept so by rigid control on the part of the trustees and under the penalty of forfeiture, would have been the result. But the administration was not sufficiently vigorous to check the protest, natural in a new country, against the principle of inheritance by tail male or to enforce the restrictions on alienation. Protests were soon raised by colonists, especially to the system of entail, and this together with their other two policies, the prohibition of the importation of rum and of negroes, the trustees were forced to defend or modify or abandon. In reference to these subjects developed the chief controversies in proprietary Georgia. But before their progress can be traced some account must be given of the government which was instituted in the province.

Owing to the fact that Georgia was to remain under the control of the trustees for only twenty-one years, and also to their dislike of control by the board of trade and privy council, they avoided the creation of a regular provincial form of government in the colony. The government which they did set up was municipal rather than provincial. It consisted, when the first body of colonists was sent over, of three bailiffs, a recorder, two constables, two tithingmen and eight conservators of the peace.[1] No mayor was appointed, and no real distinction was made between the powers of the three bailiffs. These officials, with powers both judicial and executive and without salaries or instructions, constituted the entire government of the colony at the beginning. The individuals who were appointed to these offices were selected from the rank and file of the colonists. Being therefore destitute of experience in the administration of government, they had to depend on Oglethorpe for such advice as he could give them, while he was in the colony, and afterwards they had chiefly to shift for themselves.

On his first visit, Oglethorpe's relations to the colony were temporary and informal. He accompanied the expedition

[1] Ga. Recs., II, 11; McCain, *op. cit.*

voluntarily, paying his own expenses and taking with him
no distinctly official commission. His purpose seems to have
been limited to the establishment of the colonists in their
homes, and the title which best fits him was that of attorney
of the trustees. Several special duties were entrusted to him,
as that of administering the oaths required by the British
government to be taken by the officials in the colony, of
distributing five thousand acres of land among certain of
the settlers, granting licenses to those who desired to leave
the province without forfeiting their lands. The services
which he actually performed of course exceeded in many ways
what was implied in these special commissions. During the
first five months after his arrival in Georgia he kept authority
entirely in his own hands, and it was only at the end of that
time that the magistrates, above referred to, were established in office. During that time and later Oglethorpe took
charge of all the larger affairs of the settlement. By him,
with the advice of Colonel Bull, of South Carolina, the site
of Savannah was chosen and the town laid out. Oglethorpe
opened relations with the neighboring Indians as sucessfully
as Penn had done in his province and in much the same
spirit. The site of Ebenezer was selected by Oglethorpe in
cooperation with the Salzburgers who were to settle there.
The coast to the south of the Savannah river he explored and
provision was made by him for the defence of the infant
colony. But what in certain respects was superior to all this,
Oglethorpe mingled freely with the colonists, superintended
the entire work of settlement, shared in its physical labor,
cared for the sick, settled disputes, maintained discipline.
In this step he was the father of the enterprise, to an extent
surpassing even Penn in the intimacy of his relation to it
and far surpassing in its human aspects the work of the
merely legal proprietor.

It was during Oglethorpe's first return visit to England,
that, with his full approval and partly under his influence,
the trustees passed the acts which committed them to the
principle that rum and negro slaves should never be permitted
to enter Georgia,[1] and also a law regulating peaceful dealings
with the Indians in their colony. These expressed to the full

[1] Ga. Recs., I, 31–62, 216.

the idealism which animated him, but they were so far in advance of conditions at the time and place as to be unpractical and to serve mainly as subjects of controversy. Though in themselves well meant and highly desirable, the regulations concerning rum and negroes, together with the requirement that land should be held in tail male, contributed as much as anything to arouse complaints and disputes and thus bring to an end the somewhat idyllic conditions which had attended the founding of the colony.

On the return of Oglethorpe to Georgia in the fall of 1735, he recived the same powers, with slight extensions, which were granted him on his first departure.[1]  During his first visit to the colony he had drawn bills on the trustees to the amount of over £55,000, and his frequent failure to send vouchers or letters of advice with these drafts had caused much inconvenience. But after his return to England he had been able to account for all of these payments except £1875.[2] On his departure again for the colony, Oglethorpe was given the sole right to draw bills on the trustees, and the sola bills of exchange were devised for that purpose and for circulation in Georgia, all of which had to be signed by Oglethorpe.[3] More than 280 colonists accompanied him on this voyage and as a result of the increase which they would bring to the population of the colony it was intended to found a new town. It was the preference of the trustees that a site on the Ogeechee should be selected, but Oglethorpe was resolved that the line of the Altamaha should be occupied. A short time before his arrival a colony of Highland Scotch had founded New Inverness a few miles above the mouth of the Altamaha. Oglethorpe chose a spot on St. Simon island, near the mouth of that river, for the site of his new town and called it Frederica. The selection of this site was due chiefly to military consideration, and its settlement was followed by reconnaisances and the establishment of small posts south· of the chartered limits of the province. These provoked the Spaniards and, notwithstanding treaties which Oglethorpe made with authorities at St. Augustine, helped to bring

---

[1] Ga. Recs., I, 228; II, 120, 123, 125.
[2] Ibid., 116.
[3] Ibid., 113.

about the hostilities which began a few years later. Communication between these settlements and Savannah was difficult and the former remained largely military outposts, which retained their importance as long as there was danger from the Spanish and then totally disappeared. But their settlement marks the ascendancy of military considerations in the policy of Oglethorpe in Georgia and these continued more conspicuously to absorb his attention until his career in that colony was ended.

The trustees informed Oglethorpe that, as they did not approve of expenditures outside the limits of the province, he must look to the British government for support in such enterprises. At this point began the differences between him and his official superiors. Toward the close of 1736, Oglethorpe was summoned home, partly in order to report about the dispute with South Carolina over the traffic in rum. While in England he helped to persuade the government to assume the defence of the province to the extent of raising a regiment of six hundred men and making Oglethorpe its colonel. He was at the same time made captain general of the forces of both South Carolina and Georgia. It was at this time that he began to receive for the first time a reward in money for his services in the colony, namely, the pay of a British colonel and an allowance for the command which he held in South Carolina. His accounts were audited in England and came much nearer a balance than they had done on his previous visit. The confidence of the trustees in him was variously expressed. After his third return to the colony affairs drifted on, Oglethorpe being chiefly concerned in defence and Indian relations and the civil affairs of the province being left to the strictly local officials. He might and often did interfere in business of all kinds, but now that there were several towns in the colony he could only occasionally visit even the more important of them. Affairs therefore were disordered, disputes multiplied, commands were not obeyed. Oglethorpe complained, as did other parties, and the trustees began to criticise him for his alleged mistakes and to take from him some of his control over expenditures. After the beginning of the war, Oglethorpe became so absorbed in the work of defence that it became necessary more fully to organize the civil government of the province.

During the absences of Oglethorpe his duties were intrusted to substitutes, but they were of course performed in a spirit and with results far inferior to his own. At the same time, with the growth of outlying villages, the best that could be done was to appoint for them additional constables and tithingmen and to extend over them the authority of the bailiffs of Savannah.[1] This, however, seems to have been done in only one or two cases, most of the villages, like Ebenezer, being left for years to govern themselves. When Frederica was founded a new set of bailiffs, constables and tithingmen was appointed for it and no connection, except through Oglethorpe, was established between Savannah and the settlements on the Altamaha. So chaotic were the administrative relations within Georgia that between it and Inverness, or Darien, there seems to have been no official connection. When the trustees had issued the laws to which reference has been made, as there was no governor and council to whom their execution could be intrusted, special officials were appointed for the purpose, though no instructions apparently were given them beyond what were implied in their titles. Thus, Oglethorpe was appointed commissioner for licensing Indian traders, special officers were appointed to stave and empty all brandy, spirits and strong waters, and others to license the retailing of beer, wines and ale, the sale of which was allowed by the law. The constables were specially commissioned to execute the act forbidding the importation of negroes. A register to record the grants of land was also appointed. These and the few other officers who received commissions for special purposes were appointed for the entire province and thus they tended to bind it together into an administrative whole.[2]

During the first stage of the colony's existence the most important functionary at Savannah, apart from Oglethorpe, was the storekeeper for the trust. In the hands of Thomas Causton, the incumbent, this office became more important even than it was in proprietary Virginia.[3] His duties were

---

[1] Ga. Recs., II, 43.

[2] McCain, *op. cit.*

[3] His doings may be followed in great detail in the correspondence of the colony officials with Verelst and the trustees, in Ga. Recs. XX–XXII, and in Stephens' Journal, *ibid.*, IV.

social and economic and as the keeper and dispenser of the goods which were sent over by the trustees, he was brought into relations with every colonist. During the year or so which followed settlement they were entirely dependent upon him for supplies, and he enjoyed great discretion in the distribution of them to those who had been brought over by the trust and in the prices charged to those who were independent. Under the direction of Oglethorpe, the storekeeper was also allowed to issue drafts on the trustees for supplies purchased and also for the general expenses of the province, a power which was particularly liable to abuse. In addition to his position as storekeeper, Causton for several years held the position of first bailiff at Savannah. He accumulated property and had the finest estate in the province, was indeed its foremost man when Oglethorpe was absent on his visits to England. His position and conduct gained for him the dislike of many, while his failure at times to write and submit accounts with regularity brought reproof from the trustees.[1] His expenditures for the trust also became large, occasioned by the need of improved defences as the danger of Spanish attack increased and by the larger demands for supplies in many directions. By 1738 it had become evident that Causton was running the trust heavily in debt by unauthorized expenditures. Therefore he was suspended from office, ordered under arrest and an examination of his accounts was begun. Though a long and bitter controversy followed, between Causton and his accusers, and though his accounts were found to be in such confusion that they were never wholly disentangled, he was not proven to have been guilty of fraud.[2] Though Causton claimed that the confusion in his accounts was due to the multitude of his transactions and to inadequate clerical assistance, his case adds to the already convincing evidence of the slipshod business methods which were so common among the British colonies.

The conduct of the storekeeper furnished by no means the only occasion for complaint in Georgia. The art of

[1] See a True and Historical Narrative, Colls. of Ga. Hist. Soc. II, 201.
[2] Ga. Recs., XXII (I), 318, et seq.; XXII (2), 59 et seq., and many other references in these volumes and in Stephens' Journal.

colonization was now so far advanced and the aid procurable
from neighboring colonies was so great, that the tragedies
which had attended the founding of Virginia and Plymouth were no longer to be found.  But much of the soil
of Georgia was sand and swamp and would not yield a
living return.  The labor of clearing the forest from the best
land was exhausting and largely beyond the strength of the
colonists who could not command the aid of a number of
servants.[1]  Many, therefore, especially of the quality of the
colonists who were sent to Georgia by the trust, became
discouraged, were too weak to clear and cultivate their
grants and therefore clung to the town or drifted out of the
colony.  The Scotch at Darien and the Salzburgers proved
to be the most contented and thrifty.  To the few hundreds
of colonists whom the trustees were able to take to Georgia
or to induce to settle there, the clearing of farms, building
of houses and towns, opening of roads, withstanding the
visitations of storms, drought or disease, did not prove an
easy task.  Progress was slow and when the cloud of war
appeared on the horizon, the chance of success appeared
doubtful.  A querulous tone of discouragement took possession of not a few.[2]  In spite of the courtesies of William
Bull, it was evident that South Carolina viewed the experiment with feelings of mingled jealousy and contempt, and
what with the dispute about Indian trade and Georgia's
novel policy concerning rum and negroes, taken in connection with unfavorable winds and other obstacles to navigation, it was doubtful whether the new colony could count
on the effective aid of its northern neighbor against the
Spaniards.  At the same time, South Carolina seemed to
many the land of promise and the danger was ever present
that by removals thither the population of Georgia might
be seriously depleted.

There is no doubt but that one of the greatest obstacles
to the progress of Georgia was the regulation of the trustees
providing for the descent of land according to the strictest

[1] Ga. Recs., XXI, 322 *et seq.*, 483, the statements of Brownfield, a man
of keen observation and sound judgment.

[2] Idleness and contention, according to Causton, were general in these
communities, and Georgia certainly did not enjoy a monopoly of them.
*Ibid.*, 273.

rules of primogeniture and entail. That an attempt should have been made as late as 1732 to foist this upon a new colony furnishes one of the strongest evidences of the lack of common intelligence, to say nothing of common sense, which even well-intentioned colonial administrators sometimes showed. Had there not been as chief features of the system a set of water-tight compartments known as colonies, — and later as states — a condition which to an extent also had its parallel in the departments and offices in England, the fact would have been known that in the case of the Connecticut intestacy law abundant evidence had recently been produced to show how necessary it was to depart in a new country, in the interest of the heirs in general, from the common law rule of inheritances. The experience of the colonies outside of New England was also overwhelming against the rigid enforcement of this rule, even though the principle of it had found its way into the law of some of them. But of this evidence and body of experience the Georgia trustees knew nothing. Neither, so far as we are aware, did they look about to find if there was anything to be known. Among colonial sources the nearest approach to the ideas upon the strength of which they acted in this matter appears in the charter issued to Gorges in 1637 for Maine and in the exploration and defence of its provisions which he subsequently issued. In his day, Gorges' plan was an anachronism. How much more so a century later!

When, after six or seven years, the colonists began to express their discontent in letters, petitions, pamphlets and in conversations with agents of the trustees in the colony itself, the demand for the removal of restrictions on inheritance of land, or at least for the substitution of the principle of tail general for tail male, became pronounced. Combined with this were also the complaints arising from the prohibition of traffic in rum and negro slaves and the general lack of prosperity in the colony. In order to secure better information on all matters of importance, to harmonize differences and to supply to an extent the administrative need caused by the absences of Oglethorpe and the lack of a governor, in 1737, the trustees appointed William Stephens as their secretary in Georgia. The first set of instructions which the trustees ever issued to any of their officials was given to him, and they were elaborate.[1] They did not, however, transmit authority to administer affairs directly, but to inquire and report fully on all the affairs of the colony and the condition of its inhabitants in their military, civil, religious and social relations. Confidential information was to be obtained and opinions expressed, as well as those of a more public nature. Stephens proved to be an efficient agent in these matters and his letters, together with the elaborate journal which he kept and sent regularly to the trustees, proved their most reliable source of information concerning the colony, as they are for the inquirer today. Stephens also did much to harmonize relations among the settlers and bring about a better state of affairs in the province. Upon the large questions in dispute, which have just been referred to, he had much to say which contributed to the mutual enlightenment of both the colonists and trustees.

The result of this discussion was that the trustees soon began to make concessions on the land question.[2] From an early date they expressed a special regard toward the daughters of freeholders who had made improvements on their lots. In such cases compensation for improvements would be made, provided the heiresses concerned were not already married to freeholders. According to the first detailed set of regulations concerning land, which were issued in 1735, provision was made that widows of freeholders should occupy during their lives the mansion house and one half of the lands improved by their husbands.[3] But these concessions, and possibly others that were made in special cases, did not suffice to check the growth of dissatisfaction. They still left too many prohibitions, the prospect of too high rents, and too many threats of forfeiture for the well-being of the colony. In 1738 this feeling began to find expression in complaints and protests. The Scotch at Darien, because of this and other grievances, threatened to depart from the province in a body.[4] About the same time, a petition, signed by more

[1] McCain, *op. cit.*, 148–152.
[2] Ga. Recs., I, 345; II, 271; III, 394, 397; IV, 361; V, 130, 210, 216, 230.
[3] *Ibid.*, III, 410.
[4] *Ibid.*, IV, 239.

than one hundred freeholders of Savannah and its neighborhood, was sent to the trustees.[1] The claim put forth in this was that a living could not be obtained from the land and therefore for many an outlet, if conditions were not more favorable, must be found in trade. As conditions necessary to their reasonable prosperity the petitioners demanded a tenure of land in fee simple and the introduction of negro slaves. In the second demand the Scotch and Salzburgers did not join, and a number of them sent protests against it. The trustees rejected both demands and reproved such of the magistrates as had promoted and signed the petition.

Shortly before this petition was received, the trustees further relaxed their system by the provision that an owner of land might designate any person as his successor, including female as well as male heirs and even those who were not relatives.[2] It was the belief of the trustees, confirmed in part by the representations of Stephens, that the evils complained of were due more to lack of thrift among the colonists than to the regulations concerning landholding. On the strength of this belief and of their record, the trustees appealed to posterity to judge between them and the petitioners as to which deserved the better of the colony. During the next two years or so further concessions were made, in the form of regulations which made possible holdings of two thousand acres and making possible leases for as long as twenty-one years. Some reduction also was made in the proportion of a grant which must be cultivated. These concessions, the effect of which, in true English fashion, was to make the system more complicated, in 1742 were embodied in a single order of the common council and sent to the colony.[3]

But the principle of inheritance in tail male had not yet been abandoned and free purchase and sale of land was still denied to the colonists. The rate of quit rent had not been lowered. The other questions in dispute had not been settled

---

[1] Ga. Recs., III, 422, 432; V, 75, 93, 95, *et seq.*

[2] *Ibid.*, 394.

[3] *Ibid.*, II, 393–401. It was during the controversies of this time that the pamphlet entitled, "A True and Historical Account of Georgia, etc." was prepared. Its authors were Tailfer, Anderson and Douglas, and it is one of the best statements of the views of the opposition. It is printed in Colls. of Ga. Hist. Soc. II.

and the war had added to the feeling of uncertainty in the province. When, therefore, it was determined to appeal directly to the house of commons Thomas Stephens was sent over to voice the discontent. Demands for privileges such as those of the other colonists, for the introduction of tenure in fee simple and for the reduction of quit rent to three shillings per hundred acres were made. In the discussion in the house considerable sentiment was shown in favor of the change in land tenure, but it was decided to leave all the disputed questions for adjustment between the trustees and their colonists except traffic in rum. That was approved by the house.[1] Under the influence of the sentiment expressed in the commons, the trustees now resolved to grant lands in fee simple to those who thereafter went to the colony at their own expense, but to retain certain restrictions on alienation, the amount to be held and the time within which improvements must be made. When these provisions were drafted into an act and submitted through the privy council to the law officers, they objected to it as providing for two tenures in the same province, a condition which they did not consider advisable. The matter was then dropped and tenure in tail male, with such others of the original restrictions on landholding which had not been removed, continued until 1750. Then, by resolution of the common council,[2] it was ordered that the tenure of all grants in the province be extended to an absolute inheritance and that this should be the form of all future grants. This brought the fee simple and the right of free trade in land for which the colonists had been agitating and removed one of the chief causes of discontent. In the course of the discussion of this subject the earl of Egmont was forced to admit that the restricted tenure had had an effect the opposite of what had been intended, for instead of keeping settlers in the colony it had driven them out, and now the freer tenure had become necessary in order to prevent it from being abandoned.[3]

The most distinctly moral reform to which the trustees committed themselves was the prohibition of the importation

---

[1] Ga. Recs., V, 636, 640; Jour. H. of Commons, XXIV.
[2] Ga. Recs., II, 500.
[3] *Ibid.*, 397.

and sale of rum, brandy and strong waters within their province. The idea seems first to have been suggested by Oglethorpe, who wrote to the corporation soon after his first arrival in Georgia that several of the colonists had died presumably from the effects of liquor. Taking up this in characteristic fashion as an isolated subject, the common council at once passed a resolution that the drinking of rum should be absolutely forbidden and all brought into the colony should be staved. This regulation found a place among the formal enactments of the trustees in 1735, all of which were approved by the privy council. By that time reports of the injurious effect of the traffic among the Indians served to connect the subject with legislation on trade with them. The law provided that none of the liquors specified should be brought into the province, required the destruction of any which had been brought in, and forbade the sale of any to Indians or whites. Violations of its provisions were made punishable by fines and incapacity for holding office in the colony. In the interest of peace and decency public houses and the retailing of liquor were to be steadily controlled.

But this was a counsel of perfection far beyond what was warranted by the spirit and practice of the times, both in Great Britain or the colonies. The weak administrative devices in Georgia were quite inadequate to the enforcement of a law which ran so directly counter to public sentiment as did this. Judging from the letters of Oglethorpe and Stephens and from the latter's journal, one would infer with certainty that actual prohibition was never even approximated at Savannah though drinking seems to have been less common in the southern parts of the province, while the Salzburgers were always temperate. Early in 1738 Stephens had found that at many houses liquor, and that of the worst sort from New England and elsewhere, had been smuggled in and was being sold privately.[1] He had charged the constable and tithingmen to present all such unlicensed houses at the courts, but he " could never get any such thing done." As explanations of this Stephens mentioned what were doubtless

[1] On Dec. 11, 1746, Stephens wrote that the dumping of rum had been going on ever since the act against it was passed. It was done partly through connivance; C. O. 5/641, Stephens to Montague.

two very common reasons for administrative inefficiency throughout the colonies, and these were that officials and their friends shared in the profits of the trade, and " an Unwillingness to be the Authors of Severity toward their Neighbours." About three months later the testimony of two of Stephens' servants after a drunken debauch showed that " private Rum Shops were become as common among the People, in Proportion as Gin-Shops formerly at London."[1] In a letter written more than a year later, Oglethorpe stated that juries at Savannah were acquitting the sellers of rum " in spite of Evidence."[2] One importer was commonly said to have so many friends among the freeholders that no jury would convict him, " though he tapped a Cask at Noonday."

Naturally the question of traffic in rum did not assume the prominence among the complaints which were preferred in England against the policy of the trustees as did other subjects. So far as it was urged, it was apparently brought into connection with the commercial interests of the colony. The importance of lumber as an article of export from its forests to the West Indies was dwelt upon, and it was said that this interest would be greatly promoted if rum could be imported in return. Therefore, at the very beginning of 1742 the common council ordered the secretary to write to Stephens to wink at the importation of rum and discourage seizures of it, though the licensing of its sale should be carefully regulated. This change of policy was due to positive information that the prohibitory act had not been and could not be enforced, and also to the fact that the market for lumber to the islands was restricted " because their rum, which makes port of return is prohibited." Therefore a tacit direction, without a public order, was given to cease enforcing the law, so that " it might not appear," wrote Egmont, " that we, without his Majesties' consent, undertook to repeal an Act of his passing and which we had ourselves applyed for."[3] Later, however, after the house of commons had approved a resolution, among those reported by its committee on Georgia, one that it would be an advantage to that province to per-

---

[1] Ga. Recs., IV, 62, 121, 122; XXII, 164.
[2] *Ibid.*, XXII, 165.
[3] *Ibid.*, V, 583, 635, 639, 648.

mit the importation of rum from the other British colonies, a bill to that effect was drafted and submitted to the board of trade. But it objected to certain restrictions which it contained on the importation of rum from the other colonies and Great Britain.[1] No further effort was made to modify the bill, and the original act was allowed to stand, though it was being openly ignored, during the remainder of the proprietary period.

An act for the exclusion of negroes and slave labor from Georgia provoked much more discussion than did that forbidding traffic in rum. It was the policy of the trustees concerning slavery and land titles which subjected them to the severest criticism and aroused most discontent within the province itself. It was to them that the lack of prosperity and growth in the colony was chiefly attributed by those who at the same time slurred over the part which indolence and thriftlessness on the part of the colonists had in the result. No feature of the policy adopted by the trustees more flatly contradicted the ideas of the time, especially those which found expression in the British colonial system, than did the prohibition of negro slavery. The official statements which were issued in explanation of this policy ran as follows:[2] In the preamble to the act of exclusion a justification was sought in the fact that blacks increase faster than whites and that, when the two were freely admitted as colonists, the growth of the latter was checked. When viewed, therefore, from the standpoint of defence, the presence of blacks was a source of weakness, a condition the seriousness of which was increased by the danger from slave insurrections and the ease with which a hostile state might be able to encourage such uprisings. The influence upon this reasoning of the condition which existed in the British West Indies and in South Carolina with their large excess in numbers of blacks over whites, is evident. Continuing the argument along a more narrowly economic line, the trustees observed that the first cost of a negro slave was equal to the cost of sending over a white servant and subsisting him for a year, and providing him with tools and other necessaries. It was pro-

[1] Ga. Recs., I, 406, 410, 453, 465.
[2] Ibid., I, 50; III, 376; V, 194, 195.

posed that the inhabitants of Georgia should devote themselves to the production of silk, wine and such other industries as, unlike tobacco, sugar, indigo and cotton, would not
require negro labor.  The climate also, even as far south as
Georgia, if proper care was exercised, was found by the Salzburgers and others compatible with the conditions of white
labor the year round.[1]  The real object sought by the trustees
was to provide a home for poor British subjects and foreign
Protestants who had been the victims of persecution, and to
establish a frontier for South Carolina which, owing to the
small number of its white inhabitants, was much exposed on
the south.  The filling of Georgia with slaves, whom the
Spanish would be likely to entice away or encourage to insurrection, would not promote any of these objects.  The connection between negroes and the land question was indicated
by the statement that if persons going over at their own expense were permitted to have slaves, the poor planters who
could not get them would be discouraged, and if slavery and
the free alienation of land were both permitted the poor
planter would mortgage his land to traders and planters and
thereby small properties would be swallowed up in large
estates.

These arguments were valid and their truth was not only
becoming evident at that time, but was to be confirmed by
later experience.  The difficulty, however, of maintaining such
a policy in a single infant colony at the middle of the eighteenth century was almost insuperable.  The sentiments and
policies of the times, both in Europe and America, were over-
whelmingly against such an experiment.  Could the trustees
have filled their province with colonists of such substantial
worth as the Salzburgers and many of the Scotch, and by
their labor have established the production of some of the
staples which they preferred, there might have been some
chance of success.  But the character of their own colonists
was too inferior to enable them to overcome the obstacles
inherent in the climate and soil of Georgia and in the prejudices of the times.  Great Britain at that time did not con-

---

[1] This was also the opinion of Oglethorpe and Stephens, of various
British among officers and of other observers.  See the Jours. of Stephens
and Egmont, V, 97, 98, 138, 169; XXII, 111.

tain a surplus population, available for colonizing purposes, in numbers and virility adequate to the settlement of such a colony as would have corresponded to the ideals of the trustees. Probably the average of the colonists whom they brought from England was inferior, physically and perhaps mentally and morally, to those who were then living in the colonies to the north of them. In character they resembled those whom John Smith and others denounced as the drones, or adventurers of the early Virginia settlement. The criticisms of them to be found in Stephens' Journal reminds one of the Jamestown settlers as described by Smith. It was therefore to be expected that when they felt the summer heats of Georgia and found the labor which was involved in clearing away its forests and tilling its soil, they would clamor for the aid of the African and insist that they could not compete under harder conditions than then were known by their rivals in South Carolina and the West Indies.

That was probably true, for it would have required a much higher type of men than the average then existing to have made a respectable success of Georgia on the basis of anything else than slave labor. In the course of a few years the increasing number of the colonists in Savannah and its neighborhood appeared to be becoming discontented. Stephens called these the "malcontents."[1] They met frequently at a certain tavern and this he calls their club. Some of the officials appeared as their leaders, and Stephens happened in at times to listen or join in the talk. The general tone of conversation was pessimistic. Georgia was not growing, people were leaving the province faster than they came in, there was no profit in agriculture and they must turn to trade. The colony was threatened with ruin. The evils of the land system, of course, occupied a prominent place in those discussions, but as time passed the inadequacy of white servants and of white labor in general to meet the needs of such a colony as theirs was insisted on more and more. It was claimed that the cost of production was lower in Carolina with slave labor than was possible under the economic system which had been established in Georgia. Therefore the de-

[1] See references in the index to the edition of Stephens' Journal in the Ga. Recs., IV, under "malcontents."

mand for the admission of slaves grew in volume, though
with the qualification that the number should be limited so
that the dangerous excess of blacks might be avoided.  In
this form it appeared in the numerously signed petitions of
December, 1738, to the trustees and later in the arguments
and petitions which Thomas Stephens submitted in England.[1]
In a conversation with Egmont, Stephens urged that the inhabitants of Georgia must have negroes, not as in Carolina
where they had so many that they had passed a law against
importing more, but at a moderate allowance of four or five
to one family of whites.  But Stephens had to admit that
the laws of Carolina against an excess of negroes were not
obeyed and could not be enforced and that when he was in
that province in 1737 it had 22,000 negroes and about 5,000
fighting men.  Egmont was emphatic in reference to the
probable fate of the small landholders who had no negroes,
but Stephens had the comfortable assurance concerning them
that they all might be provided for as overseers to the negroes
of planters in Georgia and South Carolina.  But he had to
admit that where there were negroes white men despised work.
To his mind, however, the doubtful features of the policy
were completely outweighed by what seemed to him the sure
prospect of a large influx of white population into Georgia
as soon as she permitted the introduction of negroes.  It is
true that a few negroes were first surreptitiously introduced
at Augusta and perhaps at other points along the Savannah
river and it was understood that more would come, with their
white owners, as soon as the prohibition was removed.  This
was certainly an important consideration as much was said
about the removal of people to other colonies and many
plantations were said to be deserted.[2]

When the question, along with the others which were raised
by Thomas Stephens' petition, came before the house of commons, the proposal to admit negroes was voted down by a
majority of nine, though Bladen, of the board of trade and
others were in favor of admitting them.  Shortly afterward
the opinion was expressed at a meeting of the trustees that
they " must come into Scheme of admitting Negroes or they

[1] Colls. Ga. Hist. Soc., II, 220;  Ga. Records, V, 475.
[2] Ga. Records, V, 451–453.

could get no money." A meeting was then arranged with
Sir John Barnard and Colonel Bladen to discuss the subject
of negroes. It was at this juncture, in disgust with what he
considered the neglect by the government of the true interests
of the colony,[1] Egmont resigned his seat in the common
council. Martyn, the secretary, under an order of the trustees, now wrote to William Stephens, at Savannah, to report
how negroes could be admitted to Georgia consistently with
the safety of the province.[2] Early in 1743, the question of
the admission of negroes was again brought up in the house
of commons, in connection with a vote of supply for Georgia.
Though some weighty opinions in favor of negroes were expressed, the petition in favor of their admission was laid on
the table and the supply was voted. Meantime Stephens had
written that in his opinion no negroes should be admitted
during the war with Spain, but that when peace should be
concluded four negroes should be allowed for one white man.[3]

After the close of the war the trustees, in an instruction to
William Stephens, reaffirmed their opposition to slave labor
and their resolve that it should never be permitted in Georgia.
But during the years which had intervened negroes had been
introduced and efforts to drive them out had been ineffectual.
In their case, as in that of rum, the immediate and dominant
self-interest of the settlers had prevailed to the nullification
of the resolves of the trustees. Now the president and assistants wrote that, in their opinion, an attempt to drive out the
negroes would depopulate the colony. Early in 1749 the
president and assistants, after formal action on the subject,
in a letter signed by them and by a great number of the inhabitants, asked that negroes be allowed in the colony under
the regulations and restrictions which were therein set forth.
In response to this the trustees petitioned the king in council
for the repeal of their act of 1735 excluding negroes from
Georgia. The repeal was effected in 1750 and a new act was
put in force.[4] Among the regulations imposed by this act

[1] Ga. Recs., V, 639, 643.
[2] Ibid., 648, 649; C. O. 5/667, July 26, 1742.
[3] Ga. Recs., V, 657, 677, 678, 681.
[4] Ibid., I, 56, 62, 506, 509, 530, 531; C. O. 5/668, Martyn to Pres. and
Assistants, May 19, 1749; C. O. 5/641, Coun. & Assis. to Martyn, Jan. 10,
1749.

was one that each planter might have four male negroes for every white male servant, that he must employ one negress in the production of silk, that no artificers except coopers should take a negro as an apprentice, while both an impost duty and an annual tax were levied on negroes. Though this interesting experiment of the trustees ended in failure, it should be remembered that it preceded by little more than a generation the movement of Clarkson and Wilberforce against the slave trade, a movement of which they must be considered as forerunners.

Oglethorpe's absorption in military affairs during his later years in Georgia strengthened his tendency toward lavish expenditure. This gradually provoked criticism on the part of his fellow trustees. Some of them complained that he suspended their orders and did many things on his own initiative, " whereby we are brought much in debt." Not only did he vigorously oppose efforts among the colonists to effect the reforms which they desired, but he tried to thwart amended orders of the trustees concerning tenure of lands.[1] On examining Oglethorpe's accounts, they found evidence of his extravagance. In November, 1739, it all resulted in their drafting a letter to him which was couched in terms so sharp that Egmont was forced to soften them, though even then they proved offensive to him. As Oglethorpe had complained that the magistrates in Georgia abused their powers and the people strove to deny him any authority, the trustees, in their letter, declared themselves " equally sensible with you that there must be a steady and regular manner of acting in Georgia, which all centers in every man's exercising faithfully the powers given and not exceeding them, more especially in not exceeding the estimates sent over or misapplying the sums appropriated to each particular service, which the Trustees expect their Officers and Commissioners appointed to make the disbursements will be punctual in." A few weeks later the trustees ordered that the sola bills for use in Georgia in 1740 should not be signed by Oglethorpe, thus excluding him " from handling our money, which was thought a necessary and prudent step." [2]

---

[1] Ga. Recs., V, 111, 117, 258, 266–270.          [2] Ibid., 287.

Oglethorpe's authority in the province, however, continued so great that the inhabitants were uncertain whether he or the trustees was their governor.[1] The magistrates sometimes took their directions from him and at other times he said he had no power to direct. In the following December, James Vernon, after observing at a meeting of the trustees, "how ill our orders are executed in Georgia, by reason of Colonel Oglethorpe's preventing their execution when not approved by him, from whence much disgrace and mischief had fallen on the Trustees and Colony." He then commented further on the mistaken idea that Oglethorpe must be consulted before any order of the trustees could be executed, depriving them of any true knowledge of the state of the colony, and urged the board to consider "whether it were not necessary to vest some person with a superior authority to act in the Province, . . . and to make that person wholly independent of Colonel Oglethorpe, whose time is so much taken up with the military concerns of the Colony that 'tis impossible he should conduct the Civil concerns of it." Vernon went on to argue that a president and council should be established in each of the two divisions of the province, the northern and southern, they thereby preserving a greater independence of the crown than would be possible with only one executive head. The appointment of one president, approved of by the king, Vernon considered would be almost equivalent to a surrender of their charter, for the trustees could not remove him without royal consent and he would always be subject to orders from the various boards in England. He expressed the belief that Colonel Stephens, the secretary, would be just the man for president of the northern half of the province, and, as to the southern division, they might compliment General Oglethorpe by naming him president. All the trustees who were present expressed themselves as pleased with Vernon's proposal and at their request he promised to submit it in outline.

During the winter and much of the spring of 1741, in intervals when they were not occupied with business in parliament, the common council was preparing to carry Vernon's

[1] Ga. Recs., V, 375.

plan into execution.[1]  On April 15, 1741, it was voted that
Georgia be divided into two counties, under the names Savannah and Frederica, the former including the settlements
on the Savannah and Ogeechee rivers and the latter those
to the southward of these.  The government of each county
was placed under a president and four assistants.  Stephens
was named as the head of the first board of Savannah county
and Oglethorpe was asked to nominate a suitable person to
hold the corresponding position in Frederica county.  Instructions,[2] both public and private, were prepared for these
officials.  In the former were included the new regulations
for granting and leasing land.  The latter, in addition to many
regulations of the character usual in proprietary governments,
contained a provision for licensed sale of liquor.  Among the
many provisions concerning executive affairs was one that
no public money should be issued except on the warrant of
the president with the consent of the assistants or a majority
of them.  Sola bills were henceforth to be issued to the president and accounts of expenditures must be sent by him to
the trustees.  The journal of the president and assistants,
together with full reports of the state of the colony, must also
be regularly sent.  These must include accounts of conditions
at Augusta and the various plantations and suggestions for
their management.  The right of appeals from town courts
to the president and assistants in cases involving £20 or more
was guaranteed, and in cases involving £100 or more appeals
might be taken to the trustees.  Constables and tithingmen
in the towns were to be appointed by the president with the
advice of the assistants.  Little power was really given to the
new officials, as they were to act in all matters under the
control of the common council of the trustees.

When the time came for settling up the new government,
Oglethorpe was so engrossed in plans for defence that he did
not nominate any one for magistrates in the southern part
of the province.  Therefore it was only over Savannah county
that for the present that government by president and assistants was established.  The government continued in this

---

[1] Ga. Recs., II, 367;  V, 432, 494, 512;  XXIV, Stephens to Martyn,
Sept. 21, 1741.

[2] C. O. 5/670, MS. Recs. of Ga., 33, Apr. 20, 1741.

form for about two years. In June, 1743, an order was issued [1] by the trustees that the president of the county of Savannah should be president of the entire province, the three bailiffs of Savannah, together with Samuel Mercer, should be the assistants, and its recorder should be the clerk of the province. By this measure the government of Georgia was organized in the form of a provincial governor and council without an assembly. It continued in this form as long as Georgia remained a proprietary province. From the elaborate journal of the president and assistants which has been preserved, it is possible to follow the course of their administration in detail.[2] In 1750 Stephens was incapacitated by age and infirmity for longer service. He was succeeded by Henry Parker and a little later by Patrick Graham.[3] The president of a single county had received £80 a year as his salary, but when he became president of the province this was increased to the modest sum of £100. He probably received some fees in addition and could hold another office, from which some income would be derived.[4] The assistants received £20 a year, with the privilege of serving in another office. The recorder received £32 and the minor officials still smaller salaries. The remuneration was much less than was received in the royal provinces, but compared fairly with what was common in chartered colonies.

The routine executive duties of this board differed in no essential respect from that of other similar bodies in the colonies. The charities of the trustees in the province, in the form of advances of money or food to disabled laborers or others, were dispensed by the president and assistants. They heard petitions on all subjects, the more important and perplexing matters being referred to the trustees. They granted permits, as for building wharves, and levied wharf rates and duties. They licensed taverns. Subject to the appointment of agents and the furnishing of permits by the trustees, the board exercised a general supervision over Indian affairs and received delegations of the tribes when they came, usually

---

[1] Ga. Recs., V, 700, 703.
[2] This fills Vol. VI of the Ga. Recs.
[3] Ibid., 332.
[4] McCain, op. cit.

at Savannah. The most important events of this kind occurred in connection with the Bosomworths and the visit of the Lower Creeks at Savannah in their interest in July, 1749.

At first the board had little to do with the granting of land and when they did make a grant it was subject to approval by the trustees. But in 1750 this was changed and from that time on the local board was given practically a free hand in this matter. Its activity in the issue of land grants increased and they were made without reference to approval by the trustees.[1] When it became necessary to found a new town, the president and assistants authorized the plan and layout of the lots, showing that the land system of localities in this new province was the same as it was in the other southern colonies. In the regulations which were enforced for the care of the herds of cattle belonging to the trustees or to the Germans at Ebenezer, or to others at the various cowpens, we have an anticipation of ranching at a much later time in the far west.[2]

The creation of the board of president and assistants also made some changes in the judicial arrangements of the province. Though the titles of bailiffs, recorder and conservators of the peace implied that their duties would be similar to those of the corresponding officers in England, their jurisdiction of necessity far exceeded that of municipal courts, or of justices of the peace, in the mother country, and roughly corresponded to that of the ordinary common law courts. They exercised both civil and criminal jurisdiction extended to the gravest crimes as well as to misdemeanors, and to all civil suits, real, personal and mixed. Thus the authority of all the English common law courts, as in the case of the supreme, general or provincial courts of other colonies, was merged in one. And yet in form and often in the lack of dignity which attended its sessions, this bailiff's courts was no more than the hustings in London. On the supposition that an English municipal court was to be reproduced at Savannah, very few instructions were given to its officials and they were left to find their way as best they could amid the duties, old and new, which were thrust upon them. Thus a

[1] Ga. Recs., VI, 353, 357, 360 et seq.
[2] Ibid., 126, 154, 170, 184, 311 et seq.

fresh example was furnished of what, in the management of the colonies, may be called the method or essence of English liberty. If one attempted to scrutinize it more carefully, possibly other and less complimentary terms might be applied to it.

When counties were formed and government by president and assistants was established three of the bailiffs of Savannah were appointed to the board of assistants. This board or council was also granted appellate jurisdiction over cases from the town court when the sums involved were £20 or over and provision was also made for appeals to the trustees in cases involving £100 or more. As the bailiffs, who were judges in the lower court, sat also among the assistants, this body was not well fitted to act as a court of appeal. This arrangement lasted only four years (1741–1745), for the town court of Frederica was suspended, as well as the appellate jurisdiction of the president and assistants. Of appeals to the privy council, there was only one instance during the proprietary period, and that was the case of Joseph Watson, an Indian trader. A Savannah jury found him guilty of using unguarded expressions the tendency of which was to incite certain Indians to murder, but it recommended him to the mercy of the court on the general ground that possibly he was not of sound mind. Causton, however, ordered Watson confined as a lunatic. So prejudiced an account of this case was sent to the trustees that they refused to entertain an appeal in this case. Watson's wife then appealed to the king in council and the trustees were requested to answer this appeal in writing. They sent to Savannah for affidavits and a full statement of the case, but meantime prepared for the council a representation of their own.[1] But before this was sent a query was submitted to the attorney general whether by sending it the trustees would be considered as parties to such complaints and a precedent would thereby be established for admitting appeals from Georgia to the privy council in criminal cases. What the opinion was is not known, but from the general attitude of the law officers, as well as from the fact that the case was at once settled out of court by an order from the trustees for the release of Watson, the inference

[1] Ga. Recs., I, 277, 285, 286; McCain, *op. cit.*, 209–212.

would be that the government stood ready to bring Georgia under its direct judicial control.

In 1751 the assembly of that year petitioned for the establishment of a court of equity, but that request was denied by the trustees because of the expense involved and of the encouragement it was likely to give to litigation, the excess of which already formed a standing subject of complaint in the correspondence of Stephens and others. It was not until 1748, just before the close of the third intercolonial war, that the establishment of an admiralty court in the province was proposed as a tribunal which could be used specially for the condemnation of prizes. At first the trustees thought they had the right to establish it, but were soon undeceived. No action, however, was taken by the British government, and proprietary Georgia remained without an admiralty court. Thus it was that the board of assistants did not attain to the judicial functions which were often performed by the council in other provinces, and for this reason the judicial system of Georgia remained very incomplete until after 1752. The appellate jurisdiction of the trustees was continuously operative. Charges against magistrates were also frequently presented before the trustees and disputes between magistrates as well came before them for settlement. These fell within the sphere of administration, but their effect should have been felt in the personnel and procedure of the courts. But magistrates were treated very leniently by the trustees and the qualifications of men who were available for the offices of bailiff and recorder in the colony were so low that a more or less impoverished type of frontier justice was the best which was then possible. There were no lawyers in the province and the widespread prejudice against them as promoters of litigation was as strong in Georgia as it was anywhere in the colonies.

As was the case at the beginning with both Virginia and New York, Georgia passed through nearly the whole of its proprietary period without an assembly. The colonists were allowed no share in local government, except so far as they held offices under the trustees. This, however, did not occasion complaint and we have seen that the grievances of these colonists were of a different order and an assembly seems never to have been demanded as likely to furnish a means of redressing them. The reason for this will be found in the fact that the expenses of Georgia were met by parliamentary grants and by rents and other forms of revenue which were strictly territorial in character. It was never necessary to resort to taxation in proprietary Georgia and therefore the occasion for an assembly was not felt by the colonists. But in March, 1750, the committee of correspondence of the common council recommended the calling of an assembly.[1] The reason which they gave was that many of the settlements had now been formed in different parts of the province and it was necessary that the trustees should be informed of the condition of these in particular and of the province in general. It was also feared that if the period assigned for proprietary rule should be allowed to pass without provision for an assembly to assert the independence of Georgia, it would not be able to continue as a separate province but would be annexed to South Carolina.[2] Provision, however, was made for only one assembly, to meet at Savannah in 1751, the date to be fixed by the president and assistants, and the session should not continue longer than three weeks or a month. The various territorial units within the province — towns, villages and districts — were to be represented in proportion to their population, Savannah to have four deputies and the others a less number. The arrangement of details concerning districts and the election in general was left to the president and assistants, and concerning these matters the board "had frequent Consultation."[3] In the act of the trustees which authorized the holding of the assembly, its function was declared to be to debate and represent to the trustees what should appear to be for the benefit of each particular settlement and the province in general.[4]

The writs of election were issued on December 15, 1750, and the assembly was to meet on the fifteenth of the following January. It is probable that the electors were the heads of families in the respective districts, and the elected were in

[1] Ga. Recs., II, 498 *et seq.*
[2] Martyn to Parker, July 11, 1750.
[3] Ga. Recs., VI, 368.
[4] *Ibid.*, I, 547.

most cases freeholders — though not in all cases — and those especially who represented Savannah, Augusta and Darien, were the leading men of the province. Francis Harris, a leading merchant of Savannah, was chosen speaker. The deliberations of the session resulted in the reporting to the president of a list of eleven grievances, nearly all of which related to improvements which were considered necessary to facilitate the trade of the port. The need of suitable officers for the guard and militia and of repairs on the court house were the only subjects of a different nature which were touched upon. The Georgia authorities themselves agreed to supply all these needs except the purchase of a pilot boat, which because of its cost they thought should be referred to the trustees. A number of requests were also made of the trustees, these being signed by the speaker and sent under the seal of the town court. Among these the more important was a protest against an annexation of Georgia to South Carolina and a suggestion that the charter be renewed; and urgent plea that private persons be forbidden to secure the reserved Indian lands near Savannah and on the islands along the coast, this being occasioned by the demands of the Bosomworths; a request that the trustees would apply for a reduction of quit rents, an urgent petition that the assembly might have the power to make by-laws, a request that a court of equity be established at Savannah, the desire that negroes might be imported from other colonies free of duty. All of the requests made by the assembly were granted except the three important ones concerning a power to pass by-laws, the establishment of a chancery court at Savannah and the free importation of negroes. It was evident from this that the trustees intended to keep strict control over the colony until their lease of power terminated. They continued the assembly, in existence, but did not allow it even the semblance of legislative power and later made the qualifications for election to it more strict. No one could be elected unless he had one hundred mulberry trees planted and properly kept on every fifty acres of land which he held, nor unless he had strictly conformed to the requirement as to the proportion of negroes to white servants in his possession. But the laying of such emphasis in this connection on the silk culture and on the restriction in the use of negroes proved useless, for no further assemblies were summoned until after Georgia had been taken over by the crown. The temporary nature of the proprietorship may be considered to furnish the chief explanation of the insignificant part played by the assembly among the early institutions of Georgia.

# CHAPTER X

In the treatment of ecclesiastical relations during the seventeenth century, as well as in the chapter on the extension of Anglicanism in the early eighteenth century, detailed reference has been made to the Independents or Puritans of the New England type and to the Quakers. Occasional references have also been made to other dissenting bodies and, especially in considering the subject of immigration, to the appearance of new sects in the colonies and the great strength which was added to many of the older ones has also been noted. Of the German sects, Lutherans, Moravians, Mennonites and the rest, perhaps enough has been said to satisfy the purposes of this work. To the Presbyterians, the Baptists and the Methodists — the last named not appearing until later — not sufficient attention has been given. But we have now reached a time when the two former constituted or were presently to form important religious bodies among the colonists. Their strength was added to that of the general body of opponents of the English church throughout the colonies and that of the Baptists to the opposition which was directed against the Puritan establishments in New England, a movement which soon began very appreciably to increase in volume.

For the sake of clearness and definiteness in the discussion of New England and its institutions,[1] the term Puritan has been restricted to those who settled that section and to the type of church and commonwealth which was there developed. Because of their clear cut views in reference to both church and civil power and of the opportunity which they had to put them into practice, the early New Englanders conformed very closely to the Calvinistic ideal. But Calvinism, of course, had a much wider extension than this, both on the European Continent and in the British Isles. Scotland was

---

[1] Osgood, Am. Colonies in the 17th Century, I.

almost wholly Presbyterian and in England the Presbyterians formed a very important part of the general Puritan body, while of their establishments in Ireland we are well aware. Under the early Stuarts there was also a strong body of Puritan sympathizers within the English church itself, men who disliked the magnifying of the power of the bishops and the enforcement of conformity to many high church practices which was begun under Whitgift and continued by such men as Bancroft and Laud. To this class belonged not a few of the members of the London Company which founded Virginia and settled the Bermudas. The attempt to found a colony on Providence Island proceeded also from the same group. Many who held opinions of this type never passed beyond the stage of protest or of mild nonconformity. In Massachusetts and Connecticut also we know that from an early period there were Presbyterians. The criticisms and demands of Dr. Child and his associates in 1646 revealed their existence with the utmost clearness. Puritanism of the New England type itself we have called Presbyterianized Congregationalism, meaning by this that the two communions closely approached one another even in their polities, while in their spirit they were substantially the same. Both had ruling elders and held synods and, with slight variations on the part of the New England churches, both accepted the Westminster Confession of Faith. In Connecticut after the Saybrook Platform had gone into effect it became even more difficult than before to distinguish between the spirit of the two systems. The exact gradation and power of sessions, presbyteries and synods as they existed in the Presbyterian system was not reproduced by the New England Puritans, but so close was the agreement of the two, both in form and spirit, that the terms Presbyterian was often freely applied to the churches, especially of Connecticut in the eighteenth century.

By the beginning of the eighteenth century Presbyterian churches were also widely scattered through the provinces to the south of New England.[1] Before the end of the previous

[1] Consult Hodge, Constitutional History of the Presbyterian Church; the volumes of Webster and Gillett on the same subject; Briggs, American Presbyterianism.

century a group of Presbyterians was living on Elizabeth river in lower Virginia. By 1710 four or five Presbyterian churches existed on the Eastern Shore of Maryland and there Francis Makemie had been laboring for many years, he also travelling far and wide as an itinerant preacher throughout the colonies. At this date there were eight churches of the same faith in Pennsylvania and the Lower Counties, three of them being located respectively at Philadelphia, Newcastle and Lewes. In New Jersey there were congregations at Freehold and Woodbridge. By the early years of the century several Presbyterian congregations were in existence in South Carolina, while in New York they early developed at the eastern end of Long Island, at Jamaica and Newtown, in Westchester county and in New York City.

Owing to their scattered condition and their inadequate equipment of church buildings and ministers, these churches were not formed upon the strict Presbyterian model. In New York, at first, the towns where such congregations were strongest seized control of the offices of vestrymen and church wardens and in that capacity, as we have seen, prevented to a large extent the execution of Fletcher's act for the establishment of the Church of England. " The American Presbyterian Church," says Briggs,[1] " began historically at the bottom. . . . It was not a reconstruction of an old Papal system into a new Presbyterian system, as in Scotland. It was a free and natural growth in accordance with the preferences of the congregations themselves. It was not imposed upon the people by civil and ecclesiastical tribunals." Such were the foundations which were laid before the immigration of large numbers of Scotch and Irish Presbyterians began in the eighteenth century. In 1706, under the lead of Makemie and with the aid of missionaries sent out from Great Britain, a presbytery or meeting of ministers for mutual edification was started at Philadelphia. For some years this consisted only of clergymen from Pennsylvania, Delaware and Maryland. It was a free missionary organization and did not claim jurisdiction beyond its own members. For their supply of ministers, the churches which composed it were dependent upon New England — graduates of Harvard and later of Yale

---

[1] American Presbyterianism, 131.

— and upon men who, upon solicitation were sent over from England, Scotland and Ireland. Thus the body became inclusive of the ideas and tendencies which were represented in all the Presbyterian churches of the British dominions. To such an extent were the Presbyterians strengthened in this way by growth at home and by immigration, that in 1717 the Synod of Philadelphia was organized and this was joined by the churches of New Jersey and New York. All the Presbyterians of the middle colonies and Maryland were thus united in one body, and presently Jonathan Dickinson, pastor at Elizabethtown, New Jersey, appeared as their ablest preacher and theologian, a staunch controversialist and a man of large ability as an organizer. From William Tennent and his Log College at Neshaminy, Pennsylvania, emanated an educational influence and missionary zeal which were to constitute another important force in spreading the Presbyterian faith. It was this communion, buttressed by the united Congregational and Presbyterian churches of New England and flanked by the Quakers of Pennsylvania and the neighboring colonies, which formed the opposition to the advance of Anglicanism throughout the northern and middle colonies.

Prior to the great Scotch-Irish migration through the Valley of Virginia and thence southward into the western sections of the Carolinas a few Presbyterian churches had been formed in the coast region of South Carolina. These were located at Charlestown, James Island, Edisto Island, Port Royal and at a few points farther toward the interior. The Scotch element was strong among them and in 1723 a presbytery was formed, known as the Presbytery of James Island. At the opposite extremity of the colonial territory, in northern New England, the Presbyterian interest was strengthened and brought into clear relief by the settlement of Scotch Irish at Londonderry, New Hampshire, and at various points in Maine. Here and there also, in Congregational centres, Presbyterian churches were formed. The result of this was the organization, in 1729, of the Presbytery of Londonderry, of which James McGregorie, the pastor of that town, was the leading founder. In the Synod of Philadelphia, as well as in one or both of the outlying presbyteries, as a reflection of controversies which were going on in the United Kingdom, the form under which subscription to the Westminster Confession should be enforced and the extent to which it should be carried soon became a mooted question. Sermons were preached on both sides and controversial pamphlets [1] were published. In 1729 action was taken upon this subject by the Synod of Philadelphia and it was in harmony with the less rigid requirements of the churches in England and Ireland. But all were pronounced in their adhesion to the Westminster Confession in its essentials, including the use of both the Longer and Shorter Catechisms. It was Dickinson who led the more liberal party in the synod, and opposed to it was a strong element which desired the acceptance of the standards with verbal exactness. Thus stood the Presbyterians prior to the Great Awakening and the rise of Methodism. In extension, organization and aggressiveness they were or were likely to become the most formidable opponents of the growth of the English Church.

Since the persecution of Clarke, Crandall and Holmes, and the organization of the first Baptist church in Massachusetts, that sect had been gradually increasing in numbers in New England.[2] Swansea, Charlestown and later Boston were among the localities where such bodies were first gathered. Thomas Gould and several of his associates in founding the church at Charlestown — which was later removed to Boston — were imprisoned and otherwise persecuted for their faith. The attitude of the churches and of the government under Bradstreet continued to be relentlessly hostile to them. The Reforming Synod of 1675, as usual, coupled Anabaptists with Quakers as dangerous heretics and disturbers of public order, whose continued presence in the colony was one of the chief occasions of God's displeasure which was manifested by a decay of the true faith and other evident judgments upon

[1] Briggs, *op. cit.*, 208 *et seq.* For the view of stricter Presbyterians, see Hodge, I.

[2] The older histories of the Baptists are by Backus, Semple and Benedict, the first named confining his attention to New England and the second to Virginia. Benedict produced an ill-digested account of the whole movement, but accurate as to details. Morgan Edwards produced authentic accounts of the rise of the Baptists in Pennsylvania, New Jersey, Delaware and Rhode Island. The recent historians of the movement are Armitage and Newman, the volume of the latter being in the American Church History Series.

New England. On one occasion, in 1680, on the complaint
that the Baptists had erected a meeting-house in violation of
law, the building was for a time closed by the magistrates.
Two or three years later William Screven, with his associates,
who had gathered a small church at Kittery, Maine, were
forced by threats of persecution to remove to South Carolina,
where they added materially to the strength of the Baptists
in that province. But Massachusetts was already in too
serious difficulties with the British government to admit of a
continuance of its former rigid attitude, and the break which
occurred with the recall of the charter brought to both
Quakers and Baptists a grudging toleration of their worship.
Until the Great Awakening, conditions in New England, outside of Rhode Island, continued unfavorable to the extension
of the Baptist faith, though toward 1720 even the Mathers
began to soften in their attitude toward it. In Connecticut
the Baptists gained no foothold whatever until well into the
eighteenth century, and then they were confined to a few
congregations in the southeastern part of the colony.[1] Rhode
Island was, of course, the original centre and home of this
body of Christians, and according to a rough estimate made
in 1714 one-fifth of the population of that colony was included within their membership.[2] The Baptists and Quakers
together included perhaps one-half, possibly a majority, of
its people.

On this continent it was first in Rhode Island that the
Baptists had opportunity to show their democratic tendencies
without fear or obstruction. The same was true of the
Quakers and together they gave to Rhode Island its chief
characteristics and through her expressed their ideals.
Though it is probable that Roger Williams was not technically a Baptist, in his essential views and characteristics he
was one with them. In their use of Scripture, and particularly of the New Testament, they were literalists and upon

---

[1] A specimen of the controversies which were carried on over forms of
baptism, the baptism of children and the lawfulness of compelling people
to contribute to the support of an established ministry, may be seen in
John Bulkeley's "An Impartial Account of a late debate at Lyme, Connecticut," New London, 1729.

[2] Memorial of Rev. Honeyman to Gen. Nicholson, May 7, 1714, Ms. Papers
of S. P. G.

certain points branches of the sect, both in Europe and America, went to extremes in this direction. Their insistence upon one particular form of baptism was also an instance in point. Their opposition to infant baptism was particularly offensive to the Puritans of Massachusetts and Connecticut. When combined with Calvinism, as has been the case almost everywhere in America, this was accompanied by a staunch adherence to the principle that the membership of churches should consist only of those who were proved to be regenerate. This brought the Baptists into direct issue with supporters of the half-way covenant and all their works. A branch of the sect, who were especially strong in southwestern Rhode Island and appeared also in New Jersey, observed the seventh day instead of Sunday, while the Rogerenes who caused much disturbance in southeastern Connecticut were reckoned among the Baptists. The organization of the early Baptist churches was informal. They laid little stress on ordination to the ministry and opened a wide scope to lay preaching. It was only after some time that their congregations came to be bound together in loose associations. In their simple democratic polity — a close imitation of what they understood to have been the condition of the churches in Apostolic times — the Baptists followed the principles of Robert Browne, from which the Independents of New England had departed. The insistence by the Baptists upon the complete separation of the church from the civil power and perfect freedom of worship allied them still again with Browne. Their scrupulosity led a large body among them to insist upon the laying on of hands as a necessary form in the admission of the new convert into the church. Upon this issue the sect early divided and those who practised the imposition of hands were known — following Hebrews vi, 1, 2 — as six-principle Baptists.

New Jersey and Pennsylvania, with their tolerant attitude in religion, offered specially favorable opportunities for the spread of Baptist churches. Before the end of the seventeenth century, Baptists, coming from England, Ireland and from Long Island, began to appear in New Jersey. A church was formed in 1688 at Middletown in the Monmouth Patent. In the next year one was formed in the neighboring town of Piscataway, and later at Cohansey, Cape May and Hopewell.

In 1688 also Baptists of Welsh extraction established themselves at Pennepak — now Dublin — in Bucks County, Pennsylvania, and a decade later a church was organized in Philadelphia.  Another congregation of much importance was that
at Welsh Tract in northern Delaware.  With the settlement
of Mennonites and Dunkers in Pennsylvania, Germans of a
kindred faith contributed largely in numbers to the strength
of the Baptist faith in the middle colonies.  Here again this
mild type of religious radicals coexisted with the Quakers
with whom they shared many qualities in common.  In 1707
a Baptist association — the first in America — was formed
at Philadelphia.  A few congregations were gathered in Maryland and in some of the lower counties of Virginia.  Slight
beginnings also were made in North Carolina.  The growth
and extension of this sect, which by 1730 had begun to secure
a foothold throughout the colonial area, added another to
the formidable list of dissenting bodies which, if they agreed
in nothing else, would surely be united in opposition to a wide
extension of the English Church and to any assumption on
its part of leadership and control.

In estimating the strength of the opposition to episcopacy,
however, one rather important point should be noted.  While
the Anglicans had the active favor and support of their church
and, to an extent, of the government at home, the Independents and Presbyterians in England had no organization for
this purpose.  The only help which their co-religionists in
the colonies received from that quarter was the sympathy
expressed by individuals or small groups.  The Church of
Scotland, however, had missionary societies which gave a certain support to Presbyterians in the colonies.  In 1718 the
standing committee of the S. P. G. of the English Church
reported [1] that a society of North Britain of the same name
had sent missionaries into the Delaware region, who had
formed themselves into a society and united with the Synod
of Glasgow.  To offset their influence it was resolved to send
a missionary of the English Church to Lewes on the Delaware.  Other references also show that the spread of Presbyterianism in the colonies was attributed in part to the direct
influence of the Scotch Church.  Later in the century the

[1] Ms. Journal of S. P. G.

Society in Scotland for Propagating Christian Knowledge, of which the well known Daniel Williams was a patron, for a time supported a few missionaries among the Indians of New England, Long Island and along the courses of the Delaware and Susquehanna rivers.[1]   Among their number was David Brainerd.  The Quakers also, through their local and general meetings, both in Great Britain and the colonies, and the active correspondence which was kept up between them, an organization was maintained and help given to Quakers in the colonies which in some respects was perhaps even more effective than that which the Anglicans received.[2]

The attitude which all these sects took toward man and the world was essentially pauline and mediaeval.[3]   They regarded man as by nature corrupt and helpless.  He had originally been created holy, but he had fallen and now could be restored or saved only by divine grace.  This was un-merited, the pure gift of God.  The world also was evil, under a curse and doomed to destruction.  The object to which the sects were directing all their efforts, for which they existed, was to save men from this world and secure for them an inheritance of bliss in another world.  Human nature and the world outside man had no interest to them except so far as they were related to these supposed eternal verities.  To their minds this was a God-centered not a man-centered world and their mental attitude toward it should not be one of in-quiry but of humility and faith.  The only reliable knowledge which was procurable about the world was contained in the Bible, which came to man by divine revelation, was inspired and as a whole should be accepted, cherished and taught as the only guide which offered humanity any salvation or way of escape.  The Presbyterians and Congregationalists of New England and other sections belonged in the main to the scholastic type of Christians, who in the later period of the Reformation had given themselves largely to the support of creeds and formulas, in the light of which they interpreted the Bible and the sayings of Jesus.  This also was the atti-

---

[1] Briggs, Am. Presbyterianism, 297–303.

[2] This point is brought out in Miss Susan M. Reed's monograph, Church and State in Massachusetts, 1690–1740.   University of Illinois Studies in the Social Sciences, III.

[3] See McGiffert, Protestant Thought before Kant, and other writers.

tude of the Lutherans and of Calvinists taken as a whole. The Anglicans occupied a similar attitude, though their interest in the liturgy and polity which they had inherited, together with a certain lack of earnestness, gave them a spirit of less intensity or greater mildness than was generally shown by their rivals. The Quakers and most of the German sects belonged to the pietistic type of Protestants. This spirit was shared by the Baptists and an element among all the radical sects was susceptible to influences of this kind. The view which the pietists took of man and the world was not different from that already described, but in their religious life they laid more stress on personal piety than on correctness of belief.

Taking therefore the sects as a whole and including the Anglicans among them, the conclusion must be that their attitude toward the world was essentially mediaeval, at least it was not modern, and that their extension in the colonies or elsewhere did not of itself mean enlightenment or progress. Rather it implied intellectual and moral stagnation and in many quarters actually resulted in that. But fortunately there were two ways of escape. One was through the perpetual conflict between sects which, in the long run, was sure to tell in favor of liberty. The other was the discrediting of the point of view taken by them all, by the shifting of interest from theories concerning the deity and his relation to the universe to the study of man in society and in his natural environment. For two centuries signs had been slowly multiplying in Europe which indicated that a change of this kind was possible. Philosophers, scientists, theorists upon the subject of religion, men of various nationalities and at different times had challenged or thrown doubt on the prevailing views and indicated that there was another and possibly a better way. Writings from the pens of the deists and others were already in existence which gave the clue and pointed the way. The writings of Locke led in this direction and they were highly esteemed by the few in the colonies who were reading them. But so unacquainted were they with this type of thought and so preoccupied with its opposite that they failed to see the real implications of his philosophy. Of works with analogous purport in other languages nothing was known in the colonies. And when the writings of the deists began to appear, coming as they did in part from obscure authors and showing a spirit of radical divergence from accepted views, they were almost everywhere denounced as false or atheistic and regarded with mingled fear and contempt. Culture in any except the traditional form was totally lacking in the colonies, and ideas which differed from this must wait for more favorable conditions before there would be any chance of their acceptance. It is with these considerations in mind that the modern man should view the religious phenomena of the seventeenth and eighteenth centuries in the American colonies. A point therefore has been reached where the subject of ecclesiastical relations can again be viewed in their connection with the English Church and the efforts that were made for its extension in the colonies.

In the year of the conclusion of the treaty of Utrecht Henry Compton died. John Robinson, who was soon to succeed him in the bishopric of London, was at the same time engaged in the negotiation of that celebrated treaty. He was then bishop of Bristol, to which dignity he had been raised in 1710, after long diplomatic service in Sweden and elsewhere on the continent. It was owing to his knowledge of British interests which had been gained in this way that Robinson, like a mediaeval bishop, was selected for this task. Soon after his return at the close of the negotiations he was appointed to the see of London and held this office until his death, in 1723. Compton had received his early training in the army and is said never to have quite lost the military bearing. Robinson had been trained in the diplomatic service. Edmund Gibson, who was appointed bishop of London on the death of Robinson and held it until his own death, in 1748, was a scholar and antiquary, the author and compiler of many learned works on the history of the English Church. Under these three prelates, Compton, Robinson and Gibson, differing widely in their training and character, the fortunes of the English Church in the colonies were largely determined. Under Robinson, already well advanced in years when he was appointed, little was done by the metropolitan to advance the interests of his church in America.

But Gibson was a man of a different type. Much more

scholarly than Compton, he shared the latter's energy as an administrator, and throughout his incumbency by interviews in London, by abundant correspondence and frequent pastoral letters, Gibson sought to inform himself concerning conditions in the colonies and to make his influence felt there. Until his time the bishops of London had drifted on without an express grant from the crown authorizing them to exercise jurisdiction over the colonies.[1]  In the spirit of Compton, but with more scholarly thoroughness, Gibson at once sought to remedy this defect.  So far as he could find, no express authority for the exercise of his jurisdiction there existed except the commissions and instructions to the governors.[2] These he considered to be insufficient, and in fact they seemed to imply that the consent of the governors might be necessary to enable commissaries to perform their duties.  Instructions to some governors implied that they might remove offending ministers.  In Barbados a governor had secured the passage of a law entirely excluding ecclesiastical processes. Therefore, Gibson petitioned the king in council for a commission under the great seal which should extend only to the clergy and to such other matters as concerned the repair of churches and the decent performance of divine service therein.  This was referred to the law officers and they expressed the opinion that the authority by which the bishop of London had acted in the plantations was insufficient, that it rested solely in the crown by virtue of the supremacy, and that such a commission as was requested was the most proper way of granting it.  Therefore, on April 29, 1728, the commission in its final form was issued.  It empowered him, by himself or through commissaries of his appointment, to exercise ecclesiastical jurisdiction in the dominions according to the laws and canons of the Church of England.  This was to include the visitation of all churches of that order, the

---

[1] In C. O. 5/390, 12, B. T. Commercial, Trade Papers, under date of 1717 is a valuable report by the board of trade on this subject.  It was occasioned by a dispute in Barbados.

[2] In answer to his queries, Garden, the commissary of South Carolina, made the most detailed reply.  Quoted from the Fulham MSS. by Cross, Anglican Episcopate, etc., 54.  The steps taken for securing the commission and the names of the proposed council of appeal are given in Acts P. C. Col, 1720–1745, pp. 88–92.

citation of rectors and curates who were incumbents and all in priests' and deacons' orders, and to inquire by sworn witnesses into their morals and conduct and punish by suspension or excommunication. To those who should feel themselves wronged by this procedure was reserved the right of appeal before certain of the privy council named in the commission.[1]

The duke of Newcastle immediately ordered a new clause to be inserted in the instructions to all the governors recognizing the bishop's jurisdiction as thus defined and requiring that all countenance and encouragement be given to it according to the laws of the respective provinces and the tenor of the commission itself. On the petition of Gibson himself another clause was also introduced providing that all laws against blasphemy, adultery, drunkenness, swearing and the like should be vigorously enforced. Gibson also issued a pamphlet, under the title of a *Methodus Procedendi*, etc., setting forth the duties of commissaries and also a plan for regulating the proceedings of commissaries in possible trials of clergymen for immoral or irregular conduct. The process was that used in ecclesiastical trials and the offences for the trial and punishment of which it was to be invoked were officiating without a license, marrying without banns or license, neglect of catechizing or other church duty, refusing to baptize or bury, immoralities of various kinds. During the years of Gibson's episcopate the church in the colonies expanded, as we shall see, in certain directions and the authority of its metropolitan continued under the commission and with the means for exercising it which had just been mentioned. But very few occasions arose where it was necessary, and at the same time possible, to exercise in full judicial form the power which was given to the commissaries. And even had it been exercised and respected, not the bishop but the privy council would have had the right of moving appeals. Therefore, notwithstanding Gibson's fidelity toward the church in the colonies, he was able to accomplish little more

---

[1] N. Y. Col. Docs., V, 849; N. J. Arch., V, 126; Cross, Anglican Episcopate in the Am. Colonies, 52 *et seq.*, 283–309, and authorities there referred to. Two patents are said to have been issued, the first having been granted by George I, and superseded by his death, and another issued by his successor.

by means of his commission than others did without it, and after his death the grant was not renewed.

Notwithstanding the accession of a Hanoverian king and the winning by the Whig party of a lease of power which was to continue for half a century, the Society for the Propagation of the Gospel in 1715, renewed its appeal for the appointment of colonial bishops.[1] It desired that two should be appointed for the islands and two for the continent and that each of the former should receive a salary of £1500 sterling and each of the latter £1000 sterling per annum. The two continental bishops should reside at Burlington, New Jersey, and Williamsburg, Virginia. Their support, it was proposed, should come from the church lands formerly belonging to the various orders of the French Catholic clergy of the island of St. Christopher, from the profits of their jurisdiction, from lands which might be purchased or granted by the king, and a tenth of all future grants and escheats in the colonies. But as the rebellion in Scotland had just broken out and conditions were in every way unfavorable, no progress in this direction could then be made. The fact also that the grant of marriage licenses and of the probate of wills in the colonies had been made to the governors indicated the preference of the government for its secular agents and robbed the clergy in advance of what would naturally have been the chief perquisites of their office. But the high churchman of later Stuart times — Nicholson, Talbot, Henderson, Heathcote, Basse and others — continued for a while longer to be active in the colonies and they lost no opportunity of enforcing the need for resident bishops.[2] The accession of George I found Nicholson in the midst of his activity as royal commissioner for inquiry into the interests of the crown in the colonies, and patronage of the church seems to have occupied the largest part of his attention. The erection of a church at Burlington and the purchase by the Venerable Society of a house and estate there for the support of one of the expected bishops attracted much attention. Jeremiah Basse sent to the Venerable Society a rather detailed history of this enter-

---

[1] S. P. G. Mss.; Acts P. C. Col. 1680–1720, p. 687; Hawkins, Missions of the Church of England, 380.

[2] S. P. G. Mss.; Hills, Hist. of the Church in Burlington, New Jersey.

prise, which included also a strong plea for the appointment of a bishop.

John Talbot continued for some years his connection with Burlington and with Anglican interests generally in New Jersey and Pennsylvania and he never ceased to describe in picturesque language the weakness of the Church while deprived of resident bishops. But he never succeeded in escaping from the stigma of Jacobitism. As a result of the controversies that arose in connection with the parish of Jamaica, Long Island, Governor Hunter wrote to Secretary Popple concerning the group of churchmen at Burlington as follows: [1] " I have been obliged to turn out that vile fellow Griffith, the Attorney General of the Jerseys, who has been all along an impudent tool of Lord Clarendon's, and that noisy fool Cox has betrayed the publick service so avowedly, that I verily believed he had orders from home to do so. Mr. Talbot has incorporated the Jacobites in the Jerseys under the name of a Church, in order to Sanctify his Sedition and Insolence to the Government. That stale pretence is now pretty much discussed, and I am easy and shall make them so in spite of themselves. Cox. Griffith and Basse are his main props. If the Society take not more care for the future than has been taken hitherto, in the choice of their Missionaries, instead of establishing Religion, they'll destroy all Government and good manners." The board of trade sent a copy of this statement to the bishop of London and he laid it before the society. By them it was sent to Talbot and drew from Basse and himself, as well as the church wardens, indignant denials of the charge. Talbot asserted that he had been a Williamite from the beginning and the church wardens pronounced the statement a calumnious and groundless scandal. Later Governor Gookin, of Pennsylvania, reported that Talbot was disaffected and had refused the oath of allegiance. The answer of the accused to this is not known, but in 1721 on his last visit to England the interest, accrued and to accrue, on Archbishop Tenison's legacy of £1000 toward the support of bishops in America was directed by an order in chancery to be paid to Talbot in recognition of his long and valuable service to the Church. After his return Talbot had occasion,

[1] N. Y. Col. Docs. V, 401.

as a member of a convocation, to sign a memorandum censuring a disreputable clergyman at Philadelphia which led to his dismissal.  This man — named Thurston — in letters to several prominent men then revived the old charges against Talbot and added to them the new story, that he had tried to exercise espicopal powers at Philadelphia.  The inference drawn from that was that, while abroad, he had been converted by a non-juror.  Color seemed to be given to that by the arrival at Philadelphia in 1724 of Dr. Welton, a violent supporter of Sacheverell, who actually had been so converted. Not knowing this, the vestry of Christ Church asked him to supply their vacant pulpit, which Welton did.  He remained in and about Philadelphia until the spring of 1726, when his status having become known, he was summoned by writ of privy seal to return to England.  The name of Talbot has often been associated with that of Welton and it has been said that he also had received episcopal consecration in the same way.  But of this there is no evidence, as there is none of the alleged exercise by these men of episcopal functions in the colonies.  Talbot died two years after the return of Welton to Europe, leaving a long record of service to the church which was so ardent and outspoken as probably to account for the equally partisan attacks which were made in such numbers against him.[1]  Of the Society's house at Burlington, we hear much in the records, of its tenants, its decay and efforts to keep it in repair, until finally in 1748 it was burned to the ground and with it disappeared the hope that on this spot might be the residence of a colonial bishop.[2]

As the years progressed, the missionaries in service in the colonies never ceased to insist on the need of resident bishops. For obvious reasons we hear less from Virginia on this subject than from any other colony.  But from Maryland and South Carolina, where opposition from dissenters and other causes was serious, the demand was insistent.  In the colonies

[1] Hills, Hist. of Burlington Church;  Chapter by Fulton in Perry, History of American Episcopal Church, I.   Many references in Perry's Hist. Colls. and in S. P. G. Mss.

[2] Another piece of property which seems to have been bequeathed to the Society, but of which it did not obtain possession, was that of the Frankfort Land Company in Pennsylvania.   Much appears in reference to this in the records of the S. P. G. from 1717 to 1740.

to the north, where the predominance of dissenters seemed overwhelming and the Church did not possess the advantages of an establishment, it seemed impossible to adjust disputes and secure united and aggressive action without an official head. Commissaries were recognized as useful and there is evidence that Vesey exerted some influence, partly for good and partly for evil, in New York. Price championed, as he was able, the cause of a rather extreme episcopalianism in Massachusetts.[1] But on the passing of both Vesey and Price, toward 1750, it was not thought worth while to continue their offices. The same was true in the case of Archibald Cummings, who held the office of commissary in Pennsylvania from 1726 to his death in 1741.[2] With the resignation of his office by Henderson about 1735 no further commissaries were appointed for Maryland.[3] With advancing years and the lack of stimulating opposition Blair lapsed into inactivity and the calm of stagnation settled down upon the Church in Virginia. Garden's official career in South Carolina extended beyond the middle of the century. His visitations were more regular than those of any other commissary and during the period of his activity — the two decades following 1730 — he was altogether the leading official representative of the bishop of London in the continental colonies.[4] In colonies like his the commissary exercised jurisdiction over clergy sent by the Society as well as over those, if there were any, who were exclusively of the bishop's appointment.

Under the stimulus of letters from the colonies and doubtless also of arguments of members who were specially familiar with colonial conditions, early in 1718 the Venerable Society resolved that the bishops who were members should be asked to consider the renewal of the society's application for the settlement of bishops in America and that subscription rolls should be prepared for raising a fund. The subject was returned to a year later and again at the close of 1722,[5] but no decisive step whatever was taken. This was during the in-

[1] Foote, Annals of King's Chapel, I, 384, et seq.
[2] Perry, Hist. Colls., Pennsylvania, 148–224.
[3] Hawks, Maryland, 222; Perry, Hist. Colls., Maryland.
[4] Dalcho, Hist. of the Church in S. C., 116–173. S. P. G. Mss.
[5] Journal of S. P. G., Feb. 21 and 24, 1717/18; Feb. 13, 1718/19; Dec. 12, 1722.

cumbency of Robinson as bishop of London. When Gibson succeeded, the chance of influencing the government in favor of the proposal did not improve and the new bishop directed his efforts toward confirming his claim to the exercise of jurisdiction directly from London. So long as Robert Walpole was chief minister the plan of a colonial episcopate slept beyond the chance of an awakening. Though Gibson actively supported the interests of the Church in the colonies, he did not attempt seriously to raise the question of the episcopate. Such progress as was made resulted from the joint efforts of the Venerable Society and the bishop in England with the coöperation of clergy and laity in the colonies, but without any more definite headship in America.

This work was carried on partly as a proselyting and missionary enterprise in the colonies where dissenters were established or in the majority, and partly in the form of control over a provincial establishment, as in Virginia, and under all the varieties of social and legal conditions which existed in the colonies. The bishop, provided he was a man like Gibson, made use of the Society of which he was the most influential member, as the chief agency for extending the work in the colonies. It chiefly administered the funds which were collected or bestowed in England or America for this purpose. It decided when and where new missions should be established, had the chief influence in selecting missionaries and schoolmasters — for in a steady proportion of cases the two went together — directed and encouraged them in their work, fixed the amount of their pay so far as it came from England and regulated their removals from place to place. Except in the cases of Virginia and Maryland, the correspondence of the Anglican clergy in the colonies was chiefly with the Society. In colonies where there was neither a commissary nor any form of Anglican establishment, the Society was looked to almost exclusively. Through the hands of the standing committee of the Society and its secretary passed nearly all important business which affected Anglican interests in the colonies. On the other hand the Society turned to the bishop, either alone or with his associates, when influence was to be exerted on the government, when candidates were to be admitted to orders or designated for work in the colonies or

schoolmasters licensed to teach there. The administration
of discipline through the commissaries and much of the influence that was exerted in the interests of order and regularity proceeded from the bishop. From time to time he
issued pastoral letters which were intended to promote work
of a certain kind, as that among negroes, and to elevate the
moral character of the clergy in general. But this does not
mean that the functions of an efficient bishop in this connection were merely formal. Correspondence was carried on by
him with missionaries as well as his own immediate appointees, and upon every variety of subject. He was consulted in reference to almost any matter by individual clergymen, by bodies of the clergy, by vestries and church wardens,
by governors and other laymen.[1] He received information,
gave direction and advice. The relations between the bishop
and the Society were analogous to that between the secretary
of state and the board of trade, though possibly with more
power of initiative in the Society than the lords of trade possessed. The two coöperated in general agreement, though
with distinct functions which they never came to the point
of clearly defining. Though they acted from a remote centre
and suffered from the disabilities which this occasioned, they
on the whole kept in sympathetic touch with their constit-
uencies in the colonies and had the aid in most of the colonies
of a body of supporters which steadily grew in numbers and
efficiency.

In all of the colonies outside of New England the Church,
with minor exceptions, had the sympathy if not the cordial
support of the executive branch of the government. As the
eighteenth century advanced this tended more to be the case.
The Calverts and members of the Penn family became Anglican, though the former caused some trouble by appointing to
livings without consulting the bishop. In the royal provinces
the crown could be trusted to keep a corps of executive
officials in existence which would be at least mildly favorable
to the ambitions of the Church. In many cases they were
strong partisans of its cause. In a number of instances the
royal appointees, even in Massachusetts, maintained this at-

---

[1] This is amply proved by the papers at Fulham Palace, fragmentary
though they are.

titude. The conspicuous activities of Francis Nicholson as a supporter and benefactor of the Church continued to the day of his death [1] and in his will he gave to her such estates of land as he possessed in America. While he was special royal commissioner in the later years of Anne he was active in her cause throughout the colonies and was appealed to from all quarters. This relation he continued to maintain after his return to England, where he was a working member of the Venerable Society.

On the other hand, the colonial assemblies were very likely to be hostile to the Church. It was in them that the strength of the dissenters was felt and their policies found expression. The clergy, the Society and the bishops not infrequently had occasion to protest against the passage of acts which were regarded as unfavorable to their interests and to labor for their disallowance in England. An instance of this kind was an act passed in New Jersey in Hunter's administration permitting Quakers to affirm. We shall meet with several instances of a similar kind in Maryland. In colonies where the Church was established the clergy was likely at times to be at issue with the entire government over the question of their support. Issues of paper money caused them hardships, as they did the rest of the population. In all the New England colonies the Anglicans were at issue with almost the entire system of ecclesiastical law. They opposed civil marriage wherever it was the law or practice. In general, however, the evidence is abundant that the Anglicans were loyal and supported institutions as they were. They were natural conservatives and sometimes were criticised on that account.

Under this form of joint management the affairs of the Church in the colonies were conducted. As was true in the domain of civil affairs, parishes and the clergy as a whole enjoyed a large degree of self government. A loose form of control, in which the secular authorities of those colonies where the Church was established bore a share, was exercised over the clergy. In all the colonies except Virginia the pressure of competition was as effective as anything in keeping them up to their duty. It was not to be expected that, with the tone of religious life so low as it then was in England, the

[1] Proofs of this abound in the Mss. of S. P. G.

average would be high in the colonies; and it was not. In the main, and especially in the colonies where the Church was not established, the episcopal ministry was a devoted and self-denying body of men. Their support was scanty — rarely exceeding and most cases falling far short of £100 a year — and the obstacles against which they had to contend were almost insurmountable. They quarreled somewhat among themselves and much with their religious opponents, especially the Quakers. Their preaching and conversation in general must have been prosaic and commonplace, but of how many among the competing sects must not the same be said? For their results the Anglicans could also rely on the beauties of the prayer book, the sense of power and security which came with an establishment and with such fidelity to ritual and the canons as the meagre resources of the colonial churches made possible. Among the missionaries men occasionally went wrong morally and scandal resulted. Now and then one proved erratic and quarrelsome and had to be repressed or eliminated. Feuds were as rife in Boston and vicinity as anywhere. But serious cases of this kind were not common. As we shall see, there was more complaint of drunkenness, neglect of duty and gross immorality among the clergy of Virginia and Maryland than elsewhere, while there were conspicuous examples of devotion among those of South Carolina and in other sections. These subjects, of course, provoked much comment and furnished one of the chief occasions for the exercise of discipline by commissary, bishop or Society. Violations of the canons [1] and needless departures from the forms of worship furnished minor causes of offence and in all except a few notable cases these were found to be excusable. The Society took measures to prevent missionaries leaving their stations for others, especially if they were in other colonies, without permission. These changes were sometimes advisable for the good of the Church, but they were often made to improve the clergyman's condition. On one occasion Nicholson recommended that such leave be not granted without the consent of the bishop, though such matters could often be adjusted by the commissaries with cer-

[1] Particularly in celebrating irregular marriages and holding service or administering the sacraments in prohibited or unusual places.

tificates from the parishes concerned.  In 1723 Governor
Burnet, of New York, by insisting that his prior collation to
a benefice on Staten Island should stand, prevented the stationing there of Mr. Wetmore by the Society and that body
took away the salary which it had appropriated for Staten
Island and used it elsewhere.  Clergymen were required at
intervals to send home, under the title of a *notitia parochialis*,
statements of the number of communicants, usual church
attendance, baptisms, extent and condition of glebes, church
buildings, and other details respecting their parishes.  They
were also required to leave the libraries provided by Dr.
Bray's society to their successors.  Complaints were occasionally made that the Society sent over too many Scotch
and Irish missionaries, for they inclined too much to the ways
of the dissenters.  In order to its successful working the
Church of course needed as complete a reproduction as possible of the European parish system.  In Virginia, Maryland,
and South Carolina it had this in differing degrees, so far as
was possible under colonial conditions.  Elsewhere the parish
in its European sense was non-existent, and with it disappeared the form of compulsory support which was of such
value to the clergy.  In those colonies they had to depend
on voluntary contributions and such stipends as the Society
could afford to bestow.  This put them at a special disadvantage when compared with the clergy of Massachusetts and
Connecticut and upon something very like the voluntary
system of Rhode Island and the Quaker colonies.

Turning now to events which affected Anglicanism in particular colonies, Virginia and Maryland first demand attention.  In April, 1719, Commissary Blair held at William and
Mary College a convocation of the clergy of Virginia.  This
was called under the direction of the bishop of London because Governor Spotswood had charged Blair with certain
minor irregularities and because a controversy had arisen
over the right of the governor to collate to benefices.  A
parish in Essex county was the one specially involved at that
time.  At this period in his administration also Spotswood was
involved in a quarrel with the burgesses and with certain
members of the council and this circumstance affected his
relations with the commissary.  To the convocation the gov-

ernor sent a letter severely arraigning Blair and appealing over his head to the clergymen of the province to correct the evils which the commissary had ignored or himself committed. Interpreting literally the words of his commission and instructions and pushing his claims as representative of the king to an extreme, Spotswood insisted that he had the right to collate, that is to present and induct, in the case of all vacancies. This he set forth in a long letter upon the case of the Essex parish which he sent to the convention. The Rev. Hugh Jones and others expressed doubt as to the validity of Blair's ordination, as it had been administered by a Scotch bishop. To all the charges Blair proposed to reply at once, but was induced to make his formal answers in letters to the bishop of London. As the convention was about equally divided between his supporters and opponents, the meeting was a lively one. In detailed statements which were sent to the bishop Blair met all the governor's charges, showing that he had been regularly ordained by a Scotch bishop, showing how and why he had permitted a clerk to officiate in his place and giving an illuminating statement of the difference between induction and collation and of the governor's powers in each. The governor, he declared, possessed the former power only when there was a lapse, but when a successor was presented by the vestry, as was the case in the Essex parish, the governor had only the right to induct. Spotswood realized that he was defeated and later wrote to the bishop of London, " I must remain passive or else I shall raise the old combination in this government and be in danger of drawing your Lordship's Commissary on my back again." [1] With this the controversial activities of Blair came to an end and in Virginia, until the appearance of dissenters in considerable numbers, quiet reigned in ecclesiastical affairs. In secular affairs, we know, after the retirement of Spotswood, a similar condition prevailed.

Religious conditions in Virginia in the eighteenth century have been more than once described and adequate materials for the purpose exist. The accounts which have been given by different writers agree in representing the spiritual life of

---

[1] Hist. Colls. (Virginia), 199–249, 321; Meade, Old Churches and Families of Virginia, I, 161; II, 393.

both clergy and communicants as low and the church as destitute to a very large extent of invigorating influence upon the people.  Though the efficiency of the Church in Great Britain at this period touched the lowest point which it has reached in modern times, it still possessed learned and able leaders and devoted men among the ranks of its clergy. There was still life enough in it for controversy, and some notable debates over questions of doctrine and practice occurred at this time.[1]  But in the colonies, and especially in Virginia, there was not life or culture sufficient even for this. Among the indifferent successes of British administration must be reckoned that of the bishops of London as metropolitans of the colonies in the eighteenth century.  In the colonies where their unassisted control was most complete the most sluggish religious conditions existed.  Virginia and Maryland furnish the most conspicuous examples of this, though in Maryland the laity at times challenged the clergy in a way which was calculated to put them upon their defence.  In South Carolina and New York active rivalry of dissenters stimulated the parsons to greater efforts, while the Venerable Society sent some of its worthiest missionaries into those provinces.  But Virginia, until the middle of the century, lacked these influences and the church in that province was correspondingly barren of achievement.

Conditions in Virginia and Maryland were to such an extent the same that they can be considered together.  Parishes in most cases were too large to be adequately cared for by a single clergyman, though the division of them or the serious reduction of their size was equally unwelcome, since then the income of the living in tobacco might be too small for the support of the incumbent.  In Virginia one parish was a hundred miles in length, another was sixty, several were forty, while a common breadth was from ten to twenty miles.  Only one parish was limited to the length of eight miles, another was ten miles long, and the rest were eighteen miles or more in length.[2]  In Maryland none of the parishes were less than

---

[1] See especially the writings of Abbey and Overton on the English Church in the Eighteenth Century, and the works of Hunt and Leslie Stephen on English Thought in the same period.

[2] This information is contained in answers by the clergy to queries in 1724.  Hist. Colls. (Va), 261 *et seq.*

nine miles long and some extended to the length of seventy miles.[1] It was therefore often necessary for people to go ten, fifteen or twenty miles to church, if they went at all, and that under the difficult conditions of travel which then existed. In Maryland, in 1725, an attempt was made by legislation to divide parishes, thereby depriving the clergymen concerned of a part of their support. In both provinces the clergy were paid in tobacco. As early as 1696 in Virginia their salaries were fixed by law at 16,000 pounds of tobacco, which, with glebes and perquisites, as the prices long prevailed, averaged from £80 to £100 sterling per annum.[2] The yield in money south of the James was less than it was north of that river, because the quality of the tobacco was poorer.

In Maryland the livings, paid in tobacco at 40 lbs. per poll, were worth about £50 sterling. Everywhere it was the custom to set aside the poorest quality of tobacco for the ministers and they complained that theirs sold for much less than other tobacco in the market.[3] As the price fell the incomes of the clergy, at best pitifully small for the support of a family, were still further reduced. In 1728, on the plea that the number of tobacco plants was being limited, the legislature of Maryland, in which there was a minority of dissenters, reduced the assessment to 30 lbs. per poll, with the option of paying in money at 10s. per hundredweight, thus giving the people the option of paying in the medium which was cheapest at the time. As bills were at the same time passed for dividing several parishes, the motive of the enemies of the church in the assembly was evident and it was taken to be a violation of the act establishing the church. Therefore, in addition to the dispatch of several strong representations to the bishop of London and others, Commissary Henderson was sent to England to procure the redress of these and other grievances of the clergy, and if he failed he was instructed to ask the Venerable Society to appoint the Maryland clergy to its missions as fast as vacancies should occur. Owing to the absence of the proprietor, Henderson

[1] Hawks, Contributions to Ecclesiastical History (Md.), 171. Hist. Colls (Del. and Md.), 190, *et seq.*

[2] Hening, VI, 88. Blair in Hist. Colls. (Va.), 150.

[3] Mereness, Maryland as a Proprietary Province, 453.

at once brought the matter before the crown. Baltimore subsequently appeared and procured a suspension of proceedings until he could take action in the case. After a full hearing he disallowed the act and instructed his governor to assent to no law by which the rights of the clergy under the act establishing the church should be diminished.[1]

And yet, in 1730 another law was passed limiting the number of tobacco plants and providing that one-fourth of the 40 lbs. per poll might be paid in wheat, barley, Indian corn and oats at fixed values. But the clergy insisted that this involved a violation of their rights of the same nature as the previous act and that it involved an unfair discrimination against them. A long and bitter controversy ensued, the elder Dulany and Henderson being especially pitted against one another in argument. Henderson and others of the clergy were assaulted and the former was hindered by his opponents in his efforts to discipline flagrant offenders against good morals. The proprietor finally assented to this act, but it remained in force only two years, after which, until 1747, no law existed regulating the quantity or quality of tobacco in Maryland. The result was that the trade there seriously declined, the clergy suffering along with the rest of the inhabitants, in consequence.[2] For many years, especially after the restoration of proprietary government, there existed in Maryland a feeling of active hostility among the laity toward the clergy, and in this respect the situation was unlike anything which showed itself in Virginia prior to the middle of the century.

Glebes were regularly provided by law in the parishes, but in many cases worthless land was selected for this use and from such glebes ministers received no benefit. Houses were in some cases built by the parishes on the glebes and should regularly be kept in repair. But in the majority of cases there were either no houses or they were not kept in repair. If repaired at all in such cases, it had to be done by the clergyman himself. Occasionally a glebe was rented by the incumbent for a small sum. So small were the incomes of

[1] Hist. Colls. (Md. and Del.), 258–287; Acts, P. C. Col. 1720–1745, pp. 252, 338. Hawks, Contributions, etc. (Maryland), 177, et seq., 208, 214.
[2] Mereness, 455, Hist. Colls. (Md.), 299 et seq.

most of the clergy that they had to live narrowly, without
books or with very few, unless perchance a small library
provided by Dr. Bray had been placed in the parish and
duly cared for by its custodians.

Upon the fact of his induction into his living or the absence of it generally depended the permanence of the clergyman's tenure. Therefore, induction was regarded by the
clergy as a matter of great importance. In Maryland, in
1724, practically all the clergy reported themselves as inducted, but in Virginia the opposite was in most instances
the case.[1] In that province in particular the vestries, acting
on behalf of the parishioners, very frequently neglected or
declined to present their appointees to the governor for induction. They simply received them, that is hired them from
year to year. Induction installed the incumbent in the living
for life and thus the parishioners would in large measure
lose control over him. Without induction an incumbent who
did not suit could be gotten rid of.[2] In this fact lay one of
the most important distinctions between the Church in
England and in most of the colonies. In the colonies the
tenure, even of Anglican clergymen, approximated to that
of the Presbyterians and Congregationalists, depending like
theirs on the will of those to whom they ministered. In not
a few instances, when vacancies occurred, parishes neglected
for periods longer or shorter to choose successors in order to
avoid the payment of their salaries. Of failure to induct
the clergy bitterly complained, saying that they were left at
the mercy of their parishioners. Still the reports of the clergy
in 1724 show that terms of residence, as a rule, were long
even in those parishes which did not favor induction, the
tenure of the clergy being in reality quite permanent. The
parishes evidently valued the relation as giving them a certain hold on their clergy and the crown was not disposed to
interfere. When, in 1748, the patronage of all livings was
by act of the general assembly transferred to the vestries,
it was approved by the crown.[3]

---

[1] Twenty-four ministers at this time reported themselves as not inducted
to six who were inducted. Even Blair was not inducted in Bruton parish.

[2] If incumbents were growing old, if in manners, ability or life they were
not acceptable, if, like Mr. Latané, they had "a small tang of French" in
their speech, they could be turned adrift.    [3] Hist. Colls. (Va.), 461, 487.

When one comes to consider the character of the clergy and the general religious condition of these two provinces, the remark of Governor Hart, of Maryland, to the effect that there were many worthy persons among the ministers of that province but there were also some whose morals and education were a scandal to their profession,[1] appears to have come as near the truth as any brief statement well could. The intelligence and devotedness of the rank and file of the English clergy of that time was not high. It shared the low moral tone which prevailed in English life. From that body, as a rule, representatives of the less available or successful types would drift into service in the colonies or secure licenses for service there. The same was to a large extent true in the civil service and similar conditions were operative in the Church. The provinces where the Church was established would naturally reflect most perfectly conditions which existed at home and also in the sphere of civil government. The record would indicate that the average of the clergy sent over by the Society for the Propagation of the Gospel was higher than that of the appointees of the bishop of London. The circumstances in which they were placed, as well as the correspondence which they had to keep up with the secretary of the Venerable Society, may well account largely for the difference. After about 1735, when Henderson resigned his office, there was no longer even a commissary in Maryland. As now there was no resort except to the bishop himself, the administration of clerical discipline must have been next to impossible. But an accumulation of testimonies from the best representatives among the ministers of Virginia and Maryland proves that drunkenness and gross forms of immorality were all too frequent on the part of members of that body. Slothfulness and negligence, as well as moral obliquity on the one hand, and on the other a feeling of general contempt on the part of the laity toward the order, due to its inferior character and the mean circumstances under which so many of its members were compelled to live, are repeatedly assigned by clergymen themselves as reasons for the inefficiency of the church. Of course, not a few devoted and able men were sent over under direct episcopal authority, but there were

[1] Hawks, *op. cit.*, 129.

too many who were not such. The fact that they were not native born and trained, like the New England clergy, also hampered them and lessened their usefulness.

In estimating the workings of an episcopal system much account has also to be taken of questions of order. Church buildings and their furnishings, clerical vestments, the orderly performance of divine service in accordance with the requirements of the prayer book and canons, the administration of the sacraments and catechizing of children and servants, the control of schoolmasters and church schools, all these and more must be present and in due order if the system was to show its true efficiency. It is needless to say that under the rough and simple conditions which existed in the colonies there could be only an approximation, more or less remote, to the usages of the Church in their perfect form. To this fact the letters of the clergy bear eloquent and abundant testimony. There was a continuous call for prayer books and minor helps to devotion. For the non-ritualistic sects, which depended solely on the Bible, preaching and a psalm book, it was in certain respects easier to adapt themselves to the simple conditions of colonial life. It was the necessities of order and clerical discipline which made the demand for resident bishops so general and imperative. It came continuously from the clergy everywhere, in the establishment and among the missionary stations. The resident bishop was necessary to complete the structure of the Church and maintain its order and the demand for one or more of these officials was a justifiable one. In the colonies outside of New England, so far as we can judge, this demand might have been met without serious opposition from any quarter. The failure of the British government to meet the demand is to be classed, with its failure to supply a coinage to the colonies and to pay salaries to its governors, as signal instances of administrative neglect. They show that the responsible leaders of the British government did not fully understand the conditions under which their imperial system could be successfully run.

In the provinces, that is outside of New England, the parish system of Europe was very generally developed. It, of course, attained its completest form in the provinces where the English Church was established. Under the establishment or wherever else the church was predominant, the entire population was regarded as connected with it and in some way under its care. They were supposed to attend its services and under proper instruction, without the throes of a semi-miraculous conversion, might become its communicants. Outward conformity, supported as far as possible by ethical qualifications, was insisted upon more than correct belief and definite or exalted spiritual experiences. Anxiety over the possibilities of evil inherent in a so-called half-way covenant could not exist under the Anglican parish system. All were in a sense in the church and the majority were not to be excluded because the minority or nucleus claimed to have had a religious experience which was deep and genuine. To the Calvinist of New England this seemed the very acme of Arminianism, in comparison with which the backslidings under the half-way covenant were merely preliminary symptoms rather than the disease itself.

When the Anglican clergyman described moral and religious conditions, he had in his mind parishes as a whole and not merely a definite religious group to the exclusion of the entire world outside. Looking at the subject from that standpoint, the descriptions which appear in the letters of clergymen in Virginia and Maryland show that religious and moral conditions among the people, even according to the standards of the time, were low. One Virginia clergyman wrote, " The inconvenience of such large bounded parishes is very great. For tho' the People are very ignorant and undisciplined, the Word of God can be Preached but seldom among them; the use of the Sabbath day is converted by them into some diversion or worldly Business, they cannot be catechized so frequently as their need requires; their sick cannot be visited." [1] Another complains of the ignorance which prevailed concerning the principles of religion and of the loose living of many, though the people at large were faithful supporters of the Church as established. In 1714 one of the Maryland clergy wrote, " There seems to be an universal disregard (a few only excepted) of holy things. I need not give a more convincing proof of this than the neglect of baptism and the

[1] Hist. Colls. (Va.), 326, 346.

holy sacrament among them. The former of these is so notorious that whole families . . . do live and sometimes die without it, and indeed seem for the most part to take no care about it. But what gives me the greatest uneasiness is that dissoluteness of manners . . . which has universally spread itself over the province, of which the frequency of polygamy etc., is a flagrant instance. These are beyond my power to redress, and the more because those who are guilty despise the checks of conscience and religion, and are above every consideration but the penalties of the laws, and here there are few to enforce their obedience." [1] The more influential families resented preaching against their sins or attempts at reproof, and because of the disdain with which clergymen of ordinary abilities were likely to be viewed by members of this class, they were likely, if faithful, to have more influence with the common people. Dr. Davies, the Presbyterian, declared that when he came to Virginia, in 1747, " religion was just expiring and a strict form of Godliness was very rare," [2] a statement which, in the sense in which he used the expression, is accepted by the ecclesiastical historians of Virginia as substantially true. Dr. Meade was of the opinion that the spiritual condition of Virginia was never tolerably good, even in comparison with the Mother Church, " over whose defects also there was so much cause to mourn." [3]

[1] Hawks, *op. cit.*, 136.
[2] Hist. Colls. (Va.), 368; Hawks, Contributions, etc.; (Va.), 100 *et seq.*
[3] Old Churches and Families of Virginia, I, 14.

# CHAPTER XI

## THE ENGLISH CHURCH AND THE DISSENTERS UNDER THE EARLY HANOVERIANS, II

Of the other provinces — the Carolinas, Georgia and New York — where the English Church was established or favored by the government, conditions were most favorable to it in South Carolina and Georgia. There the proportion of Episcopalians to the other sects combined was larger and the assistance given by the government was more regular and effective.[1] Because of the strength of the dissenters in all these provinces, the Venerable Society considered them as missionary ground and strengthened their clergy by the men whom they sent. The result of this was, that they felt the stimulus which came from correspondence with the Society, as well as from the pastoral letters and control in other forms which was exercised by the bishop of London. In North Carolina and New York the odds against the Church was very strong, in the first named province so great as to make the effort to maintain even the show of an establishment almost hopeless. But in South Carolina and Georgia its position was truly that of the favored and leading communion. Provision was made by law for salaries of the clergy, in most cases at the rate of £100 currency, with increase as the currency depreciated, for glebes and for aid from the province treasury toward building and repair of churches and houses for the clergy.[2] During most of the period under review able commissaries were resident in South Carolina. A board of lay commissioners, with the governor as a member, the successor of that board whose criticism had caused so much stir near the beginning of the century, was continued in existence,

---

[1] See Dalcho, Hist. of Church in South Carolina, 147, for a quoted estimate to the effect that in 1740 the Episcopalians in that province about equalled all the other sects combined.

[2] Stats. of S. C., III, 11.

and we are told, as late as 1734, that it joined with the commissary in verifying the credentials of newly arrived missionaries, and issued precepts to the parishes to which they
were designated to meet and elect, if a majority could be secured in support of the nominee.[1] Commissary Garden also,
beginning in 1731, held annual visitations of the clergy.[2] The
presence of Nicholson as royal governor for a number of
years in the third decade of the century gave encouragement
to the Church. Acts had previously been passed fixing the
salaries of the clergy, but during his administration, owing
to the depreciation of the currency, the passage of another
act became necessary to raise the nominal rates at which
they were paid. Nicholson secured its passage and for this
received the fervent thanks of the clergy in South Carolina
and of the Venerable Society in England.[3] His administration was believed by the clergy to have strengthened their
cause in the province and, as they recovered from the disasters of the great Yamassee War, their letters became more
optimistic and their general tone was one of encouragement.
They believed that the position of the Church in the province
was growing stronger. Some of the best among the clergy
interested themselves much in efforts to instruct and convert
the negroes in their parishes, but met with much opposition
from their masters. We hear more upon this subject in South
Carolina than in any other province.[4] Out of the discussion
of this subject which arose there and elsewhere the principle
became clear, that the effect of their christianization would
not be to emancipate the negroes from slavery, and that helped
to silence one great objection on the part of the masters to
the efforts of the few missionaries who showed an interest
in this difficult problem.

When Georgia was founded, a controversy arose between
the Trustees and Bishop Gibson over his right to license all

---

[1] Journal of S. P. G., Aug. 16 and Nov. 6, 1734. In the laws of South
Carolina also repeated references to the existence of the board of commissioners appear.

[2] Dalcho, Hist. of the Church in S. C., 116 *et seq.*

[3] Stats. of S. C., III, 11, 174; Corresp. of S. P. G. for 1722.

[4] In 1729 Bishop Gibson issued two pastoral letters, one to masters and
mistresses of families in the plantations and the other to missionaries there,
exhorting them to instruct the negroes in the Christian faith.

ministers who should preach in the colony.[1]  The former, apparently without good reason, objected to this because it would take from their hands the power of removing clergymen who proved unsatisfactory.  The Trustees even challenged the authority of the bishop, entirely on the ground that their province was founded subsequent to the issue of his commission.  Gibson threatened to bring this question to trial in the courts, but it does not appear to have been done. Though the English Church held the usual favored position in Georgia, no commissary was appointed and missionaries were sent to minister to its people, the bishop ordaining if not usually licensing them.  The procedure was not essentially different in form or results from what went on in other provinces.

Though the Georgia Trustees early applied to the Society for the Propagation of the Gospel to aid them in selecting ministers, those who first went to the colony were not nominees of the Society.  Under the advice of friends or influenced in other ways, they offered themselves for this work. John Wesley,[2] the third in this list, sailed for Georgia near the close of 1735.  He was accompanied by his brother Charles, while Oglethorpe returned on the same vessel from his first visit to England, and David Nitschmann, the Moravian, was also on board.  In learning and ability Wesley had already shown himself to be the leader of the band of so-called " Oxford Methodists," whose appearance was the first sign of an awakening of religious life within the English Church.  At that period of his life Wesley combined a highly ascetic life with scrupulous observance of the ritual of the Church and great missionary zeal.  His original purpose in going to Georgia was to serve as a missionary among the Indians. But finding on his arrival there that Samuel Quincy, his predecessor, had gone to South Carolina and left the Church vacant, Wesley settled at once over Georgia as his parish. He was the only Church of England minister in the province and continued to serve at Savannah, with two or three very disturbed and unsuccessful visits to Frederica, until he returned to England in December 1737.  He was a missionary,

---

[1] Ga. Recs., V, 46–49, 217;  McCain, Georgia as a Proprietary Province. Tyerman, Life of Wesley, I, 108–170.

but not an appointee of the Venerable Society. In all the settlements, could he have visited them regularly, there were 700 persons, most of whom were not regular communicants of the English Church.

The labors of Wesley were incessant in all that should constitute the work of a missionary. Every Sabbath he held three public services, at five in the morning, at midday and at three in the afternoon, and at night he met at his home all who desired to come for prayer and mutual exhortation. Private evening meetings, which were intended for the training of a select number in the Christian life, were held throughout the week. A school was started, in which children were taught to read, write and cast accounts, while catechising upon the principles of religion was a prominent feature of the general work.[1] The system and method which later distinguished his work appeared even at this early stage. At first Wesley seemed popular, but the regimen upon which he insisted, including as it did a vigorous conformity with the forms and canons of the English Church, was too severe for a rude frontier settlement. Wesley, too, was not a little censorious and in his frequent public discourses did not spare the faults and weaknesses — of which according to all accounts there were many — among the people of Savannah and especially of Frederica. To his austere and lofty piety they, of course, could not be brought to conform. Toward dissenters of all types he assumed the intolerant attitude of the high churchman. Presently the situation was further complicated by the love affair in which Wesley became involved with the niece of Causton, the leading magistrate. For some reason which is not clear, whether it was the resolve of Wesley under the influence of the Moravians not to marry, or some pique on the part of the young woman, the affair was broken off and she suddenly married another. Soon after Wesley found occasion to reprove her for some slight misconduct, and a few weeks later he excluded her from the communion on the ground that, in violation of a general requirement of his, she had not notified him in advance of her intention to commune.

This last act of Wesley provoked Causton, the magistrate,

[1] Wesley's Journal, Tyerman, *op. cit.*

and Williamson, the lady's husband, and a suit for damages to the amount of £1000 was brought against the young minister. To this was also added a criminal prosecution, the majority of an unusually numerous grand jury finding a true bill of ten counts against Wesley. Though this was a secular body, its indictment concerned purely ecclesiastical matters, and on that account Wesley demurred to all the charges except one. Causton, though personally interested, as magistrate supported the prosecution by all means in his power. A report of a minority of the grand jury, which declared the counts against Wesley as a whole to be inadequate as a basis for a prosecution, was not presented to the court, but is said to have been forwarded to the Trustees as a protest on behalf of the accused.[1] On seven different occasions during the three months that followed Wesley demanded a trial and the opportunity to clear himself from the charges, but on one excuse or another he was continually put off. Not being under contract to remain in Georgia any length of time, he now determined to leave and return to England, whither his brother had already preceded him. Though his enemies tried to hold him as a sort of prisoner at large, he found no difficulty in executing his resolve when a suitable time came, and sailing from Charlestown he reached England in the late winter of 1738. Before the Trustees he had little trouble in clearing himself from blame and, resigning his appointment with them, turned to what was to be the real work of his life. Both the Wesleys had suffered in Georgia from mistakes due to an effort to impose upon the miscellaneous dwellers recently brought together in a group of frontier villages, adherents of a variety of sects and the majority without the knowledge or spirit of religion, a highly developed ritual and a type of religious enthusiasm which was intolerant of their weaknesses and

[1] McCain, *op. cit.* As stated by Commissary Garden in a letter to the Bishop of London, Dec. 22, 1737, the charges against Wesley were that he had refused to christen except by dipping, that he read the litany at six instead of ten o'clock in the morning, that he refused to bury an Anabaptist, that he repelled the niece of the chief magistrate from the communion, and was called a Jesuit, a spiritual tyrant, a mover of sedition and the like. Garden added that he was much surprised at these charges, as no one could have been better liked or better reported of by the people of Georgia than Wesley. Fulham MSS.

beyond their ability to value or to put into practice. Georgia, small as it was, gave them their first real taste of practical life, and its chastening influence doubtless contributed in some measure to changes in method, as well as the development of that sublime patience, combined with tireless energy, which enabled them, and especially John Wesley, to effect so great a change in the religious life of Great Britain. Their direct connection with America now ceased, but the great religious body which they were to establish found wide and ready reception in the colonies and later in the states. Its highly wrought religious emotionalism, combined with its democratic spirit, all controlled and directed by a well ordered group of leaders and toward definite ends, has contributed as much as any sect, and more than most, toward determining the religious and social type of the American people. In this form, in the persons of their disciples, the Wesleys returned to America to abide and to add mightily to the numbers and influence of dissent, and in that way to the obstacles which were accumulating in the path of the Anglicans, as they struggled for ascendancy upon the new continent.

Just as John Wesley reached England, Whitefield — about ten years his junior, but already coming to be known as a preacher and evangelist of great power — was leaving for Georgia.[1] Whitefield lacked the austerity which at this period was characteristic of Wesley, treated lightly the canons of the Church, and by his marvellous powers of emotional speech, as well as his vast capacity for labor, easily made his way where Wesley had comparatively failed. Before he left England his sympathy had been enlisted for the poor of Georgia, and he collected and took with him a rather abundant supply of commodities to meet their needs. Whitefield remained in Georgia on his first visit only about four months, from May to the close of August, 1738. But he was well received in all its settlements and, through his intercourse with the Salzburgers at Ebenezer, had his attention called to the orphanage at Halle, in Germany, and their imitation of it. The idea of founding such an institution

[1] Tyerman, Life of George Whitefield, I, 106 et seq., 347.

in Georgia had earlier found a lodgment in his mind through a suggestion from Charles Wesley.  One of the motives which led to Whitefield's speedy return to England arose from his desire to collect money for this enterprise.  Other considerations were, the necessity that he should secure ordination as a priest and his desire — somewhat strangely — to aid in breaking down the prohibitions which the Trustees had laid upon the introduction of slaves and rum into Georgia.  He was also opposed to their prohibition of the inheritance of land by females.  When he returned to America, in the summer of 1739, it was not only with means and plans for founding the orphan house in Georgia, but to begin a series of preaching and missionary tours through the colonies which should eclipse those of Keith and Talbot and prove the beginning of the period of great religious revivals.  This was an event of sufficient importance to mark an epoch in the religious history of the eighteenth century and must have full treatment in a later chapter.

But it brought out the elements of weakness, as well as of strength, in Whitefield's character and position.  His practice of preaching freely wherever men would hear him, out of doors, in buildings devoted to secular purposes, in the meetinghouses of dissenters more often than in the churches of the establishment in which he held orders, was a gross violation of the canons.  He attacked the type of Christianity represented by the late Archbishop Tillotson and in that manual of piety, the " Whole Duty of Man."  Whitefield wandered up and down the colonies, invading the parishes of others to the apparent neglect of his own at Savannah.  All this was exceedingly offensive to Alexander Garden, the commissary, whose jurisdiction in a way extended to Georgia as well as over the Carolinas.  Therefore we presently find him preaching, apropos of Whitefield, from the text, " Those who have turned the world upside down are come hither also."  Whitefield's reply was upon the text, " Alexander the coppersmith hath done me much evil; the Lord reward him according to his works."  The combatants also resorted to the press and several bitterly controversial pamphlets appeared.  In these encounters a statement of Whitefield's that Tillotson knew no more of Christianity than Mahomet, cut a great figure;

what he meant being that the doctrines of justification by
faith alone and of the new birth did not occupy a prominent
place in current Anglican theology.[1]

When Whitefield returned to Charlestown, in August, 1740,
he repeatedly heard himself denounced by the commissary
from the pulpit and was cited to appear before him, in his
judicial capacity, to answer certain charges, " chiefly for
omitting to use the Form of Prayers prescribed in the Communion Book." The week which intervened between the date
of the citation and the sitting of the court Whitefield spent in
his customary work, breaking at almost every step the canons
which Garden was proposing to compel him to obey. When
the court met, four clergymen sat as associates with the
commissary, and there were numerous spectators. Upon the
demand of the accused Garden exhibited to him the proofs
of his office and of the claim that they were legally acting
under the jurisdiction of the bishop of London. Respecting
the claim that this jurisdiction extended to the colonies,
Whitefield expressed doubt, and referred also to the fact that
he belonged in Georgia and not in South Carolina, to which
colony Garden's appointment was properly limited. The
first hearing closed with the granting of Whitefield's request
that he might have till the morrow further to inform himself upon doubtful points. At the second hearing Whitefield
tendered an exception against Garden acting as judge, because he was prejudiced against him, and proposed six arbitrators, to be chosen equally by the two parties to the suit.
Arguments were made upon the exception by an attorney
for each party, but it was rejected by the court. Whitefield then declared, with the proper oath and deposit of
money that he would appeal within a year to the High
Court of Chancery in England. Thus ended the only trial
before a commissary's court which ever occurred in the
American colonies.[2] Whitefield lodged the appeal but, prob-

[1] Tyerman, Life of Whitefield, I, 359, 396; Dalcho, 128 et seq.; Cross
Anglican Episcopate, 80–86, 312. Answer of Garden to queries of the
Bishop of London, 1750, Fulham MSS.

[2] The pamphlets which emanated from this controversy were, "Six
Letters to Rev. George Whitefield from Alexander Garden, etc." Boston,
1740. "Three Letters from the Rev. George Whitefield, etc." Philadelphia,
1740. Garden, in his report to the Bishop of London, stated that Whitefield
proposed as his three arbitrators men who were his ardent admirers. There-

ably through some mistake, never prosecuted it, continuing to preach during the interval in his accustomed manner. After one year, the term of the appeal, had passed, Garden summoned him again and, as he neither appeared nor put in an answer, declared him suspended from his clerical office. The decree was absolutely ignored and the evangelist, who was now at the summit of his success, proceeded on his course without being affected by it to the slightest degree.[1]

As has been previously explained,[2] from a date early in the eighteenth century, North Carolina had upon paper a fully developed church establishment. A statute providing for this in a specially elaborate form was included in the revisal of 1715.[3] Nine parishes, all lying in the northeastern section of the province which was then settled, were named in this act, and lists of their vestrymen given. But two years later Governor Eden wrote that there was but one Anglican clergyman in the province and he a man of thoroughly disreputable character, who had been sent over as a missionary by the Venerable Society. A little later another missionary came to the province, but he after a time died in service, and in 1721, the same governor wrote that there was no clergyman of the English Church left in North Carolina.[4] The "nine parishes, consisting of upwards of 2500 white souls," were left destitute of the ministrations of religion except what were furnished by lay readers. In 1729 Governor Everard wrote that still there was no settled Anglican clergyman in the province, though one from Nansemond, Virginia, occasionally ministered to some in one of the northern counties. Meantime the Quakers were gaining steadily and Baptists had begun to appear and, under the lead of Paul Palmer, had

fore either no agreement could be reached or one that was adverse to the crown, and for this reason he repelled the proposal.

[1] Regularly the final step in the process would have been the excommunication of Whitefield. But Garden stopped short of that, because the statutes of Elizabeth on which the issue of that writ was grounded did not extend to America. "Unless such difficulties are removed," added Garden, "a Commissary's office or Authority will be of little avail against any irregularities of the Clergy."

[2] Osgood, Am. Colonies in the 17th Century, II, 245–6, 332.

[3] N. C. Recs., II, 207.

[4] Ibid., 293, 331, 430.

gained hundreds of converts.[1] Respecting the Quakers, Governor Burrington wrote later, that they were " considerable for their numbers and substance, the regularity of their lives, hospitality to strangers and kind offices to new settlers, inducing many to be of their persuasion." [2]

For a brief time after 1730 two English clergymen officiated in North Carolina, but before the close of 1732 they had disappeared and the province was again left totally destitute.[3] Meantime some Independent or Presbyterian ministers from New England had begun to appear, and gather congregations, and it was feared that more would follow. In 1729, when royal government was fully established an act had been passed regulating vestries, providing for the building of churches, the purchase of glebes and support of the clergy.[4] But that this also remained largely a dead letter, is proven by the speech of Burrington to the two houses in July, 1733. He called upon them to support the established worship and make competent provisions for the ministry. " The little Provision hitherto made for supporting the publick worship," he continued, "seems to be a reproach to the Country, and prevents many good People from coming here to settle." In most of the parishes churches were still lacking, and Burrington's understanding of the purpose of the legislators was that none of the things promised in the law of 1729 should be accomplished.[5] In 1736 the council in assembly acknowledged the truth contained in a scathing rebuke from Governor Gabriel Johnston for the deplorable and almost total lack of divine worship throughout the province. Not the least care had ever been taken, he said, to erect a school or educate their children. When he dissolved the assembly, some months later, he cited as one of the reasons its failure to redress these grievances.[6] Commissary Garden was doubtless right when he attributed the responsibility for this situation in part to the discord existing between the executive and the lower house, " about civil concerns." [7] A few letters, written in 1742-3 and in 1745, from two missionaries, one re-

---

[1] N. C. Recs., III, 48.
[2] Ibid., 430.
[3] Ibid., 339–343, 394, 429.
[4] Ibid., 552; XXIII, 116.

[5] Ibid., Recs., III, 541, 552, 600.
[6] Ibid., IV, 227, 231, 244.
[7] Ibid., 265.

siding in the southern and the other in the northern part of
the province, throw a vivid light on conditions and show that
they had not changed.[3]  One of these men, after describing
the great labors which were expected of him and the pittance
which vestries, composed chiefly of dissenters, were willing
to pay, exclaimed, " No Province in America, as far as I can
learn, has more need of Missionaries and none can deserve
them less." In 1746 the Venerable Society appointed Governor Johnston one of its members and took the religious
state of that province into consideration, summoning Commissary Garden to aid in the work, with what results will
appear later.

In New York, the only other province where the English
Church had even a nominal establishment, during the years
now under review no outstanding events occurred which in
a sketch of this nature call for special discussion.  The progress of ecclesiastical relations in that province has already
been traced until the controversies which grew out of the
partial establishment and of the disturbed political conditions of the early decades of the century had spent themselves.  Such disputes as followed were confined to localities
and individual churches and reveal nothing specially novel
or important.  The Presbyterian Church in New York City
asked for incorporation and secured it, though Anglican influence was cast against the demand.  The worship of a Baptist
congregation in the city was recognized.  Various local disputes in Westchester were settled to the general satisfaction
of the Anglicans.  Throughout Burnet's administration affairs
moved on smoothly and amicably, and relations were not
disturbed under his successors.  The same is true of New
Jersey and Pennsylvania where, though there was no pretence of an establishment, the predominance of dissenters
was much the same and relations were not essentially different from those which existed in New York.  The Anglican
clergy in Pennsylvania and the Lower Counties, who cared
for some dozen parishes, none lying more than about twenty
miles west of the Delaware river and bay, were not even
under the supervision of a commissary.  Yet they met together from time to time, and their reputation was certainly

as good as that of the average among the missionaries who were sent over by the Venerable Society. As there was no establishment in these colonies, the relations of the clergy with public officials were generally amicable. But the course of immigration and the persistent growth of the dissenting sects which had originally settled these colonies, were such as to make with every decade any expectation of Anglican ascendancy more and more hopeless.

It was in New England, where the efforts of the Venerable Society and its missionaries were met by a confident and defiant majority, organized in two colonies under a well compacted state church system, that the most important and dramatic events occurred. There the issues were fought with a vigor and on a scale which lends an interest and definiteness to the subject, to which in most of the provinces it scarcely attains. Says the candid historian of King's Chapel,[1] " The standing grievance between the two parties was in the fact that each really claimed supremacy of the same kind. Congregationalism was practically the Established Church of Massachusetts. . . . Face to face with this institution, to which the great majority of the people still belonged, . . . now stood a few members of the powerful establishment of the mother country, denying that any other institution could exist by English law except by sufferance, — some even denying all validity to Christian ordinances as administered in New England. The question was, which was the Established Church and which were the Dissenters? — a question whose only possible solution came in consequence of a long quarrel, but in a way which neither party either desired or dreamed."

In September, 1722, in connection with Yale College, a resounding blow was administered to the New England churches, which woke them from their dreams of security and drove the more intelligent among their clergy not only to consult the Mathers but the Bible and accessible writings on church government, for arguments against episcopacy and the doctrine of apostolic succession.[2] This was the declaration of Timothy Cutler, rector of the College, Daniel Brown, a tutor, James Wetmore, pastor of the church at North

---

[1] Foote, Annals of King's Chapel, I, 251.
[2] Doc. Hist. of Church in Conn., 62–78.

Haven, and Samuel Johnson, pastor of the church at West Haven, that they were persuaded of the invalidity of presbyterian ordination. Three other prominent clergymen joined with these in expressing doubts upon the same subject, but in the end did not renounce the system under which they had been reared.

Johnson, who in after life became the most influential of these men, gives in his autobiography [1] an interesting account of intellectual conditions in Connecticut at the time and of the process by which the change was wrought in his own mind and in those of his associates. When he graduated from Yale, in 1714, they had heard of " a new philosophy that of late was all in vogue and of such names as Des Cartes, Boyle, Locke and Newton, but they were cautioned against thinking anything of them, because the new philosophy, it was said, would soon bring in a new Divinity and corrupt the pure Religion of the Country, and they were not allowed to vary an Ace in their thought from Dr. Ames's Medulla Theologiae and Cases of Conscience and Wollebius, which were the only Systems of Divinity that were thumbed in those days and considered with equal if not greater veneration than the Bible itself, for the Contrivance of those and the like Scholastical Authors was to make curious Systems in a Scientific way out of their own heads and under each head to pick up a few texts of Scripture, which seemed to sound favorably and accommodate them to their preconceived Schemes."

No book of learning, continues Johnson, was to be had in those times which was less than a century or a century and a half old, such as the first settlers brought over seventy or eighty years before. Some few used to make synopses or abridgements of these. Johnson was thought to excel in this, having drawn up a little system of all parts of learning then known in " a Curious Cobweb of Distributions and Definitions." His interest in this continued until he lighted on Bacon's Advancement of Learning, " perhaps the only

[1] A manuscript copy of this is in the Library of Columbia University. It was used by Beardsley in writing his Life of Johnson. More information concerning the books sent over by Dummer may be obtained from Dexter's Documentary History of Yale and Oviatt's Beginnings of Yale.

copy in the country and nobody knew its Value." He at once bought the book and quickly fell to studying it. His reading of Bacon soon brought down his towering imaginations. He saw his own littleness in comparison with Bacon's greatness. He considered him over and over, so that he found himself like one emerging from the glimmer of twilight into the full sunshine of the open day. At this time also the books collected by Jeremiah Dummer, agent of Connecticut, came over and were added to the college library. They consisted of the works of the best English poets, philosophers and divines — Shakespeare, Milton, Locke, Boyle, Newton and others; and among the divines Barrow, Tillotson, South, Sharp, Scott, Sherlock, and others.[1] These were like a " flood of day." Only a few, except Johnson, Cutler and their friends, had any curiosity to consult them, but they devoured them with avidity and through their appointment as officers of the college or by settling near by, were able to continue their studies and strengthen their friendships.

Another characteristic of Johnson was his dislike of enthusiasm, a disposition which we may regard as constitutional, but which he attributed to his having noted in college how it led to conceit and spiritual pride. For much the same reasons he disliked independent church government, which made every individual think himself infallible and whose powers of discipline were often directed against mere human frailties or to revenge little private quarrels, resulting in the end in violent animosities and separations. Much embarrassed he also was by " rigid Calvinistical notions " which he had been taught to believe because every one did. But when he turned to the divines of the English Church, his mind was made easy on these points, and the Book of Common Prayer, with which he had long been acquainted, he found a most acceptable manual of devotion, the contents of which were drawn very directly from Scripture. This indicates Johnson's state of mind when, in 1720, he became pastor of the Congregational church in West Haven. In his public ministry he freely used the language of the Prayer Book and borrowed ideas, though putting them in his own language,

---

[1] Dummer states that the works of all the eminent divines among the dissenters were also in the collection. Dexter, *op. cit.*, 241.

from the sermons of Isaac Barrow. These he found very acceptable to his hearers, though they were not aware until later of the sources whence they came. The history of the early Church also formed an important subject of his study.

A similar course was being pursued by Cutler and his other friends, and they agreed in the opinion that conditions in New England differed widely from those in the primitive church where, as they read the texts in the light of Anglican interpretation, no ordination or act of government occurred without the presence of a bishop at the head of the presbytery. Pigot, who had recently come as the missionary of the Venerable Society to Stratford, was visited by Johnson and was also brought to New Haven and introduced to the group of inquirers there. The exchange of visits which followed provoked comment and led people to expect strange things, and it was this which led to the interview with the trustees, already mentioned, and the statement which then was made. As the general assembly was to meet at New Haven in October, Governor Saltonsall suggested that a debate should then be held in the college library and the whole subject discussed. This was agreed to and over the debate, when held, the governor presided. Johnson was the chief speaker on the pro-Anglican side and, in his opinion, the defenders of independency were not so well equipped with arguments as they should have been. Under the circumstances this was natural, while to the modern scholar the citations of Johnson — the position of Timothy at Ephesus, of Titus in Crete and of the angels of the seven churches in Asia — would be far too few and narrow to settle the question.[1] But an outburst of human nature in the form of an impassioned harangue from an aged minister who was present, led the governor to bring the conference abruptly to an end. The connection of Cutler and Brown with the college had already been severed and they, with Johnson, at once sailed for England. There they were admitted to orders in the established church. Brown died in England, but the other two returned as missionaries. Cutler became rector of Christ Church in Boston, the second episcopal congregation

[1] Beardsley, Life of Johnson. See Oviatt's Beginnings of Yale, p. 306, et seq., for the latest account of these events.

which was gathered in that town. Johnson settled as successor of Pigot at Stratford, Connecticut, where he entered upon a long and most honourable career. Wetmore soon followed in the same course and, after his return from England, was settled for more than thirty years over the church at Rye, New York. In 1732 Rev. John Beach, also a graduate of Yale, went over to Anglicanism and, residing at Reading, as a preacher and controversialist became one of the ablest defenders of Episcopacy in the colonies.

An interesting episode connected with the growth of Anglican inflence in New England which resulted from these events was the visit of George Berkeley, the famous philosopher and divine, to America in prosecution of his plan to found a college in Bermuda, from which to supply the colonies with clergymen and thus aid in the conversion of the Indians to Christianity. For two and one-half years (1728–9–1731) Berkeley was resident, with his family, upon his estate of Whitehall, just north of Newport, Rhode Island, writing " Alciphron " and waiting for the permission of the British Government — which never came — to proceed with the building of his college.[1] Johnson repeatedly visited Berkeley and the common philosophic tastes of the two clergymen led to a warm friendship between them. This led in course of time to the gift of Berkeley's farm to Yale College and also a notable donation of books to its library. Religious scruples were not sufficient to prevent the acceptance of these, while Berkeley's presence, and the remembrance of it after he had returned to England, served as a stimulus to the episcopal missionaries in New England and especially to Johnson. This scholarly and conscientious man, without violating the proprieties of his position, kept up connection with students in Yale who were inclined toward episcopacy, corresponded largely with other missionaries in the colonies and with his ecclesiastical superiors in England.[1] He also frequently visited New York, especially during

[1] Johnson states in his autobiography that Berkeley came to Rhode Island in order to settle a correspondence there for supplying the college with provisions. He also says that Berkeley became convinced that the college should be located at some place on the continent, probably New York.

[2] Doc. Hist. of Church in Conn. 92, 94, 97, 105, 145, 147, 148, 157; Beardsley, Church in Conn. I, 64 et seq.

Burnet's administration, whose ample library he found most attractive, though the governor's liking for the extremely Low Church theology of Benjamin Hoadley seemed almost as dangerous to Johnson as deism itself. The perilous voyage which Johnson was forced to take to England in order to secure admission to orders, as well as his observation of other similar experiences and of the loss of valuable lives which often resulted therefrom, strengthened his conviction that resident bishops were a necessity for the colonial church. Therefore he became a strong and continuous advocate of the colonial episcopate, acting as the leader among all the missionaries of his time in this cause. Though milder in his temper than Talbot, he was quite as insistent upon this point, and helped to continue the demand from the time when Talbot's voice was hushed until late in the colonial period.

In 1726, in response to a letter from Bishop Gibson, Governor Talcott, who had succeeded Saltonstall as head of the Connecticut Government,[1] complacently wrote, "The law of this colony is such that the major part of the householders in every town shall determine their ministers' maintenance, and all within the precincts of the town shall be obliged to pay their parts in an equal proportion to their estates in said towns or societies and so in the precincts of each ecclesiastical society. Under this security all our towns and ecclesiastical societies are supplied with orthodox ministers. We have no vacancies at present. When the death of the incumbent happens, they are quickly supplied by persons of our own communion, educated in our public schools of learning; which, through the divine blessing afforded us, we have a sufficiency of those that are both learned and exemplary in their lives." Of the truth of this statement the reader can satisfy himself by reference at any length to the statutes and administrative orders of Connecticut.[2] The same, of course, was true of Massachusetts, and, when one reflects, it was not so different from the system which had always been

[1] Beardsley, Church in Conn., I,

[2] Conn. Col. Recs. V, 48, 50, 87, 333; VI, 34, 248, 277, 380, 401; VII, 74, 211, 309, 334, 534. The entries in every volume concerning the formation of new "societies," i.e. parishes in the modern sense of the term, and the division of old ones, reveal with special clearness the compactness of the system.

in vogue in Virginia. Both were adapted to small and rather secluded communities which, intellectually at least, were in a static condition and tended to remain so. To the mind of Talcott, though he is credited with a milder attitude toward dissent than Saltonstall had shown, the world seemed to contain little that was desirable in the matter of religion which Connecticut did not possess.

But Anglicans, like the Baptists, were appearing in small groups here and there, in town after town. They were declining to pay church rates, were setting up services of their own and were insisting that their money should go exclusively to ministers of their own name. It was a renewal of the same conflict through which the ancestors of the New Englanders had gone in England in the previous century; but now they were in the saddle and their type of religion and culture in general had made them rather less than more tolerant. Johnson, in several of his letters, tells what happened to Anglicans when they attempted to find a lodgement within this ecclesiastical fortress, and the story is the same in the case of the Baptists. "My Lord," he wrote to the bishop in 1724, "poor people here are very much discouraged on account of the unreasonable demands of the government in exacting taxes from them to the support of the Independent teachers, for which sundry people, and those of both sexes, have been unmercifully imprisoned, contrary to the indulgence granted to them in government, by their charter, which forbids them to do anything contrary to the laws of England, and we humbly beg your Lordship's protection." In February, 1726/7, Johnson tells of visiting a number of Anglicans in prison — presumably in Fairfield — and finding the building full of them and an insulting mob outside. On this occasion an address signed by some of the prisoners was sent to the bishop.[1] Another feature of the situation, which was specially galling, was the power of the selectmen of any town, under the laws of settlement, to prevent strangers from settling among them, a power which they were said to be only too willing to use against churchmen and dissenters generally.

But in 1727, in response to a petition from the churchmen of Fairfield, the first concession was made, in the form of a

[1] Doc. Hist. of Church in Conn., 95, 108, 112, 113, 124.

law, that in towns where a society of the church of England existed and maintained regular services, the collectors should pay over to its minister the amount raised from those who lived conveniently near and attended such services, and if this should not prove adequate to his support, the rest must be voluntarily contributed by its hearers.[1]  Two years later those who proved by certificates that they were members of Quaker and Baptist congregations were also excused from paying church rates,[2] but in their case no provision was made for collecting the equivalent from their communicants.  In this case of the Quakers events which had recently occurred in Massachusetts contributed to this result, while a special petition, aided by coöperation from Rhode Island, had been presented by the Baptists.  But these laws were only the thin end of the wedge, the first breach in the wall of religious exclusiveness.  Much had still to be won.  In the law relating to churchmen no provision was made for the relief of those who lived outside the two or three towns where Anglican churches existed or soon after were founded.  In 1728 application was made to the assembly for an explanation of the law,[3] but such explanation as was given described so narrow a circle about the churches — two miles — as to leave many families or groups of Anglicans outside.  Also, when undivided lands of towns were sold, parts of funds so derived were appropriated for the sole benefit of the Congregationalists, and when in 1738 seven townships were laid out from the western lands, a large fund derived from the sale of those lands was divided among the churches of the colony in such manner that none who dissented could get any benefit from it.  Against this last measure a very numerously signed memorial was presented to the assembly by the Anglicans, but both houses negatived their request.[4]  In 1740, however, the offensive act was repealed and the income from the lands was allowed, under an earlier law, to revert to the schools of the colony, the Anglicans and others, of course, still being excluded from its benefits.

[1] Conn. Recs., VII, 106; Bea·dsley, op. cit., I, 68 et seq.
[2] Ibid., 237, 257; Backus, I, 521; Greene, Development of Religious Liberty in Conn., 216.
[3] Doc. Hist. etc., 129.
[4] Ibid., 167, 173; Beardsley, I, 106–110; Conn. Recs. VII, 123, 334.

The point has now been reached where it is necessary to refer briefly to the policy followed by the Massachusetts government under the second charter in reference to ecclesiastical affairs.[1] With the recall of the first charter the religious test was entirely abandoned, and the execution of the laws in general which had constituted the basis of the Puritan Commonwealth became impossible. On the other hand, so long as Andros and his associates were at the head of affairs, all possible encouragement was given to the Anglicans, and the Quakers were left undisturbed. The new charter, in harmony with the policy of comprehension favored by William and with the spirit of the Toleration Act broadly interpreted, provided that liberty of conscience should be enjoyed by all Christians, except papists, who should inhabit or reside within the province. Mather and his co-religionists valued this clause as a protection against encroachments of the Church of England. But by Quakers and Baptists it was understood to mean protection for them also from oppression by the Puritans of Massachusetts. If the provision was liberally interpreted, a new ecclesiastical system must develop in Massachusetts, differing radically from that which existed under the first charter and from the polity of Connecticut. The fact that Plymouth was now a part of Massachusetts might lead to the expectation that the attitude of Massachusetts toward heretics and dissenters would be somewhat softened. In some of the towns of Plymouth also lived many Quakers, and their inclusion added to the strength of these sectaries who already existed in considerable numbers along the Rhode Island border and in Lynn, Salem and several other towns in the northeast. The Baptists also, as we have seen, were making some progress, while the addition of the Maine settlements with their sprinkling of Baptists, Anglicans and Quakers, with many who were irreligious, made the people of provincial Massachusetts more varied ecclesiastically than they had been in the earlier colony.

But the traditions of the state-church system were too strong in Massachusetts to admit of an interpretation of the charter which would give to these sects equal rights with

---

[1] For the latest treatment of this subject, see Susan M. Reed's monograph, Church and State in Massachusetts, already referred to.

"that Religion which is the General Profession of the Country."[1]  The interpretation put by the Mathers upon the charter was that it secured the religion of the country in its privileged position beyond the possibility of disturbance, and it was in harmony with this view that legislation in the province developed, although the suffrage was now regulated by a property instead of a religious qualification.  As under the old charter, the only idea which was held by the Puritans was that of corporate liberty, the liberty of a closely compacted group, which knew no toleration toward minorities or individuals who were dissentients.  By a series of laws which were passed during the first five years of provincial government, all towns were required to provide themselves with able and orthodox ministers of good conversation and to see that they were suitably maintained, the court of quarter sessions of the counties being empowered, in cases of neglect, to order due assessments to be laid and collected.  In cases of total neglect, the court itself might procure and settle a minister and levy the charge on the inhabitants of the town. Under the old charter the practical identity of freemen and church members had resulted in a system under which ministers had virtually been elected by towns.  At first a similar provision was made in a province law — that ministers should be chosen by the majority of the inhabitants in town meeting and that the whole town should be obliged to pay toward their maintenance.  But now, in a number of towns, the inhabitants and the church membership were far from being identical, while in Boston there was more than one church and support by voluntary contributions was in vogue.  In order to avoid this difficulty, when it was perceived, provision was made that the choice of a minister, to be valid, must be concurred in by the majority of those who usually attended public worship and were by law qualified for voting in town affairs.  All the inhabitants and rateable estates in the town were, however, required to pay proportionably toward maintenance.  The selectmen or other assessors of towns which were wholly neglectful might be fined for the offence.  In order to bring additional pressure

---

[1] I. Mather, "The Great Blessing of Primitive Counsellours," and C. Mather, "Parentator," quoted by Miss Reed, p. 22.

upon towns where the number of non-concurrents was large, local councils of ministers and delegates from neighboring towns m.ght be called.[1] Finally, in 1702, because of resistance in the Quaker towns of Dartmouth and Tiverton, authority was given the general court to intervene in such cases, secure a minister and provide for his maintenance. This legislation was allowed by the home government to stand, though in one instance the bishop of London tried to procure a disallowance. Its effect was again to array the civil power in support of the accepted churches of the province about as effectively as under the earlier charter. For practical purposes, though with differences of detail, Massachusetts and Connecticut were again ecclesiastically upon the same basis and prepared to offer a similar resistance to the progress of dissent. Her churches, however, were not so thoroughly organized as were those of Connecticut under the Saybrook Platform.

Anglicanism was an equally dangerous foe in both these colonies. The activities of Baptists were upon a similar scale in both. But the Quakers had made comparatively little headway in Connecticut, while in Massachusetts they were increasingly numerous and aggressive. Their network of monthly, quarterly and yearly meetings, which had developed in eastern New England by 1700, with the reports of " sufferings " which were regularly submitted, gave them an effective machinery for persistent agitation. The chief contests, beginning shortly before the end of the seventeenth century, were carried on with the towns of Swansea, Dartmouth and Tiverton. In the first named the opposing body was a well organized Baptist congregation; in the others the opposition came from Quakers. In other towns in the same section similar, though not so strong, elements of opposition appeared. The local officials were partly or wholly negligent and the court of sessions of Bristol county, backed by the general court, had to interfere. The process began in 1698. The three towns named declared that they were already provided with ministers, meaning in one case a Baptist and in the other case Quaker preachers. In the cases of

[1] Acts and Res. of Mass., I, 28, 62, 66, 102, 216, 276, 505, 597; II, 26; Reed, *op. cit.*, 24 *et seq.*

Dartmouth and Tiverton unsuccessful efforts continued to be made at intervals until 1706 to procure the settlement of orthodox ministers. Then an appeal was made to the general court, under the act of 1706. Though a minister was presented by it to each of these towns, their taxes fell into arrears, their assessors were imprisoned and finally a considerable part of the ministers' support had to come from the province treasury. Prolonged struggles also occurred with other towns in the neighborhood, and from them, when viewed collectively, it became clear that the province government was being worsted in its efforts to uphold orthodoxy in this section.

But throughout these years the Quakers, in their local meetings and in the great London Meeting, were noting all the instances of oppression which their members were enduring, in the form of imprisonment, enforced payment of taxes for the support of an alien faith, refusal to accept the affirmation and the like, and were preparing to oppose such policies by petitions, appeals to the king in council or in other suitable ways. Quakers at this time stood well in England and had abundant access to men of influence in office and out. They were steadily growing on both sides of the Atlantic and the influence of the leaders of the sect was freely used to encourage their struggling brethren in New England, in Maryland or wherever else they might need support. Penn, of course, was a leader in this, but William Crouch, Richard Borden of Tiverton and Thomas Richardson of Newport, Richard Partridge of New Hampshire and others, were also very active and serviceable. They upheld the cause of the chartered colonies, procured the repeal of the Connecticut law against heretics, labored for colonial liberties in all convenient ways, and finally combined for a general assault on the legislation which restricted religious liberty in Massachusetts.

It was the Massachusetts law of 1706, renewed in 1715 and 1722, the highest assertion of the prerogative of the general court by which it could interfere and settle ministers in recalcitrant towns,[1] against which they directed their chief

---

[1] In 1722, and perhaps in earlier years, the amounts in taxes levied on the towns in question were increased.

attacks. Some expression of sympathy they obtained from
Governor Dudley. A certain amount of coöperation they
secured from the Congregational clergy in England, and
Jeremiah Dummer wrote Judge Sewall that the magistrates
of Massachusetts had an ill name in England because of
their independence and their severe treatment of Quakers and
Baptists, who were looked upon as equal with Presbyterians
and Independents under the toleration act. Before 1718
little was accomplished, because it was undertaken chiefly by
individuals. But beginning with that year joint action through
the yearly meetings in New England and the London Meeting, supported by general contributions, was resolved upon.
In 1719 a petition for relief was laid before the privy council.
But, learning that there was a chance for favorable legislation in Massachusetts itself, they turned in that direction.
The council was presently found to be favorable, but the
house of representatives stood out. As it maintained this
attitude against the reasoning of the council, in 1723 through
Partridge and Richardson the Quakers petitioned the crown
on behalf of the imprisoned assessors of Dartmouth and Tiverton and of the Quaker cause in general. The Massachusetts
agents were called in, counsel were employed and the final
result was the disallowance of the act of 1722.[1]

After further sufferings in New England and delays in
Great Britain consequent on the demise of George I, in 1728
the first law was passed in Massachusetts which was intended
to give relief.[2] Baptists as well as Quakers were included
under this act, this being due especially to the persistence of
the congregations at Swansea and Rehoboth, this sect being
destitute both of effective organization in the colonies and
of support from England. The law provided that those who
were in the habit of attending Baptist or Quaker meetings
weekly and who lived within five miles of one of their places
of worship, should be exempt from poll taxes for the support
of the established ministry and from arrest for failure to
pay such rates. The names of all members of such congregations and of those who were habitual attendants upon the
same must be annually reported to the local magistrates in

[1] Reed, *op. cit.*, 86 *et seq.*; Acts of P. C. Col, 1720–1745, pp. 58, 121;
B. T. Journal, Nov. and Dec. 1723.    [2] Acts and Res., II, 494.

order to insure the exemption.  Quakers were also required to declare before the court of general sessions their fidelity and their belief in the Trinity and in the divine inspiration of the Scriptures.  A year later the exemption was extended to taxes on real and personal estates as well as to poll taxes.[1]

By these laws the first breach was made in the Massachusetts system of religious exclusiveness.  But the victory did not bring the full relief that was demanded.  Therefore the agitation was continued, and it now received the effective aid of Governor Belcher, brother-in-law of Richard Partridge, and for political as well as personal reasons interested in putting an end to the Quaker agitation.  Moreton and Borden, who had recently been prominent in negotiations on behalf of the Quakers, soon approached the governor.  He early brought the grievances of the Quakers to the attention of the houses and by his influence overcame the opposition of the representatives.  The result was the passage, near the close of 1731, of an act, to continue in force five years, exempting Quakers, wherever they lived, wholly from taxation for the building of churches as well as the support of ministers.[2]  Lists of those who were entitled to the privilege of the act to be prepared by local assessors and duly published.  This law brought the needed relief, and due acknowledgment by the yearly meeting was made to the governor for his assistance.  Three years later a similar law was passed for the benefit of the Baptists.[3]

It is now time to direct attention again to the Anglicans, the third religious body which was dissatisfied with its treatment by Massachusetts and was trying to strengthen its position.  Their position prior to the close of Dudley's administration has already been described.  Though, because of his nonconformist connections, the conservative Congregationalists in New England had counted on the support of Shute, they were disappointed, for he joined the Venerable Society and undertook to support its missionaries.  But he was a bungler in politics and did not understand the limitations of his power as Dudley had done.  Churchmen in Marblehead, Newbury, Braintree and other country towns had long been petitioning for exemption from the require-

---

[1] Acts and Res., II, 543.    [2] Ibid.; 619.    [3] Ibid., 714.

ment to support the established ministry and churches. Shute ordered the magistrates of Marblehead not to levy any more rates upon Anglicans there for the support of " any Dissenting Minister." But his order was ignored and all were compelled to pay as heretofore.[1] The governor also took similar action upon complaints which came from Newbury and Bristol, but with the same result. After Shute went back to England, Dummer returned to the attitude of Dudley and, more than that, plainly told the Anglicans that what the local magistrates were doing was legal and that it could only be changed by new enactments. An appeal for relief was now made by four of the local clergy, among whom were Myles and Harris of King's Chapel, to Gibson who had recently become bishop of London.[2] The bishop at once wrote to Dummer asking that he would protect the clergy amid their hardships, and also sent a set of queries to be answered by the commissaries.[3] Myles answered for Massachusetts and informed the bishop that there were several laws for establishing the Independents and settling orthodox ministers who were elected by the people, and that it would be greatly to the advantage of the Church if its members were freed from compulsion to pay for the support of these ministers, as they were forced to do in many places, and some were then suffering imprisonment for their refusal to submit. But it was at this juncture that the prosecution of Checkley at Boston occurred, as well as the attempt of the Massachusetts clergy to hold a synod, and these were not unimportant episodes in the struggle between Anglicanism and Independency.

Almost contemporary with the defection of Cutler and his associates in Connecticut came the publication by John Checkley at Boston of those attacks upon the Puritan Church order and arguments in support of episcopacy which led to his prosecution. Checkley was a native of Boston who had resided and travelled abroad for a period of some fifteen years, a part of which time was spent under private instructors at Oxford.[4] On his return he opened a store for the

---

[1] Hist. Colls. of Am. Col. Church (Massachusetts), 139, 140.
[2] Fulham Mss.
[3] Hist. Colls. 144, 153, 154.
[4] Slafter, John Checkley, in Pubs. of Prince Soc.; Foote, Annals of King's Chapel, I.

sale of medicines, books and small articles of merchandise, in his native town. He also became active as a member of the small group of wits and of men who aspired to some form of culture, other than the theological, which had begun to appear in Boston. The subject in which Checkley seems to have become interested while abroad, was the history and theology of the English Church. He declared himself a disciple of its controversialists and prominent divines of the seventeenth and early eighteenth centuries. Though loyal to the reigning house, he sympathized with the attitude and spirit of the non-jurors and was an advocate of the claims of episcopacy in their extreme and least compromising form. He first made known this attitude in private conversation and then began to attack the Independents and Presbyterians in print.

In 1719 Checkley attempted to reprint the Non-Juror Charles Leslie's " Short and Easie Method with the Deists," a tract which in very pointed fashion set forth the accepted Anglican view of the origin and development of revealed religion — including apostolic and episcopal succession — as a corrective of the theory of natural religion [1] which was expounded by the English deists and also of views of the dissenters. Under order from the council of the province the publication of this work was forbidden. But, in 1722, Checkley published " A Modest Proof of the Order and Government Settled by Christ and his Apostles in the Church," which was his own defence of the doctrine of episcopal succession. In this pamphlet, following Leslie and doubtless other writings of Anglican divines, selecting appropriate texts of Scripture and, as he sat in his little Boston bookstore, training his historical imagination along certain definite and approved lines, by methods well known to sectarians and dogmatists of all types, Checkley drew a picture of a church, not of Christianity in the early centuries, which was a model of definiteness and self consistency. The gentle poet, dreamer and mystic of Galilee, whose mission in the world was to teach love in its purest and highest forms, was represented as an organizer who marshalled his disciples in the grades and ranks of an organization so perfect that in admiration of it

[1] Duniway, Freedom of the Press in Mass. (Harvard Hist. Studies), 84.

the world could be sure to forget the spirit and life, which were the only things that could give it value. Checkley's publication called into the arena a new and formidable antagonist in the person of Jonathan Dickinson, the Presbyterian divine of whom we have already heard and who was later to be president of the College of New Jersey. His "Defence of Presbyterian Ordination" was the earliest of a number of ably written controversial pamphlets as precise, narrow and scholastic as Checkley's, but giving a presbyterian view of the organization of the early church. Viewed from the scientific standpoint the arguments on both sides were futile, because the critical knowledge of the New Testament and of other writings of the time, and of social conditions as they then were, did not exist in the eighteenth century. The assumptions of partisans could not then be checked by a study of the early Christian centuries so profound as to show the uncertainty of all their cut and dried theories.

But it was probably a good thing for New England to have Checkley give publicity in such extreme form to the Anglican theory of the early church, for even such a statement as his had never before been permitted within that carefully guarded inclosure. Neither were such high Tory views acceptable to the Whig government in England, and Bishop Gibson wrote in a tone calculated to moderate the zeal of his clergy in Massachusetts. But such reaction as was to be expected followed the earliest intimations that such opinions were held and were seeking expression. In 1719, as soon as Checkley had published his first pamphlet and a minor brochure which followed it, a law was enacted authorizing two justices of the peace to tender the oath of allegiance and abjuration to any one who had incurred suspicion of being disaffected to the crown as then settled in the house of Brunswick. Twenty-seven years had passed since the statute had been passed in England which it was the object of this act to enforce in Massachusetts and until now no occasion had arisen for such a measure.[1] The similarity between Checkley's ideas and those of non-jurors, together with expressions of sympathy with them which he probably used, doubtless

[1] Slafter, *op. cit.*, I, 35.

suggested the point of attack. This might serve to silence him. But when the justices appeared and tendered him the oath, like any man who was conscious of innocence, he refused to take it. The quarter sessions then fined him £6 and put him under heavy bonds to keep the peace. Under these he remained for four years and then, to remove the scandalous report that he had been disaffected, he took the oath. It is probable that Checkley was brought to see the practical folly of holding out, by the defeat of his application for admission to holy orders when he was on a visit to England in 1722.

In 1723, soon after Checkley returned from England, he issued and sold further selections from Leslie's writings, together with some additions of his own, the whole constituting another direct attack upon the established order in Massachusetts.[1] For this he was immediately prosecuted under an order of the council and tried for libel before the court of general sessions at Boston. He was found guilty and appealed to the court of assize, this being the superior court in criminal session, with Chief Justice Sewall presiding. Sewall, and two of the judges who had presided at the earlier trial, were members of the council which had instituted the prosecution. Robert Auchmuty, in place of the attorney general, acted as counsel for the government, and John Reed, personal friend of the accused and reputed to be the ablest attorney then in Boston, was Checkley's counsel. Checkley himself was also allowed to speak on his own behalf and his speech is the only one made at the trial which has been preserved.[2] The main part of his argument, in support of which he cited the opinions of Governors Dudley and Shute, was to the effect that, according to the provisions of the laws of Elizabeth, Charles II and the Act of Union of 1707, the Church of England, and no other, was established in all the colonies. The jury was not convinced that Checkley's book was a libel and therefore brought in a special verdict,[3]

[1] "A Short and Esie Method with the Deists, Wherein the Certainty of the Christian Religion is demonstrated by infallible Proof from Four Rules, etc. In a letter to a Friend." This was printed in London and sold by John Checkley in Boston. Slafter explains the make-up of this pamphlet.

[2] It is reprinted by Slafter.

[3] It was to the effect that, if it was a libel, then they found the accused guilty; if it was not a libel, they found him not guilty.

throwing upon the court the responsibility of deciding upon its alleged libellous character. That these men, after hearing their cherished establishment declared illegal in such sweeping terms as Checkley used, would do otherwise than declare him guilty, was not to be imagined. The pleas of Reed and Checkley in arrest of judgment proved vain, the former including in his argument the claim that the libellous character of the publication should be determined by the jury and not by the court. The accused was declared guilty, fined and put under bonds to keep the peace. Though Checkley suffered and found Harris, one of the ministers of King's Chapel, strongly incensed against him chiefly because of his reactionary political views, he had struck a powerful blow for episcopacy and started a discussion which was not to cease until independence. Pamphlets and articles on both sides, written by men in a number of the northern colonies, now began to be issued from the press and a prosecution for libel of publications in defence of episcopacy could never again be attempted in New England.[1]

Since the issue of the new charter by William and Mary no synod had been held by the New England churches, though in 1715 an abortive attempt had been made to call one. But now the general convention which met in May, 1725, under the lead of Cotton Mather, felt that the time had come to revive an institution from which strength had been derived in the previous century. The ministers were moved to this proposal by the " great and visible decay of piety " and the " growth of many miscarriages," which they interpreted as judgments from the Lord sent for the purpose of distressing them. Among these we may be sure that the growth of episcopacy held a leading place. William Dummer, the lieutenant governor, and the two houses of the general court were asked to call such synod to consider remedies, " expedient to put a stop unto those or the like miscarriages." The council approved the proposal, but the house after a long debate voted to postpone the subject till the next session. Cutler and Myles, the clergymen of the two Anglican churches in Boston, took advantage of this delay to memorialize Dummer and the two houses against the synod. In this they

[1] See Foote, Annals of King's Chapel, I, 294, *et seq.*

claimed that the Church of England was more than equally concerned with the other churches of the colony, because it was the established church. As all the colonies, they concluded, were annexed to the diocese of London, nothing ecclesiastical could be done without the cognizance of the bishop and it would not be consistent with his rights or dutiful to the king to call a synod until his majesty's pleasure was known. Because of an " inherent reflection," and the " groundless insinuations " which it contained, this address was rejected by the lower house.[1]

The two clergymen now wrote to Gibson, bishop of London, upon the subject. He gave proof of his energy as the new incumbent of that see by calling the duke of Newcastle's attention to the clause in the Act of Union respecting the oath of the king and queen to uphold the Church, which seemed to imply that it was established throughout the dominions. If that was true, added the bishop, the Independent clergy were simply tolerated, as in England. He brought the matter to the attention of the lords justices, and they caused the opinion of the law officers to be taken. They reported, that they could not find such an establishment in Massachusetts as would warrant the holding of synods, but, if such bodies were to meet, it must be under the king's authority; and being only a voluntary society, they could perform no authoritative acts.[2] They also conceived that the application of the ministers to the general court was a contempt of his Majesty and an invasion of his authority, which the lieutenant governor should have withstood. After administering a sharp reproof to Dummer, the lords justices ordered him to put a stop to all proceedings such as had been intended and, if those concerned should persist in meeting, to prosecute them for misdemeanor. He was also given to understand that what had been permissible under the old charter was no longer possible under the new. The plan of holding a synod was therefore dropped and never revived during the colonial period. Never had the churches of New England received so direct a rebuff as this, the chief occa-

---

[1] Acts and Res. of Mass., X, 628.   Hist. Colls. of Am. Col. Church (Massachusetts), 172, 180, 184, 187–190.   Foote, Perry, Palfrey.   Cross, 69.

[2] Chalmers, Opinions

sion of which had been the action of Cutler, the former president of Yale.

Meantime the question of the taxation of Churchmen for the support of the clergy and churches of Massachusetts had been taken up by the Venerable Society, doubtless under the lead of the bishop, and prosecuted in connection with the question of the synod.[1] In addition to frequent letters from local missionaries referring to the penalties inflicted on their communicants, in 1725 a petition reviewing the entire system of Massachusetts legislation on church affairs and urging its repeal was sent to the king in council by Cutler, Myles, Honeyman, McSparran, Plant, Pigot and Johnson.[2] This demand exceeded what was being urged by the Quakers, but it was acted on by the Society, the laws of Connecticut being coupled with those of Massachusetts. Counsel was engaged and the law officers were asked for an opinion whether the colonies, by virtue of their charters, had power to make such laws in prejudice of the Church of England. On the strength of the opinion rendered, a representation to the king was ordered to be drawn in the name of the private persons who had sent over their grievances.[3] This came before the board of trade and some months later directions were given to ask the law officers if the king could repeal the laws in question. But at this juncture occurred the death of the king, as well as the first concession of Massachusetts to the Quakers. The result of further and continuous pressure, however, was that, at the close of 1727, the general court of Massachusetts made in favor of Anglicans the same concessions which had just been made in Connecticut in its first law upon the subject.[4] This action, together with the prominence of the salary question during the administration of Burnet, postponed further decisive action until the governorship of Belcher.

Commissary Price, with the joint vestries of King's Chapel and Christ Church, now took the case in hand, memorialized the bishop of London and petitioned the king upon the sufferings of churchmen in Massachusetts. An elaborate opin-

[1] See Journal of S. P. G., 1724, 1725, 1726, and letters from Mass. in connection therewith.

[2] Hist. Colls. etc., 191.

[3] The opinion is not in the Journal.

[4] Acts and Res., II, 459.

ion on the validity of the ecclesiastical laws of Massachusetts was now obtained from Yorke and Talbot, the attorney and solicitor general.[1]  This was to the effect that the first three acts, passed soon after the grant of the charter, had been confirmed by the crown and could not be repealed without the concurrence of the general court.  The situation with reference to the other three, so far as they had not expired, was practically the same, for they had not been disallowed within the period of three years limited by the charter.  Neither was it thought that the acts were repugnant to the charter, for the clause in it respecting liberty of conscience did not prohibit the establishment of a provincial church in a particular form and providing for worship and the maintenance of ministers as an incident thereto, provided it was done in a reasonable manner.  But even if the acts were void, the fact that they were so could only be established by judicial process.  Finally, the objection made to the law of 1727 was a prudential and not a legal one and that act, being for five years only, would soon expire.

This opinion admirably expressed the spirit of the Whigs under Walpole and left as the only alternative — which was chosen by the joint vestries — the bringing of a test case before the courts of Massachusetts.  The Anglicans were beaten in all the courts of the province and an appeal to England was denied by the superior court, but granted by the king in council.[2]  But the bishop was at the same time corresponding with the governor and,[3] though Belcher was strongly anti-episcopalian, his political aspirations and love of patronage by British aristocrats were so strong that he gave his influence in support of an act,[4] which was passed in 1735 and gave to Anglicans the same conditions of worship which had so recently been granted to Baptists and Quakers.  The further postponement of such legislation had in fact become impossible.  The Anglican leaders, both in Massachusetts and in England, had been laboring until this time to secure the disallowance of the act of 1731 in favor of the Quakers.

---

[1] Hist. Colls. *etc.*, 272, 274–288; Foote, Annals of King's Chapel, I, 455, *et seq.*

[2] Hist. Colls. *etc.*, 311;  Foote, *op. cit.*, 462, 467.

[3] Hist. Colls. *etc.*, 292.

[4] Acts. and Res., II, 783.

Early in 1736 the lords of the committee declared that all which saved it from this fate was the fact that it was a temporary measure. An additional instruction was then issued to Belcher forbidding an assent to any future law of this kind, unless the exemption granted in it was made general in favor of all Protestants. By the act of 1735 in favor of Anglicans, taken in connection with the previous laws, the exemption had been made general, and therefore this instruction signified nothing.[1] A tolerable working status had now been secured by all the dissenting sects in Massachusetts.

But as the strength of episcopacy increased, the Congregationalists drew together in opposition. This is illustrated by the controversy with Harvard College over the demand of Cutler and Myles that they should be admitted to seats in its board of overseers. For some years before 1722 both of the ministers of King's Chapel had been invited to attend the sessions of this body, but soon after Cutler left Yale no further summonses were sent. In 1727 the two clergymen, after the Overseers had voted that they were not entitled to seats, memorialized the general court for redress. Their petition was supported by another, signed by about seventy episcopal laymen. In these memorials the orthodoxy of the Church of England as a protestant body was affirmed, as well as the share which its members bore in all public charges, while the claim was urged that a school which was the " common nursery of piety and learning " should be under the charge of all. To the question, whether or no episcopalian clergymen were " teaching elders " in the sense of the law of 1642, by which the board of overseers was established, a decided affirmation was given. The reply of the general court was written by Dr. Colman, and maintained that by the expression " teaching elders " only Congregational ministers were meant, for at the time when the act was passed, and for forty years thereafter, there was no minister of the Church of England in the colony. Cutler and Myles replied, that Episcopal ministers by ordination and induction were teaching elders and must be included under the term and in the act; that by the law of Massachusetts Episcopalians had the right to form churches under ministers ordained by bishops

---

[1] Acts. and Res., II, 635; Acts of P. C. Col, 1720–1745, p. 491.

and their right to seats in the board had not lapsed, though forty years had passed before application was made for it. But before the general court appeals of this nature received a scant hearing and, in spite of still further applications, the governing board of Harvard remained closed to Anglicans.[1]

The attitude of the churches of New England toward what they considered the Anglican invasion never received better expression than in a letter sent to the bishop of London in 1734 by the associated ministers of Hampshire County.[2] Of this body William Williams was the moderator and Jonathan Edwards the scribe. Benjamin Colman, in forwarding the letter to the bishop, described the situation in his own way and with characteristic force. The position taken was, that New England was not missionary ground and that the sending of missionaries thither did not answer the professed design of the charter of the Venerable Society. New England was a Christian country, the churches of which held the same system of doctrine as the Church of England. Its towns were fully provided with ministers and the doors of their churches were open to all of competent knowledge and regular conversation. The missionaries, however, who came among them showed an uncharitable spirit by insinuating that the New England clergy, because not ordained by a bishop, was no ministry, their administrations null, their churches no churches and their people strangers to the Commonwealth of Israel. Not only was this, they said, proclaiming a tenet which came from Rome, but it was a great injustice and, by leading to endless strife, tended to cause men to identify religion with ceremonies rather than the love of God and of our neighbors and in a life of faith, repentance and holiness. Colman clinched the argument by writing, " The harvest, my Lord, is plenteous from North Carolina to New York and multitudes are perishing within that long spread of Virginia, Maryland, Pennsylvania and the Jersies; but from New York northward Dr. Bray found little Need of Missionaries for the propagating of Christianity, the Narragansett Country excepted, and in the colonies of Connecticut and Massachusetts

---

[1] Quincy, Hist of Harvard, II, 360–374; Foote, Annals of King's Chapel, I, 345–349; Perry, Hist. Colls., Mass., 210–219, 231–245, 257–261.
[2] Perry, Hist. Colls., Mass., 299, *et seq.*

none at all, as at the time I was informed." In these terms, even at the time of the first stirrings of The Great Awakening, the Anglicans were confronted by the challenge of the New England churches, which stood as a unit in opposition to them.

# CHAPTER XII

INTERNAL CONFLICTS IN MASSACHUSETTS UNDER SHUTE
AND BURNET. QUESTION OF THE GOVERNOR'S SALARY

THE probability has already been noted that, had it not
been for the pressure of war, serious internal conflicts would
have occurred in Dudley's administration. Even his astute-
ness and force of character could hardly have enabled him to
avoid collisions with a people whose predisposition against
control from outside New England was so strong as that of
the Puritans of Massachusetts. But Dudley's successful conduct of the war made his value, at least from that standpoint, apparent and for a decade the energies of the colony
were fully occupied in holding the enemy at bay or attempting to recover territory to the eastward and northward. But
with the conclusion of the treaty of Utrecht this pressure was
for a time removed, and it never again bore with such weight
of horror and peril upon New England as during the first
two colonial wars. The opportunity was thus presented for
the recurrence of disputes with the British government and its
agents in the province. Harmony in general had prevailed
along these lines since the issue of the charter of 1691. War
and the character of the royal executives had kept in the
background the questions which, when raised, must inevitably
provoke internal discord. Imperial control, as determined by
the provisions of the charter and by the principles which were
laid down in the governor's instructions, had hardly as yet
been put to the test except in the direction of war and the provision of means for carrying it on. But now that peace had
returned, the elements of conflict between the traditions of the
Puritan Commonwealth and principles of royal government
again revealed themselves. Conditions similar to those of the
later decades of the corporate colony or of the Andros régime,
though with a difference, returned and we have now to trace
the development of the struggle. It was to be carried on

under Hanoverian monarchs, with the Whig party permanently intrenched in power in England.

Colonel Elizeus Burgess, who had served in the army under General Stanhope, was the first appointee of the new Whig government to the governorship of Massachusetts. But the controversy over the land bank, which had occupied much attention during the later years of Dudley, was still in progress. Colonel Tailer, the lieutenant governor favored the land bank and the report spread that Burgess would hold similar opinions. It was also found that he would be personally unacceptable. For these reasons the opponents of the bank party, with the aid of Jonathan Belcher, who was then in London, Jeremiah Dummer, the agent and Sir William Ashurst, induced Burgess by the payment of one thousand pounds to resign his commission. Colonel Samuel Shute was then appointed to the governorship. He was a typical English Whig of the time, who had served under Marlborough in Flanders, mild and agreeable in disposition but destitute of any special elements of strength. With the exception of Lord Bellomont he was the first stranger who had been called to preside over the affairs of Massachusetts since the departure of Andros. As in the case of Phips, religious considerations influenced the appointment of Shute. He belonged to a prominent London family which was connected with the dissenters. His mother was a daughter of Joseph Caryl, the distinguished nonconformist divine of the previous century. His brother John became first Viscount Barrington in the Irish peerage and as a scholar and Presbyterian apologist, but with moderate principles, was regarded as one of the ablest men of his time. The education of Samuel, the governor, was begun under the Rev. Charles Morton, who came to Massachusetts and became the pastor at Charlestown about 1684, and whom we have met as a prominent candidate for the presidency of Harvard. In view of connections such as these it was natural to suppose that Shute would identify himself with the Congregationalists in Massachusetts, and with that in view he was welcomed by the ministers under the lead of Cotton Mather. But Shute, though declaring himself a Church of England man, really assumed a neutral attitude. He did not closely identify himself with either

Congregationalists or Episcopalians, while he especially offended the susceptibilities of Judge Sewall and others by adjourning the general court over Christmas.[1] His attitude therefore resembled that of Dudley. This was disheartening to those who had secured his appointment and doubtless proved an element of weakness in his administration. The appointment of Shute also brought to an end the term of Tailer, the lieutenant governor. He was succeeded by William Dummer, a native of New England who had been resident for some time in the parent country. As Dummer was a son-in-law of Dudley, the ex-governor interpreted it as an approval of his administration, and as events proved, like the appointment of Stoughton, it helped to perpetuate the control of Massachusetts men over the affairs of their province.

Shute arrived in Boston and assumed the duties of his office early in October, 1716. Like his successors until 1740, he was to administer the affairs of New Hampshire as well. In his instructions references to questions which had been living issues in the past but which now were losing their significance appeared in the requirement that he should persuade the province to rebuild the fort at Pemaquid, and the provision that in case of war and danger Shute should take command of the militia of Rhode Island but in time of peace it should be under the charge of the officials of that province.[2] In general his instructions contained the requirements which were customary for all the royal governors, including those to the effect that the appointee should endeavor to secure fixed salaries and a house for himself and that appropriations should be indefinite in duration, except duties on wines and liquors, which should not be imposed for less than one year. About these requirements were to centre in Massachusetts some of the most violent controversies of the immediate future, the question being substantially the same as had already agitated New York without being finally settled and which was to convulse that province again thirty years later. The first appointee whom the new Hanoverian government sent to represent it in Massachusetts was a man of medium

---

[1] Foote, Annals of King's Chapel, I, 267 *et seq.*
[2] C. O. 5/913, E. B., New Eng.

gifts, without the knowledge of finance or power of leadership which were needed in a province of that character at a time when so many critical questions demanded a hearing. The merchants of Boston who had secured his appointment as a means of defence against the projectors of the land bank did not find in him the strength and support for which they had hoped. Amid the general disappointment the spirit of partisan rancor was let loose to an extent rarely equalled even in Massachusetts, the mild mannered governor soon finding himself the principal object of attack and the younger Elisha Cooke, a truculent man both in speech and action, being the chief assailant.

In the June session of the general court prior to the arrival of Shute a committee for promoting the production and trade of the province had introduced a bill for the issue of an additional £100,000 in bills of credit.[1] This was a pure inflation measure, intended as a means of avoiding the levy of taxes and supported by the plea that the supply of money in circulation was inadequate. These bills, like the sum of £50,000 which had been issued two years before, were to be secured by mortgages on land and were to bear interest at the rate of five per cent. The bill had not been passed when Shute arrived, and in his first speech by a weak aquiescence in the popular clamor he gave his approval to the measure and it became law. Its effect of course was seriously to increase the depreciation of Massachusetts bills of credit. This frightened the governor and in the session of April, 1717, he twice alluded to the evil and besought the general court to make some provision against the " intolerable discount." [1] That the assembly intended no change in its attitude toward the salary question, was shown by its continuance of annual grants of the usual amount. And as they were made in the depreciated currency of the time, the governor protested, in November, 1717, that the £500 they had given him was in reality but £250 and, " Considering the excessive rates of all things that are necessary for my expence, it will not with decency, much less with dignity, support me in my situation." [2] A few months later, in arguing the repeal of a clause

[1] Palfrey, IV, 394.
[2] Journal of Upper House.

in the act of 1716 which authorized the commissioners to reissue any of the bills which might be paid in, Shute came out squarely for a metallic currency. " We shall' never be upon a firm and lasting foundation," said he, " 'til we recover and return to silver and gold, the only true species of money." [1]   Like all creditors, salaried persons and those with permanent incomes, Shute experienced in the most convincing fashion the evils of the existing policy as to currency issues.

Elisha Cooke, as we have seen, was a leader of the party which favored the land bank.  But before the governor had declared himself on the currency question he had raised a personal issue by insinuating that Shute was a weak man who was under the influence of the Dudleys and that it behooved the people to be careful of their liberties.[2]  Because of this or other still more personal utterances which came to the governor, Cooke was removed from the office of clerk of the superior court.  Meantime a violent dispute had arisen between Cooke and Bridger, the surveyor general of the woods. This, so far as Bridger himself was concerned, was a continuation of the controversy, elsewhere described, between himself and the people of New Hampshire and Maine over their rights as against the crown to the mast and ship timber in the forests of northern New England.  Bridger had recently returned from England, where he had successfully met the complaints of his opponents and had received a new commission.  Cooke now attacked him, alleging that he took bribes for allowing people to cut timber on the public domain while he forbade proprietors cutting on their own estates without license from himself.  This attack was made in a memorial to the general assembly, to which Bridger replied.  This, added to the sting which the personal remarks of Cooke about himself had left in the mind of the governor, proved sufficient to induce him to veto the election of Cooke to the council in the spring of 1718.  As was usual in such cases, the offending member was returned to the assembly, where he found a wider field for the exercise of his powers as tribune of the people.  Cooke in his arguments, which were frequently re-

---

[1] Journal of Upper House, Feb. 1717-18; Davis, *op. cit.*, I, 61.
[2] Hutchinson, II, 200.

peated and replied to by Bridger, sought to exclude the king and his officials wholly from Maine by claiming it as a proprietary province owned by Massachusetts.[1] It had been purchased, he said, by that colony from Gorges and there was no royal reservation, actual or possible, of timber within its limits. Bridger asserted that Massachusetts had exceeded its legal powers in making this so-called purchase, and if it had not done so it might at any time annex Rhode Island or Connecticut. In the course of the discussion Cooke also, in the spirit of the previous century, asserted that the acts of parliament relating to naval stores did not bind Massachusetts because it had a charter. These arguments cut wide and deep and because of their use the question of the rights of the king in the forests of northern New England was injected into Massachusetts politics.

When Bridger reported Cooke's argument to the board of trade, it referred the claim to its counsel, Richard West, for an opinion. West found little difficulty, either on the ground of law or expediency, in concluding that Massachusetts under its first charter had no authority to make the alleged purchase from Gorges.[2] On the other hand, by the existing charter of 1691 Maine and Massachusetts had been united in one province and the general court had been given the right to grant lands, but no more in one part of the province than in the other. In both this right was limited by the clause in the charter reserving to the king pine trees of certain dimensions, a clause which had been confirmed by a statute of the ninth of Anne. West's conclusion was that the king's rights in Maine were as fully secured as they were in any other province. But though this opinion was approved by the board of trade and was in harmony with the law, Dummer, the agent, interested himself with sufficient effect against Bridger to secure his recall. During the interval before the arrival of his successor, and later, the imperial policy concerning the timber lands of Maine was very imperfectly executed.[3] The Massachusetts assembly supported Cooke in his contentions and his boldness encouraged lumbermen to cut timber wher-

[1] C. O. 5/915, E. B. N. Eng.; Bridger to B. T. July 14, 1718; Lord, Industrial Experiments, etc., 113.

[2] C. O. 5/915; Report of West, Nov. 12, 1718.

[3] Lord, op. cit., 115.

ever they liked. Cooke also bought up hundreds of acres of the best timber lands outside of towns and offered them for sale. Seizures made by the surveyor were not condemned and it was useless in such cases to apply to the local courts. Thus in the administration of the forests affairs went at loose ends, Shute writing that the " main drift " of the Massachusetts assembly was to persuade the people that the king had no right to the woods. When a letter came from the board of trade censuring the house for supporting Cooke, it charged the governor with creating a wrong impression by reporting only one side of the case, a form of attack upon the executive in which Massachusetts assemblies in course of time became past masters.

Relations within the legislature of Massachusetts and between it and the home government became further involved as a result of financial legislation at Boston in 1718 and 1719.[1] In the former year, for the purpose in part of retiring some of the bills of credit, an impost and tonnage act was passed. But this violated the acts of trade and accepted principles of policy by allowing the importation of wines and commodities in general directly from the places of their growth, by not requiring that the importations should be in ships manned and navigated according to law, and by charging a double duty on the commodities when imported from Great Britain. The act also was a temporary one, as it was to expire in a year from the time of its passage. On report from the board of trade of these defects in the law it was disallowed, the notification of which to the assembly being accompanied with a warning as to the danger to which such legislation would expose their charter. An additional instruction had also been sent in 1717 against passing laws affecting the trade or interests of Great Britain, without a suspending clause. Shute was chided for failure to acknowledge the receipt of this instruction, and for neglect of sending home certain reports and fuller accounts of the condition of his province, which from statements in English newspapers and from other sources the board inferred to be unfavorable.[2]

[1] Acts and Res. of Mass., II, 107, 126, 138, 158; Journal of Upper House, June, 1719; Hutchinson, *op. cit.*, 204 *et seq.*
[2] B. T. to Shute, June 4, 1719, C. O. 5/915.

But before the news of the disallowance arrived, the assembly had passed another impost and tonnage bill similar to the one of the previous year. This, however, was rejected by the council. The lower house then changed the clause providing for a duty on English goods to one imposing the same on European goods. This too the council rejected as a violation of the above instruction. As the right of the council to confer upon money bills and even to amend them had not then been expressly denied in Massachusetts, the houses disputed over this subject for more than two weeks, when the governor interposed with a brief speech in the interest of harmony. The assembly then consented to the introduction of a new bill with the controverted clause left out, and finally an acceptable act was passed. The press was now becoming active in Massachusetts. A considerable number of pamphlets were published about 1720 on the question of the currency, nearly all of them being favorable to increased issues by the government or a private bank or both.[1] Sermons and publications on religious and theological subjects of course were published as usual. The house of representatives was now printing its journals and this made the governor and council measurably sensitive respecting the inclusion in the record of statements which reflected upon them.

At the close of the controversy over the impost bill the council protested against the publication of a resolve that its failure to concur had caused the loss of a considerable part of the revenue of the province.[2] Two newspapers — the " News-Letter " and the " Gazette " — were already being published in Boston, while the " Courant " was started in 1721.[3] It was at this time also that the newspapers began to publish, under the name of " advertisements," anonymous political articles expressing the views of those who paid for their insertion.[4] James Franklin and his young brother Benjamin, the publishers of the " Courant," soon exhibited a peculiar skill and incisiveness of attack upon a variety of esteemed interests and personalities. John Checkley and John

[1] See the reprints of these by Davis in the volumes published by the Prince Society.
[2] Acts and Res., II, 161; Journal of Upper House.
[3] Thomas, Hist. of Printing.
[4] Duniway, Freedom of the Press in Mass. (Harvard Hist. Studies), 91.

Colman were exploiting themes in controversial pamphlets, the former the interests of Anglicanism and the latter the distressed state of Boston, which he attributed to the lack of an adequate supply of bills of credit. It was thus made clear that by its unwonted activity the press was becoming an influence in politics. To a government in those days, and especially in a colony with a history like that of Massachusetts, this could not be viewed with indifference. Since the days of the old charter, when the censorship of the infant press was administered by the magistrates or by the clergymen designated in orders of the general court, this power had been placed by royal instructions in the hands of the governors. This practice had begun with Andros and had been continued under the second charter. Dudley, however, had neglected to use his powers in this direction and it was under the screen of his indifference that the press had begun to flourish and reveal its possibilities during the later years of his administration.[1] As the controversies of Shute's administration developed, the activity of the press, which was largely sympathetic with the lower house, increased and added to the perplexities of his situation. But the restrictions of the censorship had been abandoned in England and the pens of the Franklins were the only ones in Massachusetts which as yet gave any signs of the virulence which in the old country was customary in attacks on the government or on cherished public customs and institutions. As contrasted with the Tories, the attitude of the Whigs was one of stolid indifference to attacks of this kind, reliance being placed upon the unbroken front which a majority held together by bribery and patronage could for an indefinite time present to the assaults in any other form than those which affected the pocket. Conditions in the colonies from which the beginnings of the press emerged were only a faint reflection of these, but they were significant of changes with which British officials must reckon in a not distant future.

If the authors or publishers were to be prosecuted for criticising acts of the government it must be done by the governor with the consent of the council. With such action in view, in May, 1720, Shute submitted one of Colman's

[1] Dunniway *op. cit.*

pamphlets to the council and a prosecution of the writer was begun. But two months later this was dropped and Colman was released from his bonds. About a year later Benjamin Gray, a printer, was forced to acknowledge his fault for publishing a pamphlet in which the province was stated to be " in a flame " because of the scarcity of bills of credit, and for assuming a defiant attitude toward his prosecutors. In March, 1721, Shute, alarmed at the many factious publications, tried to induce the general assembly to provide a law for a censorship of the press. The council passed such a bill, but it was promptly negatived by the house. It so happened that in the opinion of that body one of the most " factious " pamphlets that had recently been published was " News from Robinson Crusoe's Island," [1] in which the house had been severely criticised and the governor supported. As no effort had been made to suppress this, the house naturally inferred that a law empowering the executive to enforce a censorship would be executed in a partisan spirit and be used to stifle popular discussion. The governor tried in vain to prevent the publication by the house of an " Answer " to his speeches, in which not only the question of the press was discussed but the attitude of the government on many other subjects was assailed. His failure in this also revealed with greater clearness the fact that so long as hostile relations between the governor and the lower house continued, the imposing of serious restrictions upon the freedom of the press would be impossible.

The press helped to ventilate the dissatisfaction, real or imaginary, which existed in Massachusetts at the time of which we are speaking. That there should be a certain exhaustion of resources and economic disturbance as a result of the long and costly wars which had just closed, was to be expected. But that the disturbance was greatly increased and perpetuated by the issue of bills of credit is perfectly clear. The evil which was caused by the displacement of silver and depreciation of paper furnished material for general complaint and for the agitators who clamored for further issues as the

---

[1] This was a reply to Elisha Cooke's, "Just and reasonable Vindication respecting some Affairs transacted in the late General Assembly," 1720. Its title is a commentary upon the immediate and universal popularity of Defoe's romance published in 1719 and 1720.

social panacea. It was a period of rising prices and increased cost of living. It was to satisfy the predominant debtor class that the currency policy was followed, but when they came to expend their incomes they suffered even more keenly than the creditors and the well-to-do. Connecticut and Rhode Island were now issuing bills of credit, the former having begun in 1709 and the latter in 1710.[1] During the latter years of the war Connecticut had made frequent issues, though in every case she had provided by taxation for the retirement of the bills in ten years or more from the dates of their issue. As the result of a conservative policy, by 1720 most of the bills had been retired, though a decade later Connecticut was to plunge deeply into the policy of inflation. Rhode Island proceeded directly and much more rapidly on the downward course. In 1715 she began the issue of " banks," or sums of interest bearing bills to be loaned on mortgages as security. This was an imitation of Massachusetts practice, though a somewhat different meaning was given to the word " bank," and Rhode Island carried its policy of inflation to far greater excess than any other northern colony. In 1715 she issued £40,000, in 1721 £40,000, and at intervals of a few years thereafter this or much larger sums continued to be issued. Bills rather than discussions of public policy were the chief issues of her press. They flowed over into the two adjoining colonies and helped further to inflate their currency. The excessive issues of Massachusetts, and later of Connecticut, also circulated outside their limits, though not to the extent and with the evil results of the Rhode Island bills. New England as a whole thus became deeply involved in the paper money régime, and this fact must be borne in mind in trying to interpret the course of events in any one colony of the group. New York also was not unaffected by the policy and its influence was felt through the exchanges by colonies farther south.

But the colonies were young communities, sparsely populated and with abundance of free land. Through privateering, contracts for the supply of troops, and various forms of irregular trade the wars had opened business opportunities

---

[1] See Bronson in Colls. of New Haven Hist. Soc., I, and Potter and Ryder in R. I. Hist. Tracts.

and chances for profit. During the wars trade between the
northern colonies and the West Indies had been developing
toward its later flourishing condition. Ship building had been
stimulated and in New England it was now one of the leading
industries of the empire. In a variety of lines fortunes were
being amassed. Towns and the commercial element in New
England society were steadily becoming more prominent. In
those centres at least the poverty and frugality of the early
settlers was being outgrown and foreign goods and luxuries
were being imported from many climes in ampler quantities
and varieties. Among the well-to-do expenditures were larger
than in earlier generations and gave rise to the oft repeated
charge of extravagance.[1] This course of commercial and
industrial growth, which began before the wars and was
checked by them only in certain respects, after their close
went forward with a rebound, more rapidly and powerfully
than before. It extended through the colonies at large and
prepared the way for their emergence from the more exclusive
devotion to agriculture or the other extractive industries
which were characteristic of their infancy. The signs of
change which the soft money party of the time interpreted as
evidences of distress, were rather as a whole proofs of
strength, growth and prosperity, making themselves felt,
especially after the repression of the wars. The theorists
showed by the policy which they advocated a dim consciousness of this fact, though the remedies they suggested created
far more evils than they removed. It is the restlessness which
these conditions occasioned which helps to explain the growing strength of the opposition in Massachusetts. To it was
added the signs which indicated the approach of an Indian
war and the natural jealousy of royal control, especially when
the governorship was held by a stranger who did not possess
an inspiring personality.

It was in the spring of 1720 that Shute came to a direct
issue with Cooke and his party in the province. The newly
elected house chose Cooke as its speaker. An off-hand remark
dropped by the governor when he was privately informed of
this, was later interpreted by Cooke's friends as an approval

---

[1] The currency pamphlets which have been reprinted by Mr. Davis
abound in references to this.

of the choice. Upon this assumption the house went so far as to organize for the choice of councillors without further informing the governor of the selection it had made.[1] Shute then told them that no election should be held until he was informed who was chosen speaker. When a committee notified him of their choice, Shute declared that, as Cooke had treated him ill as governor, by the authority given him in the royal charter he negatived the election and desired that they would choose another person. In further support of his action he cited a case where Dudley, in 1705, had disapproved of the choice of Thomas Oakes as speaker and stated that the board of trade had approved of this and had informed the council in Massachusetts, that it was not fit that the crown should abandon this right, which was reserved to it by the charter and the constitution of England. Shute, however, did not state the fact that Dudley had not secured the displacement of Oakes and the election of another speaker,[2] and that the house, citing a law of the province which empowered them to be sole judges of elections and qualifications of their numbers, had refused to accede to the governor's proposals.[3]

The election of councillors was now proceeded with and Shute negatived two, Nathaniel Byfield and John Clarke. He then informed the house at greater length of the reasons which led him to negative their choice of Cooke and advised them to select another speaker. After returning and debating the subject the house unanimously rejected Shute's proposal. They were at once summoned before the governor and the assembly was dissolved. Writs were at once issued for a new election and a majority of the old members were returned to the new house, which met in July. During the recess Cooke published his " Vindication," in which he dwelt at length upon the service he had rendered the crown by obstructing the corrupt practices of Bridger in the Maine woods and also claimed that he had done all a gentleman could do to remove his personal misunderstanding with the governor.

[1] Journal of Upper House, May 1720; Hutchinson, II, 211 *et seq.*

[2] Journal of Upper House, May 1705; C. O. 5/912 B. T. to Dudley, Feb. 4, 1705–6; Palfrey, IV, 294; Cooke's "Just and reasonable Vindication."

[3] They contended that the negative voice extended only to elections by both houses, as when councillors were chosen, and not to those by one house.

As to the legal point involved, he argued with ability that the choice of a speaker was not an act of the general court or of the government — the council having no share in it, — and therefore it could not be reckoned among the measures which a governor could negative. If he could negative such an act, he could quash any resolution of the house or its appointment of committees even before they came before the council for its consideration. As the charter was silent on the point, this raised a strong presumption against the governor's claim. The new assembly, wishing to proceed to business and to avoid a deadlock, chose Timothy Lindall, a person against whom no exception could be taken, as its speaker. In its reply to the governor's opening speech it however warmly condemned the advice which had led him to the course which he had pursued in the last session, and expressed the earnest hope that no assembly would ever abandon the valuable privilege of freedom of elections which had been secured when the act above referred to had been approved by William and Mary.

With this brief session began one of those captious quarrels between the assembly and the executive which recur with such frequency in the history of the province, and in this case it ceased only after the return of the governor to England. The assembly, under the same leaders as its predecessor, in order to express its resentment at what it properly regarded as an encroachment on its rights, sought every available opportunity for obstruction and for encroachment upon the sphere of the executive. A small grant to be used for the purchase of a present for three Penobscot Indians who had come to treat about the peace of the frontier was refused, and later the scanty sum of ten pounds was voted. As war with the Abenaki Indians was becoming imminent, such a policy as this was not calculated to avert it. Appropriations for celebrating the king's birthday, accession, coronation and the like were cut off. The semi-annual appropriation of the governor's salary was postponed until the close of the session and then it was reduced by one hundred pounds, though the depreciation of the currency in which it was paid was already great and was steadily increasing. The small grant to the lieutenant governor was also cut down to such an insignificant sum that he returned it in disgust.  On the ground that public notaries were civil officers and therefore by the charter subject to election by the general court, the house proposed that the council should join with it in such choice.  Because these officers had previously derived their authority from the archbishop of Canterbury, the council hesitated, whereupon the house proceeded to its election alone.  The governor, however, declined to swear in the candidate who had been selected.[1] The house showed also an exaggerated sensitiveness concerning its liberties by insisting that duplicates of all public records should be made and one copy lodged where it should direct.

In the fall session of 1720 the house, stirred by rumors that false muster rolls had been prepared of the garrisons at Castle William and Winter Harbor, on its sole initiative appointed one or more clerks to inspect the forts, garrisons and forces and see that they all had their full complement of men. The resolution of the house also required that commanders of the troops should call them out for inspection as often as these clerks should require it, that the reason of the absence of every man should be given and that no muster roll should be accepted and paid by the treasurer of the province unless it was approved by a clerk.  The house also threatened to prepare a bill to regulate the levy of soldiers and expressed itself in favor of enlistment and against the draft.  It was also voted that a committee, without application to the governor, should take account of stores at the Castle.  The treasurer was also ordered to have the stores in the fort at Winter Harbor secured, the fishing vessels in the eastern parts removed to Boston, and to provide no more subsistence for a garrison there.[2]  Though the governor said nothing as to these claims, it was plain that he could not have tolerated the activity of the officials, thus appointed, without demoralizing the service and surrendering the control over the militia which was given him by his commission.  Moreover, in judging the conduct of Massachusetts governors in reference to

[1] Hutchinson, II, 216.
[2] The reasons given for this were that the removal of the fishery from there to the eastward had made this fort useless, and that it was also decayed.

questions of this kind, it should be borne in mind that their commissions and instructions did not differ in essentials from those which were given to royal governors in general, and that the requirements of these did not necessarily square in every particular with the provisions of the charter. In case of a dispute the assembly would always follow the charter, while the governor might find a leverage against this in his commission and the general practice of England, a situation being thus created which was peculiar to a province which possessed a royal charter. Also it was not without an analogy to the situation which we have seen existing in Pennsylvania.

At the opening of the session of March 1720/1 Shute urged measures to check the depreciation of the currency, to suppress a trade carried on with the French at Cape Breton, to punish the authors of recent seditious publications, to provide a present for the Five Nations and to increase his salary. The extent to which he had failed to win the favor of the representatives is indicated by the fact that none of these proposals was approved. As to the currency, in the previous session a bill for the issue of £100,000 had been defeated in the council. This session the same measure was proposed and was again negatived in the council. As the result of a conference they agreed on the issue of £50,000 and its distribution among the towns. This, in spite of his declaration in favor of economy and a return to a specie basis, the governor signed. The year before he had reported to the board of trade that £220,000 had been issued and that it had depreciated nearly one hundred per cent.[1] As to the governor's salary of £1000 per annum in this depreciated paper, they thought it was sufficient and believed that this was the opinion of the majority of the people whom they represented. The discussion of the currency question, which was still going on apace in the public prints, occasioned the demand of the governor, supported by action of the council, that a law should be passed establishing a censorship of the press. As the pamphlet which had offended the governor and council was written in support of the soft money party, the house, which was in sympathy with its purpose, was not to be induced to favor any measure for

[1] Journals of the two Houses, Acts and Res. II, 189–200; C. O. 5/827 B. P. Eng. O. P. W., 99.

its suppression.  It told the governor that the executive and
the courts had ample power to prevent such offences and that
the spirit of licence and faction had doubtless been promoted
the year before by the publication of " News from Robinson
Crusoe's Island," which had contained false statements about
the conduct of the entire legislature.[1]  Had the inventor and
publisher of that libel been properly punished, few or none
thereafter would have dared to have put forth such false-
hoods.  The other proposals of Shute grew out of conditions
which were leading to war, and they were as summarily rejected by the house as were his suggestions which arose from
the depreciated currency of the province.

In order to rob the governor of an opportunity to issue the
proclamation for the annual fast, a custom which had existed
since the founding of the colony, the house proposed that the
council should join it in preparing a proclamation.  This the
council refused to do, as it was unprecedented.[2]  When later
the governor issued the proclamation, stating that it was done
upon advice of the council and on motion from the house, the
assembly was dissatisfied with this, denied that they had
made any such motion and ordered that none of their members should carry copies of it to their towns.  The last dispute of the session was over the seizure of certain pine trees
which had been cut in Maine under orders from a deputy
surveyor of the woods.  The house believed that the trees had
been cut for other uses than those of the royal navy, and were
being embezzled, perhaps with the connivance of the deputy
surveyor of the woods.  The council was willing to join in the
seizure, though with an express reservation of the rights of
the crown in the premises as stated in the charter and acts of
parliament.  These the house declared had no binding force in
the case, because the timber had been felled and was no longer
standing.  The house then proceeded alone to order the attorney general to prosecute.  The hand of Cooke is evident in

[1] Ex. C. Journal of Mass. Feb. and Mar. 1720/21; C. O. 5/794. Hutchinson, II, 223.  Duniway, Freedom of the Press in Mass., 95.  The pamphlet
in question was "A Letter to an Eminent Clergyman in Massachusetts Bay."
It is reprinted by Davis in Colonial Currency Reprints, II, 229.

[2] At the later hearings in England eighteen instances were cited when,
since 1691, the representatives had joined in designating fasts and thanks-
givings.  But, as was observed by the law officers, in this case they had gone
beyond their precedents.

this whole proceeding, and when he and one other obnoxious person were appointed on a committee to secure the logs for the use of the province, the council refused to join and also insisted that the king's rights as well as those of the province should be secured.[1]

At the end of the session Shute took his farewell of the assembly in a speech which reviewed some of the chief questions upon which they had differed. But, like all his utterances, it was brief, extremely mild in tone, and contained no arguments whatever upon the merits of the questions at issue. He simply stated that he would refer them to the king that he might see how his governor was treated and also what regard was paid to the royal instructions. The speech closed with a faint warning against the disadvantages they might suffer from his representations and an exhortation to loyal and peaceable behavior in the future. Had Alexander Spotswood been governor, a speech of a far different tone from this would have been delivered, or if a man like Robert Hunter had been in Shute's place we may imagine that some effort would have been made to form an interest within the house itself in support of the just claims of the executive. It might have been even more difficult to arrange than in New York; but Shute exhibited few and weak signs of political ability. His utterances implied that he wished to be regarded simply as the agent of the crown, but in failing to control his province to any degree or to influence opinion within it he failed even in his function as agent. Shute occupies a place among the numerous royal appointees of his time who reflect the low level of official life of the Georgian era. In the presence of a neutral character like his one can imagine the self-assurance mingled with contempt with which the solons of Massachusetts proceeded on their career of petty annoyance and encroachment.

With the assembly that was elected in May, 1721, the quarrel with the governor came to an issue. The choice by this house of John Clarke as its speaker, one who a year before had been negatived as a councillor, indicated that the temper of this assembly was essentially the same as that of its predecessor. Sparring began at the very outset. In order to

---

[1] Journals of the two Houses; Hutchinson, *op. cit.*

prevent the governor negativing their choice of speaker, the house notified Shute and the council jointly of this act. Under the circumstances this may well have been the best that could have been expected from the house. Shute is said to have been tempted to dissolve the assembly at once, but as the new councillors had not been chosen, such a course might have made it impossible to hold a general court for another year.[1] He therefore contented himself with notifying the house that he accepted their choice as speaker, a step which was as unexpected by them as it was unwelcome to him. The assembly then tried to seat its newly elected list of councillors without approval by the governor, a course so violent and unprecedented that it had to be abandoned. Shute approved the list, with the exception of Nathaniel Byfield.

In his opening speech the governor laid before the houses an additional instruction which he had received to the effect that assent should not hereafter be given to acts for the issue of bills of credit unless they contained a clause suspending their execution until confirmed by the king. This had now become a general instruction and over the question to which it referred no controversy of importance arose in Massachusetts at this time. But serious trouble began when, on June 19, a committee, of which Elisha Cooke was the leading spirit, was appointed by the house to vindicate the proceedings of its predecessor.[2] As the governor's speech at the close of the previous session had been published in the " Gazette," the object of the this procedure was to prepare and publish a defence of the conduct of the late house, a course which was to become more common in Massachusetts as time passed. Elaborate arguments therefore were prepared by the committee in defence of the claims of the house respecting the seizure of the logs in Maine. Had the bills proposed by the governor and council to prevent riots and prohibit the publishing of scandalous pamphlets been passed, it would have brought a lasting reproach, they said, upon the province, for its people were not rebellious or in sympathy with the pretender. Considering the hard times, they thought the governor's salary really exceeded in amount the sums which had

---

[1] Hutchinson, II, 226.
[2] Journals of the two Houses; Hutchinson op. cit.

previously been given. Far from understanding how the governor could consider himself to have been ill-treated, on their part, they complained that he had sent legislative proposals which failed of passage to the board of trade, for in local matters of government they did not consider themselves responsible to that body.

Because Dummer had informed the general court of the unfavorable sentiment entertained in England respecting its conduct, the assembly cut off his salary and voted that he should be dismissed from his agency, an act in which the council refused to concur. It was at this time that Dummer was publishing his " Defence of the New England charters," the ablest argument which was ever prepared in support of that form of colonial government for which New England had always stood. On the other side, in its elaborate report of 1721 to the king on the condition of the colonies, the board of trade recommended not only the abolition of the chartered colonies, but that the colonies as a whole should be put under a lord lieutenant or captain general, from whom the governors of particular provinces should receive their orders respecting contributions of men or money and all other matters which concerned the king's service.[1] Dummer believed that a bill would soon be introduced into the commons for the recall of the charters and it was in the hope that he might do something to prevent this result that he prepared his pamphlet. His letters show that he did not expect thanks from the assembly for this service, but he certainly did not expect removal. As another minor incident of the quarrel, an effort was also made by the house to exclude Paul Dudley from the council on the ground that he would not submit deeds to the assembly in disproof of the charge that he was not a landholder in Sagadahoc, from which section he had been chosen as a councillor.[2]

On the twentieth of July Shute dissolved this assembly. He told them in his concluding speech that he would have taken the step when their memorial in defence of the previous assembly appeared, but he hoped that they would correct or expunge it. But instead of that they had published it without

[1] N. Y. Col. Docs., V, 629.
[2] Hutchinson, II, 231.

his knowledge and as their last offence had adjourned themselves, not as hitherto from day to day, but for nearly a week. This they had done without informing Shute and, as he considered, in violation of the power expressly given him in the charter to adjourn, prorogue and dissolve the general court. The assembly admitted that the governor should have been informed of their proceeding, but insisted that the adjournment of their house was distinct from the act referred to in the charter. Shute, however, claimed that it was a high encroachment on the prerogative and made it an added reason for dissolution. No provision had been made for the support of the government for the coming year.

At intervals prior to the date we have now reached, Shute had been sending accounts of his experiences to the board of trade, accompanied by confirmatory documents. By the summer of 1721 his correspondence had become quite voluminous,[1] and he had received replies from the board approving his conduct and a not very conclusive opinion from the attorney general, Sir Robert Raymond, that the governor had the right to veto the election of the speaker.[2] When the newly elected assembly met, on August 23, these reassuring statements were laid before it. The house in notifying the governor of the reelection of Clarke as speaker informed him that this did not need his approbation, but he had already given it before this assurance had reached him. As small pox was now raging in Boston the general court voted to remove to Cambridge. This again brought up, in a different form, the question of the sole right of the governor to adjourn, prorogue and dissolve the court, and Shute let it be known that he would assent if he were asked in such form as was consistent with this claim. The house insisted that by law the general court was required to be held in Boston and it could be removed thence only with consent of the governor and the two houses. They were meeting at the time at the George Tavern beyond Boston Neck, and there they remained in very inconvenient quarters during the session of August and September. The necessity was thus avoided of acknowledging that the governor had the power to remove the court

[1] His correspondence is in C. O. 5/867, 868. B. T. N. Eng. O. P.
[2] See Journal of Lower House, August, 1721.

from Boston. The increase of difficulties with the Indians made necessary the holding of another session in November and though the court met in Boston it was necessary to remove it to Cambridge. The governor prorogued it thither, though he consented to a vote of the house that no advantage should be taken of this in favor of the claim on either side, that is, that this removal should not be used as a precedent.[1]

Though the questions at issue had not been settled and the governor had been unable to secure his salary, the discussion had assumed a somewhat milder tone and a disposition was appearing on both sides to refer the disputes to England for adjustment. But now the approaching war with the Indians began to affect the situation and the series of events reacted upon one another in characteristic fashion. Though the sources make no mention of the experience under Fletcher and Cornbury, the attitude which the Massachusetts house now assumed toward muster rolls and expenditures suggests an imitation of the claims made in New York or a consciousness of dishonesty similar to that which had existed there. That the militia companies in certain cases were not full and that there was some speculation and looseness in accounts is shown by evidence which later was brought before the house. In some cases pay was being drawn for men who were on furloughs or not in service. These cases, when discovered by inquiry and testimony given before the assembly, were promptly punished by fines, forfeiture of salaries or removal from the service of officers who were found responsible for the misconduct. That the evil approached in extent the dishonesty and corruption which had prevailed in New York is not for a moment to be supposed. But Cooke and his associates in the house, fully conscious of their aims and of the means by which to reach them, availed themselves of the war and of the financial needs of the government to push their claims of legislative supremacy to the utmost. The minor irregularities which they succeeded in overcoming were well utilized and furnished apparent justification for the policy.

In its resolve for the supply of the treasury, in November, 1721, the house sought to establish a complete control over

[1] Journal of Upper House, Acts and Res., X, 120; Hutchinson, II, 241, 245.

expenditure by introducing a clause stating that the sums should be used for the purpose indicated " and for no other end or uses whatsoever." The council objected, but the assembly replied that it was reasonable that those who granted the money should have the disposal thereof. To this assertion of legislative absolutism the council objected as contrary to custom and a practice which would be followed by evil results. If this policy should prevail, the council thought it would not be possible for the executive to so much as pay an express without a vote of the whole court. But the house stoutly refused any appropriation unless this clause was annexed and continued its attitude in later sessions. It also began making its grants in the form of resolves, so that they would escape revision by the privy council.[1] Much detail as to the uses to which the money given should be devoted was also introduced into these resolves.

The next step taken by the representatives was to interfere with the disposition and movements of the troops. They first desired that the garrison at Northfield should be discontinued, but this was voted down in the council. In the session of August, 1722, a committee of the two houses not only reported what should be the rate of pay of the troops and their supply of provisions, but where they should operate upon the frontier and the number requisite for each locality.[2] Three hundred men should be detailed for an expedition to Penobscot, and that meantime 25 men should be stationed at Arrowsick, 25 at Richmond and so on in a detailed list of that nature. The amounts which should be paid for Indian scalps and prisoners were also specified. The entire report was adopted by the two houses and it amounted to a plan of campaign. When the governor received it he replied that the king and the charter had given him the sole command and direction of all the forces that might be raised on any emergency and he would not suffer them to be under any control but his own and that of the officers whom he appointed. But this was a mere empty protest, for Shute admitted that he would issue orders respecting the forces which were agreeable to the de-

[1] Journal of Upper House; Hutchinson, II, 245; Mass. Acts and Res., II, 219, 236, 523.

[2] Journal of Upper House; Hutchinson, II, 252.

sires of the general court, while that body went on with the
further regulations which implied that it was taking entire
charge of the war. The lower house also voted that commissioners ought to be sent to Rhode Island and Connecticut
for aid and detailed steps were taken by the houses for
negotiations [1] with the Iroquois for the purpose of securing
their active cooperation. Even the employment of scouts and
their movements on the frontier did not escape the regulating
zeal of the lower house. Commanders of these troops were
required to keep journals and send them monthly to the office
of the secretary of the province. Though the governor was to
see that these measures were executed, he was reduced to the
position of agent of the houses.

The point had now been reached where the general character of this struggle, known as Râle's War, must be sketched.
It continued about four years, was confined to the New England frontier, with some skirmishes in Nova Scotia, and was
waged with the Indians of that region. Though the French
of Canada did not openly participate, their influence was
continuously exerted to bring it about and to encourage the
Indians in its prosecution when it had been once begun. This
influence was exerted not only from Quebec as a centre, but
intermediately through mission stations in Maine, one at
Norridgewock on the Kennebec river and the other at Pana-
wamske, above the site of the modern city of Bangor on the
Penobscot. The former, because of its location on one of
the routes by which the New England frontier was reached
from Canada and because of the zeal and ability of Sebastian
Râle, the Jesuit priest who was at its head, was the more important of the two. At the time of which we are speaking
Father Le Chasse was the efficient co-laborer with Râle, while
Father Lauverjot directed affairs on the Penobscot. As the
struggle of the French for the possession of North America
approached its middle and later stages the Jesuits not only
surpassed the other religious orders in activity and influence,
but their early enthusiasm for the conversion of the natives
had cooled and in its place they had become tireless supporters of the interests of their nation among the Indians.
By means of their religion they labored to bind the natives

[1] Acts and Res., X, 263, 269.

to the French alliance and then without the slightest feeling of compassion for man, woman or child, to fling them upon the exposed settlements of the English frontier. Râle was an admirable example of priests of this type, whose spirit and activities were so far secularized that he is properly to be classed with such political and military leaders as Frontenac and Portneuf, though he wore the dress and used the forms of the church. Until the end of the colonial wars, on the northeastern frontier the English had to contend against opponents of this type, and they scrupled at no means which seemed calculated to provoke the lust of the savages for blood and plunder. The mission stations at St. Francis and Biencour in Canada also furnished recruits to the warring bands of the natives.

After the return of peace following the treaty of Utrecht not only were the earlier limits of the frontier in Maine restored by the rebuilding and reoccupation of settlements near the coast which had been abandoned during the wars, but posts were established up the courses of the rivers. This was especially true of the Kennebec and its western tributary, the Androscoggin. It was by this process that an approach was made by the English toward Râle's outpost and encroachments were made on territory over which the Abenakis had hitherto roamed without molestation. The process was similar to the one that was beginning about the same time on the Mohawk river in New York. In the one region as in the other the jealousy of the Indians was aroused. The complete subjection of the Abenakis to French influence made this more pronounced in their case. Supported by their French patrons, they insisted on setting limits to the English advance. The wars, the long and cold winters and the scanty supplies of food which, mainly as hunters and fishermen, they were able to procure, were telling upon them and made the preservation of their hunting grounds a matter of life and death. Though the claims of the colonists could not be separated by bounds from the hunting grounds of the Indians, there was a general understanding that the coast region as far east as Pemaquid and extending some distance back into the country belonged to the English. But even here, so scattered were the English settlements that the Indians had free access to the coast and ranged at large through the interior. As to the territory east of Pemaquid, owing to the narrow interpretation which, as a means of avoiding the implications of the treaty of Utrecht, they now gave to the term Acadia, the French claimed it for themselves and the Indians. From all this region, though it had been subject of some of the earliest English grants, the French and Indians now sought to exclude settlement by the New Englanders. These causes all tended toward the renewal of strife.

Not only at the close of the second intercolonial war, but occasionally after that time, the governor and councils of Massachusetts and New Hampshire had held conferences with the Eastern Indians and concluded treaties with them.[1] As a rule these meetings were much less formal than those held at Albany and impressed the imagination of the savages to a less degree. The places where the more formal meetings were held were Portsmouth in New Hampshire, and Falmouth and Arrowsick Island, now Georgetown, Maine. Occasionally talks were held with a few Indian messengers at Boston or at other points to the eastward. By the end of the second war, the Indians gave such evidence of poverty and hunger that the natural temptation of the Englishman, and especially of the New Englander, to treat them with contempt was very strong. In the management of an Indian conference the New Englander assumed much the same dogmatic and argumentative attitude which distinguished him in a council for the trial of heretics. Sympathy and imagination were as absent from one function as from the other. Presents were either not bestowed at all or in very small quantity. Unlike the procedure at Albany, these conferences usually consisted of an argumentative colloquy or dispute between the governor and the Indian orator, the two addressing their conflicting statements or demands to the interpreter rather than to one another or to the audience. Shute, by the way in which he conducted the conference at Arrowsick, in August, 1717, furnished a classic example of the New England method, and the Indians finally retired in anger. Though the affair was patched up the next day, the inferiority of the English to the French in the management of Indian relations was never

[1] Colls. of Maine Hist. Soc., VI, 250–262; N. H. Prov. Papers, III, 693.

more conspicuously shown.  One does not wonder that the savages turned to men like Râle; such men were false and merciless toward their enemies but tireless in their labors and sacrifices on behalf of their devotees.  An attempt was made to establish a mission among the Maine Indians under the charge of a respectable Puritan minister named Baxter, but the kindly zeal of the Apostle Eliot was lacking and it came to nothing.

At Portsmouth, in 1713, the eastern tribes acknowledged that they had repeatedly broken their agreements with the governors. during the past twenty years, but now renewed them and professed obedience to the crown of Great Britain. They also agreed that the English should peacefully return to and enjoy all their former settlements and all the lands to which they had a right in New Hampshire and Massachusetts and their adjoining islands.  In the following year and again in 1717 this treaty was confirmed.[1]  Colonel Francis Nicholson, who for a time was in the colonies as royal commissioner and governor of Nova Scotia, participated in the earlier of these negotiations, and they were intended to have a bearing upon relations throughout the entire region as far east as the strait of Canseau.  The Indians repeatedly asked that truck houses should be established by the English in or near the settlements, where they could trade and dispose of their beaver.  Certain arrangements of this kind were made, but the trade was slight and probably irregular.  Earlier agreements had provided that cases of dispute should be submitted to the English for settlement, and as usual the terms " subjects " and " allies " were bandied about as descriptive of a situation which neither of them fitted.

So stimulated was their conceit by the support and incitements of the French, that in the course of a few years after the peace of Utrecht, the Indians again became restive. Rumors were heard of widespread conspiracies.  The Indians, at Arrowsick and on other occasions, made extensive claims to lands in Maine and were disposed to challenge the validity of the early grants of the New England Council or from other sources in that region.  Râle and the French authorities supported them to the extreme in this attitude.  Under these

---

[1] Colls. Maine Hist. Soc., *op. cit.*;  Mass. Arch., V, 51.

influences, by 1720 the conduct of the Indians had become so threatening that the renewal of war which should decide the possession of eastern and central Maine had come to be considered a necessity by Massachusetts.

Into the details of this struggle it is not necessary here to enter at length. The French government took no overt part, though it exhibited in an extreme form the possibilities of a benevolent neutrality. The Jesuits and their supporters, who were units among the French colonists, by their pernicious activity occasioned the war. So far, however, as forces actually in service were concerned, the English and the eastern Indians were the only ones concerned. As has already been noticed, considerable effort was made by the English, through conferences and other forms of diplomacy, to bring in the Iroquois, but without result. Therefore this war is to be classed with those of the seventeenth century and of later times which were waged exclusively between the British and their savage foes. Only Massachusetts and New Hampshire participated. Connecticut was asked for aid but sent none, though she did maintain her usual watchful attitude toward Hampshire county. The English, however, were able to carry their operations far beyond what had been possible for them in earlier wars in the eastern country. Instead of acting on the defensive or extending their raids along the coast or only a short distance into the interior, they now in one expedition up the Penobscot and two expeditions up the Kennebec destroyed the French mission stations, slew Râle, the chief author of the mischief, and effectually broke the hold of the Indians over the entire territory of Maine and New Hampshire for a hundred miles or more from the coast. The brave fight of Captain John Lovewell and his men against the Pigwackets, a band of the Sokokis, in western Maine, was the most heroic episode of the war. When hostilities began, the Indians destroyed cattle and crops and terrorized the eastern frontier to the confines of New Hampshire, as they had been accustomed to do in the previous wars. They attacked Arrowsick island, partially destroyed Brunswick and tried to wreck a fort on the river St. George, the most easterly outpost of the English. But when the struggle was over, the Abenakis were so far weakened that they were unable to play an important part in later conflicts. The coast settlements of New Hampshire and Maine were therefore never again exposed to the assaults and massacres from which they had suffered so much since 1676. The way was now cleared for the extension of settlement back from the coast and eastward toward Nova Scotia. During the decades which followed this process went on steadily, though slowly, and as one of its important results the province of New Hampshire attained a much needed extension inland and toward the Connecticut river.[1] Owing to the effects of Râle's war, the conditions under which the later colonial wars were waged on the northeastern frontier differed widely from those which had determined the course of the earlier struggles. It therefore marks a distinct stage in the process by which the decisive superiority of the English in that region was being established.

As the military operations of 1722 against the enemy proceeded, the Massachusetts assembly continued its encroachments upon the military powers of the governor and council. Major Samuel Moody was charged by them with indulging his soldiers in excessive drinking, with refusing assistance to the inhabitants when demanded and with failure to keep a good watch in the night season. Considerable sworn testimony on this subject was taken by the house and the governor was asked to suspend Moody and order him to attend the court at its next session to answer the complaints. Shute replied that he was surprised that they should demand the suspension of an officer before he had been heard and intimated that this affair would be inquired into in England. The house then voted that Moody should not receive any pay until he answered the complaints which had been made against him.[2]

[1] The history of Râle's War had been fully treated by New England writers, especially by Hutchinson, Penhallow, Palfrey and Parkman. A valuable special work on the share of Râle and the French in it is J. P. Baxter's New France in New England. The source material is abundant, in printed form, in the collections of the historical societies and the Prov. Papers of New Hampshire. The Ms. Archives of Mass. also contain much material. The French Archives, and Parkman Papers, in the Mass. Hist. Soc., contain the letters of Vaudreuil and others. Charlevoix's History of New France is a contemporary French authority.

[2] Journal of Lower House, Aug. 1722. Also in B. T. O. P. (C. O. 5/868)

The officer next attacked by the house was Colonel Shadrach Walton, a New Hampshire man, and this involved an effort on its part to assume control of the movement of troops and the plan of campaign. The original plan, in which the whole court had joined, had been to send an expedition to the Penobscot;[1] but during the recess of the court the attack of the Indians on Arrowsick had led to the retention of the troops in that region because of the demand for protection on the part of the inhabitants. Because Walton was in command of the detachment when this change was made, the house in November requested that all the orders which had been issued by himself and the council during the recess of the court be laid before it. Shute explained to the house the reasons which had necessitated the change of plan. The house resolved that the governor should order Walton to appear before it and give his reasons for not executing the orders. Though this demand was several times repeated on successive days, the governor refused to take notice of it. The house also appointed a committee to visit the eastern camp, but the governor, wishing to be conciliatory even under the intolerable conditions which the house were forcing upon him, ordered Walton to come to Boston, but with the express instruction to report first to himself as captain general and then to the house. On his arrival in Boston the house ordered him at once to appear before it. He appeared, but would say nothing without the governor's permission. He was then called before the council, but the house refused to share its inquiry with any other body.[2] Finally it urged that a joint committee of the houses be created to meet at intervals during the recess of the general court to concert measures for the conduct of the war. This was unanimously voted down by the council as inconsistent with the charter.

At this point, near the close of December, 1722, Shute quietly embarked and returned to England. He expressed the intention of returning in a few months, but his real purpose was to submit to the British government an account of the state of Massachusetts affairs and of his unsuccessful efforts to uphold the prerogative against the encroachments

[1] Journal of Lower House, Nov. 1722.
[2] Ibid.; Hutchinson, II, 253–260; Palfrey, IV, 427.

of the house. Under the astute leadership of Cooke and his associates, the house had practically assumed control of the war and the governor had been pushed aside. The amiable Shute had not even been able to effect a compromise and he now abandoned the contest in the province and made his appeal in England.

William Dummer, as lieutenant governor, succeeded to the task. From the personal aversion which was felt toward Shute he did not suffer. He was a Massachusetts man of good standing and judgment, and though he insisted upon some of the traditional dignities of the executive, he could not make headway against the tide which was now flowing. Under the threat of withholding the pay of obnoxious officers and of further supplies for the support of the government, he was forced to consent to the removal of Moody and Walton. Thomas Westbrooke, also a New Hampshire man, was appointed in Walton's place, but the subsequent history of the war credits him with no difficult service and fails to show that he was in any way Walton's superior. The expeditions which ended in the destruction of Norridgewock were conceived by Moulton and Harmon, while Lovewell fought the only heroic action of the war.

Parallel to the progress of the war was the continuous dispute which was kept up between the lower house and the council concerning their respective rights of control over appropriations. The journals of the sessions of 1723 were filled with long messages upon this subject, the council defending the practice during the two preceding wars and the house striving to break down this and assert its decisive preponderance in determining the objects of expenditure as well as the amounts of appropriations. From this time the governor fell largely out of view, since he was forced to maintain a neutral position. In June, 1723, a vote of supply was sent up by the lower house, but the council did not agree. It then proposed that both the votes and amendments be referred to the towns, accompanied with printed copies of " articles of grievances," which would contain criticisms of alleged misconduct on the part of the governor and council in ordering expenditures during the past year. To this procedure the council naturally objected, as well as to the form of the proposed appropriation act. Some change of form was made by the house, but still the council objected, insisting that the disposition of the money should be left with itself and the governor subject to the ordinary provision of the appropriation acts. At the end of the session an appropriation act with certain highly restrictive clauses, though not going to the extent at first demanded by the house, was passed. Near the close of the year the controversy was renewed, the house insisting that no payments should be made except after minute auditing by the court, that the council should be prevented from paying any bills while the general court was in session and that orders upon the treasurer should designate the sum and fund from which the respective payments should be made. To these innovations the council made successful opposition and during this war no further restrictions appear to have been introduced into appropriation bills. As it was, however, the house relentlessly pursued its object and pretty effectually limited the discretion of the executive over expenditures, also securing for itself a large degree of control over the conduct of the war. Thus an important step was taken toward overthrowing the balance which the home government had intended to establish by the provisions of the charter of 1691.[1]

Meantime Shute had reached England and had arraigned the conduct of the Massachusetts assembly in a long memorial to the king.[2] In this document the conduct of the house as just related was traversed, special reference being made to the questions of salary, of the speakership and the assumption of control over military affairs by the assembly. In the statement, of course, no allowance was made for the experience and traditions of Massachusetts which dated from its first charter. Reference also was not made to the changes which had come about in the English constitution, as a result of which the executive was very materially subjected to the will of the two houses. Neither was regard had to similar struggles which were going on in other provinces. But, after the manner of the executive, the perpetual obligations of a

---

[1] Journals of the Houses, Acts and Res., II, 310–315.
[2] E. B. N. Eng. C. O. 5/915, p. 366, reprinted in Hist. Colls. of Prot. Epis. Church, vol. on Mass.

constitution like that of the early Stuarts in England was assumed and deviations from it noted with severe criticism. To say that is by no means to deny the justice, to a certain extent, of these criticisms or that the lower house in Massachusetts was claiming power which should never be in the hands of a legislative assembly. But it is intended simply to call attention to the fixedness of the principles of government affirmed by the crown, while it never planned or adopted the measures required to give the colonial executive strength sufficient to perform the functions demanded of it. Naturally it was in Massachusetts that the conflict was most direct and the result most disastrous to the executive.

In his memorial Shute asserted that he found the representatives in Massachusetts possessed of greater powers than the commons of Great Britain, for they practically elected the members of the council, who were the upper house. They fixed the salaries of the governor and lieutenant governor to suit themselves. They so controlled the office of treasurer as to dictate the issue and expenditure of the public revenue. It followed that in a manner they were the whole legislature and in good measure the executive power also. As to the calibre of the members, Shute described the majority of them as men of small fortunes and mean education. By the artifice of a few leaders and the insinuations of some people in Boston the country members were made to believe that the house was barely supporting the privileges of the people, when it was really invading the rights of the crown. The inhabitants of Boston, where the assembly usually sat, — a town of about 18,000 persons — were " under no magistracy " and therefore were too much inclined to be levellers, and to give a mutinous and disorderly support to the house in its encroachments. A proof of this appeared in the fact that Boston hardly ever failed to choose among its representatives those whose election to the council the governor had vetoed. It was a common maxim that a negatived councillor made a good assemblyman. And yet Shute thought the clergy and generality of people were well affected to the king and that the wealthiest and most intelligent and upright inhabitants disapproved of the proceedings of the representatives, but as they were in the minority they could not control the elections. They therefore were excluded from the assembly and could not make their views practically effective. In addition to these general statements, the memorial summarized the particular acts of encroachment with which the house was charged, the origin and nature of which have already been described.

The board of trade heartily approved of Shute's memorial and drew the inference that the house of representatives already possessed the balance of power and was daily trying to wrest from the executive the small remains of strength which it still held and become independent. It was plain, especially in its treatment of the salary question, that the assembly had little regard for instructions. Since Massachusetts, with a population of some 94,000, was a powerful colony, it was especially necessary that it should be brought within the bounds of obedience and more firmly attached to the interests of Great Britain. But it thought this could be done only by the interposition of parliament. Under the conditions of social and political uncertainty in which Great Britain then was, a program of this sort was not practicable. The board also thought that Shute should be sent back to his province and supported there, but the time never came when this seemed likely to lead to anything but a continuance of the deadlock. The only way in which this could be overcome seemed to be by the payment of the governor's salary from the treasury in England until the people of Massachusetts should become accustomed to a perpetual and fixed provision for their executive. As Shute remained year after year in England and unpaid arrears of his salary accumulated, the board in 1726 made this suggestion to the committee of the privy council, but nothing was done.[1]

On the receipt of Shute's memorial in Massachusetts, the assembly determined to reply to it and stoutly to defend its course. This required the assistance of one or more agents. The days of the Ashursts were now past and Dummer, as we have seen, was in disfavor with the house, though not with the council. During the closing session of 1723 the subject was discussed between the two houses [2] and the proposal of

[1] Representation of B. T. to committee of privy council, Mar. 30, 1726; C. O. 5/915, p. 450.
[2] Journals of the Houses, Nov. and Dec. 1723.

the assembly finally accepted that Anthony Sanderson, of London, and Elisha Cooke, the leader of the house, be associated with Dummer in the agency. Appropriations to meet their expenditures were made and memorials from each of the houses in support of their respective views were sent to England. The case was taken up directly by the committee of the privy council with the assistance of the law officers of the crown.[1] The latter were attended by Shute and an agent for the house of representatives. The complaints and answers thereto, with proofs, were considered and a report submitted to the committee of the council. The committee then heard counsel for both sides.[2] By this time the Massachusetts case had broken down and been abandoned upon all the points except those relating to the speakership and the adjournment of the assembly. As Cooke himself was now in England, he had evidently been forced to admit that the campaign which he had carried on in reference to the Maine woods, the governor's salary, the public fast, and the interference with the military and the conduct of the war could not be legally justified. He also had to admit that the house had no authority to adjourn itself for a longer time than from day to day without first applying to the governor. Shute, it was decided, had made good his general charge and most of his specifications. His zeal and fidelity were approved and the opinion was expressed that he deserved well of the king. But the fact should be noted that he did not return to Massachusetts, nor did he receive appointment to the governorship of any other colony.[3]

Most of the questions which were at issue in this controversy were not capable of a definite legal settlement. But two of them were not of test nature and they were finally

---

[1] Acts of P. C. Col. 1720–1745, pp. 92–104. In British Museum Addtl. Mss. 15,486 (Papers from Library of George Chalmers) are three opinions of law officers on this case — one by Robert Raymond and Philip Yorke, another by Raymond, and a third by Yorke and Wearg, the last outlining the arguments of counsel at great length, especially those who appeared for the house of representatives.

[2] John Colman, of Boston, wrote home an account of this hearing, which abounds in references to the lawyers concerned and to Cooke and the helplessness of the case. 1 Mass. Hist. Soc. Colls., II, 32.

[3] This, however, was due in part to the fact that the death of George I, when Shute was about to return, vacated his commission.

disposed of in an explanatory charter which was issued by the crown in 1725 and accepted by the general court of Massachusetts early in 1726. This document gave the governor the right to approve and disapprove the choice of speakers by the lower house, and the house the right to adjourn itself for two days without leave from the governor, but not for a longer period. In the case of the speakership this was a final acknowledgement on the part of the British government that the provisions of the charter of 1691 did not fully justify the action of Shute, though it was desirable and in harmony with precedents in England that the right of the executive to approve the choice of a speaker should include also the right of disapproval. In the case of provinces which had no charters questions of this kind, if settled at all, would be settled in the commissions or instructions of the governors. Though Cooke's service in the house of representatives was now nearly ended and on his return he was elected to the council, it is probable that strong opposition would have been made to the acceptance of the explanatory charter had not the court been informed that otherwise the entire question of the relations between the crown and Massachusetts would be taken into parliament. It would probably have contributed to the permanence of the British empire in the form under which it then existed if this had been done and the issues with Massachusetts received a thorough adjustment. Had this course been followed at that time, Massachusetts could hardly have avoided a serious curtailment at least of the liberties for which she was striving, and it was doubtless this feeling which led her to accept an unwelcome charter rather than to risk defeat on more important issues.

In July, 1728, the quiet and successful administration of Dummer was brought to an end by the arrival of William Burnet, the new appointee to the governorship. He was transferred from New York, where in point of statesmanship he had an honorable rank among colonial executives. His capacity for broad views and his resolution and address in urging them had there been sufficiently proved. His name and reputation had preceded him in Massachusetts, as was shown by the fine reception which was given him on his arrival at Boston. At last a thoroughly satisfactory ap-

pointment seemed to have been made and Massachusetts had
a governor who was worthy of her dignity and pride. He
was a man of considerable literary and forensic ability, cul-
tured and more than qualified to be the social leader of the
province.

By Burnet's twenty-third instruction, pursuant to the order
of council of February 15, 1727/8, the assembly was required to settle on the governor a salary of at least £1000
per annum. It was added that in view of the long opposition
which had been made to this demand a failure to comply
would be considered " a manifest mark of undutiful Behavior " toward the king.[1]  So insistent had the instruction
on this subject to Massachusetts now become that it amounted
to a requisition; both parties were prepared to contest the
issue to the finish.  Burnet so understood it and from his
first meeting with the assembly ordered his conduct accordingly.  This made the salary question the sole issue of his
brief administration.  He resorted to diplomacy as little as
did Shute and the house remained as united as ever.  The
result was a struggle without a sign of concession on either
side.

In his opening speech to the assembly Burnet called attention to the wealth of Massachusetts and its ability properly
to support a governor.  Then, like a good Whig, he enlarged upon the balance between the three branches of the
government in England which caused its constitution to excel.
" The Wisdom of Parliaments," he continued, " has now made
it an established custom to grant the Civil List to the king
for life; and so I am confident the representatives of the
people here would be unwilling to own themselves outdone
in duty to his majesty by any of his subjects." At the close
of this speech he read the twenty-third instruction. The
reply of the house to this was a vote of £1700 to the governor to enable him to manage the public affairs and defray
the cost of his coming to Massachusetts.  Cooke, who was
again the leader of the assembly, was placed at the head of
a committee which drafted a reply to Burnet's speech, alleg-

[1] C. O. 5/916, B. T. E. B. N. Eng. p. 63. A collection of the Proceedings
of the Great and General Court or Assembly of His Majesty's Province of
Massachusetts Bay,  Printed by order of the House, 17, 29.

ing that the method of appropriation to which they adhered
in the case of the governor's salary was necessary to the
preservation of the privileges guarantied to them in the
charter. As the charter simply gave the assembly the right
to impose proportionable and reasonable taxes, this was
clearly a loose interpretation of its own devised for the
purpose of extending and confirming its power. It professed,
of course, that it had no intention of reducing the governor to
a position of dependence on the people. The large grant
which it had offered — in marked contrast to the meager
sums with which Shute was asked to be content — though it
was in depreciated currency, was apparently intended to
quiet the scruples of the governor and reconcile him to his
position. But in this they were not successful. Burnet declined the offer and in his reply stated that a support given
in so precarious a manner implied no sort of confidence in
the government and was clearly intended to take from the
executive his independence and force him into subordination
to the other branches of the legislature. He appealed to their
knowledge of the facts to state whether the governor's salary
had not been kept back till all other bills of moment had been
consented to and whether it had not depended on that consent. That this was a fact, he alleged, was well known.

The assembly, after repeating the assertion that its only
effective privilege was its control over appropriations, went
on to enlarge on the governor's power over both itself and
the council. It then drew a distinction between colonial
governors and the king by showing that the interest of the
latter in his kingdom was permanent while that of the former
was temporary. When the governor had once left the colony,
they said, neither its prosperity nor its adversity affected his
interest. If a salary should be settled permanently upon a
governor, it would be exceeding the grant of the civil list
to the king for life. The experience of other colonies of
course proves the fears of the assembly to have been largely
groundless, but that experience was unknown in Massachusetts and so the statement went practically unchallenged.
The council, at this juncture, suggested that it would not be
dangerous to grant a salary to the governor by name and for
a certain time, as had been done elsewhere, but this did not

suit the rigid dogmatism of Cooke and his faction and the proposal was rejected. In their mental and moral tone the Cookes resembled the Endicotts and Danforths in the seventeenth century and Samuel Adams at the time of the Revolution; as types of Massachusetts politicians they form connecting links between the two epochs. When the governor called their attention to the practice in other provinces and to the likelihood, if they did not yield, that they would incur the royal displeasure, the assembly expressed indifference toward the conditions in other colonies and was sure that they ought not to influence its action. Burnet's reference to the lapse of Massachusetts into the issue of irredeemable paper as a proof that the influence of the assembly was too great, may have had some weight as a criticism of government in the colonies generally, but it could not form a part of a special indictment against Massachusetts.

On August 28, and again early in September, after the court had been in session more than a month, and that in midsummer, Burnet refused to consent to its prorogation. "Unless his Majesty's pleasure has its due weight with you," he told them, "your Desires will have very little weight with me." The house now turned to the towns. A committee, of which Cooke was the chairman, was appointed to draft an address, known as "The Advice," in which the history of the salary question was reviewed as it appeared to them. This document closed with four reasons for adherence to their policy rather than to grant a permanent salary or one for a term of years, as suggested by the council: 1. The latter course was an "untrodden path," beset with danger, and one which had never been followed by themselves or their ancestors. 2. Since *magna carta* it had been an established right of all Englishmen to raise and dispose of moneys for the public good of their own free accord. 3. Any other policy would lessen the dignity of the assembly and destroy the balance of the constitution. 4. Under the province charter the general court had the right to freely appropriate all moneys. Burnet now charged the house with sending out a partisan statement of the question at issue. It was very odd, he said, to talk of the balance of the constitution being destroyed by the increase of the power of the executive when

the house of representatives had a majority of three to one
in elections of the council and while it leaves only £500 to
be disposed of by the governor and council during a recess.
Some inkling of the weakness of the assembly's reference to
*magna carta* was shown by the governor's criticism of later
acts, like the Confirmation of Charters, to show that the
grant of a permanent salary was not inconsistent with any
document of the English constitution. The house in reply
asked if the house of commons was ever told that it must
grant money in a particular way or it would be kept in session indefinitely. Burnet now tried to bring pressure to bear
by informing them that a recent bill for the issue of £60,000
in bills of credit would probably be disallowed if an act was
not passed appropriating the interest on these bills as part
of a permanent salary for the governor. The house had told
him that the interest had already been appointed for other
purposes.

At this point Wells took the place of Cooke as the penman
of the assembly, and as the discussion proceeded with a further defence of the appeal to the towns against the vigorous
attacks of the governor, the communications from the house
assumed a milder tone. A grant of £3000 was also offered
Burnet as a further inducement to concession on his part.
This he declined with the remark that it was an offer of a
higher reward "to take his Majesty's Displeasure off from
you and lay it upon myself." The Boston town meeting now
began to take an active part in the controversy. At a session
specially called it declared itself to be unanimously opposed
to the granting of a permanent salary. Burnet considered
this to be an "unnecessary forwardness" on the part of
Boston, and that it was intended as an example to be followed by the other towns. For some time also he had had
reason to think that the inhabitants of Boston had been
working upon the minds of the representatives to bring them
into their own way of thinking.[1] The town meeting had
actually instructed its representatives to vote against a permanent salary. For these reasons Burnet adjourned the general court to meet, October 31, at Salem. A discussion over
the legality of this act was now added to the salary question.

[1] Acts and Res., II, 523.

The house, of course, denied that it had been influenced by opinion in Boston and made all the capital it could out of the inconveniences to which meetings in Salem exposed it. Its argument as to the legality of the removal hinged upon the interpretation of the writ of election which was included in the election law of 1698.[1] The king in council had already decided that the writ had been introduced as a mere matter of form or example and did not take from the crown its power to summon the court on occasion to meet at another place.  The house contended that the writ was fully binding and therefore that the court could not be called at any place but Boston.  The action of Shute in 1721 was cited, but it did not yield a precedent which told clearly in favor of either side.  In the provinces generally numerous cases could have been cited which were favorable to the governor's contention, but these were not known or regarded in Massachusetts.

The house now resolved to address the king.  A memorial was accordingly prepared defending its course and arraigning that of the governor.  In this the statement was made that the governor's instruction had been obtained without the privity of the people, but if they had had the opportunity of laying their reasons against it before the king and of showing how inconsistent they believed it to be with the powers that were granted in the charter, they believed it would never have been granted.  The sum of £100 was voted to be sent to Francis Wilkes, a New England merchant resident in London, to be used in support of the appeal, but the council, which was in favor of a grant to Burnet for a term of years, refused to concur.  The money was then subscribed by principal inhabitants of Boston.  An application from the governor for a copy of the memorial was denied and no copy of it was shown to the council.  Jonathan Belcher, who had recently become friendly with Cooke, was associated with Wilkes in the agency, though he did not reach England until the business was well advanced.  By way of reprisal Burnet for a time refused to sign warrants for the payment of the salaries of the representatives, but that attitude he later found it unwise to continue.  In order to supplement his own income he also collected fees for let-

[1] Acts and Res., II, 315; Hutchinson, III, 299 *et seq.*

passes for vessels, a practice common in New York but hitherto unknown in Massachusetts, but on complaint made in England this part of his conduct was at once disapproved.

At intervals during much of 1729 the case was considered and argued before the board of trade. A number of counsel and agents appeared on both sides. Sayre and Fitzakerly, the counsel for Massachusetts, argued boldly against the validity of the king's instruction concerning salary, because it had been issued without the knowledge of the people of Massachusetts and they had been given no opportunity to express their belief that it invalidated their charter. The law officers of the crown appeared on the other side and presented substantially the same arguments which the governor had been urging. The board then reported to the king that the instruction was " proper to be enforced." The committee of the council then examined the case [1] and reported that the effect of yielding to the claims of the assembly would be to make the governor dependent on the good will of the colonists, which would lessen his authority and thus the dependence which the colony should have on the crown. Therefore a salary of at least £1000 sterling must be settled upon the governor. Finally, though the board would gladly have found some easier way, in view of the refractoriness of the province, the king was advised to lay the whole matter before parliament.[2] The report was approved and it was ordered that one of the secretaries of state should receive the pleasure of the crown thereupon. Burnet, whose conduct was highly approved, wrote to Newcastle asking that two companies of soldiers be sent over, but no further action was taken. A statement from the agents that it was not likely that the question would be brought before parliament was received in the province and printed.

In the session of April, 1729, a dispute arose between the two houses over their respective attitudes toward the salary question and the voting of supplies, and Burnet dissolved the court. The May election which followed did not essentially change the membership of either house. The council refused

---

[1] Proceedings are fully given in B. T. Journal, New England; Acts of P. C. Col. 1720–1745, p. 108; Hutchinson, II, 323.

[2] Newcastle to Burnet, June 26, 1729; C. O. 5/871, Z, 84.

to approve of an appropriation for the payment of the agents in England and the governor refused to sign a bill for the issue of more bills of credit. The irritation of the assembly was also increased by the removal of the court to Cambridge, it being the apparent policy of the governor to exhaust their endurance by removals and stubborn resistance to their demands. Such a result as that might have been possible had it not been for Burnet's death, after a brief illness, September 7, 1729. At a hearing which occurred just after the news of this event reached England, the privy council condemned the custom, which had been more or less in vogue since Shute's time of making appropriations in the form of resolves rather than acts.[1] This it declared to be a violation of the charter. It also pronounced unwarrantable the practice of reserving to the representatives the power of allowing and passing accounts before the governor had the opportunity of issuing money for the payment of them. The agents admitted that the procedure in these respects should be changed and the opinion was expressed by the committee that instructions be issued accordingly. These criticisms showed how the spirit and methods of the corporate colony were reasserting themselves in Massachusetts and to what an extent they were carrying the province beyond the principles of the charter and royal instructions.

[1] Acts of P. C. Col. 1720–1745, p. 254; C. O. 5/869, B. T. O. P. N. Eng. In this volume are the letters of Burnet, the memorial of the agents of Massachusetts against him, and much earlier material concerning Dummer's administration.

# CHAPTER XIII

## THE OUTLYING COLONIES OF NEW ENGLAND:
### NEW HAMPSHIRE

FROM whatever standpoint it may be viewed, New England appears, especially in the colonial period, to have been a distinct section. Geographically it is such, and the further back one goes in its history the more evident it becomes that it was such in the make-up of its population, in its economic structure, in the type of society and institutions which developed within it, and above all in its religious spirit and ideals. So poor were the means of communication and so limited the intercourse between New England and the other continental colonies that, prior to 1690, they knew very little of one another. New England was isolated from the rest, and so absorbed was she in her own existence that she cared little more about the other colonies than if they had been foreign states. The lack of knowledge and interest, of course, was equally great on the other side. So much easier at that time was communication by sea than by land, that with the development of commerce it seemed as if the merchants of New England would come into closer relations with the island colonies than with those of the middle and southern part of the continent. Though there were differences between the New England colonies, sufficient to account at the beginning for their separate origin and for the tenacity with which they clung to their individuality in later times, they were all found to exist under much the same natural and historic environment and had to work out their destinies together.[1] The principle of liberty, so dear to the Briton and especially to the Nonconformist, was fully satisfied by the isolation of New England and by colonial particularism in that section and wherever else it existed; the principles of authority and

[1] This is amply proved on the author's treatment of New England in his Am. Colonies in the 17th Century.

of duty, as applied to any larger political union than the colony, received very scanty recognition. To the frontiersman and the colonist this appeared arbitrary and oppressive, something which they could ill brook.

Among the tendencies which gradually revealed to New Englanders their own unity and their connection with the other colonies was the development, after 1660, of the system of imperial control. They were slowly made aware that they were being subjected to a common policy and that the pressure which they felt was brought to bear on all the other colonies as well. Among their diversities certain uniformities of treatment and obligation began to be enforced. These went along with a common language and elements of culture, and with the slow development of intercourse, to broaden the consciousness of the settlers. The New England Confederacy furnished the earliest suggestion of such a union as might be effected by the spontaneous action of the colonists. The Dominion of New England, during its brief existence, furnished an example of a union created by administrative authority. Both were crude experiments, as was shown by their methods of government and their precarious existence. But they foreshadowed changes toward which the colonies were inevitably tending and illustrated the difference between the operation of the two principles of liberty and authority or sovereignty as applied to the problem of colonial union.

The outbreak of the colonial wars set in motion anew tendencies toward union, and furnished additional opportunity for the operation both of local initiative and imperial pressure to bring about joint action on as large a scale as possible. As long as the wars continued those tendencies may be seen at work checking and balancing one another at every important step. Much of the significance of the period is to be found in following out their interaction, though it appears in all the colonies equally with New England. Military considerations told strongly and continuously in favor of union, strength, efficiency and authority. Interested upon that side were the royal officials and all who could be strongly influenced by them. But the wars were financed mainly by the colonies and this gave their assemblies the opportunity to check all imperialistic plans and utterly to

thwart many of them. It was through the assemblies that the
spirit of the localities and colonies, the traditions which had
led to their settlement and which still persisted among the
people at large, found expression. Commercial interests, religious susceptibilities and social predispositions of all kinds
had their play and in their degree influenced the result. As
the period of the colonial wars advanced, now and again,
about the mouth of the Hudson river, Delaware bay,
Chesapeake bay and the mouth of the James appear signs of
a local grouping of interests, but they never in any case
assume the importance of a section. Only in New England
were relations so distinct and permanent as properly to
justify that designation.

The nucleus and centre of the New England group of colonies was Massachusetts. From the first it dominated the
section and it continued in a position of leadership throughout
the colonial period. It was the largest colony of the group
and its location was central. In fact Massachusetts, in area
and population, always held a place among the larger colonies, while New Hampshire, Rhode Island and Connecticut
stood in the number of the smaller colonies. It had boundary
questions to adjust with all the other colonies of the section.
Boston was the chief port and commercial centre of New
England; Narragansett bay and New London never overtook
its lead. When Massachusetts received a royal governor,
while Connecticut and Rhode Island resumed government
under their corporate charters, it became in an official sense
the centre of New England. The relation between Massachusetts and the crown now became constant in all the lines
through which imperial control was exercised during the
eighteenth century. Its officials became the medium of communication in many ways between the crown and the other
colonies of the section. It was in the hands of the Massachusetts executive that the British government tried to place the
command of the militia for all New England. Even though
that failed, Massachusetts bore the chief burden of colonial
defence along the New England frontier and its action determined to a large extent that of the entire section. Its
executive was constantly in communication with the neighboring colonies, and such negotiations as New England had

with the French in Acadia and Canada were almost wholly in
her hands. The same was true, with an occasional exception
in the case of Connecticut, of dealings between New England
and the Six Nations of New York. Where joint expeditions
were fitted out, those against Acadia were always managed
chiefly or exclusively by Massachusetts, and in those against
Canada she bore the leading part among the New England
colonies, although in the last colonial war Connecticut became somewhat more prominent than she had previously
been. Boston was also made the centre from which was
exercised the jurisdiction of the admiralty courts for eastern
New England and New York for western. When royal commissions were appointed, the executives of Massachusetts or
New York were usually selected for leading places upon them.
Massachusetts officials, like those of other royal provinces,
were expected to exercise a sort of watchfulness, if not supervision, over the neighboring proprieties, and this was true of
Massachusetts as well as Virginia. The reports concerning
the conduct of Rhode Island and Connecticut which reached
the administrative boards in England proceeded to a large
extent from Massachusetts officials.

In matters religious and educational, as compared with
the previous century, Connecticut advanced relatively to a
position nearing equality with Massachusetts, while Rhode
Island maintained its independent course. All of these statements at least may be made respecting its leadership during
the eighteenth century without any desire to be partial toward
Massachusetts or to belittle the other New England colonies.
Of the sectional characteristics of that region there can also
be little doubt. If these things be true, they suggest to the
student of institutions and of the trend of political forces the
correct method of treating New England history. While emphasizing all that is essential to an understanding of the
individual peculiarities of each colony, the section should be
treated as much as possible as a unit. In the discussion of the
wars that aspect of things must necessarily be the leading
one. It should also be kept clearly in view in reference to
other matters. At the same time, of course, the relations
between New England and the rest of the colonies and the
process by which they assumed their final places in the British

imperial system must not be neglected. The great purpose, indeed, in the treatment of this growing federal system, is to reveal both its variety and its unity as mutually restricting and conditioning one another. In order to attain this object, so far as New England is concerned, it is necessary to throw Massachusetts into the foreground as the centre of the group and to treat the other colonies not merely separately and independently but also as related to her and to the general harmony with the method pursued in the history of the seventeenth century and will contribute toward an understanding of the increasing unity of development which was characteristic of the eighteenth century. Now that the history of the first two colonial wars has been sketched, and the course of development traced in Massachusetts to the close of Dudley's administration, it is time to take up the three smaller New England colonies and explain their chief characteristics and history during the period under review.

In several important respects New Hampshire was more closely related to Massachusetts than were either of the colonies of southern New England. Through her annexation of the Maine settlements and so long as the population of New Hampshire was confined to the seaboard, the territory of Massachusetts nearly surrounded that of her smaller neighbor. In earlier times, as we know, the towns of New Hampshire had been governed by Massachusetts. In the history of the wars we have seen how dependent the smaller colony was upon the larger for defence. In race, religion and general character the settlers of New Hampshire closely resembled those of Massachusetts and the majority of them would have welcomed a continuance of her government. Owing to its origin and history, it had not the sense of organic unity or of a mission which was strong in both Connecticut and Rhode Island, while its exposure on the frontier which experienced the most frequent and bloody assaults which were anywhere known in that period robbed New Hampshire of most of the spirit of independence which might otherwise have existed.

After 1690, as before, the purely internal politics of the half-dozen towns which, with a large and yet unsurveyed expanse of wilderness extending inland toward the northwest, made up the province of New Hampshire, were determined

chiefly by the contest between the people and the assignees of
John Mason. This was the inheritance which had come to it
from the method of its origin. In 1691 Samuel Allen, a mild
mannered English merchant, for £750 bought from the Mason
heirs their claim to the lands of New Hampshire.[1] The
entail had previously been docked by a fine and recovery in
the court of king's bench. Allen, and later his son Thomas,
now became the owners of the Mason claim and its persistent
defenders. During the years which intervened between the
collapse of the Dominion of New England and the arrival
of the earl of Bellomont, New Hampshire was *de facto* a
proprietary province under Allen and his appointee. Bellomont's commission included New Hampshire, but, as we have
seen, he only visited it once, in 1700, holding one session of
the assembly and remaining in the province about three weeks.
His interests were chiefly concerned with the strengthening
the fort at the mouth of the Piscataqua and the production of
naval stores. For a period of more than a decade New
Hampshire thus enjoyed officially almost complete independence of any other province. Not until the arrival of Dudley,
who was appointed governor of New Hampshire as well as
of Massachusetts, did the official connection between the two
provinces begin which was to continue with slight interruption till their final separation in 1741.

During most of the first intercolonial war John Usher was
lieutenant governor of New Hampshire. He was the Boston
stationer whom we have met in other connections as treasurer
of the Dominion of New England and whose demands for
the settlement of his claims which arose from that service
were kept before the Massachusetts and the British governments for many years after the Revolution. Usher had
married a daughter of Samuel Allen. He had earlier committed himself to the course of monarchy and imperialism as
represented by the Andros régime. But his plans had been
thwarted by the Revolution, and his repeated failures to get
his claims allowed and the unpopularity which he had incurred by his connection with Andros ruffled a naturally

---

[1] Belknap's History of N. H., Farmer's Ed., 123; Bellomont, in a letter
to the board of trade, dated June 22, 1700, states that New Hampshire cost
Allen only £250, C. O. 5/909 B. T. N. Eng. E. B.

irritable temper. As lieutenant governor of New Hampshire Usher supported the Allen claim by all means in his power, and this helped greatly to prevent his securing a revenue or any desirable improvements in government. In his letters, which were numerous and of considerable length, he became the advocate of the union again of all the colonies from Connecticut to Nova Scotia as a military necessity. His letters also formed a part of that chorus of criticism which was directed against the spirit of the New England people as shown in their preference for illegal trade and the alleged arbitrary acts of their governments. Usher listened to the complaints of royal customs officials and other royalists in New England and echoed their views in connection with his own complaints. The people of New Hampshire were few, poor and terribly harassed by war, and if the plea of poverty, so generally urged by the colonists as an excuse for small appropriations or none at all, was ever justified, it was so in their case between 1698 and 1714. Usher suffered in consequence of this and was unable to procure any salary. He became vociferous in orders and reprimands to the assembly and in public and private among the people. Though a well-meaning man, his ungrammatical and confused speech and writing, together with the contrast, evident to all, between his assumptions of authority and the insignificance of its reality, gave an air of absurdity to much that Usher said and did. To his mind willfulness and disaffection explained the refusal of the New Hampshire assembly to grant the money which he demanded. He berated them and others like schoolboys and was grossly insulted, like an unpopular pedagogue, in return. The pettiness, roughness and lack of dignity which characterized New Hampshire government in Cranfield's time was repeated in milder forms while Usher was governor.

But the fundamental reason for Usher's failure to come to terms with the people of New Hampshire is to be found in his connection with Allen. Partridge, Vaughan and usually Hincks, in the council, were determined opponents of the proprietary system, succeeding to the position held by Waldron at an earlier time. Among the body of the people the resolve never to pay rent to Allen or to any one else who was seeking to revive the Mason claim, was as strong as it ever had been. The knowledge that Usher was Allen's nominee and determined partisan made the assembly deaf to all of the governor's appeals for a salary and to many of his requests for aid in support of the government. Allen had promised Usher a salary of £250, but was unable to pay it. Owing to his total failure to obtain support, Usher repaired to Boston for long periods on the plea that he must prosecute his business there in order to support himself and family. This left the government in the hands of the council and affairs drifted loosely on, varied by spasmodic efforts to repel the enemy and to exact reprisals for their bloody attacks upon the frontier settlements. All the evidence goes to show how impossible it would have been even for one much abler than Usher to maintain the proprietary régime in New Hampshire, especially in time of war. The skill shown by both Usher and his opponents in the council and assembly in hurling scripture quotations at each other's heads only threw into clearer relief the narrowness and bitterness of their spirits.

Usher was jealous of Massachusetts and believed that the great majority of the people of New Hampshire desired reunion with her and a common restoration of the corporate form of government. He and Phips quarrelled over a charge by the latter that deserters from the guardship " Nonesuch " were being protected in New Hampshire and a countercharge that Phips violated New Hampshire territory in his attempt to arrest Captain Short and seize his effects.[1] Owing to the fact that trade and admiralty jurisdiction as between the two provinces were unregulated, disputes and complaints, especially on the part of Usher, were frequent. Vessels were reported to be trading to and from New Hampshire without clearances, and when a warrant was issued for the arrest of offenders the process servers were opposed by force. On one occasion sailors were impressed without the governor's warrant. The owner of a bark which was seized or " stopped " at the fort appealed to the general court at Boston, on the ground apparently that the jurisdiction of Massachusetts extended to the southern bank of the Piscataqua. In the fall

[1] N. H. Prov. Papers, II, 91, 100; Cal. S. P. Col. 1693-6; Letters of John Usher.

of 1693 Phips also ignored New Hampshire in concluding a treaty with Indians, some of whom lived in the latter province.

It was in the face of obstacles such as have been described that New Hampshire had to be defended against the French and Indians during the years when Phips and Usher, both inefficient products of New England individualism, were at the head of the two provinces concerned. In May, 1694, Usher made one of his characteristic speeches to the assembly. Quoting Luke, xiv, 28, " for which of you, desiring to build a tower, doth not sit down first and count the cost? " he went on to tell them that the council judged it absolutely necessary to repair the fort. An appropriation was made, though not for the fort and artillery but to pay the debts of the province and maintain sixty men on the frontier. The assembly declared that it was not able to provide for coast defence, that being an expression of a feeling, general in the colonies, that the British government should to a large extent man and defend the forts on the coast. Upon this Usher resolved to send the secretary, Thomas Davis, as a special agent, to England to lay before the government the state of the province.

At midsummer following occurred the attack on Oyster River, and much activity and correspondence followed with a view not only to sending out men from New Hampshire towns but to procuring aid from Massachusetts. Phips at first plead that the Massachusetts charter prohibited the marching of troops out of the province without their consent or that of the general assembly. This defect had been remedied by two earlier temporary acts, but these had both expired. Stoughton, who was more in sympathy with Usher than was Phips, attempted to take some decisive action in aid of New Hampshire. In September the Massachusetts assembly relieved the situation by passing another temporary act, though it was then too late to be of any special value.[1] The degree of Usher's real interest in the crisis may be measured by the fact that in about three weeks after the massacre he told the council that he was going to Boston to attend to

[1] Acts and Res., I, 18, 36, 99, 176; N. H. Prov. Papers, II, 124 et seq. For the comments of Usher see Cols. S. P. Col., loc. cit.

his private affairs. It was on this occasion that a constable resorted to the irritating school-boy tactics of impressing his saddle, for which he was solemnly bound over to keep the peace. "With submission," Usher wrote petulantly to the lords of trade, " I say that for me to spend my own estate among a lying, crooked people, who set themselves as one man to run down the governor and trample on the royal authority, is a burden greater than I can bear; and since I have no bread to eat, nor anyone to stand by me, I judge it is better for me to leave the place than that the king's commission should be thus abused." In fact neither Usher nor Phips contributed any help of value in the crisis, for the latter a few months later was forced to sail for England under charges and the evidence bearing on his case was already being collected. By the action of Stoughton, however, and the councils and assemblies of the two provinces, a joint demonstration was made on the frontier, though as usual it came too late and was ineffective. Such appropriations as were made in New Hampshire only sufficed to pay debts incurred in the past, and, as so often happened in New York, the wealthier inhabitants, in anticipation of future revenue, had to advance supplies to the Massachusetts men who remained over winter.

At the beginning of May, 1695, Usher, who had been absent most of the preceding fall and winter, returned, dissolved the assembly and ordered a new election. So small was the province that the holding of an election was a task of only a few days. The new assembly was opened in less than a week after the dissolution of the former one, and there was so little business to be done that the session lasted little more than a week. When, immediately after his return, Usher had asked the council in executive session, if anything had occurred during his absence, they answered, nothing. When he asked further if they had anything to offer for the service, the board was silent. By the new assembly no response was made to the lieutenant governor's request — oft repeated before — that an appropriation should be speedily made for the support of the government and for defence. The six months during which the Massachusetts troops were to serve in New Hampshire were ended and their return to Boston

was insisted on, as was the payment of one-third of their
wages by New Hampshire. The agreement, as made, was
that New Hampshire should provide one-half of the pay.
But when the demand was made, even at the reduced rate
of one-third, the council sharply refused its assent, stating
that Usher had never informed them of that part of the agreement. They also said that they did not know that any limit
of time was set. We may suppose that these terms were
arranged with Usher in Boston and, if so, they furnish an
interesting example of absentee government.

The soldiers were taken to Pemaquid, though in August
part of them were sent back and were used to guard from
Indian attack the men who were hauling masts from the
woods at Dover. Massachusetts still demanded their arrears
of pay and the council gave assurance that all would be made
right by the next assembly. In the brief session of September,
1695, the assembly voted £400 and according to a letter of
the council part of this was to go for the payment of the
Massachusetts troops. In October a new assembly was
elected and it also appropriated £400 for defence, including
payment of troops from Massachusetts.[1] But to Usher's
renewed proposal that they should provide for the support of
the government they were deaf, neither would they advise
how he should lay the condition and needs of the province
before the king. He wrote home that £300 of this appropriation went for arrears, and only £100 for the soldiers. More
than £1200 which was due to soldiers for wages they would
not pay at present. Proposals for the levy of additional taxes
came to nothing.

In his letters at this time Usher stated that during the three
years or more since he had been governor he had not received
a line from England as to the government. He had reported
both to the crown officials and to Allen, but all he could hear
was that they wished him to continue in charge, though they
wonder that New Hampshire could not provide for its government. This, wrote he, is like Pharaoh's command to make
bricks without straw. If the right was in the king, they
should support the government, if in Allen, they should pay

[1] Prov. Papers, II, 165 et seq.; III, 31 et seq.; Col. St. P. Col. 1693–96,
p. 609.

him quit rents and support the government, but they would do neither and nothing could be got from them but a plea of poverty.

For the winter of 1695/6 no troops were obtained from Massachusetts, the real obstacle being the arrears of pay and the tricky way in which it was claimed that New Hampshire was trying to escape from the agreement to pay part of their wages. Fortunately no attacks occurred during the winter, but they were resumed in the spring. Early in July another assembly met, but owing to a violent dispute between it and the governor about the amount of the appropriation and the use that should be made of it, he dissolved it and returned to Boston, the province being left wholly without revenue.[1] He then had to provide during several months out of his own estate for about forty men who were on garrison duty. At another session in the autumn of 1696 an appropriation of £600 was obtained, and arrears, so far as they could not be provided for out of this sum, were ignored.

At this time the strong prejudices of Usher and the stubbornness of his opponents involved him in a violent quarrel with William Vaughan and Richard Waldron, two leading opposition councillors, over the question, whether or not they had signed the association for the defence of the person of William III, and had taken the oath of allegiance. Though the councillors do not appear to have been seriously at fault, Usher suspended them from that body, and probably would have imprisoned them if there had been a prison in the province.[2] Captain Shadrach Walton, commander of the fort and a loyal supporter of Usher and the king, was sent by the lieutenant governor to England to report the condition of the province and beg for a royal garrison and proper authority to command the fort, town and province. Vaughan and Waldron sent representatives against Usher. In the last weeks of 1696 and early in 1697 New Hampshire affairs at last received a little attention from the lords of trade. Usher's last letters were read and Allen and Walton were summoned. But William Partridge, a New Hampshire merchant and shipbuilder who was already in England, seems already to have

[1] Prov. Papers, III, 38–41, 44; Cal. St. P. Col. 1696–7. p. 161 *et seq.*
[2] *Ibid.*, 515–516.

been nominated for governor by Allen and approved by the king.[1]

When, in the winter of 1697, Partridge arrived in New Hampshire, the suspended councillors seized Usher's commission, displaced his friends from the council and reorganized it with their supporters. A general change was made in officials and the Rev. Joshua Moody came again to the front. Partridge is said to have disliked these arbitrary proceedings and to have been rather an instrument than the chief actor in them. Usher returned from Boston to Hampton and there protested against the assumption of the government by Partridge until he had shown to him and his council and had properly published the commission under which he claimed to act.[2] Partridge and his supporters said that the reason he deferred the publication of his commission and the assumption of government was that he had not taken the oath prescribed by 7 & 8 Wm. III c. 22 and was told that Randolph was coming to administer it to all the governors. There was no one in New England who was authorized to administer the oaths and therefore Partridge deferred action and an arrangement was made for the council, with Hincks as president, to carry on the government in the meantime. But, on Usher's advice, Story, the new secretary, was sent to England to lay the existing state of affairs before the board of trade. The condition of New Hampshire was then considered at intervals in connection with the broader questions raised on the appointment of Lord Bellomont, until finally, in August, 1697, a letter from the lords justices was sent by Story authorizing Usher to administer the government until Partridge qualified or Bellomont arrived, and the king's authority in his person should not be trampled upon.

But though Usher published this order it was not obeyed, for his authority in the province had already practically ceased. In February, 1696/7, a proclamation was issued that the government was vested in the president and council until Allen should arrive or Partridge publish his commission.[3]

---

[1] Prov. Papers, III, 170, 184, 214, 241, 252, 299, 1696–7, pp. 74, 214, 241, 252, 368.

[2] *Ibid.*, 371, 378, 479, 485, 490, 504, 515, 517, 560, 572, 588; Prov. Papers, II, 207, 211, 215, 218, 220, *et seq.*        [3] Prov. Papers, II, 215 *et seq.*

New justices of the peace and judges were appointed and steps taken to pay off some of the debts of the province, repair the fort and provide otherwise for defence. A successful application was made to Massachusetts for forty men, who should be paid wholly by New Hampshire. A new assembly met in June, before which accounts and claims for service were duly presented and £650 were appropriated for the subsistence and pay of soldiers and the excise was continued. As the obstacles to self-government had been for a time removed, the attitude of dogged inactivity ceased and public affairs received more attention. In October, 1697 — about the time of the arrival of Bellomont in New York — Partridge published his commission. The council and assembly, as well as Partridge, wrote to the board of trade explaining the course which had been pursued, acknowledging the favor which had been shown in the appointment of Partridge and defending the members of the council who had opposed Usher.

In 1698, a few months after the close of the war, Allen arrived in New Hampshire. That was the signal for the revival of litigation concerning his claim and of certain efforts to influence the government. Usher renewed his attacks upon his opponent and hearings before Bellomont were demanded. Sampson Sheafe was appointed secretary and register and labored long to recover the records and papers from Vaughan. The assembly, however, with Pickering as speaker and Theodore Atkinson as clerk, continued favorable to Partridge. In a sort of truce both parties awaited the arrival of Bellomont and claimed to look to him for recognition and support.[1]

The attitude of Bellomont in general toward New Hampshire and the results of his brief connection with that province have been described elsewhere. But certain additional statements may be made which have a closer relation to local conditions. The arrival of Bellomont gave New Hampshire almost its first example of regular proceedings under royal government.[2] His commission was duly published. All oaths were administered to all who were under obligation to take

[1] Prov. Papers, II, 277 et seq., 288, 295; III, 69 et seq.
[2] Ibid., 332, 333.

them. The sum of £500 was granted to Bellomont, but this act had to be approved by the privy council before he could receive the money. In consequence partly of a petition of Waldron and his associates against the judges who were in office, an act was passed reorganizing the higher courts. On motion of Bellomont a bill providing for the due qualification of jurors was passed. The high sheriff, a worthless character, was removed from office. For a variety of reasons Sheafe also was removed from the office of secretary, though he was continued as deputy collector of the customs. With other supporters of the Vaughan-Waldron party, Atkinson was appointed a justice of one of the higher courts, he being thereby advanced in an official career which was to be a long and important one. In view of the danger from the French and Indians, Bellomont warned the legislature of New Hampshire to strengthen the fort on Great Island. Romer, the engineer, had reported on that fort and its needs, along with other works of defence on the New England coast. If the colonists would collect the materials, the earl would try to induce the British government to build the fort. In their reply to this proposal, signed by Atkinson as clerk, the assembly plead the smallness of the province, its poverty, the loss of life and the debt which had been caused by the war, together with the cost involved in the defence of their property rights against the claims of Allen. Yet if Bellomont would submit an estimate of the cost of materials, they would contribute toward them to their utmost ability, though the fortifying of the Piscataqua was as much a concern of Massachusetts as it was of New Hampshire. Before a month had passed Bellomont sent an estimate, made by Romer, of the materials needed and the lower house reckoned that their cost would be about £6000. Had this plan been executed it would have added to the justification for Bellomont's appointment, but a rumor of an intended Indian attack, added to the other reasons, postponed action by the assembly and the earl's premature death closed the discussion of the project until the next administration.

During the interval between the death of Bellomont and the departure of Dudley for Boston, the affairs of New Hampshire were being brought to the attention of the home gov-

ernment. William Partridge continued to administer the
government at Portsmouth, and upon an appropriation made
by a temporary act of the assembly William Vaughan was
sent to London as agent to support Partridge and the province
against Usher and the Allen claimants. Richard Partridge
coöperated with Vaughan in this agency. Usher himself was
in England urging his claims and Sampson Sheafe wrote an
important letter on the defencelessness of New Hampshire,
the need of powder and other military supplies, the cost of
defending the province against the Allen claim, and other subjects. Usher urged, among a variety of charges, that Partridge had not qualified for the office of governor as required
by law, that his administration was loose and extravagant,
and that the acts of trade were being violated.[1] Vaughan
replied with some arraignments of Usher and his government,
declaring that his conduct in every respect had been unsatisfactory, that for his personal advantage and against the
interest of the people he had supported the Allen claim and
by his rash, arbitrary and wasteful course he had incurred
the hatred of the entire province.[2] Such a man, he contended, was unfit to be governor. Vaughan also presented a
memorial on the state of defence of New Hampshire and
Maine. Certain New Hampshire laws were under consideration, as well as the condition of the records of the province.

In view of the complaints and counter charges which were
thus presented, the board of trade requested Dudley to inquire into Usher's accounts and his other affairs. Soon after
his arrival, as governor of both Massachusetts and New
Hampshire, Dudley held an assembly at Portsmouth and, of
course, found Partridge and his officials there ready for
friendly coöperation with the new royal appointee. Dudley
wrote home that he found no complaints in New Hampshire
against Partridge. Nevertheless Usher secured reappoint-
ment from the queen and returned, at the close of 1703, with
a new commission as lieutenant governor.[3] At once the old
troubles were renewed, and the complaints which Usher sent
home, as well as the letters which he exchanged with Dudley,

---

[1] C. O. 5–861, O. P. N. Eng., 1702–1703.
[2] Newman Papers, May 1703; in Rawlinson Mss. C. Brit. Mus.; C. O.
5/863.  O. P. N. Eng., May 1703.  [3] Prov. Papers, III, 229–237, 261.

again reveal in this case the utter folly of Blathwayt's system of patronage. The old flood of complaints of neglect and insult toward himself, of the neglect of the militia and fort, of the apparent disloyalty of many officials, combined with efforts to make a clean sweep of the offices and install his friends in power was renewed. Dudley replied with calmness and tact, showing him how unwise or impossible such arbitrary measures would be and restraining the angry and impatient old man in many ways, though without coming to an open breach.[1]

At the same time Dudley advised the assembly, in accordance with the commands of the queen, to come to an amicable agreement with Allen concerning the waste lands of the province. This drew from the assembly, in its session of February, 1703/4, the confession that the inhabitants could claim only that third of the province which had been settled and would not consider it a grievance if the other two-thirds was adjudged to belong to Allen, provided it might as a result of this be settled for the better security of the whole. A year later a definite agreement to this effect was prepared for submission to Allen, but his death prevented further steps of that nature being taken.[2] By this fortunate event New Hampshire was saved from a situation which every year was becaming more absurd and the importance of the Allen claim rapidly declined until it reached the vanishing point. Usher's chief hold upon New Hampshire was thus weakened and the way was opened in a few years for his complete elimination from its affairs. Until the later years of the war he continued to visit the province at intervals, holding sessions of the council and occasionally of the assembly, exhorting the members to loyal service and renewing his complaints because no salary was granted him and his services went unrecognized. A meagre appropriation was made for his entertainment while in New Hampshire, but so far as possible his presence was ignored.[3] Finally his name disappeared from

---

[1] C. O. 5/863, Letters of Dudley and Usher in 1703 and 1704.

[2] Prov. Papers, III, 272, 274; C. O. 5/863, May 3, 1705.

[3] A number of Usher's later letters to the board of trade are in Entry Books for New England. For a late expression of disgust from the council sent to England as an inclosure in one of Dudley's letters see C. O. 5/864. O. P. N. Eng. Nov. 21, 1710.

the records, and with that the Mason-Allen claim ceased to disturb the quiet of New Hampshire as, in course of time, the witches ceased to haunt the imaginations of the people of Salem.

It was under these circumstances that the merits of what might be called a personal union between Massachusetts and New Hampshire first came to a real test. Soon after the beginning of Usher's second term he proposed a general overturn among the officials charging some with disloyalty and others with incompetency. Militia officers as well as civilians were the object of his attacks. Hincks in particular, who had tried to wrest the government from his hands, he could not tolerate in command of the fort. Usher therefore wrote repeatedly to Dudley for authority to make these removals and for the grant of new commissions to the men whom he desired to put in their places. This was simply a revival of the old quarrel, was an attempt of the lieutenant governor to pay off old scores, and threatened to set the province again in a flame. Dudley, without directly claiming a right in the case, advised Usher to be cautious and referred to the fact that New Hampshire had but few men who were fit for public business. As to Hincks, Dudley referred to the various offices he had held and said that he had yet to hear of any neglect of duty on his part. Though not flatly refusing Usher's requests, he quietly remarked that he expected to sign all New Hampshire commissions, and told Usher that any request he had to make would reach him in twenty-four hours. Usher did not directly raise an issue with Dudley as to their relative authority, but wrote repeatedly to the board of trade complaining that his commission was a cipher since he was forbidden to dismiss officials or even to fill vacancies and for considerable periods of time was not consulted by the governor concerning New Hampshire affairs.[1]

With the elimination of Usher and the proprietary claim conditions in New Hampshire could become more stable. There was now a prospect that when the war should end, a normal political life might develop in the province. Another steadying influence, especially valuable during the war,

[1] C. O. 5/863. O. P. N. Eng., Letters of Dudley and Usher, 1703 and 1704; Fry, N. Hampshire as a Royal Province, 88 *et seq.*

came from the presence of Dudley as governor of Massachusetts and his visits to New Hampshire, once or oftener every year, for the purpose of holding assemblies, procuring appropriations and attending to the needs of defence. Massachusetts was under abler leadership than in the previous war, and advantage was derived, especially by New Hampshire, from the continuous presence of the governor in New England. On his first visit Dudley received a very favorable impression of New Hampshire and of its willingness to use its limited resources to the full for defence and the support of the government.[1] This opinion he continued to hold throughout his administration. The really important affairs of the province were transacted by him with the assembly on his visits to Portsmouth or by correspondence with officials. Relations between Dudley and New Hampshire throughout his long administration were not disturbed by so much as a jar. When, in 1706, charges were made against him and an effort followed to procure his recall, the assembly and clergy of New Hampshire were united in his support.[2]

For more than a decade, until after the peace of Utrecht and the accession of the Hanoverian line in England, New Hampshire continued to be the frontier province *par excellence* of New England. By the war the progress of settlement in that entire region was checked and the resources of the sparse population of farmers were strained to the utmost to maintain the frontier. No new towns were formed except by the division of the few which already existed. Almost the sole business with which Dudley and the assembly were concerned was the war and the raising of the supplies which it made necessary. The voting of the several appropriations, varying from about £500 to about £2000, the examination of claims and passing of the treasurer's accounts, constituted almost the only business of the brief sessions.[3] A salary was regularly voted to Dudley and this question did not become a political issue in New Hampshire. Revenue was

[1] Dudley to the board of trade, July 23, 1702. His letter is in the Newman Papers.

[2] Provincial Papers, III, 328.

[3] The revenue of New Hampshire was about £1000 per annum. Its ordinary expenses in peace were about the same sum, but in time of war they reached double, or more than double, that amount.

obtained from an excise on the retail of liquors, duties on imposts and on the export of lumber, the latter form of tax, however, being abandoned in 1704 and a preference expressed for a tax on polls and estates.[1] When, in the latter half of the war, expeditions were undertaken, quotas were demanded in addition to the necessary provision for the immediate frontier. Romer, the engineer, and Redknap after him, planned the necessary repairs and extension of the fort, but they could not be carried to completion. In 1709, however, a quantity of military stores was ordered by the privy council to be sent to New Hampshire.[2] Resources diminished, the public debt increased, payments fell even more into arrears than was customary. The demand for men in the service grew, while the difficulty of procuring them was steadily increased by the difficulty they found in securing their pay. Such were the conditions which led the assembly, in December, 1709, to pass its first resolution for the issue of bills of credit. The governor and council soon concurred and an issue was ordered, the bills being declared receivable in payment of taxes, subject to interest at five per cent.[3] Such issues, with various regulations as to payment, were continued at intervals, but they enabled New Hampshire to keep up its share in the war. Depreciation did not at that time become serious and the conduct of the province in this matter was not open to criticism. It was at this time, though with reference to the share of New Hampshire in the expeditions and the larger interests of the time, that Henry Newman was

[1] C. O. 5/913, E. B. N. Eng., Dudley to B. T. April 8, 1712; Prov. P, III, 291, 294; Fry, N. H. as a Royal Prov., 340 *et seq.*

[2] O. in C. Jan. 27, 1705-6, C. O. 5/864. O. P. N. Eng. S. 79; C. O. 5/913. E. B. N. Eng. Dudley to B. T., Jan, 31, 1709/10. An unusual example of thrift and efficiency, even for the colonies, was furnished by Romer in 1703, when in a report to the council he told how an appropriation of £1000, made by the province for the repair of the fort, was to be paid half in money and half in labor. The part which was to be paid in money was actually furnished in a variety of provisions. When the freeholders came for labor they brought no food with them and proceeded to eat up the provisions which had been brought in to meet the other half of the expedition. It was to stop this procedure — which was not known in the German or Scandinavian states — that Romer appealed to the council. Prov. P., III, 263.

[3] Prov. P., III, 410, 417, 420, 430. For references to the issues and reissues see Fry, 348.

appointed its agent and rendered long service in that capacity.[1]

On September 15, 1715, John Usher's name was entered for the last time as an official upon the records of the general assembly of New Hampshire.[2] As so often in the past, it then stood affixed to a speech in which he dissolved the assembly. His disjointed address was filled with the same futile complaints as of yore and it was evidently received with the same inattention. Dudley was retiring at the same time and it was known that both the provinces over which he had presided would receive new governors. Shute and not Burgess proved to be the appointee for the higher position and George Vaughan received the commission as lieutenant governor of New Hampshire. With his appointment the group which had so long opposed Usher and the Allen claim was again brought in name as well as in reality into control of the affairs of the province. In 1708 George Vaughan, son of William Vaughan, had been sent by both council and assembly as agent to England to oppose the revival of the famous suit by Thomas, the son of Samuel Allen.[3] He was also intrumental in procuring there a supply of ammunition and on his return home, a year later, was sent back to continue in his agency for some time longer. The popularity and success of Vaughan is indicated by the readiness with which provision was made by the assembly for the payment of his bills in England. He had, however, been back in the province for some years when he was appointed lieutenant governor.

An assembly was immediately elected, for it was thought necessary to prepare for the reception of a new governor. But he did not come and more than a year passed — until January, 1716/17 — before Samuel Shute, the actual appointee, arrived and opened a session of the assembly.[4] Samuel Penhallow, the historian of the Indian wars, was secretary and treasurer and a very active member of the council. Richard Waldron, John Plaisted, Mark Hunking and John Wentworth are shown by the record to have been his colleagues who were most regular in attendance. The number of members who attended was usually five, though

[1] Prov. P., III, 412 et seq., 509.
[2] Ibid., 599.
[3] Ibid., 353, 381, et seq.
[4] Ibid., 599, 658.

later it somewhat increased, especially when the council sat as the upper house of the assembly. The assembly consisted of only sixteen members, representatives of six towns and one parish.[1] Portsmouth and Hampton sent three members each, Newington and Kingston one each. Among the members may be noted Richard Gerrish, Richard Wibird, Theodore Atkinson, George Jaffery, Shadrach Walton, Nicholas Gilman and Peter Weare, as men of more or less prominence. Of these Atkinson was destined to have by far the most important career. He, with Wibird and Gerrish, were soon appointed members of the council.

Now that the long wars were ended and a decade of peace was to follow, to be interrupted by a struggle of two or three years with Râle and his Indians, that to be succeeded by twenty years of peace on the frontier, New Hampshire could again begin to expand and its inhabitants to devote themselves without fear to the pursuits of· peace. We begin to hear now of projects for the division of some of the old towns, the formation of new parishes and founding of new churches. This shows that families were pushing out into the unoccupied tracts and back into the wilderness. Petitions also gradually began to be presented before the governor and assembly for the formation of new towns.[2] For some time these were kept on file and not acted upon. In 1715 Sir Charles Hobby, one of the assigns of Allen, had died and later Elisha Cooke and probably others appeared to demand letters of administration on his estate.[3] There were other assigns also in England and the Allen claim to ungranted or waste land still haunted the province like a wraith. This probably induced caution in making grants. The boundary also, toward Massachusetts and toward Maine, was not settled and as settlement extended westward up the Merrimac valley, obstacles arising from this source were met and the boundary question was brought to the front. This first became clearly apparent when, in 1718, as elsewhere related, the group of Scotch-Irish Presbyterians arrived, who after prolonged negotiations founded Nutfield, which in 1722 was incorporated as a town-

[1] Prov. P., III, 600; Fry, *op. cit.*, 275.
[2] Prov. P., III, 707, 781, 791, 793, 799.
[3] *Ibid.*, 631, 632, 661, 664, 682.

ship under the name of Londonderry. That same year the process of westward expansion was fully recognized by the issue of four large township grants, Chester, Nottingham, Barrington and Rochester. At the same time a grant of land four miles square, west of Nottingham line, was made to the children of Samuel Allen, the former governor. The township thus granted formed a rather irregular but unbroken belt in the rear of the old towns, extending across the province in a southwesterly direction from the Salmon Falls river to approximately the limits of the town of Hudson.[1] As some of these grants extended westward of the upper course of the Merrimac river, while settlers from Massachusetts were equally aggressive from the south and were taking up land between the Merrimac and Connecticut rivers, the settlement of the boundary became at once an issue of the greatest importance. The Indian war of 1723–1725 affected mainly regions to the east and the expansion of New Hampshire westward now went steadily on, with only such obstructions as Massachusetts could put in its way. As the country along its eastern border was less accessible both from Maine and New Hampshire, its settlement was delayed and the question of the eastern boundary was not contested with the vigor shown on the south and west. This all helps to show that New Hampshire was now emerging from its earlier and comparative weakness and was beginning to share fully in the movement of expansion which was so characteristic of the eighteenth century.

Until after the arrival of Shute Vaughan's administration was satisfactory and peaceful.[2] Then trouble began. Certain of the old councillors were removed and the new appointees were taken wholly from Portsmouth. As this was a departure from a custom according to which these officers had been distributed somewhat proportionally among the towns of the province, it provoked opposition. Some of " our experienced, just and good men " also had been laid aside.[3] A dispute arose over the continuance of the impost and excise as opposed to the land tax, in which the new councillors and

---

[1] Fry, 278; N. H. State Papers, XXIV (see map in that vol.).
[2] Prov. P., III, 669.
[3] Ibid., 669, 675, 677, 680.

the trading interest, as in New York, were charged with favoring the latter form of tax because it rested more heavily upon the farmers and laborers. Most of the judges also, it was said, resided in Portsmouth and the courts were held there, though formerly they had sat as well in the other towns. In Portsmouth, too, the Anglicans of the province chiefly centered. A sectional controversy was thus being aroused, in which the council and assembly took opposite sides. A brief but sharp interchange of messages followed, during the January session of 1716/17, in which the assembly presented the above statements as grievances and the council defended the new appointees and Portsmouth as entitled to the favors they had received, because they were of the " best quality and greatest ability " and had " as good and better estates in lands and land securities than any now in said house." The crown, they said, was free to select councillors from any part of the colony and the superior advantages offered by Portsmouth as a seat of government had always been recognized. As to the form of taxation, the council had opposed the impost only when the assembly opposed an export duty to balance it, an established English custom. A disagreement between the houses, not concerning the policy of issuing bills of credit but as to the amount which should be issued, added slightly to the difficulty.[1]

By these and other occurrences Vaughan's excitable temperament seems to have been stirred and he presently became involved in a violent controversy with the lower house, with a part of the councillors and with the governor. He suspended Penhallow from the council and defied both houses in speeches which, for arrogance and inflated rhetoric,[2] it would be difficult to match in the records of the period. At their close he dismissed the assembly, and the indications must have been that disorders like those of the early years of the province were likely to follow. But Shute now interposed, suspended Vaughan, restored Penhallow and called the assembly together again — in October, 1717 — thus ignoring the dissolution pronounced by the lieutenant governor.[3] In

---

[1] Belknap, Hist. of N. H., II, 19 *et seq.*

[2] *Ibid.*, 702, 703.

[3] *Ibid.*, 704–706. C. O. 5/867, O. P. N. Eng., Vaughan to B. T., June 23, 1719.

a speech which he made in person he told how Vaughan had refused to obey an order for proclaiming a fast, and instead of proroguing the assembly, as directed, had dissolved it. From a letter of Vaughan, of earlier date, it appears that the two officials had clashed over orders respecting the collection of duties at the fort, the enjoyment by the lieutenant governor of his perquisites and the relations in general between the two.[1] Vaughan had then written for permission to go to England and submit his case to the board of trade. Shute, on the other hand, in his address to the restored assembly, declared that as governor, while he was in America and not merely during the intervals of a few days or weeks which he might spend in New Hampshire, his will as governor was superior and the lieutenant governor must conform to it. If the governor, acting under his instructions, was not regarded as the immediate and controlling representative of the king, endless confusion would result. This was essentially the attitude which Dudley had maintained toward Usher, though it had been diplomatically concealed, and at that time the board of trade had indirectly recognized it as correct. The assembly now fully indorsed this view and declared that Vaughan's conduct had been illegal and tending to confusion.[2] At Hampton, however, the opposite view prevailed and its representatives refused to take their seats unless they were returned by a new election.[3] Because these views were published by them at a meeting called for the purpose of holding a new election, the three members were summoned before the council and laid under heavy bonds for good behavior. Shute, on the advice of the council, issued a proclamation to quiet the minds of the disaffected and sent home a favorable report of the conduct of New Hampshire in general. Owing in part to the influence of Sir William Ashurst, Vaughan was not restored to his office, but John Wentworth, who in the council had opposed Vaughan's measures, was appointed lieutenant governor. Vaughan went to England and Wentworth, two years later, wrote to the board in self-defence against alleged misrepresentations of himself by the man who

[1] C. O. 5/915, E. B. N. Eng., Vaughan to B. T., July 19, 1717.
[2] Prov. P., III, 709.
[3] Ibid., 707, 710, et seq.

he now supposed was his persistent enemy.[1] But nothing serious had occurred, while peaceful relations between the lieutenant governor and his superior at Boston were not again disturbed until Jonathan Belcher and David Dunbar were brought face to face in the two provinces. With Wentworth a family which was to hold the office of governor the larger part of the time until the Revolution came into control of affairs. It was descended from one of the first settlers, and had already laid the foundation of a substantial fortune in trade. The steady but not brilliant qualities of the first Wentworth were suited to restore quiet. He held the office to which he was now appointed until his death in 1730.[2]

During the remainder of Shute's residence in New England peaceful relations continued within New Hampshire. The questions which agitated Massachusetts at that time scarcely affected New Hampshire at all. The restrictions which were imposed upon the lumbermen by Bridger and the orders of the British government in relation to naval stores occasionally raised complaints which found an echo in the assembly. It was generally believed that the officers who were appointed by the governor and council to prevent the waste of mast trees when Bridger and his subordinates were absent did the work better than those who were sent over by the British government. The announcement in 1721 that the duties on lumber had been taken off in England, was received as a favor.[3] Issues of bills of credit were demanded from time to time, not to pay the debts and meet the expenses of the government but to serve as a medium of exchange in the absence of silver. The bills were to be distributed among the towns and loaned out for a series of years at interest on security in land. This was in imitation of the land bank schemes of Massachusetts and other colonies. In May, 1717, a bill for the issue of £15,000 under these conditions was accepted by the governor.[4] During the years immediately following the results of this measure were worked out, but not to the satisfaction of its originators. In 1721 Shute communicated to

---

[1] C. O. 5/869, N. Eng. O. P. Wentworth to the B. T., received Sept. 9, 1719.

[2] Prov. P., IV, 587.

[3] Prov. P., III, 753–4.

[4] Prov. P., III, 671, 688, 692; Fry, 349.

the assembly the order of the crown forbidding governors
to assent to such issues without a suspending clause, except
in cases where they were absolutely needed to defray the
cost of government. As disturbances along the border were
increasing and making the settlement of the boundary dispute
with Massachusetts more necessary, in 1721 Henry Newman's
appointment as agent was renewed and he was instructed to
devote himself especially to the adjustment of this dispute.[1]
In 1720 irritation also developed between the two colonies
over trade between them, especially in liquors and lumber,
and there were complaints and threats of countervailing
duties.[2] Early in 1722 or a little before a conference seems
to have been held at Ipswich concerning the duties between
the two provinces, and the assembly at Portsmouth asked for
a report of what was done, pending its discussion of a proposal to repeal their impost on liquors and export duty on
boards and fish.[3] This last proposition appears to have been
made while they were discussing the course to be followed
in reference to the finances since the reception of his majesty's
order restraining the issue of bills of credit.

Râle's war, which was carried on wholly by Massachusetts
and New Hampshire and in which the settlements of the
latter province were as seriously exposed as they had ever
been in the earlier wars, brought again to the front questions
of military supplies and finance. Under a law of 1702, confirmed by the crown in 1706, New Hampshire had annually
obtained a small supply of powder from a tonnage duty in
the customary form. But in 1717 an additional instruction
directed Shute not to collect that duty longer on British ships.
This, it was afterward explained, was intended only to apply
to future acts, but in New Hampshire it was followed by the
suspension of its existing law on the subject. That necessitated a renewal of applications to the British government
for a supply of powder, the last grant of this nature having
been received in 1709. Newman's first application to the
ordinance board met with no success and Popple wrote Shute
to put the existing law in execution. When the Indian war
began the application had to be renewed, this time with a
view to a general supply of military stores for the fort as

---

[1] Prov. P., III, 779.     [2] *Ibid.*, 827.     [3] *Ibid.*, IV, 25, 310.

well as of powder and guns for use on the frontier.[1] But the application, carried by Newman even before Walpole himself, proved unsuccessful, as was reported to the assembly in 1725.[2] The ordinance office found that stores sent in Anne's time had not been paid for — it is likely that payment was not intended — and they were content to let that debt stand provided no other such grant was made without a vote of parliament.

When Râle's war began New Hampshire, of course, was on the paper money basis. As was customary generally in the colonies, the only way possible in which to provide revenues for such an emergency was to continue the levy of forced loans on the community by the issue of bills of credit. In the spring session of 1722 it was found that £2800 would be necessary to pay the debt which had accumulated since the issue of the royal instruction respecting bills of credit and to meet other accruing charges. It was voted to issue this sum in bills of credit, the same to be redeemed in 1729 and 1730 in like bills or naval stores and such commodities as should be agreed upon. The outstanding bills of the province also were much worn, and it was voted to issue new bills to the amount of £5384 in exchange for all former impressions before the year 1716. These were to be redeemed in five yearly installments, beginning in 1724, and for the redemption of both issues taxes were to be levied on polls and estates. This transaction was to be managed not by the treasurer but by trustees selected by the two houses. It was also resolved that Agent Newman should be asked what steps should be taken to secure royal assent for striking bills of credit to encourage the production of naval stores. War was declared the following summer and a further issue of £2000 became necessary. This was followed by other issues at irregular intervals and in varying amounts. Both provinces followed similar measures for financing the war, as they did for its prosecution, the chief magistrates of both drifting with the tide and availing themselves of the loophole in their instructions, furnished by the clause relating to necessity, to assent to such issues

[1] C. O. 5/915, E. B. N. Eng. 1721–1723; C. O. 5/868, O. P. N. Eng. 1721; Newman Papers; Prov. P., IV, 29.
[2] Prov. P., IV, 146, 168, 173.

of paper as were approved by the houses. In New Hampshire the muster rolls were examined by the houses and these, as well as all other claims, were passed upon by them. The resolutions of the legislatures as to redemption and destruction of bills were not lived up to and, as usual, depreciation increased with successive issues and the public debt. Money was scarce and, though New Hampshire went by no means so far as many colonies, at the beginning of 1730 between £6000 and £7000 was still due on the original £15,000 loan of 1717.

During the first year of the war Shute was in Massachusetts and the leadership, or some control of that colony over operations, was much in evidence. The people of New Hampshire remembered so vividly the horror of the last wars and realized so clearly the proximity of the Indian outposts to their frontier that the assembly objected to sending any troops out of the province.[1] They argued that the towns just across the river in Maine, which were in a situation like their own, had been exempted from sending men to the eastward and they demanded the same favor. They suggested a joint expedition to the head of the Merrimac river, from which direction they were much exposed to attack. The dispatch of a joint committee to lay their difficulties before the governor was proposed but fell through. Wentworth declared a recess for a few days to enable the members better to consider what should be done. Shute in reply to information he received from Wentworth expressed surprise that they refused to do what was so greatly to their interest. He soon followed this up with an order for the draft of fifty men from New Hampshire to join the Massachusetts force to the eastward. Treasurer Penhallow stated that there was nothing in the treasury and compliance with this order was impossible without action by the general assembly. When the session was resumed the assembly yielded, but also ordered the building of a blockhouse at Lake Winnepesaukee.[2] It was necessary in the first place to cut a road to that point and after that had been done Wentworth informed the assembly that he thought it best to postpone the building of the

[1] Prov. P., IV, 49, *et seq.*, 329 *et seq.*
[2] *Ibid.*, 61, 332, *et seq.*

blockhouse for the present. It was realized that defensive measures were not needed toward the mountains on the west, but the road may have facilitated settlement in that region after the war was over. Wentworth was more directly interested in repairing and enlarging Fort William Henry, at Newcastle, and reported for many sessions the expenditures upon that work and the progress which was being made.

Shute having suddenly returned to England, after the beginning of 1723 New Hampshire for the rest of the war and for several years thereafter was left more free to pursue her interests in her own way. Work on the fort was continued. Shute added his efforts to those of Newman in England to secure for it a grant of munitions and other supplies, but they failed in the end. The efforts of the province in the war were not relaxed amid discouraging cost and setbacks. Wentworth reported events to the assembly at its successive sessions and little except routine business connected with the war and its financing was done. So clear was the evidence that the French were giving the Indians all possible aid, and so exasperating was the knowledge of this that a joint embassy was sent by the two provinces to Canada; but they got little satisfaction from Vaudreuil except the release of a few prisoners.[1] Theodore Atkinson was the member of this commission from New Hampshire and William Dudley, who had been on a similar embassy in the previous war, and Samuel Thaxter from Massachusetts.

By 1725, the year when peace was concluded with the Indians along the Kennebec and in the west, the paper money in circulation had so depreciated as to cause a general loss of more than one-half of fixed incomes. This affected the clergy, who were the only salaried class in the colony. Those who, for example, had contracted for £100 a year could get only £50 or £60. Though they were able through the governor to make their condition known in the assembly, nothing effective of course could be done for their relief. Though a salary had been granted to Shute while he was in New England, in the form of the usual annual or semi-annual payments, during his absence his appeals fell on deaf ears. In 1727 Newman was desired to present the strongest possible

---

[1] Prov. P., IV, 163 et seq.; Belknap, II, 71, et seq.

remonstrance against directions to settle a permanent salary upon the governor, should such a design be on foot. New Hampshire, they said, was a frontier province, ever cramped by Indian wars, and yet it had always cheerfully appropriated an allowance for government, even beyond its capacity, and the same disposiiton still continued.[1]

With the return of peace, fully insured in 1727 by a treaty with the eastern Indians, the way was opened for the extension of settlement, except so far as the shadowy claims still being urged were obstacles in the way. Londonderry had now been granted representation in the assembly. Penacook, now Concord, had meantime been settled by Massachusetts, though under protest from New Hampshire. The New Hampshire government now instructed Newman to push the question of the boundary in England and bring the matter, if possible, to a settlement. In the absence of important controversies between the two houses or in other forms in New Hampshire itself, this as time passed became the most important question with which she had to deal.

As early as the spring of 1722 the assembly, which had been elected in the time of George Vaughan and which had now been in existence for more than five years, asked to be dissolved and demanded the passage of a triennial act.[2] Shute replied that he thought their request for a dissolution was without precedent, but he would consider the question and in proper time make them easy; what he immediately wanted was a supply of the treasury and provision for the discharge of the public debts. In the following June the assembly was dissolved and a new house elected.[3] In the fall session of 1723, after the departure of Shute, a triennial act was passed and Newman was ordered to devote himself specially to securing its confirmation by the crown.[4] Near the close of 1724 word came from Newman that the crown would take no action on the triennial bill because it came without the province seal.[5] Shute and others thought it doubtful if, when a properly authenticated copy should be sent, it would be approved, because of the troubles with

[1] Prov. P., IV, 249.

[2] Ibid., 24, et seq.

[3] Ibid., 318.

[4] Ibid., 366, et seq.

[5] Ibid., 146.

Massachusetts. It was also claimed that the triennial act in England had not worked well and the period of parliaments had been extended to seven years. The proposal also involved a doubtful limitation of the prerogative. The matter drifted on until 1727, when the assembly which had been elected after the death of George I proposed the passage of a new triennial act, the promoters apparently not being aware that Great Britain was then living under the septennial act. The council informed the house that a similar act, with a saving clause, had already been passed and sent home for approval. A bill, however, was drafted by a joint committee, but the assembly was dissolved before it came to a passage. By the new assembly the bill was passed, though not under the title of a triennial act, and was not disallowed by the crown.[1] It established a property qualification of a freehold estate of the value of £50 for electors and of £300 for representatives. The selectmen of the town with the moderator of the town meeting were made returning officers, and habitancy was not required either in the case of electors or elected. Because this act did not describe the localities from which representatives should be called or determine by whom writs should be issued a long controversy was occasioned by these defects at a later time.

The dissolution of the assembly, in January, 1727/8, was occasioned by a dispute which had arisen over the power of the governor and council to act as a court of chancery and appeals.[2] The dissatisfaction which that arrangement, that had existed since Cutt's time and had been complained of in Anne's reign, occasioned in most of the colonies now found rather violent expression in New Hampshire. A vote of the house for repealing several clauses in the laws relating to appeals was unanimously negatived by the council and a paragraph of the governor's instructions on the subject was sent down to the house. The house complained of the costs and difficulties attendant upon appeals to the governor and council in trials of titles to land, and resolved that no appeals in such cases should go beyond the superior court, except to the privy council when the values involved exceeded £300.

[1] Prov. P., IV 265, 288, 294, 472, 489; Belknap, II, 89; Fry, 177.
[2] Prov. P., IV, 269, 272, 476, 479.

At this vote Wentworth expressed himself as much surprised and the council declared it a " scandalous libel " and asked the house to recall it.  The assembly now passed a long resolution denouncing the chancery or court of appeals — that is, the council in judicial session — because its proceedings were neither by juries nor governed by precedents and it rendered estates precarious so that there was a general cry for relief as from an intolerable burden.  No relief could be expected from the lieutenant governor, for he had said that his instructions forbade him to dissolve any court which had already been erected.  The assembly, they continued, had been amused for years with hopes of the settlement of the boundary and a grant of military stores and sums of money had been drawn from them in support of these causes, but they were now as far from a successful issue as ever.  Therefore they resolved that some New Hampshire man, who was interested and had integrity, be appointed agent to procure, if possible, the dissolution of said court or its reform, and also the settlement of the boundary question and a grant of military stores.  As the representatives had been charged with negligence, it was voted that the proceedings of the present session be printed.  It is evident that dissatisfaction with the indifference of the home government and with narrow political arrangements which the expanding province now felt that it had outgrown found voice in this resolution. New Hampshire was a small province, but it now spoke with emphasis and intelligence upon some of the vital questions which affected it.  Wentworth and the Portsmouth coterie of councillors were hit squarely in the face by the resolutions and it is not strange that, after a little routine business had been transacted, the assembly was dissolved.

Nathaniel Weare, who belonged to the Hampton family which had previously been in opposition, was speaker of the assembly and undoubtedly a leader in the framing of the above resolution.  The election, which was soon held, resulted in little change of membership and Weare was again chosen speaker.  Wentworth negatived the choice.[1]  The assembly regarded this as unprecedented and asked for his authority.  Wentworth sent them the clause in his commis-

<hr>

[1] Prov. P., IV, 282, *et seq.*, 484, *et seq.*

sion which provided that in framing and passing laws and ordinances the governor should have a negative voice. The house replied that this language could not by any reasonable construction be extended so as to give him a negative over orders and rules of the house. They even cited Burnet's History of my Own Times in proof that the king accepted speakers in England as a matter of course. But Wentworth persisted, and after several adjournments and after Weare, tired of the controversy, had expressed a desire to be relieved of the burdens of the office, Andrew Wiggin was installed as speaker.

When Wiggin was presented, Wentworth told the assembly that the previous house had cried up liberty and property for the amusement of some who had private designs, and he hoped that the present house would cultivate principles of loyalty and obedience.[1] He had dissolved the preceding assembly because it had persisted in things to which his instructions made it impossible for him to assent, and he desired that the new assembly would confine itself to the ordinary routine business, among which was preparing for the reception of Governor Burnet, who was expected soon to arrive. The house reminded the governor in reply that it consisted mostly of the same men who had composed the other assembly and that they were wholly loyal. With this the temporary excitement passed away and only routine business, with some special attention to the governor's salary, was done during Burnet's brief administration. A salary — £600 in New Hampshire currency or £200 sterling — was settled on Burnet for his term, one-third of which he resigned to the lieutenant governor. When Belcher came into office after the close of the short administration of Burnet, this arrangement, so far as it affected the lieutenant governor, was abandoned. The assembly continued to vote the salary of the governor, it being paid usually in two semi-annual installments, but Belcher, owing to dislike for Wentworth, refused to allow him anything but the fees and perquisites which came from registers, certificates, licenses and passes, amounting in all only £50 a year.[2] Though Wentworth died soon after Belcher assumed office, this treatment offended

---

[1] Prov., P., IV, 286.          [2] Belknap, II, 97.

his relatives and friends, among whom were his son, Benning Wentworth, and his son-in-law, Theodore Atkinson, and soon made trouble for the governor.  Toward Dunbar, Wentworth's successor, Belcher adopted the same rule as has just been stated concerning salary, and this contributed its part toward intensifying the long and bitter controversy which followed between these two men.  Dunbar allied himself with Belcher's enemies in New Hampshire and soon an address, signed by fifteen persons, was sent to the king charging his government with being arbitrary and oppressive and asking for his removal.  A counter address was sent by Belcher's friends, at the head of whom was his brother-in-law, Richard Waldron, the secretary.  Probably through the influence of Martin Bladen, who was backing Dunbar and quietly opposing Belcher, Atkinson, Benning Wentworth and Joshua Pierce were appointed councillors, against which action the governor in vain protested.  This quarrel soon became involved with the question of the separation from Massachusetts, which continued to be the chief political issue throughout Belcher's administration, and an account of which is elsewhere given.  Belcher and his friends labored ardently to maintain the connection with Massachusetts, and the governor in particular to defend the Massachusetts interpretation of the boundary; the opposite party adopted fully the point of view and interests of New Hampshire and in the end successfully forced the issue to the point of a complete separation of the two provinces.

So far as other affairs of the province were concerned, the ordinary administrative and legislative routine continued, the boundary question occupying much attention, until 1732. In the May session of that year the important business which the governor brought forward was that of a supply for the treasury.  He told them that from the treasurer's brief statement they would perceive that there was no money in the treasury.  Some new method of supply, the assembly thought, must be found, as constables and collectors were generally indebted to the treasury.  An act was passed for an excise on liquors and one for proportioning taxes among the towns, but no appropriation was made.  At the close of the session Belcher remarked on what seemed the childishness of their excuse, since £1000 was all that was needed and often in time of war they had annually voted £2000 or more, when the resources and population of the province were much less than at present. The assembly was then dissolved.

With this event a deadlock began which continued until the opening of the war with Spain in 1740, repeated sessions, prorogations and dissolutions being resorted to in the meantime, but no appropriation was obtained.[1] The occasion of this prolonged struggle was the order which had been issued to Belcher that he should strictly obey the instruction not to assent to the issue of any bills of credit — except such as were necessary for the actual support of government — without a suspending clause. The assembly also was forbidden to extend the duration of their funds for redemption beyond 1742.[2] But in session after session the assembly insisted upon issues, of £20,000 or thereabouts, which were regularly non-concurred in by the council. All measures for appropriations then failed. It was a question not of the resources of the people and their ability to meet the limited need of the government, but of the power of the lower house, with its determination to imitate Massachusetts and other colonies in the paper money craze, to control the financial policy of the province.

By 1740 the boundary controversy had reached its later stage and the attitude of Belcher had been so partisan in favor of Massachusetts that his persuasions in support of any matter could not be expected to have much influence with a New Hampshire assembly. The declaration of war against Spain furnished him the opportunity to dwell upon the poor condition of the fort and the inadequacies of the New Hampshire militia law as compared with that of Massachusetts. He recommended in particular an increase in the amount of fines for breaches of discipline. Also, as the demand for masts would now increase, they could not better recommend themselves than by passing an act for their more effectual preservation. The reply of the house showed that its attitude had not changed. Earlier assemblies, they said, had been ready to vote supplies but, because of the royal

---

[1] See the journals of the two houses during those years.
[2] Prov. P., IV, 636, 641, 653, 657, 660, etc, etc.

instruction and the fixing of 1742 as the time limit for
redemption, the only possible way of relief had been closed
to them. The coupling of the council with them in the governor's appeals for revenue was also disagreeable, since the
house contained the representatives of the people and was
chiefly interested in these matters.[1] When the governor became more specific and stated that, with the exception of
the guns sent many years before by the crown, the fort was
destitute of everything necessary for defence, and now that
war existed should be properly provided for, the house balked,
as usual, at the 1742 limit and desired that a joint address
be sent to the crown to extend it. But no action was taken
by the council on this, and it expressed itself as opposed to
an issue of bills of credit for the purpose named. So another
session ended without result and this assembly was dissolved.[2]

When the new assembly met, in August, the call of the
crown for troops for the Carthagena expedition was communicated and a proclamation enforcing this call was issued.
Though no quota was mentioned and no commissions were
sent, Belcher suggested one hundred as the number New
Hampshire had contributed to the Canada expedition in 1711.
The house assumed a negative attitude. It regretted that
the subject had been postponed until so late a date, doubted
if any would enlist until they knew what encouragement they
would get, and added that at the time of the Canada expedition they were spurred on by suffering and were not impeded
by a restriction on the issue of bills of credit. It finally proposed an appropriation, but undertook to designate the captain of the force. To this the governor objected as not
squaring with his instructions. The house then desired him
to send them his instructions in full concerning the expedition, but he refused and charged the house with wasting time
on frivolous pretences. This assembly therefore was dissolved without a vote of supply or provision being made for
the transport of New Hampshire troops. Such men as went
from that colony enlisted under other governments.[3]   The

[1] Prov. P., V, 1–9, 11, 18, *et seq.*
[2] *Ibid.*, 23, 26, 28.
[3] The authority for these latter statements is not to be found in the
Provincial Papers as printed, but in the New Hampshire Papers in the
P. R. O.

only appropriation which Belcher appears to have obtained from the next assembly was £500, grudgingly given toward meeting the expense of running the Massachusetts line.

Could Massachusetts and New Hampshire have been consolidated as one province, the result would doubtless have been beneficial. So far as all matters relating to war and Indian relations were concerned there can be no doubt of the advantages which would have followed from placing the entire New England frontier under an undivided control. In other respects government would not have suffered. In the case supposed the assembly at Portsmouth would have been eliminated and representatives from what had been New Hampshire would have been sent to Boston. From the standpoint of the executive the change, so far as the councillors from New Hampshire were concerned, from an appointive to an elective basis would have been a disadvantage. But all northern New England would have again been brought into a situation corresponding to that of the Andros régime, though with full recognition of an assembly and British rights. Could the local prejudices which originated in its past history have been overcome — and in the case of New Hampshire before the boundary controversy they were not great — a stronger organization would have resulted from the union. But under the social conditions and the political ideas and experience which prevailed in the colonies at that time such an outcome was not thought of, and New Hampshire, as a result of its separation from Massachusetts, which now came, prosecuted with increased energy the settling of new towns, expansion westward, and the improvement of its finances. Business in council and assembly went on with more vigor, the improvement being shown in both the contents and care of the records. Belcher's administration — if such it could be called — had been in most respects a failure and a change could hardly fail to bring improvement. So far as external relations and the conduct of the war which was beginning were concerned, Massachusetts continued to hold the lead under Shirley quite as completely and efficiently as in the time of Dudley. In the case of the Louisburg expedition and the later futile plans of the war New Hampshire fell into line substantially as she had done in the earlier

wars. There was as little change in her methods of defending
her somewhat expanded line of settlements on the northwest.

Benning Wentworth, who was selected to be the first governor of New Hampshire of full rank, had followed the
mercantile calling of his father and had lost so heavily as
an exporter of lumber to Spain as to be plunged into bank-
ruptcy and to occupy a place among the British subjects for
whom, just before the opening of the war, redress was demanded from the court of Madrid.[1]  In provincial politics he
had always held a prominent place among the opponents of
Belcher. Thomlinson, the influential agent of New Hampshire at the time when the boundary question approached a
settlement, took up his cause, invited him to England and,
when the appointment of Dunbar to the governorship was
clearly seen to be an impossibility, procured from the duke
of Newcastle a promise that, when New Hampshire should
be separated from Massachusetts, Wentworth should be given
that office. The fees, said to amount to £300, which had to be
paid for securing the commission, were advanced by friends
in England and repaid by others in New Hampshire. As
an additional provision for his support the office of surveyor
general of the woods was procured for him.

The instructions [2] which were given to Wentworth contained as clauses which were intended exclusively for his
province a warning to take special care that no more than
£6000 in bills of credit should ever be current at one time in
New Hampshire, and that, as no quit rents had ever been
levied there, the policy to be followed in that matter should
be left to the council. A provision that certain tracts of
woodland should be reserved as nurseries of mast trees was
similar to a requirement in the Nova Scotia instructions,
but though Wentworth and others searched for such areas
none that were available seem to have been found south of
the Maine boundary. Various other special provisions were
taken, with verbal changes only, from Belcher's instructions,
and of course the general instructions were such as were given
to all governors.

Wentworth arrived and was installed in office at the close

[1] Belknap, II, 182.
[2] C. O. 5/940.  E. B. N. H. June 1741.

of 1741. He at once became involved in a discussion with his first assembly over the amount of his salary and the conditions under which it should be granted. He demanded a fixed salary, but met with obstacles. The question was involved with that of the issue of bills of credit. An act for the issue of £25,000 in bills to be let out at interest to the towns was passed. This contained the required suspending clause and it was arranged that Wentworth's salary, which was fixed at £500, should be paid in part out of this. In his first letter to the board of trade Wentworth strongly urged the approval of this act, since at least £20,000 would be needed to put the fort in a proper state of repair, build the blockhouses that were needed and the roads to the frontier that were absolutely necessary. Another bill accompanied this granting £4700 in bills of credit for supplying the treasury and discharging the public debts. As the amount of these issues was far in excess of the sum mentioned as the limit in the instructions, the board was minded not to recommend its approval, but upon consulting merchants and learning that the issue was not larger than was necessary for carrying on the business of the colony and that it would prevent the paper of other colonies from becoming the medium of trade there, it was decided to let it stand.[1]

The bills which were thus issued were known as "new tenor" and were to exchange for "old tenor" at the rate of one to four. "Old tenor" was drawn into the treasury by a province tax at the close of 1742.[2] The new bills were then made legal tender in payments to the government. It appears that the new bills were not actually issued until the fall of 1743, when the governor informed the assembly that the law for their issue had been approved by the king. A grant of stores for Fort William and Mary was promised at the same time, and Bastide, the engineer, under an order of council, came from Boston in 1743 to inspect or direct the improvements which were needed in the defences. Under the spirit of encouragement which was now abroad, recruits for the

---

[1] Prov. P., V, 137, 143, 145, 148, 152, 610, 623, 652, 668; C. O. 5/925, O. P. N. H., May 25, 1742; C. O. 5/940, E. B. N. H., B. T. July and Aug. 1742. Feb. 1742-3.

[2] Prov. P., V, 690.

West Indies had already been voted and there was activity at home in preparing for the French war which was fast approaching. Wentworth sent home a detailed statement of the military stores of the province and also, in answer to the usual queries, of its population, trade, resources and condition in general. Its population he estimated at about 20,000 and its available militia numbered 4,000 men.[1] After examining the fort, Bastide reported[2] that the guns were generally unserviceable and that there were twenty-six more than were needed. These he suggested might be remounted — apparently for show — at batteries and blockhouses elsewhere. He was furnished with votes of assembly indicating how much could be annually spent for repairs and additions. Early in 1744, William Shirley, now governor of Massachusetts, began to inquire if they proposed to take over Fort Dummer, for it was a post of such importance that, even though it was within the New Hampshire line, he did not propose to hand it over without assurance that it would be kept in a defensible state. This proposal was reserved for consideration, as it implied a more extended line of frontier defence than New Hampshire had been accustomed to.[3]

Before a sort of convocation of the two houses, called in May, 1744, between two regular sessions,[4] Wentworth laid the needs of the province, telling them that he had long since submitted the king's orders to make it properly defensible, and it gave him great concern that this had produced so little effect. He said that he had recently visited the frontier and, considering that it had taken more than thirty years to gather the people who lived there and if they should abandon the settlements a still longer time would be required to restore them, he realized that their exposed situation made it a necessity as well as a requirement of humanity to provide for their protection. The governor also referred to the need of strengthening the fort and as to that the members mentioned an appropriation for the purpose which had twice been sent to the council in the last sessions but had not been heard from again. As the present meeting was not a legal session they could not do anything authoritative, but they resolved

[1] C. O. 5/925.        [3] *Ibid.*, 226, 706.
[2] Prov. P., V, 223.       [4] *Ibid.*, 709, *et seq.*

that the governor should at once raise two hundred men for a month to " cover the frontiers," and provision for their pay would be made at the next session. To this the councillors unanimously consented.

When the next session came the program submitted included not only the stationing of troops on the frontier but the opening of the road again to Lake Winnepesaukee and the building of two blockhouses in that region, the strengthening and garrisoning of Fort William and Mary, coöperation with the other northern governments in fitting out a vessel of war to defend their coasts, the dispatch of commissioners to a conference at Albany and reinforcements to the garrison at Albany. These last suggestions originated with Shirley and the program, as a whole, was at once declared by the assembly to exceed the resources of New Hampshire. The council voted that a joint committee be appointed to provide for the repairs of the fort and the erection of other works of defence, such as the governor should consider necessary. With this the house concurred, but declared that it called for expenditures which far exceeded the resources of their province. In order to provide for it they must issue £10,000 or more in bills of credit.[1] The governor replied that they had long had the commands of the crown concerning such issues under consideration and demanded a categorical answer, as to whether or not they would obey them. But, he added, he was ready to assent to a further limited emission of paper, provided they would establish in good faith an adequate fund for its redemption.

The categorical answer Wentworth did not receive, but detailed proposals and arguments in support of them for the employment of the £10,000 and ways and means for its redemption in the course of four years. One of these resources was a tax on polls and estates and the other was the use of the interest expected from a loan for the redemption of the rest of the issue. To this latter proposal, which was typical of the loose ideas of the time as to what constituted the payment of a debt, the governor objected, as he did to the indefiniteness of the assembly as to the time during which the issue was to run. He thought that the assembly

Prov., P., V, 239, 241.

was not establishing an "undeviable fund" for purposes of redemption. In a long message the assembly tried to argue him out of this belief, using the suggestive illustration that a "stone in a building which is well laid will always bear another of equal weight," the implication seeming to be that a substantial structure could be erected out of an accumulation of debts if they were skillfully adjusted to one another. And according to the admission of the house taxation under conditions as they then were was hardly more dependable, "for no particular part of a man's estate is bound to pay those taxes till it is seized and by transferring of Estates and reward of Persons the rates are often lost [or] at least delayed in the payment." The failure to collect a large proportion of every direct tax which was levied was taken for granted and the records confirm the truth of this assumption.[1]

The governor told the houses that, if he should have to yield, he expected that a joint committee would state to the agent the necessity that he lay under, in order to avoid censure. The agent should also be instructed to apply for leave to make further issues, for though he was going to yield, he would not do so again. Meantime petitions were pouring in from the out-settlements for men and supplies and they had to be promptly sent.[2] In this way, by the pressure of war, the weak barrier which the home government had set up against the further issues of bills of credit was broken through in New Hampshire. The necessities of the campaign against Louisbourg and of the later operations of the war led to further issues and an imitation of the experience into which the plans of Shirley led Massachusetts. The original issue, in 1745, was £13,000, to which an addition of £6,000 was soon made to defray further charges, and in the autumn £8,000 more for subsisting the New Hampshire contingent left as part of the garrison of Louisbourg during the winter.[3] In June, 1746, an issue of £60,000 was voted for the proposed expedition against Canada.[4] But as it was known that these troops would be on the British establishment and that reimbursement would be allowed for clothing, transport and stores, the danger of such a policy was somewhat mitigated.

[1] Prov. P., V, 242, 245.
[2] Ibid., 247, 251, 720.
[3] Ibid., 313, 334, 342.
[4] Ibid., 813.

As in certain cases the suspending clause was omitted in the acts, Wentworth pleaded as an excuse for ignoring instructions the need of the hour, especially when they were facing the danger of an attack by the French fleet.

Preparatory to the session at the beginning of 1745, when the question of Fort Dummer, as well as that of the Louisbourg expedition was to come up, Governor Wentworth caused writs to be issued and representatives returned from six towns and districts which by the running of the southern line had been cut off from Massachusetts.[1] It was supposed that this move was intended to promote the taking over of Fort Dummer, while other settlements which were equally entitled to representation were omitted. The governor claimed, and could cite precedents to justify it, that the right of sending representatives was founded on the royal commission and instructions and therefore by executive act might be extended to new towns. The assembly, on the other hand, cited cases from New Hampshire practice which showed that there all additions to the house had been made as the result of its own votes. The triennial act was so defective that it promised no rule for the case. Though under the governor's order the secretary administered the oaths to the persons in question, the house refused to allow them to vote for speaker. The governor, in turn rejected the candidate for the speakership. But military necessity for coöperation was so strong at that time that the governor yielded for the time being, sending to the board of trade an account of what had occurred.[2] The new members were excluded.

In 1747 the question was taken up in England and the action of Wentworth was fully approved, an instruction [3] being sent to him from the lords justices to dissolve the assembly and order a new election in which he should issue writs to the towns whose members had been excluded and in reference to them uphold the royal prerogative. In accordance with the provisions of the triennial act a newly elected assembly met in January, 1748/9, and with this body the

[1] Prov. P.,V, 260 *et seq.*; Belknap, II, 267, *et seq.* 234.

[2] C. O. 5/925, O. P. N. H., Wentworth to the B. T. Nov. 26, 1745.

[3] C. O. 5/940, E. B. N. H., March and June 1748; Prov. P., VI, 888 *et seq.*

struggle in question was renewed.[1]  Richard Waldron, who in former days had been the friend of Belcher, had returned to active politics with this assembly and was chosen its speaker.  The personal bitterness of a former time was thereby injected into this controversy and doubtless explains in a measure the stubbornness of Wentworth.  Because the members from the new towns and districts had not been permitted to vote for him, the governor refused to accept the speaker.  The house therefore was unable to organize and do business.  The secretary, acting under the governor's orders, came in at intervals and adjourned or prorogued it, and this condition continued throughout the entire life of this house — until January, 1752.  The house sent up many messages in defence of its course and addressed the crown at length.  The governor replied, though with a few exceptions briefly.  Owing to the failure of the triennial act properly to define towns or other districts as units of representation and to state the powers which the assembly had exercised and should exercise over the admission of new members, the governor and the crown had the law of the case wholly on their side.  Wentworth was sure of the support of his superiors and they never thought of abandoning him.  The curious result, the opposite of the situation at this time in Massachusetts and other provinces, and of what would naturally be expected to be the case, was that the assembly was opposing the extension of representation in the province and the increase of its own membership, while the crown and governor seemed to be fighting on the other side.  This conclusion, however, will be somewhat modified by the fact that the additional instruction did not require Wentworth to issue writs of election to all districts or towns whose population seemed to justify this but only to some six of them.

In reality the interests of the home government were only slightly affected by this quarrel and it was allowed to take its course without much interference from England.  But so prolonged was it that the reputation of both governor and people suffered.  No taxes, not even an excise, could be levied or collected, the bills of credit were not redeemed and continued to depreciate, salaries and other claims were

[1] Prov. P., VI, 70–126, 886–893; Belknap, *loc. cit.*

not paid, the treasurer's accounts were not audited or muster rolls adjusted, public offices were closed and records became inaccessible. In England the people of New Hampshire, as well as Wentworth, began to lose their reputation for honesty and loyalty. Thomlinson, the agent, could not or did not complete the steps necessary for paying over the £30,000 allotted to New Hampshire in reimbursement for its expenses upon the Louisbourg and Canada expeditions. In order to meet the demands of Massachusetts for payment of the charges of maintaining Fort Dummer it was even proposed to annex a part of western New Hampshire to the province. Thomlinson had to defend himself against the charge of having procured the instruction under which Wentworth was acting. So embittered did the assembly become that it was reported to be their intention to recommend a Massachusetts man, probably Shirley, to be his successor. Such were the deplorable results of this petty quarrel which forms one of the threads of New Hampshire history between the last two intercolonial wars.

# CHAPTER XIV

## THE OUTLYING COLONIES OF NEW ENGLAND:
### RHODE ISLAND

WHILE Connecticut had a well-knit organization and was to such an extent on friendly relations with Massachusetts that she could face her enemies in England and the colonies with a degree of confidence, Rhode Island was scarcely yet assured of an independent existence. Among her people and in her institutions local and individual liberty was carried to an extreme which in a larger territory would hardly have been consistent with permanent cohesion. In her political system the towns possessed unusual independence reducing by so much the power of the general assembly and the efficiency of government. Her system of religious freedom, resulting as it did in the presence of many exclusive and jealous sects, hindered the coöperation of her people in common efforts and excluded them largely from the sympathy of the rest of New England. The presence of an important Quaker element helped to paralyze effort in time of war. The ideas which the founders of Rhode Island sought to express in her institutions in some respects augured well for a remote future, but in the earlier centuries of her existence they were fitted only for a secluded community; and that, owing to its location, Rhode Island could never be. Such was the strategic and commercial importance of Narragansett Bay on the American coast that it was a continuous object of interest and desire on the part of neighboring colonies, as well as of the colonizing European nations. Its possibilities as a naval station became apparent as soon as fleets began operating in American waters, and by the close of the seventeenth century it had become an important centre of trade.

At the same time the boundaries of the colony were far from being settled. At certain points along the coast where there are important inlets, as Piscataqua, Narragansett Bay and Delaware Bay, conflicting territorial claims gave rise to prolonged boundary controversies. Those concerned with the region about Narragansett Bay were second in importance to no others. Territorially the substantial parts of the colony were the island of Aquidneck and the Narragansett country, to the west of the bay. As a result of the destruction of the Narragansett Indians in Philip's War, and the subsequent extinction of the title of Ninigret's descendants in the Narragansett country,[1] that territory was now open for settlement. Beginnings had earlier been made, but for the next half century the occupation of that region by whites corresponded to the extension of the frontier in other colonies. Owing to a blunder in the issue of the Connecticut charter, corrected so far as possible by a qualifying clause in the Rhode Island charter, Connecticut for decades maintained a claim to all the Narragansett country and thus imperilled the very existence of Rhode Island. Various Massachusetts speculators in land and residents of the section who had secured Indian claims supported Connecticut and thus perpetuated the interest of Massachusetts and weakened the resistance of Rhode Island. This furnished an occasion for the interference of the English government and the assumption of control over the disputed territory by the royal commission of 1664 has been referred to in an earlier part of this work.[2] As the period of the Restoration progressed and was followed by the colonial wars, Rhode Island became continuously the object of serious charges of violations of the acts of trade, encouragement of piracy and neglect of defence. These, together with its boundary disputes, kept the attention of the home government pretty steadily on Rhode Island after 1680. With the absorption of Plymouth by Massachusetts a dispute relating to the entire eastern boundary of Rhode Island was inherited by the Bay Colony which, added to a contested northern boundary from Pawtucket westward, made the situation sufficiently difficult and complex. The efforts of the British government to bring the militia of Rhode Island under the control of the royal governor of Massachusetts and the disputes over jurisdiction

[1] R. I. Recs. IV, 151, 211, 232, 397, *etc.*
[2] Am. Colonies in the 17th Century, III.

which arose from the establishment of an admiralty court at Boston which was empowered to try cases at Providence and Newport, kept imperial issues and relations with Massachusetts well to the front. Such was the complicated texture of Rhode Island history, and though she was able with difficulty to retain the form of a corporate colony, she was far from being a closed whole and was almost as much exposed to outside interference as if her leading officials had been of royal appointment and through them she had been drawn directly within the sphere of imperial influences. The position of a corporate colony after 1690 was different in several important particulars from what it had been before that time.

Soon after the close of Philip's War the controversy between Connecticut and Rhode Island over the possession of the Narragansett country, which had been interrupted for a few years by the Indian hostilities, was renewed. All the parties, great and small, who had territorial interests in that region became involved, including Richard Smith, of what was later North Kingston, and William Harris, the land speculator, both of whom used their influence against Rhode Island. The result of this period of the controversy was the appointment of a royal commission, of which Governor Cranfield, of New Hampshire, was the chairman, and with him were associated William Stoughton, Joseph Dudley, Edward Randolph and five others, all of whom were Massachusetts men or men who would naturally be adverse to Rhode Island. As their commission was not shown to the authorities of Rhode Island, its assembly ordered the issue of a proclamation forbidding them to hold court and ordering them to depart from the colony. This was ignored and a report was submitted to the king which was wholly favorable to the Connecticut claim of jurisdiction and to that of the Atherton patentees to the propriety of the soil.[1] As this was in direct contravention of the Rhode Island patent, by which the Pawcatuck river and a line extending northward from its source was designated as the western boundary

[1] R. I. Recs., III, 128–149. The Records of the Narragansett Proprietors are printed in the volume known as the Fones Record, edited by James N. Arnold. See especially pp. 64–75. Arnold, Hist. of R. I., I, 471. An excellent treatment of these subjects by Brigham is to be found in Edward Field's Rhode Island at the End of the Century, I.

of the colony, it simply furnished one more example of the arbitrariness of the Cranfield-Randolph régime. Andros, while at the head of the Dominion of New England, submitted a report of the opposite tenor, in which the claims of both Connecticut and the Atherton patentees were rejected and the award of the Nicolls commission was approved. The Narragansett country was technically treated by Andros as distinct from Rhode Island, but the way was opened for its lapsing quietly back under the jurisdiction of that colony when Andros was overthrown.

After further discussion and mutual challenges between the inhabitants of Stonington on the Connecticut side of the Pawcatuck and Westerly on the Rhode Island side, a joint commission was appointed by the two colonies with very full powers. In 1703 this body reached an agreement substantially in harmony with the claim of Rhode Island, that the Pawcatuck and a line drawn north from its junction with the Ashoway should be the boundary.[1] No steps however were taken for surveying this line and the matter rested until 1719. The whole subject was then reopened as the result of a dispute over the survey of a line extending twenty miles west from Warwick neck, the determination of which was not only necessary for the settlement of certain local controversies in Rhode Island but affected Connecticut territory as well.[2] Connecticut was irritated and, by raising the question of the source of the Pawcatuck, attempted to push back the entire line ten miles to the eastward. This would have deprived Rhode Island of about half of the Narragansett country and she at once resolved to appeal to the king. Connecticut joined issue and the evidence in the case, including a map, was sent to the respective agents of the colonies, Richard Partridge and William Jencks for Rhode Island and Jeremiah Dummer for Connecticut. After the customary hearings, the board of trade, in March 1723, reported that it seemed probable, both from the terms of the charter of 1644 to Rhode Island and Providence Plantations and from the submission of the boundaries to arbitration by the agents

[1] R. I. Recs., III, 474.
[2] Ibid., IV, 273, et seq.; Conn. Mss. Boundaries; Arnold, II, 65, et seq.; Field, op. cit., 172.

within a year after the Connecticut charter had been obtained, that Charles II had been surprised in his grant to
Connecticut and intended to redress the wrong by his subsequent charter to Rhode Island; but, as the Connecticut
charter was still in force, the relief intended for Rhode Island
was of no force in law, though the proceedings of the commissioners in 1703 afforded strong proof that Connecticut
considered the claims of Rhode Island to be just and equitable.[1] Considering that the question involved was merely
one of jurisdiction and that the controversy had lasted for
sixty years, the board expressed the wish that both colonies
would resign their charters and be annexed to New Hampshire. This recommendation, the absurdity of which the
geography of New England made at once apparent, the colonies involved immediately rejected.[2] Connecticut however
recognized that her case was lost and indicated that she was
ready to submit to a final decision by the crown. Early in
1726, on a report from the committee of the council, this
was rendered by an order that the line should be run as
specified in the report of the commissioners of 1703 and that
this should be the permanent boundary between the two
colonies. The line was actually run in 1728. Thus the equitable claim of Rhode Island was fully recognized and she was
assured sufficient territory to make possible her continuance
as a distinct colony.[3]

In 1719 a minor boundary dispute with Massachusetts,
which had been in progress for nearly two decades, was concluded.[4] The grants which had been made by the sachems

[1] R. I., Recs. IV, 303. Jeremiah Dummer wrote to Governor Talcott
in 1725 that the lords of the committee thought that Connecticut had the
rigor of the law on its side, but that equity was on the side of Rhode Island.
Talcott Papers, I, 64.

[2] Ibid., 334. The reply of Rhode Island on this occasion is printed in the
Newport Hist. Mag. V, 49 et seq. It gives well their views of the services
they had rendered in defence and also on the impossibility of annexation to
New Hampshire. They refer to Dummer's book on charters as expressing
their view of their position and claims. Their governor, they claimed, was
as much a royal governor as the head of a province would be.

[3] Gov. Cranston's instructions to the Rhode Island commissioners for
finally running the line are in R. I. Recs. IV, 354. But two later acts of
assembly were necessary before the line was actually run. Ibid., 369, 400,
408–9, 414.

[4] Arnold, II, 27, 42, 62.

to Williams and his associates at the time of the settlement of Providence and which were to extend " up the streams of Pawtucket and Pawtexet without limit," had been found to encroach on the towns of Mendon and beyond in Massachusetts. The south line of Massachusetts had been run by Woodward and Saffery in 1642 and the Mendon people complained, early in Dudley's administration, that Rhode Island was encroaching upon them. Rhode Island was ready for an adjustment, but Dudley and the council at Boston were slow to act. In 1710 a preliminary agreement was reached, but it was not until after the close of Dudley's governorship that the decisive steps were taken. The line, as finally run, established the boundary on the north from Wrentham to a point two miles west of Alum Pond.

The eastern boundary of Rhode Island was settled only after a controversy more prolonged than that with Connecticut and one which at times was waged with equal bitterness. It originated from the terms of the Bradford patent which was granted to Plymouth by the New England Council in 1629. This included the territory as far west as Narragansett Bay, but of course conveyed no right of government. When the royal charter was granted to Rhode Island it included the land extending three miles east and north-east of the most eastern and north-eastern parts of Narragansett Bay. In 1665 the royal commissioners recognized the bay as the boundary pending decision by the king. After Plymouth was absorbed by Massachusetts in 1691 the controversy was carried on with that province. With it became combined a dispute over the so-called Attleboro Gore, a triangle of land which lay between a line drawn due north from Pawtucket falls and Blackstone river. Finally, in 1733, Rhode Island petitioned the king for a settlement of these claims, Partridge again acting as its agent and Francis Wilkes for Massachusetts. Proceedings were instituted and in 1736 and 1737 elaborate statements of claims were submitted by the colony and province.[1] The board of trade recommended that commissioners from the neighboring provinces should be ap-

[1] C. O. 5/1269, B. T. Proprieties; Arnold, II, 114–134; Kimball, Corresp. of the Governors of R. I., I, 65, 81, 98–104. Abundant details concerning this suit are given in the letters of Partridge contained in this volume.

pointed to determine the line. In spite of the objections of
Massachusetts this was done, though after a delay of about
two years. Fifteen commissioners were appointed, in equal
numbers from New York, New Jersey and Nova Scotia.[1]
Its sessions were held in 1741 at Providence, Cadwallader
Colden presiding. Each colony was represented by counsel
and surveyors were appointed to prepare maps and plans.
Many documents were transcribed for the use of the commission and voluminous evidence was taken. After the testimony was in pleas were made by the counsel, Rhode Island
having two attorneys and Massachusetts three, William
Shirley being one of the latter. The decision was favorable
to Rhode Island so far as both the Attleboro Gore and the
eastern shore was concerned.[2] But she was not awarded so
much as she claimed on the eastern shore and she was not
satisfied with the point which was fixed upon by the commission as the head of Narragansett Bay. Therefore she
appealed from the judgment,[3] and as Massachusetts had been
defeated on both counts she also appealed. The case then
went before the plantation committee of the privy council and
after a lapse of two years [4] was argued. The committee
reported in favor of the decision of the commissioners and
an order of council was issued in 1744 dismissing both appeals
and confirming the boundary as designated by the royal commission. A petition of Massachusetts for a rehearing of the
case after long delay was rejected in 1746 and so the eastern
boundary of Rhode Island was settled for the duration of
the colonial period. After independence the case was again
revived and a final decision reached which made only a very
slight change in the line as fixed in 1744.

In the history of no other colony did continued existence
depend to such an extent upon the establishment of boundaries as in Rhode Island. Until these questions were settled
the colonies by which she was surrounded threatened her
with extinction. This menace was a continuation of the disputes to which Rhode Island owed its origin, and as they

[1] R. I. Recs., IV, 586, 587; V, 29, 33.
[2] Corresp. of Govs., I, 201, 202.
[3] Ibid., 214, 218, 223.
[4] Ibid., 252, 255, 274, 288, 293.

were projected into the eighteenth century the territorial element involved in them assumed greater prominence than the religious disputes of an earlier time. But in their later form, as in their earlier, they expressed the jealousy which was felt by the two orthodox Puritan colonies toward their nondescript neighbor, the religious element in that feeling being by no means wholly eliminated. Rhode Island stood for the principle of the secularized state. Neither Great Britain nor any of her other colonies had reached that stage of development. Had Rhode Island been divided between Connecticut and Massachusetts, the influence of her example as a support to that valuable principle would have been lost. Rhode Island had her controversies and in point of organization was crude and inefficient, but she did not employ force or craft to influence or silence opinion, as did her neighbors on the north and west; and the disturbance which was produced by the multifarious opinions that coexisted within her borders was insignificant when compared with the conflicts which accompanied the gradual decay of the state-church system in Massachusetts and Connecticut.

In 1738, one hundred years after the founding of Rhode Island and when its permanent existence was assured, the Rev. John Callender, a Baptist clergyman resident at Newport, preached his Century Sermon which was later published, with a memoir, as his Historical Discourse.[1] This set forth in clear and simple language what the colony considered herself to stand for and the contest between herself and her two closest neighbors. Bigots, he said, might consider her voluntarism, suffering people to live peaceable lives without fines and punishment, to be confusion and disorder, but its opposite was what Roger Williams called " monstrous disorder." Callender did not undertake to defend the founders of Rhode Island, their doings and opinions, in every respect, and admitted that some had come in who had used their liberty as an occasion to the flesh; but in general an orderly and godly commonwealth had been maintained. In contrast with the dire consequences of persecution, as exhibited elsewhere, the experiment had proved a success. " It is no ways unlikely," said Callender, " some odd and whimsi-

---

[1] Colls. of R. I. Hist. Soc., IV.

cal opinions may have been broached; the liberty enjoyed here would tempt persons distressed for their opinions in the neighboring governments to retire to this colony as an asylum. It is no ways unlikely that some persons of a very different genius and spirit from the first settlers might entrench themselves. . . .; but the first set of men who came here were a pious generation, men of virtue and godliness, notwithstanding their tincture of enthusiasm, which was not peculiar to them; and notwithstanding their peculiar opinions of justification and the nature and rights of the Christian Church. They had not so many great and wise men among them, perhaps, as were in some of the other colonies, but their whole number was very small in comparison with the other colonies Nevertheless they had some very considerable men and of superior merit. It is true, likewise, their form of government was too feeble; their first Patent left them without sufficient authority in their civil officers, to check any popular humors; but yet they did, and that as early as the Massachusetts Colony, form a body of good laws, by which all vice and every immorality was discouraged or punished. And throughout the whole history of the Island and Colony there is manifestly an aim and endeavor to prevent or suppress all disorders and immoralities and to promote universal peace, virtue, godliness and charity."

" I do not pretend," he continued, " to defend all the opinions that were entertained by any of them; much less all the extravagant notions that were unjustly ascribed to some of them; nor yet to justify every word or action that might be the effect of heated zeal or raised indignation and resentment. That man who will go about to justify or condemn a party in the gross and without distinction shall never be approved or imitated by me; much less can it be expected I should defend all the opinions of so many different religious parties as were here united in civil peace. . . . If there were any of them who made shipwreck of faith and a good conscience, perhaps it would be as easy, as it would be invidious, to find parallels enough in other places to show there are other dangerous rocks besides liberty of conscience. . . . It must be a mean contracted way of thinking to confine the favor of God and the power of godliness to one set of speculative opinions or to any particular external forms of worship. . . . It would be hard to shew why liberty of conscience, mutual forbearance and good will, why brotherly kindness and charity, is not as good a center of unity as a constrained conformity to ambiguous articles. Experience has clearly convinced the world that unanimity in judgment and affection cannot be secured by penal laws. . . . It is now a glory to the colony to have owned such sentiments so long ago, while blindness in this article happened in other places, and to have led the way as an example to others and to have first put the theory into practice."

In terms of religion and of historic Christianity exclusively this is the earliest notable attempt at a definition of what Rhode Island stood for, of its mission, among the colonies of New England. It meant that the ideas and aspirations of Williams and of other kindred spirits had been embodied in institutions, in a commonwealth, and that this had survived for a century. Its record, on the whole, had been a worthy one and furnished a conclusive answer to those who had charged its founders with being anarchists and had predicted unlimited confusion culminating in disaster at the end. Such a result would have been welcomed by John Robinson of Leyden, had he been living, as a harbinger of the new light which he expected to break forth from the Word. In the light of this demonstration, the sterner spirit of John Winthrop even would have acknowledged how erroneous were many of his opinions concerning the founders of Rhode Island.

When Callender wrote, the Anglicans were already well established in Rhode Island with five churches.[1] He could enumerate seven churches or worshipping societies in Newport and in the other eleven towns of the colony twenty-five such societies with regular services and others who had occasional meetings. Of these, on the main land the Baptists had eight churches and the Quakers eight meetings besides one on Conanicut island. On the mainland there were also three Congregational or Presbyterian churches, besides one on Block island. As there were only twelve towns in the colony, the spread of churches under the voluntary system certainly

[1] R. I. Recs., IV, 120.

compared very favorably with the showing which had been made in Massachusetts and Connecticut under the careful patronage of the government. The Quakers and especially the Baptists had made the greatest progress and had found the system of freedom most favorable to their growth. It was a Baptist clergyman who now constituted himself the spokesman for the colony. In course of time he and others were to claim Williams as a member of their sect, and after Backus had published his history of the Baptists, in the time of the Revolution, that became an accepted view. Quakers ceased gradually to have that prominent connection with Rhode Island which had existed in earlier times, and to the Baptists accrued, among religious sects, more and more the honor which has resulted from the success of the Rhode Island experiment. It was with the publication of Callender's "Discourse," on the eve of the Great Awakening, that the cult of the "Rhode Island idea" may be said to have begun. Conditions were now shaping themselves in a way favorable to its acceptance outside the colony itself and by numbers far exceeding those whom Williams could reach in his own lifetime. But it was not until the Revolution and after that Williams came fully into his own.[1]

Rhode Island as a colony stood for the simple and naïve radicalism of the time, but on the basis of the meagre culture which then existed it was probably the only form that was possible. Its inhabitants, so far as they were not totally indifferent to such subjects, were Bible Christians and based their views of life and the world upon the various literal interpretations of passages from that book which were in vogue. Generations were to pass before science or historical criticism developed. As the descendents of exiles from the neighboring colonies, their security lay in peace among themselves which could be secured only by a toleration of their mutual differences. No faction or section became strong enough to impose its will on the rest. The Quaker element among them was sufficient to hold in check such tendencies as may have existed toward the use of physical force as a

---

[1] When Callender was ordained the two Mathers officiated. Cotton Mather preached the sermon and uttered an apology for the persecutions of which the Massachusetts Puritans had been guilty.

means of coercing opponents. The officials, who together constituted the government, never were able to be more than the agents of their constituents. They could not depend upon the British government for support and they were never able, as in Massachusetts under the old charter or in Connecticut, to form a combination or clique of their own which was strong enough to give them control of the province.

In Rhode Island therefore, as in no other colony, government was the agent of society and did not seek to dominate it. In the absence of a positive religious program it was confined to the negative position of maintaining independence under the charter, of attaining a certain territorial security, of defending herself as best she might toward the sea and contributing certain contingents to the forces which were engaged in general colonial defence. In time of war the chief energies of the colony were largely devoted to privateering,[1] and in peace as well as war trade was the favorite pursuit of its leading families. On a considerable scale this was carried on with the West Indies [2] — foreign as well as English — with Europe and with Africa and the East. The traffic in slaves occupied its customary place in the general course of this trade. As was to be expected, the acts of trade and the restrictions which they prescribed were treated with as scant respect as were the rubrics of the English Church.[3]

---

[1] Sheffield in his "Privateersmen of Newport," has shown that, though privateering originated much earlier in Rhode Island, it got under full headway with the Third Intercolonial War (1739–1748). The Wantons, Malbones, Browns, and Channings were then prominent among the merchant families of Newport, and among its sea captains appear the names of Potter, Hopkins, Fones, Cranston and many others. Sir Charles Wager, who rose from service on a merchantman and afterwards in the navy to be lord high admiral of England under Walpole, was the adopted son of John Hull, a Newport captain. While in office his knowledge of Rhode Island and sympathy with her people and claims enabled him to be of assistance to her in procuring cannon for the fort and in her boundary dispute with Massachusetts.

[2] Commercial relations of Abraham Redwood and others, who had migrated from the West Indies, especially with Antigua and Barbados, are abundantly illustrated by letters published in the volumes entitled, "Commerce of Rhode Island," 7 Colls. Mass. Hist. Soc. IX.

[3] A regulation adopted as early as 1711 indicates a source of trouble to customs officials which resulted from the topography of Narragansett Bay and which in later times was to lead to most serious results. This was to the effect that no open boat or lighter trading up and down the shores of

In time of war even the Rhode Islander did not scruple to traffic with the enemy and he maintained this attitude to the last. When denounced for these irregularities and for the spirit of disloyalty which they were alleged to exhibit, the governor and assembly denied the fact or pleaded simplicity and ignorance as excuses for such mistakes as they might have inadvertently committed. They said that they were unaccustomed to business and in effect that they were hardly aware of the wider obligations which their place in the empire imposed. Such was the general tone of the letters of Samuel Cranston who, during a continuous service as governor of twenty-eight years (1698–1727), carried the colony through one of the most dangerous periods in its existence.[1]

On occasion, however, especially when corresponding with the colony agent, Cranston's tone revealed the toughness of his fibre and the fact that Rhode Island would staunchly defend her chartered liberties. "We humbly pray," wrote he, "that their Lordships will believe we have a Tincture of the ancient British Blood in our veines." When in this mood he spoke of the founding of Rhode Island with much the same pride which the Massachusetts Puritan showed in his origin and ancestry. It was this combination of assumed humility and real pride which constituted the essence of Rhode Island diplomacy in the eighteenth century. It appears in the attitude of the Puritan colonies generally and enabled them to foil the attacks of the British government while they persistently followed methods and interests which were essentially their own. Rhode Island belonged to the common brood though her peculiarities gave her a very distinct personality. Her common consciousness was of slower and later development than theirs. It was not the result of a reasoned and concerted plan carried out from the start under official management, but was rather the work of individuals and groups seeking their immediate interest and

---

the bay and as far as Connecticut should be obliged to pay fees or reward for entering or clearing, and one general entry for the goods on board, taken from the master's report, should be sufficient, and for all goods that paid no custom the officer should receive no fees. R. I. Recs., IV, 111.

[1] R. I. Recs., III, 373, 394, 396, 419; IV, 55–59, 108, 279; Corresp. of Governors of R. I., I, 1–12.

meeting common perils without the guidance or restraint of an efficent government.

Rhode Island had never shown the aversion to appeals or other forms of submission to imperial control which had characterized the more distinctly Puritan colonies. This has been noted in tracing the history of her beginnings, and the same characteristic persisted through the period now under review. Her weakness and the presence of so many enemies in New England who would have welcomed her destruction furnish a partial explanation of this attitude. During the colonial wars she was the object of as much severe criticism from British officials as any colony. Randolph, Bellomont and Dudley denounced her irregularities in the strongest terms and pronounced her conduct a scandal. From the authorities in England itself she received frequent warnings and correction, and whenever a plan was on foot for the recall of charters the misdeeds of Rhode Island held a prominent place among the charges which were urged in justification of the charge. Moreover, the record of this colony makes it certain that many of these complaints were justified. In marked contrast to Connecticut, Rhode Island legislated freely upon the subject of appeals to the privy council and thereby regulated the conditions under which such action could be taken.[1] Legislation of this nature began in 1706 with an act requiring that bond should be given to prosecute appeals within a prescribed time. In 1719 appeals to England were forbidden unless the matter in controversy amounted to more than £300 current money. But notwithstanding this prohibition and the sum named in royal instructions to governors upon this subject, appeals continued to be carried by private parties to England in matters of smaller value. Therefore, in 1746, a, law was passed prohibiting appeals in cases which involved less than £150 sterling. In terms of money then current in the colony this equalled about £1,650, involving a very large increase in the legal requirement affecting appeals. In 1750 the practice was still further restricted by an act which forbade appeals

---

[1] Hazeltine, Appeals from colonial courts to the King in Council, with special reference to Rhode Island. Rept. of Am. Hist. Assoc. 1894, p. 329 *et seq.*

beyond the superior court of the colony in suits for the payment of money only. Further legislation, in 1764, fixing the limit below which appeals were not to be allowed at £200 sterling, shows that cases involving small sums were still being carried to England. By far the larger number of cases from Rhode Island which came before the privy council were of dates subsequent to 1735. They were private suits and in no case involved interests so important as those affecting Connecticut in Winthrop *vs.* Lechmere. The evidence, however, is conclusive that no opposition on principle to appeals to the king in council existed in Rhode Island.

The submissiveness of this colony to imperial control was suggestive of loyalism and there was a group of loyalists among her prominent citizens at Newport and in the Narragansett country. At this early period Francis Brinley appears most prominent among men of this type. He expressed much the same dissatisfaction with his colony as did the royal officials.[1] The Andros régime was not entirely unwelcome to Rhode Island and Andros was regarded as its friend. When he was overthrown, though Dudley was seized by Providence men in the Narragansett country, extreme caution was shown in the resumption of government under the charter. A cautiously worded letter to the people was issued by the late governor and deputy governor, one of whom was the Quaker, Walter Clarke. On May 1, 1689, a meeting was held at Newport which issued a statement of reasons for resuming government under the charter. An address, humble in tone, was sent " to the present supreme power in England." But for ten months Clarke declined to accept his former post and Coggeshall acted as deputy governor. Clarke kept the charter and another of the records until May, 1690. Then an election was held and, after some difficulty in finding a candidate, John Easton was chosen governor. Clarke refused to be actively concerned in handing over the charter, but allowed it to be taken from his custody. The records were surrendered on distraint.[2] Brinley and his friends seem not to have questioned the legality of the restored government, as did Gershom Bulkley in Connecticut, but they declared that

---

[1] See Brinley to Wait Winthrop, 6 Mass. Historical Colls. V, 20.
[2] R. I. Recs. III, 257 *et seq.*

the change was effected by the votes of only forty men. No oaths of office were administered or engagements taken, but private interests led the people generally to obey them. Among these last was the strong desire of many to settle the Narragansett country, especially the so-called mortgaged lands there.

The weakness of government at that time is evidenced by conditions at Portsmouth in the eastern part of the colony and Kingston in the west.[1] When the assembly was in session in June, 1691, it was found that neither of these towns had constables, the officers upon whom chiefly depended the keeping of the peace. In Portsmouth they had been elected, but had neglected or refused to take their oaths. In Kingston the difficulty did not arise from Quakers, but from chronic discontent which took the form of a neglect to choose any officers for keeping the peace. The assembly labored for some time to bring Portsmouth into a better method and their constables were brought before it. But only one of them could be induced to take the oath, the others refusing to serve. These were to be proceeded with according to law, which under existing conditions probably meant no action at all. To meet the situation at Kingston the assembly appointed a special constable for the entire Narragansett country, a bailiwick which was certainly too large for efficient control by a single official.

In the military system, as in everything else in Rhode Island, the principle of voluntaryism was followed. Since 1677 the trainbands of the towns had elected their militia officers. This same assembly of 1691 stated that, " forasmuch as the Colony is in great danger, to be surprised by French privateers, and such like danger, and several towns in this colony are defective of military officers and out of a posture of defense," the two colony majors were empowered, when towns had failed to act, to appoint such officers as were needed and " to effectually settle the militia." The colony attempted no reform in its method of choosing militia officers during the first colonial war. In 1705 an entry appears to the effect that great dishonor had come from this system, because of transients and " youth of small consideration "

[1] R. I. Recs. III, 575.

who chose incapable persons. Therefore it was ordered that
hereafter only freemen of the towns or colony should vote for
militia officers. By the close of the second war the assembly
was convinced that election by towns could not possibly work
well, and in 1713 it was abandoned for the system employed in the other New England colonies of choice by the
general assembly at the annual election followed by the issue
of commissions by the governor. But by the time another
year had passed the reactionaries had again won the ascendency and all the existing militia laws and orders were repealed and the system of town elections was restored.
Samuel Cranston, the governor, one of the assistants and
three representatives filed a protest against this, asserting
that the practice was repugnant to the charter and dishonor-
able to the crown, in which was vested the military power
and from which it was delegated to the assembly.[1]

In the early sixteen-nineties, as it was war time and French
privateers were raiding the coast and troops were demanded
for the defence of the frontiers, a rate of £300 was voted, But
four months later it was found that seven towns had neglected
to assess it on their inhabitants.[2] The assembly then designated three men in each town to perform the neglected
duty. But " being concerned for the ancient privileges of
every town in this Colony," the assembly added a proviso
that, if the assessment was forthwith made, the threatened
step would not be taken. When Warwick complained that
it was overrated, the assembly confessed that the rating of
towns by guess was not a suitable or certain rule and that for
the future rates should be levied, as in other colonies, as so
much in the pound of individual estates. A break in the
records makes it impossible to describe the next steps which
were taken, but in 1695 the assembly was struggling with the
same problem, a late levy of £300 having been " neglected
to be collected and paid." In 1698 a rather elaborate tax
law was passed, with the customary provisions intended to
insure assessment and collection. But a few months later we
find that obedience had been wholly neglected by some towns
and in part by others, so that the incoming of revenue from

[1] R. I. Recs. III, 534; IV, 154, 173, 211, 238; R. I. Laws, ed. of 1719.
[2] R. I. Recs. III, 273, 275, 277, 280.

it had ceased. Special town meetings were to be called to hasten payment, but in case this was not done assessors and collectors were to be appointed by the colony government.[1] By an entry in the following year it appears that this had resulted in nothing, "whereby the Collony is much straightened" and funds were not available for the necessary expenses of an agent in England. The offending towns were in the Narragansett country, and several months later they appear to have still been delinquent. In 1705 we are told that constables of several of the towns had detained in their hands a considerable part of the rates and had not delivered them to the colony treasurer as required by law.[2] Further precautions were taken, but with little prospect that the difficulty would be overcome. The collection of taxes met with serious obstacles in all the colonies and the sums paid in often fell short of the amounts voted, but the independence of its towns made Rhode Island especially familiar with this evil, and it goes far to account for the lack of means often confessed by that colony for vigorous co-operation with its neighbors. The scale of expenditure is indicated by an order of 1695 that the salary of the governor should be £10 a year, that of the deputy governor £6, and of the assistants £4 each. Members of the assembly were allowed three shillings a day during the sessions and this was payable by the towns. No fixed rate seems to have been established for the governor's salary. Occasionally his small compensation was increased by a gratuity, an example of which was the grant of £40 in 1705 to Samuel Cranston.[3] In 1721 he was granted £200 as a gratuity for his extraordinary services the past year; in 1736 a grant of £300 in heavily depreciated currency was made.

To the corporate colonies, because of their lack of a regular channel of communication with the British government, the employment of agents was especially necessary. The development of that office was their work quite as much, if not more, than it was that of the other colonies. The strengthening of imperial control brought many questions to the front

[1] R. I. Recs., III, 343–348.
[2] Ibid., 368, 371, 532.
[3] Ibid., 309, 321, 334, 525, IV; 296, 323.

which were of critical importance to them, upon the issue of
which their continual existence depended. Rhode Island was
even more deeply involved in issues of this character than was
Connecticut. Almy, Wharton, Brenton, Penn, Partridge, and
Jencks served her in this capacity, and the appropriations
which were made for their salaries and the fees and other
payments which they had to make for the colony were more
liberal than for any other object.[1] The furnishing of a quota
of a hundred men for the general defence of New England,
Rhode Island often considered to be beyond her ability, but
the voting of a salary of £100 a year for an agent, with large
additional expenses, was deemed necessary for the preservation of the colony charter and the liberties which came with
it, and it was not difficult to secure such appropriations.
The services of a man like Partridge, who was long in
service for several colonies, and himself a Quaker, may be
regarded as worth all they cost.[2]

In the corporate colonies the separation of the legislature
into two houses was not so necessary as it was in the provinces. The fact that in the latter the council was appointed
led naturally, if not necessarily, to their separation. Virginia was the only province in which it was long delayed.
But in the corporate colonies the assistants as well as the
deputies were elective. In Massachusetts their early separation into two houses was due to sectional jealousy toward a
group of magistrates from Boston and vicinity which was
compact and very persistent in its leadership. This condition
did not obtain in either Connecticut or Rhode Island, and
they were also small colonies with simple political and social
relations. Therefore in neither of them did the general court
become bicameral till near the close of the seventeenth century. The act for this purpose was passed in Rhode Island
in 1696 and in Connecticut in 1698.[3] After the separation
the governor continued to preside in the upper house, though
without the veto power over legislation. We hear of no disagreements of consequence between the houses. At times
complaints appear of the thinness of attendance on the assem-

[1] R. I. Recs., III, 321, 325, 404, 410, 464; IV, 125.
[2] His letters are in Corresp. of R. I. Governors.
[3] R. I. Recs., III, 313; Conn. Recs., IV, 267, 284.

blies. In both colonies committees were appointed for temporary purposes, but they appear with greater frequency in Connecticut. In 1696 the Connecticut assembly appointed, though only for one session, a committee with much wider duties than usual. It was " to consider and advise this assembly in such politick and prudential affairs as do concern either the promoting good order and government, in making new laws or repealing or altering laws formerly made, or in such affairs as doe concern the publick weal in promoting and advancing trade." [1] When the laws were to be revised or compiled committees were intrusted with that work.

A notable instance of the survival into the eighteenth century of primitive usage in Rhode Island was the regular practice of hearing appeals in civil cases from the court of trials or other bodies before the general assembly.[2] That body was the chancery court of the colony. After its separation into two houses, when acting as a court of judicature, they met in joint committee. In 1697 Connecticut prohibited this practice, but in Rhode Island it continued unobstructed until 1712. In that year, on an appeal to the privy council, in a case involving title to land,[3] the proceedings of the assembly in the case were utterly condemned. This led to the repeal of the law making the assembly a court of chancery and to an enactment providing for the erection of a regular court of this nature according to English methods and precedents. Provision, however, was still made for appeals by way of petition to the general assembly for " relief in any matter or thing that may be cognizable before them," and references to such appeals appear in the records at later dates. Little change was apparently made in the procedure.[4] In 1705 the assembly had been impressed with the benefits which might come from having a regular court of chancery, but apparently the dearth of legal knowledge and talent was so great that the erection of such a court was postponed. And when, in 1741, it became necessary to provide for one no effort whatever was made to designate its powers by statute. But ex-

[1] Conn. Recs., IV, 161.
[2] R. I. Recs., III, 412, 444, 481, 512, 550; IV, 29, 40, 48, 115. Conn. Recs., IV, 200.
[3] Ibid., 48, 136.
[4] Field, III, 101; R. I. Recs., IV, 268-9, 313.

press provision had been made that the laws of England should be followed in cases which were not covered by the statutes of the colony, and the existing manuals of chancery practice doubtless served as the chief guides in such cases as came before this court.[1]  Since Quakers were numerous and shared freely the offices in Rhode Island, the obstacles which had to be encountered in the administration of oaths were nearly as serious as they were in Pennsylvania or West Jersey.  As irregularity in this matter prevailed in all matters of government and was regarded as a most serious obstacle to the proper administration of justice, it came in for sharp condemnation from royal officials.

It was during the first and second colonial wars — subsiding toward the second half of the latter — that the most sweeping attacks were made on Rhode Island.  At this time also its boundary controversies were at their height.  The criticisms of Randolph and Dudley, supported by Lord Cornbury, were directed chiefly against its failure to come up to the standard of correct action in imperial concerns and were made partly at the instance of the British government.  They dwelt upon its violations of the acts of trade, its neglect of defence, its refusal to allow the control of the militia to pass out of its hands, its alleged harboring of pirates and ignoring of the admiralty jurisdiction.  Dudley also, in gross violation of the facts, asserted that Rhode Island refused to allow appeals.  He was nearer right, though his statement was inadequate, when he said that she allowed the laws of England to be pleaded in her courts only when it served her turn.[2]  To an extent this was true of the colonies generally, but the deviations were due not so much to ill will as to new and crude social conditions, to the lack of trained lawyers and judges and the inability of lay officials to comprehend the legal principles or use the procedure of the English judicial system.

Lord Bellomont carried his criticism further than the others and attacked the social conditions which he observed or believed to exist in the colony.[3]  He viewed it from the

[1] R. I. Recs., III, 425, 550;  V, 23.
[2] R. I. Recs., III, 543.
[3] Ibid., 385.

standpoint of an orthodox Anglican Whig and the severity of his temper and of his criticisms has been noted in other connections. To him, as to the orthodox Puritan, Rhode Island because of its voluntaryism [1] seemed to be irreligious. He charged it with not having a learned or orthodox ministry. In his time it was true that they had not erected or encouraged schools, though it is probably not true that the generality of its people were more ignorant than they would have been found to be in many other colonies. Bellomont viewed with aversion elections and the extent to which they were used in filling offices and thought that among such a population as the colonists they caused many evils. Voting by proxy and especially the election of militia officers he considered to be violations of the charter. So was the exercise of judicial powers by the general assembly and such a function was inconsistent with the nature of a legislative body. The numerous informalities and irregularities in the administration of government and its procedure were suggestive to him of anarchy. No directions, he said, were given to juries, the evidence was not summed up before them, little care or skill was shown in weighing evidence, arbitrary rulings or other acts, even in violation of the laws of the colony, were resorted to. The attorney general at the time was said by Bellomont to have been an illiterate mechanic. The same was true of many assistants, justices of the peace and judges. The deputy governor was declared to be totally unfit for his office. The laws were not drawn in proper form, were kept on loose scraps of paper and often could not be found when inquiry was made for them. The journals of the assembly he found to be imperfectly kept and no records were kept of the executive acts of the council. Bellomont repeatedly demanded authentic copies of the journals and the laws, but had been unable to obtain them. As a matter of fact, until 1732, it was the custom for the assembly to pass acts in substance and to leave to the clerk or recorder the task of putting them into proper form.[2] These conditions might profit-

[1] A fundamental enactment upon which this rested, as formulated in 1715, was that what maintenance or salary might be thought needful by any of the churches within the colony for their ministers should be raised by free contribution and in no other way. R. I. Recs., IV, 206.

[2] Arnold, II, 108.

ably be compared with those which existed in North Carolina or New Jersey or the Lower Counties on the Delaware. They simply indicate that, though Rhode Island was not a frontier colony, owing to its extreme individualism conditions existed within it which were similar to those of the frontier.

The charges of Dudley and Cornbury respecting the conduct of their government the magistrates and assembly of Rhode Island emphatically denied.[1] They declared that they neither encouraged illegal trade and piracy, nor harbored deserting soldiers and seamen nor protected malefactors. Settlers, on the other hand, moved freely into and out of the colony, as had come generally to be the practice elsewhere. As to the furnishing of quotas of men in aid of other colonies, they rightly contended that there was no law compelling them to do this, and yet they had furnished quotas although the defence of their colony toward the sea had always demanded their chief attention. As to control over their militia, they were quite within their chartered rights in insisting upon this, while in reference to the admiralty jurisdiction, they had complied with the king's commands though reserving the right to grant commissions to privateers in time of war. Their administration of justice they defended as legal so far as the extent of jurisdiction exercised by their courts was concerned and within the clause concerning repugnancy in matters of detail. The charge, finally, that the Quakers would not allow any persons of estate or ability in places of public trust they controverted by referring to the governor, deputy governor and other magistrates who were of that persuasion but at the same time men of known estates, abilities and loyalty.

Of the substantial truth of this defence there can be no doubt. At the same time there was a large element of truth in the charges which were brought against Rhode Island by its enemies. The apparent contradiction in these statements will be reconciled by the thought that the royal charters permitted almost everything and expressly forbade almost nothing and that it was only by filling out their content with statutes and executive orders that the chartered colonies could really be brought within the scope of a systematic imperial policy. In earlier years Massachusetts had acted with

[1] R. I. Recs., III, 547.

greater freedom than Rhode Island now assumed, but had cited her charter as containing no prohibitions of such conduct. For some decades now Rhode Island had been subjected to administrative pressure from England and some of her practices which were inconsistent with the rights of the crown she had been forced to abandon. The exercise of the admiralty jurisdiction furnishes an example in point. But the process of enforcing conformity was by no means complete and it was never possible to make it so under any pressure which Great Britain was able to exert. Hence the degree of social and corporate freedom which such colonies as Rhode Island and Connecticut were always able to enjoy and the dissatisfaction which this aroused in the minds of officials, like Randolph, Dudley or Quary, whose ideal was strict conformity to the commands of crown and parliament. This was the irrepressible conflict within the old British system, between imperial policies on the one side and colonial rights on the other, and the history of the chartered colonies that survived throughout the period furnishes the best illustrations of the latter in its extreme form. They constituted the party of states rights in the British empire.

In 1719 Caleb Heathcote, writing from Newport but having in his mind Connecticut as well as Rhode Island, complained to the board of trade that, though often commanded to do so, they wholly neglected to send their laws to England.[1] That was a fault of theirs, but to a certain extent it was corrected as time passed. The laws of these colonies were usually sent in printed form when a collected edition was published. It happened that this was done in the case of Rhode Island for the first time in the very year when Heathcote made his complaint and it was a compliance to which they could hardly have been forced so long as their charters remained intact. The custom of printing the laws, together with calls from England for copies, led more than a decade later to the appointment of an engrossing committee to draft the statutes more carefully.[2] The passage of an act for the establishing of fees, probably by reducing their rates, had in Heathcote's opinion insulted and abused the officers of his majesty's customs. But legislation of that nature, as we know, was com-

[1] R. I. Recs., IV, 259.    [2] Ibid., 472.

mon in all the colonies and it certainly could not be made a cause for the recall of the charter. Heathcote's ire in this particular case had been aroused by an attack upon Kay, the collector, and the destruction by a mob of a quantity of wine which had been seized for illegal importation. The subject of bills of credit also came in for a share of Heathcote's criticism and were to continue to be objects of attack until their further issue was prohibited by the British government.

As observed by Bellomont, the part played by elections in Rhode Island government was certainly excessive. For a long period a new assembly was elected twice every year and at times of heated controversy almost the entire membership of both houses was changed at each successive election.[1] The officials of the colony were almost as insecure in their places. For more than a generation even commissioned officers in the militia were chosen by the towns, but by legislation in 1713 and 1718 this absurd survival of primitive custom was abolished and, as required by charter, they were made appointive by the general assembly.[2] In 1741 a council of war, consisting of the governor, council, field officers and captains was established. Thus one of the many hindrances in the way of military efficiency in Rhode Island was somewhat reduced. But the influence of Quakerism, the widespread preference for service at sea and for the profits in prizes it might bring, the exaggerated attention which the colony claimed to give to seaward defence and to an enemy expected from that quarter, but who never appeared except in the form of an occasional privateer, and above all the suspicion and dislike which Rhode Island naturally felt toward her neighbors prevented her hearty and effective coöperation as a colony in the joint operations of the French wars.[3] It is a curious fact that it was much easier to hire recruits and procure volunteers in Rhode Island by appeals to individuals than it was to secure coöperation through her government. But during the second intercolonial war, while Dudley was

[1] Arnold, II, 53, 55, 57.
[2] Ibid., 52, 61, 130.
[3] A good illustration of this may be found in the statement of reasons, issued by the Rhode Island assembly in 1724, in justification of its resolve not to aid Massachusetts against Râle R. I. Recs., IV, 351.

so prominent as an organizer of defence in New England, and at the same time was campaigning as vigorously against the colonial charters, Rhode Island and Connecticut could scarcely be expected to follow his lead with enthusiasm. In the later wars she sought the common interest more willingly and naturally.

So small was Rhode Island that sectionalism could scarcely be expected to develop within her borders.[1] But some of the most pronounced symptoms of this disease appear in her history. Territorially she was not a unit, but a fringe of somewhat detached sections surrounding Narragansett Bay. Newport and the island of Aquidneck became predominantly commercial. Providence shared later and to a less degree in this development. Local trade existed among all the shore towns. But the inland towns of the Narragansett country and the northwestern part of the colony remained intensely agricultural.[2] Thus the usual economic types existed in distinct form even in this small colony, though the large stock farmers and dairymen of the Narragansett country formed a landed aristocracy which probably did not widely share the economic opinions of their less favored neighbors. So great was the influence of the towns in the assembly and such the frequency of elections that their differences were fully reflected in public policy. There was no executive authority of sufficient strength to check these influences. Therefore in connection with the issues of bills of credit and later upon other questions violent and prolonged sectional controversies arose. The colony was divided into hotly contending parties, Newport and the commercial interest being pitted against the purely agricultural towns. In connection with the former party and its affiliations with British merchants the loyalist sympathies of the colony found their origin and support.

[1] She contained only three counties and these were not organized until 1729. R. I. Recs., IV, 427.

[2] Updike's History of the Narragansett Church (the new edition, 3 vols., edited by Goodman, 1907), gives many details of a social and ecclesiastical nature to illustrate the character of that section, especially the extent to which Anglicanism, with its aristocratic leanings, penetrated there, and the economic character of these so-called planters. Channing, The Narragansett Planters.

This brings us to the consideration of the paper money craze, from which Rhode Island suffered more deeply than any other colony. The form which she gave to her issues and the arguments with which she defended them show that this policy was an expression of her radicalism. So it was in the colonies generally, when the issues were made in the form of banks for the encouragement of business and not to meet colony expenses and pay its debts. This policy was a form of agrarian radicalism, like the advocacy of similar measures in recent years in the West, and it flourished among the farmers and small traders who sought by this means to meet their imperative economic needs. The reaction of this upon long contracts and the creditor class occasioned the usual opposition among the merchants of Newport and vicinity. Rhode Island did not begin to issue bills of credit until 1710,[1] her first experiment being occasioned by the expedition of that year which resulted in the capture of Port Royal. This issue of £7000 was followed by another small emission before the close of the war. The object of these was for the supply of the treasury, that is, to meet the expenditures and pay the debts of the government. As taxation was light, such issues were continued through the decades to come and by 1747 amounted to a total of £312,000.[2] Such issues as these, to meet emergencies and supplement the inadequate money supply and financial weakness of the colonies, merchants and the British government were ready to view with a certain toleration as a necessary evil. In their case the requirements insisted upon were that the bills should be redeemed by taxation and destroyed at the time set for such redemption in the acts of issue, and that issues should not be so multiplied as to cause great depreciation and consequent fluctuations in the rates of exchange. Though proclamation money was always referred to as the colonial standard and the law which provided for it was ordered to be enforced, as the colonial wars progressed allowance had to be made for a wide divergence for its terms in practice. Instructions and exhortations to obedience took the place of

[1] Potter and Rider, Some Account of Paper Money in Rhode Island, R. I. Hist. Tracts, VIII; Arnold, II, 39.
[2] Potter and Rider, 49, 190.

absolute prohibitions of further issues, the governors and
board of trade protesting but yielding until the end of the
colonial period.

The " bank," however, was an issue of a somewhat different
character, and it made its appearance in Rhode Island in
1715. Massachusetts began issues of this nature at about
the same time. " Banks " usually consisted of large sums
and were not intended to meet the needs of government but
to stimulate trade and industry, the bills being loaned to the
people at interest on mortgage security for a term of years.[1]
The bills were legal tender and irredeemable and the mortgages furnished no security at all for the bill holders. In both
the colonies mentioned issues of this kind began after the close
of the first two colonial wars and when a period of general
peace was beginning. Connecticut also followed suit. But
in the preamble to the law for the issue of the first bank in
Rhode Island the exhaustion caused by the recent war was
given as an excuse for the measure. As a result of this, they
said, money was scarce, trade decayed, farmers discouraged
and reduced to want and business generally languishing, so
that many could not pay their debts or supply their daily
wants. The few issues already made were not sufficient to
provide for the repair of the fort at Newport and meet other
needs, or to make possible the payment of debts and give
the needed stimulus to enterprise. Therefore £30,000 in bills
were ordered to be printed and loaned out.

In 1721 another similar issue of £40,000 was made. In
order to encourage their production, hemp, flax and other
commodities were declared to be receivable in payment of
the interest on this loan. Meantime counterfeiting of the
bills had begun and the first of the customary but futile
enactments against this evil was passed. A few years later
the continuance of the bills of the first " bank " in circulation
was prolonged for ten years. In 1728, on the plea of the
decay of trade, a new issue of £40,000 was added to the
currency already out, while resolutions to call in the old bills
were not lived up to. When, in 1731, a continuance of this
policy was demanded, there was strong protest from Newport
and the governor, Joseph Jencks, recorded his dissent against

[1] Potter and Rider, 11 *et seq.*

the new loan.[1]  This act was denounced, and John Wanton, the deputy governor, who led the soft money party, called the assembly and it declared the act of Jencks to be irregular and null.  A new " bank " of £60,000 was issued.  The merchants who were opposed to this policy, including Kay, the collector, Alney, Redwood, Brown and others, with Jencks, the governor, complained to the board of trade.  They called attention not only to the fact that the non-redeemed issues already made, amounting to nearly £200,000, had so depreciated that silver in exchange for these bills had risen from eight to twenty shillings per ounce, but, with respect to the issue of 1720, the order in council forbidding the passage of such note in the future without a suspending clause and the recent instruction to Governor Belcher to the effect that Massachusetts should not have out at any one time more than £30,000 in bills of credit.  This complaint was supported by a copy of the act in question and of other public records, to which Jencks attached the public seal in evidence of their authenticity.  A protest against this was made by his opponents on the ground that it might lead to a forfeiture of the charter.  Partridge, the agent, also tried, though in vain, to prevent the dispute being carried before the British authorities, " who are no friends to the northern colonies." [2]  Questions relating to this and to the legality of his dissent were submitted from Jencks to the law officers, Yorke and Talbot.  As to his attempt to exercise the veto power, they decided that it was without authority in the charter and was illegal, but his use of the colony seal was regular and a part of his duty.  Though they admitted that the crown had no direct power to disallow laws of Rhode Island, under the clause in the charter concerning repugnancy such acts might be invalid from the beginning.

Beyond this expression of opinion no action was taken by the British government at this time.  Jencks refused to be a candidate again for governor.  The debtor class or soft money party triumphed in the next election, choosing John Wanton again to be deputy governor and his brother William as governor.  In 1733 a fifth " bank," consisting of £104,000,

---

[1] R. I. Recs., IV, 456–461; Arnold, II, 104.
[2] Corresp. of the Govs. of R. I., I, 21 et seq.

was issued. In the preamble to this act and its predecessor the pretence was discarded that they were intended to serve anything else than the craze for more paper. Reference was made to visionary plans for the production of naval stores and the encouragement of the whale and cod fishery and the building of a harbor on Block Island, while the pitiful sum of £4,000 was reserved from the issue of 1733 for the purchase of cannon and ammunition for the fort. At a later time a colony house and a lighthouse were added to the cherished objects of expenditure. There is no proof that the fort was made really defensible or any public works of more importance than was common in the colonies completed in Rhode Island during the entire period of inflation. The other New England colonies at this time were following much the same policy and the bills of all three, except when prohibited by Massachusetts, by flowing over their respective boundaries contributed to the increase of the general depreciation. In the preamble to the bank act of 1738 the spirit engendered by inflation reached its full expression:[1] " Whereas the several Emissions . . . issued by this Government have entirely answered those Ends for which they were emitted, and have tended greatly to the Interest and Advantage of the publick, by encreasing and promoting Trade and encouraging all Kinds of Business; and whereas the Times of Payment of the first Bank emitted (1715) is almost expired, and also near one Half of the second (1721), There is an absolute Necessity of an Addition to the present Medium of Exchange in order to supply those Banks, otherwise Trade and all other Business must inevitably Decay and consequently the Publick would thereby greatly suffer." The process of reasoning and acting in a circle which was plunging so many colonies more and more deeply into the abyss of inflation and repudiation was clearly exhibited in this passage and in the policy to which Rhode Island was now fully committed.

The reopening of war in 1739 restored the original plea in justification of continued emissions, and in the course of this struggle the seventh and eighth banks were issued, of £20,000 and £40,000 respectively. Large additional issues to meet public expenditures were also made, and the device of " new

[1] Potter and Rider, 45.

tenor," the name for partial repudiation, was brought into use. When the war began, as we have seen, opposition to this policy was becoming strong in Great Britain, both in parliament and among officials. An order to the colonies chiefly concerned to send over an account of their issues drew from Richard Ward, the governor, in 1740 a well written defence of the course thus far pursued by Rhode Island in the matter of currency.[1] An effort was here made to explain the disappearance of coin and the depreciation of paper which does not appear in the preambles of the acts; it was ascribed to the systematic buying up of specie by Boston merchants for use in making remittances to Europe. Before that policy was adopted, it was claimed, paper bills had been at par, but, as a result of it gold and silver had been treated as merchandise and its market value run up higher and higher, paper depreciating to a corresponding degree. If Ward had abandoned the notion that merchants in Boston or elsewhere followed this course as the result of a preconcerted or malicious plan and made his statement general, he would have approximated to Gresham's law and would have shown how impossible it was for paper and specie to co-exist under such conditions as had been created in Rhode Island. But so confirmed were Ward and his supporters that paper money was a panacea that they attributed to it the undeniable progress which Rhode Island had made in wealth, in trade and ship building, and in the supply especially of West India goods not only for her own use but for the enrichment even of Massachusetts itself. This all made her better able to fit out privateers and coöperate in defence at sea in time of war. " If this Colony," he exclaimed, " be in any respect happy and flourishing, it is paper money and a right application of it that hath rendered us so."

Partridge wrote about the bill which was introduced into parliament in 1744 for the partial suppression of paper currency.[2] Rhode Island was so alarmed by this that she ordered £550 sterling to be sent to the agent and used in fighting the measure. This was also accompanied by a very strong private protest against attempts to take away by acts of

---

[1] R. I. Recs., V, 8; Corresp. of the Govs. of R. I., I, 120, 142, 153, 158, 197.
[2] Potter and Rider, 254, 285, 289, 296.

parliament privileges which had been bestowed upon colonies by charter and long enjoyed by them. Partridge was told that in the face of such measures as these he was to " fee able and good Council and oppose the same with the Utmost Care, Wisdom and Skill." But nothing came of this and, owing to the necessities of war, the currency question drifted on. After the close of the war Rhode Island received, in the form of reimbursement for expenditures during the conflict, £6332 sterling, with which she redeemed a part of her bills.[1] In response to a command from the secretary of state an account of issues and of bills outstanding in 1750 was prepared and sent to England. According to a statement made by Governor Greene in 1750 the amount then outstanding was £525,335.[2] And yet additional issues were urged in the assembly, in opposition to which Greene delivered the strongest speech which had ever been heard in the colony upon that subject.[3] He showed what losses had been inflicted upon all creditors by depreciation and in view of this and of the amount of bills already out declared that a new issue would be an infamy. News had already come that a bill for the regulation of currencies in America was likely to be passed, and he took the ground that, as the charters were silent on this point, the imperial government probably was entitled to act and on the eve of such legislation it would be taken as the most serious affront to make a new issue. Before any further bills were put out the statute of 1751 was passed by parliament prohibiting the issue of bills of credit by the New England colonies, except to meet the emergencies of war and with the consent of the British government and provided ample funds were established for their redemption within short periods. Notwithstanding what had been declared as law on that subject in the corporate colonies, the exercise of the veto power to enforce obedience to this statute was required of governors under the heaviest penalties.[4] Larger and more frequent issues, however, were made during the last colonial war, but under circumstances which conformed in general to the terms of the law.[5]

[1] Potter and Rider, 67. There are several letters of Partridge concerning this matter in the Corresp. of the Govs. of R. I, II, 80, 89, 97, 105–115.

[2] Ibid., 118; R. I. Recs., V, 283.

[3] Corresp. of Govs., II, 116–129.

[4] Potter and Rider, 86.

[5] Ibid., 138.

# CHAPTER XV

## THE OUTLYING COLONIES OF NEW ENGLAND: CONNECTICUT

CONNECTICUT was a much larger colony than Rhode Island, though it ranked only among the smaller members of the entire group. Notwithstanding the words of its charter, it was excluded from the possibility of indefinite westward expansion. After the union of its three component parts had been effected it formed a compact whole, with practically definite boundaries. To be sure, it had boundary disputes with all the three colonies which surrounded it. But those with Massachusetts and New York were destitute of political significance, and the one with Rhode Island, while a matter of life and death to the latter colony, signified to Connecticut only the winning of an additional strip of land and the infliction of defeat upon a despised group of sectaries who stood rather ineffectively for the principle of liberty in matters religious. So far as this controversy was concerned, Connecticut was sure of the sympathy of Massachusetts, though after 1690 not of her direct assistance. In Europe such straining of technical points and insistence upon the mere letter of the law as Connecticut resorted to in this argument would have been the prelude to territorial aggression and perhaps a war of conquest. But in America, partly owing to the existence of a superior tribunal at Westminster, such questions were peacefully settled and every group which was large enough to embody itself in a colony was reasonably sure of a chance to work out its destiny unmolested.

The controversy with Massachusetts was the result of an effort to correct the line which Woodward and Saffery had pretended to run in 1642.[1] This extended, as was supposed, due west from Wrentham plain, a point three miles south of

---

[1] Bowen, Boundary Disputes of Connecticut.

Charles river, and terminated at the Connecticut river in the town of Windsor. As Springfield originally included the later towns of Enfield and Suffield, this point was not far from its southern boundary, but it lay some ten miles south of the true latitude of the Massachusetts patent. No serious attempts were made to ascertain the true line until after Massachusetts procured her second charter. People from Roxbury had meantime settled Woodstock. Connecticut had also settled Simsbury west of the river, and there had been disputes between Springfield and Windsor about their respective jurisdictions. By 1700 these local disputes had become serious and Connecticut had come to deny the accuracy of the original survey. For years complaints were made by inhabitants of Simsbury and Windsor that the adjoining towns to the north, which they claimed belonged to Connecticut, had carried off their hay and turpentine and had attempted to levy local rates upon them. Though several attempts at negotiation were made by Connecticut, they met with no effective response from Massachusetts until 1713, when the war had ended. Then commissioners were appointed by the two colonies and the true boundary was determined. But, as a preliminary agreement was made that the towns should remain to the colonies by which they had been settled, equivalent territory, to the extent of nearly 108,000 acres, had to be ceded by Massachusetts to Connecticut from its unsettled lands.[1] Later this was sold by the last named colony and its proceeds applied to the use of the college.

But dissatisfaction continued in Enfield, Suffield and other towns along the border, because they were being removed from the jurisdiction of Connecticut and placed under Massachusetts. Woodstock remained satisfied with its connection with Massachusetts until the heavy taxation which resulted from the later colonial wars turned its preferences also toward Connecticut. The point was raised, especially in an opinion which was given by three prominent New York lawyers, that a transfer of jurisdiction could be made only by authority of the king.[2] Connecticut adopted this view and

[1] Conn. Recs., IV, V, index; Hutchinson, *op. cit.*, II, 185; Trumbull, *op. cit.*, I, 479; Bowen, Boundary Disputes of Conn.
[2] Conn. Mss., Colonial Boundaries, April, 1749.

voted to receive the towns or to appeal to the king if Massachusetts refused to accede to this course.  Much correspondence followed, with reexamination of the line as agreed upon in 1713.  One of the amenities of this interchange was the remark of Governor Jonathan Law; " As for your Government's being always in the right, it looks to me rather that Mr. Tomlinson's charge upon you in his plea [in the boundary dispute with New Hampshire] that you were an overgrown Province and imposed on your neighbors, might have too much of truth in it, since New Hampshire on the North put you out of so many towns which you had granted and settled, and Rhode Island on the South." [1]  When the evidence on both sides was sent to England and submitted by the agents, Bollan and Partridge, that country was absorbed in the Seven Years' War and the opinion of the attorney general was that the settlement of 1713 had better not be disturbed.  Therefore the home government did not act.  Connecticut continued to govern the towns in dispute and Massachusetts to levy taxes on them which she never collected and to send notices of fast days and elections.  This continued until after the Revolution, when, with very slight readjustments of the boundary, Connecticut was left in final possession of the towns and the line was run through to her western limits.[2]

The boundary dispute with New York involved the final adjustment of the line under an agreement made between the governors and councils of the two colonies in 1683,[3] whereby the Byram river and a zigzag line extending some distance north of it was agreed upon.  The line twenty miles east of the Hudson was then fixed upon and Rye and Bedford, both of which had belonged to Connecticut, were transferred to New York.  This change was not welcomed by their inhabitants and for several years disturbances occurred in them which led to unfriendly correspondence between the two colonies.  This led, in 1700, to the case being presented by

[1] Conn. Mss., Col. Bound., Sept. 5, 1749.  Conn. Recs. IX, 432, 547;  X, 42, 103, 146, 389.  Connecticut regarded the controversy which Rhode Island had over its northern boundary as one with its own and sought in the records of Rhode Island evidence against the claims of Massachusetts.

[2] Bowen, *op. cit.*

[3] Osgood, Am. Colonies in the 17th Century, II;  Cal. St. P. Col., 1700, p. 124, 142, Boundaries of New York.

New York to the crown and the issue of an order in council confirming the agreement of 1683. Because Greenwich and a part of Stamford which also had been settled by Connecticut had been assigned to that colony though they lay west of the twenty-mile line, New York insisted upon receiving an equivalent. Though the assembly of Connecticut had never ratified this, she came to insist that the line should be run through to the southern boundary of Massachusetts and the controversy ended so that peace might be maintained along the border. Finally, in 1731, after a long and tedious correspondence, a joint survey was made and under the name of the Oblong a tract of 61,400 acres along the boundary line was transferred to New York.[3] Owing to the fact that the fixing of the eastern boundary of Connecticut was of such vital importance to Rhode Island it has been described in connection with the history of that colony.

Over the resumption of government under the charter in Connecticut less caution was shown than in Rhode Island, but there was much more discussion and the arguments in opposition to the course of action pursued were stated forcibly and at length. On the news of the revolution in England, the rules of passive and loyal conduct demanded that the *status quo* should be maintained until instructions came from the crown. The conditions in Massachusetts were such that this was not even considered and an extreme revolutionary program was followed out. In Connecticut and Rhode Island the collision between the colonists and the crown had not been so direct. Their old form of government had been merely suspended and its restoration still remained possible without revolution. Local officials of the towns and counties might be trusted to preserve order and both colonies might be considered sufficiently protected by their location against French attack to make serious military effort unnecessary. They should therefore refrain from calling general courts, holding elections, or seating either the old or the new magistrates in office. As their governors and other officials had been displaced by the establishment of the Dominion of New England and could no longer act, these colonies should wait until their corporate powers were restored by the crown. This would

---

[1] Conn. Recs., VII, 295.

be in harmony with the course which all municipal corporations — to which they were analogous — must follow in England. To follow a different course would be " to enter upon the king by force," which savored of treason. These were the ideas which were advocated by Gershom Bulkley in his " People's Right to Election or Alteration of Government in Connecticut Argued,"[1] published at the time of the crisis in 1689. After the crisis had passed and a different course had been followed, they were enforced at much greater length by the same writer in his " Will and Doom, or the Miseries of Connecticut by and under an Usurped and Arbitrary Power." A copy of this was sent to England by Lord Cornbury, but it was not published until a few years ago.[2] It now survives as one of the numerous examples of loyalist literature which emanated from Stuart policy and ideas. In Connecticut Bulkley had a few supporters, most prominent among whom was Major Edward Palmes, of New London. In New York, however, he had the active sympathy of the royal governors, Slaughter, Fletcher and Cornbury, and his writings may be considered a part of the campaign which was waged with such vigor for three decades against the proprieties, and especially against corporate liberties in New England. Bulkley and his friends gave their sympathy and support to the efforts which were made under their successive governors to bring the militia of Connecticut and Rhode Island under the immediate control of the crown. Early in 1694 Bulkley published a pamphlet at New York in support of Fletcher's claims and policy.[3]

James Fitch, a justice of the peace of New London, a vigorous radical and man of great activity in the politics, both local and general, of Connecticut, was Bulkley's chief opponent. It was in answer to two publications of Fitch —

[1] Colls. of Conn. Hist. Soc., I.

[2] *Ibid.*, III. The arguments which were elaborated into this book are in "Some Objections against the Pretended Government in Connecticut," a paper which accompanied an address from the malcontents to the crown, in 1692. N. Y. Col. Docs., III, 849.

[3] It was entitled, "Some Seasonable Considerations for the Good People of Connecticut." No copy of it is known to exist, but a reply to it, under the title, "Connecticut Vindicated from the Abuses of a Pamphlet," etc., is reprinted in Colls. of Conn. Hist. Soc., I.

no longer known to exist — that Bulkley issued his first pamphlet. But of greater importance was the fact that Fitch and such other local magistrates as Stanley and Steele of Hartford took the lead and summoned a court of election at Hartford for May 9, 1689.[1] When the freemen met there was doubt in the minds of many as to what course should be pursued. They had not been legally summoned, for there were no magistrates in office who had authority to do this. After a night had passed a meeting was held on the green. There was a somewhat tumultuous vote, the result of which was doubtful, and further consultation was held indoors. This the leaders had well in hand and a vote was had to restore the former governor, deputy and assistants in a body and the oaths were at once administered to them. Robert Treat was thus restored to the governorship. The general court was organized and business resumed according to the old method. William and Mary were proclaimed. The forty shilling franchise for freemen of good character was introduced and minor changes were made in the method of nominating for office. The war came immediately to occupy much of the attention both of the general court and of the magistrates.

By the beginning of 1690 two addresses to the crown had been sent, containing strong expressions of loyalty and intended to secure express recognition for what had been done. William Whiting, of London, the former attorney of the colony, was employed to solicit a favorable response to the first of these, and in the absence of any accredited agent, Increase Mather left the second at the office of the secretary of state. Presumably because of the rather too frank criticism of the Andros régime and justification of the resumption of charter government, the first address was not presented, while the second brief and non-committal statement was never formally presented. Therefore express approval of the course pursued by Connecticut was never given.[2]

This, however, was hardly necessary, for the attorney and solicitor general, in August, 1690, expressed the opinion that

[1] The only contemporary account of these events is in Bulkeley's "Will and Doom." Colls. of Conn. Hist. Soc., III, 155 *et seq.*; Conn. Col. Recs., III, app.

[2] Colls. Conn. Hist. Soc., III, 164; Conn. Col. Recs., III, 469; IV, 17.

the charter had not been invalidated by submission and that the corporation might lawfully execute the powers thereby granted.[1]

But in 1693, when the right of the colony to control its militia was seriously challenged, an address in support of this right was prepared and Fitz-John Winthrop was appointed as agent to present it. He was carefully instructed to explain the issue in all its bearings and to show of what vital importance it was to the colony.[2] He remained in England until 1697, during which time, probably in informal association with Sir Henry Ashurst, he not only successfully performed his immediate errand, but protected the colony against a repetition of the offensive instructions to Lord Bellomont. Soon after Winthrop's return Ashurst was appointed agent and continued to serve the colony for many years thereafter. Thus regular intercourse between it and the home government was resumed and maintained.

While Winthrop was absent the government of Connecticut was conducted in accordance with its traditional methods and without important change. The payment of taxes and the obligation of military service were enforced with a vigor made necessary by the presence of war. A watchful care was maintained over the towns, disputes between them concerning boundaries or within them over church affairs or the election of militia officers were inquired into and settled. In connection with its jurisdiction over the unsettled lands of the colony, as well as over trade with the Indians in land and commodities, the formation of new towns was carefully superintended by the general court. Disorder and vice in all forms were repressed, and in the fear of the Lord and the interest of the established Puritan faith the formation of new churches and the settling of an able ministry were objects of special care. So too was the maintenance of common schools in the towns, in order that all might be taught to read and especially to read the Bible. The need of a trained and orthodox ministry which should divine the truth aright kept alive also a demand for instruction in the ancient languages,

---

[1] Trumbull, *op. cit.*, I, 407; Cal. St. P. Col.
[2] Conn. Col. Recs., IV, 102, 232; Cal. St. P. Col., 1693–6, pp. 155, 243; Trumbull, I, 411; Winthrop Papers, 6 Mass. Hist. Colls., III, 18 *et seq.*

though for some years to come it was necessary to depend upon graduates of Harvard for filling the pulpits of the colony. The magistracy of the colony — governor, deputy governor, board of assistants, secretary and treasurer — was annually filled by a process of nomination by the freemen in the towns and final election of the incumbents from a list of the twenty who had received the largest vote in the colony. The governor, assistants and deputies still met together in one board, and during recesses of the general court the governor and assistants were expressly empowered every year to perform the duties of an executive. Until 1697 the general court still freely heard appeals in civil and criminal cases and transacted much probate business, but in that year appeals to it in civil cases were forbidden. Petitions for legislative or administrative action on a considerable variety of subjects were received. The group of leaders among the deputies, combined with the magistrates, kept the affairs of the colony well in hand and it acted substantially as a unit according to a tradition which, in common with Massachusetts, it had inherited from the founders of the first generation.[1] Gershom Bulkley and a little group of sympathizers, some of whom were not freemen, continued to protest against this in letters to Governor Fletcher or through other channels which were sure to convey their complaints to England. As Bulkley considered the existing government unconstitutional, all its acts to him seemed arbitrary, mere " will and doom," as the title of his book indicated. But it was not necessary for one to deny the constitutionality of the Connecticut government to feel that it was very much of a close corporation, whose mission was conceived to be not merely to guard the safety and well-being of the inhabitants of the colony, but to uphold a narrow orthodoxy and a rigid morality, neither of which was the outgrowth of broad culture or a lively human sympathy. Assaults upon this fortress could be made from outside, as had been made in the case of Massachusetts, and the complaints of Bulkley and his friends struck one note

---

[1] Abundant proof of these statements may be found in Vol. IV, of the Conn. Col. Recs. A good statement of the spirit and policy of Connecticut is in an address of the representatives to Governor Winthrop in 1699, 6 Mass. Hist. Colls. III, 41.

in the general chorus of accusation against proprieties and corporations which cherished such rigid independence, but little impression had yet been made in Connecticut.

The return of Fitz-John Winthrop and his immediate election to the governorship, an event which was about contemporaneous with the arrival of Lord Bellomont, was held not only to confirm the better traditions of Connecticut but to improve her prospects with the home government. Conservatives seem to have feared that the colony was becoming too democratic and factions too powerful,[1] and that the presence in the governorship of a member of the Winthrop family who had already rendered valuable service would steady affairs. His election was soon followed — in 1698 — by the separation of the general court into two houses.[2] The amount of business done increased. The clerk began to incorporate the text of many laws in the journal of the court and the preparation of a printed collection of laws, to be sent to the privy council, was undertaken. The title of marshal was changed to sheriff both for the colony at large and in the counties. The office of justice of the peace in the counties was created.[3] "There are two things effected since your Honor came to the Government," wrote Samuel Willis to Winthrop in 1699, "which I judge will much conduce to the wellfare of the Colony if they be continued: That the Magistrates and Deputies sitt distinct and that the Justices be stated and commissioned & not annually chosen, which will much strengthen the Government, when they are not at the dispose of the arbitrary humors of the people, and yet subject to be called to accompt by the General Court or to be displaced for delinquency."[4]

The Winthrop interest, both in local and colony affairs, was steadily opposed by James Fitch and a minority who supported him. One of the sources of this trouble lay in disputes over the so-called Quinebaug lands, which lay north of New London and later were formed into the towns of Plainfield and Canterbury. Disputes between Fitch and the Winthrops

---

[1] Letters of Willis and Woodbridge in 6 Mass. Hist. Colls. III, 31, 33.
[2] Conn. Col. Recs. IV, 267.
[3] *Ibid.*, 235, 270, 285.
[4] 6 Mass. Hist. Colls., III, 44.

over this territory occasioned frequent resort to the courts. In 1702 it was feared that Fitch and his friends were gaining an interest in the two houses of assembly which was dangerous to the ascendancy of the governor's interest and the removal of his brother, Wait Winthrop, from Boston into the colony was considered desirable.[1] In the boundary dispute with Rhode Island Fitch was believed to be betraying the interests of Connecticut, and also he was notoriously in sympathy with Palmes and Hallam, the parties in the famous suits against the Winthrops which were being appealed to England. It was feared that if the combination was allowed to grow an application would be made to fix the establishment of a British court of appeals in New England, to the great weakening of the charter government. Fitch, who was the eldest son of the first minister of Norwich and son-in-law of Major John Mason, naturally had great influence with the Mohegan Indians and large interest in their lands. As an Indian negotiator and speculator in wild lands there is some analogy between him and Robert Livingston of Albany fame. In his ardent and somewhat quarrelsome nature, which was repeatedly shown in his encounters with the Winthrops and Saltonstalls who ran Connecticut politics and prospered thereby, he somewhat resembled the elder Lewis Morris. That his activities ever imperilled the interests of Connecticut it is absurd to suppose. At most they occasioned only temporary anxieties to its ruling clique, largely in reference to their private property interests.[2]

As was true of the Puritan colonies in the seventeenth century, so it continued to be true of Connecticut in the eighteenth that its governors, deputy governors and other magistrates were usually continued in office by successive elections for many years. This was true in the case of Fitz-John Winthrop, who was continued in the office of governor until his death in 1707.[3] Gurdon Saltonstall, the former minister of the church at New London, the neighbor and able

[1] 6 Mass. Hist. Colls., III, 64, 313; V, 111; Conn. Col. Recs., IV, 391, 430, 535.

[2] An interesting sketch of Fitch is given by Miss Larned in her Historic Gleanings in Windham County. See also Caulkins, History of Norwich, 137. To Yale College Fitch gave the glass and nails for its first edifice and 637 acres of land.　　　　[3] Conn. Recs., VI, 38.

supporter of the views and policy of the Winthrops, was now elected to the office and continued to hold it with distinction until his death in 1724. During most of this time Nathan Gold held the office of deputy governor, while the names of Pitkin, Allyn, Treat, Talcott, Stanley, Haynes and others appear with the greatest regularity in the lists of assistants and of justices in the courts. Toward the close of Saltonstall's career Jonathan Law and Roger Walcott had risen to prominence. Among the representatives the names of leading families in the various towns appear with as great regularity, the speakership affording a convenient step from which to reach the council or other high official position.

Saltonstall was a man of prominent family, possessed of a fine presence and address, a good representative of the clergy of those days. His governorship, as we shall see, left a deep impress upon the ecclesiastical system of Connecticut.[1] After the death of Saltonstall Joseph Talcott, of Hartford, and Jonathan Law, of Milford, held the governorship, the former from 1724 to his death in 1741 and the latter from 1741 to 1750, he also dying in office. Talcott's ancestors had been prominent in military and administrative offices in the colony from its foundation, and Joseph, the governor, was the first native of Connecticut to hold that office. Law was a graduate of Harvard and by profession a lawyer of marked ability. Talcott was not college educated, but was active in the management of school, church and town affairs at Hartford throughout his early life. His services in the militia were particularly active. Through the positions of deputy, speaker, member of the council and deputy governor he rose by steady gradations to the office of governor. Law's ascent was similar, though with more emphasis on legal service and judicial office than on the military.[2]

[1] In Conn. Mss. Recs., Civil Officers, under date of May 10, 1717, is a long and able speech made by Saltonstall to the general court in reply to criticisms and justification of his course in public affairs. He challenged their votes at the election which had just been held, stood by his record as in harmony with the established traditions of the colony and expressed his determination not to take the oath of office if the court considered the attacks which had been made upon him to have been justified. It is needless to say that he was sworn in without a voice being raised in opposition.

[2] See the sketches of the lives of Talcott and Law in the printed editions of their Papers, Colls. of Conn. Hist. Soc.

In the careers of these three governors, Saltonstall, Talcott and Law, we have representatives of the clerical, the military and administrative and the legal types at their best in Connecticut government, and it was under their lead that this colony held on its steady course during almost the first half of the eighteenth century. Had Connecticut been at all sectional, one might have laid emphasis on the fact that the first of these came from New London, the second from Hartford, the third from New Haven county, but little or no significance attaches to that because sectionalism was almost entirely absent in Connecticut. No other of the thirteen colonies was so compact and uniform in its structure and development as this. It had no commercial centres of special importance, no landed and trading aristocracy like the colonies to the west and south of it. The gradations of wealth among her population — which was almost purely British — were moderate and the majority of farmers within it was overwhelming. Ecclesiastical unity and conformity to the general type of Puritan culture and life were rigidly maintained. The topography of Connecticut also and the way in which its settlement was completed, under the control of its government and by expansion eastward and westward from the centre, furnished no opportunity for sectional strife. With such characteristics and a highly developed system of self-government the steady and peaceful growth of Connecticut was assured.

Much that is ill founded and mythical has doubtless been written about the " blue laws " of Connecticut, but, as usual, the myth has rested on a basis of truth. To anyone who reviews the legislation of that colony in the eighteenth century concerning public and private morals it will be evident that the Puritan rigidity of the previous century in all that related to the observance of the Sabbath, family discipline, the repression not only of drunkenness and the grosser forms of immorality but of innocent and profitable diversion, was successfully maintained.[1] Both the churches and the civil power were united in this work in a way which will fully appear when we come to consider the ecclesiastical policy of

[1] A study of the Conn. Col. Recs., vols. IV to X, will furnish abundant illustration of this fact.

the period. Beyond any other colony of the time the general court interested itself in matters of this kind and both led and supported the policy of the clergy. Typical of this relation was the response, in 1715, of the general association of the churches to a recommendation of the general court to inquire into the causes of certain untoward events and tendencies which indicated that God was displeased and that " the glory is departed from us." [1] The diagnosis furnished by the clergy was that the evils were due to the want of Bibles in particular families, to the neglect of public worship and of catechizing, to defects in family government, to tale bearing and defamation, to contempt of authority and order, to intemperance and to " irregularity in comutative justice." A detailed act was therefore passed requiring officials, executive and judicial, to remedy these defects and enforce the laws which bore upon the evils of which complaint was made. There can be no doubt but that the already sober communities of this colony were presently made to feel the necessity of becoming more serious by such pressure, social and political, as the clergy and magistrates could bring to bear. This was in the midst of the administration of Saltonstall and it was only two years later when he felt called upon to defend himself against the charge of being too strict.

As compared with other colonies, there is much in the law book of Connecticut about schools and in promotion of common and higher education. The same thing is true of Massachusetts and it properly stands to the credit of both these colonies. But the knowledge which was imparted in these schools was subordinated in all possible ways to the dominant system of belief concerning things religious. It floated harmlessly about in a sea of dogmatism. It was used as an instrument to support the prevalent orthodoxy and infinite pains were taken to see that it did no harm to the cause it was intended to uphold. The schools, like the government and the churches, were devoted to securing acceptance of the well-defined system of Puritan belief and conduct. All manifestations of disorder were rigidly suppressed. In the early eighteenth century Connecticut, owing to its comparative seclusion and its homogeneity, even surpassed Mas-

[1] Conn. Recs., V, 436, 529.

sachusetts in these characteristics. Prior to about 1740 she was culturally as much a unit as Massachusetts was during the three decades or so before the recall of its charter. Her town and colony governments constituted a system of little oligarchies or well-organized groups, which worked together with a high degree of harmony for a common and well-understood end. Expansion was effected by the division of existing groups and the formation of new ones in agreement with familiar models. The general court, which comprised within itself or under its control the executive and judicial organs of government as well, possessed a compactness quite in harmony with the system as a whole. A council, specially selected and constituted, assisted the governor in the management of business during recesses of the general court.[1] By a system of nominations or primary elections held in the towns in the autumn, followed by a final choice in the court of election in May out of the list of nominees sent in from the towns, the chief executive offices were filled.[2] To such an extent were elements of opposition lacking that the holding of primary elections — the substitute here for the proxy system in Massachusetts under the first charter — did not endanger the result. So far as opinions were concerned, the average freeman was as orthodox as the leaders, though many of them did not know as much or were more indifferent. As a rule freemen were admitted in open town meeting and the lists of them were kept in their native towns or in the office of the secretary of the colony or both.[3] Adequate means also existed, or were devised, when a riotous disposition showed itself, for maintaining discipline in town meetings and punishing the disorderly. Under such social conditions as existed in Connecticut annual elections were consistent with great steadiness of policy and permanence of official tenure. The evidence of this has always been abundantly recognized in the history of the Puritan colonies. The most frequent and embittered conflicts occurred in towns over the election of militia officers and the location of meetinghouses.[4] But these

[1] Conn. Recs., V, 84, and many other entries.
[2] *Ibid.*, 31, 41, 522, 547, and similar entries throughout the period.
[3] Conn. Rec., VII, 245, 259.
[4] See abundant material concerning these not only in the Colonial Records, but in the Conn. Mss. Records, Militia.

were largely local and sectional in origin and resulted from the efforts of newly settled villages to separate or obtain equal rights with the present settlements. When these disputes were brought before the magistrates of the colony or the general court they were adjusted without serious difficulty. The general court, though it employed few standing committees, had much business brought before it by petitions and memorials from the towns, and these matters appear frequently among them.

During the second intercolonial war, with Dudley using his influence fully against the proprieties on the one side and Cornbury on the other, Connecticut and Rhode Island were kept steadily on the defensive. The story of these struggles has been told in another connection. But at the same time war was being actively prosecuted and Connecticut in particular felt her obligation to do her duty against the Catholic French and their Indian allies. Her boundary dispute with Massachusetts was not yet settled, and an attitude of wariness toward the larger colony which she had inherited from the seventeenth century had still to be maintained. This all combined to make and continue her diplomatic attitude toward the demands of New York as well as Massachusetts for aid. As has been shown in the history of the first two colonial wars, Connecticut confined herself practically to the defence of the valley immediately to the north of her, contributing however her full share to the expeditions against Canada, the plans of which originated in England.[1] The official group which steadied and controlled its affairs kept it true to this line of conduct throughout King Philip's war and the first two conflicts with the French. When Râle's War came Connecticut chose to treat it as exclusively an affair of northeastern New England and declined to join in except so far as was necessary for the protection of its own frontier.[2]

Under such conditions as have been described it was inevitable that the corporate system should be continued without essential change unless such change was forced upon the

---

[1] See e.g. Conn. Recs., V, 18.

[2] Conn. Recs., VI, 503; Talcott Papers, I, 33, 43; Con. Recs., Mss. War III, fol. 211 et seq.

colony by the imperial government. As time passed the
charter was regarded with increasing veneration as the foundation of the colony's liberties. After the accession of the
Hanoverian family to the throne the perils which for a
generation had threatened it abated for a time. But as the
question of colonial currency grew in importance and the
demand of the crown for the submission of laws and the
danger from appeals became more threatening, fears began
again to be felt that the charter was in danger. But the
outbreak of the war with Spain and then with France in the
fourth decade of the century laid that spectre, for during the
next twenty years the energies of all were devoted to the
war and the aid of the colonies was too valuable to be imperilled by a constitutional conflict. A notable list of colonial agents, including, after the death of Ashurst, the names
of Dummer, Wilks, Palmes and Partridge, watched the interests and defended the course of Connecticut in England,
rendering a service at times scarcely less important than that
of the governor. These same men also, as we know, were
often concerned in the defence of proprietary rights in general and in the cause of a whole group of colonies.

The intercolonial wars furnished the occasion for Connecticut, like the other colonies, to embark upon the issue of bills
of credit. In this policy, as in many other affairs, she
followed the lead of Massachusetts, though she did not issue
bills so early or recklessly as did the Bay Colony. The
excesses of liberty in which Rhode Island indulged Connecticut avoided in the issue of paper, as she did in other important lines of activity. As there was nothing peculiar in the
experience of Connecticut with bills of credit and as they
did not essentially modify the course of her history, there is
no occasion for dwelling upon the subject at special length
in this place. It was not until 1709, when under the influence of the expeditions at the close of the second war so
many colonies began the issue of paper, that Connecticut put
out her first bills of credit.[1] The bills of neighboring colonies
were already beginning to circulate within her borders and the
example which they had set it was easy and natural to follow.

[1] See the excellent monograph by Bronson on Connecticut Currency in
Papers of New Haven Hist. Soc., I; Trumbull, Hist. of Conn., II.

In her earlier legislation upon this subject Connecticut was conservative both as to the amounts issued and provision for redemption. The periods set for redemption were short and the taxes which were regularly imposed for the purpose were doubtless collected with tolerable promptness. Since Connecticut was at peace from 1713 to 1740, there was no excuse for any other course of conduct. Payments in kind or " country pay " was largely abandoned as the result of the introduction of bills of credit, since the laws required that rates must be paid in bills or coin. For about a decade the bills were made legal tender only in the payment of public dues. Then, in 1718, by an act that was skilfully worded in order to soften the impression it might make on the home government, debtors were declared exempt from prosecution if they tendered bills in payment of private debts contracted after July, 1709. This law was continued in force until 1735.

The advocates of paper in Connecticut increased with the growth of the craze elsewhere. Reference has been made in another connection to the origin of the " New London Society for Trade and Commerce " and its issue of a private " bank " of paper. The " society," or local, private or semi-public associations for various purposes, as we shall see, had unusual prominence in Connecticut life, and this was an example of that genus which was devoted to the issue on loan of bills of credit. Its brief existence helped to accustom the Connecticut mind to the issue of " banks " of paper on loan and the general court indulged to an extent in this practice. Though, as usual, fear for the security of her charter made her wary, the pressure of debtors and of the advocates of paper increased and frequent issues continued. Depreciation became serious, silver, in terms of Connecticut bills, rising from 8s. per oz. in 1708 to 32s. in 1745. In 1739, before the outbreak of war, it had risen to 26s. The war checked the agitation against colonial paper in England and furnished an effective argument to its advocates in the colonies. Various financial difficulties, with an increase of debtors and of the demand for more money, were occasioned and nourished by every successive issue. " New tenor " bills were resorted to in 1740. During the war which followed Connecticut was financed upon the paper basis. Unlike Massachusetts, she failed to effect a complete resumption of specie payments with the help of the sum of nearly £29,000 which was granted her as a part of the reimbursement for her share in the expedition against Louisbourg,[1] and hence was compelled to redeem her issues as best she might under the compulsion of the prohibitory act of parliament of 1751.

One of the most important features of Connecticut history in the eighteenth century, in common with that of the other New England colonies, was the expansion of settlement. This was steadily going on in all parts of the colonies where unsettled territory existed. By this means unoccupied spaces were filled and new towns formed. Where Indians still survived, their relations with the whites had to be readjusted and their claims extinguished. Thus originated the famous Mohegan controversy, which dragged through most of the century. Settlement in Connecticut expanded eastward to meet the slow advance westward in Rhode Island. In this way Windham county, which then included all the eastern part of the colony, was settled. In both colonies towns were planted first along the shore of Long Island sound and later in the interior. As population crept northward its advance made imperative the settling of the Massachusetts boundary and the fixing of the northwest limit of Rhode Island.

But the largest unsettled area lay in the western part of the colony, was known as the " western lands," and coincided approximately with the modern county of Litchfield.[2] This was a rugged and hilly country, heavily wooded, forming, like the Berkshire region to the north which was being settled at the same time by Massachusetts, the broad and high watershed between the valleys of the Connecticut and the Hudson. The Housatonic, a river of secondary importance, ran through the middle of this region. In early colonial times Indians of the Algonkin family had occupied it, but it is supposed that they suffered greatly from the slaughter which accompanied the close of Philip's war. At any rate, before the

---

[1] The exact amount paid was £28,863, 19s. 1d. Considerable information concerning the details of this transaction is given in the correspondence of Governor Law with Eliakim Palmer and Richard Partridge, the agents at the time in England. Law Papers, IV, Colls. Conn. Hist. Soc.

[2] Trumbull, II, 81–144; Conn. Col. Recs., VI, VII and VIII. Mead, Conn. as a Corporate Colony, 69 *et seq.*

beginning of the eighteenth century the region had been largely cleared of Indians.

In anticipation of the loss of the colony charter and of the evil times which came under Andros, this region was granted by the general court to the towns of Hartford and Windsor. It lay unimproved until 1719, when Litchfield was settled and organized as a town.[1] But in making this grant the court at the same time rescinded the much larger grant which had previously been made to the two towns. This stirred up opposition, especially in Hartford, and led in 1722 to the bestowment upon the county sheriff of express powers to command the assistance of all the people for the suppression of riots.[2] In 1726 a compromise was agreed to, according to which the territory was divided between the colony and the two towns. The colony took the section which lay along the Housatonic river and left to the towns the territory to the eastward which abutted more closely upon the areas which had already been settled. In 1732 and the year following, under authority of an act of assembly, the towns of Hartford and Windsor divided their portion of the western lands. In the share which went to Hartford the towns of Hartland, Winchester and New Hartford were created, from the share of Windsor were carved out Colebrook, Barkhamstead and Torrington, while Harwinton was made up equally from land belonging to both of the original towns. As actual settlers sufficient in numbers for the organization of local government within these tracts were not available for a long time to come, they were treated as areas open for settlement. To this end both Hartford and Windsor were authorized to divide their inhabitants into as many groups of proprietors as they had outlying towns. These were empowered to hold meetings, choose a clerk, appoint agents or attorneys to prosecute or defend their rights, lay rates upon themselves to meet necessary expenses and provide for the division and improvement of the lands under their charge. In contrast to the older towns of New England these towns of western Connecticut began their existence under the control of non-resident proprietors or land companies. These at their meetings

[1] Conn. Col. Recs., VI, 127.
[2] Ibid., 333. Trumbull, II, 96; Boyd, Annals of Winchester, 11.

in Hartford and Windsor administered the affairs of the remote districts as if they were dependencies.[1]

In 1727 the colony took action concerning its share of the western lands.[2]  Five townships were laid out east of the Housatonic river, Norfolk, Canaan, Goshen, Cornwall and Kent, and two on the west, Sharon and Salisbury.  It was provided that each of these should be sold at public auction in certain specified towns of the colony.  Six or seven towns were divided into fifty-three " rights " or shares and the other into twenty-five.  Of these " rights " one in each town was reserved for the use of the ministry, one as a gratuity to the first minister and one for the support of the town school.  The remaining rights were sold to the highest bidders, though certain minimum prices were set by the court, varying from £30 to £60, below which the shares were not to be sold.  Purchasers must also be residents of the colony and within three years must clear and fence at least six acres of land and build and finish a house of specified dimensions.  The purchasers and settlers came from the older towns of the colony and by the usual steps town government, with the management of the common lands, was developed.  In this way settlement was extended westward to the border of the colony.

After the destruction of the Narragansett tribe during Philip's War the subject of Indian relations in New England south of the latitude of the Merrimac river sank into insignificance.  Of the tribes which had dwelt in that region only fragments remained, some living on reservations and others not, but all falling deeper into sloth and immorality.  Objects of contempt, or at best of pity, on the part of the whites, who were powerless to do anything of real value for their redemption, the Indians of that region had succumbed, before the date of the American Revolution, before the advance of an alien people with whom it was impossible for them to assimilate.  Among the records of the time, especially in Connecticut, appears much correspondence concerning the small groups of natives who survived,[3] but this was only

[1] Conn. Col. Recs., VII, 387, 445.

[2] *Ibid.*, 343; VIII, 135, 334, 392, 421.  Mead, *op. cit.*, 71.

[3] Conn. Col. Mss., Indians; De Forest, Indians of Conn., 347 *et seq.*, 409. Many references in Conn. Col. Recs.

an incident of the steady advance of English settlement and of the process through which the Indians were passing to ultimate extinction. Those who were settled on reservations were in some respects more exposed to decay than were those who still roamed the hills. About 1740 an interesting effort was made by a party of Moravians to christianize the Indians who lived in the extreme northwestern part of Connecticut, but its chief result was the migration of a few of their converts to Pennsylvania. The education of Samson Occom, which began under the Rev. Eleazar Wheelock at Lebanon in 1743, was an isolated result of the " Great Awakening," but it was followed a decade later by the founding of a small Indian school which developed into Dartmouth College, an interesting event in the cultural history of America but of slight importance in the history of the red man.[1]

But these Mohegans succeeded in winning for their name a very prominent place in Connecticut annals. This was not due to any strength or merit of their own, for they were only a branch of the Pequots, the first tribe to receive a crushing blow at the hand of the New England colonists. But it arose from the location of the Mohegan lands in the midst of the colony and from the alliance which Uncas, their sachem, was fortunate enough to arrange with the English. This relation was continued by Owaneco and his other descendants, though after a time the line divided and rival claimants of the chieftainship became allies in interest of competing parties among the English. The Mohegan lands lay in the original New London and Windham counties, comprising parts or all of such towns as New London, Norwich, Windham, Lebanon, Canterbury, Colchester. A multitude of grants, large and small, were obtained from the Indians of land in this region, ranging over a period of nearly a century and from their indefinite and overlapping boundaries involving great confusion. Some of the grants were gifts, others were procured by fraud; many were made when the chiefs were drunk, and in general they were the tools of the settlers rather than equal competitors in a bargain. In all these respects the conditions were substantially the same as those which existed in the colonies to the west and south, except

[1] De Forest, 454; Love, Life of Samson Occom.

that the areas of land involved were much smaller. The Puritan conscience did not prohibit speculating in wild lands and it was the greed of gain from this source which gave rise to the prolonged controversy known as the Mohegan case.[1]

The parties to this dispute were Captain John Mason and his heirs *versus* the government of Connecticut. Mason was the commander of the English in their victorious struggle with the Pequots and was one of the settlers of Norwich. His descendants continued to live in southeastern Connecticut. The government of the colony during all the last half of the seventeenth century, as we have seen, was largely controlled by the Winthrop family and their supporters. During the life of the first Winthrop no opposition to this developed. But after 1689 we have seen a small group of loyalist critics of Connecticut and its chartered government develop, who naturally formed such connection as they could with imperialists in England, New York and elsewhere. Fitch, Palmes and Hallam, all of whom were members of this group, were inhabitants of New London or vicinity. There also was the residence of the Winthrops and of Rev. Gurdon Saltonstall, their ablest supporter. The estates which all these men and their families possessed came largely from Mohegan lands. In many localities, as did Fitch and Winthrop for Quinebaug lands, they became competing claimants and their disputes over land and bounds often found their way into court. The land of the north parish of New London was involved in these disputes, as was much of Norwich and larger areas in the more distant towns. The remnant of the Mohegans lived between New London and Norwich and the territory of the outlying towns had been their hunting grounds at least in their nominal possession.

As in the case of the other colonies and of the home government, the principle asserted by Connecticut was that all purchases from the Indians should be made by the colony government and grants should in all cases be derived from it. Had this been lived up to, there would have been no

---

[1] Conn. Col. Recs., throughout; Talcott Papers in Coll. of Conn. Hist. Soc., IV and V; Winthrop Papers, 6 Coll. Mass. Hist. Soc. III; Conn. Hist. Mss.; De Forest, Indians of Conn.; Trumbull, History of Conn.; Larned, Hist. of New London; Caulkins, History of Norwich.

Mohegan case, except the complaints of private injustice or of white encroachment in general which the weaker race was everywhere raising. But nowhere was the principle of exclusive government control of Indian relations lived up to, and it was the failure to do this in Connecticut which led to the disputes over Mohegan lands.

In 1640 Uncas, on behalf of his people, granted to Connecticut all the land which belonged to them, "which they may hereafter dispose of as their own," either by settling plantations or otherwise, reserving for his own use that ground which the Mohegans had planted and were actually using. As usual, the price which was paid for this large grant was ridiculously small — only a few yards of trading cloth, with some stockings and other small wares — but the English insisted that it was a *bona fide* sale. From an early time John Mason was a special friend and adviser of the Mohegans. Toward the end of his life and especially in the minds of his heirs this developed into the idea of a trusteeship. An important stage in this development was marked by transactions of 1659 and 1660, by which Uncas deeded all that remained of Mohegan lands to Mason, his heirs and assigns, forever, but Mason, as deputy governor, surrendered them to the colony. Various other confused transactions followed in later years which it is impossible to reconcile either with the view that Mason was acting as agent for the colony or for the Indians. Meantime the guardianship of the Masons over the Indians became so intimate that it tended to change their trusteeship over the Mohegan lands into ownership. Hence it was that finally the Masons and their supporters claimed with reference to these lands, that only jurisdiction had been transferred to the colony, while ownership remained with the Indians, this right to be practically exercised by the Masons and their friends. With the successive formation of towns in the section and the consequent reduction of the area of Mohegan land which was free to the Indians the situation became more acute and a settlement more imperative.

Governor Joseph Dudley, of Massachusetts, was said to be an investor in Connecticut lands, though he denied it; but, as we have seen, he was deeply engaged in schemes for the recall of charters, especially those of Connecticut and Rhode Island. He had preferred a long and serious indictment against them and was showing a persistent activity in support of it somewhat like Randolph. In both private and public affairs his relations with the Winthrops were hostile. Hallam and Palmes, who were appealing to England against Connecticut on other issues, took up also that of the Mohegans and complaints brought this matter to the attention of the British government. In 1705, without notification or warning to Connecticut, a royal commission was issued to Dudley and ten others to hear and determine the question of the Mohegan lands, subject to the right of appeal to the crown by either party. The fact that, in addition to Dudley and Deputy Governor Povey of Massachusetts, Edward Palmes, Thomas Brinley, Jahleel Brenton and Nathaniel Byfield were among its members would indicate that the animus of this body was almost sure to be hostile to Connecticut. That colony appointed commissioners to present evidence before the court in case its intent proved to be simply to inquire and report to the English government. But as it at once appeared that its design was to determine the case, the Connecticut men protested against such action as a violation of their charter and withdrew. Neither did any private parties present evidence on the Connecticut side. The commission however proceeded to an *ex parte* hearing, which lasted for one day only, and decided in favor of the claims of the Mohegans in general and especially in the case of three large grants which, since the death of Uncas, had been made in the towns of Lyme and Colchester and between New London and Norwich. A bill of £573 was filed against the colony, and with this the commission adjourned.[1]

Connecticut at once made an informal appeal against this action, in the form of a strong letter to Ashurst, its agent, but no security was given to prosecute an appeal in the regular way. As this was about the time when the bill of 1706 for the recall of all proprietary charters was being introduced into Parliament, the situation was critical. Dudley had many and influential sympathizers and he had

[1] Trumbull, I, 446; Talcott Papers, Colls. Conn. Hist. Soc., V, 20, 141–146; De Forest, 310.

doubtless managed the business of the commission substantially as had been intended. At any rate, Ashurst had to pledge security for a formal appeal himself and, with the aid of several able counsel, support the case with the best of his ability in order to save the day for Connecticut.[1] He refers to Blathwayt as having favored Dudley. The fact that Connecticut did not submit evidence to the commission, that it appeared to have dealt as a separate nation with the Mohegans, that reasonable compensation did not seem to have been given them for their lands, in addition to the informality of its appeal, told against the colony. But Ashurst won, though the colony had to appropriate a handsome sum to pay the expenses of its agent. A commission of review was granted, but as Connecticut had little interest in prosecuting the affair, it was never used. John Mason, the guardian of the Indians, became ill and eventually resigned his guardianship to appointees of the colony. The Winthrops, Saltonstall and other Connecticut magistrates strengthened their hold upon the Indian situation, while the crisis by which proprietary government had been threatened passed away. Dudley ceased to interfere with the liberties of Connecticut, and lands could easily be secured by all parties from the improvident Mohegans. Out of a tract which had been sequestered for the permanent use of the tribe, about five thousand acres were entailed upon them forever by the government of Connecticut.

When the Mohegan case became prominent again, Oweneco and several others of "royal" blood in the tribe had died and a dispute had arisen over the right of succession to the tawdry dignity of sachem. Ben Uncas, reputed to have been a younger and illegitimate son of the first Uncas, was elected sachem. But the Masons, in order better to advance their claims to land and authority over the remnant of the tribe, supported Mamohet, a rival claimant. Two factions were formed in the tribe, between which a bitter contest was waged for thirty or forty years, the government of Connecticut and the Masons supporting each its rival party. In 1735 the Masons took Mamohet with them to England, where they induced the government to issue, two years later, another

[1] Winthrop Papers, 6 Mass. Hist. Colls., III, 304–310, 324–327, 349, 377.

commission of review.[1]  Joseph Talcott was now governor of Connecticut and Francis Wilks was agent.  The latter sought to convince the board of trade that a revival of the controversy after so long a time would unsettle the established property rights of many people and was not necessary in the interests of the Indians who still had sufficient land and were satisfied.  Commissions of review were favors and not rights and the issue of one after so long a time was unprecedented.  But these arguments did not prevail and a commission was appointed consisting of Governor Clark and the council of New York and Governor John Wanton and the assistants of Rhode Island.  Of this body two New York councillors, Philip Van Cortlandt and David Horsmanden, and the governor and six assistants from Rhode Island, met at Norwich in 1738.  Philip Van Cortlandt was chosen president.  Mason and the Indians had engaged William Shirley, soon to be governor of Massachusetts, and William Bollan, his son-in-law, as counsel.  The proceedings turned almost wholly on the first question which was brought up — who was legally the sachem of the Mohegans.  Mamohet had died in England and John Uncas was now the claimant supported by the Mason party.  From the first the Rhode Island members showed themselves decidedly favorable to the claims of Connecticut.  After an examination of witnesses, the balance of whose opinions seemed to be in favor of the claim of John Uncas and that that of Ben Uncas was illegitimate, the court ruled that the latter was the true sachem.  Naturally also they negatived a motion of Shirley that a vote of the members of the tribe who were present should be taken on the question.[2]  Ben Uncas having been recognized as sachem, he discharged Shirley and Bollan and employed the Connecticut men in their places.  A motion that the Indians might be permitted to choose their counsel was voted down and Shirley and Bollan threw up the case and returned to Boston.  Van Cortlandt and Horsmanden, the leading New York members of the court, who had dissented from all its rulings, now pro-

---

[1] Talcott Papers, Colls. Conn. Hist. Soc., V, 14–23.

[2] De Forest, 328 *et seq.*; Talcott Papers, *loc. cit.*, 105, *et seq.*  An able defence of the case of Connecticut and of the general attitude of this court, by Governor Talcott is in the Talcott Papers, 195–208.

tested against it as unfair and collusive and retired. Governor John Wanton was made president and after a review of the Connecticut side of the case a decision wholly favorable to the claims of the colony was reached. The judgment of Dudley's court of 1705 was repealed.

The Mason party at once appealed and Van Cortlandt and Horsmanden sent a report of the irregular proceedings which had caused them to retire from the court. When this came before the board of trade, Wilks and Sharpe, who appeared for Connecticut in order to argue against the appeal, found an obstacle which it was impossible to overcome. The late commission had been appointed to review the action of the Dudley commission; but nothing appeared in the record to show that the proceedings of Dudley's court had been read or that any. notice had been taken of them. Whether this was the fact or that the omission, as was alleged, was the fault of the clerk, it was fatal to the contention of the agents. A new commission of review was ordered. Wilks then attempted to have Van Cortlandt and Horsmanden excluded as prejudiced parties. But it was decided to appoint the governors and councils of New York and New Jersey as the commissioners and the board thought it would be a hardship to exclude any members by name.[1]

The meetings of this commission were held at Norwich in July and August, 1743.[2] Cadwallader Colden, Philip Van Cortlandt, Daniel Horsmanden were present from New York and John Rodman and Robert Hunter Morris from New Jersey. Colden presided. William Smith of New York was counsel for Connecticut and William Bollan again appeared, this time as chief counsel, for Mason and the Indians. The case was argued ably and at length and much evidence was heard and examined. At the close three of the commissioners, Colden, Van Cortlandt and Rodman, concurred in a judgment, and Morris and Horsmanden recorded their dissent, though they far from agreed as to their reasons for it. As the majority of the court had agreed, its opinion was drawn up and filed as the judgment of the body. It was favorable in

---

[1] Talcott Papers, *op. cit.*, 327, 333.

[2] The Mohegan Petition, Mss. Library of Yale University; De Forest, 335, *et seq.* De Forest errs in reference to the Morris who was a commissioner. It was Robert Hunter Morris and not Lewis Morris.

every point to the contention of the government of Connecticut — that the original deed given by Uncas in 1640 was genuine; that Mason's surrender of 1660 — he then being deputy governor — in effect yielded up to the colony all the claims he had in Mohegan lands, provided the Indians should ever after have a sufficient quantity of land to plant on and he should retain from those lands a farm for his own use, both of which conditions had been fulfilled; that the royal charter of 1662 vested all the Mohegan lands in the governor and company and that thereafter they had only an equitable right to land enough for their subsistence and could not deed away such rights as Mason claimed to have received; that the tract of between four and five thousand acres which had been reserved under the name of sequestered lands was sufficient for the support of the Indians and that all the rest which they claimed had been legally bought from them by the English. Therefore the award of the Dudley commission was declared null, except so much as referred to the sequestered lands above referred to.[1] Horsmanden denied the authority of the deed of 1640 and believed the signatures on it to have been written by Governor Hopkins; and, even had it been genuine, the transactions subsequent to it had been such that it ought to be declared null. Morris accepted the deed as genuine, but thought that it gave to the governor and company of Connecticut the right of preemption over the Indian lands to the exclusion of other English and of the Dutch. He also held that property of the soil had been vested in Mason by the deed of August, 1659, and that in his surrender of the following year it was not his intention to convey that right, but simply to give the colony the right to govern the territory which had been conveyed to him. An appeal on behalf of the Indians was at once taken to the crown, Horsmanden sending over a copy at large of his opinion, which the commissioners refused to allow entered on the minutes.

The questions of the half-way covenant and of the consociation of churches occupied an even more prominent place in the history of Connecticut than in that of Massachusetts.[2]

---

[1] The decree of this body is printed in the Law Papers, Colls. Conn. Hist. Soc., XI, 102.

[2] The best general account of this is in M. L. Greene's Development of Religious Liberty in Connecticut. That book and Walker's Creeds of Congre-

Though New Haven, under the lead of Davenport, opposed the policy, that part of the colony which had developed from Saybrook and the River Towns committed itself to the more liberal, or, as the conservatives held, the looser policy as to church membership. Prominent men among its clergy welcomed the declaration in its favor which was made by the Boston conference of 1657 and the general court ordered copies of it to be distributed to all the churches. The custom, which was carried far in Connecticut, of the general court interfering in the quarrels of churches and regulating their affairs, had a secularizing tendency and opened the way for policies like those of the half-way covenant and consociation. After sentiment had been further growing for nearly a decade, in 1664 William Pitkin, a much esteemed Hartford official who had been born a member of the Church of England, petitioned the general court, on behalf of himself and six associates, to take into consideration the state of such as they, who were " as sheep scattered having no shepherd," and repeal any laws which forced them to contribute to the maintenance of any ministers or church officers who neglected or refused to baptize their children and take spiritual care of themselves and their families as members of the church.[1] This was substantially a repetition of the complaint made in Massachusetts by the Child memorial of 1646. And now Pitkin and his supporters referred to the king's letter of 1662, in which he had commanded that all persons of " good and honest lives and conversation " should be admitted to the Lord's Supper and their children to baptism. The response of the general court to Pitkin's appeal showed the trend of feeling in Connecticut and how conditions had changed since Massachusetts, in fear of Presbyterian triumph, had with such violence tried to suppress Child's petition. The court sent the petition to all the churches of Connecticut, with a request to consider whether it was its duty to order them to admit to fellowship all who were of honest and godly conversation and had a competent knowledge of the principles of religion and desired to join the churches and have their

---

gationalism, and the literature referred to in them, will prove a sufficient guide for the inquirer.    [1] Greene, 110.

children baptized.[1] Such children would then be under Christian care and nurture and when they grew up, if duly qualified, might be admitted to the Lord's Supper and to full membership in the churches.

With this action the decisive conflict in Connecticut began. Pitkin, on behalf of himself and several of his associates, applied for communion with the church at Hartford " in all the orderliness of Christ." This request was refused and a violent controversy arose over the baptism of children of non-communicants. In Windsor, Stratford and elsewhere similar disputes occurred. Newark, in New Jersey, was settled by conservatives from Branford, Guilford and New Haven who, under the lead of Abraham Pierson, moved thither to escape the consequences of the half-way covenant. In order to bring such disorders to an end, the general court at first undertook to call an " assembly " or synod but, as Massachusetts was too indifferent to participate, this fell through, and instead a committee was appointed of influential men in the colony to search out the rules for discipline and how far persons of " various apprehensions " might walk together in church fellowship. Upon the report of this committee, the court ordered that all persons approved as orthodox and sound in the fundamentals of the Christian religion " should have allowance of their persuasion and profession in church ways or assemblies without disturbance," but at the same time it approved the ecclesiastical system and policy which had hitherto been in existence in the colony.[2] This in effect, while holding out the prospect of toleration to dissentients, left the question to be fought out in the local churches. On the advice of the court the Hartford Church divided and a second church was founded. This example was followed in many other towns.

The policy of the half-way covenant made headway till it came to prevail in Connecticut, as it did in Massachusetts. The changing political conditions of the period of the Restoration, which made it difficult to maintain the early Puritan rigidity and exclusiveness, favored this change. The views of Stoddard with reference to the Lord's Supper were also widely influential in Connecticut. The effect of these views

[1] Conn. Recs., I, 437, 438.     [2] Conn. Recs., II.

and practices was to break down the sharp distinction between church and town which had previously existed and to merge the two more into one, thus creating a condition analogous to the European parish. There grew up about the nucleus of church members in the full sense of the term the " society," which also included the families that lived under the half-way covenant. They shared in the choice of ministers,[1] in the support of the church and the management of its property. The relation was analogous to that between proprietors and commoners in many of the towns. The merging of the two classes was greatly aided by the legislation which made the townsmen the electors of the minister,[2] while at the same time property qualifications took the place of moral or religious requirements as the prescribed conditions of admission to citizenship in the towns. The general court made the towns responsible for the payment of the salaries of their ministers and held them up to the obligation of assessing and collecting local rates for that purpose.[3] No town with impunity could neglect to maintain a settled minister. A logical step beyond this was taken in 1699, when it was enacted [4] that the individual so called and settled by the majority vote of any town, society or plantation should be accounted its lawful minister and all agreements concerning his maintenance should be binding on all the respective inhabitants. Where there was more than one society in a town, their respective bounds were regularly fixed by the general court and those whose estates lay within the bounds prescribed for each society were required to support its worship. At the same time the interposition of the general court in the founding of churches, the regulation of their affairs and settlement of their disputes was continuous and no definite limits were set to its extent.[5] Thus the state-church system of Connecticut grew in compactness and definiteness, and this was made possible in its case by a continued existence under the corporate charter, which insured the continuance of its

---

[1] C. Mather, Ratio Disciplinae, 17.
[2] Conn. Recs., III.
[3] Ibid., IV, 198.
[4] Ibid., 316.
[5] See the cases cited in the indexes to the volumes of the Conn. Recs., under Ecclesiastical Affairs.

elective officials and protected it to a large extent from interference by the British government.

That such a development as this would tend toward a growth of formalism and decay of spiritual life goes without saying. Relations became stereotyped and half secularized, a condition that paralleled in a way the spiritual and moral decline which existed at the time in England, and was similar of course to what was developing elsewhere in New England. To the modern mind the indifferentism from which sprang the half-way covenant undoubtedly appears as an advance upon the stern and intolerant dogmatism of the early Puritan age in general. It was only through such a change that the way toward toleration and liberty could be opened. The foundations of the old system were being sapped as the result of a natural human reaction and a transition to a newer and broader life was being slowly prepared. The fault of the age was that the basis of culture was too narrow and the feeling of humanity as yet too weak to make possible decisive progress to higher ideals.

Toward 1705 the movement among the clergy of Massachusetts in favor of the formation of associations for the purpose of strengthening the churches assumed more definite form. It is quite probable that in the minds of the Mathers this had a connection with their jealousies over the management of the college and the founding of the Brattle Street Church. But the fact that Colman, Willard and Pemberton sympathized with it shows that such a cause will not account for its origin. Its opponents inferred that it was an attempt to presbyterianize the church, to force the laity out of every position of influence over its affairs and to place the clergy in the saddle. With the very general abandonment of the office of ruling elder, the pastors were left at the head of the parishes and the possibility of forming a purely clerical oligarchy had increased. The clergy were the ones who viewed the inroads of secular influence and indifferentism with dismay and were ever looking about for means of checking it. To them the strengthening of clerical influence would seem a natural remedy and the prospect of a rigid and lifeless uniformity which might result would not be altogether unwelcome.

In 1704 a ministerial association of eastern Massachusetts proposed that a concerted effort be made by pastors to elevate the standard of church membership, and, in order that pastors might be better informed concerning the needs and varied experiences of their profession, that associations be extended and strengthened throughout the colony. From Cambridge a circular was sent out urging concerted action to this end. In September 1705, nine delegates, representing five associations in eastern Massachusetts, met at Boston and issued the so-called "Proposals of 1705." [1] Samuel Willard had acted as moderator and he, with Cotton Mather and Ebenezer Pemberton, were the signers from Boston. In the "Proposals" the formation of ministerial associations throughout the province was urged for the purpose of examining and licensing candidates for the ministry, watching over the conduct of pastors and churches and corresponding with one another for their mutual information and the extension of membership. The outcome of the movement was intended to be the formation of standing councils, to meet at least once a year and to consist of elected delegates, lay as well as clerical, from the local associations and churches. These bodies should "consult, advise and determine" all affairs proper for the consideration of an ecclesiastical council, and their decisions should be looked upon as final, unless aggrieved pastors and churches should present weighty reasons to the contrary, when there might be a further hearing. For gross disorders amounting to evident sins, from which it refused to be reclaimed, a church might be dropped from common fellowship by a council, though if any of the members of such church should suitably testify against its disorders, they might be retained in communion by the churches at large. In this document the plan, as outlined, was expressly called a consociation of churches.

Though at the time there was a widespread feeling in Massachusetts which was favorable to some such plan as this and a number of local associations had been formed, the "Proposals of 1705" met with no active response. Nothing ever came of them and, so far as Massachusetts was concerned, the elastic system of the Cambridge Platform re-

[1] Walker, Creeds of Congregationalism, 483–495.

mained unmodified. The reason for this is probably to be found in the political condition of Massachusetts. It was under royal government and Joseph Dudley was its governor. While he had not entirely broken his relations with the Congregationalists, he had formed new and strong ones with the Episcopalians. The council of the province was to a considerable extent under Dudley's influence. To Dudley and the council, to the Episcopalians and especially to the British government — conclusive evidence of which will appear in another connection — the establishment of church councils, or synods, among the Congregationalists of Massachusetts would have seemed very questionable and might lead to the issue of a prohibition by the crown. Owing, it is probable, to reasons like this the plan was dropped, so far as Massachusetts was concerned.

But in Connecticut, which by its charter was differently situated, it met with an instant response. Steps which looked toward the founding of a college had been taken by a number of the Connecticut clergy, beginning in 1701. In connection with this enterprise they had consulted Judge Sewall, Secretary Addington, the Mathers and possibly others of the Massachusetts conservatives. Sewall and Addington submitted the draft of a charter, and all expressed approval of the plan as offering an additional means by which not only to promote what was regarded as sound learning but to check the decay which was visible in the churches. To the Mathers, and very likely to others, the prospects of Harvard under Leverett as a school for the training of ministers were not satisfactory. With the growth of New England and the other colonies also the supply from Harvard alone was likely to be inadequate. The founding of another college, therefore, was welcome to many throughout New England and Cotton Mather, presumably for personal as well as professional reasons, became very solicitous about the enterprise. In view of the uncertain prospects of the corporate colonies at that time and of the known principle of English law that they had no right to incorporate, the movers in this plan had to proceed with caution. James Pierrepont, pastor of the New Haven church and probably the chief promoter of the college in its earliest days, felt, as many others did, that they had better keep as free from the control of the general court as possible, though of course they had to receive from it a charter which provided for a loose form of incorporation and also financial support until the institution should be able to go alone. As had always been true of Harvard, the prime object in the minds of the founders of the new college was the promotion of religion and the training of ministers of the conservative type. Everywhere education was still regarded as the hand-maid of religion and this was true with a particular emphasis in New England.

Over the location of the college there developed within the board of trustees and to an extent throughout the colony an interesting sectional struggle. Quite as truly as was later the case with the College of New Jersey, this institution was the outgrowth of the improvised but common method of train-ing young ministers in the families of prominent clergymen. After some discussion at Branford the school was started in Killingworth in the family of Abraham Pierson. Thence it was removed to temporary quarters in Saybrook. There, owing to inferior instruction and the fact that the rector could not be in residence, the enterprise languished. This gave occasion for the development of an effort, led by Timothy Woodbridge and Thomas Buckingham, both of Hart-ford, to locate it in the interior of the colony. This was promoted by the gathering of a number of students at Wethersfield under Elisha Williams as tutor, a Harvard graduate of superior gifts. Pierrepont was now dead, but the clergy along the Sound shore with the effective support of the people of New Haven now united in an effort to estab-lish the institution at that place. This move had the support of Governor Saltonstall and of the upper house of assembly, while the majority of the lower house was in sympathy with the Hartford plan. As the result of certain natural changes, the majority of the trustees came to be favorable to New Haven and there, by using funds which were at their dis-posal for erecting a building upon land which was sold to them by New Haven parties, they outmanoeuvred the Hart-ford objectors and actually got the college running at New Haven in 1717. The permanence of this decision was further insured by gifts of some 700 volumes procured in England

by Jeremiah Dummer, the agent, and the successful removal
of these from Saybrook to New Haven. In securing the name
Cotton Mather, together with Dummer and the trustees, co-
operated by correspondence with Elihu Yale, a man of New
England birth and connections, who had accumulated large
wealth in the East Indian trade. He was now a nabob and
a member of the English church, but in consideration of
goods somewhat grudgingly given, which apparently were
sold for about £560, his name was attached to the new
institution.[1] The quarrel between the Hartford and New
Haven factions continued for some years longer. It came to
involve students and tutors and before it closed occasioned
the trial of Woodbridge for defamation of character. The
successful, though brief, administration of Timothy Cutler as
rector finally brought peace so far as the sectional dispute
was concerned.

Another event of peculiar importance in church as well as
civil offices was the election of Gurdon Saltonstall to the
office of governor of Connecticut at the close of 1707. Saltonstall, as pastor of the church at New London, had been
involved in church quarrels, while he also had been in close
touch with civil affairs. While in the clerical office he had
been essentially a lawyer and administrator. There is authority for the statement that he strongly favored synods as
a feature of ecclesiastical polity and that his influence was
decisive in bringing the colony to take the next step in that
direction. At its first May session under the new governor,
the general court ordered that at the close of the following
month the ministers of the colony, with such messengers
as the churches would choose to send, should meet in their
respective counties to " consider and agree upon those
methods and rules for the management of ecclesiastical discipline which by them shall be judged agreeable and con-
formable to the word of God." [2] A committee of delegates

[1] The best authorities for this subject are the latest: Dexter, Documentary History of Yale University, and Oviatt's Beginnings of Yale. See also
President Thomas Clap's History of Yale College and his Religious Constitution of Colleges, 1754. Several references appear in vol. II of the
published edition of Cotton Mather's Diary to his interest in this project
and his correspondence with Elihu Yale. Quincy, History of Harvard, I,
226, 524-528.                          [2] Conn. Recs., V, 51.

from these bodies should then meet at Saybrook during the following commencement — for the college had not yet been located at New Haven — and there compose the results of the recent conferences and from them draw a form of ecclesiastical discipline. This should be promptly submitted to the general court to be considered and confirmed by it. The preamble of this order shows that the desire and intention of the court was to strengthen the church establishment in the colony by insuring a more prompt and sure administration of discipline.

The delegates who met at Saybrook, in September 1708, consisted of twelve ministers and four laymen. Of the ministers eight were trustees of Yale. Their perfected work was the famous Saybrook Platform,[1] an elaboration of the Massachusetts Proposals of 1705 and the most complete statement of the policy of the consociation of churches which was ever put forth in New England. The platform consisted of three parts: — a confession of faith, which was that of the Savoy Conference of 1658 reaffirmed by the synod at Boston in 1680; the Heads of Agreement, in which Increase Mather and his associates in London in 1691 had vainly sought to devise a polity upon which Presbyterians and Congregationalists could unite; and the Fifteen Articles. This statement clearly indicates the genesis and character of the document. So far as doctrinal views were concerned, it was based substantially on the Westminster Confession. In fact the Puritan movement of the seventeenth and eighteenth centuries had nothing to offer in the field of dogma beyond that Confession. The rest of the Saybrook Platform was concerned with church government and polity, and in emphasizing the trend toward Presbyterianism it advanced a step beyond what had been affirmed in the Heads of Agreement and the Boston Proposals of 1705. It set forth a somewhat more rounded and perfected system than had been outlined in either of the earlier documents.

The only original part of the Platform was contained in the Fifteen Articles. These were intended to provide a federal system of associations or councils for the church of

---

[1] Trumbull, Hist. of Conn., I, 508; Greene, Religious Liberty in Connecticut, 138. Walker, op. cit., 502.

Connecticut. The pastors and churches of the respective counties should be organized, and once a year delegates from the associations of all the counties should meet in a general council of the colony. The purpose of this organization was to facilitate the administration of discipline and maintenance of regularity and order in things ecclesiastical among the churches. By implication this included the examination and licensing of candidates for the ministry; ordination, installation and dismission of pastors; the giving of advice to churches or individuals in cases of difficulty; the hearing of appeals from the action of individual churches and local councils; the holding of church trials for heresy, scandal or any other cause. These affairs in detail would regularly be disposed of by the county associations, and only cases of general and higher interest or difficulty would be taken up in the general councils of the colony. It was intended that the persuasive and coercive power of the councils should be final and that the parties to controversies should so accept and abide by their decisions. The leading place and influence in the scheme of course was assigned to the clergy, but provision was also made for participation of elected representatives of the laity.

The final opportunity for the exercise of lay influence rested with the general court, and at the time of its issue that body was decidedly in favor of the Saybrook Platform. In October 1708, it gave its full approval to the scheme,[1] and ordered that all the churches which united under it should be acknowledged as established by law. But the right of dissent was also recognized, and any society or church which arose soberly to exercise this right should not be hindered from worshipping in its own way according to the consciences of its members. This privilege was intended specially for the benefit of those who adhered to the Cambridge Platform and was set forth in the so-called toleration act of 1708.[2] This required the taking before the county courts of the oath prescribed by the toleration act of 1690 in England and did not release the dissenter from his obligation to pay the rate for the support of the church in the town where he lived.

[1] Conn. Recs., V, 97.
[2] *Ibid.*, V, 50. Greene, 151 *et seq.*

Advantage could not be taken of this by Quakers and Rogerenes, because of their objection to the oath, but to Anglicans and dissenters of other types it offered a certain concession, though additional legislation was necessary to exempt them from the payment of church rates. This was as far as the plan for the consociation of churches was carried in New England. It was a compromise between primitive Congregationalism of the Brownist type, or even as set forth in the Cambridge Platform, and Presbyterianism. The consociations might be regarded as substantially classes or presbyteries, with complete powers of government, or they might be treated as stated councils called for consultation and advice.[1] Presbyterians would naturally interpret them in the former sense, Independents in the latter. The system could be turned in either direction as the traditions and preferences of those in control should determine.

As was to be expected from the history of Connecticut, a complete break was not made with the principles of the Cambridge Platform. The early republicanism of the New England churches, with the large provision which it made for the influence of the laity, was not wholly abandoned. Connecticut was not united in support of the new plan. Hartford and New London counties accepted the Saybrook Platform in full and without change. Fairfield county gave to it an interpretation according to which the councils would have the power of church courts, while New Haven county filed a liberal interpretation which left little beyond counsel and advice, followed by withdrawal of communion, in the action of councils upon churches.[2] Yet, until the American Revolution and later the principles of the Saybrook Platform, by a pretty general agreement of churches and general court, were enforced with vigor. The result was that the spirit of primitive congregationalism waned and a policy which was essentially presbyterian was followed. By many the church system of the colony was indifferently called congregational or presbyterian. The union of the churches proved powerless to check the decay of spiritual life, of which there had been such complaint, but rather aided the forma-

---

[1] L. Bacon, Thirteen Historical Discourses, 191.
[2] Walker, 509, 513.

tion of a crust of dead orthodoxy under which the churches slumbered until the rude awakening of the Whitefield revival.

When, in 1726, Cotton Mather was discussing with approval in his " Ratio Disciplinae " the development and workings of the system of ministerial associations and synods in New England, he referred to a satire that had been published in opposition to these, which he had not deigned to answer, but had treated with " generous silence and pious contempt." This was " The Churches Quarrel Espoused," by John Wise, the pastor of the Chebacco parish in the town of Ipswich, the same man who had distinguished himself by leading the opposition to the autocratic methods of taxation to which Andros and his council had resorted in 1687. This pamphlet Wise issued in 1710, and it, together with his " Vindication of the Government of the New England Churches," published in 1717, have given the Ipswich clergyman a place of deserved prominence among American writers of the eighteenth century. As an advocate of democracy and the rights of the people in church and state he stands practically alone in the midst of the period of the colonial wars. In his breast the spirit of the English Levellers found a response, and with many an original thought and witty and satirical touch he exposed the fallacy of those who were sacrificing liberty to a timid love for regularity and order. In spirit he was essentially a layman and protested against the threatened exclusion of the laity from influence upon church affairs and the establishment of the clergy as a permanent ruling caste. For several years after the issue of the Proposals of 1705, though he disapproved of them, he had kept quiet. But with the adoption of the Saybrook Platform he could keep silence no longer and launched his vigorous attack upon the consociation of churches, wherever it appeared. Against all such plans he defended the Cambridge Platform as an ancient inheritance of liberty, of which the people of New England should not permit themselves to be robbed. If they should pull down that fabric of their own rearing, the supporters of episcopacy would be more than ever convinced that they were fanatics and totally unreliable. A constitution which had worked so well should not be cast aside in favor of a plan which savored so much of clerical rule — a combination of presbyterianism and the papacy. It would be like turning the knights of the shires and the burgesses out of doors.

In his second pamphlet Wise took broader and higher ground, extending his argument to secular as well as ecclesiastical relations. In this he made a strong plea for democracy in church and state, as the original, natural and only true form. Adopting the current philosophy of natural law, he described the primitive state of man as free and from this deduced by means of the social compact the state, " a Compound Moral Person whose Will is the Will of all." If the apostolic church was democratic, then the right to convoke councils rests, he argued, with the churches. Councils, moreover, could have only consultative, and not judicial, power, and none among their members could claim superior authority or right of suffrage. In civil affairs he considered monarchy and aristocracy to be degenerate forms of government, the results of usurpation. In the same way, his review of church history had convinced him that its chief lesson was that of apostacy, continued and intensified through the ages, from the primitive democracy of the apostolic age. Here was a genuine voice of the eighteenth century, weak in the details of history, but strong in its assertion of the ideals of human liberty, an echo of the Puritan Revolution and an anticipation of the Revolution which was later to come in the colonies. At the time the voice of Wise seemed like one crying in the wilderness. But even then it was held to have been effective, together with other causes, in silencing the demand for consociation of churches on any comprehensive scale in Massachusetts.

Opposition to judicial appeals to England was a characteristic of the Puritan colonies. In the case of Connecticut it appeared with special prominence after 1690, when the British government was most actively developing its policy of imperial control. Under most circumstances, but especially in a time like that, the Connecticut magistrates deemed a policy of quiet and unobserved, but steady, development to be the only one which was at all likely to enable them to preserve their primitive and chartered liberty. Geographically their situation was favorable for this. Unlike Rhode Island, their territory also was not menaced by rivals. If appeals must

be resorted to, they would originate not in some supreme
need of the colony, but would be the best way of meeting
questions raised by private suits of her own citizens. The
initiative would then come from them and Connecticut would
appear in the rôle of defender of an ordered and regulated
policy.

Connecticut was concerned in only two important appeals,
the Liveen or Hallam case soon after 1690, and the Winthrop-
Lechmere case which arose toward 1730. Both originated
in or near New London and concerned, directly or indirectly,
the fortunes of the Winthrop family. Both attracted much
attention and the latter touched very deeply the interests of
colonial life at large.

John Liveen was a merchant who, while resident in Barbados, had married Alice Hallam, a widow with two sons,
John and Nicholas. In religious preference he was a
Baptist and scrupled the oath. His later life was spent in
New London [1] and on his death in 1689 he willed nearly all
his estate — reserving the use of one third to the widow
during her life — "to the ministry of New London." [2]
Though some arguments to the contrary were urged, this
meant Saltonstall's church, and it was a testimony to the
influence which that divine and the Winthrops had obtained
over the mind of the testator. The step-sons received only
minor bequests. Fitz-John Winthrop, Edward Palmes and
the widow were named in the will as executors. Palmes, we
know, was an opponent of the restored Connecticut government and the Hallams, whatever had been their previous
attitude, soon became identified with that faction. The will
came up for probate before the county court at New London
and Palmes, who had it in his custody, refused to appear,
his excuse being that the court did not derive its authority
from the crown. This plea, of course, was ignored, though
it is said that a copy of the will had to be used in settling
the estate. As the executors would not set out the share
which was to go to "the ministry," Saltonstall appeared in
court as a plaintiff and secured a decree for a division of the

---

[1] B. T. Proprieties, C. O. 5/1263.
[2] Winthrop Papers, 6 Mass. Hist. Colls., III, 95; Caulkins, History of
New London.

estate. As a means of securing obedience to this it was ordered that the executors should do nothing without the consent of Winthrop or of the county court.

Here the case rested until 1698, when the widow died. It seems that during the years which had passed the church had received its award in the form of an annual dividend. On the theory that the Liveen will was invalid and that the estate was still intact, the widow bequeathed the whole of it to her two sons, the Hallams. They now appeared as principals and tried to contest the original will. Conflicting testimony was given as to the condition of Liveen when he signed the will. An attempt was also made to show that he was no friend of the Congregationalists and that he must have intended to endow the ministry of the Church of England. Naturally these plans failed and by all tribunals in Connecticut the will was confirmed. A by-product of the controversy was the issue of a list of complaints against Saltonstall, affecting his tenure as minister of the church of New London. These he brought before the general court and obtained a resolution clearing him from blame.[1]

John Hallam having died, Nicholas Hallam now appealed to the crown, and the management of the case for Connecticut was intrusted to the agent, Sir Henry Ashurst. When this case came to the attention of the English authorities (1702-3) they were in the midst of their campaign against the proprieties, and Hallam sought to gain as much advantage as possible from the prejudices created by the question of the Rhode Island boundary, the Mohegan case, that of the militia, and by the independent course which Connecticut had followed in so many matters. " They opened such things at the Council," wrote Ashurst, " that made your case look very foul, and all the affidavits that you took in your country after the Appeal was granted, they would not allow to be read, because it appeared to be an examination *ex parte*. All that I could possibly hope for in your case I got granted, which was this; that at your charge the whole evidence should be reexamined by both parties upon oath, . . . and then to have all returned back, and then the Council have to pass

[1] C. O. 5/1263 (1700); Conn. Col. Recs., IV, 338.

their final judgment." [1] "The Canaanite being in the land, you should be very cautious not to make any laws repugnant to the laws of England, or if any such are already made, of executing them."

Winthrop was now governor and Saltonstall, partly in consequence of the issues which had been raised by the Hallam case, was passing from a clerical to a political career. He was empowered by the governor to act as his counsel in the taking of evidence for submission to the privy council. Fitch, who was presiding over the hearing, refused to allow Saltonstall to attend and thus the feud between them was intensified, while Saltonstall reported that very arbitrary methods were being used by the supporters of Hallam at the hearings. [2] The case was heard before the committee of the privy council in the summer of 1704. At first it was thought that it would go in favor of Hallam, but among the assets of the estate was a vessel of one hundred tons, called the *Liveen*, which had been appraised and sold. [3] The original bill of sale, of which Hallam was a witness, was shown, and this was taken as an acknowledgment of the validity of the will. Hence the decisions of the colonial courts were upheld.

The case of Winthrop *vs.* Lechmere involved issues of far wider and deeper significance, for the appeal endangered the stability of the land system of the colony and much that was common to all the colonies besides. One of the most natural divergencies of colonial law from the common law of England appears in the departure throughout New England from the principle of primogeniture in the inheritance of land. [4] In a new country like the colonies land was abundant and cheap, labor was scarce and costly. So also was movable property and chattels. The interest of all was to facilitate access to the land, so that the formation of new homes might be facilitated, early marriages and a rapid growth of population promoted. An easy provision for daughters and younger sons, not as annuities or as profes-

---

[1] Winthrop Papers, *op. cit.*, 120, 121.
[2] *Ibid.*, 123–125.
[3] Acts of P. C. Col.
[4] Andrews, The Conn. Intestacy Law, Yale Rev. III; Talcott Papers, Colls. Conn. Hist. Soc., IV, 143, *et seq.*

sional soldiers or in public or official life, but as farmers and productive laborers was the great need of colonial society. These were the natural and about the only outlets, for there was no army and public office was elective and monopolized by non-professionals. As was suggested at the time, England would surely not desire to force her young colonists into manufactures. In the law of inheritance, and especially that part of it which related to intestates, the treatment of land and chattels alike with a view to an approximately equal provision for all the children was well adapted to the needs of a new country. Spontaneously that principle had been acted on by the New England colonies from the first. In 1692 Massachusetts had passed an act which had escaped disallowance by the privy council — providing that in case of intestate estates after the dower or thirds of the widow had been taken out, all the residue of real and personal estate should be divided equally among the sons and daughters, excepting the eldest surviving son who should receive a double portion.[1] In 1699 an almost verbatim copy of this provision was enacted by Connecticut.[2] In view of the degree of divergence from English practice which in this and other matters had been so long tolerated, and of the manifest unfitness in the eyes of any but legalists, of primogeniture for new countries, it might be inferred that the law would be allowed to remain and that the land systems of New England would not be disturbed.

" By this custom of dividing inheritances," wrote Governor Talcott in 1727,[3] " all were supplyed with land to work upon, the land as well occupied as the number of hands would admit of, the people universally employed in husbandry; thereby considerable quantities of provisions are raised, and from our stores the trading part of the Massachusetts and Rhode Island are supplyed, the fishermen subsisted, and the most of the sugars of the West Indies are put up in casks made of our staves; by this means our predecessors were enabled to furnish themselves with almost all their cloathing, nails and most other necessaries from their neighbors at

[1] Acts and Resolves, I, 44.
[2] Conn. Recs., IV, 307.
[3] Talcott Papers, op. cit., 145.

Boston, (who transport theirs from Great Britain), and so we do this day.  By means of this custom his Majesty's Subjects are here increased, the younger bretheren do not depart from us, but others are rather encouraged to settle among us, and it's manifest that New England does populate faster than the Colonies where the land descends according to the rules of the common law.  And such measures as will furnish with the best infantry does most prepare for the defence of a people settled in their enemies country."

The evils which would follow from undermining the system were equally evident to the governor and his contemporaries. It would turn the great majority of people in the colony out of their houses and lands or some of their improvements.  The established system had existed about five generations and stocks had branched out into very numerous descendants, whose combined labors had redeemed the country from a wilderness and given the land the chief part of its value.  When the facts and claims involved came to be adjudicated according to new and strange rules, lawsuits would abound.  Many would be ruined.  Then increase of population would be checked and the productivity of Connecticut would diminish, neighboring colonies suffering in consequence.  The Connecticut law book which was sent to England soon after Fitz-John Winthrop became governor contained the law on intestate estates but, though a generation had passed, no objection had ever been made to it, and they thought they were safe.

The Winthrop-Lechmere case arose upon the death intestate, in 1717, of Wait Winthrop,[1] the younger of the sons of the first governor of Connecticut.  He left a son, John, and a daughter, Anne, the latter the wife of Thomas Lechmere, of Boston, who for a time was surveyor general of customs for the colonies.  The son was appointed administrator and he at once claimed all the real estate both of his father and of his uncle, the late governor of Connecticut, as the heir-at-law according to English precedents.  This was in harmony with the intention, often expressed by the two Winthrops during life, that their estate should not be

[1] In 1713 Winthrop had made a will but had never executed it.  6 Mass. Hist. Colls., V, 367.

divided but pass to the eldest surviving male heir.[1] It seems
that, as the generations passed, a resolve to keep its landed
property together and to transmit it by inheritance as a unit
became fixed in this family.  This approximation to English
spirit and practice, in a matter of such fundamental importance, on the part of the family which had led in the founding
of both Massachusetts and Connecticut, is a curious and
significant fact.  The independence of these two colonies in
religion and policy had been an expression of the spirit of the
Winthrops as much as of any family which had removed into
New England.  Fitz-John Winthrop had spent many of his
later years in opposing Joseph Dudley and his plans of political consolidation with the mother country.  His brother
had shared this activity.  They had defended chartered rights
to the utmost.  But evidently all that they intended by this
was a certain political and religious freedom.  In their love
of property, their aristocratic family instinct, they were
thoroughly English, and were ready even to undermine the
economic system of New England in order to gratify this
instinct.  In all this there is a profound lesson for one who
would understand the later course of New England in its
relations with the mother country.  We now have to do
with the ideas and feelings of the eighteenth century, after
religious passions had somewhat cooled, and it is interesting
to compare the type of loyalty exhibited by such men as
Joseph Dudley [2] and Gershom Bulkley with that of the Winthrops.  Both were real, though they were directed toward
different objects and were very differently expressed.  Which
was the more permanent and far reaching?  In everything
that pertained to social status the Winthrops were English
aristocrats.

John Winthrop was appointed administrator of the estate
by the county court of probate at New London and proceeded to settle it, so far as the chattels were concerned, but

---

[1] Talcott Papers, *op. cit.*, 94; Winthrop Papers, 6 Mass. Hist. Colls.,
V, 167, 169, 367, 440, *et seq.*;  The Brief in Appeal.

[2] Dudley also had the same passion to found a family with a large
estate.  "We are some of us English gentlemen," he wrote to Saltonstall,
"and such is your owne family; and we should labor to support such familyes
because truly we want them."  *Ibid.*, 170.

did not submit an inventory.[1] After six years had passed, the Lechmeres, who were in somewhat needy circumstances, suddenly demanded an inventory and Winthrop was ordered to complete the settlement of the estate. He replied by exhibiting an inventory of the personal estate, but claimed that he was not required to extend this to the land, as it belonged to him as heir-at-law. The court refused to admit such an inventory and prolonged litigation over the question was begun, which was carried through the Connecticut courts and even before the general assembly. After the letters of administration which had been granted to Winthrop had been vacated, in the spring of 1725/6, and the Lechmeres had been appointed administrators, Winthrop petitioned the assembly and threatened appeal to England.[2] As he had not brought the case before the highest court in the colony, his memorial was dismissed. He then behaved with such insolence, interrupting the governor and claiming that he was not under jurisdiction and stood upon a par with the assembly, that he was committed to the custody of the sheriff, and afterwards, escaping from his detention, was fined £20.

Winthrop then went to England and laid his case before the crown. Yorke and Talbot, the attorney and solicitor general, who stood at the head of the English bar, managed the case for Winthrop. Lechmere, whose means were limited, was poorly defended.[3] Winthrop's case was strengthened by citing alleged irregular proceedings against him in Connecticut while the case was pending. His claim also fell in naturally with the prejudices which were widely held against the proprieties. By a noticeable departure from the customary usage the case was not referred to the board of trade, but was managed wholly within the privy council. The

---

[1] The same course was pursued in the case of the property which was in Suffolk County, Massachusetts.

[2] Conn. Col. Recs., VII, 20, 43. 6 Mass. Hist. Colls., V, 460. According to the record of the assembly Winthrop was intolerably insolent and was denied permission to appeal because he had not carried his suit before the superior court. The representation made in the brief of appeal seeks to throw the onus of refusing his appeal upon the assembly.

[3] See statement by Ferdinand John Paris, who was present at the trial. Talcott Papers, *ibid.*, 77.

hearing was held before the committee of the council on December 20, 1727, and a report was adopted which went decidedly beyond what the nature of the appeal called for, Though the suit was a private one, the report demanded that the Connecticut law relating to intestate estates be repealed and that a whole series of decrees of its courts concerning the inventories of the Winthrop estate and its administration by Lechmere be set aside and that Winthrop be put into full possession of the land to which he would be entitled under English law, with the rents which had accrued during the interval. An order of council in harmony with this report was issued February 15, 1727/8.[1] Due obedience at once on the part of the colony was imperatively commanded.

By this judgment a public issue of the greatest importance not only for Connecticut but for New England at large was raised. Joseph Talcott, of Hartford, was governor, and though, curiously enough, as a young man he had petitioned the assembly against the partition of his father's real property and had claimed the whole for himself,[2] he now bent all his energies to the task of rescuing the legal and economic system of his colony from the effects of the blow which had been administered to it. The general assembly, of course, fully coöperated. Jeremiah Drummer had long been agent of the colony, but his health was now poor and, though some belated appropriations had been made to enable him to oppose the Winthrop appeal, he had apparently not been summoned to appear. Now the colony must take the matter directly in hand. Winthrop's lands were restored to him and pending the final issue of the case the settlement of intestate estates was suspended throughout the colony. Additional appropriations were made and Jonathan Belcher, of Massachusetts, was associated with Dummer as agent.[3] Belcher's mother was a Connecticut woman and from her property came a notable part of the estate which he inherited. His father, too, had spent part of his life in Hartford. Jonathan was an investor in the copper mine at Simsbury and in land at Pomfret and

[1] Conn. Col. Recs., VII, 571–579; Acts P. C. Col., 1720–1745, pp. 139–151. The petition of Winthrop in support of his appeal is there given in full.

[2] Talcott Papers, Conn. Hist. Soc. Colls., IV, XIX.

[3] Conn. Col. Recs., VII, 122, 125, 185, 192, 238, 308; Talcott Papers, loc. cit., 100, 114–123, 174, 203.

was looked upon as " at least half a Connecticut man." [1] At about the same time he was also being selected by Massachusetts as its agent for the adjustment of the salary controversy which had reached such an acute stage with Governor Burnet. Belcher desired that instructions might be given to himself alone, so that he might be independent of Dummer, his inference being that the latter had been neglectful of his duty. Such, however, was later proved not to have been the case, and Dummer's services on behalf of the chartered colonies had been too long and valuable to be ignored on the suggestion of a new appointee. Though Belcher was given separate instructions, he was warned not to blame Dummer unless it was found that he deserved it, and as the result showed, the agents proceeded harmoniously in the discharge of their duty. [2]

In the instructions to Belcher and the correspondence with him — in which Jonathan Law, the deputy governor and chief justice, shared [3] — in addition to the social and economic considerations which have already been explained, the legal bearings of the question at issue were discussed. Now that the colony was to appear as the chief litigant and in defence of a large part of its laws, it was realized that the question, what constituted repugnancy to English law, had been more directly and seriously raised than ever before. Previous to this time the act against heretics had been the only Connecticut law which had been disallowed and that at the instance of the Quakers. To Law, who doubtless had one of the ablest legal minds in the colony, it seemed at first as if the whole fabric of Connecticut law was imperilled and that they would be reduced to the condition of corporations in England. Later he came to hope that they might retain those laws which were not contrary to British statutes, that being the principle upon which they had always supposed themselves to be acting. In these two cases the boundaries between positive law and custom would be drawn at very different points. If all the lands must descend according to

---

[1] Talcott Papers, 162; Belcher Papers, 6 Mass. Hist. Colls., VI, XV *et seq.*
[2] Talcott Papers, 135–163.
[3] *Ibid.*, 120. Law had been the first choice of the general assembly for the office of agent. Conn. Col. Recs., VII, 218.

the rules of the common law, the founders of New England, like the first king of England, had " led us out of the way." But comfort was found in the dictum of Coke that all ancient grants should be expounded as the law was taken at the time of the grant, a common error making a right. " It is true that our law is of so anchient standing," wrote the deputy governor, " that one would think it to have the like foundation with the general and particular customs in England which are unalterable by anything short of an Act of Parliament." The charter had been understood by all the colony to provide that they might pass any good and wholesome laws which were not contrary to those of England. An analogy between the situation in the colonies and in England in pre-feudal times was dimly realized and the idea suggested that what was custom in England then should be allowed in the colonies now. Talcott was sure that the intestacy act was legal, but Law was not wholly convinced on that point and his advice on the whole was to sit still, as Connecticut had been in the habit of doing, unless it was deemed advisable to get an opinion from the law officers on the point at issue.

Upon taking advice in England, especially from King, the lord chancellor, the agents reported that the most satisfactory course would probably be to secure from parliament, if possible, the passage of a special statute quieting existing estates and legalizing Connecticut practice for the future.[1] But when Talcott laid his proposition before the council, it naturally occurred to them that this project might fail or bring on an inquiry which would lead to a disallowance of the ecclesiastical and possibly of more of the civil laws of the colony,[2] or perhaps might imperil the charter itself. There was likelihood also that their suit might be harmed by connecting it with the violent dispute in progress with Massachusetts over salaries. But on the other hand, it did not appear that there was any connection between the two, while no one could justly charge the House of Hanover with being invaders of the rights of the people. If it could be done without imperilling the charter, the assembly agreed that the appeal to parliament should be made.[3] The king was accord-

[1] Talcott P., 167, *et seq.*    [2] *Ibid.*, 175, *et seq.*    [3] Conn. Recs., VII, 254.

ingly asked to give leave for the introduction of the bill, and Belcher in particular thought the time was specially opportune for this because he had just been appointed governor of Massachusetts and New Hampshire,[1] with a view to the possible adjustment of the salary controversy. The petition was referred through the committee of the council to the board of trade, though without reference to the adjustment being made by act of parliament. Dummer soon after was discharged from his agency and Francis Wilks, of London, who was already agent for Massachusetts, was appointed, he, with John Sharpe as counsel, being left in charge of the business.[2] The board of trade from its counsel, Francis Fane, reported in favor of giving relief to Connecticut in the matter of intestate estates, but in return for that favor that it should be placed under a charter similar to that of Massachusetts. The charges against this colony which had been so often repeated were rehearsed again as justification for the proposed change.[3] The Connecticut government, of course, was not willing to submit to the loss of their charter in order to secure a satisfactory intestacy law, and as its next move sent over to Wilks a proposal for a new law on that subject containing as the only important divergence from the late act a provision excluding females from the inheritance of land. Wilks very earnestly assured them that this would not meet the difficulty for the intestacy law had been disallowed because it differed so radically from the common law of England.[4] No further action bearing directly and exclusively on the Winthrop case was taken in England. He did not recover his land and having expended a considerable part of his fortune in prosecuting the suit, like the later loyalists, he spent the remainder of his life in England, as a recognized fellow, it is true, of the Royal Society, but also as an embittered exile from the land which his ancestors had done so much to win for people of the English speech. Such was the end of what might be called the Winthrop dynasty in New England. The end of the Dudleys was not so very different from it, and they both remind one of the exile of the last

[1] Talcott Papers, *ibid.*, 185–192, 201; Conn. Mss. For. Corresp. B. T. Proprieties, C. O. 5/1267.

[2] Talcott Papers, 198–9, 210, 212, 221; Conn. Recs., VII, 308.

[3] Talcott Papers, 222, 232–235.　　　　[4] *Ibid.*, 241, 441.

of the Hutchinsons, and of the Olivers, too, who were of equally prominent lineage in New England.

Representations from the board of trade in 1730 and 1733 concerning the ineffectiveness of control, especially over the proprieties, drew from the house of lords in 1734 resolutions to the effect that they be required to send over complete collections of their laws and that all which were found detrimental to the trade, navigation or interest of Great Britain be repealed, any privilege or limitation by charter notwithstanding; that only emergency laws for defence in the plantations be allowed to remain in force until they had received the royal approval; and finally that the governors of Connecticut and Rhode Island be required, before they entered upon office, to take the usual oaths and enter into security to observe the laws of trade as was done by governors of other colonies. Much anxiety, especially in Connecticut, was occasioned by these resolutions and the agent was provided with means for making an active defence, if the measures proposed should ever be brought to a vote in the house.[1] No action, however, was taken in pursuance of the resolutions, and there the matter rested, so far as the Connecticut intestacy law was concerned, until 1738, when the case of Phillips vs. Savage, which had been carried on appeal from the superior court of Massachusetts, before the privy council, was decided in favor of the colony law. The fact which necessitated such a decision in that case was that the Massachusetts act of 1692, and others passed in explanation of it, had been confirmed by the privy council. But when the Winthrop appeal had come before the council, it could act in accordance with what were considered the merits of the case.[2]

As the situation in Connecticut was unsatisfactory, Governor Talcott naturally welcomed information of the decision as to the Massachusetts law, though the situations in the two colonies were not parallel. Some correspondence followed with the agent, Wilks,[3] but no decisive action was taken. Meantime a similar case, that of Clark vs. Tousey, arose in

[1] Talcott Papers, I, 296, 300, 303–306.
[2] The order in council is in Talcott Papers, II, 89. See Proc. of Mass. Hist. Soc., 1860–62, pp. 64–80, 165–171.
[3] Talcott Papers, Conn. Hist. Colls., V, 71–74, 135, 176, 189, 225.

Connecticut. It had its origin in Milford in an appeal from an order of the probate court of New Haven County dividing the entire estate of Samuel Clark in accordance with the customary law of Connecticut. The eldest son appealed on the ground that this settlement was contrary to the law of England. This litigation began in 1728 and went through the usual routine in the Connecticut courts, but an appeal to England was not taken until 1742. Thomas Tousey of Newtown, was then left as the sole defendent. The assembly appropriated £500 to aid him in his appeal. Eliakim Palmer had now succeeded to the agency and was ordered to secure the services of Paris and Sharpe, solicitors. John Read, of Boston, one of the ablest lawyers in New England, was employed to prepare the case. In the instructions [1] to the agent strong ground was taken against the doctrine that English common law extended to Connecticut, the claim being made that whereas other colonies, like Virginia and Rhode Island, had adopted it in part, Connecticut, where laws of their own were lacking, had referred themselves to the law of God. The right of a people to choose the law by which they should be governed was strongly implied, and also the old claim that the common law was limited by the four seas, but with the modification that it could be extended beyond them only by act of parliament. [2] In confirmation of the general argument an opinion rendered by Talbot and Yorke, the law officers, in 1730 was cited, to the effect that in the plantations entails could not be barred by fine and recovery as in England unless a law to that effect had been made in the colonies. The inference drawn from this was that the common law could be in force in the colonies only as the result of their own action or by act of parliament. By order in council, in 1745, the appeal of Clark was finally dismissed and the Connecticut law of intestacy, after a contest extending over seventeen years, was by implication allowed to stand. [3]

[1] Conn. Col. Recs., VIII, 463, 506; IX, 587. Talcott Papers, 87, 489; Law Papers, I, 23, 27, 51, 67, 68, 71, 72, 343.

[2] See the letters of Jonathan Law in support of this claim, and the reply of John Sharpe, Law Papers, I, 27, 72.

[3] Acts P. C. Col., 1720–1745, p. 580, 581. The name of the defendant is there spelled Towsey.

# CHAPTER XVI

MASSACHUSETTS AND NEW HAMPSHIRE UNDER BELCHER, 1730–1740. END OF THE CONFLICT OVER GOVERNOR'S SALARY. RISE OF THE STRUGGLE OVER THE LAND BANK.

UNLIKE the provinces to the west and south, New England passed through the early eighteenth century for the most part under executives who were taken from among its people. That, of course, was true of its two corporate colonies. It was almost equally true of New Hampshire. During a large part of the period the same was the case in Massachusetts, though there is no indication that the British government was consciously guided by this as a principle in the selection of appointees. Rather, one would suppose, New England would be avoided by placemen who were seeking a fortune, as a hard and unpropitious region. But whatever may have been the reason, the fact remains that though the crown, under the provisions of the charter of 1691, had the widest range of choice, Massachusetts had Englishmen as her governors only a little more than fifteen years during the first half-century of her existence as a province. Though, as we know, it was not wholly the fault of the governors, yet the fact remains that violent conflicts had disturbed the peace of two of those administrations and these conflicts form the central thread of Massachusett history for a decade.

After the death of Burnet, the home government returned to its former practice and selected Jonathan Belcher, a descendant of the original New England stock, to be governor.[1] Belcher at the time was in England, serving as one of the agents who had been appointed to support the memorial which was sent by the house of representatives in defence of its case against Burnet on the salary question. Like Dudley,

[1] For this administration, in addition to the sources for Massachusetts history in general, are the Belcher papers, containing the governor's correspondence during many of the years when he was in office, 6 Mass. Hist. Colls., VI and VII. These will be referred to as B. P. I and II.

Belcher was by no means unacquainted with Europe. " I have, my lord," he wrote to the bishop of Lincoln, " at one time and another spent about six years in Europe — twice in Hannover, before the happy Protestant succession took place; once in Berlin, Hambro, in Denmark, in several principalities of Germany, three times in Holland, and once I made progress thro the kingdoms of Great Britain (500 miles in length) . . . ." [1]  Belcher's father was a prominent Boston merchant, with interests also in Connecticut, who was often employed in public business.   The son, after his graduation from Harvard, had become associated with him in business, and from this connection had realized an ample fortune.   His energy and the effective business methods which he thus acquired were employed to the full in winning acquaintance among people of influence in Great Britain.   Like Dudley, Belcher became a courtier, but of the effusive and demonstrative type.

In the course of the eighteenth century Puritanism lost its sincerity but at the same time retained the old phraseology. Its utterances were still larded with biblical quotations and professions of piety, while its spirit had vanished and its interest had become worldly.   The impression produced by this change is one sometimes of intolerable hypocrisy.   Cotton Mather, Dudley and Belcher are representatives of declining Puritanism.   In Mather there was an element of sincerity and zeal for good works which to an extent offset his extravagance and folly.   Dudley made no unseemly professions of religion, while his efficiency wins a certain respect even for his self-seeking.   In his case it may have been a merit to have written comparatively little.   If Belcher had left only his speeches to the general court and the purely official letters which he wrote to the secretary of state and the board of trade, the impression would have been that he was a successful governor, though somewhat boastful of his achievements and much given to partisan acts which accorded well with the system of patronage then in vogue.   But into his letter books were copied also a very large number of epistles written to his son during his years as a student at the Temple, to a large proportion of the men in public life in England, to

[1] B. P. I, 54.

churchmen, to Wilks the agent and to Richard Partridge, Belcher's brother-in-law, who was associated in the agency, to Richard Waldron who was the chief supporter of the governor's measures in New Hampshire and also to David Dunbar, the lieutenant governor of New Hampshire and surveyor general of the woods. This correspondence shows that Belcher, in his zeal to found a family, was continually fawning upon the great and trying to enlist the services of his friends in the same pursuit. For years he systematically trained his son in this business and tried to use him as an aid in securing attention and favors from members of the English nobility and gentry. All the petty and ignoble means which were familar to the dispensers of patronage of the time were tried or suggested, and a rich marriage, a seat in parliament or high judicial office were held out as possible rewards of the aspiring and religiously trained youth. These letters reveal a character which approximated more closely to that of the duke of Newcastle than that of any other colonial governor. But it had a religious coloring, characteristic of New England, which made Belcher a favorite of the Massachusetts clergy and an ardent participant in the Whitefield revival. This quality the duke certainly did not share. The extent to which it was paraded by Belcher alongside of his fawning arts and dictatorial airs toward inferiors, shows that with him Puritanism had reached its lowest point, so far at least as it was revealed in official life.

As soon as news reached England of Burnet's death, Belcher sought the vacant office with all his might. Shute, to whose appointment Belcher had contributed, gave the candidacy his aid. Wilks, the agent, told Lord Townshend that nothing was more likely than that Belcher would be able to induce the people to comply with the king's instructions.[1] Belcher at once abandoned the popular cause which he had come to England to defend and declared in unctuous phrase that no one would be more tender of the honor of the crown or industrious to promote the interest of Great Britain than himself.[2] In what sense and to what extent this promise would

---

[1] Hutchinson, II, 329.

[2] See letter of Belcher to Newcastle, Dec. 31, 1729; C. O. 5/898, A. W. I. N. Eng., 1703–1736.

be fulfilled time alone could tell. But it offered a chance which the ministers accepted. Belcher had on nearly all occasions been a supporter of the prerogative and the appointment was made. Dummer was removed from the lieutenant-governorship and as the result of a shift in a minor position William Tailer again became lieutenant governor.

Belcher's appointment was made in the midst of the discussion by the board of trade and the committee of the council of the questions which had disturbed Burnet's administration. Three important instructions were given him on these questions.[1] The first of them related to the governor's salary, and it was this which Belcher published and upon which he chiefly dwelt in his opening speech to the general court, in September, 1730. The instruction was cast in the most peremptory terms and was accompanied with the threat that, because of this and many other unwarrantable practices which tended to weaken the obedience which was due from all colonies to the crown, in case of further refusals to conform the undutiful conduct of the province must be laid before parliament. Also, in case the court did not at once comply, Belcher was required to come to England and report, in order that the question might be submitted to parliament. The payment of arrears due to Burnet's children was also involved, while a letter from Wilks implied that proceedings before parliament had been merely suspended in the hope of better results in Massachusetts.[2] The salary which Belcher was instructed to demand was £1000 st., free from all deductions and to be " constantly paid." This demand he made at the opening of his first assembly, in September, 1730. The reply of the house was substantially the same as that made to Burnet. Grants were made toward reimbursing the governor for his " passage hither " and to meet the expenses of his agency, one of them taking the form of 800 acres of unappropriated land. The council voted in

---

[1] Belcher's instructions with those of the other royal governors of Massachusetts, are printed in Pubs. of Colonial Soc. of Mass. The changes which were introduced are in C. O. 5–916, B. T. E. B. N. Eng. p. 268, *et seq.*

[2] Dummer had also written in 1729, that he feared, if Massachusetts did not yield willingly, she would be compelled to yield unwillingly. Mss. of Mass. Hist. Soc.

favor of a permanent salary to continue during the governor's term, but the house could not be induced to yield. Finally the two houses agreed upon a grant of £2400 in currency and as the governor was not allowed to give his assent, they addressed the crown for permission to enable him to do so. Belcher's public comment upon this action — that it had "more the face of that duty and respect you owe the king than you have before manifested" — indicated that his attitude on the salary question would be quite different from that of Burnet. This was confirmed by his letters to Newcastle and the board of trade, recommending that the act be taken as a settlement during the present governor's administration. Near the close of the year, however, to Belcher's disgust, a pamphlet was issued, entitled "The Political State of Great Britain," in which he was represented to have entirely abandoned his earlier views and to be now the faithful agent and supporter of the policy of the crown.[1] Belcher, in a letter to the board of trade denounced the "vile author" and declared that it had poisoned the minds of the people and confirmed the existing assembly in its obstinacy.[2] The house in its spring session seemed to him to have gone backward and to have resolved to do nothing more than they had done "forty years agoe." The lords of trade on their part expressed themselves at a loss to imagine how Belcher could think this might be taken as a settlement during his administration.[3]

In November, 1731, the general court passed an act appropriating £5400 to the governor for his past services and further to enable him to manage the public affairs. In transmitting this to England Belcher totally abandoned his instruction and admitted that it was impossible to enforce it, though he dreaded the consequences should the king finally recede from orders which had been so long insisted upon and so widely proclaimed. But that his own comfort and profit were the main considerations in his mind, is proven by the argument which followed in which he pleaded the unreasonableness

---

[1] This pamphlet was published in Boston in December, 1730. A copy is in the library of the Mass. Hist. Soc.

[2] Belcher to B. T. Apr. 5, 1731; C. O. 5/872, B. T. O. P. N. Eng.

[3] Acts and Res. of Mass., II, 613, 633.

of allowing a faithful servant to suffer, and cited the conduct of nearly all the governors from Bellomont down as a justification of his urgent prayer for leave to sign the bill.[1] Young Jonathan was now drafted into the service and presented a memorial to the crown in support of his father's plea. This practically enrolled him among the agents of Massachusetts, a position which he held as long as he resided in England, to his own personal advantage as well as the comfort of his fond parent.[2] The committee of the council referred the question to the board of trade and by its report the weakness of the British government in a matter of critical importance was revealed with the utmost clearness. Its report was that, in view of the suffering which would otherwise be inflicted upon the governor and his family, he should be permitted to assent to the bill and take the grant for this time only, but that this should not be construed into a precedent to the effect of weakening in any degree the validity of the instruction as it stood. In accordance with this advice an additional instruction was prepared and forwarded.[3]

The qualification which was introduced into the instruction was mere words and nothing more. It was evident that the British government was not prepared to stand by its own declaration or to support its governor in upholding it. The cause had nearly been lost when Burnet disappeared from the scene, and by the appointment of a compromiser like Belcher [4] the government had already surrendered its case. This was well enough understood at Boston and year after year the procedure of 1731 was repeated. Until 1735 the annual appropriation was regularly made. Belcher, with assurances that no other course was possible, as each case arose, asked for permission to assent to the act; this was supported by a

---

[1] C. O. 5/873, Belcher to B. T. Apr. 26, 1731.

[2] Belcher wrote to Richard Partridge "Although my son was not deputed in form, yet I think there need be no nicety about that. He lived with me during the whole dispute with the Assembly about the 27 instruction, wrote over all my speeches and is as perfectly acquainted with the whole affair as any person in New England." B. P. I., 38.

[3] Journal of B. T. Aug. 1731; Acts P. C. Col. 1720–1745, p. 261.

[4] Belcher himself wrote at this time that he must walk circumspectly lest the king's ministers should think he was not zealous enough for the crown and the assembly should think he bore too hard on the privileges of the people. B. P. I, 38.

memorial from his son or some other in England and the permission was given. Thus the precedent was established till it was no longer necessary even to secure the consent of the crown or to note the fact that the earlier instructions were being violated.[1] If the home government hoped to maintain its ascendancy in Massachusetts, the only alternative was to provide a salary for the governor from the royal exchequer and this was the final recommendation of the board of trade.[2] But the Walpole ministry was too indifferent in such matters even to suggest such a course and thus a condition was established of which the evil fruits were to appear a generation later. As payments were continually in arrears and the steady depreciation of the currency in which they were made reduced their purchasing power, Belcher still had abundant occasions for complaint and opportunities for reminding officials and his correspondents generally of his merits as a long-suffering servant of the king and province.

But the arrears from which Belcher suffered were more directly occasioned by controversies over two other instructions — the sixteenth and the thirtieth — which related to the issue of bills of credit and to the claim of the house of representatives to the exclusive right of auditing and allowing claims against the province before they were paid. The former instruction was the one already referred to as now general, which forbade the passage of acts for the issue of bills of credit without a suspending clause; in the case of Massachusetts, issues at one time were not to exceed £30,000 for annual service and support, and in the case of New Hampshire £6000 a year was fixed as the limit.[3] The other was intended to abolish the practice of the house in regard to the allowing of claims and the making of appropriations in the form of resolves rather than acts. The controversy over the latter subject was pending on Burnet's death. The first supply act of Belcher's administration permitted the governor and coun-

---

[1] Successive letters from Belcher to Newcastle and the board of trade. These also appear in the B. T. Papers and those of the Secretary of State.

[2] B. T. to committee, Aug. 26, 1735. C. O. 5/917, B. T. E. B. N. England.

[3] Acts and Res. II, 701, 845; Acts of P. C. Col. 1720–1745, p. 326. In a letter of 1737 Belcher explained how the above sums were decided upon as the limits of annual issues in Massachusetts and New Hampshire in a conversation between himself and the earl of Westmoreland.

cil to draw warrants for payment according to their direction. The attitude of the council in this matter was naturally favorable to the claim of the governor and the crown. In order to procure, if possible, the recall of the instruction the house sent repeated addresses to England. These drew from the committee of the privy council the opinion that the privilege demanded was superior to any which the house of commons claimed in cases of similar nature.

In 1732 Belcher sent to the duke of Newcastle an able exposition of earlier practice in this matter in Massachusetts,[1] written apparently by a lawyer. In this the power of the assembly to impose and of the executive to dispose of the public taxes and revenue was asserted as in harmony with the language of the charter and a necessary division of functions in government; otherwise the work of the executive would be merely clerical. As to earlier usage, it was stated that, with the exception of a few minor instances which occurred chiefly during the later years of the second intercolonial war, there had been no attempt during the first twenty-nine years after the grant of the second charter to make appropriations specific or to allow muster rolls and other accounts of forces and garrisons. But since 1721 the representatives had insisted upon their right to examine into all these subjects and with one or two exceptions had inserted provisions in all their resolves of supply prohibiting their being passed by the governor and council without being previously allowed by the general court. The practical argument in favor of this was that otherwise the province would suffer from fraud. The reply to this was that only occasional mistakes, but no frauds, had been discovered in the past, and in case fraud should be discovered, it would be the fault of the assembly if it allowed the councillors who were guilty to remain in office more than one year.

A reference to the law officers, Yorke and Talbot, followed, which resulted in an analysis of the powers of taxation granted in the charter in full harmony with its language and reserving to the executive the discretion over expenditures subject to general, but not specific and exhaustive, clauses of appropriation. The persistence of the assembly was regarded

---

[1] C. O. 5/899, B. T. N. Eng.; Acts and Res. of Mass. II, 701.

as proof of a design to assume the executive power of government and thereby to throw off dependence on Great Britain. An order was issued declaring the king's displeasure at these repeated applications on subjects already determined and that no alteration would be made in the instruction already issued. Thereupon, after the province treasury had been kept empty for a prolonged interval to the great inconvenience of the governor and others, the assembly yielded to necessity, though it still persisted in claiming that its interpretation of the charter was correct. Though the act in which this concession was made violated the 16th instruction by providing for the issue of bills of credit without a suspending clause,[1] it was allowed by the privy council to stand till it expired. Its provisions were sufficiently detailed to secure all necessary control over expenditures to the general court. After many repeated efforts extending over three years Belcher secured an appropriation of £3000 for Governor Burnet's children.

An incident of the political changes of the early years of Belcher's administration was the loss by Elisha Cooke of his popularity in Boston,[2] so that he finally failed of election to the assembly and dropped to an extent out of public life. In Belcher's confidential letters charges presently began to appear that Cooke was his enemy, was intriguing against him and had joined with David Dunbar in making what trouble he could for the governor. With the disappearance of Cooke a period in the history of political opposition in Massachusetts may be said to have closed, and no leader who was his equal again appeared in the house until the advent of Samuel Adams.

Variety and interest were added to Belcher's administration by the doings of Dunbar and the prolonged feud which existed between him and the Massachusetts governor.[3] Reference has already been made to him as surveyor general of the

---

[1] Acts and Res. II, 691, 701; Acts P. C. Col., 1720–1745, pp. 326–334; C. O. 5/875, May 10, 1733 (Action on the 16th and 30th instructions); B. P., I, 405.

[2] Hutchinson, II, 337.

[3] A sketch of Dunbar's earlier career is in C. O. 5/5. It shows that he had seen long service in the Leeward Islands and had endured much in Spain. There is other material about him in C. O. 5/10.

woods, to which office he was appointed in 1728. This brought him directly into connection with the eastern parts as far as Nova Scotia, and this connection was strengthened by his appointment in 1731, on the death of John Wentworth, as lieutenant governor of New Hampshire. After the treaty of Utrecht, and particularly after the close of Râle's War, the English began again to push their settlements eastward beyond the Kennebec river. The results of this, as viewed from the standpoint of immigration, have been traced elsewhere, but here it is necessary to show their bearing upon Dunbar and his career. In May, 1729, the board of trade, in a report to the privy council, proposed that colonists be settled between the Kennebec and the St. Croix rivers and that a new province, to be called Georgia, be erected there, distinct from both Massachusetts and Nova Scotia. It also recommended that Colonel Dunbar should be its governor, he serving without salary until the king should think him deserving of one. He should receive power to grant lands and in addition to set apart a tract of not less than 100,000 acres of woodland in that region for the supply of the royal navy.[1] Dunbar was already in New England, with the office of surveyor general of the woods and apparently also that of surveyor of the lands of Nova Scotia. A plan which was then hatching was to extend Nova Scotia westward to the Kennebec. For this purpose the original French claim was to be used and it was to be contended that by the occupation of Pemaquid in 1696 the French had conquered that entire territory and in 1710 Nicholson had won it back, but as a part of Nova Scotia.[2] As incidents of the change the navy would receive greater advantage from the forests of the region and the territory of Massachusetts would be considerably reduced. Claims originating in earlier grants, made by the New England Council, were also being revived. The obstacle to the success of this plan lay in the fact that the charter of Massachusetts unmistakably gave to that province the territory between Sagadahoc and Nova Scotia. On April 27, 1730, Governor Richard Philips, of Nova Scotia, was instructed to take possession of the land between the Kennebec

[1] C. O., 5/4 and C. O., 5/916, B. T. to P. C. May 14, 1729.
[2] Johnston, History of Bristol, Bremen and Pemaquid, 266.

and St. Croix rivers, garrison the fort at Pemaquid and reserve 200,000 acres additional in his entire province for the uses of the navy.[1] But this was after Dunbar had taken several important steps toward the realization of a different plan.

No express authority was given to Dunbar to carry into execution the project which was suggested in the above report of the board of trade. But at first he was encouraged by the board to promote settlement in the eastern parts [2] and as a body of one hundred colonists or more was available and others were expected to come later, he established a settlement and rebuilt the fort at Pemaquid, — naming it Fredericksburg or Fredericksfort — and took other steps which were announced in his letters as the establishment of the province of " Georgia." Of this he claimed to be the governor or allowed the impression to prevail that he was such.[3] Now that Pemaquid was being replaced upon the map in this fashion the interest of Massachusetts in it at once revived. Lieutenant Governor Dummer asked Dunbar to show him the authority for what he was doing, and the latter spoke of a commission and instructions, but was able to show none. As a matter of fact, the only documents of this kind which he possessed were those under which he held the office of surveyor general of the woods.

But the men whose interests were most seriously affected by Dunbar's scheme were Samuel Waldo, Sir Bibys Lake and their associates, who were the assigns of the Muscongus Patent originally issued by the New England Council, a century before. Elisha Cooke was also interested in this and

[1] Acts P. C. Col. 1720–1745, p. 282; Johnston, op. cit., 267; Douglass Summary, I, 383.

[2] Dunbar to Newcastle, October 11, and December 10, 1729, C. O., 5/898, A more definite statement appears in a report of the board of trade to the privy council, Col. Treas. Papers, July 4, 1738.

[3] Williamson and Sullivan in their histories of Maine and Johnston in his History of Bristol, Bremen and Pemaquid, describe what Dunbar did in this connection. Dunbar's voluminous correspondence extends through several volumes of the O. P. of the Board of Trade, N. Eng. These letters taken in connection with Belcher's letters in the same collection and in his published Papers, enable one to follow the controversy in great detail. In the Papers of the Secretaries of State, N. Eng. 1733–1741, C. O. 5/898 and 899, is also much correspondence with Newcastle concerning the settlement and Dunbar's affairs in general.

other speculative ventures in Maine timber lands, and this fact, as we have seen, explains the degree of prominence which he had given to the question of the right to those lands in the Massachusetts assembly. These men depended for the validity of their claims on the Massachusetts charter, the acts of its government and the succession of grants which they had procured from early in the eighteenth century. Waldo therefore carried his case against Dunbar and Nova Scotia to England.[1] There the petitions presented were submitted to the board of trade and by it the opinion of the law officers was taken and all, in the usual course, was referred back to the king and council for final action.

Upon the attitude of the board of trade, the leading spirit in which at the time was Colonel Bladen, may be seen the effect of the earlier neglect by Massachusetts of the repeated demands that it should maintain the fort at Pemaquid and otherwise provide for the effective defence of the eastern frontier. That, as we have seen, she had refused to do and had maintained that attitude during the first two colonial wars. Was it possible that by virtue of this and of her failure to settle the region, her claim to it had been forfeited? Wilks, her agent, was examined on these and other points, and for the further information of the board queries implying doubts concerning these points were submitted to the attorney and solicitor general, Yorke and Talbot. Had not this neglect, followed by the occupation of Pemaquid in 1696 by the French, resulted in a temporary forfeiture of the territory, which in turn was terminated by Nicholson's conquest of Acadia in 1710? If so, had not the lands reverted in the crown, and now had it not power to appoint officers and grant out the territory again? The reply of the law officers was to the effect that the grant to Massachusetts, both of territory and government, was valid and that it had not been guilty of such neglect as to create a forfeiture. Magistrates and courts had been appointed and some measures of defence adopted. It was not expected, they said, that all parts of a province would be equally improved. And in case the neglect charged were true, it must be proved by legal process

[1] Acts P. C. Col. 1720–1745, p. 275; Williamson, History of Maine, II, 172.

followed by a forfeiture of the grant. As to the idea of a conquest by the French, the tract in question had not been yielded to France by treaty, and their occupation of it would have worked only a suspension of the rights of the owners and not an extinguishment of them. Upon the reconquest by Nicholson they all revived, the charter remained in force and the rights of the petitioners, notwithstanding certain informalities in their grants which were incident to colonies and conditions in a new country, should stand undisturbed. This opinion, one of the most important in the long line of those which involved colonial interests, thoroughly English in its support of vested property interests, was approved by the king in council and an order was accordingly issued revoking the instructions which had been issued to the governor of Nova Scotia and to Dunbar and commanding the latter to quit the possession of all the lands involved. This conclusion was not reached until August 10, 1732.[1]

Meantime, Belcher arrived and was installed as governor of Massachusetts and New Hampshire. Dunbar was soon brought into relations with him and with the general court at Boston by his efforts to secure legislation which would enable him to inspect the private saw mills and restrain the lumbermen in the Maine woods. Dunbar spent much time in Boston and his too facile pen and speech helped to increase the difficulties in which he soon became involved. One of the first objects of his attack was Cooke, because of the extent to which he was pillaging the king's woods. This, however, did not prejudice the governor against Dunbar, though the latter obtained no aid of value from Massachusetts in his efforts to preserve the woods and enforce the acts of parliament which were intended to encourage the production of naval stores. But what soon brought about a violent collision between Dunbar and the Massachusetts authorities was the founding of his settlement at Pemaquid and the granting of lots to settlers there in disregard of prior claims. Dunbar wrote interestingly to Newcastle on the one hand of the readiness of many to go as settlers, the general interest and the desire which existed to divert the flow of immigrants from Pennsylvania to New England; and on the other about the

[1] C. O. 5/873, 875, B. T. O. P. N. Eng.

determined opposition of the Massachusetts government and the interested claimants. Cooke, as usual, in answer to Dunbar's claim that he represented the interests of the crown, came out with the sweeping declaration that they were in possession, would not give a farthing, would as soon go to law with the king as any other man, and would sue any who should attempt to dispossess them.[1] Protests and petitions from interested parties began at once to pour into the offices at Boston. They were referred to the general court and a committee denounced the proceedings of Dunbar. Upon this Belcher was in accord with the general court and the foundation was thus laid for a prolonged and bitter feud between him and the surveyor general. The lieutenant governor and others appear to have been sent to Fredericksfort to report on the situation there. Dunbar pretended to believe that a military force was to be sent to take possession of his settlements, though Belcher denied any such intention. Some petty disturbances of the peace may have occurred which Belcher tried to magnify into a riot.[2] In his private correspondence, as was his custom in the case of all his opponents, Belcher began to apply various contemptuous nicknames to Dunbar with the purpose of bringing him into contempt. Cooke and a number of New Hampshire men innocently suffered in the same way. In due time came the order which terminated all the plans of establishing a province of " Georgia " in eastern Maine and the name was immediately appropriated by the trustees who were aiming to confirm the claims of the English against the Spanish on the southern frontier.

Bladen's influence may again be seen in the provision which had already been made to keep Dunbar in New England by appointing him lieutenant governor of New Hampshire. This office had been left vacant by the death of its incumbent, John Wentworth, at the close of 1730. As a result of petty jealousy, Belcher had already begun a quarrel with Wentworth and his friends because the latter, before it was decided which one would be appointed to the governorship, had

---

[1] Johnston, History of Bristol, *etc.*, 272; Noble, Land Controversies in Maine, Pub. of Colonial Soc. of Massachusetts, VI, and VIII.

[2] See letters of Dunbar and Belcher in C. O. 5/870, 872, B. T. O. P. N. Eng.

written letters of compliment to Shute as well as to Belcher. When Belcher visited Portsmouth he refused an invitation to Wentworth's house and compelled him to quit all claim to any part of the salary which was granted by the assembly and to acknowledge that he depended for his allowance wholly on the governor.[1] Wentworth was forced to be content with the fees and perquisites which arose from registers, certificates, licenses and passes, which amounted to about £50 sterling. The lieutenant governor himself died a few months later, but his son, Benning Wentworth, and his son-in-law, Theodore Atkinson, were made mortal enemies of Belcher by this treatment. The latter, who was the ablest man in the province, was removed from his place as collector of the customs and naval officer and was forced to divide his office of high sheriff with another. Other changes also were made to the injury of the Wentworth interest, Richard Waldron, secretary of the province, acting as the confidant and lieutenant of the governor in carrying out this policy. Into a province where the train had thus been laid for a characteristic feud David Dunbar was now introduced as Wentworth's successor. Belcher was already as strongly prejudiced against him as he was against the Wentworths, while the situation was further complicated by Dunbar's duties as surveyor general of the woods.

The appointment of Dunbar to this post was an exceedingly unwise one, though it was intended to strengthen his position as surveyor general of the woods and it also insured the sending of full reports to England of everything which might discredit Belcher or Massachusetts. Dunbar evidently had influence with Newcastle and Bladen and must be provided for as a poor, though quarrelsome, dependent. Belcher in turn denounced him to all parties in unmeasured terms and almost from the first sought by all possible means to secure his removal. He was naturally overbearing toward inferiors and those from whom no advantage was to be expected, and Dunbar was an admirable object toward whom to exhibit these qualities. Dunbar was not admitted to the council, was not allowed to command the militia and was deprived of the customary perquisites of office. In the time of Shute as

---

[1] Belknap's History of N. H., Farmer's Ed., 225.

we have seen, the claim had been put forward and acted on that the governor was constructively in the province at all times and therefore that New Hampshire could be governed from Boston and the discretion of the lieutenant governor reduced to zero. That principle of action was now revived by Belcher. This was inconsistent with any fair interpretation of the lieutenant governor's authority as set forth in his commission and instructions, and with colonial precedents in general. This intention was, that in the absence of the governor, all ordinary functions of government should be performed by the lieutenant governor and that in no case should any officials, civil or military, be exempted from obedience to his orders.[1]

Before the close of 1731 Dunbar was writing home that Belcher claimed virtually that he was present at sessions of the legislature as elsewhere and bills must be sent to him to be signed. He was ashamed that he was of so little significance and thought that Belcher was the last man in the world to whom he would choose to be subject. One of the worst instances of humiliating treatment to which Dunbar was subjected was, on going to the fort one day, to find himself excluded by the officer in charge. Benning Wentworth and Atkinson were with the lieutenant governor and formal demand was made for admission, but it was refused on most explicit orders from Belcher applicable particularly to Dunbar.[2] Belcher afterwards wrote to Dunbar a long exposition, as he interpreted them, of his powers over forts and the militia in New Hampshire, quoting his commission to substantiate it. His conclusion was that the lieutenant governor had no power over them except what was delegated to him by the governor and could not claim the command of them as a perquisite.[3] He went further and declared that, as to powers and perquisites of the lieutenant governor in general, they did not exist without the leave and order of his chief. " The licenses for marriages, registers, certificates and passes, I think," he continued, " are the principal per-

---

[1] B. T. to the King, Nov. 4, 1731; C. O. 5/917, B. T. E. B. N. Eng.

[2] This act was disapproved by the board of trade in November, 1732; *ibid.* Dunbar to Popple with affidavits, Aug. 10, 1731; C. O. 5/873.

[3] B. P. I, 334 *et seq.*

quisites in New Hampshire, and by the law of the Province you will find all these literally and strictly the Governor's." After referring to the fact that these had often been taken by his predecessors, he added, " I always thot it mean and considering there is no provision here or at New Hampshire for a Lieut. Gov'r, I think a Gov'r (in honour to the commission he bears) ought to let him enjoy all the perquisites he fairly can; nor do I, I assure you, desire to interfere with these things in N. Hampshire. But, as they are my right, they must be enjoyed under me."

The controversy over these subjects continued for years. Petitions by Dunbar and on his behalf were presented before the board of trade in England, that he might be reimbursed for building forts and settling people in the region between the Kennebec and Nova Scotia, and that his authority and salary as lieutenant governor of New Hampshire might be vindicated and restored.[1] These claims were reported upon by the board of trade and came before the committee of the council. A copy of the last mentioned petition was sent to Belcher for an answer. This, however, was not until 1735 and no further action was taken by the privy council. To views respecting these subjects expressed by the board of trade Dunbar repeatedly wrote that Belcher paid no attention.[2] But the influence of Bladen and the representatives of John Thomlinson, an able London merchant who was employed as one of the agents of New Hampshire, which were unfavorable to Belcher, gradually produced some effect. On Dunbar's return after an absence of some two years, Belcher allowed him to command the fort and resigned to him the usual perquisites of office.[3] These, with his salary of £200 as surveyor general, gave him a respectable support, though they by no means enabled him to clear off his debts. A riot at Exeter, which was occasioned by Dunbar's efforts to seize lumber at the saw mills, caused disturbance and violent disputes with Belcher over the issue of a proclamation for the arrest of the rioters. Finally, in 1737, Dunbar returned to England, where he was temporarily imprisoned for debt, but

---

[1] Acts of P. C. Col. 1720–1745, pp. 351, 611.
[2] C. O. 5/877, B. T. O. P. N. Eng. Various letters of Dunbar in 1734.
[3] Belknap, op. cit., 231.

later contributed what influence he possessed toward procuring Belcher's recall.

Very soon after Dunbar's arrival in New Hampshire an address of complaint against Belcher's administration as oppressive and arbitrary was signed by fifteen persons and sent to England, with a request for his removal. Richard Waldron, as the leader among the governor's friends, replied to this in an address of compliment to Belcher, signed with one hundred names. One of the effects of the hostile memorial, as well as the letters of Dunbar and his friends, was the appointment in England of Atkinson and Wentworth to seats in the council. A mandamus was sent for Belcher to swear them in, but they delayed responding to it as long as possible, while the governor protested against the appointments in his letters home. But finally, before the close of 1734, these two opponents of the governor were admitted to their seats in the council. Meantime they had held seats in the assembly and in the opinion of Belcher had done what mischief they could there.[1]

At the beginning of his administration in New Hampshire Belcher had no difficulty in securing a salary as prescribed in his instructions and of the amount received by his predecessor.[2] The attitude of the great majority of the inhabitants and the assembly toward Belcher was very friendly, as was to be expected from them toward a governor of New England origin and one who possessed the abilities and address of the new appointee. The same was true of his position in Massachusetts, and its attitude toward him. In New Hampshire affairs moved smoothly for a time, the quarrel between the governor and Dunbar and his friends proceeding without seriously disturbing the province. The militia needed improvement and the fort at Portsmouth, like all similar structures, was in perpetual need of repair. A public building was also needed, and the repair or rebuilding of the prison. The debts of the province should be paid and proper steps taken for the redemption of its outstanding bills of credit. These

[1] N. H. Prov. Papers, IV, 665, 668, 674, 794, 806.  B. P., I, 433, and many other references both in the Belcher Papers and in Belcher's correspondence in the British Archives.

[2] N. H. Prov. Papers, IV, 562, 565, 570, 584

were the chief internal matters which were considered in the brief sessions of the assembly during Belcher's early visits to New Hampshire. In May, 1732, Belcher told the assembly that by the brief account which the treasurer would lay before them they would perceive that there was no money in the treasury. Though only a grant of £1000 was needed, the house replied that if an additional tax was laid on polls and estates, so poor were the people that it would tend rather to fill the jails than to supply the treasury. An act was therefore passed for laying an excise on liquors,[1] but as this would not fill the treasury, Belcher dissolved the assembly and renewed his demands to its successor in the following August. The house promised a supply of £1000 if the governor and council would assent to the issue of an additional £20,000 in bills of credit. But the council would not agree to this, because of the governor's instruction forbidding him to assent to any such issues, except what were necessary for the actual support of government, without the introduction of a suspending clause.[2] The province also should not extend the duration of its funds for the redemption of its bills beyond 1742.

In a letter written early in 1734 Theodore Atkinson described the financial condition of New Hampshire as follows:[3] "The late war with the Indians was so long and vigorous that we could not maintain it by a Poll tax, which was the only way except a small excise, which in the war time scarcely amounted to one hundred pounds, we had to supply the Treasury, and the charge of the war togeather with the support of the Government amounted to twice the sum we could raise; so we were obliged to Borrow money in the Credt of the Governmt & pass acts for repaying the same in sundry successive years, . . . & all this money was *Bona fide* expended in the payment of our souldiers, which we were so generous as [to] bear what the Massachusetts called our Quota, which far exceeded our Proportion, for we sent 50 men of 500 as a travelling army through their government, and

---

[1] N. H. Prov. Papers, IV, 616 *et seq.*

[2] *Ibid.*, 636–643, 662; Acts and Res. of Mass., II, 845. The sum fixed for New Hampshire was £6,000 annually, but Belcher never assented to the issue of so much as that.

[3] N. H. Prov. Papers, IV, 835.

in all the last war had not one souldier on our frontiers nor one shilling of support from them — this, togeather with the Bounty upon Indian scalps, was the charge by which we came so much in debt, & now, those years being devolved upon us, we have the whole support of the Governmt to pay." Atkinson went on to state that this, including what was necessary for the redemption of their currency, would amount to an expenditure of £2500 a year, while the largest tax they had ever raised was £1500, that involving so much hardship that it was continued for only a year and imposed upon every taxpayer a burden more than double what one of equal means paid in Massachusetts. From these conditions arose the persistent demand for permission to issue some £60,000 in bills of credit, though how this was going to result in more than an indefinite postponement of the date when the debt of the province was to be paid, the advocates of the scheme were never able to show.

Upon this question now began a deadlock between the lower house on the one side and the governor and council on the other. To the argument that the people were too poor to bear additional taxation was added the persistent demands of the assembly for the issue of bills of credit in sums which exceeded the requirement for current expenses and for a period of years which should continue beyond 1742. Though Belcher was not specially averse to issues of currency by the colony governments, his instruction prohibited an assent to measures formulated in this way. The home government refused to yield and the governor, supported by the council, adhered to the royal instruction. The assembly on its part refused to impose heavier taxes, pleading the poverty of the province and declining trade.[1] In this way a deadlock began which continued until it became necessary to make appropriations in connection with the opening of the war between England and Spain in 1740. Repeated sessions of the general assemblies were held, but they were brief and ended in dissolutions. With the aid of Waldron and his other supporters in the council Belcher was able to conduct the routine business of the province. Occasional conferences were held with the Indians, the cost of which was borne chiefly or wholly by

[1] N. H. Prov. Papers, IV, 662, 664, 667, 673, 679, 688, 697, *et seq.*

Massachusetts. Until 1740 or later there was no visible danger of the peace of the frontier being broken by an Indian war. The militia and fort of the province could therefore be allowed to remain in the neglected condition which was habitual in time of peace. No lieutenant governor was present to clamor for a salary. Belcher had to be content with his perquisites and what he got from Massachusetts. During his absences the council, or Waldron, conducted the few affairs of government without causing irritation to Belcher. They supported him in the attitude which he assumed on the question of the boundary. The assembly and its sympathizers were chiefly interested in maintaining the agents in England, but Thomlinson appears to have served largely without pay, though he and his solicitors seem never to have lacked for money with which to prosecute the cause of New Hampshire before the boards in England.[1] The source of these funds would be difficult to determine.

Relations between Belcher and Massachusetts on the one hand and New Hampshire on the other culminated in the boundary dispute, the settlement of which was followed by the separation of New Hampshire from Massachusetts and its organization as a distinct province. This controversy had been inherited from the previous century and it survived the issue of the second Massachusetts charter. In fact that added to it, for now Maine was expressly included as a part of Massachusetts and the boundary between New Hampshire and it on the east had also to be adjusted. The origin and status of the question in the seventeenth century have already been described.[2] By the charter of 1691 the colony of Massachusetts, as well as the other colonies and districts which were combined into the enlarged province, was to comprise the territory that was included within its earlier boundaries. The line three miles north of the Merrimac river was again

---

[1] See the interesting extracts from the correspondence which passed between Thomlinson and Atkinson, N. H. Prov. Papers, IV, 833 *et seq.* Early in 1734 Atkinson wrote that sometime they hoped to pay the agent, but for the present all such proposals were blocked by the governor and council, who, he charged, were working in the interest of Massachusetts. *Ibid.*, 836. Early in 1737, however, £500 seems to have been appropriated for the agent. *Ibid.*, 720, 820.

[2] Osgood, Am. Colonies in 17th Century, I, 371 *et seq.*; III, 186, 311, *et seq.*

specified as the northern boundary of Massachusetts and it was to extend westward as far as the colonies of Rhode Island and Connecticut extended.  This was a crude and indefinite statement, especially in view of the fact that Connecticut, according to its charter, extended through to the south sea. But it brought into prominence the fact that the northern boundary of Massachusetts must be defined to a point at least somewhere near the Hudson river.  Since the establishment of New Hampshire as a separate province it had become impossible for Massachusetts to maintain its extravagant claim to all the territory lying east and south of a line drawn eastward from near the outlet of Lake Winnepesaukee.  But it now revived that claim so far as it applied to territory lying west of the upper course of the Merrimac river, and to justify it reference was made to an opinion of the chief justices, Rainsford and North, in England in 1677. Massachusetts asserted that its northern boundary should be a line parallel to the Merrimac and three miles north and east of it to the junction of the streams which formed its source, and thence the line should extend due west to the point which should be fixed as the longitude of the western boundary of the province.  By this interpretation a strip of territory fifty miles broad, which now comprises the southern part of New Hampshire and Vermont, would have belonged to Massachusetts.

When New Hampshire was made a royal province no attempt was made to run the line.  Massachusetts towns, especially Salisbury, Amesbury and Haverhill, extended their borders north of the Merrimac and beyond the three-mile line, so that conflicts over jurisdiction arose between them and the inhabitants of Hampton, Kingston and Londonderry, which lay well within the boundary of New Hampshire.  On the one hand parties who wished to avoid jury duty or the payment of taxes were able to do so, and on the other parties were wrongfully arrested and punished — both as incidents of confused and undefined jurisdiction.  Governor Belcher wrote, at a later date, " The poor borderers on the lines . . . live like toads under the harrow, being run into jails on the one side or the other as often as they please to quarrel. They will pull down one another's houses, often wound one another and I fear it will end in bloodshed. . . ."[1] As Massachusetts was so much stronger than New Hampshire and its settlers the more numerous, they usually carried the day in cases of conflict.

Beginning in 1693, New Hampshire made repeated efforts to have the line run. Committees were appointed, but Massachusetts was unwilling to co-operate. In 1696 Governor Usher had the line run as far west as settlements then extended. This Massachusetts refused to recognize and the perils of the wars, added to her continued opposition, made any approach to decisive action impossible until after peace had been restored. In 1719 another futile attempt was made by New Hampshire to settle the dispute. She then instructed Henry Newman, her agent in England, to lay the question before the lords of trade and the king, and voted £100 to meet his expenses. The view which was expressed concerning their southern boundary was that it should be a line extending due west to the utmost limit of Massachusetts, while the only question at issue in the case of the northern boundary was whether, beyond the head-waters of the Newichwonnock river, its direction should be due northwest or a little west of north.

Affairs however drifted on without further action until 1726. Early in that year Massachusetts granted a tract of land on both sides of the Merrimac at Penacook — now Concord. This act was in strict accordance with the theory of Massachusetts respecting its northern boundary and so it was maintained in answer to a protest from Lieutenant Governor Wentworth that the grant lay within " the very bowels " of New Hampshire and included the most valuable part of that province.[2] A warning addressed to the Massachusetts settlers who were felling trees and laying out lands proved futile and then the government of New Hampshire appealed in earnest to the crown. Massachusetts also instructed its agent to defend its claims and furnished him evidence upon

[1] N. H. State Papers, XIX, 234, 236. This volume contains a mass of papers on the boundary controversy. The Massachusetts papers are here in large part and the rest are in manuscript in the Mass. Archives. The best accounts of this controversy is in Fry, New Hampshire as a Royal Province, 241, et seq. (C. U. Studies).

[2] N. H. Prov. Papers, IV, 206; Fry, op. cit., 244.

which to do it.  In November the board of trade requested
the king to order the governors of both provinces to desist
from laying out new towns or making grants of land in the
disputed territory.[1]  The board was then expecting reports
from commissioners of the two provinces upon the basis of
which the dispute might be settled, but though such boards
had been designated they never acted, because Massachusetts
now chose to insist that the entire question had been referred
to England.  Action was thus blocked and during the years
which followed Massachusetts continued to make township
grants in the disputed region.  In 1727, on the plea that it
would shorten her inland frontier and lessen the charge of
defence, she appointed a committee to lay out a line of towns
between the Connecticut and Merrimac rivers.  Another was
also planned to extend along the upper course of the Merrimac and a third to extend from the Newichwonnock to
Falmouth on Casco Bay.[2]  New Hampshire was moved by
this to grant all her unappropriated lands east of the upper
course of the Merrimac, and Bow, one of the towns thus laid
out, overlapped much of the Penacook grant.  By these steps
the danger of collisions between rival settlers was greatly
increased and the necessity for an adjustment of the question
was therefore becoming imperative.

When Belcher was appointed governor he was instructed
to recommend to the assemblies that they should choose commissioners from the neighboring provinces with power to
adjust the dispute over the boundaries.  Massachusetts took
action first and, as the result of the acquiescence of New
Hampshire in its choice of two candidates, the board consisted of Governor Talcott of Connecticut, Governor Jenks of
Rhode Island and Adolph Philipse of New York.  The interest
of Belcher, of course, was with Massachusetts, while he also
controlled the council of New Hampshire.  Whether or not
his influence was used at this time to prevent an agreement,
none was reached.  The provinces failed to agree upon forms
of procedure and also upon a proposal that an equivalent
should be given in lieu of lands which either party had held
or improved under ancient grants.  As this suggestion was ap-

---

[1] C. O. 5/915.  B. T. E. B. N. Eng.; Acts P. C. Col. 1726–1745, p. 127.
[2] Hutchinson, II, 299;  Journal of Upper House.

parently intended to favor Massachusetts, New Hampshire rejected it. The commission never met, the practiced hand of Elisha Cooke being visible in this result.

The next move of the New Hampshire assembly was to appoint John Rindge, a Portsmouth merchant who had large connections in England, as agent to reopen negotiations there. With this appointment the council did not concur. Rindge submitted to the king in council a petition which contains the ablest statement ever made of the case of New Hampshire.[1] But, having soon to return to America, Rindge left Captain John Thomlinson, a London merchant who had frequently been in New Hampshire,[2] to prosecute the case in his stead. Thomlinson, who himself showed great diligence and insight, secured the services of Ferdinand John Paris as solicitor. A copy of Rindge's petition was transmitted to Wilks, the agent of Massachusetts, to be forwarded by him to his principals for an answer. This took time, and it was not until the middle of 1735 that the board of trade was able to report that Massachusetts had agreed to the settlement of the controversy by a royal commission. To this the committee of the privy council assented, but the spring of 1736 was well advanced before the commissioners were named.[3] They consisted of the five eldest councillors of New York, New Jersey and also of Rhode Island, provided the Rhode Islanders named were still in office. The close of 1736 had arrived when the instructions of this body were drafted, and their commission passed the privy seal the following April.

Meantime Massachusetts, of course with the assent of Belcher, had been hurrying on town grants and private grants so that her claim to the territory west of the Merrimac river might be fortified by occupation and possession. In 1736 thirteen townships were laid out between the Penacook grant and the Connecticut and along the eastern bank of that river. These, together with the townships previously granted, formed an irregular quadrilateral extending from Northfield and Dunstable, which till now had been the northern frontier towns of Massachusetts, to and including Boscawen and Charlestown in New Hampshire.[4] Collective grants, known

[1] N. H. State Papers, XIX, 235.
Belknap, Farmer's Edition, 229.
N. H. State Papers, XIX, 256, 260, 262, 265, 274, 277.　　[4] Fry, 254.

as the Narragansett towns, were also made to heirs of those
who had fought in Philip's War.  Nearly 1100 claimants appeared in response to this appeal.  There the survivors and
heirs of the Canada expedition of 1690 were enrolled for the
same purpose and a large number of grants were made for
their benefit.  As the determination of the crown, whatever
it might be, was not likely to affect private property, Massachusetts people seemed sure to gain from this process, while
indulgence in land grabbing, the result of which was intended
to be the settlement of towns, was bound in the end to be
beneficial, though it was a specially offensive exhibition of
the aggressive spirit of Massachusetts toward her weaker
neighbor on the north.

The royal commission met at Hampton, New Hampshire,
in August, 1737.  A delay of about a week was occasioned by
the neglect of Massachusetts promptly to prepare its case.
Belcher also, by what was later termed by the lords of the
council in England an act of partiality in favor of Massachusetts, prorogued the New Hampshire assembly to the tenth
of August, so that it could not attend to the immediate
preparations for the hearing.  But the case and the evidence
supporting it for each province were duly submitted.  The
commissioners rendered their decision on the second of September.  The question of the northern boundary occasioned
little difficulty and the decision respecting it — which was
favorable to New Hampshire — was of slight practical importance.  It was the southern boundary which lay in the
midst of settled territory and which from the first had been
the chief subject of contention.  In reference to that line the
commission decided only one point, that being the locality
on the coast where it should begin.  But as to the direction
it should follow, the commissioners decided that this would
depend upon a legal interpretation of the terms of the second
Massachusetts charter.[1]  If by that patent all the territory
included in the grant of 1629 was guaranteed to Massachusetts, its interpretation of its northern boundary was considered to be justified.  But if this should not be the judgment
of the crown, the line should run along the lower course of
the Merrimac to the point, at Pawtucket falls, where it

[1] N. H. State Papers, XIX, 301.

curved northward, and thence should extend due west until it met his majesty's other governments.

At the time this decision was rendered the assemblies of the two provinces were in session in the neighborhood. The New Hampshire assembly Belcher at once prorogued for more than a month and, when it came together, the council opposed an appeal and refused to concur in a proposal to raise money for the purpose. The commissioners, however, received the list of exceptions which were filed by the lower house as equivalent to an appeal, and the agent was instructed to press for a decision in England. Belcher then dissolved the assembly and another was not called for nearly a year. This was a familiar procedure on the part of governors to prevent action which was not considered desirable, and Belcher employed it with smooth facility. The general court of Massachusetts was continued in session until it had perfected the resolutions and other measures which were necessary to an appeal. After receiving the appeals of the two parties the commissioners adjourned and submitted the question to the crown.[1]

That the board of trade and committee of the council, before which the question now came, were wholly unbiased, no one who is familiar with the previous history of Massachusetts and of its relations with New Hampshire would contend. The history of Massachusetts told against her in any such reference, and the conduct of Belcher did not help her cause. She possessed a charter and New Hampshire was a royal province of the regular and favorite type. Viewed from the standpoint of the home government, the earlier and the present encroachments which Massachusetts had made upon her territory were indefensible. They were not even justified by military considerations, for New Hampshire made no objection to co-operation or to the passage of troops through her territory. By encouraging New Hampshire it was thought that the king would secure more complete control over ungranted land in New England and the prospect of securing

---

[1] N. H. State Papers, XIX, 393 *et seq.* In the entries under dates in September 1737 and later in vols. IV and V of the N. H. Prov. Papers the doings of its general assembly concerning this affair may be traced. The more important proceedings of Mass. are printed in Vol. XIX of the N. H. State Papers. The rest are still in manuscript.

a little revenue in the form of quit rents might be improved. Massachusetts realized that she labored under these disadvantages and therefore had fought for delay until the issue had finally to be met. The decision of the king in council — and it would seem to have been simply a registry of one arrived at well back in the previous century — was that the line should be run straight from the mouth of the Merrimac to his majesty's other governments.[1] The contention of New Hampshire as to the northern boundary was also confirmed. The judgment was announced early in 1740. The town of Dracut later petitioned against the decision on the ground that it so divided their estates and parish as to cause great inconvenience. Thomas Hutchinson was sent as agent to England to present their case and also petitions from other towns which had recently been laid out north of the line, that they be restored to Massachusetts. But these petitions failed to impress the committee and after considerable delay, in 1746 they were dismissed.[2] This decision was due to various considerations, among them being the fact that Massachusetts was a chartered province and in the town grants which she had hastily made there was no reservation to the crown of quit rents or pine trees. There was left over for further adjustment claims to a large tract of unsettled land west of the Connecticut river, respecting a part of which arrangements were entered into between Massachusetts and Connecticut. From this originated the later controversy over the so-called New Hampshire Grants.

New Hampshire had now obtained more territory than she had claimed; but what was of greater importance, she had secured an opportunity for westward expansion and tolerable conditions of existence as a distinct province. The time had therefore come for its final separation from Massachusetts by the appointment of a governor of its own. But in order to explain how this came about we must retrace our steps and follow the career of Belcher through the later years of his governorship in Massachusetts as well as New Hampshire.

[1] Acts P. C. Col. 1720–1745, p. 598.
[2] *Ibid.*, 601. N. H. Prov. Papers, XIX, 523, 534, 537. Belknap, Farmer's Edition, 251–262.

In the earlier years of his administration the question of the efficacy of royal instructions, when they ran counter to the will of a colonial assembly, especially of its house of representatives, was brought to the test. Upon the subject of the governor's salary the instruction had been practically abandoned, but the one which related to the control of the lower house over expenditure had been maintained. A much more prolonged struggle occurred over the third instruction, the purpose of which was strictly to limit issues of bills of credit. This was a more difficult question to adjust than either of the others, more obscure in its nature and one that deeply affected the social and economic interests of the province. It was therefore not so capable of definite adjustment as were the other questions which have just been mentioned. From the first Belcher had announced his resolve to live up to this instruction and the council on the whole supported him. The assembly, however, persisted, addressed the crown and house of commons in vain, and attempted the passage of a number of supply bills which failed to secure the governor's assent. The revenue therefore fell heavily into arrears, and in 1733 Belcher assented to an appropriation act which provided for the issue of £76,500 in bills of credit. This was intended to provide for expenditures which had been incurred during two or three preceding years. Two other acts were also passed within the space of seven months which provided for additional issues, making a total of £106,571, and in none of them was the suspending clause inserted.[1] This drew from the board of trade and privy council an additional instruction to Belcher forbidding him in the future, on pain of immediate removal, to assent to bills which provided for issues in excess of £30,000 in any one year or for the reissue of old bills or the continuance of bills in circulation beyond the dates mentioned in the acts of emission. Belcher in reply explained how he had believed himself to have acted in harmony at least with the spirit of the previous instruction and corrected the opinion of the board to the effect that reissues of bills were always equivalent to new issues. But he also declared his intention in the future strictly to obey the commands of the home government upon this subject.

[1] Acts and Res., II, 690, 698, 707, 744.

The effect of this policy, taken as a whole, was to reduce the medium of exchange of Massachusetts to an amount which was quite inadequate to its needs. As an incident of the controversy also appropriations had been so reduced that the government had not the means to pay its current expenses. Debts were accumulating and suffering was the result. According to the terms of their issue practically all the outstanding bills of credit must be called in by the beginning of 1742, thus leaving the province almost destitute of a medium of exchange. It was at this juncture that the project of a land bank was revived as a means of affording needed help.[1] In recent years two plans of this kind had been launched — though quickly suppressed — one in Connecticut and the other in New Hampshire. The Connecticut scheme had originated with the " New London Society United for Trade and Commerce," founded by Daniel Coit, John Curtis and others. Those who desired to form this society first petitioned the general assembly for a charter in 1729, and prominent among the privileges asked for was that of issuing currency upon the credit of the company, which should circulate under conditions similar to those attaching to bills of credit of the colony. A charter was not granted, but three years later, in 1732, the petitioners having omitted all reference to the issue of currency and limited their objects to the promotion of trade, fishing and other industries, they were incorporated by act of the general court.[2] But in a few months this company revealed its true nature by commencing to issue bills of credit on a considerable scale. These were based solely on mortgages of real estate deposited by members and bill holders, and they were believed to threaten a further and serious inflation of the currency.

For this reason Governor Talcott, in February, 1732/3, called an extra session of the general assmbly and ordered the society to appear and prove by what authority they had emitted and sold bills and to show why they should not be compelled to refund the sums for which they had sold the bills and submit to dissolution as a society. The general

---

[1] Davis, Currency and Banking in Mass., I, 121 *et seq.*; II, 102 *et seq.*

[2] Conn. Col. Recs., VII, 390; Caulkins, Hist. of New London; Talcott Papers, Colls. of Conn. Hist. Soc., IV, 268, 270, 281.

assembly, after considering its charter and inquiring into the use which had been made of it, resolved that its conduct in issuing bills of credit was illegal, that it should put out no more bills and those which it had issued should be redeemed, and that the society should forfeit its charter. It did not consider that by the deposit of mortgages a true capital stock had been created and declined to give its support in any form to the financial scheme of the society. This program was carried out and by an act of assembly the New London Society was dissolved.[1] When it was later proposed that the company should be revived, the assembly admitted — what was true at the outset — that a corporation had no right to incorporate and that in granting the original charter it had exceeded its powers.[2] An act was passed appointing a court of chancery to settle up the affairs of the concern. By business operations the society seems to have accumulated some property and with this, helped by a generous loan from the colony, it was able to call in and redeem its bills, though several years passed before references to the process of settlement disappear from the record.

In 1731 certain Boston merchants, led by Jacob Wendell, petitioned the general court for permission to issue £50,000 in bills to be loaned on real estate as security and redeemable in the course of ten years.[3] The governor refused to assent to the bill and the project never came to anything. But two years later these same merchants formed a partnership and issued on their own credit £110,000 in bills, known as merchants' notes, redeemable in the course of ten years in coined silver at 19s. an ounce. These notes were readily received because of belief in the credit of those who issued them. But owing to the fact that they were redeemable at a fixed rate in silver, they were soon hoarded and passed out of circulation.

These projects led certain New Hampshire merchants, in 1734, to issue bills which were redeemable in bills of the various New England colonies or in silver or gold. They bore interest at one per cent. About £6000 sterling was issued.

[1] Conn. Col. Recs., VII, 422.
[2] Ibid., 499.
[3] Davis, Banking and Currency in Mass., I, 123; II, 122.

The assembly of Massachusetts passed an act prohibiting the circulation of the bills in the colony, but this was disallowed by the privy council, because they considered it would be a great hardship publicly to discredit persons who were engaged in this undertaking as well as a disservice to New Hampshire to prohibit the circulation of these bills which might be of advantage to the said province.[1] Belcher, however, in speeches to the New Hampshire assembly and in his letters, denounced the plan as unwarrantable and a fraud and issued a proclamation for the enforcement of the Massachusetts act against them before its disallowance. The New Hampshire assembly defended the notes and their issues against the governor's attacks and contended that the royal instruction was not aimed at negotiable notes among merchants and traders.[2]

By many and devious paths the people of New England were trying to secure a circulating medium which was adequate in quantity, stable in value and of such material that it could be conveniently used. There was no science of finance at that time and only a very slight accumulation of experience in the world which would throw light on their peculiar difficulties. The British government insisted that they should conform to a lofty and rigid ideal, but withheld from them the means which might enable them to reach it. Rhode Island, their near neighbor, in the exercise of the liberty which it still possessed under its charter and of that far wider liberty of indulging at will in the vagaries of the time, complicated the situation by pouring out from its presses a mass of irredeemable paper to circulate not only within her own limits but far and wide in the adjacent colonies, adding thus to the evils of depreciation under which they were already staggering. Under the influence of the royal instructions and of the hoarding of the merchants' notes, the increase of Massachusetts currency, about 1734, seems to have been temporarily checked. But depreciation continued, as indicated by the rise in the price of silver and a high rate of exchange. The presence of Rhode Island notes furnished a partial explanation of this phenomenon.

[1] Acts and Res., II, 747.
[2] N H. Prov. Papers, IV, 685, 688; Davis, Banking and Currency, II, 128.

During the latter half of the decade of the thirties many plans were proposed in Massachusetts and crude efforts made to return to a specie basis and silver was frequently mentioned as the metal in which, by some process or other, the outstanding bills must be made actually redeemable. Plans were discussed in the general court and outside. Many pamphlets were published, a few of which really threw some light on the situation. In the general court the Hutchinsons, father and son, occupied themselves much with these questions and always in the interest of sound currency. The elder Hutchinson is credited with the introduction of a bill in 1734, the object of which was to provide for a new issue of bills to be redeemable in silver, and for these the old bills should be exchanged at a ratio of about three to one. This bill was, however, defeated. In 1736 the younger Hutchinson — afterwards the governor — is supposed to have published anonymously a pamphlet in which he advocated the same plan in a more detailed form.[1] This plan required as a prerequisite that the bills of other colonies should be forbidden to circulate in Massachusetts.

A little later, Dr. William Douglass, one of the leading physicians of Boston, a man of penetrating intellect and caustic pen, began a vigorous attack on paper currency and the heresies of its supporters. His first pamphlet was published anonymously under the title of " An Essay concerning Silver and Paper Currencies," and is supposed to have appeared in 1738. Two years later Douglass published in Boston his " Discourse concerning the Currencies of the British Plantations in America,"[2] which has since had wide vogue. It is reckoned as " one of the very best of the eighteenth century discussions of the money question." The secret of its value lies in the fact that the author did not view the subject from the standpoint of the narrow and partisan

---

[1] "A letter to a member of the Honourable House of Representatives on the present state of Bills of Credit." This is in Davis' Colonial Currency Reprints, III, 152. See also his discussion of it in Proc. of Mass. Hist. Soc. 1899.

[2] Both these pamphlets are reprinted by Davis in his third volume, and the latter has also been ably edited by Bullock in Economic Studies (published by the Am. Econ. Assoc.) Vol. II. Douglass was also the author of the well known work, The Summary Historical and Political of the British Settlements in North America, 1755.

interest of the debtors who constituted the majority of the people of the colonies, but in its relation to the trading communities of the world at large. From that source he learned the correct doctrine that the commodity selected by common consent to be the medium of exchange or trade must be the least changeable of all in value, and that was silver. There therefore could be no other proper medium of exchange but silver, or bills of exchange and notes of hand payable in silver at certain periods and redeemable to ready money in silver at any time. After reviewing the chaotic condition of the currency in the colonies, Douglass affirmed, though in doing so he ignored or denied a number of potent facts, that at the beginning they were comparatively well supplied with silver and it was not its scarcity, but the clamor of the debtors, the idle, the extravagant and those whose poor judgment had allowed them to be misled, which had caused the issues of paper and had carried them to such excess that now rates of depreciation in the various colonies ranged from seventy to nine hundred per cent. It was the inflation of the currencies, he continued, and not the unfavorable balance of trade, the excess of imports over exports, which had driven the coin out of circulation. He attacked the idea that government finds money for the people and asserted rather that it was the people who by their trade and industry provided not only for their own subsistence and the support of the government but found " their own Tool and Medium of Trade." Upon the evil political and social effects of the paper money craze Douglass dwelt with great force, and wondered why it was that the colonizing states of Europe should permit their dependencies, by laws and practices of very questionable morality, to so degrade their medium of exchange and thereby cheat their creditors both in Europe and in the colonies. The fiat money scheme of Rhode Island and its mistakes came in for pitiless condemnation, and the way of return to specie payments by means of contraction of the currency and the payment of debts was clearly pointed out.

Douglass preached a strong and invigorating doctrine, and it was the first time it had been heard in such effective force in the colonies. In its appeal to reason and common sense and its suggestion of views which a wider experience and a deeper culture have since made a commonplace, the protests of Douglass may well be compared to those of Chauncy and others against that other outburst of emotionalism, the White-field revival, which was prevailing at the same time. At the close of his pamphlet Douglass briefly reviewed the plans which had been suggested for a return to specie payments in Massachusetts. Of all these which had as their object the substitution of silver for mere promises to pay, or for the unavailable security of land, he approved, whether they emanated from the action of the government or from the private initiative of groups of reputable merchants. One of these, which was incorporated into the annual appropriation acts, beginning with 1737, was a provision for the payment of taxes in so-called new tenor bills, which should be exchanged for earlier issues — now called old tenor bills — in the proportion of one to three. Payments might also be made in coined silver at 6s. 8d. per ounce,[1] which was the par value of silver. But as that metal was then rated in the old bills at 27s. per ounce, the difficulty of floating the new bills at the prescribed rate is evident. Subscriptions for the new bills were solicited from respectable merchants, which were in the nature of loans to the government — of which there had been several instances in earlier years — but under the conditions which now existed these were only moderately successful. It did not check the depreciation of the currency or tend even to restore it to normal value. The influx of Rhode Island bills alone would have prevented that, and where an attempt was made to exclude them by law, Massachusetts saw herself restricted by the royal instruction to £30,000 in heavily depreciated bills, which, since she must call in her earlier issues to the amount of £170,000 in 1742, was quite inadequate to her needs. Hutchinson came a step nearer what proved finally to be the solution, by proposing that 220,000 ounces of silver should be borrowed in England for ten years at four per cent interest — a fund being provided by a duty or excise for the payment of this debt — and this should be used for the redemption of the bills and providing a stable medium of exchange. But this proposal was rejected.[2]

[1] Acts and Res., II, 875, and references for the acts of the succeeding years. Davis, *op. cit.*, I, 124, 126, 140 *et seq.*
[2] Hutchinson, II, 352; Shirley Corresp., I, 47.

As none of the plans for a return to specie payments proved possible, and at the beginning of 1742 the legal term of existence of bills of credit to the amount of £270,000 would expire, by 1740 financial disaster seemed impending over Massachusetts. It was at this moment that John Colman, with widely extended support throughout the province, revived the project of a land bank. Belcher made most determined opposition to it, so there was no prospect at all of securing legislation in its favor or the incorporation of its supporters. The question, however, was carried into the general court and there for many sessions it held the chief place, as it did in the attention of the province at large. About this question developed a struggle which affected Massachusetts more deeply than any which had occurred since the days of Andros; in one of its aspects it even suggested a revolt such as occurred a generation later.

By the close of 1739 Colman, as a result of diligent effort, had secured nearly four hundred subscribers to a plan for issuing bills to serve as a medium of trade and based for security on mortgages of real estate. It was in essentials the same plan which Chamberlayne had advocated in England in the previous century and Colman himself in Massachusetts in 1714. A prospectus was issued and by advertisement the number of subscribers was finally increased to eight hundred. They were drawn largely from people of small means throughout the province. The original board of directors included Robert Auchmuty, Samuel Adams (the father of the revolutionary leader), Samuel Watts, John Choate, Thomas Cheever, George Leonard and Robert Hale, all men of prominence in their towns but none with a much wider reputation, with the exception of Auchmuty. It was therefore the more democratic element in the colony which supported the land bank. The result which it sought to attain was in harmony with the ideas of this class. Each subscriber was only required to pay forty shillings on each thousand pounds of his subscription and in addition he must furnish satisfactory mortgage security for his entire loan and on this pay interest at the annual rate of three per cent and repay the principal in twenty annual installments of five per cent each. As the result of a vivid stroke of the imagination the capital stock of the concern was declared at the outset to be £150,000. Colman had an idea that a capital could be accumulated out of the reserved profits, but from what these were to be derived was never made clear. The only "business" contemplated was the issue of bills, called "manufactory notes." These were to be put into circulation by loans to the subscribers. In them, as well as in various enumerated commodities, the principal was to be paid back by the subscribers. These bills were thus to be issued by a company without capital, were not redeemable until twenty years after date and were then payable in commodities.

To counteract the wildly speculative influences which were backing Colman's scheme, a group of Boston merchants and citizens, including Edward Hutchinson, Edmund Quincy, James Bowdoin, Samuel Sewall, Andrew Oliver, Joshua Winslow and others, formed what was known as the "Silver Scheme." Their plan was to issue notes, like the merchants' notes of 1733, which should be redeemed in silver, and mutually to agree not to receive, except at a discount, the bills of other colonies which were not redeemable in gold or silver, and not at any time to receive the notes of the land banks. Their notes also were given only a limited circulation among reputable merchants and their friends and the possibility of inflation from their use seemed excluded. It was between these two associations, with their respective policies and backers, that the battle was now drawn.

In the general court the house of representatives supported the land bank and the cause of what was virtually irredeemable paper currency; the governor and council stood firmly in opposition to this and favored a course which looked toward the resumption of specie payments. They, too, were sure of the support of the British government upon this issue. In the session of May, 1740, the struggle really began, the court being bombarded by memorials, and petitions from the supporters of the respective schemes — especially of the land bank — in the various counties. The newspapers furnished avenues, as never before, for the expression of opinion. On the motion of the council a joint committee was named by the houses to consider both plans, but owing to the fact that the members from the house refused to attend, the committee never accomplished anything. From the first the house showed a determination to go its own way and ignore the council. On June 18, while the two plans were before the committee, the house voted that persons concerned in the land bank should not be forbidden to issue bills as they had planned. This caused general alarm among the opposite party, and after the close of the session the governor issued a proclamation cautioning the people against receiving or passing these bills, which tended to defraud men of substance and to disturb the peace. The directors of the silver scheme soon began the issue of bills and somewhat later announced that holders of these bills might receive their value in gold or silver on demand. Belcher, in his speeches to the assembly, in his letters to the board of trade and the duke of New-castle, and by means of proclamations, now began to de-nounce the land bank in the strongest terms,[1] and to give a correspondingly strong support to the silver bank. By Sep-tember, however, the directors of the land bank had so far perfected their scheme as to commence the issue of notes. In the newspapers arguments began to be published by sup-porters of both plans that they would not receive the notes which were issued by their opponents. It is curious to note that they applied the system of tests, to which they had always been so accustomed in the religious sphere, to this question of economics. We now have appearing the idea of orthodox and heretical as applied to a question of economic belief and practice, and the heretics, as usual, were charged with moral obliquity. They were said to be violating the principles of common honesty. Belcher wrote that, with opinion moving in the direction which it then seemed to have taken in Massachusetts, he would not trust the honor of that province for a pair of old shoes. Both at that time and in the future we shall find the attitude of the test and of orthodoxy — or, speaking sociologically, the taboo — applied to all sorts of questions, religious, social, political, with the resultant conflicts along lines of intolerance and extreme opposition, which give rise to conflicting parties and social groups, whose activities are so highly valued as a means of progress and

[1] Belcher Papers, II, 340, 348, 359, 360, 388-9. Davis, I, 130, *et seq.*, gives the best account extant of the controversy over the land bank.

enlightenment in the Anglo-American type of civilization. Their methods and spirit in most instances are certainly the exact opposite of those which are inculcated both by science and morals, and the paths through which they lead toward enlightenment and progress, to state it mildly, are very devious and uncertain.

It was in perfect accordance with this spirit, as well as with the methods of political action which were then in vogue both in England and the colonies, that Belcher, supported by the council, should undertake at once to crush the land bank party by the use of his power of patronage, by removals of its supporters from offices local and general and the appointment of its opponents to the vacancies thus created. Early in November he issued proclamations to all who held offices, civil or military, under his commission, warning them not in any way to encourage the circulation of the notes of the land bank on pain of removal.[1] This, of course, is always a brutal and therefore a mistaken policy, and it failed in this instance. Four of the directors of the land bank who held the office of justices of the peace at once sent in their resignations. But Belcher, not content with this, formally removed them. Several other justices of the peace in outlying counties were also removed. Many militia officers either resigned or were removed, and discontent because of this policy of the governor became widespread. Inquisitorial proceedings on the part of the government were not lacking. The registers of deeds were called upon to return the mortgages which had been pledged as security to the land bank, and in this way a list of its subscribers was secured. This was freely made use of to increase the pressure on office holders. The colonels of regiments were ordered to report the conduct of officers subordinated to them, and justices of the general sessions were instructed to use their power in various ways, as in the granting of licenses, in opposition to the land bank and its bills. In January, 1740/1, an order was issued by the council that no one should plead before it as an attorney who passed, received, or in any way encouraged the circulation of the manufactory bills. As all probate business was done before the board, lawyers who supported

[1] C. O. 5/882, B. T. O. P. N. Eng. Nov. 5 and 6, 1740.

the land bank were cut off from that most important line of practice.

By May, 1741, these measures had occasioned rumors to circulate, and here and there a sworn affidavit to be made, that organized resistance was preparing in some of the towns. A report was made that such a movement was contemplated in Weymouth and that it might be extending to several other towns on the south shore. The time generally rumored for such a demonstration was near the end of the month, when the court of elections would be held. Threats of this kind indicate that the pressure was checking the circulation of land bank bills. This impression is strengthened by the special efforts, made by its directors, early in 1741, to promote the circulation of their bills, and by plans to establish local banks of similar character in various counties. But the election passed and the new general court met without disturbance. The house was shown to be as staunch in its support of the land bank as its predecessor had been. Samuel Watts, a director and one of the justices of the peace who had been removed, was chosen speaker. The governor rejected the choice and another candidate was chosen and accepted without a struggle. Thirteen of the councillors were also rejected by the governor because of their connection with the land bank. Because of the evidence which these acts showed of the spirit of the house, Belcher immediately dissolved it and ordered a new election, the writs to be returnable on July eighth.

When the new house met, it elected John Choate as speaker, a man who had been very conspicuous as a supporter of the land bank. His election of course was vetoed and one John Hobson, a friend of the bank but not a subscriber, was chosen in his stead. Other choices also were made which were equally offensive to the governor and council. It was at this juncture that the action of the British government upon the crisis became known in Massachusetts and began to exert its effect. In addition to the letters of Belcher and statements which Wilks and also Hutchinson — who was then in England on a special errand — may have made to the board of trade against the policy of the land bank, English merchants had petitioned against it. This brought it to the front in connection with the subject of the colonial currencies in general, which had for some time been attracting attention. The board reported to the privy council against the scheme as being very dangerous and that in connection with it the people and assembly of Massachusetts were giving another exhibition of their independent spirit. Though the governor's opposition to this was approved, he was making little headway. The board suggested that the attorney general of the province should be directed to prosecute the supporters of the bank; but it was realized that, as it was impossible to secure legislation against it in Massachusetts, parliament would have to act. This was the opinion of the law officers in England, and all other measures were regarded as merely palliatives.[1]

We have seen that in 1736 the privy council, acting in agreement with a report of the board of trade, had expressed the opinion that the notes which were being issued by the New Hampshire merchants were not harmful. In 1735 Wilks, the attorney general, had expressed himself as unable to find any objection to the scheme for a land bank, as proposed in Massachusetts. No effort was made by it to make its notes legal tender and there was nothing at the time which made them in any way illegal. Had the project been launched in England, its supporters would have been subject to prosecution under the act 6 Geo. I, c. 18, the so-called " bubble act," which had been passed as a means of suppressing the speculative companies which had come into existence at the time of the excitement over the South Sea Company. This act did not extend to the colonies, and the English merchants who now were petitioning against the land bank urged that it be so extended, as it was generally held that this was the only way in which the evil that threatened trade and credit in Massachusetts could be checked.[2] This course was adopted and by act of parliament (14 Geo. II, c. 37), the statute in question was extended to the dominions

[1] Acts of P. C. Col. 1720–1745, pp. 85; Report of B. T. to P. C. Nov. 14, 1740, C. O. 5/917.

[2] On Dec. 21, 1740, Ryder and Strange, the attorney and solicitor general, rendered an opinion that nothing could be done to put a stop to the land bank except by a positive law; C. O. 5/882. In the petition from Massachusetts we see certain Americans asking parliament protection in domestic colonial matters.

and its prohibitions were made effective there in September, 1741.

The "bubble act," however, was originally passed to meet conditions quite different from those which existed in Massachusetts at the time of the land bank. In order to secure the monopoly of the stock market for certain existing corporations, all transactions by joint stock companies having transferable shares, without special authority by statute, were declared unlawful, and a public nuisance. The offenders were threatened with punishment under the nuisance act, would further incur the penalties of premunire and would be liable for treble damages to any merchant who suffered harm to his trade through them. Proceedings under it were to be held at Westminster, Edinburgh or Dublin. In extending the act to America the operations of the land bank were described and these undertakings with all the things prohibited by the "bubble act" were declared illegal and void. Prosecution of them could now take place in the colonies. But as the land bank was not a joint stock company and did not have transferable shares, and as the description of its operations in the preamble was far from accurate, the statute was only roughly applicable, if at all, to the association which it was intended to destroy.

Owing to the attitude which he had assumed toward New Hampshire in the boundary controversy and toward some of its leading men at an earlier time, Belcher had become unpopular in that province. Atkinson and Wentworth, with the aid of Thomlinson, the agent, and Dunbar, were tireless in their efforts against him. Samuel Waldo who, besides his interest as a land speculator in Maine, was agent for Gulston in procuring masts for the navy, was active in the same cause. A forged letter was sent to Sir Charles Wager, first lord of the admiralty, representing that Belcher was allowing the lumbermen freely to waste the king's woods, with many other false statements about his policy and claims.[1] Though Belcher was easily able to prove that this was a forgery, other complaints were urged in which it was made to appear that he was responsible for the defenceless condition of the prov-

[1] Belknap, *op. cit.*, 255; C.O. 5/899. Letters to the Secretary of State. Dated May 5, 1739.

ince and was neglectful of its government. The correspondence of the governor shows that he was fully conscious of this opposition against him. When the decision in the boundary case came it confirmed the resolve of the home government, in the interest of the authority of the crown in New England, to appoint a separate governor for that province. Benning Wentworth, who had been in England for some time soliciting for the place, was so appointed. The policy which had been adopted with the appointment of Dunbar was also continued by the designation of Wentworth as surveyor general of the woods.

In Massachusetts at the same time Belcher had come to so complete a break with the mass of the people over the question of the land bank that it was evident he could not peacefully settle up its affairs. Martin Bladen, who was among the most influential members of the board of trade, had never been fond of Belcher and, as we have seen, had quietly supported Dunbar in his opposition to him. He now was decidedly of the opinion that Belcher should go, and the influence which the governor had so painfully labored to promote and nourish in England was quite too weak to save him from dismissal. The rival aspirant was William Shirley, and Belcher's letters show that for some years he had been growing increasingly suspicious and jealous of this rising lawyer and official. Shirley was of English birth and education and had come to Massachusetts in 1731 with a letter of introduction to the governor from the duke of Newcastle. He had a large family to support and sought such minor offices as came in his way, while he gradually built up a practice as a lawyer. At first Belcher befriended him, as a means perhaps of recommending himself further to Newcastle. Shirley was appointed advocate general before the court of admiralty for New England and later came to hope for the collectorship of the customs at Boston, a more lucrative office. The office of clerk of common pleas and the naval office, as well as offices in Virginia and New York, were sought by him. His position as advocate general brought him into connection with the king's woods and the interests of the navy in New England. By the assembly he was appointed a member of the Rhode Island boundary commission. In 1736 Shirley's wife was sent to England, partly at the instance of Belcher, to secure for her husband a salary from the exchequer. She, being also of English birth and an adept in pulling wires and soliciting for office, pleaded so long and successfully with the duke of Newcastle, the cause of her husband, herself and their nine children that she presently earned from Belcher various titles which were not intended to be complimentary. Meantime, in his confidential letters, Belcher began applying much stronger epithets to Shirley himself and warned his correspondents, especially in England, to watch closely the steps which were being taken on his behalf. In 1738 a letter was sent to the duke of Newcastle in denunciation of Belcher and open advocacy of Shirley as his successor, and to this was attached the forged signature of James Bowdoin.[1] As soon as he was informed of this Shirley hastened to disclaim all knowledge of its origin, and to attribute it by implication to the governor as a means of destroying Shirley's influence with the duke.

In the midst of the struggle over the land bank the war with Spain began and a requisition was sent to the continental colonies for a contingent of troops to strengthen Vernon and Cathcart's expedition of 1740 against Carthagena and Porto Bello. The opponents of Belcher represented that his unpopularity had become so great that he probably could raise only a few troops. By this time applications, supported by Bladen, were being made for Belcher's removal and for the appointment of Shirley as his successor. Newcastle wrote to Shirley asking him to assist in all possible ways in raising the troops.[2] Shirley responded, with his usual and somewhat officious zeal, to this request and recommended to Belcher three men who, if commissioned as officers, would be likely to raise companies of volunteers. He also was active in procuring supplies for the expedition, keeping Newcastle informed of what he was doing and assuring him that the chief aim of his life was to " Pursue the united Intrest of his Majty and the Country." It was not surprising that he should presently receive a curt note from Belcher respecting his recommendations for appointments on the expedition.

[1] C. O. 7/899, May 1738; Lincoln, Corresp. of Shirley, I, 13.
[2] Lincoln, op. cit., I, 18.

" You must be sensible," wrote the governor, " if every gentle-man in the Province of your order should take the same freedom you have done, such applications must give me a great deal of trouble. You'll therefore, avoid anything of the like nature for the future." [1] To the individuals whom Shirley had named or those who supported their applications, Belcher bluntly declared that he would not make the appoint-ments, because of the source from which their recommenda-tions came.

But this was only the petulance of a man who knew that his official days in Massachusetts were ended. When the above letter was written Belcher had already received in-formation that he had lost both his governments and that Shirley had been chosen as his successor in Massachusetts. With Massachusetts in the distracted condition in which it then was and a war just beginning, the development of which no one could foretell, it was rightly judged that a change of governors was desirable, and that notwithstanding the fact that Belcher had been faithful in the discharge of his duties and even in the raising of recruits for the West Indies had met with all the success which could fairly be expected. In his defeat — which he attributed to the malice of his enemies — Belcher had recourse to two sources of consolation and these were the main props of his life. One was to humble himself before God and in silence to acknowledge that he had sinned, and the other was to visit England in the hope that, when the ministry was better informed concerning his sacri-fices and difficulties, they would make some further provision for him. [2] Newcastle was an " easy boss " and there was so much in common between the two men that the ex-governor had no difficulty in reading his superior aright. In due time the correctness of his forecast was shown in the appointment of Belcher as governor of New Jersey.

[1] Lincoln, I, 20–28; Belcher Papers, II, 310.
[2] Belcher Papers, II, 403, 408.

# CHAPTER XVII

## INDIAN RELATIONS DURING THE SECOND QUARTER OF THE EIGHTEENTH CENTURY

WHILE the raids of the young Iroquois warriors against the Catawbas, or other tribes of the south, were disturbing the frontiers of Pennsylvania and Virginia and thus bringing the colonies into a wider coöperation in Indian policy, the occupation of Niagara, and afterwards the building of the English fort at Oswego, were mooted questions in the north. By their efforts in these directions the French were renewing the projects of La Salle and Denonville, taking a further step westward than had been indicated in the building of Fort Frontenac and preëmpting the chief strategic point between that post and Detroit, which already had been settled in the midst of the lake region. The English, on their part, were advancing their actual frontier to the Great Lakes and were beginning to carry into execution the territorial policy which was implied in the Iroquois deed of cession of 1701.

Rivalry in the fur trade had now become more than ever the controlling motive on the part of both nationalities which were contending for expansion along the New York frontier. The predominant interest of Albany in that industry had long been evident, and now that war had ceased it clearly appeared, going to the extent of a large direct trade in British manufactures with Canada. By means of the lower prices of their goods and their increased activity the British were also establishing wider trade connections among the Indians of the northwest. British traders were pushing further into the interior, and appeared at last to be supplanting the French. They were at any rate challenging the leadership which, until this time, the French had enjoyed in the fur trade of the northwest. To this result the Hudson Bay Company was also contributing, and the French were in danger of being encircled by a ring of hostile competitors. But, meantime, their spirit had become more secular and commercial than it had been in the previous century, and priest as well as trader and explorer were now uniting in one common movement for retaining the lead which they had so long held and pushing their triumphs even further into the interior. It was from conditions such as these that the founding of Niagara and Oswego and the rivalries of Governor Burnet's administration proceeded.

Steadily after 1715 evidence accumulates, both from the British and French sides, that competition for the Indian trade was becoming more intense. In view of this the Six Nations frequently warned the British to make better use of the weapon of cheapness, which they might wield with such effect. A deputation of Oneidas complained at Albany at the beginning of 1716 of the dearness of goods. They said that on the price of goods the covenant chain chiefly depended and that, unless goods were cheaper, it would cause the ruin of both the Iroquois and the British. On this and later occasions they also complained, that both they and the far Indians were imposed on and cheated when they came to Albany to trade, and were discouraged from coming oftener.[1] But notwithstanding these complaints, British trade and influence were on the increase and the French with every year became more painfully aware of it. In 1717 Alphonse de Tonty, while crossing Lake Ontario on his way to Niagara and Detroit, met a considerable flotilla of canoes filled with western Indians and peltries bound for Albany. By skilful use of brandy, the commodity with which the French contended against English rum, most of the savage crew were diverted to Montreal or Detroit.[2] This encounter is characteristic of the struggle which went on, but with a slow and steady gain in favor of Albany. When Burnet's legislation increased the difficulty of direct trade between Albany and Canada, the superior cheapness with which the British could furnish Indian supplies told more effectively on the result. Even in 1716 Vaudreuil wrote that the only article of French merchandise which the Indians preferred to that of

---

[1] Wraxall, *op. cit.*, Jan. 1715/16, June 1716.
[2] Severance, *op. cit.*, 111.

the English was powder.[1]  He therefore besought the crown
to be liberal in permitting the establishment of posts in the
Indian country, in issuing licences for traffic there and in
permitting the moderate use of brandy in connection with
that trade.

Extended reference has already been made to the revival
by the French, in 1706, of the project for the establishment
of a trading post at Niagara, and of its being laid to rest
as a result of the unfavorable report of Cleranbout d'Aigre-
mont.  Though Joncaire continued to live much of the time
among the western Iroquois and to strengthen his influence
there as he was able, the plan for the occupation of Niagara
did not reappear with prominence until about 1716.  The
growth of commercial rivalry with the English then brought
it to the front under such conditions as gave it practical
result.  Associated with Joncaire in the promotion of French
interests among the Iroquois was Charles Le Moyne the
second, now lieutenant governor of Montreal and later to be
the second baron of Longueil.  The great achievements of the
family to which he belonged, as well as his own ability, were
guaranties that the influence of his advice upon the government would far exceed that of Joncaire.  In 1716, on his
return from the Iroquois country, he called the attention of
M. de Ramezay, the governor of Montreal, and the Intendant
Begon, to the need of a small establishment at Niagara.[2]  He
insisted that, by means of it, the French and their allies
among the Iroquois would control the trade of the region
between Lake Huron and the Ottawa river, inhabited by the
Chippewas and other tribes.  The *coureurs de bois* could also
be better controlled from that centre, the Iroquois would be
conciliated, and trade which now went to the English would
be in great part regained.  This proposal was communicated
to Vaudreuil, but he was not willing to establish the post
until the Iroquois should ask for it.  Under this condition
the council of the Marine in France approved the plan.
This was the suggestion, rather than the earlier and far
more prolonged work of Joncaire, which was to lead a few
years later to the permanent occupation of Niagara, a result

[1] N. Y. Docs., IX, 870.
[2] N. Y. Docs., IX, 874;  Severance, 108.

which doubtless was due not merely to the insight but to the superior social standing of De Longueil.

In the meantime rumors circulated among the Iroquois and the British of what the French were doing or intended to do. Some of these reports located their new enterprise at Irondequoit bay, at the mouth of the Genesee river. In July, 1719, an Onondaga chief reported at Albany that the French were already building a fort near the falls at Niagara. This was just as Governor Hunter was sailing for England, and during the interval which was to pass before the arrival of Burnet the government of New York was under the charge of Peter Schuyler as president of the council. In consequence of the report concerning Niagara, two Albany commissioners were sent, in April, 1720, to the Seneca country to negotiate.[1] They reminded the Indians of the violation which the French, by this and other acts, were committing against the Iroquois deed of grant of 1701, and that the result of such events would be that the Iroquois would lose their hunting grounds and be entirely surrounded. By intrigues they were being hushed to sleep, while the French took possession of the heart of their country. In their lackadaisical fashion the Indians, even the Senecas, admitted this to be true and with their usual empty formula of words promised thereafter to consult only the British concerning these matters. But their reference, in closing, to the vain confidence which they had put in the English assistance when in the past Denonville and Frontenac had invaded their country and destroyed their villages, revealed in part the cause of their distrust.

Even while these words were being exchanged, decisive steps were being taken by the French.[2] In pursuance of orders from the French court in 1718, that a number of magazines should be built around Lake Ontario, Vaudreuil and Begon had sent Joncaire "to try the minds of the Senecas and to see if they could be induced to consent to the building of a house upon their Land, and to maintain that settlement in case the English should oppose it." Joncaire

[1] N. Y. Docs., V, 528, 541–545; Wraxall, *op. cit.*, July 6, and Aug. 3, May 22, Aug. 31, Sept. 10, 1720. Many references to this and other features of Indian relations during this period also appear in the Ex. C. Min. of New York.

[2] *Ibid.*, 588; Severance, 115 *et seq.*

had spent the winter of 1719 among them and with the aid of presents had already got their consent before the conference just referred to was held. Early in the summer of 1720 Joncaire went to Niagara and on the site of the modern Lewiston, at the entrance to the portage, hastily constructed a cabin of bark, upon which were displayed the king's colors, and "honored it with the name of the Magazin Royal." Of this Joncaire was made commandant and truck master.

On the close of their conference with the Senecas, the two Indian commissioners from Albany sent Lawrence Claessen, their interpreter, with three sachems, to protest in person at Niagara against the French encroachment. They found the structure built and La Corne, the trader who was stationed there, asserting that permission had been given by the young Seneca warriors to erect it.[1] This the sachems who were present denied. Returning by Irondequoit, Claessen found a French blacksmith established there. When they reached the Seneca castle they found Joncaire, and the two agents in a sharp exchange of words forcibly declared their purpose in each case so to control the Indian trade that his colony should reap the chief benefit from it. The Frenchman relied on his possession of the strategic portages involved and the Dutchman on the superior cheapness of his wares. The sachems joined in a chorus of disclaimers of the charge that they had consented to the building of the house at Niagara, and suggested that the British have it destroyed. In the following September the magistrates of Albany wrote to the president and council at New York, that the Six Nations were in a "staggering condition," and hence the French partly by threats and partly by presents and fair means had obtained "such an awe and influence over them."[2] Some of the Senecas, it was reported, were even preparing to remove to Canada, while the rest of the cantons, though well enough affected toward the English, did not dare to oppose the French, as had just been shown by their allowing them to occupy Niagara, the only passage to their hunting grounds and the one by which the far Indians would come for trade with them and the English. In view of the contempt with

[1] N. Y. Docs., V, 550.
[2] *Ibid.*, 570.

which the French had viewed the decayed fortifications on the New York frontier and the indifference with which the residence of their agents among the western Iroquois was viewed by the English, the Albanians looked forward to the next war with dread, lest they might be wholly driven from the frontier. They therefore urged not only that stone forts be built at Albany and Schenectady, but that a forward movement be started by the English, as a result of which posts might be established on the southern shore of Lake Ontario. This was the situation when Governor Burnet assumed office.

In his first long letter home, Burnet, after having consulted De Lisle's new map of Louisiana and Canada, enlarged upon the encroachments of the French and especially upon the post at Niagara and its expected consequences. Then he wrote to de Vaudreuil protesting against the occupation of Niagara as a violation of the treaty of Utrecht and of alleged orders that no steps should be taken until the boundary had been fixed by agreement in Europe.[1] To Burnet it seemed to be the purpose of Joncaire's doings to nullify entirely that treaty both as to free trade for the Indians and as to its declaration that the Five Nations were subjects of the English, going even to the extent, if necessary, of removing a large part of them to Canadian soil. To the diplomatic consciousness of the Canadian governor the English could have no claim to Niagara which would compare to that of the French, who had possessed it " from all time." Its occupation however, by the French he chose to interpret as involving no interruption of Indian trade, as no Indian had been compelled to trade with the French, and they would enjoy the same privilege of going to the English as had previously been theirs. Joncaire and De Longeuil had been adopted into their tribes. To de Vaudreuil the Iroquois stood wholly in relation of allies both to the French and English; as to their receiving of priests or blacksmiths or their removal to or from Canada, these would be left by him wholly free to follow their own preferences. In war also it had been the desire of the governor, and of the tribes also, that they should remain perfectly neutral. To such a colorless void

---

[1] N. Y. Docs., V, 517; IX, 889 *et seq.*

did M. de Vaudreuil's agreement reduce the whole course of French and Indian relations, that one step more would have brought him to a denial of the existence of Niagara itself.

The reply of Burnet and the British to this easy interpretation of Indian relations, was the passage of the laws which checked direct trade between Albany and Canada and thus deprived the French of the advantage of cheap English goods, while at the same time they extended relations as fast and far as possible with the western tribes and sought to bring them direct to Albany for trade. In the autumn of 1721 the young Peter Schuyler was instructed by the governor to settle with a company of young men for a twelve-month in the Seneca country.[1] He was to establish a trading post at Irondequoit, or some other convenient place, in the territory of the Senecas, notify the far Indians of it and by all lawful means draw trade thither. As an attraction, he was to insist upon the superior cheapness of English goods, and was also to assure them of the firm promise of the Five Nations, that they would " Secure and Keep the Path Open and Clean " for them whenever they should come to trade with New York. Even French *coureurs de bois* were to be drawn, if possible, into the trade, by the cheapness of English goods. The merchandise which Schuyler and his associates took along with them were to be bought and sold upon a joint stock, but they were not to hinder any other British subjects who might wish to trade there on their own account. Finally, if possible, a tract of land fifty miles broad and of indefinite westward extent above the falls of Niagara, was to be bought from the Indians. That this plan in general was executed we know, and that it met with encouraging success is also evident, for in the summer of 1723 allowances were made by the governor and council for the support of officers and eight privates, a smith and interpreter, to serve in the Seneca country, and that instructions were given to this company similar to those which had been given to Schuyler. Canoes were also provided and presents for the Indians, while a reward was offered for the one who on his return should be found best versed in the language of the Senecas.

[1] N. Y. Docs., V, 641; Ex. C. Min. Sept. 4, 1721.

The result of this rather systematic effort, was to divert a considerable body of trade to Albany, as was shown before many months had passed, by increased numbers of far Indians appearing there or on their way thither with peltries. At the close of May, 1723, so many Indians had arrived in the city, that a conference with them was held, at which their dialects were interpreted by a Seneca, he in turn being rendered into Dutch by Lawrence Claessen. Among the advantages for trade which the strangers were told they would find at Albany were two wooden houses, built for Indians to lodge in, so that they might deliberately buy and sell there without being exposed to the extent which had been customary in the past to the influence of the trader's rum and his deceitful arts.[1] A few weeks later Burnet wrote to the board of trade in a spirit of satisfaction concerning the results of his policy which was characteristic of his sanguine temperament. The previous spring, he said, about twenty far Indians had visited Albany, but this year the number had been increased to eighty, and he had learned that about fifty more were on their way. It was also at this juncture that Cadwallader Colden was gaining the hold upon office and public affairs which he was so long to retain. He was now surveyor general and at Burnet's request he prepared two papers, one on the climate and the other on the trade of New York, both of which were sent to England with the governor's commendation.[2] In reference to trade Colden explained all the features of Burnet's policy, with their favorable results, and ventured the opinion that by such arts of peace and for less than one-tenth of the cost of the late expedition against Canada, that colony would be rendered so useless to the French that they would be obliged to abandon it.

The precision with which Burnet's policy, in the aspects of it which we are now discussing, fell in with the ideas of the board of trade is evidenced in many ways. The whole tenor of the board's report of 1721 on the state of the continental colonies was in harmony with it. Comprising within their view the entire frontier from Nova Scotia to Florida,

---

[1] N. Y. Docs., V, 684, 693–697.
[2] Ibid., 685–692. Colden also prepared a map of New York; ibid., 704.

they recommended that Englishmen should be encouraged to intermarry with the natives, that missionary work among them should be promoted, presents sent and bestowed more regularly, the widest possible alliances with them concluded, and the fullest use made of the advantages which Great Britain possessed in the domain of trade. As to territory, it was the opinion of the board not only that the mountain barrier of the Alleghanies should be defended against the French but that settlements on a small scale west of this should be encouraged. To this end, with the consent of the Indians, forts should be built on Lake Erie, at Niagara, at the heads of the Susquehanna and Potomac rivers, while the defence of the Carolina frontier should receive the special care of the government. The influence of Spotswood's ideas upon certain features of this program is unmistakable, while in most respects it was a response by way of imitation to the policy which French expansion on the continent had already made familiar to the British officials.[1]

The next moves in the competitive enterprise for trade and territory on the lake frontier were made by the founding of Oswego on the part of the British and the building of the stone fort at the mouth of the Niagara river by the French. The French enterprise was carried through in 1725 and 1726, under the immediate influence of news that the British were preparing to settle at Oswego, and of the actual sight of a large number of them at the mouth of the Chouaguen river.[2] To Joncaire was intrusted the main task of conciliating the Five Nations, while De Longueil, in the autumn of 1725, secured the consent of the Onondagas to the actual construction of the fort. This so-called consent, it will be noted, was given by only one of the five Iroquois tribes and that not the one on whose territory the stone house was to be built. Moreover, all the preparations for building the house had been made by the French before even this pretence of action on the part of the Indians had been sought. The house, or fort, was actually constructed during the spring and summer of 1726. As usual, the British had delayed action until spurred on by the initiative of the French. At a conference,

---

[1] N. Y. Docs., V, 623–627.

[2] N. Y. Docs., IX, 949–953, 976 *et seq.*; Severance, 146 *et seq.*

held in the autumn of 1726, the achievement of the French at
Niagara was fully discussed between Burnet and the Indians,
especially in its bearing on the grant or concession which had
been signed in 1701.[1] Now a new deed was drawn and signed
by sachems from the three western cantons — the Onondagas,
Cayugas and Senecas — according to which they put all the
hunting grounds described in the previous deed under the protection of the English and in addition ceded to the crown,
for the purposes of protection and defence, a tract sixty
miles broad along the entire southern shore of Lake Ontario,
and thence westward to about the longitude of Cleveland,
Ohio. This was expressly declared to include all the castles
of the aforesaid three nations. It was signed, sealed and
delivered in the presence of Philip Livingston, Peter Van
Brugh, Myndert Schuyler and Lawrence Claessen, and was
recorded in the office of the secretary of the province of New
York. Another important step was thus taken in the process
of extending a British control or protectorate over the Six
Nations, and under the authority of this Oswego was founded
in the following year. The French success at Niagara was
gained at a strategic point and, like all that they did, was
bold in conception and skilful in execution. But it involved
no large concessions of territory and was not located where
it could be supported by a solid advance of frontier settlements. The opposite was true of the British post. Oswego
bore a normal relation to the advancing New York frontier
and was not to be merely an outpost for trade flung forward
into the wilderness. It bore such geographical relations to
the Mohawk valley in general that in time it could be supported by settlements in the rear and permanent land communication with it established. These two settlements were
therefore typical of the ways in which the two peoples made
their advances toward the interior of the continent. The
Indians were treated, so far as possible, as pawns in the game,
but the influence which the British had over the Six Nations
was much more substantial and effective than that of the
French. It could readily advance through a protectorate
to complete subjection, a prospective result which the French
could never make real or even probable.

[1] N. Y. Docs., V, 781–801.

As soon as Burnet heard of the building of the fort at
Niagara he sent a letter of protest to De Longeuil and received a reply, to the effect that they were not contravening
the treaty of Utrecht and were working with the full consent
of the Indians.[1]  Thereupon Burnet wrote to Newcastle and
the board of trade, giving the substance of this reply and
stating that the French had obtained the consent only of
the Onondagas, who were not the possessors of the land at
Niagara.  The Six Nations, he said, joined with him in the
urgent request that the crown would demand of the French
king the demolition of this fort, the erection of which was
a violation of the treaty and was intended to destroy the
Indians who, it was claimed, had made the cession.[2]  Newcastle at once communicated this protest through Horatio
Walpole, who was then the British ambassador at Paris, to
the French court.  But the slight prospect there was of its
being needed is indicated by the fact, that at the same time
the French government was planning not only the repair of
the trading house at Niagara portage but the building of a
fort and house, as soon as means were available, on the site
where the English were just about to found Oswego.  As soon
as news reached De Beauharnois, the new governor general of
Canada, that the English had occupied Oswego, he sent a
summons to its garrison to withdraw and complained to
Burnet of the infraction of the treaty of Utrecht which was
involved in its occupation.  Burnet replied with a full explanation of that treaty as it was understood by the English,
and a defence of his enterprise at Oswego as in full harmony
with it.  In its answer to the representation from London
the French government coupled the alleged encroachments
of the English upon their territory in Maine and Nova Scotia
with those in New York, and asserted that they all were
violations of the treaty of Utrecht and were indefensible.[3]
That the Iroquois were subjects of the English, or that any
Indian nation could rightly be treated in that way either by
the French or English, they denied.  Notwithstanding the

---

[1] During the interval between the death of De Vaudreuil and the arrival
of De Beauharnois, his successor, De Longueuil was commander in chief in
Canada.

[2] N. Y. Docs., V, 802–804;  V, 963, 996.

[3] N. Y. Docs., IX, 964–985.

language of the treaty, they maintained that in the discussions of the Congress there was no thought of determining who were subjects or allies, but that was left to be worked out by commissioners who should later be appointed. In a way analogous to their interpretation of the bounds of Acadia, the French also claimed that the territory of the Iroquois was confined to their villages and fields, and that the so-called hunting grounds were totally indefinite and over them no claim could be established which would avail against the right of the subjects of King Louis to all the territory along the St. Lawrence and the lakes which fed it, as well as the streams which were their tributaries from the south.[1] The English therefore were carrying on operations entirely on French territory and had not even pretended to undertake them until after the treaty of Utrecht. Beyond the statement of these mutually contradictory claims the discussion did not advance at this time, and both parties maintained their hold upon the points which had been gained.

Oswego was both a trading house and a garrison and its existence affected both the problem of trade and that of defence. Among the acts of Burnet's administration which were disallowed by the crown in 1729 because they unduly restricted the trade through New York with the Indians, was one for defraying the cost of maintaining the post at Oswego.[2] Apart from the extremely detailed and restrictive provisions for the execution of the act, the privy council probably objected to the fact that the funds for the support of Oswego were to be raised by taxes on Indian trade. When it became necessary to pass a substitute for the act which had been disallowed, sectional feeling again developed. As the benefits of the. Indian trade fell chiefly to Albany and its vicinity, the southern counties and those of Long Island objected to a general tax for the support of Oswego, which should rest equally upon all parts of the province. The erection of a company to take over the Indian trade and become responsible for the support of the garrison was pro-

---

[1] A good statement of this claim and its consequences for the British colonies if established, was made in 1739 by Governor Clarke in a letter to the board of trade. N. Y. Docs., VI, 143.

[2] Acts P. C. Col., III, 211.

posed as an alternative. Governor Montgomerie urged a land tax, while it was with great difficulty that the assembly was persuaded to refrain from again taxing the Indian trade.[1] After appropriating for the purpose the revenue which for a year should arise from a tax of three shillings upon every inhabitant who wore a wig, the council and assembly sent a strong address on the subject to the board of trade. The governor also wrote at length upon the importance of every reason for maintaining the post at Oswego. The board, after consulting merchants, expressed its willingness to approve a license tax, for example, on the Indian trade, though it deprecated the opposition to the support of a post so important as Oswego by the province as a whole. Encouraged by this, the burden of supporting Oswego and its garrison was at once imposed on the Indian trade.

It was the desire to control this trade, together with the influence over Indian relations in general which went with it, that furnished the principal motive for the founding of Niagara and Oswego. But the next advance, which was made by the French, was determined by territorial and military considerations. This was the occupation of Crown Point (Fort Frederic) on the west side of Lake Champlain, the building of a fort and stationing of a garrison there and, as the years passed, the strengthening of this place as a point of vantage against the British.[2] As Crown Point lay within the country of the Iroquois, this was regarded not only as a violation of the treaty of Utrecht but as a serious encroachment on British territory. The move received the attention of officials in London and diplomatic representations concerning it were made to the French government. When Governor Cosby met the Iroquois in conference in 1733 he told them that it was expected they would not suffer the French to build forts or trading houses in any part of their lands and to this they mildly assented.[3] Beyond these fruitless declara-

---

[1] Col. Laws of N. Y., II, 372, 484, 535, 688; N. Y. Docs., V, 905 et seq.; Ass. J. I, 621.

[2] Wraxall, op. cit., Nov. 26, 1730; J. of N. Y. Ass., I, 632; 1 Pa. Archs., I, 298; N. Y. Docs., V, 931, 933; IX, 1034, 1038; B. T. J. Mar. 28, 1732.

[3] N. Y. Docs., V, 965, 967, 972. In May 1731 the Indians had told Gov. Montgomerie that they would not permit the French to make any settlements south of Lake Ontario.

tions nothing was done and before many years had passed reports were circulated that the French were about to establish a post on Wood Creek and thus secure control of the waterways as far south as the Hudson river.[1] It was in order to check this move that the plan was formed to settle a colony of Scotch on the lands northeast of the Hudson which Governor Fletcher had granted to Godfrey Dellius.

Under the governors of New York who succeeded Burnet no opposition was made to the resumption of free trade relations with Canada, and in August, 1735, the Indian commissioners in a conference with the Caughnawagas from Montreal, at which the governor was not present, solemnly agreed to maintain liberty of neutral trade and intercourse with them. That Governor Cosby was fully aware of the advantage which the French were believed to derive from this, is proved by his statement at a conference the next month, " that Canada could not have been subsisted had it not been supplied from Albany."[2]   Meantime as events drew toward the reopening of war in Europe, rumors and threats multiplied on both sides of the establishment of posts between Oswego and Niagara, Irondequoit and Sodus Bay being frequently mentioned. With the extension of British settlements along the Mohawk valley and the securing of additional grants of land by Albanians and others from Indians whom they sometimes made drunk for the purpose, the feelings, especially of the Mohawks, on this subject became more and more aroused and the preparation was made for the passionate outbursts which were later heard from the lips of their chief, Hendrick.[3]   The activity of the French, and especially of the younger Joncaire, among the western Iroquois, and efforts to induce the Shawnees to remove into that region, were significant of the future trouble, and concerning them the British had some knowledge and more suspicions.   By 1740

---

[1] N. Y. Docs., VI, 131, 143–146.

[2] Wraxall, *op. cit.*, Aug. and Sept. 1735.

[3] *Ibid.*, entries for 1731 and 1732.   New York Docs., VI, 58 *et seq.*, relating to a grant on Canada Creek, in the Mohawk country, which Storke and Van Brugh Livingston were trying to secure in 1736.   At the beginning of 1741 the Senecas ceded a tract of land around Irondequoit to the British but it was not settled because of the fear of a French war.   N. Y. Docs., VI, 204, 220, IX, 1027, 1097.

the British and French were estimating the force which they could bring to bear on Lake Ontario. Lieutenant Governor Clarke, who was one of the best informed men on the British side, wrote to Newcastle that the French had two brigantines on that lake, of about fifty tons each, which they used for the transportation of men, merchandise and munitions of war to their forts. Clarke's advice was that the British should build there two vessels of size and force superior to those of their rivals, and in case of war use them for the destruction of the French vessels and capture of the posts on the lake.[1] His view took in also the serious menace to the British which came from the chain of French posts through the Mississippi valley, the importance of Louisbourg and the necessity, if possible, of averting Indian raids from the New England frontier. A plan for the capture of Louisbourg, by the co-operation of the British and colonial forces, was among the ideas which he cherished at the opening of the Third Inter-colonial War, but his letters made no effective impression on the British ministry.

During the two decades of which we have been speaking central Pennsylvania was being settled by Germans and Scotch Irish. As a consequence of this and of the settle-ment of the valley of Virginia the route which for genera-tions the Six Nations and the tribes of the south had used in their raids of attack and reprisal was being occupied by the farms and villages of Europeans. The creation of a frontier by filling these empty spaces, made possible the development of a common Indian policy, the beginnings of which have already been traced. Pennsylvania now appears perma-nently on the scene, and from the middle position which she occupied helped materially to bring New York and the south-ern provinces, and the northern and southern Indians as well, into joint action. Joint conferences, in which a number of provinces, and also a number of Indian peoples participated, became more common, and some of the most important of these were held in Pennsylvania. Albany to an extent lost its leadership in this matter and Lancaster, along with other places in Pennsylvania, became its rival. Virginia and Mary-land even tried to draw the northern tribes into conferences

[1] N. Y. Docs., VI, 183, 207–209.

within their limits. It is maintained with much force that, for some time before the appearance of William Johnson, Conrad Weiser, the Palatine, and a citizen of Pennsylvania, was the most influential interpreter and Indian negotiator among the British.[1] As the Fourth Intercolonial War approached delegates from New England occasionally joined in conferences at Albany and the tendency to consider the interests of that frontier in common with those of New York was strengthened. Attention must now be given to the broadening of the Indian and frontier problem as it has been thus indicated.

Between the conferences of 1722 and about 1730 nothing of special importance affecting relations between Pennsylvania and the Six Nations had happened. When, in 1729, young Conrad Weiser settled among the Palatines at Tulpehocken, he brought with him a knowledge of the Mohawk tongue and an appreciation of Indian affairs in general not common among colonists. In 1728 Shikallemy, an Oneida chief, was sent to Pennsylvania to guard the interests of the Six Nations in their sales of land in that province and also to have an oversight of the relations between the Delawares and Shawnees — who were tributary to the Iroquois — and the government of the Penns. For two decades this Indian, with his residence during the later part of the time at Shomokin — the forks of the Susquehanna — shared in all the negotiations of importance and exercised a sort of leadership over the dependents of the Iroquois in that region.[2] With him Weiser was closely associated, and together they contributed distinctly toward the unifying of Indian relations. On many occasions, especially in Pennsylvania, the value of their services was recognized, and Weiser came to rank high as a diplomat in Indian affairs from New York to Virginia.

By 1730 Pennsylvanians like Logan had become fully aware of the seriousness of French claims in the Mississippi valley. On one occasion Logan produced before the council a map from which it appeared that they claimed a great part of

[1] It is the object of Watson's Conrad Weiser and the Indian Policy of Pennsylvania, to prove this.
[2] Weiser, Mississippi Basin, 239.

Carolina and Virginia and made it appear that the Susquehanna was the western boundary of Pennsylvania.[1] Now that the French had planted forts on the Mississippi, their principle that all the territory drained by its tributaries was theirs would give them the entire valley of the Ohio and bring them within the western boundary of Penn's province. The Shawnees, continuing their wanderings, had already settled in the Alleghany region and were thus brought directly under French influence. This furnished additional occasion for anxiety concerning the western frontier. According to the testimony of a number of Indian traders, among them Edmund Cartlidge, one Cavalier was agent of the French in the Alleghany region and Delawares, as well as Shawnees and a number of other tribes there, kept up regular communication with Canada.[2] It was these considerations which led Logan to prepare for the holding of a conference with the Five Nations, in order that, through their control over the Shawnees, the latter might be kept firmly attached to the English and be induced to return to some place nearer to the English settlements. The Delawares and other Indians were offended by the encroachments of the white settlers and by conflicting claims. All these causes now combined to bring the Indian question prominently to the front. The Six Nations were therefore invited, through Shikallemy, to send envoys to Philadelphia. This they did in 1732, and the presence of Thomas Penn, one of the proprietors, added dignity to the occasion.[3] In this conference, which lasted for a week and was closed with a public session in the presence of a crowded audience in the Great Meeting House at Philadelphia, the two subjects which were discussed were the relations between the Six Nations and the French and the effort which should be made to win back the Shawnees. The envoys reiterated their fidelity to the English, whose goods were cheaper, and their lack of confidence in the French, though they were at peace with them and sometimes visited Canada. As to the Shawnees, the Indians insisted that British traders must be recalled from the Alleghany region so that supplies

---

[1] Pa. Col. Recs., III, 402 et seq.
[2] Pa. Arch., I, 299–306.
[3] Pa. Col. Recs., III, 425, 435 et seq.; Watson, op. cit., 21.

of goods could no longer be easily procured there, and then they could order the Shawnees to return, with some prospect of success. This was agreed to, and during the following year the Iroquois and the governor and council of Pennsylvania tried to induce the Shawnees to settle east of the mountains. But their efforts failed after coming near to kindling a war among the Indians, and the complaints about the trade in rum, followed by occasional outrages on the Virginia frontier or elsewhere, continued as serious as ever.[1] Chiefs who had come to treat with the English often, while under the influence of drink, raised such disturbances in the streets of Philadelphia that the sale of liquor in any form to them had to be strictly forbidden.[2] Occasionally the Indians, in a spasm of virtue, smashed the kegs and poured the liquor on the ground, but as a rule their demand for it continued steady and the traders were as regular in furnishing the supply.

The opening of direct relations between Pennsylvania and the Six Nations brought the question of land titles to the front in a way which was fraught with danger in the future. William Penn had been careful to extinguish Indian claims by purchase and his treaties had been made with the Delawares, Shawnees and other minor tribes which had occupied the territory of his province. These tribes however had previously been conquered by the Five Nations and over their lands and persons that confederacy held a certain overlordship. The earliest recognition of this fact by the English appeared when agents of Penn induced Thomas Dongan, while governor of New York, to purchase from the Five Nations lands of indefinite extent lying along the course of the Susquehanna river. In London, in 1696, such claims as Dongan secured by this purchase were transferred to Penn.[3] The original Dongan deed having been lost, in 1701 Penn obtained a confirmation of it from the Susquehannas, Shawnees and Potomac Indians and a surrender of all the title of the Susquehannas to land along that river.[4] At best such a title was shadowy, the validity of it was later denied

[1] Pa. Col. Recs., III, 460, 580, 619.
[2] Ibid., IV, 87. 1 Pa. Arch., I, 549–552. Winsor, Mississippi Basin, 172.
[3] 1 Pa. Arch., I, 74–76, 80, 121, 122; Shepherd, Pa. as a Proprietary Province, 97 et seq.
[4] 1 Pa. Arch., I, 133, 144–147,

by the Conestoga Indians, and the young proprietors soon began to regard it as precarious. It was this feeling which induced them to seek from the Six Nations a cession of their claims to all territory in Pennsylvania which was now being rapidly occupied by white settlers. This question, along with others, came up in 1736, when more than one hundred Iroquois visited Philadelphia for the purpose of confirming the treaty of four years before.[1] Logan was the president and the sachems were at first entertained at Stenton, his home, but later met the council in the Great Meeting House, though smallpox at the time was raging in the city. Logan, Weiser and Shikallemy were the managers of this conference and its important result was the extinction by purchase of the superior rights of the Iroquois to the Susquehanna lands, extending west as far as the Blue Mountains or Endless Hills. A date two weeks later was affixed to a deed from these same sachems by which they also ceded their claims to lands along the Delaware river from the mountains southward.[2] They also promised that thereafter they would sell no more land in the province except to the children of William Penn. But a part of these same lands had already been sold to the Penns by the Delaware Indians themselves and the sale was confirmed by a series of deeds beginning as early as 1686. This was the so-called " Walking Purchase " and lay in what later became Berks county, about the junction of the Delaware and Lehigh rivers, called at the time the Forks of the Delaware. It was to extend as far as a man could walk in a day and a half, though it had not yet been walked. Therefore, in 1737, the proprietors secured from the Delawares a confirmation of this grant and an agreement that the tract or tracts should be measured out according to the requirement of the deed.[3] The Indians complained of the unfairness of the whites in the measurement of this tract, and a controversy over it continued for some years. Meantime a few minor conferences were held with Shawnees and Delawares at Philadelphia, in the effort to attract them back into the province, but without

---

[1] Pa. Col. Recs., IV, 79–95; Watson *op. cit.*, 25 *et seq.*, Shepherd *op. cit.*, 99 *et seq.*

[2] 1 Pa. Arch., I, 494, 498.

[3] *Ibid.*, 541. Shepherd, 101–102.

result. For a time also Conrad Weiser fell under the influence of the community of Seventh Day Baptists at Ephrata, and abandoned Indian affairs and the secular life altogether. But Governor Thomas appointed him to the office of justice of the peace, and the growing attraction of its duties, together with certain differences which arose between him and Conrad Beissel, the leader of the Ephrata Community, led Weiser to break his connection with it and return to his Indian affairs. This occurred toward 1740, and by that time the Moravians had settled in Berks county and were beginning their missionary work among the Indians. In this Weiser assisted them by teaching several of them the Mohawk tongue, accompanying them on some of their missionary journeys and instructing them as to the best method to be followed in converting the Indians.[1] Soon after 1740 Weiser returned to his work as negotiator and interpreter and this meant that relations between Pennsylvania and the Six Nations would again be opened and that their influence would again be felt in the affairs of the Middle Colonies.

In 1742 delegates from the three central Iroquois cantons, accompanied by a large number of their tribesmen, appeared at Philadelphia. The conference which followed had long been preparing and was the most important one which, up to that time, had been held in the province. Its immediate purpose, as stated in the records, was to enable the Iroquois to receive payment for the lands west of the Susquehanna river which, six years before, they had sold to the English, but had declined at that time to take the goods which were due for that part of the grant. Weiser acted as interpreter and Canassetego, one of the greatest orators of the Six Nations, led the delegation from the Onondagas. Among the Germans, Weiser had already begun to oppose Quaker rule in Pennsylvania and to support Governor Thomas and his policy. So keenly alive was Weiser to French encroachments, while at the same time the prospect of another war with France was imminent, that he could hardly avoid supporting a policy of active defence. The governor and all opponents of the Quakers were also committed to this course. The bringing of the Six Nations more prominently into Pennsylvania affairs

[1] Watson, *op. cit.*, 44–55.

was a part of this same policy, though it involved a departure
from the course followed by the Quakers and the first proprietor. They had cultivated friendship with the Delawares,
Shawnees and minor Indian groups within the province and
had avoided dealings with distant peoples.[1]

So far as indicated by the words of their orator, the Six
Nations never showed themselves more proud and confident
than on this occasion. Governor Thomas also bore himself
well and everything indicated that Pennsylvania was being
drawn from its isolation into the general stream of colonial
politics. Both parties asserted with the utmost confidence
that no sales or purchases of Indian land within Pennsylvania
would be recognized, unless they were made under the authority of the Six Nations and " Brother Onas," the governor.
When, during the banquet, Thomas inquired into their relations with the French, Canassetego replied with jaunty confidence that the governor of Canada paid great court to them
at this time, told them he was sharpening the hatchet against
the English and asked them to remain neutral. " But ten of
his words do not go so far as one of yours. We do not look
towards them. We look towards you, and you may depend
on our assistance." With characteristic exaggeration he declared, that they had long been " in the strictest League of
Amity " with the English and exclaimed, " Why should We,
who are one flesh with You, refuse to help You whenever You
want our Assistance? " And when Canassetego asked the
governor how the war with the Spanish was going, the tone
of the Englishman's answer was quite as confident and boastful. " The Governor told them the King of Great Britain
lived on an Island and being surrounded with the Sea his
Chief Strength lay in his Ships, in which he was so much
Superior to his Enemies that they were seldom to be met
with on the Broad Ocean, but skulked and hid themselves,
only venturing out now and then, and whenever they did
they were almost sure to be taken. And that the King of
Great Britain with his Ships had beat down or taken several
of the Spaniard's Great Forts in America." In view of the
actual history of Vernon's expedition against Porto Bello
and Carthagena, this summary must be pronounced some-

[1] Pa. Col. Recs., IV, 557–586; Watson, op. cit.

what highly colored. But it suited well the occasion, and the savages expressed themselves "pleased to hear their Brotheren were an Overmatch for their Enemies, and wished them good Success."

The goods which had been provided in payment for the lands west of the Susquehanna were next delivered, accompanied with the strongest expressions of friendship and alliance from the governor, showing that he desired to put a literal interpretation on the language which the Indian orator had spoken. But the speech made by Canassetego on receiving the goods was set to a different key. It showed that the Iroquois were fully conscious of the fact that the Indians were being forced from their hunting grounds by the advance of settlement, that it was more difficult to secure game and that they were steadily waning in power. The existence of a famine was given as the excuse for the failure of the Senecas to appear at this conference. Therefore they pleaded that the payment was too small, that when it was divided it counted for little and the goods soon wore out, while "the Land was Everlasting." The Indian was comparing in his mind the few goods he received with the value to the European of the great stretches of country which he ceded. Thomas, in reply, called his attention to the other side of the picture. Is the value of the lands, he said, "not entirely owing to the Industry and Labour used by the white people in their Cultivation and Improvement? Had not they come amongst you, these Lands would have been of no use to you any further than to maintain you, and is there not, now you have sold so much, enough left for all the Purposes of living?" It was, however, thought advisable by the Pennsylvania government to add a moderate present to the sum which by treaty they were bound to pay. The authorities of that colony more than once had made investments in good will, and drawn dividends in the form of peace.

The governor then brought before the conference the trouble which had been caused by the Delawares over the lands of the "Walking Purchase," and their refusal to remove because of the presence of squatters there, and the claim that they had been cheated when the tract was measured. Certain representatives of the Delawares were present at the conference and, whether inspired by Weiser, Shikallemy or other negotiators of influence or moved by a savage pleasure in humiliating a former enemy, Canassetego administered to these Delawares the most stinging rebuke which it was possible for one Indian to offer another. He called them women, told them that the Iroquois had made them so, that they had no power to sell land and deserved to be chastised, to be shaken by the hair of the head till they recovered their senses and became sober. He denounced them as dishonest for presuming to sell land without consulting their superiors, the Six Nations, and with trying to break the chain of friendship with Brother Onas by not recognizing the validity of a deed of sale for this land made years before. He bade them be gone, not only from the conference but from the land on the Delaware and never again, to their latest posterity, to dare to sell land or meddle with territorial affairs. The Delawares slunk away with bitterness in their hearts, and this, with other slights to themselves and the Shawnees, prepared the way for a bloody reckoning for Pennsylvania a decade later.

The proud Iroquois had now proved their claim of overlordship over the Delawares and Shawnees to the point where they insisted that all large sales of Indian lands in Pennsylvania should hereafter be negotiated with them, and the government at Philadelphia had acquiesced in this. Canassetego even reproved Thomas and his council for failing to remove squatters from the valley of the Juniata, and told them that their officials were in league with the trespassers. The next move of the Iroquois was to assume a similar attitude toward Maryland and Virginia. In reference to both these provinces the claim was made in 1736 and repeated at the congress of 1742. It was based on the assertion that the western part of both Virginia and Maryland belonged to the Iroquois by right of conquest, and that for decades white men had been trespassing on lands along the lower course of the Susquehanna river as well as along the Potomac and the Shenandoah.[1] Correspondence between Pennsylvania and Maryland over this and other grievances was at once begun. After a few months anxiety was caused by an encounter be-

[1] Md. Arch. Council, 1732–1753, pp. 271–274.

tween white settlers of Virginia and a party of Iroquois raiders.[1] Conrad Weiser was at once ordered to confer with Shikallemy at Shamokin. Two such conferences were held, at which Shawnees, Delawares and Iroquois were present. According to the statements there made, it seemed that the Virginians were the aggressors. Weiser reported the result to the governor and council at Philadelphia, and Thomas adopted that view in his letters to Governor Gooch. In order to avoid reprisals and serious disturbances along the frontier, Weiser was sent to Onondaga, in the summer of 1743, with a present from Virginia for the Six Nations and instructions to conciliate them and invite them to a conference the following year at some prominent place, where disputes about land and all other disturbing questions might be settled. At a formal council, preceded by personal talks between the leaders, this plan was agreed to by the Indians.[2] War between them and Virginia was avoided and arrangements were made under which the great conference of 1744 was held at Lancaster, Pennsylvania. Had the earlier precedents been followed, this question would have been settled at Albany. Governor Gooch did inform Clarke of the skirmish, and also referred to the claim which the Iroquois were making on Virginia lands. After considerable delay an interpreter was sent from Albany to Onondaga, but he reported simply on the excuses made by the Indians for the raid, and got no information as to its cause and the responsibility for the attack. The suggestion that Virginia should send envoys to Albany met with no response. Clarke's term as governor came to an end just at this time and, with the arrival of Clinton, attention was fixed wholly on the war and the local struggle which accompanied it. In this way New York lost an opportunity and, under the lead of Weiser and his associates, Pennsylvania came fully to share with her in the control of Indian relations.

The conference at Lancaster was attended by commissioners from Maryland and Virginia, as well as by the Penn-

---

[1] N. Y. Col. Docs.,VI, 230 et seq.

[2] Ibid., 655–669. The report of this which Weiser submitted to Governor Thomas is one of the best accounts of an Indian council and negotiation which has been preserved.

sylvania authorities and by delegates from five of the Iroquois cantons, the Mohawks taking no part in any negotiations with the colonies to the south.[1] It involved a notable development of joint action in Indian affairs along the western frontier, centering in Pennsylvania instead of New York. It confirmed still further the lead of the Six Nations in all concerns of their race, at least as far south as the Carolinas, and in honor of the occasion they sent their leading sachems and orators to Lancaster.

At one of the earlier sessions, Canassetego, in a brilliant passage of Indian eloquence, described the evolution of the covenant chain, and reminded his hearers that on the soil of America they were but children of yesterday as compared with the antiquity of his own race.[2] Addressing the Marylanders, he exclaimed, " What is one hundred years in comparison to the length of time since our Claim began?  Since we came out of the Ground?  For we must tell you that long before One hundred years Our ancestors came out of this very ground, and their Children have remained here ever since; you came out of the Ground in a country that lyes beyond Seas, there you may have a just Claim, but here you must allow Us to be your elder Brethren, and the lands to belong to Us long before you knew anything of them.  It is true that above One hundred years ago the Dutch came here in a ship and brought with them several Goods, such as Awls, Knives, Hatchets, Guns and many other particulars, which they gave us, and when they had taught us how to use their things, and we saw what sort of People they were, we were so pleased with them that we tyed their Ship to the Bushes on the Shoar, and afterwards liking them still better the longer they stayed with us, and thinking the Bushes too slender we removed the Rope and tyed it to the trees, and as the trees were liable to be blown down by high Winds, or to decay of themselves, We from the affection We bore them, again removed the Rope and tyed it to a strong Rock, and not content with this, for its further security We removed the Rope to the Big Mountain and there tyed it very fast and rowled Wampum about it. . . . After this the Eng-

---

[1] Pa. Col. Recs., IV, 698-737.
[2] Ibid., 707.

lish came into the Country and, as we are told, became one
People with the Dutch; about two years after the arrival
of the English an English Governor came to Albany and
finding that great friendship subsisted between us and the
Dutch, he approved it mightily, and desired to make as
Strong a league and to be upon as good Terms with us as
the Dutch were, with whom he was united, and to become one
People with us, and by his further care in looking [into]
what had been passed between us he found that the Rope
which had tyed the Ship to the Great Mountain was only
fastened with Wampum, which was liable to break and rot,
and to perish in the course of years. He therefore told us
that he would give us a silver Chain which would be much
stronger and last for ever. This we accepted and fastened
the Ship with it and it has lasted ever since."

This outburst was occasioned by the opening speech of the
commissioners from Maryland, in which they confidently asserted that by virtue of the right and sovereignty of their
king they had held the land of their province free and
undisturbed for a hundred years. For written proof of this
they relied on a treaty of 1652 with the Minquas or Susquehannas for their claim to both sides of Chesapeake bay,
and for the region north of it on the deed which the Iroquois
had granted to Dongan and the later transactions by which
Pennsylvania had confirmed its title to all the Susquehanna
lands.[1] Canassetego was not unprepared for this argument
and his version of those transactions, as he commented ironically on the " Pen and Ink work that is going on at the
Table," was this: " Before the Europeans came, though we
had only bows and arrows and hatchets of stone, we had
plenty of land; but we are now straitened and sometimes in
want of land and liable to many other inconveniences since
the English came. When Penn desired to buy Susquehanna
lands of us, the governor of New York told us not to sell to
him, for he would make bad use of it, but instead to grant it
to New York so that we could have it back again when we
wanted it. It should be kept for our use and the governor
of New York would never allow anyone else to possess it.
We trusted him and put our lands in his hands, but some

[1] Pa. Col. Recs., IV, 704; Watson, 99.

time after he went away to England and carried Our Land with him, and there sold it to our brother Onas for a Large Sum of money; and when at the Instance of our brother Onas we were minded to sell him some lands, he told us that we had sold the Susquehanna Lands already to the Governor of New York and that he had bought them from him in England, though when he came to Understand how the Governor of New York had deceived Us, he very generously paid Us for our lands over again."

This method of settlement was the one which Maryland resolved to follow. It simply involved the not uncommon practice of paying twice or even three times for Indian lands. In this case the sachems had threatened reprisals if their demands were not conceded, and the outbreak of an Indian war, when one with the French was beginning, was by all means to be avoided. In return for a payment of goods to the value of £300 a formal deed of release of Iroquois claims to Maryland lands as far west as Cresap's hunting cabin, two miles above the uppermost fork of the Potomac, was drawn and duly signed, Weiser acting as interpreter and witness.[1]

The Virginia commissioners duly impressed upon the minds of the savages that, in their case, they were dealing with the king himself through his direct representatives. The Indians claimed that the valley of Virginia had been conquered by them from other tribes and was theirs by that right. This the Virginians denied and asserted that this territory was unoccupied when their people began to settle in it. They also cited the treaties from 1684 to 1722, in which cessions had been made and the right of Virginia to her lands had been recognized by the Six Nations. But when it came to the interpretation of Spotswood's treaty of 1722, its ambiguity became evident. Its provision which forbade the Six Nations to pass the great mountain that formed the western boundary of Virginia, was interpreted by the Indians to mean the Blue Ridge and by the Virginians to mean the Allegheny range. It was the intention of the Indians that their trail through the valley to the south should be left open, and they had

[1] Pa. Col. Recs., IV, 715, 719, 723. Darlington's Edition of Christopher Gist's Journals, 219.

moved it as far toward the Alleghenies as they were able. But " we had not been long in the use of this new Road before your People came like Flocks of Birds and sat down in both sides of it, and yet we never made a Complaint to you, though you must be Sensible those things must have been done by your People in manifest Breach of your own Proposal made at Albany. . . . That Affair of the Road must be looked upon as Preliminary to be settled before the Grant of Lands. . . ." In answer to this demand the Virginians fell back upon the superior authority of their written records, which were already in the possession of the king. As to the road, they said that they intended to remove the necessity for it by making peace between the Six Nations and the southern Indians, but if they insisted on having a road, the Virginians would agree to one if the Indians in using it would behave in an orderly fashion, like friends and brethren. As to peace with the southern Indians, the sachems declared that one had been concluded with the Cherokees, but the Catawbas were so treacherous that war with them must be continued until one party or the other was destroyed. That the Iroquois felt a comfortable assurance as to which party this would be, was indicated by the remark that the Virginians should not be troubled " at what we should do to the Catawbas." The wagon road which had been made through the valley was the one that they wanted retained; and in reference to the alleged cause of the recent skirmish there, they called the attention of the Williamsburg government to the fact that some very ill-natured people were living in their upper settlements, who would not allow the Indians that were passing through to " have reasonable victuals when they were in want." Goods to the value of £200 and £300 in money were paid by the Virginians to the sachems in extinguishment of their claims to all the lands which by his majesty's appointment are or should be included in the colony of Virginia. With a handsomer gift of money from Pennsylvania, the Indians were dismissed and one of the most famous conferences of the colonial period came to an end.[1]

The Third Intercolonial war had now begun and Indian

---

[1] Pa. Col. Recs., IV, 709 *et seq.*  Darlington's edition of Journals of Christopher Gist, 219.

policy was controlled by that fact. The centre of activity again shifted to New York. A conference of minor importance was held at Albany by Governor Clinton in June, 1744, and another, more generally attended and of much greater significance, in October, 1745.[1] On both these occasions commissioners from Massachusetts and Connecticut were present, though they did not take formal part in the conference of 1744. The conference of 1745 was attended by Kinsey, Lawrence and Peters on behalf of Pennsylvania and Weiser was present as their interpreter, with an unusual opportunity of ascertaining the real drift in Indian affairs. New England from the first had been involved in the war and was urgently in favor of securing the active participation of the Six Nations and of New York. This they considered necessary in part for their own relief, and at Albany in 1744 they submitted proposals for coöperation on the part of all the northern colonies, both by sea and land, against the French. This contemplated an offensive, as well as a defensive, war. The New York authorities in general favored this, but without any definite idea as yet concerning joint action by the colonies. The Quakers of Pennsylvania, who still controlled the assembly, were of course opposed to participation in the war, while Governor Thomas, the council and a minority in the assembly, favored a war policy. Toward this end Weiser was also working. The Six Nations tried to maintain a neutral, or at least a defensive, attitude. At Albany, in 1744, they spoke only of defence, especially for the security of Oswego. Pennsylvanians had come to fear that in case of war the French and their Indians might assail the western frontier. This feeling they had been brought to entertain not only by the existence of French forts along the Great Lakes and the Mississippi, but by the activity of the French half-bred, Cavalier, among the Shawnees on the Ohio, and by the reported influence of the Catawbas, the hereditary foes of the Six Nations, in the same region.[2] By these influences a part of the Shawnees were drawn away to the French, though the Six Nations held the rest of the tribe

[1] N. Y. Docs., VI, 262, 267, 289; Pa. Col. Recs., V, 7 et seq.
[2] Pa. Col. Recs., IV, 757, 759; 1 Pa. Arch., I, 661–665; Watson 125 et seq.

to the English alliance. As a result, no hostilities occurred in the Ohio region, and the Shawnees after the war acknowledged that their conduct had been wrong and futile.[1] But Pennsylvania neglected the opportunity to conciliate them and, because of additional slights, the savages cherished their grudge till the time should come for revenge. Weiser and Shikallemy were deeply involved in negotiations with the Six Nations over these matters and also in the general effort to prevent any of the members of the Confederacy going over to the French. It was becoming deeply and permanently divided on that subject, the Senecas, on one excuse or another, neglecting to attend conferences with the English and the Mohawks, under William Johnson's dawning influence, being little more than dependents of New York. The customary visits to Canada were continued and De Beauharnois, the governor general, by presents and exhortation, was doing his best to win the tribes over to the French. Delegates from several of the cantons had visited Montreal in August, 1745, and the report was abroad that they had been induced to take up the hatchet for the French.

At the Albany conference of October, 1745, New York was first occupied in quieting the fears of the Indians which arose from rumors — apparently started by Joncaire — of a joint movement on the part of both the French and the English for the destruction of the Indians.[2] As on so many earlier occasions, these were proved to be false; but the discussion of them gave an opportunity for Hendrick, the Mohawk chief, to vent his wrath at British encroachments on Indian lands and rights. The commissioners from Pennsylvania had been instructed to confer with the Indians chiefly about affairs which concerned the western frontier and to use their influence to prevent them from actually joining with the French.[3] When it came to the drafting of the speech which Governor Clinton was to deliver on behalf of the commissioners in general, it was decided to urge the Six Nations to

[1] Pa. Col. Recs., V, 311 *et seq.*

[2] There are several references to this in the Minutes of Ex. Coun. of N. Y. (Ms.), and also to the restiveness of the Mohawks over the question of their lands. The Pennsylvania report of this conference is in Pa. Col. Recs., V, 7 *et seq.*

[3] *Ibid.*, IV, 776.

join in the war against the eastern Indians. To this the Pennsylvania delegates objected, because of the danger that it would bring on a war along the entire frontier, and also because they had no authority to commit their province to the expenditure which would necessarily follow from such a policy. Therefore it was agreed that Pennsylvania should confer separately with the Indians, and the meeting with them occurred after the principal conference had ended.

The success of the New Englanders at Louisbourg had become known just before the Six Nations visited Canada. It was also dwelt upon in the opening speech of Clinton at the conference and it, together with the chance which it revealed of further British victories, probably had an influence on the Indians. In Canada they seem to have demanded nothing except to be left alone, that their country might be free from the ravages of war. Though they took a war belt home with them, it was to consider in a general council at Onondaga what course they would pursue. Likewise, when Clinton proposed that they should join actually with the British, they replied that they would accept the hatchet and keep it in their bosom. This attitude of neutrality they maintained against the pressure which was exerted by both sides, the arguments and presents which were offered by the two parties neutralizing one another. Even the reports of outrages committed by the French Indians in western Massachusetts, which were reported by the envoys of that province before they left for home, led to no change of attitude. Clinton also was unwilling that the Six Nations should engage in war outside New York without the consent of its assembly. To the Pennsylvanians the Iroquois declared that they looked upon this war as confined to the English and French, and they did not intend to engage on either side. When the Europeans made war they made peace at pleasure, but no one knew when an Indian war would end. Among the things which they said they told the French was this, that the present war should be fought out on salt water and that the trade at Oswego in particular should not be obstructed. With this the Pennsylvanians were doubtless content, though they did not receive any assurance of peace between the Six Nations and the Catawbas.

In less than a month after the close of the conference a
party of French and Indians destroyed Saratoga, on the
Hudson, about fifty miles above Albany, and it was reported
that thirty persons were killed and sixty taken prisoners.[1]
The village of Hoosick, east of the river, was also destroyed.
Albany was now exposed and the frontier for many miles
along the Hudson and Mohawk was abandoned. Indian
parties approached nearer and French agents, especially
Joncaire, were busy among the Six Nations. Clinton also
was at loggerheads with the assembly and it was difficult, if
not impossible, to secure appropriations. In January, 1745/6,
Arent Stevens, the interpreter, was sent on a visit to the
tribes of the Confederacy to tell them that the governor had
taken up the hatchet and to ask them to join in the war. This
they flatly refused to do, alleging that they and the Caughnawagas were of the same blood and they could not make
war on one another. When Stevens reproached them with
breach of covenant, they desired that the governor would not
so consider it, and they would not if the English refused to
assist them in their wars.

It was in the course of 1746 that Clinton broke with the
Indian commissioners and began calling William Johnson
into increasing activity in the affairs of the Six Nations.
Johnson was of Scotch-Irish descent and a relative and pro-
tégé of Commodore Sir Peter Warren. Warren had married
a sister of James De Lancey and was rising steadily in rank
in the British navy. Johnson had settled in the Mohawk
country and soon revealed great aptitude for dealing with the
natives and winning their confidence. He was also deeply
engaged in trade with Oswego and the West Indies, in contracts for the supply of the garrison at Oswego, and in land
speculation. By his hearty good fellowship and the ample
entertainment which he furnished them at Johnson Hall, he
was able usually to attract the Indians to himself rather than
to be forced like so many Frenchmen to seek them out in their
native wilds. The plan for the joint attack on Canada in
1746 made the securing of the co-operation of the Six Nations
a matter of great importance. The council of New York
advised a conference, at which large presents should be be-

[1] N. Y. Docs., VI, 306.

stowed by a number of colonies. It was held at Albany in the summer of 1746, but so indifferent were the Indians that a month passed after the arrival of Clinton before enough Indians appeared to make a conference possible.[1] Some of their chiefs had been visiting Canada. The sensitiveness of the Mohawks concerning their lands reappeared. They declared that Philip Livingston, secretary of the Indian commissioners, held land of theirs which he had never bought from them. The commissioners were in bad odor with the Indians, as well as with the governor. This fact and the need of a special effort had led to the employment of Johnson as a special agent to Onondaga and afterwards to the Mohawks. He learned to speak their tongue and was adopted into the tribe. Through his influence the Mohawks put themselves actively at the head of the British party in the Confederacy, and they made him their captain in war. It was in this way that the Mohawks and the English sympathizers among the other tribes were induced to attend the conference of 1746 and take up the hatchet.

But owing to the failure of plans for the joint expedition, operations were confined to the exploits of scouting parties, the Indians in which were fitted out mostly by Johnson. By the beginning of 1747 Johnson was at the head of Indian affairs in New York, and was given practical charge of the defence of its northern frontier until the close of the war.

In the south the undivided control of South Carolina over Indian relations continued until after the settlement of Georgia. The journals and correspondence show that rumors and fears at times prevailed that a war would break out with the Creeks. The strengthening of posts on the frontier was then discussed and acts were passed modifying in detail, but not fundamentally, the system of administration which had already been established. Letters from the traders and agents, with all other information, was fully submitted by the governor to the houses and discussed by them. The advance of settlements toward the interior by the founding of Saxe Gotha, Fredericksburg, Amelia, Orangeburg and Savannah Town, peopled chiefly by Scotch Irish and Ger-

---

[1] N. Y. Docs., VI, 317; Stone, Life of Sir William Johnson, I.

mans, brought settlers nearer to the Indian country and made the problem of interior defence more imperative. The French also were slowly extending their influence and rumor pictured it often as far more active and dangerous than it really was. The determination of the Carolina government at this time was not to allow large numbers of Indians to come into the settlements for trade, but to carry the goods to them and bring back the packs of skins and furs from the Indian towns. Traders penetrated to the Mississippi and beyond, and their reports, conflicting and reflecting the desires or prejudices of the writers, always to a large extent inaccurate, furnished the best information attainable about the French and Indian country. The reports of the productivity of its soil made it at least attractive as a possible field for colonization.

In Nicholson's administration a largely attended conference was held at Congaree Fort, near the modern Columbia. But among early negotiations the most famous were those of 1730 with the Cherokees. The object of these was to check what had been reported as a dangerous assertion of French influence over all the western tribes. Sir Alexander Cuming, who had been interested not only in South Carolina but in Berkeley's plan for an Indian college in Bermuda, was sent among the Cherokees to revive their over-hill trade with the English. He travelled more than five hundred miles through the Indian country, brought them to what he claimed to be an acknowledgment of the sovereignty of England, and in the end took several headmen of the Cherokees with him to London, thus rivalling the achievements of Schuyler with his Mohawks twenty years before, and of Oglethorpe with Tomochichi and his associates from the Creeks four years later.[1] Friendly relations between the English and the Cherokees were strengthened by this event, and for twenty years to come they were maintained by South Carolina, being confirmed from time to time by conferences held by Gov-

[1] Oglethorpe's journey in 1739 of three hundred miles into the country of the Creeks was highly celebrated at the time and is comparable as an achievement with the less famous journeys of Cuming and Glen. Alexander Hewatt, Historical Account of the Rise and Progress of the Colonies of S. C. and Ga. in Carroll's Historical Collections, I, 278.

ernor Glen after his arrival, near the opening of the third war with France. But relations with the upper Creeks and Cherokees never became so intimate as those between the British and the Iroquois in the north. To an extent also the Cherokees played the same double game between the two European rivals as did the Iroquois; but in the south the Europeans were too weak and remote for relations to assume the definiteness which they had on the northern frontier. So far as we know, the tribesmen also were not so fully confederated as were the cantons around Onondaga, and did not have so well developed a policy of their own.

The founding of Georgia as a distinct province on the southern frontier modified to an extent the administration of Indian affairs, as it did other relations in that region. Georgia lay within the country of the Maskoki people, and the Lower Creeks were its immediate neighbors. Georgia was now the province which felt first and most directly the effect of restlessness among the Indians which was caused by Spanish influence. She at once established her own trade relations with the natives and by agents, traders and conferences began to develop an Indian policy of her own. It was similar in form and purpose to that of South Carolina, but was a rival of it and the older province soon realized that the control of these affairs was no longer exclusively in its own hands. She found Georgia traders and officials establishing themselves south and west of the Savannah river and claiming the right to exclude Carolinians from access to the Creeks of that region.

An act for maintaining peace with the natives, which was passed by the Georgia trustees in January, 1734/5, placed the management of Indian affairs in the hands of commissioners appointed by the common council and forbade any to trade with them without a license and bonds. The commissioners were authorized to hear complaints and award damages. Oglethorpe was made sole commissioner, but later Stephens was associated with him in the office.[1] Though this measure was intended only to apply to Indians who lived within the bounds of Georgia, when extended to the upper waters of

[1] Ga. Col. Recs., I, 30–43, 388.

the rivers or beyond it must necessarily curtail the liberty which traders from South Carolina had hitherto enjoyed.[1] As rum was extensively used in the Indian trade, the regulation of Georgia prohibiting its importation into that colony also interfered with the practice of the South Carolinians, and also with their claim to the free and joint use of the Savannah river. Fort Augusta was presently founded on the southern bank of the Savannah and became a very important centre of Indian trade, a rival of Fort Moore or Old Savannah Town on the Carolina side of the river. It was by the opposition of Patrick MacKay, who had been commissioned to build a fort in that region, to the presence of Carolina traders in the up country, and by the seizure of rum at Savannah as it was passing on boats up the river for use in the Indian trade, that the merchants and officials at Charlestown found their operations impeded by Georgia.[2] In June, 1736, at a session of the assembly which was hastily called, an ordinance was passed providing that traders who suffered damages from the execution of the trade regulations of Georgia should be compensated from the South Carolina treasury to the amount of £2000 each. After some correspondence with Georgia on the subject, complaints were sent to England and the case was taken up by the board of trade and committee of the council with the Trustees.

Georgia contended that the execution of a law which she had rightfully made was being impeded by another colony. The proposal of South Carolina that she should license all the traders who came to her with recommendations from Charlestown, Georgia declared would soon result in the transfer to them of the greater part of her Indian trade. On the other hand, the contention of South Carolina was in favor of her prior rights and of the advantages of a large degree of freedom as between the colonies in Indian trade.[3] The privy

[1] The point of view of South Carolina in reference to these subjects was well stated in a "Report of the Committee appointed to examine into the Proceedings of the People of Georgia with respect to the Province of South Carolina." This was published at Charlestown in 1736.

[2] C. O. 5/364, O. P. S. C. July-Dec. 1735; C. O. 5/435; S. C. L. H. J. 1736; Colls. Ga. Hist. Soc., III, 35; S. C. Gazette, July 3 and 10, 1736.

[3] Acts of P. C. Col. 1720–1745, p. 512; C. O. 5/401, S. C. E. .B June and Sept., 1737; Egmont's Journ. Ga. Col. Recs., V, 30, 45, 50, 55, 63, 66, 546; S. C. State, III, 448.

council advised the two provinces to reach an amicable agreement and to that end instructed the trustees to provide for licensing all properly accredited traders from Charlestown and to cease fining them. The above ordinance of South Carolina, which it had irregularly passed, was disallowed and both provinces were instructed, through their respective governor and trustees, to pass laws for settling the question to their joint benefit and satisfaction.[1] The opinion of the earl of Egmont was, that this would throw the Indian trade of Georgia into Carolina hands and would result in the issue of so many licenses as to destroy the trade of Carolina itself. Oglethorpe, when he was trying to secure the aid of the Cherokees against the Spanish in 1739, reported that they had been so weakened by the ravages of rum and smallpox, both of which had been brought among them from South Carolina, that they threatened revenge and had sent to the French for assistance.[2] Affairs continued without further attempt at regulation until 1741, when an agreement was reached between the trustees and Governor Glen, according to which Carolina should license one-half the Indian traders in Georgia and that one-half of those who were reserved to be licensed by Georgia should have equal liberty to trade in Carolina. As two years were to pass before Glen arrived in his province, it is not probable that much practical result followed this agreement. But MacKay, the offending official, had long since been removed and the prohibition of the importation of rum was abandoned by Georgia. The war made reprisals between the two provinces dangerous and there is no proof that any more such occurred. Still the Georgians believed that South Carolina felt very jealous and irritable toward her and that she took occasion to show this in other ways than in the absorption of a large part of her Indian trade. When, in 1745, a detailed statement was received by the board of trade from Colonel John Fenwick, of South Carolina, on Indian relations throughout the south, the dispute between the two provinces concerning the rights of their traders was still in progress.[3]

So weak were the Spanish in Florida, and so little aid was

---

[1] C. O. 5/364, S. C. O. P. May 25, 1738.
[2] Colls. of Ga. Hist. Soc., III, 87.
[3] C. O. 5/371, O. P. S. C. Apr. 1745.

given by the natives to the English in that conflict, that the war with them had no important effect on Indian relations. The opening of war with France, however, stimulated fears of French and Indian attacks. Governor Glen evidently enjoyed conferences with the natives and especially visits to their country. One notable tour of several hundred miles he made in the Cherokee country.[1] Presents were given and treaties concluded, and of his activity in these directions Glen was fond of writing home. One would judge from what was done and written that, in 1746, Indian relations reached a more serious crisis than at any other time during the war. Because of what was regarded as the critical situation of affairs, a special session of the assembly was called about the middle of April.[2] A large number of letters from agents, traders and others concerning the Indians were laid before the houses. They were to the effect that the French were trying to win the Creeks, Cherokees and Catawbas away from the English interest. Glen had already sent a messenger to the Cherokees to summon the headmen of that nation to meet him at Ninety Six. On the way thither he said he should meet some of the Creeks and Chickasaws at Fort Moore. A conference committee was appointed and, after examining the evidence submitted, it declared itself convinced that the French at Quebec and New Orleans had developed a large plan to seduce the above mentioned Indian tribes from the English alliance. They were believed to be uniting these tribes into a confederation against the English and for an invasion. It was agreed that the governor should proceed with his plan for conferences and that two hundred horsemen should be raised to attend him. About fifty gentlemen with their servants also accompanied him as volunteers. Of the conferences which were actually held, among the Catawbas and at Ninety Six, no account has been preserved, but on his return the governor said that they had been reasonably successful and would check French influence for a time. Presents, of course, were bestowed and an effort was made to impress the savage imagination by a show of the strength of the province, though in no

[1] C. O. 5/372, O. P. S. C. Glen to B. T. Apr. 23, 1748; C. O. 5/385, Glen to Newcastle, May 2, 1746.

[2] C. O. 5/453, L. H. J. Apr. 1746. C. O. 5/376, S. C. O. P. May 2, 1746.

case with such success as had attended Cuming in 1730. The danger was probably by no means so great as was represented, but the incident is cited from the fragmentary records of the time as an example of what was done when the activity of South Carolina in negotiation with the Indians was at its best. The erection of one or more forts, especially in the country of the Cherokees, was under discussion for years, but it was not until after the middle of the century that the decisive step was taken in the building of Fort Prince George and Fort Loudon, the former near Keowee in the Lower Cherokee country and the latter far to the northwest at the junction of the Tellico and Tennessee rivers.[1]

As the war progressed and rival efforts for control over the Indians increased, the presents which were annually bestowed grew also. By the close of the war South Carolina had come to appropriate £1500 in currency annually for this purpose.[2] The British government also made frequent grants for the same object, her presents being sent through agents for both South Carolina and Georgia and designated for the different tribes along the border.[3] In 1748 and 1749 Abraham Bosomworth acted as agent of the two provinces in procuring and distributing the presents from the crown, William Stephens being associated with him for Georgia and John Dort for South Carolina. Bosomworth's brother, Thomas, a clergyman, had secured appointment as Indian agent in Georgia. He had married Mary Matthews, a "princess" of the Creek nation, who from the time of the founding of Georgia and earlier had rendered valuable services to the English.[4] She had been reared and christianized in South Carolina and at the time of the arrival of Oglethorpe and his colonists was living not far

---

[1] See *e.g.* Glen to B. T. July 15, 1750, C. O. 5/372. Glen states that he had already purchased land for this purpose.

[2] S. C. Hist. Colls., II, 298.

[3] C. O. 5/389, A. W. I. S. C. 1748–1751. Papers of Sec. of State. C. O. 5/385 Secy. of State, 1744–1753, Account of presents sent in 1749. Glen stated in 1750 that English govt. had decided to spend £3000 annually on presents for S. C. and Ga.

[4] Ga. Col. Recs., I, 537, 540, 557, 558; VI, 205, 252, 256–286, 289, 305; Stevens, Hist. of Ga., I, 226 *et seq.*; Jones, Hist. of Ga., I, 284 *et seq.*; Logan, Hist. of Upper South Carolina, 176. Mary's Indian name was Coosaponakesa. Musgrave, her first husband and by whom she had one son, was himself a son of the Col. John Musgrave who negotiated a treaty with the Creeks in 1716.

from Savannah. In promoting trade and amicable relations with the Indians and in giving aid to the settlers in other forms her efforts, and those of her first husband, Musgrove, may be considered to have been more valuable than those rendered by Pocahontas to the early settlers of Virginia. In consideration of these Oglethorpe, in 1743, paid £200 and is said to have promised to procure for her from the British government a more adequate compensation. Naturally nothing came, and in 1747 Bosomworth, the third husband of the Indian princess, with the support of Colonel Heron, who was stationed at Frederica, and some others, undertook to extort from the government a sum of more than £5000 for unrequited services. In consideration of this it was said that Mrs. Bosomworth would undertake to secure for the English the permanent friendship of the Creek nation. A poor introduction to an undertaking of this sort was an attempt on Bosomworth's part to bring some slaves into the province in violation of the policy of the trustees.

In order to coerce Georgia into the acceptance of these terms, Bosomworth, who had now entirely abandoned his clerical calling, not only aroused the prejudices of his wife against the English but organized a demonstration of the Creeks against Savannah. As the Bosomworths at this time lived on the Altamaha and had the sympathy of some of the officers at Frederica, this movement proceeded from the southern part of the province. For a time it seemed to threaten the outbreak of another Indian war, like that with the Yamassees. Bosomworth had induced Malatchee, a mico or chief, to proclaim himself head of the nation and then to deed to the Bosomworths three islands, off the coast of the province, and a tract on the mainland near Savannah, which they had previously claimed as a part of their reward. Memorials setting forth their claims and also those of Malatchee were sent to the duke of Newcastle. Mary now, at the instance of her husband, proclaimed herself empress of the Creeks and independent of Great Britain. She and they were therefore sovereign in Georgia, and demanded that the English should abandon all they possessed south and west of the Savannah river and above tidewater. This, which was in harmony with claims the Creeks had long cherished, was

agreed to in a council of the Indians, and a large body of
them accompanied the Bosomworths to Savannah with the
evident intent of overawing the government.  Though the
Indians were armed and President Stephens had only 170
men capable of bearing arms with which to meet them, he
put the town in the best posture of defence that was possible
and met the Indians with a bold front.  With Bosomworth
he refused to parley and the chiefs, when approached, insisted
that Mary should speak for herself and them.  They were
aroused on the one side by a rumor that Mary was to be sent
as a prisoner to England, while, by a report that Stephens
had been murdered, the armed citizens were provoked to
arrest Bosomworth.  His wife then became frantic with rage
and made such wild statements that Stephens also imprisoned
her.  Negotiations then could be carried on with the chiefs
and Stephens, in addition to persuasion, resorted to the magic
influence of a banquet and presents.  Even Malatchee soon
appeared to be quieted by them, though the sudden appearance of the queen once more and the reading of a statement
of her claims threatened to produce an outbreak.  But this
was avoided by the presence of mind of the officers, working
on the excitable and vacillating minds of the savages.
Stephens was then able to persuade them that Bosomworth
was trying to deceive them into supporting false and baseless
claims of his wife as a means of securing power and riches
for himself.  Under the influence of this treatment the Indians
became quiet and in due time took their departure.

The Bosomworths later acknowledged their fault and were
pardoned, but their claims were pushed in England until, in
1759, Mrs. Bosomworth obtained £450 for goods expended in
the king's service, and arrears of salary as agent and interpreter at the rate of £100 per annum for sixteen and one-half
years.  One of the islands which they claimed, and on which
they had settled, was also granted to them.  The trustees,
however, approved of the action of Stephens and the colonists
in every particular, and were specially insistent that no reserved lands should be disposed of except by treaties between
themselves and the Creek Indians.  With this passed one of
the most interesting episodes in the history of Indian relations.  It had no bearing on relations with the French, and

notwithstanding all the rumors and fears the third colonial war passed without a serious disturbance of the peace of the southern frontier.[1]

In letters which were occasionally sent to the southern provinces by Governors Clarke and Clinton of New York proposals were made for general conferences of all the colonies, the object of which should be to secure a peaceful adjustment of relations between all the Indians along the British frontier. This was regarded by Oglethorpe as "one of the noblest designs and most advantageous," among other reasons because it would remove from the southern tribes the fear of the "back Enemy," that is, of attacks in the rear by the Five Nations, and this would facilitate their coöperation with the English in their operations against the Spanish and French.[2]

[1] The affairs of the Bosomworths fill much space in the records of the time. In addition to the Georgia materials already referred to, full accounts may be found in South Carolina sources: Ex. C. J., C. O. 5/457, July 1749; *Ibid.*, C. O. 5/464, May 1751; *Ibid.*, C. O. 5/467, June 1752; L. H. J. and U. H. J. C. O., 5/465, Apr. 1752, Feb., March and May 1754; C. O., 5/389, Secy. of State, S. C. C. O. 5/373, O. P. S. C. Talk delivered to Upper and Lower Creeks, May 28, 1751, and their replies renouncing the claims urged by the Bosomworths.

[2] Colls. of Ga. Hist. Soc., III, 119.

# PART THREE

## THE GROWTH OF THE SPIRIT OF INDEPENDENCE DURING THE PERIOD OF THE THIRD AND FOURTH INTERCOLONIAL WARS
### 1740–1763

# CHAPTER I

## THE GREAT AWAKENING

ONE who reads carefully the letters of the Anglican missionaries in the colonies, after he passes the year 1730 or thereabouts will become conscious of a change of tone. Before that time the prevailing note was one of discouragement. So few and scattered were they, so meagre their support and so great the obstacles which they confronted that they generally felt the task to be too heavy for them. But such progress was made, such was the increase in the number and ability of the laborers and the strength of churches founded at so many strategic points within the colonial territory that, after the date mentioned, a tone of confidence becomes perceptible. This may have been due in part to the vigor that was infused by Bishop Gibson, but must also have been the result of a consciousness of progress made and results achieved. The Anglicans had made their presence felt in all the colonies, but the fact that a foothold had been secured in New England and certain concessions won from the legislatures of Connecticut and Massachusetts afforded just reason for encouragement. It must now be apparent to all observers that the Church had won a permanent place in colonial life and must be reckoned with whenever issues affecting her interests were raised. This position, such as it was, had been won without very much assistance from the British government and certainly without effective administrative control. It was a growth, and its attainment added another element to the colonial fabric, the presence of which indicates that primitive conditions were being slowly outgrown.

This, with all related phenomena was characterized by the New England clergy as the growth of Arminianism and interpreted as a proof of the decay of true religion, a falling away from the ideals of the fathers. After the death of the Mathers this complaint continued, though no one appeared who rang the changes upon the theme so persistently as those two worthies had done.  Toward 1730, however, the situation was made much more serious than ever by the appearance of deistical literature in the colonies.  We hear complaints from Anglican missionaries as well as dissenters of the advent of this literature and the spread of deism, socinianism and atheism.  Pennsylvania was perhaps the scene of worst inroads.  From time to time concerted efforts were made by the Boston pastors and others to check the backsliding by a general revival.  For this purpose they even looked with pious favor upon a visitation of the smallpox and of a throat distemper which proved very fatal among children.  The effects of severe thunderstorms were watched and notable results were expected from the earthquake of 1727.  But all signs failed and the people remained indifferent.[1]  Similar conditions, though of course much worse, existed in all the colonies outside of New England, and certain local stirrings in the region of New Brunswick and Freehold, New Jersey, at first under the preaching of the excellent Dutch minister Theodore

[1] The authority for these statements is Thomas Prince, An Account of the Revival of Religion in Boston, the Christian History, edited by his son, No. 100, and in Gillies, Historical Collections.  John White's New England's Lamentations, Boston, 1734, to which was prefixed a recommendatory epistle signed by the leading Boston pastors, contains a good statement of the orthodox view of the decay of religion and of what Arminianism was supposed to be.  G. P. Fisher, in the introduction to his edition of Edwards' Essay on the Trinity (p. 30), remarks upon the weakening of Calvinism in England as reflected in the writings of Watts and Doddridge.  This was due in part to the influence of Arminius and Grotius and especially to that of Locke.  In the sphere of doctrine it involved the breaking down of the theories of predestination and election, made faith the cause and not the effect of election, and sought the origin of faith and salvation in a free act of the human will.  This, said the writer, was inconsistent with the plan of God to save man purely by the act of His sovereign power and opened a door for boasting.  It weakened the discipline of the churches and caused general indifference and confusion.  The remedy insisted on in this pamphlet was the revival of the office of ruling elder, which many more of the churches had now dropped, and a return to the letter and spirit of the Cambridge Platform.  Incidents of the reform would be a better treatment of the ministers and an increase of their salaries to make up for the effects of the depreciation of bills of credit.  These are signs of the break-down of primitive Calvinism and the only remedy, of course, which the conservatives could see was a renewed allegiance to the past with its appeals to the old interpretations of the Bible and the ecclesiastical system set forth in the Cambridge Platform.  But a return to the past was impossible and the revival which was soon to come, temporarily checked stagnation and posited the issue in a modified form.

Frelinghuysen, and under John and William Tennent, were the only signs of improvement.

But within a few years after the Church had reached the position in the colonies which has just been described, its membership, as well as conservatives among all the dissenting sects, found themselves nearly submerged by a wave of religious enthusiasm which swept over the continental colonies and Great Britain as well and introduced the period of evangelicalism and modern revivals, with the doctrine of the new birth which they have all emphasized. Of such importance was this movement — known in America as the Great Awakening — that it has generally been considered to mark an epoch in the religious history of the eighteenth century. Its history, in whole or in part, has been written and its phenomena described by many pens and from various points of view.[1] All students of the careers of Jonathan Edwards, Gilbert Tennent and George Whitefield, the three leading personalities who were connected with it, have found it necessary to discuss it from their respective points of view. Church historians, thus far conservative in opinion, have traced its development and described its phenomena, sociologists and psychologists have found in it ample material from which to illustrate the primitive traits which came to the surface when crowds are subjected to strong excitement and moved by passion and a common impulse. Students of religion as a profound and mysterious experience of the human soul find in it some of their best accredited material. Curious inquirers, whose purpose it may be to interpret the mind of the American people, will rank this high among the early phenomena which furnish a clue to the elusive thing of which they are in pursuit. It was an event of general human significance, while it abounded in details of the pettiest and most transient character, and the whole was cast in the mould of colonial America. It was the first great and spontaneous movement in the history of the American people, deeper and

---

[1] Trumbull, Hist. of Connecticut; Prince, Christian History of New England; Tracy, The Great Awakening; Tyerman, Life of Whitefield; Chauncy, Seasonable Thoughts on the State of Religion in New England; Dwight, Life of Jonathan Edwards; Works of Edwards; Allen, Jonathan Edwards; Larned, Hist. of Windham County, Conn.; Greene, Development of Religious Liberty in Conn., etc., etc.

more pervading than the wars and yet far less prolonged, an event which in its origin and continuance lay outside the sphere of influence of governors, councils and boards of trade. Administrative regulations did not produce or control it, and although it occasioned notable political changes in New England, in its origin it was as far removed from politics as could be imagined. As an expression, or rather suggestion, of American ideals there was nothing at the time that would compare with it in importance except those utterances and events which reveal the high value set by the people upon individual liberty and self-government. Magna Carta, the colonial charters, and the Bible, taken together in idealized form, embodied the truths best known to the colonists, and from them came their highest aspirations.

The Mathers had now passed to their rest, but Arminianism and the half-way covenant, the arch-enemies of Calvinism and of the severe and exclusive piety of the earlier time, were still the fashion in New England. Of the half-way covenant in an extreme form Solomon Stoddard, of Northampton, was the leading apostle. He had defended it in his " Appeal to the Learned," though in spite of its calmness and restraint his personality or some more mysterious influence had occasioned a succession of revivals in his church. But in general the words of Trumbull, the historian, are accepted as fairly descriptive of the religious condition of the Puritan colonies at this period: " Though the preaching of the gospel was not altogether without success, and though there was tolerable peace and order in the churches, yet there was too generally a great decay as to the life and power of godliness. There was a general ease and security in sin." " The forms of religions were kept up, but there appeared but little of the power of it. . . . The young people became loose and vicious, family prayer and religion was greatly neglected, the Sabbath was lamentably profaned. . . . The young people made the evenings after the Lord's Day and after lectures the times for their mirth and company keeping. Taverns were haunted, intemperance and other vices increased and the spirit of God appeared to be awfully withdrawn. It seems also that many of the clergy, instead of clearly and powerfully preaching the doctrines of original sin, of regeneration, justification by faith alone, and the other peculiar doctrines of the gospel, contented themselves with preaching 'a cold, unprincipled and lifeless morality.' " [1] The modern critic would say that human nature was beginning to assert itself and the way was opening toward a richer and more varied future as the bars and manacles of the Puritan prison house rusted away. But to the great mass of men, even at the middle of the eighteenth century, it did not appear in this light. To them it seemed a decay, a falling away from the ideals of the fathers, a sinking to a lower social level, and no type of culture was known to them which could make anything seem tolerable except a more rigid adherence to the Calvinistic ideal of the Puritan commonwealth. Under the lead of revivalists of unusual power, a spasmodic effort, which extended not only throughout New England but over the colonies at large, was now made to escape from the religious lethargy of the mid-eighteenth century, and this was known as the Great Awakening.

The revival began in 1734 in Northampton, Massachusetts, Jonathan Edwards, thirty-one years of age and the grandson of the revered Stoddard, was then pastor of the church in that interior town of the Connecticut valley. Though he had shown great precocity as a youth and a student at Yale, nothing had yet occurred to distinguish him from Cotton or the Mathers as a typical New England preacher and divine of the more ascetic and learned class. After his graduation in 1720 and during his later service as a tutor in Yale, he had access to the same books which produced such an awakening influence upon the mind of Johnson. In a list kept by Edwards of books " to be read or to be inquired for " appear a goodly number of the English classics of the time. Edwards also relates that, when he read Locke's " Essay Concerning Human Understanding," it was with a delight greater " than the most greedy miser finds when gathering up handfuls of silver and gold from some newly discovered treasure." The influence of Locke upon Edwards' type of Calvinism has been noted, as also the coincidence of his idealism with that of Berkeley, though without evidence of his having borrowed from that source. Unlike Johnson, however, there is no indication that Edwards was attracted by the writings of the

[1] Trumbull, Hist. of Conn., II, 135, 137.

divines of the English Church. His mind remained closed to its claims and to the appeals of the Prayer Book. To both men the writings of the deists were anathema, and the mathematics and astronomy of Newton with such primitive fragments of natural science as were to be gleaned from Bacon and others of that time were wholly inadequate to convince the unwilling of the truth in the rationalist point of view. Therefore Edwards' reading did not liberalize him at all, but rather the opposite, while Johnson's awakening simply made him a successful Anglican divine.

But Edwards' asceticism was tempered by an early and most happy marriage with Sarah Pierrepont, the daughter of the New Haven clergyman who was so influential in the founding of Yale. Her capacity for deep religious enthusiasm in some respects exceeded that of Edwards himself. The mystical and poetic element in Edwards' nature was strong, giving color to his style as well as to his philosophical and theological views, making prominent in his experience and teaching a sense of the immediate divine presence and influence. This related him in a way to the best among the Quakers and to those who had been labelled Antinomians in the previous century, giving to his preaching an unusually quickening power. A most acute logical mind and vivid imagination, both trained in the grooves of Calvinistic theology, completed his equipment and were destined to make him the most powerful intellectual force in New England during the later eighteenth century. This distinction he achieved, though his life was spent in comparative isolation and the most productive part of it actually on the frontier.

And yet to a modern mind the narrowness of Edwards' outlook and the limitations of his culture are pitiful. The fact that a mind naturally so powerful and an endowment so rich as his should have been so completely imprisoned within the stone walls and iron gates of later New England puritanism makes his career a tragedy. One can feel that such an environment was as good as men of the type of the Mathers deserved; at least they did all in their power to perpetuate it. But one cannot read Edwards' flowing style and note the beautiful imagery which adorns his writings, or feel the sweep of his argument, without knowing that he was

worthy of better things.  To the historian perhaps the most
significant of his writings is his "Work of Redemption,"
though it has hitherto been passed over almost in silence.[1]  It
sets forth his philosophy of history, commonplace to be sure
and implicit in the minds of thousands because it is as intensely biblical and Calvinistic as Milton's two immortal
poems.  His purpose was to show that the work of redemption, the purpose of which is to overcome the effects of the
fall of man, is the central theme of history.  The comparatively simple evolution of a God-centered, not a man-centered
world was his subject.  The birth and resurrection of the
Christ was that toward which all earlier history converged
and in the light of which all later events should be viewed.
All recorded time he divided into three periods:  from the
fall of man to the incarnation of Christ, from Christ's incarnation to his resurrection, from thence to the end of the
world.  Of the three periods the second, though so short, in
importance exceeded both the others.  "Space of time from
the resurrection of Christ to the end of the world is all taken
up in bringing about or accomplishing the great effect or
success of that purchase."  In a work of nearly four hundred
pages, the substance of which was originally delivered in
sermons at Northampton in 1739, this subject is developed
with precision and force.  The great enemy of the divine plan
and of the church before Christ was heathenism; since the
early Christian centuries its great foe had been the papacy.
Of the modern period the Reformation was the central land-
mark, and the writer's sketch was filled in with references to
persecutions, heresies, schisms and the futile struggles of
Antichrist, the beast of the Apocalypse, to withstand the
blows which had been administered by the hands of true
Christians.  No party or kingdom or cause had ever met such
opposition and successfully withstood it as had the Christian
Church, and this was accepted as proof of its divine origin,
while the added declarations of prophecy are cited as assurances of its ultimate triumph.  This was the historic back-

[1] This is printed in vol. II of the first American edition of Edwards'
Works, Worcester, 1808.  It differs from Augustine's City of God in
being purely expository and not apologetic, and is evidently much more
complete and systematic than any mediaeval attempts to treat the same
theme.

ground of Edwards' thought and his hearers had no other with which to compare it. To his mind and theirs also the most surprising triumphs of grace were still to be won in the new eastern world and especially in New England, that favored land of the gospel, where the true faith had so prevailed in the past.

" And it is worthy to be noted," says Edwards in another work,[1] " that America was discovered about the time of the reformation but little before: Which reformation was the first thing that God did towards the glorious renovation of the world after it had sunk into the depths of darkness and ruin under the great antichristian apostasy. So that as soon as this new world is (as it were) created, and stands forth in view, God presently goes about doing some great thing to make way for the introduction of the· churches latter-day glory, that is to have its first seat in and is to take its rise from that new world."

To the Puritan consciousness a period of alleged spiritual decline always appeared to be an evidence of divine displeasure, a " judgment," and the only remedy was a renewed turning to God in the spirit and according to the methods approved in the past. It had been so in the days of Salem witchcraft, and the crisis which the churches were facing forty years later was only a continuation and expansion of that which they had faced when the early charter fell. Edwards was more deeply conscious of the crisis than any of his contemporaries and his remedy was correspondingly thorough. It consisted theologically in the most emphatic reassertion of Augustinianism and Calvinism in their ultra form. This he first indicated in a lecture which he delivered in Boston in 1731, published under the title of " God glorified in Man's Dependence." The views which he then expressed were elaborated in his later utterances and especially in his famous treatise on the " Freedom of the Will." They consisted in such a lofty conception of the divine nature and sovereignty as to dwarf both external nature and man in comparison therewith. God was conceived as the universal substance underlying all external phenomena and by implica-

---

[1] The Revival of Religion in New England, Works, III, 156.

tion also all the operations of the human mind.[1] The only real existence was the divine and the nature of the deity, as he conceived it, was absolute, even arbitrary, will. Predestination and election were simple corollaries of this principle, and to man was reserved the power of self-determination only in certain lower spheres of action. This was his challenge to the Deism and Arminianism of his time, a denial more complete and sweeping than any Calvinist had previously uttered.

For the purpose of practical application from the pulpit his theory was supported to the full by the Puritan mythology of the time — hell, with its torments, as the inevitable doom of the sinner, and heaven, with its light and glory inconceivable, as the reward of the pure and holy. The rewards of the blest could be secured not by an outward, though sincere, conformity, but by genuine conversion, followed by a deep and true Christian experience. These were Edwards' intense convictions and he enforced them with a logic and power of illustration, a beauty and copiousness of diction, which made his appeal unusually effective. So far as the personality of Edwards was responsible for the Great Awakening, this, briefly stated, was his position and the source of his power.

Before an appeal such as his, New England congregations were to a large extent helpless, for they had no conception of man or the universe to set up in opposition to him. They had always been taught to hold man in low esteem. Everywhere the emphasis was laid on authority, on trust and belief, and the possibility of independent inquiry, to say nothing of its methods, was unknown. Nature was a sealed book and human nature, except as interpreted in the light of a rigid Calvinistic orthodoxy, was equally unknown. It was consciously or implicitly held that the great mass of humanity was destined to an endless existence of misery unless saved therefrom by an act of grace which their wills alone were powerless

---

[1] Allen, *op. cit.*, 60. "His Calvinism," says McGiffert concerning Edwards, "was the least scholastic and the most profound, both philosophically and religiously, to be found in any school. It was not the greatness of God but the nothingness of man that he was primarily interested to enforce and all his theology was dominated by this aim." McGiffert, Protestant Thought before Kant, 76.

to induce. Their minds, both in their conscious and sub-conscious activities, were filled with images and suggestions derived from this idea. They were particularly susceptible to emotional appeals, in which images and warnings derived from this source were used. Salvation, pictured as an escape from eternal torment and admission to a state of blessedness which in every respect was its extreme opposite, furnished an equally powerful appeal. When men, women and children were brought together in crowds, the force of such appeals was magnified many times. Fear, rising at times to terror, was the emotion roused by the first appeal, and joy, equally extravagant, was the response to the second. Under their influence ordinary inhibitions were thrown off and we have the well known phenomena of revivals — " the violent spasmodic action, the contortions of the body, the shouting, the trembling, the hypnotic rigidity and, at the other extreme, the sinking of muscular energy, the trance and the vision." [1] By a process of mental contagion not only assemblies of people, but whole communities extending over large areas of country, could be thrown into a state of abnormal excitement and kept there for a longer or shorter period, with mass " conversions " as a result. It is true, as represented by Edwards, Prince, Colman, Blair and other well balanced participants in and supporters of the movement, that the majority of those who were touched by the appeals of the revivalists did not show the symptoms of excitement in the extreme forms which have been described. There were all grades and varieties of experience. But in all real cases appeared the familiar signs of conviction of sin, ended by a subjection of the will, which in turn was followed by a sense of forgiveness and peace that was supposed to come from a divine source. While this process of conversion was going on and until its effects wore away, the attention of individuals and of communities was largely or wholly withdrawn from ordinary affairs of this world and fixed on an imagined future state or the preparation for it. Anxiety for others existed, but it was that they might share this experience and hope and was totally regardless of the well-being or improvement of society, except so far as it might result from the observance of a limited number

---

[1] Davenport, *op. cit.*, 216.

of moral precepts laid down in the decalogue and expounded chiefly in the New Testament. This was the circle within which the Great Awakening and all similar revivals have moved, and it clearly indicates the limits of their influence and usefulness.

In this place further description of their well-known phenomena is unnecessary. Their interest lies chiefly in the domain of social psychology, and such political and ecclesiastical results as followed this movement will appear in the sequel. But in its inception nothing could be further removed from the political sphere than this revival. Throughout their lives the activities of its two great leaders were as completely divorced from politics as those of any men could well be. But under the relationship which then existed between church and state such a religious and moral upheaval as this could not occur without important effects upon the body politic.

Without special missionary labors on the part of Edwards or others, the revival which began in Northampton extended to the other towns of the valley and to many sections of Connecticut, though not appreciably through eastern New England. Edwards' " Narrative " and his later " Thoughts " on the revival gave the interested public an account of its phenomena, with the calm, though very sympathetic, criticisms of its chief apostle. The excitement had abated and to all appearance would not have extended further, even in New England, had it not been for the return of Whitefield to America on his second visit, in the autumn of 1739. The experiences of the previous year in England had determined the course of his life. His marvellous powers of emotional appeal as a preacher to vast audiences had been shown in all parts of the realm. He had travelled far and wide and poured forth sermon after sermon, preferably upon his favorite themes of sin, regeneration and the new birth, as if from an inexhaustable reservoir. Their intellectual quality was low and they involved endless variations upon a few simple themes. But they were delivered with extraordinary oratorical power, with a moving and affectionate appeal,[1]

[1] One of the most appreciative accounts of Whitefield's style of address is given by Prince in his Account of the Revival of Religion in Boston. So far as we know, the effective revivalists of that time did not joke or tell

and were eminently fitted to arouse the emotions of the multitudes of common people who flocked to listen.  Some also of the higher classes, notably women and those in search of new sensations, became his supporters.  He was only twenty-four years of age and, as has been well said, immeasurably inferior to Edwards in everything except the artifices of the pulpit.  In rank he was a humble clergyman of the parish of Savannah, in Georgia, and for the building of an orphan house in that province he was already raising money far and wide.[1]  Because of what was considered his effrontery in asking for the use of some of their churches, he fell out with the clergy of Bristol.  He then began preaching out of doors, in chapels, or wherever the people would flock to hear him.  Thereupon the clergy and churchmen generally began to attack him and he felt the first effects of persecution.  But it was powerless to check his wonderful success and popularity, so that when he returned to America he was already one of the most famous men in the British Isles.  At last a genuine revivalist, such as the world had never before seen, had appeared, incessantly active, with limitless endurance, with energy enough to move continents, bent upon rousing the masses from their moral and spiritual lethargy by the emotional use of the simple and well known themes of the gospel.  Whitefield's achievements, together with the work of the Wesleys which was just beginning, were portents of a profound religious change throughout the English speaking world.  Of the two, Whitefield, with his Calvinistic belief, was best fitted to work in the colonies.

Beginning in Philadelphia, his place of landing, Whitefield

---

stories or use slang.  Their appeal was direct and scriptural.  Edwards and Tennent spoke, one with great solemnity, the other with crushing force.  The young Jonathan Mayhew, however, expressed an opinion of Whitefield which was the extreme opposite of these and one upon which many modern critical hearers would probably find it difficult to improve.  "When he was lately in Boston," wrote Mayhew, "many persons attended him, but chiefly of the more illiterate sort, except some who went out of curiosity.  I heard him once; and it was as low, confused, puerile, conceited, ill-natured, enthusiastic a performance as I ever heard."  Foote, Annals of King's Chapel, II, 261.

[1] This, Whitefield said, was suggested to him by Charles Wesley, who had concerted the scheme with Oglethorpe.  But the original which was copied was the institution established by Francke at Halle, in Germany.  Tyerman, I, 347, 441 et seq.

at once entered upon his evangelistic tours, extending from one end of the colonial territory to the other, far exceeding in their extent and effectiveness those of Keith thirty years before. After preaching to multitudes in Philadelphia, he journeyed to New York, preaching at places on the way and everywhere meeting with equal success. At this, the beginning of his career, he met the Tennents, of Log College fame, and formed a specially sympathetic acquaintance with William, the father, and with Gilbert, who became one of the most famous of the sons. Returning through Philadelphia, Whitefield passed southward in a continuous overland journey to Charlestown, South Carolina. In Virginia he preached scarcely at all, and among the scattered settlements of Maryland and North Carolina only in the intervals of long and tiresome journeys. His journey from Charlestown to Savannah was made by water. Staying in his parish for only a short time, he returned by sea to Pennsylvania and travelled again through a part of the middle colonies. From the beginning of his missionary journeys through the colonies he had thrown off entirely the restraints of the canons and preached in all places where a hearing could be obtained. Therefore it was that, on his second return to the south, as has already been related, he was summoned to meet Commissary Garden in court. He had now become practically a dissenter and it was among them that he met with the warmest reception.

In September, 1740, Whitefield, in response to invitations, landed at Newport, Rhode Island, and began his tours of New England. He soon reached Boston, with its group of active and mutually jealous churches, the great meeting place of the section. Its people, like the Athenians of old, were curious to see and hear, and presently the town and the surrounding country was aroused to a pitch of excitement upon religion such as had not been witnessed since the time of the Antinomians. As the fire spread from town to town the Mathers, had they been living, would have hailed it as the end of the long and dreary period of decline and spiritual drought. To Colman, Sewall, Foxcroft, and the other ministers, it was the divine visitation for which they had long been waiting. The emotional nature of Governor Belcher, in which there was a certain kinship between him and the evangelist, was deeply moved from the first and, with repeated attendance upon his ministrations, prayers and effusions of tears, the chief magistrate contributed both personal and official recognition to the whirlwind campaign. The Boston ministers, except those of the English church, welcomed Whitefield to their pulpits, though the crowds were so large that he found his favorite rostrum upon the Common. Boston was now large enough to give a suggestion, in its response to the appeals of Whitefield, of that liking for such thrills and outpourings which it has continued to exhibit ever since. With the visits of Whitefield we have the first demonstration on a large scale of one of the most important social characteristics not only of Boston but of a democracy in general.

After visiting a number of the towns in the neighborhood of Boston, including Cambridge, Whitefield journeyed northward as far as Portsmouth, preaching on his way. He then returned for a brief additional sojourn at the capital and then started westward for the valley of the Connecticut. In that region the most significant event was his visit to Edwards at Northampton. He preached repeatedly in Edwards' pulpit, during which exercises, says Whitefield, not only was the congregation much moved but the pastor wept — on one occasion during the whole time of the service. When Whitefield started on his return southward, Edwards, with others, accompanied him as far as East Windsor, Connecticut, the birthplace of the Northampton pastor and still the residence and parish of his father. It is said that on the way Edwards expressed opinions which differed from those of the evangelist concerning impulses and also concerning the charge which Whitefield had already begun making in public, that the great body of the ministry of all the sects was unconverted.[1] This, it will be noted, was substantially a repetition of the charge which Anne Hutchinson and her friends had made in their day. In view of the effect which this produced in her time and which it was to produce before the end of the Whitefield movement, it is certainly not surprising to be told that the friendship of the two men, as the result of this conversation, was somewhat chilled, though not destroyed.

Whitefield, after parting with Edwards, continued his jour-

[1] Dwight, Life of Edwards, 147.

ney southward, preaching with the usual success in many Connecticut towns, addressing the students of Yale College, as he had done those of Harvard. Thence he proceeded, again repeating the experiences of his earlier visits, through New York, New Jersey and Pennsylvania and onward to Savannah. As a result of his continuous appeals, he had raised a considerable sum for the orphanage and his interests in Georgia henceforward chiefly centred in that. His first and greatest missionary tour through the colonies had now ended with the breaking of the ground and the starting of the movement.

Whitefield now returned to Great Britain, where he continued his gigantic labors for three years. Then he again visited America, where he remained for a period of four years — 1744 to 1748. During that time he continued to travel widely through the continent, laboring incessantly and winning multitudes of converts, gaining more of a foothold in the southern colonies, even including Virginia. But he was now hindered to an extent by ill health and was forced, as we shall see, to contend against powerful opposition, especially in New England. In order to combat this he had to resort to the press and to divide his labors between those of the pen and the voice. Though in the use of the former Whitefield made a fair showing, his great superiority lay in the spoken word. From the pulpit he could quell all audible opposition and sway the multitudes as he willed. At this and the later stages of his career he also on many occasions exhibited the most heroic and indomitable spirit in overcoming his bodily weakness, as well as a truly Christian temper in the treatment of his enemies and the acknowledgment of his own mistakes. These acts go far to counterbalance the harsh judgments to which the errors and extravagances of Whitefield's conduct naturally give rise. When, to these proofs of heroism and manliness, are added the testimony of Franklin and Edwards and many others, supported by all that we know of what was reasonable and beneficent in the revival as a whole, though much that was deplorable will be noted, it will be seen that purely negative and cynical judgments concerning the phenomenon must be ruled out.

Before the close of his life Whitefield paid three more

visits to America, spending upwards of four years longer in the colonies. Worn out by his abundant labors, death overtook him at Newburyport, Massachusetts, in 1770, on the eve of the Revolution, and his ashes repose in New England, for the redemption of which, as he conceived it, he so lavishly expended his energies. Edwards had died at Princeton twelve years before. When these men passed away, though their spirit and theological views were long to dominate America and especially New England, the deists in England had already challenged the fundamental tenets of Calvinism and the faint beginnings of a movement may be discerned which, if it ever comes to a complete fruitage, will make such phenomena as this eighteenth-century Great Awakening forever impossible.

The point has now been reached where it is necessary to describe the opposition that was aroused by the Great Awakening, the various controversies and struggles which it occasioned and the influence which it had upon the state-church system in the various colonies. Those who are not specially interested in theological polemics, or in hypnotism, hysteria and abnormal psychology, will find in these reactions of the movement its chief interest. And even when viewed upon this secular level, it will be found to have been an event of much importance, for it administered the first severe blow to the cause of church establishment in the colonies, whether that policy was of the Congregational or the Episcopalian type. From this standpoint it will be found well worthy of study. Though it occasioned much sordid controversy and its influence in many ways was unfavorable to true culture and freedom, it did stir the shallows in the minds of many colonists and led to readjustments which were to prove beneficial.

The worst features of the revival may best be illustrated by reference to the career of James Davenport,[1] who was pastor of the Presbyterian church at Southold, Long Island. Though at the beginning he was highly esteemed by Whitefield and others, under the excitement of the time he and a neighboring minister, named Barber, soon developed into fanatics of the most extreme and intolerant character. While they were reading the Bible new light seemed to break forth

[1] Tracy, *op. cit.*, 230 *et seq.*, and other authorities.

from certain texts with overwhelming force upon their minds
and this they interpreted as a divine inspiration to leave their
parishes and become itinerants as Whitefield was doing.
Davenport accompanied Whitefield upon a few occasions and
was always warmly received by the evangelist. This still
further inflamed his conceit and soon his zeal as an imitator
carried him well beyond the excesses of his model. As he
travelled about the country, especially in New England, he
was guilty of some of the worst extravagances of the time in
the pulpit, haranguing, shouting and painting lurid pictures
of hell as a means of increasing the agonies of his hearers and
multiplying the number of converts. But he was specially
distinguished for his attacks upon his brethren, the clergy.
One after another of those in whose parishes he preached,
were denounced by Davenport as unconverted. The great
body of church members he also assigned to the same class,
reserving the term " brothers " for those whom he considered
regenerate and excluding all others from the communion.
The minister of Saybrook, Connecticut, and three other neighboring clergymen, he declared to be unconverted, though he
had just asked to be admitted to the pulpit of at least one of
them. After Mr. Noyes, of New Haven, had permitted him
to use his church, the revivalist also affixed the same brand to
him. Thereupon a meeting of the church was called, which
was also attended by some of the officers of Yale, and it was
voted to exclude Davenport from the use of the church
building.

In the spring of 1742 the Connecticut assembly passed a
law against itinerancy, which further increased the anger of
Davenport and his associates.[1]  Because of his conduct and
that of Pomeroy, in the town of Stratford, they were arrested
on complaint of two citizens and brought before the assembly. After an examination which lasted for two days and
which was accompanied by much disorder, the assembly resolved that Davenport was " under the influences of en-
thusiastical impressions and impulses, and thereby disturbed
in the rational faculties of his mind, and therefore to be pitied
and compassionated, and not to be treated as otherwise he
might be." He was therefore ordered to be sent back to his

---

[1] Conn. Recs., VIII, 454, 482, 483.

abode on Long Island, and the order was duly executed. Pomeroy was released without punishment. For a moment it seemed that the problem was solved.

But though Davenport's parishioners had long since complained of his absences, he soon left them again and appeared in Boston. The association of ministers of that section at once published a " Declaration " in reference to him and his conduct, in which approval of his earnestness and of his genuine services was aptly mingled with caution as to his excesses.[1] Benjamin Colman's name stood at the head of its list of signers, and it well expressed the spirit of this sympathetic, but cautious, friend of the revival, though it stated that the ministers were resolved not to admit Davenport to their pulpits. This, together with disturbances at his outdoor meetings, probably made him more extreme, so that on Copp's Hill he told the Lord that he would not mince the matter any longer, for it was known between them that most of the ministers of the town of Boston and of the country were unconverted and were leading their people blindfold to hell. He also appealed to the Lord to pull them down, turn them out and put others in their places. Davenport for these and other sayings and doings was indicted by the grand jury and, refusing to give bail, was detained for trial. When he was arraigned, several of the ministers sent a note to the court requesting that he be tenderly dealt with. The verdict was that when he uttered the words alleged the prisoner was not *compos mentis* and therefore was not guilty. He was not expelled from Massachusetts, but continued preaching there for some time after his trial. Until the spring of the following year he continued his half insane antics in public, when his excitement seems to have abated. In 1744 he published a " Retraction,"[2] in which he confessed that he had been led astray by following impulses and impressions, in encouraging private persons to preach, and particularly in his wholesale denunciation of ministers as unconverted and urging their congregations to separate from them. With this Davenport's special activities in connection with the

---

[1] Tracy, 242, *et seq.*

[2] Tracy, 249. The Retraction is printed in full in Prince, Christian History.

Great Awakening ceased, but the effects to which they had contributed, especially in eastern Connecticut, continued and will call for further description.

But in point of censoriousness Whitefield and Tennent offended almost as seriously as did Davenport. At an early stage in his American career Whitefield began the publication of his journals, artlessly revealing his inmost religious experiences and flinging broadcast the charge that most of the New England clergy did not experimentally know Christ. The habit of making such charges he had formed in England and he now continued the practice in communities which prided themselves upon being the religious *élite* of the world. The men who had welcomed him to Boston and others of equal merit might consider themselves under the ban. Harvard and Yale he also condemned, as he had done the English universities, saying that they were seminaries of paganism, that " their light is now become darkness, darkness that may be felt." These charges, especially against the clergy, Gilbert Tennent urged with much greater harshness in Boston and elsewhere throughout the earlier years of the revival. At Nottingham, Pennsylvania, he preached a famous sermon, widely circulated in print, which was an elaborate comparison of the clergy of the time to the pharisees and to Judas and an application to them of the harshest denunciations used in scripture.[1] He denounced them as letter-learned pharisees, plastered hypocrites, having the form of godliness but destitute of its power. This was a veritable philippic and in set terms justified those congregations which should abandon such ministers and seek true shepherds.[2]

It was conduct such as Davenport's and the extravagant outbursts of emotion on the part of multitudes of converts which brought the revival into disrepute with conservatives

[1] This is outlined by Hodge, Const. Hist., II, 152.

[2] Tennent was attacked in the press for his harsh language and his proceedings in general in New England. One of these attacks was in a pamphlet by one John Hancock, entitled, The Examiner against Tennent. To this Tennent replied in The Examiner Examined, Boston, 1743. In this, while still defending his previous course, he attempted to soften the impression it had made by claiming that his sincere purpose was to extend the kingdom of God and righteousness and not to stir up contention. We shall see how Tennent was compelled still further to change his attitude.

throughout the colonies. The savage attacks made by White-field and Tennent on the clergy and the colleges were in most cases so unjust as to provoke keen resentment and stir up active opposition. Itinerancy was a novelty which threw parishes into confusion and ran counter to all established relations between ministers and their congregations. Preaching and exhorting by laymen and by the uneducated was equally irregular and fell in with the other anarchical features of the movement. When popular evangelists came into a neighborhood, the regular pastors found themselves abandoned by a large part of their congregations and, in cases where this became permanent, rival churches were established, with the inevitable accompaniment of bitter and long continued jealousies and quarrels. As by a powerful revolutionary disturbance in the body politic, long established ties were broken, customs and institutions were attacked, the public peace was disturbed, and leaders who had hitherto enjoyed general respect were assailed and threatened with professional ruin. Out of conditions such as these developed the conservative opposition to the revival and the efforts to keep society stable and prevent it from yielding to the assaults of the innovators.

The element in society, of course, which it was found impossible to move, the most stolid of all, was the persistently ungodly, those who remained indifferent to all appeals or who lived in regions too remote to feel the effects of the revival. In most sections these probably constituted the majority of the population. In general it may be said that the colonies south of Pennsylvania and the Lower Counties were only superficially affected by Whitefield's preaching. Population was so scattered and means of communication so poor that he never attempted to visit more than a few accessible towns in those colonies. The clergy as a whole did not actively respond to his appeals and therefore no corps of helpers was developed to extend his work in those sections. Language, of course, proved a barrier against work among the Germans of Pennsylvania and the Dutch of central and northern New York. The slaves as a class were scarcely reached at this time and the same was probably true to a large extent of the indented servants. The converts came chiefly from among the free colonists and from those who lived north of Mason and Dixon's line.

Of the protestant sects, the Anglicans were most united and determined in opposition to the revival. They were ultra conservative. The reason for this is to be found in part in their dislike of Whitefield because of the flagrant contempt with which he treated the orders and canons of the church. The enthusiasm and gross breaches of decorum with which the revival was accompanied provoked in their minds mingled feelings of contempt and disgust. The bishop of London issued a pastoral against enthusiasm and this was everywhere read and observed by the faithful. With very few exceptions, Whitefield was excluded from episcopal churches. When he first arrived in Boston one brief interview occurred between him and the episcopal rectors and then they went their respective ways. When one reads the letters of the episcopal clergy during those years he finds that, in all the colonies and from Alexander Garden down, they write in a chorus of criticism and denunciation of Whitefield and of the movement which he was leading. Some of the best descriptions of its main features from a hostile pen were written by Timothy Cutler respecting the revival as he observed it in Boston.[1] Vesey was even more pronounced in New York, and in Connecticut Johnson surpassed all his brethren in his gentlemanly but firm opposition to the movement in all its features. We have it from his autobiography that he was early opposed to enthusiasm, and one effect of the revival was to turn his mind to the more systematic study of ethics as a corrective for its extravagances of conduct. So united were the Anglicans in their opposition, that the revival had no tendency to divide their ranks or to develop a schism among them.

The extent to which Whitefield turned to the dissenters, and the warm welcome which he received from them, were not among the least of the offences which the Anglicans reckoned up against him. Among the dissenters whom he seriously influenced, the Presbyterians were as prominent and theologically as conservative as any. But they as a body,

---

[1] Hist. Colls. *etc.* (Massachusetts), 345–348. The comments of the episcopal clergy may be found in all the volumes of this series and in the manuscript letters of the S. P. G.

together with the Congregational clergy and laity of New England, welcomed Whitefield on his first tour and continued in large measure to support him to the end of his career. We have seen how favorable was the attitude of Boston to his coming, and that was generally repeated wherever he went. Presbyterians and Congregationalists, who were so closely allied and in Connecticut almost amalgamated, were Calvinists and to them appealed the strong Calvinism of Whitefield. The Arminianism, toward which the Wesleyan movement in Great Britain inclined, was less welcome to them. It, with other things, continued to exist as a barrier between them and the Methodists, as that sect developed. The Quakers were not specially moved by Whitefield. Their calm and quiet spirit and methods were not like his. They doubtless listened in large numbers, at Society Hill in Philadelphia and elsewhere, but went away distrustful of the violent type of conversion to which his preaching led. The Baptists, as we shall see, profited greatly by the revival, with the general course and results of which they found themselves in very complete agreement.

But as time passed and Whitefield's journals were published, his indictment of the clergy was urged and the practices to which reference has been made were indulged in on an increasing scale, opposition developed among both Presbyterians and Congregationalists. These two bodies became divided in their attitude toward the revival, and from the conflict which followed proceeded the effects of the movement on ecclesiastical and secular politics. The parties which were formed were popularly known in New England as " Old Lights " and " New Lights," and among the Presbyterians of the middle colonies as the " Old Side " and the " New Side." The former term indicated the conservatives to whom the revival in its more violent aspects was unwelcome, the latter those who accepted and approved of it as a whole. The division which arose over this issue among the Presbyterians of the middle colonies will first demand attention.

In 1729, after considerable controversy in which Jonathan Dickinson was the leader of those who took the broader view and John Thomson, of the Newcastle Presbytery, was the chief spokesman on the other, the Synod of Philadelphia adopted the Westminster Confession of Faith and the Larger and Shorter Catechisms, as " good forms of sound words and systems of Christian doctrine " and as the " confession of our faith." [1] As is inevitable when a definite creed or platform is adopted, the members of the body subject to it divide into strict subscriptionists and their opponents. As years passed and particularly at the time of the Great Awakening, it became difficult for the churches to secure an adequate supply of ministers who were sound in the faith and had sufficient learning. The graduates of the two New England colleges were for the most part absorbed by the churches of that section. William Tennent, in his Log College at Neshaminy, trained his sons and a few other devoted young men for the Presbyterian ministry in the middle and southern colonies, and when the Great Awakening came these were of a type which fitted them to be ardent leaders in that movement.[2] In 1738 the synod resolved, in order to prevent the admission of uneducated men to the ministry, that every candidate must be furnished with a diploma of graduation from some European or New England college or a certificate of competent scholarship from a committee of the synod. In the previous year members of one presbytery were prohibited from preaching to congregations under the care of another presbytery without a regular invitation.[3]

Upon these two points disputes arose. In 1738 the presbytery of New Brunswick, in New Jersey, where the Tennents had worked, licensed John Rowland to preach and later ordained him without subjecting him to the tests as to scholarship which were required by the synod. Later it also licensed in the same way Robinson and Finley, both of whom became distinguished evangelists. This conduct directly raised the question of the obligation of a presbytery which was associated with other similar presbyteries to conform to the regulations adopted by the body in and under which they were all conjoined. But the synod was of very recent origin, relations were fluid and passions were being stirred by the

[1] Hodge, op. cit., I, 151 et seq.; Briggs, op. cit., 208 et seq.
[2] These were Tennent's four sons, Samuel Blair, John Blair, Samuel Finley, William Robinson, John Rowland and Charles Beatty. Arch. Alexander; Biographical Sketches of Founders and Principal Alumni of Log College. [3] Hodge, II, 124.

revival in its early stages. The Tennents were forerunners of this, as well as its leaders in that section. They were eager to develop a godly ministry and, while arguing the question on the basis of church law, also made it a matter of conscience. Personal and family interests also were brought in, for it was charged that the regulation was intended to operate against the Log College. Thomson and his associates on the other hand, contended that the synod was the highest judicatory of the church, was the guardian of regularity and itself could examine, license and ordain.

In 1740, after much agitation, an attempt was made at the meeting of the synod to settle the question. But Gilbert Tennent and Samuel Blair threw firebrands into the assembly by reading papers in which it was declared that its members — the men who were listening to their voices — were unsound in doctrine and unconverted in life. They were therefore stiff upon small points, it was said, zealous for outward order, while they were ignorant of the true needs of the people and were opposing God's true servants and work. " Rules," said Tennent, " which are serviceable in ordinary times, when the church is stocked with a faithful ministry, are notoriously prejudicial when the church is oppressed with a carnal ministry." These were the sentiments which he was soon to repeat with such tremendous emphasis in his Nottingham sermon. The charges were made without attempt to prove them, though on the floor of the synod the complainants were urged in the strongest manner to accuse certain individuals and bring these cases to an adjudication. But that would have been impossible and was wholly inconsistent with the purpose of the agitators. Both Tennent and Blair urged congregations to separate from their unconverted pastors, and that process went on in certain localities. Several cases, notably that of Alexander Craighead, were brought up of intrusion into neighboring parishes or congregations.

In 1741, so strong had feeling become, that in a disorderly session from which the New York members were absent, and by a very small majority, the New Brunswick presbytery and its supporters were excluded. As the two factions were of about equal strength and determination, it proved to be a schism which was difficult to heal. The small majority —

only a fragment of the synod — which had excluded Tennent and his friends at once passed an order making strict subscription of the Confession and Catechism obligatory upon all ministers and elders, thus discarding the liberty, implied in the language of the adopting act.[1]  In 1742 the New York members attended the synod and Dickinson was chosen moderator, with a view to restoring harmony.  But, though the debate and efforts toward agreement were continued for three years, they proved futile.  In 1745 the presbyteries of New York, New Brunswick and New Londonderry, Pennsylvania — Blair's parish — united and formed the synod of New York, with its meeting place at Elizabethtown, New Jersey.  It is interesting to note that in the articles which were adopted at the founding of this synod all of the objectionable practices of the " new side " party were renounced. They agreed to be bound in their assemblies by the majority vote of the ministers and elders, that charges against brethren should not be propagated as scandal but dealt with in accordance with the well-known methods of discipline, that orthodoxy and a competent degree of knowledge should be required of those who should be admitted to the ministerial calling, that divisive and separating practices should not be encouraged.  Somewhat later Gilbert Tennent, in a pamphlet entitled " Irenicum," renounced his former attitude of extreme opposition and violent criticism and admitted to the full the merits and good intentions of his opponents.  " While some," he said, " were earnestly contending for the credit of the late extraordinary religious appearances, with design that they might spread far and wide; others were strenuously contending for the order and government of Christ's kingdom, lest they should suffer and be quite unhinged in the uncommon situation and ferment that obtained among the churches.  But though the things controverted, considered calmly and in a true distinct light were small, yet the heat of debate about them ran very high.  This, together with evil surroundings, severe censurings, and rash judgings of each other, carried to and fro by the unwearied industry of tale-bearers and tattlers,

---

[1] Briggs, 267.  Hodge describes the controversy in detail, with quotations from the opposing manifestoes, but with the conclusion that there was no principle really at issue between the parties.

who are generally busy on such occasions, increased mutual prejudices and suspicions to a melancholy crisis, and occasioned the unhappy rupture of the church's union, which has subsisted among us for some years." In spirit as well as in importance this is far more than comparable with Davenport's retraction, and the changed attitude of both, after the excitement of the revival had passed, suggests the friendship of rival statesmen not only after, but during, a heated political conflict.

The schism as well as the revival, however, had more lasting consequences than would be indicated by such reversals of conduct by individuals. The efforts of Tennent and others to restore harmony were only in part successful and their influence extended slowly. Congregations in many places in the middle colonies were partially or wholly broken up and separatist churches were formed. Because of its opposition to revivals, the Old Side was paralyzed for the time and the growth of its churches stopped. Candidates for its churches were few and the appeals which it sent to President Clap, of Yale, brought few men and those of ability inferior to the young ministers who were flocking to the other side.[1] Because of the schism, a proposal which might have resulted in the union of the Dutch and German Reformed Churches with the Presyterians was frustrated.[2] But as this would have given Presbyterianism of a reactionary type the decided predominance in the middle colonies and in parts of the south, it was probably fortunate for the cause of liberty that the union did not take place. As it was, owing to the energy of the New Side party and the ability of its leaders, Presbyterianism was widely extended in the middle colonies, Virginia and North Carolina, a movement the results of which will appear in a later chapter. The schism continued until 1758, when the synods of New York and Philadelphia were united and the two factions buried the hatchet.

The attitude of the clergy of eastern Massachusetts and New Hampshire toward the revival was officially expressed by two meetings which were held respectively in May and July, 1743, at Boston.[3] The former of these was the general

---

[1] Gillett, History of the Presbyterian Church, I, 96.
[2] Briggs, 284.　　　　[3] Tracy, 286 *et seq.*

convention and by it, after a heated debate and a rather close vote, a set of resolutions was adopted which condemned various errors of doctrine and practice, such as reliance upon secret impulses rather than the word of God, itinerancy, encouragement of lay and unlearned exhorters, ordaining persons who were not assigned to particular parishes, censoriousness, the practice of congregations separating from their pastors, disorderly conduct whether from excess of joy or sorrow, and also failed to express approval of the revival as a whole. The friends of the movement, of course, were not satisfied with this and, after such correspondence as would call out a larger attendance and a far more general expression of opinion, another meeting was held. The members of this body expressed warm approval of the revival as to its magnitude and the genuineness of its results, though they admitted that some irregularities and excesses had been committed, and this testimony they all signed.

The issue was also somewhat discussed in the newspapers, but the most important publications, in which the nature of the revival was reviewed from the standpoints of the two parties, were the " Seasonable Thoughts on the State of Religion in New-England," by Charles Chauncy, pastor of the First Church in Boston, and Jonathan Edwards' " Thoughts on the Revival of Religion in New England." These in fact were the most important contemporary criticisms of the revival which were published in the colonies, and may be said to have been the only ones that were systematic enough to be of permanent value.[1] Chauncy, whose publication was the later of the two, replied to a few points made by Edwards, but in only a general sense was his book a rejoinder to the treatise of the Northampton pastor. In form and spirit the two publications fitly represented the best in the attitude of the Old Lights and the New Lights in New England.

Both writers were equally orthodox and from the stand-

[1] The issue between Edwards and Chauncy was not drawn in the direct and harsh terms which were common in those days. Edwards did not expressly refer to Chauncy at all, and Chauncy referred to only a few passages in Edwards and that often to approve. Edwards published first (1742), Chauncy's book coming out the following year. But their earlier publications and their respective attitudes toward the revival marked them out as the two most representative exponents of the opposing views that were held.

point of culture had much the same outlook. The one, however, had been reared under the broadening influences of a
seaport town in eastern Massachusetts, while the other was
spending his life adjacent to the frontier and in small communities where there was nothing to relieve the intense re-
ligiousness which he had inherited from both parents and
which had been further emphasized by all the experiences of
his life. Chauncy was calm, logical, unimaginative, the
framework of his argument standing out with all the dis-
tinctness of a scholastic treatise or a Puritan sermon of the
previous century. In form as well as substance it was a
systematic and powerful attack on enthusiasm. Its genuineness as a Massachusetts product was shown by a preface in
which detailed reference was made to the experience of the
colony in its early days with Antinomianism. Chauncy drew
his information from the famous pamphlet on that subject
which had been issued under the name of Thomas Welde.
The close analogy which Chauncy found between the condition at that time and at the present was pressed home with
the statement, "It may not be amiss to observe here, as
the Church of which I am pastor was the only one in Boston
at the time I have been speaking of, so this was the Church
to which most of the grand Opinionists belonged, and from
hence it was that Disturbance went forth into the Country.
Many of its members depended upon the immediate Witness
of the Spirit for an Assurance of their good Estate, . . .
which indeed was the Root of most of the Errors and
Confusions of that Day."

Chauncy viewed the revival from the negative and adversely critical standpoint. From the start, and throughout
the great body of his work, he dwelt upon the dangerous
tendencies of the movement — itinerancy, bodily agitations,
impulses and impressions, censoriousness and all the rest.
These were analyzed and dwelt upon at length, constituting
together, though written with calmness and without passion,
a marshalling of the evils of the movement such as no
Episcopalian or Presbyterian in the colonies attempted. The
tendency of the revival as a whole toward the "vilifying of
good works" came in for a liberal amount of attention. The
Bible, the well-known standards and practices of the New

England churches and, to an extent, the experiences of Protestantism in general, were put under contribution to support and illustrate the argument. Principles set forth by Cotton Mather, by an early convention of the Massachusetts clergy and by the late convention, wherein it criticised the revival, were quoted at length to show the agreement of the views then presented with those of the writer. The proclamation of a fast by Governor Law, of Connecticut, in 1743, was also cited for the same purpose. Chauncy wrote as a clergyman, with a full sense of his dignity and exclusive rights within his church and parish, which was an essential part of the New England ecclesiastical system. Itinerancy, lay exhorting, an unlearned ministry, the breaking up of congregations and parish relations, orgies of passion, whether of gloomy or of glorious hues, were intolerably offensive to him. He was one of the most representative Arminians of his time, a man who had some confidence in the essential goodness of human nature and in the efficiency of the human will. His mind was not burdened with a sense of the decay of religion and of the need of a general revival. Such quickening as might and ought to occur should be rather local in character and under the control of the regular clergy of the parishes. Men with the even and well-balanced nature of Chauncy were prepared, with broadening culture, to escape from the trammels of Calvinism and to welcome the growth of a critical spirit, to turn from an undue contemplation of the deity and the analysis of his operations and qualities, to the study of man. For such as he, tough, prosaic and limited, there was the possibility of a certain outlook into a future where interests other than the religious and theological should assume importance before the minds of men.

Though in general subject matter and in certain classifications Edwards' book agreed with that of Chauncy, in literary form and in spirit no two writings could be more unlike. The reader of Edwards' pages is raised from the level of the prosaic into the realm of the emotions and the imagination. The language upon almost every page quivers with a holy passion. The mind of the writer was aglow with the contemplation of the deity, and the grandeur and beauty of the spiritual as compared with the material realm. A zeal for holiness in its most exalted forms seems to have possessed his being. This carried him into the domain of the affections and the will, raising him above the level of the critical intellect. His consciousness of this fact shows that the views which later were to be set forth in his famous treatises on the religious affections and on the will were already formed in Edwards' mind. It was from the level of these, making use of scripture in its highest reaches of inspiration, that Edwards desired the Great Awakening to be judged. No partial judgments, based merely on human relations, would suffice for a manifestation like this. This came from God, from heaven, it let men into the blessed experiences of that realm of spirits, of purity and holiness, and showed them a sure way of escape from sin and its consequences of eternal torment. From this exalted level alone, in the view of both worlds, could the revival be adequately judged. Its faults and weaknesses — for Edwards admitted that there were such, and his catalogue of them did not so much differ from that of Chauncy — would then appear in correct perspective. They were simply the result of human weakness when brought under such mighty and transcendent influences. For bodily agitations in extreme forms, even for censoriousness, and all other attendant evils except impressions and impulses which had an antinomian tendency, he was ready to make allowance as flaws in a work which was essentially divine and fraught with infinite possibilities of good. Of the surprising effects produced by the religious affections when deeply aroused, Edwards had seen many instances, not the least being the experiences of his own wife. His rhapsodical descriptions of these, extending through pages of this work, show that his soul was carried away with the contemplation of the state of blessedness of which they were taken to be a proof. " The soul remained in a kind of heavenly elysium, and did as it were swim in the rays of Christ's love, like a little mote swimming in the beams of the sun, or streams of his light that come in at a window; and the heart was swallowed up in a kind of glow of Christ's love, . . . so that there seemed to be a constant flowing and reflowing from heart to heart. The soul dwelt on high and was lost in God and seemed almost to leave the body. . . ."

In other passages, though not in imagery so terrifying as
that of the famous Enfield sermon, Edwards set forth the
certainty of eternal torment for the unregenerate, including
those who died in infancy.  This to his mind was the inexorable consequences of the lost condition of man by nature
and of his powerlessness for good except under the influence
of the divine spirit.  Here, to his mind, lay the meaning of
the universe, of life, death and immortality.  Between the
possibilities of heaven and hell, subject to the inexorable
decrees of God, human life hung suspended, and therefore
any movement like this revival which should awaken members to their danger and open to them the gates of paradise,
was to be welcomed and furthered by all powers human and
divine.  From this arose the idea of the tremendous importance of conversion.  "I am bold to say," wrote Edwards in
one place, "that the work of God in the conversion of one
soul, considered together with the source, foundation and purchase of it, and also the benefit, end and eternal issue of it,
is a more glorious work of God than the creation of the whole
material universe."  No man since Milton had beheld and set
forth in language such exalted visions of the universe as conceived by Paul, Augustine and Calvin, as did Jonathan
Edwards.  His nature was profoundly imaginative and poeti-
cal, as well as logical, and in him the dream of New England
Puritans found its highest and final expression.  That his
view of the revival as a religious phenomenon was far higher
and truer than Chauncy's, no one can deny.  But in its relations to the progress of mankind in its slow evolution from
primitive conditions and ideas, it was far more reactionary.
The ideas which Edwards sought to perpetuate were already
antiquated, and the type of reform in which they were bound
to result, so far as society in general was concerned, was
temporary and superficial.  Before five years had passed,
Edwards himself was complaining that the effects of the revival had passed away and coldness, like that which preceded
it, had reappeared.  A project soon emanated from Scotland
for the union of its churches with those of New England in
continual prayer for the return of the blessed season, as a prelude to the millenium.  To this plan Edwards devoted another

treatise,[1] in which he made extended use of the visions in the Apocalypse to justify the belief that the capture of Louisbourg, the destruction of D'Anville's fleet and other successes of the British, and disasters which had recently overtaken the French and Spanish, betokened the approaching fall of the kingdom of Antichrist and the coming of the final divine consummation. This is perhaps the closest approach that we have from the pen of Edwards to any interpretation of contemporary history, and the descent from his visions of divine glory to such absurdities indicates the great gulf which lay between his theology and any reasonable interpretation of human affairs.

In Massachusetts, under its royal governor, William Shirley, agitated as it was by the struggle over the land bank and with accumulating evidence that a war with the French was approaching, no official notice was taken of the Great Awakening or of the disturbances which it caused in the life of the churches. Indeed, there is no evidence that the churches desired any action by the civil power, though Congregations were to an extent broken up and the general sense of public decorum was violated on many occasions. The agitation of the time was allowed to die away without resort to civil compulsion in the form of public orders or legislation in any form.

Attacks by the conservatives upon Whitefield and his followers, conceived in the spirit of Chauncy and of the convention to which reference has already been made, were continued for several years.[2] These were replied to by Whitefield himself and by his supporters. Sermons were preached and individual statements were made on both sides. Articles were printed in the newspapers. A number of local conventions of ministers, one meeting at Exeter, New Hampshire, others at Boston, Cambridge, Weymouth and Marlborough, expressed unfavorable opinions of the movement. These dissensions expressed in the main the feeling of disquiet and hostile reaction which an established class or a settled com-

---

[1] An Humble Attempt to promote Explicit Agreement and Visible Union of God's People in Extraordinary Prayer for the Revival of Religion and the Advancement of Christ's Kingdom on Earth, pursuant to Scripture Promises concerning the last Time.

[2] Tracy, 330, *et seq.*

munity always shows in the presence of innovations. No
new ideas were brought out and the records of the debate
served only to show how the movement had spread throughout
eastern New England, and that the country towns were often
more prejudiced against it than was Boston.

At the close of 1744 the faculty of Harvard College replied
to the printed criticisms of Whitefield upon its spiritual condition by a much more detailed and equally censorious attack
upon him. They charged him with having uttered " a most
wicked and libellous falsehood " concerning the colleges and
rehearsed the entire catalogue of charges which were generally
being made against him personally and against his methods of
work. By this statement no light is thrown on the spiritual
condition of the college, the point to which Whitefield had
called attention, and it serves chiefly to show that the revival
had passed into a bitterly controversial stage. Whitefield, who
was in the country at the time, replied, as he was forced to do,
to the many attacks upon him. He admitted that he had made
some mistaken and exaggerated statements, but defended the
methods and results of his work against all assailants. To
the Harvard manifesto he made a detailed reply and one
highly honorable to himself as a gentleman and Christian.
In his remarks upon the colleges he claimed only to have
meant that they shared in the general declension of religion,
the existence of which all admitted. He disclaimed all intention of unduly disturbing the churches and ministers or
of setting up a party for himself; but he claimed the right
to preach and for the people the right to hear, and if the
pulpits were shut the fields were open.

Outside of New England the Old Light party among the
Presbyterians had no connection with civil power and hence
could not call any of the colonial governments to their aid.
But in Connecticut the Saybrook Platform and the general
court, with its long established custom of freely interfering
in church affairs, furnished a well organized machinery which
could easily be used for the suppression of dissent. Institutionally and in every other way Connecticut was still living
in the seventeenth century. Its unrestricted power of legislation and its exemption from liability to appeals in such
ecclesiastical cases as were likely to arise, made it possible

for things to be done within her borders which would be very unsafe in Massachusetts. These circumstances go far to explain the struggle, violent beyond that in any other colony, sordid in some of its features but heroic in others, which was occasioned by the Great Awakening in Connecticut.[1]

In this colony the Old Light stood by the Saybrook Platform, the half-way covenant, and the church-state system which had come down from the previous century, with all that it implied. As elsewhere, they had welcomed the revival in its early stages, but when its extravagances became unduly prominent, especially as illustrated by Davenport, with itinerancy, lay exhorting and the discerning of spirits, they began to protest. And when they protested they at once fell back upon the government to enforce their demands and prohibitions. The vicious circle in which Massachusetts Puritans had been proud to live, when they were persecuting Antinomians and Quakers in the seventeenth century, was still complete in Connecticut, and another chapter was added to the seemingly endless story of coercion and resistance. Though toleration had been extended to Quakers, Baptists and Anglicans, the strongest possible coercion was now applied to members of the established churches, fellow Christians with whom the members of the majority had long worshipped, because of their share in commotions that were the inevitable consequence of the awakening which the churches had long pretended to desire. So common did the break up of congregations become that the New Lights in this colony were ordinarily called Separatists or Separates. The revival took strongest hold in the eastern section of the colony, where settlements were newer and more secluded from outside influences. There disturbances were more general. To the west of the river, Fairfield county was liberal in its attitude toward the revival. New Haven county, with Yale College as its leader, was the centre of conservative strength, and with it Hartford county in general sympathized.

---

[1] The authorities for this are Col. Recs., VIII and IX; a mass of manuscript material which is classified at Hartford under Affairs Ecclesiastical. Trumbull, Hist. of Conn., II; Greene, Religious Liberty in Conn.; Larned, Hist. of Windham County, and Historic Gleanings in Windham County; Tracy, The Great Awakening. A Collection of Papers of Separate Churches (Ms.) in possession of the Conn. Hist. Soc.

In October, 1741, Thomas Clap, president of Yale, signed his name, along with those of several Old Light clergymen, to a paper asking the general court or assembly to call a consociation of the churches of the entire colony, to meet on the 24th of the following month at Guilford.[1] This was approved, the call was issued and the general consociation met, the only assembly of its kind that was ever held in the colony. The long series of resolves which it adopted, though in perfunctory terms they expressed gratitude for the revival, were chiefly filled with warnings and safeguards against the "stratagems and devices of Satan" by which at such crises he sought to delude the unwary and thus bring reproach on the work of God. It is clear that it was not enthusiasm *per se* which the ministers in this assembly feared, but its effects in destroying the unity of their parishes and imperilling the control which they had always held over their little oligarchical town groups. Regularity was the watchword. Great care should be used in the selection of ministers, so as to secure only men of learning, wisdom and prudence, and they should be upheld unless they were guilty of some gross offense. The Word of God, together with the Saybrook Platform backed by the laws of the colony, were appealed to as the standards to which they proposed to adhere. The invasion of parishes by preachers from outside, without invitation, or in opposition to the settled ministers, and the separations which were resulting therefrom, were the evils aimed at. But if a considerable number of people in a parish were desirous of hearing another minister preach, and he was sound in the faith and otherwise unobjectionable, they might be gratified, provided suitable application was made to the resident pastor and other ministers should not advise him to the contrary.

But mere resolutions proved insufficient to check the disorders. At this juncture occurred the death of Governor Talcott and the election of Jonathan Law, of Milford, who not only was a lawyer but was thoroughly imbued with the spirit of New Haven county. The assembly of May, 1742, having been memorialized by twenty-one of the clergy and asked to take their difficulties into consideration, a law was

[1] Conn. Mss., Eccl., VII, Conn. Recs., VIII, 438.

passed which, so far as itinerant preachers and Separatists were concerned, nullified their church privileges and exposed them to severe penalties without the possibility of redress.[1] Ordained ministers or licentiates, who should preach in parishes without due invitation, should be denied the benefit of any law made for their support. The same disability should be suffered by all the ministers in any association who should undertake to examine or license a candidate or decide any controversy that belonged under the jurisdiction of another association. No assistant or justice of the peace should sign any warrant for the collection of a minister's salary without a certificate proving that no information had been lodged against him for preaching in another's parish without invitation. Unsettled or unordained ministers who preached in parishes without invitation should be bound over in the sum of £100 not so to offend again, or be laid under such other penalty as the county court should decide. Any person from outside the colony who should so offend should be arrested and sent from constable to constable till he was expelled from its bounds. In 1743 the so-called toleration act of 1708, because Separatists were taking advantage of it, was repealed and dissenters were required henceforth to apply to the assembly for relief.[2]

This legislation deserves extended analysis, because it was ingeniously contrived to deprive offending parties, and the Congregationalists, of their civil rights. It was passed in the midst of a bitter struggle and was not only the answer of Connecticut to the extravagances of Davenport, but also to the demand of many of its best citizens for greater elasticity in the church system in order to make room for the expression of a deeper religious life. These were also the last severely persecuting statutes which have been passed among English speaking peoples, and such distinction as comes from such an achievement belongs to the colony of Connecticut. That the nature of it was clearly understood at the time, was shown by several admirable protests which were filed against the act of 1742. The associated ministers of the western division of Fairfield county condemned the principle of the act as wrong,

---

[1] Conn. Recs., VIII, 454. Trumbull, II, 162.
[2] Conn. Recs., VIII, 521.

on the ground that it invoked the civil power to correct disorders which were purely ecclesiastical.[1] The keys of ecclesiastical discipline, they affirmed, were not committed to the
civil magistrate. If it were so, legislators and officials might
disallow everything in public worship which did not agree
with their opinion. Where then was Christian liberty, and
what need was there for the act of toleration? Except in
very rare cases, they did not believe that the preaching of
laymen occasioned disorders which called for the interposition
of the civil power; they could be dealt with by the churches.
They considered it a hardship to be forbidden to preach for
brethren, even in their own associations, without first obtaining the consent of the majority of their churches. They considered this to be inconsistent with the congregational system,
and with what was implied when the right hand of fellowship
was given to ministers at their ordination. They called attention to the crying inconsistency of allowing Anglicans and
others freely to exchange pulpits while they were strictly confined to their own parishes. To conclude, they warned the
magistrates that the executing of the law would not reclaim
the disorderly, but would probably add to the number of
those who sympathized with them; and, as for themselves,
they felt it might be necessary to act contrary to the requirements of the law, thereby exposing themselves to the liability
of having false and malicious informations lodged against
them and of having to resort to the common law, as against
this statute, for the collection of their salaries. The eastern
association of the same county filed an argument which was
drawn on similar lines.[2] Protests like these, together with
the acts of local bodies and the defiant speech and consequent
sufferings of many individuals, showed that the spirit which
had animated the fathers was alive and had been quickened
into greater activity by the revival.

Agitations and conflicts occurred in many towns, resulting
in the division of churches and the founding of new ones; in
the rise of a new or newly invigorated group of preachers, some
of whom had been laymen and were less learned in the ancient
tongues and in traditional views of the Bible and theology

---

[1] Conn. Mss. Eccl. The names of Moses Dickinson and Noah Hobart
were signed to this on behalf of the association.      [2] *Ibid.*

than had been common in New England; in greater insistence upon a genuine Christian experience and life among church members, and upon the enforcement of stricter conditions for admission to membership and to the communion. Wherever separation prevailed, a fatal blow was given to the half-way covenant, and through the doctrine of the new birth a sharp line of demarcation was drawn between the church and the world. The democratic and evangelistic element in religion was emphasized, and efforts were made to break through the barriers between parishes and associations. The autocracy of the settled ministers was attacked, and the union of state and church was assailed. Toward all these changes the Baptists were receptive, and not a few Separatist congregations were absorbed by that sect. In general the Brownist elements in Congregationalism were pushed to the fore. These phenomena, of course, appeared wherever the revival extended in the colonies, but nowhere were the lines drawn so sharply, as the result of a conflict so intense, as in Connecticut.

The officials of Yale College, under President Clap, stood in the forefront of this struggle on the conservative side, though there was much enthusiasm and a very rebellious spirit among the students. The New Lights set up at New London a school for training exhorters, teachers and ministers, called the "The Shepherd's Tent." In order to put an end to this, an act was passed forbidding the erection of any school, college or seminary of learning without the license of the assembly and the authority of law.[1] It also provided that no person who was not a graduate of Harvard, Yale or some foreign Protestant college or university, should enjoy the benefit of the laws respecting the settlement and support of ministers. After this enactment we hear no more of the "Shepherd's Tent," and its fate, when compared with that of the Log College in Pennsylvania, illustrates the superiority of the Quaker province from the standpoint of religious liberty. The New Haven church was rent by a long conflict over its pastor, Noyes, and the Separates seceded and formed a new body. With this the college authorities were somewhat closely concerned.

The preaching of Eleazar Wheelock was very effective in

[1] Dexter, Doc. Hist. of Yale, 356; Conn. Recs., VIII, 501; Greene, 255.

promoting the revival of Windham county, and among all the towns that were moved the struggle was most violent in Canterbury.[1] There the majority of the church became Separatist, Elisha and Solomon Paine, two of the ablest men in town, being the leaders and afterwards rising from the position of laymen to be Separatist ministers. After investigation by a committee it was voted that this church had never accepted the Saybrook Platform. The conservatives fell back upon the " society " or parish and claimed that it had the right to override the decisions of the church. The conflict between the two, over listening to lay exhorters, over admissions to membership and the calling of pastors, continued with much disorder and for a long time. One incident among many was the imprisonment of Elisha Paine. Another was the expulsion from Yale of John and Ebenezer Cleveland, nephews of the Paines, because they had attended Separatist meetings and listened to lay exhorters, while spending a vacation at home in Canterbury, and would not make what was regarded as a proper submissive apology therefor;[2] under prompting from the civil authorities, the college made severer rules in order to prevent any Separatist wolves from finding a place among the flock which it was training according to the strictest standards for the gospel ministry. It had also expelled David Brainerd because of a sharp criticism he had passed upon certain members of the faculty for their opposition to Whitefield. This attracted Edwards' attention to the young man, with the result that his saintly life and death were later heralded throughout the world. The expulsion of the two Cleveland boys also advertised the quarrel in the Canterbury church and furnished the Separatists with additional martyrs. The college reached the limit of its activities for the suppression of free thought when it tried to suppress a reprint of Locke's Letter on Toleration, which the senior class was preparing to issue at its own expense. The attempt of the faculty to overawe the students by threats of expulsion was checked by the resolute threat of one of them to appeal to the king in council.

The separation finally became permanent at Canterbury

---

[1] Larned, Hist. of Windham County, 402 *et seq.*
[2] Dexter, *op. cit.*, 368 *et seq.*

with the ordination of Solomon Paine as pastor of the new church. In Stonington, Groton, Hebron, Enfield, Branford, Milford, and in many other towns, similar conflicts occurred, some as spirited and as successful for the New Lights, and others resulting in compromises or only partial successes. The distinguished Samuel Finley, afterwards president of Princeton, was imprisoned and driven from the colony for preaching at Milford and New Haven. Rev. Philemon Robbins, of Branford, was subjected to the meanest and most persistent persecution by a small clique among his parishoners, supported by the association of New Haven county, because he had preached to a congregation of Baptists at Wallingford.[1] But the Old Lights and the government, though they caused a good deal of inconvenience and some suffering to individuals, were unable to throttle the Separatist movement and in the end had to recognize openly or by silence the churches to which it had given rise.

From a revision of its laws, published in 1750, and in the preparation of which a committee led by Roger Wolcott, Jonathan Trumbull and Thomas Fitch, had been occupied at intervals for eight years, all the ancient persecuting statutes were dropped. But the laws authorizing the Saybrook Platform and the levy of taxes on Separates were continued.[2] Therefore imprisonments, especially of Baptists, for refusal to pay taxes for the support of Congregationalist ministers continued after that date. Late in the decade of the fifties (1758–1760) a most stubborn fight was waged in and about the church at Wallingford over the settlement of Jonas Dana, whom the majority of the members called from eastern Massachusetts to be their pastor. He was a young man, and by the time the council for his ordination had been called, a minority in the church had come to be dissatisfied with him. Questions of his orthodoxy were raised and the consociation of New Haven county was invoked. It decided against Dana, but he and his supporters refused to yield. The ministers of Hartford county were also called in. A notable group of controversial pamphlets were published, of which the ablest were written by Noah Hobart of Fairfield, and William Hart

[1] Trumbull, II, 197 et seq.
[2] Conn. Recs., IX, 497; Greene, op. cit., 273.

of Saybrook.  Hobart supported the claims of the consociation and Hart pleaded for the liberty of the local church.[1] Probably no better contemporary expositions, favorable and unfavorable, of the workings of the church system under the Saybrook Platform exist than are contained in these publications.  The struggle occurred among Congregationalists, and long after the excitement of the Great Awakening had died down.  The majority in the Wallingford church contended solely for the liberty of the local body against a system which, in the hands of facile theorizers like Hobart, threatened to destroy its independence.  By vote of the consociation they were excluded from the communion of the churches and so remained until 1772.  The minority were allowed to form a separate church and were freed from the obligation to pay taxes for the support of Dana.  This struggle is to be classed with those of the Separates and with the influence of the French War in diverting attention from religious issues, as among the causes which weakened the hold of the Saybrook Platform and set limits to the power of consociations in Connecticut.

Various rough estimates were made, sometime after the event, of the numbers who were converted during the Great Awakening, these varying from 25,000 to 50,000.[2]  Though these must be guesses, the numbers mentioned may not be so far from the truth.  But in estimating the significance of the revival, another unknown element of still greater importance is the permanence and strength of the new principles in the lives of the converted.  We know that the excitement abated after two or three years, and that other absorbing events supplanted it in the public mind.  In 1751 Edwards wrote, " I cannot say that the greater part of supposed converts give reason by their conversation, to suppose that they are true converts.  The proportion may, perhaps, be more truly represented by the proportion of blossoms on a tree, which abide and come to mature fruit, to the whole number of blossoms in

[1] Hobart, "The Principles of Congregational Churches, etc."  Hart, "Remarks on a late Pamphlet by Mr. Hobart, etc."  Other pamphlets on the subject were also written by these men, and a "Faithful Narrative of the Proceeding," by Jonathan Todd.  Trumbull treats the episode very fully, supporting the consociation in his Hist. of Conn., II, Chap. XXV.

[2] Tracy, 388 *et seq.*

the spring." But whatever was the number of converts, and however unevenly they may have been distributed, it is certain that society in many sections experienced a notable shaking up religiously and when the wave had passed some things had been changed. This of course, was especially true in New England. A more active type of piety was abroad than had been known for generations, if such had ever existed. This was the Methodist spirit, though doctrinally it was Calvinistic. More ministers, as well as laymen with this spirit, were working in colonial society. From this sprang the later missionary enthusiasm. Education profited by the founding of the College of New Jersey and by the starting of impulses which were to lead to the founding of Dartmouth College. Of the effect of such a movement on public and private morals, where alone is to be found the only real justification of revivals, if they have any, it is of course impossible to make any estimate. The lapse of time, and the very partial and prejudiced statements which were made at the time, preclude even a conjecture. But there was one effect in New England which, though it came slowly, can be traced in its beginnings to the revival, and that was the abandonment by the Congregational churches of the halfway covenant and the reduction of their membership to those who gave evidence of actual conversion. This was a change of no small moment, for it brought those churches back into harmony with the spirit of the fathers and helped greatly to determine the character of New England Congregationalism ever since. By means of it the spirit of Arminianism was exorcised.

Though the impulse to this change came from the revival, it was the example and writings of Edwards which so impressed it upon the churches as to secure at last the triumph of the cause. His great treatise on the " Religious Affections " (1746) first enforced the doctrine that positive holiness was necessary to church membership. In 1748, after long consideration of the subject, he resolved openly to break with the principles of his grandfather, the revered Stoddard, and to impose strict requirements for admission to membership in his church at Northampton.[1] This was in

---

[1] Dwight, Life of Edwards, 298 *et seq.*

direct conflict with what had been the practice of this and all neighboring churches for at least half a century. It was also preceded by an attempt of Edwards to inquire into the conduct of certain young people, scions of leading families, in the alleged use of obscene literature. The result of this double assault on the susceptibilities of the community was an outburst of hostile feeling toward the pastor. A church quarrel of the first magnitude followed. Edwards stood to his guns and managed his side of the case with rare ability. Town as well as church authorities were called in, and his opponents made up in persistence and stubbornness for what they may have lacked in knowledge of the points at issue. Edwards published his " Humble Inquiry concerning the Qualifications requisite to a full Communion in the visible Christian Church," which became the text book of later opponents of the half-way covenant. In addition to distributing a few copies of this, Edwards desired to expound his opinions from the pulpit. This was opposed, but later he succeeded in delivering several weekday lectures on the subject which were thinly attended by his own people, but heard by large numbers from the surrounding towns. It was the complaint of Edwards throughout that his people refused to hear his side of the question. The contrast between the spirit now shown and the loving harmony which had prevailed a few years before furnishes one of the best possible proofs of the superficial effects of revivals upon human character.

Councils were resorted to as a last means of restoring harmony or, if that was shown to be impossible, to advise that the pastoral relation should be severed. The church insisted that the members of this body should be chosen wholly from the county and Edwards that he should be permitted to select a part of his half of the membership from New England at large. Over this a long dispute occurred, which involved the holding of a preparatory council. Finally Edwards' contention was allowed and in the council which finally met four churches from eastern Massachusetts were represented. Two years had now passed since the controversy began, and the council, after a few vain efforts to bring about a reconciliation, was able to see no course open except to recommend, if the church desired it, that Mr. Edwards be immediately dismissed from his pastoral office. In favor of this the church voted by a large majority. The council ratified the decision. Less than two weeks later Edwards preached his farewell sermon to the church where he had rendered such faithful and distinguished service for nearly a quarter of a century. Its theme was the certainty that, though congregations might refuse to listen to their ministers on earth and the two be separated, they would meet at the last day and before the judge of all the cause at issue between them would be heard through and decided. Considering the time and place, it would be difficult to imagine a more skilful handling of this theme than that which it received at the hands of the Northampton pastor. Suffering great loss and discouragement, this distinguished man then retired with his family to the frontier settlement at Stockbridge, to preach to the Indians and the few whites who might come to hear him. But the leisure which he found there was used for perfecting his system of philosophy by the publication of the famous treatise on the " Freedom of the Will." Though his life was prolonged for only a few years and ended in apparent defeat, the revival insured the ultimate triumph of his cause, while his writings and the men whom he had been able to influence by his teachings raised his reputation to a commanding height. The type of Calvinism of which he was the exponent was to hold sway in New England for more than a century and to enjoy a wide international reputation. The practice of the churches, including after a time that of the fellowship at Northampton which had cast him out without a hearing, conformed with his ideas, so that the name of Jonathan Edwards came to stand for what was highest and most enduring in the great revival of 1740.

# CHAPTER II

## ECCLESIASTICAL RELATIONS AT THE MIDDLE OF
## THE CENTURY

WITH the decline of the excitement which had been occasioned by the Great Awakening, no appreciable improvement in the morals of communities was observable and people generally had not been made wiser in the conduct of their lives. Many at the time and afterwards believed that the spirt of kindliness in human relations had suffered a decline and that censoriousness had been promoted. In the teachings and exhortations of the time the emphasis had been laid on God, as he was supposed to be, and on relations with him, while this world and mere human relations had not been thought worthy of much attention. A frenzied effort was made to prepare men for a predicated future existence, to the neglect of the only methods by which life upon this planet can really be improved. This was the course which men had for the most part pursued throughout the Christian centuries, and the colonists, under the lead of their clergy, were following in a peculiarly excited manner one of the most reactionary traditions of which the human race has ever been the victim. After the revival and its excitements had passed, men knew no more than previously of the nature of the world they lived in or of the way to adapt their lives to it. The complaints of moral and spiritual decline which soon reappear prove the barrenness of the revival in any results which told for substantial human progress. Its purpose had not been to remove ignorance or broaden and deepen knowledge of human society, or to discover faults in the political or economic structure and methods of the time and to seek their correction. Nothing permanent was done by it to relieve the sordid monotony of colonial life, and thereby to save men from the gross forms of immorality which always accompany such conditions of existence. It brought in no inspiring literature for the masses and left the education of the time as narrow and illiberal as it had been before. There had been an intense desire to improve men, to save them completely and eternally, but the emphasis had been laid wrongly and, except in the case of a small minority who were naturally endowed with the capacity to become religious experts, the men who lived through this crisis remained essentially unchanged. To effect the genuine elevation of men in these or any communities — and under the best conditions the process must be very slow — a complete reversal of the point of view was necessary. A man-centred world must be substituted for a God-centred world and all the resources of human knowledge and virtue concentrated on the problem of existence here and now. Religionists, then and always, have expended their energies in bombarding the heavens and so have failed to hit their mark. An all round attack on human ignorance, carried on upon the level of the earth and with a determination to know man and nature as they really are, though less dramatic and far less pretentious in its appeal, opens the only paths which may lead to success. The first faint signs of this were appearing in the writings of philosophers and deists, but they were viewed with horror by most men of the time.

Among the religious bodies of the period to which the revival had directly brought no increase of strength or numbers, was the Anglican. Such permanent converts as were made had gone chiefly to the Presbyterians, Baptists and Congregationalists, while the way was being prepared for the appearance of the Methodists. But from Anglican sources had risen an unbroken chorus of hostile criticism of the revival, and such gains among their membership as could even indirectly be attributed to its influence had come from those who, in a revulsion of feeling against the confusion of the time, took refuge in the Church as an asylum where at least dignity and order reigned. During the period of the excitement the missionaries of the Church had continued their work according to the customary methods and with the usual results in the founding of new churches, especially in New England, and they increased faster than the means at the command of the Society for paying the salaries of their ministers. Connecticut was so far away that Price could not perform his duties as commissary there and the elevation of Johnson to that office was suggested, though even after the retirement of Price the suggestion was never acted upon.

Checkley's publications had started a long controversy over the relative merits and authoritativeness of episcopacy and presbyterianism or independency. This took the form of sermons, letters and pamphlets, and a very few articles in newspapers. In the early stage of this debate Thomas Foxcroft and Edward Wigglesworth, the latter a professor at Harvard, took the leading part in defence of the New England churches.[1] Later Jonathan Dickinson, who was so prominent among the Presbyterians of the middle colonies, stepped to the front and was ably supported by Noah Hobart, of Fairfield, Connecticut. By this time — between 1740 and 1750 — the Episcopalians in Connecticut had found their leaders, and Johnson, Beach and Wetmore took up the cudgels in support of their church. The controversy narrowed down to exchanges of more or less embittered pamphlets between these men, and continued until the death of Dickinson, in 1747. After 1760 Charles Chauncy appeared as a prominent disputant on the Congregational side. The discussion ranged widely over doctrinal subjects, bringing into view the high Calvinism of Dickinson in contrast with the moderate Arminianism of Johnson. It was a sermon preached by Hobart at an ordination in Stamford that reawakened the controversy and was followed by the chief publications on the episcopal side.[2] The Presbyterians advanced and defended their theory of the essential identity of bishops and presbyters in the early church, that there were no sharply divided classes among the clergy and that no peculiar or

[1] Thomas Foxcroft, The Ruling and Ordaining Power of Congregational Bishops and Presbyters Defended, Boston 1724. Edward Wigglesworth, Sober Remarks on a Book lately reprinted at Boston entitled "A Modest Proof," etc., Boston 1724.

[2] Hobart, "Ministers of the Gospel Considered as Fellow Labourers," Boston, 1747. Hobart was a grandson of the pastor at Hingham, Massachusetts, who was prominent in the famous controversy between that town and Governor Winthrop in the previous century. Hobart's leading pamphlets were, "A Serious Address to the Members of the Episcopal Separation in New England," Boston, 1748; and "A Second Address, etc." Boston, 1751. James Wetmore's reply to Hobart's Sermon was entitled "A Vindication of the Church of England in Connecticut against the Invectives in a Sermon preached by N. Hobart, 3 Dec. 1746, etc." Boston, 1747.

superior powers were bestowed upon any among them. The idea that the source of power in the church might be the local congregation, or a number of these joined in a loose league, either did not appear at all or was not stressed in this discussion. It wholly related to the position of the clergy and their relation to Jesus as the supposed founder of the church. The essentially clerical, that is, official or aristocratic, viewpoint of the disputants is therefore evident. Beach in particular attacked the foundations of the New England ministry by asserting that at the beginning they had been ordained by mere laymen or by such as had only received priest's orders, through neither of which channels could apostolic power be conveyed. Such ordinations, he said, were a mere novelty, a matter of yesterday and implied no succession. He insisted that the Massachusetts clergy had become Separatists before they left England, and in the eyes of all the episcopalian disputants they of course ranked as schismatics of a most decided type.

Hobart, on the other hand, maintained that it was impossible to prove an uninterrupted line of episcopal succession, and that absolute proof of the existence of a distinct order of bishops in the early church was necessary to make such a view credible. Of the break at the Reformation he was also ready to avail himself to the full extent. Dickinson attacked the liturgy, the use of vain repetitions, the hierarchy and church courts, these all being human devices, similar to, if not derived from, the Church of Rome. Such customs and doctrines should not be imposed upon any, though the Anglicans were too much inclined to use compulsion in such matters. To the minds of Johnson and his associates the institutions thus attacked were the very ark of the covenant. The words schism and schismatic were used or were prominent in the thought of the disputants, even if they were not actually employed in their writings. In addition to exhausting their limited resources for the interpretation of conditions in the early church, each side of course emphasized to the full extent his interpretation of present conditions and failed to see the force of his opponents' arguments or strove to belittle them. The Presbyterians complained because they were called dissenters in New England, and denied that the colonists had brought the established church with them or that subordination in civil affairs implied a similar relation in the ecclesiastical realm. While the Episcopalians made much of the Act of Union as a proof of the opposite, Hobart described this as a new argument, to which Dr. William Douglass had called their attention and they had then seized upon it as a refuge. The evident lack of ecclesiastical unity in Great Britain, which followed from the recognition of the Scotch Church as established, was not lost sight of nor were the more or less authoritative statements which had already been made by Englishmen that there was no national establishment in the colonies, but a condition of equal liberty to all Protestants. But in the opinion of a man like Beach there could be no true church without episcopal succession and, though he believed the law supported the contention that the English Church was established throughout the dominions, this was rather a corollary than a fundamental proposition in his system. Though Johnson went deeply into the arguments against Calvinism as a doctrine, his treatment of the policy to be pursued moved rather on the lower level of everyday expediency. He was striving to furnish correct ministrations for those who already were Anglicans and for others who might wish to come over from the dissenters and conform. In the matter of order and regularity, the Church had the advantage and certainly dissenters had as much right to come over and join it as people had to go in the opposite direction, and to such as came the Anglican clergy had the right to minister.

By certain of the writers on both sides more or less of innuendo and abuse was used, but never by Johnson. The mental attitude of all, however, was dogmatic. They were engaged not in attempting to discover the truth, but in the defence of views which they had already accepted in definite form. They approached all the subjects with which they dealt as partisans, as convinced supporters or opponents of creeds, and from the scientific standpoint the differences observable between them are largely those of temperament. Hence the hopelessness of the debate and of all debates carried on in this spirit. With the knowledge then at hand, and with their methods, no agreement could be reached and, so far as the contestants and their generation were concerned, the lines of separation were only more sharply drawn. As the result of this first debate between Anglicans and dissenters in America they reached, it is true, a certain understanding. This took the form, unfortunately all too common in human relations, of continuing their disagreements and of a resolve to live, with reference to one another, as critics and hostile rivals. This exhibition of their spirit, too, was furnished to the world immediately after the Great Awakening, an event which was supposed to renew the true Christian spirit, and bring heaven down to earth. To many, instead, it seemed to redouble strife and contentiousness. This debate certainly does not confute that idea, but rather indicates that the spirit and temper of men had not been appreciably improved by the revival.

But involved in this controversy was a question of more direct practical bearing than any thing which has yet been mentioned. That was the rightfulness of the efforts of the Society for the Propagation of the Gospel to proselytize New England or to treat it as missionary ground. The steady growth of Anglicanism in that section was forcing that question to the front, and as a matter of course it was included among the issues which were discussed in the writings to which reference has just been made. In his first two publications Hobart dwelt in a particularly offensive manner on the alleged moral inferiority of Anglicans to their opponents, to the lack of discipline over their clergy and laity, to the looseness, irreligion and undisguised profaneness of which they were guilty. He contrasted the morals of New England in the old days with those of colonies where the English Church was supreme and with those which prevailed about him, now that Anglicanism had found its way in. He warned his hearers and readers against allowing their children to fall under such influences. The missionaries of the Venerable Society, he added, though incorrectly, furnished the earliest examples of itinerancy and separatism in the colonies. From these remarks the transition was easy to a denunciation of the Society itself because of its intrusion into New England.

In his " Serious Address to the Members of the Episcopal Separation in New England " Hobart declared that the Society was expending more than £1000 yearly in maintaining missionaries in New England, while it had not a single missionary in Virginia or Maryland and but two in North Carolina. Maryland, however, was in greater danger from Catholicism than any other colony, and North Carolina was generally allowed to be irreligious and profane. It was in such communities as these and among the Indians that, according to his interpretation of its charter, the work of the Society was intended to be done. But, instead, it maintained only one man at Albany, who preached part of the time to the Mohawks, and two Indian teachers. One catechist was engaged in teaching negroes in New York City, and elsewhere only a little work was done among them. By way of contrast, though Connecticut had approximately 150 Congregational ministers, the Society had about eight missions in that colony, two schoolmasters and one catechist. The result, he contended, was injurious to the cause of religion and negligible at best so far as morals were concerned. Later, in his "Second Address," Hobart returned to the subject and advanced the idea that this departure of the Society from the purpose of its charter was probably due to the High Church spirit of the later years of Anne. This was soon followed by the conversion to Anglicanism of Cutler and his associates, which was "a most fatal accident" and hurtful to the peace of the churches and the interests of practical religion. According to him it put an end to the plans of the Society for converting the heathen, and committed it fully to the design of promoting the Church where other churches had long existed and flourished. Since that time, he contended, other fields had been systematically neglected for New England, and in order to promote this the Society was being misled by exaggerated statements concerning the number of churchmen already in New England, their character and standing and their need of churches. Although the supposition was that the missionaries were simply caring for church people, they were really carrying on systematic proselyting. Hobart's arguments, as a whole, were directed against conformity to the Church of England, not only for the reasons already stated but because of the expense which its maintenance would bring upon the people and of the probability that it would

would bring the colonies into ecclesiastical dependence on England.

The provisions of the Society's charter were broad enough to cover all the varieties of work which its missionaries were doing. It authorized the Society to provide learned and orthodox ministers for administering God's Word and the sacraments among the king's subjects in the colonies, and to make such other provision as was necessary for the propagation of the gospel in those parts. The maintenance of the missionaries of the Society and of the public worship of God was also considered as highly conducive to the restraint of atheism, infidelity, popish superstition and idolatry, so far as they existed in the plantations. Beach, who was as strenuous a disputant as Hobart, claimed on behalf of the Society all the rights that were implied in this language. He stated that it was their intention to support missionaries in New England, and that this did not hinder their being sent elsewhere. Johnson wrote a preface to Beach's first publication and they both claimed — as was true — that the occasion of their entrance into New England was the existence there of some thousands of church people who must either violate their consciences by worshipping with the dissenters or be entirely deprived of religious privileges.[1] Johnson, though in milder language, claimed equality of right with the other churches in New England, and rights for Anglicans there similar to those which they enjoyed in the other colonies. He also could not refrain from telling the New Englanders, that their churches were imperfect because of their lack of valid ordination and of a liturgy.

It is, of course, unnecessary to dwell longer on the charges and counter charges which were bandied back and forth between these disputants. They were ecclesiastical partisans of a type with which the world is very familiar. Though Johnson was in tone the mildest and most gentlemanly of the group, he was also the most astute and successful as a protagonist. As a pastor and preacher he was faithful and able, a man who won respect by his blameless life. But he

---

[1] The two leading pamphlets by Beach were, "A Calm and Dispassionate Vindication of the Professors of the Church of England, etc.," Boston, 1749, and "A Continuation of the Calm and Dispassionate Vindication, etc." Boston, 1751.

knew where the key to success, especially in New England, lay, and that was in winning over a goodly representation of educated young men to the Anglican faith and establishing them in missions for which provision in part was made by the Venerable Society. This, in the long run, would tell more than the immediate addition of thousands to the rank and file of communicants. It was reproducing his own experience in others. So long, therefore, as he remained pastor at Stratford, he kept up a certain connection with Yale and nursed into steadily growing activity an Anglican influence among the students there. This was effective propagandism, and Johnson's letters to the bishop and Society contain the record of what he accomplished and hoped for as the result of these and his other activities.[1] It would have required an especially able resident bishop to accomplish as much as this modest gentleman. It was far more significant than the mere administration of discipline or looking after petty violations of episcopal order.

If one reads also the correspondence of Cutler, from Boston, he will find him especially rejoicing when he was able to report the addition of dissenters to his flock. A typical statement of his was to this effect: " An accession also hath been made to our Communion of 12 persons well apprised of the nature of that Ordinance, ornamental to their profession and, I believe, conscientiously mindful of it. Eight of them were Dissenters by Education and have inoffensively come into the bosom of the Church, of whom 6 belong to a town called Sudbury, . . . where the 3 Clergymen of this Town have preached at the request of many and to good acceptance, and are like to continue this service; and I hope this will increase an affection to the Church there and spread it in the parts adjacent and prepare members for the settled advantage of the Ordinances of it, especially if their good beginnings may have the countenance and assistance of the Honorable Society." [2] The purpose of Price in promoting the interest at Hopkinton was similar to this, though the element of personal and social comfort was prominent in the mind of the com-

[1] See Hawks and Perry, Conn. Church Docs. and Mss. Johnson Papers in C. U. Library.
[2] Hist. Colls. of Am. Col. Church, Mass., 359.

missary. The correspondence of the Anglican missionaries could be quoted at great length to this same general effect, but it would be to no purpose. The evident truth of the case is, that this was one of the familiar struggles for place and ascendancy between supporters of rival ecclesiastical systems. In New England the Congregationalists or Presbyterians, call them which you choose, had a little ecclesiastical preserve, respecting the founding of which they were very proud and over which for more than a century they had maintained very exclusive control. During that time they had furnished one of the most finished examples of intolerance, both in theory and practice, which the world has ever seen. Rivals were now forcing their way in, and it was perfectly natural that the original occupants should resent it and that a first class sectarian conflict should be the result. The advent of the Anglicans brought with it the first challenge to the dominant Calvinism of the region, which came from a source whose social standing and learning the New England clergy were forced to respect. It also had the countenance of the British government, and both these reasons made it unusually significant. The pressure of the Anglicans also helped in certain ways toward the emancipation of the New England mind, though since both sects appealed equally to the past and to authority for their justification, its influence in that direction could not be in any way decisive. The rivalries of a certain number of competing sects, though no one of them exhibited much but an exclusive and dogmatic spirit, was better than blank uniformity, with the rigid exclusion of all differing forms of faith, and that was about as far as the narrow culture of the eighteenth century made it possible to go.

Had the practice of the half-way covenant continued general among the New England churches, a certain approximation between them and the Anglicans, except in matters of church government and ritual, might have been possible. Their attitude toward the world would at least have approximated more closely. But, as has been suggested, after the expulsion of Edwards from Northampton, and as the result of the emphasis which, during the revival, had been laid on conversion, the churches abandoned the half-way covenant and in that respect returned to the practice of the early settlers of New England. Thus the triumph of Edwards was final and decisive, and the influence of the principle for which he stood extended wherever the New Lights, under whatever name, gained a foothold. The effect of this was to draw the line of separation between the church and the world very sharply. By this means the highly valued purity of the churches and their membership has been to an extent guaranteed, but at the cost of restricting their members to a select minority of the communities within which they have existed. This was not the ideal of the Anglicans or of the established and hierarchial churches of Europe, into which all subjects of the crown or the state were held to be born. Standards of belief and conduct, as actually enforced, were correspondingly low and conditions elastic. Numbers were kept up and standards maintained by other means than revivals. But under the opposite system rigid requirements were set up and so far as possible maintained, and to uphold standards and increase numbers evangelism and the frequent recurrence of revivals was deemed necessary.

In the midst of these contentions Thomas Sherlock, who had been appointed as successor of Gibson in the see of London, brought again to the front the question of the colonial episcopate. In 1748, soon after he was made bishop of London, he waited upon the king and laid before him the necessity there was that one or more bishops should be appointed for the plantations.[1] The king consented to the submission of the proposal to the ministers. Sherlock's idea, as he expressed it, was that at such a distance from the colonies he could accomplish little, and, if he could not secure assistance, he would prefer to limit his activities to his own province of London. When, in September, 1749, Sherlock wrote to Newcastle to this general effect, the duke, inferring that personal considerations were moving the bishop to make the proposal, answered rather sharply that it involved important public interests, had been long under consideration and, having been laid aside, should not be resumed from motives such as had been suggested. This brought from Sherlock a disclaimer of personal motives and a diplomatic suggestion that other con-

[1] N. C. Col. Recs., VI, 12; Cross, Anglican Episcopate, 114 et seq., 320–345; Hawkins, Missions of the Church of England, 389.

siderations, — perhaps of a political nature and well understood — had prompted his statement.  But without setting
these forth, the bishop declared that there never was a church
in the world in the condition the Church of England then was
in the plantations, " obliged to send from one side of the World
to the other to get ministers ordained to officiate in their
Congregations."

In 1749 one Spencer was sent as an agent to America to
sound the colonists upon the subject of the episcopate.  He
found that they feared lest such an establishment would infringe on the privileges of the people and the rights of the
proprietaries.  Spencer sought to remove these objections by
stating that the bishops would have no more power over the
laity than the commissaries at present possessed, but that
the advantages of the office would be confined to the appointment of suitable candidates to the ministry and the exercise
of control over them.  But he seems to have found difficulty
in making the colonists believe that the powers of the suffragans would be thus limited.  The appearance of this agent,
as well as letters from Sherlock and the expression of sentiments favorable to a colonial episcopate by Secker, bishop of
Oxford, in the anniversary sermon before the Venerable Society in 1741, caused the feeling to spread both in England
and the colonies that bishops would soon be appointed.  This
led to protests, presumably from dissenters in England, which
had the support of the house of representatives in Massachusetts.[1]

In March, 1749/50, Sherlock wrote again to Newcastle that
he intended to lay a representation on the state of the Church
in the colonies before the king in council.  The lord chancellor
had already approved its style and tone and, though the
bishop now sent a copy to the secretary, he expressed a determination to secure an expression from the council upon
this question.  Newcastle proposed that it first be discussed
by the ministers.  But in April the plan was laid before the
council, and owing, it is said, to the king's departure for
Hanover, the consideration of it was postponed.  Near the
end of May Horatio Walpole, himself a privy councillor, after

[1] Cross, op. cit., 115; Perry, Hist. of Am. Episcopal Church, I, 406;
Hist. Colls., etc., Va., 373; Sherlock to Doddridge, May 11, 1751.

having read Sherlock's communication, wrote to the bishop at length in opposition to his plan.[1] Walpole argued that there was no evidence of a desire on the part of the colonists in general for resident bishops, but rather that they were satisfied with existing arrangements. On the other hand, if it should become known that such a plan was likely to be seriously undertaken, the pulpits and press of the dissenters would be aroused in opposition to it. A heated controversy, such as religion always provoked, would follow, with the issue of many pamphlets and libels. It would be said that this was only the first step toward the establishment of full episcopal authority. The controversy, he thought, would extend to the low and high church parties in England and would call out, both there and in the colonies, attacks upon the government and its policy. From this letter we also learn that Sherlock had proposed to the Venerable Society that the governors be asked to give their opinions on the proposal and that, in the letter which it was proposed to send them, a guaranty was given that the appointees should have no coercive jurisdiction. This step Walpole unqualifiedly condemned and asked how such a guaranty could be given, or one that the maintenance of the bishops would not be a burden on the colonists. He also called attention to the confusion which would result if the governors were consulted, and if a general discussion of so delicate a subject was provoked while it was under consideration by the council. Letters which were now exchanged between Walpole and Newcastle show that the secretary shared Walpole's views, and also that the S.P.G. had decided not to take the step proposed.

In 1750 the famous William Butler, bishop of Durham, in addition to Secker, came out in support of Sherlock's plan. Butler stated that the bishops, if sent, would have no coercive power over the laity but only disciplinary power over the clergy, such as the commissaries had exercised; that they would not to the least degree interfere with the dignity or authority of the governors or any other civil officers; that their maintenance would not be a charge on the colonies; and that they would not be settled in places where, like New England, the government was in the hands of dissenters, but

[1] Cross, 322–332. Prot. Epis. Colls., I, 145.

authority only would be given them to ordain and inspect the
Anglican clergy who were stationed in such colonies.[1]  These
proposals, which did not differ essentially from all those that
were then being considered, were so drawn as to meet all the
supposed objections to the plan, and certain of the missionaries
in New England wrote that they could not recollect any objections which had been urged by dissenters except those just
referred to.

Until 1752 Sherlock held out, not only refusing to take out
a commission such as Gibson had received, but neglecting to
assume charge of his ecclesiastical duties in the colonies.
His purpose in this had been to force the question of a colonial
episcopate to an issue and, by means of what was hoped would
be a general demand, to secure the appointment of suffragans
in America.  The effort had now failed and Sherlock, without
a commission, assumed his duties as metropolitan of America,
protesting that he had neither power nor influence in that vast
country, that he was so far distant that he never expected to
see the people of his charge, and he should be tempted to decline the office entirely were it not for preserving the appearance of an episcopal church in the plantations.  That Sherlock, though he submitted to the will of the civil power, never
changed his opinion upon this subject, is shown by his utterances in the later years of his episcopate and his criticism of
the commission which had been issued to Gibson.[2]  " As the
Bishop of London cannot be supposed to reside in America,"
he wrote in 1759, " he can do nothing by himself.  As soon as
he has appointed Commissaries the Bishop can neither direct
nor correct their judgment.  No appeal lyes to the Bishop,
nor indeed can there; for in judgment of Law the Commissary's Sentence is the Bishop's sentence and the Appeal must
go to the higher Court.  But this shows at the same time how
very improper it is to give such power to a Bishop of England
which he cannot execute, but must be obliged to give it over
to somebody else as soon as he has it.  So that the Bishop,
receiving with one hand what he must necessarily give with
the other, remains himself a Cypher, without any authority,
power or influence."  Such a commission, he declared in a

[1] Prot. Epis. Hist. Colls., I, 143.
[2] N. Y. Col. Docs., VI, 360–369.

letter to the board of trade, he judged it not proper for him to accept.[1] But he admitted that, if the jurisdiction had come to him by custom, as it had done to Gibson's predecessors, he would have made no difficulty about acting on it. The reason, however, for his lack of scruples in the one case and for his extreme scrupulosity in the other, when the office was as destitute of real power in the one case as in the other, the bishop never made clear. The date when Sherlock attempted to carry through his plan naturally leads to the inference that it was part of the general policy of more systematic colonial administration which Lord Halifax and others were at that time promoting, but that it was not thought wise to avow the fact.

In 1752 came an urgent appeal from Maryland for the appointment of commissaries there, lest the dissenters, availing themselves of the prejudice against the clergy, which was so strong in the assembly, might so reduce their salaries as virtually to overthrow the establishment.[2] Some leader was greatly needed to bring about concerted action among the clergy in support of their rights. But no action was taken by Sherlock either for Maryland or any other colony except Virginia. The line of commissaries was continued there, but elsewhere the office was allowed to die out. But in 1754 Sherlock wrote to Johnson, in Connecticut, advising that the episcopal clergy throughout the colonies endeavor, by friendly converse with leading dissenters, to convince them that nothing more was desired than that the Church should enjoy the full benefit of its own institutions as others did. "For so long as they are uneasy and remonstrate," he continued, " regard will be paid to them and their friends here by our ministers of state.[3] And yet it will be a hard matter for you to prevent their being uneasy, while they find you gaining ground upon them. . . . Our friends in America will furnish us, I hope, from time to time, with all such facts, books, observations and reasonings as may enable us the better to defend our common cause."

The low level reached by the authority of the bishop and

---

[1] N. C. Col. Recs., VI, 13.
[2] Hist. Colls., etc., Maryland, 327.
[3] Beardsley, Life of Johnson, 179.

his commissary toward 1760 is illustrated by two cases of discipline, one arising in Virginia and the other in Pennsylvania. The former involved the removal of a clergyman, named Brunskill, from his parish because of grossly immoral life. This was done after a hearing by order of the governor and council, because Thomas Dawson, who was then the commissary in Virginia, had not received a commission and therefore did not consider that he had authority to act. Though the governor and council had taken action in such cases in Blair's time, and Dinwiddie considered that his instructions, as well as Virginia law, gave them authority to do so, Dawson and some of the clergy were alarmed at such a violation of the canons and reported the case to the bishop. The governor also stated what had been done and why, and said that he would not have interfered if the commissary had possessed the proper authority. The legality, or at least the necessity, of this procedure was evidently not denied by the bishop and, if the Virginia clergy were thereafter disciplined, it was by lay authority.[1]

The other case involved an attempt on the part of a group of parishioners of Christ Church, Philadelphia, to force William McClennaghan upon the aged Robert Jenney, the rector, as his third assistant. One assistant was in residence and a second, — later the famous Jacob Duché, — was on his way back from Europe and arrived while the dispute was in progress. Provost William Smith also returned from England about the same time and took a prominent part in support of the rector. Jenney and his friends naturally considered that a third assistant was not needed. But McClennaghan, who had had an erratic career and was a recent arrival, by his imitation of Whitefield and the New Lights in the pulpit and association with the Presbyterians, had caught the fancy of the more democratic element among the parishioners. The clergy and their supporters insisted — and appealed to the province charter and to general usage in justification — that no one could officiate regularly or act as assistant without the consent of the rector and a license from the bishop. The

---

[1] Hist. Colls. etc., Virginia, 451–458. The law referred to by Dinwiddie did not refer to the governor and council as such but to them as composing the general court. It had cognizance of both civil and ecclesiastical causes.

latter McClennaghan did not have and could not get, because of his wild and eccentric conduct. A nominal assent was extorted from the infirm rector almost by duress. The affair as a whole was an attempt to force a man, who was really a New Light Presbyterian and who violated nearly all the canons and offended by his manner and doctrines, into a prominent Anglican pulpit. The effort of course failed. McClennaghan had to leave, taking his admirers with him, and is said later to have removed to New Jersey.[1]

While the efforts of the Anglicans in the colonies to elevate the episcopate to a position of greater influence among them were meeting with so little success, the blast which Jonathan Mayhew, in 1750, delivered from his pulpit in Boston boded ill for the effects of such a policy if vigorously pushed in the future. Seizing upon the occasion of the anniversary of the death of Charles I (January 30, 1749/50) Mayhew preached three sermons, the last of which he published under the title, " A Discourse concerning Unlimited Submission and Non-Resistance to the Higher Powers, With some Reflections on the Resistance made to King Charles I, and on the Anniversary of his Death: In which the Mysterious Doctrine of that Prince's Saintship and Martyrdom is Unriddled."[2] This trenchant discourse was directed against high churchmanship on both sides of the Atlantic, as shown in certain of its extreme views and characteristic superstitions. It recalled the crisis which the Puritans had faced in England from the time of the Hampton Court Conference until the Toleration Act. Since the close of the previous century there had been abundant appeals to the spirit of the fathers, as shown especially in New England and on its ecclesiastical side. But this sermon had a decidedly political tone, recalling the spirit of Milton and the struggle of the seventeenth century as a whole, against political as well as ecclesiastical domination. But it was intended more directly to recall to the public mind the spectre of Laud and to rouse the fighting spirit in New England against such high-flying notions as Checkley had

---

[1] Hist. ·Colls. etc., Pennsylvania, 320 *et seq.*;  N. Y. Col. Docs., VII, 406–417;  Cross, 134.

[2] This pamphlet is reprinted in Thornton's Pulpit of the American Revolution. See also Bradford, Life of Mayhew, 103 *et seq.*

advocated and men like Cutler loved to encourage on all suitable occasions. " Civil tyranny," wrote Mayhew in the preface to his pamphlet, " is usually small in its beginning, like ' the drop in a bucket,' till at length, like a mighty torrent, it bears down all before it, and deluges whole countries and empires. Thus it is as to ecclesiastical tyranny also — the most cruel, intolerable and impious of any. From small beginnings, ' it exalts itself above all that is called God and that is worshipped.' People have no security against being unmercifully priest-ridden but by keeping all imperious bishops, and other clergymen who love to ' lord it over God's heritage ' from getting their foot into the stirrup at all. Let them be once fairly mounted and ' their beasts, the laity,' [1] may prance and flounce about to no purpose; and they will at length be so jaded and hocked by these reverend jockeys, that they will not even have spirits enough to complain that their backs are galled, or, like Balaam's ass, to ' rebuke the madness of the prophet.' "

Upon such an issue of this the situation in Virginia was to an extent the reverse of that in New England. There the Episcopalians, though without a resident bishop, were in the saddle. It had always been so, though it was the Episcopalian laity rather than the clergy who were really in control, and among the former there had always been an element which had Puritan leanings, while as a whole they were strongly inclined to local freedom. Down to the time of the Great Awakening the Quakers had been the only dissenting body of any size with which it had been necessary to deal in Virginia, and that issue had been fought out in the seventeenth century.[2] Under the declaration of indulgence issued by James II, the later toleration act and a law of 1705 the Quakers became entitled in Virginia to hold church property, regulate their church government, hold religious meetings and affirm instead of taking the oath before the courts. Refusal, however, to perform military service was punishable by fine, and over that subject there was a controversy as late as Spotswood's time. In 1699 it was provided by law that dis-

---

[1] This was quoted from Leslie.

[2] Bruce, Industrial History of Virginia in the 17th Century, I, 222–251; McIlwaine, Struggle for Religious Toleration in Va. in J. H. U. Studies, XII.

senters who were qualified according to the provisions of the toleration act should be exempted from the penalties which were inflicted for failure to attend service in the parish churches, but they must attend their own services at least once in two months.[1] It was under this law that the Presbyterians, Josias Mackie and Francis Makemie, obtained in Norfolk and Accomac counties their licenses to preach and hold services. But payment of taxes for the support of the established church was required from all. The number of dissenters also was so small — a congregation of French Huguenots, three small meetings of Quakers, and four of Presbyterians in 1705 — that the authorities could afford to ignore them.[2] The tobacco of Accomac was poor, and such counties were avoided by the Anglican clergy. In general, until the middle of the eighteenth century, southeastern Virginia was the section where the strength of dissent, both Quaker and Puritan, was the greatest. But the absence of Makemie from the province, followed by his death in 1708, resulted in the decline of the Presbyterian interest there until after the Great Awakening.

By that time the immigration of the Scotch Irish and Germans into the Valley, and adjacent counties of Virginia, had brought in a large and steadily increasing body of dissenters. But at first they had no organized churches or church privileges, and were not in a position to demand any. In 1738 John Caldwell, on behalf of himself and others, applied to the Presbyterian Synod at Philadelphia with the request that some provision be made for furnishing the dissenters of upper Virginia with the ordinances of religion. This came from the Scotch Irish. In response the Synod sent one of its members with a letter to Governor Gooch, who himself was a Scotchman, asking that freedom of worship might be allowed these new immigrants, and assuring him of their loyalty to the house of Hanover. Gooch replied that, if they behaved peaceably and conformed to the rules laid down for such cases in the act of toleration, Presbyterian ministers who should be sent among them would not be molested.[3] Thereafter a num-

---

[1] Hening, III, 171, 360; Foote, Sketches of Virginia, 49.
[2] Foote, *op. cit.*, 51, quoting in part from Beverley.
[3] Foote, *op. cit.*, 103 *et seq.*

ber of clergymen from the north visited these congregations in the Valley of Virginia, organized churches and some settled among them. In 1744 governments were organized in Augusta and Frederick counties, which included all the settled territory of Virginia west of the Blue Ridge, and vestries were formed which, as in New York, were largely composed of dissenters and insisted that the parish churches, though nominally Episcopalian, should be open also to Presbyterians.

As the Great Awakening progressed, the spirit of the New Lights began to spread through the section between tide-water and the Blue Ridge. By 1743, as a result of reports of Whitefield's preaching and of the revival, people here and there in Hanover and adjacent counties began to feel that they had not been hearing the real gospel preached in the parish churches. Samuel Morris, a layman, began reading Luther on Galatians, Flavel, Bunyan and similar writers to such of his neighbors as would come to hear. Some of Whitefield's sermons also were procured, and later Whitefield himself paid a brief visit to the region. Interest was aroused, discussion followed, and the spread of dissent within the establishment began. Private houses became too small to accommodate those who attended these meetings and houses not for preaching but for reading — reading houses — were built. So secluded had been the lives of these Virginians, that they knew of no dissenting sect and therefore were at a loss what name to assume. But seeing that Luther was a great reformer, they concluded at first to adopt the name Lutherans.[1]

At this juncture the New Side Presbytery of Newcastle, Delaware, sent William Robinson, a disciple of the Tennents, to visit the Presbyterian settlements in the Shenandoah Valley and along the James river and in upper North Carolina. While on this tour, by special invitation he visited Hanover and adjacent counties and so strengthened the dissenters there that they placed themselves under the Presbytery of New-castle. Robinson, who was highly esteemed, was succeeded by John Blair, a brother of Samuel Blair, whose narrative of the revival at New Londonderry, Pennsylvania, is so well

---

[1] "Not in the usual sense of that denomination in Europe," wrote Samuel Davies, "but merely to intimate that they were of Luther's Sentiments, particularly in the article of Justification." Foote, 191.

known, and he by John Roon. The last named minister began attacking the Anglican clergy and holding them up to
ridicule. This occasioned the sending of complaints to the
governor and council at Williamsburg and reports that society in the middle counties was being seriously disturbed.
The reasons which had moved the governor to a tolerant
attitude toward the settlers in the Valley — that they were
nearly all dissenters and their presence there involved a
notable extension and strengthening of the Virginia frontier
— did not apply to the converts who were now being won
from the Church in the central counties. That involved an
invasion of an ecclesiastical preserve analogous to New England, though in the two cases the position of the parties was
reversed and the Anglicans lacked the efficiency and strenuous
dogmatism of the Puritan. The New Side preachers had
neglected to procure licenses and their meeting houses were
not registered. Those therefore who attended their meetings
were subject to fine. But it was not until active proselyting
began, accompanied by attacks on the establishment, that
the government began to take action.

In April, 1745, Gooch at the meeting of the general court
charged the grand jury " to make strict inquiry after those
seducers," to the end that the people might be protected
against them and they silenced by such methods as the law
directed.[1] The purport of the charge was that in the interest
of public peace and order, as well as that of the true faith,
the insolent attack must be stopped, but in checking them he
proposed to act in harmony with the letter of the law. The
jury made certain presentments, among them one against
Roon, though he had already taken a final leave of Virginia.
When a copy of the governor's charge reached the Synod at
Philadelphia, it of course disclaimed all connection with the
New Side evangelists and expressed the hope that " those who
belong to us and produce proper testimonials, behave themselves suitably." In his reply to a letter from the Synod
describing this attitude, Gooch expressed his abhorrence of
the practices of the itinerant preachers, but declared that
missionaries producing proper testimonials, complying with
the laws and performing divine service in some certain place

[1] Foote, 135; Burke, Hist. of Va., III, 119.

without disturbing the peace, might be sure of his protection.[1] The Conjunct Presbytery of Newcastle and New Brunswick, soon to become members of the Synod of New York, now sent two of their leading preachers, Gilbert Tennent and Samuel Finley, as messengers of peace to the governor and the Presbyterians of Virginia. They were kindly received and permitted to preach in Hanover and elsewhere. Samuel Blair and William Tennent also visited Virginia and they were followed, in 1747, by Samuel Davies, who became the genuine apostle of Presbyterianism in that province and led in the formation of the Presbytery of Hanover.

By this time prosecution of Presbyterians and the levy of moderate fines upon them for violations of the Virginia law incorporating the toleration act had begun. The licensing of dissenting preachers and churches, as well as trials for violations of the law, were now taken over entirely by the general court, sitting at Williamsburg. The judges of this court and the provincial council, the personnel of the two being substantially the same, assumed a more rigid attitude toward the dissenters than did the governor, and one that was not justified by the toleration act as administered in England. Peyton Randolph was the attorney general and had charge of the government's cases against the accused. William Dawson, the commissary, was the chief spokesman for the Church, especially in laying its case before the bishop of London. After Davies had resolved to settle somewhat permanently in Virginia he developed with great ability the course of argument by which the Presbyterian cause was defended. He wrote to Drs. Doddridge and Avery, the highly respected Presbyterian leaders in England, his view of the situation in Virginia and of the legal rights of the dissenters. By them his statements, so far as they deemed it wise, were transmitted to the bishop and his comments were received in return. At times also Davies faced the attorney general, before the governor and council, and won the compliments of his hearers by the ability of his pleas. All this time he was preaching to a number of congregations in Hanover and adjoining counties, with a winning power that promised better permanent results than the appeals of Whitefield. His argu-

[1] Foote, 138 *et seq.*

ments also in support of the legal claims of the Presbyterians were so clear and logically acute, and were set forth with such beauty and spirit as to prove that his success in the law might have been as great as it was in the ministry.

The attitude of the council was clearly indicated by its refusal of a license to John Rodgers, who accompanied Davies to Virginia. As Rodgers had been sent by the presbytery and was ready to take the required oaths, this action was rightly interpreted as evidence of a determination to prevent more dissenting preachers from coming into the older settled counties of the province. As the settlers beyond the Blue Ridge were practically all dissenters, this policy was not applied to them. Their preachers, moreover, came largely from the Old Side Synod of Philadelphia and lacked the evangelistic spirit and views of those who were sent out by the presbyteries of Newcastle and New Brunswick, which united into the Synod of New York. Davies and all the others who worked east of the mountains came from this source and were of this type. They showed the spirit of the Tennents and the Log College, and Davies in particular was soon to become deeply concerned in the founding of the College of New Jersey or Nassau Hall, which was to become Princeton University. The presence of Presbyterians of the Philadelphia type could be comfortably tolerated in Virginia, but the aggressive assaults of the other party, especially when delivered in the interior of the province, were felt to be dangerous.[1]

Davies, however, did not claim a natural right to preach the gospel in Virginia, as the Baptists did at a later time, but based his arguments on the act of toleration. The Anglican authorities, especially in Virginia, attempted to prove that he was not really a Presbyterian but merely an enthusiast — a Methodist — and that his standing was that of an itinerant who had come in from a remote colony uninvited and was trying to draw the people away from the parish churches where the gospel had always been adequately preached. The coming in of others like him they intended, if possible, to prevent. As Davies had been licensed they could not exclude him, but they insisted that his activities

[1] See Foote, 164 et seq.; Hist. Colls. Va., 368 et seq., and McIlwaine for the situation as it was at this time.

should be confined, like those of each parish minister, to a single congregation or at least to as few such as possible. Davies insisted that he was not an itinerant and certainly not an enthusiast, but an accredited Presbyterian minister and a preacher of the genuine gospel, for the lack of hearing which the people of Virginia were perishing eternally.

In order, so far as possible, to hold in check the growing popular demand to hear Davies and the other evangelists who paid brief visits to Virginia, the general court restricted the licensing of congregations and the building of meeting houses for them. But such was the pressure that, by 1750, seven meeting houses, situated in five counties, had been licensed for Davies. Complaint respecting this was sent to England, as involving the setting up of itinerants, the licensing of buildings not yet erected and the consequent spread of schism far and wide. The reply of Davies to this was, that the members of his congregations were so scattered that the full number of places licensed was necessary for their accommodation. It was also impossible to procure ministers enough from the north to supply each congregation and therefore, in trying himself to officiate for them all, he should not be regarded as an itinerant. He claimed to be doing substantially what the clergy in their large parishes did by means of their chapels of ease. His dispersed congregations really formed but one church, and without the number of meeting places which they had they would be deprived of the benefit of the act of toleration. It also appeared that in England, when congregations duly applied for the licensing of their places of worship, the authorities were bound to grant the requests, and that duly licensed clergymen could preach in any of these places without securing special permission. Though the general court and clergy in Virginia for a time held to the strict interpretation of the province act of 1699, and introduced a bill in 1752 further to define the status of dissenters, they received no special encouragement from England. The bishop disclaimed all intention of severity. An opinion was issued by Sir Dudley Ryder, the attorney general, which was favorable to the claims of Davies, and the board of trade wrote to the Virginia authorities warning them

against giving just cause of offence by unwarrantably restricting the free exercise of religion, " so valuable a branch
of true liberty and so essential to the enriching and improving of a trading nation." [1]  For a century this had been
substantially the attitude of the British government, and it
now prevailed in the end against the spirit of narrow exclusiveness which existed among the Anglicans of the province.  After the outbreak of the last intercolonial war, when
the frontiers of Virginia were devastated by the attacks of
French and Indians, the necessity of uniting the people as
much as possible for defence outweighed every other consideration, and in the midst of this conflict the controversy
over the subject of toleration for Presbyterians was largely
obscured and forgotten.  The struggle of the Baptists for freedom of worship in Virginia as a natural right, and one which
led to more violence on both sides, belongs to a somewhat
later time.

The case of William Kay, minister of Lunenburg parish, in
Richmond county, not only illustrated anew the arbitrariness
which the vestries and the great planters, who so often controlled them, might show toward the clergy, but also the
chance there was for the injured party to right himself
through appeal to the general court and to the king in council.[2]  The decision was held to confirm the right of ministers,
though not inducted, to continue in possession of their glebes.
The local magnate who in this case attacked the clergyman
was the well known Landon Carter, and his ire had been
roused by a sermon which Kay preached against pride.  This
case, after being at issue for some five years, was finally
settled in 1753.  By a well attended convention of the clergy
in 1754, called by the new commissary, Thomas Dawson, a
warm letter of thanks was sent to the bishop of London for
the vigor he had shown in support of Mr. Kay, and also in
favor of the appointment of Thomas Dawson, the new commissary, as a member of the council.  They also protested
to the governor against an order of the council excluding
clergymen from the office of justice of the peace.[3]  The

[1] Hist. Colls. etc., Virginia, 379.

[2] Ibid., 386 et seq., 403.

[3] Ibid., 422, 424.

assaults which the dissenters were making upon the Church would naturally strengthen the sense of corporate unity among its clergy. The case of Mr. Kay, as well as signs observable in society generally, must have impressed at least the more acute among them with a feeling that the laity were growing more independent and that the easy going conditions of the past might not always continue. In such a state of feeling nothing was more natural than for the freeholders to seize upon such plausible excuse as might present itself for curtailing the already narrow incomes of the clergy, and use legislation for the purpose. Even if that was not the motive, the clergy would be almost sure so to interpret it and to affix that stigma to any serious change, except in the upward direction, which might be made in their salaries. This was one of the important conditions out of which developed the famous Parson's Cause, and the train for the explosion was being laid at the time of which we speak. We have met with a like situation, and one even more acute than this, in Maryland two decades earlier.

In 1748 the legislature of Virginia completed one of its periodical revisions of the laws of the province. In this was an act repealing all earlier ones for the collection of parish levies and providing that the annual salary of every minister should be 16,000 pounds of tobacco and casks, with an allowance of one-fourth for shrinkage. This had been substantially the remuneration of the clergy since the close of the seventeenth century, and in 1751 the act was approved by the king. It then became subject to the clause in the royal instructions which provided that such a law could not be altered or repealed except by an act containing the usual suspending clause. At this point the fast and loose methods in which both executives and legislatures dealt with instructions began to affect this question. Exceptions in certain cases were made to the law, and then the provisions of the law were wholly changed, and · this without a suspending clause or waiting for the approval of the crown. In 1753 an act was passed providing that the ministers of the parishes of Frederick and Augusta should be paid in money at the rate of £100 Virginia currency per year. In 1755 the justices of Princess Anne and Norfolk counties were required to fix a price on tobacco not under 10s. per hundredweight and all payments there were to be convertible into money at that rate. In 1755, the year after the convention of the clergy above referred to, it was provided that for ten months payments which had previously been made in tobacco might at the option of the buyer be converted into money at 2d. per pound or 16s. 8d. per hundredweight. This was the famous two penny act, and it affected not only the clergy but all officials and other creditors of the government. But the laymen were usually planters, in some cases large planters, and might compensate themselves by the rise in the price of tobacco. The act also did not apply to the counties where provision had already been made for compensation.[1] The excuse for this legislation was an expected shortage in the tobacco crop.

Two letters of protest from different bodies of the Virginia clergy were sent to the bishop of London and a separate epistle in a milder tone was written by the commissary. Rev. John Camm, of the college and York-Hampton parish, took the leading place, in the press and later as agent to England, in advocacy of the cause of the clergy. A general grievance of which they complained was that, owing to the methods of levy and payment, their salaries were always about a year and a half in arrears. But against the particular law in question they urged that it discriminated against the clergy by robbing them of the advantage of years when the price of tobacco ranged high and that too after a long period when the price had been uniformly low. Owing to local drouths and frosts and especially to the war, the crop was short and a correspondingly high price was expected. In their hope of profit from this the clergy saw themselves disappointed by the new law. But it turned out that the rate fixed in the act did not differ much from the market price and so the complaint was dropped.

But again in 1758, in anticipation of another partial failure of the crop, the legislature passed a similar act to be in force for a year.[2] As the price of tobacco now rose to about 50s. per hundredweight, while the clergy received only 16s.

---

[1] Hening, VI, 88, 369, 502, 568; Hist. Colls. etc., Va., 434, 440, 447.
[2] Hening, VII, 240. Hist. Colls. etc., Va., 458 *et seq.*

8d. in money, they lost heavily. They therefore sent Camm as their agent to England to procure, with the aid of Sherlock and of Paris as his solicitor, the repeal of the law. Abercrombie, the agent of the province, under instructions from the assembly, appeared in support of the measure.[1] The board of trade reported in favor of the disallowance of the act, basing its argument on the unfairness of the measure toward the clergy and on the violation, in passing it, of the royal instruction concerning the suspending clause. On these grounds it was declared repealed. When the act of 1755 was passed Dinwiddie was governor, but Fauquier was in office when the second measure became law.[2] He unjustifiably attacked Camm, when the latter returned with notice of repeal, and a heated pamphlet controversy followed upon the merits of the issue as a whole. Landon Carter and Richard Bland, the former, as we have seen, being no friend of the clergy and the latter the author of the two penny act, upheld the cause of the assembly and Camm that of the clergy. Carter attacked the bishop for suggesting in his letter to the lords of the committee that the assembly was disloyal and had encouraged dissent. He also abused Camm. Bland, who wrote the ablest pamphlets, claimed that the clergy really got a salary of £144 under the act, instead of £80 or £100 which the assembly intended they should have and which they had received in earlier years. He also insisted that Virginia was in such straitened circumstances in 1758 that some such legislation as was passed was necessary. In the last of his pamphlets, which was published in 1763, Bland asserted in their strongest form the rights of Virginians as Englishmen, and made a very notable attack upon the binding authority which was claimed for instructions.[3] This argument, which was widely read in the province, gave great political significance to the discussion.

Immediately after notice of the disallowance was published, the first point which was brought sharply into dis-

---

[1] Va. Mag. of Hist., X, 347.

[2] Both of these governors violated their instructions by assenting to the acts, and Dinwiddie is reported to have said that he did it to please the people.

[3] Wm. and Mary College Quarterly, X, 31. See also the article of Dr. Tyler in the same number.

pute by the two parties was this: Did the disallowance
destroy the force of the act from the time of its passage,
or did it take effect only at the date of Camm's return,
when it was proclaimed in Virginia? The clergy contended
for the former view and the assembly and its supporters for
the latter. The law had actually expired before notice of
its disallowance reached Virginia. If the contention of the
clergy was correct, it had not been in force at all and the
obligations as to salary which existed prior to it continued
valid during that year. According to the opposite view it had
been in force during the entire year for which it was passed
and sums in excess of the salaries which had then been paid
could not be collected. Certain fragmentary notes among
the papers of Lord Hardwicke, which apparently refer to this
case, indicate that the question just stated was discussed
probably before the committee of the council which ordered
the repeal of the law.[1] The point there raised by the attorney
general was, whether the act ought not to have been declared
void *ab initio* with the idea that, if that was done, its effect
from the time of its enactment would have been destroyed.
Doubt was expressed whether it was in the power of the
privy council to do such a thing, the idea being that a
judicial process would be necessary. The attorney general
urged that the council had as high authority in such a case
as any court of judicature, and cited instances of its action
upon laws of various colonies which might serve as precedents. He also emphasized the limitations derived from
reason, the laws of England and royal instructions which
restricted the powers of a colonial assembly. Wedderburn
took the opposite ground, and Lord Hardwicke apparently
jotted down various queries upon the subject. But the act
in question was simply disallowed or repealed [2] and, as
shown by a long line of valid precedents, the effects of such
action was not retroactive. The law of 1758 must be considered to have been in force until the publication of its
disallowance in Virginia.[3]

[1] Brit. Mss. Addit. Mss. No. 36218, fol. 38. See Hunt's article in Pol.
Sci. Quarterly, Dec. 1916; Hist. Colls., Va., 510.

[2] The common formula was used: "disallowed, declared void and of no
effect."

[3] The committee of correspondence of the Virginia Burgesses, in its

But the clergy took the opposite ground. In the brief which they submitted in England they went further than that, by not only insisting that the governor was restrained by his instructions from assenting to the act but that it was " void in itself, being contrary to the principles of justice."[1] It was upon this issue and against the contention that, by the constitution of Virginia, the governor and assembly were authorized to pass any law not repugnant to the laws of England, that suits were brought by a number of the clergy before county courts and by Camm before the general court to recover, in the form of damages against the collectors, the balance of their salaries. In King William county the jury brought in a verdict for the collectors. In York county the jury awarded damages against the collectors, but the justices, holding that the law of 1758 was in force and valid, refused to allow judgment to be entered up. The clergymen appealed to the general court. In Hanover county the act was declared invalid and a special jury was called to fix the amount of damages due to the clergyman, James Maury. A decision by the general court in Camm's case was not reached until 1764, when by a vote of five to four, the act was upheld and judgment was given against the plaintiff. Camm appealed to the crown, intending to make his a test case for the clergy as a whole. The assembly, with a similar idea, made appropriation for the defense of the collectors. The case was argued at length, and Camm's appeal was dismissed[2] on the technical ground that the original suit should have been brought as an action of debt instead of trespass. As this decision was not reached until near the close of 1765, when the stamp act troubles were at their height, the political motive was probably decisive in allowing this case, in which so much controversial matter was involved, to be shelved by a technicality.[3] The general court of Virginia, therefore, dis-

instructions to Montague, the agent, in 1759, gave away their case, and Bland was one of the signers of this paper, though a few years later his opinion was so strong upon the other side. Va. Mag. of Hist., X, 348.

[1] Hunt, *op. cit.*

[2] Acts P. C. Col., 1745–66, p. 399.

[3] In the Hardwicke Papers, Addtl. Mss. No. 36220, are the briefs of plaintiffs and defendants in the Camm trial. Hunt, in the article referred to, sums up the arguments for and against the law.

missed the three pending appeals from the counties, and the
clergy had to content themselves as best they were able under
a complete practical defeat.

Three years earlier than this, in November, 1762, before a
special jury called to fix the damages due Mr. Maury in
Hanover county, Patrick Henry, then a young and unknown
lawyer, not only undertook to argue the law of the case, but
made an impassioned attack on the clergy. Though the court
before which he plead had already passed on the law, and it
was no longer before the justices or jury, they listened to
his argument. He voiced the growing dissatisfaction, brew-
ing especially strong in Virginia, with the power of the crown
to restrict by disallowance and in other ways the sphere of
the assemblies. He may have had in mind the annullment of
a law *ab initio*, but it is not necessary to suppose that his
argument was limited to that. If he started from the theory
of compact as determining the relations between the crown
and the colonies, he would be opposed to the repeal by the
crown of any law which, like this, was of acknowledged
public utility. But not content with voicing this feeling,
which would have won general approval among the leaders
of New England in the seventeenth century, Henry launched
into an attack on the Anglican clergy. In this may be
recognized an echo from his Scotch ancestry and also an
expression of the spirit which was abroad in Hanover county
and the entire adjacent region. The rapid growth of the
dissenters there testifies to its existence. Davies stated that
he never openly criticized Anglican forms or church government, but the type of religion which he sought to spread
among the people was by implication a continuous rebuke
to the respectable but lifeless Antinomianism of the Church.
Davies had written that the attitude of the parish clergy
toward the real gospel was one of " serene stupidity." Henry
struck at the clergy from another angle, and his language was
much less restrained than that of the Presbyterian divine.
He denied that they were moved by holy zeal or practiced
the benevolent precepts of the gospel. They neither fed the
hungry nor clothed the naked, but like harpies stood ready
to snatch from the poor their last earthly possession. This,
of course, was extreme rhetorical exaggeration, and it was

cruelly unjust to the great body of the clergy. But when one combines Davies and Henry and what they represented, with the attitude of assembly, officials and courts, as shown in the Parson's Cause, the impression is clear that the Church in Virginia at last was facing opposition which might lead to a crisis.[1]

At the period of which we are speaking, the interests of the English Church in its broader aspects, as the patron of higher education and of sound learning, as then understood both in the sciences and the philosophical and literary studies which were chiefly based on the ancient classics, were advanced by the founding of the College, Academy, and charitable schools of Philadelphia and of Kings College of New York.

Much earlier in the century a proposal had twice been made to found a college in New York. The first occasion was when the Queen's Farm was deeded to Trinity Church early in Lord Cornbury's administration. At that time originated the idea that a college building should be located on that land. The second occasion arose during the residence of Berkeley in Rhode Island, when it was suggested that his proposed college should be located not in Bermuda but in New York. But in neither case was action taken, and the people of the province were allowed to drift on in a condition, especially in the interior, of deplorable ignorance and neglect of learning. The historian Smith is authority for the statement that for many years there had been only two " academics " in the province, except those who were in holy orders, and that as late as 1747 he could reckon up only fifteen who had received the bachelor's degree.[2] " Commerce," he wrote, " engrossed the attention of the principal families, and their sons were usually sent from the writing school to the counting house and thence to the West India islands." A little later Cadwallader Colden used even

---

[1] This episode is treated in all the histories of Virginia and especially by Wirt, Tyler, and Henry in their biographies of Patrick Henry; also by Eckenrode in an able monograph on the "Separation of Church and State in Virginia" in the Report of the Va. State Library for 1910. See also an article by L. G. Tyler in W. and M. Coll. Quarterly, XIX, and Maury, Memoirs of a Huguenot Family.

[2] Smith, History of New York, ed. of 1829, Vol. II, 94.

stronger language, though it was doubtless colored to an extent by political disgust and animosity.[1] But it is interesting to read his opinion that " The only principle of Life propagated among the young People is to get money, and men are only esteemed according to what they are worth, that is, the money they are possessed of." Colden had a plan for founding a college at Newburg upon land which had been granted to the first Palatine immigrants, but which they had long since abandoned for other and distant homes. But notwithstanding the great need of enlightenment in the interior of the province, no competitor for the site of a college at that time had any chance of success against New York City.

Such, in his opinion, were the narrow and selfish views of the assembly and public men, that Colden had very little confidence in the effectiveness of any support of a college which might come from that quarter. But, even while he was writing, the first steps were being taken which were to supply financial support for such an institution. By an act of 1746, followed by two supplementary measures in 1748, authority was given to raise by public lottery a fund for the founding of a college in the province. In 1751 an act was passed vesting in trustees the sum of £3443, which had been raised in the way and for the purpose indicated. The board, which included the eldest resident councillor of the province, the speaker of the assembly, the judges of the supreme court, the mayor of New York City, and the province treasurer, consisted of six Episcopalians, two of the Dutch Church, and William Livingston, who was considered to be a Presbyterian. Provision was made in an act of July, 1753, for continuing the excise, that £500 from that source should be annually devoted to the payment of salaries and other uses of the seminary which the trustees should think needful. Another lottery was authorized the same year, and gifts were received from various individuals in the colony and England.[2] As soon as the board of trustees for the fund which was theirs to

[1] Colden to Hezekiah Watkins, Dec. 12, 1748, printed by G. H. Moore in his address on the Origin and Early History of Columbia College, pp. 37 et seq.

[2] Col. Laws of N. Y., III, 607, 679, 731, 842, 899, 930. A list of early gifts is printed by Moore in his address, p. 17.

accumulate was known, a spirited opposition against the place was started by the dissenters, especially of the Presbyterian communion. William Livingston was the leader of this protest, and it was directed against the apparent intention of those who were founding the institution, that it should be controlled by the English Church, or, as they said, that it should be a " Trinity Church College."

William Livingston, belonging to the second generation in descent from Robert, the founder of the family, was a son of Philip Livingston and Catherine Van Brugh.[1] In his veins Scotch and Dutch blood was mingled. His father had enjoyed and probably increased the large estate accumulated by the versatile Robert, and had held the offices and performed the social duties which fell regularly to the lot of a landed magnate in the interior of New York. But altogether the chief service rendered by himself and wife was that they reared a large family of sons and daughters, several of whom were destined to wide and useful service in the colonies. Through them and their descendants the Livingston family rose to the distinguished place which it held during the latter half of the century. Of these William, the fourth son, was the most brilliant. During the decade between 1731 and 1741 he and three of his brothers were graduated from Yale. Though that seminary failed in their cases to overcome the secular spirit which they had inherited in New York and to make them clergymen, it may be supposed that the young William at least found something there which nourished his inborn love of criticism and dissent. On his return to New York he entered the law office of James Alexander and completed his legal training without a term of residence in the law schools of England. He read widely outside the books of his profession and aimed at achievements in a distinctly literary and satirical vein. In 1746 Livingston became connected in law practice with William Smith and later with his son of the same name and with John Morin Scott, all of them Whigs or Liberals in politics, and through that connection, as well as his natural inclinations, he became permanently identified with that group in public life.

[1] Sedgwick, Life of William Livingston.

It is altogether probable that Livingston had read the deistical writers, though the attitude of the "Independent Whig," that irritating attack on the Established Church and its clergy, which had been published some years before in England, agrees better with the ideas which he later expressed in print. He was a pronounced non-sectarian. In 1744, respecting that subject, he wrote, "Let us resemble the bee, that collects the purest nectar out of a diversity of flowers that we may not quake, but exult, at the second sound of the trumpet, when we shall not be asked of what sect we have been, but be judged according to our works."[1]

At the close of November, 1752, Livingston began the publication of the "Independent Reflector," a non-partisan periodical devoted to the discussion and criticism of subjects of local and general interest. His purpose, as its editor declared, was to expose public vice and corruption, to vindicate liberty and human rights and to show how detestable were slavery and oppression.[2] "In a Word" he wrote, "I shall dare to attempt the Reforming of the Abuses of my Country, and to point out whatever may tend to its Prosperity and Ennoblement." In the long list of subjects which Livingston discussed or proposed to discuss many were not in any sense controversial, but related to such affairs of the city and of every day life and morals as might form the subject of comment in this or any publication of the time. But there were other subjects, political and religious, current opinions upon which Livingston desired to attack and it was for this purpose that the paper was started. Its issue was therefore a sign that the spirit of Zenger and his supporters was reappearing, this time also within the circle of the provincial aristocracy. War, it is true, was seen to be approaching and with it the problem of securing united action among the colonies. Livingston's later writings show that he was not forgetful of these questions. But the issue which he proposed chiefly to discuss in the "Independent Reflector" was that of the college.

At Yale under Clap he had seen and felt the evils of a

---

[1] Livingston published his creed in the "Independent Reflector," No. 46, and Sedgwick gives it in part, *op. cit.*, 86.

[2] See No. 1, on the design of the paper.

narrow sectarian education, and now his assault was delivered against colleges, wherever they were, which stood for
that idea.  To colleges which could be described as "schools
of the prophets" he was unalterably opposed.  To the unduly
partisan nature of the colleges in New England and New
Jersey he attributed the sway of the Congregationalists and
the "incurable languor" of episcopacy in New England.  The
Episcopalians, he said, were fully alive to reasonings of this
kind when they were directed against colleges in the hands of
other sects, but a similar policy when pursued under their own
control seemed to them only reasonable moderation.  This
remark he could have fully supported by reference to the
English universities and their narrowly sectarian attitude.
That policy he believed it was the intention of those who
were being put in charge of the new enterprise to perpetuate
in New York, a province the great majority of whose inhabitants were outside the Church.  This would be an attempt to perpetuate a condition which had been artifically
created under Fletcher and Cornbury, when by the ministry
act they had tried to palm off upon the people of New York
a pseudo-church establishment.  The bitter animosities of
that period were for the moment reawakened by Livingston's
attack upon the plan for the college.

Livingston's remedy was a radical one, and his advocacy
of it was doubtless the result of theoretical opinions far in
advance of his time, but of the truth of which he had become
convinced.  He declared in favor of secular education, and for
the transfer of it from the control of the clergy to that of the
laity.  The service of the community as a whole, and not
merely of a sect, should be the purpose.  The spirit of inquiry and not of unquestioning belief, of liberty and not of
submission, of patriotism and zeal for the public good and not
of dogmas supported by scholastic disputations, should be
inculcated.  He was opposed even to the establishment of a
professorship of divinity in the college.  "A public Academy,"
he said, "is, or ought to be, a mere civil Institution, and
cannot with any tolerable Propriety be monopolized by any
religious Sect."  The design of such bodies was entirely
political, that is, for the benefit of society as a society, without any intention of teaching religion, which was the province

of the pulpit. If the college should be organized on this plan, it would serve as a powerful liberalizer in the province, but if in accordance with the opposite idea it would bring the heaviest disaster. In order, therefore, to keep it out of the control of a sect, Livingston urged that it be created by an act of the legislature and maintained as a state institution. He was opposed to its incorporation by a royal charter, for such a grant would give too exclusive power to the trustees. If the college was created by statute and placed under the inspection of the civil authority, it would be more permanent, better endowed, less liable to abuse and more capable of answering its true end. In August, 1754, the subject of the college again came before the assembly. A majority of the house seemed favorable to a " free college," and a bill was introduced for its organization.[1] Petitions in support of such a plan were presented from several of the counties, and some of the Dutch petitioned for a Calvinistic professor of divinity.

While this action and these bold assertions were signs of a spirit which was beginning to appear in the colonies and in a way were an outgrowth of the secular feeling which had always been strong in New York, their immediate effect was to provoke violent counter attacks in the " New York Mercury " and to hasten action on the part of the trustees and Trinity Church. In the spring of 1754 the corporation of Trinity offered the trustees a tract within the King's Farm on which to erect a building, provided the charter which they intended to procure should contain provisions to the effect that the president should be a communicant of the English Church and its liturgy should be used in the morning and evening services of the college forever. This grant, with its condition, was accepted, and in the following October a charter was issued by Lieutenant Governor De Lancey and the council. This provided for a governing board consisting of the archbishop of Canterbury and the first commissioner of trade as honorary heads, the leading officials, for the time being, of the province, the mayor of New York City, the rector of Trinity, a minister respectively of the Dutch Reformed, Lutheran, French and Presbyterian churches of the

[1] This bill is printed in the Journal of the Ass., II, 413.

city, the president of the College and twenty-four other lay-men. Henry Barclay, rector of Trinity, wrote to Samuel Johnson at Stratford, immeditaely after the grant of the charter; " He [the lieutenant governor] has given us a good majority of Churchmen, no less than eleven of the Vestry being of the number. There are but eight of the Dutch Church, most of them good men and true, and two Dissenters. . . . We have a majority of twenty-nine to twelve." [1]

Against this decision Livingston publicly protested, calling attention to the fact that probably seven-eighths of the free-holders and inhabitants of New York were not of the Church of England, and claiming that the money which had been appropriated by the legislature had been intended for a free college. In a long list of queries he denied the justice, and sought to throw doubt on the legality, of the action of the trustees in accepting the land from Trinity Church and securing a charter, thus seeking to exclude further action by the assembly. Another protest, signed by James Alexander and William Smith, was presented in council. To the charges of the opponents of the charter Benjamin Nicoll, step-son of Samuel Johnson and an able lawyer, replied in " A Brief Vindication of the Proceedings of the Trustees." He did not undertake to answer all the queries and objections of Livingston, but took the ground that the agitation he had started was largely needless and artificial. The notion of a " Trinity Church College " he treated as a figment of the imagination, considered the liturgy as good as any form of prayer for the purpose which could be devised. He believed that the moderate type of Christianity for which the Church stood would recommend itself to most who would be likely to patronize a college. In the attack of the Presbyterians he also professed to see a desire to check the movement in New York, so as to favor the prospects of the College of New Jersey. The purpose of the lottery and excise acts, Nicoll claimed, was to raise money for the founding of a college, upon the implied supposition that it must be by charter from the crown, as without its concurrence no corporation could be made. The governor and council who had acted upon the petition of the trustees considered it regular,

[1] Beardsley, Life of Johnson, 196.

and it was to them and the assembly that the board was obliged to account. Later the trustees had reported to the house, Livingston filing a separate report of his own, which as it stood on the minutes would be a standing reproach to him.

In the so-called " Watch Tower " articles, printed in the " Mercury," after the suspension of the " Independent Reflector," the discussion was continued far into 1755, the writers often descending to personal abuse. But it resulted in no change. By action of the provincial executive the college had been established under the conditions which the episcopal majority desired, and action by the assembly to disturb this settlement could not be obtained. The elaborate bill which embodied Livingston's ideas was dropped and a measure substituted which only provided for the holding of a lottery for the support of the college.[1] When Sir Charles Hardy arrived as governor, by a gift of £500 he helped to clinch the decision. As soon as it was decided to procure a charter Samuel Johnson was asked to accept the presidency of the college. He was already somewhat advanced in years and not robust in health. He was also strongly attached to his work in Stratford and to his interests in New England. But after persuasion he accepted, being at the same time appointed assistant minister of Trinity Church.

When he received the appointment Johnson was exchanging letters with President Clap, of Yale, in which he protested against the rule by which the New Haven college refused to permit sons of Episcopalians to attend services on Sundays in their own church.[2] The whole nature of Johnson, as head of a college, was opposed to a rigid sectarian attitude. Samuel Whittlesey, a prominent Presbyterian of Connecticut, was the first man who was called to a mastership, though because of his health he declined to accept. In the advertisement which was issued respecting terms of admission, courses and the beginning of instruction in the new college, it was stated that there was no intention of imposing on the students the tenets of any particular sect, but to inculcate the principles upon which all Christians were agreed. As to peculiar tenets, everyone would be left to judge for himself.

[1] Ass. J., II, 413–422; Col. Laws of N. Y., III, 994, 1027, 1127.
[2] Beardsley, Life of Johnson, 201.

Regular attendance at church on Sundays would be required, but students might select such places of worship as their parents or guardians thought fit to order or permit. As to the daily services, a collection of lessons, prayers and hymns taken mostly from Scripture and expressive of common Christianity was prepared and, after approval by the trustees, was used for this purpose. During the few years when Johnson was president, and apparently thereafter until the Revolution, this mild policy was followed. It was rather colorless and did not appeal to the stronger impulses which were gathering in the community, but it might fairly be regarded as an advance upon the militant sectarianism which Clap was trying to perpetuate at Yale, or upon most which Harvard could show prior to that date. The worst fears of Livingston certainly were not justified by the result, and in favor of his alternative, namely control by a legislature, the record of such bodies, added to their total lack of experience in such matters, certainly offered little that was encouraging.

# CHAPTER III

REOPENING OF THE STRUGGLE WITH THE BOURBON ALLI-
ANCE. THE THIRD INTERCOLONIAL WAR. 1739-1748

So far as events in western Europe and its adjacent seas were concerned, there had been a lull for nearly thirty years in the conflict between the combinations of powers of which Great Britain and France were the leaders. During the interval Cardinal Alberoni had tried to revive the energies of Spain and overthrow the settlement of Utrecht; a combination of northern powers which under the lead of Charles XII of Sweden had menaced England had been formed and quickly collapsed; the question of the Polish succession had led to territorial changes in Italy and central Europe; but these all were minor events which led to subsidiary readjustments and did not change the European system in its more important features. This period of comparative peace — exceptional in the Europe of those days — was due to the policy of the duke of Orleans as regent, and later of Cardinal Fleury, in France and to that of Sir Robert Walpole in England. It marked the reaction which followed the age of Louis XIV and the exhausting wars which had been caused by his long continued effort to establish the predominance of France and thereby to overthrow the political adjustments which had been reached at the Congress of Westphalia. France needed rest and time for recuperation, while dynastic considerations also inclined the regent toward peace. England felt a similar exhaustion, while peace furnished to the new Hanoverian kingship its only guaranty against the attacks of the Stuart pretenders and opportunity to establish its hold upon the throne.

With the accession of the Hanoverians the Whig Party came into power and that under circumstances which insured its overwhelming predominance in parliament and the country for half a century. The fortunes of this party were closely

involved with those of the new dynasty and the policy of
both, as formulated by Walpole, was peace and the development of the commercial and financial resources of the realm
and dominions. Party government, with its accompaniment
of the cabinet system and the methods of control which were
then systematically followed, was so fully established that
the crown even became an instrument of policy more than
an end in itself. Both the theory and spirit of monarchy
declined in Great Britain and the rule of a well-compacted
aristocracy, composed of the great Whig families, took its
place. This was a system to which the Revolution of 1689
naturally led and under it Great Britain became — what she
remained for two centuries — one of the most aristocratic
nations in the world. At that time the party system was
fastened upon her and ever since her internal policy has
been evolved by roundabout and hesitating steps, as the result
of the action and counter-action which has accompanied
party conflicts.

By 1715 it had become evident that the most important
questions affecting western Europe were those which arose
from commerce and over-sea expansion. The industrial revolution, which came in due time, was largely a resultant of
these. As a consequence of the evolution of the previous
century, Portugal and Holland had been passed in the race
and England, France and Spain were left as the great colonizing powers. Spain had won at the outset vast and rich
dominions which she was seeking to exploit under a system of
strict monopoly. But she had reached the limit of her development and was already in decline. She had not become
an industrial state. Her efforts to develop a fleet and genuine
maritime efficiency had never been successful. France and
Great Britain therefore remained as the leading contestants
in this domain. France, though open to the sea on two sides
and actually producing seamen in the west and north of the
greatest ability, was still chiefly a land power. From the
beginning she had been deeply involved in the territorial and
dynastic conflicts of the continent. Her insular position, on
the other hand, saved Great Britain from being wholly or
chiefly absorbed in the wars of the continent. In point of
climate and for all the purposes of intercolonial trade and

naval development, she was most fortunately situated. She lay athwart the entrance to the seas of northern Europe, while she was accessible to the Mediterranean and to all the coasts of the Atlantic basin. The conflicts of the seventeenth century had left her free from serious danger of invasion, while she could easily reach the coasts of her adversaries. Her interests on the continent were protected by a group of buffer states in the Low Countries and Scandinavia and by a system of alliances which she supported less by troops than by subsidies. From her island seclusion England was already weaving a web of commercial and naval posts and interests which was to surround the globe.

The War of the Spanish Succession had turned the attention of both the rivals more toward the Mediterranean. When the results of that war were gathered up, it appears that Spain was the chief sufferer. The occupation of Gibraltar and Minorca by England, supported by the Methuen treaty and the stationing of a permanent squadron in the Mediterranean, proved the beginning of connecting links of the greatest importance extending between the British Isles, the west coast of Africa and Spanish Americas on the one hand and the near and remote east on the other. By her gains from France in this war Great Britain also took important steps toward encircling the Atlantic Ocean with her possessions and already the rough sketch of her maritime empire might be seen. Her occupation of Gibraltar, that greatest of all precedents for the seizure and retention of naval stations on foreign territory, has continued as a badge of the impotence of Spain. For a time Spain struggled and protested, then acquiesced and long since has come to regard the presence of the foreigner as keeper of her gateway into the Atlantic as a part of the order of nations. The transfer, at the same time, of the *assiento* to England opened the way into Spanish America for British goods and slaves and through them occasions for further conflicts, encroachments and gains in the future.

But this same war also secured to a French Bourbon the throne of Spain, and this involved almost the certainty of coöperation and a permanent alliance between the powers. The union of the two crowns was averted, but the way was

prepared for the Family Compact, secretly concluded in its
original form in 1733, and the consequent union of the fleets
and resources against the German Powers on the one hand
and England on the other.  In this way the three prominent
sea powers were adjusting themselves for the next period in
the struggle for ascendency which was soon to open.  Great
Britain must now face the united navies of France and Spain
and if a decisive triumph over them could be won her
ascendency as a sea power would be permanently established.
The armies and general resources of her rivals, however,
were not concentrated in opposition to hers, but largely
diverted to the support of their interests in Italy and Germany.  That diverted interest from their navies, kept France
predominantly a land power and enabled Great Britain to
carry through successfully what may be called the middle
stage in the development of her empire and navy, which was
marked in the west by the expulsion of the French from
North America and in the east by the conquest of India.  We
are approaching the time when the stage was being set for
these great events, and in the process of keeping the attention
of France to a large extent diverted from the sea and
from the needed support of her colonial interests Frederick
II, of Prussia, had a large share.  His seizure of Silesia, connected as it was with the delicate question of the Austrian
Succession, began a series of readjustments in Central Europe
which were destined to absorb the chief attention and energies
of France for three quarters of a century.  Long before that
time had passed the naval and colonial ascendency which
might have belonged to the Bourbon alliance had been forever lost to them.  The miscalculations of Louis XIV had
been repeated.  A few hundred square miles of territory
along the Rhine or in Flanders had weighed more heavily
in the balance than all America and India.  Such over-
estimation of Europe and its issues was of course characteristic of the eighteenth century and of very much later times.
England shared it with the other states, but her insular position, with the attention to trade and a navy which came
naturally with it, and the support of the wealth amassed by
the industrial revolution, enabled her, though a small state
with a non-military population and an inefficient govern-

ment, to win an empire of unprecedented extent and unique character. She did this by following lines of least resistance and availing herself of the opportunities afforded by the absorption of her chief rival in the wars of the continent to occupy without great expenditure of force many regions which at the time were considered of little value but later, either as a part of her scheme or as the result of the expansion of European interests, have come to be regarded as among the most desirable places of the earth. This process, moreover, was not the result of deliberate planning but proceeded from hand to mouth, as it were, the government availing itself of bargains as discovery, trade settlement or war brought them to its counter. By this policy of the tradesman among the nations, suiting the action to the immediate opportunity, the British Empire was slowly built up, the navy and the mercantile marine being the chief connecting links between its scattered and heterogenous parts.

The reopening of the struggle between Great Britain and her rivals was due to irritation caused by the illicit trade of the British in the seas of Spanish America and by the reprisals which were visited upon the offenders by the Spaniards. Under the treaties of Breda and Madrid English ships with a license from the king of Spain or if forced by storms or other perils, might enter Spanish harbors to furnish or refit, provided they notified the governor and came singly or in groups of not more than two or three at a time. This exception gave occasion for much intercourse with the Spanish colonies as did also the fact that in their voyages to their own colonies the British usually passed through Spanish seas. Piracy, encouraged as usual by the island colonists, was a still more fertile source of trouble for the Spanish, and this in various ways was supported by the British and their colonists for commercial advantage and as a means of forcing an entrance into the rich dominions of Spain. The enforcement of the privilege of the *assiento* under the treaty of Utrecht furnished additional opportunity for encroachment on Spanish rights. About 1730 the claim of the English to a right to cut logwood on the bay of Campeachy and to gather salt on the island of Tortuga, together with the controversy about the southern boundary of Carolina, became additional causes of irritation.

Against these encroachments and the contraband trade of the English, which was steadily on the increase, Spain made use of the right of search and seizure, to which, as a right exercised first in European and then in American waters, she was entitled under the earlier treaties. Her *guarda costas*, or coast guardships, analogous to those employed by the English, she made use of for the purpose. As their grievances against the British increased, the Spanish not only seized ships in ports but on the high seas and acts of increasing violence and cruelty were committed on both sides. The English considered themselves unjustly taken if they were not captured when actually engaged in illicit trade, but to the Spanish all English vessels were objects of suspicion. Seamen who were captured were taken to Spain and kept in prison for indefinite periods by delays of the Spanish tribunals. Stories of cruel treatment suffered during such imprisonment were circulated in Great Britain and gained wide credence. At the same time the complaints of British merchants of the losses they were suffering at the hands of the Spanish became more insistent and detailed. By the treaty of the first Family Compact France promised to aid the efforts of Spain to check the abuses from which she was suffering in her trade relations with England. The effect of this was to make Spain still more rigid in her policy, while ere long signs began to appear that France was abandoning the friendly attitude which she had maintained toward England since the establishment of the Regency. With 1737, under pressure from the merchants, negotiations over the points at issue between England and Spain became active, and soon after the question became the subject of prolonged and heated debates in parliament. Petitions on the subject of Spanish depredations began to pour in and demands to be made with increasing urgency for the submission of papers to the houses, so that the nation might be informed as to the course of negotiations. As Walpole was ready to acknowledge the claim of Spain to the right of search and was trying to avoid war, his opponents among both the Whigs and Tories charged him with betraying the rights of England and her seamen and merchants. His foreign policy was denounced as pusillanimous, war was demanded and a systematic effort was made by means of this cry to drive Walpole from power.

In 1738, though with great difficulty, Spain was brought to agree to a convention providing that plenipotentiaries should meet at Madrid and regulate the pretensions of the two crowns both in Europe and America, and the boundary between Carolina and Florida, and that the claims due the British from Spain should be adjusted and paid. As this looked toward a peaceful settlement, the convention was vigorously attacked by the war party in parliament and outside. Spain was so irritated by the despatch of a British fleet to the Mediterranean and so resolved upon her course for other reasons, that negotiations under the convention broke down and a declaration of war became necessary for Walpole, in October, 1739. With increasing difficulty the minister was able to maintain himself in office for a little more than two years longer, when he was forced out by a combination of the Whig factions which opposed him. As the war developed and France and the powers of central Europe became involved, Henry Pelham and his brother the duke of Newcastle, became the leaders of this Whig coalition and under their mediocre leadership the war was carried through to its end.

The initial operations of the war consisted of the expedition sent against the coast of South America and the island of Cuba under Admiral Vernon, an opponent of Walpole, assisted first by Lord Cathcart and later by Brigadier General Wentworth, as commanders of the land forces. As a reinforcement to the troops sent out from England, volunteers were called for, without the specification of quotas from all the continental colonies except Georgia, and South Carolina. Orders to raise these were sent to the governors and ex-Governor Spotswood, of Virginia, was appointed to the command of the force and placed in general charge of the measures to be taken to raise it.[1] Spotswood, now an old man in impaired health, soon started northward to visit New

---

[1] For the responses to this see Belcher Papers, II, 312, 331; N. H. Prov. Papers, V, 47–53; Conn. Recs., VIII, 324; Talcott Papers, II, 251–305; R. I. Recs., IV, 573, 576. N. Y. Col. Docs., VI, 147, 162–170; N. C. Col. Recs., IV, 427; and further references below.

York and other colonies to perfect arrangements and promote recruiting when he suddenly died, in Maryland, early in June, 1740. Governor Gooch, who from the first had taken active charge of raising the recruits from Virginia, now succeeded to the command and accompanied the force to the West Indies. Colonel William Blakeney, of the British army, was sent to the colonies as adjutant general of the expedition and coöperated in the task of equipping and subsisting it. According to the reports of the governors, the response to the appeal for recruits was prompt and even more than adequate in all, or nearly all, the colonies to which orders were sent. The hope of plunder which was aroused by the proposal of an expedition to the Spanish dominions was sufficient to enlist a quick response, which was not offset by any adequate idea of the dangers of the climate. The number of companies raised could not properly exceed the number of commissions for officers sent over, and in some colonies, for example Massachusetts, a considerably larger number of men were ready to go than could be accommodated in the companies for which commissions were provided. Some of these were allowed to go, and were provided with certificates of enlistment to be presented to the commander when they should reach the West Indies. In the Quaker colonies, however, such aversion appeared toward the plan as was natural, and there the expected numbers were secured either with difficulty or not at all. In Pennsylvania a warm dispute arose between Governor Thomas and the assembly over the right to enlist indented servants without the consent of their masters. Among the seven companies which were raised in that province a considerable number of servants were included, to the great loss, it was claimed, of their masters. The governor claimed that if the assembly offered a bounty, enough freemen would have been secured and all servants could have been rejected. In the end the superior right of the king to the service of all his subjects was recognized and the servants were not returned to their masters, though the assembly made provision toward paying for them.[1]

[1] Pa. Col. Recs., IV, 427–468. Conditions in New Jersey are described in the letters of Governor Morris. See papers of Gov. Lewis Morris, 87–120, N. J. Arch., VI, 99.

In the colonies generally the steps taken by the governors in order to secure recruits consisted in announcing by proclamation the instruction of the home government and then designating certain persons who from experience would be suitable to command the companies to raise the men. In Virginia musters were ordered to be held by commanders of the respective counties. As it was the plan of the British government to pay the troops from the date of enlistment, such advances as were made by vote of assemblies or by the governors to meet initial expenses of this nature were reimbursed by Colonel Blakeney in the form of bills on the paymaster general in England, which were sold at the prevailing rates of exchange in the colonies. Clothing, tents, arms and ammunition were also furnished by the British government. Transports were hired by the colonies and they went, at least for the most part, under British convoy. In Virginia [1] and one or two New England colonies small bounties were granted by the assemblies, but generally the pay and hope of plunder were relied upon as adequate to secure the required number of volunteers.

Outside of Pennsylvania, where a violent controversy was aroused between the governor and the assembly over the subject of defence in general and the Quakers made a determined effort in support of their cherished principle, this requisition was promptly and quietly met and, as has been said, in several instances more than the expected number of troops were raised. [2] In Virginia the business was carried on more promptly than elsewhere, pay being advanced to the troops from an early date and transports hired though at higher rates than were customary in England because they could not count on securing freight for the return voyage from the West Indies. [3] In other colonies, prior to Blakeney's arrival, because of lack of money to subsist their men, they had only been able to take the names of the persons who were willing to serve and not actually to enlist them. Owing to lack of specie in Virginia also, merchants could not cash government bills. The receiver general said he had not money and

[1] C. O. 5/1324, B. T. O. P. Va.

[2] C. O. 5/1270, B. T. Proprieties; Shepherd, Pa., as a Prop. Prov. 523 et seq.          [3] See letters of Gooch to Newcastle, C. O. 5/1337.

yet the men must be paid and while waiting for weeks and months for the arrival of the recruits from the north their ardor cooled and one hundred deserted. To meet the crisis Gooch himself had to advance £1200.

Though this requisition was successful far beyond anything that had been attained by the same policy in the earlier wars — a result which was due to the fact that the British government bore all or nearly all the expense — the expedition upon which the three thousand or more colonials who had been raised were sent, proved a tragic failure. Owing to the incapacity and blundering chiefly of Wentworth, not only did the British fail to capture Carthagena and Santiago de Cuba, against both of which they advanced, but their operations were delayed until the beginning of the wet season and to the tropical diseases which were induced thereby a large part of the land forces succumbed.[1]  Of the colonials only a few ever returned to their homes. By the middle of September, 1741, Gooch was back in Virginia recovering from the effects of the tropical climate and from a wound. He then wrote to Newcastle voicing for the first time, on behalf of himself and his subordinate officers, their complaints at the harsh treatment which had been meted out to them when on service with British regulars. Gooch had gone as quartermaster general and considered himself entitled to a seat in the council of war, but during the prolonged stay at Jamaica, he was systematically snubbed by Wentworth. Not until they were about to sail for Carthagena did Wentworth condescend to visit Gooch and show him a little more consideration. After the seige, in which Gooch was wounded, his good conduct forced Wentworth to acknowledge that he deserved all that he had expected. Certainly Gooch, who was one of the best of officials, thought it hard to be so treated after what Newcastle had written to him, and he had so long held the governorship of Virginia. With truth he could claim that he had done more than any one else in the northern colonies to promote the success of the expedition. In its furtherance he had spent more than his income and had incurred heavy

[1] See article on Admiral Vernon, by J. K. Laughton, in Dict. of Nat. Biog.

debts and now found that he had returned quite disabled in health.

As to the officers and men, they now felt for the first time the sting of that sharp discrimination between regulars and themselves which became a subject of such general complaint in the next war. Twenty-one of the colonial captains, in a memorial to Wentworth, complained that contrary to promises which had been held out to them, a captain younger than any of them had been advanced over them. They also complained that they and their men had been ill used by being placed on men-of-war instead of transports, that their subsistance money had been paid in Jamaica currency at a valuation twenty per cent lower than its actual value. Promises made through governors, they claimed, had not been kept and this would make the raising of troops in the colonies more difficult in the future. The complaints of the officers concerning their rank and the currency Gooch supported, but he could not induce Wentworth to promote any of them, though their behavior in the opinion of the governor, had been such as to entitle them to promotion in any service.[1] Thus ended in useless waste of life, and general disgust among those who were aware of the facts, the only intervention of the colonies in the military affairs of the West Indies.

The location of the Florida boundary was a standing subject of controversy between the Spanish and English governments. The English claim, as usually stated, extended to the south of the St. John's river, which is about midway between the thirtieth and the thirty-first parallels. But this could not be guaranteed by the treaty of 1670, since at that time no British settlements had been established south of St. Helena sound, near Beaufort, South Carolina. The Spanish therefore claimed that the settlement of Georgia, and specially the establishment of ports on the Altamaha, were in violation of their territorial rights. In 1736, they demanded the evacuation of all posts south of St. Helena sound,[2] while at about the same time Oglethorpe by a reconnaissance was seeking to locate the actual frontier on the mouth of the

[1] C. O. 5/1337.          [2] Stevens, History of Georgia, I, 149.

St. John's, though the charter limit of his own province was the Altamaha and no British settlements south of that region had yet been established. To the great irritation of the Spanish, Oglethorpe planted a military outpost, under the name of St. George's fort, on the north bank of the St. John's and stationed guard boats to patrol that river. On their part the Spanish had no settlements north of St. Augustine and no military outposts north of the immediate vicinity of the St. John's river. The overlapping boundary claims, as is well known, furnished permanent cause for hostile acts on both sides. In these the Indians were deeply involved, while the disturbed conditions operated as a continual menace to the stability of the slave system in both Georgia and South Carolina. Charges of intrigues with the Indians, of the extension of protection to runaway negroes and of the promotion of slave insurrections were bandied about between the two nationalities concerned. Though the balance of responsibility for these evils would be difficult, if not impossible, strictly to determine, the weight of evidence inclines strongly against the Spanish. They were even charged with indirectly inciting a dangerous slave insurrection at Stow, in South Carolina, in 1739.[1] The minor conflicts at sea, which so disturbed the Caribbean, also extended to the Florida and Carolina coasts, where attacks and seizures were made by both parties. It was unsettled conditions such as these which furnished a prominent cause of the war between England and Spain and, as soon as the hostilities began, brought the southern frontier into greater prominence than ever before. This furnished an additional illustration of the fact that relations had broadened since the earlier wars and that events and decisions could not much longer be confined within the narrow limits of the earlier time.

Because of the dangers revealed by these circumstances, the existence of which was also confirmed by repeated negotiations with the Spaniards, Oglethorpe visited England in 1737 and came back with a regiment which he had been authorized to recruit there and with an appointment as general and commander-in-chief of the forces of South Carolina and Georgia. His regiment came over in two detach-

[1] McCrady, S. C. under Royal Govt., 185.

ments; the largest of which accompanied Oglethorpe and reached Georgia under the convoy of two men-of-war in September, 1738. He had been instructed to ascertain and report the movements of the Spaniards in Florida, and yet to give them no provocation to attack and permit no encroachment upon them. He was also to put all the forts in the best condition for offence and defence and make such disposition of his force as would best secure the colony from unexpected attack. The southern end of St. Simon's island was now fortified and a road built connecting this fort with Frederica. At Frederica itself the whole town was inclosed with a fortification which Oglethorpe described as having been constructed according to "Monsieur Vauban's method." Thus the defensive works about the mouth of the Altamaha were extended and the larger part of the new regiment was stationed there. A visit to South Carolina in the following April for the purpose of assuming command over its forces, and a journey of three hundred miles later in the summer through the wilderness to Coweta, the principal town of the Creek nation, in order fully to insure their fidelity to the cause of the British, were other important measures in Oglethorpe's plan of defense against the Spanish.[1] His plans were conceived and executed with all the zeal and ability shown a little later by Governor Shirley, of Massachusetts, at the opposite extreme of the frontier, and their execution required of the leader much more personal exposure. Oglethorpe also had the advantage over the Massachusetts lawyer of training in the armies of Europe and under its most famous commanders, and came to the colonies with greater military reputation than had been attained by any one else who had held the post of governor or commander in any of the continental colonies.

When the general returned to Savannah from his visit to the Indian country he found despatches announcing that war had begun between England and Spain. Messengers were soon sent to the Creeks and Cherokees to rouse them to activity. Oglethorpe himself soon repaired to Frederica, while an outrage committed by Spaniards who had landed on Amelia island suggested reprisal which finally took the form

[1] Colls. of Ga. Hist. Soc., III, 81, 82, 100.

of a plan for the capture of St. Augustine. It had long been evident that there could be no hope of peace along the border until it passed into the hands of the British. An account of the operations of 1740 and 1742, which shall omit all unnecessary details, will reveal at once the faults and the merits of Oglethorpe's plans and their execution.

St. Augustine was defended by a garrison of about 600 Spanish troops, aided by a small body of militia and Indians.[1] The fort or castle was a square bastioned structure with thick walls of soft stone twenty feet high. It contained fifty pieces of mounted cannon, a part of which were brass twenty-four pounders. The town itself was protected by intrenchments and a covered way was in process of construction between the castle and the town. Sufficient troops were stationed elsewhere in Florida, especially on the Gulf coast, to raise the total to somewhat over 1300 men. The distance overland from the lower course of the St. John's to St. Augustine was about 45 miles. The easiest method of transport would have been by boat up the St. John's from St. George's fort, the place of rendezvous of the British, to some point nearly opposite St. Augustine, thus requiring only a short overland march. By previous reduction of Picolata, the only Spanish outpost on its left bank, the control of the river had been left in the hands of the British.[2]

In the later months of 1739 Oglethorpe applied to the lieutenant governor and assembly of South Carolina for aid in his projected expedition and informed them of the pre-

[1] Colls. of Ga. Hist. Soc., III, 108. A somewhat larger estimate is in S. C. Hist. Colls., IV, 24.

[2] The topography and other details of this campaign may best be followed in the report of the general assembly of South Carolina published in Colls. of S. C. Hist. Soc., IV and fully outlined by McCrady, S. C. under Royal Govt., 199 *et seq.* The accounts from Georgia sources are in first volumes of the histories by Stevens and Jones, supported by references in Oglethorpe's letters, in Ga. Hist. Colls., III. Of the controversial pamphlets which were published after the expedition, two supported the contention of the Carolinians and one that of Georgia and the friends of Oglethorpe. Of the first two James Kilpatrick was the author, and their titles were "An Impartial Account of the late Expedition against St. Augustine under General Oglethorpe" (London 1742), and "A full Reply to Lieutenant Cadogan's Spanish Hireling and Lieutenant MacKay's Letter concerning the Action at Moosa" (London 1743). The defence of Oglethorpe was by Lieutenant George Cadogan and was entitled "The Spanish Hireling Detected" (London 1743).

liminary steps which he had taken. Among these had been
a raid or two into northeastern Florida, which, to offset any
gain which had resulted, had certainly put the Spanish on
their guard against surprise.[1] To the first two estimates for
men, munitions and supplies which were submitted by the
general the assembly replied that the cost exceeded their
ability. Finally, in March, 1740, Oglethorpe visited Charlestown and secured the assent of the assembly to a somewhat
reduced estimate, on the strength of a report that St. Augustine was short of provisions, supported by the knowledge that
if the offensive was to be assumed it must be done quickly
before the beginning of hot weather and also before supplies
and reinforcements could arrive from Havana. As to the last
mentioned contingency, the presence of Vernon's and Wentworth's force in the Spanish seas may be supposed to have
operated as a deterrent upon plans which the Spanish in Cuba
may have had for the relief of St. Augustine.[2] Though the
province was exhausted by a recent visitation of the small
pox, the assembly of South Carolina was so impressed with
the possibility of removing what they chose to regard as the
chief source from which proceeded incitements to slave insurrections, that they responded rather liberally to Oglethorpe's demands. They voted a regiment of 400 men, a
troop of rangers, provisions for the same and for 500 Indians,
with a present of a gun, hatchet and blanket for each, a
considerable quantity of supplies and munitions and an armed
schooner.[3] Two hundred men, in addition to a company of
nearly fifty, were subsequently levied. The Carolina troops
were placed under the command of Colonel Vander Dussen.
From Georgia a force of about equal size with this was contributed, the nucleus of which was a detachment of 500 men
from Oglethorpe's regiment, to which were added 100 from
the militia.[4] The total land force somewhat exceeded 2000
regulars, militia and Indians. In addition, one forty-gun
ship and four of twenty guns each of the British navy were

[1] One raid occurred in January 1739/40. Colls. of Ga. Hist. Soc., III, 107

[2] The inaccessibility of Spanish sources makes it almost impossible to
treat these events from any other than the British standpoint.

[3] For preparations in So. Car., see C. O. 5/438, U. H. J. S. C., Feb. and
later months, 1740.

[4] Stevens, I, 170, 171; Jones, I, 329.

present ready to coöperate, though, as it proved, they were
unable to stay beyond the early days of July. The commander of one of these vessels was Captain Peter Warren.
About the time when the British expedition was starting,
St. Augustine was reinforced by the arrival of six half-galleys,
manned by 200 regulars and armed with 9 small brass cannon.
Two sloops loaded with provisions also came in. But even
with these reinforcements, the Spaniards scarcely numbered
one-half of the British force.

With such superiority of force and six weeks ahead during
which to invest the town by sea and land and push the siege,
it would seem as if success might fairly have been expected.
But instead, early in July, the forces retired without having
invested the town or achieved anything which could be called
a siege. The naval force returned to the West Indies or to
their cruises and the land troops to their respective colonies,
where they were disbanded or placed again on garrison duty.
Toward the end of the operations many of the Carolinians
had deserted. The cause of this fiasco became the subject of
controversy between the two colonies, the South Carolinians
asserting that it was due to the failure of the general to form
or attempt to execute any workable plan for besieging the
town, while the Georgians laid the blame on the delay of
South Carolina in sending aid and the poor quality and inadequate strength of it when sent. It is true that the Carolina
troops were somewhat late in arriving, but all the last half of
May was wasted by Oglethorpe in fruitless marches back
and forth between the lower St. Johns and points lying toward St. Augustine, and in attempts personally to reconnoitre
the town. At the beginning of June an advance in force toward the town and castle was made. But, instead of allowing
an assault to be made, with a fair prospect that the town
would be captured and that this would soon be followed by
the surrender of the castle, Oglethorpe distributed his force
in detachments at a number of points on the mainland to the
north and on Anastasia Island to the southeast of St. Augustine. This might indicate a large plan of investment by sea
and land. But the land force at least was not large enough
for this and its artillery was not brought sufficiently near to
town or castle to produce any effect. The warships did not

approach near enough to the town for a bombardment, while the Spanish half-galleys made it too dangerous, it was thought, for the ship's boats to effect a landing. At Fort Moosa a detachment under Colonel Palmer, which had been left unsupported in a post which was of no strategic importance, was forced to surrender after considerable loss of life at the hands of the Spanish. The commissariat was so mismanaged or neglected that detachments repeatedly found themselves in danger of being left without any food at all. Oglethorpe was the only officer who appears to have acted as general commissary, while many of his doings would indicate that he was also performing the duties of a scout as well as those of commander-in-chief. The Indians early became disgusted and went off. Vander Dussen and his men stood by the enterprise to the end, so that, except for some desertions, its failure cannot be attributed to lack of harmony between the forces of the two colonies concerned. This statement cannot, however, be made concerning the naval force. Without an effective coöperation of the sea and land forces such an operation as that against St. Augustine could not succeed. But Captain Peoree, the commander, and his force seem to have held aloof, to have been unwilling to risk anything and to have gladly found an excuse for abandoning the enterprise at least a month before the beginning of the hurricane season. This act sealed the fate of an expedition which, however well planned, in its execution conspicuously lacked a directing mind and was dissolved into a series of aimless manœuvres which may have furnished an interesting spectacle to the enemy, but nothing more.

Two years passed, and by that time the peril from the early expeditions of the British into the Caribbean and adjacent waters had sufficiently abated to open a prospect of safety for a joint expedition from Cuba and Florida against Georgia. Moreover, that such a counter-move as this should be attempted was almost inevitable after Oglethorpe's raid against St. Augustine. A force, variously estimated by the British at from 3000 to 7000 men, was mustered for this purpose.[1] A considerable fleet of vessels, large and small,

[1] Jones, Hist. of Ga., I, 344, 359; Harris, Memorials of Oglethorpe, 255. Charles Hicks, a merchant, deposed before the council of South Carolina that

transported and convoyed this force, the Cuban armament suffering somewhat from a storm on its way from Havana to St. Augustine. Although, since the last expedition relations between Georgia and South Carolina had been somewhat strained,[1] yet in response to a call for help a squadron sailed from Charlestown consisting of four of his majesty's guard-ships — two of 22 guns each and two of 8 guns each — and eight provincial vessels of armament ranging from 22 guns to 6 guns respectively.[2] This force was under the command of Captain Charles Hardy, but it did not arrive in time to share in the action, though the knowledge that such a squad-ron was in the neighborhood may have hastened the departure of the Spaniards. The object of the raiders was said to be the destruction of the posts along the coast as far north as Port Royal, which, they said, had been taken from them in time of peace. Oglethorpe had only a force of about 600 men with which to meet them; but the Georgians knew well the network of sounds, creeks, islands, forests and marshes which formed the topography of the coast in the vicinity of St. Simon's island and Frederica, the immediate objective of the Spanish attacks. The defensive works at these places were also of some value, though the fort on St. Simon's had to be abandoned, and the advance of the Spaniards was checked before they reached Frederica. As compared with the campaign of 1740 the situation was reversed. Upon the Spaniards now rested the difficulties of transporting their troops and supplies a long distance, of effecting a landing and defeating

---

the Spaniards had 45 sail in all, carrying about 1200 regulars, 400 to 500 negroes and mulattoes, and the rest volunteers and convicts from Vera Cruz. C. O. 5/369, B. T. O. P. S. C. Feb. 17, 1742/3. See also C. O. 5/441, Oct. 28, 1742, and Feb. 7, 1742/3.

[1] It appears from an entry in the Upper House Journal, May 20, 1742, that Fury, the agent, was persuaded by Glen — before he sailed for South Carolina as governor — and by others, not to print the report of the assembly from which we have drawn so much evidence that the failure of the expedition against St. Augustine was due to mismanagement on the part of Oglethorpe. A letter of Glen to a committee of the lower house in April, 1744, throws additional light on this subject. Lord Wilmington read part of the report and thought it would injure the province. General Wade thought men of his profession would think the expedition was ill described. Glen thought the report too long to attract attention in London.

[2] For preparations at Charlestown, see Ex. C. J. and N. H. J. for early summer of 1742, C. O. 5/441, and C. O. 5/443.

the enemy on a difficult coast, with which they were imperfectly acquainted. Though, as against defences of the colonial type, the possession of a naval force usually gave a decisive advantage, it was not so on a coast like that of southern Georgia. The Spaniards at first passed without difficulties the vessels and two small batteries on St. Simon's island and compelled their evacuation. But when the enemy landed for an advance on Frederica, one detachment was attacked in the woods with great spirit by Oglethorpe and a body of Highlanders and Indians and routed. Another party met a similar fate by falling into an ambush at a place which went henceforth by the name of "Bloody Marsh." The loss of more than 200 men and several officers in these encounters discouraged the invaders and occasioned dissensions among them, so that the Cubans separated from the rest and in the end, after committing some ravages, they all embarked and sailed away homeward. On this occasion the inefficiency and lack of persistence of the Spaniards were exhibited even more conspicuously than the shortcomings of the British had been two years before; while in his defence of Frederica, Oglethorpe and his men showed great dash and bravery, all appearing at their best.

This effort to secure the effective coöperation of a sea and land force had not been more successful than that of two years before, and after the return of Hardy to Charlestown without having even pursued the enemy to St. Augustine, controversy over his conduct arose between the captain on one side and Lieutenant Governor Bull and the council on the other. Delay in the preparation was attributed to desertions of seamen, which was encouraged by the colonists, and to the necessity of resorting to impressment. Contrary winds, it was said, prevented the pursuit of the Spaniards southward, while the fact that the largest Spanish vessels, on leaving, stood straight out to sea led to the supposition that they would turn north against Port Royal and Charlestown, and it was to protect them that Hardy returned immediately to port. Hardy assumed a lofty tone toward the governor and council and for a time they communicated only in writing while elaborate charges against the captain were prepared for submission to the authorities in England. Oglethorpe also com-

plained of alleged neglect of Georgia by her neighbor, and
the case of one Sterling who as quartermaster on the late
expedition, was imprisoned in Georgia for making charges
against her magistrates, served to enliven relations between
the colonies for some time.  Meantime for months a Spanish
invasion of South Carolina was looked for as imminent, and
the fear of this gave rise not only to extended plans for recruiting in North Carolina, but to an urgent plea for aid from
the West Indies.  This was directed by Bull to Vernon and
Wentworth, and in the fall of 1742 a small force was actually
sent from Jamaica to Charlestown, but as there was then no
immediate prospect of an invasion it soon returned.  In these
plans the entire coast of the Carolinas and Georgia was
treated as a unit, Charlestown was regarded as the central
point to be defended and the use by both combatants of naval
forces from the West Indies for the protection or attack of
this coast has also been noted.  But as 1743 opened it became
evident that the Spanish were not in a condition for large
offensive movements,[1] and the only event was a raid, in
March, by Oglethorpe and a small force from Georgia against
St. Augustine.[2]  The weakness of this post was well known,
but the efforts of the Georgians were by no means equal to
its capture.  A few months later occurred Oglethorpe's final
return to England, and with this formal military operations
on the southern frontier ceased for the rest of the war.  The
interests which centred attention on the western frontier can
best be considered under Indian relations.

The events which have just been described show that the
continental colonies were now being called into activity on
a larger scale on the southern frontier than at any earlier
period.  As soon as the war opened in France, in 1744, a
similar result followed on the northeast.  It was now that the
struggle for the control of the Gulf of St. Lawrence and of
the fisheries connected therewith began in earnest.  The expulsion of the French from Newfoundland in the previous war
had been followed by the removal to Cape Breton island —
now called Isle Royale — and the founding of Louisbourg on
its southern coast.  That harbor was selected because it was
open to the Atlantic and never closed by ice in winter, and

---

[1] See Ex. Council Journal of S. C. for 1742.      [2] Jones, I, 361.

by the expenditure of large sums upon works, the construction of which was continued for decades, it was made the stronghold of the French upon the North American coast.[1] In connection with a strong navy it would command the southern entrances to the gulf and river St. Lawrence. Its garrison and the officials who were appointed to govern the island were also intended to watch over French interests throughout that large part of Acadian territory which, according to their interpretation, had not been ceded to the British by the treaty of Utrecht. As, according to that interpretation, the cession included only the peninsula of Nova Scotia, which lay south of the Bay of Fundy, this might properly include territory at least as far west as the St. Croix river and extending northward along the coast as far as the gulf of St. Lawrence. Those parts of Acadia which lay west of these points fell more naturally under control from Quebec. The Micmac and Malecite tribes of Indians who inhabited the eastern parts of this region were allied in origin and interests with the Abenakis of Maine. They all lived under a common subjection to French influence, which now came to be exerted from Quebec and Louisbourg as its two centres and was chiefly transmitted through the activities of Catholic priests who were stationed at important points throughout the region. Costabelle and St. Ovide, the governors at Louisbourg, saw to it that French interests were upheld throughout the islands and in eastern Acadia, as Vaudreuil and his associates did along the New England border and the Great Lakes. The frontier was treated by the French as a unit and the same policy was applied throughout its entire extent. The policy which led Râle and his Indians of the Kennebec to lay waste the New England frontier was applied in Nova Scotia as well, all being ultimately guided from Paris as a centre.[2]

Annapolis and the country surrounding it to the breadth of three miles, which was surrendered to Nicholson and his force in 1710, lay like a small island in the southeastern part

[1] Murdock, History of Nova Scotia, I, 340; Kingsford, Hist. of Canada, III, 131.

[2] See utterances of Canadian officials and of the crown in N. Y. Col. Docs., IX, 878, 895, 939, 948, 956, 1002, 1107.

of this vast territory. Nova Scotia, as defined by the French after the treaty of Utrecht, was larger than Annapolis, but still it included only a very small part of the region claimed by the English and especially of that wider expanse over which roamed the savage allies of the French as they passed from one mission station or trading post to another. The weakness and almost insignificance of Nova Scotia in those days becomes still more apparent when one reflects that for a generation after the treaty of Utrecht not only were no efforts made to reach an agreement concerning its boundary, but the province itself was neglected and no new settlements in it were made either by emigrants from New England or from Europe. This attitude of indifference was maintained by the British government during the period when Louisbourg was being fortified by the French and in the presence of a native French population variously estimated from about 2500 to 12,000.[1] A part of the French lived near Annapolis, but by far the larger body of them were located in the northern peninsula, near the basin of Minas and Chignecto bay. Though the mere existence of Nova Scotia made the situation in eastern New England differ from those earlier times when Pemaquid was the remotest outpost, yet no more striking proof exists of the neglect of colonial interests by the early Whig administration than is afforded by the history of Nova Scotia for nearly forty years after the treaty of Utrecht.

It is not necessary in this place to explain in detail the policy which was followed toward the Acadians who were permitted to remain in Nova Scotia. It has been the subject of much controversial writing and editing, as a result of which the truth has been made pretty evident. The attitude of the British government, as revealed in the treaty of Utrecht and the letter of Queen Anne to Governor Nicholson was one of acquiescence in their going or staying, and that applied as well to the whole body of them as to a part. The choice was left to the Acadians, though they must exercise it within a specified time, and if they should remove they might sell their lands, and take their movable effects with them. But

---

[1] Among the many estimates, probably one of the most accurate is that of Casgrain for 1748 based on a description of Acadia by Le Loutre, in Documents inedits sur l'Acadie, I, 44.

in the absence of British settlers it is hard to discover the parties to whom their lands could be sold. During a period of two years the French who lived within the neighborhood of Annapolis were subject to the somewhat more precise requirements of the capitulation of 1710, but by the end of the war all the Acadians stood on practically the same footing. When with the passage of time, the situation cleared so that the parties concerned could more clearly discern their interests, it appeared that the Acadians had no real desire to remove, and neither did the French desire to have them. Though at one time the Acadians might have consented to a removal to Cape Breton, they never enjoyed the prospect of clearing the forests and making themselves new houses in that island. The soil where they lived was richer and more cultivated than what they were likely to find elsewhere. Of the adventurous spirit they possessed little or none whatever. Naturally British vessels were not provided for their removal and neither they nor the French authorities had interest or initiative enough to furnish the conveyances and overcome the other obstacles which attended the not very long journey from the head of the peninsula of Nova Scotia to Cape Breton.

Under these conditions the simple-minded Acadian peasants became from an early date the sport of political interests. The British saw that if they departed Isle Royale would be strengthened and only a few straggling colonists of their own nationality would be left to support and defend Nova Scotia against its enemies. Samuel Vetch saw this at the outset and with the passage of every decade the fact became clearer. On the other hand, the French desired to retain a hold upon the peninsula of Nova Scotia which they had been compelled to cede to the English by a treaty which they did not intend should be permanent, and made use of the Acadians as a convenient instrument for the purpose. To allow them to remain and take the oath of allegiance without qualification would defeat this object. Therefore the course pursued was to acquiesce in their remaining and at the same time quietly to uphold them in their natural inclination to avoid the taking of an unqualified oath. The obligation from which the Acadians always insisted that they should be excused was that of bearing arms in the service of the British and so against their own countrymen. Their priests, who chiefly managed the public affairs of these peasants, found this a convenient subject upon which to exercise their casuistry and practice their subtile diplomatic arts. The neighboring Indians assured the habitants that they were far more welcome to remain than would be English strangers to supplant them. The rapid growth of the Acadians in numbers and the strengthening of their settlements, especially in the northern part of the province, made it more difficult to remove them or to bring them completely under the obligations of English law. So weak was Nova Scotia as a province that a compromise was all that was attained.

Between 1715 and 1730, especially after the accessions of George I and George II, attempts were made to induce the Acadians to take the oath without qualification. But on one excuse or another it was avoided and all the efforts failed. In 1730 Governor Phillips induced most of the Acadians to take an oath the form of which was criticized by the board of trade as so ambiguous that the priests might easily convince their flocks that they were not bound to obey it. However, no other oath in written or printed form was ever taken by them. The French also continued to assert that their oath at this time contained an exemption from bearing arms and in virtue of this they were henceforth spoken of as the " Neutral French." In recent times evidence has come to light which goes to show that Phillips made the Acadians a verbal promise that they should enjoy this exemption. The memory of this they cherished and the fact in a general way was admitted by later governors. As such a promise could bind no one, except as a moral restraint upon the governor who made it, this promise, if it was made, simply formed another link in the chain of events which was drawing the Acadians onward to the tragedy of which they were being made the victims. No further efforts had been made to induce them to take the oath when war with France reopened in 1744 and Nova Scotia became at once involved in the struggle.[1]

[1] Controversy has done much to obscure as well as to illuminate the history of the Neutral French. So far as documents are concerned, Akin's

In the spring, as soon as news of the declaration of war arrived, the English fishing station at Canseau was seized by a force from Louisbourg. Later in the year and in the spring of 1745 three successive forces of Indians and of French and Indians appeared before Annapolis and attempted to reduce the post. The priest, Le Loutre, was leader of the body of Indians who came first. The first body of French troops came from Louisbourg and were under the command of Duvivier, the officer who had captured Canseau. Though the fort was in poor repair and its garrison numbered less than one hundred men who were fit for duty, the assailants were unable to capture the place. Reinforcements and supplies — though the men were very imperfectly armed — arrived in time from Massachusetts, while the assistance expected by sea for the French did not appear in time.[1] The expeditions of the French came overland through Chignecto and the region occupied by the " Neutral French." During the period of nearly thirty-five years since their conquest they had prospered under the mild British rule. No rents or taxes had been demanded from them. They had also been permitted to choose deputies to arbitrate petty disputes among themselves and to represent them in conferences with the British authorities. They had enjoyed perfect religious freedom and had prospered industrially. The administration of the English governor, Mascarene, had been especially mild

---

Nova Scotia Archives should be supplemented and corrected by the use of Abbé Casgrain's Documents Inedits. The French view of the episode will be found set forth in Casgrain's "Eclaircissements sur la Question Acadienne," in the Proceedings of the Royal Society of Canada, Vol. VI; in Romeau de Saint-Pere, Une Colonie Feodale en Amerique; and in Edward Richards' Acadia, Missing Links of a Lost Chapter in American History, two vols. In addition Akin's Nova Scotia Archives, which was edited in support of the English side of the controversy, and several volumes of the Collections of the Nova Scotia Historical Society contain material bearing on the subject Kingsford in his History of Canada, Vol. III, and Parkman, Half Century of Conflict, are the leading exponents of the English view. Murdock (History of Nova Scotia) is non-committal.

[1] A highly critical view of the conditions existing in Louisbourg, of the inefficiency of Duquesnal, the governor, and of the interest of the naval officers in trade, all of which and more contributed to this failure and to the disaster the following year, is contained in the Lettre d'un Habitant translated and published by G. M. Wood, under the title of "Louisbourg in 1745."

and he had treated the priests with scrupulous politeness. Under this treatment the Acadians had become reconciled to English rule and furnished little aid to Duvivier against Annapolis.[1] His harsh requisitions came as an unwelcome invasion and met with as little response as it was deemed safe to give. He was forced to rely chiefly upon the Indians for aid and therefore failed. The third force, under Marin, the trader, consisted of 600 Canadians and Indians. They found Annapolis so strengthened that they did not attempt a siege, but a part of both of the French and Indians were sent off upon a belated attempt to reinforce the garrison at Louisbourg. It, however, seemed exceedingly doubtful if the British would be able to hold Annapolis during another summer. Could the French of Louisbourg have sent vessels of war past the English cruisers which were watching that port and had they reached Annapolis in time, its capitulation must have followed. The work of 1710 would then have been undone, the New England frontier would have suffered a serious contraction, the Indians would have been encouraged to renew their attacks and conditions resembling those of 1700 would have returned.

But the peril to the fisheries from French cruisers and privateers operating from Louisbourg as a centre was what most forcibly struck the understanding of the New England merchants. So long as Nova Scotia remained so weak, the existence of Louisbourg was a most serious menace to New England interests, more so than was the existence of St. Augustine to the peace of Georgia and the Carolinas. William Shirley was sufficiently alert and in touch with all the interests, political and commercial, of New England to understand the situation from the outset. In the summer of 1744 he wrote to Commander Warren about the desirability of coming with his squadron to the relief of Annapolis. In the following November he wrote at length to the admiralty in England about the danger to which Annapolis had been exposed and the heavy loss which its capture would inflict on the northern colonies.[2] Even earlier in the autumn he had written to Newcastle about the state of affairs in Nova Scotia and Cape Breton, the doings of French and British privateers

---

[1] Murdock, II, 42.　　　[2] Admiralty Sec. In-Letters, 3817.

in those waters and especially of the possibility of capturing some French East Indiamen who were likely to touch at Louisbourg on their homeward voyage.[1] This information had much of value concerning Louisbourg and conditions existing inside the town and fortress there came to Shirley from British troops captured by the French and returned to Boston under flags of truce early in the fall of 1744. From his letters it would appear that the governor was the most alert and the best informed man in New England concerning the French and English posts to the eastward, what had happened there recently and what seemed likely to happen in the near future. In January, 1774/5, Newcastle wrote that the king had decided to order Warren — the same officer, though now with higher rank, whom we met five years earlier before St. Augustine — to operate with his squadron in the waters about Nova Scotia and Cape Breton in order to protect Annapolis and distress the enemy, and Shirley was ordered to afford him all proper assistance and concert with him such measures as seemed necessary.[2]

It has often been said that William Vaughan of Damariscotta, son of the former lieutenant governor of New Hampshire, graduate of Harvard but in later life land speculator and trader in fish and lumber on the Maine coast, first suggested the expedition of 1745 from New England against Louisbourg. This distinction has also been claimed for Colonel John Bradstreet and for Judge Robert Auchmuty.[3] But whatever these men may have done or suggested, the real moving spirit in the enterprise was the governor. For months his attention had been closely fixed on affairs in that region, and such was his ambition, resourcefulness and love for devising military schemes, that one need not suppose him to have lagged behind any one in forming a plan of this kind. By or before the middle of December, 1744, the general assembly in Massachusetts, in consulting about the best methods of carrying on the war, had judged that it would be advantageous if that province and New Hampshire should

[1] Lincoln, Corresp. of Shirley, I, 145.
[2] *Ibid.*, 156.
[3] Parkman, Half Century of Conflict, II, 83. See also references in Hutchinson, Douglass, Belknap and Palfrey, and also Goold, in Colls. of Me. Hist. Soc.

act in conjunction and had expressed the desire that a joint commission should be appointed for the purpose. Shirley wrote to Governor Wentworth on the subject and the latter approved the plan.[1] Somewhat later Massachusetts actually appointed its members of the committee, but the assembly of New Hampshire did not fall in with this project, though at the proper time it faithfully performed its share in the enterprise.

Before the time had come for finally arranging terms of coöperation with New Hampshire, Shirley surprised the house at Boston by asking it to pledge itself to secrecy respecting the matter he was about to lay before it. It readily acceded. On January 9 he then presented his famous message urging that an expedition be sent against Louisbourg.[2] The motive to which he appealed was the commercial one, that this would more effectively promote the interests of Massachusetts in trade and the fishery than anything which could be done. He did not argue that an expedition in order to bring this result, should end in the capture of the fortress. He thought it would be justified if it broke up the out-settlements of the French, destroyed their cattle and magazines, wrecked their fishing stages and so weakened their defences as to leave the harbor exposed. Conceived in this way, the expedition would be of the same nature as the raids of Colonel Church in the preceding war, though on a larger scale. Shirley estimated that two thousand men might accomplish what has just been described. A joint committee was appointed by the two houses and after debating the subject for two days it reported that Massachusetts alone could not raise a sufficiently large force and therefore they urged the governor to ask for a grant for the project from the crown.[3]

This was equivalent to a rejection of the plan and the governor now turned to the merchants for help in further stimulating action.[4] Petitions, inspired by the governor, were circulated, especially in the trading communities of Salem, Marblehead and Boston. Within a few days a numerously

[1] Corresp. of Shirley, I, 154.
[2] Gen. Court Recs. of Mass.; Corresp. of Shirley, I, 159.
[3] Hutchinson, Hist. of Mass., II, 366.
[4] See Parkman, II, 86, for the story of his interview with James Gibson

signed petition from Marblehead was presented to the council
and it was sent down to the house accompanied with another
message on Louisbourg.  Shirley stated that he was informed
that the favorable attitude toward the expedition, which was
shown in this petition, existed throughout the maritime sections of the province, and recommended that a hearing be
given to the petitioners.  This was done by another joint committee.  While this body was considering the petition from
Marblehead, the governor sent another message to the house.
When compared with his first message, this revealed a noticeable enlargement of ideas.  He now spoke of a force of three
thousand men, which should be raised not only in Massachusetts but in the other New England colonies and New York as
well, and that the fortress itself might be taken if this force
could remain masters of the field until troops and ships sufficient to reduce the island could arrive from England.[1]  This
message was turned over to the committee which was considering the petition from Marblehead, to which several
members were added, among whom was William Pepperell.
At the same time a petition was received from a great number
of merchants and others of Boston describing the annoyance
which the English suffered from the French at Cape Breton
and asking that the expedition be undertaken.  Pepperell
reported from the committee that their meeting had been
attended by two who had lately been prisoners at Louisbourg
and by others who as traders were well acquainted with the
place.  They stated that the garrison there consisted of only
500 or 600 regular troops and that among the inhabitants
there were not more than 300 or 400 fighting men; that they
had only a small quantity of provisions, no strong vessels in
the harbor and that the place was less capable of defence
than it would probably ever be again.  The committee therefore found in favor of an expedition for the reduction of the
place and that the governor be asked to call for 3000 volunteers and that all the other New England colonies, New
York, New Jersey and Pennsylvania be applied to for quotas.
This report was accepted by both houses, though the majority
in its favor in the house of representatives was only one.[2]

[1] Gen. Court Recs.;  Corresp. of Shirley, I, 167.
[2] Gen. Court Recs.;  Shirley Corresp., I,  169;  N. H. Prov. Papers, V, 266.

Though the majority was so small, the controlling element in the province were so active in support of the plan, that preparations for it were made with energy and success. This was to be a major operation of New England under the lead of Massachusetts and the administration measures which were taken in preparation for it were not essentially different from those employed under Dudley in the previous war. A supply bill of £50,000 was passed and bills of credit issued as usual. Instead of a commissary being appointed, a joint committee of the houses was designated to secure not only provisions but proper transportation for the troops. They expended from the general appropriation sums for special purposes under authority from the general court. In the purchase of supplies the products and vessels of Massachusetts were to have the preference. An embargo was laid to continue until after the expedition sailed, but it did not prevent news of the plan reaching the enemy. Because of the need of them for a cargo, the governor was asked by the houses to ask the commanders of the guardships in Massachusetts waters for their aid and with the aid of the committee he was also to procure the services of other designated vessels. Except for securing seamen just before the expedition started, enlistment and not the draft was the method used for filling the ranks, and from experience gained in raising troops in 1740, it was voted to pay down to the recruiting officers 2s. 6d. for each man whom they enlisted. An act to encourage enlistment was passed. One month's pay was advanced to the recruits on enlistment and 5s. per week was allowed to every man for subsistence. Though on the whole recruiting proceeded rapidly, in its later stages bounties were offered. Firearms from the province magazine were delivered to those who had none, the captain of each company giving a receipt for as many as his company received, the receipts being security that the arms should be paid for out of the soldiers' wages. Cannon were taken from the forts.

Shirley also applied himself diligently to procuring aid from the other colonies. Letters were sent to the governors of all the colonies as far south as Pennsylvania. John Choate of the house and Thomas Barry of the council were appointed to visit Connecticut, New York and New Jersey. Hutchinson was sent on the same errand to Rhode Island. In Connecticut a special session of the general court was called, late in February, and in this and a later session full preparations were made for the dispatch of men, armed sloops and transports and stores for the soldiers.[1] The steps taken to procure volunteers and equip and pay them were much the same as those taken in Massachusetts. Deputy Governor Roger Wolcott was appointed to command this contingent, with the rank of major-general. The contrast between the attitude of Connecticut now and in the earlier wars, when she could not be induced to send a force of any strength even to the New Hampshire frontier, is worthy of notice.

Rhode Island was still involved in the controversy with Massachusetts over her northern boundary. She had not yet paid the debts incurred for the disastrous expedition of 1740. She had eight or ten privateers out cruising and did not expect so much from the fishery as did the two provinces to the north of her. Yet she voted to raise 150 volunteers.[2] A special act was passed and the usual encouragements offered for enlistment. It was also voted to fit out the colony sloop with 26 guns, 130 seamen and supplies of all sorts to serve until the beginning of July. These steps were taken on the supposition that Shirley had full authority from the British government for his enterprise. But when it was found that he had not, zeal abated. The old feeling of dislike toward Massachusetts so far prevailed that the troops were finally disbanded, though the sloop went as a convoy of the Connecticut transports. The men, too, were raised again, but arrived too late to join in the siege. New Hampshire, with her accustomed acquiescence, her interest in the enterprise also being as great as that of Massachusetts, voted a handsome contingent.[3] There was some dispute over the terms under which the bills of credit for this expenditure should be regulated, but this was adjusted and £13,000 were finally issued. All the other provinces to which application was made excused themselves, though New York sent ten cannon

---

[1] Conn. Recs., VIII, 83 et seq.
[2] R. I. Recs., V, 100 et seq., 145 et seq.
[3] N. H. Prov. Papers, V, 266, 272, 276–296.

— 18 pounders — which were of special value in the siege, and New Jersey and Pennsylvania sent some provisions which arrived after the siege was over.

The selection of a commander was not the least difficult part of Shirley's task. The honor belonged naturally to Massachusetts, because she furnished more than three-fourths of the entire force. But neither she, nor any of the colonies concerned, possessed men who had had military experience on any but the smallest scale. Not for thirty years had any expeditions like those which had formerly started for Canada been fitted out, and then Francis Nicholson had been considered the only available commander. In Râle's War and the expedition of 1740 to the West Indies there had been no opportunity for the development of such talent as was required for such an enterprise as was now being planned. The only governor who was inclined to claim the honor was Benning Wentworth, of New Hampshire, but in the opinion of Shirley his gouty legs ruled him out. The governor's choice fell upon William Pepperell, of Kittery Point, and all things considered, it was as fortunate a choice as could have been made. In origin and execution this expedition was substantially a civilian enterprise, and Pepperell was no more absurd as its commander than was the lawyer Shirley as its organizer. Though Pepperell had never led a regiment in battle or on the march, he had long been the colonel of one of the militia regiments of York county and had been zealous in his efforts to make it more efficient. He was a man of wealth, active and highly respected throughout northern New England. He was genial and popular in his manners. According to existing methods, he had large business experience and good connections. These qualifications were valuable in the work of preparing for the expedition and in its general management. Pepperell's name also was an asset of great value to the recruiting officers, at least throughout Maine and New Hampshire. Judging by the standards which necessarily obtain in colonial communities, as well as by the history of the expedition, the appointment of Pepperell must be regarded as especially fortunate. It was in harmony with the relations in which the colonies stood to one another that the commanding officers were commissioned by all the three.

Seven weeks only were consumed in the organization of the expedition. When complete it consisted of a total of 4300 men. Of these Connecticut contributed 516, New Hampshire 304 in her own pay and 150 in the pay of Massachusetts. The rest, to the number of about 3300, were raised by Massachusetts. In Maine the enthusiasm for the service was greatest, she contributing about one-third of the Massachusetts contingent, and sending out more than one-third of her entire male population which was of military age. This is to be accounted for in part by the popularity of the commander, but more by hatred of the French intensified by prolonged and terrible sufferings at their hands. The New England " navy " was commanded by Captain Edward Tyng and consisted of six vessels from Massachusetts, two sloops each from Connecticut and Rhode Island and one sloop from New Hampshire. The largest vessel was a frigate — the *Massachusetts* — of 24 guns. Three other vessels carried 20 guns each and the rest carried a less number. The New England vessels had about 204 guns all told, and 12 swivels. The heaviest cannon they had were 22 pounders. Two large men of war of the French fleet would equal them all in number of guns and far exceed them in weight of metal; in short they would have the " navy " and the transports under its protection at their mercy.

Hence arose the imperative necessity, if possible, of procuring the aid of Warren. On January 29 Shirley had written to Warren, at Antigua, that the expedition had been decided upon and expressing the hope that the commodore would support it with a sufficient force to make possible a blockade of the harbor of Louisbourg by the middle of March.[1] Warren, who was an uncle of William Johnson of New York fame, had married a sister of James De Lancey and had invested largely in lands on the Mohawk, was strongly inclined to help, but as orders to do so had not arrived from England, on the advice of a council of his officers, he was forced to decline. A letter to this effect was sent to Shirley, the discouraging effect of which was sure to be so great that he did not dare to make it public. But a few days after Warren had sent his dispatch to Shirley, the order mentioned

---

[1] Admiralty Sec. In-letters, 3817.

above came from Newcastle, and on its strength he started northward with his three ships, the "Superbe," "Mermaid," and "Lancaster." The first of these carried 60 guns, and the last two forty guns each. Before he reached the New England coast he met a fishing schooner from the officers of which he learned that the expedition had sailed. The master he took on board as a pilot and, after writing to Shirley of the course he was taking, started direct for Cape Breton.[1] Before the expedition started, hopes were entertained that the cannon in the Grand Battery at Louisbourg might be captured and turned against the French, an event which actually occurred. This, together with the discovery of some cannon which the French had buried on the beach, went far toward furnishing the English with artillery, of which they were almost destitute and without which a successful siege would have been impossible.

In estimating the motives from which this and all similar enterprises of New England sprang and which helped to carry them through to such success as was attained, the religious and emotional element must not be overlooked. This expedition followed close on the heels of the Great Awakening which had stirred again the religious emotions of those communities, and had by so much stirred their anti-Catholic prejudices. This, combined with the emotional reactions caused by the French and Indian atrocities, kept alive a state of feeling from which a glorification of a raid against a French stronghold as a crusade could most naturally proceed. The Rev. Thomas Prince exclaimed, "The heavenly shower was over; from fighting the devil they must turn to fighting the French." In the eyes of the clergy and their sympathisers these events were in a large measure providential and this feeling had its influence in promoting the general acclaim with which the appointment of Pepperell to command was received. His standing as a church member was high and unimpeachable, much higher than that of Phips when he was appointed to command the expedition against Quebec. For the success of an officer of that character prayers were offered and sermons were preached in multitudes of homes and churches with the highest assurance that they would bring divine aid. Fasts were held which when the victory

[1] 1 Mass. Hist. Colls. I, 18.

had been won, were turned into thanksgiving. One of the strongholds of the papal antichrist had been captured and its altars levelled. Pepperell had asked Whitefield whether or not he should accept the command, and Whitefield had expressed doubt about the success of the plan and told Pepperell that he must be prepared for reproach if he failed and for envy if he succeeded. Later, however, at the request of Henry Sherburn, commissary of the New Hampshire regiment, he suggested as the motto of the flag, "*Nil desperandum, Christo duce.*" [1] "I doubt not but the cause is God's so far as we can well say any cause of this nature well can be," wrote the Rev. John Barnard. Deacon John Gray, of Biddeford, reached the highest point of enthusiastic expectation when he exclaimed, in a letter to Pepperell, "Oh, that I could be with you and dear Mr. Moody in that single church to destroy the images there set up and [hear] the true Gospel of our Lord and Saviour there preached." [2]

William Douglass, the Boston physician, in commenting on the expedition, criticised it as an enterprise which was "much above our capacity," it had a lawyer for contriver, a merchant for general, and farmers, fishermen and mechanics for soldiers.[3] He viewed its success as the result of good luck, which might at any time have changed and brought defeat at the end. Then, as it was wholly a colonial undertaking, its cost would not have been reimbursed and, as was the case after Phips' Canadian expedition, the people would for generations have been burdened with the debts incurred and would have cursed those, who had caused the disaster. The effects of such plans on the finances and currency of the colonies were always vividly present before Douglass' mind and that led him to view it from a more modern and critical standpoint. The same was true of Hutchinson, who also called attention to the good fortune which attended even the preparations and to the extravagant enthusiasm which was aroused.[4] This certainly helped to promote another period of inflation of the currency with its attendant evils.

[1] Parsons, Life of Pepperell, 51.
[2] The Pepperell Papers, 6 Mass. Hist. Colls., X, 106, 116.
[3] Douglass, Summary, Historical and Political, I, 336.
[4] Hutchinson, II, 369. Belknap, at a date subsequent to the Revolution, continued the criticism of the enterprise in its absurd aspects, which has culminated in our own day in the work of Parkman.

The crudity and inexperience which Douglass saw revealed in this expedition, and which were shown as well in all colonial enterprises, conspicuously appeared in Shirley's instructions to Pepperell. In the preparations for the expedition, Shirley had shown great diligence and much foresight. He interpreted with skill the information given by the returned prisoners concerning dissensions in the garrison and the comparative weakness of Louisbourg, notwithstanding its great apparent strength. From this may have arisen Shirley's idea that it would be possible to take Louisbourg by surprise and sudden assault and that in instructions to the general he could specify every important step in the process of accomplishing this.[1] Other governors and officials, in giving instructions to commanders, had necessarily left details to be worked out on the spot; directions had been general. But Shirley ignored the difficulties of a rocky coast, in a stormy season, with ice and fog to contend with in addition to a powerful enemy, and thought Pepperell could go straight to the works, could land, surprise and capture the town in a single night. It is due to the governor to say that provision was made in his instructions for the failure of surprise and the eventuality of a siege, but even with this allowance the document is a peculiar one and may be unique in the annals of military administration.

It is not necessary in this place to give a detailed account of an event which has been many times described and which is among the most familiar in our colonial history. But a brief reference to some of its most striking features will show how clearly Pepperell was able to live up to his instructions. The forces from the three colonies reached Canseau at different times during the months of March and April; those from Connecticut were about a month behind those from New Hampshire. For about three weeks after his own arrival, Pepperell was forced to remain at Canseau, because there was so much ice along the shore of Cape Breton as to make it impossible to land. " The weather continues thick and dirty with the wind at Northeast," indicates another source of perplexity. But Pepperell found every moment of this time

---

[1] These instructions in revised form are in Mass. Hist. Colls., I, 5. A first draft are in the Mass. Arch.

valuable, as the troops had not yet been drilled or formed into detachments, nor their arms properly examined and prepared for use.[1] It was found that many of the arms were defective as the extra stores had not arrived, the gunsmiths were set to work repairing them but at the best some of the men had to proceed with a very poor equipment. Such drilling and organization as they got was the result of the brief stay at Canseau. In the presence of such facts as these the idea of a capture by surprise vanished. As they evidently were facing a siege, the question of provisions became pressing. The supply which had been brought with them was inadequate and a dispatch was therefore sent back to Shirley to hurry on an additional supply. Shirley was already attending to this and induced the committee of war to purchase enough for an additional month beyond the time for which supplies had already been collected. While the troops were lying at Canseau two brigantines loaded with rum and molasses were taken as prizes and their cargoes were added to the stock of provisions.

From Warren Shirley learned, of course, that the British government was favorable to the enterprise, though it had not expressly authorized it. This encouraged him to proceed in the hope that aid might still come direct from England. On April 23 Warren arrived off Louisbourg and friendly relations were at once established between him and Pepperell and these, on the whole, were maintained during the siege. Thus one of the most serious dangers to the undertaking was avoided. In his letter to Warren at Antigua Shirley had suggested that he (Warren) might take command of the expedition.[2] When the squadron arrived, Shirley informed Pepperell that the command of the entire sea force before Louisbourg would be transferred to Warren, since that seemed to be the meaning of the letter which Newcastle had sent the previous January. " Had I not received these precise orders," wrote Shirley to Pepperell, " I should have insisted upon my command given you over the sea forces, . . . against every person whatever, and you must be sensible that this is not a preference given to him by me, but only acting

---

[1] Pepperell's letters to Shirley, in 1 Mass. Hist. Colls., I, 15 *et seq.*, show what occurred on the voyage and at Canseau.     [2] *Ibid.*, 36.

in obedience to his Majesty's orders."[1]   It is thus clear that
Shirley in his zeal had laid the train which might have caused
a bitter quarrel.  But the good sense of the two commanders
prevented it.  During most of the siege Warren's attitude
was such as he declared it would be in one of his earliest
letters to Pepperell; " You may be assured I will use my
utmost endeavors to prevent any succors getting in to Louisbourg and to be in every shape as serviceable to the present
expedition as possible."[2]   When, in the midst of the siege,
in a moment of irritation because of lack of proper cooperation, Warren informed Pepperell of Shirley's original
intention as to the command, the latter did not allow his
equanimity to be disturbed and so general harmony was
maintained to the end.

Shirley had imagined that the passage from Canseau to
Chapeau Rouge or Gabarus bay could be made in one day
and that during the following night a landing could be effected
and the town captured by assault.  By the latter days of
April the ice had cleared away sufficiently to admit of the
landing of the force on Cape Breton island.  A new blockhouse meantime had been built at Canseau and a small
garrison was left there to facilitate communication with New
England and to give warning of the approach of reinforcements for the French from Nova Scotia or Canada.  It took
Pepperell's force a day and a night to make the passage from
Canseau to Gabarus bay, on the southern shore of Cape
Breton, west of Louisbourg, where the landing was to be
made.  Though the enemy at once raised an alarm and sent
out a force to oppose the landing, it was not of sufficient
strength seriously to obstruct it.  It took two days to land
the troops and nearly a fortnight longer to land the artillery,
military stores and provisions.  The landing of these was
attended with great difficulty, as it had to be done from the
open sea upon a beach over which the surf ran so high
that sometimes for days nothing could be landed.  As the
flat boats which were used in landing often could not reach
the shore, the men were obliged to wade high in the water in
order to save everything which would be damaged by being

---

[1] Shirley Corresp., I, 156; 1 Mass. Hist. Colls., I, 19.
[2] Pepperell Papers, 131.

wet. The men had to dry themselves as best they could without change of clothing in the cold air of that latitude; the nights were very chilly and generally attended with thick fogs. Scarcely any tents had been brought, and hence the men had to improvise shelter with old sails stretched over poles or spruce boughs piled over rude huts. It is no wonder that under such conditions sickness prevailed and the desire to return home soon became prevalent. Yet the open winter which had facilitated preparation was followed by a spring without a storm of such severity as to hinder the expedition, and as the season advanced the weather improved.

After the cannon had been landed they had to be dragged through a morass between the landing place and the hills back of the town. As the place was exposed to fire from the town, this all had to be done at night. At first the men harnessed together and sinking up to their knees in mud, dragged the cannon through. But finally a New Hampshire shipwright, who was also a lieutenant-colonel, overcame the difficulty in part by having sledges built of plank on which the cannon were drawn. The men worked on with great patience and enthusiasm until they had planted a goodly array of cannon and mortars on the ridges a mile or less from the fortifications. At the very beginning of the siege the troops were cheered by the occupation of the Grand Battery, which was located at the interior of the harbor opposite its entrance. Attention had early been fixed on the importance of securing this, while the French, because of the poor condition of its defences and of the number of men who were required to hold it, had resolved on its abandonment. Vaughan and his men who took possession of the works found a valuable supply of ammunition and other ordnance stores and of cannon of large size which the French had spiked but had not put beyond the possibility of repair and later use. This gain was invaluable in several respects to the besiegers.

The remaining defences of Louisbourg were the Island Battery, at the entrance to the harbor, with thirty 28-pounders, mortars and several guns, and the strong fortifications surrounding the town itself. This was situated on a neck of land extending eastward into the harbor, and reducing the channel at its entrance to a width of less than half a mile. Extending across the base of this tongue of land, a distance of about 1200 yards, was the strongest line of defence of the fortress. The ramparts, built of stone, were from 30 to 36 feet high, with a ditch in front 80 feet wide and 30 feet deep. A marsh extended out from the glacis of the fortress and added greatly to the difficulty of storming the place. After the siege was over about ninety cannon were found in this fortress. The garrison consisted of 560 regulars and between 1300 and 1400 militia, levied from the inhabitants of the town and the settlements on the island. By the exploit of Captain Donohue, at Tatmagouche harbor, a force of about 300 Canadians and as many more Indians, which had been hovering about Annapolis, were prevented from reaching the vicinity of Louisbourg and molesting its besiegers.[1]

Conditions within Louisbourg were not favorable to a long and vigorous defence. A few months before there had been a mutiny among the regulars in the garrison, and such was the distrust of the fidelity of the soldiers and the lack of courage among soldiers and officers, that no sorties were attempted. Duchambon, the governor, and commandant, was not a strong man, and his predecessor had been inferior in quality to him. The readiness to abandon the Grand Battery revealed distrust and lack of courage on the part of the garrison. Though well supplied with food and ammunition, they are charged with having wasted the latter. Now that the blockade was complete, no more could be obtained and toward the last the supply ran low. A large French sloop, the "Vigilant," was captured by Warren and furnished the British with an additional supply of ammunition. Therefore, when all the elements of the situation are taken into account, it would appear that Shirley's undertaking was not so rash as some of his contemporaries and others would have us believe.[2]

The main operation of the siege was the bombardment of the town and its defences by Pepperell's main force from the hills in the rear. Though some of the mortars burst and the gunnery was anything but scientific, it proved effective, as the weeks passed and the batteries were advanced nearer and

[1] The Journal of Captain William Potes, XXVI, 29 et seq.
[2] Evidence from the Lettre d'un Habitant confirms this view.

nearer, in making breaches in the walls which the garrison were unable to repair. There was abundance of energy and enthusiasm, but very little discipline. Frolics were of frequent occurrence in the camp behind the lines, the good nature and popularity of the commander being a substitute for rules and articles of war. According to colonial custom and his instructions, Pepperell held frequent councils of war and consulted his colleagues in reference to all important measures. It was on its advice that a plan to storm the fortress was "deferred for the present." The alternative to a storming party was an attempt to silence the Island Battery, which commanded the entrance to the harbor, so as to open the way for the advance of Warren to close quarters so that he could coöperate with the land forces in a general bombardment. An attempt to capture the Island Battery by a surprise assault at night failed, with a loss to the British in killed, wounded, and prisoners of nearly two hundred men. They later succeeded in planting a battery behind it on Lighthouse Point and its fire silenced the guns on the island.

It was now near the middle of June. Breaches had been made in the walls on the landward side and the garrison and inhabitants were suffering severely from privation and the steady fire of the enemy. Many buildings had been injured or wrecked by the fire of the besiegers. The way was also open for a combined attack by the land and sea forces, and the two commanders had reached an understanding that this should be attempted. The French knew that such an attack was altogether likely and they feared its disastrous results. Warren could have brought more than 300 guns from his squadron to bear on the town at once, while the stock of ammunition in the fortress was nearly exhausted. The people of the town petitioned Duchambon to capitulate and he yielded. On June 15 a suspension of hostilities pending negotiations for surrender was asked and granted. Duchambon then proposed several articles of capitulation, some of which were rejected. The articles, as finally agreed upon, provided that the garrison should march out with the honors of war and, as soon as possible, should be transported to France; that they should not serve against the English for the space of one year; that the commissioned officers of the garrison and inhabitants of the town should be permitted to remain in their houses, with free exercise of religion, till they could be removed. The Island Battery was then occupied as security and the next day the British squadron entered the harbor and the land forces the town. Though the town could not have been taken without the coöperation of Warren's squadron, the siege had been the work of the land forces. As was proper, Pepperell received the keys of the town and fortress and in due time delivered them to the Governor, when he visited Louisbourg in the autumn. But a rumor spread that the surrender was made to Warren and this occasioned violent protests from New England. The *Habitant* is authority for the statement that jealousy existed between the two commanders over this point, but it did not mar the external regularity and friendliness of their conduct up to the very end.[1]

The expedition of 1745 against Louisbourg should be compared not so much with combined military and naval operations in Europe as with similar colonial expeditions of earlier or contemporary dates. Its relative merits and success can best be seen when it is brought into comparison with the expeditions of the earlier wars against Port Royal, with Phips' expedition against Quebec, and with Oglethorpe's expedition against St. Augustine. When viewed in relation to these it stands forth conspicuously as by far the greatest success which the colonists had yet won in arms. In comparison with the failure of both the land and naval force — though under officers of European training — before St. Augustine in 1740 it merits distinction. The same can be said with equal truth when it is compared with the larger operations of the first two wars. Abundant evidences of inexperience, with many a ludicrous incident, appear in its history, but above them all is to be seen an instinct which seized upon the right moment, foresight in preparation and a diligent spirit of coöperation among those who were concerned, which merited success and won it. It was the only important victory, and certainly the most dramatic one,

---

[1] For Shirley's accounts of the siege see Shirley Corresp., I, 273, and his "Letter to the Duke of Newcastle with a Journal of the Siege of Louisbourg, etc.," London, 1746.

which had yet been won by the British in the colonial wars. It was almost the only event which gives to the third war any significance in the annals of the continental colonies. How rich an atonement it was for the earlier indifference of Massachusetts toward the proposals for the fortification of Pemaquid! The impression made by the victory is indicated not only by the frantic rejoicings with which it was welcomed in New England, but by the reception with which the news was greeted in New York and Philadelphia. In England also it was welcomed with bonfires and rejoicings, while almost every city presented congratulatory addresses to the king in honor of the event. The royal approbation of their services was expressed by direct order of the king to the officers and soldiers who had participated in the siege. Pepperell was created a baronet — the first time such an honor was conferred upon a native of the American colonies. Warren was promoted to the rank of admiral and was appointed governor of Louisbourg,[1] though during the interval until the arrival of his commission he and Pepperell administered the duties of this office jointly. Shirley received a colonel's commission and he and Pepperell each were authorized to raise and command a regiment of the British line in America. These honors show that the capture of Louisbourg was the first British victory of the colonial wars which was considered of sufficient importance to deserve recognition. It served to a degree to offset a too long list of wasted efforts or disgraceful blunders, or perhaps to indicate the turning of the tide and the approach of a period of decisive success.

But the usual discouragements were to follow. Though all the French were removed, the town of Louisbourg proved a breeding place of disease for the troops who were left there for its defence. Seven hundred of the New England troops who were found unfit for further service, were sent home, but the rest were retained to garrison the place until commands should come from England. Then two regiments from Gibraltar were ordered to be transferred to Louisbourg, but such delays ensued that these regiments actually spent the winter in Virginia and did not reach their destination until the next spring.[2] A mutinous spirit at first developed among

[1] Parsons, Life of Pepperell, 122.    [2] Ibid., 123; Shirley Corresp., I, 316, 317.

the New England levies, who had enlisted for the siege and thought they should be kept no longer. But Shirley visited Louisbourg and quieted this disturbance by raising the pay of the troops. Small reinforcements were later sent and some supplies. But as the summer progressed fevers and dysentery developed in the garrison and assumed the magnitude of a pestilence, so that by spring nearly nine hundred had died — about four times the loss of life on both sides during the siege. This furnishes an additional illustration of the well-known fact that in those days, and much later, the fatalities of camp and garrison life exceeded those of the battlefield. If we take this into consideration, we see that New England after all paid a good price for the capture of Louisbourg.

But to the ardent mind of Shirley this victory opened the prospect of great events. On the one hand it seemed to him almost certain that the French, by great operations both on land and sea, would seek to recover it, and, if they succeeded, Nova Scotia would fall into their hands and the frontier of eastern New England would suffer. Forecasts of this nature abound in his correspondence, especially with Newcastle, during a year or more to come. His fears seemed confirmed by signs of renewed activity among the Indians and French, one of these being the destruction of the small outpost at Saratoga, on the upper Hudson, in November 1745.[1] When his mind was turned to the British side of the picture, he realized as clearly that the fall of Louisbourg might and should be followed by the capture of Quebec and the end once and for all of the disturbance of the northern frontier. In this connection the strengthening of Nova Scotia and the reduction to complete obedience of the " Neutral French " was ever before his mind. This last proposal did not meet with a favorable response in England, but the suggestion that in 1746 a joint expedition should be sent against Canada was acceded to by the British government. The orders with which we have been made familiar in the history of the later years of the second intercolonial war — especially of 1709 — were again

---

[1] Schuyler, Colonial New York, II, 115. For the opinions of Shirley, see his Corresp., edited by Lincoln, I, 293 *et seq.*, and extracts from his letters, printed by Parkman in the appendix to the second volume of his Half Century of Conflict.

issued to the colonies as far south as Virginia.[1] The usual correspondence between the colonial executives and action by their assemblies followed, as a result of which two forces were collected.[2] One of these consisted of the New England levies, and, if the men voted by the assemblies to be enlisted were all raised, would number five thousand. These were to rendezvous at Louisbourg, when they would be met by a squadron and a force of regular troops and taken up the St. Lawrence to Quebec. The command of this expedition was to be entrusted to Warren, the land troops being under General John St. Clair (Sinclair). The other body of troops, consisting of levies from New York and the colonies thence southward to Virginia, numbering twenty-nine hundred, were to rendezvous at Albany and proceed under the command of Governor Gooch, against Montreal.[3] These forces, or most of them, were duly raised and kept for many months under arms at the expense of the colonies, vainly looking for the contingent from England. It did not come, for the force of which it was to have been composed was diverted to a fruitless expedition against the French coast. It was not until the beginning of the summer of 1747 that definite orders came from England for the disbandment of these levies and the laying aside for the present the plan for an invasion of Canada. Meanwhile, in the late fall of 1746, Shirley had tried to organize a similar joint expedition against Crown Point, but this too failed of accomplishment.

But the French also devised ambitious plans, the failure of which was more disastrous than were the results of the low record of efficiency attained by the Pelham administration. In June, 1746, the largest French fleet which had yet been

[1] A copy will be found printed in Md. Arch., XXVIII, 360. See *Ibid.*, 365 *et seq.*, for references to action taken in consequence.

[2] These are referred to more or less fully in the standard histories and are detailed at considerable length by V. H. Paltsits, in a paper of the Am. Antiq. Soc., 1905. The full details can be followed in the journals and archives of the respective colonies and of the secretary of state in England. The correspondence of Shirley throws most light on the execution of the plan in general.

[3] The health of Gooch was such as to prevent his taking command. Governor Thomas, of Pennsylvania, was then talked of as a possible successor, but his health would have prevented his accepting. No commander except Schuyler, of the New Jersey regiment, was ever actually in charge of the troops while they were stationed at Albany. Penn Mss. Thomas to T. P. Nov. 3, 1746. Off. Corr., IV, 75. P. L. B., II, 187.

sent to the North Atlantic coasts was dispatched under the command of the Duc D'Anville. It numbered eleven large men-of-war and some thirty smaller armed vessels and privateers. Transports accompanied the fleet carrying a land force of somewhat more than 3000 men. The immediate object of this expedition was to recapture Louisbourg and conquer Nova Scotia. It was then to attack the New England coast and ports farther south and finally visit the West Indies. At Chebucto harbor, now Halifax, it was to be joined by four large ships of war which had lately been sent to the West Indies. The English colonies were at once filled with rumors that this force, after accomplishing its immediate purpose would ravage their coast and destroy their port towns at least as far south as Boston. The fear of this operated as a powerful motive for enlistment in the intended expedition against Canada, and aided in reconciling the colonists to remaining under arms after the prospect of aid from England had vanished. But the French met with mishaps and disasters from the first, due in large part to the neglect of proper precautions in the outfit of the expedition. While at sea ship fever and dysentery broke out, of which it is said that in all more than two thousand perished. By this the force was so weakened that it could hope to accomplish nothing. The ruin of the expedition was completed by storms with which it met off the coast of Nova Scotia. The admiral died of apoplexy, his successor committed suicide, and what remained of the force returned to France under the command of De la Jonquière.[1]

While such was the fate of the over-seas expedition, considerable activity, for the purpose of defence as well as offence, was aroused in Canada. The fortifications of Quebec were much extended. But before this was undertaken a force consisting of nearly 700 men, under the command of De Ramezay, was sent from Canada to Acadia to support the French interest there.[2] This was stationed at Chignecto near the isthmus which connected the peninsula of Acadia with

---

[1] A French account of this expedition is printed in the Docs. Inedits., edited by Casgrain, I, 70–108; N. Y. Col. Docs., X, 27. The reactions of Shirley to the news from the eastward can be seen in his letters during September and October.

[2] See Docs. Inedits., II, 16–75.

the mainland, in the midst of the country which was most thickly settled by the " Neutral French." From this point communication was easy with Bay Verte on the east, Chebucto on the south and Annapolis on the west. The country of the Micmac Indians, firm allies of the French, lay adjacent on the north. The fidelity of the " Neutral French " to the cause of their compatriots was counted on. It had been strengthened and assured by the influence of the Abbé Le Loutre, the most influential Frenchman now in Acadia, a priest who was now repeating in that region the kind of work which Râle had so long prosecuted in western Maine. He and Father Germain, whose station was on the St. John's river, were tireless in their semi-political work and in their efforts to combine all the resources of the French for the recovery of Nova Scotia. Now that Louisbourg had fallen, their efforts were redoubled to hold the intermediate region between Isle Royale and Annapolis and in the end, by war or diplomacy or both, to recover the whole. Le Loutre visited Quebec for this purpose and it was on this errand that De Ramezay, with his troops, was sent to Acadia. Thus the struggle over the possession of that entire region widened and deepened.[1]

Shirley, with the help of Governor Mascarene, was kept informed of these doings, of the danger and weakness of Annapolis. An attack upon it was expected by land as well as sea, and the weeks during which the arrival of D'Anville's fleet was expected were anxious ones for those in whose hands rested British interests to the eastward. Warren and Pepperell had returned to New England and Commodore Knowles had been left in command at Louisbourg. His impression of the place, its climate and general availability for naval and military purposes was very unfavorable and this was conveyed with the utmost fullness and emphasis in his letters to his superiors in England.[2] He thought that the defences should be destroyed, the harbor filled up and the place abandoned. The alternative to that — and it was suggested by Shirley and perhaps by others at this time, though not with the view of its taking the place of Louisbourg — was the

[1] N. Y. Col. Docs., X, 3–19.
[2] Murdock, Hist. of Nova Scotia, II, 98.

fortifying of Chebucto harbor and the building of a town there. Every move in the plans which the struggle — now becoming acute — for the possession of Acadia developed, made the attitude of the Acadian-French a subject of greater importance. They themselves understood this, refused to deliver provisions to the English in Louisbourg, and their support in a crisis was fully counted upon by the priests and the other French in Canada. It was in accordance with the harsh nature of Knowles that he should urge their removal in a body from Nova Scotia. Shirley was not ready to go to this length, but advised the exclusion of the priests and some of the ringleaders among the French sympathizers, promising indemnity to the rest if they should take the oath of allegiance. The king also, through Newcastle, desired that the Acadians should be informed in some " authentick manner " that there was no intention of removing them.[1] The building of a fortified town on Chebucto harbor, Shirley held, would help confirm the hold of the British on all Nova Scotia. The colonizing of the region in part by immigrants from New England was a favorite plan with him. As occasion offered, he sent reinforcements to Annapolis, and induced other New England colonies, so far as he was able, to coöperate in these measures.

It was in pursuance of this general policy and as an offset to the activity of De Ramezay, that Colonel Arthur Noble with a small body of men from Massachusetts, was sent, in the winter of 1746/7, to garrison Grand Pré. Levies which had been raised for a similar purpose in New Hampshire and Rhode Island, failed to reach their destination. Noble's force, said to have been about 500, was billeted in the houses of the village, but the French at once informed De Ramezay of what was occurring and furnished him with the necessary guides. With a force of 300 French and a body of Indians — but including among his men some of the best fighters among the Canadian *noblesse* — De Ramezay set out upon a long midwinter march to surprise the English. So deep was the snow that Noble had thought himself protected and the

---

[1] Shirley Corresp. I, 388. Shirley had previously written to Mascarene that he knew of no plan of the government to remove the Acadians. C. O. 5/900, O. P. N. Eng. Sept. 16, 1746.

surprise was complete.  The attack was made some hours before dawn in the midst of a blinding snowstorm and the English after losing a considerable number in killed and wounded were forced to surrender.  This, with the capture of Fort Massachusetts the previous August, near the opposite end of the northern frontier, were the most notable achievements of the French in *la petite guerre* during this war.  As was always the case, they were indecisive.  This was especially true in Nova Scotia, for the following spring Grand Pré was forced to receive another garrison from New England and the Acadians found it even more dangerous than before to respond to what had now become the express command of De Ramezay, that they should openly take up arms for the French.

It was while events were rapidly nearing a crisis, but before a decision upon any point had been reached, that this war was closed by the treaty of Aix la Chapelle, signed in October, 1748.  Again it was European conditions and those alone which dictated the peace.  Great Britain had been successful at sea, but on land she was engaged in a costly and indecisive struggle concerning questions of slight importance to her.  With the expulsion of the Pretender her interest in the European struggle had ceased to be vital.  And now, in order to procure peace, in accordance with the principle of the general restoration of conquests, Louisbourg was sacrificed.  Shirley and the New Englanders were forced to see the results of their great effort thrown away and the French again in possession of Isle Royale.

# CHAPTER IV

MASSACHUSETTS UNDER SHIRLEY.   MID-CENTURY PROB-
LEMS OF COLONIAL ADMINISTRATION, 1740–1754

THE difficulties with which the new governor of Massachusetts had first to deal were chiefly financial in character.
When he came into office, in the late summer of 1741, the
public was deeply aroused over the subject of the land bank
and the efforts of the government to suppress it.   Never since
the time of the English Revolution and the uprising against
Andros had the province been so stirred by any public question.   The decisive but brutal measures of Belcher and the
British government had administered a blow to the bank
which in the end was to prove fatal — that was already apparent; but the fortunes of very many who had made themselves responsible for the redemption of its bills were involved
and the loss or ruin which these parties all over the province
now had to face, taken in connection with the sympathy of
their neighbors and friends and the widely extended consciousness, especially in the country districts, that the medium
of exchange was in a most unsatisfactory state, produced an
intensity of popular feeling which threatened an explosion.
There was activity in the towns and meetings of the subscribers to the bank were held at which heated debates doubtless occurred.   The currency and the various schemes which
were mooted for its increase, restriction or general improvement were subjects of animated discussion in the press.[1]   In
order to estimate aright the emotional state in which the
public mind then was the fact should also be borne in mind
that the Great Awakening had not yet fully spent its force
and in the newspapers and pamphlets it shared attention with
questions of currency and finance.   It was also felt that war
with France was not many years off and that it would put

[1] This can be proved from the files of all the Boston papers, but especially
from those of the "News Letter," "Journal" and "Post Boy."

additional strain on the rickety financial structure of the colonies. These were the chief questions and this the state of the popular mind with which Shirley had to deal.

The change in the person of the governor helped materially to relieve the situation. Belcher, like most other purely Massachusetts men, had been actively involved as a partisan in all the questions which were agitating the province. He was as ardent in his support of Whitefield as he was in his opposition to the land bank. But Shirley, though he had lived long enough in New England and had sufficient insight to understand and conform himself in large measure to its spirit, was still an outsider, and had the ability to view its controversies with a certain objectivity. He was a man of secular spirit, a lawyer in the European sense and, therefore, stood wholly outside the religious enthusiasm of the time and place. He had taken no part, at least of prominence, in the controversy out of which the land bank had originated or in the measures thus far taken for its overthrow. Upon the state of the currency in New England he had not yet expressed himself at length, though the letters which he soon began writing to the board of trade showed that he was intimately acquainted with its condition and was able to review the effect of the existing laws upon its amount and relative values with all the detail and exactness of a lawyer's brief. Though all of these questions, and in addition that of the governor's salary, had to be attacked at the same time and underwent development contemporaneously, that of the land bank was most rapidly approaching a settlement and for this reason should be the first considered.

Soon after Shirley assumed office operations under both the land bank and the silver scheme were suspended, and because of the general solvency of most or all concerned in the last named enterprise, no special difficulty was experienced in settling up its affairs. But the affixing of the brand of illegality to all the contracts and agreements of the land bank company had a much more serious and extended effect. Its outstanding bills had, if possible, to be redeemed and expenses and losses met. Among the subscribers there was no lack of insolvents, fugitives from the colony and those who to escape payment put their property out of their hands. Subscribers who lived in the towns which as the result of the adjustment of the boundary had been set off to New Hampshire also escaped payment. The obligations which, from these causes and in addition to their own loans, fell upon the honest subscribers were heavy and often ruinous. An effort was made to wind up the affairs of the bank without legislation. After several months, in April, 1742, an order of the general court was passed for the appointment of a committee to report the amount of bills outstanding so that they might be called in. As this did not recognize any of the contracts of the company, the governor assented to it.[1] Also, like so much that was practically legislation in Massachusetts, this was put in the form of a resolve, so that it need not be submitted to the privy council. The committee was appointed and, after working through the summer, it was found, as was to be expected, that many of the partners neglected or refused to bring in or destroy their bills. The council then ordered the attorney general to prosecute such delinquents. Some suits were begun, but little was accomplished, while subscribers who had paid their shares continued exposed to the prosecution of any holders of bills who chose to attempt to recover from them, while they could not collect what was due to the company because the act of parliament had declared all its contracts void.

In order to secure for subscribers some relief, an act was passed at the beginning of 1742, which, having been submitted to the king, became law after passing a second time in the autumn of that year. In this law a commission of three was named and given power, after examination of persons and papers and subject to approval by the general court, to assess partners for their share of the bills of the company, to bring suits for recovery when necessary and take other stringent measures to force an actual settlement and prevent fraud. Appeal could be had to the courts on questions of fact or by those who considered themselves aggrieved. Inasmuch as contracts and agreements of the company were recognized by this law as valid, the act of parliament was to that extent ignored. The unpaid obligations to which the law applied

---

[1] Davis, 3 Pub. of American Economic Association, II(2), 196; Shirley Correspondence, I, 85.

amounted to only £2318, and 83 partial or total delinquents were the total number involved. The commissioners began their work in November, 1743. Their proceedings, resulting in assessments upon total or partial delinquents, were exceedingly prolonged and tedious, and met with opposition and avoidance of all kinds. They were able to collect little and when, in 1747, the town house at Boston was burned, the books and papers of the commission were totally destroyed. The general court now had to take up the matter again. By an act passed late in 1748 it authorized an assessment of all the delinquent partners which should be sufficient to redeem all bills, make good deficiencies and cover all expenses. This was to be approved by the general court and then warrants of distress were to be issued against those who should still neglect or refuse to pay. In 1749 the assessment called for by this act was submitted to the general court, but some of the partners succeeded in getting it rejected by one of the houses and it became invalid.

The business now reverted largely to the general court and dragged on there till, in April, 1751, a committee of this body reported in detail the sums due to the company from the directors and their heirs. As a result of its recommendations another, and more effective, act was passed [1] requiring the payment with interest of the assessments under the threat of further warrants of distress. But ten years had now passed since the task of winding up the affairs of the bank had been undertaken. Its bills were no longer in circulation and all or most of them had been destroyed. But a residuum of debts or loans which these represented, together with expenses and interest, remained unpaid. With this commissioners and committees struggled in vain or with very little success. Through the sheriffs returns were made to the warrants of distress, " dead," " insolvent," " out of the province," " cannot find the estate," " sold and gone to Albany." Not a few investors in the bank were ruined by the litigation which was forced upon them by the effort to settle up its affairs. In August, 1758, the sale at public auction of the estate — dwelling, malt house, land and other buildings adjoining — of Samuel Adams, now deceased, was advertised. But in the

[1] Acts and Resolves, III, 551.

same issue of the " News Letter " his son, of the same name and the man who was destined to become the most persistent opponent of the supremacy of parliament who appeared in the colonies during the Revolution, inserted a notice warning any intending purchasers that the proceeding was illegal and that he would prosecute any who should trespass on the estate. These are illustrations of the varied obstacles which officials had to meet in their efforts to straighten out this tangled affair. In despair of being able to secure by legal process the funds which were necessary to discharge the debts of the bank, in 1760 an act was passed authorizing the holding of a lottery. Tickets were issued and five years were allowed for the completion of this process. A still further extension of time had to be obtained and at the end so many of the tickets remained unsold that the lottery netted only about £556 out of the £3500, which it had been proposed to raise by this method.

This narrative has already carried us far beyond Shirley's administration and well into the period when questions of the Revolution had come to be of absorbing interest. Yet in 1767 much attention was devoted by the general court and its committees to plans for securing the payment of earlier assessments upon the directors of the land bank. Robert Auchmuty denied the jurisdiction of the general court in the premises, but it appointed a committee which held a number of sessions and with the presentation of its bill for services the subject of the land bank disappears from the records. The administration and judicial system of Massachusetts at that time was not vigorous and efficient enough to bring about a settlement of the affairs of this company and it was only the death of the parties who were chiefly interested that, after the lapse of a quarter of a century, carried the subject to oblivion.[1]

It was during only about two years at the beginning of his administration that the influence of Shirley upon the question of the land bank is clearly visible; but that is sufficient to reveal his attitude toward it. It was not that of the brutal partisan, like Belcher, who would resort to any means to destroy a hated enemy, and that quickly. Shirley desired to

[1] See the detailed account by Davis in his Monograph on Banking in Mass.

see the concern wound up, but that it should be done equitably and with a due regard to the varied interests involved.[1]  He took the attitude of the lawyer, with a leaning toward sentiments of equity.  Hence he insisted that recourse in all cases should be left open to the courts, that no party should lose the benefit of a trial at law, if he desired it.  For this reason, in 1743, he objected to a bill for the more speedy termination of the land bank, because of the extraordinary powers which it gave to the commissioners of breaking and entering, of assessing sums upon delinquent debtors and of selling their property without an opportunity for appeal.[2]  He insisted that resort should not be had to anything like writs of assistance, but only to the ordinary writ of attachment, and that the commissioners — the administrative body — should be kept responsible to the general court, with the right of recourse to a jury trial for the establishment of facts.  Thus by this lawyer-governor the British-American system of administration, held in check by the legislature and the courts, was set at work on the problem of winding up the land bank.  It was to be done in such a way as to guarantee individual rights, and endless opportunities were offered for interposing checks and obstacles.  We have seen what the result was — the bank was never really wound up.  Numbers were incidentally ruined, but many also escaped the payment of their honest debts.  The movement originated in an effort to bring relief to the poorer classes and to debtors, to farmers, shopkeepers and artisans, as over against the merchants of the coast towns and of Great Britain.  But when the collapse came the honest investors or holders of the bills suddenly found themselves in the position of creditors who could not realize upon their investments, in fact because of the delinquencies of many with whom they had been associated.  Thus in the process of liquidation a new alignment of debtors and creditors was brought about and in the general issue one of these fared, perhaps, as badly as the other.  Therefore, in spite of the desires of Shirley, and of others like him, the community simply muddled through, with a result which in many respects was anything but equitable or even legal.  But

---

[1] Shirley Corresp., I, 79.
[2] Davis, *op. cit.*, 200; Shirley Corresp., I, 108.

for the final result Shirley was not responsible, for almost as soon as the muddling process was begun his attention was diverted to other things. and before it had reached its middle course his connection with Massachusetts had ceased.

The issue of bills of credit was a subject with which Shirley was much more closely connected, and that for a longer time, than was the closure of the land bank. His instructions required that the bills already out should be called in and destroyed at the times specified in the acts under which they were issued, and that no more than £30,000 in such bills should be at any time current in the province.[1] Early in 1739 a law of the province had been passed restraining the circulation of bills of the neighboring colonies. The doom of the land bank and of the silver scheme was also sealed and an increase of the circulating medium from those sources could no longer be expected. Such gold and silver as was in the province was not in circulation, but was used as merchandise for the purpose of making remittances to England. Therefore, Massachusetts seemed to be shut up to the prospect of a monetary supply of £30,000, which was quite inadequate to its need. The usual large arrears of uncollected taxes existed in the province and also a large sum of outstanding bills for the redemption of which no provision had been made.[2] Bills of old and new tenor were circulating together, without distinction as to values in private transactions, but received at different rates in payments to the government. The feeling in favor of new and excessive issues of course was strong, though the tendency had been held somewhat in check under Belcher. The treasury was empty and the defences of the province were in the usual state of decay. War existed with Spain and it was probable that before many years France would become involved. Shirley was peculiarly alive to these aspects of the situation, while he had been instructed anew to secure for himself a permanent salary of £1,000, clear of all

[1] Shirley, Corresp., I, 47–49; Davis, Currency, 3 Pubs. of Am. Econ. Assoc. I(4), p. 152 et seq.

[2] An excellent review of the situation as to bills of credit in Massachusetts and its origin, showing the governor's grasp of the subject, is in a letter or report of his to the board of trade, under date of Dec. 23, 1743. C. O. 5/884, O. P. Mass. Much of this is printed in Palfrey, History of New England, V, 102 notes. Other letters and speeches of Shirley also show the governor's competence in the discussion of finance.

deductions. This was £350 in excess of the amount Belcher had been receiving in the later years of his administration. These were the elements of the situation which had to be met.

A bill was passed for an additional emission in the usual form, but declaring that 5s.2d. in the new bills should be equal to an ounce of silver. To this for several reasons Shirley objected. A bill was then passed for an issue of £30,000, as suggested in the instructions, including also a provision for redeeming through taxes the outstanding bills, to the amount of £105,525. This bill was accepted by Shirley and afterwards approved by the privy council. The bills issued under it were known as new tenor, while those of 1737 were thereafter called middle tenor. A second act was also passed, upon which the governor congratulated himself, since it appeared to secure such an adjustment of debts as would protect creditors from the losses to which they were continually exposed in consequence of depreciation. This was a subject to which Shirley devoted much thought and which he expounded in letters and speeches of undoubted ability.[1] The occasion for the passage of such a measure was furnished by the expiring of the act of 1712, renewed in 1732, which made bills of the old tenor legal tender. This compelled creditors to receive the bills at their nominal value, however great may have been their depreciation since their issue, or between the time when a debt was contracted and when it was paid. The evil was equally great when creditors were compelled to receive bills emitted in later years and which at the time of their issue were depreciated below the rates at which the currency stood at the times when the loans involved were made. This accurately described the stages of depreciation through which currency in all the colonies sank under the influence of successive emissions, accompanied as they were with chronic neglect to collect the taxes which had nominally been levied for the purpose of redeeming the bills, and with oft-repeated reissues of bills which had been called in and should have been destroyed. In proportion as creditors lost by this process debtors gained and injustice ran riot.

The remedy which the governor sought for this evil was

---

[1] See the letter above referred to and printed in Palfrey, and his speech to the assembly in April, 1743.

analogous to the practice of the courts in " chancering " payments upon bonds and mortgages which had run for some time. It consisted in devising a sliding scale of payments of private debts, adjusted to the progressive degrees of depreciation of the bills of credit. A provision of this kind was made in a law to ascertain the value of money and bills of public credit and in two appropriation acts passed in 1742 and 1743.[1] The first mentioned act provided that, once in every six months, the general assembly should determine the rates at which bills should pass in relation, at the standard value of 6s.8d. per ounce, to silver and bills of exchange on London. Seeing that the general assembly would be unfitted for such a task, provision was made for recourse to a committee of the council, and on its failure to a committee designated by the justices of the superior court. Their findings would furnish the courts with a rule for making up their judgments as to the true value of debts. The assembly naturally was unwilling to pass such a measure, and Shirley induced them to consent by agreeing to the above mentioned emission of £30,000 in bills of credit. But, as was to be expected, he found the assembly, the council and the judges all indifferent to the execution of the plan. The judges, in particular, Shirley prodded till they promised to address themselves to the task. But this plan, like all such schemes, was complicated and with successive emissions and consequent changes in the values of bills, the estimates made had to be periodically readjusted.

The complexity of the problem was also increased by provisions in the above mentioned acts that debts might also be paid in any one of a long list of commodities, the products of the colony. Debtors in particular insisted that these, as well as silver and bills of exchange, should be included in the " chancering " process. The declaration of war with France, as we shall see, also brought in its train largely increased emissions of paper, followed by further heavy depreciation. Continued negotiations between the two houses, of the governor with both houses, and of these with the judges and with such councilmen as were appointed members of the committees

---

[1] Acts and Resolves of Mass., III, 11, 32, 68; Shirley Corresp., I, 102; Davis, *op. cit.*, 172 *et seq.*; Hutchinson II, 361.

of adjustment, were therefore necessitated. Many committees were formed, many resolves were passed by one house or the other and some additional legislation was enacted as the result of activities upon this subject which were continued throughout the third intercolonial war. So numerous and influential were the debtors and so sensitive were they to such increases in the amounts of their debts as would really approximate to the depreciation in the value of paper, that the committees which had the adjustment in charge did not dare to fix rates at all comparable with the extent of depreciation. Says Hutchinson in reference to the plan, " This was a scheme to establish an ideal measure in all trade and dealings, let the instrument be what it would. . . . How to ascertain the depreciation from time to time was the great difficulty. To leave it to a common jury would never do. There was some doubt whether a house of representatives would be wholly unbiased. At length it was agreed that the eldest councillors in each county should meet once a year and ascertain the depreciation. . . . That at best must have been a very partial cure." After mentioning large classes of debts to which the scheme could not be made to apply, the writer refers to another fundamental defect. " The councillors appointed to estimate the depreciation never had firmness enough in any instance to make the full allowance, but when silver and exchange had risen 20 per cent or more, an addition was made of four or five only." The reason for this was that the " popular cry " was so strong against it. " The act neither prevented the depreciation of bills, nor afforded relief in case of it." This statement so well summarizes the result as to make it unnecessary to follow the oft-repeated efforts to execute the scheme which appear in the records until nearly 1750, when the subject drops out of sight. The plan does credit to Shirley's understanding of the essential character of the problem and it shows a grasp of the subject of which we have no hint in any other colony or on the part of any other governor; but the execution of the plan involved difficulties which far exceeded the abilities of men of that time and place to overcome. Therefore it takes its place, along with the closure of the land bank, as an administrative failure.

As a result of one of the usual contradictions in human

events, Shirley, while he was laboring to relieve the province from some of the worst evils of the paper régime, became an inflationist himself and was the occasion of an increase of the evils he was seeking to cure. As we know, he was an ardent supporter of the policy of war against the French in Acadia and elsewhere. As soon as war was declared between France and England in Europe he plunged into the fray with great enthusiasm. Even before that occurred, under his lead considerable sums were expended in strengthening fortifications. The rebuilding of Pemaquid, now called Fort Frederick, was taken seriously in hand. When the war began and provision had to be made for frontier defences, when troops were sent to Acadia and the expedition against Louisbourg was undertaken, much larger sums were needed. Shirley had already obtained permission from the British government for the issue of £8,000 in excess of the £30,000 which by his instructions was declared to be the amount of bills of credit allowed to circulate in Massachusetts. This additional sum was to be used for finishing the works at Castle William, Fort Frederick and other places and for no other purposes whatever, and the bills were to be retired during the years 1744 and 1745.[1] These conditions were in harmony with the special request of Shirley which gave rise to the concession.

As early as 1742 Shirley had informed the board of trade that the £30,000, the issue of which was allowed by his instructions, was at best only sufficient for a peace establishment and that in case of a rupture with France the necessity of maintaining 1000 or 1200 men in constant pay would call for other emissions. Therefore he hoped that in such cases the crown would consent to dispense with his instructions prohibiting further issues and would permit the emission of such sums as the needs of war should be found to require. The total suppression of bills of credit he viewed with apprehension, fearing it would result in checking trade with Great Britain in forcing colonists into manufacturing, and that it might almost bring government to a standstill. In the summer of 1744 this request was granted and his twelfth instruction was suspended for the duration of the war, provided the

---

[1] C. O. 5/918, E. B. N. Eng. April and June, 1743; C. O. 5/883, O. P. N. Eng., Nov., 1742.

money to be raised in connection with the issues of bills during that time was used for the necessary defence of Massachusetts Bay only.[1] Early in 1745 Shirley was also warned by the board of trade that the issue of paper money in the colonies was regarded as a grievance to British merchants and prejudicial to commerce and that, if time had permitted, a new bill for its restriction would have been introduced into parliament. Therefore he must take care, when assenting to such issues, that good and sufficient funds were provided for their redemption within a reasonable time. As usual, however, under the pressure of war and the incitement of the governor's military enthusiasm, this caution was disregarded.

Not only were further emissions considered necessary for putting the province in a better position of defence after war began with France, but provision had to be amply made for the expedition against Louisbourg and for the later expeditions which were planned against Crown Point and Canada in general. The result was that between June, 1744, and June, 1748, nineteen acts were passed for the issue of bills of credit. Of these five were passed in 1745 and seven in 1746. The sums authorized to be issued by each of the respective acts ranged between £8,000 and £100,000, and the total amount of all the issues was nearly £700,000. As, notwithstanding the later issues, bills of the old tenor were practically the medium in which values were measured, and it was heavily depreciated below the nominal rates at which these later issues were made, we may say that in such terms the issues amounted to nearly £2,794,000. Of this in 1749 £1,800,000 were outstanding.[2] In these issues silver was rated at 7s.6d. per ounce and old tenor at four to one. But as the emissions continued, depreciation went on apace, so that by the end of the war it reached eleven or twelve to one.[3] In none of the colonies except Rhode Island was inflation of the currency carried further or developed more rapidly than by Massachusetts during this decade. Such issues became so much a matter of course as a means of mortgaging the future to meet immediate needs that,

[1] C. O. 5/883, O. P. Mass. Nov., 1742; C. O. 5/885, Sept. 6, 1744; C. O. 5/918 E. B. N. Eng. Aug. 9, 1744, Feb. 21, 1745.
[2] Davis, *op. cit.*, 169.      [3] Hutchinson, II, 390.

apparently, without authorization from any quarter, the council of officers in the garrison at Louisbourg after its surrender, ordered the issue of £10,000 in Massachusetts bills of old tenor, to be used in paying off the workmen employed in repairs till money could be had in exchange for them.[1] Such legislation also as had been passed for the exclusion of the bills of other New England colonies from the province had proved inoperative and they were steadily contributing toward the increase of depreciation.

From such a financial slough as this into which Massachusetts had been plunged, in part by the necessities of war, escape through the ordinary method of taxation and redemption was clearly impossible. Partial repudiation had already been effected by the change in the rating of silver from 6s.8d. to 7s.6d. per ounce, and the province was facing repudiation on a much larger scale unless, after the war, measures of the most heroic kind could be applied. But fortunately a new way of escape was opened, and to an extent by good fortune Shirley's reputation as a financier was saved. This was through a plan for reimbursing from the British exchequer the expenditures of the New England colonies in the expedition against Louisbourg. This was a policy which came to be applied on a much larger scale in the last intercolonial war and will demand separate treatment in that connection. But it was now initiated in the case of Massachusetts, and also of the other New England colonies, which had borne the chief burden of the war, and because of the decisive influence which it had on the currency system of the Bay Colony it demands treatment here.[2]

For some years the attention of parliament had been drawn to the necessity of regulating the issue of bills of credit in the colonies. The capture of Louisbourg was due almost wholly to colonial initiative and was, as we have seen, the most successful achievement of the British in North America since the beginning of the French wars. In less than a fortnight after the surrender of the fortress, the house of

---

[1] Pepperell Papers, 6 Mass. Hist. Colls., X, 37; Davis, 170.
[2] Journals of H. of Commons, Apr. 5, 1748; Minutes of Treasury Board, Vol. 29, 1748, 1749, et seq.; Mass. Arch., Vol. 20; Acts and Res. of Mass., III; Davis op. cit. 201 et seq.; Hutchinson, II, 391.

representatives at Boston voted to prepare a petition to the king for relief from the burden of debt thus incurred. For a year and more Christopher Kilby had been serving the province as agent in England, and had been instructed to give careful attention to any inquiry which might be made into the state of the currencies of the colonies in order that no injury might be done thereby to Massachusetts. In the fall of 1744 a bill on this subject was under discussion in parliament and a copy, or at least the contents, of the measure were communicated to the assembly. This induced the council to vote that the governor should prepare a full account of the experience of the province with paper money and send it to the Secretary of State. One purpose of this was to show the difference between the position of Massachusetts in this matter as compared with that of other New England colonies which had plunged more deeply into this policy than she had dared and perhaps with less excuse. But the house was unwilling to intrust this task to Shirley and, therefore, caused the drafting of a petition from the two houses to the king and authorized William Bollan, son-in-law of the governor, who was just sailing for England, to join Kilby as agent in presenting it and securing relief. Bollan took with him a mass of detailed evidence concerning the number of men, stores and vessels which were contributed by Massachusetts to the expedition, showing a total expenditure of £261,000. Some typical muster rolls of companies were included, but not all, owing, it was said, to the danger and difficulty of taking so many papers to England. To authenticate the account as a whole it was attested by the commissary general, signed by the governor and the province seal was attached. But the board of trade found errors in the computing and, while it accepted the statement as substantially true, it could not accept its details as amounting to vouchers.[1]

This novel application depended for its success upon the attitude which might be assumed toward it, not only by the

[1] C. O. 5/916, E. B. N. Eng. Apr. 7, 1747. In an exchange of messages between Shirley and the assembly in 1754, occasioned by a demand of the governor for a grant in recognition for special services, he laid great stress on the influence in procuring reimbursement which his narratives and account had at the time. See L. H. J. Jan., 1754. In contemporary sources this does not appear so clearly.

house of commons but by the treasury board. This seemed at first to be favorable, but war was in progress and naturally a decisive result in favor of the colony could not be expected until the struggle was ended or its close was in sight. The matter dragged along for months, with the usual alternations of hopes and fears on the part of the agents. Bollan was pretty confident of getting something, but whether it would be all that was asked for seemed very much in doubt. As time passed Kilby fell into the background and was dismissed from this part of his agency.[1] Bollan, as the result of his superior knowledge and his interest in the subject, assumed charge of the business. The order in council for reimbursement to Massachusetts was issued, January 15, 1746/7.[2] The usual watch-dog attitude of the treasury board became evident by its postponing payment and by insisting that the sum paid should be equal to the present value of the bills. As depreciation had been continuous and rapid, this was much less than their value in sterling at the time when the debt was incurred. In February, 1747/8, Bollan replied to statements made by Pelham, of the treasury board, enlarging upon this point and claiming that the debts which had been contracted still retained their original values and if the reimbursement was made on the basis of the present value of the bills, the province would lose half the sum expended; also that payment in the lower sum would not more than meet the cost of holding Louisbourg and provide nothing for its capture. At the beginning of the following April, however, the commons resolved that the reimbursement was reasonable, and payment at the higher rate, as demanded by Bollan, was agreed to.

Two years passed after the grant was assured before the sum due Massachusetts was paid. The delay was largely owing to the lords of the treasury, who at first insisted that the payment should be made in installments extending over several years. To this the agent objected and insisted that as soon as the grant was made the whole amount was due to the province, which from that time stood toward the king in the relation of a creditor. Later still another condition

---

[1] For Shirley's account of Kilby down to 1750, see Shirley Corresp., I, 475 *et seq.*

[2] C. O. 5/885, O. P. Mass.

was added, that the person who was appointed to receive the money must give security of a character and amount which would satisfy the board. To this Bollan made strong opposition, not only because of the cost which was involved but of the implication which it carried that the claim of the province and of its agent to receive the grant was not a complete one. It was adding, he asserted, a restriction which was not implied in the act of grant. As Bollan had been appointed before the act of parliament, it was urged that his powers were not sufficient, and the law officers also found that they were not properly authenticated.

Meantime a discussion of the possibility and methods of a return to specie payments went on in Massachusetts. Early in 1748 Hutchinson submitted to the house a memorial proposing that the specie to be granted by the British government should be used for the redemption of the larger part of the outstanding paper and that, as the result of a loan, enough Spanish and Portuguese money should be imported to redeem the balance. Massachusetts would thus be brought to a specie basis. In the house this proposal was received with favor, and it was extended there by the added suggestion that a committee be appointed to secure, if possible, the coöperation of the other New England colonies in a plan for the retirement of bills of credit throughout the entire section. An attempt was even made to hold a conference on the subject. But this plan failed because the amounts of specie due to the other colonies, especially Rhode Island and Connecticut, as their shares in the reimbursement, were so small as compared with the sums of paper which they had outstanding as to be ineffective for the purpose.[1]

In the spring session of 1748 a bill, based on Hutchinson's proposal, was read in the Massachusetts assembly, but not passed. In a speech to the assembly in its fall session Shirley referred to a bill for sinking the currency by means of the reimbursement as having been passed and sent to England, and that he believed it had induced the ministers there to

[1] The result was agreed to in committee of the whole and, after being reported to the houses, was put into the supply bill. The grants were made at the same time to all the New England colonies. £183,649 to Mass., £16,355 to N. H., £28,864 to Conn., and £332 to R. I.

decide that the money should be paid in such a way as to put an end to bills of credit in New England. When this statement, which it is supposed was made for effect, became known to the board of trade, they called upon Bollan to explain why he had concealed from them action so important as this. He had received a copy of the bill as introduced, with authority to use it as he saw fit, but, of course, no act had reached him, since none existed, and he doubted the ability of the province to borrow enough (£50,000) to complete the redemption of the bills of credit. Bollan therefore had to admit the facts of the case, including the probability that the governor had made the incorrect statement in order to exert a favorable influence on the cause of redemption of specie payments. As the board of trade was sympathetic with the purpose of the governor, no further criticism of his conduct seems to have been made.

In consequence of the delay in securing the payment, however, a new complication, arising from the continued and rapid depreciation of the outstanding bills, came in further to imperil the result. It was reported, whether truly or not, that speculators were buying up bills at their lowest values in silver and holding them for redemption at a higher rate. Certain merchants in England who were interested in trade to New England called the attention of the authorities to these reports with the effect of delaying the time of making the payment. Kilby, Bollan's associate, also favored this attitude, and also seemed ready to acquiesce in the proposal of certain ministers to adjust the amount of the reimbursement not to the value of the currency at the time of the expedition against Louisbourg but to their much more depreciated value at the time when payment should be made. Against this both Bollan and Massachusetts strenuously protested, and because of his sympathy with it, Kilby was dropped from the agency altogether and Bollan was left to manage the affair alone.[1]

The subject, meanwhile, was not allowed to sleep in the Massachusetts assembly. At the beginning of 1748/9 there was a prolonged struggle in which the country party, which had supported the land bank and feared the pressure to which

[1] Shirley Corresp., I, 496.

the contraction of the currency would expose debtors, fought for paper money and against the use of specie. Hutchinson, who was speaker, led the hard money members. Finally, after the bill for resumption had been once lost, by the change of votes of two of its most prominent opponents the final success of the measure was secured.[1] As the money was not paid over until the close of the following June, and as it was not yet known in Massachusetts what course the British government would take, the act was conditional and related to a future contingency. Like the earlier statement of Shirley, it was intended to facilitate the payment of the money, as well as to fix the conditions under which specie payments should actually be resumed in the province. It named Sir Peter Warren, William Bollan and Eliakim Palmer of London as the individuals who should give a discharge to the treasury board when the money was paid, and requested that the money should be paid in foreign coined silver and carried to America in one or more of his majesty's ships. The act also declared that resumption should be effected in the province during the year following the close of March, 1750. The terms on which bills of the different tenors should be redeemed in silver pieces of eight were also specified. A tax was imposed sufficient to redeem the bills which were in excess of the reimbursement expected from England and the provisions made in various acts of emission for redemption at dates later than March, 1751, were declared void. All contracts made subsequent to March, 1750, must be satisfied and debts paid in silver at 6s.8d per ounce. After that date the receiving or paying of bills of credit of any neighboring colony was prohibited by severe penalties and a rigorous test oath upon this point was required to be taken by officials. A proviso, however, was added, that these clauses should become void if the neighboring colonies should take steps to redeem their bills.

When this bill, with an explanatory statement from Shirley,[2] reached England, the board of trade and Lamb, its counsel, together with the lords of the committee, made

[1] Hutchinson, II, 394; Acts and Resolves of Mass., III, 430; Davis, *op. cit.*, 234 *et seq.*

[2] Shirley Corresp., I, 462.

some criticisms upon its wording and provisions. These chiefly related to the rates at which the paper was to be redeemed and to the fact that the bill declared void parts of certain acts of emission which had received the royal approval. But in view of the beneficial purpose of the measure and its conformity with the provisions of law regarding proclamation money, it was approved by the crown.[1] The payments were made by the British government, the fees for the transaction being heavy but yet fixed at as low rates as could fairly be expected. In September, 1749, the specie reached Boston, and in due time, with the help of some additional legislation, the process of resumption was completed. So evident to all was the advantage of having the debt of the province largely paid by the home government that the disturbances or even riots which some expected did not occur. The expenses attendant upon the transaction helped to exhaust the supply of specie in the treasury before all the bills were redeemed, and the veto of Lieutenant Governor Phips, together with a protest of Oliver and Hutchinson, were all that saved the province from a perpetuation of currency in the form of interest-bearing certificates. But the necessary amount of specie was secured by a loan and the resumption carried through without meeting any further obstacle. Writing of the resumption act of 1748/9, by which Massachusetts was committed to that policy, Shirley said, " I am persuaded these motions would not of themselves have prevailed in the House of Representatives, had not their present Speaker, Mr. Hutchinson, in concert with whom alone this Act was originally Planned, and all measures previously settled, by his extraordinary Abilities and uncommon Influence with the Members, managed and conducted it through the Difficulties it long laboured under in passing the House." [2]

Among the financial questions of Shirley's administration that of the governor's salary was of far less importance than those of the land bank and the retirement of the currency, though discussions of this subject between him and the lower house occurred at intervals throughout his entire administration. Belcher had been forced to content himself with £680 for the greater part of his governorship. In his twenty-third

[1] Acts of P. C. Col., 1745–1766, p. 85, et seq.    [2] Shirley Corresp., I, 467.

instruction Shirley was required, if possible, to secure £1,000
clear of all deductions, as a competent sum. If he could not
secure this as a fixed grant for his term, he was permitted
to accept it in the form of annual grants, provided this was
disposed of in every case as the first business of the session.[1]
At first the assembly refused to grant more than approx-
mately the sum which Belcher had been receiving. But
Shirley declared that this was inadequate, below the dignity
of his office and little in excess of the ordinary expenses of
Boston merchants and their families. He pleaded also the requirement of the British constitution that the different
branches of the government must be kept independent the
one of the other. But the unanimous opinion of the assembly
continued to be, as it had been in the past, "that to settle
a salary as proposed would be of dangerous consequence to
the liberties and privileges of His Majesty's subjects of this
province." [2] The amount, however, they increased until, in
1742, it reached the sum of £1,000 per annum. At that point
it was kept throughout his adminstration. In the course of
the discussion the force of royal instructions was briefly referred to, but upon this subject the opinion of the house
continued to be that they were not binding upon it though
they were binding on the governor. After the beginning
of the war the depreciation of the currency proceeded so
rapidly that the nominal amount of the salary, as of all
other payments, had to be correspondingly increased. In
1748 the grant made was £2,000, and later it was increased
somewhat beyond this sum. In the later years of his administration Shirley pleaded strongly for certain grants additional to his salary, in recognition of special services which
he had rendered to the province. The services upon which he
laid stress were those connected with his visit to Louisbourg
after the surrender, his procuring some cannon and other
ordnance supplies from the crown and services rendered in
the eastern parts of the province. For these, after repeated
applications, he received small grants from the assembly, £200
or £300 in each case. But the period of struggle over the
salary question had long since passed and whether it was

[1] *Ibid.*, I, 52, 87; L. H. J. Jan. 1741/2 and later years.
[2] L. H. J. Nov. 31, 1742.

Shirley or Phips, the lieutenant governor, who complained that his remuneration was inadequate, the assembly determined its amount and there was no serious question of its right so to do.

The naval operations off the northeastern coast of America in the later stage of the third intercolonial war brought the British fleet and its needs closer home to the colonists of New England than had been usual in the past. In the matter of impressment there was much activity and the effect of this was felt by the seamen and the coasting vessels of Massachusetts. Craft of this nature brought supplies of wood and other commodities from the eastern parts or the north and south shores to Boston. Their crews, as well as men found about the wharves of the town, sailors, craftsmen, apprentices and laborers were specially exposed to seizure by the officers or agents of any British warship which happened to be lying in the harbor. Early in 1742 men had been taken off a wood boat, a fishing boat, and a coaster, and a master carpenter, who was also a freeholder of Boston, had been seized. The captain of the " Astræa," by whose officers these men had been seized,[1] was compelled by the governor and council to give them up. In August, 1745, the selectmen of Boston complained to the lieutenant governor and council that for a considerable time a schooner had lain off the harbor and fired on all coasters coming in and going out and had taken several men from them.[2] They were probably taken on board his majesty's ship, the " Bien Ann," whose crew had been reduced by desertions, the men, it was claimed, being concealed in Boston. It was the numerous desertions, encouraged by people of the localities, from warships which lay in colonial waters that furnished the excuse for the exercise in cases like these of the brutal right of impressment. Evils like flogging in the navy, as well as the superior profits of privateering, led to the desertions, and so the chain of evils resulting from brutality on the one side and gross breaches of contract on the other continued to work themselves out.

In the autumn of 1745, the captain of his majesty's ship

[1] L. H. J. Nov. 20, 1741/2.

[2] Ibid., Aug. 23, 1745; Selectmen's Minutes, Aug. 21, Rep. of Boston Rec. Comm., XVII.

"Wager" applied for the impressment of "a considerable number of men" to make up his complement.[1] The lieutenant governor was advised by the council to issue the order, but for only five men. In addition to the usual restrictions the sheriffs of the three counties concerned were ordered to take none with them in the execution of the warrant except inhabitants of the province and persons of good character, and they were not to take any men who had been on the late expedition against Louisbourg. All this furnishes clear evidence of growing sensitiveness on the subject of impressment. In the course of impressment for the "Wager" two men in Boston were murdered and two officers and a man of the warship were held responsible for the outrage. But before they could be arrested they took refuge on the man-of-war and it sailed for the West Indies. The council desired the lieutenant governor to write to the governors of the island colonies and also to inform the admiralty board in England, with a view of securing the surrender of the accused for trial. Naturally, no further reference appears to this case, but in the following February the captain of his majesty's ship "Shirley," to whom orders for impressment had been issued, together with the deputy sheriff of Suffolk county, were assaulted by a mob on the streets of Boston, and a number of seamen, armed with cutlasses, threatened to kill the captain and others who were concerned in impressments.[2] Somewhat later a memorial was presented to the house of representatives by the town of Boston, complaining of the issue of writs of impressment by the governor and council. This was denounced by the council as insulting and tending to stir up strife, but defended by the house as a regular form of procedure for procuring a redress of grievances. The "tragical consequences" which accompanied impressment, even when managed with caution, were insisted upon, and also the determination of the house to secure the rights of its constituents. The simple truth was undoubtedly expressed, when the house said that if impressment was carried further it must prove distressing to the people of the province and especially Boston.[3]

---

[1] C. O. 5/818, Journal of Ex. C. of Mass. Oct. 26, Dec. 3, 1745.
[2] *Ibid.*, Feb. 17, 1745–6.     [3] L. H. J. Mar. 14 & 21, 1745/6.

By this time the sensitiveness of the Massachusetts public had been increased not only by the collapse of the land bank, but by the heavy debt and taxation caused by the war, by the heavy losses of life at Louisbourg after the siege, by the stagnation of business of which there was general complaint, and by the fact that Rhode Island and other colonies were profiting so much by privateering and trade while Massachusetts vessels and seamen were to such an extent requisitioned by the government. These matters, aggravated by the "insupportable grievances" resulting from impressment, formed the burden of a petition from the Boston town meeting to the house of representatives in March, 1745/6.[1]

We hear nothing further on the subject until after the arrival, in November, 1747, of Commodore Knowles with his squadron from Louisbourg. While he was refitting and assembling the merchantmen he was to convoy, many desertions occurred among his men. To fill their places a general press warrant was issued and seamen from boats throughout the harbor and on shore were swept in.[2] Three townsmen happened to be taken with the rest, though it is said to have been the intention of Knowles to release all such on application. But the feelings of the seamen and common people of Boston, who were exposed to seizure in such raids as this, had been so wrought upon by recent occurrences that, on November 17,[3] an explosion of mob violence occurred in the town such as had not been seen since the overthrow of Andros and was not to be repeated until the passage of the stamp act. The mob, consisting of 300 or more, easily overpowered the sheriff, seized all the British officers and seamen they could find, appeared before the governor's house and drew from him the information that the press warrant was issued without his knowledge. They then broke the windows of the council house and demanded the release of the impressed men, efforts of Shirley to quiet them being futile. He had ordered out the town militia, but scarcely any responded, a result which caused much chagrin. A

[1] Rep. of Boston Rec. Comm., XIV, 84.
[2] Forty-eight men were impressed.
[3] Shirley Corresp., I, 406, 412, 421; Pubs. of Colonial Soc. of Mass., III, 213–239; Hutchinson, II, 386.

proclamation was issued calling upon all to aid in suppressing the riot and a call was issued to the militia of the neighboring counties. But Shirley considered it safer to retire to the castle.

Like Montague at a later time, Knowles cherished a lively contempt for colonists. When he heard of the doings of the mob, in a passion he ordered his ships made ready for action and prepared to fire upon the town. From actually carrying out this rash resolve he was persuaded by the suggestions of his men and the warnings of the governor, and in the end released nearly all who had been impressed, before he went to sea. After the withdrawal of the governor the general court and town authorities were left to deal with the insurgents. They by solemn resolutions declared their abhorrence of such riotous proceedings and their resolve to support the executive. Public feeling after about four days quieted down and, piqued by the governor's call upon the troops of neighboring towns, the militia of Boston turned out and escorted him back to his house. Though impressment was occasionally resorted to during the next war, it was done legally and awakened no special resentment.

An event like this naturally provoked public discussion. Two letters from Governor Shirley to Secretary Willard were published in the "Post-Boy" and another account of the riot appeared in the "News Letter." In one of Shirley's letters the conduct of the town militia was criticised. This occasioned the holding of town meetings and the drafting of a petition to the governor in vindication of the character and attitude of the towns people.[1] At this point Dr. William Douglass took a hand in the discussion by publishing, as a part of his "Summary, Historical and Political," a number of rather severe strictures on the character of Commodore Knowles. Besides representing that he was of low origin and rose through the unaccountable whim and favor of his superiors from the meanest posts in the navy, Douglass stated that he was not really brave and that on various occasions in the colonies had shown himself to be both inefficient and a

---

[1] Shirley Corresp., I, 406 Post-Boy, Nov. 2 and Dec. 14, 1747; Rep. of Boston. Rec. Com., XIV, 129; Noble in Pubs. of Colonial Soc. of Mass., III, 217 et seq.

petty tyrant. Knowles, when informed of his publication, sued Douglass for libel. The case ran through the courts of Massachusetts, Douglass winning upon the verdict of a jury in the inferior court of common pleas, that decision being reversed by the superior court of judicature. Under a writ of review the case was heard again and Douglass recovered costs from Knowles. Knowles then appealed to the privy council, but the case does not seem to have been heard there. He was appointed governor of Jamaica, the affair was apparently dropped, and so a final decision was not reached.[1]

In New England, as elsewhere, the process known as expansion had been in active progress, especially since the peace of Utrecht. We have met it in discussing immigration, Indian relations, the fur trade and war. Closely involved with it were the boundary disputes, as a result of the slow progress of which the limits of the colonies came to be fixed. During the thirty years of comparative peace which followed the treaty of Utrecht a gradual drift of population westward and northward, as well as into sections within the colonies which hitherto had remained unsettled, went on with the result that the frontier in a measure was extended and spaces behind it were filled up. Institutionally in New England this process was facilitated by the multiplication of township grants and the peopling of these sometimes by immigrants from Europe, but generally from the already settled parts of the colonies. It was the process of the seventeenth century extended and developed. By this process in Worcester county, the region in central Massachusetts which had previously been so sparsely settled, several new townships were established. In both Connecticut and Massachusetts a similar process went on in the hill country west of the Connecticut valley. Towns were settled in the valley of the Housatonic and to the eastward of it, while from the region of Albany and of the Livingston Manor in New York, population was creeping eastward to meet the advance from New England. The Hoosac valley furnished one of the avenues of approach from the Hudson in this movement. We have already seen how, first from Massachusetts and later from New Hampshire as centres, new townships were formed between the Merri-

[1] Acts of P. C. Col., 1745–1766, p. 107.

mac river and the upper Connecticut, thus extending the
frontier toward the Green Mountains, while large territorial
grants of New York were preparing the way for an advance
of settlement toward Lake Champlain and the mountains
from the south. In Maine the progress of settlement had
been checked by Râle's war, as well as by the bloody conflicts of the intercolonial wars which preceded and followed
it, and only slight advance along the coast to the eastward
was made prior to the peace of 1748. No part of the entire
colonial territory suffered so heavily at the hands of the
French and Indians as did this region. The settlement of
Halifax on the extreme east was an answer to the challenge
of the French north of the Bay of Fundy, but some time was
to pass before the long stretch of country between it and the
Kennebec region was occupied by English settlements.[1]

The effect of the advance of the British frontier, taken
in connection with the planting of the French military post
at Crown Point and with the activity of the French at St.
Francis and in the northeast from St. John to Louisbourg,
became evident in the Third Intercolonial War. The conflicts
which it involved extended over the entire line of territory
from Louisbourg on the east to Lake Champlain on the west.
The encounters at Number Four and in the region of Fort
Dummer in New Hampshire, at Fort Massachusetts in the
Hoosac valley, and the attention which was given to efforts
against Crown Point, show the extent to which the frontiers
had approached one another since the treaty of Utrecht and
serve in part to differentiate the Third War from any which
had preceded it. Apart from the financial questions which
have just been discussed, it was the problem involved in the
defence and development of this frontier which chiefly occupied Governor Shirley's attention and determined the
course of his administration. The interests and activities
of Massachusetts under his lead were central and to an extent controlling in New England and, as we know, they
reached out to Louisbourg on the east and Crown Point on
the west. They also involved negotiations to secure the

---

[1] The best sketch of this development is in Mathews' Expansion of New
England, which is based upon a study of town histories and of the histories of
the colonies and sections involved.

active coöperation of the Six Nations against the French. On the British side Shirley and Massachusetts played altogether the leading part and it was the aggressive spirit of this lawyer-governor which largely determined the scope of the activities of his colony at this time. Not since the days of Dudley had so strong an imperialist been in a position directly to influence affairs in New England. As the result of the changes which have just been outlined, relations had greatly broadened since Dudley's time and the scope of Shirley's activities was correspondingly wider than had been that of his predecessor. Dudley also was hindered by the suspicion and jealousy felt toward him by his contemporaries. Shirley had very little opposition of this nature to contend against and secured wide support for his plans with perhaps a minimum of antagonism. This was due in part to the combination of aggressiveness and tact for which he was distinguished and also to the fact that conditions in both Great Britain and America had become such as to favor, if not to necessitate, a positive attitude such as Shirley assumed; and that he caught and to a high degree reflected the spirit of his times. With the death of Cotton Mather the last irreconcilable reactionary of prominence had disappeared and though in a non-technical sense New England was long to remain Puritan, Massachusetts produced no more leaders who pinned their faith wholly to the corporate colony and the Puritan Commonwealth. In the related fields of religion and politics this meant an important gain for a man in Shirley's position.

The administration which we are considering covered the period of the Third Intercolonial War and continued well into the Fourth. It also synchronized with the ascendancy of the Pelhams in British politics, with the years when the duke of Newcastle reached the height of his influence in foreign and colonial affairs. It closed before Pitt attained great prominence and therefore before the blows were struck which were to bring the Newcastle régime to an end. Shirley and his work belong to that phase of British development which is identified with the reputation of the duke, when political and social life sank to the lowest level which was reached even in the period of the " four Georges." Shirley in some of his doings exhibited the qualities of that period. He was a tireless office seeker and probably applied for the governorship of more colonies than any other man on record.[1] He was by nature a courtier and paid his addresses to the duke, his patron, with a constancy which was exceeded by no one. About his loyalty to the whig system of government there could be no question, and to the support of the imperial policy which it was upholding he devoted all the energy which he possessed. Much of this might also be said concerning Clinton of New York, Gooch of Virginia, Dobbs of South Carolina, contemporaries of Shirley in colonial governorships. They were also products and representatives of the period in which they lived, but the student at once sees that they were of decidedly lower types than Shirley. He ranks with Bellomont, Hunter and Spotswood — if he was not superior to them — and certainly stands in the first rank among colonial governers of the old régime. Like the rest, he is to be judged not so much by what he accomplished, which naturally, under the political and social conditions that existed in both the mother country and the colonies, could not be great, but by what he conceived to be possible and desirable. It is true that the results of his most dramatic achievement, the capture of Louisbourg, were nullified by the treaty of Aix la Chapelle, but that did not cause him to abandon plans by which Cape Breton would again be brought within the British frontier.

Shirley belonged to that group of men, best represented in England by the earl of Halifax, who were preparing for the effort which was to overthrow French power in America and India and thus bring the British maritime empire out into the clear light of day. Pitt was of course the leader of this group, but men of a lower order than he better represent the real spirit of the movement as an evolution out of the past. These men broke less completely with the Walpole and Newcastle tradition and were more clearly connected with the routine of administration than Pitt could ever claim to have been. In the colonies Shirley was the best representative of this group. His letters contain some of the best expositions

[1] The list included at least Massachusetts, Nova Scotia, New York and the Leeward Islands.

of its policy and his official career was devoted without stint to the realization of its ideals. To his correspondence, as in earlier times to the representations of the board of trade, one may turn for some of the best statements extant of the aims of aggressive British imperialists as they were at the middle of the eighteenth century. Though they were directed chiefly to problems of the northern frontier, they reveal more thought upon colonial problems in general than the letters of any other governor on the continent.

At the request of Clinton, in 1748, Shirley diagnosed the evils from which the government of New York was suffering.[1] The assistance of Colden in the preparation of this paper is acknowledged and he attributes to the encroachments of the assembly too late an origin; but the nature and extent of some of them are clearly stated, though the suggestions as to remedies are singularly weak and ineffective. But they are what the crown and its governors had been repeating for more than half a century. Shirley accepted the inevitable in his own province and could hardly be expected to propose any radical or impossible remedies for a neighboring colony. But more indicative of the spirit and times of Shirley was his insistence in the conference with the Iroquois in 1748 and on other occasions that, under order from the king, he and Governor Clinton were jointly to take care of all the northern colonies.[2] This had special reference to the steps which should be taken to keep the Six Nations true to the British alliance. It was directly connected with the crisis in affairs which was threatened by the French occupation of Crown Point. To Shirley's mind and in his time this was the event of chief importance near the western end of the northern frontier, as the situation in Nova Scotia was at its eastern end. On August 18, 1748, Shirley and Clinton sent a joint letter to the board of trade,[3] in which they declared that Crown Point, built in time of peace, was an encroachment on British territory which furnished a secure retreat for their war parties and interposed a serious obstacle to expeditions which the English might send against Canada. They hoped that the French might be persuaded to demolish it, but, if

---

[1] N. Y. Col. Docs., VI, 432; Shirley Corresp., I, 441.
[2] Ibid., 426–430.　　　　[3] Ibid., 449–455.

not, the British must needs build rival posts on the passes to the south of it as a protection to the frontier.

As was true later, in the time of the Revolution, New England was sensitive to the presence of an enemy on Lake Champlain. From that point the entire frontier of New Hampshire, Massachusetts and New York was exposed to attack. In defending that frontier these provinces served the colonies to the south as a barrier against the enemy. This suggested the entire problem of colonial union and coöperation, as illustrated in the earlier wars and in Shirley's own efforts to organize expeditions against Crown Point and Canada. Shirley discussed this on the basis of the quota system which had been tried in the reign of William. He did not propose any departure from that system, though he was fully aware that the colonies would not voluntarily conform to it. He also called attention, especially at the later date, to the great changes which had come about since William's time in the relative population of some of the colonies, especially the growth of Pennsylvania and Connecticut and their ability to bear higher quotas, as compared with Massachusetts, than at the earlier date. Massachusetts had surrendered several towns to New Hampshire and Rhode Island, and her losses at Louisbourg and in the colonial wars had generally been heavy. The quotas should, therefore, be revised to correspond with existing conditions and enforced by fresh instructions.[1]

A question of detail in connection with the defence of the northern frontier which provoked some discussion during the Third Colonial War was that of Fort Dummer and Number Four. The former was situated west of the Connecticut river and a few miles north of the Massachusetts line; the latter was on the east bank of the river about forty miles further north, and has become the modern Charlestown. Fort Dummer was built under Massachusetts jurisdiction, partly for the promotion of the fur trade, and both parts were settled by people from that colony. As they were isolated and on a favorite line of French and Indian attack, their position was very exposed. When it was decided that Fort Dummer lay within New Hampshire, in 1745 Governor

[1] Shirley Corresp., I, 455; II, 20–29.

Wentworth, under an order from the crown, submitted to two successive assemblies the question of providing for its defence, but they refused to add this burden to their other expenditures in the war, alleging that the place was too remote from their other settlements and communication with it would be difficult and costly. The same arguments were applied to the case of Number Four, and it was claimed that the defence of both posts was more in the interest of Massachusetts than of New Hampshire, since they were a protection of the settlements to the southward rather than those beyond the Merrimac and far to the eastward.[1] Massachusetts therefore had to continue such support as was given to these outposts, Number Four in particular being the object of many and most violent attacks by the Indians. After the war she tried to get the cost of this support deducted from the reimbursement made to New Hampshire, but failed.

To the mind of Shirley it seemed most unfortunate that a frontier so long and exposed as this should lie within a poor and small province like New Hampshire, while Massachusetts could with difficulty be induced to defend it, and that very imperfectly, because it lay outside her limits. But this was the situation which the system of detached and jealous colonies everywhere presented. It was, therefore, his idea that the boundary between British and French possessions should be established and then that the frontier should be treated from the military standpoint as a unit and protected by a line of forts which should be under joint control.[2]

Upon his services in Nova Scotia, at the eastern limit of the frontier, Shirley especially prided himself. In 1750 he wrote to the duke of Newcastle that during the late war the care of that province had principally devolved upon him.[3]

---

[1] N. H. Prov. Papers, V, 301–304, 310, 320, and many other references in index; Belknap (Farmer's edition), 286; C. O. 5/885, O. P. Mass. (Sept. 6, 1744; June 26, 1746; Nov. 30, 1748); Shirley Corresp., II, 31.

[2] Shirley Corresp., I, 341, 503, II, 22, 66.

[3] *Ibid.*, 499. These statements are substantially an elaboration of the claim set forth by Shirley in his speech to the Massachusetts legislature on November 29, 1744. In this he said that the ships and men sent to Annapolis — 120 men were voted — had prevented an attack by the French and discouraged any effort to stir up revolt in the rest of Nova Scotia. In the absence of a French naval force this all proved to be true. Mass. L. H. J. June 12 and November 29, 1744.

The correspondence of Mascarene with the ministers at home had been transmitted through Shirley's hands and without his advice no steps of importance had been taken. Troops had been freely sent from New England for the protection of Nova Scotia, and twice — in 1744 and 1746 — Shirley claimed to have preserved it from imminent danger of falling into the enemy's hands. The facts certainly show that these statements contained a large element of truth. Shirley's correspondence also shows that during those years his attention was closely fixed upon the French neutrals and the danger which their presence in Nova Scotia involved.[1] As early as 1746 he expressed himself in favor of the removal, at least of the most dangerous among them. But as no intimation came from Newcastle or his associates of an intention to adopt such a policy, Shirley was careful to limit his proposals to those who actively supported the enemy. When Knowles urged the removal of the entire body of Acadians, Shirley deprecated such a policy as calculated to destroy the effect of his own moderate counsels, as well as those of the home government.

When the war was over, Shirley had Captain Morris, who commanded one of the New England companies at Annapolis, prepare a map or plan of the Bay of Funday, including also the isthmus to Bay Verte.[2] His purpose in this, as he wrote to Newcastle, was to prepare the way for the planting of British settlers among the French of that region, being convinced that the latter would not make good subjects of the crown. By means of these settlements and the intercourse in trade and other relations which must result therefrom, Shirley believed that the influence of the priests and of the French government would be broken and the English language, laws and customs introduced. French Protestant ministers might be utilized for this purpose. British settlements and families, in number well exceeding those of the French, should be interspersed among the latter and forts should be built at strategic points, so that communication with Louisbourg might be cut off. Some such plan as this, Shirley informed Newcastle, must be adopted or the

---

[1] *Ibid.*, 298, 321 n, 328, 336, 351, 354, 371, 388.
[2] C. O. 5/886, O. P. Mass., Feb. 18. 1748/9.

Acadians, a compact body of French Roman Catholics, would sooner or later become strong enough to subvert the king's government in the province or, as a third possibility, the entire body of Acadians would have to be removed — a policy which would be attended with very hazardous consequences and should be avoided if possible. At this very time and upon the request of Newcastle, Shirley proposed a plan of civil government for Nova Scotia.[1] It was based upon the charter which William and Mary had granted to Massachusetts, but a long proviso was added that, until a sufficient number of English were settled in the province and the French had became sufficiently acquainted with the English language and government to serve on juries and in the assembly, the province should be administered by a governor and council. In view of these utterances it will probably be admitted that Shirley had thought out this problem more clearly than any one else who expressed himself upon it, but the British government, unfortunately as usual, allowed affairs to drift and finally, as the result of action taken on the spot and when the crisis became acute, the most brutal course short of wholesale massacre was adopted.

The Massachusetts governor also devoted some critical attention to the acts of trade. In a letter of February 6, 1747/8, to the board of trade,[2] Shirley laid before them defects of these acts arising from omissions and ambiguous expressions, of which judges of the provincial courts took advantage in order, by prohibitions, to break in upon the jurisdiction of the admiralty courts and defeat the purpose of the trade laws. Of this increasing evil Shirley heard frequent complaints from the customs officers, and a detailed statement upon the subject had been prepared and transmitted by the advocate general. The evil, it was believed, could be checked only by expressly giving the courts of admiralty jurisdiction over the plantation trade in all its branches and under the acts intended for its preservation. In this same letter Shirley also enlarged upon the evil of trade with the enemy under flags of truce. So far had this practice gone in Rhode Island that in eighteen months sixty vessels were said

---

[1] Shirley Corresp., I, 470–477.
[2] C. O. 5/885, O. P. Mass.

to have gone thence to Cape François and other parts of St. Domingo and Martinique. The return of a single French prisoner on one of these vessels was considered sufficient to give countenance to this trade. The aid which it afforded the enemy, as well as the extent to which it exhausted the supplies needed for provisioning British ships were so evident that at the beginning of the war an act had been passed in Massachusetts, making any commerce with the enemy penal.[1] But as similar measures were not adopted by other colonies, the traffic continued and Shirley perceived that an act of parliament was necessary. All this is indicative of conditions which were to develop on a larger scale in the next war and to have momentous results.

An official with Shirley's abounding activity could hardly avoid making some enemies and provoking some complaints. Toward the close of the first decade of his administration he became aware of complaints on the part of members of the treasury board and in the war office. These grew out of transactions connected with his regiment and with the expenditures occasioned by the levies for his intended expedition against Canada. With Kilby, the former agent of Massachusetts, and with Samuel Waldo, Shirley had disputes growing out of their public relations. Reports of these complaints led him to defend himself at length in letters to Newcastle.[2] In these not only did he assert, though he had had many complicated accounts to settle, that he had not been guilty of any breach of trust, but he could reflect with pride on the fact that, unlike many of his predecessors in the Massachusetts governorship, he had had no quarrel or misunderstanding with the assembly. At about the same time in the course of an address to the assembly, Shirley summed up the achievements of his administration thus far as follows:[3] " War is a calamity whenever it befalls a country, but this one has been attended with unparalleled success and most signal deliverance to this province and, as is most unusual, has left a country less in debt than when it entered upon war." The reimbursement, he continued, had put an end to

[1] Acts of 1745/6, Ch. 6.
[2] Shirley Corresp., I, 458, 493.
[3] C. O. 5/885, O. P. Mass., Nov. 15, 1748.

paper money, a great evil in peace and insupportable in war, and had substituted a stable medium which would be a lasting foundation for prosperity.

These statements, though made in rather sweeping and optimistic terms, may be taken in connection with the suggestions of policy and the actual achievements which have already been described, to indicate fairly the worth of Shirley's administration in New England up to the time when, in 1750, he went abroad as royal commissioner to settle, if possible, the boundary between the British and French territories in and adjacent to Nova Scotia. There for a series of months his attention was devoted to marshalling anew the historical evidence and arguments which supported the British claim to the territory in dispute. He thus had occasion, with his associate Mildmay, to emphasize still further the view, to which he had committed himself, that Nova Scotia was the key to British interests and dominion in America. When, years later, he came to write a formal account of the transactions of the late war,[1] Shirley threw boldly into the foreground the claim that Nova Scotia and Cape Breton made up the key to the eastern colonies, the barrier of the British against the French throughout the entire St. Lawrence region; that upon their possession depended the control of the fisheries, the security of New England and naval control in the north Atlantic. Under the influence of these ideas — whoever originated them, they gained their prestige by his support — the government now awoke from its indifference to the fate of those coasts. The result was the triumph of British arms in North America, and thereby the attention of officials was so centered on this coast that later it reacted against the larger interests of the interior and the western frontier.

The fact that the opinions of Governor Shirley rather than the achievements of his province have demanded so much of our attention, is justified by the necessity of explaining the policies by which British efforts were coming to be directed at the period of crisis which was now approaching. The earliest and in certain respects the best statements of those

---

[1] Memoirs of the Principal Transactions of the Last War, *etc.* dedicated to the Duke of Newcastle. This was published anonymously but has generally been attributed to Shirley.

policies and of the ideas underlying them are to be found in the letters of William Shirley. He was the man who saw these things and had the resolution to put them down on paper and support them by action more effectively, during the decade between 1740 and 1750, than any other person. He is therefore to be regarded as a forerunner of what was to come, a connecting link between the period of Walpole and Newcastle and that of Pitt and Wolfe. The ablest among the royal governors were usually better imperialists than were members of the British cabinet. The reason for this was that their vision of interests in America was less obscured by the complications of European politics than was that of the immediate advisers of the crown. Of the advantage which this gave certainly Shirley furnishes a most conspicuous example, though his expositions, like those of many in the past, might have fallen on deaf ears had it not been that in the fullness of time conditions were ripe for Halifax, Pitt and the policy which they and their associates were to carry through to decisive victory.

Fortunately, it is not necessary, in order to understand the relation which Massachusetts assumed toward the policies which have been outlined, laboriously to follow through the legislative history of Shirley's administration. In the sphere of military affairs the response which was made by the general court to his proposal of the Louisbourg expedition is in general representative of the whole. Unlike the deadlocks which to such an extent paralyzed military activity in New York, the spirit of coöperation prevailed to a high degree in Massachusetts. The contrast in this regard between the two provinces had been great from the first, but was even more decisive than usual during the Third Intercolonial War. This is in part explained by the pressure of war upon New England, but in this case it was due also in large measure to the efficient leadership of Shirley. It was also of great importance that the question of the governor's salary had been settled, or at least that it was not allowed to interfere with the problem of defence. The journals of the two houses, with the record of governor's speeches and replies, of reports of committees, motions, resolutions, votes, conferences which they contain, show that a high degree of harmony was maintained between the executive and the legislature.[1] The council, of course, as always, exerted a mediating influence. The governor also, while actually leading and usually formulating policy, maintained a conciliatory attitude toward the assembly. He asked the advice and assistance of the legislature and submitted to their rather slow, though on the whole efficient, action. In the lower house the committee for defence worked over and digested proposals for the building and repair of forts, expeditions and the men and money needed for these, and in most cases its recommendations were accepted by the house with little or no debate. In response to messages of the governor measures were commonly introduced the following day or even on the same day, having usually passed through the hands of the committee for defence, and three or four days more would often suffice to secure their passage through both houses. Though amendments were made, on one side or the other, there was a notable absence of bickering and evidence that a reasonable spirit of compromise prevailed. From the machinery, thus adjusted, came in the form of acts and resolves measures for levying soldiers, for prevention of the arrest of soldiers and seamen for debts, for prevention of mutiny and desertion, supplying troops with arms, blankets, subsistence and the like, better regulating of garrisons on the frontiers, and all the details of administration in time of war. Owing to the pressure of this business, matters of a private or civil nature were dealt with rather more summarily. Occasionally a special committee was appointed to investigate some matter, or a vote was passed to defer the establishing of wages and subsistence of men raised for the defence of the frontier, especially of the remote forts in New Hampshire. These were dilatory tactics and were on the whole exceptional. The actual result of the coöperation of the governor and legislature through the committee for the defence, and also through other special committees appointed to join the governor in the inspection of the north, or other similar tasks, was to make the committees essentially executive in function, though appointed by the legislature. The legislature in substance, if not in theory, recognized that the logic of the situation demanded untrammeled executive action, and

[1] See especially the Journal of the Lower House from June, 1744.

Shirley was content with the substance. He was not inclined to quibble over prerogative, provided the legislature refrained from attempts to encroach upon his actual rights as governor and captain general.

Shirley in his speeches to the assembly discussed policies with fulness and power; some of the best statements of his views are to be found in these utterances. On December 5, 1744, there was intrusted to a committee of the lower house, which had been appointed to consider a proper method for the payment of soldiers in service, also the consideration of the garrisons necessary to be employed, especially in the eastern parts. It reported that two hundred men be forthwith dismissed and that various other adjustments be made in the garrisons in that region, specific numbers being mentioned in every case. This report was accepted by the house and a committee appointed to establish the wages for the men concerned and to acquaint the governor with the resolution of the house upon this matter and desire him to give his orders accordingly. This drew at once from Shirley a message in which he told the house that they had entirely mistaken their province in this affair. They and the council had the function of raising money for the support of troops, " but as to the part of the militia out of which they are to be drawn, the posting of those soldiers when raised, and the duty upon which they are to be employed, the determination of it appertains only to the Captain General, who by the royal charter, . . . as well as by His Majesty's commission, has the sole government of the militia." He believed that there was no precedent for such an encroachment upon executive authority in Massachusetts since it had been a royal province. He could not bind himself to obey ' a resolution which included the raising and disposition of the forces, as well as the establishing of their pay, and he hoped the board would be sensible of its mistake. By successive votes which were passed in the course of the next few days it appears that the house yielded to the warning of the governor and left with him the disposition of the troops, while it authorized the payment of a sufficient number for the eastern garrisons. Later, in 1745 and 1746, it is observable that the governor retained troops on the frontier for months beyond the time for which provision had been made for them by the general court. No protest was made, because the court saw that such a course was necessary and that the governor was acting with patriotism and intelligence. On the other hand, the assembly instinctively delayed providing for additional levies until a crisis made the need for them imperative. The soldiers were always complaining of the low rates at which their wages were fixed by the assembly, while the rapid depreciation of the currency increased difficulties of this nature. Against such predispositions and obstacles as these the governor had always to be struggling. A long, costly and defensive war rather than a short and offensive one was the result.

These incidents reveal the line of cleavage between the spheres of the executive and legislature in the provincial system and the spirit in which at this time a conflict over their respective powers was avoided in Massachusetts. It shows a certain political maturity which could be by no means always matched in other colonies and reveals the secret of the success of the administration we are considering. The multiplication of details concerning military administration which are already reasonably familiar could do no more.

Men of the type of Shirley inevitably laid great emphasis on colonial union, though under conditions that would not weaken imperial control over the colonies. Under the pressure caused by the advance of the frontier on both sides, officials and all imperialists became more and more insistent upon this point, as the middle of the century approached. One of Shirley's last appeals to the Massachusetts general court before the end of the Third Intercolonial War was set to this key.[1] " It has ever been my apprehension " he said, " that a disunion of councils among His Majesty's colonies on this continent, and their acting upon separate schemes of interest, without a strict regard to the general good of the common cause, would in the course of a long war prove destructive to the whole; as it naturally turns what ought to be their superiority and advantage over the enemy to their weakness and misfortune." After calling attention to the fact that failure on the part of the southern colonies to act pre-

[1] L. H. J., May 27, 1748.

vented action by the northern ones, he continued: "For this reason I have laboured ever since the beginning of the war to promote an agreement between all the colonies to join in it, more especially by endeavouring to convince the southern governments, not only of the reasonableness· and justice but of the wisdom also and good policy of a close union of our councils and strength against the common enemy. But if such a union of the colonies can't be effected, I hope those governments that are immediately exposed to the incursions and devastations of the enemy . . . will not be given over to so fatal an infatuation as to suffer themselves to be destroyed by a much inferior force to their own, because other governments which ought to assist them neglect doing their duty."

This was one of the best expressions of Shirley's feelings on the subject of colonial union as they were at the close of the third war. His experiences in Europe, including the attention which it had been necessary for him to give to the study and defence of the British contentions as to territorial rights in North America, had only confirmed his opinions. The commissioners had met and argued in the spirit of advocates of the extreme claims of their respective governments. In much the same spirit were all intercolonial relations between rivals at that time conducted. This all served to stimulate the sentiment of national pride which lies at the root of imperialism and to fan these emotions till they led to aggressive action and finally to war. Both the French and British were equally involved and the result was a succession of wars which could end only with the complete triumph of one nation or the exhaustion of both. It was to this policy, with all its consequences, that men like Shirley were fully committed. It was their stock in trade and by it, with its most serious limitations as well as its elements of power, they are to be judged. But the masses of a people are only with great difficulty and to an imperfect degree fired with emotions of this type. In social groups so isolated and so individualistic as those of the British colonies it was quite impossible to attain such a result. But Shirley worked for it and may be called the leading exponent of it among the governors of his time. All the royal officials supported the idea according to their place and degree. But Shirley, as a connecting link between the last two colonial wars did more than any other official in the colonies to formulate and spread the idea in its later form. Franklin was the only colonist whose services in this direction were comparable with those of Shirley. Though Shirley was not present at the Albany Congress of 1754, he supported it, though chiefly from the standpoint of Indian relations, in an able speech before the legislature of Massachusetts, and as is well known he and Franklin after the Congress was over exchanged views upon the plan of colonial union which it put forth.[1] It was too much like the corporate colonies of New England to suit the lawyer and royal governor, whose ideal was rather the dominion, though with a tax-granting assembly, or — what would perhaps have been still more satisfactory to him — the admission of representatives from the colonies into parliament and then the exercise of the full sovereign power of legislation and taxation of this imperial body throughout the realm and the colonies alike.

[1] Gen. Court Recs., XV, 198–201, Apr. 2, 1754. Sparks, Writings of Franklin, III, 56. Shirley Corresp., II, 103, 111.

D1320276

THE SHAAR PRESS

THE JUDAICA IMPRINT
FOR THOUGHTFUL PEOPLE

THE
SHAAR
PRESS

# ABANDONED

## A NOVEL BY
## M. KENAN

author of *The Betrayal* and *Wildlands*

© Copyright 2022 by Shaar Press

First edition – First impression / May 2022


**ALL RIGHTS RESERVED**

*No part of this book may be reproduced* **IN ANY FORM,** *scan, photocopy, electronic media, for use with digital retrieval systems, as an audio or video recording, or otherwise –* **EVEN FOR PERSONAL, STUDY GROUP, OR CLASSROOM USE –** *without* **WRITTEN** *permission from the copyright holder, except by a reviewer who wishes to quote brief passages in connection with a review written for inclusion in magazines or newspapers..*

**THE RIGHTS OF THE COPYRIGHT HOLDER WILL BE STRICTLY ENFORCED.**

This is a work of fiction. Names, characters, places, and incidents are either the product of the author's imagination or are used fictitiously. Any resemblance to actual persons, living or dead, or locales is entirely coincidental.

Published by **SHAAR PRESS**
Distributed by MESORAH PUBLICATIONS, LTD.
313 Regina Avenue / Rahway, N.J. 07065 / (718) 921-9000

Distributed in Israel by SIFRIATI / A. GITLER
POB 2351 / Bnei Brak 51122

Distributed in Europe by LEHMANNS
Unit E, Viking Business Park, Rolling Mill Road / Jarrow, Tyne and Wear, NE32 3DP/ England

Distributed in Australia and New Zealand by GOLDS WORLD OF JUDAICA
3-13 William Street / Balaclava, Melbourne 3183 / Victoria Australia

Distributed in South Africa by KOLLEL BOOKSHOP
Northfield Centre / 17 Northfield Avenue / Glenhazel 2192, Johannesburg, South Africa

ITEM CODE: ABANDH
ISBN 10:1-4226-3171-0 / ISBN 13: 978-1-4226-3171-3

Printed in the United States of America
Custom bound by Sefercraft, Inc. / 313 Regina Avenue / Rahway N.J. 07065

*A single moment of spontaneous courage*
*requires a lifetime of preparation.*

*(Anonymous)*

# PART 1

1

RELATIONS BETWEEN ISRAEL AND INDIA WERE GENERALLY good, but the region in which they had spent the past week was predominantly Muslim and reminded Shaul of his last, and far from pleasant, visit to Jordan. Their driver, a tall Sikh who had served for seven years with the Indian paratroopers and another seven as a security officer in the Indian embassy in Tel Aviv, was not happy.

"You can do whatever you want," he said. "I only follow orders." He paused to take a long breath. "But if you take my advice—you'll make all your phone calls afterward. Let's get out of here. Now."

*Now.* Pinchas looked around at the rented room, strewn with items that testified to a human presence. "Give us three minutes and we're gone," he said. He glanced at Shaul. "You agree?"

"Two and a half." Shaul, whose slashed cheek was still bleeding, rose to his feet and, in a single motion, swept up all the *sefarim* that lay on the table. "Let's not take any chances."

Three personal bags. A large bag of canned goods. The bags with their tallis and tefillin. A worn cloth bag packed with *sefarim*. The Sikh, more anxious than both of them combined, brushed the entire load up in his arms at once. "We're out of here," he said. "Yes?"

Pinchas and Shaul exchanged a swift glance that allowed each to see the fear in the other's eyes.

This was Shaul's third visit to India, yet he had never seen the Sikh don his security turban. Until now, Jarnail, with his enormous muscles, had served as nothing more than an expert driver who provided entertaining tours. The change that took place as he was transformed into a military man was worrisome.

"We're out of here," Pinchas agreed, scanning the small room quickly and checking under the bed and in the cupboards.

"We're leaving now," said the driver, the last word sharp. "Pinchas, you're first. Go outside, don't make eye contact with anyone, go to the car, open the back door and get in. I'll leave second, start the car and wait for you, Shaul, to run out of the house and join us. Is everyone clear?"

Oncologists, they say, are afraid of tumors. Firefighters view every flickering flame as a potential inferno. And security guards? Were they exaggerating when they thought that a furious mob was about to attack them? It was reasonable to assume that the answer was yes. Very reasonable. But outside—it could not be denied—a group of dark-eyed street youths were already gathering.

Pinchas left first, squinting in the sun's powerful glare as he moved toward the startlingly green vehicle that had carried them faithfully all the way from Mumbai. He opened the back door as ordered, recoiling from the superheated air that rose to greet him. Though the car was parked partially in the shade, the sun had managed to raise the temperature in that metal cage to boiling. The sight of the youths standing around and watching him silently might have persuaded him to lower his head and get inside.

No one thought that the job of a kashrus *mashgiach* was easy. But until two o'clock this afternoon, it had seemed as though everything was going to be simple. The manager of the factory that processed cooking oil was eager to please, the workers lived up to the image of Indians as smiling and alert, and matters had been moving along as expected.

They had been due to complete the *kashering* tomorrow morning, start work in the afternoon and have the whole job over and done with in the next three days—leaving behind thousands of bottles of Indian peanut oil, with Hebrew lettering adorned with a *mehadrin min hamehadrin* symbol of kashrus.

That was the plan.

And then Shaul became aware of the whispers.

Pinchas passed a hand across his perspiring brow. Life did not always go the way people thought it should. If it did, he and Sari would have held a baby in their arms a decade ago. And still, one was always surprised anew when sticks were thrust into the wheels of his life.

The Sikh started the engine. Shaul, the guilty one, rushed over to join them, the rag he held to his cheek stained with blood. And then, a moment before they would have been out of sight, one of the youths lifted his arms and threw a rock at the car. No, not a rock. A cinder block.

The rock hit the window on the driver's side, creating a network of cracks. But that was a minor problem. Much worse was the fact that two of the youths were hurrying into the center of the road to block their way.

Jarnail mumbled angrily under his breath and turned the wheel sharply, so that his beautiful European car smashed into the rubbish bin on its left. The vehicle rose onto the narrow pavement and, tires screeching in protest, managed to get back on the road and speed away.

"We did it?" Shaul turned around.

The Sikh glanced at the rearview mirror, either at them or at the road behind them. "Maybe we did," he said slowly. "That is, those young men aren't here. Now all we have to do is stay away from the police."

The police!

Pinchas and Shaul had been working together for less than six years, but they already had an astonishing ability to communicate without words.

"Why the police?" Pinchas asked at last.

Jarnail laughed. "Don't be naïve, Pinchas," he said softly. "After all, our Shaul almost killed a person."

"The person almost killed *me*," Shaul protested automatically. "He shoved a cartful of glass bottles at me. You were both there. You saw everything!"

"Well, that's what the police will want to check out," the Sikh said. "This is India, as you know. Police officers don't always understand everything right away. Not even very simple things.

"And if you have an established kashrus organization behind you that would agree to pay a hefty bribe to spare you from languishing in an Indian jail, the police will not be satisfied with a mere several thousand rupees."

Silence filled the car.

"It could take the police chief some time to grasp the monetary potential here," Jarnail said encouragingly. "Or else he may be in the middle of his dinner. In any case, we have thirty kilometers until we leave this region's jurisdiction. And in another seventy kilometers, we'll be out of the whole province's jurisdiction. So you two pray, I'll drive, and with G-d's help all will be well."

"*B'ezras Hashem*," Pinchas murmured, patting his pockets in search of his *Tehillim*. Shaul, after a few moments of silence, said, "I didn't do anything, Jarnail. That guy pushed three hundred bottles at me and then slipped on the broken pieces. As far as I could see, he just sprained or broke his leg and got a few cuts from the glass. That's all."

"They could bring in another man's death certificate, along with a pathologist's report saying that the injuries were definitely deliberate." Jarnail's voice filled with loathing, the centuries-old hatred between Sikhs and Muslims echoing in his words. "And they could also *not* do that, of course. It all depends on how much you're willing to pay." He smiled at them in the mirror. "It's all still hypothetical, right? At this point, it's just another fifteen kilometers until we're out of the region."

Fifteen kilometers was not so much. But the road was narrow and winding, and a cow could appear at any moment and languidly block their way.

Pinchas davened under his breath, while Shaul opened the booklet of *pesukim* about *bitachon* that he carried everywhere with him. And Jarnail pressed the gas pedal, expertly pushing the car to its limits.

For long moments, each of them was lost in his own world and not a word was heard. The air conditioning worked with a slight whine, cooling the air in the vehicle along with their pounding pulses.

Suddenly, the car turned sharply to the right, making their heart-beats accelerate again.

"Jarnail?" Shaul asked, sitting up and groping for his booklet, which had flown out of his hand.

"I just went onto the shoulder of the road." Jarnail sounded slightly detached, remote. "Too bad you weren't wearing your seat belts."

The shoulder was a precipice leading down a terrifying slope. The men hastened to buckle their safety belts. "Is something wrong?" Pinchas asked, trying to turn his head to look behind them.

"Right now—no. But I don't want to take a chance."

Pinchas and Shaul exchanged a glance. If not for the fact that this was Jarnail, who had accompanied them on their visits to India for several years now, they might have suspected him of trying to increase his driver's fee on the grounds that he'd saved them from some mythical disaster. But Jarnail, until now, had proved himself trustworthy.

Still, maybe it was a good idea to let someone in Israel know that they were in trouble.

2

THE SMALL SATELLITE PHONE FELT WARM IN PINCHAS'S hand, but a strange wave of coldness flowed over his heart as he put it to his ear. He'd always done the right thing. He'd never, not even in his turbulent adolescence, been in trouble. On the contrary, from a young age he'd been the proverbial "good boy" who knew how to mediate arguments, soothe the grown-ups and solve all problems. An uneasy feeling had swept through him when Shaul asked him to call Rabbi Schwab in Israel and update him on their situation.

From their place in the back seat, Pinchas and Shaul could see the wheel jumping under Jarnail's fingers as he held it tightly. Their seat belts afforded minimal protection against the car's bumpy progress.

"Jarnail?" Shaul's voice rose sharply, warning and objecting. He was cut off when another pothole caused his seat belt to squeeze his ribs. "Jarnail?" he tried again, holding on with whitened fingers. The Sikh made no answer. The danger of the car overturning became much more pressing than the prospect of the extended jail sentence that Jarnail had warned him about.

"Call Schwab!" The air burst from Shaul's lungs as the car slid down a muddy incline. "Call him already, Pinchas!"

*Call so that they'll know to send a medical team if we disappear. So they'll know where to start searching. Otherwise, no one will find us here.*

Although the air conditioner was doing its best, beads of sweat dripped from Jarnail's blue turban and down the back of his neck, to collect in the blue fabric of his shirt. The adrenalin coursing through Pinchas's body sped up the tempo of his thoughts. An awful picture rose in his mind of Sari receiving a call from the Kupat Cholim clinic with the news they'd been waiting so many years to hear… only to get a second call in which Rav Schwab, in his brief and businesslike way, informed her that her husband had disappeared in India, or had perhaps been injured or even killed in a car crash.

*They won't send Schwab. They won't send him.* That was the sole comfort his mind could provide at that moment. *They'll find a professional woman to break the news gently.*

They slid further along the slope, speeding toward the river flowing at its foot, until the car suddenly stopped.

In the small, crowded car, silence reigned. For a minute, Jarnail rested his head on the steering wheel. Then he straightened up and glanced back at them in the mirror with a broad smile.

"We just saved ourselves thirty miles," he said. "And by good fortune, we've entered the Maharashtra Province. You know, it's a pity to drive in a roundabout way when you can shorten the trip by going in a straight line."

"Ah." Shaul was the first to activate his vocal cords. "Yes, a real pity."

The driver's thick eyebrows knitted together as he tried to interpret Shaul's tone. Succeeding, he looked a bit affronted. "I'm not talking about just any thirty miles!" he said. "Did you want to get involved with the police?"

"No," Shaul admitted. "But I also didn't want to leave my wife a widow."

"Neither did I," Jarnail said with a shrug. "But as you see, that didn't happen."

His logic wasn't impeccable, but Pinchas sensed that continuing the conversation would lead to the faithful Sikh's feelings being hurt. "We didn't know you were such an accomplished driver," he said weakly, his heart still thumping from the recent fright.

Jarnail shrugged again. "It's not an inborn talent," he said. "I had training."

"Training in what?" Shaul, still shaken, sounded sharper than he intended.

"To serve as an escape driver," Jarnail said, turning the engine back on. "You know about my military background, right? I was in a special unit and then worked for seven years as a security guard in our embassy in Israel."

"Certainly, certainly." Pinchas forced a smile at the man in the rearview mirror. "How could we forget when we hear your beautiful Hebrew?"

"It actually improved after I returned to India and started working with Israeli businessmen and tourists."

Jarnail fell silent as he concentrated on driving along the muddy riverbank. The roar of the engine shattered the peaceful scene, causing several cows to lift their heads in surprise, children to throw glances at them, and people wading in the shallow water, dragging fish nets behind them, to stare wide-eyed at the green car as it vanished from sight almost as soon as it had appeared.

"All right," Jarnail said after a few more minutes' driving. "I think we're out of the danger zone. Do you want to call your boss and tell him what happened?"

The phone rang as though in response to his question. "Rabbi Schwab must be getting back to me," Pinchas said, bringing the phone to his ear. But the wails that rose from it couldn't belong to his employer. Pinchas's eyes darted about uneasily, trying to gauge if the sounds were able to reach his fellow passengers.

"Sari, I'm in the car," he said. When his hint wasn't picked up, he added, "Shaul and the driver are here with me. I'll call you a little later, okay?"

Pinchas's wife was apparently unhappy with this suggestion. Hastily Pinchas said, "No, no, of course I don't want you to have to deal with this alone. I'm just with other people here in the car, okay?"

"We need to stop for lunch anyway," Jarnail said from the driver's seat. "Or has the tension made you two lose your appetites?"

"I'm hungry," Shaul pronounced.

"I'll get right back to you," Pinchas said, closing the phone with a click. "You don't have to stop for me," he said, looking dejected.

"We're stopping for lunch," Shaul said quickly. His heart went out to his friend. Some women are prone to cry over nothing, but a sixth sense told him that once again Pinchas and his wife's dreams had been shattered. Though he hadn't stolen his own ten children from anyone, he felt uncomfortable sitting beside Pinchas right now.

Jarnail hummed a tune with an indifference that was almost too marked. After another moment's travel, he braked. "Here," he said.

"This looks like the perfect place for a meal. Nice scenery, shade, everything we need."

With an effort, Pinchas smiled. He felt even worse when he saw their attempt to pretend they had neither heard nor understood a thing. "Good," he said. "Should I help you set the table?"

"No, thanks," Jarnail said, mopping his perspiring brow. "We'll manage."

"Go on, make the call you promised," Shaul told Pinchas. "We'll take care of the food in the meanwhile."

"Thanks." Pinchas blinked hard, despite himself. Then he plodded over to some bushes and retreated from the others, his expression woebegone.

⟶ ⟞⟎⟎⟍⟍⟎⟍⟎⟍ ⟵

"Is someone in his family unwell?" Jarnail asked quietly.

"No." Shaul wasn't prepared to share his friend's troubles with their driver. But Pinchas, in the mistaken belief that he had moved far enough away from them to speak to his wife out loud, told Jarnail everything.

"So the doctor yelled. That's *his* problem for being so uncouth." Pinchas was trying to sound strong and encouraging. "So you didn't take the right dose. So what? Medicine won't decide whether or not we have children, right? We're just doing our *hishtadlus*. You don't have to cry. Yes, I know it's hard, I know. I also feel like crying."

It was unpleasant to listen to a conversation not meant for their ears. Shaul wondered if he should hurry after Pinchas and ask him to either move further away or lower his voice. Or maybe such a request would only embarrass him.

"When HaKadosh Baruch Hu wants to send us a child, that's when it will happen," Pinchas said in response to what he'd heard from the other end of the line. As his friend's voice began to sound more distant, Shaul decided to stay where he was and let the echoes fade away on their own.

But the spot was so quiet that even after Pinchas had moved away, his words continued to float back: "Do you want to tell me that there's anything that Hashem can't do? That for Him, there is the slightest difference between giving us a baby or giving one to Shaul and his wife?"

Oops. Shaul's ears tingled.

"It's really pretty here," he murmured to Jarnail. "I think I'll go have a look at the scenery." Without waiting for the Sikh's reaction, he hurried away in the opposite direction to escape his friend's voice.

Every person has his own path in life. His own challenges. He shouldn't feel so bad right now, conscience-stricken and filled with guilt over the fact that he didn't know how to properly appreciate the existence of each of his children. While the test of wealth may be more comfortable than the test of poverty, it brings its own challenges. He was trying, really trying, to live his life the way he should, even if he was sometimes impatient with his children's antics, wasn't always the perfect father, and had to travel abroad at frequent intervals.

When Pinchas's voice had melted into the green expanse, Shaul saw no point in strolling any further. He sank down onto a handy boulder, dropping his aching head onto his closed fists.

3

THE PARCEL OF LAND IN WHICH JARNAIL HAD PARKED HIS car could reasonably be considered one of the most beautiful in the world. Dozens of shades of green were intermingled with bright splotches of pink, red, and a warm, cheerful orange. But little of that beauty was able to penetrate Shaul's thoughts.

Not every *yeshivah bachur* spends his time worrying about what kind of parent he'll be when he grows up. Shaul was one of the few who had devoted considerable time to that question and had been convinced—absolutely—that he would be one of the best fathers in the world. A father who would be both compassionate yet firm in his views, who would be both attentive and inclusive, who would know how to give criticism but would mostly offer compliments. It wasn't pleasant to admit to himself that he would also be the kind of father who would be prepared to do literally anything so that his child wouldn't lack the fifty shekels he needed to take a yearly outing along with the rest of his class.

Well, in this, at least, he had stuck to his principles. Bitterness touched his lips. He did do everything—including sleeping on mattresses stuffed with fleas in China and fleeing a lynching in India. His children didn't lack for anything—except a father who was present in their lives. His own father had been home every Shabbos, and young Shaul hadn't been forced to be tested on the *Mishnayos* that he'd learned in school by a neighbor he barely knew.

He sighed. Obviously he wouldn't have chosen this line of work

as his first option. It would have been far more pleasant had he managed to find a position as an eighth-grade rebbi in the local elementary
school. He would have been a great teacher. But in light of the fact that
he had not succeeded in finding a position in that field, and that reb-
beim are not the only ones who need good people skills and an ability
to problem-solve, it seemed that Shaul was born to be a kashrus *mashgiach*. It was part of his mission in life. And until now, he had fulfilled
it fairly well.

His cellphone vibrated in his pocket. Shaul sighed. They really
needed to update Rabbi Schwab on the latest developments... But it
was only Gadi, his young brother-in-law.

"Yes, Gedalia?" he said wearily into the shiny little device. "How
are you?"

A rapid torrent of words poured into his ear in response. Within
sixty seconds, he was apprised of the latest business deals that Gadi
had successfully closed since they'd last spoken.

"Nice, very nice," he said, feeling a million years old. "So good to
hear. And how's everything at home?"

When Gadi spoke of his home and children, his voice didn't have
the same energy and positivity as when he discussed his business
affairs. Even so, one definitely was given the impression that Gadi's
life was all light and perfection. None of his children, for instance,
ever caught a cold. None of them ever needed speech therapy or help
with reading. Or maybe Gadi hadn't yet encountered such challenges
because he had only four children so far.

"Are you listening, Shaul?"

He recalled the many long talks on *emunah* they'd had on Friday
nights, soon after Shaul had married Gadi's older sister, Ricki, and
Gadi had still been a *yeshivah bachur*. And then there were the learning sessions in *Nefesh HaChaim* every Motza'ei Shabbos. But two years
after getting married, Gadi had left the *beis medrash* and earned a BA
in computer programming and a master's in business. Immediately
afterward, he'd launched his first start-up, which was hugely successful. And then another. By the time the third one rolled around, according to the rumor in the family, his bank account already held a seven-
figure sum.

"Of course I'm listening. Was there any particular reason that you
called?"

"Yes, actually there's something serious I want to talk to you about."

"Be my guest." Almost of its own volition, Shaul's hand went to his injured cheek. It throbbed, and the pain became worse when he touched it. But the pain cleared his thoughts. "Though I have to tell you that this has been a very long day, and I'm exhausted right now."

"I'll make it brief," Gadi promised. "I understand from Ricki that you're in India and that you have a two-day break between jobs coming up. So I had a brainstorm. I think it might be a good idea for her to book a flight and meet you there. I'm prepared to cover the airfare and sign on a bank loan so that she can finally open the business we've talked about a million times."

Shaul coughed. "That's very kind of you, Gadi," he said patiently.

"It's not kindness. She's my big sister! And the two of you did so much for me when I was in yeshivah."

There was a nostalgia in his brother-in-law's voice that Shaul found surprising.

"So what business are we talking about?" Shaul prodded.

"Don't you remember when I brought up the idea of importing fabrics from India? And you agreed it was a good one? Ricki's always had a flair for fashion, and everyone who knows her is always asking her advice about design. Now here's her chance. And if it's a problem of financing, I'm prepared to help. Her passport is up to date, right? She could be in Mumbai by Monday afternoon, just when you get there."

Birds were prancing all about as though they couldn't see the black-clad man sitting motionless on the boulder. The grass near his feet rippled with the passage of a large gray lizard.

"Shaul?"

Shaul had plenty to say. But none of the sentences racing through his head seemed the correct thing to say out loud right now.

"In order to start a successful business, you need a business plan," he said at last—and regretted it at once. It would have been better to refer to "personal issues" and not give Gadi an opportunity to start describing his great wealth and the plethora of his successes, which he had achieved as a result of "having courage at the right moment in time."

"The least successful business is the one that is never started." This time, for some reason, Gadi didn't use himself as a personal example. "Listen, Shaul. It seems that if no one drags you by the ears, this will simply never happen. So I'm prepared to be your sponsor. The important thing is for Ricki to start doing something with herself already."

Indignation on his wife's behalf burned in Shaul. "You don't think Ricki's doing anything with herself?" he asked, his voice low and cold.

"You understand perfectly well what I meant. And don't start making a speech about her raising ten children, because until eleven months ago she was raising nine children and also working full-time at Intel. Your tenth baby, with all due respect, does not create eight hours of work a day by any measure."

Shaul swallowed. "Have you ever tried raising ten children, Gadi? Ten children whose father is out of the country half the time?"

"No. But that's not really the point. Like you, I want Ricki to be happy. And in order for her to be happy, she needs other things to think about than cooking chicken, changing diapers, and checking kids' heads for nits. Don't you agree?"

Shaul had neither the strength nor the desire to argue. But it didn't look like he had a choice. "If you think that raising children is all about chicken, diapers, and nits, then you have a real problem, my friend." He tried to maintain a genial tone. "I've had a crazy morning. Let's continue this tomorrow."

"No problem. But I'm getting her the visa for India now."

Shaul stood up and discovered that one of his feet had fallen asleep. "Do whatever you want," he said, too tired to protest. "But it's a pity to waste the money. Ricki doesn't want to open a fabrics boutique or a bridal salon."

"She wants more money," Gadi said. "Every woman does. And she wants satisfaction and a feeling of success. The two of you can buy whatever merchandise in India you want. The main thing for her is not to stay at home all day in a ratty old kerchief and stained housedress. She was never that type."

Shaul's lips tightened again, but he didn't say a word.

"I'm getting her a visa," Gadi repeated. "As for the rest, we can talk tomorrow."

"Fabrics can be bought in Israel," Shaul said a minute later, having mustered what little energy he had left to lodge a final protest. But the phone was silent. Gadi had disconnected.

---

"You're both in a bad mood," Jarnail said as they gathered for lunch. "I understand that you're disappointed over the episode with the oil.

But look at the bright side: you prevented them from feeding their customers oil with fraudulent kashrus symbols, and that's wonderful. And we've moved out of the danger zone. You can lift up your heads and smile. The danger is past. The story is over."

"*Baruch Hashem*," Pinchas mumbled, taking tiny bites of the tuna sandwich Jarnail had prepared.

"*Baruch Hashem*," Shaul agreed in a low voice, not raising his eyes. He didn't want to see the open sorrow in Pinchas's face or the visible track leading from the corner of his right eye down to his beard, clear evidence of at least one tear shed while Shaul had been arguing with Gadi over nonsense.

"You're taking this hard," Jarnail insisted. "But as an Israeli once told me: 'Smile—everything is for the best.' He told me that a big rabbi said that. You two probably know who I'm talking about."

"We do," Shaul confirmed.

But it was all apparently too much for Pinchas. Abruptly, he stood up and said, "I'll be right back."

With the branches rustling vigorously behind his back, he walked into the bushes and vanished from view.

4

JARNAIL GAZED AT THE SPOT WHERE PINCHAS HAD disappeared. Then he looked at Shaul and sighed.

"The water will be hot soon," he said, in an attempt to make a conversation. "Then we'll be able to make some coffee for you, chai for me, and tea for Pinchas when he gets back."

Shaul sighed as well and chewed the rather dry bread. Jarnail threw in a third sigh and then asked, "How long has Pinchas been married?"

"Nearly eleven years now."

"Eleven years. That's a long time."

"Very long." Shaul's heart was heavy.

"And the doctors—they have no ideas for them? Are there no treatments?"

Shaul happened to know that the doctors had no explanation for Pinchas and Sari's silent home. But he merely lifted his eyes to the Indian and smiled. "We Jews call such a conversation 'lashon hara.' Pinchas wouldn't want to know that we're talking about him behind his back."

Jarnail shrugged. "I'm not a gossip," he said. "But my wife's sister went to an old woman who gave her some herbs that helped her right away."

"You can tell him that. But not now. Let him calm down a little."

"Of course, of course." Jarnail finished eating his portion and looked hungrily at the remains of the tuna in the can. Although Shaul generally couldn't be too generous with the limited food they had brought from Israel, this time he couldn't resist. The fellow had worked hard today. He deserved an extra sandwich.

Jarnail appreciated the gesture. "Are you sure I can have it?"

Shaul nodded. "Go ahead."

"Thank you very much!"

"My pleasure." Shaul took his phone out of his pocket. "I'm going to call my boss now."

"Tell him about the car," Jarnail reminded him. "I'll need to replace the window, knock out the dents, and paint the metal. The repairs could cost fifteen thousand rupees easily."

"Sure, I'll do that," Shaul said, already walking away.

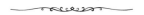

"Hello, Rabbi Schwab. How are you?"

Rabbi Schwab was doing well, *baruch Hashem*. He asked after their welfare.

"We're all right," Shaul said, choosing his words with care. "But there was a bit of drama at the factory, and we got a little beaten up by some worker who tried—" He paused as Rabbi Schwab reacted to this news. "Yes, actually beaten up. Pinchas got punched in the stomach, and I was cut by broken glass. No, it's not a very big cut. It's already stopped bleeding. . . This was"—he checked his watch—"a little more than two hours ago. We had to run from there after the worker who attacked us slipped on some of the broken glass and was hurt. His friends decided to avenge him and tried to attack us."

Shaul looked over at Jarnail, who was making dramatic gestures toward his car and added, "Jarnail was very efficient and got us out of there just in time, just as some punks threw a cinder block at us that cracked his car window, and he dented the car when we fled." He chuckled. "No, I'm not trying to break anything to you slowly. Anyway, we're out of the danger zone and—"

A scream shattered the silence. A loud, high-pitched scream, the likes of which Shaul had never heard before. It was so loud that it reached even Rabbi Schwab's office in Jerusalem.

"That's Pinchas!" Shaul leaped to his feet. "I'll get back to you, Rabbi Schwab."

Another scream, but this time it was broken into short bursts.

"Shaul!" Pinchas yelled. "Shaul, come here!"

"He went that way." Jarnail's gun, usually tucked away, was already in his hand. He used it to point.

The monsoon season had ended not long before, and all of nature was green and burgeoning. But all the beauty didn't make the path any easier to traverse. They pushed through the bushes, suffering scratches from branches in their way and stumbling over rocks hidden beneath the dense foliage. They directed their steps toward the nonstop shouts of "Shaul! Shaul! Shaul!" coming from Pinchas.

"We're coming, Pinchas. We're here!" Shaul beat back the bushes. "Don't move if there's a snake."

"It's not a snake." The voice came from the other side of the screen of plants, indicating that Pinchas, too, was trying to close the distance between them. "It's not a snake at all, Shaul. It's a baby. A little baby."

---

A baby?

Jarnail and Shaul exchanged a brief stare.

"A baby?" Shaul stooped beneath the branches of a particularly thorny tree. "What are you talking about?"

Pinchas suddenly appeared among leaves of millet taller than he was, his jacket, soiled with dirt and leaves, bundled oddly in his arms. "There was a baby girl there, tossed on the ground."

People sometimes went insane from grief. But that didn't usually happen so suddenly. "What do you mean, there was a baby girl?" Shaul asked gently. "And where is she now?"

Pinchas's face was pale, his eyes wide. "Here," he said, holding his grimy jacket out to Shaul. "I covered her so she wouldn't be cold."

A baby?

Hesitantly, Shaul took the jacket and unfolded it, wondering what he'd find inside.

It was nothing strange or marvelous. Pinchas had told them the simple truth.

"She's so small." Incredulously, Shaul gazed at the round, creased face, the tiny nose and the hair covered with a layer of white. "She... she was just born."

The baby breathed slowly, quietly, her minuscule body shivering inside the folds of the jacket. The bluish tinge of her lips told him that

Pinchas was right. She was cold, despite the warm weather. Carefully, he rewrapped the child and held her close. "Come," he said, feeling a sense of hysteria rising up to engulf him. "I think she needs to eat. Now."

"Eat what?" Pinchas asked.

He was a father of ten. Pinchas and Jarnail were prepared to follow his lead without hesitation. But the sad truth was that he had never personally tended to such a small infant. Ricki would be with the baby in the hospital, and afterward she'd go to her mother's. Even when she came home, she'd always preferred to let him take care of the older kids. The newborn was all hers.

Shaul took a deep breath. "I think that first we should give her boiled water with a little sugar."

"How?" Pinchas asked. A good question.

"With a spoon," Shaul said with a confidence he did not feel. "With a spoon, little by little."

Flies were already buzzing around their abandoned tuna, but the water was bubbling peacefully over the fire as though nothing had happened.

"Can a newborn have sugar?" Pinchas wondered.

"I don't know." Shaul sat on the orange folding chair, clasping the tiny bundle. "I have no idea. But one thing I'm sure of: If we don't give her something to eat, she could die of starvation." He touched the baby. She was covered in blood and dirt, and her hands were freezing. "Pinchas, give me a cup of water with three teaspoons of sugar. Jarnail, please go find us some milk."

"And leave you two here alone?" Jarnail shook his head. "Sorry. Impossible."

"Here's the water." Pinchas's hands were shaking. "What do we do now?"

"We feed her," Shaul replied quietly, leaning the baby's head against his arm. "Did you mix in the sugar? Good. Now, while I hold her, you give her the water. Did you mix in some mineral water, so it won't be too hot?"

Pinchas's hand froze in midair. "I didn't think of that," he admitted sheepishly. "How much water should I add, do you think?"

The infant let out a woebegone mewl.

"Add two-thirds cold water," Shaul instructed. "But after you pour out the old water and start pouring in the new water, add more sugar."

"More sugar," repeated Pinchas. His hands were shaking so badly that it was Jarnail who ended up doing the job.

"Here," he said, sitting down on the grass beside Shaul so that his face was level with the baby's, ready to help. "What now?"

But Shaul was through with giving orders. Though at first it had looked like he'd have to hold the baby with one hand, the cup in the other, and the spoon in a third, he managed to position the baby's head in the crook of his left arm, hold the cup in the same hand, and manage on his own.

"Is she swallowing?" Pinchas appeared above them, watching the white plastic teaspoon making its way from the cup to the little mouth.

"She's swallowing," Shaul said softly. "Look—she likes it."

"That's…awesome." Pinchas's voice was hoarse. "Give her more, poor thing."

The spoon moved again. The drops of sweetness gave the newborn enough energy to open her eyes and gaze at them with what seemed like gratitude.

"It's good for her," Jarnail said with astonishing gentleness. "She has so few demands that she's satisfied already."

"Yes," Pinchas agreed, then asked, "Does anyone have any idea how she got here?"

"She didn't 'get' here. She was left," Jarnail replied dryly.

"Obviously," Pinchas said. "But who could do such a thing to such a tiny baby?"

The Sikh's brow furrowed. "Unfortunately," he said, "that's not even a question."

5

YOU'RE NOT SUPPOSED TO RAISE YOUR VOICE NEAR A newborn. At least, that's the rule in a world where one boils pacifiers and scrubs one's hands with alcohol before approaching the bassinette. But despite the fact that he'd broken any number of rules in giving a newborn infant mineral water with sugar, Shaul didn't want to raise his voice. In a near-whisper, he asked, "What are you talking about? Is there a war going on between different sects and groups that you told us break out in India from time to time?"

Jarnail rubbed his broad nose. "Isn't it true that in Israel when someone really annoys you, you tell him something like 'Be well,' or 'A *kapparah* on you'? Words that are fundamentally positive, but you're actually saying them because you're angry at the person?"

Pinchas and Shaul didn't understand the sudden change of subject. They nodded, wondering why the man had chosen this moment to give them a lesson in semantics. "Yes," Pinchas said. "Why?"

"Here in India, we say, 'May you have ten daughters, and may all of them find good husbands!'" Jarnail explained with a long look from his dark eyes. "A son helps at home. He works in the field, supports the family if the father is sick, takes care of the parents when they grow old and can't work for themselves. Daughters just drain away money. They don't work, they do eat, and a good match costs a fortune. People in India don't want daughters. They are prepared to do anything not to have daughters."

His words were swallowed up in the silence of the verdant nature surrounding them.

"Anything? Meaning—*anything*?" Shaul asked hoarsely, placing another spoonful into the baby's mouth. She swallowed soundlessly, her lips moving with enchanting delicacy.

"Anything and everything," Jarnail said starkly. "Her parent was nice enough to just leave her on the ground and walk away. How do I put it? There are worse parents than him in the world."

"But—" Pinchas's eyes were very wide. "This is their daughter! Their child! How could they do that to their own child? Doesn't he even care? Does he think that some angel will come down and give her milk and honey?"

Jarnail apparently didn't grasp the connection between angels and milk and honey, but he didn't let that stop him. "Look, I'm not in favor of these things," he said, holding out his palms as though to ward off the attack. "I happen to have two daughters at home. But it's been this way for hundreds of years. When the British arrived in northern India, they thought at first that Indians are very modest folk, which was why they never saw any girls in the streets. Later they realized that it was because in certain regions"—he paused to seek the right phraseology—"there are hardly any girls."

Pinchas groped his way over to the empty chair, automatically shooing away the flies hovering around his sandwich. Slowly, he sat.

"I'm sorry," Jarnail said. "I'm sorry, Pinchas, that you had to come across this right now."

But Pinchas was too shaken to gather the import of his words. "It's... it's inhuman," he said. "Don't they know that murder is the most terrible thing in the world?"

"It's human if human beings do it," Jarnail argued. "And the poverty in India, as you've seen for yourselves, can be devastating. Poverty can drive men out of their senses. They don't know how they will manage to raise this girl and how they will give her what she needs in life. They think it a pity for her to suffer all her life for nothing." He fell silent for a moment. "And some don't think of death as such a bad thing. After all, souls never get lost. The baby's soul simply leaves its body and will return in another body, in another incarnation."

The infant was eating with gusto, and gradually her color and her temperature seemed to improve. "Nice of them to find some sort of justification," Shaul said, bringing another spoonful of sugar water to the tiny mouth. "Really nice."

Jarnail shifted his weight from one foot to the other. "You have to understand that they are not bad people. They simply know that they are not able to raise this girl and give her what she needs. They don't have enough money to raise her and marry her off."

"And they don't think it would be better for her to stay unmarried all her life as long as she's alive?"

"They think that she will not want to marry a bad man from a bad family because her father has no money to marry her to a good man from a good family."

Pinchas shook his head. "Soon you'll say that they do it out of love."

Jarnail gave a short bark of laughter. "You will surely agree with me that it's not good for a girl to grow up where she's not wanted. To know that she's a burden, that her parents are raising her only because they have no other choice."

As they stared at him, he spread his hands. "But to say that it is love? No, I won't say that. But it's not honorable for a father to let his daughter remain a spinster or marry her off to a bad man from a bad family. And then there is the fact that she consumes resources but does not bring in any income—"

"Look at people with terminal conditions," Pinchas said harshly. "How they plead for just one more breath. Can't someone explain to them that no one wants to give up a chance to live just because she won't be happy all the time?"

"The government is trying to institute change," Jarnail said. "But... it's not as simple as it sounds."

"All right," Shaul broke in. "Enough. I don't think we need to go into detail about this nightmare. The question is what to do now."

"We finish lunch," Jarnail said. "And you need to call your boss. He's probably somewhat shaken up."

"I was talking to Schwab when you screamed," Shaul explained to Pinchas. "It sounded terrible."

"It *was* terrible." Pinchas took off his glasses and mopped his face. "I almost stepped on her. A second before I put down my foot, I suddenly saw that it wasn't a piece of plastic but a tiny baby! I was sure I'd lost my mind." He replaced his glasses and immediately took them off again. "If I had stepped on her, I would never have been able to forgive myself."

"I can understand that."

The baby in Shaul's arms had fallen asleep, and his efforts to introduce another spoonful into her mouth were in vain. The little lass had finished eating, at least for now. He looked at her, at the little closed eyelids, the thin eyelashes, and nearly invisible eyebrows, and was swamped by memories that seemed to come from a different existence. The look and fragrance of his own babies when he'd held them for the first time. In these circumstances, though, the images caused him deep pain. He and his wife would boil their children's pacifiers if they so much as touched the floor, while this child had been lying on the ground for who knew how long...

"Listen," he said urgently. "I think that I—that is, we—need to give her a bath now. She's all scratched up, and we have no idea what sort of bacteria were thriving in the mud she was lying on."

"A bath!" Jarnail echoed. "Here?"

"I have shampoo in my bag, and you have a jerry can of water in the trunk of your car. We have those tablets for purifying water. That seems to me part of the minimum we are obligated to do for her. A newborn is vulnerable. Easier to heat up a pot of water than to try to find an antibiotic IV for her because she contracted something while lying on the ground."

Jarnail looked back and forth between Shaul and Pinchas. "I am here to help you with whatever you need," he said at last, his voice heavy. "And I am prepared to boil water if that is what you want. But may I ask what you plan to do with her afterward?"

"After her bath? We'll give her a nap, of course." Shaul's answer was sarcastic, but Jarnail didn't hear the barb in his words.

"After the bath," he said, "and after her nap—what then?"

Shaul looked at Pinchas, who looked back at him.

"Good question," Pinchas said at length. "Don't we have to report a thing like this to the police? Maybe...maybe she wasn't really abandoned? Maybe she was kidnaped?"

"Not likely," Jarnail said. "But I don't mind filing a report. The question is whether you two want to take the risk of going to the police and having them arrest you for that injured guy in the factory."

"That guy attacked us!" Shaul insisted. "He merely slipped on some oil that had spilled."

"You keep reminding me of that," Jarnail said, nearly losing his patience, "even though you know that I remember it just fine. The question is, are you ready to take the risk of explaining all that to some greedy superintendent at the police station?"

"You said we were out of the danger zone."

Once again, Shaul managed to keep his voice down in consideration of the infant asleep in his arms.

"Yes, I did. And I believe that it's true," Jarnail affirmed. "But I did not mean that it would be a good idea to get involved with the police. It's one thing to drive quietly down the road and another to go in there and put your passport down on the desk." He drew a deep breath. "Besides—excuse me for saying this, Shaul—it's not nice of you to get angry at me. I didn't do anything wrong."

6

SHAUL SIGHED. "YOU'RE RIGHT, JARNAIL. YOU'VE ONLY BEEN helpful." He lowered his eyes to the baby. The baby's hand, thin and soft, stuck out of Pinchas's jacket. He tried to wrap her more securely in the woolen cloth that was never meant to serve as a blanket. "I'm just a little frustrated, and also a bit shaken up. It's not directed at you. It's directed at the situation."

Jarnail blinked. "When you say 'the situation,' are you referring to the Ribbono shel Olam?" He pronounced the last words in Shaul's Ashkenazic-Yekkish accent.

Both Shaul and Pinchas looked stunned. "Why would you say that?" Pinchas asked.

The Sikh shrugged. "I'm just trying to be logical," he said. "After all, who created this situation? Is it not the Ribbono shel Olam?"

An awkward silence fell. It was a bit disconcerting to receive a lesson in *mussar* from a Sikh whose hair—when it wasn't covered by a turban—reached nearly to his hips.

"You're right, of course," Pinchas said at last. "Hashem creates every situation. But Shaul isn't angry at Him, Heaven forbid. It's just hard to know what we're supposed to do now. And that makes him tense. He wants to do the right thing, but he doesn't know what that is, since you say it's impossible for us to go to the police."

"I didn't say it is impossible," Jarnail protested. "I just expressed my opinion that it would be foolish, and maybe also unnecessary. The chances that someone kidnaped this child in order to cause her parents misery are like the chances that we are all lying in our beds and dreaming right now."

"A small chance, but it exists." Shaul rose to his feet. "Let's think about it while giving this little one her bath. A pity to waste time."

But bathing a newborn baby under field conditions didn't leave them much time for thinking. After they pulled out their suitcases to look for soap, a clean towel, and something with which to wrap the child, then heated the water, cooled it off, and then heated it up a bit more and managed to wash her, they ended up with soaking sleeves and shoes and none the wiser about their next steps. Shaul had never before appreciated the expertise he'd acquired in his years of fatherhood. To tell the truth, compared to Ricki's expertise he always felt clumsy and ungainly. The way he'd met the challenges he had faced this past hour surprised him and afforded him a modicum of satisfaction.

"So what do we do now?" Jarnail's job was to drive them along India's winding roads, and he was itching to do that now. "Are you going to the police?"

"Is there a chance that someone has been quick enough to have our passports tagged as problematic this soon?"

"I don't think so," Jarnail said slowly. "To be honest, I don't think there is even a police station in this area. There are only tiny villages, and they solve their problems on their own."

For some reason, neither Shaul nor Pinchas believed that they would enjoy the way those villagers solved their problems, or that it would help them deal with the problem that had landed on their heads.

"So where *is* there a police station?"

"In the city," said Jarnail. "If you'll give me a moment, I'll bring a map…"

He was quick and efficient, already on his way to the green car that had been pristine only that morning, to withdraw a thick book of maps that he always kept in the car's glove compartment.

Pinchas glanced at him, and then at the baby, wrapped in a soft purple towel. He asked Shaul in a whisper, "I don't know why, but I have a sense that he's really not happy that we're taking care of her."

"I think he's just annoyed about the delay," Shaul whispered back. "And he thinks that she's liable to cause us a big headache and plenty of trouble. Besides—" He fell silent when Jarnail appeared at their side.

"Here we go." Jarnail flipped through the spiral-bound pages. "I think we're located just about here, see?"

Pinchas and Shaul looked at him without saying a word. He realized that he had interrupted them. "Are you in the middle of something important?" he asked graciously.

Jarnail was a courteous man, and though they had become friendly, he was ever cognizant of his position as guide rather than friend. Not for the first time, Shaul sensed that the man's humble demeanor was only a pretense, behind which lurked a sensitive person with a feeling heart who wasn't happy with the role he'd been forced to play.

"We were talking about the baby," he said. Searching for a different topic, he found himself asking, "Don't you think she's terribly pale?"

"Pale?" The Sikh looked at the child as though seeing her for the first time. "She looks all right," he said when he'd completed his scrutiny. "I think she's just light-skinned. Maybe her parents were Brahmins. I don't see any cause for worry. You fed her and she ate her fill. She'll be all right, don't worry."

He nodded his head, as though confirming his own words, and then thrust the map between them and pointed. "Here, I think this is where we are. This is the road we came from, and here is the river we drove beside, and this is the mountain range over there to the northeast. See?" His finger moved along the map. "And here is the city. If we don't find a proper road, it will take us at least two hours to get there. There are plenty of villages in the area. The baby could have come from any of them. But it's reasonable to guess that she came from the nearest one. In my opinion, it's this one." His fingernail scratched a line on the map.

"Will they know in the village who did this?" Shaul asked.

"They will know, of course. But they will not tell an outsider anything."

"What about you? Won't they speak to you?"

"They won't talk to me either. Besides, what will you do if you find out who the father is? Give him money to raise his daughter? The money will run out, and he'll remain the same person: a man who has no interest in raising a daughter."

"Maybe we could deposit money in the bank for her dowry," Pinchas suggested hesitantly. "Like a savings plan that she can access when she's older."

Jarnail sniffed. "I don't know how much these uneducated people understand about banks and savings plans. But I think this whole discussion is unnecessary. They won't tell us anything. They will be afraid that we're from the police."

"So we're basically left with two options," Pinchas concluded. "Take her to the police station in the city—or take her to the police station in the city. Is there a third option that I'm not aware of?"

"The city is far away, and we need milk," Shaul said in a practical vein. "With all due respect to the water and sugar that we gave her, it's not enough. The more I think about it, the more I realize that this deep sleep of hers may be a blessing. But it could also be telling us that she's extremely weak. I want to know that we gave her the best treatment possible."

Jarnail's lips tightened with the same displeased and frustrated expression they had seen before. Shaul was about to speak when Jarnail said, "Whatever you want to do is fine with me. Just make sure, please, that your boss is updated about the situation and is fine with it, too."

He was right. They debated which of them should be the one to explain the complicated situation to their exacting employer. Shaul, who had begun the conversation earlier, was finally forced to accept that it was up to him. He handed the baby to Pinchas and then, over the course of eight and a half minutes, tried to explain to Rabbi Schwab what had taken place at the factory, starting with the innocent rustle he'd heard each time he passed the packing room, through his discovery of a cart filled with bottles of oil sporting falsified labels, and ending with the furious and hysterical attack he'd suffered at the hands of the worker responsible for the fraud when he learned that his deception had been revealed.

Only after he obtained his boss's confirmation that their behavior throughout had been appropriate and proper did Shaul clear his throat and say, "Actually, we have another problem right now. A problem that weighs approximately six and a half pounds."

NOT MUCH WAS CAPABLE OF SURPRISING REFAEL SCHWAB. IN his time, he'd received a ransom demand from Malaysian pirates, negotiated with Lee Kuan Yew, a former prime minister of Singapore, and persuaded him to help release from jail a kashrus *mashgiach* suspected of tossing a piece of gum on the ground, bargained with Dutch mobsters in broken English, provided collateral for the freeing of *mashgichim* in China, and, over the course of his forty-five years in the Vaad HaKashrus, fielded any number of urgent calls from every corner of the globe.

But even after all these years, he could still be shocked. He abruptly dropped his pen onto his desk with a clatter when he heard that the urgent problem of the two *mashgichim* at the other end of the line was how to obtain a quart of milk.

"What?" Refael tapped his pen on the edge of his desk. "I don't understand what you're saying."

"Maybe because I don't know exactly how to tell you what I need to tell you." Shaul gazed at the baby in Pinchas's arms. "Pinchas found a baby—"

"What do you mean, he found a baby?" Refael broke in.

"We stopped for lunch, and Pinchas nearly stepped on a newborn baby that someone had left in the bushes," Shaul said matter-of-factly. "We gave her water and sugar and put her to sleep. We thought you might be able to advise us what to do now."

The cluttered office suddenly seemed suffocating. Refael stood up and went to the window. "What does Jarnail say?" The pragmatic and efficient Indian had made an excellent impression on him.

"Jarnail says that the baby's parents apparently abandoned her deliberately because they have no money to marry her off when she grows up." Saying the words made that cruel act sound even more foolish than when Jarnail had described it. "He says that the chances that she was actually kidnaped or lost are practically nil."

"And what else does he say?"

Down below, the busy Jerusalem street hummed with life, and a minor traffic jam had prompted an irritable bus driver to honk his horn unceasingly.

"He's not thrilled with the idea of our going to the police. There's a chance that someone will take advantage of the factory worker's injury to try to blackmail us. It's better if we don't walk into a police station right now."

"Then let him go in." Rafael slammed his window shut and switched on the air conditioner.

Shaul covered the phone's mouthpiece and looked at Jarnail. "The boss suggests that *you* take the baby to the police station," he told the Sikh.

Jarnail shook his head. "Not a good idea."

"He says it's not a good idea," Shaul transmitted to Jerusalem. "He's afraid that if a complaint is made against us, there will be one against him, too."

"So let him find some guy and pay him a few rupees to take the baby to the police station. Really, Shaul. Don't make a mountain out of a molehill."

"That's not a bad idea," Shaul said slowly. He looked at Jarnail, who was moving his lips without speaking. "What's the matter?" he asked.

The Sikh shrugged. "Nothing." Then the roiling frustration inside him burst out. "All right, let's go crazy. Let's feed her mineral water with sugar, bathe her in water that's not too hot and not too cold, and then travel to who knows where to get her some milk. And then, in the end, we'll dump her in some filthy police station where they'll see her as an annoyance, just like her parents did. So why go to all this trouble?"

"It's a police station," Shaul said, taken aback. "They can't...that is...there are laws! They're human beings!"

Jarnail was annoyed. "What do you want me to say?"

Shaul's shoulders slumped, and he removed his hand from the mouthpiece. "Jarnail says he's afraid the police won't take care of the baby the way they should. Maybe we should take her with us to Mumbai and give her to one of the orphanages there."

"How far are you from Mumbai?"

"Pretty far. We'll probably have to stop to spend the night somewhere. But I think we can do it. We can make arrangements for her."

"Then why did you even call me?" his boss complained. "What did you want, an expense account for milk?"

Reluctantly, Shaul chuckled. "I wanted the advice of a smart Jew," he said. "Aren't I allowed?"

"You're allowed," Rabbi Schwab grumbled. "My advice is, first of all, to tell Pinchas to watch where he looks. What we don't see won't cause problems."

This sounded rather cynical to Shaul, but he had known Refael Schwab for years, and he could attest that he was a good person. So he asked, "Meaning?"

"Meaning that there are a million children in India who die every year, and a hundred million more children who suffer from malnutrition. With all the good will in the world, you can't save them all. Or maybe you can, if you daven hard enough on Rosh Hashanah. But right now...you've got yourself a problem."

"We're well aware of that." Shaul looked at Pinchas, holding the baby with amazing gentleness. "So what do you think we should do now?"

In Jerusalem, Rabbi Schwab ran his fingers through his graying beard. "To tell you the truth, Shaul? Something I don't tell just anyone?"

This didn't sound promising. Shaul offered a grudging "Yes?"

"My opinion is that, in contrast to eighty percent of our *mashgichim*, you don't need my help. You can manage on your own. I know you'll find a way out of this mess. Don't worry."

This was a compliment of a magnitude that Shaul hadn't received since he became engaged and heard his *rosh yeshivah* label him "one of the best *bachurim* in our yeshivah, a *ben aliyah* who will, b'ezras Hashem, be a *talmid chacham*." As he had been then, he was keenly aware of the steep price tag that came with the praise.

"So you're basically telling me to go it alone," he said slowly.

"No, of course not. You know that the Vaad HaKashrus stands

behind its *mashgichim*. We don't leave any wounded behind on the battlefield. But I trust you and I'm confident that you are capable of solving this problem yourself. If you decide that I've made a mistake, you are welcome to call me again at any time."

*Aargh.*

"Are you with me, Shaul?"

"Absolutely. I'm thinking about what you just said."

Rafael Schwab combed his beard with his fingers again. "I think a simple 'thank you' and 'goodbye' will suffice. Go tend to your baby, and I'll tend to the mess at the oil factory. I'll see if I can move up the date for your job at the food-coloring factory. As for the rest, call me again if you need help. Agreed?"

"Yes," Shaul said, the word emerging from between his clenched teeth. "Agreed."

---

"Well?" Pinchas asked expectantly. "What did he say?"

"He thinks that we're capable of handling this ourselves." Shaul forced himself to relax the fists that he'd unwittingly been clenching. "He says that we have everything we need to get the job done."

Pinchas looked right and left. He lowered himself carefully onto one of the three folding chairs and asked, "And what *do* we need?"

"I think he was talking about common sense. But if you want to call and ask him"—Shaul took a deep breath, inhaling the scent of the grass and moist soil—"you're more than welcome to do so."

The baby emitted a shuddering cry that quickly turned into hysterical wails. "Maybe she's hungry again," Pinchas said in alarm. "Should we give her more sugar water or try to get some milk?"

"Sugar, *bentching*, and milk," Shaul said briefly. "And let's hurry. Otherwise, we'll have to stop on the way to daven Minchah."

Jarnail's map wasn't precise, but it was the best they had. He had come by it through the help of a friend who worked in India's military office. As they returned to the car, the odor of its musky interior enveloping them, Shaul prayed that the village would be where the map said it was and that its inhabitants would agree to help them care for the infant—and even rent them a place to sleep for the night.

"The man who brought the baby here," Pinchas asked after fifteen minutes of silent driving, "came all this way on foot?"

"On foot or on a bicycle, or on a wagon harnessed to an ox." Jarnail's eyes were fixed on the narrow, dusty track.

"And that doesn't mean that there's another, closer village that doesn't appear on the map?"

Jarnail glanced at him in the rearview mirror. "His route was shorter. He could have crossed through the millet fields while I have to drive around them. But don't worry. We'll get there, too, in the end."

8

AN ENORMOUS OX WITH TWISTED HORNS WAS THE FIRST sign that they were on the right road. Harnessed to the beast was a tall wagon shaped like a basket. On a pole resting on the ox's neck sat a small man with grizzled hair and a face as wrinkled as a nut. He seemed utterly unfazed by the appearance of the green car or the honks that Jarnail sounded to induce him to move his ox and wagon to the side of the road.

"He's smoking," Jarnail said, giving up on the horn. "He'll apparently move when he's finished his cigarette. I have no desire to argue with him." He unbuckled his seat belt and turned around to face them. "I'm going out to talk to him for a minute. Wait here."

Despite his height, Jarnail reached only to the wagon's wheels. The old man peered down at him from above, speaking with a superiority that the emperor of India must have exuded when meeting the lowliest of his subjects. A moment or two of conversation ensued before Jarnail returned to the driver's seat.

"I told him that your wife died," he announced without looking at them, "and that you have a newborn baby girl and need help."

"You told him *what*?" the two men exclaimed in unison.

"Choose which wife." Jarnail started his engine and slowly followed the ox and wagon.

Shaul looked at Pinchas, who shrugged and shook his head in disbelief. "Why…did you have to say that?" he asked, his eyes on the ox's tail waving as the animal plodded down the track.

"Why do you think?" Jarnail asked. "Maybe because we have a day-old baby in this car, and you two are trying to act like a father and mother to her, and we *really* need help?"

Shaul sighed. He would never understand how the Indian mind worked.

Pinchas wasn't so resigned to the situation. Nervously, he cracked his knuckles. "But why give an opening to the Satan? Couldn't you just have told the truth and asked for help?"

The ox moved slowly between the millet fields, their sheaves as tall as a man. The car straggled after it.

"You can never tell with people." Jarnail crossed his hands behind his neck and gripped the steering wheel with his knees. "If, for instance, that old man decides that his son or grandson doesn't need another daughter, it would be foolish to turn him into our enemy right from the start. But if this is your baby, you're not a threat to anyone. You're also not calling anyone cruel or wicked. If someone in the village feels remorse, he can always offer to take the baby from you and raise her as his own."

They fell silent. The long silence didn't trouble Jarnail. He hummed a lilting Indian tune to himself as he steered the car at the ox's placid pace. Such a placid pace that the men working in the millet fields saw the car making its way toward the village and ran ahead to spread the news.

* * *

The village was comprised of one street lined with rounded mud huts adorned with round windows. Their roofs looked like small hats made of yellowed grass. All its inhabitants, as well as several from the nearby villages, had gathered to welcome the strangers.

"We're here." Jarnail switched off the engine and announced the obvious. "Who is the father, gentlemen?"

Pinchas wasn't a father and had never been one. It didn't seem right to Shaul to give him that title for the first time while involved in this deception over a tiny Indian baby. "I'm ready," Shaul said. "That is, I wouldn't have concocted this story in the first place..."

Pinchas lifted his eyes. "It's all right," he said. "I found her, and I take full responsibility. Give her to me."

Shaul didn't feel good about handing his partner the small, soft bundle. "A hand under her neck," he reminded Pinchas, sounding to himself like an echo of his wife. "She can't hold up her head by herself yet."

Jarnail glanced at them in the mirror. "Let's hurry," he said. "It's not nice to disappoint the audience. Besides, you said you needed to say your prayers."

The last argument was very persuasive.

---

The circle of men received them in profound silence. Gravely, without expression, they listened to Jarnail's short speech, which ended with a gesture at Pinchas, who was looking a bit pale as he clutched the baby to his chest.

"Nod your head," Shaul whispered. "You know, on a slant, like the Indians are doing."

The nod brought the men to life, turning them from immobile wax figures into warm-blooded men who pounded Pinchas on the back and arms in an effort to express their condolences and sympathy.

"They're asking what kind of help you need," Jarnail said. "And they are very sorry for your loss, Pinchas. I asked for milk for the baby and a place to sleep. I don't think we need more than that for now."

"I'd like to watch the milking," Shaul said quickly. "It's a religious matter. Find some way to explain to them, please."

"You want to see the milking for the baby?" Pinchas asked in an undertone. "Why?"

"Our pot," Shaul whispered back. "We'll have to pasteurize the milk for her."

Jarnail's request was met with vigorous nodding, indicating the villagers' readiness to help them. An Indian man in the prime of life took Shaul's arm in a proprietary fashion and went with him to find a cow.

The sum of money that Jarnail offered for lodgings convinced more than one villager to offer his home. In the time needed to fill an empty water bottle with milk, an agreement was reached. The entire group, some one hundred and fifty strong, escorted Jarnail to see the three suggested houses and choose the one that was cleanest and best ventilated.

After moving the car close to the fence decorated with strange Hindu symbols that made the two *mashgichim* uncomfortable, the Sikh took their camp burner from the car and set it down on the ground.

As the men gazed curiously at Shaul, working at the burner to heat the milk, Jarnail delivered a speech to the circle of men about the need to filter drinking water through seven layers of cotton, to boil milk before drinking it, and to wash their hands before eating a meal. From their amused expressions, it was clear that they didn't take his words very seriously. These bedtime stories that foreign women liked to tell their children didn't frighten them at all.

There is no need to boil milk in order to pasteurize it, but Shaul had no other idea how to be sure that the milk had attained the proper temperature. He waited until bubbles appeared, to demonstrate that the milk had reached the boiling point. After the milk was finally boiled, he diluted it with fifty-percent mineral water, only to find that it was still too hot.

When Shaul's children wanted to cool off a cup of cocoa, they put it in the freezer. But his grandmother used to pour the cereal she'd cooked for him from vessel to vessel in a neat stream until the cereal had cooled sufficiently. As the baby howled, impatient for her meal, he poured the hot milk from one disposable cup into another, again and again, as the audience watched with interest as though he were performing some sort of esoteric magic trick.

Pinchas rocked the baby helplessly. "How long will it take? A long time, do you think?"

"I have no idea." The day had been so long and exhausting in every way that Shaul felt like the simple act of boiling milk was too much for him. "I'll tell you when I know."

The baby screamed, and Jarnail gave them both a look that held no amusement. "I don't know how you feel about babies under your care," he said wearily, "but maybe I should just look for some mother here who will agree to take care of this one overnight?"

9

A N ADOPTIVE MOTHER, EVEN FOR JUST ONE NIGHT, WAS AN
excellent solution for the three exhausted men and one abandoned
baby. Someone experienced, with the right equipment—from diapers
to blankets—could give the infant the basic care that most babies in the
world receive without appreciating their good fortune.

Had she been his own child, Shaul wouldn't have been prepared to
hand her over to an Indian woman, however good-hearted, who had
never heard that water must be filtered or milk boiled before feeding
it to a newborn. But she wasn't his own child, or Pinchas's. Despite
the lies that Jarnail had disseminated, and despite the fact that Heaven
had made him and Pinchas responsible for her fate, this was an Indian
girl who would grow up in India and drink polluted water and unpas-
teurized milk all her life. Seen that way, his desire to give her the best,
Western-style care for one more day was ludicrous.

"Yes," Shaul said slowly. "That's a good idea. Thank you."

Jarnail nodded, and then turned to address the crowd standing and
watching them. He spoke a few sentences in Marathi, the local lingo,
and waited for an answer that wasn't quick to come. He repeated his
question in a more pleading tone, and then added a rebuking one. The
grizzle-haired village elder who'd brought them there joined in the
scold.

Finally, one of the young men came forward. He said a few words
whose meaning seemed to be "I'll take her," or perhaps, "Where's the

money you promised?" Jarnail hastened to rummage in his deep pockets and pulled out his wallet.

There was a short negotiation, apparently regarding how much of the payment would be tendered in advance and how much would be paid tomorrow, when the baby would be returned to them whole, healthy, and well fed. A few bills changed hands.

"Three dollars today," Jarnail said without looking at them, "and two dollars tomorrow. That comes to about three months' salary for them—even half a year's worth."

Shaul didn't begrudge the five dollars that Jarnail had spent, nor did he mind paying such a fortune to the Indian for one night. But Pinchas asked, "Nobody wants her?"

Jarnail shook his head slightly. "We'll talk later," he said. "Please bring the girl, Pinchas."

The small bundle passed into the young Indian's arms. Clutching his payment in his hand, he nodded graciously to the young "widower" and retreated with the child.

Shaul remained behind, holding two paper cups, each half-filled with milk. His heart was heavy. Anxious.

"Now go pray," Jarnail said to them. "I'll try to get the house ready for us. We'll have to bring in two more beds, and you'll probably want me to cover the idols. In short, there's work to do."

The sun was dipping definitively into the west. They washed their hands, preparing to daven amid the lovely village scenery. Even the numerous curious eyes following their every move didn't succeed in ruining their *tefillah*, as the fragrance of millet and cinnamon wafted around them and the tremulous trills of birds filled the air.

---

The village had no electricity. When night fell, Jarnail's powerful flashlight became the brightest illumination in the whole place. The cold white light that washed the peeling plaster walls didn't gladden them.

"Do you want something else to eat, Pinchas?" Jarnail sometimes sounded like a Polish grandmother. "You hardly touched a thing!"

"I had two big sandwiches earlier." Pinchas's eyes were on his *sefer*, but both Jarnail and Shaul noticed that he hadn't turned a page in ten minutes.

"That was a long time ago," Shaul remarked, trying to sound lighthearted.

"I'm full." Pinchas lifted his eyes from the page. "And tired. Thank you both for your concern. Tomorrow is another day."

Shaul glanced at his watch. In Israel, his children would be getting ready for bed. He should call them now, listen to the events of their day, and wish them—as he did every day—a good night. But right now he didn't want to give Pinchas another reason to feel dejected. Maybe it would be better to skip the call just this once. By tomorrow, Pinchas would have calmed down a bit.

On the other hand, these phone calls were a regular part of his daily schedule. Pinchas would surely realize, at some point, that he had deviated from his routine. And he would be hurt.

"I think I'll go out and get a little fresh air," he said, rising heavily to his feet. "I won't go far, Jarnail, or look for more babies in bushes. Don't worry."

Outside, the frogs were croaking, and the scent of cinnamon was more pronounced than it had been during the daytime hours. A breeze stirred the branches of the tree that stood in the center of the large courtyard surrounding the house. Shaul found himself a bench, pulled his phone from his pocket, pressed the right number, and a moment later was sitting not in the heart of serene nature but deep, deep in the cheerful, bubbling cauldron of family.

* * *

Miri had to bring some candy to preschool tomorrow that began with the letter *lamed*, and she had a hard time trying to explain to her father exactly what kind of candy she wanted. Moishy had argued with Chaim, his best friend, over the course of which his glasses had been broken. Batya, his turbulent teenager, had to give a speech the next day about *tefillah* and had found fault with every idea her mother had come up with. Tzviki, who had only recently learned how to pronounce the word "Abba," said that word over and over and over again, bursting into tears each time one of his siblings snatched the phone from him to say a few words to their father.

Apart from all this, he had to explain to Benny, his twelve-year-old, how to free a stuck float valve in the toilet tank, lecture Benny's sister for not doing her homework three times in a row—as per a note she'd brought home from the teacher—and, for dessert, try to remember where he'd put the guarantor's note he'd signed for Mendelowitz five minutes before he'd left home.

It was all so ordinary, yet filled with a charm and a sweetness that, had he been there in the heart of the storm, he would not have been able to discern at all.

"Okay…good night, then," he said at last. He had noted that Ricki wanted to speak to him while the ten young souls clamored for her attention.

"Just a second," she said, moving away from the center of the commotion, or perhaps even entering another room and closing the door behind her. "I have something else to tell you. I think I found a job."

"Through your brother, Gadi, as an importer of fabrics from India?" Shaul joked.

"Gadi? No, he has nothing to do with this. It actually came through my friend Esther Reichberg."

"*She* gave you the idea about the fabrics from India?"

"Why are you talking about fabrics? I don't get the joke."

"Gadi called me today, told me that he's getting you a visa for India and an airline ticket," Shaul explained briefly. "He will also lend you the necessary funds to open an upscale fabrics shop or bridal salon."

"Gadi and his ideas." Ricki was amused. "But that's not what I'm talking about. I found a job! A wonderful job. Do you know the Magshimim Institute? The head of their computer department left, and they want me to come work for them. As far as they're concerned, I can come in tomorrow to learn the ropes."

Had Shaul not been sitting, he would have sat down now. "That *is* news," he said. "Are you happy?"

"The hours are from nine to two," Ricki said, her voice more upbeat than he'd heard it in a long time, "and the salary is good. I'm happy. I'm *very* happy!"

"So am I," he said as a mountain of worry that had been resting on his shoulders crumbled all at once. "It was hard to get by without your salary."

She was silent, waiting for additional words of appreciation. Shaul interpreted her silence as resentment over his inability to bring home enough to allow her to raise their children in peace.

"I hope the job is fulfilling as well as good," he said, feeling slightly deflated.

"Fulfilling?"

He felt misunderstood. He didn't mean to say that managing a household and raising children should be any less meaningful than racing out to an office at the crack of dawn. If anything, it should be more fulfilling. But if he was locked inside four walls day after day, without seeing a soul, he'd have very quickly gone out of his mind.

"I meant to say that I hope you'll find it refreshing, going out to work."

"Refreshing?" The puzzlement in Ricki's voice deepened. "Don't tell me that Gadi has infected you, and now you also think that women go out to work to be refreshed—or to find themselves."

The greatest gift Hashem had bestowed on them—apart from their ten children, of course—was their ability to be open with each other.

"*Baruch Hashem*, you have plenty to do at home," he said, still feeling guilty because he couldn't help Ricki the way she deserved. "I just wanted to say that it will be good for you, I think, to be able to express other sides of your personality besides the ones that are always running around between the dishes and the laundry."

"There's something in that," she admitted. "But you know when? When I start working outside"—her voice became suddenly hoarse—"the laundry won't disappear. I'll just have to work twice as hard."

If only he had it in his power to promise her that he would return to Israel and not leave her and the kids alone ever again. If only he could, at least, enable her to have regular cleaning help.

But he didn't have that power. He lowered his eyes. "Maybe one day—"

But he never got to make his promises because, in that far-off kitchen, someone had just spilled his cup of cocoa on the floor. Ricki said a hasty goodbye, leaving him missing his family as he hadn't missed them in a long time.

10

IT WAS GOOD TO HAVE SOMEONE TO MISS. HE KNEW HE WAS
fortunate to have a family to long for. But that didn't make the
longing any easier to bear.

Two years earlier Shaul would have tried to subdue the longing by
calling home again and speaking to his children once more. Since then,
he'd learned that you don't miss people any less that way. On the contrary, it just reinforces their hold on you.

He hadn't told Ricki about the baby. Not a word. All the talk about
broken toilets and the note from Toby's teacher had stolen his attention.

"I understand why Pinchas is sad." The light spilling from the house
turned Jarnail into a black silhouette. "But what is bothering you?"

"Nothing." Shaul moved slightly, making room for the Sikh to sit.

"It's been a long day."

"Long," Shaul agreed.

"The episode at the factory this morning," Jarnail tallied. "Pinchas's
disappointment this afternoon. And then the baby and everything."

"And everything," Shaul agreed.

But Jarnail was pursuing his own train of thought. "I'm asking
myself," he said slowly, "if Pinchas has no children, and at the exact
moment when he is gripped with sorrow over that, G-d puts a baby
right at his feet—don't you think that's a divine message that he should
adopt her?"

"That he should *what*?" Shaul wasn't usually hard of hearing.

"On one hand, a father who wants a baby. On the other side, a baby who has no father. Don't you think it would be the simplest thing to restore balance to the world and make two souls happy? Eh?"

It was a very hard question to answer, seated beside a good-hearted Sikh. But after an instinctive desire to send Jarnail to discuss it with Pinchas rose up, Shaul decided that it wouldn't be nice to have Jarnail add to his friend's pain.

"I think that Pinchas isn't yet ready to consider adoption," he said carefully.

Jarnail wasn't convinced. "He has been married many years. There are international adoptions," he added. "Many Americans and Europeans who have no children, or who have just one, come to India to adopt a child."

"I don't understand these things." Shaul clasped his palms between his knees. "But I don't think it's our business. Let's allow Pinchas to run his own life."

"That is a little cruel," Jarnail said. "Until now, I thought that Israelis were different. That you are a warm and caring people."

It was a very well-aimed insult, intended, apparently, to motivate him to action. But Shaul shook his head. "Forget about 'Israelis,'" he said. "You and I know each other a fairly long time now. You know that I care about Pinchas, right? And still, I don't think it's a good idea to suggest that he adopt the baby."

Jarnail popped something into his mouth and chewed in silence. Then he said, "You usually have good instincts. This time, though, I'm telling you it's a mistake. G-d sent Pinchas that baby as a gift."

Shaul shrugged. "Human beings shouldn't be arrogant enough to try to understand the ways of G-d, Jarnail Singh Kapoor."

"Pah! If you aren't arrogant enough to try to understand the ways of G-d, why do you come supervise those Muslims to make sure they fill their bottles only with oil that was made in machines that you personally cleaned?"

"That's different." Shaul stood up. "That's not an attempt to understand G-d's will through all kinds of signs and coincidences. It's a strict adherence to the instructions for life that G-d wrote for us in the Torah."

"All right," Jarnail said, dragging out the words. "So He wrote about peanut oil and food coloring in His Torah, but nothing about Pinchas and the baby?"

Oops. In the past, Shaul had explained at length to Jarnail that every detail of a Jew's life is dictated by the Torah. Now he found himself wondering how to extricate himself from the simple trap that had caught him in its teeth.

"It's not connected, Jarnail," he said, speaking more tiredly than he actually felt. "Pinchas himself knows that a childless couple can adopt a child. You wouldn't be telling him anything new."

Jarnail rose to his feet. "If someone knows that it's prohibited to smoke near a source of gasoline, and he smokes there anyway— wouldn't you say something to him?

"It's not the same thing."

"Yes, it is," Jarnail insisted. "Besides, here is a different example: If you have money in your pocket and your friend needs a loan, what is it better to do—lend him the money or wait for him to come to you and ask?"

"That example is a little closer, but it's still not the same thing. Excuse me a minute, please. I have to make a call now."

"Certainly," Jarnail acquiesced. "I didn't intend to disturb you."

"It's all right." Shaul sat down and looked down at his small cell-phone, searching for Gadi's number. He needed to tell him that there was no cause for worry, that Ricki had found a job suited to her talents and personality that would also provide a regular paycheck.

He had the phone to his ear and was waiting for the ringtone when Jarnail placed a heavy hand on his shoulder and signaled for him to be silent. Someone was coming.

⚬⚬⚬

They had no enemies here. On the contrary, the villagers had welcomed them with genuine friendliness. But it couldn't be denied that the few valuables they were traveling with would constitute a fortune to these people, who earned about five dollars for three months of hard labor.

Also, if Jarnail was to be believed, there were criminal elements out to rob foreigners throughout India.

But the group that was approaching the house at a rapid clip hadn't come to take but rather to give. Or to be precise—to return. Both the three dollars and the baby, which one of them was carrying in an unadorned straw bassinet, held far away from his body with an expression of loathing.

"What happened?" Jarnail spoke in a quick, furious Marathi. "We had an agreement. If you don't want her, someone else would have taken the baby!"

"She brings bad luck." The oldest member of the group spoke, his voice quivering and not from age. "She is cursed. She is dangerous."

"The baby?" Jarnail's eyes narrowed. "Do you know her family?"

All five men shook their heads vigorously.

"Then how do you know anything about the kind of luck she brings?"

The young man who had volunteered his wife as a nursing mother said, "The cow. Our cow hasn't been feeling well ever since we brought the girl home."

Cows were a serious matter, at least in the eyes of Hindus. "I don't think there's a connection between the child and the cow," Jarnail said. "She is a small baby who never did anybody any harm."

"Her mother died," said the old man, throwing Jarnail's lies back in his teeth. "And now our cow is sick. What else do you want to happen, Sikh, before you'll agree that the child is cursed?"

This reference to Jarnail's faith didn't augur well. He bit his lower lip. "I'm sure your cow is just a bit worn out."

"I hope that is true," said one of the previously quiet men. "But if anything happens to her..." His finger slashed his neck twice, his meaning unambiguous.

"Nothing will happen to her," Jarnail said firmly. "Sometimes cows, like people, don't feel well. A day or two passes, and everything is fine."

He grasped the bassinet with one hand and the dollar bills with the other and sent the men on their way in the manner of a school principal fed up with his students' nonsense. But the moment the men disappeared among the village huts, his confidence dissipated like ice on an Indian summer's day.

"I don't think I know G-d's ways or understand why this had to happen twice in one day," he said to Shaul. "But if we escaped once today, we now need to escape again—and twice as quickly. Three weeks ago, about forty-five miles from here, some villagers lynched two Muslims who had insulted a cow.

"We need to leave—now."

11

"I WANT TO KNOW ONE THING."

They had left the village on foot, pushing Jarnail's car along the dirt track rather than turning on the ignition and calling the villagers' attention to their departure. Since then, they'd been traveling for hours along dark and menacing roads.

"Just one thing," Pinchas continued. "How can you insult a cow?"

Jarnail, who had been humming a tune with his eyebrows up in the middle of his high forehead, stopped his humming long enough to say, "I wasn't there." He paused. "Fortunately."

"At least they gave her back to us dressed and diapered," Shaul remarked, squinting at the child slumbering peacefully in the bassinet, which was now upholstered with a soft towel. "And they gave us the bassinet. Maybe we should have paid them for all that instead of taking the money back."

"They can split the money we gave the owners of the hut that we didn't end up sleeping in," Jarnail said harshly. After humming a few more bars, he said, "Someone please talk to me or I'll fall asleep."

Distances in India are staggering. Since he was honoring their request that he not turn on the radio during their travels, they were forced more than once to help him stay awake.

"What do you want to talk about?" Pinchas asked.

"I don't know." Jarnail sighed.

"All right." Pinchas adjusted his yarmulke on his head. "I'll tell you a story."

"A story about a cow?" Jarnail grinned.

"Actually, I do have a story about a cow," Pinchas said, rising to the challenge.

"A sick cow?"

"I want to tell you a story about a cow that decided to keep Shabbos." Pinchas's hand stroked his beard. "But, okay, I also have a story about a sick cow. A story with a lesson that everyone can use."

But Jarnail's thoughts weren't trending toward life lessons just then. "Did your cow die at the end of the story?" he asked.

"Just a minute," Pinchas pleaded. "Let's not ruin the suspense. I'll start at the beginning. There was once a pious Jew whose name was Rabbi Yehoshua…"

Despite their slow rate of travel, the car bumped unsteadily over stones in the road, rendering Pinchas's voice slightly clipped. "So Rabbi Yehoshua HaLevi asked Eliyahu HaNavi to let him walk with him—"

"Just a second," Jarnail said. "You're talking about Eliyahu, the prophet who performed the miracle on Mount Carmel? Didn't the Sages of the Talmud live many years after he did?"

Pinchas bit his lip. Jarnail was intelligent and had a surprisingly good memory, which was making him feel uncomfortable. "Yes. True. You're right. But…" Before trying to explain a revelation of Eliyahu to the Sikh, he said, "Don't you think it would be a good idea to stop and rest a bit? We're far enough from that village, and somehow I don't think we'll cause a traffic jam."

Jarnail gave a snort of laughter. "Looks like you're right. I'm driving on inertia. There's no reason not to stop now. I'll take out my sleeping bag while you two use the car."

Knowing that Jarnail didn't mind sleeping out in the open, Shaul and Pinchas felt comfortable accepting his generous offer. Together they arranged the car for sleeping, repositioning the backs of the front seats and setting the baby's bassinet in the space between them. But just as their preparations were complete and Shaul had covered his eyes with his arm, ready for a sound slumber, a whimper rose from the basket.

"Shaul?" Pinchas was alarmed. "She's crying!"

"Give her the pacifier," Shaul mumbled, from exhaustion. Then he turned toward the bassinet and said, "Just kidding."

"Maybe she's hungry. Or wet." Pinchas cracked his knuckles. "Where did we put the milk?"'

They had put the milk at the rear, in a bag that was impossible to extricate with the seats in their present position. They raised one seat and then the second, before they discovered that the superorganized Jarnail had placed the milk bottle in the basket beside the baby. But even after she ate, had been changed into clean clothing, and burped on Shaul's shoulder—she still cried.

"Maybe she's just spoiled." Pinchas was weary and discouraged.

"Spoiled?" Shaul laughed. "You're right, Pinchas. I've never met such a spoiled baby in my life."

Pinchas stared at him for a moment. It was fifteen seconds before his lips twitched into a small smile. "So...maybe the opposite," he said, pain in his voice. "Maybe she's just missing her mother."

The words echoed in the interior of the car, mingling with the baby's wails.

"What do you suggest?" Shaul's hand patted the baby's back without much visible success.

"I don't know. I have no experience. But—"

Shaul's lips tightened. "I've never been a mother either," he said a bit sharply. "I'm doing everything I can. What about you?"

"I..." The moon's white glow lent Pinchas's face a sickly, pale cast. "You've just been managing so well so far..." He held out his arms. "Try to get some rest. I'll look after her, don't worry."

"She should sleep now." Shaul turned toward the driver's window, away from Pinchas and baby, fatigue blunting his senses.

"She'll sleep, " Pinchas said in a slow, soft voice. "Let's see what we can do for you, little lamb. What would my grandmother have done with you right now?" he continued in the same gentle voice. "She would tell you that it's okay, you're allowed to cry. It's just your way of connecting to the world. And you're right—the world hasn't welcomed you so nicely, little lamb. It's perfectly understandable that you feel like crying."

Pinchas sounded so unlike himself that Shaul had to restrain himself from turning around to look at him. But his soothing voice and patience were doing the job. The infant's high wail diminished to a feeble whimper and gradually died away. Thanking Hashem for the silence, Shaul fell instantly asleep.

Shaul woke when the strong Indian sun pierced his eyelids. Surprised that he'd slept so long, he turned toward the other seat— and stopped. Pinchas was sleeping there, one hand clutching the baby to his chest and his second hand on her cheek.

The sight gave Shaul a pang of muted pain. Afraid that Jarnail would wake up and see it, too, he shook Pinchas's arm to rouse him.

"Good morning." Shaul forced a smile. "We should get up and daven…"

Pinchas smiled, dazed. Then, slowly, he straightened up, still holding the newborn with great care. "It worked," he said, surprised. "She fell asleep!"

"And she'll probably wake up in a few minutes and want more milk," Shaul said. "Where did you put her bottle yesterday?"

"Let's hope it didn't go bad." Pinchas was worried.

"I don't think so. It's hardly been twelve hours since the milking." Shaul opened the bottle and sniffed. "You smell it, too," he suggested, "just to make sure. But I'm not worried."

"She's so small," Pinchas reminded him. "We have to be careful not to let any germs get into the milk."

Shaul nodded. "It looks all right," he said again. "I'm not worried."

"I am, a little." Pinchas peered sideways at the mineral-water bottle. "But we have no choice, right?" He answered his own question with a sigh, and then said, "I'll keep holding her so she won't wake up. You go daven Shacharis, and then we'll switch."

This change in their roles, and the way Pinchas had undertaken responsibility for the baby, baffled Shaul. "What if she starts screaming?" he asked.

"Then I'll feed her. It shouldn't be more complicated than *kashering* an assembly line in an oil factory. I think I can manage."

"Excellent." Shaul opened the door on his side of the car. "So I'll go daven now."

He straightened up and looked around, expecting to see Jarnail busy preparing sandwiches for their breakfast. But Jarnail was nowhere to be seen. The only evidence of his presence was his empty sleeping bag lying on the ground under a nearby tree.

No one had kidnaped him. And he hadn't abandoned them to their fate. Shaul was certain of both those things.

Still—it was strange.

Where was Jarnail?

A GREAT DEAL HAPPENED DURING THE FORTY-FIVE MINUTES that Shaul spent davening. The baby abruptly woke amid heartrending cries, as though she wanted to make up for the fact that she had denied the world the sound of her voice all night. Pinchas managed to pour three-quarters of the milk in the bottle onto the floor of Jarnail's car. But after he extricated himself from the vehicle and sat cross-legged on the ground outside, he and the baby became an excellent team. He fed her and she sucked with vigor, gazing at him with big eyes that were many times more mature than her age.

"Good girl. Drink up, little lamb," he murmured, in a marvelous imitation of his mother. "Yes, open your mouth, sweetheart. Now swallow it down. Good, you did that wonderfully! Here's another spoonful. And another..." A stream of milk appeared beside her mouth, and he dabbed it carefully with his finger. "You are so small and so special," he said. "I wonder how far you'll go in life because you've had the privilege of having *chalav Yisrael* today that was milked for you by a tzaddik like our Shaul. Who knows what special *kavanos* he put in that milk?"

Someone cleared his throat behind him.

"Jarnail." Pinchas wondered how much of his babbling the other man had overheard. "How are you?"

"All right." The Sikh crouched beside him. "Did you sleep well last night? I woke up early, saw that all three of you were sound asleep, and decided to take a little walk."

"You know, your Hebrew is very good," Pinchas exclaimed, as if the notion had just struck him. He also discovered that rising to one's feet while holding a sleeping baby in one's arms requires a certain degree of agility.

"I was a security guard at the Indian embassy in Israel for seven years," Jarnail said.

"Yes, yes, we heard about that."

Jarnail touched the baby's soft cheek. "She's a sweet one, isn't she?"

Pinchas hesitated. "I don't know many babies," he said, choosing his words carefully.

"You don't have to know many babies to love one baby. I heard you talking to her. You told her that she was special."

"She's just so small and dainty," Pinchas said.

"Dainty," Jarnail agreed, looking at the child. "That word suits her. She's a dainty little girl. Have you told your wife about her?"

Pinchas swallowed. "Not...not yet."

"A pity," Jarnail said. "Tell her, and maybe even invite her to jump over to India to see the baby for herself."

"Jump over to India?" Pinchas asked. "A little jump over the ocean, eh?"

"The world gets smaller all the time," Jarnail said. "And India and Israel have a good relationship." He drew a deep breath. "Since we cut short our stint in the peanut oil factory you have a week's vacation, and I still have some connections at the embassy. If she wants to come to India, I could try to see if one of my former colleagues is willing to talk to the ambassador to arrange an immediate visa so she could fly out today."

"That's very nice of you," Pinchas allowed. "But a flight costs nearly four hundred dollars. Besides, my wife is a teacher. She can't leave her students in the middle of the year and fly off to India, even if it would be a beautiful vacation."

They looked at one another. "Perhaps I did not explain myself well," Jarnail said. "I did not mean that she should come to India to tour the country and see the sights, though I don't think that's a bad idea. I suggested that she come here to see the baby."

Pinchas stared at him, his eyes as large as two soup bowls. "Back home we used to say that you don't have to buy a whole cow if you want a glass of milk," he said. "In our modern world, all I'd have to do is take a picture of the baby, Jarnail, and show it to her."

"Will that be enough?" Jarnail's face was alight. "Oh, Pinchas, I'm so happy!" He grabbed Pinchas's arm with both hands. "I can't describe how happy I am. I think this is the right decision."

Pinchas shook his head. "Maybe I'm a little tired," he said, "or I ate something strange last night. I really don't understand what the great happiness is about."

Jarnail's smile withered and died. "I suggested that you bring your wife to India to look at the baby in person and see how sweet she is. Dainty and sweet."

"Yes," Pinchas agreed. "I understood that part. But I don't understand why I need to bring my wife to India to see the baby. It's not like she's never seen a baby. Do you know how many babies there are in our neighborhood?"

Jarnail fell silent.

Pinchas looked at him and suddenly shook his head. "No," he said. "You don't mean to tell me that you think I should adopt—" He shook his head again. "No, Jarnail. It's not relevant. But thank you."

"You've been married for many years," Jarnail said with brutal directness. "If G-d sent you a baby, what does it matter how she joins your family?" He nodded. "Look how healthy and strong she is. I understand about babies. I have three of them at home, and I'm telling you, this is a special one. Sweet and delicate. Don't say no before you think about it."

"Good morning, good morning!" Shaul, radiant after his davening, approached. "Where were you, Jarnail? Pinchas, what's wrong?"

Pinchas inhaled deeply. "It's nothing. Everything's fine." He stared at Jarnail, challenging him to speak up.

"Everything is fine, Shaul," Jarnail confirmed.

Pinchas lowered his eyes and breathed a sigh of relief. They fell silent, listening to the birds chirping merrily around them, each lost in his own thoughts.

13

ISRAELIS HAVE A HARD TIME GRASPING THE IMMENSITY OF India. The province of Maharashtra alone, which is just one of the twenty-eight states that make up India, has twelve times more residents than all of Israel and is thirteen times its size. So it was no surprise that the trip to Mumbai dragged on and on. And on.

Though the trip was pleasant at first, with only the hum of the air conditioning to accompany their thoughts or their learning, at some point the temperature changed. The car began to bump over potholes in a way that didn't allow them to concentrate on what they were learning. And the baby, too, began to wail, loudly and from the depths of her heart.

She had eaten a little more than two ounces a couple of hours earlier. When Shaul consulted with his wife, Ricki, she said that the baby couldn't be hungry. All other attempts to calm the child were met with the same tears.

"She must have a stomachache," Shaul said, quoting his wife. "An infant's digestive system isn't completely mature. Cow's milk isn't ideal for a baby's diet."

But even though they all understood that this was what babies were like, a mantra that one of the three men repeated every few minutes, the wails of suffering grated on their nerves and put their patience to a serious test.

"I'm turning on some music," Jarnail said. "Maybe that will help her calm down. Only music, without words. Okay?"

"Do you think music will help?" Shaul jiggled in his seat, attempting to comfort the baby in his arms.

"There's a chance. We Indians love music. It'll do her good."

"Then I'll sing to her," Pinchas volunteered, politely rejecting Jarnail's idea. "Give her to me, Shaul."

Shaul handed over the baby. Pinchas, with surprising deftness, held her close with his cheek to her head, swaying from side to side as he sang a song in Yiddish, his mother tongue. By the fifth time he'd repeated the refrain, Jarnail was able to sing along.

Pinchas wasn't a trained singer by any means, and Jarnail, too, hit plenty of false notes. But the baby's musical sense, like her digestive system, was apparently not fully developed yet. She was content.

Although he was happy about the silence that had returned to the car, and although the sight of a turban-clad Sikh joining a bearded Jew in singing "Rozhinkes mit Mandlen" to an Indian baby was one that would ordinarily have amused Shaul greatly, he was finding his sense of humor sadly depleted these days.

Pinchas needed a *yeshuah*. He would be such a good father. A wonderful father.

---

Babies eat every three hours. Though it seemed to them as if three hours had passed very quickly, the sun had made its usual passage from east to west and was sinking into the horizon in a blaze of color. Anxiously, Shaul asked, "How much longer until we reach Mumbai? We'll get there today, right?"

Jarnail tightened his lips. "If there are no surprises, then yes. We'll get there today. We will not have to sleep outside again."

"Meaning?" both Pinchas and Shaul asked in puzzlement.

"Nothing. I'm just worried that we will arrive very late."

The men looked at one another. "The police station is open twenty-four hours a day, isn't it?" Shaul asked cautiously.

"Yes, of course," Jarnail replied. "But...I do not intend to walk in there and link my name to this baby."

"Don't you have a friend you could call who would do the job for you?"

Until now, all through their joint travels, Jarnail had always had friends he could call on to handle the job at hand, whether it was ana-lyzing the chemical makeup of samples from a food factory to drag-ging a car out of the mud.

"I'll try to find someone." Jarnail's voice was heavy. "The problem is that most of the guys who might undertake such a job have traveled out of town for a friend's wedding."

He wasn't lying, Shaul decided. But it was also obvious that Jarnail didn't intend to stretch himself to help them deliver this baby to the authorities. In his view, Shaul knew, the best thing to do was to con-vince Pinchas to keep the baby and sweeten both their futures. He was convinced, apparently, that if the two were together for long enough, Pinchas would be incapable of separating from the baby and would decide to make her his daughter.

But Pinchas, good man that he was, had already dismissed the thoughts that were in his friend's head. "So what do you suggest?" he asked without a shadow of suspicion.

Jarnail sighed. "The truth? I've been mulling over that question for hours, and I don't have too many ideas."

"What are the options?" Pinchas asked innocently.

"I thought you two would take her to a hotel," Jarnail admitted. "But by law they will have to take a picture of your passports, and they won't be happy if you bring an unregistered baby anywhere."

"We could smuggle her inside," Pinchas said thoughtfully. "She's so small that we could hide her without a problem. The question is what happens when she screams in the middle of the night... I wouldn't want the hotel staff to break down our door in a panic."

Jarnail gave a short laugh. "Yes, that could be unpleasant. And it would also make things complicated for the two of you. They'll won-der why you have an unidentified baby in your room instead of bring-ing her to the police like a good citizen."

"Actually, why not?" Shaul asked, trying to soften his tone. "Aren't we being a little too fearful?"

"Leave the worrying to me, Shaul. That's what I get paid for. And believe me, they pay me well," Jarnail said.

"Well, aren't *you* being a little too fearful?" Shaul asked bluntly.

The Sikh didn't answer at once. He also didn't appear to be offended. He mulled over the question and then said, "No, I don't think so."

"You really think that they may have taken out an arrest warrant for us because of the incident at the factory?" Shaul asked skeptically.

"The Indian police don't have anything better to do with their time?"

"Of course they do." The Sikh's sense of humor was also in abeyance today. "I simply do not want the same idea of a bribe that may have entered the mind of an officer there to enter the mind of an officer here. It doesn't matter if they accuse you of attacking a worker over there or with kidnaping a baby here. The main thing is for you to pay—and pay a very great deal. You don't live in India, Shaul. Trust me when I tell you that you don't want to get in trouble. Okay?"

"*Sha, sha*," Pinchas begged. "We shouldn't talk this way near children. My mother always says that they start crying when the atmosphere in the room is tense."

"This is not a room, it's a car," Shaul pointed out needlessly. "And I don't understand what you're trying to say, Jarnail. You keep bringing up problems and then telling us not to worry."

Jarnail shook his head. "Tonight you'll come home with me," he said. "We'll deal with the rest tomorrow."

"How?" Pinchas asked softly.

After a few moments' silence, Jarnail said, "We'll talk about it when the time comes. I have a few ideas."

"And what will we do until tomorrow?" Shaul pressed.

"Come home with me," Jarnail repeated. "My wife will tend to the baby, and you two can sleep."

"That's very generous of you." Shaul was astonished.

Jarnail's smile held a touch of bitterness. "Yes," he said. "I've never mixed my work with my private life before. But that's how it is—I'm a good man."

Pinchas's hand touched Shaul's knee in silent warning. "Thank you, Jarnail," he said. "We appreciate it very much. G-d loves people who do kind deeds for others. I'm sure He will repay you for your kindness."

The Sikh lowered his head, eyes on the black asphalt. Bleakly he said, "To tell the truth, up till now I haven't seen much profit from being a good person."

"G-d's kindness can be hidden at times." Pinchas stroked the baby's hair with one finger. "And sometimes we don't know the difference between good and sweet. We expect to see a quick profit. Too quick. But there is justice and there is a Judge, Jarnail. You never lose out by doing a good deed."

The Sikh sighed. "Perhaps," he said. "And now, please let me concentrate on my driving."

14

JARNAIL'S REMARK ABOUT THE DAMAGE HE'D SUFFERED ON account of his good heart, and the sudden silence that had descended on him immediately afterward, ruffled Shaul's peace. It wouldn't be pleasant, but he would have to speak to the boss and request an appropriate bonus for Jarnail in light of his new role as babysitter and innkeeper. And maybe there would be enough extra payment to encourage the young man to focus a bit more on finding a good place for the little foundling instead of wasting time on dreams that Pinchas would adopt her as his daughter.

Jarnail drove in silence. The baby slept in Pinchas's arms. Pinchas himself seemed to be drowsing as well. The car slid quietly over the highway leading to Mumbai.

One of the largest cities in the world, a close competitor to New York and London, she welcomed them with an overpowering, pungent odor all her own—a potent combination of twelve million people who created seven thousand tons of garbage each day, mingled with the smell of the sea. The odor accompanied the city's residents from the day they were born until the day they died, and it managed, despite the closed windows, to penetrate the car as well. Outside sprawled an opaque sea of horrendous poverty, of neighborhoods without running water, their windows dark and partially hidden behind gigantic, illuminated billboards.

"I take it we're getting closer." The garish colored lights were making Shaul queasy. He rubbed his forehead in an effort to remove the fog that was slowing his thoughts.

"Very close," Jarnail confirmed. It seemed to Shaul that Jarnail was struggling to hide a small smile. "Very, very close—though not in Israeli terms, of course."

"Meaning?"

"We'll be at my house in about an hour and a half," Jarnail said cheerfully. "You'll be comfortable there. My wife already bought everything the baby will need."

"Thank you, Jarnail. You're amazing. I'll talk to Rabbi Schwab about compensation, don't worry."

"I'm not worrying," Jarnail assured him. "Besides, like you, I don't think money is the most important thing in life."

This sounded better than the gloomy note Jarnail had sounded before sinking into silence. But the weight on Shaul's heart refused to lift. He leaned his aching head on the cool window and closed his eyes.

"The city looks different at night, eh?" Jarnail apparently thought that Shaul was gazing out at the city lights, at the sumptuous stores with their sparkling display windows side by side with piles of garbage and rows of people wrapped in rags, lying motionless on the ground. They looked as if they were dead but certainly hoped to rise with the dawn.

"The city?" Shaul opened his eyes and looked out. "Yes, you could say that."

"It was worse twenty years ago," Jarnail said. "At night you could see rivers of rats racing from the city to the poorer sections, and the mosquitoes would eat people alive. Today the streets are sprayed against mosquitoes every night, and the rat problem is not as prevalent as it once was."

"Nice," Shaul said, somewhat appalled.

"We're making progress. India is slowly developing. But look at those people sleeping in the streets. Villagers who hoped to come to Mumbai and scoop up gold. So many children. For them, the improvement is too slow. They will not be alive when India finally finds its equilibrium and reaches the level of comfort that exists in the West."

Shaul stole a glance at Pinchas. Whether or not his friend was actually asleep, he seemed disinclined to join in the conversation. "That's really sad," he said carefully.

"It's more than sad," Jarnail snapped.

"True." Shaul felt as if he was walking on broken glass. "It's terrible. But you know something, Jarnail? Most international adoptions are not that successful. It would be a lot more logical for every Indian with a steady income to adopt one hungry child than to send millions of children to Europe and America, where they would be cut off from their native environment and would always feel different, maybe even inferior, to those around them."

Jarnail threw Shaul an appreciative smile. "There's something to that," he said, and returned his eyes to the road. His silence made Shaul hope that he didn't intend to trouble them further with his ethical arguments, at least not as long as he himself was unwilling to take the baby into his own home and adopt her as his daughter.

Although Jarnail was silent, his heart pained him. He had saved this baby's life. Without him, it was highly probable that she wouldn't be here now. It saddened him to think that he lacked the power to spare her the mountain of difficulties she would have to scale all her life. He could only—and, at that moment, nothing felt more natural—pray for her.

And so he did.

---

Even the longest trip ends at last. Jarnail's green car proceeded through elegant streets where the buildings were made of stone and glass and were surrounded by flourishing, landscaped gardens.

"This is where you live?" Pinchas asked in surprise as a gatekeeper in a crisp white uniform came to check their ID. The man greeted Jarnail warmly and then opened the gate leading to the building's parking garage.

"This is where I live," Jarnail said. "On the twenty-seventh floor. From the balcony, you have the nicest view in the city."

Here?

A security guard at the embassy?

A driver and bodyguard?

Pinchas and Shaul exchanged glances, each reading the question in the other's eyes. Jarnail, for his part, coolly ignored their curious expressions.

"There is a doorman here who can help us with our luggage," he said, "but I'd prefer that he not see the baby. The elevator is not far. I think we can manage."

Memories of their hasty escape three days earlier flitted through the minds of the two other men. At the time, Jarnail had carried all their baggage in his arms. The three of them could certainly manage to handle the addition of a newborn baby in her bassinet.

"Come."

As always, Jarnail held the door open for them. Issuing gracious instructions, he led them and their belongings to a spacious elevator lined with a velvety surface that shot them in seconds to the top of the elegant residential tower.

"My wife's parents live over there." The Sikh pointed to a door on the right. "And we go here." He pointed left. "Welcome to my humble abode."

The humble abode, they saw a moment later, was graced with decorative molding and discreet spotlights. The place was spotlessly clean and decorated in pleasing colors.

A woman emerged from the depths of the house and approached. "Welcome," she said in a heavily and oddly accented Hebrew. Then she switched to one of the Indian dialects to issue a number of instructions to her husband.

"Padmasri says that my den is ready for you," Jarnail translated a few minutes later. "If you'd like to give her the child, she will be glad to care for her until tomorrow."

"We thank her very much for her kindness."

Against the background of this opulence, Mrs. Kapoor's offer seemed even more generous than it had earlier.

"Padmasri loves babies," Jarnail said. "And she is happy to host my friends." He took the bassinet from Pinchas's hands. "She will take good care of her and will not let her cry," he promised, transferring the child to his wife. "Do not worry."

Real estate in Mumbai is among the most expensive in all of India. Jarnail's den could easily have accommodated Shaul's entire family for a Shabbos meal. In fact, they could have all sat around the gleaming wooden desk standing at one end of the room in front of an executive chair upholstered in black leather so that it resembled an armchair.

"You have everything you need here." One of the bookcases swiveled on a hidden electric hinge to reveal a small but well-equipped bathroom. A small refrigerator filled with fresh fruit and bottles of mineral water was tucked under the desk. "Make yourselves at home. Sleep well. I will knock on your door at eight o'clock tomorrow morning. If you wish to speak to me before that, you can call. I sleep with my cellphone under my pillow."

He regarded them hesitantly, as though he wanted to add something. His eyes, Shaul saw, went to a spot above their heads and lingered a moment.

"Well, good night," Jarnail said. "See you tomorrow."

What had drawn his attention?

The moment the door closed behind him, Shaul turned around to study the wall and the row of pictures hanging on it. His eyes narrowed in disbelief.

**15**

PINCHAS HAD NOTICED NEITHER JARNAIL'S SWIFT GLANCE nor Shaul's suspicious one. He slumped tiredly onto one of the neatly made beds and said, "Wow."

"An excellent description," Shaul said, turning slowly. He looked at Pinchas, who was staring up at the ceiling, and asked, "Why 'wow'?"

Pinchas continued to gaze at the recessed spotlights above his head. "All kinds of reasons," he said without looking at Shaul. "The quality of this mattress, for example." A moment later he added, "And everything we've been through these past few days." He was quiet again. "Why did you say 'an excellent description'?"

Shaul hesitated. It was late, and Pinchas sounded exhausted—and not just physically. No need to give him something else to cope with tonight.

"Nothing," he said. "It's nice here."

Pinchas sat up. "Very. And a little surprising."

"A *lot* surprising," Shaul agreed.

Pinchas scratched his nose. "I'm tired," he said. "Do you mind if I say *Krias Shema*?"

Shaul clicked his tongue to show how little he minded. As Pinchas began to get ready for bed, Shaul turned back to the picture. He studied it with open animosity.

That's the way it was. You could know a person for years. Think that you really understand who he is. And then, in the end, it turns out that he's a liar.

Jarnail was a liar. That was clear to him now, as certainly as the man with the mane of hair and the striped tie standing beside him in the gold-framed picture was former Prime Minister Ehud Barak.

"The baby's crying." Pinchas placed his folded clothing on the dresser. "Do you hear her?" He grimaced. "She's so tiny…"

He cared. Shaul could see that. And it was no superficial caring. Not knowing how to respond, he ventured, "Would you consider adopting her, the way Jarnail keeps urging?"

Pinchas didn't reply at once. Long seconds later, he said, "I want a child of my own, Shaul. Is that too much to ask?"

"For Hashem, nothing is too much." Shaul sat at the edge of the executive chair. "So many people are davening for you that I'm sure it will happen sometime—hopefully soon. But I think that Jarnail intends to put you under a lot of pressure to persuade you to adopt the girl. Is there a possibility that you would do it?"

Pinchas's laughter sounded like an old man's. "I can't explain to you what I felt when I saw her lying there on the ground." He closed his siddur, absently replaced it in his tallis bag, and zipped it up. "But my wife… We've talked about this. She doesn't want to adopt. That's a red line for her."

"You know that halachically it can be done?"

"Of course. The *beis din* converts the child, who has to confirm the *geirus* at the age of twelve or thirteen. But my wife…it just won't happen."

Pinchas looked around, obviously wanting to change the subject. "Where is my siddur? I took it out of my bag a minute ago."

"You put it back." Shaul gazed fixedly at a spot on the wall. Without looking at Pinchas, he said, "Please tell Jarnail tomorrow what you just told me. The minute you see him. Tell him that maybe he didn't understand you, but your wife isn't prepared to listen to any talk of adoption so there's no reason to pressure you. Tell him that clearly. Maybe then he'll manage to find someone to take her to the police station. Right now my impression is that he's counting on you and not in any rush to help us make arrangements for her."

"Tell him?" Pinchas looked around. "All right. I'll tell him… What is that picture with the Israeli flag on the wall? Is that from when he worked for the Indian embassy in Israel?"

Shaul accepted the change of subject. "Uh-huh," he confirmed.

"Then he really did work there." Pinchas still sounded distracted. "When he brought us into this fancy apartment, I thought he'd lied."

Shaul kept his silence.

"All right." Pinchas opened his siddur again with a sigh. "I'm going to say *Krias Shema* and *HaMapil*. And I think you should do the same."

But Shaul didn't intend to say *HaMapil* that night. He knew himself too well. Until he understood the world he was living in—he wouldn't fall asleep.

*Who are you, Jarnail?*

The Sikh was an intelligent man—that was undeniable. But what about the rest? After all, it wasn't likely that the prime minister and former defense minister of Israel would agree to take a formal picture, against the background of the national flag, with a security guard.

Or maybe they would, if the anonymous guard had done a priceless favor for his host country or performed some act of heroism. But if that were the case, surely Jarnail would have found an opportunity to tell them about it at some point...

Shaul swiveled to and fro in the upholstered executive chair. If there had been a mitzvah to judge Jarnail favorably, he could undoubtedly have concocted all sorts of unlikely scenarios in which a minor security guard performed an act of heroism linked to secrets that had not yet been made public, forcing Jarnail to remain silent about the episode that had led to the photograph.

The chair paused in its swiveling before the beaming face of Ehud Barak. The simplest explanation was that Jarnail hadn't been a security guard at all, but a diplomat. But if that was the case, why had he decided on his return to his native land to take a job as a tour guide and security guard who hefted people's suitcases and fixed excellent sandwiches in his spare time?

The younger and more smiling Jarnail of the photograph gazed down at him, an indecipherable gleam in his dark eyes. The closed lips didn't reveal a word about the crime he may have committed that had expelled him from public service.

Shaul's teeth dug into his lower lip. Committing a crime and being fired was a possible explanation for this sharp turn in his career direction. A young man whose future in diplomacy had been cut off suddenly, compelling him to seek a way to use his skills in the private sector.

But he'd been a young man with financial backing—enough to buy an apartment in this beautiful residential tower and to pay its monthly maintenance fees. Such a man could surely find more interesting ways to spend his time than working as a driver on the roads of his native land. Above the bookcase, crowded with volumes in an impressive array of languages, hung a wooden clock that gave the time in London, Paris, New York, and Mumbai. What time was it in Israel right now?

Shaul stared at his cellphone, and the cellphone stared back at him. Although a link to all those who were dear to him was just an arm's length away, the thought didn't dispel his loneliness.

Pinchas was in a deep slumber, his regular breaths punctuated by a faint whistle. Somewhere beyond the door, the baby was bawling. From the window, Jarnail had said, one could have the loveliest view in Mumbai. But right now the horizon was black.

The room was furnished in good taste. Though he didn't know much about such things, it seemed to Shaul that any five-star hotel in London, Paris, or New York would have been proud to offer its guests such a room. Still, he would have much preferred to be sitting on one of his scratched kitchen chairs, listening to the rattling of the fridge and looking at the floor's cracked tile. And he would have preferred occupying his mind with matters other than secrets that had no solution.

He sat frozen in place, the gears of his mind turning in search of an explanation that would put everything in its proper place. Finally, he shook his head and rose to his feet. It didn't look like he was going to find any answers tonight. But the question marks had banished his tiredness.

That would give him several wonderful hours of peace and quiet in which he could simply sit and learn.

# 16

AT 3:30 A.M., SHAUL REALIZED THAT HE HAD FALLEN ASLEEP, his body on the leather executive chair and his head on his Gemara. He gave it a soft kiss and was on his way to wash his hands when he heard the baby crying. Still? He wasn't sure. Perhaps she had fallen asleep, like him, and, like him, had just woken up again. But he felt uncomfortable having Jarnail's wife coping with her alone.

She had agreed to do so, and he was tired, said the small, logical voice in his head. But Shaul often found himself acting in ways that defied logic.

One ring, and Jarnail picked up. He sounded sleepy.

"I hear the baby crying," Shaul said quietly.

"Yes," Jarnail said. "I don't know what's bothering her. My wife said that she doesn't need to eat for another hour and a half, but she still keeps crying."

"Do you want me to take over for a while? Want to bring her here to me?"

Jarnail might have refused. But he was silent for a moment. Then he said, "The truth? I'd be glad to."

"So you'll bring her to the room?"

"You can come to the living room and sit on the couch with her. That's what I've been doing this past hour."

"I'm on my way." Shaul went to the door, stepped into the hall, and from there to the softly lit living room.

"Did her crying wake you?" Jarnail was apologetic.

"No. I sat down to learn a little and I fell asleep at the desk," Shaul admitted. Then, since it was going to be necessary to bring up the topic and air the facts, he added, "Your chair is very comfortable. And the room is amazing. I was looking at the pictures on the wall—"

Jarnail's smile was a bit sad. "Nothing escapes you, eh?"

Shaul smiled back and said, "That's my job. To pay attention to small details."

"You are good at it," Jarnail complimented him.

"I'm not so sure."

Shaul took the baby and laid her on his arm in a position that their pediatrician had recommended when his daughter Batya had been especially colicky. "If I was really that good, I would have realized a long time ago that you are more than just a talented guy with especially broad horizons."

"There are also simple people with life wisdom," Jarnail protested. "And you should know that I did not come from a rich family at all. My wife brought the apartment as part of her dowry. That is why we are here."

"You told us that a good son-in-law is a valuable thing," Shaul remarked, rocking the baby on his arm back and forth while patting her back. "But judging by the dowry you got, you were not just a successful son-in-law but an exceptional one."

Jarnail shifted his weight from foot to foot. "Yes, I was successful when I was younger."

"You are still successful today," Shaul said. Then he asked, "When you were photographed with Ehud Barak, was he prime minister or defense minister?"

Jarnail placed a hand on his heart. "Only defense minister," he avowed.

"And what were you? Not a security guard at the embassy." It was a statement.

"I was the deputy military attaché."

A military attaché. The *cheder* in Bnei Brak where Shaul had received his early education hadn't taught him about all the ins and outs of government, but he did know that a military attaché was the person responsible for security links between his country and the host country. The post was apparently considered a very high-level one.

"You never told us that," he said.

Jarnail gave a short laugh. "I didn't want Rabbi Schwab to reject me for being overqualified," he said. "You know that expression, right? If you're too talented, and served in too-lofty positions, no one will hire you as a driver."

"You're much more than a driver," Shaul said, and smiled. "You know that, don't you?"

"Yes," said Jarnail. "And don't think that I don't like it."

Various words ran through Shaul's head. None of them seemed right.

"I should let you get some sleep," he said at last. "But maybe you could just tell me why you left the military?"

"Because I was a good person." Jarnail leaned against the back of the sofa. "I already told you that being good doesn't always pay, didn't I?"

"You did," Shaul confirmed. "And I promised to let you get some sleep…"

"Yes," Jarnail said. "You did."

"So—good night."

"Good night," Jarnail replied. "Here is the stroller… There are disposable cups on the counter and cold water in the fridge."

He took a slow step or two away, then shook his head and turned back.

"The government of Israel and the government of India do business together worth billions of dollars. But if you expose the fact that your country is losing millions because someone in the system is taking bribes, they don't always appreciate it. Sometimes you even report it to the wrong person. The one who received the kickbacks and put it in his own pocket. Then you're in real trouble."

He spoke rapidly, in his excitement switching to English halfway through. When he was done, he looked as though all his energy had been drained.

Shaul couldn't bear to see him that way. "You're a brave person," he said.

"Or a foolish one," Jarnail said. "Wise people don't lie on the railroad tracks when they are trying to stop the train. And if they do lie down, they don't fall into a depression afterward, when the train crushes them." He breathed deeply. "Never mind," he said. "You wanted to know, and now you know. Yes, I was depressed after they got rid of me. Maybe I still am, and you just can't tell because of the medication."

"If I can't tell, then it must be behind you," Shaul said stoutly, stunned by these revelations. Energetic, efficient Jarnail lying in bed like a tree fallen onto its side? It was hard to imagine.

Jarnail gave a short chuckle and moved closer to the sofa. "There are people who would claim that until I return to a job that suits my education, experience, and abilities, it's a sign that I'm still suffering the consequences of the depression."

"And what do you think?"

Jarnail nodded. "I actually prefer a simpler life now. I want no connection to politics or money. I want to work with people, quietly, on my own terms. Without politics, without big money. Just being a good person."

"You have a family," Shaul commented. "A wife and children... And they have apparently become accustomed to a very high standard of living."

"True," Jarnail agreed. "It's not easy to support a family in India through work in the public sector. Certainly not a family accustomed to luxuries."

The baby chose that moment to burst into loud wails, providing a perfect distraction. Shaul had no choice but to say, "It's not simple. Not simple at all. What did they officially fire you for, if I may ask?"

"They threatened to charge me with treason." The mere memory made Jarnail's lips turn white with fury and pain. "But after they realized that if I went to prison, I was going to take them with me, they settled on unsuitability for the job—even though the very fact that I exposed their corruption proved that I was perfectly suited to it."

"You've been through a lot, and you're still a young man."

"He who climbs high falls far," Jarnail said. "The moment I returned to India, I tried to find other work that would suit my talents and abilities. But those who had fired me also managed to cut off any job opportunities that I might want. And that hurt terribly. More than you can imagine."

17

THERE IS SO MUCH THAT WE DON'T KNOW ABOUT THE PEOPLE around us. Not even those whose smiles project contentment and who seem as laid back as a river on a sultry day.

"I'm sorry to hear your story," Shaul said. "I didn't know."

"I'm sorry I had to live through it. And I didn't want you to know. I don't want pity, Shaul. I'm still the same person I was three hours ago."

He was the same person, undoubtedly. But Shaul suddenly saw additional layers to which he'd been oblivious before.

"I think you were very brave when you tried to fight the corruption in your office," he said cautiously. "And I'm sorry to hear that you were hurt as a result."

"You can also be sorry that the corruption, in the end, was not prevented," Jarnail suggested. "Or maybe, as an Israeli, you ought to be happy that your country received a bit more tax income and can provide better services to its populace."

Shaul gave the expected chuckle. "I'm not talking as an Israeli to an Indian. I'm talking man to man."

"I'm tired, so I'm probably going to be a bit too blunt," Jarnail said. "But I believe that despite the fact that we respect one another, you are still Israeli and I am still Indian. And that's the way it will always be." There was no smile on his face—or in his eyes. Instead, there was bitterness. "And that's even before we talk about your view as a religious man who sees himself as the crown of creation."

"What?" Jarnail's last words surprised Shaul so thoroughly that the word flew unthinkingly from his lips.

"I don't only speak good Hebrew. I can also read it. When I was in Israel, I bought several books on the main street of Bnei Brak. That was part of my job as a military attaché: to learn the culture and thought process of the country I was living in and to understand how that culture can affect the host country's political and military outlook, as well as the relations between the host country and my own."

Shaul gaped at him, wondering how Jarnail had looked when he'd visited the *sefarim* store and which intelligent shopkeeper had helped him choose the volumes that would provide answers to his questions.

"What?" Jarnail said, surprised by the long silence.

"Nothing." Shaul roused himself. "I'm tired, too. So maybe I'm also going to be a bit blunt, and ask if, at any time during our mutual travels, you sensed contempt from us because you are Indian and we are—as you put it—the crown of creation?"

"You've both been very nice," Jarnail said. "I have no complaints."

"You brought up a point that bothers you," Shaul said. "That's okay. It's good to ask real questions and to get real answers. It makes the journey of life easier. Judaism is not fascist, Jarnail. Everyone can be the crown of creation if he wants to be. And we don't claim a monopoly on spirituality: every human being has a soul."

"They explained that to me already. That Jews do not see themselves as a nationalistic group, but rather as a religious one, and that anyone can join. But it's not precisely that way. You push away converts and those that are allowed to join you are not so easily accepted."

"We push away converts in order to see if they're serious in their intentions. I have a family tree at home that goes back to King David, who was the descendant of a Moabite woman who converted to Judaism. If you look at how Judaism speaks of King David, and the mission that G-d gave him in the world, I think you'll come to a slightly different conclusion that the one you just had."

"King David?" Jarnail was astonished. "Is that really true?"

"Absolutely. Have you heard of the mitzvah to love the convert?"

"Yes," Jarnail admitted.

Shaul tried unsuccessfully to conceal a yawn. "It's late and we're both tired right now. Not the most conducive state for a serious discussion. Let's talk tomorrow."

"Tomorrow starts in three and a half hours, and you, at least, will be a lot more tired than you are now." Jarnail had retained his sense of humor. He glanced down at the carriage and then at Shaul. "If she's asleep, then you can lie on the couch and doze," he said. "In my experience, she doesn't sleep very long."

She didn't sleep very long, and Shaul didn't sleep at all. His mind was too full of a jumble of half-formed thoughts and he was having a hard time working them out alone. He pulled his phone from his pocket and looked at the screen. It was the middle of the night in Israel, too, but Ricki's brother, Gadi, was a night owl who was often in contact with people abroad at a time when the rest of his fellow Israeli citizens were sound asleep.

The bedrooms were far enough from the living room. But Shaul stepped out onto the large balcony and went to its furthest corner just in case.

"Gadi?" He felt a certain relief that his brother-in-law was awake and prepared to take his call.

"Yes, Shaul." Gadi's voice sounded cool and remote.

"Did I wake you?" This conversation wasn't urgent enough to justify that.

"No." The coolness was still pronounced. "I've been sitting here waiting for your call."

"I'm sorry."

"So am I. And I'm not only sorry, but also insulted. That visa cost me money, and so did the airline ticket. I don't know what the two of you think, but my money doesn't sleep in a money-market account. I sold some shares of a successful stock so that I could give you some financial backing. So that you could buy plenty of merchandise and furnish the store in good taste. But forget about the money—I gave this whole business at least an hour and a half of my time today. And neither of you even bothered to take five minutes to pick up a phone and tell me that Ricki found a job! Is that nice, Shaul? Is that how a *talmid chacham* behaves?"

Gadi always dragged in the *"talmid chacham"* theme when he was particularly hurt. In the early years, Shaul would protest that he hadn't yet attained a level worthy of that label. Since he'd started working and understood that Gadi used it only to hurt him, he had stopped protesting.

"Wow," he said instead. "I…I don't believe this, Gadi. I feel terrible. It's just that—"

"Yes, Ricki told me that the baby you found has been keeping you busy." Gadi sounded mocking. "But, you know, it *is* possible to call to tell your beloved brother-in-law that congratulations are in order and to update him about a few other small matters at the same time."

This, apparently, was a reference to the never-forgotten time when Gadi had been informed that a nephew had been born to him almost forty-five hours after the event. Shaul swallowed this in silence as well.

"I apologize," he said. "It's not just a 'baby.' The story is a little more complicated than that... Still, I should have been focused enough to call you. I feel really bad about that. I'm sorry."

"Okay, okay. It's not the end of the world."

Gadi didn't sound very convincing.

18

SHAUL LEANED ON THE BALCONY RAILING, WONDERING what to say now. The lights of Mumbai glittered around him like endless rows of diamonds, melting into a dark horizon that could be either the sea or one of the terribly destitute city neighborhoods that were bereft of even the most basic utilities. Given Jarnail's comments about the stunning view to be had from his apartment, the first option was probably the correct one.

"You're judging me harshly, Gadi," he said at last, quietly, to his brother-in-law in Israel. "And I understand why. I shouldn't have forgotten to call to update you. But you know something? Over the years, we've talked so much about so many ideas for improving our financial situation, and none of them came to anything. There was no real reason to think that you were serious this time."

"We talked about a date!" Gadi said. "We said that you're in India now and have several free days when you could go around with her and choose merchandise! We weren't talking about some vague or distant plan!"

"You're right." Shaul ran his thumbnail along the railing. He could say that they had also had conversations like this one more than once in the past. But there was no point. Not even a tiny one.

"I'm sorry. When we spoke, I wasn't very focused because of my injury and our escape. Then came the baby, and these villagers threatened to kill us if their cow died because of her…"

"Because of the baby?"

"Yes. They said she brings bad luck or something. That she was the reason their cow was sick. I was holding the phone in my hand to call you when they brought her back in a bassinet."

"The cow?"

"The baby." Shaul smiled slightly. "I apologize if I sound a bit scattered. But it's the middle of the night here. And the past few days haven't been easy ones. Again, it's no excuse. I shouldn't have neglected to update you."

"Or Ricki." Gadi was bitter and sharp again.

"Yes," Shaul admitted. "I realize now that you were serious, but I thought you would call her yourself and get the details you'd need for getting her a visa... I never imagined that right after talking to me, you would see the matter as settled and go into action."

"Well, I had brought it up before, and it was obvious to me that she liked the idea and that you were both just being your usual impractical selves and too embarrassed to ask for help. I figured you just needed the financial backing, and you'd jump at the opportunity."

Shaul pushed his glasses higher up on the bridge of his nose. Gadi knew how to press all his buttons, but he couldn't let himself be dragged into this dance right now. Let Gadi take pleasure in thinking of them as impractical.

"How much did the visa cost?" he asked.

Gadi laughed. "If you're asking about the visa, you might as well ask about the airfare. It cost about the same as the visa, only in dollars. And it can't be canceled. The flight is tomorrow."

This wasn't good. "I'm really sorry," Shaul said yet again. "How much was the airline ticket?"

Gadi's laughter was mocking. "I'll absorb the loss," he said. "I was planning on giving you the price of the fare as a gift anyway. So, like the vase you gave Aunt Gita, you won't be using my gift. No problem."

Where did this successful young man, who had grown up surrounded by so much love, get such copious quantities of contempt? And while Aunt Gita had been an angry and critical old woman, was there any need to drag her up from the grave in order to hurt his own brother-in-law in the middle of a hot Indian night?

A thin wail rose up from the darkened living room. The baby was crying again.

"I'm sorry," Shaul whispered as he hurried inside. "I have to go.

The baby is crying, and I have to take care of her before she wakes up the whole family."

"What family?"

"Jarnail's family—our driver. It was impossible to go to a hotel with an undocumented infant."

A pacifier is a wondrous invention. Shaul was happy to find it lying beside the baby in the carriage. As he tended to the baby, something else occurred to him.

"Gadi, do you happen to know what the position of military attaché in a country's embassy entails?"

"Military attaché...military attaché... Here's the definition I found: 'A military attaché is an expert in military matters.' That's obvious. 'The military attaché is responsible for relations with the army of the host country,'" Gadi continued. "'He represents his government on matters relating to security issues, represents the military industry of his country in the host country, and serves as a consultant to his country's ambassador on security-related matters.'" He paused. "Should I continue?"

"If it's not too much trouble."

Shaul felt a real need to know everything he could about Jarnail, whom he'd come to consider a friend.

"All right. 'Officers who are appointed to represent their government abroad generally take a preparatory course for their new jobs as diplomats, which lasts approximately three months,'" Gadi read. "'On occasion, the position of military attaché in certain countries is considered a senior one. For example, the post of IDF military attaché at the Israeli embassy in the United States is held by an officer with the rank of major general.'" The words tumbled out at a rapid pace. "'It's customary to use a military attaché for purposes of intelligence, which is why an exceptional intelligence officer is often appointed to the job.'"

Gadi paused. "Why do you need all this information, Shaul? Did someone suggest a *shidduch* for Rini with some military attaché somewhere?"

"You know that Rini's not ready for *shidduchim* yet. No, I met someone who was once a military attaché." Shaul preferred to stick as close as possible to the truth. "I wanted to understand a little more about it."

"Ah." Gadi sounded distant again. And he had a right. From his point of view—without knowing the entire situation—Shaul was simply not taking his feelings into consideration.

"Gadi." Shaul wanted to return to the balcony, but the baby wasn't calm, and he felt obligated to continue standing beside her, rocking the stroller. "Gadi, I've just lived through the craziest week of my life. I don't know how to tell a story dramatically the way you do, but believe me that it was an awful week. That military attaché is somehow connected to all this. But I simply can't expand on that right now."

"Shaul's adventures in India," Gadi said. "All right, your apology is accepted. I know that you didn't mean to waste my time and money. You simply didn't realize how much I care about your and Ricki's situation." This was another form of insult, but Shaul knew that Gadi hadn't meant it as such.

His brother-in-law wasn't finished. "Look, I'll find out more about military attachés for you. It sounds as though they're spies in the guise of diplomats. How does that fit with your guy?"

A spy disguised as a diplomat fit well with a diplomat disguised as a driver. Shaul sighed. "It fits. But I can't talk right now."

"Because he put a bug in your phone?" Gadi joked.

"No, no. It's nothing like that."

There was a full bottle of milk tucked into the side of the carriage. Although no more than an hour and a half had elapsed since Shaul had been appointed nursemaid, he decided that it was time to check if the baby was hungry. "I hope I'll find time in the morning to call and tell you everything in an organized way."

"Okay. You'll try to find time to call me, and I'll try to find some Israeli who wants to buy the ticket off me and fly to India tomorrow. We'll see which of us is more successful."

"Let's hope we both succeed," he said slowly. "And I'm sorry again, Gadi. For everything. There were no bad intentions."

"If I'd thought that there were bad intentions, I wouldn't have answered your call, either now or in a year from now," Gadi said. "Okay, no need to talk about it anymore. I told you that your apology is accepted."

His apology had been accepted, and the baby had eaten. Shaul knew nothing else until he opened his eyes and discovered a trio of Indian children standing in front of the sofa, gazing at him with interest.

# 19

EVER SINCE THEY'D MET JARNAIL, HE'D ALWAYS WORN SIMPLE cotton shirts, either blue or brown, and thick-soled black boots that went well with his parachutist past. This morning, though, he wore a crisp white shirt, pale gray pants, and ordinary shoes that reminded Shaul of Gadi's Shabbos shoes. And when Jarnail spoke to his children, his tone was different from when he drove them around.

Shaul had often wondered, over the years, about the seeming contradictions in the man's personality: the odd juxtaposition of the just-plain-folks fellow with the man of powerful intellect and broad horizons. This morning, he realized that Jarnail's simple guise was only an illusion. Still, he wasn't at all sure that he liked this new elegant Jarnail as much as he liked the man in the blue shirts who didn't mind sleeping under the sky and sitting behind the wheel of his green car.

But the loving hugs that the children gave their father, and the way he lifted them high into the air—almost to the ceiling—tickling them until they screamed with laughter and promising that, yes, today he would fix their sandwiches for school, and that he would be home today, tomorrow, and maybe even the next day, mitigated Shaul's uneasiness. Even if part of Jarnail's story was a vigorous distortion of reality, he was still apparently the same person.

Politely, unwilling to disturb the family, Shaul retreated with the baby to the suite that the night before had been modestly referred to as Jarnail's office. He woke Pinchas, who asked drowsily after the baby, and urged him to hurry and daven Shacharis. Afterward, he showed him the picture of Ehud Barak on the wall, the one that Pinchas had been too tired to notice, and updated him on the night's revelations.

"That explains a few things." Pinchas, too, wasn't really surprised.

"Yes," Shaul agreed.

They looked at one another.

"All right." Pinchas shifted his weight from one foot to another. "This doesn't change anything for us. He didn't lie. He just distorted reality a little so that he could get the job."

"Being a military attaché instead of an embassy security guard is not exactly 'distorting reality a little.'"

Shaul liked Jarnail, too, and he wasn't at all happy to serve as his prosecutor. But he couldn't ignore the facts.

"He lied, Pinchas. Let's see what the world looks like after we accept that fact."

"To me, it doesn't look so bad." Pinchas took in the tasteful room. "In fact, it looks pretty good. I can understand Jarnail. I'm not sure if we would have behaved all that differently in his place. He hasn't harmed us. He presented the reality that most resembles the reality that he didn't want to talk about." He nodded. "And don't forget that we're the ones who need his help. Let's find a place for the baby today and put everything else aside."

---

Jarnail's friends might be at a wedding somewhere in Mumbai, but he had managed, as always, to locate the person they needed. They were finishing their breakfast when he came to them with a satisfied smile.

"My cousin has a worker in his factory who grew up in an orphanage in the center of the city. He says it's an excellent place. They have a wing for boys and another for girls, they never lacked for food, and the staff is generally competent. Finish eating and we'll go over there."

Shaul hid a small smile. Until yesterday, he would have pictured Jarnail's cousin as a grease-stained laborer, eating from a plastic container that had seen better days and discussing his miserable childhood with his friends as he ate. This morning, the same words painted a slightly different picture in his mind. He could only guess at the worry the worker on the production line had felt when summoned urgently to the manager's office, and how hard he'd found it to believe that he'd been sent to the big boss's office just to tell him how he had been treated in the orphanage where he was raised.

Pinchas wasn't so sanguine. "What do you mean, generally competent?" he asked, his voice sharp.

Jarnail lifted his shoulders until they nearly touched his ears. "The majority of them are competent," he said, "like in any home. Didn't your parents ever behave less than perfectly reasonably with you?"

Pinchas said nothing. Jarnail spread his hands. "It's a good place. They don't compel the children to go around begging for alms. They teach them a trade. The man I told you about is a welder. That's a respectable profession. And the girls learn how to cook and sew." He nodded as though agreeing with his own words. "Can we leave in fifteen minutes?"

---

Dressed in Jarnail's daughter's clothing, the baby in the bassinet resembled a little doll. Her deep, peaceful slumber reinforced the image.

"HaKadosh Baruch Hu knows what He's doing." Pinchas placed the basket on the floor of the velvet-lined elevator.

"Obviously," Shaul replied. "That's not even a question."

"Yes." Pinchas nodded. "You're right, of course." He looked again at the bassinet and stifled a sigh.

"You can still change your mind," Jarnail said. "International adoptions are very routine."

Pinchas let out a sad laugh. "You're a good man, Jarnail. Thanks for your caring and concern. But that won't work for me. Really, thank you."

"She's a strong, healthy baby," Jarnail said. "I—"

Pinchas's upraised hand stopped him in midsentence. Jarnail maintained his silence until they were parked in front of the orphanage.

"We're here," he said, turning around. "This is the place. Doesn't look too bad, eh?"

Pinchas shrugged, looking at the low stone fence and the two-story building with barred windows and peeling paint. "It's all relative," he said. "Your apartment is nicer."

Jarnail smiled. "Come." He released his seat belt. "Let's do this fast and be done with it. I hope we can put this story behind us within a quarter of an hour."

---

Children were playing in the unpaved yard under the gaze of a white-haired woman sitting heavily on one of the benches. Shaul felt that the children were too skinny and too dirty for such an early hour of the day. On the other hand, how much can you expect from kids playing in the sand for even ten minutes?

"The entrance is over here." Jarnail was carrying the bassinet that held the baby. "The place really looks all right, doesn't it?"

"Yes," Pinchas said decidedly.

But Shaul was having misgivings. He didn't like the cow dung scattered throughout the yard where the children were playing without anyone thinking to sweep it away. He was bothered by the colorless, unadorned walls. The fact that Indians generally favor bold hues made this place look even bleaker. He wondered if, in all of Mumbai, there was no orphanage that was in slightly better condition.

The administrator, with whom Jarnail had spoken on the phone earlier, received them with a wide smile. He assured them that he could report the baby's discovery to the police in their stead and urged them to take a short stroll through the building.

The man was obviously proud of his institution. In strongly Indian-accented English, he pointed out the linoleum, which looked as if it had been laid down in the 1940s, and which he boasted "made it possible to wash the floor easily and to minimize bugs and disease." Proudly he showed them the kitchen with its running water, scratched counters, and insect-infested flypaper. He boasted about how much dairy they gave the children, about the varied menu, and the high standard of hygiene. He wound up with a tour of the babies' rooms: two vast halls filled with white metal folding cribs featuring colorful sheets and filled with toys and babies ages newborn to one year, watched over by three women in local dress. It couldn't be denied that the babies appeared contented.

"A nice place," Jarnail said. "You can see the thought that goes into every detail."

The institution's chief administrator sighed. "We try, we try. It is not easy. The government gives us a very limited budget, and children need a great deal. A great deal of heart, of thought, of…money."

Pinchas was silent. So was Shaul. And Jarnail. Fearing that he'd been misunderstood, the administrator elaborated. "There are places that send children out to collect donations. Others bring work in, and the children from ages four or six learn how to fold boxes or package beads. We don't do that. We give them a childhood."

"Yes," Shaul said politely. "One can see that you try."

"We receive used toys and clothing sent to us from outside India," the administrator said. "But toys and clothes are a very small part of what it costs to raise a child. If you have children of your own, you probably know this, too. They must be given food—good, nutritious food. They must be given medicine when they are ill. We need a large staff, including teachers and caretakers, as well as cleaners and a cook."

He paced the hall, his voice echoing off the empty walls. "You want to leave me a baby to raise for…how long? Sixteen years? I know what my accountant tells me about our financial situation. With all the good will in the world, I don't think that I can take on this additional burden."

"Meaning?" Jarnail asked. He threw his companions a quick look that said, "Leave the negotiations to me."

"Thirty thousand dollars," the administrator said. "And I am not extorting you. That is what this little girl will cost me, in addition to the money I receive from the government."

# 20

IT WAS AMUSING. DID THIS MAN, WITH HIS ROUND FACE AND little mustache, really think that they were about to fork over thirty thousand dollars for him to take a baby that was not theirs and raise her in his venerable institution? Shaul's lips quivered with suppressed laughter as Jarnail switched to Marathi and tried to persuade the man to be reasonable.

But the orphanage's director insisted on speaking English, explaining to them—and not to Jarnail—that he didn't feel obligated to take this baby and that without proper payment there was no chance of his doing so. His orphanage was filled to capacity. If they were unable to pay, he could certainly go to the nearest police station and leave the baby there. The police would know what to do with her. No worries.

As he said this, his lips formed a tight, oily smile that made Shaul clench his fists to the point that he could feel the blood pounding in them. Pinchas reacted even more strongly. He simply reached out, picked up the bassinet, and wordlessly turned and walked away.

"Pinchas!" Shaul wheeled around. "Pinchas?"

Pinchas didn't answer. He just kept walking, down the stairs to the first floor and down the next flight of stairs to the ground floor. Only there, in the yard, did Shaul manage to catch up with him.

"Pinchas!" he said, grabbing his friend's shoulder. "Pinchas, what are you doing?"

Then he stopped talking. Tears were dripping from Pinchas's eyes, one after another.

It isn't often that one sees a grown man cry, and the sight shook Shaul to his core. "Pinchas," he said gently, "what's the matter?"

Pinchas wiped his eyes with his free hand. "He's terrible, that Jarnail. He did this on purpose."

"Did what?"

"Everything." Pinchas turned. "Here he comes. He has no shame at all."

"Shame over what?"

"Don't be naïve, Shaul." Pinchas passed his hand over his damp eyes again, making sure the tears were gone. "Don't you understand that he's been playing us all along, trying to convince me that I have no choice? That it would be cruel to leave this sweet little girl in the hands of people like that director?"

Something hard and unpleasant lodged in Shaul's stomach. He didn't like Pinchas's suspicions, or the way it had been expressed. But, stated less harshly, it was entirely possible that Jarnail *was* trying to bring about a certain end. To create an emotional state that would prepare Pinchas to adopt the child—for her sake and his.

"You may be right," he said softly and quickly to spare Jarnail the insult. "But we can manage without him. I speak English, and we have a phone and some cash. We can figure this out ourselves."

Pinchas stole another look over his shoulder. "We may have reached the point where we have no choice," he said coldly. "I don't believe anything he says anymore."

A man shouldn't be judged in his hour of distress. Shaul very much hoped that he wouldn't have to explain this to Jarnail. On the other hand…maybe there was a certain truth in Pinchas's words. It needed to be cleared up now. They couldn't follow Jarnail's lead if his motives were suspect. Shaul's shoulders slumped fractionally with the burden.

"He is insolent!" Jarnail crossed the courtyard and joined them, almost as agitated as they were. "He is terribly insolent, that fellow! He didn't say a word about money when I spoke to him this morning. Do you believe me when I say that I would not have brought you here had I imagined such a thing?"

Pinchas tugged meaningfully at his nose while Shaul said carefully, "Pinchas feels that you're trying to exert psychological pressure so that he'll adopt the baby. And he doesn't like it."

"I definitely think it would be good—" Jarnail began seriously.

Pinchas lost the last shreds of his self-control. "You think!" he cried hoarsely. "You think! What do you know anyway? I told you that my wife isn't prepared to adopt! I told you! How many times do you think I can say the same thing? I think it's time you stayed out of my business!"

A startled flock of birds burst from the tree above them. Jarnail took a step back.

"Let's get in the car and turn on the air conditioning," Shaul said. "It's hot out here."

"Order us a taxi, Shaul," Pinchas said in a trembling voice. "Order us a taxi that will get us away from here."

"I will order one." Jarnail's tone was even.

"We don't need favors."

Pinchas's hand was shaking, too, whether from frustration or from the extended effort of carrying the bassinet.

"You're losing your composure, Pinchas." Droplets of sweat were dampening Shaul's neck. "Try to calm down, okay?"

Pinchas took a deep breath. "Believe me, I'm trying. But you can't push someone off a roof and then yell at him not to fall."

"Let's get in the car," Jarnail said, a voice of calm in the midst of the storm. "We can wait for the taxi there."

"No." Two pink patches stained Pinchas's cheeks. "I'm waiting here."

"Enough," Shaul said. "Pinchas, enough. Please."

"You're telling me enough? For the past three days, you haven't said a word to him! Did the two of you want to break me? Okay. You broke me. I hope you're happy with the results."

"Obviously we are," Jarnail said in the same even tone. "It's nice to see you all worked up like this."

The barb seemed misplaced to Shaul, but it worked on Pinchas like a glass of cold water dumped down his neck without warning. He fell silent and with measured movements bent down to release the baby from the straps of her bassinet. He lifted her and patted her back while murmuring a completely unnecessary "*Sha, sha.*" Then he said calmly, "Where's that taxi? Did you order it yet?"

Their eyes met and held for a moment—blue eyes burning with pain and outrage, and dark brown, almost black ones, also insulted and downcast.

"I will order one." Jarnail looked down at his phone. "But tell me that you believe me when I say that I did not know he would try to squeeze us for money like that."

Pinchas shrugged. "I could say a lot of things. But I'm not a liar."

Had he placed the slightest emphasis on the word? Shaul wasn't sure. Neither was Jarnail. But the hot air had just become even more oppressive.

"We are friends, Pinchas," Jarnail said heavily. "Even if I made a mistake—and I see now that I did—I did it out of love."

Pinchas breathed deeply. "I'd rather stop talking now," he said. "Okay? If I talk, I'll say things that I'll regret afterward. You hurt me deeply, both of you. And I—"

"Both of us?" Shaul asked. "Excuse me for asking, but what exactly did I do?"

Pinchas shook his head. "I don't know, Shaul. And the truth is, I also don't feel so well right now. I'd prefer not to talk about anything. My head hurts, and I feel terrible."

Shaul believed him.

"Do you want to talk to Rabbi Schwab?" he asked. "I mean, if you don't trust either Jarnail or me, he seems to be the last resort."

Pinchas turned paler while the pink patches on his cheeks darkened. "Give me air," he said. "That's all I'm asking. Give me air, please."

"There's air in the car." Shaul took the baby from his friend's arms. "Get in. Jarnail and I will stay outside if that makes you feel better."

Pinchas looked down at his empty arms, and then at Shaul. "My wife's pain," he said. "My parents' pain. Her parents' pain. Do you know how hard it is to carry all that on my back? What do I want? What am I asking of HaKadosh Baruch Hu? Just a child of my own. Just one child."

"You'll have it," Shaul said. "You'll have it, Pinchas."

"Really?" A crooked smile touched Pinchas's lips. "Do you promise? Based on what?"

"Based on a man who has been traveling to all kinds of holes in the world to support a large family." The heat was maddening. Maybe that was why Shaul's eyes were sweating now, too. "Hashem has provided for us all these years, and my family has never lacked for anything they needed. I promise you that your time will come, Pinchas."

"If you say so." Pinchas ran a hand over his face. He suddenly roused himself, as though grasping their situation. "So what happens now?"

B ACK WHEN THEY'D FIRST BECOME ACQUAINTED, THEY had given Jarnail a CD filled with soulful Jewish music for them to listen to on the road in place of the Indian ballads he so loved. Jarnail had been polite, but after playing the disc for the first time he had never listened to it again. Now, though, as they settled into the back seat, he put the CD into the player and pressed Play.

"It's hot," Shaul remarked, simply to say something.

"Very," Pinchas agreed. He twisted around to reach their cooler and extracted one of their water bottles. "What do we do now?"

Jarnail turned to face them. "Whatever you two want to do."

Shaul nodded. "What do we want to do, Pinchas?"

"Want? I don't want anything right now...except for Minchah in Zichron Moshe, if someone could get me over there."

"Should we call Rabbi Schwab again? Ask if it's possible to bring you home?" Suddenly, Shaul started laughing. "My brother-in-law is looking for someone to buy a ticket from him. Ben Gurion to Mumbai, for tomorrow. He'd probably agree to give Rabbi Schwab a special price to send someone here in your place."

"Your brother-in-law?" Pinchas asked.

"He bought a ticket for my wife." Shaul shook his head, still laughing. "He thought I could help her buy fabric here so she could open a shop in Israel."

Laughter is contagious. Pinchas smiled, even though he didn't really get the joke.

"Actually, I'm serious," Shaul said. He straightened. "I have an airline ticket to India for tomorrow. Do you want to return home and let them send someone else here in your place?"

The smile vanished from Pinchas's face. "On what pretext?" he asked. "I'm okay, Shaul. Don't worry. It was a momentary breakdown. I'm over it."

Silence filled the car as Shaul's thoughts tumbled over one another and Jarnail opened and then shut his mouth with a silent snap.

"What?" Pinchas asked. "What did you want to say?"

"Nothing," Jarnail said quietly.

"You wanted to say something, so say it. Better for you to include us in your thoughts than try to arrange our lives behind our backs." Anger was back in Pinchas's voice and eyes.

"I can't even run my own life. Why should I think I can run yours?" Jarnail retorted. "And if you want one hundred percent honesty, I just wanted to say that my therapist would have said that until you understand *why* you had that breakdown, you can't really say you're over it." He shook his head. "And don't say that now I'm causing you to have another breakdown—because your interpretation of my actions may have hastened it, but the true breakdown came from inside of you."

"The seats of this car are very comfortable," Shaul pointed out, "but they still don't deserve to be called a couch. Besides, Jarnail, you don't get paid enough to throw psychological advice into the package. Let's be practical, please. Pinchas, Minchah in Zichron Moshe isn't relevant right now. What else would make you happy?"

"A sip of cold water," Pinchas said. "Could you please straighten her head, Shaul?"

Shaul rearranged his grip on the baby while Pinchas took a drink of water. "Let's be practical," Shaul repeated. "Pinchas, we need a new plan. What do you suggest we do with this baby?"

Pinchas took a deep breath that sounded almost like a sigh. "I... Jarnail, can you please find us the numbers of a few more orphanages? Shaul, are you prepared to call them to arrange a meeting?"

"I can call for you. That would be smarter." Jarnail was hurt. Shaul could sense that despite the courteous mask. "I can do it in English, in Shaul's presence, if that will calm you, my suspicious friend. Simply because I am an Indian, a call from me will not be received with suspicion the way a call from Shaul would, with his nice Canadian English."

Pinchas opened and corked the bottle repeatedly. "You must have something like the Yellow Pages," he said. "Some sort of telephone directory. Please just get us the first five numbers, okay? If you'll give me a pen, Jarnail, I'll write them down."

"Good thing there are still people walking around with pens," Jarnail said, pulling a silver pen from his shirt pocket. "And I'm glad you believe that I will give you the first five numbers and aren't asking to see that I do not make some sort of sneaky selection to choose, say, the orphanages located in the worst sections of Mum—"

"Jarnail Singh Kapoor," Shaul said softly, trying to telegraph his empathy while at the same time asking for a bit of sympathy for the emotional Pinchas, "let's stay practical, please. Pinchas is in a lot of pain. You know that, which is why you so much wanted him to adopt the baby. Don't add to it, please."

"We all have pain," Jarnail said, staring at the small implement in his hand. "Everyone. I take pills to avoid feeling mine, so it looks like Pinchas is still better off than me—unless he also takes pills that we don't know about."

It was meant as a joke, Shaul assumed. But no one was laughing. Silence weighed heavily inside the car.

"I don't take pills," Pinchas said at last. "But if someone throws you over a railing, you fall. That's the power of gravity. And I'm prepared to present my argument to your therapist."

"Hmmm." Jarnail smiled. "You know what he would say? He will tell you that people have wings, and they are meant to spread them and glide on the wind when they feel the earth falling away beneath them."

It was a profound sentence, and one Shaul knew he would ponder later. Out loud, he said only, "Falling away beneath them! Your Hebrew is excellent, Jarnail. It never ceases to amaze me. My mother, *aleha hashalom*, couldn't speak Hebrew that well after twenty years in Israel."

Jarnail shrugged. "When you grow up in an area where they speak five languages, you have two choices: either you never speak any of them properly, or acquiring new languages becomes easy for you."

"Anyway, it's impressive," Shaul said. "I assume that you read any number of books in Hebrew to acquire such a vocabulary."

"The Yellow Pages, for instance," Pinchas said. "We want to make progress, Shaul. Please."

"All right," Jarnail said. He pulled out his phone and searched for the site that provided a telephone directory for Mumbai and its environs. "The first number is for an orphanage located in a really bad neighborhood. So bad that I won't go in there with my car, and I'm not sure if there is a taxi that would take you. Do you want to write down the number?"

Wordlessly, Pinchas shook his head.

"Okay, let's move on to the next one. It is located at the other end of the city, according to the number. You can write it down, but let's not call it as our first option. It's quite a drive."

"Fine," Pinchas agreed. "Next?"

"The next orphanage belongs to the Anglican Mission," said Jarnail. "They aren't too far from here. Take down the number."

"No," Pinchas said instinctively. "I don't want an orphanage run by missionaries. Move on to the next one."

"But she's not Jewish." Jarnail was astonished. "And those kinds of places generally have plenty of money. I don't know why I didn't think of it myself!" He looked at the expression on Pinchas's face and shrugged. "Okay, you're the boss. There are a lot of other options here. So let's—" He glanced up. "Shaul? Are you all right?"

Shaul had grown very quiet for the past few minutes as Pinchas and Jarnail tried, in vain, to find an orphanage where they could leave the baby.

"Me?" Shaul cleared his throat. "I—" He coughed again. "I—"

"You...?" Pinchas urged.

Shaul passed a hand over his eyes and straightened up. "We can't do it."

"Do what?" Pinchas asked sharply.

"We...I...can't abandon this baby."

22

THE CAR WAS IMPOSSIBLY QUIET. THE ENGINE WAS EMITTING
its usual growl, and the air-conditioning unit kept hissing out cool
air. But to Shaul's ears the silence was profound and cutting. As though
a large glass wall separated him from the engine, the air conditioner,
and the two men sitting in the car looking at him.

While Jarnail and Pinchas argued about orphanages, images had
started flashing through his mind. An abandoned newborn baby in
the grass under the beating sun. Young children, barely out of diapers,
begging in the streets and rooting in trash bins for scraps of food. The
British encountering a country with a dearth of girls because no one
wanted them.

What if they did find an orphanage that would raise this baby?
What if a family would adopt her? What kind of life would she have as
an unwanted girl in an impoverished, overpopulated country? True,
millions of children grew up in India healthy and fine. They found
their way. But they had saved this baby's life. In his eyes, that made
her theirs.

Would he ever consider giving away one of his own children?

He couldn't do it. They couldn't do it. He wouldn't allow it to
happen.

"We saved this baby's life," he said, his voice ringing out strangely
over the silence in his head. "I feel that we have a responsibility for her.
It just doesn't feel right."

Jarnail raised his thick brows. When they had reached the middle of his forehead, he asked, "What are you proposing?"

"I don't know," he said. Shaul shook his head, and the world reverted to its usual, noisy self. "No—I do know. One of us has to take in this baby. We can't abandon her to an orphanage and certainly not to the police."

Pinchas's lips tightened until they turned white. "If you mean to tell me that I have to adopt her because of your feelings," he said very quietly, "then I'm sorry, Shaul, but I respectfully decline. And considering that I've made *my* feelings clear, I consider this subject well and truly closed."

Frustration, pain, anger, and everything that had burst out of him earlier bubbled under those quiet words.

"I'm not saying that." To avoid looking at Pinchas, Shaul stared at his fingernails instead. "I'm just saying that I don't feel comfortable leaving her to some unknown fate in a country that has made it loud and clear that girls are not wanted. I feel that we have a responsibility to her now, since you found her."

"From where do you derive that?" Pinchas's voice was so calm as to sound nearly lifeless.

Shaul straightened his head to look at him. "Look, there's obligation and what's required according to the letter of the law. And then there is what's right. To me, all this—trying to find a way to pass her off like a football, looking for an orphanage that is 'competent'—just isn't right. It isn't right!"

Jarnail kept his foot on the gas without saying a word. The exhaust blew away leaves and dirt as he executed a U-turn and began to climb the road they had descended so easily before, where they had been certain that they would be able to bring the story of this infant to a good conclusion within a quarter-hour's time.

"Maybe we should call Schwab," Pinchas said minutes later, as Jarnail's car entered the stream of heavy city traffic. "He has a lot of connections. I hear what you're saying, Shaul. But who says we have to be the ones to adopt her? There are plenty of couples who would welcome a new baby with open arms. Schwab might know someone who could take her."

Shaul nodded. "Good idea. Of course, it would mean finding a way to bring her back with us to Eretz Yisrael. But we'll jump that hurdle when we get to it. So go ahead. Do it."

"Me?"

Shaul shrugged. "Yes, you. This is your question. You found her."
He glanced at Pinchas, whose lips were turning white again. "I'm here
to help you in any way I can. But if I'd been standing two steps away
from you when you picked up a diamond worth millions of shekels,
I'd have no rights to it. Same here."

Pinchas smiled a little sadly. "You know what I like about you?"
he asked. "You always make everything so simple. What needs to be
done—you do. Eh?"

Shaul smiled gently, almost shyly. "It always looks that way to other
people," he said. "We only know our own struggles. For the other guy,
it always seems so easy."

They made a good team and had worked together for a long time.
When one worked so closely with another person, it was impossible
not to uncover certain basics about each other's lives. It took over-
hearing only forty-five calls to *gemachs* for Pinchas to understand that
Shaul was the one taking responsibility for marrying off his sisters-
in-law, whose father had died too soon and whose widowed mother
couldn't bear the entire burden alone. At a certain point, Pinchas also
realized that those sisters-in-law had a well-to-do brother who could
have covered those expenses quite easily.

Gadi, Shaul's brother-in-law—his wife's brother—was generous.
He had given each of the girls fifteen thousand shekels as a wedding
present. It was a fine gift—but it was Shaul who took responsibility
for all the rest, with the same quiet practicality he used in checking his
tefillin straps each morning to make sure they were not damaged.

"It's *not* easy for you?" Pinchas asked rhetorically. "You look at the
situation, figure out what Hashem wants from you now, and then do
it, right? You don't know what it is to be angry or afraid. I know it's
true. I've been watching you for a long time."

Shaul laughed. "What a compliment!" he said. "But no. I'm
human, don't worry." He wanted to say more, but the phone in his
pocket began to vibrate. With a sigh, he pulled it out. "Hello?" he said
wearily.

"Shaul? It's Gadi. Listen—I thought of an amazing idea."

Shaul could tell that his brother-in-law was bubbling with energy,
bursting with the high spirits that always came along with a sizzling
new notion. The call pierced the tense bubble inside the car with a
humorous, almost bizarre, incongruity.

"Hello, Gadi." In light of the fact that he had caused Gadi no small expense and waste of time in obtaining an unnecessary airline ticket and visa, Shaul didn't feel right about simply telling him he'd call back later. "How are you? I'm in the middle of—"

"Listen to what I just thought of!" Gadi did not let him finish his sentence. "I don't know why I didn't think of it the minute I spoke to Ricki yesterday. But listen to my brainstorm: If Ricki found a job, why don't you take the money I want to lend the two of you and *you* start the business?"

"Me?"

"Yes, you. Who else?" Gadi was ebullient. "It could be perfect... That is, assuming that your decision to travel all over the world is not some form of escape from your responsibilities to your family."

Gadi, Gadi, Gadi. It was only Gadi. No need to get excited about anything he said. Even if it hurt badly. Shaul should even be grateful to him for puncturing the pride that may have collected in his heart after Pinchas's praise.

"I'm not running away from anything," Shaul said shortly. "But I don't know whether it suits me to start a business and be independent. And I also don't know if I have the ability to take on another debt right now. Ricki and I need steady paychecks." He threw an apologetic glance at Pinchas, with a shrug that said, *I can't just hang up on him.* "Anyway, I'm in the middle of something right now. I'll give this some thought and get back to you this afternoon, if that's all right with you."

"Sure thing, Shaul. But don't keep me waiting for too long. The offer won't be on the table forever."

---

"Those are the Hanging Gardens of Malabar Hill," Jarnail said, looking at both of them in the rearview mirror. "A beautiful place. You can get out, get some air. Give us a chance to regroup. Why don't I meet you back here in another hour and we'll discuss plan B?" He ended on a questioning note.

"Yes," Pinchas said. "Thank you."

"We'll leave the baby with you," Shaul suggested. "Is that okay?"

Jarnail nodded doubtfully. "I wanted to run over to visit a friend who lives around here. I'd be glad if the two of you could take her. There is a stroller in the trunk. I pulled it out of storage, where we had tucked it away when my youngest grew out of it. Padmasri reminded me that we still had it. Good thing, too."

The park was, indeed, beautiful. Green, quiet, and very spacious. They walked through it in silence, two men and a penniless baby in a splendid, borrowed stroller.

"I'll call Rabbi Schwab," Pinchas said at length. "Though I always get confused when I speak to him."

Shaul nodded, knowing exactly what his friend meant. Their employer's shrewdness often had an intimidating effect on others that could muddle one's thinking. But it couldn't be helped. They needed his advice.

"And I prefer to do it in private, if you don't mind."

Shaul nodded again, suddenly feeling tired and a little sad. Somehow this whole business had opened a tiny rift, a thin crack, between them. Barely visible, perhaps, but it was there. Though it was the fault of neither of them—they hadn't gone looking for abandoned babies—he wondered whether that rift would ever close.

"Call me when you're done," he said, gazing at the green expanse lying ahead. "I'll be waiting for your call."

23

THE PARK IN WHICH JARNAIL HAD DEPOSITED THEM WAS breathtaking in its beauty, but Shaul didn't choose to enjoy the scenery. Instead he found a quiet, green corner, parked the stroller in the shade of a tree, and settled in for an hour of learning. Then a group of Western tourists decided to plant themselves on the grass in front of him to do yoga exercises in the fresh air.

Fifty feet further on, he sat down again, took out his Gemara, and had just located the right page when someone touched his shoulder, making him jump. A local beggar, covered in ugly, oozing boils, wanted him to move over and make room on the bench. After a polite moment or two, so as not to hurt the beggar's feelings, Shaul looked at his watch, pretended to be alarmed at the time, seized the stroller, and escaped.

On the third bench, sprinklers suddenly began shooting streams of water all around him. He wasn't surprised to find that the fourth bench wobbled unsteadily. Still, he stayed, his Gemara resting on his knees and one hand rocking the stroller.

Birds chirped all around, the sun sent beams of dazzling light through the limbs of the tree above him, the breeze carried the fragrance of jasmine, and the baby slumbered soundly in her stroller. Two minutes later, Shaul's head slumped forward and he fell asleep.

He slept while the exercisers passed in front of him on their way to the parking lot, and he didn't stir when the birds came down from the trees to peck peacefully at the cake crumbs lying on the ground near his feet. Some dream caused his eyelids to flutter as the beggar limped along nearby.

Only when his cellphone rang did he open his eyes in confusion. Realizing where he was, he hastened to take the call.

"I'm glad you like the park," Jarnail said jovially. "But we said an hour, and it's already been an hour and a half. Do you want to stay here? Should I call again in another hour?"

"I apologize." Shaul straightened his spine and stretched. "I fell asleep sitting on one of the benches. I'll call Pinchas and see what he's up to."

"He's not with you?"

"No. He wanted to make his calls in private, so we parted ways. We arranged to meet up again at the exit."

"Well, he's not here." Jarnail's voice sounded a little troubled. "And I can save you a call. His cellphone's not picking up."

"He charged it just yesterday," Shaul said, getting to his feet. "Maybe he wanted quiet and turned it off for a while."

"There's no place for me to park," Jarnail said. "Hurry, please."

"Maybe you should try to find someplace to park," Shaul suggested, pushing the stroller ahead of him on the cobblestone paths. "This place is enormous, and I have no idea where Pinchas is right now."

He looked around, seeking a clue as to his friend's whereabouts. There was no flicker of black among the trees. "It may take me some time to locate him. Who knows? Maybe he fell asleep, too."

"Maybe." Jarnail was doubtful. "I'll look for parking and join you."

———————

The stroller moved along the paths that wound among the trees, clearings, and flowerbeds. Shaul had to pause when his phone rang.

"Did you find him?" It was Jarnail again, breathing hard on the phone.

"Not yet." Shaul hesitated, but Jarnail didn't pick up on it.

"Okay. Then we'd better divide up the territory. Where are you?"

Shaul took a deep breath. Jarnail was always stressed, always worried, but this time, he was going too far. "Let's not march into battle just yet," he said gently. "I don't think anything bad happened to Pinchas. Right now he's speaking with Rabbi Schwab on a very sensitive topic.

Let's give him the time he needs and wait patiently until he recovers somewhat."

Jarnail said, "May I remind you that I've already waited quietly for half an hour, which is not an insignificant amount of time. I think I see you, by the way."

"Half an hour may be a lot of time for sharpening a pencil, but very little for swimming an ocean." Turning around, Shaul spotted Jarnail on the other side of a long hedge and raised a hand in greeting. "Let's give him a little more time."

Jarnail motioned that he was going around the hedge. "You're the boss," he said into the phone. "My day belongs to you. That's what I'm being paid for. I'm in no hurry to go anywhere. I have all the time in the world."

"You're a good man," Shaul complimented, turning the stroller just as the energetic figure of the Sikh driver appeared in front of him.

"Thank you." Jarnail thrust his phone into his pocket. "So you don't want to look for Pinchas for now? Is that your decision?"

"For now," Shaul said.

Jarnail nodded. "All right. You know him better than I do. I respect your opinion." He shook his head as if to indicate that had he been in charge, he would have decided differently. "A nice day," he said, changing the subject. "But hot."

"India is hot," Shaul agreed. "But nice."

They both chuckled.

"Is this heat good for the farmers?" Shaul asked.

"It's not bad for things that grow naturally." Something darkened in Jarnail's voice. "But you must know what's been happening to Indian agriculture in the past hundred years. It's become too Western. First we switched from our traditional foods to food that, in the opinion of the British, was tastier or simpler to grow. Then financial considerations prompted farmers to become dependent on the big grain producers." He shook his head. "What can I say? If you don't act, you don't make mistakes. Look what happened in Israel, with all the matchstick trees planted by the Jewish National Fund..."

"What do you mean?"

"They tried to bring European scenery to the hills of Israel. Instead of planting dates or pomegranates, they filled the hills with barren trees that are highly flammable. That's the reason the fires on the Carmel and the Jerusalem hills spread so rapidly."

"Really?" Shaul hadn't known this. He wondered if the information was correct.

"That's what I heard." Jarnail peered around. "Do you want to go back to the car or find a bench to sit on?" He narrowed his eyes. "Look to your left. Is that Pinchas?"

It was. Unless a few other *mashgichim* had arrived in Mumbai recently. Pinchas was sitting on a stone wall, his back rounded and his posture dejected.

"Do you want to go over to him?" Jarnail asked quietly.

Shaul nodded slowly. Pushing the stroller ahead of him, he crossed the lawn.

---

"Pinchas?"

"Yes." Pinchas neither lifted his head nor turned his face.

"Is everything all right? Did you speak to Rabbi Schwab?"

"Yes." The same hoarse voice. Strange.

"And what did he say?"

"It took me three-quarters of an hour to convince him that leaving the baby at a police station is not an option. That we wanted to look into the idea of adoption in Israel, where she has a chance at a better life. He said he'd check it out and get back to me."

Pinchas fell silent, clearly mulling something over.

"Pinchas, what is it?"

Pinchas's sigh was heavy enough to shake the surrounding foliage. "I can't do it either."

Shaul's head started to pound. Was Pinchas saying what he thought he was saying?

"I could tell that Rabbi Schwab wasn't too hopeful that he'd find someone in Eretz Yisrael to take an abandoned Indian baby. And you're right. We saved her. We've been keeping her alive until now. We can't quit the job in the middle, right? Hashem placed this baby in our path for a reason. Maybe..." He faltered as his voice broke. "Maybe I am meant to be raising her as my own. Maybe that's what HaKadosh Baruch Hu wants from me right now." He took a deep breath. "Anyway, that's what I was feeling when I hung up after speaking with Rabbi Schwab."

Shaul rubbed the stroller's leather handle, wondering whether to speak or remain silent. When the silence stretched uncomfortably long, he tried, "And?" In light of Pinchas's attitude toward the little one in the stroller, it didn't seem as if the idea of adopting her should cause him such mental anguish.

"And?" Pinchas echoed. He stopped breathing for a moment, and then said, "And I called my wife. I told her everything. And what happened next was exactly what I thought would happen."

Finally, he turned around. The pain in his eyes was so great that Shaul nearly recoiled from it.

"What did you think would happen?" he whispered.

"Did you see how I reacted in the orphanage today? The same thing happened to her. She collapsed." He inhaled noisily. "She told me that she can't bear life as a childless woman. She wants to get divorced. She said that her father already went to speak to their rav, who said that it's an extreme measure and not a good idea. But if I want to adopt a baby, she thinks the situation is too much for her to handle. And that it would be best if we separated now."

He pressed his lips together to prevent them from trembling and passed a quick hand over his face, either to collect his troubled thoughts or to wipe his eyes.

Shaul's heart was breaking. "Women say all kinds of things when they're angry," he ventured.

"I know," Pinchas said. "But I spoke with her father, too. He was the one who called me."

# 24

SHAUL KNEW THAT PEOPLE CONSIDERED HIM A BRAVE MAN. They had told him so, thumping him on the shoulder, when he had undertaken to jump from a sixth-floor balcony onto a ledge on the fifth floor, and from there to the neighbor's window, to soothe three hysterical children whose mother had gone to the grocery store and locked the door behind her from the outside, apparently certain that they would sleep soundly until her return.

When he had told his mother-in-law that he was taking full financial responsibility for the weddings of his sisters-in-law, there were those who called him "insanely brave."

But when he had to approach a suffering man and say the right words of encouragement, all his courage dissipated without a trace.

"*Oy*, Pinchas," he said. "That's so sad."

Pinchas laughed. A dry laugh. "Yes," he said. "It is."

He should say something else, Shaul thought. But what? Should he say that Pinchas's wife was making a huge mistake, or would that only serve to exacerbate his friend's pain? But what else could he say? Was Pinchas capable of hearing him state that there was a good chance that ten years from now this moment—painful as it was—would be revealed as the source of a great deal of good?

"However you position a sick person, he will hurt," a very compassionate man had once told Shaul. "There are times when anything you say can be interpreted as unfeeling or insensitive."

So Shaul chose silence. Almost of its own volition, his hand reached out and brushed some dust from Pinchas's shoulder. The shoulder twitched, and Shaul's hand fell.

"I knew for a long time now that this moment would come," Pinchas whispered. "Often, when it's been hard for her, she would cry that maybe, if we can't have children, even though the doctors have no explanation, it's a sign that our marriage was a mistake."

"HaKadosh Baruch Hu doesn't make mistakes," Shaul said.

"True." Pinchas sighed. "But still. And her parents… Her mother is all right, but her father…" Another sigh. "He's a character."

Shaul spread his hands and said, "If she's spoken about it in the past, maybe this time it's also just frustration? She didn't make this decision calmly and analytically, right?"

"Calmly?" Pinchas laughed. "Not so much, no."

Dots were connecting in Shaul's mind. "Just a minute," he said. "Your phone isn't out of charge, is it?" He looked at Pinchas's hand, holding his phone, and shook his head. "No," he said. "Not that I think you're obligated to continue listening to your father-in-law's ranting. But to hang up on him? That wasn't the right move, Pinchas."

"It's a good thing we're a team, since you always know the right thing to do," Pinchas retorted.

Shaul didn't know if this was a feeble attempt at humor or an upwelling of bitterness and pain. After Pinchas's outburst that morning, Shaul tended toward the latter theory. He fervently hoped that the compassionate man whose words he had recalled was right, and that this was the fault of the suffering and not himself. That he hadn't rampaged among the delicate crystals in his friend's heart with all the sensitivity of a bear.

"The truth is, I don't know what's the right thing to do," Shaul said. "Only what's not right."

Pinchas made an ambiguous gesture. "In that case, maybe you should have talked to my father-in-law. Maybe you would have managed to calm him down."

Shaul hesitated again, wondering whether he should make another joke about himself and his advice. In the end, he heeded his more mature self. "Give me the phone," he said. "I can try to calm him down."

Pinchas's sigh sounded like a tree being uprooted. "That's what you think," he said. "There are some people who, the more you try to calm them, the louder they yell. My father-in-law is like that. Things would have been much simpler and better if he hadn't interfered so much in our lives.

"He never liked me from the beginning," Pinchas went on. "Even when we got engaged, he told someone that he thought he'd made a mistake in choosing me. Why should you get involved? Better not to have any dealings with him."

"It's nice of you to worry about me. But I won't be insulted if he yells. I promise."

Pinchas dropped his eyes to the stroller, studying the edges of the thin blanket covering the baby. "What would you tell him?" he asked tiredly. "He's not a person who's prepared to listen to anyone except himself."

The phone in Shaul's other hand vibrated. The screen informed him that Pinchas's irritable father-in-law had remembered that there was another way to reach his son-in-law, even if said son-in-law had decided to turn off his phone.

"Hello," Shaul said politely.

"Hello. I'm looking for Pinchas."

Shaul took a deep breath. "Yes, I saw your name on the caller ID," he said in a friendly voice. "You're Pinchas's father-in-law, right?"

"Yes, yes," the man said impatiently. "Can I talk to him?"

Shaul thought fast. Had Ricki been here, she would have urged him to try to see the other person's point of view, to think of the distress he was feeling, and maybe also the fear that was prompting him to act the way he was. But he had never been very good at imagination.

"Actually, I wanted to call you," he said briskly instead. "I understand that you gave Pinchas…hmmm…some bad news this morning. I assume that you're simply upset, and now that you've calmed down a bit, you want to apologize about the whole thing, right?"

The silence at the other end of the line spoke volumes.

"What is there to apologize about?" the man asked at last.

In Sedom, they asked a person who'd been beaten to pay the one who struck and injured him; after all, bloodletting is a health remedy. Shouldn't the person who received the benefits pay for it? For some reason, the rest of the world thinks otherwise. But if this father-in-law didn't understand that there's a right way and a wrong way to do things, it wasn't to be expected that Shaul would succeed in teaching him in a single phone conversation.

"Are you going to let me talk to Pinchas or not?"

"I'll gladly let you talk to Pinchas," Shaul said, ignoring his friend, who was standing in front of him shaking his head from side to side. "I just want to know if your daughter explained to you that Pinchas feels a responsibility toward the baby girl. He feels that this is what he has to do. That it's the right thing to do."

"He did tell her some such nonsense," the father-in-law said dismissively, "and that's fine with me. But my daughter doesn't wish to be involved in this business. That's all."

"I'd like to ask you one question." Shaul's palms were suddenly damp. "Had Pinchas called your daughter this morning and told her that he'd been in an accident and needed her help—would she have come?"

"You're getting involved in matters that don't concern you, young man."

"If only I were a young man. If only this matter didn't concern me. You don't leave a wounded man, right? Do you accept the idea that marriage involves mutual responsibilities? A partnership between a couple isn't something that should be suddenly broken the minute the situation turns into something we don't like."

The ground was starting to shake. "We asked our *rav*—"

"You asked your *rav*, and after talking it over with us, you understood that there's no reason to rush and every reason to wait," Shaul broke in, trying his best to erase every vestige of emotion from his voice. "Something unexpected happened that upset you. Is that any basis for deciding on an immediate divorce? Does that sound reasonable to you? If Pinchas had, *chas v'shalom*, been in a car accident and lost a foot, would you also have decided that that was the right time to declare that his marriage was over?"

"You're talking about things that aren't relevant," the father-in-law said, slowly and clearly. "Where's Pinchas? I need to talk to him."

"I think that you need to go back to your *rav*." Shaul, too, could speak slowly and clearly. "Tell him what a diamond your daughter got. What a precious Jew, filled with *emunah* and feeling, with such fine *middos*. And what *yiras Shamayim* he has, to the point where he is prepared to undertake to raise this baby because that's what HaKadosh Baruch Hu is asking of him. And ask the *rav* if it isn't right and proper that your daughter, who has received so much from Pinchas over the years, should help him and take part in this mitzvah."

"Even if it is right and proper, that's not something she's going to do," the father-in-law snapped. "My daughter is not going to raise some non-Jewish child simply because her husband decided that's the right thing to do. Besides, since you're talking—why don't you undertake this great and holy mitzvah yourself?"

# 25

"YOU SAID YOU WOULDN'T GET INSULTED," PINCHAS SAID. "I said what?" Shaul's senses had become dulled, his thoughts slow.

"You said that you wouldn't get insulted by my father-in-law."

"I wasn't insulted."

Shaul inhaled deeply, taking in the fragrances of the beautifully landscaped park, a sea of sweet, soft smells that suddenly made him feel queasy.

"You don't look like someone who isn't insulted." Pinchas gave a crooked smile. "Maybe you're doing this on purpose because you know how good it is for someone to worry about someone else? Distracts a person from his own concerns?"

"I'm not that clever." Shaul's brain hadn't yet returned to its normal functioning.

"You don't look so good," Jarnail said, appearing behind them. "I think you'd better have a drink."

"Me?" Shaul turned to meet Jarnail's eyes. They were very brown eyes, really dark, but on the innermost point he saw a soft, golden dot.

"Drink," Jarnail requested. "I don't want you becoming dehydrated. India is a hot country."

"Really?" Shaul asked. "How haven't I noticed that until now?"

He got his water bottle out of the bag he'd hung on the stroller's handle and saw that Jarnail had been right. Since leaving home for the orphanage, he'd drunk less than one cupful. He said the *berachah* and took a long drink of lukewarm water. Water was good. It washed away the bad feelings and unclogged the gears of his brain.

Slowly he lowered the bottle, closed it, and put it back in the bag. This afforded him a few more seconds to think.

"Pinchas," he said, "tell me something. Have the two of you tried? Really tried?"

Pinchas stared at him as if he were a toad that had sprouted wings. Shaul regretted having spoken before he'd properly formulated his thoughts. "I mean, in terms of *shalom bayis*," he said.

Suddenly, he felt as exhausted as if he'd just finished *kashering* a complete production line. "Forgive me for interfering, Pinchas... But I had a friend who suffered from a cough in the spring. One year it was so bad that he coughed up blood. Though everyone begged him to see a doctor, he refused because he said this was nothing new." Shaul suppressed a sigh. "By the end of the summer, he was dead of lung cancer."

"Poor fellow," Jarnail murmured. Shaul sensed that he understood his intention.

"An earlier diagnosis doesn't always help," Shaul said in his deceased friend's defense. "Maybe Heaven wanted to remove months of suffering from him and his family. That's a definite possibility. But I don't want to talk about him. I want to talk about you."

"About me?"

"With your permission."

"What is there to say about me?" Pinchas could reveal glimpses of dark humor at times.

"There are no secrets between us, right?" Shaul said. "We all agree that you arrived at this moment for a good reason. Even two. You have a manipulative and problematic father-in-law, and you have no children. Each of those factors, on its own, could rock the stability of a marriage."

Pinchas shook his head glumly.

"But each of them alone can also strengthen you as a couple," Shaul continued quietly. "And if that doesn't happen, it's worthwhile asking why. Have you ever gone for help?"

Pinchas hung his head, his blond *peyos* falling forward so that he looked as delicate and helpless as a child. "There's no point in talking about any of that now."

Shaul sighed. "You should have gone," he stated. "Go ahead—call your wife. Ask her what would happen if this baby were out of the picture, and you agreed to go for counseling. When you have an answer, get back to me. Okay?"

"And how, exactly, is the baby going to get out of the picture?" Pinchas asked bitterly.

"Leave the worrying to the adults," Shaul chided. His children, had they been present, would have recognized the forced humor he sometimes used when a situation became particularly challenging. "You can occasionally do what you're told without asking questions."

Their eyes clashed for a moment, and it was Shaul who lowered his first. He stared at his dusty shoes, which hadn't been polished since the previous Friday back home, and saw a tiny black beetle winding its way among the trodden blades of grass. When he looked up again, Pinchas was gone. Only Jarnail was there, giving him a measured look.

Shaul gave him a tense smile.

Jarnail cracked his knuckles. "Did I understand you correctly, Shaul?" he asked. "You want to adopt the baby yourself?"

The question, spoken out loud, only underlined how illogical the idea was.

"I have debts to the tune of approximately a million and a half shekels, Jarnail," Shaul said. "And ten children. The oldest is seventeen and the youngest is not yet twelve months old. There's no space in the children's room for his crib. When he moves into the children's bedroom at the end of the summer, my oldest son—who will be going away to yeshivah—will spend his Shabbosos at home sleeping in the living room." Shaul's voice trailed off.

"So what you said before—" Jarnail began. He shook his head. "I do not understand anything."

Shaul closed his eyes and covered them as though about to say *Shema.* "Neither do I." He rubbed his forehead and then looked down at the baby, who was beginning to stir in the stroller. The sun beat down on his neck. "We'll have to feed her soon," he said. "Can you prepare a bottle for her, Jarnail? I have a call to make."

---

Ricki answered almost immediately, sounding excited and out of breath. "How nice that you remembered!" she said. "It was wonderful.

Simply wonderful. I think I'm going to like this place. We signed a contract. I start work in a week and a half."

"A week and a half," Shaul echoed.

"Yes." Ricki was ebullient. "Isn't it great?"

"You sound happy," Shaul whispered, gazing around at the beauty surrounding him: flowers in so many different colors, an abundance of green, a yellow bird jumping onto a branch almost within reach of his hand.

"*Baruch Hashem, baruch Hashem,*" Ricki replied.

The world around her came through her cellphone: the sound of cars beeping, the annoying rattle of an old bus, and, in the distance, more birdsong.

"Do you remember my telling you about a baby we found?"

The question was unnecessary, but Ricki replied anyway. "Of course." She sounded distracted.

"Where are you?" he asked.

"There's a basket of socks on sale here," Ricki said. "The ones with the silicon stripe at the bottom. You know the ones I mean, right? I wanted to buy some for Tzviki. He took his first three steps yesterday."

"He's quick." A smile rose to Shaul's face whenever he thought of his baby.

"Miri also walked at eleven months—but he *is* quick. You should have seen how proud he was of his accomplishment."

Shaul's heart constricted and expanded. Expanded with sweet longing, constricted with love. Pain. His children were growing up without him. The price he was paying for the right and proper decision that he'd made years ago was a steep one. Very steep.

"Ricki—" he said. "Can we talk seriously for a few minutes?"

"Did something happen?"

"The baby we found…"

"Yes? What about her? Did you find someone to take her?"

"No, I…we…weren't satisfied with the conditions in the orphanage we went to. Leaving her at a police station is not an option, for various reasons. Ricki, I feel responsible for this baby. She's so vulnerable, and life in India, particularly for girls, is so harsh."

"I see. So…what are you saying?"

He waited, allowing the words to echo in her consciousness.

"Just a minute." She finally got it. Two pairs of socks dropped back into the basket. "Are you saying what I think you're saying?"

# 26

HOW LONG DID RICKI'S SILENCE LAST?

For Shaul, an eternity seemed to stretch before he heard her voice again. "So let your partner adopt her," she said. "That could be wonderful for him. Tell him that there are many couples who had children of their own after adopting a child."

Shaul took a deep breath. "Everyone has thought of that idea," he said quietly. "A childless couple, a child without parents—it sounds ideal. But...his wife doesn't want it."

"Do you want me to try to convince her?" Ricki sounded relieved. "I'd do it gladly."

"I..." Shaul hesitated. "I don't think it will work. She is very, very sure—"

"We had a nice talk at Chanukah when they came to visit us," Ricki said quickly. "I can at least try, Shaul!"

Shaul chose his words with care. "Pinchas's wife is absolutely against the idea. She prefers to get divorced rather than adopt. And she means that seriously."

"Divorced! I can't believe it!"

Shaul was silent.

"All right," she thought out loud. "Then we have to put an ad in the *Yated Ne'eman*: 'Newborn infant, healthy and sweet, needs religious adoptive parents.' I'm sure we'll get applicants."

"Ninety percent of them will drop out the minute they hear that we're talking about a sweet and healthy non-Jew," Shaul said. "And ninety percent of those who are left will drop out when they hear that it's not a blue-eyed non-Jew but a girl from India. And ninety percent after *that* will just ask for a lot of information or not be suitable candidates for adoption. And the two people who are left after all that will be a curious journalist and a police detective who will want to arrest both of us for peddling children. And then we'll have to put another ad in the *Yated*: 'Ten well-brought-up children from a good home need a stable family.'"

"Enough," she begged. "Stop. Don't joke about things like this."

"You're right," he admitted. "I'm sorry. I'm very tired."

"What other solutions have you rejected?" she asked. In school, on the job, everywhere, she had always been considered clever. To her delight, her husband was always one step ahead of her. Smarter, more knowledgeable, with a better understanding in nearly every area.

He mopped his forehead and bit his lip. Ricki would have understood how he felt had she been there to see him, but all she heard was the silence.

"What about an institution here in Israel?"

"To do that, we'd have to first get her out of India legally, and then bring her legally into Israel, and then convince the authorities in Israel that she deserves to be raised at the expense of the state—in a religious institution, of course."

"Let's take this one step at a time," she said. He was the smarter one, but she was more practical. "How can she be taken out of India legally?"

"That would be fairly easy, I think." He fell silent.

She was silent, too. Married couples can sometimes understand one another even without words. But understanding was just the first stage of the process. Ricki shook her head even though there was no one to see her.

"All right," she said at last. "I know that you're not supposed to joke about such things, but listen, Shaul, if you're going to say what I think you're going to say, then I—"

"It's no joke," he said quickly. "But yes. I think I'm going to say what you think I'm going to say."

Ricki swallowed hard. "You mean, we should adopt her temporarily? Just temporarily, right?"

"If we adopt her in order to take her out of India, there won't be anything temporary about it."

"All right. Then that idea's impossible," she said. "The mere thought of it makes it hard for me to breathe."

She did sound a little short of breath. "Take a deep breath, Ricki," he said. "Please. Maybe sit down for a minute, and we'll talk about it, okay?"

"I don't have to sit," she said. "I need to hear that you're not serious. We have ten children. *Ten children.* Do you think I have the strength to raise another baby now, with Tzviki only eleven months old?" Tears sprang into her eyes. "Shaul, do you know what a baby is? Do you know what it is to get up three, four, five times every night? When you think about introducing another child to our family, you have to consider the consequences. I just signed a contract for a new job. The best job I could have dreamed of. And even without that—I don't have the energy for another baby. Not now."

She was crying in earnest now. He didn't have to see her to know that she was wiping the tears with the back of her hand, even as new tears came to take their place.

"Ricki—"

"No. Don't say 'Ricki.' You always say, 'Ricki,' and I give in. But not this time. Absolutely not. How much can one woman carry on her back? Do you think I have infinite strength? Do you really want another baby right now? There aren't enough babies in our house?"

"You're right," Shaul said in a low voice. "About all of it. But this is the right thing to do. If I leave this baby here in India to an uncertain fate, I won't be able to live with myself. It will gnaw at me for the rest of my life. You understand that, right?"

His words unsettled her. She abandoned the sweet little socks, dropping them back into their basket, and went out to weave among the parked cars. "Why does it have to be you? Why do you always have to do the right thing?" Her hoarse voice sounded strange over the phone. "Anyway, I think the responsibility belongs to Pinchas. He's the one who found that baby!"

Maybe she didn't have to sit down—but he did. Desperately.

"So many questions," he said, seating himself slowly in front of a huge bush trimmed in the shape of a giraffe. "Where do I start?"

She sat, too, on a stone wall, staring down at a green Jerusalem frog. "Wherever you want," she said. "Pinchas and his wife are good Jews, right?"

"Right," he agreed.

"Then why can they get out of this, and we can't?"

"Because we're better Jews?" he suggested.

"And you think that tiny flame of pride is supposed to warm me for eighteen years, until I bring this little stranger to the *chuppah* with a top yeshivah boy?"

"If you really do that, you'll have many more things to be proud of," he promised her. "Ricki, to raise a child is to serve Hashem. It's a big deal."

"It's arrogance." She preferred to attack rather than to listen, and she knew it. "It's ugly to elevate ourselves at someone else's expense. To say that we're better than Pinchas and Sari and that we, as opposed to them, are capable of doing the right thing."

"Sometimes the truth is ugly," he remarked, staring at the suddenly unappealing giraffe bush. "But I'm not elevating myself at all. I have no idea what their challenges are, *baruch Hashem*. I also have no idea what they're capable of. I know myself, and I know you. And I think that with Hashem's help, we can do it. And do it well."

"Why can't Jarnail do it? Wouldn't he be the best choice? Wouldn't she be better off staying in her own country being raised as an Indian?"

"Jarnail hasn't offered or even hinted at the possibility. I get the impression that his family situation is complicated. And he himself is dealing with some personal challenges. He could easily provide the baby with all her material needs. But emotionally… Let's just say that this is not a good time for him to be adopting babies."

The sounds that reached Shaul's ear told him that Ricki had started crying again. "I'll try to help," he said. "I'll get up for her at night. If that's what you're afraid of, I'll undertake that job, *bli neder*. You can count on that."

"Nice," she snapped. "The problem is that by the time you wake up, our upstairs neighbors won't be able to sleep anymore. And what happens when you have to travel abroad again?"

Shaul closed his eyes, and everything around him suddenly vanished. The world turned dark. "I thought about that," he admitted, "and you're right. It's really hard for you. So I've made a decision: If you agree that we take in the baby, I will leave the Vaad HaKashrus, Ricki. I won't travel anymore."

They were not young, unbalanced kids. They were two mature people who had thought a great deal, consulted others, and chosen the least problematic of all the possibilities before them. He hadn't expected his wife to jump for joy at hearing this decision. On the other hand, he hadn't expected this blast of frigid air either. It lasted for a full minute before she said, "You're willing to do all this for the sake of one Indian baby? You're going to let her destroy our whole life?"

"I'm insulted," he said with the same forced humor he'd used on Pinchas earlier. "Would it really destroy your life if I'm home and can make Kiddush for you?"

"Oh, come on," she chided. "You know very well that Kiddush is a bonus. I'm talking about earning a living. We need your salary. We have so many debts. You don't have a chance of earning that kind of salary if you stay here. Right?

"We do so much," she whispered. "I'm afraid you'll have to pass this one up. Okay?"

27

THOUSANDS OF MILES OF ARID DESERT AND THOUSANDS OF miles of salt water lie between Yerushalayim and Mumbai. The silence on the phone lengthened that distance. It rose above the atmosphere, was grasped by satellite sensors, and then got sent back down to earth.

"When you say 'pass up,' what do you mean?" Shaul asked at last. "I know you. You don't want us to do the wrong thing just because it's easier."

"Of course not," Ricki agreed. "I like doing the right thing as much as you do, don't worry. But to bring her into our home, crowd the children even more, and be even more careful with every shekel—that *is* the right thing to do?"

"I'm in India now," Shaul reminded her, as though she might have forgotten. "Somehow, in comparison with the poverty I see here, the six-year-olds I see going through the garbage to find scraps of metal and plastic to sell—I can't manage to feel that our financial situation is so bad, or even a factor in the decision."

The wretchedness that Shaul had described with wrenching feeling after his first visit to India flooded Ricki's mind. "Still," she said, "you know that wealth and poverty are relative terms. You feel poor if you have less than your neighbors, not if you have less than people in India. Isn't that true?"

"Very true." The bushes in this part of the park, shaped into all sorts of animals, was very far from the poverty they were talking about. "I just wanted both of us to be aware of the reality. In America, people don't want children if they won't have the money to send them to university, but I don't think there are many youngsters who would have preferred not to exist for that reason."

"So?" She had to get home to prepare lunch. "What does that have to do with anything?"

"I don't think she would feel that we've let her down if we can't give her a perfect future."

"You're such a good person." Something in Ricki's heart melted. "You're already thinking about that baby and the complaints she may have against you... But I'm not there yet. I'm thinking about the children we have at home right now."

"And what are you thinking about them?" In any matter related to feelings, Ricki had a clear advantage over him, and Shaul knew it. "Do you think they would really be miserable if there was one more baby in the house?"

"There's no room in the house for one more crib," she pointed out. "And, no, they wouldn't be miserable. But they have needs and wants, a little more than the needs and wants of people born into the poor caste in India. Their wants are legitimate in the country where they live, and to provide them you need money. And for money, you have to fly abroad and leave me alone at home. And I'm not capable of staying home alone and raising nine children and two babies on my own."

"I understand," he said slowly, thinking as he spoke. "Ten, yes— eleven, no. A baby who weighs about six pounds is a straw big enough to break the camel's back. Well, no one is asked to do more than he's capable of doing. So I will simply stay in Israel and help you to help me do the *chesed* that has been given to me."

"But you can't stay in Israel if you have to travel abroad to make a living," she reminded him. A glance at the digital timetable near the bus stop told her that her bus wouldn't appear for another fifteen minutes. She allowed herself to move back into the shade and relative privacy. "Is it possible for you to find a job here with the same salary? And if so, why haven't we looked for it until now?"

"From a logical standpoint, there's not much chance that I'll find a job in Israel with the same salary," he agreed heavily. "But you know? After my natural desire to protect my family and to support it and myself, I think that my job is to carry out Hashem's will. And Hashem's will is to 'satisfy the desire of every living thing.' It makes much more sense for me to do my job and leave His job…to Him."

"You didn't say that eight years ago."

"Because then it would have meant evading my debts. Today, faced with a situation like this, and knowing that it will not be especially easy or pleasant to change my whole lifestyle—I feel that this falls under the category of genuine *bitachon*, not irresponsibility. It also sounds more sensible to me than taking responsibility for my own livelihood and explaining to Him that I can't obey His will."

She was sitting in a good spot. No one passed by. No one could overhear her. Yet Ricki couldn't sit still while the blood pumped so powerfully in her veins. She got to her feet and stepped carefully along the edge of the road leading down to the parking lot's bottom level.

"People will think we've gone mad," she said. "What a crazy idea, to adopt a child when we have ten of our own!"

"You mean to say that if we had no children and were heartbroken about it, this would look like the right step?" Shaul asked sharply. "Simply because then this baby would be fulfilling our emotional needs and helping us feel better? You don't think it's a little cruel to view children as entertainment for their parents, or as the means to fulfill all sorts of emotional or social whims? If we don't need them—then their mission in the world suddenly has no importance?"

"I didn't say no importance," she stammered. "But you have to agree with me, Shaul, that the ideal situation would be a combination of the couple's needs and those of the children."

"The ideal situation is the situation that Hashem puts us in at any given moment." He started walking along the park paths without noticing where his feet were taking him or noting landmarks to lead him to the exit. "I don't have to remind you that it was you who taught me that nice sentence, right?"

The sentence had come from Miss Wallach, her much-admired teacher in seminary. She would often quote it during the early years of their marriage.

"I was once better and more idealistic, apparently."

Her eyes burned, not from an inner fire but from an unfortunate combination of hard contact lenses and tears.

"Once, you talked the talk more," he said. "Today you talk less but do more. That's what I think, anyway."

"Are you saying that in order to bribe me?" she asked. But the parking lot, crowded with gleaming cars—a luxury that she and Shaul would most likely never be able to afford—told its own story about the truth of Shaul's point about the choices they had made over the course of their life.

"Listen, Shaul." Energy suddenly suffused her. "Let's be practical for a minute. I understand that you're afraid to put ads in the paper. But there must be couples who would be thrilled with an offer to adopt a baby without going through a million hoops. Give me forty-eight hours…"

There was logic in what she said. "You remember the airline ticket that Gadi bought you?" he asked anyway. "He got you a visa, and there's a ticket for tomorrow morning."

"We can always buy another ticket," she said. "You don't adopt a baby for the sake of saving four or five hundred dollars."

He laughed. "But it would be a pity to lose the five hundred dollars for no reason. I think that if you don't succeed in finding someone by tonight, you should use that ticket and fly to India."

Ricki's lips stretched in a smile. "You're talking like a *mashgiach* who's already visited half the countries in the world. For me to travel from Yerushalayim to Haifa is a challenge."

"In a certain sense, India is closer," Shaul said. "All you have to do is get to Ben Gurion Airport. The rest happens on its own."

# 28

SERVING LUNCH TO SEVEN LIVELY CHILDREN WHO'D returned from school calls for true artistry. Ricki liked to picture it as a complex dance. Her right hand opened the fridge to take out cucumbers, while her left opened the drawer to take out a knife. Her foot pushed one chair closer to the table, while an elbow carefully pushed back the container of sugar that someone had left out that morning, rescuing it from falling. Then, in a crescendo, she chopped the cucumber for a salad, exclaimed over a good mark on a test, stirred the soup, and assured one daughter that everyone in kindergarten loved her in the hope of stopping her tears. Turned the patties in the frying pan while wondering about the rhythmic thumping from the living room. Tried to make sense of the geometry question thrust under her nose and hoped that she didn't err in saying that the teacher made a mistake in marking it wrong. As an impressive finale, she managed to find some Bamba for the baby and rescued her cellphone from falling into the sink.

But the silence that came afterward, that moment of peace when they were all eating—that was a rare gift from Heaven.

Yet there was no peace today, because fragments of her conversation with Shaul kept running through her head.

"Ima will be right back," she told her children instead of taking her place at the head of the table. "Toby, you can watch them for a minute, right? I'm just going to my room to make a quick phone call."

Toby's expression was doubtful. Ricki gave the eleven-year-old an encouraging smile: "I know you can do it." Still, on second thought, it might be a good idea to provide some help. She thought for a moment and then added, "Whoever eats nicely will get chocolate lentils. Ima will be right back."

These stolen moments of quiet were all too rare. Someone or something would be demanding her attention before long. Impossible to conduct a real phone conversation right now. But the call she was planning shouldn't take long. What did she want, after all? To get a phone number for Dassi, who had taught high school with her, and for Efrat's sister-in-law. She'd make the serious calls later, after Rini came home and agreed to take the younger kids to the park.

"You're the sixth person to ask for Dassi's number this week." Ricki's friend Esther chuckled. "It's nice to see how close the teachers have remained after all this time."

"Mm-hmm," Ricki agreed distractedly, listening to the sounds coming from the kitchen.

"Everyone is so happy that she finally had a baby!" Esther added.

"Dassi had a baby?" Ricki was stunned.

"You didn't hear?" Esther was no less surprised. "Then why did you ask for her number?"

"To suggest a *segulah* that I heard about today. Something rare that happens only once in a century," Ricki said, only because she hoped that her words would be taken as a joke.

"Oh, really?" As expected, Esther was amused. "All right. I can give you plenty of other phone numbers if you want."

If she wanted? Did she want to call strangers with her odd proposal? No, she didn't want. But she needed to do it anyway. And Esther was prepared to help.

Ricki took down the names and numbers as her friend added details about the people hiding behind them so that Ricki would grasp the whole picture. And although the conversation seemed to Ricki like an underwater dive that lasts too long, when she ended the call and filled her lungs with air, there were still no unusual sounds from the kitchen demanding her rapid return.

What now? Her fingers acted on their own, taking advantage of the silence. Gadi answered at once.

"What?" he asked.

"About the trip to India," she said cautiously. "Is the offer still on the table?"

"I thought you found a job."

"Yes. I signed the contract this morning. I'll be running the computer department at the Magshimim Institute." Even now, as she thought about the well-lit office that would be hers starting next week, she felt better than she had in a long time. "But there's a chance I'll fly out tomorrow anyway."

"Shaul took my suggestion that he open a business seriously, and you're going there to help him pick merchandise?" Gadi sounded happy. "I'm thrilled, Ricki. You're a good wife. You don't deserve to live alone."

"I don't live alone," she said.

"Yes, with ten children no one is ever alone." Ricki liked to think that he didn't realize how much his words stung. "Shaul probably won't buy fabric, eh?"

"Fabric?" It took her a minute to remember the wonderful plan Gadi had devised for her. She smiled. Her brother was sweet. He remembered her energetic sewing projects as a high school girl and thought that today, twenty years later, she was still just as enamored of sewing.

"What else?" he asked.

"I don't know if he's planning something like that." She decided to be as clear and straightforward as possible. "But since there's a ticket and you got me a visa, I thought maybe I'd fly to India to help him with the baby."

"Fly to India," Gadi repeated, amused. "You sound like a woman of the world, big sister."

She had kept her passport handy since her trip to Canada to visit Shaul's grandmother before the elderly woman had passed away. "India is closer than Haifa," she said, repeating Shaul's joke. "All you have to do is get to the airport. The rest happens on its own."

"That's what *I* always say," Gadi shot back. "You two are the ones who don't understand why I want to see Niagara Falls if I've already seen Ein Gedi and the Banyas."

"What does Niagara Falls have to do with India?" she asked innocently.

"Nothing at all. But if you want, after India I'll send you there."

"You're generous, little brother." She fell silent for a moment. "It's a round-trip ticket, right?"

He laughed. "Yes, don't worry. You'll be home within a week. I'm not going to leave you stranded."

"What about Tzviki?"

Silence. Then: "Where does Tzviki come into this?"

"What do you mean? What do you think he eats? I haven't left him for more than twelve hours at a stretch since he was born."

More silence. 'He's a year old now."

"Eleven months," she corrected him.

"So let him drink formula," the baby's uncle decided. "On my tab. It will cost me a lot less than another airline ticket."

"Very funny."

"You're the funny one, Ricki. Hysterical."

"In short," she said, swallowing a sudden lump in her throat, "there's no ticket for Tzviki."

"There's no ticket for Tzviki," her brother affirmed. "I'm not as bad as you think, Ricki. I would have gotten him a ticket had I known. But there's nothing to be done now."

"Why not?" she asked, swallowing her pride along with the lump.

"Because the flight is full," Gadi said impatiently. "It's not the bus to Bnei Brak. You can't travel standing up."

A crash sounded in the kitchen, as though an entire drawerful of pots had been dumped on the floor. "I see," Ricki said, heading quickly to the kitchen. "I'll have to think about what to do, Gadi. Thank you."

"You're welcome." Gadi sounded tired.

"Are you all right?" she asked, stepping out into the hall.

"Yes," he said. "Thanks for asking. My health is fine."

"What *isn't* fine?" She hoped that only pots had fallen. Ah—no. A Pyrex dish had cracked all along its side. Oh, well.

"Our relationship. Look how much I'm willing to do for you—and now you're angry at me again."

"I'm not angry," she said, starting to gather the pots into a pile, frustration gathering in her heart. Somehow he always managed to turn herself and Shaul into the bad ones. On the other hand, maybe she really was still angry at him, deep inside, because after their father died tragically of a stroke he hadn't agreed to Shaul's request that they split the financial burden that had been created. She had never managed to forget how he'd turned his back on them.

"I'm glad to hear that. Anyway, the flight leaves at two-thirty a.m. That means you have to be at the airport by twelve-thirty."

Ricki took a deep breath. That didn't leave her much time at all. "I hear," she said. "The ticket and the visa are in your office? Can I send one of the kids to pick them up?"

"So you're really going."

No, she wasn't. "Possibly," she said. "I still don't know."

"And when will you know?"

She placed the pots on the counter and gazed around at the cheerful mess that was her kitchen at the end of a meal. Miri was tugging at her skirt while Toby tried to clear the table among the chaos. She had to get off the phone.

"I think I'll know when the wheels of the plane lift off from the ground," she said. "I'll be in touch, Gadi. Don't worry."

He was silent for a moment. "Okay," he said finally. "I'll be in the office at four. I'm taking a break right now."

29

G ADI HAD NEVER WANTED TO RESEMBLE HIS FATHER—
and yet, he did. They had the same eyes, blue and sparkling.
The same height, far above average, and the same broad shoulders.
Also, starting from a certain age, the same potbelly and the same
annoying tendency toward high cholesterol, which worried Gadi a
great deal.

His father had suffered a stroke at the age of fifty-two. Since Gadi
didn't intend to resemble him in that point, he found himself obliged
to distance himself from his comforts. To abandon his beloved steaks
in favor of outlandish quantities of lettuce, to stretch his muscles until
they screamed, and to work up a sweat on the treadmill in an effort to
reduce his cholesterol. Apparently, it liked lettuce and had no intention
of going anywhere.

At first, it was a nightmare. An expenditure of time and energy that
he could scarcely absorb. Lately, he'd actually begun to look forward
to it. Not because of the endorphins that, according to his doctor, were
released during physical exercise and lifted his mood, but because of
the psychologist: a guy he'd happened to meet at the gym whom he'd
found himself confiding in.

"It's not working," he said as they left the gym together.

The psychologist, who was at least twenty years his senior, nodded.
"Not everything goes the way we want it to," he said in an excellent
Hebrew with a heavy French accent.

"I tried to do exactly what you said, to try to help my sister and brother-in-law with only their interests in mind so that we could turn over a new leaf in our relationship."

The psychologist nodded again as he mopped perspiration from his brow. "Yes, I remember that we spoke about that."

"But it's not working. I invested time, I invested money, I was full of good will—and all I got in return was humiliation. My brother-in-law thinks I'm too pushy, and my sister is angry at me because the cherry on top of the whipped cream on top of the ice cream I gave her is not exactly in the right place."

The psychologist—somehow Gadi never managed to find out his name, and he was too embarrassed to ask now—opened his bottle of mineral water with a practiced twist. "It's nice that you're trying so hard," he said. "You have a heart."

Gadi grimaced. "Maybe I have a social disability," he said. "Do you think a person can be so successful in life and still have a disability?"

The other man slowly made a *berachah*. "Obviously," he said afterward. "Do you know how many successful people have disabilities?" He took another sip. "Or, more accurately, we all have disabilities. One person's may be larger and the other person's smaller, but that's what we're here for: to work on our *middos*."

"I'm talking about disabilities," Gadi clarified, "not *middos*. Something like, say, attention deficit disorder."

The psychologist tilted his head and slanted a look at Gadi. "If a person has ADD and learns how to succeed in life in spite of it—that's what I call working on one's *middos*."

"Working on *middos* is what *Mesillas Yesharim* is about." Gadi opened his locker and took out his gym bag. "It doesn't say anything there about ADD."

"Have you checked?"

Gadi laughed. "Actually? I haven't."

The psychologist nodded. "You missed out. And no, I don't think you have disabilities. But you know, it might be a good idea for us to talk more at length."

Gadi ran his tongue over his teeth. "How much does a meeting with you cost?" he asked politely, prepared to retreat at once with the excuse of too much work and a crowded calendar.

"It costs," the psychologist said. "But I don't accept friends as my clients. If I did, I would be a very lonely man."

Friends. Although the man could almost be his father, Gadi was gratified to hear that word. "So how—" he began. "That is, you said that we need to talk more at length."

The psychologist sighed. "See?" he said. "Life is full of contradictions."

"A psychologist should know how to cope with that."

The psychologist laughed. "There's a coffee machine outside," he said. "You can buy me a cup."

---

Shaul had no desire to fill Jarnail in on the details of his talk with Ricki, or to tell him his plan. He was glad to see that Jarnail had no such expectations.

"I think it's starting to be too hot for her here," the Sikh said. "She's so small. If her life were normal, no one would take such a young baby out into this kind of heat. It's not healthy for infants." He looked around, troubled. "It's not a good idea to bother Pinchas, right?"

"No," Shaul agreed. "But Pinchas has money and a phone. He can call us when he's finished his business, or he can always call for a cab."

Jarnail nodded, but the crease between his brows was deep. "So let's get her home," he said.

As Shaul transferred the baby to the car, he felt that she was, indeed, very warm. "Has she eaten?" Shaul asked, an alarm bell ringing in his brain.

"No. She slept, and I prepared a bottle. But she hasn't wanted it yet." Jarnail turned around.

"I'm afraid she's becoming dehydrated." The responsibility he felt made Shaul's heart constrict. "We have to make sure she drinks."

"Her bottle is in the bag." Jarnail extended his hand toward the bag lying on the back seat. "Right there. Give her to drink."

But the little chick in Shaul's arms refused to open her mouth, even with drops of sweet milk tickling her lips.

"Put your finger in her mouth and then put the bottle's nipple in," Jarnail advised.

Shaul tried this and then looked up. "Have you ever heard the saying 'You can bring a horse to water, but you can't make it drink'?"

"She's not drinking?"

Shaul clicked his tongue.

"Can a person die of dehydration with a bottle full of liquid in his mouth?" Jarnail wondered. "That doesn't sound logical. It contradicts all the laws of self-preservation."

"People drown because they open their mouths to breathe in the water," Shaul pointed out. "And she's not drinking. Those are the facts."

"What are we supposed to do now?"

Shaul looked down at the baby. She looked so peaceful and calm. If he'd been back home, and Ricki was the one holding the baby while he was in the driver's seat, he wouldn't have taken the baby to the emergency room for such a reason. "Let's take her home," he said softly. "We can try to feed her with a medicine dropper or a spoon."

"You're worried about her."

Shaul didn't want to answer, and Jarnail respected his silence. It filled the car for long minutes, dispelled only by the flow of the air conditioner and the street sounds outside.

"Shaul," he said finally, his hesitation clear.

"Yes?" Shaul returned his look in the rearview mirror.

Jarnail's eyes went back to the road. "You know that I would have offered to take the baby if I could," he said in an oddly tentative tone. "Perhaps if it had happened at a different time in my life..." He took a deep breath. "I just want to say that it's very good and noble of you to offer her a home. I'm sorry that I am not as good or noble."

Shaul didn't answer. What could he say in any case? He gazed down at the infant in his arms. "I think she's drinking now," he said, surprised. "Yes! There are bubbles in the bottle!"

"Good," Jarnail said. "I'm glad to hear that. But did you hear what I said?"

"This is not an easy situation for any of us, Jarnail. No one can force you to do anything you can't do. I'm just glad that I'm in a position to step in and be able to do what I feel is right." He paused. Then: "I just hope my wife can feel the same way."

30

$S$HE HAD SENT HER CHILDREN TO THE PARK TO ENSURE
that her important phone calls could be conducted in the
respectful silence they deserved. Then she wrote down a few
introductory sentences. In the deep and unusual silence that reigned in
the apartment after she'd finished supplying some five hundred thirty-
three urgent requests considered absolutely mandatory for spending
an hour in a public park and closed the door behind her offspring, she
could hear the fast beating of her heart.

Her finger trembled as she pressed the phone number. Her voice—
to her own ears, at least—had a croaking quality as she said, "Hello,
am I speaking to Chaya? My name is Ricki. I'm a friend of Efrat, your
sister-in-law."

"Yes?" Chaya's voice was cool. Ricki wondered if relations between
Efrat and Chaya were so bad that, as a friend of Efrat's, she'd been
immediately classified as unworthy of being spoken to. Or maybe
she'd just caught Chaya at a bad time.

"I think we have other acquaintances in common," she continued,
with spurious good cheer. "Was Shani Fogel in your class?"

"Yes." Now Chaya's voice held a smile. "But that was years ago. I
haven't spoken to her in at least seven years. How is she?"

"The truth is, I also haven't seen her for a year," Ricki admitted.
"We worked together, but..." She had been about to say, "I went on

maternity leave and stopped working," but was able to stop herself soon enough to change it to "But I left that job."

In the ensuing brief silence, Ricki scanned the page she'd prepared, skipping rapidly over the lines of self-introduction and saying, a little awkwardly, "I'm calling about something a little…" She had written, "surprising," but now her dry lips formed the word "unusual."

"Do you have time to talk, or am I disturbing you?"

"I'm listening."

It wasn't an especially encouraging response, but Ricki plunged onward. "My husband is a *mashgiach* for a kashrus organization, and he's in India right now. During his stay there, in a rural region, he found an abandoned baby girl. It was explained to him that poor people often abandon their infant daughters because they don't have the means to raise them."

"And you want to suggest that I adopt her."

Chaya's quick grasp stunned Ricki. "Yes. That is—"

"Aren't you ashamed?" Chaya's voice was restrained, but Ricki could hear the explosion erupting underneath. "Do you not have a drop of sensitivity? I will never understand how people give themselves permission to intrude on a person's privacy with every idea that enters their head without thinking about the pain they are causing. They just pick up the phone and say whatever they want. Any idea that enters their head!"

"It's not what you think—" Ricki tried.

"I don't know who you are," Chaya broke in. "And the truth is, I'd rather not know. Because I don't really care to know people like you. No sensitivity. No real caring. No understanding of the suffering a childless couple goes through and the pain that every foolish idea gives them. None. And you'd better not call to apologize on Erev Yom Kippur and hurt me again, okay?"

The slight trembling that had attacked Ricki's fingers as she had dialed the number spread to the entire arm holding the phone. "I never for a second meant to—"

"Does it matter what you meant?"

Chaya taught in high school, she recalled. No wonder Ricki felt like a backward student.

"You didn't understand me," she gathered the courage to say. But when she tried to continue, she found that the connection had been severed.

*Wow.*

Ricki took one deep breath, and then another. She shook her head to shake off the pain in her throat and the saltiness in her eyes. For some reason, out of all the thoughts in the world, she thought of Gadi, the brother just fifteen months younger than she.

But Gadi *really* didn't think much before he spoke. At least, that's the way he'd been when he was young. Had things changed over time? She rubbed her eyes and stood up to wash her face at the sink. The water soothed her momentarily. Then she started crying in earnest.

What had she done that was so bad? She'd called to offer someone a proposal that could make her life happier. Maybe she couldn't understand the pain, or share in it, but had she committed such a serious crime?

She pondered the question and concluded that it hadn't been a crime. The Ribbono shel Olam knew that she meant well. And yet, despite her good intentions, she had hurt someone badly.

What to do now? She must find that baby a home. She needed a solution.

Slowly, she returned to the kitchen table and sat down in front of her papers. She stared at her pathetic script and the phone numbers that Esther had given her.

She could try to call some of the other women on the list and hope that not all of them were as quick to be hurt as Efrat's sister-in-law. But, on third thought, she decided that even if she could technically do so, the chances that over the course of nine phone calls, she'd succeed in finding one person less sensitive to the idea, ready for it in a technical sense and also spontaneous enough to undertake it overnight, were so small as to be unreasonable.

Shaul was right. Out of all the people she knew...the two of them were the ones best suited to this mission. But even if that were so, their home, made of stones and plaster, was not so well suited.

What to do?

Maybe she should try a different approach. Instead of reaching out to strangers with her odd proposal, she could talk to people who knew many such couples and would know which of them would rejoice at her offer.

A short search in the telephone directory gleaned the names of several relevant organizations. She called the first of them and heard an automatic recording that informed her of the hours of operation and added that the office was closed that day. She dialed the next number. After two or three rings, she reached a woman who sounded very empathetic and compassionate as she listened to the story of Shaul and the baby, but didn't understand how her organization could help.

"You know many childless couples," Ricki said. "You can certainly find one who would be happy to adopt this baby. My husband says she's very sweet." It felt strange to try to sell a human being as if she were merchandise. "She doesn't look like the stereotypical Indian. She's fair-skinned and could integrate into society here without a problem."

"But we don't deal with that, dear," the empathetic woman said. "We don't handle adoptions at all. It's simply not what we do, you see? We provide medical advice and emotional support, along with financial help if needed. But not advice about adoption."

"All I need—"

"I understand what you need. But we don't do that, dear. Each organization has its own focus."

"As a person? A private person?" There was nothing degrading or virulent in the woman's words. Still, Ricki felt mortified to the point of tears. "Can you help me as a private person? To connect me with couples who might be glad to adopt this baby?"

"As a private person, I wouldn't have any access to the organization's files," the empathetic woman said genially.

"Oh," Ricki said helplessly. "But—"

"No, dear. No buts. Thank you for calling. Goodbye."

When she called the third place, the secretary said with brisk efficiency that she had never come across such a question and would pass it on to the director, who would get back to her soon. Within no more than three weeks.

"Three weeks!"

"Yes. The director is abroad right now."

"Doesn't he have a cellphone or a computer? You can't send him an email or transfer me to someone else in the organization?"

"He's so busy that I don't think he'll have time to consider this matter until he returns to Israel," the secretary said. "Meanwhile, I can only send him urgent questions."

"This *is* urgent," Ricki said. "Very urgent. My husband is with this baby in India, and he doesn't know what to do."

The secretary fell silent. It sounded like she might be chewing gum.

"Okay," she said at length. "Call me at the end of the week, and we'll see what we can do."

The responder at the fourth organization was as sensitive as Efrat's sister-in-law. Although she said nothing about requests for forgiveness on Erev Yom Kippur, she told Ricki that her idea of calling up women and suggesting that they adopt a baby from India didn't come from a good place. She urged Ricki to get some help.

Ricki slowly put down the phone. She was nearing the conclusion that if she continued with these calls, she would indeed need some urgent help.

Still, she wasn't ready to give up. She decided to try again.

31

Deciding is one thing. Acting is another. Although it was clear to her that she must continue making calls until she found the baby a home, Ricki couldn't make her fingers press the keys of her phone.

Instead, she stood up, searched for two shekels in the small coin drawer, and ended up taking five coins that she found there. She listened to the sound they made as they fell into the *tzedakah* box. The sound seemed muffled, indistinct, as were her *tefillos*.

"Help me not to insult anyone and to do the right thing," she murmured. She felt detached, as though her heart were made of thick, recycled plastic. "Give me the wisdom to succeed in this mission. And save me from making mistakes."

Having already invested five shekels in opening the gates of Heaven, she decided to use them to their fullest. She added: "And please help all the childless people in *Klal Yisrael* merit their own children soon. Especially Shaul's friend and Efrat's sister-in-law, Chaya. Let them rejoice in their own children soon, really soon, and give them hope and joy until then."

That was that. Time to return to the kitchen table, and the page of phone numbers, and the unpleasant task that awaited her.

But she stood where she was, near the *tzedakah* box, leaned her head against the wall as though it were the Kosel, and waited. Hashem heard *tefillos*. Even those that emerged from a dry heart. He heard her, and He would help her. She just needed to wait for the right idea…

Her mind, empty of ideas, tried to drag her thoughts to the pile of laundry, the dishes, and the ironing. She shook her head to push those thoughts aside and continued to wait patiently… Until, from somewhere, into the empty void she'd created, a surprising thought gently floated. She ought to have proceeded in precisely the opposite way!

She threw a hasty glance at her watch. The first year of marriage is still the first year of marriage, even for couples who are no longer young. Ever since her mother had remarried, three months after Tzviki's birth, she'd become so busy. But she could provide Ricki with a phone number even if Uncle Reuven, as they'd instructed the children to call him, was at home.

"Is it urgent?" her mother asked without saying hello.

Although she'd been prepared for it, Ricki's heart clenched. "I just need Shoshana Zweig's phone number," she said. "And it *is* urgent. I'm sorry if I'm calling at a bad time."

"You can call whenever you need to, sweetie." Her mother flipped through the pages of her old phonebook. "Are you writing this down, dear?"

Ricki wrote down the number. Then she called Shoshana, a childhood friend of her mother's, and chatted lightly with her, reporting on her mother's wonderful health and how she looked fifteen years younger than her age. Her mother had even started taking guitar lessons, a lifelong dream of hers. Only then, politely, did she request the number of Shoshana's daughter Leah, who had adopted four brothers shortly before Ricki's Toby was born.

Leah's husband was a well-known figure and Leah herself was a warm and lively personality, so Ricki assumed that plenty of people who were interested in adopting turned to them for guidance and support. Leah could easily connect her with a couple who wished to adopt a child so fervently that they would be willing to get on a plane tomorrow.

This idea was better than the ones before. Leah was enthusiastic. "I have two ideas for couples who will surely want the baby," she said. "Stay near the phone. I'm calling them now."

Stay near the phone?

Instead, Ricki took the phone with her into the kitchen, where she washed the dishes while humming with great relief. There are few things more pleasurable than succeeding in an impossible mission and being a messenger to bring others good fortune. She had solved Shaul's problem, solved the baby's problem, and in her merit a Jewish couple would soon be really happy.

How wonderful!

———————

Pinchas had disappeared. Five hours after they returned to Jarnail's lovely, air-conditioned apartment, and two hours since they'd tried to call him and heard a laconic voice inform them that the number wasn't available and asking them to try again later—Shaul began to feel uneasy.

It wasn't like Pinchas to block his calls. It wasn't like Pinchas to go off without telling him where. It wasn't like him to be so irresponsible and neglect to think about those he'd left behind.

Could he have been robbed? Was he waiting for them in the park right now without his phone and wallet? Even so, it was for exactly that reason that they always made sure to have enough local currency in their inner pocket—so they'd be able to get help if needed.

The baby, who had eaten, cried, slept, and eaten again, now slumbered on Shaul's shoulder as he restlessly paced the room. Jarnail wouldn't object to driving him back to the park to look for Pinchas. But assuming that nothing dramatic had happened, it was understandable that Pinchas might feel the need for some time alone in light of what he had been through that morning…

A light knock on the door heralded Jarnail's arrival, armed with a container of ice cubes. "The children went to their cousin's birthday party," he said, just as though a deep freeze hadn't reigned in the car on their way back from the park.

"He should have called by now."

"Maybe he's simply not aware that so much time has passed." Jarnail's eyes narrowed. "A broken heart can make time act strangely."

"You're not worried?"

"No, not really." He smiled. "I know that you're feeling responsible for the way Pinchas has been reacting, but Pinchas is not a child. He's just eleven years younger than you are. That's not much."

Responsible? He supposed he was feeling responsible.

Jarnail's smile widened. "How about putting the little one down in her stroller?"

Shaul obeyed. When he turned around, he saw that the smile on Jarnail's face had disappeared.

"Eh?" he asked.

Jarnail remained still for long enough to make Shaul wonder whether the depression that the Sikh had admitted to suffering from was not only depression, but some other, more serious emotional disturbance that had decided to manifest itself right now.

"Did something happen?" he asked again, feeling slightly threatened.

Jarnail's face looked as if it were carved from basalt. "You Jews are certain that only your Torah is true, right?"

The words "you Jews" had an unpleasant ring to them. Jarnail's face was none too friendly either. For a second, Shaul lost his power of speech, and his mouth became dry.

"Yes," he said. "Absolutely. If a table is a table, then a chair can't be a table. When G-d gave the Torah to three million Jews on Mount Sinai, He showed them prophetically that He is the only G-d there is and promised that He would never trade in the Torah that He gave Moshe for any other one. This is the absolute truth. And I tell you this with love."

"So that my soul won't go to purgatory?" Jarnail's tone was ambiguous.

Shaul wasn't sure if this was a genuine question or a form of mockery.

"Because we've been acquainted long enough for me to know that you are a believing person who wants to live life on the highest possible level," he said. "A person who cares about fulfilling his mission on earth in the best possible way. And because you asked, and I think that we're on terms of friendship that do not allow me to evade or ignore your question, but obligate me to answer you in the sincerest possible way."

Jarnail made a noise that was meant to be hearty laughter but failed.

"You are a strange one, Shaul," he said. "Not many men would consider insulting another person's faith, upsetting his equilibrium, and hurting his feelings to be acts of friendship done for his benefit."

Their eyes measured one another.

"People love to have it easy," Shaul said with a shrug. "They love themselves, and their serenity, and are not prepared to endanger it when they know that what's good for another person to hear is not the easiest thing to say. You asked, and I believed that you deserve to hear the truth. That's all I can say."

"And you believe that you did me a favor."

Shaul considered the question for a moment. "To tell the truth," he said, "maybe I made a mistake. Maybe it would have been better for you to continue living in ignorance. Maybe I shouldn't have put you in a situation where you'd know the truth and deny it. But since you asked the question, I felt that you deserved an answer."

"That maybe I am doing the right things but not for the right reason?"

"Yes. Exactly."

"I see," Jarnail said cynically. "And I assume that in your view, I am now supposed to thank you for your candidness."

Shaul lifted his brows and inhaled deeply. "I'm not the type who waits for thanks," he said briskly. "But even if I were, I would understand that I just hurt you. So no. You don't have to thank me for anything."

32

VEGETABLE SOUP, FRENCH TOAST, A CUCUMBER AND tomato salad, and chocolate pudding constituted a weekday supper that was more elaborate than usual. The children, returning home from the park, were surprised to see it on the table.

"It's not Rosh Chodesh," reported Benny, who was always on top of the calendar.

"No," she confirmed. "I just felt like serving a nice supper."

"In honor of what?" Miri asked.

"In honor of all of you. In honor of how much I love you all," she said. "So who's washing first, guys? The French toast is getting cold."

Smiling, she watched as they washed their hands, sprinkling droplets of water on the floor that she had washed that morning before leaving to sign a contract for her new job. She thanked Hashem for the simplicity with which they allowed themselves to ignore her oft-repeated instructions about hand towels and for helping her to refrain from telling them that in other parts of the world the children's life struggles were made up of more than the burning question of who gets to sit in the corner seat.

"You made all the calls you had to make, Ima?" Rini, approaching her eighteenth birthday, had been brought into the picture a couple of hours earlier when she had come home from school and had taken the story of the little Indian baby to heart.

"Yes, I did." Ricki picked up Tzviki. "I don't have a final answer yet, but things are moving in the right direction, *baruch Hashem*."

"Great." Rini was happy. "Can I go over to Shiffy to study history now?"

Ricki looked over her shoulder at the cluttered kitchen and the living room with its piles of laundry. "Of course you can," she said cheerfully. "When will you be back?"

"Is ten-thirty okay?"

Ten-thirty was fine, but it meant that Rini had finished helping out at home for today.

"Yes," Ricki said, stretching her smile a bit wider. "Go now and come home at ten-thirty. I want you to do well on the test."

Rini hesitated. "Are you sure?"

"Positive."

In truth, the test wasn't that important. But it was important to her, very important, that her children feel safe. That despite their father's globe-trotting, their home nest would remain secure and protected.

"Great." Rini was obviously relieved. "Okay, I'm leaving now. We have tons of material to study."

And then she was gone. The kitchen floor had sprouted a puddle the size of three cups of cocoa and the adjoining hallway was a garden of child-sized chocolate-pudding footprints. The floor now looked as though it hadn't been washed since last Erev Pesach.

Ricki took a deep breath, put herself on automatic, and set out to do battle for her sense of humor, her children's *chinuch*, her home's cleanliness, and for having her five youngest in their beds by eight o'clock in good spirits and without their mother having to raise her voice too often.

Although she succeeded in all these objectives, there was no time afterward to catch her breath. At eight on the dot, Gadi knocked on the door. After greeting him with surprise, she viewed her house through his eyes and curled up into a tiny ball.

"You forgot to send someone for the visa," he said. "And you didn't answer your cellphone." He looked around. "You probably don't remember where you put it in all this mess."

"This blessed mess," she said. "Thanks so much, Gadi, really. This is so nice of you! Do you have time for a cup of tea?"

"I do," he said, "but you don't. You're supposed to be leaving the house in five hours."

"Where are you going, Ima?" Benny adored his wealthy uncle and was a little too enthusiastic around him. It was inevitable that the boy would show up and try to join in the conversation.

"Go show Uncle Gadi what you made with the Lego he gave you." She urged him forward, and after her son danced off, she said quietly, "Nothing is final yet, Gadi. And the kids don't know anything about this whole story. They don't know what Shaul found. I'm still working on finding a different solution. There may be someone who's interested."

"No, they're not," he said firmly. "No one but you two would be that crazy."

"I'm waiting for an answer—"

He laughed. "I'll save you time and tell what's going to happen. I'm doing this for your benefit, right? So you'll have time to pack."

She usually became annoyed when he issued such peremptory statements, especially when it included slapping herself and Shaul with various doubtful labels. But the experience she'd been through today, and the way her good intentions had been interpreted, made her view things in a different light. "There's a good chance you're right," she said. "A really good chance."

He smiled, a slightly boyish smile. "Come on, I'll help you tidy up in here," he said. "Do you remember how we used to clean up the house in an hour before Ima came home from work?"

That had been an eternity ago. Nearly.

"I'm good at cleaning and organizing," he said almost shyly. "I can help you. And then you'll have time to pack your—"

"Here, Uncle Gadi!" Benny was back with the nine-hundred-piece Lego ship he'd built all on his own. "Isn't it great? I love Lego. It was such a great present!"

"You'll get another one for your bar mitzvah." His uncle thumped him on the back.

For a moment, the two of them leaned companionably against the coffee table in a way that made Ricki's heart skip a beat. She wasn't at all certain she wanted Gadi to be her son's role model. And what kind of idea was it to give a boy Lego to mark the day he became a bar mitzvah?

"And also a *Mishnah Berurah*," Gadi suddenly added—apparently for her sake. "So if anyone else wants to give you a *Mishnah Berurah*, tell them your uncle's getting it."

After pinching the boy's cheek and administering another resounding thump on his back, Gadi sent the pink-cheeked lad off to restore his creation to its place. Gadi looked at his sister. "Well? Are you giving me a mop and broom?"

"If you want to help, you can wash the dishes," Ricki said half-jokingly. But he accepted her suggestion at face value and went to the kitchen. Ricki followed.

Then her phone rang.

---

"You spoke to both families?" she asked, leaning against the counter as Gadi gave her an opaque look. "And you have no other leads? Are you sure?"

Silence as Ricki heard Leah's disappointing answer.

"Yes, of course, I understand the sensitivity."

Another moment of silence.

"You're amazing. Thanks for your good will."

"Like I said." Gadi didn't even wait for her to disconnect the call.

She didn't bother to respond.

"Okay," he said. "There's plenty of time to get ready. It's only eight-thirty now. You can do this, big sister."

"Can I?" She looked around. How did one leave ten children for a week with only a few hours' warning? How did one do a thing like that? It made no sense!

"I'll drive you to the airport," he said generously.

"I'll take a taxi," she replied hoarsely. "But that's actually the least of my problems right now."

"So what's the first one?"

She swept a hand over her eyes, trying to collect her wits. "I don't even know where to start."

"Do you have formula in the house for Tzviki?" He was trying to be practical for her. "Do you want me to go to the supermarket and buy some things?" He hesitated. "I know that you have *hechsher* preferences, so I wouldn't want to go alone. Should I take Benny with me? Would that work for you?"

"Okay, thanks." She was dizzy. Which friend had Rini gone to? Chany? Henny? Maybe she should tell her to come home now. And where would the children be for Shabbos?

Benny and Gadi had disappeared, she realized vaguely.

She wasn't really flying to India so suddenly, was she? She couldn't. It was too much. Shaul would have to understand that this whole thing wasn't for her. She was finished. Completely finished. Besides, she couldn't leave the house in its present chaotic state without preparing clothes for the kids and filling the freezer with ready-made meals.

She couldn't? Really?

Two years ago an electric bike had hit Shalom as he crossed the street on his way home from yeshivah. Shaul had been in Sweden then, and she had left the house with a crumpled fifty-shekel bill in her hand—to return three days later, with one shekel left.

When you have to, you do it.

That was a fact.

Ricki put her ice-cold fingertips to her forehead and took a deep breath.

Back then it had been her maternal instinct that had driven her, pushing aside all habit, all the usual arrangements, her ordinary grasp of what was right and good. This time, she would act as a daughter. The daughter of the Chosen People who stands up unhesitatingly when she sees the banner unfurl with the words *"Mi laShem eilai!"*

And the mess in the house?

Her breath caught in her throat. It wasn't merely a mess, but a hundred times that.

But Rini was seventeen and a half, and Shalom had just turned sixteen. Ricki's sisters would presumably pitch in, too.

Maybe, at the end of it all, the children would even look back on this week as an adventure.

33

$\mathcal{S}$HE HAD TO PACK A SUITCASE. FORTUNATELY FOR RICKI, despite the confusion that gripped her in the face of this dramatic turn in her routine life, this goal, at least, was made simple because of all the suitcases she'd packed for Shaul in recent years and the packing list they'd prepared together the first time they'd had to meet this challenge.

Something about her youthful handwriting on the yellowing paper hanging on the inner wall of the wardrobe made this trip feel, for a moment, like an adventure.

*Passport and visa*

Those were the first two items on the list. Thanks to Gadi, all she needed to do was put them both in the pocketbook she'd be using.

*Money*

There was cash in the house. Shaul made sure of that before each trip. But she wanted to leave it for the children. Instead, she put her credit card in her purse. In the airport she would withdraw shekels and dollars on the assumption that Shaul would supply rupees after she landed.

Onward.

*Check weather in destination city*

Okay, that was one thing she didn't have to bother about. Shaul, in India, had already provided that information. She reached into the top shelf of her closet to take down the summer clothes she'd worn to work two years earlier that had lain peacefully on their shelf ever since.

What could be easier than climbing onto a stepladder and pulling down a pile of clothing? Yet she found her insides clenching as though she were somehow threatened. A minute later, the feeling turned out to be all too justified. Not a single article of clothing from that stack fit her present size. Not one.

This wasn't surprising. Her tenth child wasn't yet a year old, and it had become harder and harder to shed the "baby fat." Still, it made her feel drained, empty as a shell. Although the logical part of her mind pointed out how odd it was that this specific detail made her feel like collapsing onto her bed like a high school girl at the height of adolescence, another part completely ignored this wise observation.

Gadi's voice, as he strode into the house as though it were his own, only strengthened her sense of unreality. Benny trailed in his wake.

Her mother was far away, busy with her new life, and her father was even more distant. There wasn't the slightest chance that either of them would appear here right now, knock on the door, and save the day. And because the responsibility for maintaining her equilibrium rested on her shoulders alone, even the privilege of feeling sorry for herself was denied her. She was forced to dry her tears, walk back to the wardrobe with a firm step, and take down the clothing she'd worn last summer, right before Tzviki's birth.

She would go on a diet when she returned from India. Now she had to maintain her composure and cope to the best of her ability.

In the second stack of clothing—maternity clothing—she found a few pretty tops, though their baggy style made her feel mortified as she packed them into her suitcase.

*Let it be a kapparah for my sins*, she encouraged herself. Besides, she'd be leaving home in a coat, and once in India she wouldn't be meeting anyone she knew.

"Ricki?" Gadi was knocking energetically on her door. "Is everything all right? I brought you food. Do you want to put it in your suitcase?"

"You're so nice," she said sincerely as she inspected the contents of the large bags he presented her with a festive air. "You didn't spare any expense, huh? So nice of you!"

"I'm sure you would have done the same for me," he said.

"I'm not sure I'd have been capable," she confessed. "With all the needs of this house—"

"What are you talking about?" he scolded, half serious, half teasing. "You couldn't drop in to see me for two or three hours, but you can fly to India without the slightest warning?"

There's one child in every family, talented and charming, who challenges his parents more than all the others. Benny was Ricki's challenge. In his presence, she had to weigh all her words and reactions carefully. Ricki opened and closed her mouth twice, seeking the right words. Gadi, meanwhile, told his nephew lightly, "Abba and Ima want to start a business. Ima has to fly to India to help Abba choose merchandise."

Business. Merchandise. Benny's eyes—he was only twelve, after all—sparkled with excitement. "Really, Ima?" he said. "Abba wants to leave kashrus and open a store in the new shopping center?"

It was easy to see that he was all in favor of the plan. He had no idea how she was cringing inside.

"Nothing is final," she managed to say.

---

"Nothing is final," she told Rini an hour and a half later. "Don't trouble yourself with unnecessary concerns. If there's anything you need to know, I'll keep you informed."

"What, there's a chance you won't bring her home?" Rini's voice had dropped to a whisper, her eyes darting right and left.

"Maybe. Absolutely. Abba just asked me to use the ticket that Uncle Gadi had already purchased and come. Maybe I'll also have a look at some merchandise and see if there's any reason to open a sweet little home business." She smiled with an effort. "Don't say anything to the kids, okay? I'm counting on you to keep this quiet."

"Hel-lo!" Shalom was home. As he walked through the door, he almost tripped over the suitcase. "What's this? Abba came home?"

"No! Ima is going!" Benny yelled from the next room, destroying any possibility of a gentler and more delicate update. "She'll be back next week."

"Did something happen to Abba?" Shalom entered the kitchen even before Ricki managed to go out to meet him. "An accident?"

"*Chas v'shalom!*"

He gave her a measuring look. "Then why—"

"It's a little complicated," she said. "Uncle Gadi was putting a lot of pressure on Abba and me to check out the possibility of buying merchandise in India for sale in this country. Abba happens to have some free time this week because the kashering of the peanut oil factory was canceled, and Uncle Gadi bought a ticket for me without asking anyone…"

"Okay." Shalom wasn't a young man of many words. This time, for a change, she was glad of that. "Do you need help with anything or is everything ready?"

"I'll need both you and Rini to be in charge," she replied with a measure of cheerfulness. "Benny will be your right-hand man. Rini will be in charge of the food, Toby will help her with the kids, and you and Benny are responsible for the cleanup each evening and also before Shabbos. Rini will also be responsible for the laundry. Each of you will iron the shirts you need to wear."

She looked back at Rini. "I spoke to Shuli and Yael. They'll be in touch with you and will help however they can. The freezer is filled with soy products, and there's plenty of pasta in the pantry. If you cut up some tomatoes and cucumbers for the kids, that will be healthy enough for one week. I didn't have time to do a laundry load, but that won't be a problem for you. Penina and Dovid will come to be with you for Shabbos."

"You organized things so quickly!" Rini was surprised.

"Uncle Gadi says that you and Abba are an insane couple," Benny decided to announce just then.

"Is that what he said?" Ricki asked, trying to buy some time.

"You heard him," Benny said. "He said it to you, too."

"Not exactly." Ricki waved a dismissive hand. "You didn't really understand, sweetie."

"It's slang," Rini informed her brother. "Remember when you asked him how Niagara Falls was, and he said, 'Insane'?"

A cautious smile appeared on Benny's face. "Ah," he said. "Yes. I remember that now."

Ricki silently thanked Hashem for the existence of slang in the world He'd created. She looked at the boy pouring himself a glass of water and then returned her gaze to her house. "I wanted to call your teacher, Rini, to ask her to have consideration for you next week. It's too late now. I'll call her from India. I put her number in my phone."

One minute. She didn't have a calling card to let her make calls from outside the country! How could she have forgotten about that?

"Is something wrong?" Shalom asked.

"No. Nothing."

She clenched her teeth. Up until twenty years ago, people managed to survive without cellphones. It wasn't pleasant. It wasn't easy. But it also wasn't catastrophic. After all, she was about to become a mother of eleven! She couldn't allow trivialities like the style of a blouse or the absence of a cellphone to spoil her mood.

# 34

NIGHT FELL OVER MUMBAI IN A BLAZE OF GORGEOUS COLOR. The city was wrapped in hues of crimson and purple, but Pinchas hadn't yet returned. And his cellphone, which had been charged the day before, still didn't pick up, for some reason.

"What are you doing, Shaul?' Jarnail's powerful body filled the doorway.

Shaul's lips moved soundlessly for a minute. Then he lifted his head. "Saying *Tehillim*," he replied quietly.

"That means that you are very worried about Pinchas."

Shaul sighed, confirming Jarnail's assumption.

Jarnail hesitated for a moment, passing a hand over his smooth black hair. "I'm not worried," he said. "He most probably just needs some time and space to cope with things. I think that's understandable."

"Yes," Shaul agreed. "I didn't say he doesn't. But still, you can't deny that the guy doesn't know English or Marathi, and that he's been out on his own for such a long time, which isn't like him at all."

Jarnail sighed. "I will tell you the truth even if you get angry at me over it. But you know me and my anxieties, right? I always prefer to prepare for the worst. That is why I did the same thing for my children."

"The same what?" Shaul was confused. The baby in the stroller squirmed uneasily, as though sensing the tension in the air.

"I attached tiny stickers to your shoes that serve as transmitters to help me find you easily if you were lost or something bad happens. Pinchas is all right. Look—" He flipped his cellphone around and held it under Shaul's nose. "You see the yellow dot on the left side of the map? That's Pinchas. He's still in the park."

"Either he or the sticker," Shaul corrected. "Which yellow dot are we talking about?"

"Left side, on the top." Jarnail looked at the map and furrowed his brows. "He was there ten minutes ago," he said. "Just a second." He enlarged the area displayed on the screen. "Oh, there he is," he said with relief. "He must have taken a taxi. That's not a walking pace." He nodded to himself. "You can try calling him again. But even if you don't, I believe that he will be here within twenty minutes or half an hour."

"*Baruch Hashem.*" Shaul expected to feel relieved, but for some reason the feeling didn't come. "Your idea with the stickers is a good one. But it would have been more respectful if you'd told us about them."

Jarnail smiled sheepishly. "I was afraid you would say there's no need," he explained. "If you two had opposed it, I would still have attached the stickers. And that would really have been rude."

Shaul chuckled. "It's lucky I like you," he said. "That's all I can say."

"Thank you." Jarnail was even more uncomfortable now. "So you're not angry?"

Shaul shook his head. "I prefer transparency," he said, "but it's all right. I'm just glad Pinchas is safe. Where is he now?"

Jarnail looked at the map again and grimaced. "Call him," he said in an odd voice.

"What happened?" Shaul asked as he put his phone to his ear.

"They're going in the wrong direction." Jarnail's eyes were glued to the screen. "Taxi drivers do that sometimes. They take tourists on a long and unnecessary route in order to demand a higher fee afterward."

"His phone still isn't picking up," Shaul said, his phone glued to his ear.

Jarnail was hesitant. His head bobbed in time with an inner ambivalence. Finally, he spoke. "As I said, sometimes taxi drivers do this kind of thing. But..." He looked at the screen again. "I'm giving him ten minutes to get on the right road," he said firmly. "If Pinchas doesn't contact us by then, I'm going to treat this as a problem."

"Meaning?"

"Let's give it ten minutes," Jarnail repeated. "Maybe things will work out on their own." His face wore the same tense expression it had worn when he helped them escape from the peanut oil factory, and his eyes were blank. No longer the amiable driver, he had become a full-fledged soldier.

"I'm just going out to make a few calls, if you don't mind."

No, Shaul didn't mind. But he, too, would have an important conversation in the meantime.

With the Ribbono shel Olam.

———

It took slightly longer than ten minutes, but when Shaul had completed his fourth round of the fifteen chapters of *Shir HaMaalos*, Jarnail walked into the room dressed in a short jacket with a bulge at one side that looked suspiciously like a gun.

"I reported the new developments to Rabbi Schwab," he said. "He does not want to contact the embassy yet about a suspected kidnaping. That is his choice. I can't interfere with that. Maybe you can. Do whatever you think best. In the meantime, I am going out with a few fellows to see if there is any way to help. My wife will be home soon—"

Shaul stood up. "I'm going with you."

"You are not." Jarnail was adamant. "You'll stay here and—"

Shaul smiled politely. "We are coming with you. I'm not staying here alone."

"You—meaning you and the baby? Really, Shaul. You're treating this whole thing as a joke."

Shaul was silent.

Jarnail thought the situation over.

"I will check if my mother-in-law's maid is available," he said at last. "If she agrees to look after the baby, I'll agree to have you join me. At your own risk."

———

The three men whom Jarnail had summoned to help appeared to be several years younger than he was. Jarnail introduced them as "previous students of mine" before he switched over to the local idiomatic Hindi to speak with them. Although Shaul suspected that this switch was designed to keep him from understanding what they said, the foreign tongue clarified his own mission right now. It allowed him to focus on the words of David HaMelech without distraction—apart from the worry roiling inside him like a thousand hungry worms.

"We're going to follow that yellow dot," Jarnail updated him as they filed into his car. "It's moving too fast, and right now it's about fifty-five minutes ahead of us. In short, we need your prayers." He clenched his teeth. "We could still be wrong," he reminded Shaul. "It could still be a taxi driver who's pulling some stunt, or else Pinchas decided that he wants to breathe fresh air and get away from us for a while or something. But...you know..."

Yes, he knew. He opened his *Tehillim* again, starting from the beginning.

"We're in good shape," Jarnail said as they stopped for a red light an hour and a half later. "Ordinarily, we'd have no idea what was hap-pening. We'd still be sitting in my house waiting to hear from him." He tilted his head back, glancing at Shaul. "If only I had a way to get hold of a helicopter. Then we wouldn't be sitting here in traffic."

"Do you want me to call Rabbi Schwab? Convince him to contact the embassy and get some support?"

Jarnail hesitated. "Do what you think best," he said. "But maybe, considering Pinchas's state of mind when we parted from him, it doesn't pay to create a mess. We may be harming Pinchas by involving your boss in every little thing." He switched to English. "These fellows think he may simply have wanted to get away from us for a while. You and he are used to living at close quarters, but these three think it is only logical that he would want some time to himself."

The three men nodded their heads.

"Besides—" Jarnail turned around again. "If this were a kidnaping, we'd be seeing the yellow dot moving into one of the areas of the city where the criminal element thrives. Meanwhile, thank G-d, it's still in a decent area."

This *was* good news. "Why didn't you tell me this before?" Shaul asked.

Jarnail licked his dry lips. "Let's focus on the half-full glass and do our best to fill the second half as well. I hope this logjam will open up soon."

Hope is a good thing. Shaul grabbed it with all ten fingers. And because he was trying to convince himself that everything would be all right, and because there was no point in having Ricki be consumed with worry during the six hours' flying time, he didn't say a word about Pinchas's disappearance when he called her to finalize the details for their upcoming meeting at the airport.

E VEN THE MOST TIRESOME TRAFFIC JAMS IN ISRAEL DON'T hold a candle to those in Mumbai. The interior of Jarnail's car grew more and more oppressive with the passage of time, and because at least one of Jarnail's "students" was smoking so heavily that the cloying smoke clung to everything, the situation became more and more unbearable.

The car would drive for a few feet and then stop, move another couple of feet and stop again. The repeated braking, along with the stench of the cigarettes, combined with the aftershave of another of the young men traveling with them, gave rise to nausea. Shaul had to close his *Tehillim*, lean his head back, and murmur a few chapters from memory. Then even that effort became too much.

"Do you have a bag, Jarnail?" Shaul's head ached, and the cold air from the air conditioner only increased his distress. "Do you have a bag?" he asked again. When it was given to him, he felt so ill that even the word "thanks" emerged almost inaudibly from between clenched teeth.

"This is crazy," said one of Jarnail's pals. "Can someone explain to me why we're stuck in this traffic, while they managed to avoid all this and are racing through the streets like weasels?"

"What I don't understand is why they're traveling in such a round-about way," a second said. "Do they think someone is tailing them physically? If I kidnaped someone, I would take away anything he has that could serve as an electronic beacon and then travel directly to my hideout."

"I wouldn't kidnap anyone," the third said with a yawn. "Better to rob a bank. More money, less work."

"Jarnail." Shaul opened one eye and straightened up. "Tell me, could the answer to all your questions be a bicycle?"

They all turned to look at him.

"Could we be following a bicycle?" Shaul explained slowly. "A bike or motorbike would have less trouble with heavy traffic. Maybe that's why they're managing to widen the gap between us all the time?"

The three young men looked at him and then, as if on a signal, turned to Jarnail, who rubbed his nose and asked, "Are you thinking that no one kidnaped Pinchas? That he simply went out for an outing through the streets of Mumbai riding a bicycle? Or that he asked to hitch a ride on someone's motorcycle? That doesn't sound like the Pinchas we know." He paused, and then added heavily, "And bikes are not exactly the ideal way to take a kidnaping victim from place to place."

Jarnail's argument was on the mark, as usual. Somehow, Shaul managed to link this view to the acid roiling in his stomach.

"If that's the case," he said, "then we have to go back to the park."

"Where?" one of the young men asked.

"To the park. Where we last saw Pinchas. I think he's still there." He tried to produce a smile at Jarnail's raised eyebrows. "I don't think we're following Pinchas, but only his shoes," he said with a last attempt to conquer his queasiness. "Apparently, someone stole them. And his cellphone."

A spate of Hindi washed over him, along with a total inability to hold back the wave boiling up inside him.

"Maybe you're right," Jarnail said as Shaul vomited the contents of his insides into the bag. "Or maybe not. It's worth checking." He returned to Hindi, and when Shaul had finished his business, said briskly, "Amitav will stay with us. The other two are getting out and taking a taxi. They'll follow the yellow dot. I gave them all the cash I have. Do you have any more?"

He had. He passed the bills to the young man seated beside him, while the one next to Jarnail energetically plied his cellphone until he was satisfied. "Okay," he said. "He's showing up on mine, too, though in orange."

"Update us on developments every fifteen minutes," Jarnail said as the two men opened their doors and stepped out among the cars.

"Every fifteen minutes," affirmed the one with the busy cellphone. "No worries."

Both doors slammed at the same time, so resoundingly that the car shook.

---

"Pinchas! Pin-chas! Pinchas?"

The park looked different at night. The beast-shaped bushes looked ready to pounce and make short work of them.

"Pinchas?"

The three walked down the park paths, calling his name out loud.

"Pinchas? Where are you?"

Jarnail walked beside Shaul, tall and quiet. "My commanding officer in the army used to say, 'We are not the architects of success,'" he remarked. "We are not responsible for the results, only for trying to do the work well. If we don't find him, you don't have to feel bad about bringing us here. Your idea was a logical one."

"Thank you." Shaul lifted his voice as high as he could. "Pinchas! Pinchas, are you here?"

No voice answered him, but Jarnail's flashlight caught a strip of white cloth peeking out from under an elephant's heavy shadow. Shaul turned sharply and leaped over the fence with a vigor that surprised Jarnail.

"Pinchas?" He stuck out his hand to touch him—to make sure he was breathing. "Pinchas," he repeated, shaking his friend. "Pinchas, are you all right?"

Pinchas opened one eye and quickly closed it again, blinded by the light. Slowly, he lifted himself like a man whose bones ached. "It certainly took you long enough to come and find me," he said. "What time is it?"

"Nighttime," Shaul said. "Are you all right, Pinchas? We were so worried about you."

"*Gever al chataav*," Pinchas said. *A man for his sins.* "What else can I say?"

"He's confused," Jarnail whispered.

"No," Shaul answered, just as quietly. "He's quoting a verse. I understand what he means to say."

"They mugged me," Pinchas said, leaning on them to drag himself out of his improvised hiding place. "There were three of them, and they had some sort of metal pipe." He shivered despite the heat. "I didn't want to give in at first. I thought they would run away if I yelled…" He tottered, and Jarnail and Shaul helped him to his feet.

"Did they beat you?" Jarnail's voice was hard.

Pinchas chuckled, but the sound was nothing like his usual warm laughter. He passed a hand over his head and then looked at his fingers. "It's all clotted by now, apparently. But it hurts." His eyelids fluttered. "It's a miracle I'm alive. Where were you two until now? I didn't think you'd leave me like that. I was sure you'd be back in an hour at most."

"We thought you turned off your phone on purpose, and we wanted to give you some breathing space," Shaul said apologetically. "Then we followed your shoes…" He grabbed Pinchas's arm, helping him over the low fence. "It's a long story. Sit down for a minute. Catch your breath."

Pinchas measured the distance to the nearest bench with compressed lips. "I have a cut in my ankle," he said. "It might need stitches."

Jarnail held his phone to his lips, reporting to the other three searchers that their quarry had been found. "We'll take you to a clinic straight from here," he said when he disconnected. "You'll get good treatment, don't worry. You have excellent medical insurance."

"At least that," Pinchas said, closing his eyes. In the flashlight beam his face looked very pale and smudged with dirt.

"You need to wash your face." Shaul handed him his water bottle. "And you probably need to drink, too."

"Yes." Pinchas's eyes were still closed, and his arm lay on the arm of the bench in a way that made Shaul suspect it was also injured.

"That was a scary experience," he told Pinchas with empathy.

"Yes," Pinchas agreed. "But also encouraging."

For an instant, Shaul wondered if Pinchas *was* confused. "Encouraging?"

"Uh-huh." Pinchas's voice was muffled, his face twisted. "Don't you know the chassidic story? After they take away even his shoes, he has no place else to go but up… From here on in, we ought to start seeing miracles."

36

PINCHAS WAS VERY QUIET THAT EVENING. HE WAS QUIET on the way to the emergency clinic. Apart from answering concrete questions, he didn't say a word, even when the doctor put twelve stitches in his ankle and five at the back of his scalp. And he continued his silence as the nurse poked his arm repeatedly in an effort to find a suitable vein for his IV line.

"Say something," Jarnail urged.

Pinchas smiled slowly. *"Todah laKel al hakol,"* he said. *Thank You, Hashem, for everything.*

"Yes," Shaul agreed. "That mugging could have ended very differently. You got off easy."

Pinchas smiled again and leaned his head back. *"Baruch Hashem u'varuch Shemo."* Then he closed his eyes. Although he didn't open them, it was obvious to those in the room that he wasn't asleep. He just wanted to be with himself.

"The doctor says that he's all right." Jarnail looked worried as he spoke. "He says there's no need even for a tetanus shot and that Pinchas was not beaten that badly. They gave him fluids only because I insisted."

"True," Shaul said.

"But he doesn't look right." Jarnail's voice held a hint of hoarseness. "He's too calm. It's not logical."

"It's…special." Shaul chose a different word. "I think it's amazing."

He leaned against the hospital wall, wondering if Jarnail, too, had noticed the faint radiance that seemed to shine from Pinchas's face since they'd brought him here.

"That's an evasion," Jarnail barked. "It's not healthy, Shaul. A person needs to express his feelings, not ignore them. Just think about what he went through today! First the situation with his wife, then the mugging, and then waiting for us all alone in the park, in the dark... Do you think it's normal, the way he's reacting?"

The nearly aggressive note in the question surprised Shaul. "What would you have wanted to happen?" he asked.

Jarnail shrugged. "What would I want? I would have wanted none of this to happen. But I'm not G-d and I don't have that power. So 'what do you want' is not the right question."

His words made rational sense, but Jarnail's voice was full of anger.

"Then what is the right question?" Shaul asked carefully, glancing over his shoulder at the open door and Pinchas in his hospital bed, an IV line snaking into his arm.

"It's not good to repress things," Jarnail said, more calmly now. "A person needs to process reality and deal with it, not ignore it and believe that all will be well. A person has to get angry! A person has to cry. To let himself shatter into pieces so that he can gather them up afterward and put himself together again as a new person."

"Is that what your therapist says?" Shaul asked.

Jarnail passed a hand over his face, smoothed his beard, and replied, "Yes, as a matter of fact."

"And yet you still can't cry."

Jarnail gave a bitter bark of laughter. "You know me too well. Yes. It's hard for me to let go and give up control."

"Then that, I believe, is the root of the difference," Shaul said. "Pinchas never *had* control. Today, he's had a little time to remember that."

Jarnail's eyes narrowed. "I don't understand what you're getting at," he drawled with feigned indifference.

"He's radiant," Shaul said. "Didn't you notice?"

"The lighting in here is strong, and he's fair. So—"

"Maybe," Shaul agreed. "It's certainly possible. And maybe the fact that he fasted today, and sweated a lot, made his skin devoid of toxins. But I think there's another explanation. You are a believing person. I think you know much more about Judaism than you've ever let on. So I think you can understand what I'm thinking."

"That he has accepted the judgment," Jarnail said quietly. "And placed himself in the Creator's hands."

Shaul nodded.

"That it's clear to him that it's all for the best." Jarnail's voice dropped another notch. "And that there's no coincidence in the world. Nothing just happens."

Shaul nodded again.

Jarnail's lips moved. "How nice for him," he said, straightening up suddenly. "I'll be right back, Shaul. Wait for me here."

---

"Are you all right, Pinchas?" Shaul pulled one of the greenish chairs closer to the bed and sat down.

"Me?" Pinchas smiled. "Yes, *baruch Hashem.*" He stirred cautiously and grimaced as the IV needle pained him. "*You* don't look so good."

"I'm a little queasy, my head hurts, and I'm dizzy," Shaul admitted. "I think the chummus I ate at lunch might have gone bad."

Pinchas's expression showed empathy with Shaul's plight. "Sit down. Rest a little. You guys worked hard for me today."

A smile split Shaul's face. "If some *darshan* were to ever hear this story, he could make something of it. He could say, 'Why is it that, when a person tries too hard, he moves further away from his goal instead of reaching it?' If not for Jarnail's tracking stickers, we would have returned to the park much sooner."

Shaul's features twisted as a fresh wave of nausea overtook him. With a wave of his hand, he escaped to the corridor.

"Are you all right?" Pinchas asked when Shaul had returned and apologetically resumed his seat.

"Yes," Shaul said. "When I see you here, alive and well, I'm just great."

"And the baby?"

"Jarnail's mother-in-law's maid is taking care of her. She's fine." Shaul's voice was soft. "It will take these liquids at least another hour to be absorbed into your body. Let's both rest. We need it."

"Yes." Pinchas sank more deeply into his pillow, completely worn out. "You're right. Resting sounds like the right idea."

But even when Pinchas fell asleep, Shaul's mind refused to turn itself off. Despite the nausea and the dizzying fatigue, his body remained tense and alert. It took nothing more than the scrape of Jarnail's shoes to startle him upright.

"You're back," he whispered. He looked at the man and the large bag he was holding. "What's that?"

"For Pinchas," Jarnail whispered back. "The boys we sent to follow the signal from his shoes decided that once they were already out and about, it would be a good idea to return Pinchas's shoes and jacket... His hat is here, too, though it got crushed. I don't think he'll be wearing it again."

At Shaul's expression, he shrugged. "The boys were determined to finish what they'd started. And Pinchas needs his clothes. They also brought him a bit of compensation." He rummaged in the bag. "It's a Cartier watch. From what I can tell, it's the real thing. I think it's worth a great deal." After a beat of silence, he added, "The guys who took Pinchas's belongings were Muslims. This may not have been a simple mugging."

"They *were*?" Shaul asked with trepidation.

"They still are." Jarnail grinned. The restored clothing and the meting out of justice had marvelously improved his spirits. "Just a bad choice of words. My boys are law-abiding citizens."

Shaul looked at him.

"Well, mostly..."

But Shaul wasn't really listening. "Jarnail, tell me something," he said without stopping to think, simply searching for a way to change the subject. "What is the cheapest and best merchandise to be had in India?"

"People," Jarnail answered promptly. "Why?"

"People?" In light of their adventures in recent days, this answer didn't sound appropriate.

"Have you ever heard of outsourcing? How huge firms from all over the world hire other firms to do all kinds of things for them, from answering phones to computer programming?"

"I've heard of it."

Jarnail nodded. "It's an enormous industry that is flourishing here in India. Millions of Americans who call customer service for their refrigerator or cellphone receive very good service from Indian operators who learned how to speak English with the right accent. India is running the US these days. Without us, it's liable to collapse." He smiled at his own joke, and then added gently, "But Israelis don't speak English, so if this is not a theoretical discussion, then a more relevant idea for you would be programming. Many university graduates with excellent grades would be happy to lease you their expertise in exchange for a salary that, in Israeli terms, is literally small change."

Queasiness rose up in Shaul again, but he refused to give in to it. "I was thinking more of an import-export business," he said. "Something to buy here and sell there. I..." He paused for a moment to overcome what his body was trying to do to him. "I don't have a large budget."

Jarnail looked at him and smiled. "You know something?" he said. "We work well together. Maybe we can form a partnership."

$37$

THE TRIP STARTED OUT ON THE WRONG FOOT, DESPITE RICKI'S
efforts to get it right. It was Gadi's fault for trying to be so
accommodating and efficient.

"You don't need a coat," he decided. "Why drag along that extra
weight? For the two steps from your house to my car and from the car
to the terminal? Do you have any idea what a bother it will be when
you get to Mumbai? Better leave it here."

He was right. She left her coat behind. She also gave him her suitcase to carry. Which meant that she had nothing to hide behind when
Bluma, her neighbor, came out of her apartment carrying two large
trash bags.

"Ricki!" she called happily, regarding her with surprise. "How are
you?"

"*Baruch Hashem, baruch Hashem.*"

Bluma studied her again. "It's been a long time since we met," she
said significantly. "May I assume you'll be coming home with full
arms?"

For one confused moment Ricki wondered if Bluma had merited
*ruach hakodesh*. Then she asked herself how the secret, which even her
children were unaware of, could have leaked out. Finally, with understanding, came a profound discomfort. But Bluma, to her credit, had
analyzed what she saw with the eyes of logic. The "baby fat." The
maternity clothes. Besides, where could a mother of ten be going in the

middle of the night with a big traveling case? Either to the airport or to the delivery ward. And a trip abroad didn't seem to fit the lifestyle of a woman like Ricki, who so rarely even ventured out of the city.

"Ricki?" Gadi's voice floated up from below, impatient. "Didn't you just say that we need to hurry?"

"Go, go, dear." Bluma's smile was sincere, if oily. "I don't want to hold you back, *chas v'shalom*. My cousin was once stuck at home—"

"*Ricki!*"

She wanted to say something to Bluma. To explain… On the other hand, there was a chance that she *would* be returning from India with full arms. Now that Bluma had opened the door, why not be proactive in minimizing the inevitable gossip?

"Ricki?"

"I'm coming." She nearly tripped down the stairs. "I'm coming. Don't worry."

"May you have *besuros tovos*!" Bluma called after her. "Only *besuros tovos*!"

Gadi was taller than she was, and his steps were longer. By the time Ricki reached his car, he had managed to load her suitcase into the trunk and unlock the doors. "What did she want?" he asked.

"Nothing."

For the children's sake, she'd armored herself in the pretense of high spirits, praising them for making it possible for her to enjoy a vacation with their father, until even she was almost convinced that she would enjoy this trip. But the remnants of her good cheer had vanished with the good wishes she'd just received on the stairs.

If it had been just anybody… But Bluma had undertaken to be a representative of the Mishmeres Shalom movement in an honest effort to force herself to stop gossiping about all the neighbors. An effort that had, to date, not been all that successful.

*Maybe I'll benefit from the encounter*, Ricki reflected. That was certainly possible. But the only word she wanted to utter was a childish "Ugh!"

"Here." Gadi held out a sour candy.

She loved sour candies. But she wasn't a child. Candies wouldn't make everything all better. Besides, she wouldn't be able to get it past the lump in her throat. "No, thanks."

"You like these," he reminded her.

"I'm just not in the mood," she said. "I'm so stressed about this trip…"

"I thought one is never supposed to be stressed. After all, everything Hashem does is for the best!"

At most, he meant to tease her. But his words pierced her like a needle under a fingernail. She'd been marveling at herself all day. At her willingness to create a dramatic upheaval in her life simply because it seemed like the right thing to do. And now HaKadosh Baruch Hu had sent someone along to burst her balloon.

"Ricki?" he asked. "Did I say something wrong?"

He had tried so hard today. Gone out of his way to be pleasant and friendly. Ricki couldn't ignore that surprising fact or stop herself from wondering at its cause.

"No," she said, swallowing her feelings with an effort. "On the contrary, you said all the right things."

"So your tears are tears of joy. I get that." His car was new and gleaming, gliding elegantly through the streets.

"I'm crying?"

She wiped her eyes and found, as she'd expected, that they were dry. With a tiny shake of her head, she realized that she'd fallen into his trap. But even if Gadi had laid this small trap for her, she had no intention of letting him drag her further into the mud.

"If I didn't know that I have nothing you want, I'd think that you want to ask me for something," she said. "You've been so nice today."

Gadi smiled. "So I can tell my psychologist that I'm making progress?"

"You see a psychologist?" The thought of Gadi sitting in an armchair and devoting fifty minutes to a conversation about thoughts and feelings seemed as absurd as the fact that she was setting out for India and might return with full arms.

"Not exactly."

Gadi looked at the road, one hand holding the wheel and the other fiddling with the buttons of his CD player, searching for the perfect song for this moment. "He's more like a friend of mine. But I spoke to him about you today, and about me and Shaul. I think the conversation did me good. It helped me see the world from a different perspective."

She was considering how to compliment him on this brave step without causing him to regret having confided in her when he said, "You know something? It might be a good idea for Benny to speak to someone."

"Who?"

"Your son, Benny," he said. "He's a good boy, but I see that life is not easy for him. Just like it wasn't easy for me when I was his age."

*Ribbono shel Olam. Ribbono shel Olam.* For a moment, the world went black. Then, somehow, Ricki found the strength to open her eyes and say, "You're very different, you and Benny."

"Yes," he agreed. "Different, but also alike. Who is this kid Ari that he's always getting mixed up with?"

"A boy." Ricki wasn't interested in expanding.

"The son of some doctor, he told me."

"Yes."

Someone else would have taken a hint from her curt answers. Not Gadi. She turned her head to the window.

"Wow," Gadi said. "You really *are* stressed about this trip."

She murmured something indefinite that wasn't precisely a lie and allowed him to understand the situation as he saw fit.

"Okay," he said presently. "You're sure you don't want a candy? I bought them specially for you. Benny says you love them."

"Did he say that before or after the two of you talked about Ari?"

She took three of the candies but couldn't bring herself to unwrap even one of them.

"Before, I think," Gadi said. "Or it might have been after. What difference does it make?"

"None, apparently." She rolled the sweets between her fingers. "Thanks for today, Gadi. You helped me so much. And the ticket you bought… It turned out to be the right thing at the right time."

He smiled. "Hashem must have known that I had good intentions."

His eyes focused on the highway, and she listened to the music, an unfamiliar tune filled with nostalgia and longing. She liked it. As though he intuited this, Gadi pressed the button to turn the music off.

"Ricki," he said, "about my original idea, that you and Shaul open a business. I want the two of you to at least consider it. You found a job, that's true. And it's true that it doesn't suit Shaul to deal in fabrics. But there are scores, if not hundreds, of other products that can be imported from India. Just use this week to think about it, okay?"

Ricki shook her head. "You don't start a business on a whim, without a business plan," she said, explaining something he ought to know better than she did. "And you gave us the money to help us, not to cause us problems. We'll have to return your loan someday, and you know how businesses are at the start of the road. The merchandise we'd buy with your financing would only force us into more debt."

"You can't profit without investing," Gadi said firmly. "And this is the only way for you two to get out from under your mountain of debt. If you continue as salaried workers, you don't stand a chance. You need to start thinking big. And I'm here for you, ready to help."

These weren't Gadi's words, Ricki was sure of that. It was that psychologist's.

And with all due respect, she didn't think they could depend on that psychologist to be there for them when they ran into trouble.

38

BY MIDNIGHT, SHAUL AND JARNAIL WERE SITTING ON A bench in the hospital corridor to allow Pinchas to sleep while the IV dripped into his arm. Jarnail's mother-in-law's maid had gone home. Seeing no other option, she reluctantly took the infant with her. In the same period of time, Shaul had three phone conversations with Ricki. The first was to make sure she hadn't forgotten to pack anything. In the second, he heard that she was making her way to the airport but had no SIM card to let her make calls outside the country. The third call told him that she had passed through security and reassured him that she knew exactly where he'd be waiting for her.

He also vomited twice in that time, took one pill for his headache and then, an hour later, another one. He accepted the fact that he was no longer a youth of twenty and must start conserving his energy, especially while he filled the role of sole parent to a newborn baby.

"We're helping you plenty!" Jarnail protested when Shaul shared this thought with him.

"But I'm the one who's taking responsibility." Shaul was slumped on a chair, limp and dizzy with exhaustion.

"Responsibility is fatiguing," Jarnail agreed. "Let's talk about something more pleasant. What do you think about my idea? Would you want to form a partnership?

"Open a computer-programming business?" Shaul smiled and shook his head. "I don't know, Jarnail. It sounds like too much for me. Besides, we'd need an organized business plan for such a thing, no?"

Jarnail shrugged. "My father-in-law says that if he'd known the words 'business plan' when he was young, he'd still be washing floors in the office of his first boss. Today he's worth about twenty."

"Twenty million rupees?"

Jarnail laughed. "Twenty million dollars, my friend." Once again, Jarnail shrugged his big shoulders. "True, he had a great deal of luck. But as the saying goes, it's not enough to find your fortune—you also have to wake it up."

"If my grandmother could hear you, she would say it's a good idea to check what kind of mazel you're arousing before you tug its ears," Shaul said, closing his eyes. "It could be very painful to arouse the wrong mazel."

"A wise woman, your grandmother," Jarnail said. "But seriously, Shaul. You're an unusually capable person. Your job is too small for you. With your head, your attention to detail, your memory, your responsibility, dedication, and ability to motivate a team—you could make big money."

"I don't want big money." Shaul spoke slowly, eyes closed. "I want to live a life of meaning. To work at something that helps the world…"

"Like food coloring," Jarnail said mockingly. "There's great value in helping people be able to bake colorful cookies for their children's birthdays. That's immensely meaningful."

Shaul cracked open an eye. It was red and burning. "There is great value in giving Jewish children the sense that they can enjoy pleasures in life, pleasures like colorful birthday treats," he said forcefully. "G-d's work is made up of details. So even if I'm making you laugh, it's clear to me that my efforts have meaning."

"Enough meaning to make it worth being so far away from your children?"

Shaul squirmed. "My family needs my salary," he said quietly, his eyes closing again. But his expression indicated that Jarnail had touched an exposed nerve.

"If you start a business, you could earn a salary four times as high," Jarnail pressed. "Stop turning the words 'business plan' and 'meaning' into a barrier that prevents you from doing the right thing. If you need a business plan, we'll make one. If you need meaning, we'll find it. But only after we decide that we're doing this."

With an effort, Shaul straightened up. "Let's talk about it tomorrow," he said. "I really don't feel well."

"We're in a hospital," Jarnail reminded him. "This is where you go when you don't feel well."

"No." Shaul breathed deeply. "I don't think it's that bad. Just an upset stomach. I need to sleep."

"You can take a taxi to my house. I'll wait until they release Pinchas and bring him home."

Shaul shook his head. "I prefer to wait here with you."

Silence fell between them. It was deep and roiling with emotion, punctuated by the noise characteristic of an ER.

"Programming is your wife's profession," Jarnail said presently. "She works in high-tech, am I right?"

"Yes. But there's a big difference between being the manager of a crew for someone else and being the person who runs the whole place and seeks out clients." Shaul closed his eyes and leaned back. "Responsibility is a heavy thing, Jarnail. And you know the way we live in Israel. We don't have the option of employing maids in exchange for room and board, the way they do here. My wife already has an empire to run. Even before adopting this baby."

"Another good excuse. When I speak to someone as right as you— sometimes I feel the need to swallow my tongue."

Shaul's consciousness was floating among clouds of exhaustion several inches above his body. After a wave of nausea brought him back down to himself, he asked tiredly, "What's your interest here, Jarnail? You worked in Israel for seven years and mingled with the high brass. I saw the picture you had taken with Ehud Barak, and I'm sure you have many more photos of important people in your professional album. Even if you think that an Israeli-Indian partnership is the most successful idea on the market, why take a *chareidi* without even a high school diploma, not to mention a university degree, a man without connections or money? Why go into partnership with him, of all the people in the world?

"Honestly, I like you. We work very well as a team. But if this is nothing more than a hallway chat and the idle talk that comes from exhaustion—then it seems to me that it would be in your best interests to think it through again."

Jarnail suddenly looked a little pale. This cleared Shaul's brain enough to prompt him to touch the other man's arm gently. "Hey, I didn't mean anything bad. Did I say the wrong thing?"

Jarnail's tongue passed over his dry lips. "I gave you a thumbnail sketch of what I went through—that whole business with the bribe. Right?"

"Yes."

"So here's the thing." Jarnail sighed. "I trust you. Enough to let me step out of the shell that I keep around me in order to survive. I'm also happy at the thought that what we do together could help you and the baby we found. That's it, more or less." He swallowed. "I also think that my father-in-law will agree to invest a considerable amount of money in a business, which will give him hope that I'm finally coming out of my depression."

"You're not depressed," Shaul said. "You don't look, sound, or act like a person suffering from depression."

Jarnail smiled. "It's certainly not a clinical depression. But my therapist says—" He rose to his feet. "Doctor, I'm glad to see you. When can we leave?"

The doctor flashed a very white smile. "Right now!" he said gaily. "Here are your papers, gentlemen. I hope we never meet again."

"Not all wishes come true," Jarnail said five minutes later, as they stood in the parking lot and Shaul threw up again. "Should we go back inside, Shaul? The number of times you've vomited in the past three hours concerns me."

"No, no," Shaul protested. "Of course not. My wife is landing in six and a half hours. I have to be there on time. And in order to do that, I need a little sleep."

"But in order to sleep you need something for the nausea." Jarnail threw a doubtful glance at the hospital building.

"I have something in my bag. It's part of the standard stock of medicines I always take with me." Shaul opened the car door decisively. "Let's get moving. It's time for bed."

# 39

LIFTING OFF WAS A LITTLE FRIGHTENING. IT MADE HER stomach churn. The illuminated night view from the plane's window minutes later was impressive, but it soon gave way to black sky. Boredom led the passengers to take an interest in one another.

"You don't look like someone who's on her way to India to go backpacking," remarked the gray-haired woman seated beside Ricki.

Ricki smiled. "Neither do you."

"I'm going to see my son," the woman said. "He's been in India for three years and isn't even thinking of coming back for a visit. So I said, 'If the son doesn't come see his mother, then the mother will go see the son.'" The words were affectionate, but the woman's lips were hard and thin. "Do you know the saying 'Small children weigh down your hands, and big children weigh down your head'? I'm supposed to be happy for him because he likes it there, but I'm not sleeping at night."

Ricki's heart went out to her. "Being a mother isn't simple," she said with empathy. "It was only when I became one myself that I understood that I'd never appreciated my own mother enough."

The gray-haired woman laughed. "You probably have a lot of children."

Ricki smiled and said, "They should all be healthy."

"How many?" the woman wanted to know. She folded the newspaper she'd been holding and placed it on the small tray table open in front of her.

"It's hard to count them because they're always moving," Ricki said with another smile. "How many do *you* have?"

"Three. And believe me, even that's too much." The woman stretched her legs. "I told my daughter, 'One child is lovely. Another one, for backup? Fine. But three is too much.'"

"Backup?" Ricki wasn't sure she understood the woman's meaning.

"We are a nation at war. Maybe the first one will be a soldier and die. So you need another child, as backup. But three is too much. Look at me. Almost sixty, and I have to fly to India along with all these backpackers to make sure my son is okay… Not that I don't love Shai. When he was born, I told everyone, 'We'll name him Shai because G-d gave him to us as a gift.' But he was never an easy child."

What was she supposed to say to that? "Our generation is not an easy one," Ricki said cautiously.

"I don't know." Her neighbor shrugged. "I don't think it's the generation. It's not easy raising kids. How many do you have?"

Ricki murmured something noncommittal.

"Come on, are you afraid to say how many? Is it more than five?"

"Yes, *baruch Hashem*."

"More than eight?"

"*Baruch Hashem*."

"More than ten?"

"No. Not yet."

"Not yet? What do you mean 'yet'? Don't tell me that you're hoping to have more than ten kids! What do ten kids have that one doesn't have? You're lying. Even if you don't know it—you're lying."

She was so sure of herself, so bitter and domineering. Ricki thought she understood why Shai had run so far away.

"When you get back to Israel, give me a call," she said. "Come over and meet my children and tell me if they're not amazing. After that, we'll talk."

The gray-haired woman muttered something that sounded unpleasant. "What's an 'amazing' child?" she demanded. "Don't they wake you up at night? Don't you always have to do laundry for them? Aren't they sometimes insolent? Do you never cry because of them? No. *You're* amazing!"

Ricki chuckled. "I'm not amazing. Obviously, I work hard. And obviously, wonderful as they are, they're still growing up. Nobody is born perfect."

"Nobody dies perfect either."

"There were a few who managed to die perfect," Ricki said. "Anyone can get there."

Her neighbor grimaced. "You're talking as if you're reading from a book," she declared. "Saying what you were taught, not things that you thought of on your own. They told you that ten children is a good thing, so you're telling me that. It's not coming from you. Not from your heart."

There was a long flight ahead of them. Ricki was sorry she'd been friendly and opened herself up to this conversation. "Is living a good thing?" she asked. "Or is it better to die?"

"Of course it's better to live," the gray-haired woman said. "What kind of question is that?"

"That's what you say, because that's what they taught you. But you don't really know. You learned some sayings and are quoting them as if they came from you."

The woman laughed. "I've been an ER nurse for decades," she said. "It's no saying. People want to live."

"You're an ER nurse, and I'm a mother of ten. And I'm telling you that I'm not just spouting sayings. If I had only nine, my world would be missing something. I wouldn't know that, of course. Maybe I would think that my life was complete. But each child makes your world a little wider. Each one makes your heart a little bigger and teaches you a little more about love."

The gray-haired woman opened her newspaper. Her tight lips drooped a bit and her wrinkles stood out before she snapped, "I don't believe you. Period."

"A pity."

"Convince me."

Ricki chuckled. "Do I have to?"

Her neighbor chuckled, too, but there was little benevolence in the sound. "You don't like to prove to people that you're right? Do you want me to go on thinking that you're raising ten children only because you have no choice?"

Ricki shook her head. "Wow," she said, stunned by this woman's nerve. "How old is Shai?"

"He's twenty-seven," the woman said. "He's been in India for six years now, ever since he finished his army service. After three years, he came home for one visit, but half a year later he went back. Believe me,

I have no idea what he finds to like over there. A filthy place, India."

"They say the Indians aren't critical," Ricki said. "That life flows there, without a constant need to prove yourself. Maybe that's what he needs. Maybe that's what he found there."

The woman's eyes flashed. "You probably think you're the first person who's told me that."

"And you probably think that you're the first person who wonders how it is that those *chareidim* have such big families and even claim to like it, declaring that each new child they bring into the world is a reason for rejoicing."

"You're not a typical housewife. You're sharp."

"Actually, I am," Ricki said. "That is, right now, I am. But I'll be perfectly honest with you. I'm also a computer programmer. For the last year I've been at home, but I hope to go back to work in a few weeks."

"Then you're not the classic *chareidi* woman."

"Maybe you don't know us as well as you think you do," Ricki retorted.

The woman lifted her brows. "That was meant as a compliment."

"Lovely."

The woman laughed. "You are a terrible liar."

Ricki took a deep breath. "When do they come around with food?" she asked, trying to signal her desire to end the conversation.

"I think there's still time. But you can ask the stewardess if you want."

"No, I'll wait."

"Anyway, they say the kosher meals aren't as good."

Ricki laughed again. How to conclude this talk?

"Look how sweet my oldest daughter is. She got me a book of Sudoku puzzles. She said I never have time to do them. But now I'll have a few quiet hours to enjoy it…" She pulled her bag down from the overhead compartment—and gasped when it fell on her head. "Oh no! I think the strap is torn!"

"Try tying it like this." Their hands met for a moment as the gray-haired nurse tried to create a slipknot in the stiff strap. "No," she said, letting her hand drop. "It won't work. But I have another idea…"

She removed a designer keychain from her own pocketbook and used it to connect the strap to the luggage. "It's just a copy," she said, "not the real thing. Otherwise, I wouldn't have given it to you, of course. But you can have it now."

"That is really good of you," Ricki said. "Thank you."

She pulled out the paperback puzzle book. "What a sweetie. She gave me her entire Sudoku collection."

"Really sweet," her neighbor agreed. Then, to Ricki's satisfaction, she wrapped herself in a deep silence, which wasn't broken except for a few polite words until the plane's wheels touched the ground.

"You should just know," the woman said before they stood up to disembark, "that I don't believe you. You didn't give me proof."

Ricki looked with despairing eyes at the line stretching up toward the airplane's exit. "All right," she said. "I'll give you one. I am coming to India in order to adopt a little girl."

The gray-haired woman's jaw dropped. "You're kidding."

The impatience of the passengers waiting their turn to be free of the cramped plane and get onto solid ground was contagious.

"No, I'm not kidding. And about the keychain—maybe you should give me your address, and I'll send it back to you."

"No, no need," the gray-haired woman said. "Instead, pray for Shai. He's a good boy. What a waste."

"We pray using the mother's name," Ricki told her neighbor's back. "What is your name?"

"Zahava."

"Shai ben Zahava," Ricki said. "All right. I'll pray for him."

$\mathcal{S}$HAUL SLEPT DEEPLY AND DIDN'T WAKE UP EVEN ONCE TO throw up. He also didn't wake when the alarm clock that he'd placed under his pillow began to vibrate. Nor did he stir when his cellphone emitted an urgent reminder—or when Pinchas shook him vigorously and reminded him that he had to go to the airport.

"Shaul!" Pinchas tried. "Shaul!"

But Shaul kept on sleeping.

He'd been very tired the day before, Pinchas remembered. With a yawning glance at the clock, he decided that his friend could sleep a bit longer, at least until the alarm did its job. But when he woke again and saw his friend still asleep, he felt a little apprehensive.

"Really, Shaul!" he urged. "Don't you remember that you have to go to the airport?"

No reaction.

"Shaul, are you ready?" Jarnail whispered, opening the door and poking his head inside.

"Nope," Pinchas updated him. "He's sleeping like a stone. No matter how hard I try to wake him—he won't wake up."

"There's no such thing." Sidestepping the bowls and cups lying on the floor for *negel vasser*, the suitcases, and his guests' personal belongings, he gripped Shaul's shoulder and said, "Shaul! Open your eyes, please!"

Shaul didn't even bother to turn over onto his other side. He continued his peaceful slumber.

Jarnail's lips tightened. He gave Shaul a good pinch.

"Ouch!" Pinchas said. "What are you doing?"

"Waking him up," Jarnail said dryly. "Are you with us, Shaul?"

"Not now..." Shaul mumbled.

"What's not now?" Jarnail was either angry or pretending to be. "You ordered a ride to the airport. Your wife is coming, right?"

"No," Shaul said, his eyes unfocused. "Her father died. She can't come."

"Her father died ten years ago!" Pinchas expostulated. "Shaul? Are you in the middle of a dream?"

Shaul's voice was groggy. "I want to sleep."

"He's very tired," Pinchas said cautiously. "All that running around yesterday wore him out. And he had that stomachache and vomiting..."

"I was also very tired yesterday," Jarnail grumbled. "Shaul, if you don't sit up this minute, I'm going to pinch you again."

<hr />

El-Al flights to Southeast Asia allow each passenger a total of fifty-one pounds of luggage. Ricki had filled her suitcase generously, packing a plethora of *kosher l'mehadrin* products aimed at making their week more pleasant, small gifts for Jarnail's family, and basic equipment for a baby girl.

"It's always better to take too much than too little," she explained to her children when she asked them to sit on her suitcase so she could close the zipper. But when it was time to grapple with that same suitcase and drag it off the baggage carousel, she felt that she might at least have left behind the candy she'd brought for Jarnail's children.

"Do you need help, ma'am?" A tall, good-hearted porter swung her bag off effortlessly and placed it on the floor with a thump. Good. Ricki took a deep breath. At least that problem was solved. But when she started moving toward passport control, she found that the suitcase that had slid so easily over the tiles in Ben Gurion Airport refused to cooperate now. With an effort, she managed to drag it a few feet out of the endless distance that needed to be crossed. There she stopped to measure her progress and to waver between despair at the huge effort required and fury at the inconsideration of luggage manufacturers.

*You're a mother of ten children,* she told herself encouragingly. *You managed to carry all of them around without a problem. So what's one suitcase?*

This encouragement helped her over the next ten feet, after which she decided that it's very easy to raise ten children. Fact: They'd never caused her as much frustration as this suitcase was doing with its crooked wheel. With children, she thought, mopping her perspiring brow, you can at least try speaking logically.

Maybe that's what the suitcase needed, too?

Awkwardly, she turned the bag over and checked the wheels. One of them was indeed completely crooked. She hit it with the heel of her hand, earning a scratch for her efforts. Then she used the heel of her shoe and found that lightweight summer shoes are not very effective as hammers.

For a moment she considered opening the suitcase and removing some of the cans. But the thought of exposing all the items she'd packed to the scrutiny of her fellow travelers was too embarrassing. Rummaging in her pocketbook, she came upon her useless phone and then noticed the keychain that her pleasant seatmate, Zahava, had given her.

It was made of metal and appeared strong. It also had one sharp corner that could be thrust between the crooked wheel and the piece of metal that held it in place. There! Within seconds, and without undue effort, her suitcase was gliding along as though nothing had happened.

With wonder at the greatness of the Creator, Who uses one affliction to heal another, tearing the strap of her purse in order to give her the tool she needed to fix the suitcase wheel, she went to stand in line at passport control. Afterward, she slowly advanced toward the precise spot where Shaul had promised to meet her.

When she saw that he wasn't there, she was convinced that the mistake was her own. She must have turned right instead of left, made for a black bench instead of a red one, or even flown to Calcutta instead of Mumbai.

But this *was* Mumbai. And because she didn't trust her memory, Shaul's instructions were written, blue-on-white, on the back of a napkin. They told her that she was in the right place. She was supposed to wait right here. Under the clock, between the ice cream store and the emergency exit, near the red bench.

So where was he?

Not here.

This wasn't like Shaul. Perhaps there had been some miscommunication between them. Or the traffic that exhausted him on every visit to India had worked against them this morning. She would wait patiently until he came. And imagine that she was sitting here, doing nothing, simply because she was waiting for the next flight out, scheduled to lift off hours from now.

The problem was that imagination had always been her weak point.

The passengers from her flight had long since scattered, and no one who looked Jewish or Israeli passed near her. Her efforts to communicate with members of other nationalities, to ask them to make a call for her on their cellphones, didn't elicit the reaction she'd hoped for.

Did she look like a thief? She found that hard to believe. Just as she found it hard to believe they were in such a hurry that they couldn't wait a minute, just one minute, to help her find out where her husband was.

At least they'd agreed to meet by a bench. Ricki sat down on it and drew her suitcase near. It glided easily on the gleaming floor, reminding her just how precisely the world was run and how every challenge was designed only for a person's benefit. In this world or the next.

This problem, too, must be some sort of gift. Although, perhaps because she wasn't sufficiently creative, she hadn't the slightest idea how this frustrating wait could be transformed into something that would be pleasant to remember later. But since there are no bugs in programs written by the Creator of the world, and He would have had no difficulty sending Shaul to her exactly on time or letting some nice woman pass by and agree to let her use her phone—apparently, for reasons she couldn't fathom right now, her best option was to wait on this bench. Which had been fashioned, it seemed, with the goal of being as uncomfortable as possible.

Time passed slowly. She tried to avoid filling these minutes of enforced idleness with too many worries. Soon she would have a baby girl to take care of. A tiny creation who would need her to be constantly alert to her needs, who would demand endless quantities of strength, patience, and attention. It was quiet now. No one was bothering her. There was no reason not to enjoy the tranquility and contemplate the kaleidoscope of figures racing around her.

All these conclusions were logical, and she tried to implement them.

To extract what she could from the position in which the Creator had placed her and learn whatever lessons she was meant to learn. But after a while she was fed up with all this contemplation.

How had people managed years ago, when she was a high school student, and people didn't yet have cellphones? Had they worried less in those days, or had they been more patient?

Or maybe—the cynical programmer inside her said—there were simply more public phones around then…

Public phones!

Ricki straightened abruptly. What did Shaul call the areas where travelers could stay between flights? Communication centers? No, she remembered, it was called a "cellphone lot." This airport was enormous. Surely there must be one of those here… But how could she go find one and leave this bench empty? The minute she disappeared, Shaul would doubtless come racing up and become deeply alarmed not to find her here.

The desire to spare him anxiety kept her in her place for another twenty minutes. Then she lost the last of her patience.

If he worried—he worried. She had to find a phone. Now.

41

WHAT MAKES A JOKE FUNNY? SOME PEOPLE SAY IT'S THE intrinsic illogic of the situation described and its ensuing strangeness. In that sense, it was impossible to deny that the situation was amusing. Responsible, energetic Shaul, ready for any mission, the first to wake in the morning and the last to go to bed, who called his wife three times to make sure she was managing well and knew exactly where to wait for him, was lying in bed and refusing to wake up, while his two friends stood over the bed pleading with him to open his eyes and go pick up his wife from the airport.

"He's delirious," Jarnail said, scratching his beard.

"Yes," Pinchas agreed. "Shaul, you're not serious, right? It's not Purim today. You didn't drink anything... *Nu*, get up already!"

"I'm going to pinch him again," Jarnail said.

"In yeshivah, we used to pour a cup of cold water over the boys." Pinchas looked around. "There wasn't a single guy who didn't jump out of bed after that."

"I don't want to ruin the mattress," Jarnail said. "Shaul, do you feel all right?"

Shaul mumbled something indecipherable.

"Exactly," Jarnail agreed. "Get up right now, or I'm going to give you the pinch of a lifetime!"

Shaul didn't respond.

"Enough already," Pinchas said. The joke no longer seemed so amusing. "We need to be at the airport in less than an hour. We'll be late, Shaul. It's not *my* wife who's flying in today."

"Shaul," Jarnail said, beside him, "don't come complaining to me later when you have a bruise."

"Something's wrong with him," Pinchas said, shoulder slumping. "This doesn't make sense."

Jarnail made a gesture whose meaning was unclear but seemed to signify something about the futility of man. Then he gave Shaul a proper pinch. A pinch to wake an elephant.

But Shaul merely groaned and mumbled something about ants.

"He's not running a fever," Jarnail said.

"Look." Pinchas touched Jarnail's shoulder. "Look at his skin. How weird it looks. How it doesn't move back into place…"

Jarnail followed Pinchas's finger, and his eyes grew dark. "We are two blind men without eyes," he said. "Two fools without brains." His hands shook as he whipped out his cellphone. "I don't know what's happening with this visit of yours. You two must have started your trip on a luckless day. But Shaul isn't sleeping. He's dehydrated, Pinchas. I'm going to order an ambulance. We'll take him to the same hospital we took you to yesterday."

"Ambulance?' The word slowly penetrated Pinchas's brain. "What do you mean, dehydrated?"

"You know exactly what I mean. He never drinks enough anyway, and yesterday we were out in the sun for hours. Afterward, he experienced nausea, threw up repeatedly, and now his mind is cloudy… I'm a fool for not realizing it earlier." He looked around in despair. "I'll call for an ambulance. There's an excellent private company near here. You'll go with Shaul, and I'll go to the airport to get his wife."

Pinchas slumped. "Let's first try giving him something to drink," he said feebly. "Maybe that will help."

"We should have done that yesterday…" Jarnail said something into his phone in one of the nine languages he had mastered, then answered a few more questions before saying, "Thank you," and restoring the phone to his pocket. "They'll be here in fifteen minutes," he said. "Meanwhile, you can certainly try giving him something to drink."

But Shaul, as expected, didn't cooperate. The water dribbled down the side of his mouth and was absorbed into his pillow.

"They'll give him IV fluids and he'll revive," Jarnail promised. "In a few hours, everything will be fine. You'll go with him, yes? I'll go get his wife."

"I don't speak English, Jarnail! You can't let me go with him without the ability to communicate."

"I'll tell the ambulance crew everything they need to know." Jarnail searched for the pouch containing Shaul's papers. "Listen—this is the number of your insurance plan in Israel. You need to call them to make sure they'll cover the cost of his treatment. There shouldn't be any reason why they wouldn't. Yesterday they authorized your visit to the hospital."

"I'm not going alone, Jarnail. Shaul deserves to have a good interpreter with him."

"His wife doesn't have a cellphone. You heard what he said yesterday. We have no way of getting in touch with her. We can't just let her wait."

"Yes, we can, if it means her husband will get the best possible care." Pinchas was determined. "Do you have someone else to send for her? Maybe your wife? Would she agree to help?"

"My wife?" Jarnail's lips lifted in a half-smile. "No, my friend. For all the understanding she's shown for my nonsense, I can't ask that of my father-in-law's daughter. No."

"So, someone else? A reliable taxi driver?"

Jarnail's brow furrowed. "I never do business with taxis. But maybe my wife's second cousin would agree to help." He held a brief dialogue with himself and then said, "No. I think it's preferable that I ask the young man who's in charge of cleaning this building. He can drive my car."

Though this wasn't the time for such thoughts, Pinchas wondered about the life of a man who was once a rising star and who today chose, consciously, to place himself on a par with a janitor. And whether it might not be their responsibility, as people who owed him a debt of gratitude, to help him get out of this tight corner once and for all.

---

The ambulance crew was efficient and pleasant, and the young man whom Jarnail had called evinced a willingness to help. The paramedics carried Shaul's stretcher through the dimly lit parking garage while the janitor opened the door of the green car that had been returned, repaired, the day before. He got in, placed the key in the ignition, and turned it.

"You get in first," Jarnail told Pinchas as they approached the ambulance.

A moment later, there was a mighty explosion in the parking garage. It was loud enough to make the paramedics and Pinchas crouch down and cover their ears with their hands. Only Jarnail spun around, gaping at his car as it went up in flames.

There was a fire extinguisher in the garage. There were paramedics. There was also an ambulance filled with emergency equipment. But the explosion was too powerful. Not a single one of them was able to help the young man who had entered the car two minutes before, cheerful and smiling.

"He just…died?" Pinchas's eyes bulged from his face like two blue marbles.

"It was meant for us." Jarnail was breathing heavily, his shoulders rising and falling with each breath. "*We* were supposed to be inside."

People appeared at the garage's entrance. Shrieks began to be heard, and the odor of burning plastic made it hard to breathe.

"How—?"

"They booby-trapped the car," Jarnail explained. "But this garage has security. This is not supposed to happen."

"But why—?"

Jarnail thought for a moment, then smacked his forehead. "My boys who were looking for you and gave you the watch in compensation?" he said. "I'm afraid that whole business punctured someone's pride." He shook his head. "It's hard to absorb," he mumbled. "It was just a watch!"

Pinchas was having difficulty swallowing. "We have to get Shaul out of here," he whispered. "He needs treatment. But this is terrible, Jarnail. Really terrible."

Someone approached Jarnail. A man a head and a half shorter than Jarnail with a rapid gait and sparkling eyes. "My father-in-law," Jarnail said quietly. "Dad, this is Pinchas, the rabbi from Jerusalem."

The millionaire transferred his burning gaze to the shaken Pinchas and said in English, with Jarnail translating the words into Hebrew, "My son-in-law has told me very interesting things about you and your friend. What happened to your car, son? It doesn't look too good."

Jarnail responded with a flow of quiet words that was almost completely drowned out in the commotion of the people filling the parking garage. His father-in-law answered in kind. They didn't like each other much, Pinchas decided from the tone of their speech and their body language, but there was a certain mutual appreciation. A kind of respect.

More neighbors crowded onto the scene. The natural Indian tendency to express emotions thoroughly and out loud, together with the echoes bounding off the garage's walls, the smell of scorched plastic, and the mute image of the young man who had been, until a few minutes before, a living being, made every second spent there distressing in the extreme.

In all the pandemonium, it was no wonder that no one heard Shaul's cellphone ring. Again and again and again.

# 42

RICKI'S FEET WERE ACHING BY THE TIME SHE FOUND AN airport employee whom she could bombard with questions. The waiting area she sought was located, she learned, in an entirely different part of the airport, but the young woman was prepared to let Ricki use her cellphone to try to reach those who were supposed to pick her up.

Shaul didn't answer her call.

This, Ricki decided, was the time to become frantic. To worry that something had happened to him. That he was lying injured in a mangled car at the side of the highway and no one was stopping to help him. It was time to start entertaining horrific images of covered mirrors and low chairs. But the woman who had allowed Ricki the use of her cellphone was standing by impatiently, giving her suspicious looks that caused the back of Ricki's neck to prickle and kept her from being swallowed up in a wave of panic.

"They're not answering," Ricki told her with an apologetic smile. "I'd like to try again."

But the second attempt, and the third, were no more successful than the first. She began scrolling through the contacts in her own useless phone, searching for Pinchas's number.

"Are you okay?" The young woman spoke with stiff and pointed geniality.

"I'm going to try a different number," Ricki told her, bringing the phone to her ear. "Just one more minute, please."

But here, too, there was no answer. Ricki clenched her teeth until her jaw ached, returned the phone to its owner, and wondered what to do next.

Two hours had passed since she'd landed, after a long, sleepless night. She needed a place to rest, where she could use a phone without begging people for favors. And how nice it would be if she could drink some cold water and sit right under an air conditioner...

"Which hotel do people use when they're waiting for a connecting flight?" she asked the woman in the airport uniform. "And how would you recommend that I get there from here?"

---

The odor of singed plastic and scorched auto paint filled the parking garage with pungent fumes. "There's nothing more for us to do here," the paramedic told Jarnail. "We want to take the patient away. Is one of you coming with us?"

"Both of us," Pinchas said firmly.

"Your English is improving," Jarnail said with a grin.

"It has no choice," Pinchas retorted. "Let's get out of here."

Jarnail rubbed his eyes. "I..." he began. Then he made up his mind. "Okay. Let's go."

"One in front and one with the patient," the paramedic said.

Both of them moved forward, both feeling the same degree of connection.

"You," the paramedic said, grabbing Pinchas's arm. "You're with the patient. And you get in front," he instructed Jarnail. "Next to the driver."

The man shouted something in a local dialect at the other paramedic, who was in the driver's seat, then took his seat in the rear of the ambulance and slammed the door shut.

"We'll be at the hospital in twenty minutes," the paramedic said to Shaul, who was lying on the stretcher with open eyes. "You're feeling better, yes?"

Shaul didn't answer.

"He already received almost half the bag of fluid," the paramedic reported. "And he opened his eyes. He'll improve soon."

"*B'ezras Hashem*," Pinchas mumbled. For the seventh time that morning, he stuck his hand in his pocket to reject an incoming call.

"Who is it?" Jarnail asked.

"My wife," Pinchas said shortly. "Apparently, it's very urgent for her to let me know the date she arranged for us to meet at the *beis din*. This is the seventh time she's called this morning."

Jarnail turned around from his seat in the front and looked at him. Pinchas shrugged. "You want me to take the call?" he asked. "Does this look like the right time and place?"

Jarnail lifted his brows and then lowered them meaningfully. Pinchas shrugged again and leaned toward Shaul. "Shaul, can you hear me? You apparently became dehydrated. We're on our way to the hospital."

"Good," Shaul said.

It was a logical answer in one way, but illogical in another. Pinchas sighed.

"Ask him what his name is," the paramedic said. "Let's see if he's coherent."

Pinchas leaned close again. "Do you remember your name?" he asked Shaul, holding tight to one of the ambulance's hand grips and doing his best not to go flying as the ambulance barreled through the streets in the wild fashion typical of the city.

"My wife," Shaul answered. "Where is she?"

Jarnail and Pinchas exchanged a glance.

"Okay," Jarnail said. "First of all, Shaul, good news. You've started to recover, and you're talking coherently. We were very worried about you this morning. We tried to wake you up, but we couldn't. That's how we got here." He was prepared to continue chattering until Shaul's eyes closed, and he dropped off. But Shaul broke in. "Someone has to go to the airport," he said slowly, pronouncing each word individually. "I arranged with her where to meet. Near the red bench."

"So, he *is* coherent," the paramedic said. "Nice. That's really good news."

Without understanding either that sentence or the one that followed, which Pinchas guessed was about Shaul's blood pressure being unstable and the need to keep him calm, Pinchas realized that he'd guessed correctly when he heard Jarnail say, "We'll get you to the hospital and immediately go pick her up. There's nothing to worry about, Shaul. Rest a little now. Everything's going to be all right."

"She was supposed to land at eleven-fifty." Speech demanded a great effort for Shaul. "What time is it now?"

Jarnail glanced at his watch and discovered that time moves more quickly when you're trying to put out a car fire and calm frantic people. It was past two-thirty. How had he let the time get away from him like that?

"We'll go get her soon," he said out loud. "Rest, Shaul. We want to be able to tell her that you're in good shape."

When Pinchas saw this argument persuade Shaul to close his eyes and stop trying to manage things, he felt a wave of sadness almost like the one that had filled his heart the day before. It was hard to see Shaul, usually so vibrant, in such a weak and vulnerable state. As though to heap more sadness onto his sorrow, the phone in his pocket rang again.

"Answer it," Jarnail said.

But Pinchas didn't feel capable. "I'll answer in your place," Jarnail offered, twisting his big body so that he faced the rear. "I'll ask if it's urgent. You're usually such a gentleman, Pinchas. What do you call it? A *mentch*. It's not like you to let someone call so many times without answering."

Pinchas's throat worked behind his beard. Then he pulled out the phone and handed it to Jarnail. "Do what you think best," he said. "Maybe this really is the right thing."

The small phone was nearly swallowed up in Jarnail's big hand as he turned back around and accepted the call.

"Yes?" he said. "No, this is Jarnail. He's busy at the moment. He'll get back to you later. I understand that it's urgent, but Shaul is not feeling well and we're in the ambulance with him right now." Silence. "All right. I'll tell him. Goodbye."

"Your wife," he reported, returning the phone to Pinchas. "She was crying. She said that you don't have to rush, just get back to her when you can."

"What happened?" Pinchas asked.

"When you call her back, I suppose you'll find out," Jarnail remarked. "It was nice of her to say that you don't have to rush. That's consideration."

"Or else it means that I very much need to rush, and she's trying to blur the facts," Pinchas said. "My grandfather happens to be very sick, but that's not a new situation." Lines popped out on his forehead. "That shouldn't make her cry."

As if of their own volition, his fingers moved over the buttons on his phone. His face was like a carved mask as he waited for his call to be answered.

"Yes?" he said, his voice low and tense. "Did something happen?"

He listened in silence for a few seconds, and his light eyes narrowed. "What? You're not kidding me, right?" Silence. "I don't believe it. Have you gone for another blood test? And this is after that whole business with the medicine! Ribbono shel Olam… I can't believe it… No, no, you didn't ruin anything. Don't cry. You can ask Shaul: I told him that when you hit rock bottom, you can only go up." Another silence, this one very long. "Wow. Everything should go well from here on in. Hashem will help. Yes, of course. I'll call you the minute I can speak privately."

"In five minutes, we'll be at the hospital," the paramedic said in Hindi. He hadn't understood a word.

"Excellent." Jarnail looked straight ahead, as if he had heard nothing. "Shaul, did you catch that? We'll be at the hospital in five minutes."

But Shaul, though he *had* heard, preferred to lie back on the stretcher with his eyes closed. And Pinchas, who felt as though his heart had suddenly swelled so much that it was pressing on his ribs, leaned his head against the ambulance wall, tears filling his eyes and his lips moving silently.

43

SHAUL'S STORIES ABOUT JARNAIL HAD PAINTED A PICTURE in Ricki's mind of a warmhearted man filled with goodwill. That image stood in stark contrast to the cold British politeness with which he evaded all her efforts to understand the "series of mishaps" that had left her stranded in the airport, going crazy with worry and discovering powers of survival and independence that she hadn't known she possessed.

"Is Shaul all right?" she asked again, for the fourth time.

"Certainly, Mrs. Sofer. You just spoke to him a moment ago. He simply needs some treatment that can't be put off. If you'd be so kind as to give me the address of the hotel you are in…"

She had no idea what the hotel's address was. Her sixth sense strongly claimed that this courteous creature was lying. "Where are you all now?" she asked. "I think it would be easier for everyone if I simply take a taxi."

"Unfortunately, I must point out that some of the cab drivers in Mumbai are not sufficiently trustworthy. Therefore, I would not recommend taking that step. I think—"

"I think you're lying," she found herself saying. "What happened? Was Shaul hurt in a car accident?"

"Heaven forbid," he said. "We simply ran into a chain of unfortunate mishaps this morning and—"

His slow, formal Hebrew was driving her out of her mind. "Where are you now?" she asked sharply. "I am not prepared to wait here for an hour and a half while you cross the city to get here. I am going to ask the receptionist here in the lobby to call a cab for me, and I am coming to you."

She sounded extremely stubborn and energetic, but the tone of voice she used to raise the children while Shaul was far away from home was once again successful at masking her true feelings.

People fly to Turkey and China all the time to tour or to order merchandise. This adventure was not, in absolute terms, all that monumental. But it was a little too big for *her*—at least it was now, when she was so exhausted from the long hours of waiting at the airport. When, on top of all that, she had to try to guess at the truth hiding behind Jarnail's lies, her ragged nerves sending out high-speed electric currents that were making her tingle with distress.

Could Shaul have been kidnaped? And was Jarnail working with the kidnapers? And were they now trying to draw her into the trap, too, so that they could demand a higher ransom? After all, who could resist contributing to a ransom when they heard about ten children who'd been left without a mother or father…

It was fatigue that was rendering her so creative, she thought. She breathed deeply, running her hands along the carved armrests of her armchair. "I'd like to speak with Shaul again," she said, demonstrating her own graciousness. "Can you give him the phone, please?"

"He's a little busy right now."

The people of India, she'd once been told, are capable of repeating the same sentence for hours and thereby achieve a state of deep serenity. But while the line "He's a little busy right now" might be calming to Jarnail, it was giving her the feeling that she was about to go out of her mind.

"So let him stop what he's doing," she said. "I want to talk to him now."

"I'm sorry, but that's not possible. He's in the middle of an important conference. He will get back to you when he's done. In the meantime, if you could give me the hotel's address where you're located at present?"

The man's obstinacy was exhausting. She was almost ready to give up, when generations of anonymous mothers lined up behind her and made her strong. "I think that we have three possibilities here. You can choose whichever one you prefer. Either I wait until Shaul is done and he calls me back to explain what's going on, or you do that for him, honestly and without skipping a detail, or you can give me the address of the hospital he's in and I'll find my own way there."

She slipped the words "the hospital he's in" lightly, letting them be swallowed up among the rest without letting on that she was quaking inside. If she was simply being paranoid, Jarnail would protest those words.

He didn't protest, and she felt dizzy. "Where is Shaul?" The quiet firmness had disappeared from her voice. To her own ears, at least, she sounded fairly hysterical. "I want to talk to him now."

"He'll get back to you when he finishes speaking with the doctor." Jarnail apparently realized that he'd fallen into a trap. "He feels perfectly fine, Mrs. Sofer. It was simply a mild case of dehydration."

No mild case of dehydration would have prevented Shaul from meeting her at the airport on time. That much was clear to Ricki. She said merely, "What is the hospital's address? I'm heading there now."

"He's all right," Jarnail said. "You spoke to him yourself."

"Yes," she said, her mind simultaneously scattered and sharp as a pin. "Will you give me the address, as I asked?"

---

"Explain to us both again," Shaul's wife said. "What, exactly, happened to your car?"

"It exploded," Jarnail said patiently. "I'm no expert on crime, but it looked as though someone booby-trapped it."

"Booby-trapped," repeated Ricki.

"He attached a bomb that would detonate when someone started the engine," Jarnail explained. "He assumed that all three of us—or at least I—would be inside." He shrugged, his eyes moving from Shaul, seated in his bed with the headrest elevated, to Pinchas, leaning against the chest of drawers beside it. "The two of you saw the building. It has twenty-four/seven security and is covered by security cameras." His voice was apologetic. "Such a scenario never happened to me. It's something that simply doesn't occur."

Shaul's breaths were coming fast and shallow. Pinchas, his partner on this trip, seemed completely detached from what was happening around him.

Ricki sighed. "But it did happen," she said.

"Yes." Jarnail shook his head and folded his arms across his chest. "A professional operation that points to a highly organized gang."

"A gang that's prepared to kill a person for a watch."

"Unfortunately, certain kinds of people are prepared to kill one another for less," he said. "Anyway, I sent someone to investigate the value of the watch. It's a Cartier, as I told Shaul, but it may be set with diamonds, not semiprecious stones as I first thought."

"What difference does that make for us?" Ricki asked sharply.

Jarnail sighed. "Are you familiar with the term 'protection'? My father-in-law pays all sorts of people so that his various business enterprises will function smoothly, without interruption, and his interests in the city will be safeguarded. How to put this delicately? He is very unhappy that his son-in-law's car exploded underneath the house. He feels betrayed."

"And what does that have to do with us?" Ricki asked again.

As far as she was concerned, none of this mattered right now. She just wanted to see Shaul's kidney function return to normal and then leave on the first El-Al plane out of here. Something that would not be so simple considering that in order to win Shaul's cooperation with the plan, she had to find a way to smuggle a baby in her luggage...

"I spoke with my father-in-law," Jarnail said slowly. "He is a refined man who appreciates peace. He is working to bring about some kind of reconciliation. We will apologize for taking the watch, and they will apologize to you, Pinchas, for what happened yesterday, and to me for bombing my car. He wants it to take place today."

"Here? In the emergency room?" Ricki asked. It didn't take a sensitive ear to pick up the sarcasm in her tone.

"The emergency room is as good as any other place." Jarnail glanced at his wristwatch. "We can ask the doctors to provide a conference room. And I'm sorry, but it looks like that's what will happen—because, as I understand, they're not planning to release Shaul today."

"The day is long." Ricki didn't like the note of hysteria in her voice.

"Doctors have protocols," Jarnail said. "After the kind of trauma Shaul's body experienced this morning, it's better for all of us that he remain under observation until we're sure he's okay."

"That man," Shaul said hoarsely. "What about him? Who will participate in the 'reconciliation' in his name?"

"Which man?" Jarnail asked.

"The one who died." Shaul sucked in some air. "In your car. He has a family, no?"

"Most people have a family." Jarnail rubbed his broad forehead with his fist. "All right, Shaul. I'll speak to my father-in-law. We'll see what we can do for his family. Apart from that, are we agreed? Can I tell them to come here?"

44

ON THE LONG DRIVE TO THE HOSPITAL, RICKI HAD BEEN troubled by images of Shaul lying on a rickety bed under an old ceiling fan that squeaked as it turned. But the hospital, when she arrived, proved a pleasant surprise. It was large and modern. Something about the colors and fabrics made her wonder if it had been designed by the same architect who designed Hadassah Hospital back in the day. Perhaps because of the normalcy of the place, Ricki found it hard to imagine that the hospital would agree to allow them the use of a conference room for a group of criminals who wanted to effect a reconciliation with those whom they had nearly maimed or killed.

But Jarnail knew the place and its rules, and he seemed satisfied that the meeting was possible. Ricki shrugged. Either way, the matter didn't concern her.

"Whatever you say," Pinchas said. His manner gave no indication of whether he had fully absorbed what had been said.

Shaul carefully maneuvered the tube attached to his arm and sat up. "If you're asking our opinion, apparently we can also say no."

A quick, small smile rose to Jarnail's face. "If your medical condition does not allow for visitors…" He said solemnly in English.

Shaul nodded his understanding. "I think that is correct," he said. "My medical condition does not allow for me to receive visitors. Absolutely not."

"All right," Jarnail said. Then he added, in English, "Father, do you hear? I just spoke to them now, but Shaul is still feeling unwell. Tomorrow would be better, or even the day after. Not today."

Those Bluetooth earphones. Ricki shook her head, only partially amused. It would have been nice of Jarnail to let them know in advance that there were others privy to their conversation.

"All right," Jarnail said presently. "We are alone again. My father-in-law acquiesced to your request, Shaul. The meeting will be put off for another day."

"Good," Shaul said, and sighed. "I think that a little rest with the curtain closed and quiet wouldn't hurt right now."

"That's not enough," Ricki intervened. "Considering that if your kidney function doesn't improve in the next twenty-four hours, they'll have to consider dialysis, I want us to start thinking about a flight home." She took a deep breath. "Despite the fact that this hospital adheres to international standards and all."

"No problem," Jarnail said. "I'll work on the insurance, but one of you needs to call the boss. Tell him that there's no one to handle the kashrus of the food-coloring factory."

"Rabbi Schwab?" Ricki asked. "I'll do it. I'll tell him we're going back to Israel—"

Shaul lifted a hand. "No."

"What do you mean, 'no'?" Women are weak, according to an Indian saying, but mothers are strong. And Ricki's maternal side was showing in full force now.

"We need to deal with adopting the baby," Shaul said. "We're not going anywhere."

"I don't think you're thinking clearly just yet, Rabbi Sofer. You're not ready to make decisions."

"Ricki."

She fell silent. "You're crazy," she said, shaking her head.

"That's what the Kotzker Rebbe was looking for: a quorum of crazy people," Jarnail said. "No?" He cringed under the unexpected barrage of looks that shot his way. "He was an inspiring figure, the Kotzker Rebbe," he said apologetically. "I once read a nice book about him."

Shaul grinned. "From that bookstore on Rabbi Akiva Street."

"Yes," Jarnail said. "Exactly."

"They were probably thrilled to have some Sikh guy come in and buy out half the store," Pinchas remarked.

Jarnail chuckled. "A Sikh's money smells just as good as anyone else's."

"Okay." Ricki wanted to move things along. "Let's focus, Shaul. You agree with me that your life takes precedence over that baby. Especially since we can always come back to India to adopt her. Right?"

"Right," Shaul agreed. "If it's a matter of *pikuach nefesh*, it certainly takes precedence. But I don't think it is."

A silence fell between them, and hospital noises filled the void.

"We can violate Shabbos even on suspicion of *pikuach nefesh*," Ricki insisted. "No?"

"Let's let time do its job," Jarnail advised. "Shaul will rest here and give his body a chance to recover. In the meantime, we'll plan for the possibility that things won't go exactly the way we want. Okay?"

Shaul's muscles slackened as he let himself fall back onto his pillow. "Okay," he said. "The first thing to focus on is our appointment at the agency that deals with international adoptions. We have only a week. In adoption terms, that's nothing."

Somehow, amid all the chaos that had ensued the day before, Jarnail had made an appointment with the adoption agency as soon as he heard that Ricki was coming.

"Yes." Jarnail roused himself. "Certainly." He glanced at his watch again and grimaced. "Our original appointment is an hour from now. I'll call them and push it off till tomorrow."

"But not because I'm in the hospital," Shaul warned. "We don't want them to use that as an excuse to cause problems."

---

How many hours had it been since she'd last slept? Jarnail and Pinchas had left the room to make urgent phone calls. Ricki sat beside Shaul's bed and felt the exhaustion creeping slowly over her, turning the hospital commotion into a monotonous buzz that grew ever weaker, dimming the glaring neon lights and wrapping her senses in a thick woolen blanket that provided a blessed detachment.

But an instant before the process was complete, Jarnail tore through the metaphorical blanket and sent a shower of sparks into the air. "We have a small problem," he said. "The woman at the adoption agency that was supposed to meet us in an hour won't be in the office either tomorrow or the next day. She's willing to push off the appointment for an hour to give us time to get there today, but she won't agree to meet with us tomorrow. I even offered to pay her to come into the office especially for us. No use."

"In a city of twelve million people, there must be more than one agency that handles adoptions," Ricki said, glad that her voice sounded alert and energetic.

"Yes, there are," Jarnail said. His voice held a clear note of doubt. "But we need one with a certain amount of flexibility, that will grasp our special situation and not create problems."

"What kind of problems, for example?" Shaul asked, still hoarse. He rubbed his arm around the place where the IV needle was inserted into his skin.

"All sorts." Jarnail waved a hand as though to chase away a fly. "You need to understand, Shaul, that adoption is not the whim of a moment or something that people do in a week's time. Under ordinary circumstances, it takes months. And you're hoping to complete the process within a week. And not just a week, but a week consisting of six days, since you intend to rest on Shabbos. So you need shortcuts, and you want a specific baby. You want quick service. You have a great many demands, right? So you need to go to an agency that is prepared to provide all that without asking questions or creating problems." He smiled, though he looked worried. "I'm sorry," he said, "but those are the facts."

"They have no appointments available tomorrow," Shaul clarified.

"Or the next day," Jarnail confirmed.

"All right." Shaul took a breath. "You didn't cancel today's appointment, right?"

Jarnail emitted a short bark that sounded like laughter. "I knew you'd ask that. So I didn't cancel it. No."

Ricki wanted to protest. She wanted to scold. She wanted to say that she couldn't agree to this under any circumstances. That Shaul should remember that he had been in real danger that morning and that he must learn to take care of himself.

But along with the wave of anger there rose in her a wave of simple pride in this man, with a beard that had long since begun to turn silver at the edges, yet he retained his youthful energy, determination, and disregard for himself and his needs. Just like on their first date, when he decided to climb a tree to save a cat trapped in its upper branches, where it had sought refuge.

Shaul looked at the IV stand, whose bag was half empty. "Very good," he said. "How long does it take to get there?"

"It's about a thirty-five-minute drive," Jarnail said. "But—"

"Do you remember the cat on our first date?" Ricki asked, slightly embarrassed because the conversation wasn't as private as perhaps it should have been. "Do you remember how it tore your jacket? How it might have been more practical and less expensive to call the fire department to come get the cat down instead of climbing up yourself? Not to mention the shots against rabies that you had to have because it scratched you…"

"That's because it was a tiger, not a cat," Shaul said with a smile. "In our house in Montreal, I was tops in our neighborhood at saving cats—and not one of them was as wild as that one."

Jarnail was smiling, too. "You really climbed a tree to save a cat in the middle of your first date with your wife?"

He hadn't just saved the cat. He had also crossed a muddy patch of ground to reach the tree where the cat had been wailing so piteously. Ricki, hurrying after him, remembered to this day how her Shabbos shoes had looked when the adventure was over. And how it was clear to her, by evening's end, that they might as well set a date for the wedding three months later.

No. You couldn't say that she didn't know what she was getting into when she agreed to build a home with him. And although she was much prouder of him today than she'd been then, there was still a bit of disgruntlement in her voice as she said, "All I'm asking is that you don't make any hasty decisions. Let's take a few minutes to think about this whole thing from every angle."

Shaul nodded, forehead wrinkling as he thought. "Let's see what they have planned for me," he said presently. "If I've received the fluids they wanted to give me, from their point of view I can get some fresh air in the courtyard downstairs and stay there until morning, when the doctor comes around. I don't see any problem with taking a short drive in between."

"A short drive of thirty-five minutes each way," Ricki corrected him. "*If* there's no traffic. And that's without taking into account the amount of time the appointment will take."

"Ask the doctor, Jarnail," Shaul requested. "Tell him that we have an urgent appointment that could affect my whole future. That we're talking about a life hanging in the balance and that it would be a real tragedy for me to miss it. Try to get his unofficial permission for me to leave on my own recognizance and to return here in time for the next doctor's rounds."

"If necessary, maybe we could stay here another week," Ricki said as Jarnail left on his mission. "I don't want you to put yourself at risk for such a thing."

"The children need you at home," Shaul said. "We can't leave them on Rini's and Shalom's shoulders for two weeks. Even a week is a long time. And I'm really all right. I received the fluids I need and I feel fine."

"You're still very pale. And your kidney function isn't back to normal yet."

"You heard the doctor. It's a process that takes time."

"That's why I want you to fly home. I don't want you to undergo dialysis here. Who knows what kind of diseases you could catch? It's dangerous."

"Do you think kidney function is like a bad back?" Shaul inquired. "That it gets better if a person lies in bed without moving? All I'd be doing is going on a trip in an air-conditioned car and breathing a little fresh air. Ask any doctor: a good state of mind helps a person heal."

At that moment, Jarnail returned wearing a broad smile. Their outing had been approved.

The meeting got off to a good start. Ricki shook the hand of an older woman. Jarnail described their trip and the moment they'd found the baby girl. He told how Shaul had protected her and devotedly cared for her all through the journey, and then Shaul presented the folder of documents that Ricki had packed in her suitcase: proof that they owned their own apartment, bank statements going back six months, health certifications—admittedly a bit old—signed by their family doctor, which they had obtained when trying to reduce the cost of their mortgage, and a set of pictures to show how happy and wonderful their family was. Ricki's heart swelled as she looked at them from the side.

"Where is the baby now?" the woman asked when the three had finished saying everything they had to say.

"I left her with our housekeeper," Jarnail said. "We'd be happy to bring her here tomorrow."

"We will need her to come here in order to register her in one of the orphanages with whom we work," the woman said. "And we will need, of course, a notarized translation of all these documents. You must surely understand that apart from the figures in the bank accounts, I don't understand a thing they say."

All three of them smiled.

"Apart from that, everything seems to be in order," she said. "Which child in the picture is yours, by the way?"

"Children," Shaul corrected. "All of them."

"I asked, which of these children in the picture is yours," the social worker said again, tapping one of the photographs for emphasis. She was clearly certain she had misunderstood.

"What do you mean?" Ricki asked. "They're all ours. All of them."

"*All* of these children?" The woman's teeth showed in an expression of scornful astonishment. "You have so many children? Then—no. I am sorry. About ten years ago, the government of India passed a law that international adoptions are only possible when the adopting family has a maximum of three children of their own. I don't know why we did not cover this point earlier, but you cannot adopt her."

45

OVER THE WINDOW IN THE SOCIAL WORKER'S OFFICE hung an orange curtain embroidered with blue beads. Hanging from the ceiling, a large fan hummed steadily except when it interrupted itself with what sounded like a faint groan. From time to time—perhaps from the social worker's bag—the scent of fried dough wafted into the air. Ricki's fingers left patches of dampness on the folder of documents she was holding.

"What do you mean?" she asked, leaning forward. The adrenaline surging through her body had heightened every one of her nerves.

"I believe you understood me very well, my dear," the woman said, adjusting the necklace around her throat. "Unfortunately, despite the fact that I'm certain the two of you would be wonderful parents to the sweet baby you found, the law makes it impossible for you to adopt her."

"Will she have it better in one of the orphanages that sends children to Nepal and sells them to the highest bidder, who turn them into lifetime servants?" Jarnail asked, a slight threat in his voice that Ricki, with her supersharp nerves, was able to pick up easily.

"Oh no. Heavens, no." The woman sat up. "But that is the law, Mr. Jarnail Singh Kapoor. There is nothing we can do about it."

"Except for sending kids to Nepal," Jarnail whispered unpleasantly.

"No," the woman snapped. "I know that there are all sorts of rumors flying around, but we do not do such things. It's not true."

Jarnail folded his arms so that the metal bracelet that he, like all Sikhs, wore, stood out. "The way I've heard it, those rumors have a very real basis," he said. "And because everyone present in this room is aware that this baby has no expectations of a bright future if she remains in Mumbai, and she has a chance of receiving a good education in Israel with a loving family, I ask you: What can we do now?"

The social worker lifted her shoulders. "You are the son of our secretary of legal affairs," she said. "You're the one who can influence this legislation, not I. I can only bemoan the close-mindedness of the legislators who, instead of worrying about the three million Indian orphans in the lowest caste, prefer to play political games with the countries of the West. What is preferable for a child—to be a servant in a stable wealthy home or to starve to death on the streets of Mumbai?"

The moment his father was mentioned, Jarnail's face hardened and shut down. The groaning fan didn't succeed in banishing the tension in the air.

"In my opinion, this conversation has moved a little off track," Shaul said carefully. "Let's go back and check the facts—"

The social worker on the other side of the desk shook her head. "There's nothing to check," she said, and tapped the family pictures with one pointed nail. "These are your children, correct? You have how many? Nine? Indian law prohibits handing Indian children over to non-Indian families that have more than three children. That is the reality, and there is nothing to be done about it."

Her tone softened as she said, "I can see how much you love the baby. I understand that the circumstances are unusual, and I sympathize with your pain. But the law is clear on this point."

Noise arose from the street, shouts and honks. "The law was instituted for good reason," she added, raising her voice over the cacophony. "There were some very distressing stories of people with good intentions who thought that adopting a child is no more complicated than adopting a dog or a cat."

For some reason, this ignited Ricki's wrath. "Parents of more than three children generally know what's involved in raising a child," she said with forced calm.

"Their *own* child," the social worker said pointedly, waving an instructive finger in front of Ricki's face. "Their own child, Mrs. Sofer. Raising someone else's child is a whole different story. More complicated. Then we are talking about a child who has experienced abandonment, who is not sure of his parents' love for him, who demands proof that he is wanted, and, consciously or unconsciously, puts his adoptive parents to the test to check if they really love him."

She nodded, as though agreeing with her own words. "Yes, and that's even before we talk about the fact that human behavior has not only environmental causes, but genetic ones as well. An adopted child can be very different, in every way, from the family that adopts him."

She stacked the documents that Ricki had placed on the table into one tall pile. "You have to understand that adoption can be very successful, but it demands a great deal." Firmly, she pushed the pile toward the Sofers. "And honestly, even without reference to this law, I must say that it doesn't seem to me that parents of a family this large will find the energy for everything that is demanded of them." She clasped her hands. "The challenge before you, to raise your nine children, is no less significant a kindness than saving an anonymous third-world baby."

"The point is, she's *not* anonymous," Shaul insisted. He didn't bother to correct her and mention their tenth child. "This is a baby I already saved once. I can't just send her away."

"I feel for you, honestly," the woman said. "But it seems to me that everyone will benefit if you give her to one of the excellent orphanages that we have in Mumbai and come once a year to visit her. A monthly bank deposit of a hundred or two hundred dollars and loving friends from across the sea will guarantee the child good treatment from the educational staff and optimum chances for growth with none of the effort that adopting and raising her would entail.

"Besides"—she paused for a moment to emphasize her point—"I must point out that though there are those who would regard adopting a hungry baby as a wonderful thing, you cannot forget that raising your own children is also an incredibly important mission. Your children have no one to care for them but you two. You are the only ones who can fill their emotional and physical needs. Therefore, I urge you, focus on that and leave this baby to someone else."

The woman stood up, lending a finality to her words. "I'm sorry I was not able to help," she said. "I wish you a good day and every kind of success."

Since none of them took the hint to stir from their places, she opened the door for them and waited patiently until they had passed through it.

In silence, the three descended the stairs to the street, which at this hour was filled with white-collar workers in brown, gray, or black suits rushing here and there with briefcases in hand.

"What do we do now?" Shaul asked.

Jarnail shrugged. "I'm sorry that I was not aware of that law. I didn't have a clue. On the contrary, I heard about an American family with five children that adopted two Indian brothers twelve years ago. I didn't know that things had changed since then."

Shaul tried to smile. "Everything is ordained in Heaven, and everything is for the best," he said. "The question is, where we do go from here?"

"I don't know." It was not often that Jarnail was stymied. He said, "Forgive me for saying this, but there was some truth in what she said."

Shaul leaned on the wall of the building, his head touching the gilded plaque of a lawyer's office. "Yes," he said. "I didn't imagine it would be easy. But I'm certain that I didn't encounter that baby for no reason. HaKadosh Baruch Hu had a reason for putting her into my hands. And just as I wouldn't abandon one of my children because someone tells me that raising them won't be easy, I'm also not prepared to abandon her."

"Neither am I," Ricki said. "I agree with Shaul. And I also believe that every rule has its exception. Is there no loophole in this law that we can use?"

"We can check." Jarnail did not sound enthusiastic. "But I can tell you sincerely that this law seems designed to prevent exactly what is happening here: the moment a religiously-motivated couple with a missionary zeal takes on more than it can handle."

Shaul shook his head. "If I were an Indian citizen, would this be easier?" he asked, ignoring Jarnail's words. "Maybe it's worth our while to find out what that would entail."

For some reason, this amused Jarnail inordinately. "I love you, Shaul," he said. "And I join the Rebbe of Kotzk: If there were a few more madmen like you in the world, it would be a much, much better place. But before we turn you into a citizen of India, I think it would be a good idea to pay a visit to the hospital. I promised the doctor that I'd return you to him within three hours."

46

THE TAXI DRIVER WHO WAS WAITING FOR THEM APPEARED surprised, and even a bit disappointed, at their speedy return. "Is everything all right?" he asked.

"More or less," Jarnail said, slamming the door. "We're going back to the hospital now."

"Would a bribe help here?" Shaul asked.

"A bribe to whom?" Jarnail wondered. "Do you know how many people are involved in an adoption? She's just a clerk. After her there's a whole chain of people whose palms would have to be greased."

"We have cash," Ricki said quickly. Before she could regret it.

"No." Shaul's head hung down, either from fatigue or despondency. "Gadi lent us the money for a specific purpose. I think we'd have to get his okay to use it for anything else."

Ricki could picture Gadi's face when she told him that she needed fifty thousand shekels to adopt a baby in India. She had to bite the inside of her cheek to keep from laughing.

"Where's the baby now?" she asked. "I'd love to finally meet her."

Jarnail sighed. "I don't know if that's a good idea, Mrs. Sofer," he said. "There may be no point in getting attached to her now. It looks like we've hit a dead end. Unless, as Shaul is planning, you all move to Mumbai for the next twelve years."

"Why twelve?" Shaul asked.

"Indian citizenship can be obtained by someone who is not here illegally and who lived in India for all of twelve months before he issued his request, and for a total of eleven years out of the fourteen years before that," Jarnail read aloud from his phone. "That's wonderful, isn't it? If you do that, you can adopt her the minute she becomes a bas mitzvah. Shaul, that will satisfy all your religious requirements to perfection." He turned around to look Shaul and Ricki in the eye.

Ricki concentrated on her breathing. Jarnail was mocking them, that much was obvious. But Shaul, despite his current weakness, didn't need her to protect him. She turned toward the window and looked out.

"Enough, Jarnail," Shaul said tiredly. "Let's fight some other day, okay? Today I need you to be patient and sympathetic. All right?"

"Your wife doesn't want the baby," Jarnail said starkly in English. "She's doing this only because you asked. Is that a stable basis for committing to raising a child for the next twenty years? Do you have any idea how much frustration and anger that baby will have to contend with simply because she is not really wanted?"

"What's he saying, Shaul?" Ricki asked, turning away from the window.

"He says that my wife doesn't really want the baby," Shaul repeated, exhaustion emphasizing dark circles around his eyes. "She's doing it only because I asked. And it's impossible to raise a child for twenty years just because someone asked. It's not fair to the child. It will make the child grow up feeling rejected."

Ricki was silent for a moment, considering this. "I wouldn't have done this without you," she said. "Such an idea would never have occurred to me, and I wouldn't have considered it my problem. But let me meet her and care for her for a year, and then just try to take her away from me... I think I'd make you regret that you ever tried. Giving gives birth to love, and I'll give whatever is needed. I don't think there's any reason to worry."

"Giving *what*?" Jarnail asked.

"Gives birth to love," Shaul answered quietly. "It's a teaching from a book called *Michtav MeEliyahu*."

"Ah. I think I may have heard of it..."

Shaul looked at him sharply. With a sudden flush, Jarnail turned away from them and stared out at the road.

"Hey," Shaul said after a moment's stunned silence. "You're really seriously into Judaism, eh?"

"I...I love wisdom. Especially divine wisdom. For now, that's all it is."

*For now.*

The words rang in Shaul's ears, causing the air around him to tremble as though someone nearby had played some especially low notes.

*He loves Divine wisdom.*

"Wow," he said, finding nothing more intelligent to say. "Wow."

"I do not intend to convert," Jarnail stated emphatically. "You don't have to worry. My wife, my children, my father-in-law... No, I'm not really considering that possibility."

"Okay," Shaul said mildly, prepared to leave it at that.

"You should rest a little, Shaul," Jarnail said, eager to change the subject. "You need rest."

As if on cue, Shaul's phone began to vibrate loudly.

He pulled it out with the forced movements of one whose muscles are filled with sour milk. "It's from home," he said, putting the phone to his ear.

"Hello," he said with tired friendliness. "I don't understand. Who is this? Why are you crying?" Silence. "Calm down so I can understand what you're saying." Silence. "Benny, I can't understand a word. Except for the name Ari. Drink some water and call me back in half a minute."

"Benny's crying?" Ricki was surprised. That was an unusual happening.

Shaul nodded his head and closed his eyes. "Ari is making trouble for him," he said. "They sent him to the principal or something. I didn't catch the rest."

"According to Benny, Ari could be an author when he grows up," Ricki said dryly. "He knows how to make up stories, he has a well-developed imagination, and he's a little sadistic. That's what you need to be a good author, no?"

"Why sadistic?" Shaul wanted to know.

"Just look at what all authors do to their heroes," Ricki said. "They take innocent, good-hearted people and give them impossible challenges." She grimaced. "I'm fed up with that boy. He's hurting Benny. And his parents, excuse me for saying so, don't know how to raise children. If it were up to me, he'd be kicked out of the school tomorrow."

"You're tired," Shaul said. "You missed a night's sleep, and you're also worried about me. Everything will look better tomorrow. Jarnail, maybe we should take her back to her hotel first?"

"If I were to go to sleep every time Ari makes trouble for Benny, I'd have been asleep for most of the past two years," Ricki huffed. "Seriously, Shaul. That boy..."

"Benny's no tzaddik either," Shaul reminded her. "And I have a feeling that if you call Ari's mother, you'd be surprised to find that *we're* the ones in urgent need of parenting classes."

Suddenly, Ricki felt uncomfortable at having Jarnail overhear what they were saying.

"It will be okay," she said. "I really am tired."

"Tell me..." Jarnail joined the conversation without a trace of hesitation or diffidence. "In about twelve more years, when little Sarah calls you crying because some friend did something to her, will you also defend her like a lioness? Or will the two of you talk about 'hot Indian blood' and say, 'We didn't know what we were getting into when we took her'?"

"A nice name, Sarah," Shaul remarked. "When we reach that bridge, we'll call and update you. Till then, don't change your number."

Ricki was a little insulted at having the baby's name chosen for her. "We sometimes say that our own children have hot blood," she retorted. "Or that when they were born, we didn't know they'd turn out so mischievous at the age of twelve. And even if a personality has a genetic connection, that doesn't mean education can't influence it."

Jarnail nodded. "I'm asking because it interests me, not because I have preconceived notions or anything like that. So is the stubbornness that the two of you are showing a matter of upbringing or genetics?"

"Wow," said Shaul. "The third 'wow' in one conversation. But I don't know how to answer you. When Sarah is twenty, we'll invite you to her wedding. You can see how stubborn she is and reach your own conclusions."

Jarnail laughed silently. "Act as you see fit," he said. "I only tried."

"It's good that you tried. That way you'll sleep better at night," Shaul said encouragingly. "Are we going to the hotel now?"

Jarnail straightened slightly: "We're going to Sarah," he said. "She is feeling a little neglected after three days without her mother. I think the time has come for the first family meeting."

47

ADOPTING A BABY FROM INDIA HAD NOT BEEN AMONG THE things that Ricki had planned for the current year, nor for the coming five years. Or even forever. So she was the first to be surprised at the unexpected eagerness in her own voice as she asked, "Do we have time to go to her? Is it possible? Don't we have to get back to the hospital now?"

"Don't you want to rest a little first?" Shaul asked, also taken aback by the excitement in her voice. "She's being cared for by an experienced woman, Ricki. You don't have to worry."

A woman's emotions, even as logical and intellectual a woman as Ricki, are a complex and bewildering thing. "I'm not worried," she said. "I'm just..." She searched for the right words. "I'm just..."

"Just?" Shaul tried to help.

"Just..." she said for the third time, shaking her head. "I don't know how to explain it, Shaul. I want to go see her now. That's all."

"We have time," Jarnail said. "I thought the meeting at the adoption agency would take at least two hours. It took less than twenty-five minutes."

"All right," Shaul said, lifting a hand. "I'm in favor." Then he closed his eyes and sank into a broken, intermittent sleep, rousing each time the cab driver braked suddenly or swerved. Things that, in Mumbai-style driving, happened frequently.

Ricki's visit to India until now had encompassed only four stops: the huge, modern airport, a hotel owned by an international conglomerate, the best hospital in the city, and one of its largest and most spacious business centers.

The working neighborhood they entered now was her first and most powerful encounter with the real people's India. And the encounter, which included a group of children who were either beggars or simply curious, and who surrounded her pleading for money in English and found her nearly slipping on a puddle of oily water that glistened a metallic green, left her slightly shaken.

"Is this a poor neighborhood?" she whispered to Shaul.

"No, of course not," her husband whispered back. "It's a lower-middle-class part of town. Didn't you see the illegal city near the airport? *That's* a poor neighborhood. They don't even have running water."

"Do they have it here?" she asked with trepidation.

"Don't you see the water tanks on the roofs?"

She nodded. Through narrowed eyes, she took in the peeling buildings, the laden clotheslines, and the smoke rising from a bonfire that burned at the edge of one of the courtyards.

"Here," Jarnail said, passing them in a few long strides. "This is the building. We go in through here."

The stench in the stairwell was even worse than the one outside, and an oppressive dimness lent the place a menacing air.

"Third floor," Jarnail said. "Shaul, are you okay? Do you have the strength to climb?"

"Slowly and carefully," Shaul replied. "And in the knowledge that every staircase comes to an end."

Jarnail gave a short, polite laugh. "I've never been here before," he said, as though apologizing, between the second and third floors, for the lack of an elevator. "But I'm sure Mama Takor's house itself is quite clean."

He was right. The small apartment sparkled with cleanliness, achieved apparently not only by the woman herself but by her two daughters, bashful teenagers who spoke a broken English. They each took hold of one of Ricki's arms and led her gaily to a corner of the living room where, behind a pile of mattresses that the family used at night, lay the little girl for whose sake she had traveled thousands of miles. The baby slept peacefully on the lined floor of a vegetable crate.

She was so small. So tiny. Carefully wrapped in a purple-blue cloth, her little fists framing her cheeks, she looked like she was posing for a world-renowned infant photographer.

Although mothers, for some reason, tend to melt at pictures of tiny babies lying in wooden crates lined with colorful scarves, one minuscule foot sticking out, when the crate is the newborn's actual bed and the scarves are the only thing separating the baby from the crate, the picture quickly loses much of its charm. Ricki dropped her pocketbook and lifted the baby into her arms. The child, unaware of the moment's significance, slept on.

"*Shalom*," Ricki whispered, placing a cupped palm on the baby's soft cheek. "Hello, little one."

The infant's delicate, almost transparent eyelids flickered in her sleep, and her lips moved.

"She's dreaming," Ricki said. "You can tell that she's dreaming. She's perfect. Such a tiny bird."

Her fingers stroked the thin, silken hair. "Let's hope you'll like it with us," she said. "That we manage to overcome all the hurdles and bring you home with us. So daven, tiny one, and we'll keep on trying."

The baby opened her eyes and looked at her as though she understood. Ricki's heart skipped a beat. "HaKadosh Baruch Hu has all kinds of wonderful ways to run His world," she said. "Do you see the shape of her ears? It's exactly the same shape as Toby's and Shoshi's were when they were born."

They fell silent, gazing at the delicate lines of the baby's face as the child closed her eyes again. A moment later, she found her fist and began sucking it hungrily.

"She'll cry soon," Ricki predicted just as the girl who had run into the kitchen earlier hurried toward her holding a cracked, grayish bottle with a rubber nipple on top.

"My mother said this morning that we're to give her milk now."

Ricki looked at the ancient, grimy bottle with distaste. "Is this the bottle you've been using the whole time?" she asked Shaul in dismay. "Do you know how many germs are breeding inside the cracks in that nipple?"

"Of course not!" he said. "On the way, we fed her from cups, and when we reached Jarnail's house he brought us a different bottle. A pink one."

Jarnail translated the question into the local dialect, but the girls—or so they claimed—knew nothing about a pink bottle. This was what their mother had told them before she left for work: to give the baby milk from the bottle.

"Okay," Ricki said. "All right. No problem. How much are we supposed to pay them for babysitting, Shaul? I have cash."

"I already paid them in advance." Jarnail didn't seem overly upset by the state of the bottle. "She can definitely stay here for the next few days."

"She's not staying," Ricki stated.

"Mama Takor and her family can take care of her for you until you leave India," Jarnail explained softly. "I paid them for that in advance."

"We'll pay it all back to you, of course," Shaul said quickly. "But from what I understand, my wife is interested in caring for the baby herself from now on."

"She will have many days and nights to do that when the adoption is authorized," Jarnail pointed out. "And as I explained when we reached the city, there is no way to bring an unregistered baby into any respectable hotel. After the adoption papers come through, you won't have that problem. In the meantime—"

Ricki's eyes went to the baby, and something that only she saw there filled her with a courage that made her lift her head and say, "In the meantime, we'll have to find some sort of solution. Because if this baby is ours, then she's coming with us. That's all."

"She's not ours yet," Shaul reminded her gently.

"Legally," Ricki agreed. "Not emotionally. My heart wants the best for her right now."

"I don't think she'll have it so bad." Shaul lowered his voice until it was nearly inaudible. "Maybe they wanted to keep the bottle... But look, she's getting good care."

Ricki shook her head. "There's good, and there's good," she said. "If this were our baby and we lost her papers, we wouldn't let her stay here, would we?"

48

A FAN WHIRLING SOMEWHERE IN THE APARTMENT EMITTED loud squeaks. A dog barked in the courtyard below, and a man was shouting in the stairwell.

"This is not your baby, Mrs. Sofer," Jarnail reminded her. "Not yet. Although I very much hope and want to believe that we will find a way to bypass the law that prevents you from adopting her, I think you're moving too fast."

"Meaning?" Ricki sounded like a suspicious lioness.

"There is a chance that you will be able to overcome this hurdle," Jarnail said. "We will try everything. If necessary, we'll go all the way up to the prime minister and the Supreme Court. But it's a process that can take five years, not something that can be resolved in a day."

Ricki's brows snapped together.

"Don't you agree with me that the baby is being well cared for? She's clean, she's fed, she's sleeping well… True, the bottle is old, but it's clean, and I'm sure they boiled it before they used it for the baby. You have seen her, as you asked. Now, please, put her back in her crate and let us return here in a few days."

Jarnail's tone of voice was one that could have made even stone lions obey him. But Ricki didn't budge.

"Ricki?" Shaul prompted.

Ricki gave him a crooked smile. "I'm not a very stubborn or opinionated person," she said. "I think that we can still count on the fingers of one hand the number of times that I didn't listen to you in important matters… But this time I'm saying no."

"What do you mean?" Shaul asked.

"I am not leaving this baby here. Just as I wouldn't have left Tzviki here, even though I believe they would have boiled the bottle for him, too."

This, Shaul understood, was intended as a barb. Jarnail lacked that understanding. "So what do you suggest that we do?"

"Exactly what we would have done if we had brought Tzviki here from Israel and his passport was lost. We wouldn't have abandoned him because we couldn't bring him to a hotel, right?"

"Are you suggesting that we take the baby to the embassy and ask them to issue her a new passport in place of the one that was lost?" Shaul asked.

Ricki shrugged. She looked down again at the baby, and then said quietly, "That's actually an idea, Shaul. It's an idea. Mr. Kapoor, how much would it cost to bribe a secretary in the hospital where Shaul was admitted, so that she'd prepare documents saying that I gave birth to this baby today?"

Shaul brought a hand to his mouth to stifle an uncharacteristic snort of laughter. "Ricki! Be serious!"

"In two weeks, Tzviki will be one year old," Ricki said, her gaze thoughtful. "I have all the papers from our medical insurance, all organized in folders in a cabinet. I can ask one of my sisters to fax them to me. We'll only need to find someone to go through the papers, and each time the date appears, to change the number."

"Hmmm," said Jarnail.

But Shaul shook his head. "We can't do such a thing," he said. "First of all, it could be stealing, if the hospital sends your travel insurance company a demand for coverage."

"No," Ricki said. "I was bored during the flight, so I read all the paperwork. My medical insurance is minimal. It won't cover this."

"Second, I'm sure this is a crime," Shaul said. "It would break the law."

"Okay," Ricki said. "I'm not like you, walking to the corner of the block to find a pedestrian crossing. If there's no choice, you look right and left and cross. That's all."

"It's not the same thing." Shaul rubbed his forehead. "Forgive me for saying this, but I don't feel so well…"

"Oops," Jarnail said. "You're really not supposed to be standing."

There was no Western-style chair in the room, so Jarnail helped Shaul onto the pile of mattresses. "How are you feeling? Just don't become delirious again."

"A little dizziness…nausea… Ricki, I'm not really capable of making decisions right now."

"Then it's a good thing I'm here," Ricki said. "Tell them 'thank you' for me, Mr. Kapoor, and let's go."

Jarnail said something to the girls, then turned back to Ricki. "I told them that we're taking the baby for a few hours and that we'll be in touch with them over the course of the day. I'm afraid, Mrs. Sofer, that you're making a rash decision. There's no reason to be in such a hurry. Besides, you need to care for Shaul right now. You have enough on your head."

"Come, Shaul," Ricki said instead of answering. "Do you have the strength to stand?"

Shaul nodded. "Yes. No need to get excited. I'm just feeling a little woozy."

He tried to smile, but he was so weak and exhausted that Ricki was flooded with nightmare visions of the nephrology ward, of lingering by the door of the operating room in the hopes of a kidney transplant and being overwhelmed by despair when it turned out that the transplant was unsuccessful and the kidney had been rejected.

But these were only imaginings, she knew. Abnormal kidney function was common after dehydration. And if there was some spiritual lien against them right now…good deeds are the best defense against a harsh judgment.

"I want eye drops for her and vitamin K for blood clotting. Like they give babies in Israel," Ricki said as the taxi wove through the streets. "And I'd be happy if a pediatrician could take a look at her and check to see if anything else is needed. Antibiotics, for example, after all the places she's been. How do I find a good pediatrician?"

"Do you want an answer from Jarnail the person, or from the man who was hired to accompany your husband and protect him to the best of his ability?"

"Both," Shaul whispered, eyes closed.

"The Jarnail who wants to protect you says absolutely not," the Sikh said. "He says there's nothing to talk about. That Mrs. Sofer must stop acting out of emotion. In the end, I believe you will get what you want, but you have to be patient. You need to respect the process. There's no point in getting so attached to a child that you'll be leaving behind in a week's time. That will only cause pain and suffering to everyone involved and will cause us to waste resources."

"A bribe for the hotel clerk?" Shaul suggested.

"We can send Pinchas to the hotel, and the two of you can stay with me. Though, after this whole mess, I don't know how comfortable that would be for my family."

Shaul and Ricki were silent. "Maybe we can find a third solution," Ricki finally said. "We don't want to make anyone uncomfortable, Heaven forbid."

"And what does the other Jarnail say?" Shaul asked, the words coming slowly. "He's the one who interests me more."

Jarnail gave a sad smile. "The other Jarnail says that he admires you both. And that he wishes there were more people like you in the world. And that tomorrow or the next day we will meet the most appropriate people in the city who could help. The ones who are coming to apologize to Pinchas. This is exactly the right time to ask for a favor. I'm sure they have someone in the hospital, and forging documents as your wife suggested would be easy for them. But I would not want to involve the two of you in this way. I wouldn't want to cause you to break the law…" His voice trailed away. "Trafficking in children is no joke."

"Trafficking?" Ricki asked. "You need a buyer and a seller for that, right? We just want to rescue a baby from a miserable life."

Jarnail shrugged. "If you're caught, I assume that your lawyer would use that claim to convince the judge to have mercy. But it would not be possible to ignore the fact that you knew the law and broke it— trampling on the laws of two countries."

"Then we'll have to be very careful not to get caught," Ricki said. "Okay, we understand. We'll try very hard. And now, please arrange an appointment for me with a pediatrician. I want vitamin K and eye drops."

"I'll take care of it," Jarnail said. "Shaul's needs and yours take precedence, from my perspective, over the needs of this baby. Even though I am prepared to make sure she is well."

"My need right now includes the care of a good doctor, vitamin K, and drops." Ricki could be very single-minded. "If you can find a way to help me, I'll be very happy."

"Shaul?" Jarnail asked.

"I don't feel well and it's hard to think," Shaul said, looking queasy. "But Ricki is a smart woman. I endorse her decisions... Help her, Jarnail. As for the things you said—we'll hope for the best."

49

PINCHAS NEITHER NOTICED WHEN SHAUL AND JARNAIL
left the hospital nor noticed when they returned. For three
hours, he wandered the hospital grounds, moving from one patch of
shade to the next and talking on the phone about the future and about
the past. With a courage that was unusual for him, he raised topics that
should have been raised a long time ago. His mistakes. Her mistakes.
The mistakes they'd made together…

He shouldn't have agreed to work abroad, knowing that she would
be left alone. So alone.

She shouldn't have insisted on visiting her parents so often, knowing that on each visit she absorbed another drop of poison that ate
away at the underpinnings of her home.

They agreed on these two points. They were filled with the will
to move forward, trying to bridge the knowledge that he would not
have traveled so far had he not been suffocating from the toxic cloud
that she brought home with her. And she would not have gone to her
parents' so often had she not, even when he *was* in the country, been
forced to spend so many hours alone at home.

"*B'ezras Hashem*, a year from now everything will look different,"
Sari said. "Maybe we'll think this whole discussion was unnecessary."

"Shaul says there are always challenges." Pinchas often quoted his
friend. "That no challenge that you try to ignore will simply disappear.
It only changes shape."

"Maybe, instead of spending so much time at their house, I should have studied some sort of profession like you told me," she admitted after a moment's silence. "Maybe that would have given me a sense of meaning, something to keep me busy. Then I would have needed my sisters' company less, like you were always telling me."

"Maybe," Pinchas said. "We'll never know. But that doesn't seem to me to be the main issue. It's more like the part that takes on different shapes." He took a deep breath. "The real issue is our personalities. I, for example, am too afraid to admit to problems and pain."

This was more than just an example. It was also an apology, as they were both aware. "I realized that on this trip. I'm always trying to cut corners. Hoping that in a little while everything will be fine. That the problem will disappear. When I had no way to comfort you, I felt helpless and ran away. I should have stayed and admitted to the pain. Admitted that there's a problem and that it's a big one. Not be afraid to look reality in the eye and say…"

He couldn't go on. "You see?" he said when he managed to get his vocal cords working again. "See? I still can't do it."

"Maybe I should have been ready to try harder," his wife said quietly. "Not to look for easy solutions all the time. Going to my parents so I wouldn't be alone was just an easy solution." A breath. "I'm sorry."

"It's all right," he said. He bit his lip, wondering if now, too, he was escaping the pain and afraid to look it in the eye.

"It's not really all right," she said in his place. "I think I always knew that. But I convinced myself that it was the only solution. That there was no choice."

Both of them fell silent. An expensive, cellphone silence.

"Pinchas?" she asked. "Are you still there?"

"Yes," he said. "Always. I'm asking myself why we didn't talk about this five years ago."

"We tried," she said. "It didn't work."

"We should have gone for help."

Suddenly, he was angry. Not at her, and not at himself. He was angry at them both, as a couple. At the situation. "What were we thinking? We should have asked for help."

"We spoke about it a few times. Once, we even looked into someone, and it was expensive," she reminded him. "Too expensive for us. And I preferred to buy a new couch. And you always agreed with me that, in light of everything, the situation wasn't really that bad."

"But it was. The fact is that in the end we came to a place that we should never have reached. To a place other couples don't reach."

This time it was he who recovered first and broke the silence: "A Jew who looks backward has to believe that his choices were also decreed by Heaven," he reminded them both. "And we're still young. This is an excellent time to turn over a new leaf."

"Could you find work in Israel?"

He loved his job. Loved the trips and enjoyed seeing the world. "Will you visit your parents less often?" he asked in return.

She was silent.

They were both silent.

Suddenly they broke into healthy, shared laughter. "We'll have to find the money for a professional," she said when they finished laughing. "We're all right. But there are still some things that are hard to do alone."

"I'll find a job in Israel," he declared, assuming that this would be something that the professional would insist on in any case. "But it won't happen overnight. And don't complain to me if the salary isn't as good."

"I'll try to go to my parents less often," she said, trying to cooperate. "But..."

He knew what she meant. He understood, despite everything, what she found there. A household that was always bustling, her sisters' merry companionship, big, bubbling pots on the stove, joking, caring, and warmth. Although recently, the warmth had turned hot enough to scorch, and the family's sense of humor more than occasionally turned on him, leaving bleeding scars in their wake.

"We need a professional," he agreed. "I'll find him for us, and I'll get hold of the money. We deserve that as a couple, and we'll deserve it even more, *b'ezras Hashem*, as a family..." The words rang strangely in his ears.

"*B'ezras Hashem*," she echoed softly.

After several more minutes on the phone, he promised to call again that night and ended the call. They had spoken for three and a half hours! How had he lost himself that way? How had he left Shaul alone for so long?

The hospital's corridors were maze-like, and he lost his way. He tried to ask passing people for directions but obeying them only made him more lost. After he ran hopefully over to a Sikh who turned out to be a complete stranger, he sat down, defeated, and called Jarnail for help.

"Stay where you are. I'm coming."

"Just try to explain to me—" Pinchas asked.

"No, no, I'm coming." Their devoted guide seemed eager to leave wherever he was. "Wait patiently. I'll be right there."

It turned out that "right there" could take a long time. But Pinchas waited patiently until Jarnail appeared, looking tired and disheveled.

"It's been a long day," he said in response to the question in Pinchas's eyes. "I don't know what your and Shaul's lives are like outside India, but I don't usually spend my time rescuing abandoned babies, escaping from muggers, debating with social workers, and engaging in negotiations with forgers."

Forgers? This was new to Pinchas, and he said so.

"This trip of yours is like a barrel rolling down a mountain in the Himalayas." Jarnail sighed. "Everything is happening so fast. We were at the adoption agency, and they disqualified Shaul's family. Too large. Indian law doesn't allow parents of large families to adopt an Indian child. I messed up, and I only found out about it now."

A stone lodged on Pinchas's heart. His baby. He had picked her up. Although Shaul had hastened to help, if he couldn't find a way to keep his promise, the baby should return to him…

"I—" he began.

"We understand one another," Jarnail said. "The three of us get along beautifully. If only my brothers and I were on the same page, the way I am with Shaul and you. But Shaul's wife came, and she's shaking things up. Nothing interests her except taking the baby *now*. She wants me to find a forger who will make a set of Israeli papers, and for me to bribe a clerk in the hospital to issue a false birth certificate for the baby. She wants to get that baby into her hands right now."

"Really?" Relief washed over Pinchas like a wave. "How wonderful!"

"Wonderful?" Jarnail frowned. "What, exactly, is so wonderful?"

"The fact that she wants the baby. Is there a way to help her—legal or illegal? Just to wrap up the incident as quickly as possible?"

Jarnail shook his head in disbelief. "I didn't think you'd say that," he remarked. "I hoped that you would help me calm the two of them down, to find a loophole that would let us leave the baby here for now. If I were to kidnap her, for example, without their permission and give her to someone who would pass her on in such a way that they'd never find her—wouldn't that have been easiest for everyone?"

50

JARNAIL'S QUESTION CONFUSED PINCHAS. IF THE BABY WERE to vanish just the way she had appeared, there was no question that life would be simpler for them all—except for the child herself. If Jarnail undertook to make her vanish, it could definitely serve as a kind of solution…

But considering that it was he, and not Shaul, who had found the baby and was obligated to be concerned about her, he was not the one who could hint to Jarnail to make her go away.

"You're quiet," Jarnail said.

"I don't know what to say." The corridor was broad and hushed, layer upon layer of stone separating it from the outside world.

"I didn't want to be involved in all this," Jarnail said. "There is a limit to how far I'm prepared to go for the two of you. If I didn't have pity on the baby, I would probably have reached that limit already. But now—enough. No further."

"That is your right," Pinchas said hesitantly.

"It certainly is," Jarnail said with a grim smile. "But you and Shaul will not manage without me…"

Pinchas smiled. "True."

Although he would later muse that perhaps this wasn't the right moment to change the subject, Pinchas asked, "How is he now?"

"Shaul?" Jarnail rubbed his forehead with two fingers. "The doctor is satisfied. He says that Shaul is recovering beautifully. I am a little less satisfied, because he looks terrible."

"He's been through a lot in the past twenty-four hours," Pinchas offered.

"We all have." Jarnail's voice was gritty. "I don't want to get involved," he said again. "I don't want my wife to get involved. Most of all, I don't want my father-in-law to get involved...or even to have anyone *think* that he's involved. I care about you and Shaul, and I like you, but there's a limit. I can't do more than that."

"And kidnaping a baby and selling her to some stranger would be okay?" Pinchas tried to use humor, but his quip came out far too sharply. The cutting words, though subtle, drew blood.

"Shame on you." Jarnail was wounded to his depths. "To talk like that after everything I've done for you two!"

"It was a joke..."

"There are things you don't joke about. For shame! I was talking about giving her to an orphanage!"

"I didn't mean anything by it," Pinchas protested. "Jarnail, you're looking for a reason to quarrel. If I thought there was a chance you'd dispose of the girl in an improper way I wouldn't standing here talking to you right now. I joked about it because it's obvious to me that you have more integrity than that. Believe me, I had no intention of insulting you."

"Maybe, and maybe not." Jarnail's face was dark. "But it does not matter now. I understand Shaul's wife's idea. I think it has a chance of succeeding. But that's all. I don't want to be involved."

*Then don't,* Pinchas wanted to say. To slip away, as usual. To say that they would manage somehow. But even he was incapable of saying that. They had no chance of managing without Jarnail. They didn't have a sliver of a chance of getting out of the imbroglio in which they'd found themselves.

"Shaul is sick, and I don't speak English," he said at last. "What do you expect us to do? What would you do if you were in our place, alone in a foreign land?"

Jarnail shrugged. "I don't know. Good question."

His indifference surprised Pinchas. "Soon you'll say that they don't pay you for this, so you don't feel obligated to do anything."

"They really don't pay me for this, and the service I've provided over the last few days is far above and beyond my job description."

"Which you need so badly to make ends meet," Pinchas snapped back. "Forget it, Jarnail. You've already shown that it's not money that motivates you. Be serious for a minute. I don't want to pressure you or to beg, but it doesn't seem right for you to abandon us now."

"I am not abandoning anybody. I'm just saying that there are normal, culturally acceptable solutions for dealing with abandoned babies. Use one of them instead of trying to recreate the world. It shouldn't be too complicated."

Pinchas shook his head incredulously. "There are many interpretations of what is 'culturally acceptable.' Many of which are not necessarily positive."

"How about 'normal' or 'commonplace?'"

"Ninety-nine percent of the creatures in the world think it perfectly acceptable to eat one another, either alive or after death. And most of them would not recoil from eating their own children. So you want me to kowtow to what is 'normal' and 'accepted'?"

"Ninety-nine percent of the world's creatures?" Jarnail's nose wrinkled.

"Arthropods, mollusks, and fish make up the majority," Pinchas said. "That's what it said in a nature book I read when I was a boy. But the number ninety-nine may be inexact. When I return to Israel, I can check it for you."

"Again, you're raising an argument that's not relevant," Jarnail responded. "I'm not asking you to behave like a spider, or even like a monkey. I'm asking you to behave like a respectable human being. And respectable human beings obey the law. They don't go around the law when it seems useful or easier for them or supports their worldview."

Three orderlies pushed and pulled a hospital bed bearing an old, wrinkled man. They moved past, forcing Jarnail and Pinchas to one side of the corridor. The old man coughed, the instruments beeped, and the man's hand waved in the air as he grumbled to those carrying him along. The entourage continued on its way until it moved out of sight around the corner, leaving a thin, dark, frightening, and invisible trail in its wake.

"Old age," Pinchas said. "The hope of every respectable human being."

"What are you talking about, Pinchas?"

"No one wants to die young. But if old age is mankind's hope, isn't it terrible to think that this is all there is? An aide, a wheelchair, and a bib?"

"A bib?" Jarnail shook his head. "Pinchas, speak clearly. What are you trying to say?"

"That man was once healthy and vigorous like us. Maybe he was even respected and famous. He probably didn't want to die young. So now he achieved his goal—and that's what it looks like," Pinchas said. "Whatever associations that arouses for you is completely your own business."

"Look." Jarnail mopped the drops of perspiration that had gathered at the edge of his impressive turban. "It is obvious to me, just as is it to you, that man is much more than merely a physical being. And I also accept the argument that it is illogical that the entire purpose of creation was to give a person a body, however perfect it may be, which will survive for a while and then break down and eventually cease to exist. And I'm even willing to go one step further and say that I agree that taking a child and teaching him that there is a soul, and teaching him how to earn eternal life, is a great thing.

"But what can we do if, despite all that, this whole business of forgery really does not appeal to me? I am really sorry, Pinchas, but yes, I want my time with an aide, a wheelchair, and a bib. Indian prisons are no picnic. And with my family background, I am fairly certain I would never get out of one alive."

51

"**I**UNDERSTAND THAT, AND I RESPECT IT," RICKI SAID QUIETLY, cradling the baby in her arms and casting a glance behind her at the bed peeking out from behind the hospital curtain. "Your considerations are completely understandable, and I thank you both for everything you've done until now."

"It's only me," Jarnail said. "Pinchas is not connected to this. He tried, to the best of his ability, to persuade me to pitch in with this project. But I don't want to. It's dangerous."

"I understand," Ricki said again, her right hand stroking the baby's back as she held the infant with her left arm. "Again, thank you for all your help."

Jarnail nodded at her graciousness. "I'm sorry," he said. "I..." For a moment, he was at a loss for words. He shrugged. "I think I'll take Pinchas and go home. The doctors here speak an excellent English. I don't think you'll need an interpreter. In case you do, I am available on my cellphone twenty-four hours a day."

"Thank you," Ricki said again.

Jarnail's lower lip protruded. "I'm afraid you have nothing to thank me for," he said with weighty courtesy. "Forgive me."

Ricki was silent. She continued to stroke the baby's back, her gaze fixed on a hidden point down the hall.

"Is there anything else that I can do for Shaul before I go?" Jarnail asked.

Ricki's hand stopped its motion. "Maybe there is," she said. "I need a phone number where I can reach the people who are coming to meet us tomorrow."

"Excuse me?" Jarnail asked. Then he shook his head. "I don't have it."

"Can you get it?"

Jarnail sighed. In a low, heavy voice, he said, "Yes. But that will be my last connection with this matter. Afterward, I will be forced to resign from your Vaad HaKashrus. There are matters that a person with a rational mind tries to avoid."

"Thank you," Ricki said. "Can you take care of that now?"

Jarnail took a breath. "All right. But after that, you and Shaul will be on your own."

He was trying to get her to give in, Ricki thought. He would do anything to make it impossible for them to succeed. But why? What had happened? At first, he'd seemed eager to help. The Jarnail who loved Shaul and wanted to protect him was apparently stronger than the Jarnail who wanted to work together with him.

Could the problem lie with her? In the fact that she, and not Shaul, had taken over management of the problem?

But the flight from the hospital had weakened Shaul to the point where he could hardly make the simplest decision, and infants at this age grow so quickly and change literally from day to day. A baby of ten days doesn't look exactly as it did on the day it was born. If she wanted to register this child on her and Shaul's passports as their newborn daughter, she must deal with everything that it entailed—yesterday. There was no time to wait until tomorrow.

"I'll be glad to have the number," she said. "Thank you."

Minutes later, the number was in her hand, jotted down in rigid, firm digits as though their writer wished to express his views through them.

All right. From here on in, they would manage on their own. After all, Jarnail was only a messenger. HaKadosh Baruch Hu would send others in his place.

She inhaled deeply. Looking again at the firm, foreboding numbers, she let her breath out very slowly.

She wasn't a phone person and never had been. Shaul never understood why she set aside, until his return home from one of his trips, simple arrangements that could have been handled in a single phone call.

But now...

She glanced at the baby who, for lack of any other space, was sleeping on her knees. Every child, they say, matures us a little more. If this baby could compel her to call the head of the local mafia and conduct a negotiation with him, then she had matured quite a bit over the past twenty-four hours.

With a small, cynical smile that only she herself understood, she punched in the series of numbers and put Shaul's cellphone to her ear.

Her English wasn't perfect. There were gaps in her vocabulary. She sent up a wordless prayer that she would manage despite that.

"This is Shaul Sofer's wife," she said, trying to sound like an efficient secretary. "I understand you have a meeting tomorrow with my husband."

The man at the other end of the line said something that she assumed meant "Yes."

"I understand that the goal of the meeting is to settle a dispute," she added. "But I must tell you that everything that happened the other day has affected my husband's health. Right now he is in the hospital, and his condition is complicated..." Her heart quailed as she said this. She hoped she wasn't creating an opening for bad things to happen. "There's danger of kidney failure. We will want a meaningful gesture on your part in order to close this chapter."

It was a long speech, and she had barely breathed through it, so her final words emerged a bit fragmented.

"What type of meaningful gesture?" The man at the other end was matter-of-fact and emotionless.

"Simply to adjust a few documents that we will fax to you. They need to be updated from last year to the present one."

"How many documents?"

She hesitated. "About twenty pages," she said. "All we need is to have the date changed from 2018 to 2019. And to change the gender from boy to girl. That's all."

"Write down this number."

"Just a minute," she requested. "Apart from that, I also want a discharge letter from the delivery ward, with today's date."

A moment of silence.

"Discharge of a baby boy or a baby girl?"

"A girl."

"That will cost you twenty thousand dollars."

"We think we deserve a more…reasonable price."

"That's the price after the discount."

"We expect to get the documents for free," she said, searching for a ladder she could give the man so he could climb down from the fee he'd quoted. "And I assume that we will be able to view this as the end of the business with my husband's partner, who was mugged and left for dead by your people."

Silence.

The baby stretched on Ricki's lap. Ricki rocked her, afraid lest she start screeching at this delicate moment.

"Write down this fax number," the man said, "and include all the details you need to appear on the documents. It should all be written clearly."

*Thank You, Hashem.* She dared to breathe again. "I'm writing the number," she said. "The material will reach you soon. Will the papers be ready by tomorrow?"

A light laugh reached her ears. Had she pushed too hard?

"We'll bring them with us," the man said. "Wish Mr. Sofer a speedy recovery."

She'd done it. She'd done it! Ricki's heart was bursting with happiness. She had spoken to that frightening man and bent him to her will!

But now…

She also had to speak to her sister.

And tell her…

That she had decided to adopt a baby from India…

As her eleventh child.

And that was one conversation that *really* terrified her.

———————

In Israel, Ricki's sister Minna was in the middle of a particularly rowdy bedtime session. "Talk fast," she begged. "I can hardly hear you in all this commotion."

Fast? Ricki lifted her shoulders until they almost touched her ears. "Okay, here goes: I need you to go over to my house now, get a few papers, and fax them to me."

"Chanshi, bring that to me. No, no, don't touch it! It's dangerous!"

"Listen, Minna, these are classified documents. And I need them urgently."

"What's so urgent?" Minna demanded.

"Mrs. Sofer?" The tag on the gray-haired man who had just entered the room said that he was the physician in charge of the ward. "Minna, I have a doctor's visit right now," she gasped. "Do me a favor and take care of this yourself? I need those papers urgently. They're on the highest shelf in my closet, in the green binder. Write down this number."

"I'm writing, but—"

"No buts," Ricki said. She blurted out the number and then, without waiting for an answer, firmly disconnected the call.

# 52

THE DOCTOR ONLY WANTED TO GIVE HER HIS PERSONAL phone number so that she could contact him if an unexpected problem arose in the middle of the night. She appreciated the gesture and thanked him, assuming that it was linked to Jarnail's family status and perhaps also to the hope of a healthy tip on the side.

"Are there supposed to be unexpected problems?" she asked.

"Unexpected problems are not usually expected," he answered respectfully. "But based on statistics, the night should be a peaceful one. Your husband's condition is excellent."

She studied the sleeping Shaul, who didn't look excellent at all, and then returned her gaze to the doctor. "What about his kidneys?" she asked.

"Ah. The numbers are still a little on the high side, but we expect to see them drop. They will be fine within a day or two. No reason to worry."

Really? She gaped at him in astonishment. The doctor with whom she had spoken that afternoon had sung a completely different tune. He had spoken about dialysis. And this ward physician wasn't worried?

"The doctor we spoke to this afternoon said there might be a need for dialysis," she said.

The doctor twisted his lips. "We are considering a discharge from the hospital, not dialysis," he updated her. "But we are ready for any development. If he needs dialysis, we have an excellent facility

here. But as I said, right now his future looks completely different."
He glanced meaningfully at his watch. "In any case, as I said earlier,
if anything unexpected happens, you are welcome to call me at any
time."

The doctor departed, and her phone rang.

It was Gadi, as full of himself as usual, and perhaps even more so.

"Tell me, are you normal? You think you'll be able to convince anyone that that Indian baby is your own? There is not a chance that she'll
fit into your family."

Ricki shrugged. "It's so good to have a brother who knows everything," she said. "What else do you know, Gadi? I'm listening."

He was silent, and then sighed. "All the girls are in a frenzy," he
said gaily. "Minna called me in hysterics, saying that you're in a hospital in India and asking her to fax you all kinds of documents ... I don't
think it's right of you to scare her like that."

"I didn't say—" Ricki began. Then she got it. "Oh, Gadi! I asked her
for the papers because I really need them here for a procedure. But it's
Shaul who's been admitted."

"Shaul? Admitted to the hospital?"

"He was dehydrated," she said shortly. "He'll be all right. The head
doctor on the ward told me that Shaul will be discharged tomorrow.
All I told Minna was that the doctor had come in, so I had to hang up."

"Then she misunderstood," Gadi said. "She thinks *you're* in the hospital, and you asked for all those medical documents... Your sisters
are saying *Tehillim* for you now, and Ima is in total shock. She says that
*berachah* only comes to things that are hidden from sight, and that we
don't have to talk about everything, and that's just fine with her. But
you should have found time to update her."

"*Oy,*" Ricki groaned.

"Yes, *oy,*" Gadi agreed. "You should have thought before you
spoke."

"What did you tell them?" she asked cautiously.

"I'm a devoted and loyal man," Gadi declared. "I didn't tell them
anything. I just said that I would never have urged you to fly to India
in such a condition."

Ricki was silent.

"Ricki?"

"Gadi," she said, "tell me. Would it be completely wrong for me to
take advantage of their mistake and ask you to tell them that—mazel

tov!—we have a new daughter?"

He snorted in amusement. "Why do *I* get that honor?" he asked.

"Because Shaul is asleep and can't call anyone. And if I talk to them, they'll realize right away that something is off."

"And why did you call me before Ima?"

"You called me, if I'm not mistaken."

"That, at least, is true."

"When you tell them that we have a baby girl," Ricki said, "you can say it with complete honesty."

"A sweet little girl," Gadi said. "She doesn't look like anyone in the family, but sweet, she is."

"She is a bit small," Ricki said, ignoring the barb. "Smaller than all the babies I've had until now. About six pounds, or maybe a little more. And she has the same exact ears as Toby and Shoshi. When we get home, I'll show you a picture."

"And her nose is like mine," Gadi said merrily.

Ricki looked at the baby. "Well, she does have two nostrils. In that respect, her nose is exactly like yours."

"I'll tell them you said so."

"Tell them," she agreed. "And thank you."

He was quiet. "Are you sure about this step you're taking?" he asked at last. "And who will tell your children, forgive me for asking?"

"I'll talk to the children myself. And tell Ima and the girls that we're in a fine hospital, completely Western and very up-to-date. It's a place where Mumbai's millionaires go to receive treatment. Calm them down about that so they won't be nervous for me. Okay?"

"All right," Gadi said. "I can do that. I'm just not sure it's the right step. A lie has no legs. In the end, they'll know everything."

*In the end or in the beginning*, Ricki thought. But after the matter became a fait accompli and no argument or discussion could change it, everything would be a lot simpler and a lot easier.

Besides, right now she would have to supply all the explanations herself, and life had already shown her that she wasn't so adept at explaining things to her sisters. Much better to wait a bit until Shaul could provide the explanations in her place.

Would her mother be insulted?

Her mother, afraid of *ayin hara*, always urged her daughters to conceal every blessing and not talk overmuch. But the present situation was extreme. What, then, to do? Ricki turned the question over in her mind. Until she realized that Gadi, with his perfect manners, wasn't waiting for her any longer. As far as he was concerned, the conversation was long over.

A return call to Israel elicited the information that Gadi was presently engaged in another call. The spread of the news had apparently begun. She must call Rini who, as opposed to Ricki's own generation, was aware that her mother had flown to India in order to adopt a newborn baby girl. She needed to tell Rini to be careful about how she chose her words.

⁓⌒⟨⟨⟨⟨⟩⟩⟩⌒⁓

Talking with her children and hearing their cries of happiness, along with talk of the taffies that would be distributed the next day in school, returned Ricki to the previous year and significantly solidified her decision. Along with that feeling came an overwhelming exhaustion.

"I want to rest a little now," she said. "Good night, my darlings. We'll talk again tomorrow."

After a draining day following a long plane flight and a sleepless night as she tended a baby, less than a week old, who knew how to make her needs known, Ricki allowed herself to switch her phone to silent mode, crank the recliner backward to its lowest position and, settling the baby securely beside her, sink in a good, deep slumber.

When she awoke at nine, Shaul was still sleeping.

At eleven-thirty, when she awoke again with a start and remembered that she had never sent the details the criminal needed to prepare the discharge papers for herself and the baby, Shaul was sitting up in bed.

"There are thirty unanswered calls," he said, seeing that she was awake. "Most of them from my family and yours."

His family! Ricki colored to the tips of her ears. "All kinds of things happened while you were asleep," she said, abashed. "Jarnail decided that he's quitting. I spoke with the man from the crime gang and got his agreement to forge the papers that we need to register the baby on my passport. Then I talked to my sister Minna and asked her to fax me some documents. At just that moment, the ward doctor came in, and I hung up on her. Somehow, out of all that, my whole family thinks that I just had a baby. But I forgot to tell your family. I'm sorry."

Shaul listened to her account, which she related again, more slowly and from the beginning. "I told Gadi not to lie," she said, defending herself from the guilt that she was feeling. "I told him to just say that our family has a new little girl. And that she weighs about six pounds and that her ears look like Toby's and Shoshi's, as I already told you."

"Six pounds?" In the midst of all the excitement, Shaul latched onto one small, factual detail. "Are you sure she weighs so little?"

"It's not so little," Ricki replied in the baby's defense. "Our other children were born big, but six pounds is—what's so funny?"

"'Our other children,'" Shaul quoted. "I...I didn't think this would be so easy for you. You're even more righteous than I thought. It's simply...unbelievable."

53

HAD THERE BEEN ANY SPECIAL RIGHTEOUSNESS IN HER decision to open her heart to this little girl? Ricki looked at the pretty baby slumbering silently in her arms.

"I don't know," she said out loud. "That is, I don't think it's any more righteous than undertaking to raise child number eleven that's your own flesh and blood. There's even a wonderful shortcut here— to receive a baby that HaKadosh Baruch Hu sends you already three days old."

Shaul scratched his beard. "I'm trying to follow your reasoning," he said. "So far, I haven't been so successful."

Ricki tried to explain. "People appreciate the unusual," she said. "It excites them. Having a baby after nineteen years of marriage, or child number nineteen in a family—those are special. But ordinary child number six or eight? Well, okay, mazel tov. Please don't make too much of a fuss."

"People do get excited over extraordinary things," Shaul agreed.

"Right." Ricki shook her head. "But a seventh child or tenth should be just as exciting as a child born after nineteen years. When Tzviki was born no one got too excited about another Sofer *neshamah* entering the world. If what I'm doing now is more unusual, so what? The Torah gives precedence to the usual over the unusual."

"I get your point," Shaul murmured thoughtfully. He glanced at his cellphone. "My father," he said. "Probably calling to wish us mazel tov."

"On the occasion of the addition of a baby girl to our family," Ricki confirmed. "Yes. That's what we'll tell everyone."

Shaul nodded and accepted the call. Ricki was happy for Shaul's father, who was no longer young by any standard, for having the chance to hear his son so cheerful, alert, and enthusiastic. But when the heartfelt conversation was over, the phone vibrated again. Rabbi Refael Schwab was on the other end and wished to speak to him urgently.

"At a quarter to twelve at night!" Ricki's sixth sense urged her to tell him to reject the call. "And you're sick! Do you have to talk to him now?"

"I don't reject calls for no reason." Shaul took a deep breath, put the phone to his ear and said, "*Shalom*, Rabbi Schwab… *Baruch Hashem*, I don't know yet if I can be pronounced completely healthy."

Silence as Rabbi Schwab responded.

"I think most of that took place while I was sleeping. I have only a partial knowledge of all this. What underworld? They bombed Jarnail's car because he sent some guys to get back the things they stole from Pinchas, and the guys took a watch in compensation. None of it had anything to do with me."

Another silence.

"You are using very strong language, Rabbi Schwab, and I don't know if I can accept that. Are you suggesting that I simply leave him with the baby and flee?"

Again Rabbi Schwab spoke.

"Yes, that's true. Indian law permits him to adopt her and not me. But his wife isn't interested, and my wife *is* prepared to undertake the responsibility."

Silence.

"Pinchas's wife was extremely firm in her views. And no, I don't think she'll soften. I'm not interested in trying that approach."

Silence.

"Yes, this was an extraordinary combination of events. But no, I'm not certain that this was what HaKadosh Baruch planned for them. I think He planned for us to honor their choice in this matter."

Unpleasant echoes of an irate baritone voice wafted from the phone. Ricki couldn't make out the words, but the tone made her bite her lip and nervously tap her fingernails on the arm of the chair in which she was sitting.

"Jarnail is a much more complex person than he appears at first glance, Rabbi Schwab. Pinchas already told you that we discovered that Jarnail is the son-in-law of one of the richest men in Mumbai, and that he was not actually a security officer but a—" Silence. "It *is* relevant. Because he tells us what he's comfortable telling us and ignores what makes him uncomfortable. And I think that for all sorts of reasons, he decided now to present you with a picture completely distorted from the reality. Those people—no, I'm not shouting at you, *chas v'shalom*. I'm just trying to speak clearly."

Silence.

"All I'm trying to tell you is—no, I'm not denying reality. Yes, I'm aware that the Vaad HaKashrus can't make it possible for such a thing to happen."

Again, he fell silent. Ricki, following the conversation with trepidation, noticed how Shaul's face lost the healthy color it had gained during his rest and how the tiny lines at the corners of his eyes were deepening and the corners of his mouth hardening behind his mustache.

"Okay, Rabbi Schwab," he said at last, his voice silk wrapped in steel. "I understand. It's totally fine. No, I have nothing else to say. Okay, thank you very much." He swallowed. "Have a nice night."

"What?" Ricki asked, the moment she was sure the call was disconnected.

Shaul shook his head. "Nothing important," he said. "No reason to worry."

"Aha," Ricki agreed. "But what happened?"

"Jarnail sent in a long, detailed letter of resignation," Shaul said, gazing at a spot behind her back. "He explained that he's not prepared to take part in trafficking babies or having documents forged by members of the criminal underworld. Therefore, with great sadness, he is forced to end his working relationship with the Vaad HaKashrus."

"There are other drivers in Mumbai," Ricki said wisely.

"Aha." He imitated her perfectly. "Of course, Rabbi Schwab is under terrible pressure. He isn't prepared to take the risk that the Vaad's good name will be connected to illegal undertakings."

"Hmmm," Ricki said. "And so?"

Shaul placed his cellphone on the nightstand beside his bed. "Nothing important, as I said. *Parnasah* comes from *Shamayim*. The Vaad HaKashrus was just the pipeline. And when I asked you to adopt this baby, I promised that I'd be home more to help."

Ricki stared at him. "You're joking," she said. "You're laughing at me."

"I'll receive compensation," Shaul said. "Severance pay. Whatever the law requires. They're very efficient. You don't need to worry."

"I..." Ricki drew in an audible lungful of air.

"I..." Ricki looked at the baby. "Am I to blame?"

"You've made a huge effort to carry out Hashem's will in a situation that didn't give you a large window of time," Shaul said. "It is a beautiful and special matter." He was quiet for a moment. "And I also don't see any alternative that we could have chosen," he added after some thought. "Like you say—if it were Tzviki, would we have given him up because my boss threatened to fire me?"

Ricki looked mournfully into the baby's face. "Maybe it's a good thing that HaKadosh Baruch Hu sent someone to burst my balloon and make me land on the ground. This is not Tzviki. This is a little non-Jewish baby."

"HaKadosh Baruch Hu turned over the whole world to link her fate with ours," Shaul said gently. "A special *neshamah*, one in billions, who had to be born as a non-Jew in India and grow up in Eretz Yisrael as a Jew. I'm sure that we'll have a lot of *nachas* from her, Ricki."

## 54

THE NEXT MORNING, RICKI OPENED HER EYES WITH SUBDUED spirits and an aching back. She spent about twenty minutes watching Shaul, who stood with his back to her, davening Shacharis. She could find within herself not a trace of a desire to get up.

Babies are exhausting creatures, and the sleep she'd missed on the night flight to India had also taken its toll. And when she remembered that Shaul had been fired in last night's phone call, she sensed the remnants of her positivity evaporating like the last drops of water in a hot skillet.

"It's not fair," she said the minute Shaul finished removing his tefillin. "It's really not right. You've known the man for years, and you've never given him any reason to question you. All the hard work, all the traveling and being away from your family. And this is how it ends? How can he treat you this way? Is that how a rabbi behaves?"

Shaul's lips quivered as he tried not to laugh. "No," he said. "It's the way an efficient administrator behaves. A man of order and organization. A person who memorized a list of thousands of powders and extracts and hundreds of factory addresses. And who runs one of the most complicated logistical networks in the country."

"You need to speak to his superiors," she said. "To the *rabbanim* of the Vaad HaKashrus. How could a place like the Vaad HaKashrus fire a Jew simply for trying to do the right thing?"

"I hear." With measured movements, Shaul replaced his tefillin in their case. "But we have to figure out if that's a wise move, Ricki. Considering that I promised you I'd be home more in the near future to help with the baby, I don't know if there's any reason to pressure the Vaad HaKashrus to give me back my position and send me on jobs from Helsinki to Shanghai. It might be better to graciously accept the compensation they're offering and take advantage of a vacation that's come around at just the right time."

"They still can't fire you like that!" Shaul's serenity was frustrating Ricki. "It's not right! You've worked there for so many years! And you did your job with such exceptional devotion!"

"I understand perfectly why he fired me," Shaul said as he folded his tallis into precise squares, "and why he couldn't say a single positive thing to me during that phone call if he's afraid that he may one day have to recount that conversation in a court of law. Everything is fine, Ricki. You don't have to let it upset you."

"Do you think he recorded the conversation?"

"Obviously. I told you, he's an efficient man."

"And all efficient men record their phone calls?" she asked with feigned innocence.

"All efficient men who run big organizations and who have to make sure that no one will claim they said *A* when they actually said *B*." Shaul zipped up the velvet bag and inserted it into its plastic case. "He is a very cautious man," he remarked, as the door opened and a group of doctors trooped in. "And say what you will, that's a definite asset in his position."

It was a good way to conclude the discussion, and Ricki was prepared to let Shaul's final words echo in the chambers of her mind while she tried to understand what the doctors were saying among themselves. Although she couldn't grasp the details, the general direction was definitely encouraging. Tests had been done. If, as the ward physician had told her last night, there were no surprises, the patient could be discharged as early as today.

"Before noon?" Shaul asked.

The doctors raised their brows at this interruption. "It's still too soon to talk about that," said the youngest among them. And the oldest asked, "Why specifically noon, Mr. Sofer?"

"I have an important business meeting at twelve-thirty," Shaul said calmly. "I'd be happy if I could make it on time."

"It's not always—" the youngest doctor began, but the older one interjected, "If your blood work comes back in order, Mr. Sofer, we will try to accommodate you to the best of our ability."

"A meeting at twelve-thirty?" Ricki asked when the white-coated group had left the room.

"The famous 'apology' conference. Did you forget?"

"And where will I be then? And the baby?"

"The two of you will go shopping in one of the air-conditioned malls around here. First thing we need to do is get a carriage for this little one."

"We have one at home," Ricki reminded him.

"But home is thousands of miles away. Besides, after Tzviki was born, you announced that that was the last time you were using it."

She *had* said that. Still, when Tzviki had graduated to a stroller, she hadn't had the heart to throw away their solid old baby carriage. Thriftiness or nostalgia? Either way, the carriage was resting securely in their storage room.

"In short"—Shaul was unable to follow the train of her thoughts—"buy a good carriage as befits our daughter. And some nice clothes, and gifts for the children back home. And doesn't the mother herself deserve a present?"

"The mother?" For an instant, Ricki thought about the baby's mother, wherever she was, and wondered if she had participated in the decision to abandon her child. Or had she woken up in the morning and found the cradle empty?

"Buy yourself something, too," Shaul clarified. "A small token of appreciation to yourself for all the devotion you demonstrated since you arrived here, and the devotion you're ready to demonstrate from here on in. It's far less than you deserve."

"And who's going to pay for all that?" Ricki didn't know why she was being so cynical. "Gadi's credit card? I'm not sure he shares your appreciation."

"Our own credit card." Shaul smiled. "My boss is an efficient man, as I think I've mentioned. Ten paychecks are going to be deposited in our bank account all at once, at the start of the coming month."

———————

"Something doesn't smell good, Ronit. It doesn't smell good at all."
Ronit took a deep sniff, breathing in the consulate's fragrance of

furniture polish and floor wax. "Everything smells fine to me," she said. "What do you smell?"

The older woman grimaced. "I'm talking about that couple. Something about this story smells fishy to me. She is not that baby's mother, I'm certain of it."

"They have all the paperwork," Ronit said cautiously, peeking through the two-way glass at the not-so-young Orthodox couple sitting there, a baby in a pale-gray carriage between them. "Follow-up from the health clinic, papers from the hospital, a receipt, discharge papers—everything's in order. Where do you see a problem?"

The older woman grimaced again. "I don't see, I smell. Did you look at the color of that baby's skin when you interviewed them?"

"Her father is not exactly pale, Smadar. Besides, think logically for a minute: Why should a couple with ten children come to India to get another one?"

"Financial allotments for the child, maybe?"

"How much is she worth per month?"

The older woman lifted her shoulders. "Honestly? Not much. When I was still getting allotments for my children, I used to say that it didn't cover their needs for even one day."

"See? So what do you want?"

"She doesn't look like a woman who got out of the hospital three hours ago. She told you that they bought the carriage immediately after they left the hospital, right? How did she have the strength to go shopping? With my children, I headed straight home from the hospital. I hardly managed to make it to the elevator."

"*Chareidi* women are strong," Ronit said, throwing a glance at the tranquil couple on the other side of the glass. "Every time I read the newspaper I think about that. How they—women just like me—manage to have such large families and also hold down jobs…So what is it for one of them to go straight from the hospital to buy a carriage? Nothing!"

The elder of the two clerks cast a somewhat hostile look at the Orthodox couple on the other side of the glass. "I don't believe that. We're all human beings, and we're all cut from the same cloth. I'm telling you, something doesn't smell right."

Ronit shrugged. "Smadar, let's move ahead without preconceived notions. They've brought all the necessary documentation, and they want a passport for their new daughter. I don't think you have the authority to put them off."

"If something smells false to me, I can certainly tell them to come back tomorrow," Smadar argued. "What would you say if I told you that in my opinion that baby doesn't look as young as they're making her out to be?"

Ronit grimaced. "I hope you're not going to tell me that little girl is a year old."

Unwillingly, Smadar laughed. "No, not a year old. But she could be more than a week old, not a day or two. I think we'll hold on to their paperwork for further study and tell them to come back tomorrow."

55

THERE ARE PEOPLE WHO LOVE SURPRISES AND THE excitement of firsts. Shaul had something of this tendency. Ricki, on the other hand, preferred the known and the familiar. First-time experiences, even if they weren't inherently fraught with danger, had her fearful of making mistakes and losing control. Ever since they had entered the embassy building, she had been apprehensive of falling into a trap that someone had set for her or slipping on a puddle of water that someone had deliberately spilled for her downfall.

What would happen if everyone turned out to be right and she was the one who was wrong? What if they discovered the whole story any minute now and accused her and Shaul of kidnaping?

Would the embassy leave them in the hands of the Indians? Or would it be possible for them to return to Israel and stand trial there?

And what would happen to the children if both she and Shaul were forced to be away from home for a long period of time?

These thoughts were useless. She rocked the carriage mechanically and tried to remind herself of what she knew very well: There is no power capable of hurting or helping a person. Everything that happens happens because it's the will of HaKadosh Baruch Hu.

At the very moment that she managed to connect to this thought and let it relieve her of her fears, the baby burst into loud wails. Louder than any that Ricki had heard from her since they'd met.

She picked up the baby, still trying to hold on to that strengthening thought and the safe, protected feeling it gave her. But she couldn't do it.

"Okay, okay," she murmured. "Your screams are also *hashgachah pratis*. Wonderful *hashgachah pratis*."

But saying this didn't give her heart the same sense of lightness that she'd felt just a moment earlier.

Shaul lifted his eyes from his *sefer*. "Is she hungry?"

"She ate less than two hours ago. And she doesn't turn her head when you touch her cheek. It's not hunger."

Frustration rose up in Ricki. They were so much in need of heavenly mercy just now. Why was the Creator sending them a distraction at this particular point in time? Didn't they merit compassion and assistance?

---

"There's a newborn baby on the ground floor?" the ambassador, Shuki Alfasi, asked the military attaché seated across from him.

The attaché lifted his head and pricked his ears. "Yes, that's exactly what it sounds like."

The ambassador picked up his desk phone. "Sharon," he said, "what's going on? Did we open a nursery in the embassy?"

He listened for a minute to his secretary's response and then chuckled. "You actually think that I should go downstairs and have a picture taken with them?" He chuckled again. "I thought only the president has to kiss babies as part of the job. Okay, I'll go down there. Bring the camera."

He turned back to the military attaché. "The youngest citizen ever to visit the Israeli Embassy in Mumbai," he explained. "Sharon says I should take a picture with the baby for public relations. Want to come?"

The attaché indulged in a silent laugh. "If only to see you holding a baby, a hardened bachelor like you. Maybe I'll take a picture with her, too..."

"Where are you two going?" The economic adjunct hadn't had much work lately, and the sight of the two men leaving the office laughing aroused his curiosity.

"To take a picture with the youngest Israeli citizen who ever visited this embassy," Alfasi told him. "Her parents brought a two-day-old baby here to get her a passport, and Sharon wants a photograph for public relations."

"I'm coming, too."

∼⧼⧽∼

"Smadar." Sharon was the first to arrive on the ground floor, camera in hand. "Everyone's coming to take a picture with the baby. Quick, issue a passport for her so the ambassador can hold it in his hand while holding the baby in his other one."

"But—"

"No buts," Sharon said firmly. Her weight of two hundred ninety-five pounds and a height that scraped six feet, along with a stinging tongue and thirty-one years of working at the embassy, had turned her into the most feared personality in the building. "They brought all the required papers, yes? And a photo? So go on—issue the passport."

"Smadar thinks there's something underhanded about their story," Ronit said. It was unclear whether she was supporting her colleague or slandering her. "It smells fishy to her."

"How did they let the mother fly in her condition, for example?" Smadar planted her fists on her hips, ready for battle.

"The same way they let *me* travel, without asking me a thing," Sharon said mockingly. "Would you believe it?"

You didn't start up with Sharon. Smadar muttered something under her breath.

"Did you say something?" Sharon asked sweetly, following her into the inner room. "Because I didn't hear you so clearly." She turned to the couple seated there with a broad smile.

"So you are the ones who brought us the youngest citizen ever to need our help! Can I see her? What a sweetheart!"

It was staggering to see the woman with the military bearing melt at the sight of the infant. "Can I hold her a minute?"

A moment later she was cooing and clucking, causing the wailing child to fall abruptly silent. "Ah, she also loves Dodah Sharon, like all the little ones," crowed the intimidating woman. "How adorable! How sweet!" She threw a radiant smile at Ricki. "You don't mind if we let the ambassador take a picture with her?"

The ambassador had just appeared on the threshold.

"Shuki, you have to come here and see this adorable child!"

Ricki glanced at Shaul, who lifted his shoulders and eyebrows as if to say, "What can we do?" Ricki nodded. "Just make sure to support her head. An infant this age can't hold her head up on her own."

"You hear that, Shuki? Support her head carefully. There, behind her neck. Good, good. Smadar, is the passport ready? Great! Come, get in the picture, too. What a great picture! Mr. Ambassador, give the father the passport, please. Nice! No, just a minute. It came out a little blurry. Father, give the passport back to the ambassador for a second. Mr. Ambassador, hand back the passport to the father—but with a smile. Yes! Just like that. Thank you!"

Sharon perused the pictures one more time. "Good," she said. "Now let the ambassador have a picture alone with the baby. And another one with the father. Abba, you hold the baby for a minute." She looked at the photo and nodded to herself. "That's it," she announced in a satisfied tone. "We're done. Apart from the passport, do you need any other kind of help?"

"We're all set." Shaul restored the baby carefully to her carriage. "We'll go to the hotel now and fly back to Israel at the beginning of next week."

"Check to see from what age they let you fly with a newborn," the ambassador cautioned. "Make sure it's all right with the airline."

"I will," Shaul agreed. "Thanks for the advice."

"And if you need anything else—we're here," Sharon said, pulling out her business card. "Have a wonderful day."

After thanking the others politely for their help, they were escorted out to the street by the highest-ranking officials in the embassy. The military attaché helped Shaul carry the carriage down the stairs. He clicked his tongue when he saw that the waiting taxi had no car seat for transporting a baby. "Buy one," he begged the couple. "The drivers here in Mumbai are wild. There are some things you can't skimp on. Planning ahead saves trouble later." And the ambassador held the door for them and made sure that they were securely seated before he gently closed it again.

"Wow," Ricki said after the taxi had pulled away.

"Wow," Shaul agreed. "But the important thing is, we have a passport."

56

"WHAT DO PEOPLE DO ON VACATION?" RICKI ASKED some sixteen hours after they parted from the astonishingly friendly staff of the Israeli Embassy in Mumbai. "We slept, ate, shopped... What now?"

Shaul lifted his eyes from his pocket Gemara. "We can always sleep again and eat again," he suggested. "Or learn a little..."

Ricki pulled aside the green curtain and looked down at the cars winding their way below. "I'm homesick," she said with sudden hoarseness. "Do you think Tzviki will be angry at me when we get back? Do you remember how angry Batya was after my appendix operation when she was about his age?"

Batya had indeed been angry. Despite the number of years that had passed since then, Shaul remembered her childish resentment. How she would turn her head away from Ricki and refuse to look at her.

"Even if he's angry, he'll come around in the end," he said gently. "You bought them presents, right?"

A chime from the dresser cut off her words. "A call from home," Shaul said. "Hello! Who is this?"

He listened for a moment while she strained in vain to catch what was said.

"All right," he said. "Thanks for calling, Rini."

He disconnected and carefully smoothed the hairs of his mustache. "That was Rini," Ricki said encouragingly.

"Yes," he confirmed. "They called from the *cheder*. They know we're busy and so on, but they still asked, if possible, that I call Benny's rebbi now."

Ricki's blood froze.

"What happened this time?" she asked. "What did sweet little Ari do now?"

Shaul bit his lower lip. "Let's not rush to blame anyone. Every coin has two sides. Benny is also not perfect, as we both know. If I put the call on speakerphone, will you be able to keep quiet and not interrupt?"

It was a harsh ultimatum. Ricki sighed. "That's no way to talk to a new mother," she scolded. "But, okay, I'll try very hard. If you'll let me call the rebbi later and talk to him."

"You're the mother. I'm not denying your instincts. I just don't like to talk with two voices."

Ricki looked at him as he searched for the rebbi's cellphone number among his contacts. He suddenly looked his age. Neither of them was young anymore. The past two years of dealing with Benny and his shenanigans had demanded that they make a concerted effort to work on their *middos* and exacted a not inconsiderable emotional toll.

"Hashem will help," she said. "Benny's a good boy, even if he has his challenges and didn't get along with last year's rebbi…"

"Yes," he said. "Sometimes I wonder how much of all this aggravation is caused by my being an absentee father."

A white elephant stood suddenly in the center of the room, waving its trunk and lifting its ears.

"You are not an absentee father," Ricki said, a little too emphatically. "Even when you're not at home, you're always with us. In everything."

Shaul's sigh was almost soundless. "I tried to do the right thing," he said. "But maybe it would have been better to open my own start-up, like Gadi keeps encouraging me to do."

She didn't like the way he sounded. "We'll talk," she said, flapping a hand to chase away the elephant, or at least reduce its dimensions. "Right now we have to call the rebbi, if I'm not mistaken."

"Yes," he agreed, finally pressing the button that would connect him to Benny's teacher, creating a virtual bridge between a four-star hotel in Mumbai and a small faculty room in Yerushalayim.

"Speakerphone," she reminded him in a whisper.

With a nod, Shaul pressed another button, making it possible for her to hear the annoying digital ringtone signaling that the rebbi hadn't yet picked up the call.

But a moment later, when he tried again, the rebbi's slightly hoarse voice filled the hotel room.

"*Shalom*, Rabbi Fink," Shaul said politely. "I received a message from home with a request that I call you."

"Yes, yes, Rabbi Sofer." The teacher's voice, too, was more cordial than he'd expected. "First of all, mazel tov. We heard that you had a baby girl."

"Thank you, thank you," Shaul said distractedly.

"May she grow up to merit marrying a *ben Torah*, a *chuppah*, and good deeds," the rebbi continued. "Much *nachas* from her and from all the children."

"Amen," Shaul said. "Thank you. Did something happen in school this morning?"

"Nothing connected to Benny," the teacher said. "That is, not directly." A cough. "That is…well…to tell the truth, the reason I asked you to call immediately is because I want to apologize."

"Meaning?" Shaul prompted, stepping gingerly on the narrow glass bridge.

"We should have listened to both of you more," the rebbi said. "Especially to the rebbetzin. And I'm sorry that we didn't, and for all the suffering that was caused to Benny recently. We never imagined that a twelve-year-old could be so—how to put it? Devious."

"I don't understand," Shaul admitted.

*ARI*, Ricki wrote on a slip of paper, forgetting their earlier agreement. *THEY FINALLY REALIZE THAT ARI IS PLAYING PRANKS AND SAYING THAT BENNY DID THEM.*

"Benny has always claimed that we accused him unjustly of all sorts of unusual things that happened this year. We didn't believe him," the rebbi said in a pained voice. "For example, the glue on the chairs in the faculty room. It was a failure on our part that we didn't believe him." He breathed deeply. "We knew that Ari Blau was bothering him, but we never for a moment thought it was anything beyond the usual." Another sigh.

"We never imagined that someone was actually incriminating Benny and turning him into a scapegoat for every bad thing. But today there was another incident, very unpleasant. Seemingly, and by the testimony of three boys, Benny was the guilty party. But a janitor, on his own initiative, decided to check the security cameras."

Ricki brought a hand to her mouth, stifling the sob that threatened to burst forth. She couldn't stop the tears.

"And Benny wasn't to blame?" Shaul's voice cracked.

"The boys lied," the rebbi said heavily. "Benny wasn't even in the yard when it happened. He was alone on the roof, just as he claimed." He was silent for a moment. "The boys aren't allowed up on the roof," he added. "But this time, of course, we're going to overlook that."

Benny on the roof. Alone. Ricki needed a tissue. The boy who, until two years ago, was the most popular kid in the class! She had noticed that he never brought home friends anymore. But she'd thought that it was the age, and the long hours of school, and the fact that their home was so crowded and there wasn't enough privacy.

There was no tissue to be found. She hid her face in one of the cloth diapers that she'd purchased for the baby.

She had believed her son when he'd said that Ari was not all right. But *they* hadn't believed him.

"It's possible that Benny was involved in a number of the incidents for which he was blamed, but right now we're almost completely certain that the serious pranks had nothing to do with him." Now it was the rebbi who was walking the fragile glass bridge.

"Apart from the testimony of the security cameras, we don't know anything for sure. Right now, nothing is clear…apart from the fact that the parents of the three boys who were involved in today's incident have been asked to come down to the school and that the instigator will have to find himself a new school."

"I'm afraid I don't completely understand," Shaul said. "What are you trying to say?"

The teacher was silent. Then, clearing his throat, he said, "Well, as things look—and we're still shaken by this whole story—there was a strong negative force in the class that carried out pranks and arranged for the clues to point to Benny as the culprit. And because Benny, as you know, is a boy who tests boundaries all the time, we didn't believe him when he denied culpability and pointed to the true culprits." Another silence. "We did Benny a great injustice," he said. "Unfortunately, I wasn't wise enough to understand it at the time. I will talk to him. But I wanted to update you first."

"Thank you." Shaul's voice was reedy. "I…don't know what to say."

The rebbi murmured something unclear and then said, "We here, all of us, don't know what to say. This is the first time something like this has ever happened in the school since it was founded more than thirty-five years ago.

"Children are resilient," Rabbi Fink said. "And Benny is especially strong. I'm sure that he'll recover from this, Rabbi Sofer. And we here, on our part, will give him all the support possible."

"Hashem will help." Shaul passed a hand over his eyes. "At this stage, as you can understand, I'm very shaken and don't know exactly what to say."

"I've been sitting in the principal's office these past three hours and haven't been able to go back into the classroom," the rebbi said with startling candor. "And I've been teaching for over thirty years."

Ricki looked at the baby of all of six pounds lying in the hotel crib and wondered if the miracle that had happened to Benny today had taken place in her merit.

57

THERE ARE MOMENTS WHEN WORDS FAIL. THE EMOTIONAL turmoil that had overtaken the rebbi, who hadn't been able to walk into his classroom for the past three hours, underlined for Shaul the magnitude of the situation.

Was Benny a strong boy? Shaul didn't agree with the simplicity with which the rebbi had said so. Benny looked brave and tough, that was true. But an ocean could stretch between an outward appearance of strength and the inner reality. Who could have imagined, for instance, that practical, broad-shouldered Jarnail was so fragile that losing his job could plunge him into a depression?

"I don't think it's a good idea to depend on Benny's strength," he said very carefully. "Benny has just lived through two very hard years. On top of the bullying he was dealing with, none of the adults around him gave him the trust he deserved. That could break a grown person. We'll all have to give a great deal of thought and effort to rectify"—he wanted to say "the injustice" but changed his mind—"his trust in the world."

Shaul wasn't sure how the school staff would be able to restore the boy's trust in the system and in his classmates, a trust that had been eroded over the past two years of what he privately considered a gross injustice.

"We'll also have to speak with Benny after you speak to him," he added when there was no response from the other side. "Can we talk to him in about an hour on your cellphone?"

"Of course," the rebbi said. "The school counselor is already here, and he's talking to an educational consultant we sometimes use. I'll call you once we finish talking to Benny and let him speak to you."

"Benny," Shaul clarified.

"That's right. You want to talk to Benny, of course. But it would be very worthwhile to speak to the consultant afterward."

The rebbi sounded a little defeated. "I feel terrible that this happened on my watch," he said. "But apart from being suspicious or unbelievably naïve, I don't know what I need to learn here. This morning they laughed at Benny for 'drawing pictures like a girl' and bringing red paint to school. Could I have guessed that they had stained his sleeve with paint and brought it to my attention so that five hours later—even before anyone said a word—it would be obvious that it was Benny who'd painted the graffiti on the back wall of the building?"

Ricki suddenly felt the need to breathe fresh air. But the air that came in through the window she opened carried the sour-rotten smell of the city and only increased her nausea.

"There's something to be happy about in all of this." Shaul sounded clear and calm. "Although you're limited, as you yourself admit, Hashem sent you another way to discover what you couldn't figure out for yourself."

The rebbi was silent. He cleared his throat to alleviate the choking feeling. "We'll be in touch. When are you returning home, by the way?"

"We'd be thrilled to return right now," Shaul said. "Unfortunately, it will only be at the start of next week."

"Can we change our ticket?" Ricki asked the moment the call was over.

"Mine, maybe," Shaul said. "But not yours. A round-trip ticket with a stay of less than a week is expensive."

"So we can buy a new ticket," Ricki said. "Let it cost what it costs."

Shaul nodded. "I'll see what can be done," he said. "But do you remember what they told us at the embassy? We have to check with the airline and find out from what age they let an infant fly. I'll do that right now."

In actuality, however, he didn't do a thing.

Neither did Ricki.

The silence that filled the room was thick enough to touch.

"I feel sorry for Ari's parents," Shaul said at last, breaking the heavy silence.

Ricki lifted her chin noncommittally. "They were to be pitied until today," she said. "Until now, their son did whatever he wanted and managed to escape punishment each time. Maybe now that they're aware of the reality, they'll manage to teach him how to behave. Then they won't need to be pitied so much."

"I'd like to think that Ari's parents are doing their best. You never know what's going on behind the scenes."

Ricki bit her lip. "When you put it that way, it sounds terrible." She sighed. "As angry as I am at that Ari, I prefer to think that his situation is not all that awful."

"A boy who is capable of—" Shaul began. He didn't finish.

"I just don't want Gadi to hear about this." Ricki opened and closed the zipper of her bag. "He'd enjoy the story too much."

"Gadi is our last worry right now." Unsurprisingly, the mention of his brother-in-law made Shaul a bit impatient.

"Not exactly." Ricki searched in her bag for something good to eat, but all she found was the key ring that the nurse on her flight had given her. "We're not in Israel, and if Benny wants someone to talk to, Gadi may be the one he turns to."

"I'll say a word to Benny." Shaul wasn't overly worried. "He's a smart boy. He'll understand."

"I just don't want him to think that the school's failure was so great that he can't talk about it."

The cellphone on the table erupted into a little dance. Shaul glanced at it and made a face. "Jarnail," he said to Ricki. "I don't have patience for him right now."

<hr />

Shaul looked at the phone without touching it. It was hard for him to disregard the fact that Jarnail had turned his back on them when they were vulnerable. And the fax that he had sent to the Vaad HaKashrus had led directly to Shaul being fired.

"So don't answer," Ricki advised. "Better than picking up and dumping all your frustrations on him."

"I don't think there's any danger of that." Shaul knew how to keep his feelings to himself. "And I don't like to filter callers."

"So answer it," Ricki said. "You can always tell him that you need to get off because your wife needs help."

Shaul picked up the phone. "Yes, Jarnail?" Shaul was polite, if dry. "How are you?"

"All right." In contrast to his manner with Shaul until now, Jarnail's tone was clipped. "I called because my father-in-law wants to talk to you."

"Meaning?"

The Sikh, wherever he was, must have shrugged his massive shoulders. "He was very impressed by your behavior at the apology meeting with the gang members. He likes you. I think he wants to offer you a job."

Since Shaul could think of nothing especially impressive that he'd done or said during the brief meeting with the members of Mumbai's Islamic mafia, he suspected that this job offer was Jarnail's way of apologizing for his being fired. There wasn't much in this very indirect apology to make him feel happy.

"Thanks for thinking of me," he said politely. "But I don't think I'm interested in flitting around continents on a regular basis the way I've been doing until now."

Jarnail gave a short laugh. "Technically, India and Israel are on the same continent," he reminded Shaul. "And it's worth your while to meet my father-in-law. At worst, you can always say no after you hear what he has to say."

"Thanks, Jarnail, but no thanks." Shaul was decided. "I'll be looking for work in Israel. At most an hour's drive from my home. I have no interest in hearing any other suggestions right now—although I certainly appreciate the concern."

"Look." Jarnail's voice grew sharp, tense. "Even the president of the United States found time to meet with my father-in-law when my father-in-law wanted to see him. He's an important man. And he didn't say anything explicit to me about a job. He just said that he wants to meet you. Can't you give him an hour? Are you that busy?"

# 58

JARNAIL'S FATHER-IN-LAW, MR. ISHIR ATTWAL, WAS A SHORT, quiet, smiling man who also—in a strange way—projected power. He certainly harbored no doubt about his worth. No doubt about the esteem with which others held him. And he had complete confidence in his ability to change the lives of those whom he favored.

All this was broadcast instantly and without a word simply by the way he shook Shaul's hand and courteously invited him to sit.

"Jarnail told me that you'd want to drink only bottled water," he said. "They'll bring it here at once."

"Thank you," Shaul said, crossing his ankles beneath the upholstered chair.

"I was favorably impressed with you in our short meeting," the older Indian man said. "But I don't really know much about you. Would you like to tell me a little bit about yourself?"

In job interviews, this question is given great weight and people toil to prepare well-expressed answers to show the prospective employer how suited they are to the available position. But Shaul hadn't come here to be interviewed, nor had he prepared an answer in advance. He found himself slightly at a loss.

"My name is Shaul Sofer," he said. "I'm forty-one, married, and the father of ten—"

"Eleven, I understand." There was a small smile in the other man's voice.

"Eleven. Correct. I still haven't absorbed the new status."

The millionaire in the executive chair behind the big desk nodded his head and let the small smile show itself.

"I'm an Orthodox Jew and I live in Israel—in Jerusalem. For the past nine years I've worked as a kashrus supervisor. That's essentially a kind of logistical inspector who makes sure that the food products in various factories throughout the world are manufactured in accordance with Jewish law."

The Indian nodded again. "And you've spent a great deal of time in India."

"Relatively speaking," Shaul confirmed. "That's how I came to know Jarnail. He is an intelligent person with a special personality, far above average. I admire him and like him very much."

Ishir pressed the tips of his fingers together and said, "He admires and likes you, too. That is essentially why I invited you here today."

He straightened in his big leather chair and leaned forward. "Has Jarnail told you what he's been through these past few years?"

"Only recently," Shaul replied. "And perhaps not everything."

"Jarnail apparently exposed some large-scale corruption taking place at the highest levels of the Israeli and Indian armies," the wealthy man said in a measured voice. "And in doing so, he came under fire by some very powerful and dangerous people. He lost his position on the embassy's diplomatic staff, and certain parties managed—with the aid of libel and bribes—to block his advance in political and government spheres, as he'd hoped for."

Mr. Attwal stopped for a moment and took a deep breath. "I prefer to look at the bright side. The wasps' nest that he stepped on could have led to his death. Had I not been his father-in-law, that might have happened. I thank G-d that he is with us, and I want to see him happy again. Something which, unfortunately, has not happened much in recent years."

He lowered his head to rest his chin on his steepled fingers for a few long seconds of silence.

"The only time I've heard or seen him really happy these past few years has been the time he's spent working with you and your partner here in India. Your companionship has brought him to life, infused him with energy, led him to make plans and to speak with enthusiasm... I don't want it to end. That is why I asked you here today."

He looked directly at Shaul, who looked down and said,

"Unfortunately, it doesn't look like I'll be returning to India anytime soon. I left my place of work—"

The man sitting opposite him waved an impatient hand. "I know that. Jarnail told me. He didn't take the news well. I'd like to find a different way to allow the three of you to work together. It is important."

Shaul was at a loss.

"I don't know if there's a way to do that right now," he said. "I left my previous job, so it looks like—"

"You are a logistical supervisor, correct?" Ishir Attwal leaned forward. "I can create an enterprise for you—a computer software firm, a factory, anything you want. My staff will accompany the founding process and guide the three of you in your joint project until you're standing on your own feet. You will receive a munificent salary and excellent benefits. But the reason behind all of this must, of course, remain a secret." His two forefingers tapped one another. "Jarnail is like a son to me," he said. "It is important to me that he is happy. That he find himself."

From somewhere a picture rose before Shaul's eyes of Jarnail dancing in front of a *sefer Torah*, tzitzis flying. He blinked in an effort to banish the image from his brain. "What, exactly, do you mean by 'finding himself'?" he asked, returning to reality.

"To actualize his talents and abilities," the rich man said. "We all suffered a blow when we understood that he would not be able to continue on the political career path most suited to him. But…how do you say it? The sun does not move backward. There is nothing to be done about that. Now I just want him to be happy. To have a reason to get up in the morning. I want his eyes to shine when he speaks of the future and for him to make plans. I want my daughter to have a husband who serves as head of the home, not a worm that sits on the couch and says, 'Whatever you want is fine with me, dear.'"

Shaul's eyes widened in surprise. "That's not the man I know," he said. "That description sounds very far from reality."

"True. When you two are around, he behaves differently—much more like the person he once was. That is exactly why we are having this conversation."

Shaul had no idea of Jarnail's future plans. No idea whether his interest in Judaism would one day move out of the realm of random curiosity and what his father-in-law would think if that were to happen. And could it even be possible, he thought in sudden surprise, that the real difference in Jarnail's mood didn't come from his and Pinchas's presence as much as the distance it put between himself and his father-in-law?

"You are thinking about something," the rich man said. Not for naught had he achieved what he'd achieved.

"About a few things," Shaul admitted.

"Take your time."

"Actually, I don't have that much to think about," Shaul said. "Your offer is surprising, but I promised my wife that I would stay close to home in the near future."

"The children need a father figure," the older man agreed.

"Yes." Shaul was taken aback by the quick support. "Exactly."

"Jarnail's children need a father figure, too. That is one of the reasons this whole story pains me so much."

The love with which the children had enveloped their father, and the way Jarnail had lifted them into the air, floated through Shaul's mind in a series of images.

"They are wonderful children," he said quietly. "I'd be happy to help—" He was about to add the word "but" when the man in front of him raised an imperious hand to stop him.

"Take this," he said, pulling a leather-bound folder from a drawer in his desk. "It contains four proposals that my experts have prepared. These are the initial proposals—general outlines for a possible partnership between the Indian and Israeli parties. Due to lack of time, none of them has been checked in depth. Think about it, talk to Jarnail, and get back to me."

"I—"

"None of the proposals demands your continuous presence in India. Two of the four enterprises are even based in Israel. Don't say no now, young man. Go home, think about it, weigh the matter, take a look at the salary and conditions I am offering, and we will talk again tomorrow, at this time." He took a business card from a crystal stand dotted with tiny gems. "My personal assistant will be expecting your call," he said. "I do not think you ever in your life have had, or will have, this kind of opportunity."

Shaul looked at the folder without touching it. "It seems to me that you underestimate your son-in-law," he said. "He'll understand immediately what you're trying to achieve here."

The man shrugged. "He knows that I have a good sense about

people and opportunities. If he wants, he can convince himself that I saw you as a person worth cultivating."

"He can convince himself," Shaul repeated.

"Or," Attwal said, "he can decide to look away from the why and focus on the what. I cannot do all the work for him."

# 59

RICKI'S MOTHER AND SISTERS HAD EACH CALLED SEVERAL times in the past two days to ask how she was feeling. Ricki, who couldn't remember such interest in her well-being since the birth of her firstborn daughter, was rather amused. Her amusement dwindled when she began to receive calls from neighbors and friends who had never called to wish her mazel tov after an ordinary birth.

How had they all obtained Shaul's cellphone number? Apparently, it was passing from hand to hand and arousing the conscience of good Jewish women who called, one after another, to express their support and to ask about the quality of the vaccinations given to babies in India, the standard of cleanliness in the hospital, and the number of nurses manning the nursery. She was able to answer some of the questions with ease because of her experience at Shaul's bedside. Others forced her into evasive maneuvers, saying things like "There are all kinds of hospitals in India" or claiming that the baby needed her or that she was tired.

She *was* tired. But how much sleep does a woman need when she's far from home and, instead of caring for ten youngsters, is tending to just one calm baby?

The folder that Shaul brought back from his meeting arrived just in time. Reading in English exhausted Ricki and made her eyes ache, but the material in the leatherbound folder prompted her to turn its pages as the night deepened and the hour grew late.

"This is incredible," she said, flipping to the last page.

No one answered. Shaul, who'd accorded her the respect of going through the material first, had fallen asleep with his head on his open pocket Gemara.

It was late, one-thirty a.m. Her experience on the previous nights had taught her that the baby would be waking soon. Ricki felt a pang. Why had she let herself stay up so late?

On the other hand—what was the hurry? Apart from davening Shacharis and tending to the baby, no special challenges awaited her the next day.

Carefully, she stood up and placed the intricate folder on the hotel table. She lingered for a moment, gazing at the darkness outside and the fragments of light scattered through the city.

She missed her home. It had been years since she'd been so far from her children. Their phone conversations didn't comfort her. Men, she believed, are made differently. Still, it seemed to her that when Shaul used to call home at all hours and try to keep some sort of conversation going—he had felt the same way.

She breathed deeply, trying to chase away the faint depression. The ways of the Creator are hidden from mortal man. Maybe this whole episode, with all its details and permutations, had been necessary in order to enable them to make the change they had never believed would come: to bring Shaul home and allow them to slowly repay all their debts…

There was no question that if one of the proposals that Attwal's people had assembled were put into action, the turnaround in their lives would be well worth the homesickness and the distance.

The baby whimpered. Ricki went to her, lost in thought.

"You need a name," she told the child. "We could have named you Bracha, for the blessing you brought us. But that's my grandmother's name, so it's impossible. And we can't use Batya, even though that's a beautiful name, because that's your older sister's name."

She looked down at the baby, names flitting through her mind. "Maybe Naama?" The baby gazed at her, riveted. Babies can't speak, but they know how to listen. "Naama is a pretty name. I like it. But your father doesn't care for it." She twirled a strand of the fine, soft hair around her finger as she continued speaking her thoughts out loud. "Tamar? She was also a *giyores*, I think. What, you don't like the name? Why are you crying?"

She laid the baby on her shoulder and began circling the room until the cries stopped. "I won't call you Sarah," Ricki decided, sinking into an armchair, "even though it's a lovely name that suits you, because the first person who came up with that idea is a man who, at the moment, I don't like so much. So what's left?"

*The man you don't like so much is about to become a prominent figure in your lives,* said a quiet voice at the edge of her mind. In the silence of the night, the words came through very clearly. *Take that into account when you get excited about the ideas in that folder.*

"All right," she told herself, slightly annoyed. "You don't choose a boss because you think he's a wonderful person. You choose him because he offers a good salary. Shaul gets along with him—that's the important thing. Besides, even I don't think he's a bad person."

*Even though he abandoned Shaul and stood against the two of you just when you needed help? And even though Shaul was fired because of him? You're being blinded by the money, Ricki. Stop for a minute and think straight.*

She stopped, weighed everything that she knew about Jarnail, and tried very, very hard to think straight.

"I don't know him well enough," she said, airing her thoughts out loud. "But Shaul sees him as a kind of friend, and Shaul is a smart person. Besides, there's a chance that he was just trying to look after us. That he didn't want us to plunge into something that could end badly. Most people in the world would have tried to prevent us from taking such big risks for a strange child. As for the firing, I don't think he planned for that to happen. It just…happened."

*And if other things like this happen, after Shaul invests his heart and soul in a partnership? True, he'll be getting a salary. But how would the two of you feel if they were to throw Shaul out after five or seven years of hard work?*

They would feel bad. She knew they would. But five years of economic breathing space wasn't something to sneer at.

*And if it doesn't happen after five years, but after one?*

The exhaustion that had stayed away all evening caught up with her now. She couldn't think anymore. She had no more strength to concentrate. She would summarize what she'd read for Shaul, and let him decide.

"So it's the proposal for exporting agricultural technology and information to India that attracts you?" Shaul was seated with the folder, lines of concentration etched on his forehead. "What are its advantages?"

"First of all, compared to the other ideas in the folder, you bring extra value to this one. Your first years in the kashrus field, especially before *Shemittah*, gave you an understanding of the difficulties that farmers face and a common language with them."

"An understanding only from the kashrus perspective," Shaul pointed out. "That's not enough."

"Okay. But it's a lot more than you know about diamonds or high-tech. Besides..." She was a bit embarrassed. "As opposed to diamonds or high-tech, marketing agricultural technology is an act of *chesed* that can save many people from hunger. And both the diamond industry and high-tech take advantage of cheap labor, the exact opposite of *chesed*... Do you understand what I'm saying?"

Shaul nodded, flipping through the pages in the binder, eyes narrowed in thought.

"I don't know how they did all this research so quickly," Ricki said, "but they did an incredible job. Look at all the information about similar initiatives that were started up in various places in the world. It seems to me that there's an extraordinary potential for profit here— without demanding too much from you. Just to liaison with the various scientists and inventors in Israel, who should be thrilled at the chance to sell their merchandise to India."

She fell silent, and Shaul continued reading. "I'll still need to fly abroad from time to time," he said afterward. "Don't live in a fantasy bubble, Ricki. It's impossible to work in an international business and remain at home three hundred sixty-five days a year. Besides, neither of us has the slightest idea about what could cause these kinds of ideas to fail. The fact that we're impressed by the professionalism of the material means nothing."

"Attwal's people are supposed to be highly experienced." Ricki was still enthusiastic, though Shaul's skepticism was slowly bringing her down to earth.

"Undoubtedly. But they're not out for our benefit, right? We have a mutual interest with Attwal, true. But we have to consider this proposal in a fundamental way and study all the factors ourselves. I'm not the type who makes important decisions without forethought."

"Absolutely not." Ricki's eyes wandered to the crib, and a small smile rose to her lips.

"Right. Absolutely not." Shaul's eyes were smiling, too. He nodded at the baby. "Adopting her was a decision with the most far-reaching consequences I ever made, and I spent thirty-eight years preparing for it—since my first day in *cheder*."

# 60

MENTIONING THE BABY REMINDED RICKI OF THE QUESTION that had troubled her in the night. "She needs a name," she said. "We don't have to wait for an *aliyah* to the Torah, right?"

"All taken care of," Shaul surprised her. "While you rested I took the baby to immerse her in a kosher *mikveh*. I did it in the presence of two other *frum* Israelis I had encountered in the hotel lobby yesterday. This *zeese* baby is now a Jewish child. At the time, I needed to give her a name. Please don't be annoyed with me. There was no time to consult you. So I did what I thought best." He paused.

"Go ahead."

"I thought of Ahuva." He was embarrassed.

"Ahuva? As the antithesis to what she's experienced until now?"

His bewildered look told her how far she was from the truth.

"I meant because she was abandoned by her parents," she hastened to explain.

"*Chas v'shalom.*" Shaul waved a hand. "I thought just the opposite— how loved and wanted this little soul is by HaKadosh Baruch Hu. For her sake, He had Pinchas and me violently chased from the oil factory and brought us to some remote field so that we'd find her and take her from the place where she'd been left and give her, from day one, kosher food and a good upbringing."

This trend of thought surprised Ricki.

"But in that case," she said with a lowered voice, as though the baby was already capable of understanding every word, "if she's so beloved—why didn't HaKadosh Baruch Hu give her to us in Bnei Brak?"

"We can't know the answer to things like that. We never know why a specific *neshamah* is the recipient of a certain mission or challenge. It doesn't matter. We aren't meant to dwell on such questions. What does matter is how HaKadosh Baruch brought everything about so that at the right moment I would be in the right place to adopt her."

"In short, you named her Ahuva," Ricki concluded. After a moment's thought, she said, "That's all right with me. Ahuvi is a sweet nickname. What should we tell the kids? That Uncle Gadi already gave her a name in shul?"

"We'll have to think of how to phrase it," Shaul said. "But that's not a bad idea."

"Call him now," Ricki urged. "And then, before we raise too many hopes, call Jarnail and hear what he has to say."

"I probably should call Pinchas, too, though my instinctive expectation would be that he would call me. I thought he'd be more attentive…" He pressed his lips together, regretting the words as soon as he'd uttered them.

"Maybe he's embarrassed," Ricki said. "Maybe it's not easy for him to think about what you've had to go through because of him… Neither of you imagined that this story would end with your being fired. Now he's feeling guilty and doesn't know what to say."

"Hm? Maybe…" Shaul sounded a little less resentful. "Maybe."

"There couldn't be any other reason," Ricki decided. "Unless his wife suddenly changed her mind and wants the baby, and he's angry at us for taking her."

Shaul smiled. "No chance of that," he said. "And no reason to worry. I'll call him. He's probably in the middle of work and won't answer me now, but at least he'll see that I called."

But Pinchas answered at once. He shared his frustration over an especially complicated issue he'd discovered at the factory and then asked hesitantly, "How is the baby?"

"She's eating nicely and sleeping nicely," Shaul answered, glancing at the crib. "And she has a name—Ahuva."

"May you and your wife raise her to marry a *ben Torah*, to the *chuppah*, and to good deeds," Pinchas said.

"*Amen.* May you, too, celebrate a *simchah* soon." They were both extraordinarily polite.

"*Amen*. Thank you." A short silence. "Are you angry at me?"

"I was afraid that's why you didn't call… No, I'm not angry at you. Everything comes from *Shamayim*. I am completely okay with the decision I made. Don't worry."

"I tried talking to Schwab," Pinchas said unexpectedly. "I even tried to speak to a few other people in the Vaad about giving you back your job. But Schwab is being stubborn—"

"Don't start up with him," Shaul advised. "Keep on calling him Rabbi Schwab like everyone else."

"I won't call someone a rabbi who fires a friend because he took on a huge responsibility that he felt was the right thing to do!" Pinchas was adamant. "Besides, right now it would be good if he'd fire me. In any case, I'm going to resign when I get back home."

"Why?" Shaul asked automatically. Then he regretted asking. It was logical that the good news at home would bring him back. "Did Jarnail's father-in-law speak to you?" he asked.

"Whose father-in-law?" A large car roared by in the background.

"Jarnail's."

"I haven't heard from Jarnail since he resigned. I thought he'd at least finish up this job with me. He sent over some Israeli to take his place. Said something about Jarnail catching a cold." Pinchas had to shout as the background noise increased. "I can hardly hear you. I'll call you later."

"Apparently Jarnail has been out for two days," Shaul said, replacing his cellphone in his shirt pocket. "They say he has a cold, though when I spoke to him last he sounded fine."

"He must have a guilty conscience," Ricki said. "In his case, it's justified."

"All he did was try to protect himself from becoming involved in criminal activity," Shaul explained to her. "He couldn't have known that his actions would result in my being fired." He nodded in support of his own words, and took out his phone. "I'll call him right now."

Jarnail did sound like he had a cold.

"I never thought you could catch a cold in India," Shaul tried to joke. "You sound awful."

"Certainly you can, if you have air conditioning." Jarnail's voice was subdued. "But I don't really have a cold."

"What, then?"

Jarnail's heavy breaths seemed amplified over the phone. "I…feel very bad. I always thought of myself as a good person. And these past years, I thought that the person who exposed me and caused me to lose my job at the embassy was a very bad person. Suddenly, I realized that I did the exact same thing to you. And it broke me. If I don't even have the moral high ground—I have nothing. I feel like a zero."

"Don't talk about yourself that way," Shaul begged. "It's not justified. You may have brought me benefit and not harm."

"Because of my father-in-law?" There was cynicism in Jarnail's tone. "How nice of him to rush in to correct my mistakes, eh?"

"He didn't say anything like that," Shaul said.

Although he knew that his next sentence could frustrate his chances of becoming a bit more well off, he added, "In any case, I promised my wife that if she agrees to adopt the baby, I will stay close to home and help raise her. So your actions led to my receiving a compensation package that will tide us over in the near future."

61

WHEN SHAUL WAS SEVENTEEN, ONE OF HIS YESHIVAH friends fell into a depression. Sadly, he stayed in bed for three months before he was diagnosed, and another three and a half months passed before he agreed to take medication that brought him back to the land of the living. Jarnail's voice reminded Shaul suddenly of those days, leaving him feeling young and helpless.

"You are a nice person, Shaul," Jarnail said, his voice coming slowly. "A good person. It's nice of you to lie for me." The words betrayed a profound exhaustion. "But even if that were the truth, how would that help me? I still made a mistake, and it was a huge one."

"You didn't intend for them to fire me," Shaul pointed out. "Correct?"

"I don't know what I intended. I'm very tired. I think I'll go to sleep now, okay?"

"No, you are not going to sleep now." Shaul filled his voice with the authority he'd once used to budge obstinate workers and conceited factory managers.

Silence.

"There is an enormous difference between someone who does a deliberate act to ruin another person's life, and someone who didn't intend it but mistakenly took the same action."

More silence. Shaul didn't even know if Jarnail was listening.

Then: "What if it *was* deliberate? What if a tiny part of me wanted to see if you would remain faithful to your truth even if no one will back you up?" There was a bit of life in his voice now. Negative energy will inject life, too. At the moment, Jarnail was motivated by the power of self-blame.

"Did you want that?" Shaul asked, countering the question with a question.

Silence.

"Did you?"

Jarnail sighed. "That may have been part of it. Yes. My wife did not believe me that you are really that good. I also thought that maybe you had an agenda, or that maybe another child—after you already have ten—is not such a complicated undertaking."

Shaul laughed lightly. "If you have ten children of your own one day," he said, "you'll see that it's not that way at all. There is no such thing as 'ten children.' There is one child, and another child, and another…ten times. But, yes, I can see how people on the outside might not always understand that." After a moment's silence, he added, "But even if we assume that you wanted to test me, Jarnail, that's still very different from the desire of those who caused you to lose your job and tarnished your name. They wanted to destroy your life, not see the measure of your devotion when tested. It's completely different in every way."

Silence. Silence. Silence.

"Are you there, Jarnail?"

"Yes."

"So what do you think about what I just said?"

Silence.

"Jarnail?"

"That you are a good person. A good and special person. There's no need for you to come work in my father-in-law's businesses. You should be a Rebbe—a Rebbe to many chassidim."

Shaul bit his lip, trying with all his might not to laugh. "Jarnail," he said, "let's be serious…"

"I am serious." Jarnail sounded completely subdued. "You should be a Rebbe, and I should become a trash collector."

Shaul took a deep breath, wondering how to respond to that.

"Listen, Jarnail," he said at last. "A person has to listen to a Rebbe, right? A Rebbe knows what he's talking about."

Silence.

"So, as a Rebbe, I'm telling you that you need to get up from the couch now, or the bed, or wherever you are, and go do a good deed. An act of kindness, without expectation of reward. In that way, you will have an atonement for causing me to be fired."

"An act of kindness without expecting anything back?"

"Yes. Exactly."

"And that will serve as an atonement?"

A shiver of trepidation stole into Shaul's heart. What did he know about the judgments of Heaven? And who was he to promise this non-Jew atonement for what he'd caused?

"I've already forgiven you," he said, "and I'll ask my wife to do the same. But I think that an act like that, stripped of any selfish interests, is a proper way to repent for the self-interest you demonstrated when you tried to put me to the test."

"I shouldn't have done it." Jarnail was filled with guilt.

"True. You shouldn't have done it. But, as I told you, it actually brought about a certain positive outcome, since I was planning to leave my job anyway."

"And don't forget my father-in-law's proposal," Jarnail reminded him.

"Yes. That, too." Shaul was happy to change the subject. "What do you think of it? Have you looked through it?"

"Through what?"

"Your father-in-law's proposal."

"No, I didn't look through it." Jarnail's bad mood was slowly—very slowly—dissipating. So slowly that Shaul wasn't at all sure it was dissipating at all. But Jarnail sounded better now than at the start of their talk.

"I'd like to discuss it with you. Can you get yourself together and call me back in about an hour?"

"I don't know…"

"No excuses, Jarnail. In one hour, you are to be sitting at your desk and having a proper business conversation with me."

"I also have to do the kind deed you mentioned," Jarnail said. "Give me an hour and a half, if you don't mind."

"Fine. An hour and a half, including everything."

"An hour and a half, including everything," Jarnail confirmed. "There are many unfortunate people in the world. It seems reasonable that by then I'll have found someone to help."

"Good." Shaul was satisfied. "Go on, then. I'll be waiting for your call."

He disconnected and stuck the phone into his jacket pocket. "You'll manage with the baby on your own?" he asked Ricki, as though this was his wife's first child. "I want to run over to the embassy and show the folder to the economic attaché there."

"I'll manage with the baby," she said. "But shouldn't you call for an appointment first?"

Shaul shook his head. "People don't like to make same-day appointments. It gives the impression that they're always available. But if I happen to be in the neighborhood…"

He picked up the binder and absently used it to fan himself. "Do you think, in the meantime, you could reach El-Al and find out their policy about flying with infants? I don't want to overburden you, but—"

"I didn't really just give birth, don't forget. I'll be glad to help," she said. "I'll deal with the return tickets. You're in charge of all the rest."

<hr />

Ben Gurion Airport was different from their home in every way. And yet something about the air of Eretz Yisrael filled Ricki's eyes with tears and made her acutely aware of just how homesick she had been. She checked for the fifth time that the presents for the children were in Shaul's large carry-on.

Her cellphone, roused to life upon reentry to the domain of its parent company, surprised them an instant later.

"Ricki?" It was Gadi. "If you're answering, you must have landed already."

"What's the matter?" She was alarmed.

"Nothing that I know of." She pictured him shrugging his shoulders. "I just wanted to let the two of you know that I'm waiting for you outside. Don't miss me at the exit."

"Wow!" She was surprised. "That's so nice of you!"

Right now, according to tried and true tradition with regard to their relationship, he was supposed to say something cutting about people who didn't own a car and didn't allow themselves to take a private taxi, thus forcing good-hearted folks to serve them. He surprised her yet again when he said nothing of the sort.

"I wanted to be the first one to see the little girl," he said. "Besides,

I need to shake Shaul's hand and congratulate him on his new job."

*How he's changed!* Ricki thought in astonishment. And it wasn't only because of Shaul's new job and its added perks. Even before she'd left the country, she'd been able to discern a new note in his voice...

Her heart clenched in silent prayer. Only a year and a half separated them, just eighteen short months. She wanted all the best in the world for her brother. If only, just as so many new chapters were opening up for them, a new page would open up for Gadi as well...

"Shaul!" Gadi, not content with a handshake, gave his brother-in-law a warm hug. "Mazel tov to you! How happy I was to hear the news! Unbelievable, isn't it?"

*Why unbelievable?* Ricki thought indignantly. *Shaul is a talented man!*

"Yes. A miracle." Shaul, in contrast to his wife, was able to take Gadi's words at face value.

"Well, I wish you all the luck in the world!" Gadi thumped Shaul on the shoulder and turned to regard the slumbering princess. "So this is Ahuvi," he said gaily. "Hello there, miss! I'm your uncle. Nice to meet you, my newest little niece."

Ricki, without knowing where it came from, burst suddenly into a torrent of tears.

62

THE TWO MEN STOOD HELPLESS BEFORE RICKI'S STORM OF weeping.

Ricki's tears intensified. "I don't know why I'm crying. It's just ... a new baby ... so much responsibility. I'm not a *tzaddekes*," she sobbed. "I'm not like you..."

"You're better than me!" Shaul protested.

"Not true. You know that's not true."

It was very embarrassing to cry in public, in the middle of the airport, with hundreds of people hurrying by, brisk and focused, all around them. Even more embarrassing with tears coursing down her cheeks and not a single tissue at hand.

"You never mess up like me. You don't have mood swings or ups and downs. But I—"

People were turning their heads to look at her as she sobbed, some of them with concern and others with simple curiosity.

Gadi lifted his shoulders until they nearly reached his ears. He picked up her suitcase. "Come on," he said firmly. "Let's buy you a small bottle of cola and a bar of chocolate. It'll do you good."

"How will that help me? Can chocolate change reality?"

"No, just your perspective," Gadi said. "I mentioned that I have a new friend. A psychologist."

What neither compliments nor promises had been able to do,

curiosity accomplished. Ricki mopped her eyes with her sleeve and said, "You did say something…"

"He loves to talk about perspective." Gadi plucked one of the two big suitcases out of Shaul's hand. "He's this little Frenchman, and very smart. He has a funny parrot that talks on an unbelievably high level. Hey! That could be a great excuse to bring Benny to him. Benny loves animals!"

Benny. A psychologist. A friend of Gadi's. A Frenchman. Ricki cringed the way she often did in her devoted brother's company.

"Maybe," Shaul said. "Maybe that's a good idea."

"Benny will love him," Gadi said enthusiastically.

"Love who?" Shaul asked. "The parrot or the psychologist?"

Ricki couldn't help it. With the tears still wet on her cheeks, she started laughing.

"Both of them." Gadi looked at his sister. "I'm glad you're in a better mood," he said. "Well, how was India? The first time in your life, Ricki! Tell me about your experiences."

"It was…" Ricki tried to cooperate. "Stunning. In the non-slang meaning of the word. It's such a different world that it gives you culture shock."

"And she didn't even see anything," Shaul put in. "She went from a Western-style hospital to a Western-style mall—"

"And dropped in on the way to a poor neighborhood to pick up a baby whose parents abandoned her in a field," Ricki finished with a slight acerbity. "Besides, it's enough of a culture shock to see the hungry children begging at traffic lights."

"There are poor people in America, too," Gadi said. "But over there, people are afraid of them instead of feeling sorry for them. Or else they act as if they don't exist…"

Ahuva, in her carriage, let out a small—and, to Ricki's ears, sweet—squeak.

"Is she hungry?" Shaul asked.

"No. She's just talking." Ricki adjusted the blanket, gazed into the baby's face and sneaked a quick stroke of her cheek, which had fleshed out over the past week.

"You're acting just like a mother!" Gadi exclaimed, genuinely moved.

"Because I really am her mother, even though—" Both Gadi and Shaul sensed the emotional turmoil within her.

"Listen, Gadi," Shaul said urgently. "I heard a *vort* on this week's *parashah* that will interest you very much."

Gadi. *Vort*. On the *parashah*.

This time, Ricki managed to hold back her laughter. Gadi's eagerness to listen to the *vort*, and his efforts to carry on a sensible conversation about it with Shaul afterward, persuaded her to allow them to distract her until Gadi's car came to a stop in front of the building's entrance, where a group of children were crowded in front.

"The baby! The baby's here!" Shoshi, three and a half, was extremely excited. She bounced up and down on her toes. "Our baby Ahuvi is here! My uncle's bringing her in his big car!"

"I-ma! I-ma!" Tzviki warbled. He held out his arms, ignoring the two older sisters who were urging, "Say 'Ahuvi,' Tzviki. Say 'Ahuvi!' Show Ima that you can do it!"

"I want to hold her!" Miri pushed forward, pushing the boys aside. "When Tzviki was born, you told me next time! And now I'm very big!"

"Abba!" Eliezer and Moishy crushed Shaul in an enormous hug. "Ima said you bought us presents!"

"Batya, Rini!" Ricki's heart filled with warmth as she looked at her two big girls. "The children look so happy and are dressed so nicely!"

"I also have lunch ready," Batya said proudly. "Meatballs that are really something. With yellow rice. I know you don't like to eat things that the neighbors send."

"How sweet you all are, my wonderful girls."

She hugged Batya and noticed the caution with which Rini was peeking at the carriage, shoulders hunched with the weight of keeping the secret. She also saw the relief in her daughter's face when she straightened up again and declared, "She's an adorable baby!" She stopped and took a deep breath. "And the carriage is beautiful, too! The kind all the young mothers have…"

"I can't see her!" Shoshi complained, holding on to the handles of the carriage and rising onto her tiptoes. "I can't see the baby, Ima! Pick me up so I can see her!"

"I'll pick you up." Shaul lifted up his most fair-skinned child. "Do you see her now?"

"No! Only her hair."

Heads crowded around the carriage, peering inside and arguing about who the baby slightly resembled and who she resembled the most.

"Benny is still in school?" Ricki asked anxiously. "Why isn't he here?"

"He's upstairs," said Rini.

"Upstairs?" Gadi repeated. Until now, he'd stood aside watching the happy scene with a fond uncle's smile.

"He bought the baby some kind of mobile and is having a hard time putting it together." Rini shrugged. "I told him that he can do it later, but he wants it to work the first time you put her in the crib. So Shalom stayed home with him to help."

Shalom was a good brother. And Benny was very generous. He'd always been that way. Ricki wanted to see him, to look into his eyes and see, with a mother's sixth sense, how her young adolescent had weathered his recent storms and if he really, as he'd sounded on the phone, was feeling upbeat and well.

"Let's take her home," she said. "Sweeties, move a little. Let the baby breathe."

She took the carriage and wheeled it inside the building, her children's chatter enveloping her like a big hug.

"I'm going." Gadi waved a hand behind them.

"You don't want to come upstairs with us?" Shaul turned back, his hands grasping those of Moishy and Eliezer.

"This is your time as a family," Gadi said with an enormous smile. "See you."

It was, indeed, their time as a family. A big, happy family. Ricki allowed the children to lead her through the decorated door into the dining room, where the table was festively set. Silently she thanked the Creator of the world for her ten wonderful children—and also for the eleventh child who, according to Shaul, must certainly have a very significant mission to fulfill in this world.

# PART 2

## ...Eight months later

63

OF ALL THE CHILDREN IN THE HOUSE, BENNY WAS THE one most enamored of Ahuvi—and she returned his love two-fold. At first she would smile only at him. Later, she would play peek-a-boo games only with him, and they would laugh together. Now, at nearly eight months, she was able to express herself unambiguously and to throw herself from any arms that were holding her right into those of her big brother. He bore all her idiosyncrasies with good humor, even when she pinched his nose or lovingly scratched his face.

"You're sweet," he would tell her, lifting her above his head and enjoying the sound of her giggles. "You're cute, you're a good girl, and I'm almost ready to take you on a big trip."

"A trip?" Tzviki preferred his big sisters' more experienced arms, but these magic words touched his independent spirit. "Tzviki go on trip, too!"

Benny debated. The double stroller was massive and complicated, much harder to manage than Ahuvi's carriage. But Tzviki had been his brother even before Ahuvi, and besides, he would appreciate the adventure more than the baby, who was still too young to understand anything.

"Okay," he said. "If you're a good boy and Toby gets you ready fast, I'll take you, too."

"Where to?" voices called from adjoining rooms, putting Benny and his patience to the test.

Benny scowled as he placed Ahuvi in her infant seat. "Nowhere! I'm just going to Francois to feed his parrot—"

"Today is Monday," Toby announced, making a face. "Your appointment is on Wednesday, isn't it?"

Benny hated the word "appointment." And Toby tended to use it often, for some reason, making it hard for him to maintain his thin veneer of denial.

"My appointment is on Wednesday, Miss Nosy," he said, practicing his ability to use humor to turn lemons into lemonade and various other expressions that he couldn't remember at the moment. "But today is not an appointment. Today I'm going to visit the parrot. Because Francois went to some sort of convention, and he doesn't like to leave the parrot alone all day."

Toby wrinkled her nose. "Do Ima and Abba know about this? They let you go to his house by yourself?"

"Imagine that," he said sarcastically. "Besides, if Ahuvi and Tzviki are with me, I won't be alone."

She fell into a long and laden silence.

"I'm coming with you," she said at last. "Is it my fault that I don't need a therapist? I like animals just as much as you do."

"You volunteer at the child-care center," Benny reminded her resentfully. "And you help the kids take care of the pets there! All I do is take care of one parrot. Aren't you ashamed to be so jealous?"

Toby lifted her shoulders. "I bring you a book from the library every week," she reminded him. "And I always believed you when you said that Ari was lying about everything and that it was awful that no one believed you. Don't I deserve to go with you to see the funny parrot one time? Just one single time?"

Others older and stronger than Benny had succumbed to Toby's manipulations. The personal suffering he'd experienced had been transformed, with the help of Dr. Francois Dreyfus, into a powerful desire to be good to others and to help them.

"I didn't ask permission," he mumbled. "If Abba says it's okay…"

But their father was in the United States, engaged in a marathon series of meetings with firms that supported farmers throughout the world, trying to solicit funding for irrigating fields not in India, but in Africa, in areas where residents were suffering from nearly constant hunger.

Benny had seen the pictures in the prospectuses that his mother's sister had designed. Children about his own age, dressed in tricot shirts that looked as if they'd been salvaged from a trash bin and so skinny that their arms looked like long, dark broomsticks sticking out of their short sleeves. He couldn't help but admire his father for finding a way to help them. And yet…it would be nice if his father were home now.

"It's a big *kiddush Hashem* when a Jew helps people like that," his father had told him two days earlier when Benny expressed resentment that he would once again have to study for his monthly Gemara test on his own. "Besides, don't forget that before Ahuvi was born, I was abroad for a much longer time and much more frequently than just twice a year."

This was true. And Benny appreciated the differences that the little duckling in the infant seat had brought into their lives. Right now she was exerting all her charm in an effort to get him to come back and play with her again.

"All right," he said, addressing the baby. But the satisfaction he saw on Toby's face told him that she thought he was agreeing to her plea.

Nuts.

He couldn't refuse her now. Especially since he knew for sure that Francois wouldn't mind.

So let her come, too. He had to be thankful that she made an effort to bring him interesting books from the library…

After a call to their mother, who was presently at a graduation ceremony for the students in one of the courses at her job, to make sure the family outing had her approval, Benny picked up the spare key that the doctor had given him and placed it with youthful pride in his jacket pocket. A bus pass from the drawer. Bottles, diapers, all kinds of paraphernalia that, had Toby not been coming along, would never have occurred to him. A phone call to find out what time the next bus was due at the stop—in two minutes it would be pulling in. And they were on their way, running and panting, pushing the stroller and carriage that they had decided to bring in the end.

"There's the bus!" Toby was hysterical. "The next one's not for half an hour!"

Running wildly, they managed to close the gap and climb gasping through the bus's rear door. They sank onto an empty row of seats with relief, each holding a lively little one in their arms.

"I once thought that psychologists live in all kinds of weird neighborhoods," Toby said when they exited the bus a half-hour later.

"Neighborhoods with tall trees and low houses. This neighborhood looks normal."

"It *is* normal," Benny said, touching his pocket to make sure the key was still there. He wound his way among the buildings with an expertise he had not possessed the first time he'd come here.

Toby hurried after him. "Walk a little slower," she pleaded. "Tzviki's stroller is heavier."

"We're here." Benny turned right and stepped onto a narrow path that circled the building. "He lives on the ground floor. The entrance to his clinic is through a door in the garden."

"Doesn't he have any family?" Toby asked.

"He has three sons who live out of the country," Benny said, unlocking the door. "And also a few grandchildren. But his wife died a short time before Uncle Gadi met him. I once asked him if he wanted to get married again. He said that he wishes people would wait with their suggestions at least until the first year has passed."

"You don't ask those kinds of questions!" Toby was aghast. "It's not polite to talk that way to a grown-up."

"He's different," Benny said, entering the house. "He likes when you talk honestly to him. That's what he always says." Benny pressed the switch and light filled the room. "Paolo?" he called. "Where are you? Benny came to visit you!"

"Wow!" Toby caught her breath. "So that's the parrot you're always talking about! He's gorgeous!"

The parrot *was* gorgeous, with his long red tail, beady black eyes, and dignified step as he emerged from his open cage and hopped from chair to table and from table onto Benny's outstretched arm, rubbing his beak against the boy's finger in greeting.

"Say 'shalom,'" Benny urged.

"Shalom, shalom, how are you?" the parrot squawked. "Nice to meet you. How was your week?"

"Oh, he talks with a French accent!" Toby said, hiding her laughter behind her hand. "Look, Tzviki! Isn't he a nice parrot?"

Three-quarters of an hour passed very pleasantly. Benny treated Paolo to some parrot treats that Francois had provided in advance and enjoyed showing off the bird's unique talents to his excited sister.

It turned out to be a good idea to bring her and the little ones, he thought as they left. But three minutes later, as they stepped into the street which was now totally dark, the direction of his thoughts abruptly changed.

"Who do we have here?" A very familiar figure—too familiar and at the same time not familiar at all—stepped out of the shadows and into the circle of light.

Ari. Wearing very different clothes from those he'd worn when Benny saw him last. His hair was overgrown, and his eyes burned malevolently.

"Here's our brave Benny! And his little brother and sisters! Guys, remember the tattletale who ruined my life? Look, he came to visit and brought along his whole family!"

# 64

ARI BLAU ALWAYS MADE BENNY FEEL SMALL AND WEAK, LIKE the bird in the story that fell into a puddle and had to stay there, cold, wet, and trembling.

But he had grown lately. His father had said so. And so had his mother. Even Francois had said it. He had power. He didn't have to freeze up in fear and lose his tongue when faced with confrontation. He could find inner strength at other times, and he must find it now, draw it out of himself.

But how could he do it here?

Had he been alone, he would have picked up his feet and run. It would have been neither wise nor brave, but at such times—at least in his view—the most efficient solution was the best one.

The problem was that he wasn't alone. Toby was here, and she was a year and a half younger than he was. His job was to protect her. And there were also Tzviki and Ahuvi, whom he must surely protect. Could they run away fast enough while pushing both babies?

Benny's tongue seemed to swell in his mouth, and a sudden cold crept down his arms.

"Look how he's shaking," one of the shaggy-haired boys mocked. "Look at him shaking, Ari!"

Where was the switch? The switch to access inner strength?

Benny's shallow breaths were coming with a real effort. The cold inside him was so great that he felt his knees turning to jelly. Where was the switch that would turn on the inner strength? What would a great, righteous, wise man do now?

*He would take responsibility and let the others run away*, he thought.

It's not like they would do anything really serious to him. At most, they would beat him up—give him a black eye or a broken arm. How bad could it be? In the end, it would pass and be forgotten. And everything would go back to being good again. Something that would not happen if, for example, the carriage overturned because of him and Ahuvi got hurt.

He released the carriage's handle and said slowly, "You know very well, Ari, that it was the janitor who looked at the security cameras because he was upset about having to wash the graffitied walls. It had nothing to do with me."

With each word, he moved a little further away from Ahuvi's carriage. To one side, and forward, toward the very scary boys.

*Please, Hashem, let Toby be smart and use this time to escape. At least with one of the babies. Give her common sense, Hashem. Please.*

"You're a lousy tattletale," Ari said. "They kicked me out of the school because of you!"

"No," Benny said forcefully, continuing his advance. "They kicked you out because of you. Because of the choices you made."

"Bah!" one of Ari's friends said scornfully. "What's he saying?"

Was he far enough from the carriage? Benny was afraid to turn his head to check.

"If you'd regretted it, you wouldn't be talking like this now," he insisted. "You would see that the whole thing was—"

Ouch. He doubled over. The punch to his jaw hurt more than he'd thought it would. It hurt. Hurt a lot! But it was okay. He wasn't a baby. He could deal with a few blows. It would soon be over. Soon be over. He covered his face with his arm. Waiting.

"Mr. Blau?" came a voice from behind him. "This is Benny Sofer's sister. I'm here, near your house, with two babies, and your son is beating up my brother. I wanted—"

Silence fell all around.

"You want to talk to him?" Toby's voice was clear and loud. "I should give him the phone?" She covered the mouthpiece with her hand. "Your father," she said to Ari. "But I can tell him that I got mixed up and it's not you—if you and your friends get out of here right now."

"Let's go," Ari said to his friends. "My father is always mad at me anyway. And I know where you guys live." His eyes bored into Benny, who was still holding his jaw. "If I want, I'll come there tomorrow and beat you up." He turned to his friends. "Come on," he said. "It's not nice to hit him near the babies."

Toby nodded her head. "Mr. Blau?" she said, putting the phone back to her ear. "I think I got mixed up and it's not your son. What? Stay on the line for a minute, I'll go closer and check…"

But she didn't come any closer. She just watched the four hooligans move away and then shut the phone without saying goodbye. Her voice, so clear before, shook badly as she said, "Let's get out of here."

They ran. Hysterically, without paying attention to a bump in the sidewalk, which made Benny fall and bang his nose hard. Ahuvi, nearly eight months old, received a hard bang on the head.

But it didn't matter. Nothing mattered. With blood streaming from his nose, staining his shirt and Ahuvi's clothing, he put the crying baby back in her carriage and kept on running. Fast. Fast. Fast. As fast as he could go, turning his head from time to time to make sure Toby was managing to keep up with him.

"Benny"—she was starting to breathe hard—"where are we going? We need the bus."

Bus? He looked around at the quiet street, filled with flowering foliage. It was completely unfamiliar. "I don't know where the bus stop is." He allowed himself to stop, dab at his bleeding nose, and pop a pacifier into Ahuvi's mouth. "I think we're lost."

The pacifier calmed Ahuvi but Toby, to his shock, burst into tears. "The cellphone isn't charged," she gasped. "What can we do if we're lost?"

"We'll ask somebody," he said automatically. "But…you spoke to Ari's father! How could it be that the phone isn't charged?"

She tried to laugh. "He believed me," she said. "It was funny, right?"

But she wasn't laughing. Instead, she began to cry even harder, hugging Tzviki, who had managed to free himself from his stroller straps.

Funny? Nothing about this situation was funny.

"Let's all calm down," he begged. He heard his father's voice echo in his words. "Toby, in half an hour we'll be home. I'll make sure of that. You don't have to cry."

"It was s-scary," she wept. "So scary…"

*It's still scary*, Benny thought, feeling small and unprotected in the vast darkness, lit only by the streetlamp. "You were smart and brave," he told her out loud. "Look inside. Try to find the strength inside you and be brave again. Help me find the way home. Okay?"

"Strength inside me?"

"That's what Francois says. The idea is to find the place of strength inside yourself and let it shine."

Toby wrinkled her nose. "Psychologists have weird ideas," she said, sounding more like herself. "How does that work? Just a second. Look—a woman's coming out of her house. I'll run over and ask her if she can help."

Two minutes of talk persuaded the elderly woman to fetch the giant wolfhound from her house and escort them to the bus stop. She held tightly to the dog's red leather leash. "We'll stay to watch over you until the bus comes," she said firmly. "Unbelievable what happened to you poor children. When I was young, even street gangs didn't treat babies that way!"

Benny didn't like dogs. Toby was afraid of them. But in their present situation, they both agreed—without exchanging a word—that the dog was preferable to people right now. They stood bravely in the wolfhound's presence at the dark bus stop until the bus came and endured in silence the old woman explaining to the bus driver that "a gang attacked these children" and demanding that he "make sure the babies get home safely."

The driver, surprisingly, took the job seriously—to the point where he didn't allow them to get off at their stop, but halted the bus opposite their building and waited, along with his full complement of passengers, until they had crossed the street and were swallowed up inside.

Only there, catching a glimpse of himself in the mirror, did Benny understand the driver's behavior.

65

IN SHOCK, BENNY STUDIED HIS REFLECTION IN THE MIRROR IN the building's lobby—the red, grotesquely swollen eye and the big scratch he'd received when he fell on the sidewalk, extending from his cheekbone to his collar. Bruises were forming under his eyes and his nose looked swollen. He saw the prominent bloodstains that adorned his face and neck. Then he studied Ahuvi again.

Although he'd held her in his arms all the way home, only now did he notice the red abrasion on her small, smooth forehead and the droplets of blood that had fallen from his nose onto her clothes and the carriage. Only now did he understand why people had been so quick to lend a helping hand.

"What makes you think every person can have special strength?" Toby considered this the right moment to express her views.

"You proved it yourself!" Gingerly, he touched his eye. "Yours is made out of words. You used it to scare off Ari and also when you talked to the old woman. You know how to use words in a way that will help."

"And you?" she asked.

Good question. Francois asked it often, suggesting all kinds of possibilities that didn't completely satisfy Benny. But now, standing in front of the mirror, he suddenly found the answer.

"I know how to bow my head," he told her. "When necessary, that can be a very great strength."

"And when it's not?" she asked.

He chuckled at his reflection in the mirror. "When it's not—it's not. Just like you sometimes have to know how to keep quiet."

Toby opened her mouth to say something and then closed it dramatically. "When you give me permission to speak, let me know," she said behind clenched teeth.

"You can say whatever you want." He lifted his shoulders. "I just meant that any gift has to be used the right way. You have yours, and I have mine."

"I don't like that you're seeing a psychologist," she said in an almost inaudible voice. She threw him a daring look in the mirror. "It gives you all kinds of strange ideas."

Her words pained Benny. "You're acting like a little kid," he said shortly.

"Why? Because I said something you don't want to hear?"

The stroller and carriage were bumping up from stair to stair. "Because you say things without thinking. Do you want me to start talking about your marks in English right now?"

"No." She didn't get the connection.

"So why would you think I'd want to hear you talking about my private business?" He was breathing hard between words, not from anger, but from the effort of lifting the heavy carriage. "And right in the middle of the building!"

"Now you're the one who's yelling," she pointed out.

"And you're being too stubborn to understand," he puffed.

The day's tension had them both in its grip and threatened to plunge them into an awesome quarrel. The kind that would cause their father to spend a great deal of time on a transatlantic call to rebuke and instruct.

Benny realized this first. "Let's not fight," he said, standing the carriage upright on the last landing. "If you want, we can talk it over with Ima later. Now it's important that we walk into the house calmly. We have to explain that in spite of all the blood, nothing happened."

Toby glanced at her wristwatch. "Ima isn't home anyway," she said acidly. "The big ceremony from her work isn't over yet."

"Okay." Benny took a deep breath. "That's even better. By the time she gets home, we'll have time to clean the carriage and put my shirt in the wash." Another breath. "Let's not tell anyone that it was Ari, okay? I don't want everyone to start feeling sorry for me again and think I'm some kind of *nebach*."

"Ima says it's foolish to hide secrets inside," Toby said.

"We won't," said Benny. "We'll just say it was some young hood-lums. Why does she have to know that it was Ari?" He reached for the doorknob. "If you manage to keep quiet this time, just for a change, I'll give you the binoculars that Ima brought me from India when Ahuvi was born."

Toby had been dreaming about those binoculars ever since. She nod-ded her head vigorously. "Okay," she promised. "I won't say a word."

In front of their faces, the door was suddenly flung wide open. "Finally!" Rini cried. "I was getting really worried!" Her eyes nar-rowed. "What happened to you? What's all this blood?"

"We ran," Benny said, "and we tripped, and I got a nosebleed, and it went all over Ahuvi and the carriage. Will Ima be angry?"

"Ahuvi fell?" The girl gasped. "*Oy, vey!* Look at the scrape on her forehead!"

"She fell out of the carriage," Benny said. "It overturned. It was a miracle."

"And then we got lost, and a lady who was about a hundred years old took us, with her dog, to the bus stop and waited with us until the bus came." Toby found it hard to leave out the gory details. "You should have seen that dog, Rini! Gigantic!"

"A dog?" Rini recoiled slightly. "Come in the house. Batya! Come take the babies. I'll clean the carriage."

"I can do it," Benny said, following her into the kitchen.

"You. You're always getting in trouble." Rini loved the carriage, which was new, attractive, and up-to-date. A carriage you could be proud of. Now, she feared, it would start looking secondhand. Although she was generally a patient big sister, this time she was very upset.

"You couldn't be a little more careful before you tipped the baby out of the carriage?" she chastised. "Don't you have eyes to see where you're going? What kind of fool runs with a carriage? Do you realize she could have gotten a concussion? Would you want to be responsible for her having to suffer her whole life because of you?"

Her words were painful for Benny to hear. But he swallowed them, standing small and pale.

"I'll go change my clothes," he said. "I don't want Ima to see that I got my shirt dirty."

It had been a lovely evening. Ricki returned home tired but happy. Filled with a satisfaction that she hadn't felt when sitting in front of a computer from morning to night, writing more and more lines of code. She had never thought of herself as especially sociable, but in this job that Hashem had arranged for her, the direct contact with the students and their dreams, questions, and fears, and even standing in front of a crowd—which at first had frightened her—all of it energized her.

She would return home now, and despite the late hour prepare meat borekas with baked potatoes and a big, green salad for tomorrow's lunch, transfer the laundry to the dryer, and start a new load. Then she would call Shaul to hear how it was going for him over there in the USA and if he had managed to impress the committee the way he'd hoped.

These were ambitious plans, maybe too ambitious considering that the hands of her new watch were inching past midnight. But it wasn't the list of things to do that made her short of breath, but the many stairs leading up to her apartment.

If Shaul's business succeeded, maybe, maybe, they could allow themselves to finally move near the end of the following year. Some place on the ground floor, an extra room, maybe a garden, would make life easier for all of them and allow for a little breathing room.

It was nice to hope, nice to make plans. And nice, too, to feel such satisfaction from her work.

As she stood in her doorway, one hand on the mezuzah and the other grasping her key, Ricki whispered words of thanks for the wonderful period her family was experiencing. She added a quiet prayer that the blessings would continue on into the future.

"Hi!" Rini came out of the living room to greet her. "How was it?"

"You're still awake?" Ricki asked in surprise.

"Too much homework," Rini complained. "And I also washed the dishes, and I had to clean the carriage. That Benny and Toby! They took Ahuvi and Tzviki along to go take care of that dumb parrot."

The term "dumb parrot" was Rini's way of coping with the fact that her brother regularly visited a psychologist's office.

Ricki nodded her understanding. "They asked permission," she said. "And Toby so much wanted to see the parrot just one time…"

"I know." Rini shut her looseleaf binder with a bang. "Not that I understand why she feels the need for a parrot in her life, but that's not important. What I wanted to tell you is that they apparently had some sort of silly race on the way, and Benny fell and got a big nosebleed, and he got Ahuvi and the carriage dirty."

"*Oish.* Apart from that, are they all right?"

"Ahuvi got the worst of it. You should see the scrape she got!"

"Ahuvi?" Ricki's eyes widened. "What, she also fell?"

"I told him. I told him!" Rini flared. "I told him that it could be dangerous. That a baby less than a year old who falls can get a concussion or some other terrible thing. But she's okay, Ima. You don't have to worry. She didn't throw up or anything. She's completely fine. It's just the carriage. As much as I scrubbed, I couldn't get it clean."

Girls and their world. Ricki shook her head. "I'll clean it up. But first I'm going to see how they're doing."

Ahuvi was sleeping peacefully, and the small night-light showed no sign of anything out of the ordinary. Ricki stroked the soft cheek before going to check on her sleeping sons on the enclosed porch.

66

BENNY LIKED GETTING TO PLACES EARLY. INCLUDING DAV-ening in school. He was energetic and independent, and if Ricki didn't wake up in time to wish him a good day, he got himself ready quickly, fixed two slices of bread with some cheese in between, and left the house on tiptoe with a wonderful sense of honoring his parents that always left Ricki feeling drained out. She didn't like this hushed departure, the fact that no one wished the boy a good day and good luck or made sure he took along a fruit or spread something on the bread slices. She would have been happy if Benny, like his older brother, needed her and her blessing in the mornings.

This morning, after the alarm clock once again failed to wake her on time and she finally roused to find that Benny had left the house some time earlier, deepened the hollow feeling and gnawed at her more than on other days.

Yesterday the boy had returned home injured. Apart from his older sister, who had roundly scolded him for dirtying the carriage and then rather offhandedly offered him some iodine, no one had checked to see if his eye was all right. She hadn't had the chance to talk to him about what had happened or to remove from his shoulders the burden of guilt over the fact that, because of him, Ahuvi had fallen out of her carriage.

"You're afraid that he feels guilty, is that it? You would have liked to comfort him?"

Geula, the secretary in charge of registration at the institute, was Ricki's age and had been in her grade at school. Working together had reminded them that they'd liked one another some twenty-odd years before, when they'd entered high school.

"No, I don't think that's the point." Ricki stirred her coffee vigorously. "It's certainly not pleasant for him, but he knows it was an accident and that nothing happened to Ahuvi, *baruch Hashem*... I think what bothers me most is that he doesn't feel the need to talk about it."

"Boys generally don't like to talk about their feelings," Geula said. "I ask my son, 'How are you?' and he says, 'Fine.' I tell him, "Do you want to add any details?' and he says, 'Fine, *baruch Hashem*, thanks.' That's boys for you. Don't you know that by now?"

Ricki chuckled, but the laughter died away too soon. She didn't like to talk about what had happened to Benny before Ari had been asked to leave the school. She didn't think that telling outsiders about it would be constructive for Benny, for them, or for anyone else. To this day, she had never found a reason to tell Geula anything about it. Somehow, without that piece of information—that her son had suffered terribly over a period of two years and hadn't shared much of what he was going through with his parents—it was impossible to understand what bothered her about Benny's mature attitude and his tendency to keep forging ahead without communicating much about the events of his life, let alone his feelings.

"I want to be sure that I'm a part of his life," she said at last, pouring the last drops of milk into her mug but not sipping from it. "After all, things can't always be all right—school is excellent, the food is great, his friends are fine... When a child always gives you one-word answers, don't you sometimes worry that he's hiding something?"

"If it's important to him, he'll talk." Geula was very sure of herself. "Believe me, as a person who grew up with five brothers, when something is bothering them, you hear about it, and plenty loud. I don't think you have any reason to worry."

Ricki smiled politely and tactfully switched the topic of conversation to something work related. She didn't have five brothers. She had one. And no, he had never yelled, even when he walked on coals and they burned the soles of his feet. Sometimes he'd use sarcasm, and sometimes he simply closed in on himself or went on long walks without saying a word to anyone.

Recently she'd been trying hard not to make comparisons between

Gadi and Benny. Even if two people were born with similar character traits, that didn't mean they were the same, did it? There is a great deal of room for family and educational influences, and every child's life is different. But this time she couldn't easily silence the worm of worry.

Maybe boys weren't chatterboxes by nature. And maybe Benny wasn't at all like Gadi and this was nothing more than her motherly imagination that was seeking something to worry about because it was hard to accept that everything was all right. But she returned to her desk even more troubled than before.

How difficult it was to be a new immigrant. Gadi couldn't help pitying Francois Dreyfus, who had already called him four times on the same subject. The first time it was to ask delicately whether Gadi was prepared to be one of ten men willing to come with him to the gravesite of his deceased wife. The second time it was to tell him that he'd found eight other people who'd be happy to come and to arrange the date and time. The third time he'd called to remind Gadi to join the next day, and the fourth was in order to ascertain that Gadi was, indeed, planning to make it to the cemetery on time.

Gadi found the tension a bit exaggerated. Especially in light of the fact that Francois was usually such a tranquil person.

But what wouldn't you do for a friend? You'd even leave the office ten minutes before the time you'd planned to start out, appear in the parking lot of the cemetery on time to meet the other eight strangers, and smile at them politely.

"Good. Everyone's here now, I think." Francois was still tense. "Do you want to introduce yourselves, maybe?"

What was the point of introductions in a cemetery parking lot? Gadi thought it was completely unnecessary. One could certainly recite Kaddish for a strange woman in the company of eight men you'd probably never see again.

"It's a bit warm," one fellow with very blond hair complained. The others did as they'd been told and mumbled their names. The names flew past Gadi's head as he made no attempt to remember them. But one name caused him to straighten up and stare at the speaker sharply.

Dr. Yosef Blau.

Was it possible?

How many religious doctors named Blau lived in Yerushalayim? Not many, apparently. Besides, the guy looked a little like his son, from what Gadi remembered from the single glimpse he'd once had of the boy.

The fact that Francois counted Yosef Blau among the people to whom he was close—the nine chosen ones who'd been invited to his wife's grave—and at the same time was treating Benny, who'd been so grievously hurt by Blau's son, didn't make Gadi happy. Not happy at all.

The whole thing struck him as wrong. Unethical. A conflict of interests.

"I don't see the problem," Francois said on the phone some five hours later. "True, I'm friends with Yosef. He's a fine person. His son caused some trouble and distress for your nephew. But how is that connected to me?"

His ingenuousness infuriated Gadi. "Distress?" he said. "That's all you have to say after you've been treating my nephew for seven and a half months and seen how that boy ruined his life?"

"First of all, your nephew's life is not ruined at all. It's spread before him, filled with wonderful opportunities. It's Yosef's son whose life is a little off course right now," Francois said patiently. "Second— again—why should my relationship with Ari Blau's father in any way influence my work with your nephew? Ari isn't my grandson. He's just the son of one of my friends."

"I understand that that's your opinion," Gadi said coldly. "But I think you should have informed us of that fact at some point."

"Us?" Francois retorted. "What's your connection to all of this? Do you think I have an obligation to report to all of my patients' relatives? Because I haven't heard of any such obligation."

67

GADI NEVER FELT LONELY. WHEREVER HE WENT, HE MET new people, did them a favor or two, offered a few compliments, laughed with them, and instantly won them over. He liked to believe he had friends in every town and city in Israel.

Until he met Francois and realized that the easy acquaintanceships he'd made were very far from the real thing—which he might never actually have known at all.

Because of that, and though he'd never been afraid to express his views to his friends, or held back from demanding justice and truth when it seemed necessary to him—right now he bit his lips angrily and remained cold and mute.

No. He wouldn't let the Blau family hurt him or his family again. He would remain silent and not let this discussion ruin everything.

"Yosef is a wonderful person," Francois continued in his effort to calm Gadi. "If you know how much *siyatta d'Shmaya* he's had with his diagnoses, and how many people owe him their lives, you would think differently of him. I'm sure of that."

*Why*? Gadi wondered. *What connection was there between professional ability and a person's innate value?* Somehow, he wasn't sure how, he managed to say, "I see that you feel that way. All right. Everyone has his own take on things."

"Exactly," Francois agreed cheerfully. "Everyone has his own perspective."

"Right," Gadi choked out over the lump in his throat. "Different people, different perspectives."

"That's what I said. I'm really glad we understand one another so well."

"I'm glad, too. Very glad." The need to swallow his feelings and not express them in any way, not even with sarcasm or by putting a hasty end to the conversation, was very hard for Gadi. So hard that his breathing became shallow and wheezy.

"Very good," Francois said approvingly. "It's important to have mutual understanding between friends."

Gadi clenched his fists until his nails dug into his flesh. Francois was a clinical psychologist. He was supposed to understand people and their feelings. Couldn't he tell that Gadi wasn't being genuine? Was a phone really such a barrier that Francois didn't pick up on the signals?

"In any case, I'll have to let my brother-in-law know that you're a friend of Dr. Blau's," he said. "You don't mind, do you?"

"No." Francois sounded serene. "Not at all. I don't see any problem here or a conflict of interest."

Hearing this, Gadi pressed his lips tightly closed. He didn't feel on solid enough ground to suggest that there might be a conflict of interest in Francois's friendships with both Blau and himself. And he hated himself for it. He ought to say what needed to be said and end the discussion there. But instead of shooting back something sharp and sophisticated, he found himself saying only, "All right. Okay. L'hitra'ot."

---

The worlds of philanthropy and UN subcommittees were unfamiliar to Shaul and Jarnail, but Steve, an American Jew who wore a *kippah*, was a recognized expert in the field that they were cautiously trying to enter. In his enthusiastic opinion, their presentation had made a good impression, the technical data was excellent, and the reactions of the subcommittee members before whom they'd made their pitch was very encouraging.

"You need patience. A lot of patience, at every stage," the consultant explained for the umpteenth time. "There's no chance of getting an answer right away. But it would be worth your while to take a deep breath. If my instincts aren't deceiving me—and they usually don't—within a few weeks you'll have a contract in hand."

"*Baruch Hashem,*" Shaul said, glancing out of the corner of his eye at Jarnail, dressed in a handsome business suit that muted his giant-warrior aspect and brought out the depth of his eyes and his intellectual mien. The change of employment had done him good, no question about that. But Shaul wondered how it had impacted him from a spiritual standpoint. The deep talks they used to have had nearly ceased these past few months. That made him sad.

"The cooperation between you two is something special," Steve went on animatedly. "An Orthodox Jew and an Indian diplomat working together on behalf of the hungry of Africa. You have to admit, it sounds very good... I even have someone, an internationally known journalist whose chosen topic of interest is the war against hunger, who would like to interview you both. An interview with him could jump-start your chances to be granted the contract, and maybe even a few others. Can I set up a meeting? How about this evening at seven in the hotel lobby?"

"Of course," Jarnail said. "Who is the journalist? Maybe I know him."

"Jeremy Forsythe," Steve said.

Jarnail whistled. "Wow. That really is a golden opportunity. We'll have to go over the presentation again, Shaul. He knows his stuff."

"Will there be a place to show it in the lobby?" Shaul asked. "Wouldn't it be better to rent a conference room?"

"You're right," Steve said. "That's a good idea. You two take care of the room, and I'll take care of Jeremy. We'll meet again at seven?"

"*B'ezras Hashem,*" Shaul said.

Steve gave him a smile. "This is important," he said. "Our America has become a bit anti-Semitic lately. It's good for them to see a rabbinical figure like you in a positive light."

One of the warm blessings that Shaul had received from his rav when he'd gone to consult with him and to tell him about the dramatic changes in his life had been that he should continue to make a *kiddush Hashem* both openly and privately. He hoped that this interview—apart from its financial benefits—would prove positive from that angle as well.

He sat with Jarnail for an hour preparing for the interview. Together, they formulated the human anecdotal material to be mentioned in the article. They also reviewed the way they would explain the origins of their friendship in a way that wouldn't embarrass either Jarnail or his family, nor divert the journalist's attention from irrigation to kashrus.

When they were done, Jarnail undertook the responsibility of preparing the conference room that they had rented from the hotel for the upcoming interview. Shaul went to join a minyan for Minchah in a small shul that Steve had found for him, where Jews who worked in the area davened.

At six forty-five, as he stood davening, his cellphone began to vibrate silently in his pocket. By the time he was finished, he found that Steve and Jarnail had called him no less than seven times. They sounded very tense.

"They moved it up," Steve said. "And they're in a rush. Come quickly, okay?"

He hurried. But distances in the city weren't small, traffic was heavy, and he arrived in the conference room at one minute after seven. He was stunned to see video equipment set up and waiting.

He hadn't realized that the word "interview" meant this kind of production. Had he known that, he would have thought seven times before granting his consent, and there was a good chance he wouldn't have agreed to it at all. But it was too late to retreat now, not unless he wanted to invite denigration toward himself and the people he represented in his black suit, white shirt, and long beard.

He took a deep breath, prayed for *siyatta d'Shmaya*, and with his most pleasant smile introduced himself to Mr. Forsythe, a man with a shock of graying hair who shook Shaul's hand affably and asked him to call him Jeremy.

Jeremy was a skilled interviewer. Jarnail had already warned Shaul about that. He made his subjects feel secure and then led them, slowly and in the friendliest way, into the trap he'd laid. But given that both of them believed in their mission and were backed up by data proving that the irrigation system they were peddling really was capable of bringing significant benefit to the agricultural growth of countries suffering from drought, Shaul didn't anticipate any particular trouble.

"I have just one question left," the interviewer said as they prepared to wind things up. "Considering the threats to agriculture in the State of Israel, wouldn't it be more appropriate for you to tend to problems on the home front instead of trying to fix the whole world?"

Threats to agriculture in the State of Israel? Shaul knew nothing about such threats. But he knew that silence and a show of ignorance in front of the cameras wouldn't help his business at all.

"I see that you aren't updated," Forsythe said with a small smile. "In that case—"

"Permit me, Jeremy," Jarnail intervened mildly. "Shaul is a man of vision and action. I, on the other hand, have a great deal of experience in the areas of government and security. As a person well versed in such things, I believe it best for each person to focus on his area of strength. The State of Israel has an outstanding security apparatus, and I'm certain that if such a threat exists, they will succeed in neutralizing it. We will naturally be happy to offer them our services, if and when they ask for it."

"I didn't think of that. I didn't think of that."

Once the interview was over and they parted from the crew, Jarnail permitted himself to vent.

"It never occurred to me that it was because of that whole Iranian story that they were so eager to interview us today."

An Iranian threat? The question marks were piling up to the point of critical mass, and Shaul didn't hesitate to betray his ignorance.

"What's going on?" he asked, suddenly anxious for his family at home. "Can you just tell me what you're talking about instead of dropping all these frightening hints?"

## 68

"OH, IT'S JUST NONSENSE." WITH A WAVE OF HIS HAND, Jarnail dismissed the whole matter. "The *Daily Telegraph* ran a piece this morning about the Biotechnology Research Institute in Khorramshahr, one of the big cities in Iran."

"Well?" Shaul pressed, sensing that Jarnail's nonchalant remarks concealed something.

"There's a quote there from a 'very senior source' that speaks about one of their latest developments—a virus that will attack everything that grows in the Land of Israel, destroying agriculture and even the fruits and vegetables that have already been picked and warehoused."

Shaul raised his brows. "Interesting," he said. "Interesting and strange. If you're already engineering viruses, why engineer a virus that will attack agriculture and not people?"

"I don't really understand these things, but it could certainly be difficult to engineer a virus that can overcome the human immune system. Much easier to make something that will attack plants."

"Maybe," Shaul said, still thoughtful.

"Another possibility is that this was the most successful information Iran managed to steal from a biological lab of a more developed country," Jarnail continued with a smile. "And a third: the information is false, and they just want to sow fear in the Israelis. So they looked for something that wouldn't get the UN on their backs, along with the whole international community."

"That option seems the most likely."

"Speaking as someone who worked in the field—absolutely," Jarnail agreed. "I believe that when a country really wants to fight another country, and it has cutting-edge weaponry, they don't talk about it, and they don't allow the other side to start thinking about ways to defend against it. This is not the age of the Cold War, and the balance of power between Israel and Iran is not such that it would be worthwhile for Iran to expose itself to international sanctions."

This sounded eminently logical to Shaul. "In any case, we can always import vegetables from abroad," he said after a moment. "We do that regularly during *Shemittah*. Apart from higher prices and lower quality, there's no real damage."

"According to the 'senior source,' that wouldn't help this time," Jarnail said. "The virus would attack produce that has already been picked and cause it to rot within hours."

"So we'll import frozen vegetables," Shaul said stubbornly. "Or fresh vegetables vacuum-packed."

Jarnail chuckled. "Too bad I didn't tell you this news earlier. We could have told Forsythe that we're working on an initiative that will solve the problem." He yawned. "I still have a few things to do this evening," he said. "Shall we meet tomorrow?"

Shaul nodded. "I'm going out to Maariv," he said. "There are no minyanim in this area, so I'll be late getting back. If anything urgent happens, I have my cellphone."

"Excellent," Jarnail said, and yawned again. "Pray well, and I'll see you tomorrow."

Shaul watched him go with narrowed eyes. "Jarnail?"

"Yes?" His partner turned around.

"What's so worrying about that story? We've known each other a long time, and there's something in your voice that isn't completely dismissive of it."

Jarnail smiled, a mixture of surprise and embarrassment. "True," he admitted. "You have a discerning ear." He was silent for a moment. "I'm troubled by the Israeli response," he said. "Their tone was too sharp. I would even say that it was a bit aggressive. Normally they would react more or less the way you or I did. But they sound...how shall I put it? Ready for battle."

"So that makes you think that they have inside information about the existence of that virus, that it's not just a trial balloon that Iran sent up."

"Something like that," Jarnail said. "Or Israel is looking for an excuse to attack Iran, so they sent someone to work on the *Daily Telegraph* representative—to sell him a story about an Iranian virus in order to give them a pretext for such an attack." He shrugged. "Throughout the world, in all sorts of dim offices, people are sitting and trying to figure out which of these possibilities is the correct one. But I was fired, if you'll recall, and passed responsibility for the well-being of the world onto other shoulders."

"You can still pray for the world," Shaul reminded him.

"Yes." Jarnail smiled. "I even do that from time to time, believe it or not." His tone didn't invite further discussion, and Shaul didn't want to probe.

"Wonderful," he said. "So I'll go pray now, too."

"And you'll stay a while to learn," Jarnail added, "and you'll come back late. And if I need something, I can call you on your cellphone."

"At least I'm predictable, as opposed to various sinister figures in Iran." Shaul threw a hasty glance at his watch and said, "It's late. I'm out of here."

* * *

It was late. Ricki glanced at her watch. If this traffic jam didn't clear up soon, she'd have to send one of the children to pick up Ahuvi from the daycare center. And even though she was picked up four times each week, Ricki thought it was important for her to show up herself at least once a week. To meet the caregiver, say a good word, and take a look at the environment in which her little girl spent most of her waking hours.

People were talking about a truck that was stuck further up the road. Someone especially pessimistic spoke of an accident with casualties. But just as she was about to call to send one of the kids out to Ahuvi's day care, there was a sudden easing of the traffic. A moment before zero hour, she got off the bus and inhaled the hot air with relief. A brisk two-minute walk, and she was there.

She climbed the stairs to the fourth floor instead of taking the elevator, taking advantage of the chance to burn a few calories. She knocked on the door, readying herself to offer a big smile to the woman who would soon open it.

"Sha-lom!" Varda, who greeted her with her own big smile, was a small, energetic woman who managed, apart from running the play-group, to volunteer regularly for a *kiruv* organization and to sell health products, vitamins, and socks in the storage room that she'd fixed up and painted with her own two hands. "How are you, Ricki? How nice to see you! She's a little tired today, the sweetheart."

"Really?" Ricki was surprised. This morning, Ahuvi had seemed cheerful and full of energy.

"Yes," Varda said. "There was a substitute here this morning because we took my son to *cheder* today for the first time. She said that Ahuvi slept for two hours, and now, after lunch, she cried until I had no choice but to put her down for another nap. I hope she'll sleep tonight... Wait a second. I'll bring her."

While she was gone, Ricki looked at the small, well-kept apartment and was filled as usual with a mixture of admiration and pangs of conscience. Where did Varda get all her strength? To work at two jobs while raising a large family, all while keeping up with the demands of running a playgroup... And, for dessert, she'd decorated the house to mark her little one's *upsherin*!

"Nice, no?" Varda, returning with Ahuvi in her arms, was clearly proud of the decorations. "We're making him a small party tonight. My parents and siblings are all planning to come. We're having a *seu-dah*, and my husband is finishing a *masechta*... It's hard to believe he's three years old already. We've had so many miracles with him. You know about his two close calls with crib death..."

No, Ricki didn't know. Her eyes widened in surprise.

"Miracles, miracles," Varda said. "We all live with miracles. Say goodbye to Varda, Ahuvi? What, you don't want to?"

No, Ahuvi didn't want to. She lay in Ricki's arms, small and tired, as though she hadn't slept for a week. Her eyes closed in exhaustion.

"She's not running a fever," Varda said.

"No." Ricki's lips touched the baby's forehead, confirming that diagnosis. Ahuvi's forehead was dry and cool, though she had just risen from a nap.

"Good," Varda said. "She's allowed to be tired. You'll be more wide awake tomorrow, sweetheart! By the way, Ricki, have you been checking her iron? Sometimes an iron deficiency can cause fatigue and weakness..." She thought a moment, as though debating whether to push the notion more assertively. Then she decided: "We received a shipment of vitamins for children. I have samples to give out to selected customers... Maybe I'll give you a few for her?"

She called out to someone inside the house, and a child brought out a small, decorative cardboard box. "Give her one now, and another one tonight," Varda said encouragingly. "By tomorrow, she'll be good as new."

69

ASICK BABY CAN BE VERY DEMANDING, WAILING AND INSIST-
ing on endless attention. But like a paramedic on the battlefield,
Ricki worried more about those who were silently sick, lying in their
cribs with eyes closed, deeply asleep.

Ahuvi, she noticed, tended toward the second group. And her
motherly heart was afraid that this was a consequence of the hours
she lay alone in a field and experienced the world for the first time as
a cold and hostile place where no one heard her cries. The silence coming from the crib bothered her. It bothered her a lot.

Again and again, she went over to check the little girl's temperature
and other vital statistics. By the book, she should have been reassured.
The baby was sleeping well, her breathing was even, and there was no
change in her body temperature. When she awoke from time to time,
she made eye contact, smiled wearily, reached out a hand for her pacifier, and even offered her cheek for a kiss.

But this exhaustion. It was strange.

"Maybe she's coming down with something," Ricki said, half to
herself and half to her oldest daughter. "Maybe the rash will come out
tomorrow…"

But that evening, when she happened to come across the nicely
packaged box of vitamins and read again the spate of endorsements
from "satisfied customers," she decided to try the mixture. The instructions page said to mix the powder in food or water. An experienced

mother, Ricki had no trouble inserting the mixture into a bit of formula and injecting it directly into Ahuvi's mouth. The results, as Varda had promised, surprised her. Though not in a good way.

The vitamins didn't sit well with Ahuvi. At two a.m., after an exhausted Ricki was forced to wash her off for the third time and change all the bedding in the crib, she decided not to try the powder again. Even more—she would let Varda know the outcome of the treatment.

"Ima?" A sleepy voice came from the boy's room. "Ima, is that you?"

"It's me," she said quickly. "There are no burglars in the house, Benny. Don't worry."

"I didn't think it was a burglar. I just heard somebody throwing up, so I wanted to make sure you were up."

"I'm up." And very tired. "You have good hearing. Go back to sleep now."

"Who threw up?" Benny appeared at the kitchen door.

"Ahuvi," she reported. "This was the third time tonight. She's not feeling so well. Let's hope she feels better tomorrow."

He took a deep breath and straightened up. "Could it be," he asked anxiously, "because she fell out of her carriage?"

The direction of his thoughts surprised her. "She was fine in the morning," she said, forehead wrinkling in thought. "If it was a concussion, I think she would have reacted badly closer to when she fell. It's been more than twenty-four hours between the fall and when she started throwing up."

"Really?" He was still troubled. "Maybe you should call the doctor anyway? I don't want anything bad to happen to her."

"Benny, I really don't think they're connected. She started throwing up only after I gave her some vitamin powder. If it was connected to anything, it was that. Not to the bang on her head."

"Really?" he asked again. His eyes still looked doubtful. "Ima, do you remember Elchanan, who came here once? He fell off his bike and got hurt. For three days he complained, but everyone said he was just spoiled. It was only on the third day that they found out he broke his hand."

"Oy." Ricki thought about Elchanan's mother, whom she hardly knew. "That couldn't have been easy."

Benny made a face. "I can take Ahuvi to the doctor myself tomorrow," he said. "I'm responsible for her falling, so…"

"You're a good boy," Ricki said sincerely. "But I don't think there's any need. Besides, if it does become necessary, a boy your age can't take a baby to the doctor. And just so you know, if there was a fear of concussion, we couldn't wait until tomorrow. I would have to take her to the emergency room right now."

"I can take care of things here," he said quickly. "I'll lock the door, and I'll calm everyone down in the morning. I'll make their sandwiches and take the little ones to preschool."

"I'm not going, tzaddik." She was firm. "But just so you won't worry, I'll call the clinic's hotline and hear what they have to say."

But she was second in line when she called, waiting for twenty long minutes, and then first in line for another long period of time. She fell asleep on the couch, the phone clutched in her hand. And when she woke up, at some indeterminate hour before dawn, she found that the connection had been severed.

Call again?

Ricki considered herself a worrier. An over-the-top worrier, to be accurate. Letting herself be dragged along with Benny's fears last night, when it was clear to her that there was no connection between the two incidents, seemed like a big mistake now.

The vomiting had begun more than twenty-four hours after the fall.

And the fall itself had been from a height of less than a foot.

So where was the reason for worry?

Children could throw up simply because they were teething. Not to mention that they didn't always successfully digest vitamins that their well-meaning caretaker handed out. At four-thirty in the morning, there didn't seem much more to say.

Everything looked all right. Too bad she wouldn't be able to send Ahuvi back to her playgroup today and would be forced to miss a day of work.

"It's definitely not the vitamins," Varda said when Ricki called her later that morning to let her know that Ahuvi would not be coming to playgroup. "And now that you mention it, I remember that her stomach was a little upset these past few days. Maybe she doesn't need vitamins, but something to help her digestion. I'll consult with my supplier. She's very knowledgeable about children's dietary supplements. So you're not bringing her in today, yes? A baby who's been throwing up has to stay home at least twenty-four hours, according to the Ministry of Health."

This wasn't the reaction Ricki had expected, but she accepted it in weary silence. "I still think she threw up because of the vitamins," she said. "Check to see if other mothers have complained about that. It would be a pity if your product got a bad reputation."

Maybe she shouldn't have said that. The moment the words were out of her mouth, she sensed the air between their cellphones grow frosty. The Varda who ended the call with a few pleasant words was completely different from the warm, talkative babysitter Ricki knew.

She had invested so much in the woman over the years, trying to establish friendly relations that would overflow onto Varda's attitude toward the child Ricki was leaving with her. And now to ruin it all because of an exaggerated degree of concern?

Ricki was angry at herself. Perhaps it was because of her exhaustion, or the early hour, but after the anger and frustration came the tears.

Tzviki, that sweet little chick who hadn't yet been taken to *gan*, watched her cry with interest. After a moment's thought, he left the room and returned with a box of tissues in his pudgy hands. He handed it to her with a worried look and then stared at her steadily until she'd taken one and mopped her eyes.

Ricki managed a laugh. "Everything's all right, sweetie," she promised him. "You don't have to worry. I was just in a bad mood. You still don't know what that is, right?"

No, he didn't know. But he did know about *gan* and now that, in his considered opinion, she had recovered sufficiently, he began to demand what he wanted and didn't subside until she gave in. After a few basic preparations, she went out with him and Ahuvi and started walking.

The day was flooded with sunshine, the birds were chirping, and after her son was swallowed up among his friends and she'd started for home, a thought popped into her head: since she was already outside and had come this far, and the clinic was so close by—why not drop in to see the doctor anyway? Just to receive his official assurance that there was no cause for worry.

Why not?

Maybe because she hadn't made an appointment?

According to the receptionist, that was a very good reason, indeed.

But Ricki argued pleasantly with her until she succeeded in persuading her to at least give the doctor her question in writing.

Two minutes later, she had the scrawled answer in her hands to show Benny and anyone else who might be interested. It seemed that there was no reason to worry. If the vomiting and loose stomach continued, and the baby looked unwell or was suffering from other symptoms of dehydration, Ricki should bring her back to the clinic.

70

THE VISIT TO THE CLINIC SOOTHED RICKI'S FEARS. REFLECT-
ing that an upset stomach wasn't considered dangerous, she
allowed herself to enjoy the unexpected day off. A little leisurely sitting
at the breakfast table, a little tidying in bedrooms and closets, cooking
a more elaborate midday meal than usual, and chatting with a friend
on the phone, something she hadn't had a chance to do for months
without curious listening ears nearby.

But she wasn't prepared for the news she received during that
phone conversation.

"What do you mean, 'How am I getting ready for the war'?" she
asked her friend Tehilla, who had always been something of a pessi-
mist. "Has a war broken out that I don't know about?"

As Tehilla related a long story about an engineered virus that would
attack all growth in the land of Israel, including fruits and vegetables
in refrigerators, it was hard for Ricki not to laugh out loud. "I didn't
think you were the type to believe such nonsense," she said. "Doesn't
Iran have any more original ideas?"

"It's actually a very original idea," Tehilla remonstrated. "It's so
original, it's almost unbelievable."

"It sounds like a bluff made up by a bad liar," Ricki said.

"I have a second cousin whose brother-in-law is a senior officer in
military intelligence," she said. "He told them that the article in the

newspaper is true and that the prime minister is taking this threat very seriously."

"Okaaaay," Ricki said. "If the senior officer says so, he must know." A sound from Ahuvi's crib summoned her. "Meanwhile, I have worries that are a little more pressing. My baby is throwing up again."

"Give her rice water," Tehilla said. "You know how to make it, right? Just cook rice in a lot of water—more than you would usually use—and then, when the rice is ready, strain out the rice and pour the leftover water into a bottle and give it to her. They say it saves millions of babies' lives in countries like India."

Was this supposed to be a hint? As had happened numerous times in the past eight months, the word "India" had the power to paralyze Ricki.

"Interesting," she managed to say. "I'll try it. But I thought that rice is less for vomiting and more for other stomach issues."

"We use it for vomiting, too," Tehilla said firmly.

"I'll try it," Ricki repeated. Then she added, "I'm wondering if it's not an allergy. Yesterday I gave her a vitamin supplement—"

"No supplements! Any vitamins you need can be found in fruits and vegetables. That is, as long as there'll be any of those left in the store after this threat from Iran. My advice is to buy large quantities now, cook them, and freeze them. I'm smelling trouble, and my nose has proven itself before."

---

Tehilla wasn't the only one who smelled trouble. In Rini's high school, too, the girls were seeing black. Rini, who belonged to a certain category of oldest children, didn't go directly home but instead to the fruit and vegetable store, where she spent all the cash she had with her—money earned over long, exhausting hours—on twelve big bags of produce, which she had to ask her younger sisters to help her carry home.

"You should have seen the store!" she said breathlessly when she reached the apartment. "The lines were incredible. If I'd gone home first to ask permission, there wouldn't have been anything left to buy." She opened the fridge and pulled out a bottle of cold water. "I had to hold myself back not to scream at someone and fight with her over the last box of plums. Believe me, I held back, but it was simply unbelievable. She *saw* that I just put it down for a minute because my hands were full—and she took it anyway!"

"Good for you." Ricki studied the overflowing produce on her table with disbelieving eyes. "How much did it cost?"

"About three hundred shekels." Rini made a *berachah* and drank down two-thirds of the water at once. "Is that too much? Did I overdo it? There were people there buying much more than me!"

"Maybe they have more children," Shoshi said.

Ricki tried not to laugh. "There's not likely to be too many people in the neighborhood with more than eleven children," she said. "This is a bit expensive, Rini. I would have preferred if you'd consulted with me beforehand. But now, after the fact, I appreciate your caring and sense of responsibility."

"If it's too much, you don't have to pay me back the whole amount," Rini said defensively. "I just thought—"

"You're wonderful," Ricki praised her daughter, still dumbfounded by the quantity of fruits and vegetables heaped on the table. "Just… next time I'd be happy if you'd make a short call to me to talk it over. Okay?"

This wasn't exactly the effusive thanks that the eighteen-year-old had expected. But Ricki felt that she'd given all she could just then.

"If something really happens with this virus, we'll all be very happy that Rini bought all that," Batya declared in support of her sister. "Besides, Ima, you always say it gives you a feeling of abundance when there's plenty of fruits and vegetables in the house. We can use the fruit to make the kind of compote you make on Pesach, and ice cream and cake…"

"They told me in the store that carrots can be frozen," Rini said. "You peel them and freeze them, and later you can take them out and put them directly into whatever you're cooking. Onions can be sauteed and frozen. People were buying bags and bags of them. And garlic—"

"*B'ezras Hashem*," Ricki said, "we'll do all that. It's a good thing I'm off from work today."

"You don't sound enthusiastic."

"No," said Ricki. "I…simply don't think there's a connection between an article in the newspaper and reality. And even if the reality is that Iran has that virus, that doesn't mean they're planning to release it inside our borders tomorrow."

"But will our army attack, the way the prime minister threatened?"

"Will the army *what?*" This piece of information had not yet reached Ricki.

"The prime minister said that the army won't hesitate to attack," Rini said, quoting her friends. "And Iran said that if the State of Israel enters their territory, it will pay a high price. And someone at the UN said that he very much hopes the Middle East isn't poised on the brink of a war."

Ricki's head ached. "I very much hope that your friends don't know what they're talking about," she said, more sharply than she'd intended. "There has been plenty of talk about war since I was born, and 99.9 percent of it came to nothing…except making a profit for the stores."

"I asked my friend who's having a sale in her house to bring us emergency lamps and batteries tomorrow," Rini suddenly remembered. "Should I call her and tell her we don't need them? She said it's an excellent lamp that can run without electricity for up to twenty-four hours. And the batteries stay charged for a long time. She said that instructions from the Home Front Command is that people should have emergency lamps and batteries and that people are going to be stuck without basic equipment if they don't buy it fast."

Ahuvi, throwing up again, spared Ricki the need to answer.

---

"Shaul." Jarnail was troubled. "Tell me something. Do you have savings?"

Shaul raised his brows. "Do you need a loan?"

"No," said Jarnail. "I'm just wondering what your family will say about a trip to India. There's so much to see there."

"And why would my family need to go to India?" The amused tone vanished from Shaul's voice.

"I made a few calls for you because I care about you and that's no secret. It seems that the threats are serious this time. Your prime minister and the Iranian president are broadcasting very concerning messages."

"Because of that virus?"

"Yes," Jarnail said. "I don't want to sound like a doomsayer, but there is a chance that you're on the brink of a serious war. So if you want to make a small trip to India, I'd be glad to help however I can. And if India is too far, my father-in-law has a vacation estate in southern England. I believe he'd agree to let you stay there for a few weeks."

# 71

BENNY LIKED HIS VISITS TO FRANCOIS. HE LIKED THE TEA that the gray-haired man fixed for him, the outspoken parrot, the fragrance of the rosemary bushes that surrounded the house, and the way Francois listened to him, his body leaning slightly forward, his eyes large and attentive.

But today Benny wasn't eager to go. Ricki couldn't understand why. "If you don't want to go, don't go," she said. "This is a gift that your father and I are giving you with love—not a punishment. Call him up and ask to cancel the appointment."

"Me?" Benny's face suddenly looked shrunken, as though the skin had been pulled too tight over his bones.

"You're the one who wants to cancel, right? So what could be more logical than your making the call?"

"I don't like talking to adults on the phone. Could you call, Ima? Please?"

"No." She gave him a brief, tired smile. "This is your business and your responsibility. I'm sorry, Benny. You'll have to deal with it bravely." She turned her back to him, and then turned around again. "Unless you have a good reason that you want to share with me."

"What?" Benny shook his head. "No."

If the countertops hadn't been covered with produce in need of rapid attention, if Ahuvi's vomiting hadn't exhausted her, and if Benny's unwillingness to talk on the phone hadn't reminded her of her own difficulty when it came to dealing with problems over the phone—maybe Ricki would have asked herself exactly why Benny had responded with that no. Had he meant that he didn't have a good reason or that he preferred not to share what was bothering him?

Although she was generally very sensitive to his reactions, this time, with everything going on, his "no" slipped past her radar. And when, an hour later, Benny appeared at the door ready to leave the house—she was happy with her decision.

"*L'hitra'ot*," she said cheerfully. "I think you made the right choice."

"I hope so," he said a little coolly. With a weak "*l'hitra'ot*," he closed the door behind him.

Ricki looked at the door for a moment and then sighed. Some of the children resembled her, and some of them were more like Shaul. She managed to understand all of them without much difficulty, at least most of the time, and could often even anticipate their reactions. But Benny was a mystery to her.

He was so like her, so like Shaul, and so like Gadi. Each time, she saw a different person looking out through his eyes. And she could never be sure who would be peeking out the next time.

---

There was no reason to be afraid that he'd meet Ari and his bushy-haired pals. No reason to be afraid that they always stood on the same corner, waiting just for him. Their encounter had been a coincidence. They hadn't been lying in ambush for him, they hadn't laid a trap, and they certainly couldn't know that he would be coming back two days later at a different hour.

Despite all these logical arguments, Benny felt as if someone had filled the bus's seat with tiny thorns that didn't let him sit comfortably. Even when he stood up, the discomfort remained. The trip seemed longer than it ever had before.

As it turned out, his fears were unfounded. The walk from the bus stop to Francois's house was short and quick, and no scary shadow threatened him on the way. Ari and his friends were nowhere to be seen.

Feeling about twenty years younger than his thirteen years, Benny knocked on the door and hummed to himself until it was opened. "Hi!" he called gaily to Francois, who appeared tired and preoccupied. "How are you?"

*"Baruch Hashem, baruch Hashem."* The man's French accent was more obvious than usual, lending his words a kind of musical quality. "And how are you?"

For some reason, he wasn't sure why, Benny sensed that the question had been offered with less caring than usual. "I'm fine," he said, studying his grown-up friend with alert eyes. "Are you not feeling well?"

"I'm a bit troubled," Francois admitted. "But that shouldn't affect our time together."

"My aunt always says that the words 'should' or 'shouldn't' is a sign of weakness," Benny said, quoting his aunt. "She says that sometimes, when a person tries to do what he should, he's really trying to do what he's not capable of doing."

The psychologist laughed. "Let's check out my capabilities," he said. "If you're not satisfied, we can stop any time you like."

"At least I can take care of the parrot," Benny said.

"Ah, yes!" Francois roused himself. "I didn't thank you for what you did for me when you came to take care of Paolo two days ago. I was so worried about who would take care of him while I was away at the conference, and you saved the day. Paolo is satisfied and happy, the cage is clean, and everything is perfect."

The positivity had returned to the doctor's voice. Benny was glad.

But when they sat down on armchairs near the small round table, and Paolo found himself a place on Benny's arm, the boy noticed that the man's eyes were troubled again.

What could be causing that? Something on the table?

But the table was bare. Only Francois's appointment book lay there.

In the book, Benny knew, Francois kept all the checks he received. Maybe he'd lost some checks? Was that why he was worried? Benny wasn't sure if it was polite to ask.

"So how was your week since the last time we met?" Francois asked.

"My baby sister fell down because of me," Benny said, the emotions beginning to roil inside him.

"Ah," Francois said. "Little Ahuvi?"

"Yes." The word emerged with a sigh. "Everyone thinks she just fell down because I wasn't careful. But that's not what happened."

Francois nodded encouragingly.

"I didn't tell my mother why she really fell," Benny said. "But I didn't actually tell a lie. She just thought she understood, so she didn't ask."

"And you didn't want to tell her."

"No." Benny stroked the parrot's short feathers.

"That happens sometimes," Francois remarked. "People don't want to tell what really happened."

"It's stupid," Benny said angrily. "It's stupid not to tell about things. I hate not telling things!"

"Yes, you told me that," Francois said. "We've spoken about that a few times. You hate not saying things—and still, you often don't say them."

"Because I also hate feeling dumb! And pathetic!" Benny's eyes narrowed. "And I guess I hate feeling that way even more than not saying things."

Francois nodded in understanding. "Oh! I must really be distracted today. I didn't offer you a drink! You are my guest who comes from far away…"

"I'm not thirsty right now." Benny's fingers continued to smooth the bird's feathers with a gentleness that was absent from his words. "I'm frustrated."

"Someone else was here today," Francois said. "A grown man, much older than you. He was frustrated, too. He also got tangled up in lies, and his lie grew bigger and bigger. Now he doesn't know what to do. If he tells the truth, many people will be angry at him and will probably fire him from his job and demand that he pay back a great deal of money. Maybe they'll even put him on trial, and he'll have to go to jail."

"I didn't tell a lie," Benny said, sitting up straighter. "I just didn't explain more than Rini understood on her own. If no one asked me—I didn't have to tell."

"You didn't have to tell?" Francois repeated.

Benny sank back into his armchair. "Do we always have to tell everything?" he asked. "Don't you ever keep anything to yourself?"

It wasn't a rhetorical question, and Francois answered gravely. "There are things that I have to keep to myself," he said. "All the secrets that my clients tell me, for instance."

In Francois's small, tasteful room, in the company of the amusing parrot, it was easy to believe that his mother and father would understand that he wasn't a "magnet for trouble" or "weak and helpless" or in need of "special attention." At home, however, matters were a lot less clear.

Especially since Ahuvi wasn't all right. Not at all.

---

"It wasn't a concussion." Ima was a little impatient when he ventured to raise the topic again. "I already explained that to you twice. It's just an upset stomach."

But Benny had seen babies with upset stomachs before. This was different. Scarier. Stronger.

"She's not smiling," he said. "I want you to take her to the hospital, Ima. I want them to check her. To make sure nothing happened to her. If…if something happens to her because of me…"

"I went to the doctor, Benny." Ricki had never been very good at coping with unreasonable fears. "He said that it doesn't look like a problem to him. He wrote that down for me. His note is in my pocketbook, if you insist on seeing it."

"But…she's different," he insisted. "This is not the Ahuvi that we know at all. I tried for two hours to make her laugh, and she didn't laugh even once!"

"You didn't try to make her laugh for two hours," Ricki corrected him. "Twenty minutes would be more accurate. And she smiled twice. By the way, when you had an earache last winter, you also didn't laugh at anything."

He looked down at his shoes, which had been new not long ago but now looked all scuffed up. "When will she feel better?" he asked, too drained to turn the conversation in the direction it was supposed to go according to his original plan.

"An upset stomach can sometimes take ten days to go away." Ricki mustered her patience again. "But it usually takes less. I believe that by tomorrow, when Abba is due to come home, she'll have stopped throwing up and will feel better."

Although the first part of her prediction came true, and the vomiting stopped the next day, Ahuvi didn't recover. Ricki, growing tired of telling her children that everything was well and under control, found herself becoming very worried.

All the things she told the children were eminently logical. But her motherly heart quailed at the sight of the limp little girl.

Was she getting old? Growing soft? Losing her ability to handle stress? Friends said that this kind of thing happened. That along with age and wisdom came worries and anxieties, along with a lack of confidence unsuited to one's experience and expertise.

She needed Shaul to come home. Soon.

***

"You know much more about babies than I do."

Less than three-quarters of an hour after returning home, Shaul had been summoned to the crib. "Why do you suddenly want my opinion?"

"Look how quietly she's lying there," Ricki said. "Doesn't it worry you? She doesn't even hold out her arms when we take her out of the crib."

"But her arms are all right." Shaul stuck his finger into the baby's fist and was rewarded with a weak response. "She just wants to sleep, no? I don't understand why we're bothering her."

Maybe he was right. Ricki covered Ahuvi with her blanket and stroked her cheek good night.

"An upset stomach isn't always a simple thing," Shaul added afterward. "You're the one who says that we have to be patient with our bodies."

True. But babies recover faster than adults. Ricki bit her lip. Maybe he would go back to the doctor with her tomorrow and get an expert opinion? That's what the clinic was for, right?

But their regular doctor was away for army reserve training. And the substitute knew neither Ricki nor Ahuvi, who was usually filled with life. When Ricki complained that the child was pale, he couldn't conceal a smile. What exactly did the mother mean? Her daughter looked superbly tanned.

"I think you're too worried, Ima," he said dismissively. "The baby isn't dehydrated, and her reflexes are fine. Give her time to recover. We live in the instant-gratification generation, but you can't speed everything up. You just have to be patient."

Patient?

Okay. Ricki didn't think she was lacking in that commodity. She would wait patiently.

***

Patience is a relative term. The two days she spent watching Ahuvi deteriorate further, from a bright, alert child who loved to play and sway back and forth on her hands and knees to a small, weak baby who lay on her stomach and barely lifted her head, broke something inside Ricki.

She was responsible for this baby. She had undertaken to care for her. And somehow, "wait patiently" didn't seem to her the most efficient way of caring.

After a long Shabbos spent contemplating Ahuva's appearance and atypical behavior, Ricki cleared away the remains of Shabbos and searched for a phone number. The usual number for the medical clinic gave her the location of their night clinic. The doctor there, to her annoyance, was the same conceited substitute she'd met during her daytime visit. And his attitude toward the problem was just as superficial this time around.

"The child is not okay," Ricki insisted. "Look how weak she is. She can hardly lift her head. Could this be some kind of aggressive bug, for example, that appeared in her digestive system and has now moved into other areas of her body?"

"If you want a blood count, we'll take a blood count." The doctor's superior smile was insufferable. "But in my opinion, it would be a pity to cause the little girl to go through that pain."

Genuine pity, Ricki thought, would act firmly and decisively right now. But the results of the blood work only increased the doctor's arrogance.

"Your daughter is fine, Ima," he said. "Go home and put her to bed. Give her time to recover. That's all."

Why had she come here alone? Why hadn't she asked Shaul to accompany her, now that he was finally back home? True, she was capable of handling things on her own. She had demonstrated that beautifully during the long years he'd spent abroad. But he had promised to help her personally with this child and to contribute to her care even more than he had with the older ones. She needed him here, gracious but firm as only he knew how to be.

With tears flowing from her eyes, Ricki left the clinic and blindly entered the taxi. She should have been more insistent, more assertive, more threatening. She should have—

"Is everything all right, ma'am?" The white-haired cab driver was concerned.

"Yes." She took a breath. "But my baby doesn't feel well."

"What did they tell you at the clinic?"

"That it's nothing."

"So it's nothing," he soothed her. "They have excellent doctors there."

And he wasn't the only one. Her mother and two of her sisters were of the same opinion when she called them for advice.

"It could be the sense of tension throughout the country in general that's making you afraid," her mother said. "All this talk of engineered viruses and war is not good for anybody. Make her some good herbal tea. And you know what? Reuven's daughter is studying macrobiotics right now. She says that warmed-up lettuce is very, very calming."

Warmed-up lettuce? Ricki's eyebrows went up, but wouldn't express any skepticism in connection with her mother's stepdaughter. And considering all the produce with which Rini had filled the house, she certainly could afford to waste one lettuce.

"I'll try that," she said. "Thank you."

---

Another day passed and then another. Monday night, after putting her children to bed with pursed lips and relative quiet had descended on her home, Ricki took a deep breath.

"I have a birthday coming up next week, right?" she asked Shaul rhetorically. "Well, I've decided what I want for a gift."

He was surprised by her declaration.

"I want an expensive gift," she continued, before he had a chance to speak. "Really expensive. I want a gift that costs over five hundred shekels. I want us to take Ahuvi to the emergency room right now."

Shaul ignored the dramatic introduction. "You know what an emergency room is like," he said. "And you saw the doctor's reaction to your complaint. Do you really want to pay that amount of money to sit for three or four hours and then return home just the way you came?"

Ricki did some more deep breathing. "I actually do think I want that," she said at last. "Why do you care? It's just money. Let's do this so that we'll know we're really doing our best for Ahuvi."

"Money, time, your exhaustion tomorrow..." He fell silent for a moment. "And the insult and the frustration. Do you remember the state you were in when you came back from the clinic? Let's wait another few days. I know there's nothing like a mother's intuition, but you may be worrying for nothing."

A mother's intuition. Ricki bit her lower lip and shook her head. She loved Ahuvi and cared about her, but she wasn't at all sure she had any of that in this case.

Would it be this way all her life? Would she find it hard to set boundaries for an adolescent Ahuvi as naturally as she'd done for the other girls in the family? Would she always be afraid that she might be treating her differently? And what about when the time came to find her a husband?

These were distant worries, true. But they managed to quiet some of her present ones.

All right. She would continue to wait patiently, the way everyone wanted her to.

W EDNESDAY WAS A PACKED DAY. IT STARTED WITH A LONG
and fatiguing staff meeting at work, continued with OT therapy for Shoshi, her four-year-old, then passing through the neighborhood supermarket and trying to empty the laundry baskets before
the great and terrible Thursday arrived, and ended with welcoming
Benny home from his weekly session with the therapist when, as happened frequently, her son wanted to share some of his thoughts and
experiences with her.

It wasn't a day for a maternal crisis. It really wasn't. But at six forty-
five on Wednesday evening, as she got Ahuvi ready for bed, Ricki felt
one coming on.

She asked no one. She consulted with nobody. She didn't care how
much the ER would cost. She simply took a sweet pink outfit out of
the drawer instead of the pale-blue pajamas that had once belonged to
Tzviki, and prepared Ahuvi for an outing. She packed a few necessaries in the diaper bag for the baby and put in a *Tehillim* for herself.

Then she called the nearest taxi service and ordered a cab. Only
then, with the baby in her arms, did she leave the room and inform her
older children of the drastic change in plans.

They should be nice to Benny when he came home. They should fix
Abba a plate when *he* came home.

"I need to go now."

"Where to?" Batya asked.

"I want another doctor to take a look at Ahuvi." She deliberately avoided more ominous wording. "There's something about her weakness that doesn't make sense to me."

"But there are no doctors at the clinic now!" Batya protested. "Are you going back to the night clinic?"

"No. My taxi will be here any minute, sweetie. I need to run. I have my cellphone with me. We'll talk later."

"Ooookay." Batya wasn't happy. "Fine." She followed her mother to the door. "But tell Moishy and Toby to help me! I can't take care of everything myself!"

"There's ice cream in the freezer, behind the ground meat," Ricki said. "When everyone's in bed, take one for yourself, okay, sweetie? I have to go now."

Downstairs, near the mailboxes, she met Shaul, who looked surprised to see her. "Where to?" he asked.

"The emergency room," she said. "There's food for you at home. I'll keep you posted."

His brows came together. "Meaning?"

"You think that I don't have to take her, and I think that I do. So I'm wasting my time as I see fit and allowing you to use your time as you see fit," she said a little too briskly.

"I'll eat something and come with you."

"My taxi is on its way. I can't wait for you."

"So I'll just run upstairs and get an apple—"

"No need. This is probably just me worrying too much. I'll go alone. It would be a pity to waste your time." A car stopped in front of the building. "That's the taxi," she said.

"Tell him to wait a minute. I'll just get an apple." Shaul shook his head. "Did something happen? Was something different today that made you feel you have to run out right now?"

"Nothing," she said. "But this has been going on too long. It's not normal. And I'm worried. Period."

He tipped his hat back. "Okay," he said. "I respect that. You're the mother."

"I'll keep you posted." She started for the car.

"No," he said. "Wait. Tell the driver to start the meter and wait for me. I'll be right there."

"No," she said stubbornly. "I've been at the pediatrician, and I've been at the night clinic, and both of them sent me home. I don't want you to waste your time. Besides, you haven't even eaten supper yet, and you have a *chavrusa* afterward. If they decide to admit her, I'll let you know."

"Are you sure?" He hesitated.

"Yes. Absolutely. Don't worry. We both know what an ER is like. Just sitting around and wasting time."

The taxi honked impatiently.

"I'm going," she said, wheeling the stroller onto the sidewalk. "Have an easy night."

"You, too," he said. He walked toward the stairs and climbed up to the second floor. Then he retraced his steps and ran out into the warm night. "Ricki!"

But she wasn't there anymore.

---

"Why hasn't anyone seen to the child in bed 14?" the ER doctor bellowed at the nurses who stood gossiping near the medications room. "I told you half an hour ago that she's dehydrated and needs a saline drip and a blood culture!" Thinking about the cafeteria, due to close soon, he asked the charge nurse, "What's new since then? Anything special?"

"One strange story," she said. "A baby, eight months old, with extreme muscle weakness and signs of trauma in her legs and forehead. The mother says that she fell out of her carriage a few weeks ago, but it seems a little suspicious to me. She also has another sign on her hand—looks like a bite…"

"Hmm," the doctor said.

"The mother says that she didn't notice it before. But she has another child at home who's nearly two and has starting biting lately."

"Hmm," the doctor said again. "She didn't notice, eh? Okay, the first thing is to take a blood count."

"I don't like it," the nurse said. "Especially since she claims that this weakness has been going on for more than a week. Where was she until now?" She lowered her voice. "The father didn't come with them, and the mother looks completely worn out. This is her eleventh child. There's a child just before this one, and another one two years before that… She mumbled something about her husband being out of the country and that he just came back two days ago. I don't like it. The whole picture. Certainly not the signs of trauma. I think it would be worthwhile for you to go check and see if my impression is correct."

"Hmm," the doctor said for the third time. "Okay. I'll go see her."

---

Benny jumped down from the bus onto the sidewalk with youthful energy, holding tight to the plastic bag that contained his secret note-book. He'd had a lot of successes this week, and Francois had been so happy to hear about them. Especially since they were due to him. Otherwise, it would never have occurred to Benny that a person can control his own thoughts so well…

It was a good thing that his father and mother had more money now, he thought, skipping up the last flight of stairs, and that they could afford to send him to a psychologist even though he didn't really need him anymore. And—

He stopped.

There was someone in Francois's yard. Sitting on the doorstep. Ari Blau?

No. The fear was stupid and unnecessary. Ari had simply been pass-ing through the neighborhood last time. There was no need for Benny to be afraid of him every time he came here.

But the fear stuck in his throat anyway and made him take a step back and find a different angle from which to gain a better view of the yard and the figure inside it.

It wasn't Ari. But what was that kid doing here, anyway? Benny craned his neck until he nearly detached it. This was *his* hour—Wednesday at seven-fifteen. No one was supposed to be here except him! Francois had told him that at the start, when he used to come here with his father, afraid he might meet someone who knew him and would think that his seeing a psychologist was weird.

The boy took off his hat and fanned his face with it. *It's not so hot,* thought Benny. Was it possible today wasn't Wednesday? Was this even his hour?

Yes, it was Wednesday. He was sure of that.

Benny left his vantage point and rubbed his neck. That kid had made a mistake, not him. What to do? Just go over and tell him?

"Francois?" came a voice from the yard. "Is that you?"

Okay, it looked like he had no choice. "No, it's me," he said, going down the narrow stairs. "What's the matter? Francois isn't here?"

The boy, who looked a bit odd close up, fanned himself with his hat again. "He didn't open the door," he said. "I came at six—that's my time. I knocked, but he didn't answer."

"Maybe he's not there," Benny said with astute logic. The thought that Francois had disappeared when they had an appointment made him feel betrayed.

"It's strange," the other boy said. "The light's on, and the air conditioner. And that awful parrot—"

"Paolo is not awful!" Benny said automatically.

"He has long claws and a beak that can break bones," the boy retorted. "So what if he can talk? Does that mean he's not an animal? Are we supposed to treat him as if he were a person?"

"He is an animal," Benny agreed quickly. "But he's very cute!"

"No, he isn't," the boy insisted. "Anyway that awful parrot is there, the air conditioner is on, and the door isn't closed—"

"It is, too, closed." Benny looked at the door.

"Now it is," the boy said. "Because I closed it. But when I came at six, it wasn't."

"It wasn't closed?"

"Exactly."

Benny rubbed his nose, deep in thought. All kinds of people came to see a therapist. His father had told him so when he'd cried and protested that he didn't have to come here. And this boy apparently belonged to the "all kinds" category that Benny wanted no part of. But it didn't really matter so much right now. What *was* important was finding the answer to the question: What were they supposed to do now?

73

THE YARD WAS QUIET. SO QUIET THAT A FURTIVE CAT THOUGHT she could cross the space at a run. The strange boy jumped and yelped.

"Cats carry diseases," he explained to Benny. "Parrots, too. People and animals shouldn't live in the same place." He fanned his face with his hat. "Maybe Francois caught something from his parrot and is lying unconscious on the floor right now."

The notion horrified Benny. "Let's go inside and check," he said in alarm, putting his hand on the doorknob.

"Wait! It's not your apartment. You can't just barge in without a reason."

"But you said that maybe Francois—"

"Yes, I did." The boy grimaced. "But the probability is small."

Benny wasn't entirely sure what the word "probability" meant, but he thought he remembered Rini, his eighteen-year-old sister, using the word a lot this past year. Something to do with her math class. He decided to call home and ask for advice.

"Do you have a cellphone?" he asked the other boy. "I want to call home and ask someone what we should do now."

The boy shook his head. "I prefer not to give my phone to other people," he said. "When people talk, they send out a spray full of viruses and bacteria, which can stay on the phone for a very long time."

"Okay," said Benny, taking another step back. "I get that."

"I could call for you and put the call on speakerphone," the boy offered graciously. "Okay?"

"Yes." Benny was careful to open his mouth the bare minimum. "I want to call my parents. I'll give you the number—"

The home number was busy. Nobody picked up on his mother's cellphone. And his father—

Benny lifted his sleeve and peeked at the brand-name wristwatch he'd received as a gift from his Uncle Gadi. Abba would be with his *chavrusa* now, his phone turned off.

"Okay," he said. "Let's try something else. We'll call my uncle. He's a good friend of Francois's."

The boy passed his tongue over his dry lips. "All right," he said. "What's the number?"

Gadi, to Benny's delight, answered almost at once. His impatient "hello" echoed through the small yard.

"Uncle Gadi? You're on speakerphone. It's Benny. I'm calling from another kid's phone."

"Benny!" Gadi said. "Good evening to you. What made you suddenly remember your old uncle?"

"You're not old," Benny said courteously. "And I remember you lots of times. Whenever I get frustrated with the watch you bought me and when I—"

"Okay, okay," Gadi said. "It's all right. I'm sure your mother would tell me if something terrible happened to you, so I'm not really worried. What can I do for you?"

"I'm in Francois's yard," Benny said, "and there's another boy here who's been waiting for him for an hour already and Francois never opened the door. And what's even stranger is that the boy says the door was open when he came. And there are lights on inside and the air conditioner, too. As if someone is supposed to be home... Do you think something could have happened to him? That maybe he fell down and banged his head and lost consciousness?"

"Unlikely," said Gadi. "There's probably a more simple explanation."

"So should we go inside, and go from room to room to make sure nothing happened to him?" Benny was a little embarrassed at the thought. "If he just fell asleep, it could be awful."

And if, against all odds, he was lying dead, Gadi thought, that would be awful, too. Ricki would never forgive him for giving that advice to her son.

"You could knock on one of the neighbor's doors and ask for help," he suggested. "Maybe a grown-up can go into the house with you? I have a meeting that's starting in a minute—"

"This is not a regular neighborhood." Benny lowered his voice, choosing his words with care. "I don't know anyone here. I can't know what kind of people are behind the door I knock on to ask for help."

Gadi sighed. "All right," he said. "I'll be with you in ten minutes."

Ten minutes is a long time to be in a small, dark yard together with a strange boy. Benny told him, "I think I'll go wait for my uncle in the parking area."

"Whatever you want," the boy said. "I'm staying here so that if Francois suddenly opens the door, I'll be before you. I've been waiting more than an hour already."

This didn't sound fair to Benny. He saw no reason for this kid to take his scheduled slot and compel him to hang around waiting. But he decided that arguing about it now was pointless. Proud of his own maturity and wisdom, he left the place silently and headed for the parking area.

"Boy?" An old woman's voice stopped him. "Hey, you!"

He turned around and found her sitting on a tiny balcony, looking out. "You go to Francois, right? Wednesdays at 7:15 is your time."

"What?"

"I remember you from last week. You've been here for half an hour already," the old woman continued. "This is the first time he didn't open the door, eh?"

Had he been ten years old instead of thirteen and a half, Benny would have asked whether she tracked everyone who came and went in the building. But the last three years had definitely matured him. He realized on his own that there was no need to ask her that.

"I wasn't here earlier. I had to go to the doctor and the pharmacy," the old woman informed him. "When I came home, I had to eat and rest a little. But since four-thirty, everyone who came here went away without going inside. The boy who came before you, I didn't see when he left. It must have been when I went to the kitchen for a minute to check on the cake."

"No, he's still here," Benny said without thinking. He felt at a loss. "What…what's going on?"

"This has never happened before," she said. "And he's been seeing people here for two years already. He didn't look sick this morning when he came home from shul. And even if he suddenly didn't feel well, what would be the problem with picking up a phone and letting people know that they should come back next week?"

---

Dr. Nir Glick approached the woman who was rocking her baby's carriage with monotonous regularity. The motion irritated him. Like his ex-wife, this woman didn't understand that it was completely unnecessary to rock a sleeping baby. Then they complained that the child was spoiled and they demanded endless help instead of raising the child with clear guidelines from the start.

He was tired. It had been a long day. Too long. And he was annoyed at discovering that he'd forgotten to change his scrubs after taking blood from a preemie. Had he been walking around for three hours with blood on his sleeve?

"Good evening," he said to the woman with the carriage.

"Good evening," the woman said, standing up. "You're the doctor?"

"No, I'm the janitor," he said, and immediately regretted it.

*Get a grip,* he scolded himself silently. *Just two minutes here, and you can go eat.* He was certain that this wouldn't take long. *She's probably just another overanxious mother.*

"Dr. Glick," he introduced himself curtly. "So what's the problem that brought you here?"

"I came here because my baby isn't behaving normally." The woman's finger stroked the carriage's handle nervously. "She's usually an active, smiling baby, and this past week she's been very apathetic. She hardly lifts her head, and she's certainly not trying to crawl…"

Dr. Glick gazed at the baby, who happened to be awake, and shook his head. "She is a bit listless," he admitted. "The nurse said something about a fall from her carriage?"

The mother nodded. "And she's had an upset stomach all week. I took her to the pediatrician and to the night clinic. They said she's just feeling weak and it will pass. But this is not a normal weakness. She's my eleventh child. I've seen plenty of upset stomachs in my time."

Her confidence annoyed him. "There are all kinds of stomach upsets," he responded with a trace of arrogance. "What's the story with her fall from the carriage?"

"It happened twenty-four hours before the vomiting started," the woman answered with a discomfort that seemed suspicious to him. "I asked the doctor about it, and he said there's no connection. The fall was from a low height, and an upset stomach is an upset stomach…"

"Okay," Dr. Glick said. "I understand your thinking. But I like to check things out thoroughly. I think we'll run a few tests, and we'll ask the pediatric neurologist to take a look at her, too. Then we'll be a lot smarter than we are now."

It had taken three and a half minutes, not two. Still, as he hurried to the cafeteria, Dr. Glick was satisfied with how he'd dealt with the case.

74

THE THINGS THE OLD WOMAN ON THE BALCONY HAD SAID made Benny feel more uneasy than ever. She was right. It was completely out of character for Francois to disappear this way, so insensitive, so inconsiderate, leaving clients anxious, the air conditioning running, and a parrot flying around outside its cage.

"When you list everything like that, it does sound like something to worry about," he said, unaware of how much like his father he sounded.

Something must have happened to Francois. Something horrendous. And every minute that he stood here waiting for Uncle Gadi chafed. He had to go into that apartment himself and see what had happened.

"I think I'll go back to his apartment and try to find out if anything happened to him," he mused. "He's not such a young man."

"But not very old either," the woman said. "You know what I've been sitting here and thinking this past hour? That things can happen to young people, too. No one has any guarantees."

Benny took a deep breath. "So…I'm going to check."

The mission shouldn't be too complicated. He'd simply go over to the door, press the knob, and go inside, exactly the way he'd entered the previous week, when Francois had gone away for that one-day conference and asked him to care for Paolo while he was gone.

The strange boy was waiting for him by the door, among the bushes that might soon wilt and die if the Iranians carried through on their threat. Though he shouldn't be thinking about that now, Benny felt the prewar tension in the air make the burden on his shoulders even heavier.

"What happened?" the boy asked.

"I'm going in to see if Francois needs help," Benny said decisively. "He lets me. I came here last week to feed the parrot when he had to go to a conference. I'm sure he won't mind if I go in now."

The boy didn't budge. Benny twisted the knob and entered the apartment.

The cold surprised him. A bone-penetrating chill from the air conditioner that had been working for hours without a break. And he didn't like the look of Paolo, who perched on Benny's shoulder and began pecking at his black velvet yarmulke. The bird, if such a thing could be said, looked worried.

"Francois is not here?" he asked the parrot. An instant later, he realized how ludicrous the question was. Raising his voice, he called, "Francois? Are you here?"

No response. He took another step, then two. Something shattered beneath his shoe. It was a man's wristwatch.

"Francois?"

Nothing. No answer.

"You're not here, right?" Benny peeked into the small utility room that led off the living room, ventured another peek into the kitchen, and then paused uncomfortably. This was where the public area ended. Beyond that hall were Francois's private rooms. Benny had never been there before.

Someone coughed behind him, and he jumped. But it was only the strange boy.

"There's an old lady," he said. "She says she owns this apartment."

"This one?"

"Yes," said the old woman, walking in with a jangling ring of keys. "My husband was the contractor who put up this building. How many years ago? Maybe thirty-nine? No, forty-three, I think. Or maybe... Well, it doesn't matter. What's the story? Is he here?"

"I didn't check the inner rooms."

Benny felt an enormous relief when his uncle's booming voice suddenly called from the entrance, "What is this? A conference?"

"I'm the landlady," the old woman said. "I came to see if the locked door needed to be opened."

"My appointment was at six," the boy said. "I'm not leaving. I already paid him last week—in cash."

"They say that every minute counts in an emergency," Benny said defensively as Paolo's sharp claws bit into his shoulder. "And I knew that Francois lets me come in. So I decided to check."

"Okay, okay," Gadi said, crossing the room with long steps. "So he's not here, right? Or in the kitchen…or here…"

He advanced unhesitatingly across the invisible boundary that separated the clinical area from the private living quarters. "This looks like a storage room. Let's make sure he's not here…"

He disappeared inside, and Benny hurried after him as though afraid that his uncle, too, would vanish among the odds and ends.

"Turn on the light," Gadi said, poking his head out of the storage room. "No…he's not here either, from what I can see. Let's go check the last room and the bathroom."

"There's another room," the old woman said. "A kind of big closet that you enter through the next room."

But the closet held nothing except carefully pressed clothes and a fragrance that gave Benny a powerful urge to sneeze.

"He's not here," Gadi said when they emerged. "And you say the front door was open?"

"Also the air conditioner," Benny said. "It's set on high, much colder than Francois usually likes it."

Gadi grimaced. "Very odd," he said. "Maybe I'll make another round of the rooms to make sure he's really not here…"

"In Bnei Brak, there was a kid they were looking for, and in the end they found that he'd gone to sleep under the bed," the strange boy told Benny. "Tell your uncle that he has to look more thoroughly. Maybe Francois wanted to clean under the couch, or something rolled under there, and just then he got a heart attack and died instantly."

"*Chas v'shalom,*" Benny said quickly.

"That's right," Uncle Gadi agreed. "*Chas v'shalom.* Tell me, kiddo, do you have a problem with your back?"

"No," the boy said questioningly.

"So why don't you check under the couch yourself?"

The boy froze, as if someone had just suggested that he take a hike to the North Pole and back. Then, moving stiffly, he forced himself to go to the couch. He bent down and peeked underneath.

"Okay," he said, his voice muffled. "He doesn't seem to be here."

He rose slowly, brushing invisible dust from his knees.

"Do you have any other ideas about where to look?"

"Once, the fedayeen murdered a whole family, except for one child who hid in the washing machine," the boy said. "But he was a kid. Francois could never hide there."

"Maybe he went in and couldn't get out," Gadi said with deep seriousness. "Maybe that's why he disappeared. Do you want to check it out?"

The situation wasn't funny at all, yet Benny could hardly keep his lips from quivering.

The old woman wasn't laughing. "That doesn't sound logical," she said, her keys jangling incessantly like a set of bells. "But go know what a person will do in a time of danger. Let me show you where the washing machine is." She turned toward the utility porch. "By the way, young man," she told Gadi, "I remember the day that happened. It was a sad day for everyone in this country. I admired the mother for her incredible resourcefulness, and I had such pity for that little baby."

This anecdote robbed Benny of any desire to laugh.

Francois—in case anyone wondered—wasn't in the washing machine. Or behind it. Or beneath the beds in the bedroom. Or in the linen closet, which was filled with boxes decorated with French writing.

"There's no place here to hide," Gadi summarized. "He's not here."

"I paid him for the appointment last week. In cash," the boy said. "And I need it. We stopped in the middle of a topic."

"But he's not here," Benny pointed out, feeling a sudden, profound pity. "Call him tomorrow. Maybe he'll be able to give you another appointment sooner."

"The police must be called," the old woman said, "to ask if any fifty-eight-year-old man was involved in a traffic accident today. Maybe he's already in the hospital. He has no family here. And only a few close friends. He needs caring people to help him. Should I call the police?"

"I can call," Gadi said. "But what do I tell them?"

"Tell them that there's a missing psychologist who didn't show up for appointments with his clients and isn't in his apartment. As his friend—you *are* his friend, right? I've seen you come to him outside his office hours—you're very worried because this behavior isn't typical of him. And you want to know if a man of that age was hurt in a road accident today." She paused to catch her breath, and then continued, "If not, you want to report a missing person and ask for help."

"They'll tell me to wait forty-eight hours," Gadi said dismissively. "And that makes sense. It's very possible that he received some sort of news that upset him and made him leave in a hurry and that he'll be back soon."

The words were hardly out of his mouth when they heard a throat being cleared in the doorway, and a man's surprised voice saying, "Excuse me?"

**75**

TIMING IS EVERYTHING. THE SOUND OF THAT CLEARING throat, and the slightly annoyed "Excuse me?" thrown into the room at that moment, caused all four of those present to whirl around to face the doorway like thieves caught in the act. Even Paolo fluttered up in alarm, to perch on the light fixture.

But it wasn't Francois who stood in the doorway. It was a stranger, tall and broad-shouldered, with an impressive square chin and a smallish knitted *kippah* that was held in place on his cropped hair with bobby pins.

"Yes?" The old woman recovered first. "How can I help you?"

"I...." The man's eyes darted here and there, from the boy fanning his face with his hand to Gadi with his chin jutted out to Benny who, had he dared, would have hidden behind his uncle. "I came to see Francois. I'm...I have an appointment."

"He's not here," Gadi said. "He's not seeing clients today."

"I made an appointment," the man said, taking a step inside the room. "No one informed me that it was canceled. Are you his family?"

The boy grinned. "Do we look like it?"

"I don't know," the stranger said. "This is my first time here. It's not right that he didn't let me know. Did something happen to him?"

"Maybe," Gadi said. "At this stage, we have no idea. We'll tell him to get back to you to make a new appointment."

"He disappeared," the old woman put in. "When did you make your appointment?"

"When did I make my appointment?" The man rubbed his nose and wrinkled his brow. "At eleven-thirty today or thereabouts."

"When I was at the clinic," the old woman told the others. "I left the house at eleven forty-five and returned about two-thirty. It's a bus ride, and there was a long line when I got there, and in the end they told me that the receptionist had called me by mistake. The service in these health clinics today is not the best. I think I'll write a letter to the minister of health."

She sounded like an old woman, but Benny noticed her eyes scurrying sharply to and fro. So he wasn't surprised when she said, "How did you manage to get a same-day appointment—and outside his usual office hours?"

"He agreed to see me because I explained that it was extremely urgent," the stranger said.

"Okay," Gadi said. "Let's move. I think it would be a good idea for you to lock the door, Mrs.—"

"Freida," the old woman said. "You can call me Freida."

"I think you should lock the door now, Freida," Gadi said. "And anyone who wants an appointment and didn't get one will get it, G-d willing, when Francois comes back. I will speak to him personally about it."

"What are you to him?" the stranger inquired.

"His brother," Gadi said. "His younger brother."

"Ah," said the stranger, visibly surprised. "You don't sound French."

"I grew up in Israel," Gadi said. "He lived in France. That's the small difference. But people say we're very much alike. Haven't you noticed that we have the same nose?"

"A Jewish nose," Benny said, who got his uncle's jokes.

"That's usually said a little more politely—but yes. That's what I meant," Gadi agreed. "So we'll be leaving now, Freida. We'll be in touch. I'm going to deal with this matter."

"What matter?" the stranger asked.

Gadi gave him a long look. "Forgive me for saying this," he said evenly, "but I don't think this is any of your business."

"A person comes to an appointment that was set up in advance," the stranger protested, "and he's told that it's been canceled. You don't think it would be basic politeness to explain to him what happened?"

The old woman spoke up, before Gadi could. "Francois has disappeared. He left home sometime between when you made your appointment and four-thirty, when I went out on my balcony to hang out the laundry. And he didn't leave word for any of his clients."

"That's negligence," the tall stranger said. "Is he like this in general? I just want to know."

"Absolutely not!" Benny said loyally.

"He's been living here for two years and three months," the old woman said, "and this is the first time."

"Did you call the police to find out if he was in an accident?" the stranger asked. "Because if what you say is true, Freida, then this is really unusual."

"Exactly." After Gadi's coolness, the landlady was happy to meet someone who agreed with her own ideas. "That's what I think. We need to call the police. It's just a phone call. So why not? Eh?"

"I'll call." The stranger pulled his cellphone from his pocket. "Should I talk to them first and then let you take it from there?"

"No, no," the old woman protested.

"Cellphones can have germs," the strange boy said.

"But I'm not—" The person manning the desk must have picked up at that moment, because the man stopped midsentence and began talking on his phone.

The results weren't very different from what Gadi had expected. The police had no information about any man aged fifty-five, plus or minus, who'd been injured in a traffic accident, or, as Freida hastened to ascertain, as a victim of a mugging. Regarding his being absent, if there was no significant reason for worry, it would be forty-eight hours before the police would become involved.

"So we learned nothing new," Gadi said when the call disconnected.

"We learned plenty," the other man said. "The anxious younger brother can let go of at least some of his worries. Right?"

Gadi smiled dryly. "I think it's time to break up the party," he said with great authority. "Mr.—"

"Yair Steinberg," the stranger said.

"And you are...?" Gadi's head gestured toward the boy.

"Sruly Roth."

"Yair Steinberg and Sruly Roth, I thank you for your worry and your caring. If you leave me your phone numbers, I'll be glad to be in touch to update you about Francois."

Sruly mumbled something at a rapid clip and almost inaudibly. By the third repetition, Gadi managed to commit the number to memory.

Mr. Steinberg pulled a business card from his pocket. "I'd be glad to be of service to you any time," he said with an oily smile. "I have a bit of experience in these matters, by the way."

The tastefully designed card, on which appeared Yair Steinberg's name and the numbers where he could be reached on his cell, at home, and at the office, provided his profession as well: "Licensed Private Investigator."

"Okay," Gadi said, putting the card in the pocket of his suit jacket. "If necessary, we'll be in touch. Thank you."

"My pleasure," Steinberg said. "Well...good luck. Sruly, do you need a lift? Where do you go from here?"

"I don't accept rides from strangers," the boy said, looking alarmed. "Thank you for the offer, though. Thank you very much."

"That's fine," said Steinberg. "Thank you, too, Freida. Good night."

"G'night," Benny mumbled, slightly insulted that the man had ignored his presence. As if he hadn't been the first brave one who dared enter the apartment to search for Francois!

"*L'hitra'ot*," said the private eye, waving in farewell. Then something happened that none of them had expected.

Paolo, Francois's pet and Benny's friend—the terrifying parrot with a beak that could crack bones, who had spent this entire interval perched nervously on the light fixture—shot suddenly downward in a flurry of wings, landed on Steinberg's head, and tried to pluck out the man's eyes.

"What? What's that?" The investigator's hand waved about, trying to trap the creature, which had now sunk its claws into his neck. "What's the matter with this crazy parrot? Get him off me! Get him off me *now*!"

"Paolo!" Benny cried, shaken. "Paolo, come to me!"

But Paolo, always so well mannered, shrieked like a wild animal and continued its attack on the stranger.

"Paolo, enough!" Gadi tried to pull the bird off the man's neck and received a nip that made him retreat with a cry of pain. Sruly Roth bent over and put both arms protectively over his head as though trying to survive an earthquake. Freida, unalarmed, grabbed the tablecloth and used it as a whip to beat both the parrot and Steinberg. "Go to your cage, parrot!" she shouted. "Go to your cage, you wild thing!"

The flailing tablecloth knocked off Steinberg's glasses, but since it also chased the parrot away, he was grateful. "What a creature!" he panted, accepting his glasses from Gadi with a nod. "What…what was that about?"

Silence answered him.

Not even Freida could explain the bird's unusual behavior. Only Sruly, who hadn't yet fully risen from his crouch, offered, "My cousins had a parrot like that when I was little. They loved it, but it bit me right here." He pointed to the inside of his arm. "I kept telling Francois that he shouldn't keep such a parrot here, because keeping a bad animal in the house brings bad mazel. But he told me that his Paolo is a good parrot. And now look what happened!"

It was a long speech, and Sruly was breathless at its end. "I think I'll go home now," he said weakly. "Call me if you need my testimony or something. But I need to go now. All of this has made me feel ill. Excuse me."

## 76

$S$RULY WALKED TO THE DOOR CAUTIOUSLY, MAINTAINING eye contact with Paolo, who stared back sullenly from his cage.

"I think I'd better leave, too," Yair Steinberg said. "Does anyone know if this parrot has rabies? Did he even get his shots? He bit me twice, in case you didn't notice!"

"He only tried to," Sruly amended from the door. "And I once asked Francois, and he said that he makes sure he gets all the shots he needs."

"I'll bet he also said that he cuts that bird's nails," Steinberg said scornfully, "which he obviously hasn't done recently." He rubbed the back of his neck. "Do any of you happen to know which veterinarian he uses? I want to call him and make sure I don't need shots."

No one said a word.

"Maybe he wrote the number in his appointment book," Sruly suggested from the doorway. "He kept all his important numbers there, at the back."

"Okay," said Steinberg. "Anyone know where the appointment book is? Or did he take it with him?"

The book was under the table. Benny saw it clearly. For some reason, he didn't want to share this information with the others. Freida was silent, too. Only Uncle Gadi said, "I don't think parrots can have rabies, Yair. Go put some iodine on the scratches. That's what I intend to do."

"Iodine," Steinberg murmured. "Good idea." He was quiet for a moment. "Give me your number," he requested. "I'll let you know if I get any medical updates."

Gadi's brow knitted as he considered how to respond. Benny bit his tongue behind his sealed lips. Uncle Gadi didn't like to give strangers his personal cellphone number. But in the end, Gadi gave in.

"I'll keep you posted," Steinberg promised. "May we share only good news."

"*Amen, amen*," Freida chimed in. "All the best."

---

"Okay," Freida said in a lowered voice she obviously thought was a whisper. "Now it's all clear. Apparently that investigator really did speak to Francois this morning and frightened him terribly. That's why he up and ran."

"Without even turning off the air conditioner or locking the door," Gadi added. "A wild dash to escape."

"Private investigators can be like hunting dogs," Freida asserted. "They focus on what they think is a trail of clues and don't give up until they find blood. That's how they earn a living. We need to judge them favorably: like everyone else, they need to earn a living. But if you're on the right side, and a character like that tries to slander you, you might feel the world closing in. You might feel the urge to simply get up and run."

She sighed and then said briskly, "And if you *do* have something to hide… With all due respect to Francois, and how we all think that he's a wonderful person, he's probably made mistakes in his life, just like everyone else. The visit he expected from the private detective shook him. And this is the result."

"A harsh result," Gadi said grimly, "and an unexpected one. I think I'll take the appointment book with me. That guy wanted it badly. It doesn't seem safe to leave it here."

"It's under the table," Benny volunteered. For the first time, it seemed, Gadi remembered his nephew's presence.

"Ah, Benny," he said. "Not an easy experience for you, eh?"

Not an easy experience? Benny thought about that. "What do you mean?" he asked.

"First, you discover that your psychologist has disappeared," Gadi said sympathetically. "And then you find out that he may be a suspect in some crime… Not easy."

"Being investigated by a private eye doesn't mean that someone is a criminal," Benny protested. "Anyway, you can't accuse someone before you even know what he's suspected of doing. When Francois gets back, he'll explain everything. I'm sure of it."

"If he gets back," Gadi said.

He entertained dark thoughts about the reasons his older friend had decided to move to Israel. Leaving behind a thriving clinical practice back in Paris, he and his wife had come to this country to make a new start. Maybe it had been more than simple longing for the Holy Land that prompted their move...

"I have his children's phone numbers, I think, in the apartment's rental contract," Freida said. "But I don't give out that kind of information. I did it once—and once was too much."

"I'm certainly not the right person to do it," Gadi said. "I'm... not sensitive enough, according to most people. But if we reach the point where we know that we have to talk to them, Benny's father is a Canadian who speaks French and is also very good with people. He could make the call for us. Want to grab the book for me, Benny?."

Benny fetched the appointment book. "There are secrets in here," he said uncomfortably as he passed it to his uncle. "The names of his clients, which is something really private. Also checks and cash. Every time he receives payment, he puts it into the appointment book."

Gadi opened the book. "True," he said. "There's a little cash here, and also checks."

"How much?" Freida asked. "If we know the amount, we can figure out how many people he saw today and what time he left."

"How will that help?" Gadi wanted to know.

"We can't know that yet," the old woman said. "But lacking any other information, it would be useful to know how much there is. So that no one can say afterward that one of us put some of the money in his own pocket."

Gadi flipped through the bills and shook his head. "There's too much here," he said. "Either he received a big payment from someone all at once, or he's less organized than we thought and kept more than one day's takings in this book."

He counted the money again as he spoke, and then said, "Nearly three thousand shekels in cash and a few more checks. Not all of them made out to him alone."

"Whenever Jews had to run, they always ran with all the cash they had," Freida said. "It's a little strange that he'd leave this money behind." She sighed. "I'll talk it over with my husband and see what he has to say about the whole story. Do you want to come up with me? He'd be happy. Moishe doesn't get many visitors, and he can't leave the house on his own anymore."

---

She had been in the emergency room with children before. More than once. But Ricki had never felt so attacked as she was now. First Tziona, the skinny nurse who examined Ahuvi and found evidence that she'd been hurt. Then that cynical, conceited doctor.

Maybe she was just being overly sensitive because Ahuvi was her adopted child and somehow that made her doubt her motherly instincts where she was concerned. And maybe it was the tension concerning the situation with Iran that was making people behave this way, sharp and suspicious. Though she believed that the two countries would find a way to resolve the problem, she still sensed a small black snake slithering along beneath the optimism, sending up clouds of dust as it moved to and fro.

And maybe it was just the reason she found herself here in the first place. Those others times, she'd known what the problem was that had brought her to the ER. She'd understood how it would be treated and how long the treatment would take, more or less. But in this situation she felt like a fish out of water. This was no broken leg or dehydration. This was something else. Something unusual. She had never heard of a healthy, alert baby who suddenly began to regress practically overnight. The fact that Ahuvi's problem was hiding somewhere deep in the medical tomes didn't make her happy at all.

"Hello."

A voice with a thick Arabic accent made her shoot to her feet.

"Dr. Zahir Nassar, pediatric neurology," he introduced himself. "And this is Ahuvi, yes? How is she? Why did you bring her to the ER today?"

He was so human, so friendly, that tears sprang into Ricki's eyes.

There is something so cruel and sad about hatred between brothers. About alienation between two members of the same nation. The neurologist's appearance deepened Ricki's sense of melancholy and loneliness.

"Ahuvi is eight months old," she said. "Until a few days ago, she was very active and smiley. Clever. She had an upset stomach for a week, no fever or signs of dehydration. Then suddenly—"

"And what are the signs of dehydration, Mrs. Sofer?"

The unsympathetic doctor had appeared suddenly behind the neurologist's back. As before, the tone of his voice wasn't friendly at all.

77

FREIDA WASN'T THE KIND OF ELDERLY WOMAN YOU COULD easily refuse. Gadi found himself unwillingly dragged along to her apartment on the first floor.

The apartment surprised him. It wasn't filled with old, crocheted doilies, faded and dusty. Instead, the place was furnished along sleek, modern lines and completely devoid of nostalgic ornaments.

Freida noticed his curiosity. "It was all designed by Moishe, he should be healthy," she said, jangling her keys. "It's nice, no? Those spotlights over there and the color of the flooring? He's talented, Moishe is. Everything he touches turns to gold…"

She disappeared into the next room for a moment, leaving them alone. Then she returned, pushing a small, wizened man in a wheelchair.

"First of all, introductions," she said. "Moishe, this nice boy is Benny. He was the first one to decide to take action and enter Francois Dreyfus's apartment to check if something happened to him. And this is Gadi, who is a friend of the psychologist's. He came here specifically to find out what happened to him."

There was something in the compliments she handed out that made Benny and Gadi stand a little straighter without realizing it.

"There was another boy—poor thing. A little odd. He left already," she added in a lowered voice. "The kind who's afraid of everything. And there was also a man, a private investigator, who claimed to be a client at first. The therapist's parrot was very angry to see him there. Very angry."

Moishe said something, his voice so distorted that Gadi and Benny couldn't make out the words. But Freida nodded her head. "Yes, it attacked him. Exactly. So I thought that maybe Francois ran away from home because he thought the detective was after him. But if he was running away, he would have taken all the cash he had on hand, right? Yet we found a lot of cash tucked into his appointment book."

Moishe said something else.

"Maybe that's it!" Freida agreed. She turned to address her two guests. "Moishe says that maybe Francois left the money there for us—that is, for the rent. The rent is due in two days, and he was always an honest man."

Moishe couldn't have had enough time to say all that, but apparently a word or two were sufficient for her to build upon.

"You can take the money if you give me a receipt for the amount you take."

Gadi was glad to be rid of the responsibility for safeguarding Francois's cash.

"Of course," Freida said. "The question is, Moishe, what to do now. The private detective already called the police. They have no information about an injured man of his age, and they're not in a hurry to open a missing-persons file. And maybe that's a good thing, if he decided to run away because the private investigator came…"

Once again, Moishe articulated.

"Not do anything?" Freida protested. "But think of him, the poor man. Maybe he needs help! Someone to listen to him, to lend him a hand. The way he ran away like that, so suddenly…"

Moishe said something else, and Freida sighed. She answered him in Hungarian and then turned to the others. "He says that if Francois wants our help, he knows where to find us. And if he didn't ask…" She sighed again. "People don't always know what's good for them," she pronounced. "But you have to respect their wishes anyway, right?"

Gadi nodded in full agreement. People certainly didn't know what was good for them. The fact that you had to respect their wishes anyway was a lesson that he was slowly learning over time.

Benny gave a little cough and said, "Reb Moishe, there's also Paolo. Francois would have taken him along. He wouldn't have left him alone. Even when he went away for just two days, he asked me to come play with Paolo so he wouldn't feel lonely. Would he leave him behind now and not even make sure he gets food and water? I don't know, Reb Moishe, but it doesn't sound so logical to me."

"That parrot is certainly a spoiled pet," Gadi added with a small grin. "But, Benny, when a person feels the need to escape for his life, he doesn't always have the time to think about pets."

"But maybe that's not what happened," Benny protested. "Maybe he just went out for a minute and didn't plan to be delayed at all. And then something happened. Francois is a good man. He wouldn't leave his parrot like that."

"And he would leave the cash on the table? And the air conditioner running?" Freida interjected. "Clearly he behaved erratically and in a way that wasn't like him at all."

"Maybe we should call his children," Gadi said.

The old woman objected. "He's a grown man. Anyway, what could they possibly do that we can't?"

Moishe asked a short question, just a word or two.

"Of course!" Freida appeared to be insulted. "What do you think? The minute I saw that his first client left without going in, I called to find out what happened. Francois didn't answer. I can try again, but if he really ran away, the first thing he'd do would be to remove the battery from his cellphone. He knows that with today's technology, you can track a person through the location of his phone."

Gadi put his own phone to his ear. "Maybe he really did that," he said after a moment. "No one's picking up." He sighed. "We're going home, Benny. Come on, I'll drop you off."

"What about Paolo?"

"I'll take care of him," Freida said. "Parrots, like chickens, sleep at night. So there's no reason to worry about him right now. I'll go to him tomorrow."

"Maybe Francois will be back by then and will take responsibility like he's always urging everyone else to do," Gadi said. Seeing the wounded look Benny gave him, he felt a little ashamed of himself. Why had he assumed that Francois had known no trouble in his life?

"I'm sure Francois didn't run away." Benny turned away from his uncle and looked at the two elderly people. "I'm positive."

But one of the things Benny had learned long ago was that grownups weren't all that interested in his opinion.

The fact that the doctors moved so rapidly to admit Ahuva to the hospital surprised Shaul. The tears in Ricki's voice as she told him made him tense up, and his fists and muscles were clenched painfully all the way to the hospital.

What wasn't Ricki telling him? What had brought on that intense, emotional reaction?

He leaped out of the taxi and almost ran to the hospital entrance. He made for the elevators at a rapid clip and waited in rising impatience for one to come. He was almost assaulted by a man with a familiar face.

"Shaul!" Pinchas cried. "How did you know? You shouldn't have come!"

*Yes, I should have*, Shaul thought. He had brought the child home. He had promised to help raise her.

"No, you shouldn't have come," Pinchas said, "but it's really nice that you did! I'm so excited!"

"Are you going in or coming out?" someone asked.

Pinchas stepped out of the elevator, causing the doors to shut right in front of Shaul's nose. He was oblivious to Shaul's distress at the delay.

"So nice of you!" he repeated. "You're a loyal friend."

Shaul was bewildered. He had been a loyal friend when he'd agreed to solve Pinchas's problem and undertake the burden of raising the child, with all the endless demands that entailed. To tell the truth, there had been once or twice recently when he'd even complained to himself, in his secret heart, over Pinchas's lack of interest in Ahuvi.

But Pinchas wasn't talking about Ahuvi. That much was clear.

"I don't understand," he said with great caution, trying not to jump to conclusions.

"You mean, we met here by accident?" Pinchas was incredulous. "The two of us, out of all the people in the world? And all this time, I've been telling my wife that it was obvious that many of the obstacles were smoothed away for us because of your promise."

His promise?

"In simple words?" Shaul asked. Because there were some questions that he wasn't prepared to ask outright.

The gleam in Pinchas's eyes grew even brighter. "Twelve hours ago," he said. "Two girls and a boy."

78

PAOLO, IT SEEMED, HAD CAPTURED BENNY'S HEART. THE boy didn't seem at all upset that the bird had attacked an innocent man. And when Gadi had intervened, it attacked him, too.

"He just gave a warning bite," Benny defended his feathered friend. "Look, you don't even have a mark! You can't call him wild just because he attacked someone he thought was dangerous."

"I can call him whatever I want," Gadi corrected him, maneuvering the car expertly. "At most, you could say it's not nice of me to call him that."

"Okay, okay. But he's still a good bird, Uncle Gadi. He's always been nice to me. And Francois loves him. He wouldn't have left him like that."

"So you want to claim that he was kidnaped? That they forced him to leave the house at gunpoint? That the private eye saw it all and didn't protect Francois, which was why the parrot attacked him like that?"

Benny winced at the cynical tone. "Maybe," he whispered. "There's something illogical in the other possibility you suggested. What kind of terrible thing could Francois have done already? Something so terrible that simply knowing that the private eye knows about it would make him drop everything and run away?"

Gadi laughed. "Plenty terrible," he said. "We don't really know him all that well…"

"But my parents checked him out carefully!" Benny protested. "They wouldn't send me to just anyone!"

*Oops.* Gadi took a deep breath and contemplated the minefield into which he'd inadvertently stepped. Although he enjoyed, to a certain degree, proving yet again that nobody in this world is perfect, Benny was emotionally involved here. He had trusted the psychologist. He had learned a great deal from him, and with his help had coped with no small number of challenges.

While he didn't consider himself either a diplomat or a noted educator, as a businessman Gadi prided himself on his ability to adapt to any situation and to adjust his speech to the other person's capacity to absorb what he was saying.

"Listen, Binyamin," he said gravely, using his nephew's full name to emphasize the gravity of his words. "I hear what you're saying. There are a few points here that I didn't think about before. I'll try to call other friends of Francois's tonight and ask if they have any ideas as to where we might look to find out what happened to him or where he is now."

"You know his friends?" Benny was suspicious.

"Yes. I happened to meet some of them. We went together to his wife's gravesite."

"And you'll really call them?"

"Not all eight of them…" Gadi uttered a short laugh. "But don't worry."

Benny was silent for a moment. "'Not all eight' could also mean 'none of them.'"

"No, no. I seriously intend to try. Don't worry." Gadi turned the car into the building's parking area. "Go home and forget about this until tomorrow."

"I get out of *cheder* at six," Benny said. "That's a long time from now. And I'll be worried… No one I know ever disappeared before." He sighed. "If you have a very important message for me, will you ask my father to call me in *cheder*?" he asked. "No matter what the message is?"

*He's a smart boy*, thought Gadi. Aloud, he said, "If that will help you learn with peace of mind, then gladly."

"Good," Benny said as he opened the door. "Thanks, Uncle Gadi." He paused, and then added, "I once heard Ima tell Abba that you are very loyal. I see that that's true. Francois is lucky to have a friend like you."

"Really?" Gadi gave a crooked smile, embarrassed. He wasn't at all sure how loyal his thoughts had been this past hour. "Thank you."

"You'll make those calls, right?" Benny urged. "You're not just saying that?"

"Word of honor," Gadi said, thumping on his heart and immediately regretting it. Now he'd have no excuse. He would be obligated to contact Yosef Blau, update him on what had happened, and work with him.

---

Two daughters and a son!

Shaul was speechless as he pumped Pinchas's hand vigorously with both of his own. "Mazel tov, mazel tov, mazel tov!" he said. "I'm so…so thrilled I met you now!"

His voice was slightly hoarse, though he didn't consider himself an emotional man. "This is…absolutely wonderful. How are they?"

"They're in the NICU," Pinchas said. "But they're much bigger than we expected, and their prognosis is excellent. It's such a miracle, Shaul. Each one of them is so perfect. And the three of them together…" He breathed deeply. "This morning I felt like I could almost fly with happiness. Now I'm starting to touch the ground. But it's still unbelievable."

They shared a moment of quiet, filled with the words they didn't need to say.

"My cellphone broke yesterday," Pinchas said at last. "Otherwise, you would have heard from me earlier… I had no numbers on me."

"It's okay. What I mean is—it's wonderful! May you have tremendous *nachas*, Pinchas, and merit raising them to Torah, *chuppah*, and good deeds, together with many brothers and sisters."

Pinchas laughed. Then, abruptly, he stopped laughing. "Just a minute. Why are *you* here?"

"A little thing." Shaul didn't want to puncture Pinchas's perfect happiness even the tiniest bit. "I came to bring a package to a relative."

"They should be healthy," Pinchas blessed warmly. "From where I am now, I can see that HaKadosh Baruch Hu does everything for a good reason, with mercy and love. I hope that you'll feel it soon, too."

"*Amen.*" The elevator opened again.

"I have to run," Pinchas said.

"Go ahead. Get used to it," Shaul chuckled. "You can expect a lot of running from now on…"

With a huge smile on his face, he entered the elevator. The news he was bringing Ricki warmed his heart and lifted his spirits.

There was no coincidence in the world. He could so easily have missed Pinchas. The fact that HaKadosh Baruch Hu had arranged for them to meet sowed fresh hope in Shaul that their troubles, too, would soon turn out to be nothing.

⁓⁓⁓

"They were right when they commented in the baby's case file that her parents seem apathetic," one nurse told another, her immediate superior. "Would you believe it? I walk into the room, and the little girl…well, you saw her! And the parents are laughing and chattering about some friend who just had triplets… Is that what you'd expect from parents who were just told that their child apparently suffers from epilepsy? Does that sound human to you?"

"I spoke with the mother, and she doesn't seem to have absorbed what Dr. Nassar told her. You know him. He always puts things too delicately. She thinks it's just something they have to rule out according to the protocol and that epilepsy always comes along with convulsions and seizures… Poor things. Give them time to digest it. Besides, there's no known correlation between epilepsy and parental negligence. If that really is the problem, the two are not connected. We'll just have to assign a social worker to make sure they're taking good care of the child."

"Tziona is an excellent judge of character," the other nurse said with slight disapproval. "If something troubles her about a patient, we should pay attention."

"But remember that she's also had many unfounded suspicions, and the older she gets, the worse it becomes," the head nurse said calmly. "It's important to remember that it's a good thing she points things out to us when necessary. It's good to keep an eye open and to be sensitive to anything suspicious or out of the ordinary. There have been times when she's saved babies and children from a cruel fate. But unless we have proof, the parents are considered loving caretakers, just like any other set of parents on the ward."

"Is that why they put them in room 8?" the first nurse asked, lowering her voice. "Because of the security cameras?"

"Ssssh," said her superior. "We don't yet have authorization to use the cameras, and there's really no reason for it. Let's take it slow."

THE GOOD NEWS ABOUT THE BIRTH OF THE TRIPLETS, AND the stunning timing of their hearing about it, gave them more than a smidgen of hope. It imbued Shaul and Ricki with the same exalted feeling they'd had when they undertook to raise Ahuvi.

But now, twenty-five minutes after Shaul's appearance in the ward, Ricki said despondently, "I hope it's nothing, and that in the end it will turn out to have been just a bug that will disappear after a few days of antibiotics. But…" She stood up and went to close the door. "But I'm very on edge. Ahuvi is a sweetheart. A really special soul. But…we don't know anything about her. The doctors asked me about genetic problems in the family. What was I supposed to say?"

Shaul bit his lower lip. "The truth," he said quietly. "That you don't know of anything specific."

Ricki sighed. "That's what I said," she admitted. "But—"

"There is no genetic problem that passes from generation to generation since Adam HaRishon," Shaul stated. "Every disease erupted at some time, in some person. Even if this is a problem that would be categorized as genetic, they'll figure it out in the end."

Ricki squinted at the closed door, looked at the baby sleeping quietly in her carriage, and said hoarsely, "You know what I'm thinking about? Tay-Sachs."

Shaul stiffened. "Does that sound like what she has?"

"No. I didn't mean that. But…what do you think?"

"I don't know enough," he said, twisting his fingers. "I have no idea. But does that condition even exist in India?"

"That's exactly what I mean," Ricki whispered. "There are illnesses typical of Ashkenazic Jews, right? And those illnesses are not typical of Indians from—what is that place called? Maharashtra?"

"That's right," Shaul affirmed. After a moment's silence, he added, "It's reasonable to expect that they have these kinds of conditions, too. Every closed system will have its characteristic genetic diseases."

"And not all of them are incurable, right? There are some that can be treated if they're identified in time?"

"I'm not a doctor. I have no idea."

"When you leave the delivery room, you are given a page with all kinds of markers for conditions like that, which can be arrested if found in time," Ricki remembered. "Maybe…maybe Ahuvi has some kind of disease typical of Indians, but the doctors here wouldn't even think of checking for it simply because they have no clue as to her origin."

"Sssh," Shaul pleaded.

"Yes," she agreed. "Absolutely. I remember Jarnail's warnings. But we have to find a way to deal with this problem. From what I understood from the doctors, right now they don't have a clue about what's wrong with her."

"We've been in the hospital less than three hours," Shaul said, trying to place the problem in its proper perspective. "I believe that most medical issues are not diagnosed that quickly." He took a deep breath. "Let's wait a bit longer."

"And after we wait? What do we do if we continue groping in the dark?"

"We'll send her medical file to India for a consultation," Shaul said quietly, "and we'll see what they have to say."

The idea calmed Ricki for three or four minutes. Then she smoothed the blanket around Ahuvi and said, "Why don't we do that right now? Isn't it a pity to waste precious time?"

"We don't have enough information," Shaul said. "What have they done for her until now? Taken her vitals and blood count? Let's wait until we know more."

"If we had a hint from India about what kind of information would be useful, we could direct the doctors toward those tests," Ricki insisted. "Besides, it will take time to locate the right doctor and get in touch with him. It's worth our while for you to ask for Jarnail's help right now."

---

"Jarnail?" Shaul would have preferred to have this conversation far from unwanted listeners. Neither in the hospital, nor at home. "I have two pieces of news. One good and the other not so much…"

"Hm?" Wherever he was, Jarnail's brows lifted. "What do you mean?"

"I have two pieces of news, and one of them is very joyful. The second is…how should I put it? Troubling. Which one do you want me to tell you first?"

"Start with the happy news."

"So…Pinchas gets a huge mazel tov. He had a son—"

"How wonderful!" The vaunted Indian warmth poured from Jarnail, who sounded as if he'd leaped out of his seat and touched the ceiling. "I'm so happy to hear that! I'll call him immediately!"

"Just a minute," Shaul said. "He also had two daughters."

"Two daughters!" Jarnail was stupefied. "*Triplets*? But why do you call that troubling? Girls cost money, that's true, but you shouldn't—"

Shaul laughed. Jarnail wasn't joking. "That's not what I meant," he said. "The two girls and the boy are all included in the good news. Pinchas is overjoyed."

"So what is the troubling part?" Jarnail became tense. "I haven't been keeping up with the news lately."

Shaul felt tired. "My news isn't connected to an Iranian virus or talk of war. It's something else."

He sounded uncomfortable even to his own ears. He was fully aware that he was about to ask Jarnail to throw himself head and shoulders into the smuggling of Ahuvi from India. A subject of which he wasn't enamored, to use an understatement.

"Not connected to talk of war?" From the sound of it, Jarnail had walked away to a quieter spot. "What happened?"

"Ahuvi is in the hospital," Shaul said, his heart heavy. "She has a strange weakness and lassitude, and right now the doctors don't know what's causing it. First thing in the morning, they're going to check out the possibility of epilepsy, but she hasn't had any seizures so that doesn't appear to be the problem."

"Poor thing," Jarnail murmured.

"Yes," Shaul agreed. "She really looks miserable. The reason I called you is because my wife is very afraid that we're dealing with some kind of genetic disease that's not known in this country. As you know, nearly every group in the world has certain genetic conditions unique to it."

Jarnail was quiet.

"There are conditions that can be treated if discovered early enough," Shaul continued. "We don't want to waste time. If I write down the details, do you think you could find a good specialist who would be prepared to look at her file and give us his opinion?"

"In principle, yes," Jarnail said slowly. "But wouldn't it be a good idea to say something to the medical team in Israel? At least that this child was born in India and you're afraid she was switched with your own baby soon after her birth? That won't incriminate you in any way."

"Come on, really?" Shaul said. "If we had any real fear that our baby had been kidnaped and switched, is it logical that we've sat here quietly until now and done nothing?"

"Not so much," Jarnail acknowledged.

"I don't mind spinning that story to the Indian specialist you find," Shaul said after a moment, "though from his perspective, we're talking about an Indian baby that was adopted by an Israeli couple. No need to add any details."

"Okay." Jarnail's capitulation was a little surprising. "But thank Heaven, I don't know any pediatric specialists or genetic consultants. It will take me time to find someone. And considering the lateness of the hour, I'll only be able to get the medical file to him tomorrow."

80

THERE WAS NOTHING MORE REASONABLE THAN PICKING UP a phone and calling Dr. Yosef Blau to update him about their mutual friend, Francois Dreyfus. But reason and the heart don't always cooperate with one another. He'd been so angry at Francois for not telling Shaul that he was friendly with the Blau family and accepting Benny as a client despite the conflict of interest. And now he was about to do something similar...

But the disappearance of a man one summer afternoon wasn't something he could ignore. And so, after he'd parked his car but before he went into his house, he looked up Blau's number and called him.

"Am I speaking with Dr. Yosef Blau?" he asked when the call connected.

"Correct." The doctor was gracious.

"This is Gadi Phillips. We met when we went to Mrs. Dreyfus's grave together."

"Yes."

A trickle of coolness had entered the doctor's voice. Gadi assumed, with an acid smile, that the doctor, too, wasn't happy about his friendship with Francois, seeing it as a kind of deceit and disloyalty. This discovery actually afforded Gadi a sense of relief.

"I went to Francois's apartment today, and I noticed something strange," he told the hostile man at the other end of the line. "All the lights were on, the air conditioner was running, and not only was the front door unlocked, but it wasn't even closed."

He paused to breathe. "And another point. According to one of the neighbors in his building, an elderly woman who sees everyone who comes and goes, he didn't inform any of his clients about his absence. They continued to arrive all day and went away disappointed."

"Strange," said Dr. Blau.

"It's not like him, right?" said Gadi, using one of the tools he'd acquired in his younger days in a sales course: getting the customer to agree with you about something, it didn't matter what.

"It's not like him," Blau agreed. "But life has taught me that sometimes there are simple explanations for seemingly complicated events."

"Sometimes," Gadi said with emphasis.

Blau sighed. "So what do you want from me? The right address would be the police, wouldn't it?"

"True," Gadi said. "We called them. To our relief, they have no information about the victim of any sort of crime or accident that fits his description. And they won't start investigating him as a missing person before at least two days have passed."

"That's because they assume that the person whom the callers label missing will return home on his own within a short time," Blau said meaningfully.

"And what about those who fall on the wrong side of the statistics?" Gadi asked. "I understand that the police have limited resources, but I thought that as his friends we ought to do something."

Blau took a deep breath. "Look," he said, "there are people who call me a 'medical detective' because I can often pinpoint the correct diagnosis that eludes other doctors. But I'm not actually a detective, understand? I have no special information or abilities that can be used to locate missing people. Besides"—he finally paused for breath—"Francois and I haven't been in close contact. I don't know if it's appropriate for me to get involved."

"I think there are issues that should be overlooked when a friend is in trouble," Gadi said with faint sarcasm. "I'm sure that if he was kidnaped, for example, he would have no objection to your saving him."

"Kidnaped," Blau echoed with a bark of false laughter. "You like to read thrillers, eh? When was the last time you heard of a grown man being kidnaped in this country?"

For some reason, Gadi's excellent memory didn't help him this time. "So what do you think could have caused him to disappear?" he asked. "And I just want to say, before we continue, that there was someone else who showed up at the apartment. A private investigator who'd made an appointment."

"The most likely reason for a person to leave home in a hurry, without turning off the lights or air conditioner, would be a medical crisis," Blau said matter-of-factly. "But if Francois was sufficiently in command of himself to call for help and get himself out of the house, it's reasonable to suppose that he was also sufficiently in command to ask one of his friends to accompany him."

"But help for what?" Gadi insisted.

"Ever heard of a heart attack? Or how stress or fear can cause a person to think that he's having one?" Blau retorted with his own note of triumph. "Maybe you think there's an exciting mystery here, young man, but I'm sorry to tell you that I don't agree."

Young man! When Francois's elderly neighbor had said it, it had been natural and understandable. And generally, when other people used the term, Gadi felt complimented. From Blau, it sounded like an insult.

"I think you're treating this whole thing too superficially," he said heavily. "I'm asking you to ignore any difference you may have had with Francois and think about this situation again."

Now Yosef Blau was insulted. "You think I'm refusing to help because I quarreled with him? What did you say your name was? I don't think we know each other well enough to exchange insults."

*What did you say your name was?*

Gadi squinted in the dark. Blau didn't even know who he was? Had all the hostility that Gadi had heard in his conversation been the fruit of his own imagination? Was this the way the fellow spoke to everyone who called him?

"My name is Gadi," he said at last.

"Gadi what?"

"What's the difference?" Gadi asked. He had freely volunteered his name at the start of their talk, but he'd never enjoyed bowing to authority.

"Apparently, not much. I think this conversation is over," Blau said. "Have a good evening. I'm sorry I couldn't do more to help."

"Maybe you'll rethink the matter?" he said. "Will your conscience be completely at peace tonight when you know that you refused, because of some quarrel or offense, to step out of your comfort zone and help a friend in trouble?"

"Why don't you go to all the emergency rooms in Yerushalayim, introduce yourself as Dreyfus's son-in-law, and say that he hasn't been answering his phone and that when you last spoke you didn't catch where, exactly, he was located?" Blau suggested. "Because privacy standards in Israeli hospitals are in great need of improvement, chances are that you'll manage to find him and cause him a great deal of embarrassment. People don't like when others run after them and dig into their secrets, my detective friend. If Francois Dreyfus wanted you with him in the emergency room or the cardiology ward, he would have found a way to reach you."

With that, the connection went dead. Dr. Blau had ended the call.

Gadi listened to the silence and then looked at his phone's screen, at a loss. He didn't remember the names of the other men whom Francois had introduced to him at the cemetery, and for some reason he didn't think the respected doctor would be happy to supply that information. Still, if only to prove to the man that he was not impressed by his callous treatment, he pressed the button to redial the number.

In vain.

Blau knew how to teach a lesson, too. His message informed Gadi that he was unable to accept the call right now.

Wonderful.

Gadi thumped on the steering wheel.

If that arrogant Blau was right, and Gadi had allowed himself to be swept away by the imaginings of his distressed nephew, that odd boy, and the nosy old neighbor, who had treated the apartment like a crime scene, then he really could leave the whole thing alone. Francois hadn't felt well and had left home a little absentmindedly. That was why he hadn't closed the door or turned off the air conditioner. And because he hadn't planned to flee to any place, he hadn't needed the cash that had been lying on his table.

With all due respect for Francois—and he did respect him—they weren't close enough to warrant Gadi's tramping around from hospital to hospital, trying to pry his whereabouts from the staff.

He sighed.

And if the other scenario was the correct one, and Francois hadn't suffered a heart attack but rather an attack of terror because of the private detective's impending visit, it would be a good idea to go back to the house now, return the appointment book, and leave a note explaining where the money was.

It had been a long time since Gadi had felt so foolish.

He lifted his eyes, gazing sadly at the window of his dining room, bathed in soft yellow light. Then he called home to tell his wife, Shuli, that although he'd been sitting outside their building for the past quarter hour, he would still be late for dinner.

81

SHULI RECEIVED THE NEWS WITH REMARKABLE CALM. "Okay," she said. "I wanted you to pick up a few things at the supermarket anyway."

"The supermarket?" Gadi was surprised. His organized wife's schedule was exacting, and Wednesday was the day she went grocery shopping.

"You know Shmulevitz, from my office?" she said. "Her husband works at the Ministry of Defense, very high up. And she hinted to me that it would be a very good idea to stock up on groceries right now... It's not just spam, all the information that's flying around these days. We're soon going to be in a state of emergency. It will pay to be prepared."

"You already bought a ton of vegetables," he said with a sigh.

His credit card wouldn't crumble over a few sacks of carrots, but he didn't like the way their guest room had been transformed into a produce warehouse.

"Vegetables," Shuli agreed. "But will you be willing to eat nothing but veggies for a month or two if war breaks out? My friend's brother says that people don't understand how volatile the situation is. If Israel decides to attack Iran, it's clear that Iran won't sit back with folded hands."

Yes, that was clear. But...

"There is no 'situation,'" he said. "The rumor about a virus that will cause all growing things to rot is ludicrous. Something that even children's comic books wouldn't see fit to print. It's a farce, Shuli. A story that some journalist's tired brain came up with in the middle of the night. That's as obvious to me as the fact that Israel won't attack Iran without a reason. And if it's obvious to me, it's even more obvious to them."

"You know what? I'm taking my credit card and coming down," Shuli replied, not exactly on topic. Her words were accompanied by the sound of the front door opening and closing. "By the way, remember before Pesach when we wanted to buy a new freezer?"

"Yes. But you couldn't decide how many shelves you wanted."

"Well, I've decided," she said. "And I found an excellent model on sale."

"Whatever you want," he said. "But there's not going to be a war. Remember that I said that."

"If there's no war, at least there'll be a freezer," she said cheerfully. "Aren't you glad that something finally pushed me to make a decision?"

"We can give the old freezer to your brother," he said. "They'll be happy, no?"

"I'll ask," she promised. "I'm getting into the elevator now so—"

"Where, exactly, do you need to go?" Shuli asked as she got into the car. "I didn't understand what you said about Francois."

"He's missing," Gadi said, tired of having to tell the tale yet again. "All kinds of people I've spoken to have convinced me that it looks strange and suspicious. That maybe he was hurt, arrested, or kidnaped. Now I feel stupid."

"Why?"

"Because Blau, his friend, explained to me that there are very few kidnapings in Israel. This is not Mexico." Gadi merged the car into the stream of traffic. "Francois probably didn't feel well and took himself to the emergency room, forgetting under stress to close the door and the air conditioning." He was silent for a moment and then added, "Or to tell his patients that he wouldn't be at the clinic. There was a boy there who waited for two hours today. Benny was also upset and didn't know what to do with himself. If I were his father, I would be pretty nervous right now. A psychologist can't do a thing like that. It's unprofessional."

"If Francois had a stroke, it's uncertain whether he could have called anyone," Shuli pointed out wisely. "Poor man. It's such a pity he didn't want to listen to any *shidduch* suggestions. Just think how miserable it is to go to the emergency room alone."

"You don't have to get married to have someone with you in the ER." Gadi drove with his eyes on the road. "But Blau claims that Francois would be angry if I tried to track him down. In his opinion, it's more reasonable to assume that he didn't have a stroke or heart attack. He thinks Francois had an anxiety attack because of the private detective who wanted to meet with him."

Shuli didn't demand to hear the entire story from the beginning. She simply sighed and said, "And?"

"And, in his opinion, he'll be released from the hospital sometime tonight, and when he gets home, he'll be alarmed to find that people were in his house and took his appointment book along with his cash... So I want to go there, put back the appointment book, and leave him a note with an explanation and an apology so he won't have to be frightened for nothing."

"You're a good friend," Shuli complimented her husband. She put her hand on the black-bound volume that Gadi had placed between their two seats. "This is the appointment book?"

"Don't touch it," Gadi requested. "It's privileged information. The names of the people he sees and instructions about them..."

Shuli chuckled. "Do you think I'll find the names of our girls' teachers there, or an old high school friend of mine?" To Gadi's alarm, she opened the book.

"Shuli!" The car swerved dangerously.

"I think you let Blau scare you for nothing," Shul said. "I think that when people go to the hospital, they do manage to close the door and turn off the lights. Or if not, then one of the paramedics who take him out do that."

"So?"

"So we need to find out who was the last person who saw him today, and whether Francois looked pale or weak or troubled," Shuli said. "Let's start with his eleven o'clock appointment. His name is Bernstein. Call him, explain the problem, and ask him if he knows where Francois went."

"That would be the most tactless thing I've ever done in my life—and I've done some tactless things," Gadi said. "Really, Shuli. Think for a minute..."

"I am thinking," Shuli retorted. "It seems to me that this is a special situation where the usual rules don't apply. But if you're not comfortable with it, I can make the call myself. The twelve o'clock clients were a couple. I'll call and ask for the wife."

"Okay," he said, retreating from his position. "Do what you think best. But not now, okay? Go to the supermarket and buy groceries, like you planned. I'll go on to Francois's house to see if he might have come back."

"I'll shop afterward," his wife insisted. "I'm coming with you. And if he's not back, I'll call the clients and ask if he was acting odd."

---

Francois hadn't returned. The woman whom Shuli requested to speak to so politely was alarmed by Dr. Dreyfus's disappearance and happy to cooperate. They'd been at his office between noon and one, she said, and the session had been excellent. They had sensed nothing out of the ordinary.

Shuli thanked the woman profusely and promised an update with good news. Once again, she opened the appointment book to see who the next client had been.

"Gavriel Kaplan," she said. "Do you want to call him?"

Gadi glanced at the parrot, who stared darkly back. "I don't like this," he remarked. "But you're right: If he did have a stroke and is in the hospital, somebody has to find him—and the sooner, the better. If my mother hadn't been so helpless when my father was hospitalized…" His voice faltered and disappeared. "What's the number?" he asked presently, businesslike as ever.

She gave him the number. His fingers danced over the keys and then brought the phone to his ear.

After two minutes of silence, he shrugged. "Voice mail." He put the phone down on the table. "No point leaving a message."

Shuli nodded. She checked the clock that sat on the table. "Interesting," she said. "Very interesting."

"What's interesting?" Being in someone's apartment with the owner absent was beginning to make Gadi nervous.

"What people having a heart attack find it necessary to do before going to the hospital," Shuli said. "I would have guessed all kinds of things. Before turning off the lights or the air conditioner, would it be important to set their clock?"

"Meaning?"

"This clock isn't broken," Shuli said firmly. "It's stopped at 1:49 because someone pulled out the clock-setting tab. See? I push it in, and the numbers start changing. I pull it out, and it stops again…"

"Ten minutes to two," Gadi said. "In the middle of Gavriel Kaplan's session. Interesting. I'll try calling him again."

"Are you sure you should?" Shuli was hesitant. "If there's something criminal going on here, he shouldn't know we're on to him."

"We're not 'on' to anyone," Gadi said. "If we believe there's criminal activity here, we'll call the police and give them the information."

The words were hardly out of his mouth when his phone vibrated. The last number he'd dialed appeared on the screen. "He's calling us," said Gadi. "I'll take the call and ask him for information, just like you asked the woman you spoke to earlier. I won't say anything about your suspicions."

*Your suspicions.* Shuli looked at the clock and then turned another page in the appointment book. She skimmed through the past few weeks and bit her lip hard.

Just as she'd expected: today was the first time the name "Gavriel Kaplan" appeared. He was a new patient, and Francois had never met him before.

# 82

THE MINISTRY OF DEFENSE HAS A LARGE BUDGET, NOT ALL OF it earmarked for field units. Accordingly, the furniture in the conference room is updated periodically. Avi Goetz, who remembered more than a few improvements that had taken place in this office, wondered whom he should approach about switching the chairs yet again. The last set hadn't been a success. During long meetings, his back began to ache.

Once upon a time, he would have tossed a remark to that effect to the minister of defense himself and seen the job done by others. But lately he'd begun to feel too old to let drop that kind of remark. He had the sense that the others thought he was not up to doing his job—his official title was head of the Iran department in the Military Intelligence Research and Analysis Division—though he was quite robust for a man of fifty-seven, which made his doctor very happy.

He sat down on the chair, leaned cautiously back, and opened the folder he'd brought with him. The discussion was apt to be stormy and fateful. A review of the material couldn't hurt.

"Avi?"

He lifted his head, surprised to see the chief of staff standing beside him. "You're early," Avi said. "That's unusual for you."

The chief of staff grinned. "The truth is, I'm not early. I asked them to let me know when you came in. I wanted to talk to you before the fun begins."

Avi smiled politely and nodded, wondering how to interpret this.

"I spoke with the Mossad chief," said the man who as a boy had eaten lunch at Avi's house and asked him for help solving square root equations. "He says that most of the information we have on the Iranian virus came from you. I wanted to hear it from you, face to face."

"First of all," Avi said in a lowered voice, "remember that we're not sure we're really dealing with a virus. This could be a fungus or a chemical that paralyzes cell activity in plants. We don't have enough data. With all the electronic and human eyes we have in Iran, we're still a little blind."

"I know, I know," said the chief of staff. "The loss of Sorsy and his three boys was a great loss indeed."

"Yes," Avi agreed. "But let's not whine, let's try to work with what we have. Our information about the Biotechnology Research Institute in Khorramshahr came to us from a reliable source. One of our agents. He's a complicated fellow who dreams of a free Iran but has proven himself trustworthy over the years."

"I have a friend," the chief of staff said. "That is, not a personal friend, but a friend of my brother-in-law's friend, who managed to reach me yesterday. He's a senior agronomist at the Weizmann Institute. He read the article in the *Daily Telegraph* in its original English, and he also spoke to the reporter. Something seems off to him. The reporter doesn't understand how this virus is supposed to work. And when the reporter himself doesn't understand what he's talking about..."

"I think that if the friend of the friend of the friend was a biotechnologist or a nutritional biotechnologist, his area of expertise would interest us more," Avi said with gentle firmness. "For some time now, we've been getting crumbs of information about the Iranians preparing something 'big and creative.' You remember Sorsy saying that last year?"

"Three weeks before they cottoned on to him," the chief of staff affirmed. "Of course I remember."

"In any case"—Avi returned to the folder—"we have information from two different agents. We have intelligence about unusual money transfers to the institute in Khorramshahr. We also have an endless email correspondence by employees there, which an expanded team has been analyzing this past week. Apart from that?" He scratched his chin. "The journalist, of course, has refused to reveal his sources, but we've identified one of them. An important figure in Iran's agricultural ministry. A very important figure."

The chief of staff had to assume that the source was the Iranian minister of agriculture himself. "That's not enough meat," he said thoughtfully. "Not enough meat."

"In this case, a carrot analogy might be more fitting." Avi's humor was dry. "Analysis of the Iranian reaction is not in my department. The boys there claim that the feeble denial proves that the leak was intentional."

"I know." The chief of staff turned, showing him his back. "I know. But I don't want to be the man responsible for starting a war with Iran if that war does not end well. From my perspective, and I say this sincerely, I'd have preferred another six months before we launch such a major operation."

Now Avi understood the goal of this conversation.

"And you'd like me to give you a little space?" he asked quietly. "To say that it would be worth our while to investigate and cross-check our facts?"

"If it's true."

He'd been a boy once, Avi remembered. A young boy from a poor family, on fire to be at least as successful as his friends who came from the right side of town. And he'd never been bashful about asking for help. But...there was a limit.

"We can cross-check our facts forever," he said. "But it's not always the right thing to do. Wars don't come by invitation. If Iran is threatening to attack, we have to be the ones to make the first move. If we become fearful, that will be to our detriment."

Sounds of laughter reached them from the corridor. The prime minister walked in along with his entourage.

"I'm not afraid," the chief of staff had time to whisper. "But—"

*But you belong to the younger generation*, Avi thought. A generation who didn't truly understand how dangerous and determined our enemies were. Who thought about their retirement or about the prime minister's seat instead of focusing on their present job.

They had information. Good information. It was made up of reports from a trusted agent, from money transfers and equipment transfers, and the *Daily Telegraph* columnist had his own sources, some of them quite high up. The US, Great Britain, and Germany had already announced that they would not tolerate a biological war against civilians and were giving the prime minster and the minister of defense their full support. So…why wait?

It was ten more minutes before the meeting commenced at last. Twenty-five minutes after that, he had a chance to say his piece.

And he said it. He invested the short speech with all his oratorical talent and the weight of his full professional reputation. He presented the facts and explained them in such a way as to erase any doubt. He answered questions and then took his seat, exhausted. He listened to what the others had to say only because he was obliged to do so.

There were risks. He nodded when one of his colleagues spoke about the expected Iranian response. Of course there were risks. But, as in any game, it was better to be the one who made the rules. Even if war wasn't something to be played at, it was still better to be the ones who issued the first blow and not let the Iranians seize the upper hand.

When the prime minister gave the green light for a deep assault onto Iranian territory, he was annoyed to see that the chief of staff wasn't happy.

<hr>

Other hospitalizations, with other children, stood out in Ricki's memory as long, boring experiences filled with waiting periods devoid of activity between one dose of antibiotics and the next.

But no one had given little Ahuvi antibiotics, at least not yet. Instead, a very energetic nurse came to inform Ricki of the neurologist's views, and the set of tests that Ahuvi was scheduled to take in the coming hours.

"First we'll give her an EEG," she said. "That's a simple, noninvasive test. They'll place electrodes on her scalp to track electric signals in her brain in order to see what kind of epilepsy she has."

"What do you mean, 'what kind'? Who says she has epilepsy at all?"

"The neurologist spoke to you, didn't he?"

"He didn't say she had epilepsy! He said he had suspicions!"

"Okay," the nurse said in a tone that was supposed to be comforting. "Obviously, he won't provide a diagnosis without in-depth testing. But she is not the only child who has ever come here in this condition. And Dr. Nassar has a great deal of experience."

*She's just a nurse*, thought Ricki, breathing hard. *Just a nurse*. The doctor had explicitly spoken about "suspicions," that there were all sorts of other possibilities.

"Are you with me?" The nurse was anxious to finish up. "In any case, we want to do an EEG. They'll attach electrodes to her scalp and track the signals they receive from them to identify changes in brain activity. Okay?"

"Yes," Ricki said wearily. "And if there's no change in brain activity?"

The nurse looked at her critically. "Then we'll talk to the doctor again. Any more questions?"

*Where is Shaul?* Ricki wanted to ask. Shaul had stepped outside to make some calls. He was supposed to be back by now. What had delayed him for so long?

"I want to wait for my husband," she said. "Does the test have to be done right now? Can't we wait until he gets back?"

"It's not a good idea to wait," the nurse said, tilting her head. "Every minute is precious. We want to help your little girl, Ima. Right?"

83

RICKI BREATHED DEEPLY, RECRUITING ALL HER CONGENI-
ality and assertiveness, although she wished she knew where,
exactly, she'd found those things so simply and naturally back in
Mumbai.

"I don't understand the connection between my question and your
answer," she told the nurse. "Of course we want to help our daughter.
But I'd like to have my husband present during the test. Why can't we
wait for him five or ten minutes?"

"Because the young man in charge of this test was supposed to have
gone home two hours ago," the nurse replied, in a tone that wasn't
friendly at all. "It's only because there were electrical problems on this
floor last week, and all the slots were backed up, that he stayed until
now. And it's only because Dr. Nassar put pressure on him that he
agreed to take Ahuva now instead of waiting until tomorrow." She
tossed her head sharply. "We're going above and beyond for Ahuva.
All we ask from you is a little cooperation."

"Cooperation" was a word with a nice ring to it. A friendly, sociable
word. Ricki didn't know why, but coming from this nurse, it sounded
so aggressive. She searched for the right words in response.

"Don't give us the impression," the nurse continued, "that we care
about your child more than you do. Okay?"

"*Oy*, Ricki"—Shaul didn't know how to cope with such a torrent of tears—"I am so sorry. Forgive me. But what happened? Were the test results bad?"

"We don't have the results yet." Ricki tried to calm herself. "That is, the technician will give the results to the neurologist who ordered the test, and he'll talk to us. But he was annoyed that he had to stay here so late, and he spoke to me so rudely. And before that, the nurse yelled at me…" She caught her breath. "I must be tired, I don't know." Again she tried to collect herself. "What is wrong with the staff here today? Did they all just get word of an across-the-board decrease in salary?"

"Maybe," Shaul said. "I'm really sorry that I was delayed outside with calls and you had to go through all that alone."

"Why were you delayed so long?"

"I wasn't delayed 'so long.' I was delayed for less than half an hour. First I spoke to Jarnail, as we agreed, and I asked him to find us a geneticist to review Ahuvi's file. Then I took a call from Benny, who was hysterical because he went to see Dreyfus today and the man wasn't home. There was some sort of blowup with the parrot and a private investigator and an elderly neighbor who decided that Dreyfus had been kidnaped—"

"Kidnaped!" Ricki echoed in astonishment. "Why would someone kidnap a psychologist?"

"I have no idea. But Benny is really upset about the whole thing. He said that last week Dreyfus was on edge during their meeting, and he thinks it might be connected." Shaul's shoulders lifted nearly to his ears. "I had to let him talk, right?"

"Of course." Ricki wiped her eyes. "Of course."

She looked at Ahuvi and smoothed her long, black hair, sticky from the gel that had been spread on it for the EEG test. She sighed. "It's just the timing that was off. Benny always keeps everything inside. And now, suddenly, at the worst moment, he decides to talk to you."

Shaul smiled. "There's no perfection in this world," he said. "By the way, when we spoke…"

There was something in his tone that told Ricki his next words would be loaded. She closed her eyes. "Yes?"

"When we spoke, Benny blurted something about the incident when Ahuvi fell out of her carriage last week." Shaul chose his words. "It turns out that her carriage didn't simply overturn because of a pothole."

"Then what?"

"Ari Blau was there with a few of his friends, and the carriage turned over when Benny ran away from them," Shaul said. "He didn't want to tell us because he doesn't want us to think he's still a pathetic little kid who's afraid of everything."

"Toby was with him," Ricki said, stunned. "I don't believe she managed to keep something like that to herself!"

"She received the binoculars that we bought Benny in Mumbai as an incentive," Shaul said. "Along with all the candy he got on Shabbos."

"Little businesswoman... I'll have a serious talk with her when we get home."

"Absolutely," Shaul said. "And maybe I'll do it before you. But that's why I was delayed. Understand? And that was even before my talk with Gadi, who is no less upset than Benny. It turns out that Dreyfus managed to somehow signal the time that he left home, and it was exactly the hour when the neighbor who always sits and watches the building's entrance was called away to the clinic—by a new secretary who doesn't actually work there at all."

"Just a minute. Just a minute."

Ricki had no room in her heart for any new worries. She was filled with anxiety for Ahuvi, the slight tension that arose whenever things didn't go smoothly in Benny's life, and Israel's security concerns. Still, she didn't like gray clouds and question marks.

"Can you explain it all more slowly, and from the beginning?"

"Benny went for his appointment with Francois Dreyfus—"

"And he wasn't there. And Benny was frustrated and upset."

"He also felt a little betrayed, I think," Shaul commented.

"Could be," she agreed. "What happened then?"

"An old woman came, who sits on her balcony all day and keeps an eye on people coming and going. She claimed that everyone who came for an appointment with Dreyfus that afternoon ended up leaving just the way they'd come."

"Okay," Ricki said. "And then?"

"Shuli, who went back to the apartment later with Gadi, discovered that Dreyfus's clock had stopped working at ten minutes to two, in the middle of a session with a new client. At that time, the old woman was not on her balcony, because she'd received a call asking her to come to her doctor's clinic urgently because of some irregularity in her blood work... But all the blood work was fine, and the doctor didn't understand who had called her to the clinic or why. She returned home annoyed."

"So now they're convinced that while she was gone the client kidnaped Francois?" The corner of Ricki's mouth rose in a twisted smile. "It doesn't sound convincing. Most likely it was just a series of unrelated events."

"A suspicious series of events," Shaul said. "Doesn't it seem that way to you?"

Ricki's face clouded. "Even so, things like that happen. The fact that $x$ happened after $y$, or at the same time, is no proof of anything. We— or rather, I—was convinced that Ahuvi's upset stomach was linked to her listlessness, and the doctors here are firm in saying that it's not."

Shaul was silent. Then he asked, "What do I tell Benny? I haven't called him back because I wanted to talk to you first. He's worried about Dreyfus. For him, Francois is like a wise, benevolent uncle. I can't expect him to ignore the fact that Dreyfus has disappeared. I can't ignore that myself."

"Maybe you should explain, gently, that the relationship between a client and his psychologist isn't like a relationship between friends. Maybe we should have explained that to him earlier, when the relationship expanded beyond their official sessions."

"You're talking about his going there a few times to take care of the parrot?" Shaul asked. "But...it was a therapeutic matter, to give him a chance to care for a creature that relied on him and liked him. I think you're just in a bad mood."

"No 'just' about it," Ricki said. "I'm in a bad mood for very good reasons. But you're right. I don't need to spread my bitterness to anyone else." She fell silent for a moment. "What do you want me to say? That I'll try to imagine what I would have done had I gone to visit my mother's apartment, and she wasn't there?"

"Yes." Shaul nodded. "And that it happened after she'd arranged a time for you to come. And that all kinds of other strange things were happening at the same time—like the old neighbor's story, for instance."

"I wouldn't be too concerned about the neighbor's story," Ricki said slowly. "I would try to concentrate on the medical aspect. Check the city's emergency rooms to see if she had gone there for some reason. But my mother is...my mother. No one in the world has a reason to kidnap her. I can't say that with the same level of certainty about

Francois Dreyfus. Psychologists deal with unbalanced people, right? So maybe someone crossed the line between 'slightly unbalanced' and 'completely unbalanced' and decided that he needs to have his psychologist close to him forever?"

"And he kidnaped him so that he'll always be on hand to listen to him and say, 'Ah!'" Shaul joked.

"The world is crazy," Ricki said with a shrug. "You never know."

"The world is crazy," Shaul agreed. "But…" He turned around.

"This is Dr. Nassar, the neurologist," Ricki said. "Dr. Nassar, this is Ahuvi's father, Shaul."

"It's a good thing you came," the neurologist said. "We need to talk. I see that this room is empty. Maybe we should do it right now."

84

WHEN SHAUL WAS A CHILD, DOCTORS WERE GROWN-UP
and dignified. Today, strangely, they sometimes looked young
to him. Too young. And Dr. Nassar belonged to that group. His cheeks
were smooth and round, his hair plentiful and thick. He was no more
than thirty years old, or at most thirty-two, Shaul thought with a certain degree of criticalness. How long had he been working in his field?
When had he finished his residency?

"Unfortunately," the doctor said, "there are a fair number of children who come to us throughout the year with a clinical picture that
resembles your Ahuva's. Although we tried to check for more remote
possibilities as well, the staff's diagnosis is fairly straightforward. I
must tell you, before anything else, that although the diagnosis sounds
frightening, when it begins in babyhood there is a very good chance
that the disease will not stay with the child throughout his life. Apart
from that, there are excellent medications today that help prevent
additional and more damaging attacks and allow the child to live as
happily and healthily as everyone else."

"You're talking about epilepsy," Ricki said. "Have the carnitine levels come back yet?"

"Not yet," the doctor said. "But problems with carnitine production
are extremely rare. Extremely. In contrast, one out of every hundred
people has epilepsy—that is, one percent of the population. I want to

treat Ahuvi as early as possible, because in her condition…how shall I put it? It's very important to prevent irreversible brain damage."

"She's has no seizures," Shaul said. "So how can epilepsy—"

The doctor adjusted his collar, as though about to deliver a lecture to an audience. "As both of you are surely aware, information in the brain is transmitted via electric and chemical impulses along defined pathways." His right hand described a kind of path in the air in front of him. "In an epileptic seizure, something happens. A disturbance is caused in this vital and delicate balance, and the disturbance prevents the brain from functioning as it should. Frequently, the body reacts with hallucinations, sudden mood swings, and sometimes a detachment from one's surroundings. This, apparently, is the kind of epileptic disturbance that Ahuvi is suffering from."

"Who says?" Shaul demanded. "That is, I understand that such a phenomenon exists. But what does it have to do with Ahuvi?"

The doctor adjusted his collar again. "What is your profession?" he asked.

It wasn't easy for Shaul to categorize what he did in one word. "I market irrigation products to third-world countries," he said, offering the short version.

"Nice," the doctor complimented him. "It's a field I am so unfamiliar with that I can't think of analogy I can use." He turned to Ricki. "You are a homemaker, correct?"

Her days as a homemaker were the most beautiful Ricki had ever known. She missed them. But right now, it was important for the doctor and the rest of the medical staff who treated her with such conceit to know that she didn't conform with their assumed stereotype.

"Actually, no," she said. "I manage the computer department at an institute for higher learning. I trained as a programmer."

"Ah, that I understand." He smiled. "At least, a little… In any case, I assume that both of you, in your jobs, have encountered problems that you solve through eliminating negatives. If it's not *A*, and it's also not *B*, and *C* hardly ever happens, then we have nothing left but to understand that the solution is *D*."

He waited for an answer. They nodded.

"In the ER, they performed a CT and a focused MRI scan on Ahuvi in order to make sure there was no injury or growth that was causing her lethargy," the physician continued. "We thereby eliminated options *A* and *B*. Option *C*, which is a carnitine deficiency, is extremely rare. I've seen it only once, a decade ago, and although we carried out the appropriate blood test, my professional experience allows me to assume that that's not the problem. In light of everything we've eliminated so far, all we have left is to accept that despite the lack of proof from the EEG, the solution is still *D*—that is, general idiopathic epilepsy, the kind that appears in childhood."

"All medical knowledge is centered on four possibilities?" Ricki asked sharply. "The moment I can say *A,B,C,* and *D,* I can receive my degree in neurology?"

"Ricki, I think—" Shaul didn't think that the embattled stance of a worried lioness was the most productive one in the present situation. But the doctor smiled.

"Apparently not, Mrs. Sofer. You would have to know a few other things, such as when it's correct to begin suspecting one of these possibilities, and when and how to eliminate growths, cysts, internal hemorrhage, and other problems that can imitate the symptoms of epilepsy. But just as a throat infection can be either viral or bacterial, and a pediatrician doesn't need to call a cabinet meeting to know that an inflamed and suppurating throat is typical of an infection caused by the streptococcus bacterium, an experienced neurologist can establish, with a high probability of accuracy, that a child with the symptoms that Ahuvi has is suffering from epilepsy."

"Even though the EEG was normal." Shaul hurried to get ahead of Ricki.

The doctor turned his dark, serious eyes on him. "Yes. The EEG gives us abnormal results during an attack, but the attacks don't always come when we need them." He sighed. "As I said before, with proper treatment there is a very high chance that Ahuvi can return to herself and develop nicely, just like other babies. That's why it's important to start treatment today. Meaning, right now."

He didn't notice, or perhaps chose to ignore, the glance that the couple exchanged. "If you have any questions, you can come to me and—"

Ricki broke in. "We want a second opinion."

"Gladly," the doctor said. "But I find it hard to believe that you can get one tonight."

"We'll wait for morning."

"Not a good idea," the doctor said. "Every minute is important. I don't like the state Ahuvi is in. Her periods of lethargy and detachment are too long and too close together. I don't want us to reach a place where she suffers irreversible damage to her brain."

"I understand," Ricki said. "But we still don't think it will hurt to get a second opinion. Unless you're threatened by that idea..."

"Ricki—" Shaul warned.

"I understand that you're very upset by this whole situation," the doctor said. "But it's a shame. Mrs. Sofer. Try to take a breath and calm down. I hope and pray that your precious Ahuva will respond well to the medications and go home in a few days, perfectly normal. This is not as difficult as you're making it out to be."

"I—" Ricki shook her head, looking down at the baby's carriage and its precious passenger. "I just want a second opinion. And I'm not prepared to start medical treatment until I get it."

"But isn't it a pity to wait another ten or twelve hours until you get your second opinion, which could cause damage?" the doctor pressed. "I think that would be a serious mistake, and—"

"We already sent a request for an opinion to a specialist abroad," Shaul said, opting not to mention the exact location. "I'll try to speed things along. But it's worth our while to wait. Maybe there are other directions to explore that..." He hesitated. "That didn't come up here in Israel because of a lack of exposure to them, for example."

"We are a country with nine million residents," the doctor said, smiling drily. "And although that's not much compared to countries like Germany or the US, I still think we have enough knowledge to give Ahuvi excellent care. I'll say it for the third time: It's not a good idea to delay treatment. The damage that can be caused by this kind of epilepsy, in light of Ahuvi's low level of responsiveness and her apathy, can be irreversible."

Shaul lowered his gaze to his fingernails. "I hear what you're saying, Doctor," he said slowly. "I'd like to speak to my wife, if I may."

"Certainly." The doctor stood up. "I'll leave the nurse instructions about the medications she needs. I'm sure you will act responsibly."

Respectfully, Shaul stood, too. "Thanks very much for your patience, Dr. Nassar. Really, thank you."

The doctor looked at him. "Don't refuse the treatment," he said, his tone pleading. "That would be a pity."

# 85

HE WAS A DOCTOR, BUT HE WAS ALSO A PERSON. THERE WERE times when all the experience he'd amassed pained him as if he were a young student newly embarked on the study of medicine. And there were other times that exhausted him, wrung him out. Caused him to regret that he'd wanted to be one of the good guys, one of those who doled out life instead of taking it away. Better to have studied computer science.

What were those parents thinking? What?

"Everything all right, Zahir?"

Dr. Zahir Nassar and Dr. Nir Glick weren't especially close, but they worked together, and their relationship was characterized by mutual professional respect.

"The parents in room 8," Dr. Nassar said briefly. "The ones who brought in the baby with the hematoma and the lethargy."

"The *chareidim*." Dr. Glick nodded. "From the start, I noticed that they were problematic."

"Stubborn," said the neurologist.

"Arrogant," the pediatrician said.

They both were quiet.

"From the start, the mother didn't make a good impression on me," Dr. Glick continued. "The ER nurse also suspected that the baby's injuries had been inflicted deliberately."

"But they said that her carriage overturned, and all the bruises do seem to have been inflicted at the same time," Nassar said, unwilling to go there without solid proof. "And the mother took her to the doctor when the problems started. To me, the situation looks different. They look to me like the kind of people who work hard to look good... The father is busy saving the world, and the mother is trying to climb all sorts of professional mountains. For them, children are just a social obligation, a check mark on the list of their successes. That's why they refuse to accept that something could be wrong with their child."

Dr. Glick gave a short laugh devoid of charm. "I'll bet that after you manage to convince them that their daughter has a real problem, they'll want to give a natural practitioner a chance."

Once again, both men fell silent.

"I want to approach the hospital's legal department," Nassar said finally. "I want us to go to court and request that the parents be forced to give the girl the medication she needs. I'm not prepared to let them risk irreversible brain damage just to preserve a family's reputation and other such nonsense. Two weeks ago, that baby was as healthy as any other baby. Now, if we don't treat her quickly, her development could be delayed."

"Are you sure of that?"

"Sure enough to go to the legal department and back this case with my reputation. The problem is, the results of the forty-minute EEG were normal. With a judge who doesn't understand, that could lead to problems. And we have no technician here until the morning, so I can't order an immediate EEG to monitor her brain activity."

"It's amazing that you managed to get him when you did," Glick said slowly, his mind working. "We can try to give them a warning before you take practical steps. Sometimes that's enough. People understand that every crisis has its limit."

Nassar looked at the closed door of room 8 and ran a hand through his hair. "It may work," he said. "But you do it. I'm not good at threats. Or lies."

---

"Why did you attack the doctor that way?" Shaul couldn't understand it.

"I didn't attack him." Ricki lifted Ahuvi from the carriage and hugged her. "I just explained that we came to him via the public medical system, and the fact that you have a beard and I wear a *sheitel* doesn't give him the right to talk nonsense. We want the best care for our daughter. No one gets to gamble at her expense. No one can build a tower of bubbles on her back or use her as a guinea pig in scientific experiments."

"You really think that's what the doctor plans to do? He looks like a good doctor."

"I don't trust him." Ricki bit her lower lip. "Shaul, our doctor at the clinic treats a diagnosis of a sore throat more seriously than this. From the start, I saw that he was leaning toward a diagnosis of epilepsy and not even trying to consider other possibilities."

"Maybe there are none," Shaul said gently.

"If that's so, why do they spend so many years in medical school? I was right when I said that I could learn neurology in five minutes. I—"

"No, you weren't right. You just ended up insulting him. You were angry, resistant, and you came off sounding unreasonable." Shaul paced to and fro in the room, hands behind his back.

"You agree with the way he gave his diagnosis?" Ricki was stunned. "You don't think it's a sign of terrible contempt for a person's life and health?"

"He said that it's a very widespread diagnosis. That, for him, it's like diagnosing a strep throat—"

"Even for a strep throat, they take a swab before they prescribe antibiotics!" Ricki's voice rose.

"If no infection is visible to the eye," Shaul said, trying to remain equable. "Ricki, we both want this to be something else—the kind of infection that can be healed with a few days in the hospital. But sometimes you have to accept the decree of *Shamayim* and bow your head."

"We thought she was going to be something special," Ricki whispered, blinking. "We thought she had a huge mission in the world and that we have to help her fulfill it."

"We still think that," Shaul said, pausing in his pacing. "It's still true. People with epilepsy can lead full, functional lives. Nothing has changed, Ricki. It's not over, Ricki. This is just one chapter in a larger story. You've hardly even seen the beginning, and you already think you know the end?"

Ricki ran a finger along Ahuvi's delicate eyebrows, then down her nose and around her lips. "I love her so much," she whispered. "I want the best for her. And it doesn't look to me like that doctor is giving her the treatment he'd give the grandson of the Queen of England. You can go ask him if you want."

"I think it makes more sense to ask him about the dangers of taking these medications and find out what the consequences will be for Ahuvi's health if it turns out it's not epilepsy," Shaul said briskly. "And to weigh that, percentage-wise, against the dangers of her present situation if she does have epilepsy and we don't give her the medicine."

"And you'll rely on whatever he tells you, blindly?"

Shaul took a deep breath. "That's what generally happens between doctors and patients, no?"

"Not when the patient's life is at stake. Shaul, I don't want to start suspecting that it's because it's Ahuvi and not..." She didn't want to name any of their children but depended on him to understand. "You're not taking this seriously enough!"

"Ricki the lioness," Shaul said. "When you enter that maternal fighting stance, there's no talking logically to you."

"Of course you can," Ricki retorted. "On the contrary, out of all the people in this room, I'm the one who spoke the most logically! All I want is the opinion of an Indian neurologist. If he has nothing to tell me, then I want a senior physician, the chief of the department here in Israel, to confirm the diagnosis. Only then will I agree to give Ahuvi the medication."

"He said that every minute is precious! That you could damage her brain by waiting!"

"And he said nothing about the side effects if his diagnosis turns out to be wrong!"

"True." Shaul took a deep breath, suddenly calm, as though an internal button had been pressed. "You're right about that. He didn't treat that possibility seriously enough. I'll go talk to him again."

---

In the business world, success calls for courage and nerves of steel. Gadi had more than once proved to the world that he was liberally armed with both. But now, in the relative dimness of his friend's home, as the possibility of a kidnaping once again began to seem real, he felt something that couldn't be called anything except cowardice. When the telephone on the table began to ring, he clenched his fists and bit his lip nervously.

"It's him again—the one o'clock appointment," he said. "I didn't answer him the last time he called…"

"Don't answer now either," Shuli recommended. "We have nothing clever to say to him, right?"

"On the understanding that it wouldn't be clever to tell him that we figured it all out and that he should bring Francois home before he gets in trouble."

"Hello? Hello?" The parrot reacted to the phone's summons.

The bird's French accent made Gadi shake his head. "We can't deal with this alone," he said. "We need a professional on our side. Who do you think might know a good private detective?"

"Maybe Shaul," Shuli said cautiously. "Do you remember him telling us about a private investigator who did a big job for his Vaad HaKashrus?"

"It's not 'his' Vaad HaKashrus, and he's in the hospital with Ahuvi," Gadi reminded her. "I don't know if he has the time or the patience for this right now."

"This could be a matter of *pikuach nefesh*," Shuli said. "Life or death. Call him. If it's not a good time for him, he doesn't have to pick up."

86

$S$HAUL'S PHONE BEGAN TO VIBRATE AND HUM, JUST WHEN
it seemed to him that he'd managed to convince Dr. Nassar to
present to him, in an orderly, scientific manner, all the risks involved in
each of the medical options that Ahuvi's condition presented. He thrust
his hand into his jacket pocket, pulled out the phone, and silenced it.

But that small pause, despite the apology that preceded it, took its
toll. The doctor's mood had changed. He was no longer amenable to
treating Shaul like a colleague in the investigation and simply reiterated his medical opinion yet again. This time he added a few open
threats about the harm they could be causing their baby daughter,
along with several implicit threats about how the hospital could take
action to prevent that from happening.

Shaul, with a suppressed sigh, tried once again to work his personal
magic and employ his powers of persuasion, which had been known
to prompt tougher men than Dr. Nassar to change their minds.

It took time. And energy. Despite the optimal temperature that
reigned in the hospital corridor, Shaul found himself perspiring from
the effort involved. In the end, he managed to persuade the doctor to
sit down with him in the doctor's small office to talk about facts and
figures and even to draw some graphs for his edification.

Oddly, the same pointers that the doctor used to try to convince
Shaul that the treatment was crucial for Ahuvi had the opposite effect.
They convinced Shaul that as long as they lacked clear proof that Ahuvi

suffered from epilepsy, it wasn't a good idea to embark on a long-term treatment regimen, when it wouldn't be possible to ascertain whether she actually needed all the medications they would be administering to her in the coming years.

From there, he and the doctor conducted a conversation in which neither heard the other.

Over the course of a decade's work around the globe, Shaul had learned how to maintain a gracious demeanor even during moments of crisis. But graciousness wasn't enough right now. The effort of staying calm in the face of the doctor's warnings made him break out in a sweat all over again.

"We'll try to get a consultation as soon as possible," he said at last when he understood that the dialogue—at least from the doctor's point of view—was going nowhere. "At the moment, I can't agree to allow our baby to receive medication when there's no proof that she needs it."

"No proof, yes. But there's also no proof that you're not dreaming right now," the doctor retorted. "There are all sorts of signs that you're awake, but no way of achieving certainty. Sometimes a person has to be satisfied with the evidence and not look for proof."

"I understand," Shaul said with great respect. "But it seems to me that I need a few more hours to think about this approach. Maybe in the end I'll come to the conclusion that you're right."

"And maybe that will be too late!" the doctor snapped.

Shaul mopped his brow. In his youth, he'd read many books about the Holocaust. At an age when his friends still played with marbles, he'd found himself wondering how parents could decide whether to escape to the forest with their children and risk being mowed down outside the ghetto walls or remain inside in the hope that the situation would improve. Now, in the doctor's air-conditioned office, he once again had the feelings that had filled his heart then: fear, helplessness, and despair.

"We'll try to make the most intelligent and correct choice," he said. "Besides, in the morning the test can be administered again."

"Yes," said the doctor. "True. But it's not certain that we will find absolute proof. I explained that to you, right?"

The conversation was going in circles. Shaul rose to his feet, shoulders bent under the weight of responsibility. "You did explain that, Doctor. Several times," he said, drained. "And I thank you very much for giving me so much of your time. I'll try to get back to you as soon as possible with an answer."

"Mr. Sofer," the doctor said gravely, "you're a serious person. You have good sense. I've been very impressed with that. That's why I'm asking you to look inward and check to see if your calculations are pure and scientific or if you're following a groundless mixture of intuition, hope, and dreams."

Groundless intuition. Hopes. Dreams.

The words reverberated in Shaul's mind, and the pain in his heart intensified.

His talk with the doctor had lasted over an hour. It took another three-quarters of an hour to relay it all to Ricki and left them both with a big, unanswered question.

"Maybe you should try calling Jarnail again," Ricki urged. "He has so many contacts. Maybe if he understands how urgent it is, he'll manage to find a geneticist and a neurologist who would talk to us now."

But no one answered Jarnail's phone. Shaul felt his shoulders slump a little lower.

"What are you thinking?" Ricki asked.

"That maybe we should tell the doctor the truth." Shaul's voice was low. "They must have their own ways of checking these things out—all sorts of programs where they enter symptoms and get a list of relevant diseases. They have a wealth of information at their fingertips."

"Will he take the trouble of digging through all that for us or decide that there's no reason to take the trouble because the problem is clear and known?"

"I'm not a *navi*."

"But you understand people," she said. "Besides, are you sure he won't take advantage of the fact that we don't really have legal custody over her to force us to have her treated for epilepsy, or go to the police if we don't?"

"There are confidentiality policies on what patients tell their doctors," Shaul reminded her.

"Patients. Not their parents… I'm not sure the law protects us here, Shaul. Or, rather, I know it doesn't. I read about it once."

"And what happens if the Indian specialist says he knows what

Ahuvi has and that it's a condition typical of people from her place of origin?" Shaul asked almost rhetorically.

"If that happens, we'll obviously tell the truth about her. But I wouldn't be sure that he'd run and tell on us. It would be a whole new situation."

"Okay." Shaul sighed. "Then there's nothing else for us to do tonight apart from trying to reach Jarnail and check if there's any news."

"And daven," Ricki advised.

Shaul laughed. "Of course. So maybe I'll do that. I'll take a taxi to Zichron Moshe and daven with a minyan."

"And then go home," Ricki said. "There are ten children there who need you."

Shaul nodded. "I'll come back here the minute they leave for school. Call me if you need me before that. I'll get in a cab and come immediately."

<hr />

In the taxi to the *shtiebel*, Shaul checked the seven unanswered calls that appeared on the screen of his cellphone. There was one from Steve, their man in New York, but Shaul didn't feel up to taking part in a business talk just then. One call from home, and another five from Gadi.

Five calls!

Something exciting must have happened. He hoped it was only exciting, and not awful.

Troubled, he tapped in his brother-in-law's number. The lines on his forehead deepened when he heard a message say that the number was unavailable at the moment.

Gadi, his dear, extroverted brother-in-law, was *always* available on his phone. Even when he slept, he kept the phone under his pillow.

Shaul tried again. Then, allowing himself to assume that Gadi's phone had fallen into a puddle, he tried his sister-in-law's number.

He shouldn't have been worried when she, too, didn't answer. It was logical to assume that a couple traveling in the same car would both find their phones out of service in the same area.

Still, knowing that Gadi had been working alone to solve a possible case of kidnaping this evening, Shaul began to harbor a very strange feeling.

Maybe it was because he was tired. Or because he was already anxious over the whole Ahuvi situation.

But the feeling that engulfed him had a name.

It was called fear.

# 87

THE DRIVE TO ZICHRON MOSHE WAS LONG ENOUGH FOR HIM to call Gadi's home, speak to his oldest son, who had just returned from yeshivah, and tactfully ascertain whether his parents were home or if they'd called within the past hour.

He wasn't surprised when the answer was negative.

"Hello, mister? We're here," said the aging cab driver. "Don't you need to get out?"

"Yes, thank you." Shaul counted coins into the man's rough hand, then impulsively asked, "Tell me—what would you do if your brother-in-law suddenly disappeared?"

"Your sister's husband?" the driver asked.

"No, my wife's brother. He told me today that he thinks his friend was kidnaped, and now, when I called his phone, no one picked up. His wife didn't answer her phone either. And their son said that they haven't come home."

"Wow." The driver scratched his chin. "Does his car have a locator? Maybe that would help."

"I think it does." Shaul remembered a conversation on the topic during one family *sheva berachos*. "But I don't have his car's license number in order to check."

"Maybe the son knows," the driver suggested.

"I'd rather not involve him right now."

"The police?"

"I don't think they'd jump out of their seats to help me."

"Does he have a lot of money?" The driver turned around to face the back.

This sudden interest raised Shaul's hackles. He answered carefully, "I believe it would be possible to raise money to help him if he really was kidnaped. Anyway, the friend who he thought was kidnaped this afternoon doesn't have a lot of money. He's a new immigrant."

"What a story," the driver said sympathetically. "Good luck to all of you. You need to get out here?"

"Yes," Shaul said despondently. "Thank you."

---

"The French have passed some intelligence to us that we don't know if we can fully rely on," the prime minister reported to the head of the Mossad. "They say the story of a planned biological attack is a bluff and that the Iranians simply want to goad us into attacking them so that they'll appear justified in the eyes of the world when they launch a pan-Arabic attack, like the one that precipitated the Yom Kippur War."

"On Yom Kippur we were unprepared," the Mossad chief reminded him. "Don't let the terminology and history intimidate you."

"I'm not." With his usual flair for the theatrical, the prime minister placed a hand over his heart. "But I want us to review the file again. Look, Motty, the chief of staff isn't convinced that we're ready for war right now. A number of our senior people have retired in the past six months, and Arnon died of a heart attack. He'd be far more at ease if we had the option of delaying this war for half a year."

"You're the prime minister," said the head of the Mossad, spreading his hands. "Do as you think best. I did my job and brought you the intelligence."

"That's exactly what I want to talk to you about." The prime minister leaned forward. "I want you to review the material again, slowly. And this time, I'd like you to not only pay attention to the conclusions, but to take a look at the raw information."

"In Farsi?" the Mossad chief asked ironically.

"Not necessarily. I'll trust your translators to know their job." The prime minister smiled. "But help me become convinced that we're right. That the French are either working with the Iranians or being deceived by them. Give me some recordings, some material before it was analyzed, pictures, satellite images before their information was culled. Information that will help me sleep at night and feel confident that I'm not a fool if I take this country into a war whose outcome is unclear because of something that we all agree sounds very, very strange."

"We all agreed that it sounds strange, and we all went over the facts and weighed them—"

"I want you to go through it all one more time. To tell the truth, I'd prefer that after reviewing it and finding nothing new, you make an effort to get me intelligence that will convince me it's expedient to go to war now. All right?"

The Mossad chief sighed. "Soon you'll make me hope you'll decide that war is unnecessary before the next election."

The prime minister's smile was nuanced. "I think it would actually be good for me. Still, no matter what they say about me, I will not go out to war for such reasons. Let's be professional, Motty. Let's go over the facts again."

"You want the raw material," the Mossad chief reminded him. "I don't have it here."

"So send someone to get it. And maybe also the guy who found it," the prime minister urged. "It's important."

But even after the raw intelligence arrived, no one was able to reach the man who had obtained it.

"He's not available," the Mossad chief explained.

"You allow your active agents to be unavailable?" the prime minister asked. "Or does this mean we have a problem?"

"Sometimes they're unreachable because they want to be," the Mossad chief said slowly. "In any case, we have the intelligence we need. There's no reason to think we have a problem. It's all recorded right here."

---

"This villa is one big Faraday cage," Francois told Gadi. "There's no point trying to call anyone. I tried doing that at least three hundred times since Yair persuaded me that I have to talk to his boss and brought me here."

Gadi had no idea what a Faraday cage was. But the large, lavish house was indeed one big cage. One that he had no idea how he'd ended up in.

To be more accurate, he did have a technical idea. A moment after he'd called the number of Francois's one forty-five client—the last person who, according to their calculations, had come to see the therapist—the private investigator had called him to say that he'd found Francois, who was injured but refusing to go to the hospital.

Had he been foolish for believing him? For not grasping the link between the call he'd just made and the man who'd called him, from a different number, a moment later?

Had he been foolish for following the man to this big house and allowing him to imprison him inside?

"What's a Faraday cage, Gadi?" Shuli asked from her spot on a couch at the other end of the room.

"It's a device that blocks electromagnetic waves," Francois answered in Gadi's place. "A metal cage that makes calls from cellphones impossible."

"Like an elevator," Gadi remembered suddenly. "We have that kind of safeguard at my office for some of our computers."

"Someone took a huge house in such an expensive part of town, and covered the whole thing with iron bars to prevent anyone from making a call from there?" Shuli was finding this hard to swallow. "Is there some criminal gang in Israel that can create such cages for people?"

Francois looked at both of them tiredly. "I just want to turn your attention to the fact that we are imprisoned and apparently being filmed twenty-four hours a day. Nava will decide how to handle us according to what he sees us doing here."

"Nava?" Gadi asked. "Who's that?"

"Yair Nava. The person who brought you here."

"He called himself Steinberg," Gadi said. "He said he was a private investigator, that he made an appointment with you, and that he found you and you were injured but refusing to go to the hospital or call the police."

"He has many names." Francois was extremely tense. His silver hair showed a little crusted blood. "And many identities. Too bad you didn't ask to speak to me yourself."

"I did ask. He said that he'd gone outside to talk to me because there was no reception inside the house."

"Well, that's true," Francois remarked. "When Yair is able to, he tries to stick to the truth."

"So he hurt you in order to stick to the truth?" Gadi asked. "And my mistake was in not asking him how he kidnaped you and why?"

"Honesty is a commendable trait," Francois said.

It seemed to Gadi and Shuli that though he was directing the remark to them, he meant it for the recording device.

"It's a sign of a very high personal standard."

Shuli was silent as she looked around with interest at the tasteful décor. The villa's location was upscale, as were the furnishings. Very different from everything she'd read in suspense novels about kidnapings and kidnapers.

"He did seem to be an intelligent, upper-class individual," Gadi said, playing along. "Elegant, responsible, stable..."

"You're not fooling anyone with your exaggerated compliments," a voice blared suddenly from a hidden microphone. "You've forced me into a situation where I have no choice. You brought this on yourselves. What do you think I'll do now?"

"We forced you how?" Gadi was irritable. "Did we do something bad? We didn't have a single clue to lead us to Francois. You revealed everything. And you brought us here!"

"Don't lie. Mirage said that you already know everything."

"Mirage?" Gadi asked. "Who's that?"

"Do you want to answer that, Yair?" Francois asked. "Or do you prefer that I explain?"

The microphone that had sprung to life earlier went silent.

"Who's Mirage?" Gadi pressed. "Is he the one responsible for our being here?"

Francois gave a weary smile. "You could say that. But we'll wait until Yair decides to explain on his own. In the meantime, as long as I'm his doctor, I'm obligated to maintain full confidentiality on his behalf, right?"

Although he had addressed the question directly to Yair Nava, there wasn't any response from the microphone.

88

AVI GOETZ ENTERED THE PRIME MINISTER'S OFFICE WITH A
small laptop armed with an impressive set of security codes. He
used it to share with the prime minister the raw intelligence he had
gathered regarding the "biological war," as the impending Iranian
attack had been dubbed in the media.

Aware of the man's abilities—he was probably destined to sit in
the Mossad chief's chair one day—the prime minister greeted him
warmly. Some of the warmth dissolved as he asked, "Where is the man
who met the agents?"

"Nava?" Avi said. "He was granted a twenty-four-hour leave for
personal reasons."

"*Now*?" the prime minister fumed.

"We didn't know that you would need him, sir. We thought he'd
been working hard these past two weeks and wanted to let him
recharge his batteries."

"But now that you know I need him, don't you have any way to
reach him? Doesn't he have a cellphone? The best intelligence service
in the world and you can't even locate your own people?"

The Mossad chief suppressed a sigh, and Avi nodded. "We believe
that he forgot his cellphone at home, under his pillow," he said with a
small smile. "He reported that to us himself at eight-thirty this morning. Though his supervisor suspected that the oversight was deliberate, he gave his permission for Nava to go on leave. He called again at

noon to ask if there was any news, but we had nothing to tell him. The next time he called, at seven, he asked if we needed him for anything and said he would be home before eleven forty-five if we needed to contact him."

"He shouldn't have been given permission to leave," the prime minister grumbled. "That was a mistake."

The Mossad chief was silent for a moment. Then he sighed again and said, "Well, I'll chew out Nava's supervisor later. In the meantime, we'll be glad to show you all the main points—"

"Not only the main points," the prime minister requested. "I want the full picture."

The Mossad chief tugged at his tie in a gesture that indicated his growing impatience, but he maintained his composure. "I'll try," he promised. "Avi, do you want to start?"

"First, a few words about Nava," said Avi. "He is a second-generation agent in this organization. The son of Amihud Nava, a legendary handler of agents. Yair inherited his father's talents. The charisma that enables him to capture the heart of anyone he comes in contact with, the ability to win trust and to make people feel appreciated… He is forty-three years old today, and over the years he's managed to win over all the agents he's had contact with, except three. We send him to crack the hardest nuts we have in the basket.

"As the threat from Iran has grown over the years, we've had him focusing more and more on activity in this area. The intelligence he's brought us has been top quality and helpful. He also obtained it at far less expense than could be imagined," the Mossad chief commented. "At some point we tried to have him transferred to an instructional capacity so he could guide young agents. But he doesn't like teaching. Considering that we had no substitute to replace him in the field, we were forced to give up that idea."

"He received three badges of distinction over the course of his career," said the prime minister. "So they tell me. Why only three, if he was so successful?"

The question made the other two laugh. "Three is not an insignificant number," the Mossad chief said at last. "And I think there was a bit of politics involved as well. There are those who don't like the risks he takes or the way he plays loose with the system."

"Meaning?" the Prime Minister asked.

"As the prime minister knows, we generally like to set up a triangle composed of an agent, a handler, and a soldier. The agent is the one who brings the intelligence, and the handler maintains contact with him and creates the warm personal relationship that guarantees cooperation. The soldier is the one who provides security for their meetings. Nava claims that he's capable of looking after himself. And I must say that on both occasions when he was attacked, he proved that he can. Over time, the organization followed his lead and allowed the soldier to keep his distance and give Nava the sense of independence he seems to need."

"That's the risk you mentioned," said the Prime Minister. "What about the looseness?"

"Okay." Avi Goetz appeared embarrassed. "At the start of his service, Nava was rebuked—sometimes severely enough to be marked down in his file—for not filling out his reports in enough detail. Over the years, the problem was solved simply by his dictating his reports to a secretary, who fills them out in his place."

"You've met him halfway in many ways."

"He warrants it," the Mossad chief said. "We all appreciate his talents."

"Because his charisma works on you, too, just like on the agents he handles?" the prime minister joked.

He was surprised when the man seated opposite him lifted the corners of his mouth in a smile and said, "If that's so—it's even more proof that he deserves it, right?"

---

Sometimes a person feels as if the gates of Heaven are firmly shut against his prayers, even if it's just a feeling without any basis in truth, and it's actually just another test that has been decreed from on high. Shaul's heart was heavy when he finished davening. Ahuvi's situation was far from simple, and it was impossible to know how it would develop from here. Gadi had vanished, evoking new worries, and Eretz Yisrael was facing a threat from Iran. And now he couldn't even concentrate on his davening.

What kind of person was he, to permit this one-time chance to daven Maariv tonight slip right through his fingers just when everything was so uncertain and he was so in need of help?

True, he was very tired. His workday had begun with overseas calls before dawn. Then learning, davening, long hours of office work, more calls, more learning, and—for dessert—a visit to the hospital pediatric ward. But would he permit himself the same absentmindedness when speaking to the Indian specialist? If not, what did that say about his *emunah*?

The self-flagellation hurt, and he left the *shtiebel* for the chilly street more exhausted than when he'd gone in. He lingered on the sidewalk, wondering what came next.

Apparently, his first step should be to try calling Gadi again, to hear with relief that the man was home and to laugh at his own inflated fears.

"Tell me, do you think I'm a four-year-old who needs to ask permission before I leave the house?" his brother-in-law would retort. Shaul was already planning his response when, once again, he heard the annoying recording that said the number wasn't available right now.

Hesitantly, because of the late hour, he called the Phillipses' home. His call was answered again by Yossi, Gadi and Shuli's fourteen-year-old son. No, his parents hadn't returned. No, they hadn't called either.

"Do you need them urgently?" the boy asked politely. "Because I'll be going to bed soon. But I can leave them a message to call you back if it's urgent."

"Yes, leave them a message and go to sleep." Shaul didn't want to alarm the boy. "Write that Ahuvi is in the hospital and that your father should call me. I need to speak with him."

"What does she have?" Yossi asked.

"Let's hope it's nothing. It will be okay."

"I'll daven for her."

"That'll be great."

"So…let's only hear good news, Uncle Shaul."

"Only good news," Shaul echoed heavily. "*L'hitra'ot.*"

So Gadi wasn't back yet. Shaul hoped he'd laugh away his brother-in-law's fears when he returned. But Shaul was prepared to take the risk of continuing to trust his instincts.

Every man has his strengths. Shaul's "nose" had proven itself reliable many times over the past decade. The last time, in the peanut oil factory, Pinchas had literally laughed at him when he insisted that the wall near the basement was actually a hidden door.

On that occasion, there had been no verbal way to explain his gut instinct. But he had been right. Behind the door he'd found hundreds

of bottles of oil stamped with their *hechsher* and ready for shipment—
and an employee who became violent when he realized that the *mash-gichim* had stumbled on his fraudulent plot.

This time, unfortunately, it seemed to him that his suspicions were based on more.

"Don't forget that you can be wrong at times, too," he told himself almost out loud in an effort to banish the feeling of responsibility and concern that threatened to strangle him. But his only mistake in this area that he could remember had taken place three years before, in China, when he was convinced that the owner of the canned-goods factory was hiding something that the Vaad HaKashrus was obligated to know. In the end, after exposing himself to unnecessary risk, he discovered that the factory owner did have something to hide, only it wasn't relevant to the Vaad: he had set up a lab for producing counterfeit money, which he was running in one of his warehouses. Fortunately for Shaul, no one spotted him as he lay on the hot metal roof, and he was able to wait until the clatter of the machinery covered his descent. He told Pinchas and another *mashgiach* who was there that they'd been right. There was nothing there.

Somehow the memory of that mistake wasn't significant enough to let him ignore his worry over his brother-in-law or to allow him to return home and give his weary bones the rest they craved.

89

THERE WAS NO PLACE LIKE ZICHRON MOSHE FOR MEETING
forgotten acquaintances, but Shaul was so preoccupied with the
complexities of his life that he hardly managed a smile for Eli Levy,
who'd been a grade behind him in *yeshivah gedolah*. Eli, in contrast,
seemed relaxed, contented, and ready for a long, friendly chat.

"You're still working in kashrus? Like you were the last time we
met, five years ago?" Eli asked.

"No," Shaul said, producing another smile. "I actually left that field
nearly a year ago. Today I work as a liaison between Israeli manufacturers of irrigation equipment and customers abroad."

"Does it pay?" Eli asked with interest, forthright as ever.

"So far, yes. *Baruch Hashem*." His old friend's nosiness amused
Shaul.

"I'm sure you're good at it. You're patient and good with people,"
Eli Levi complimented. "I'm sure it helps that you speak English
fluently."

"And how are you?" Shaul mimicked. "Still working as a *sofer stam*,
the way you were when we last met five years ago?"

Eli chuckled. "Yes, yes, still a *sofer stam*. But it's not an easy market.
So I'm also doing other things. I studied to become a mortgage consul-
tant, and I also do some public relations work for the health services.
And—eh? What is it?"

"Nothing." Shaul forced his muscles to keep his lips curved upward, though they were strongly protesting. "It's just that my daughter is in the hospital right now. I just came from there…"

"What does she have?"

"That's the thing. It's not clear. She's eight months old and had an upset stomach for about a week and a half. Suddenly she started to be lethargic, staring into space, detached from everything. Her muscles aren't firm." He swallowed. "The doctors in the hospital are convinced that it's epilepsy, even though there's no proof that they're right. I'm looking for a top specialist who'd be prepared to look into other possibilities." He paused, and then added, "And if it's someone trustworthy, discreet, and not antireligious—in other words, not someone who looks at the parents of eleven children and notably decides that they must be primitive creatures—then it'll be a bonus."

Eli Levy glanced right and left. "Listen, you didn't hear this from me, okay? But there's one doctor, a brilliant guy, who might be able to help you."

"Why haven't I heard it from you?" Shaul asked.

"Because he handles medical malpractice suits and finds all kinds of mistakes that the doctors make. And they took away his license two years ago after he gave a patient a medication that wasn't approved in Israel for his condition. The patient recovered, but the doctor lost his license."

"Why?"

"They claimed it was medical negligence since he didn't mark the medication on the patient's chart. But that was only vengefulness, in my opinion. Because of the medical malpractice suits. I happen to know that all kinds of doctors still send him people. Quietly, under the radar. Just to review the file and see where other doctors might have made a mistake before something bad happens… Understand?"

"Yes." Shaul took a deep breath. "That really sounds like what we need."

"Then I'll give you the details. But don't give anyone my name. Just the doctor's name, Dr. Blau."

Blau!

Shaul's ears rang.

"What?" Eli Levy had always had sharp eyes.

"He's religious?"

"Yes. Do you know him?"

"My son and his son learned in the same school. And it didn't go well."

"Nonsense." Eli waved a hand. "No one remembers childish quarrels when it's a question of a baby's life. Right?"

It was reasonable to suppose so. But the sense of discomfort wasn't merely big. It was enormous.

---

Sometimes, when his wife would disappear into the pages of a book for too many hours, forgetting domestic obligations, Gadi would wonder if any of the things she read with such devotion could be of the slightest use in her life.

She'd never even tried to prove the purpose of the emotion-laden literature she devoured. For the fifteen years of their marriage, until he'd met Francois, Gadi hadn't attached much importance to emotions.

But when he mentioned the suspense and detective stories she liked to read, she would occasionally say jokingly that she was acquiring vital information about how to cope with all kinds of situations.

Now, as she sat on the sofa in the handsome living room that had become their prison, she hoped that Gadi didn't remember that comment made in jest. Even if she'd read about numerous heroes who managed to concoct bombs out of cleaning materials, turn pens into weapons, or use other mundane objects to open locked doors or summon the rescuers waiting outside—she didn't have the slightest idea how to turn those tales into reality.

Anyway, there was no rescue squad waiting for them outside. No one knew where they'd gone before they'd disappeared. She had left the house in such a hurry that she hadn't taken the time to explain anything to the children. She'd just asked them to go to bed nicely, that was all. And whoever had prepared this place and turned it into a Faraday cage, as Francois had said, had also made sure that there were no cleaning materials lying around to foil his plot.

But maybe it was worthwhile to check...

"Shuli?"

"If we're supposed to make ourselves at home, like he said, I want to fix us something to eat," she said, distorting the truth slightly. "I'm hungry, aren't you?"

In light of Shuli's perpetual habit of strict dieting, this announcement astonished Gadi. But he managed to gather that there was something lurking behind the words and watched as she sauntered over to the windows and tried to open them, then went to the kitchen. He turned to Francois. "Is he dangerous?" he asked in a low voice.

"What?"

Gadi's voice had apparently been *too* low. "I asked if he's dangerous. This Yair," Gadi said quietly.

"Yair?" Francois considered. "No. Absolutely not. He's a person who's sensitive, caring, smart...with a few character quirks, true. But his good qualities are strong enough to overcome anything."

Were these words addressed to the microphones set into the walls?

Perhaps they were. But Gadi sensed that Francois meant what he'd said.

"And Mirage?" he asked.

Francois spun around to face him, surprised.

"Is Mirage dangerous?" Gadi asked again.

"Mirage," Francois repeated heavily. "Is Mirage dangerous?" He coughed. "The truth is...he might be."

The words echoed through the beautifully appointed living room, whirled around the chandelier, and sank down to land on one of the solidly framed landscapes.

"Don't say anything to my wife," Gadi warned.

"Obviously," Francois said. "Obviously."

---

The rich lode of suspense literature that she'd read was useless. That was what Shuli concluded after a prolonged tour of the kitchen and a search through drawers and cabinets didn't yield even one sharp implement apart from a bunch of disposable knives. The sum total of cleaning supplies comprised a bottle of floor cleanser and one pink rag.

But she didn't only read suspense novels. She also read stories about great people, particularly about women who persisted despite challenges that life presented them. Shuli did something that the heroines in those books often did, although it had always seemed a bit cheesy to her when she'd read it.

Alone in a strange kitchen, cold and well equipped, near a table attached to the wall with screws, she spoke with the Creator of the world, straight from her heart. She told Him about her life. About different choices she could have made. About good words she hadn't said and all sorts of clothes that she had worn. She cried a little. And not because she was trying to be like those heroines.

And she felt that the Master of the universe was listening. He was close by. And He loved her.

## 90

J ARNAIL MADE HIMSELF COMFORTABLE IN HIS SEAT AND stretched his legs out to their full length. There were advantages to being wealthy. Such as the ability to travel first class when there was no room in business class and you had a burning need to get to Israel as soon as possible.

So much had changed in the last few months. For one thing, he and Padmasri were thinking about moving to the US. His wife claimed that if they moved to the US and became acclimatized there, her father would be able to accept the new changes in their lives and handle them in a reasonable fashion, without cutting them off from all the luxuries they'd enjoyed until now.

Now that Pinchas was a father, and with Shaul in a difficult predicament on top of that, he had decided to jump on a plane and offer his assistance from up close. Here, too, Padmasri interjected her voice of reason and had advised that there was no sense in buying helium balloons in Mumbai, or any chance that he'd be permitted to bring them onto the aircraft.

So maybe it wouldn't be so scary to become a Jew. Maybe it would be less difficult than he'd imagined.

Jarnail reached for the cup of wine that had been placed in front of him along with his meal. Then he decided to refrain. If he'd be able to do so in a month and a half, he could withstand the temptation right now. He took out the box of food that Padmasri had prepared for him and felt a strange elation as he chose cold rice over the delicacies served in first class.

And although he had no doubt that Shaul hadn't been referring to people like him when he'd said that there was vital significance to putting a *hechsher* on candies and food coloring, when he thought of his children and the changes that would take place in their lives—he understood for the first time what Shaul had meant. And believed that he was right.

But he would only be able to tell him so in a month and a half, when he and Padmasri completed the process.

Padmasri believed that Shaul would be insulted that Jarnail hadn't let him be involved and would be further insulted when he heard that Pinchas *had* been included in what Jarnail was going through. Still, he was firm in his desire to present Shaul with a fait accompli. Maybe because he wanted to see his friend's shocked face, or because he was afraid that Shaul might convince him somehow that G-d would be happier if Jarnail remained a non-Jew, who believed in Hashem and kept the seven Noahide laws. There was also a chance that what was sealing his lips was the fear that their conversion would sever the source of income for Shaul and his family.

"*Parnasah* is from Heaven," Pinchas had reminded him from time to time in the phone calls they'd conducted at odd hours. "Your thoughts don't have to be troubled by that, Jarnail. Throw your burden on the Creator and all will be well."

"The good does not always come right away," he'd remarked once, knowing that Pinchas would grasp his meaning more fully than most people.

"And not always is what we think good actually good," Pinchas had replied soberly.

Jarnail felt a sudden desire to see Pinchas's eyes, which were probably shining more brightly than the stars in the sky right now, and hear him thank G-d for sending him good that was also sweet. He also wanted to stand beside Shaul and promise him that he, too, would taste that same sweetness soon.

But even money could not shorten the flight. There were still six long hours before the plane was due to land at Ben Gurion Airport. Jarnail made use of the indulgences provided in first class and tilted his seat back so he could sleep.

There was no question about it: People who were Jewish from birth didn't know how to appreciate the gift they'd been given. To think that from childhood, they were aware that they could toss up the keys and know that there was Someone to take them and arrange everything for them in the best possible way.

"Tell Shaul," Padmasri had urged as he'd stood at the door with his suitcase and carry-on. "Say something to him so that later you can at least say that you tried to give him a hint…"

All sorts of possible hints flickered through Jarnail's mind as he sank into a choppy midflight sleep filled with meaningless dreams.

---

"Jarnail's not answering his phone," Shaul reported to Ricki from the taxi that was taking him home. "Neither one of his phones is picking up my call. But when I came out of Maariv, I met an old friend who recommended a brilliant doctor. He said it would be worth our while to consult him about this whole thing."

"This whole thing?"

Shaul compressed his lips. "I hope that Jarnail will get us a medical consult on the phone tomorrow morning, as I asked him to. But I thought we could also consult Blau—"

"Consult who?"

Ricki had sharp senses, and when he was tired, he tended to make unnecessary slips.

"The doctor my friend recommended," he said feebly.

"And who is this doctor?" Ricki would not yield.

"A doctor who works mostly on medical malpractice cases. He has a reputation for being successful at pinpointing mistaken diagnoses."

Ricki was silent for a moment. "Does he have a first name?"

"My friend didn't give it to me." Shaul was glad to use this escape hatch.

"You said his name was Blau. From the way you're acting, it seems that this is *our* Blau. Is that true?"

"That's a reasonable assumption."

"And he'll agree to help us?"

"I'll find out tomorrow."

"Not until tomorrow?"

"I can't call him now and wake him up…"

"In Canada, people are fast asleep at eleven forty-five p.m. Here in Israel, as you know, that's not a given."

Shaul sighed. "Even in the best case, there's a chance he'll hang up on me. If I call him at midnight—"

"Eleven forty-five," Ricki corrected him. "Shaul, the doctor keeps saying that we have to treat Ahuvi as soon as possible. We don't have time to play polite games. Besides, as opposed to doctors named Blau, there are plenty of babies named Sofer."

Shaul considered this.

"Doctors are used to getting calls from panicky people at all hours," Ricki pressed. "I don't think there's room for doubt here."

This was true. He nodded. "All right. I'll call him now."

"Good luck," Ricki said. "Talk to you later."

---

Shuli was lingering in the kitchen, and the silence felt oppressive to Gadi. "Mirage is the name of an aircraft, isn't it?" he asked rhetorically. "I didn't know people also have that name."

Francois leaned his head back. "Mirage is the name of an aircraft," he affirmed, eyes staring at the ceiling. "The English word 'mirage,' which, incidentally, originates from French, is also a kind of optical illusion that makes a person see reality in two ways. But it's also a Jewish-Iranian family name. It is—how should I put it?—a very interesting coincidence."

Interesting? Gadi wasn't sure. Still, he smiled politely. "I didn't know either of those things," he said. "You have a rich general knowledge."

"If you like trivia, I can tell you lots of interesting things," Francois said. "But what I told you is what's important."

Gadi was still puzzled. "That Mirage is the name of a Jewish-Iranian family," he repeated, "and also the French word for an optical illusion."

"The kind of illusion that gives rise to a double vision of reality," Francois said again. Then, changing the subject: "Have you davened Maariv yet?"

"No," Gadi admitted. He raised his voice, directing his next words to the faceless voice. "Yair, you're religious, right? You know how important it is to daven with a *minyan*, right? How about taking us to Zichron Moshe so we can daven. There are still *minyanim* there at this hour. Then you can bring us back here."

Silence.

"He may already have gone," Francois said. "I'm pretty sure he's not sitting on the other side of that wall eavesdropping on us all day."

"These days you don't have to sit in any particular spot if you want to eavesdrop on a person," Gadi told the therapist. "He can program his recording equipment and cameras to send all the material they gather right to his cellphone."

"That makes sense," Francois said. He suddenly looked old. After a moment, he roused himself to say, "The Mirage aircraft was the pride of France when I was a boy. The Mirage 4 had a double mission: Officially, it could carry atom bombs at a speed faster than sound. The second was to show the world in general, and the Soviets in particular, that there was no chance that Paris would ever fall again."

"As she did in the First and Second World Wars?" Gadi asked politely.

"Yes. But that's not our subject. We're talking about the Mirage of my childhood, not about world wars."

Gadi blinked. Francois didn't sound like himself.

"When have you last had something to eat?" he asked delicately. "Do you want me to get you a drink?"

"I'd love a good cup of tea. But last time I checked, there was no kettle in the kitchen."

"If there's no bread, you eat cake. If there's no tea, you drink water," Gadi said. "Tastier, healthier, better."

Francois laughed. "Human nature is fascinating," he said. "Two men are sitting in captivity, and instead of trying to figure out how to escape, they're telling each other jokes."

"So far, I told only one joke," Gadi pointed out. "But I can think of more."

"Instead of that, how about if we continue with the trivia?" Francois said seriously. "I know a great deal about the Mirage. I read up on it when I was a boy..."

## 91

FRANCOIS WASN'T AN OLD MAN, BUT NEITHER WAS HE young any longer. Although his hair had only partially silvered, he appeared elderly and frail to Gadi now, with bags under his eyes and age spots on the hands that rested weakly on his knees. His closed eyelids masked the spark of life that had drawn Gadi to him. The man who'd lost his father before the age of twenty-three felt a pang of alarm in his heart.

"Everything will be all right, Francois," he promised. "Don't worry. We'll get out of this. Hashem is great."

"Yes, that's certainly true. And His greatness is not connected to any outcome we might hope for," Francois remarked logically.

"People like to say that," Gadi said. "They like to say that it's not connected, but sometimes, Francois, that's just an excuse not to believe strongly enough that Hashem is good to everyone."

"Are you trying to say that there is no pain or suffering in the world? No sorrow?" The psychologist opened his eyes. "I encounter endless pain and sorrow in my clinic. Endless."

"Of course. That's obvious." Gadi waved a dismissive hand. "I'm not stupid, and I'm not trying to claim that everything in life is fine and dandy. All I said was that sometimes, only sometimes, people say those words at a challenging time because they don't have enough faith. Why do we have to justify the decree in advance? We only need to know that the Creator wants to bestow good, that there's no limit to

His love, and that if He desires it, everything can be transformed into good in an instant."

"You've turned into a Rebbe," Francois said. Although Gadi was by nature sensitive and suspicious, he found no trace of mockery in the other man's voice.

"No, not a Rebbe," he said. "I know I'm no great tzaddik. But... look at the way I grew from nothing. From a young man with zero, I became rich within fifteen years. You know better than anyone that my life has not been all sweetness and honey—but I do believe that Hashem can do anything. And when He wants something, there is no power that can prevent Him from helping."

"I believe that, too," Francois said soberly.

"In that case," Gadi said, "we can continue having a pleasant chat about the Mirages that you loved as a boy while Hashem arranges everything for the best."

Francois gave a short bark of laughter and then took a long, slow breath. "Yes, we were talking about Mirages. Did I tell you that their creator was a Jew? His name was Marcel Dassault, if I'm not mistaken."

Tension was fraying Gadi's nerves, and the other man's slow, measured words annoyed him.

"Was he religious, this Dassault?" he asked.

"I have no idea. It's reasonable to assume that he was not. But he had a good Jewish head. He devised an aircraft that no radar has ever been able to pick up. Planes that no enemy of France ever saw when they flew above them at top speed. Beautiful planes, big and stealthy. So fast that no one ever saw it. All the children in France admired them—and the adults, too. Charles de Gaulle—he was our president then—established the *Force de frappe*, a strike force that used the Mirage as its central pivot."

"Interesting," Gadi said politely, though in truth he was completely disinterested, and he groped for a change of subject. "How about if I bring you something to drink now?"

"I'm okay, I'm okay," Francois said. "And I want you to listen. This is part of my history. Part of my childhood."

*Human beings are amazing creatures*, Gadi thought, recalling Francois's earlier words. Here were two men sitting in captivity, and instead of thinking about how to escape, they tell each other about planes from their childhood?

Really?

He knew himself capable, in the right mood, of doing something that foolish. But Francois? This wasn't like him. Not at all.

"I'll bring you a cup of water, and we'll keep talking," Gadi said firmly. He crossed the living room and walked into the kitchen where, at the table, his wife sat in tears. "Are you okay?" he asked.

"Yes," she said, her voice surprisingly strong in contrast to her red eyes. "It's just…" She was embarrassed. "I talked to Hashem and cried a little. Don't worry, they were good tears."

"At least this captivity is bringing out our better sides," he answered, with a touch of his usual cynicism. "You're talking to Hashem, and I'm giving Francois hearty pep talks. Do you have any idea where I can find disposable cups?"

"In the second drawer," Shuli said. "And I wouldn't mind"—she inhaled—"a hearty pep talk myself."

"I just reminded him that Hashem is good," Gadi said, turning on the water faucet the way, according to the stories, Soviet Jews would do when they wanted to confound the authorities' bugging devices. He also lowered his voice. "He's acting strange. I think he's trying to hint something to me, but I don't understand what. Could you please come back to the living room and help me try to figure it out?"

---

When Shaul was small, perhaps eight years old, and his family had lived in Montreal, when playing ball one day he had broken a window in the home of an old man who was always yelling. He was an anti-Semite who lived across the way. It was scary, it was mortifying, and he'd run away, feeling as if his heart, beating with all its might in his throat, was almost choking him.

Then his father had taught him how a grown-up behaves.

"A grown-up is not afraid of doing the right thing," he'd said, holding Shaul's small, trembling hand in his big one. "You're eight years old, Shaul. You're old enough to deal with a little unpleasantness. Take your money box and go knock on his door. Tell him that you broke his window and that you're prepared to pay to fix it."

His father hadn't come with him to the neighbor's house. He'd stood in the lobby of their building, watching Shaul cross the street like a man walking the plank, press the bell with a shaking finger, and wait for the old man to answer.

The man had been angry at first. Shaul could still remember the fear he'd felt in the face of his neighbor's furious words and big, hairy hands. But the words his father had practiced with him softened the old man's heart, especially, it had seemed to Shaul, when he saw the money box. He'd emptied it completely, but afterward began to smile at the boy each time they met in the street. The anti-Semitic shouts with which the old man used to persecute the neighborhood children ceased.

The loss of his savings, which he'd been setting aside to buy a set of *Mishnayos*, and one frightening and unpleasant experience had been a costly but worthwhile price to pay. Shaul tried to remember the lesson he'd learned as he called Dr. Blau to ask for his help now.

But the comparison between his childhood memory and the present reality was greater than Shaul had initially believed.

He waited for Blau to pick up his call, but he didn't answer. The doctor might have silenced the ringer before he went to bed. Or maybe he didn't answer calls from unfamiliar numbers after work hours. He would have to go knocking on the man's door. He had no other choice.

A call to the telephone information gave him the address of the Blau family, and his taxi driver was happy to change course.

"Can you wait five minutes?" Shaul asked as he paid the man for the ride. "They may not even open the door. In that case, I'll come right back. If not—you can go on and I'll manage on my own."

"*Ein baayah*," the driver said, speaking in a glaring Arabic accent. "No problem."

Shaul exited the cab with a heavy heart and studied the building. Every floor had at least one lit window, he comforted himself. There was a reasonable chance that someone in the Blau family was still awake.

"Yes?" asked the overgrown teenager who opened the door. "What?"

Was this Ari? The boy whom the entire staff of the *cheder* had adored less than a year ago? Shaul found it hard to absorb the change that had taken place in the boy who'd been expelled from the school. But he couldn't think about that now. "I'm looking for Dr. Blau," he said very politely. "Is he here?"

"No," said the youth, whose coarse features didn't fit with the well-lit, plant-filled room behind him. "He's not home. And I know who you are! You're Benny's father, right?"

92

HE WAS BENNY'S FATHER. ABSOLUTELY. BUT THE DIRECTNESS of the question confused Shaul. "I know who you are, too," he said without thinking. "You're Ari, aren't you?"

The youth grimaced. "Guilty as charged."

Though it was meant, apparently, to be a lighthearted quip, an arrow was thrust right between Shaul's ribs. How miserable a person had to be if merely confirming his identity was, for him, a confession of guilt!

"I came to see your father about something else," Shaul said. "It's urgent. But now that we've met…I don't know if I have anything to apologize for, because the school reached its decision without us. I wasn't even in the country at that time. But I realized just today how unhappy you were two years ago, when you started bothering Benny. You'd apparently gone through a difficult time."

"When?" the boy asked aggressively.

"When you started playing pranks on Benny. When they rescinded your father's license to practice medicine."

"What's the connection?" Ari was even angrier. "You don't understand anything."

Maybe he didn't. Shaul was at a loss. The connections he'd drawn between the information Eli Levy had given him and Ari's behavior may have been too hasty. But the dates were too congruent to be mere coincidence.

"Anyway," he said, faking a cough to give himself a second to collect his thoughts, "I think you're a strong boy. And it's clear to me that you'll get wherever you want to go."

Ari's lips curled again. "You can be sure of that. But I don't need compliments from you."

His tone was dismissive and insulting, but Shaul accepted it with understanding. "When do you think it will be possible to speak to your father?"

The boy shrugged. "Maybe tomorrow morning."

"How early can I call?"

"Ten."

"Ten?"

"He doesn't usually answer the phone before then. He's learning."

Shaul inhaled and let his breath out in a sigh. "I came here about a matter that's practically life and death. They said there's a chance that he's the only one who can help me. Can you ask him to call me?"

"Call Benny's father?" The question was loaded. "Honestly, I don't know how happy he'll be."

"I'm sure he'll agree to help us," Shaul insisted. "I'm convinced of it. Just give him the message, please."

"If I see him," Ari said evasively. "I'm going to bed soon, and he usually leaves the house before I wake up."

"Maybe you can leave him a note?" Shaul suggested. "On his tallis bag?"

"Maybe," Ari said. With that, before Shaul had a chance to insert his foot in the doorway to prevent its slamming, it shut in his face.

Knock again? Insist? Explain how urgent this was?

Shaul sighed. What he really wanted to do was turn around and walk away. But parenthood has its obligations. Shaul knocked again. In vain.

With a heavy heart, Shaul looked at the closed door and turned back to the stairs. Ari hadn't actually said that he wouldn't leave a note. His reaction only meant that the boy enjoyed exercising his power. To feel strong.

Slowly, he descended the stairs. He wondered if his duty to Ahuvi obligated him to wait for Dr. Blau to come home, or if it was better to go to sleep and gather his strength to cope with tomorrow's challenges.

He reached for his cellphone and tried again to reach his absent brother-in-law. But Gadi was still unavailable.

Gadi's four children would wake in the morning to find there was no adult at home. They would panic when they realized that both their parents had disappeared and wouldn't know which of their relatives to call. If they woke their grandmother, Ricki's mother, with the news, that could be really bad. His mother-in-law suffered from high blood pressure and had already had one heart-related episode.

Maybe it was more important that he take the reserve key that Gadi had once given him and go sleep on their sofa.

He sighed.

He would do it. Afterward.

Right now, talking to Blau was of paramount importance. He would wait until the doctor returned.

---

Shaul was a patient man. He also knew a slew of pages in the Gemara by heart. The only problem was that at a certain point his feet began to ache.

He bore the situation for twenty more minutes, shifting his weight from leg to leg, before he realized that he had no choice but to sit down on the steps to give his legs a rest.

The next thing he knew two strong hands were shaking him vigorously and an alarmed voice called, "Reb Yid? Reb Yid?"

He'd fallen asleep. On the stairs. Mortified, Shaul scrambled to his feet.

"You're alive!" exclaimed the older man with the Gemara tucked beneath his arm. "When I saw you lying here on the stairs, I was terrified."

"I'm sorry." Shaul was sure he was blushing. "I'm just waiting for the doctor. Dr. Blau…"

The man nodded. "What do you need?" he asked. "He doesn't see patients at home."

"I need advice," Shaul said briefly. "My daughter is in the hospital, and I need his opinion."

"You know that they took away his license." The other man lowered his voice.

"His license, but not his ability," Shaul said with a smile. "He comes highly recommended as a second opinion."

"Yes, they say he's a genius," the older Jew agreed. "He has an office on the other side of the building, in the parking area."

"Thank you." With a nod, Shaul hurried downstairs. The street was dimly lit, and the tall trees surrounding the building made it even darker. Shaul used the flashlight on his phone to try to determine which of the three "other sides" of the building the man had been referring to. The search wasn't as simple as it should have been, since someone had decided to build a chicken coop on one side of the structure, while a second side boasted a pile of heavy construction materials and lumber scattered dangerously about. On the third side, though, Shaul managed to locate the entrance to the building's storage rooms, which people sometimes turned into private offices. A square of illumination, winking at him in the distance, gave him hope.

At that moment, the light went out.

Shaul halted. He squinted in the dark, waiting for the sound of a door opening and the sight of the doctor walking toward him.

But neither of those things happened.

Instead, he heard a thud, as if something had fallen, followed by what he could only call a groan. Though it was entirely possible that Dr. Blau had simply bumbled into something on his way to the door, Shaul's tension over Ahuvi's condition and the three disappearances caused him to dart toward the door with a sense that even a moment's delay could lead to tragedy.

"Dr. Blau!" he called, struggling with the immovable doorknob. "Dr. Blau, can you hear me?"

Silence. Profound silence.

But someone was there. Shaul was convinced of that. Someone who had turned off the light, then bumped into a table or something so that it had toppled over, and then groaned.

"Dr. Blau?" He knocked again, and pressed his ear to the door. "Do you hear me?"

No response. But Shaul's ear picked up the sound of rapid breathing on the other side of the door.

"Dr. Blau," he said, "if you don't answer me, I'm going to break down the door and come inside to see if you're all right..."

Silence. Followed by a jerky voice. "Everything's...fine. Go away."

*Everything's fine? Go away?* Shaul wrinkled his nose.

"Dr. Blau?" He knocked again. "Are you sure you don't need help?"

A pause. "Yes. I'm sure."

"Then maybe you can open the door for me? I need your help..."

Shaul tried to infuse his voice with all the warmth he possessed. It apparently made no impression on the man on the other side of the door who, after the usual pause, said, "I can't right now. Go away."

But Shaul hadn't come here in order to retreat. "Dr. Blau, it's urgent. A matter of *pikuach nefesh*... Someone sent me to you. It's really urgent."

Silence.

As though there was no one at all behind the locked door.

Shaul scratched his chin thoughtfully, trying to make sense of the strange situation he'd stumbled into. Maybe Blau was too conceited to let a stranger see him sitting on the floor with a sprained ankle. But although this possibility was more logical than any of the others scrolling through his brain, he didn't accept it.

He glanced right and left, remembered the pile of building materials, and hurried there on tiptoe. He succeeded in making his way back without making a sound, a heavy plank of lumber in hand.

"Dr. Blau," he said, "I'm worried about you. If you don't open the door, I'm going to break it."

Though he addressed the door, his eyes were on the window. It would be easier to shatter and less expensive to repair. Entering that way would be a good idea.

"Dr. Blau?" he said. "Dr. Blau? This is the last—"

Another thud sounded from within. Just as he lifted the plank to break the window, it opened right in front of his face and the upraised wood struck a figure, dressed from head to toe in black, who had shot out through the window.

The blow, which had been intended to shatter the glass, landed with force on the shoulder of the man in black, but didn't stop him. He evaded Shaul's hands and disappeared in the direction of the street.

"Dr. Blau?" Shaul looked back at the door. "Dr. Blau? Is everything okay?"

A groan.

Shaul bit his lip. After a second's hesitation, he called the police, gave them the address and details of the incident, and requested urgent assistance. Then he pushed a plastic-covered couch close to the window, climbed up and peered inside.

"Dr. Blau?"

His heart skipped a beat at the sight of a figure sprawled on the floor. In one courageous, but perhaps thoughtless, leap, he was inside.

He closed the window behind him, turned on the light, and

crouched by the sprawled figure. There was a cut in his shirt, but it was completely superficial. Apparently, what had stunned the man was a blow with a heavy implement to the side of his face.

"Dr. Blau..." Shaul filled a washing cup with water and squatted beside the man, dabbing water gently on his face. "Are you okay? Should I call for help?"

"No, no," the man groaned. "No, thank you."

A person saying "thank you" is conscious enough, it seemed. Shaul's heart rate slowed slightly. "Can I help you sit up?" he asked. "Do you feel well? I called the police."

"Cancel it," the man said. "Cancel it."

It was too late. Blue lights were already flickering outside, and Shaul's cellphone vibrated: a nearby patrol car, requesting exact directions to their location.

The police officers, one of Ethiopian origin and one Russian-born, were very pleasant. They questioned the injured doctor mildly about the break-in, shaking their heads sternly when they heard that the man had found it easy to get inside because the door had been unlocked. They were sorry to hear that the intruder had worn gloves and a mask and glad to hear that he'd left without taking anything. Seeing no need for medical assistance, they canceled the ambulance they had summoned in the wake of Shaul's call and recommended that Dr. Blau go down to the station the next day to submit a formal complaint.

"I suggest that you leave together with them and go upstairs to your apartment," Shaul said as the policemen prepared to depart. "You shouldn't stay down here in case he comes back."

"Good idea," said one of the officers.

The other one added, "You said you have no enemies. If he just came in randomly to search for valuables, we can probably assume that he won't be back."

"I'll stay here, thanks." The doctor's smile was strained. "I'm not going to let anyone chase me out of my office... When do you think it will be safe for me to come back here?"

Shaul smiled. "When you've replaced the door and put security bars on the window, maybe?"

"Two good ideas," said the police officer who had previously urged the doctor to leave. "That way you'll be protected."

"Maybe I'll work at home for a few days," Dr. Blau said. He scanned the room, whose walls were covered with medical tomes sporting titles in English. Then he picked up a small carton containing a few binders and grimaced when pain prevented him from carrying it.

"I'll help you," Shaul volunteered, taking the box from the doctor. With the two officers escorting them, they left the office and started for the building.

***

"Why did you come here anyway?" Dr. Blau asked as Shaul placed the carton on the table in the dark dining room of his home.

"To ask your advice about my daughter's medical condition," Shaul said hesitantly. "May I?"

Blau gave a forced smile. "The truth? It's not worth it at this moment. You may have saved my life, but I don't think I'll be able to focus right now. Do you have any medical records for me to peruse? Do you want to leave it with me, and I'll read it when I've recovered a bit?"

"I can write down the details of the case now," Shaul said, feeling slightly embarrassed. "If you'd just give me a pen and paper..."

A moment's searching brought Dr. Blau back from the kitchen with a small bottle of pain relief medication, from which he extracted two pills and swallowed them with another grimace.

"I can't find any paper," he said. "Do you want to summarize the case for me? Let's start from the beginning. How old is your daughter? What is her condition now?"

"Eight months," said Shaul. "And she...she's not really reacting. She's not focusing, she's very weak, doesn't lift her head—"

"Did she have a stomachache?"

"Yes. For a few days. My wife thought—"

The doctor raised one finger. "We're both tired," he said. "So let's cut to the chase. In the hospital, they checked out the common things. You came to me for the things that are less common. So tell me, has anyone mentioned botulism? That's a toxin that settles on the nerve connectors and can affect an infant's intestines."

"They talked about epilepsy," Shaul said.

"Epilepsy?" Blau wrinkled his nose. "Maybe. But tell them to check for botulism. And call me again in the morning." He rubbed the side of his face. "I can't understand what was in those binders to cause someone to break into my office with such violence..."

"There are people who are prepared to go very far to protect their good name," said Shaul. "Maybe you ran into a person like that at some point?"

"Maybe..." Blau murmured. "Anyway, about your case. I think it's worthwhile telling the medical team to look for botulism—urgently. Time is a factor here. That could be a good direction to explore."

"Absolutely. Thank you so much," Shaul said from the depths of his heart.

"Thank *you*." Blau passed a hand over his face again. "First, for saving my life, and second, for giving me a direction to think about. Someone happened to speak to me just last week about some complicated medical suspicion..." He fell silent again. "We'll talk tomorrow," he said, walking Shaul to the door. "Do you have my cellphone number?"

Shaul nodded.

"What's your name, by the way?"

There were many Sofers in the world, as Ricki had said just a few hours ago. But Shaul was the one who saw the expression that crossed the doctor's face at the sound of his name.

"Do we know each other from somewhere, Rabbi?" the man asked in a less friendly voice.

"We don't know each other personally," Shaul said with a shrug. "We can get acquainted now."

The doctor gave him a long look, and then sighed. "As I said, you saved my life tonight. And maybe my idea will save your daughter's life, so we'll be even. Let's leave it at that."

"Yes," Shaul agreed. "I'll call you tomorrow."

"If there's a need," Blau said.

"Let's hope there won't be any need, and she'll be completely healthy," Shaul said. "Feel good—and thanks for the advice."

"You're welcome," said Blau, looking completely drained. "Good night."

---

Jarnail fell asleep in the taxi the moment it left the airport and began making its way toward Jerusalem. The flight had exhausted him. When the driver asked him, "Where exactly do you need to go?" he unthinkingly blurted Pinchas's address. He had come here in order to take part in his friend's joy.

"Well, that's right here!" the driver exclaimed. "It's a good thing I woke you, eh?" Before Jarnail was fully awake, the taxi stopped. He paid his fare and got out, carrying his travel bags and cringing in the predawn cold typical of the city.

It was only after the taxi had driven away that he realized how ludicrous the situation was.

It was 5:30 a.m. Pinchas was peacefully asleep and he—carrying a bouquet of flowers he'd bought in the airport—was preparing to knock on his door to shower blessings on his head.

The situation was laughable, but Jarnail was too tired to laugh. He was also at a loss.

What to do with himself now?

The small street slumbered around him. At this hour, not even taxis were circling aimlessly.

He needed a taxi. Yawn. He needed to go to the hotel he'd stayed in the last time he was here. Another yawn. Just as his face split in a third, enormous yawn, a light went on in a window on the first floor.

Pinchas was up!

A small smile touched Jarnail's lips. He wouldn't have planned this, but now that he was already here, maybe he'd give Pinchas a bit of a surprise. . .

Should he simply stand at the door and wait for him with a bouquet of flowers and warm, heartfelt congratulations?

The thought of Pinchas's astonished expression amused him—and the actual expression that he witnessed eight and a half minutes later amused him even more.

"What are you doing here?" Pinchas was overjoyed. Jarnail had never seen a happier man. "How did you get here?"

"On a plane." Jarnail held out the flowers. "I had to congratulate you face to face as soon as possible."

"Wow." Pinchas was very moved. "And what a bouquet!"

"The biggest and most beautiful I could find…" Jarnail said. "It cost as much as three of them."

Pinchas chuckled, embarrassed. "So Shaul told you?"

"Yes. I understood that you were too discombobulated and busy to do it yourself."

"Yes." Pinchas laughed silently. "But…you came straight here from the airport?"

"Yes." Jarnail lifted his shoulders sheepishly. "I told you, I wanted to congratulate you as soon as possible, so my subconscious gave the taxi driver your address instead of the Ramada Hotel... Just tell me in two words what it feels like to be a father, and I'll leave for the hotel."

"It's... incredible," " said Pinchas.

"I'm happy," Jarnail said. "I'm so happy for you, Pinchas. So, so happy."

They stood side by side, in a mutual peaceful silence.

"I wanted to pray with an early *minyan*," Pinchas said hesitantly, "so that I could get to the hospital early."

Jarnail nodded his understanding. "Of course, I won't hold you back. But—"

"Yes?"

"Since I'm already here"—Jarnail hesitated—"would it be all right if I came to shul with you? I've been davening Shacharis for two months already, but I've never done it with a *minyan* yet."

Pinchas was uncertain. Jarnail read as much in his features and in the way he rubbed his nose. But just as he opened his mouth to say that he understood if today wasn't the right day, Pinchas said, "Gladly, Jarnail. But take into consideration that this is a small and not especially impressive *minyan*, okay? There are much more powerful experiences of praying with a *minyan*."

———

"I think it *was* powerful," Jarnail said fifty-five minutes later after all the members of the minyan finished saying mazel tov to Pinchas. "Even though, as you said, it was a small minyan." He paused a moment. "I'm a fairly intellectual kind of person," he said. "But when they said *Birkas Kohanim*, there was something in the air. I felt it."

The words were still on his lips when his phone emitted a familiar chime

"Shaul!" he said in alarm. "Why would he be calling me now?"

"Jarnail?" Shaul's voice over the phone was tense. "I need your help."

"Is this about the doctor?" Jarnail asked. "Don't worry—"

"No, not about the doctor. Something else." Shaul spoke tightly. "I called because I've gotten mixed up in a strange business here..."

93

MORNINGS WERE COLD IN YERUSHALAYIM, AND THE COLD, together with the odd note in Shaul's voice, made Jarnail shiver. "What is it?" he asked. "What happened?"

"Do you know what a tall tale is?" Shaul asked rhetorically. "It's a kind of story that stretches the nerves and the limits of reality. When I was a boy, I had a friend who liked to tell a story like that, about a family that lived on the first floor of a building. The father said that he was going up to the top floor. He went up and didn't come back. So the mother went to check where he was, and she didn't come back. Then the oldest son went to find them—and *he* didn't come back. And on and on…until the youngest child, who was left all alone, decided to go up, too. And when he reached the elevator, he found them all sitting there, eating watermelon."

Jarnail's brows came together as this tale tumbled into his ears in one long breath. "Nice story," he said, wondering.

"I don't know about that," Shaul said. "First of all, it wasn't very nice that no one came down to invite the youngest child to eat with them. And second—it was nice only at the end. Not in the middle, when people are disappearing all around you."

"Explain, please," Jarnail snapped.

Pinchas, standing nearby, was able to hear some of what Shaul had said but not enough to fully understand. He wrinkled his brow as Jarnail adopted his "security guard" voice.

"My son went to see his psychologist last night," Shaul said, "and discovered that he had disappeared. Because my brother-in-law, Gadi, is friendly with the man, my son decided to fill him in and ask for his help. My brother-in-law went, walked around the apartment a little, tried to figure out where the man had gone, and then brought my son home."

"Yes?" Jarnail urged.

"Two hours later, I noticed that my brother-in-law had called me several times in a row. But when I tried to call him back, there was no answer. Since then, his cellphone hasn't been available to take calls. He also never returned to his apartment last night." Shaul lowered his voice. "His wife's gone, too. The children will be waking up soon, and I'm worried."

"You sound worried," Jarnail agreed. "They…they're not the type to do such a thing, are they?"

"No. They might leave the children sleeping alone in the apartment for an hour or two, but never for a full night. And not if their cellphones aren't working."

He breathed deeply. "But wait—that's not the end of the story. Last night, I went to find a doctor who was recommended to me for Ahuvi. He wasn't home, and I couldn't reach him on his cell. I gave his son my number and asked that his father call me back as soon as he could. Then I found the doctor, and I actually saved him from some guy in a stocking mask who had broken into his office. I walked him home and got the advice I needed. But now they just called—the doctor's wife and son—to ask if I ever got to see the doctor, since he never came home last night. He—"

"Disappeared," Jarnail finished.

"Exactly. When I spoke with the son, it turned out that the last place they knew he'd gone the night before—that is, before I met him and the guy in the stocking mask—was the home of the psychologist I just told you about. He knows him, too."

Jarnail cleared his throat. "Strange."

"Yes," said Shaul. "Strange is an understatement. What do I do with all this?"

Jarnail considered the question for a long moment. "First of all, don't send Benny to school this morning."

"Benny? I never even thought of that! And it's already six forty-five—he may have left the house!"

"Call and try to stop him," Jarnail said. "That's the most urgent thing right now."

Because it did sound urgent, Shaul didn't even say thank you or goodbye before he disconnected.

A moment passed, and then two. Something about the silence began to seem odd.

"Let's hope that Shaul hasn't disappeared now," Pinchas remarked. "Call him."

Jarnail was already tapping out the number.

---

"He already left." Shaul sounded discouraged. "I sent my daughter after him to the bus stop. She's supposed to call me when they get home." His voice dropped to a whisper. "My nephew also woke up. I told him that his parents had to go away, without giving too many details. Do you think I should let him go to school?"

"Yes," said Jarnail. "So far only those who'd been in the psychologist's apartment are missing, but not their relatives. Correct?"

The beep of an incoming call prompted Shaul to disconnect again without a word of apology. He was soon back and in low spirits. "He wasn't at the bus stop. My daughter said that a bus had just passed by. Apparently, he was on it."

"Call the school," Jarnail said. "Let them contact you the minute he gets there." He paused to think and then added, "And on second thought, it may be a good idea for your nephew to stay home, too. So you won't have to stay there to babysit."

"But what do I do? Where am I going with this story? Do you think the police will take me seriously? Or will the two or three hours that I sit there be a waste of precious time?"

Jarnail glanced at Pinchas and sighed. "I'm not an Israeli, Shaul. I'm not familiar with the police here. I don't know what their procedures are."

"But you're the only person I know who has any kind of experience in this area. Tell me what you think."

"In Mumbai, there wasn't much point going to the police," Jarnail said slowly. "The Israeli police, of course, are much more efficient. I don't know what to say, Shaul. I simply don't know. Try to reach your son's school. In the meantime, I'll try to figure something out."

"Thank you," Shaul said. "Thank you very much."

"My pleasure," Jarnail responded, but the line had fallen silent. He turned to Pinchas, who'd been filled in on the details of the story along with snippets from the cellphone. "What do you think?"

"What could prompt people to disappear like that?" Pinchas answered the question with a question.

"It could be a panicky criminal," Jarnail said, "who knows he's made a critical mistake that may enable people to identify him. Or…a madman."

"Crazy people aren't this illogical," Pinchas offered. "I mean, where's the logic that would lead someone to kidnap everyone who was in a certain apartment? That sounds really strange."

"Maybe he thinks, for instance, that everyone who entered that apartment is an Iranian spy who came there for an annual spy conference," Jarnail suggested. "And that's why he thinks he's obligated to get them all out of the way." He rubbed his forehead. "I think we need to involve the police. But—I have an idea—the one who ought to call is the boy. Shaul's nephew. Let him report that his parents have disappeared. The police won't ignore that. They'll come immediately."

He called Shaul and shared his idea with him. "The police are more sensitive to cases that involve children," he explained. "When they come, he can tell them everything that he heard from you. When they need you, they'll come to you. That will be better for everyone."

"Isn't it…" Shaul hesitated. "Isn't it a little cruel to drop this on my nephew and then vanish?"

"It's worse not to try to speed matters up to find his parents," Jarnail said firmly. "Take advantage of the fact that the other kids are still sleeping and explain to him that this may be nothing."

"He won't believe me," Shaul said in distress. "He's a smart boy."

Jarnail was silent for a beat. "Does your wife really have to be with the baby?" he asked. "In such an emergency, can't the nurses keep an eye on her?"

"I'll ask her," Shaul said, his voice even heavier. "Although I must say that the staff hasn't been acting as if they like us much…"

"This is an emergency," Jarnail said sympathetically. "She can explain that to them, and they'll understand. They're human beings."

"One can always hope," Shaul said with a sigh. "Okay, what else?"

"It would be a good idea to send someone to pick up Benny from school," Jarnail said. "But you can't be in three places at once. I'll ask

Pinchas if he can do that for you."

"Don't involve him in this," Shaul said. "Let him be happy… He's waited for this happiness a long time."

"A long time," Pinchas agreed, taking the phone from Jarnail. "Give me the address, Shaul. I'll go."

"Are you part of this conference?" Shaul asked, stunned.

"Jarnail landed here two hours ago," his friend replied. "He surprised me at the door, and we went to *vasikin* together. He's amazing."

"You went *where* together?" Shaul's astonishment deepened.

"Never mind. Remind me which school Benny goes to," Pinchas said, trying to cover his tracks. "I'll go there right now."

"And I'll come to you." Jarnail took the phone and put the call on speakerphone. "If you'll tell me where. You're on speakerphone. No secrets now."

"You are both good friends." Shaul was moved. "I thank Hashem for sending you to me. I was feeling very alone."

"Let's hope that they'll all be found soon, and we'll get a slice of watermelon," Jarnail said encouragingly. "There may be a simple explanation for this whole thing."

Really?

Was that possible?

94

DESPITE THE COMPLICATED SITUATION, SHAUL SMILED when he saw his two friends waiting for him in a car near the entrance of Gadi's building, where he had spent a fitful night on the Phillipses' couch.

"Thanks for coming," he said. "And so quickly."

"Thank Pinchas," Jarnail said. "I don't know if I would have come here only for you and Ahuvi. But when I heard about the triplets, I suddenly felt a powerful need to be with both you and him, so I jumped on a plane and came here."

"A private plane?" Shaul entered the rental car and took the back seat.

Jarnail chuckled. "No, I'm just the son-in-law of a wealthy man, not the wealthy man himself. But I traveled first class, because I *am* his son-in-law, and there was no room in business class. Now tell me, what's happening, Shaul? What's been going on in the last ten minutes?"

"Benny is at school." Shaul sounded relieved. "I spoke to his teacher. He'll warn him not to go out to the yard during recess and will keep an eye on him until the end of the day."

"What happens when school is over?" Jarnail asked.

Shaul gave a mirthless laugh. "By then, we'll stop the kidnaper, find all the kidnapees, and send them home," he said. "Won't we? My niece's class has parent-teacher meetings tonight, and her mother has to be there on time."

Jarnail sighed. "Let's try, for a moment, to separate ourselves from the emotional aspect," he said. "That's never helpful. We need to try to be as clear and practical as possible." He paused, silent. "Where is the apartment where everything began?"

"It's a twenty-minute drive from here."

"It wouldn't be wise to just go in," Pinchas pointed out from the driver's seat. "If there are cameras, for instance, we'll ruin any chances of acting in the future."

"If I had a weapon," Jarnail said thoughtfully, "I would go in and wait for someone to come and challenge me. But I have no weapon. I have nothing…" He lowered his eyes to his thigh, but the dagger that the believing Sikh carries with him everywhere was gone.

"We wouldn't want to put you at risk," Shaul said. "We don't know if the people who vanished were only kidnaped, right?"

"At this stage, nothing is certain," Jarnail said. "They may all be sitting there eating watermelon, as you so wisely pointed out in our phone conversation. We need to get to the apartment and see what it can tell us."

"And place ourselves in the sights of anyone who might be staking out the place."

"That's why I wish I had a weapon," Jarnail said. "You wouldn't happen to know someone who can supply me with one, along with some bugging and tracking equipment, do you?"

Both men shook their heads.

"All right," said Jarnail. "Listen—I have an idea. Not an especially brilliant idea, but it's a place to start. I have a friend at the embassy. He was my second-in-command and inherited my position." There was a slight, but marked, change in his tone. "He owes me a few favors. I'll call him at around eight a.m. Any earlier would be impolite, and he might not be so willing to help."

"How will he help you?" Pinchas didn't understand. "Will he tell you where you can get hold of a weapon and spying equipment?"

Jarnail laughed. "No, I'll ask him for help, which I'll pay for." He lifted his shoulders and then said, "I'm not used to talking about such things too explicitly, but because you two aren't good at riddles—I'm going to ask him to give two or three guys from the embassy's security team a day off, plus money for a little trip."

"A trip to Yerushalayim," Pinchas guessed.

Jarnail smiled. "No, Tzefas."

"Tzefas!" Pinchas echoed. Then he said. "I get it. Okay. Fine."

"And meanwhile," Jarnail said, "until eight, you two can go to that apartment and take a look around. I'm going to the Kosel."

"Where?" Shaul was certain he hadn't heard right.

"To the Kosel," Jarnail repeated. "King Solomon requested that the prayers of non-Jews should always be accepted there, no?"

Silence filled the car from window to window.

"Did I misunderstand something?" Jarnail was at a loss. "I thought that if…" He was silent for a moment, and then continued, "In any case, it worked for me twice already. Once when I prayed to climb out of my depression. Two weeks later, someone called me from your Vaad HaKashrus and introduced me to you two. And the second time was when I came to Israel about ten months ago to pray for you, Pinchas. I asked G-d to give you at least three children, like He'd given me." He paused. "Two daughters and a son. That says something, doesn't it?"

"Wow," Pinchas said. "Amazing. Thank you, Jarnail. I didn't know that."

Jarnail shrugged. "You are important to me," he said. "I wanted you to be happy."

"Wow. I'm touched. Really touched." Pinchas was feeling so emotional that the situation began to border on the uncomfortable.

"Listen, Jarnail!" Shaul tried to lighten the atmosphere. "If your prayers are so well accepted, I'm going to start sending you names of people throughout this country to daven for. Forty days at the Kosel…"

Jarnail snorted. "I know, I know," he said. "I told Pinchas that you're the only one who has a chance of finding a reason that would convince me not to convert. But that's it. They already rejected me numerous times. You don't have to do it again. You can just wish me luck. Okay?"

Shaul was silent. Then he said, "I wish you the very best of luck, Jarnail."

"*Amen*," Jarnail said fervently. "Now here's an update for you, Shaul. If all goes as it should, it will happen soon. Let's concentrate on what's urgent. Shaul, remove my laptop from my travel bag, open the CD compartment, and take out the purple sticker you'll find there. Yes, that's it. Put it in your sock. Now I can track you from anywhere to anywhere…"

A sound interrupted them. "That's my cellphone," Shaul said, thrusting his hand into his pocket. "It's probably my wife… No, it's

Benny's teacher." His face darkened. "Hm, what does he want?" he asked as he brought the phone to his ear.

"Abba?" Benny gasped into his ear. "Listen to something that I just thought of. The last time I was with Francois, he acted very strange. He was kind of confused. And he explained to me that someone had come to him who'd gotten mixed up in a lie, and the lie had grown, and he didn't know what to do about it. Because if he told the truth now, a lot of people would be angry at him, and he'd probably get fired from his job and have to give back a lot of money."

"Yes?" Shaul encouraged him.

"Then he told me that unlike regular people, he has to protect his clients' secrets and can't tell them to anyone." Benny caught his breath. "So, Abba, maybe that guy, the one who lied, killed Francois because he was afraid that in the end Francois would give away his secret to someone, like the police?"

"First of all," Shaul said, trying to calm both his son and himself, "there's no need to assume the worst-case scenario. We hope that everything's okay and that Francois is well."

"But, Abba, listen a minute, okay?"

"I'm listening."

"I feel in my heart that this is right."

"That the guy who lied to a lot of people, and is afraid to tell the truth now because he's afraid he'll lose his job, is the one who kidnaped Francois?"

"Francois was really confused," Benny repeated stubbornly. "And now I realize that he understood that the lie he heard is just too big. Don't you always tell me that someone who tells a lie has no idea what other *aveiros* will come after that? That's what Francois realized, too. That's why he was stressed. Because he realized that it put him in danger."

His son was thirteen and a half, and he loved suspense stories, of which his father was less than enamored. But even if it was those adventures that were speaking out of the boy's throat, it was still the first and only thread they had to follow in unraveling this mystery.

Shaul decided to take it seriously.

## 95

J ARNAIL AND PINCHAS LISTENED TO SHAUL IN SOBER
silence.

"This is certainly something worth checking out," Jarnail said energetically. "Drop me off here, and then go to the apartment to look for
the psychologist's appointment book. We'll be in touch the moment
you find it."

"You're still going to the Kosel?" Pinchas asked.

"Yes." A quick smile lit the man's dark eyes. "Isn't that what you
would consider the minimal effort? *Hishtadlus*, you call it, am I right?"

For Jarnail, the matter was simple. Both Pinchas and Shaul experienced a pang of nostalgic envy.

"We'll daven here," Shaul said after a moment's silence. "May your
*tefillos* be accepted, Jarnail."

"*Amen.*" The man glanced at his wristwatch. "At eight, I'll call the
man at the embassy to ask for backup, and then I'll call you to find
out what's happening. Meanwhile, you two drive to the apartment,
go inside—"

"We don't have a key," Pinchas remarked.

"Benny told me that there's a neighbor, the landlady, who has a
key," Shaul said. "It'll be all right."

"Excellent," said Jarnail. "So go to the apartment, find the appointment book, and make a list of the clients who were there last week, on
the day he spoke with Benny—"

"That would be Wednesday," Shaul said.

"Wednesday," Jarnail repeated. "Good. Okay, let me out, Pinchas." Pinchas obediently signaled and moved to the curb. "In any case, if you find that the page was torn out, don't despair. That would actually be a good sign. A sign that we're looking in the right direction."

---

"I really should let my wife know that I won't be coming anytime soon," Pinchas said, lines of worry on his brow. "I wanted to surprise her and come early, but she won't be expecting to see me before nine..."

"Let's hope there will be some positive developments by then," Shaul said. "And if we're realistic—even without positive developments, there are mitzvos that can be done by others and mitzvos that can't."

Pinchas smiled. "That's true," he said. "But let's hope for the positive developments. Where am I supposed to be heading, Shaul? Give me an address, okay?"

Shaul rattled off the address, and Pinchas entered it into Waze. They rode in silence, listening together to the instructions that the GPS issued, until they parked near the old apartment building with its surrounding foliage.

"I'll go in alone," Shaul said. "You stay here. In case..." His hand stroked his beard. "There's no reason to risk both of us. I'll go in with my cellphone on, and you'll be here, listening. Okay?"

"It's not likely that anything will happen," Pinchas said encouragingly. "But okay, I'll wait here and say *Tehillim* with my cellphone on. No need to worry."

"Thanks." Shaul took a deep breath. "It's all so strange," he said, opening the car door and taking another breath of morning air. "May Hashem help. And may all be well."

"*Amen*," Pinchas said. "Go on, Shaul. You're the one who always says, 'If you don't start, you don't finish.' Right?"

---

"I can't give out the key to anyone who asks!" said the irate elderly woman neighbor. "Everyone tells me that they're a friend of Dr. Dreyfus's, but I don't know if I'd want to let so many friends walking around my living room if I suddenly disappeared."

"I'm Benny's father. He's the boy who was here yesterday," Shaul said politely. "And my brother-in-law—the tall, dark-haired man who was with him—never came home yesterday. We're afraid the two events may be connected."

"He came back here again yesterday," the old woman said, the lines of her face softening slightly. "With his wife. A nice woman. She was very taken with Moishe's eye for design, he should be well. I gave them the key and asked them to return it."

"Did they?" Shaul asked tensely.

"They left it in the mailbox, as I told them to," Freida said. "I know because later, at around ten-thirty, another friend of Francois's knocked on the door. A man with a beard, longer than yours, and wild *peyos*—"

Shaul shook his head. "I don't know him."

"He knocked and knocked until I opened the door." Freida was annoyed. "Such a lack of manners! But he apologized. And he looked like a nice person. So I agreed to let him take the key from the mailbox. But he never came back. The key wasn't there in the morning when I went down to get the newspaper."

"Could his name be Dr. Blau?" Shaul asked. "Because if it was, he also didn't come back last night," Shaul said. "And his family is worried."

"He didn't look like a doctor. He looked like a chassid," Freida said. "But I suppose that doesn't mean he couldn't be a doctor. So maybe he was."

"Do you have another key? I wanted to go down and see if there's anything in the apartment that could help me find everyone who is missing."

"There's nothing to find there," the old woman said firmly. "Just a parrot with a big mouth—"

"A parrot that bit someone," Shaul remarked, his son's tale fresh in his mind.

"He bit the private investigator," Freida nodded. "I didn't like him from the start, that detective. Too arrogant, wearing shoes that had obviously just come out of the box and choosing every word he said too carefully."

Shaul contemplated this unflattering description. "Do you mean to say that he looked like he was in disguise?" he asked.

"Disguise!" The old woman lifted a shaky finger. "That's the word I couldn't put my finger on whenever I thought of him. Those shoes, you know? And his pants—so clean, cleaner than even a real Hungarian could get them."

Shaul nodded sagely. "Did he leave you a phone number?"

"No, he didn't. He wasn't the type who shows respect to elderly women. But he did exchange numbers with your brother-in-law. And he wanted to give the other boy, the one who was a little strange, a ride to his home."

"To whose home?"

"To the strange boy's home. But he didn't want to go."

Shaul wasn't sure he understood. "Who didn't agree? The other boy?"

"Yes." She nodded her head three times. "Poor boy. Hashem should help him and all of *Klal Yisrael*."

"*Amen*." Shaul tried to focus his thoughts. "So let me summarize what I know so far," he said. "My brother-in-law Gadi and his wife were here, and they put the key in your mailbox before ten-thirty—"

"Which was when the maybe-doctor came with the wild *peyos*," Freida confirmed.

"And he didn't put the keys back," Shaul continued.

The old woman nodded.

"And the private detective that the parrot attacked looked to you like he was wearing a disguise because his clothes were too new."

"Too clean," she corrected. "People today don't know how to clean like that anymore."

"What about dry cleaning?"

"Do dry cleaners polish shoes?" Freida retorted scornfully. "I know what I'm talking about. Those were clothes that he'd washed a few times so they wouldn't look new. Like in times of deprivation, when there were those who would do that so that others wouldn't be jealous of them for having money for luxuries." She nodded her head. "I didn't think of that until you said it. But—in disguise. Yes. That's the word I was grasping for, but I couldn't grab hold of it."

"Are there any security cameras in the building?" Shaul asked, thinking of the police who had perhaps reached Gadi's home by now. "Or some other way to identify the man?"

"Maybe in the grocery store," the old woman said. "On the other side of the street, directly opposite us."

"I saw it when I came here," Shaul said. "Okay. I'll go down afterward to check. And about the apartment, do you have another key? I still want to take a look. There's something I need to check."

"I have one last key," the old woman said. "The very last."

"I'll return it to you, don't worry."

"Fine." She sighed. "Okay. But don't forget."

The key was somewhere on a top shelf, based on the sounds of the stepladder that Freida dragged in from the balcony. Shaul thanked her for her trouble and promised not to forget to return it.

"Bring the key here, to my house," Freida said. "Don't put it in the mailbox. And if I don't open the door, maybe if I happen to be in the middle of davening, then wait patiently for me to finish."

He promised and returned to the ground floor while exchanging a few words with Pinchas, who agreed to step into the grocery to see if there were security cameras. Shaul inserted the key in the keyhole and grimaced.

"I don't feel comfortable about bothering her again," he said. "But this isn't the right key. It doesn't fit in the hole."

# 96

FREIDA CLUTCHED AN OLD SIDDUR WHOSE COVER WAS WORN and whose pages were brown and yellowed. Her annoyance at being interrupted made Shaul feel like he was back in his boyhood days.

"What do you think?" she asked. "That I'm completely senile? That I don't know the difference between keys? How many keys do you think I have here? What do you think I am, a tycoon who has any number of apartments for rent?"

"I'm talking about this key," he insisted.

"The green key—*nu*, I'm also talking about that. Let me see it. Yes, that's the key. Why do you say it doesn't fit in the keyhole?"

"Because it doesn't."

"Are you sure you checked the right door?"

"Yes, the brown door on the left."

"And maybe it's open, and that maybe-doctor left the key in the keyhole on the inside?"

"It's locked. I checked."

She sighed. "Okay," she said, in a tone that sounded a lot like a fed-up mother. "I'll go down myself."

Despite the tense situation, Shaul was amused to find himself feeling like a child again. He waited patiently for the results of her investigation.

"It really is locked," she agreed. "Could that man be inside? Did you try ringing the bell?" She pressed the bell with a shaky finger and left it there until a shuffling sound was heard from within. A sleepy voice asked, "Who's there?"

"Francois Dreyfus's landlady," Freida snapped. "And his friend."

The door opened at once—a little too quickly for Shaul's taste. Dr. Blau, looking thin and tired, with a long, brown beard and bushy *peyos* escaping from behind his ears, appeared in the doorway. "How can I help you?" he asked courteously.

"Who are you?" Freida asked.

Hesitation. "I'm Dr. Blau," he said at last. "Is there a problem?"

"Your family is looking for you," Shaul said quietly. "Your phone isn't on, and they're very worried."

A blink. "Is it morning already? Ribbono shel Olam, I've been here how long? Seven hours?"

"Eleven," Freida said. "Not that I'm counting. But you came here at nine last night, and now it's nearly eight."

"I went home in the middle," Blau said, giving Shaul a look that warned him against giving away secrets. "Then I came back here, because I got a…hmmm…a second wind and wanted to try and figure out what's going on here." He glanced at his watch. "Ten to eight!" he said, stunned. "How can it be?"

"Call home," Shaul urged. "They're very worried. To tell the truth, after I told them that someone attacked you last night, they apparently contacted the police. It would be a good idea to call them now."

"My cellphone shuts off automatically at eleven forty-five at night," Blau mumbled, though it wasn't clear whether he was addressing them or himself. "I didn't notice that so many hours had gone by."

"You fell asleep?" Freida asked. "Is that why you came here?"

"No. I went through his files," Blau said with a sigh. "His appointment book doesn't seem to be organized, so I had no choice but to go through the notes that he wrote down for himself during his sessions."

He rubbed his eyes and put his phone to his ear. "His handwriting is awful, and my French is rusty," Shaul heard him tell his wife. "It took time, and I didn't notice that it was daytime already. You know what happens to me when I'm trying to solve a riddle…"

He disconnected and gave a small, sheepish smile. "Forgive me for troubling you," he said, spreading his hands in apology. "So unpleasant." He nodded at Shaul. "Do you have the results of the tests yet?"

"Not yet." Shaul's lips were tight. "Not yet." He took a deep breath.

"I didn't actually manage to convince them that it's important. Maybe you can give me a little more information that will help my wife explain it to them."

His head was starting to ache. His broken sleep on his brother-in-law's couch hadn't succeeded in banishing yesterday's fatigue. "It's really a long story," he said. "I don't know who to worry about first. My brother-in-law Gadi, whom you met once, went out searching for Francois, and he disappeared, too…"

"Your daughter is still in the hospital?" Blau interrupted.

"Yes."

"You informed them of my possible diagnosis, correct?"

"Yes."

"Then they must be taking care of her there. She's not in mortal danger."

"But—" Shaul slowly digested this. "Okay," he said. "The second thing on the agenda is Francois's disappearance, and that of my brother-in-law and his wife. They were here yesterday and took the key from the landlady—"

"Yes," Freida confirmed. "That's right."

"And then they vanished."

"That's right. She told me yesterday that there was a couple in the apartment," Blau remembered. "I think he left his license here."

Blau turned and pointing, directing Shaul's gaze to the license that was lying on the table. Shaul's heart turned to ice.

"That's not a good sign," he said.

"No," Blau agreed. "I'd say it's a very bad sign, indeed."

---

The bright daylight blinded Shuli, whose eyes were raw from copious weeping. She had never cried so much.

She wanted to go home. She wanted her children. She and Gadi had always been law-abiding citizens. How did this happen? How had they fallen into this trap?

"Sssh." Gadi motioned at the older man dozing on the sofa. "Sssh."

They hadn't slept all night. Francois persisted in talking about childhood memories and all sorts of nonsense. About France's military history and the country's fear of a third world war, and the Mirages that were developed to defend France from the Soviet Union.

He'd talked and talked, and she couldn't help admiring Gadi for his patience. On the other hand, Gadi had always been good at pretending to pay attention while not actually absorbing anything.

Sometimes she suspected that he could sleep with his eyes open.

It was six-thirty in the morning now. Yossi had probably woken up already. He'd be wandering around the house drowsily, getting ready to leave for yeshivah. When would he begin to realize that things weren't all right? That there were no adults in the house?

It would be preferable, of course, if that took place as late as possible so he wouldn't have a chance to panic. But what happened if he left the house, thinking she was simply tired and had decided to sleep in, and it was the girls who woke up to find that their parents had vanished without a word of warning?

Yossi was an even-tempered boy. He wouldn't become hysterical. But even he, upon calling them both and getting no response, would start to be frightened. And what would happen then?

There was no answer to this question. She could only hope that they would be smart enough to call one of their aunts or uncles and not try to cope with the problem on their own.

She, the mother who had always been so much in control, could do nothing now to spare them alarm or anxiety. Not a thing.

She could daven.

Yes. Of course.

But even the longest Shacharis eventually ends, and she was left again with the suffocating need to do something useful.

She would make breakfast. But with what?

The refrigerator shelf held ketchup. There were crackers in a cabinet. That was it. Undertaking the role of homemaker, Shuli prepared cold coffee and cracker-and-ketchup sandwiches for them all.

"Breakfast is ready," she announced, in a voice she tried to keep steady. "We won't gain anything by being hungry.'

She watched the psychologist walk slowly toward the kitchen, and then her husband, who also looked prematurely aged. She was thankful that there were no mirrors. She couldn't imagine how she herself looked after the long, nightmarish night.

The men ate quickly and were still hungry. She rummaged through the cupboards in the hope of finding something else that they could eat cold. Something without empty sugar calories that would lift their moods for a few minutes only to have them plummet again.

Eventually, she uncovered a package of whole-wheat cookies and brought them to the table in defeat.

"Dessert," she told them, starting to clear away their dishes.

"Thank you, Mrs. Philips," Francois said in his marked accent. "The food was excellent."

The French politeness was grotesque when applied to crackers and ketchup, not to mention cold coffee in which coffee granules floated at the top, refusing to dissolve. But something in his rigid hand and pleading eyes made her look down at the plate he was holding out to her. On the plate, in shaky ketchup letters, were two words:

*MIRAGE = ILLUSION*

He had explained the same thing to Gadi multiple times throughout the night, so she found nothing new in the words. She took the plate and threw it in the trash, her eyebrows scrunched to the point of pain.

They had begun the discussion of planes and the Soviet Union through talking about their generous "host," Mr. Mirage, an Iranian Jew.

What was the therapist trying to say? That Mirage was an illusion? And if he was, what then?

---

Avi Goetz, head of the Iran department of the Military Intelligence unit, had completed his morning exercises and was doing his last stretches when the phone rang. Perspiring from the exertion, but proud that he was in better shape than most men his age, he went to his desk and wrinkled his nose at the name that appeared on the caller screen. Rafi. The chief of staff. Or, in other words, the one who had tried to use him in order to avoid admitting that the army under his command was unprepared for the upcoming war.

"Yes, Rafi," he said with sugary friendliness. "How can I help you?"

Rafi hadn't attained his lofty position because he was a fool or because he couldn't read subtext. He also wasn't a coward or one to retreat from unpleasant tasks. So although he was well aware of the currents hidden beneath Avi's friendly words, he only said mildly, "I didn't call too early, did I?"

The question was almost insulting for someone who, for nearly forty years, had been rising at five a.m. But the conversation continued along pleasant lines as Avi said, "Certainly not. What can I do for you?"

"This time I'm calling to offer help," Rafi said. "That is…" His tone sounded even more friendly, as if they were good buddies who regularly confided in each other, as he said, "The guy you brought to the meeting with the prime minister yesterday. The handler. Is he tall and dark?"

"I assume that at least twenty percent of the residents of this country are tall and dark," Avi said dryly. "Dark hair is a dominant gene in Israel."

"But height isn't," Rafi replied with slight acerbity. "He was wearing a blue shirt, right?"

"Correct."

Rafi took a deep breath. "I'm going to ask something insulting, Avi, but I mean it completely for the good and completely seriously. Tell me—is he all there?"

"What?"

"This fellow who handles our agents. Nava, or whatever he's called," Rafi said. "I saw him in the hall—"

"Yes?" Avi urged.

"He looked nervous—"

"We're all nervous at times, especially before important meetings."

"Yes, true. But something seemed off…"

"No one asked for your opinion."

"So don't ask. I'm offering. Listen, about fifteen minutes before the meeting started, I went to make myself a coffee two floors down. I saw him standing and talking on the phone. And that was weird, because there's no cellphone reception there."

"Who says?"

"The chief of staff of the State of Israel."

Avi's nostrils flared. "Maybe his phone is more powerful than yours."

"No such thing."

"Then he was probably rehearsing what he was going to tell the prime minister," Avi said angrily, "and he didn't want anyone to know that he was doing it.

"Really, Rafi. There's a limit. You don't want to go to war. That's legitimate. No one wants it. We wouldn't want a chief of staff who loves conflicts. But don't try to wiggle out of your job for absurd reasons! Don't you know that we, and all of those who work for us, undergo a thorough psychological screening?"

"And you didn't exempt him from that? For political reasons?"

Avi shook his head in disbelief. "Are you serious? No, we didn't exempt him. No chance of that. But if you insist, I can check."

"Check and get back to me, okay?"

"I...I have no words."

The chief of staff fell silent for a moment. "I just want what's best, and in the most professional way. Something about that guy is off. Do you want to help me, or should I go over your head and launch my own investigation?"

"No, no," Avi said a little too quickly. "Not that I understand what you're after, but I'll check. I'll check."

When the call ended, Avi remained thoughtfully in place. After some consideration, he scrolled through his phone's menu options and called Nava.

"What?" Nava sounded a bit confused.

"Yesterday," Avi barked. "Two floors beneath the conference room. You spoke on the phone. To whom?"

There was an instant of silence.

"The truth?" Nava asked rhetorically.

"Yes?"

"I...was davening Maariv."

"G-d accepts phone calls?"

Nava chuckled. "No, but it looked better than standing facing the wall in the middle of the hall."

"I'm not sure about that," Goetz huffed. "Do me a favor and next time look for a shul. We are a Jewish state. You can find a shul anywhere. Don't mess me up with secretive phone calls, okay? The chief of staff saw you talking in a place where there's no reception, and he blew a fuse."

"There *is* reception there," Nava said.

"No, there isn't."

Silence. "I'm sorry," Nava said after a long pause. "I blew it. Sorry."

"Don't do it again. In another time and place, that could have cost you dearly." He made a face. "Who's honking there?"

"Just a traffic jam." Yair Nava moved to the side and turned off the car. "Okay, I hear. It won't happen again."

"Good. You'll be expected in the office at ten-thirty."

"Yes, I'll be there." Nava's tone of voice remained neutral, emotionless.

"Good," Avi said again. "And daven at home, eh?"

"Yes," Nava said. "Don't worry."

---

"Are you all right, sir?" A uniformed policeman leaned into the window of the silver car. "Are you feeling okay?"

Yair Nava lifted his head slowly from the wheel. "Yes, thank you. I'm fine."

"You don't look that good." The officer was kind but firm. "You slowed very suddenly and pulled over. You're pale. What's your name?"

"My name? Neiman. Yair Neiman." He breathed deeply. "But I'm all right." His voice was indistinct. "It's just…I got some bad news. A good friend of mine…" He paused. "Died."

"Oy," said the policeman. "Do you have any water in the car? Do you want me to bring you something to drink?"

"I have some. I'm really fine, don't worry. I just…took it to heart. But I'm over it now."

The officer looked at him and nodded. "When you feel completely better, please start driving again. This was a bad place to stop."

## 97

THE POLICEMAN STRUTTED AWAY FROM THE CAR, AND NAVA rested his head on the steering wheel again. His throat felt like burning acid. Everything was closing in on him. The world was closing in on him. The corner he'd been pushed into felt crushing. He was the king of fools, a nitwit with a head full of straw. Why had he let his sister talk him into seeing a psychologist?

Who needed them anyway?

Hadn't he been living a full life before? Hadn't he done plenty of good in the world before?

So he was over forty and hadn't yet managed to get married. So what?

In his profession, that was normal. It's hard to marry when you have to constantly keep your personal information under wraps and spend whole chunks of time in other countries, some of them friendly and others less so.

It was a sacrifice for his people and his country, and he had made it with love.

So…why had he gone to Dreyfus?

Why had he been so foolish and talked about himself honestly for the first time in his life?

And what was he supposed to do now?

A natural instinct for survival, highly developed in him, made him lift his head from the wheel and see that the annoying policeman hadn't yet driven away. There was no choice. He had to move.

With stiff fingers, he turned on the ignition and merged into traffic. His blood pounded powerfully in his ears, and he sensed his blood pressure shooting skyward. Too bad he was healthy and fit. There was no logical reason to hope that a sudden heart attack would come along and rescue him from his suffering.

"*Chas v'shalom,*" Mirage said.

Nava turned his head and looked at him. "That's all you have to say?"

"It's dangerous to live with a death wish," said the man beside him. "It can lead to doing irresponsible things. And in your field, one mistake can cost a person his life."

Nava passed his tongue over dry lips. "First of all, I think I've already done some irresponsible things... And second, my life isn't the most important thing here. There are a few other things hanging in the balance."

"Like what?" Mirage asked. He was short and stocky, and his glossy dark hear fell over his broad forehead.

"The State of Israel," Nava said. "Because of my reports, they're going to start a war, and no one can be sure of its outcome."

"Nonsense." Mirage waved a dismissive hand. "Wars aren't started because of one person's reports."

Nava was generally a modest person, but this time he sighed. "I'm not just 'one person,' Mirage."

"True." Mirage was his opposite in many ways. He was lighthearted and almost without a conscience. He was also a loyal and devoted friend who always showed up in times of trouble—not like him, who'd been out of the country when his father had a stroke, out of the country when his niece drowned, and out of the country yet again when his mother passed away the previous year.

"You are not just one person, Yair. Besides, we're two."

"At least that."

The road was long and straight, and Yair gripped the wheel, automatically keeping the right distance between his car and those before and after him.

"I feel lost," he said. "I feel like there's no way out."

"There's always a way out."

"That's what people always think before they find themselves swinging at the end of a rope."

"No, they didn't think that way. I promise you. There was a minute when they gave up—when they threw their hands in the air. And then the worst happened."

He paused a moment. "Listen, Yair. I'm going to repeat my proposal. Over the years, you deposited a great deal of money for me in the bank account that you opened. I don't need it. I have enough of my own. Take as much as you need to build a new life for yourself, with a new identity… That's the simplest solution to the problem."

"The simplest is not always the best."

Yair pressed the button to turn on the car's music system and set the volume on high. He loved music. Ever since he was a boy, he loved to lose himself in it. To forget everything. To be nothing but the next note floating in the air. Not a boy who already knew that his father's life was in perpetual danger. Not a son determined to fill his absent father's place and to protect his fragile mother. Not the youth with the chronic cough who wasn't accepted into his preferred unit, despite his father's connections. Just that: a single, high note, floating above it all and reaching for the stars.

"Yair?"

He didn't answer. His eyes were fixed on the puffy clouds that adorned the pale-blue sky.

"Yair?" Mirage grabbed the steering wheel, ignoring all rules of safety.

For a moment they struggled, and not only for the wheel. But the struggle reached no conclusion, because the car, controlled by two hands and two hearts, veered wildly and rammed into the security rail.

---

Long ago, when Ricki's grandmother had been a young woman who'd uprooted herself from the United States to settle in the sands of Eretz Yisrael, she would write long letters to her parents, pouring out her misgivings and receiving, two months later, advice and suggestions for handling problems that had already become irrelevant.

When Ricki's mother had been a young woman who remained behind in Eretz Yisrael when her parents traveled to South Africa for *parnasah* reasons, she would jot down reminders of the topics she wanted to discuss with them during their expensive biweekly calls…

only to find, in real time, that a significant number of the points she'd wished to cover were no longer that urgent.

And Ricki herself, in a world where nothing was more understood or available than remote control, grasped completely on this sunny morning that there is no substitute for being fully present in the place where one is needed.

But what was one to do when she was needed in two places at once?

She needed to be with Ahuvi, whose condition showed no improvement. And she needed to be with Gadi's children, whose parents had become involved in some as yet unknown predicament.

Apparently, Gadi's children came first right now. That was what her mind told her. But had her assistance been needed to help bring Gadi or Shuli themselves home, she would have done all she could. When it was just a matter of staying with the children to wait and to soothe— the options seemed a little less clear.

Who said that only *she* could calm the children and assure them that all would be well? Why couldn't one of her other sisters be summoned to fill that role?

Impossible. She knew that. This was such a complicated and sensitive affair. To bring more people into it could endanger even more of her family. Perhaps Gadi's home was being watched.

She couldn't take a chance. No one would suspect a nice *chareidi* woman who came to help her sister even though her own child was hospitalized. No, she would go to Gadi's. It was safer for everyone.

She scrolled through her phone contacts, trying to decide which of her sisters to turn to for help.

"Minna?" Just as she'd done back in India, she chose the same one. "Did I wake you?"

"What's wrong?" It was obvious to Minna, a mother of five, that Ricki wouldn't be calling at such an hour for no special reason.

"Can you talk privately for a minute?"

"Is it Ima?"

"No, no. But I have to talk to you."

"This sounds bad. Just a minute…"

The minute was used to issue instructions to Minna's under-eight offspring. Then Minna stepped onto the porch and closed the door behind her. "Talk," she said. "What happened?"

"It's a long, strange story," Ricki said slowly. "But I'll give you the bottom line. I'm in the hospital with Ahuvi since yesterday and

Shaul…" She paused to find the right words, which prompted Minna to ask, "Shaul? What happened to him?"

"He's okay. He's not the problem." Ricki paused again. "Listen. Shaul spent the night in Gadi's house. He went there because… How do I explain it? In short, he had to keep an eye on the kids, because Gadi and Shuli…"

"Bought last-minute tickets again and flew out of the country?"

Ricki bit her lip. She didn't want to speak explicitly, but Minna refused to understand.

"When was the last time Shaul babysat for Gadi's kids because Gadi took a trip abroad?" she asked ironically. "Minna, Gadi and Shuli have disappeared. They…they seem to have gotten mixed up in something. We don't know exactly what, though Shaul has some guesses."

"Financial problems?"

"No, no. It's nothing like that. But listen, I have to go be with Gadi's children, and I also have to be here with Ahuvi…"

"Okay," Minna said. "I get it. I'll come take your place."

"In the hospital," Ricki clarified.

"Yes, of course. But what do you mean, 'disappeared'? What…what happened?"

"Get your kids off to school and take a taxi to the hospital at my expense," Ricki said. "I have no clear information to give you. They disappeared. That's all I know. Let's hope nothing happened to them."

"You checked that they weren't in an accident or something?"

"I didn't check," Ricki confessed. "I assume that Shaul did. Let's talk about it all afterward. I need to go, and I want to know if you'll come here to take my place."

"I'll come," Minna assured her. "I'll send the kids another way to school and come. You can calm down."

And Ricki was calm, not knowing that Minna—in contrast to herself—didn't always manage to send her kids out to school and kindergarten at eight o'clock on the dot.

98

THE CHILDREN WERE UP. THEY HAD SURELY TRIED CALLING both their parents' cellphones and knew that something was wrong. Shuli only hoped that they had called her parents, who might become hysterical but would be able to cope, and not Gadi's mother, for whom such a call could end in tragedy. And if only they had the sense to say a little *Tehillim*...

She shoved the used paper plates into the trash can, along with the message that Francois had written in ketchup. As she did, she made sure to keep the message from the lens of any hidden cameras in the apartment.

*MIRAGE = ILLUSION*

Mirage was an illusion? What did that mean?

She tidied the disposable plates and empty containers with too much care, trying at the same time to make order out of her confused thoughts. Slowly, she returned to the table.

"Dr. Dreyfus," she said, "I know that it's not considered polite to talk to a professional—" at this the psychologist's eyes grew wide as he stiffened and sat up in what she could only call alarm— "and ask him something in his field of work without paying. But considering the situation..."

"No, no," Francois said. "You can ask anything you want, Mrs. Phillips. I once told Gadi that I don't accept friends as clients. But I'll gladly help in other areas."

"So you didn't know Yair beforehand," Gadi said.

"Yair?" Francois sobered, the fingers of one hand drumming on the table. "I...I don't like to talk about my patients."

He was afraid, Shuli understood. Afraid that talk of Yair's problems would annoy the man and prompt him to take hasty steps.

"I think that Yair took into consideration the fact that he might become the exception to that rule when he locked us up here," Gadi said wryly. "The minute he attacked you and kidnaped us, he stopped being in a position to complain."

Francois moved his finger slightly from right to left. This, Shuli realized, interpreting the minute gesture, was not the way. They must be careful.

"The fabric of the relationship between psychologist and client is a delicate one," Francois said, tensely adjusting his collar. "It's important not to let it unravel."

This remark provoked Gadi, who was about to protest but then snapped his mouth shut. Psychologists were sometimes called upon to assist in negotiations to free hostages. It would be foolish to damage the relationship that existed between the doctor and his imbalanced client, although something in that relationship had clearly not worked out too successfully, seeing that the psychologist himself was one of those held hostage.

Yair wasn't dangerous, the doctor had said yesterday. That was definitely encouraging. But...Mirage was.

Suddenly, in a flash, Gadi grasped what Francois had been trying to hint to him all night.

Could it be?

Was it possible?

"We have a nephew," Shuli was saying, her voice brisk. "His name is Benny. A really sweet boy, thirteen years old."

"Yes," said Francois.

Gadi appreciated him for not allowing his voice to betray that he'd been seeing that sweet boy professionally for more than six months.

Because Shuli was well aware of this, it was reasonable to suppose that she was trying to accomplish something. Gadi had no choice but to tilt his chair back, stretch out his legs, and watch the unfolding scene in silence.

"Anyway," Shuli continued, having decided to cloak her questions in the guise of being about her young nephew whom Francois was treating, "Benny keeps complaining that he has a friend who makes trouble for him. A boy named Ari."

"Yes," Francois said again.

"The problem," Shuli said with a wrinkled brow, "is that I recently checked it out with a friend of mine who works as a secretary in the school, and she says there's no one in his class by that name."

"Maybe there once was," Gadi couldn't resist inserting.

"She says there never was," Shuli said.

The words were a rebuke, which he accepted. He would let her speak. Even more, he would try to understand what she was trying to achieve with this strange distortion of reality.

"The boy complains that another boy is bothering him," said Francois, "and the school says that there was never such a student there. Could he have been in a different class?"

"No," Shuli said. "Benny came to our house yesterday, during afternoon recess, to pick up a package for his mother. In a casual way, I asked him a few questions about the troublesome boy, and he said again that he was in his class."

"The simple explanation is that the secretary made a mistake," the psychologist said after a moment. "That's the simplest way to solve this riddle."

"She checked twice," Shuli said quietly. "And she said there is no such student. And there never was."

Francois took a deep breath. "Look, Mrs. Phillips," he said. "There is a phenomenon in which a child can have an imaginary friend. If I'm not mistaken, sixty-five percent of children ages three to five have a friend like that."

"But Benny isn't three years old. He's thirteen!"

Francois gazed at his fingernails. "And you are certain that there is no boy by that name in his class?"

"Positive."

"Look, I'm not supposed to give you advice about some other child. In principle, however, it would be worthwhile for his parents to check what's going on here. Sometimes a person is aware of the fact that he is saying something that's not true, and talking about problems that don't exist, in order to get attention."

"And other times?"

"Sometimes the human mind behaves in unexpected ways and deceives a person," Francois said heavily. "There are many strange phenomena in which, for example, someone sees colors when he hears music, or smells certain fragrances, or hears sounds that don't exist. He can even see or sense, with all five of his senses, things that are not there."

"Things that don't exist?" Shuli asked.

"Like friends?" Gadi put in.

"Yes," said Francois. "Or enemies. The second is more widespread."

"Wow," Shuli said. "How can such a situation be checked out?"

"With great care," said Francois. "With extreme care. Because becoming aware of the actual reality can shake a person badly and cause him to react in an unhealthy way."

*Such as, for instance, locking his psychologist in a Faraday cage in the shape of an apartment*, Gadi thought, but managed not to say.

"Imagine, Mrs. Phillips, that someone would come to you today and tell you that your husband or children are only an illusion. That your mind created them for you so you wouldn't feel lonely."

The notion made Gadi recoil. "I'm right here," he said with a wave of his hand. "And I'm no illusion."

"That's one of the favorite lines of imaginary friends," Francois said with a flash of humor. "The only point in your favor, Gadi, is that there are not many illusionary figures that reveal themselves to two people at the same time."

"Or that you can see in a security camera," Shuli said. "Or withdraws money from the bank. Or—"

"Actually, that does happen," Francois said. "A person can withdraw the money himself, use it to make purchases, and afterward be convinced that he received those purchases as a gift."

"Wow," said Gadi. "That sounds...crazy. Really crazy."

Francois spread his hands. "That's how it is."

"Wow," said Shuli. "Wow, wow, wow." Then she added, "Poor Benny."

"He must be spoken to carefully," Francois emphasized. "It's probable that he knows by now that there's some sort of problem. Maybe, as I said earlier, he is even aware that he's lying in order to receive attention or other benefits."

"And maybe not?" Gadi asked.

"And maybe not," Francois admitted. "Or...he may be aware of it at times. Sometimes he's sure that his classmate exists, and at others is aware that he is an illusion. What can I say? Of the three possibilities, this one seems to me the one that puts a person in the worst emotional state of them all."

———

"I still don't understand what you did here in this apartment all night," Freida scolded.

"I'm going over Francois's notes," the doctor with the long beard said with a certain degree of impatience, "in order to see if there is some clue regarding who is the client he spoke to me about last week. The client who suffers from hallucinations and threatened him."

"If that were so, wouldn't Dr. Dreyfus have called the police?"

"That is a wise direction to investigate," Pinchas said. "I know someone who has connections with the police."

"Who?" Shaul asked.

Pinchas gave a bark of laughter, different from his usual, almost timid laugh. "My father-in-law."

"No," said Shaul. "I don't think it's a good idea to call him now with a question like that, at a time when you're—"

"Uh, I didn't mean *I* was going to call," Pinchas said. "I meant that you should call."

"And I can tell him that I'm a friend of yours?"

"You can. Besides, he knows that already."

"What kind of connections does he have?" Shaul asked.

"You don't need to ask him that, and you don't need to know. He has someone there who can help. That's what you heard from me once, which is why you're calling him today."

"Okay," Shaul said. "Thanks."

"You two are very polite!" Freida cried. "It's 'please' and 'thank you' all day long. Go call already. And you"—she turned her gaze on Dr. Blau—"tell me, did you or did you not find something in those notes?"

"My French is really bad," Blau admitted. "I can barely make out his handwriting, and I'm using a dictionary to help me... It's going to take time."

"This younger generation." Freida sighed. "Didn't they teach you anything in school? Give me the book that you're talking about. I'll tell you what that poor doctor wrote."

T HE BOOK THAT DR. BLAU HAD SPOKEN OF WAS A LARGE, hardcover notebook whose every page was filled with scribbled notes in a fairly illegible handwriting.

"A lot of material," Freida remarked, eyeing the notebook. "Let's see... Where are my reading glasses?"

They were dangling from a chain around her neck. Carefully, she perched them on the tip of her nose. "Where can I sit down?" she asked. "There are a lot of pages here. What exactly are you looking for? Delusions? It will just be written here?"

"I have no idea," the doctor said. "But I hope that we'll know soon." He smiled at the elderly woman. "This is also what I do in my own work. I read mountains of material searching for the odd fact, the irregular detail... It's impossible to know in advance what that will be. You can only pray."

"That's always a good thing to do," Freida agreed. "But do you want me to simply sit here and translate page after page?"

"That would be ideal," Blau replied with a smile.

"That will take a long time!" Freida retorted. "And Moishe is alone at home! Maybe we can go up there?"

"The parrot will be happy about that," Blau said. "He didn't like my intrusion..."

"The parrot!" Freida looked at the winged creature perched on top of the bookcase, gazing mournfully down at the group below. "That reminds me of something else. The bird was very nervous when we came here the first time and discovered that Dr. Dreyfus was gone. It attacked that private investigator who came in. Bit him hard."

"A private investigator?"

Freida felt around in the pocket of her dress, which was adorned with large wooden buttons. "I already told the one who went outside to talk on the phone. There was someone here who said he was a private investigator, and I didn't like him. Partly because I don't like people who are too nice for no reason. And partly because his clothes looked like a costume—brand-new garments that he'd messed a bit so that they wouldn't look too new."

"I think I see what you mean," Blau said, studying the small business card. "A private detective? Did he say why he came here?"

"No," said Freida. She sighed. "But you know what? I wouldn't call him. The brother-in-law of the man who went out also called him before he disappeared. I know that, because I happened to be sitting on my balcony, and I heard him talking to him on his cellphone. People today aren't at all careful about their privacy."

Blau's forehead wrinkled, and blue vein bulged in his temple. "Just a minute," he said. "Let's figure this out. The private investigator was a client?"

"He said that this was the first time he'd come here." The old woman shrugged. "But the fact that he said it doesn't make it true, as I'm sure you know. Would *you* say that you were being treated by a psychologist? Not everyone would admit to that."

"So our prime suspect is a man of about what age?" Blau asked.

"Maybe thirty-five or forty, I think. But you, Mr. Detective—"

"Yes?" Blau asked.

"Aren't you curious about what Gadi wanted from that private investigator?"

"I certainly am."

"He told him something about a clock that stopped at ten minutes to two," said Freida, "and that it seemed to him that Dreyfus had done it on purpose. And do you know what annoys me, now that I'm already telling you the story? The secretary of the clinic called to ask me to come for an urgent appointment. I got agitated and took a taxi, and when I got there, no one knew what I was talking about. No one at all."

"Yes?" Blau urged.

"I came home at two-thirty. Otherwise, at that hour…I'm always out on my balcony. Do you see the chutzpah? To treat an old woman that way? To frighten her for nothing?"

Silently, Dr. Blau nodded. "Doesn't Francois have a weekly appointment book?" he asked in frustration.

"He had one. Black," said Freida. "And there was money inside—checks and cash. That was the first clue that made the guy named Gadi assume he'd been kidnaped. But *I* thought that he'd left the money to cover the rent."

"And where is that appointment book now?"

She shrugged. "Who knows?"

"I need a pen and paper," Blau said, patting his pockets. "Let's write down in an organized fashion what we know to this point."

---

"He was really nice, your father-in-law," Shaul said, walking back into the apartment. "He gladly agreed to help us, and even said a lot of nice things about you."

Pinchas's face hardened slightly. "Let's not go into that," he said. "But, yes, I think he's trying to change."

"What did you ask him? Remind me," requested Blau.

"To check whether Francois submitted any sort of complaint to the police of being threatened or harassed," Shaul said.

"It may be worth our while to ask for one other thing." Blau flipped through the hard-covered notebook. "We have a suspect. That is, going on the assumption that clients generally come to their psychologist at a fixed time every week. We have someone who came regularly at 1:45 on Wednesdays. His name is Yair Neiman. Maybe he can provide a little background on this guy?"

"Okay," Shaul said. "I'll try."

Once again, he stepped outside. He left behind an open door and a heavy silence.

"Moishe is alone," Freida said again. "And we're sitting here in a house that's not ours, and that's not right. So I suggest that we take the notebook and anything else we need and go up to my apartment. I'll give you all some coffee and cookies. Sugar helps you think better."

"I need to be going soon," Pinchas said apologetically. "I have to go to the hospital to be with my wife and children." A flush of emotion suffused his face at the last word. "But if there's anything I can do to help…"

Dr. Blau shook his head. "You've done a great deal," he said graciously. "We'll be in touch if we need help."

———⁓❧⁓———

"Excuse me?"

A short young woman wearing a modest kerchief approached the nurse's desk.

"Excuse me, the baby in room 8 has been crying for a long time and no one's coming."

"Room 8?" The nurse raised her head from her cellphone. "Yes, the mother said something about having a family emergency. She said someone will be right over to take her place."

"But it's already been a long time," the young woman insisted. "I gave her a pacifier twice already—"

"You're not supposed to give pacifiers to babies who are not yours," the nurse scolded.

"I'm also not supposed to let them cry for thirty-five minutes straight," the small woman mumbled. "She's very unhappy, poor thing."

"Mrs. Sofer abandoned the child and went to work?" another, larger nurse broke in. "Am I hearing right, Sophia?"

"No. She said there was an emergency in the family, that her substitute was on the way, and that the baby was asleep."

"What's more of an emergency than her baby's condition right now?" the nurse asked. "I think it's time to bring in the social worker."

An expression of alarm crossed the young woman's face. "Maybe I just imagined that she'd been away that long," she hastened to say. "Maybe I'm just too sensitive to a baby's crying."

"Women need to be sensitive to a baby's crying," the large nurse said. Then, afraid she might have something that was not politically correct, she added quickly, "Men, too, of course. In this case—" She stopped again, lest she cross a legal line regarding patient privacy. "Thanks for reporting to us. Someone will be with her right away."

———⁓❧⁓———

"Forgive me for interrupting."

Dr. Zahir Nassar, the neurologist, opened the door to the office of the head of the pediatric ward. He almost retreated when he saw that the head nurse was in the room. Then, maintaining his stance, he said, "Just one thing—urgent. Sofer from room 8. They're refusing treatment for the baby. Just like those *chareidim* we had here last month. But this time, I think we need to dig in our heels—"

The ward chief took a deep breath. "I don't think we need to draw a parallel between the two cases," he said. "I'd like to hear the facts without commentary."

The neurologist nodded. For the next seven minutes, he spoke. Then he concluded, "And not only have they refused treatment, but now both of them left the baby alone and disappeared."

"That could work in our favor in court," said the head nurse.

The ward chief sighed. "Going to court to force treatment is an extreme and unusual step. Instead, let's send in the social worker to issue a warning. If that doesn't work, we'll move on to the next stage."

100

BEFORE ZAHAVA, THE HEAD NURSE, RETURNED TO HER office, she went to see the nurses on the ward to wish them a good day and remind them that someone was keeping an eye on them to make sure they didn't slack off. In the midst of her brief pep talk, interspersed with various slightly lengthy critical observations, a young woman came panting breathlessly onto the ward and asked where room 8 was.

"I'll show you," Zahava offered before any of the other nurses could say a word. "Come. It's this way."

She walked close to Minna as they traversed the corridor. "The baby has been alone for a long time," she remarked.

Minna was still trying to catch her breath from her race through the hospital's halls. "Yes," she admitted guiltily. "I feel really bad for letting my sister down. I was sure that I could be here forty minutes ago."

"Ah," said Zahava. Her tone held a combination of kindliness and criticism.

The young woman leaned closer, lowering her voice. "We have an emergency in the family," she said. "That's why my sister went and left the baby for me to watch. Otherwise, she would never, ever have left her. She's such a mother hen."

Zahava forced a smile. "Here is the room," she said, walking inside with the sure step of a hostess in her own home. "And this is the crib—" Something caught her eye and made her stop.

"Ahuvi, my sweet," Minna cooed at the baby. "How are you feeling, precious? It's so hard to see you lying in this place…so small, and so quiet. Won't you give your Aunt Minna a smile? Aren't you happy to see me?"

She paused in her motherly rambling to glance at Zahava. "Is there a problem?" she asked, sounding completely different.

"No," said Zahava. She pressed her lips together until they nearly disappeared. "No problem at all." She was on her way to the door.

"Little sweetie-pie!" Minna pulled a chair close to Ahuvi. "Your mother is so worried about you! She told Aunt Minna to come quickly. I'm sorry, darling, that I made you wait so long."

There was a polite cough from behind her. Nurse Zahava.

"Tell me," she asked Minna, her expression troubled. "Your sister… hmmm… Was she in India about eight months ago?"

"What?" Minna's jaw dropped.

"Your sister," the head nurse repeated, her returning self-confidence making the words emerge in the tempo of automatic gunfire. "She was in India sometime in this past year, right?"

"I…" Minna almost said, "I'm not answering any questions without a lawyer present," but quelled the urge at the last minute. "Why?" she asked instead.

Zahava lightly touched the metal key ring hanging from Ricki's bag. "I think I met her on the plane. I gave her this key ring, and I regretted it greatly later on. It was the last gift my mother gave me before she…" A short pause. "Before she had her final heart attack."

Minna's heart softened. "Yes," she said. "She went to India—how long ago? Eight months." She smiled. "In fact, Ahuvi was born there."

The nurse's face was like a mask of stone as she said, "Ah." She fell silent, and then said, "I don't know what to say about your brother and all that, but when you see your sister, tell her I'd be glad to have my key ring back." She hesitated. "When do you think she'll be back?"

"I have no idea," Minna said honestly. "I hope that things will become clearer soon—and that we'll hear good news, of course."

Zahava folded her hands and pursed her lips like a bird's bill. "I understand. Tell her that she should get in touch with me as soon as she can. Do you have a cellphone? Please take my number."

*You can never tell with people,* Minna mused, as she added the name to her contact list. Had anyone asked her, she would have said that this woman was hard and unfeeling, a real woman of steel. But look at how she reacted to a key ring that her mother had bought her! Unbelievable. Just unbelievable.

"Dr. Silver?" Zahava emerged from the ward. "Dr. Silver, are you here?"

"I'm here," the ward chief said from the depths of his office. "What happened?"

"Sofer," she said, breathing hard as if she'd just climbed a mountain. "It's not what we thought at all..."

"Meaning?" the ward chief asked slowly, as measured as ever.

"They're... How shall I put it? Righteous people of the world, perhaps?" Zahava sank into a chair. "Do you remember when I went to visit my son in India? I met the mother on the plane. She told me that she was on her way to adopt a baby."

The ward chief blinked. "The baby that was admitted here?" He tapped on his keyboard with uncharacteristic haste. "It doesn't say anything about that here."

"*Chareidim* love secrets," Zahava said, shaking her head. "They're probably afraid that no one will want to marry her if they know she wasn't born Jewish. But that's probably why they insisted on consulting with a doctor they trust. A doctor who knows their family secret. Maybe he helped them with the adoption or examined the baby over there, in India."

The ward chief grabbed his head with both hands. "She's their eleventh child! Were they getting bored?"

Zahava hesitated. "I don't remember the details of our conversation," she admitted. "But it seems to me that the father simply took pity on the baby after he found her abandoned."

"Unbelievable," the head doctor said. "Simply unbelievable."

"People can be amazing," Zahava agreed. "I hope, for their sake, that the child doesn't have epilepsy."

"Zahir is convinced that she does."

"Look over her file," Zahava urged. "Check to see if we might be missing something. I want to be satisfied that this case was handled properly."

"All our patients are handled properly," the doctor said stiffly.

"There's proper and there's proper. I want a consultation with a geneticist who is an expert in the Mumbai region. And I want another top neurologist's opinion and—"

She hesitated.

"Yes?"

"You've kept up a good relationship with Dr. Blau all this time," Zahava said. "So maybe…"

Dr. Silver shook his head. "I can't do that. Officially he's lost his license."

"Well, he did involve himself in medical malpractice suits against doctors who also work for us."

"Still…" The ward chief stuck out his weak chin. "Revoking his license was a very disproportionate punishment, in my opinion. We could have just given him a scolding, or if someone really wanted to teach him a lesson, suspend him for three months. Maximum, a year."

Zahava said nothing.

"He has appealed the decision," Dr. Silver said, "and I'm prepared to make a deal with you. I'll tend to the child, and you tend to the hospital director and get him to support Blau's appeal."

"He won't do it."

"Every hospital knows that when it's important enough, it will happen." Dr. Silver shrugged. "I don't think it should be any harder than being granted the equipment you requested last year."

Zahava was silent for a moment longer.

"Call me at eleven and tell me what you've done for that baby," she said. "Then we'll see what I can do for you."

---

The car struck the guardrail too lightly to deploy the airbags, but it made Yair Nava lose his equilibrium.

He'd had an accident! And why? Because of whom?

Because of Dreyfus! This was the result of the thousands of shekels he'd poured into that charlatan's pocket. Instead of helping him solve the minor problems that had brought him for therapy, the man had turned his life into one big pit of chaos.

Fury burned in him. Red, flaming, dangerous.

He should never have listened to the advice of a man like that! He should never have paid attention to him!

He was going to put him in his place right now. Show him that he shouldn't have interfered. That he should have kept his distance.

"That's right," Mirage encouraged. "Go teach him a lesson! Do you have your gun?"

# 101

SHAUL DIDN'T KNOW EXACTLY WHAT PINCHAS'S FATHER-in-law did for a living, but his contact person at the police was very helpful.

"Tell me, *yungerman*," the father-in-law bellowed into the phone five minutes later, "what are you dragging my son-in-law into less than twenty-four hours after he became a father?"

Had it really been less than twenty-four hours?

Shaul felt as drained as if twenty-four months had passed.

"He's not here anymore," he said tiredly into the phone. "He went to the hospital to see his wife and children. He just suggested you could help."

Pinchas's father-in-law roared again, "Whose number are you looking for?"

"The number of a private investigator named Yair Neiman." Shaul wasn't prepared to offer any unnecessary details that might burden Pinchas in the coming days.

"A private investigator?" The cellphone reception was excellent. Shaul felt as if the man were breathing right into his ear. "He's an agent with our intelligence unit, your Yair Neiman."

"Really?" Shaul was surprised.

"It's not written anywhere, black on white. But, sometimes, what's not written down says more than what is."

Shaul understood. "You have no information on him?"

"He apparently doesn't exist." The older man's voice softened slightly. "Yair Neiman is a second or third identity. He's probably carrying a few sets of identification with him."

This should have been encouraging news. For some reason, though, Shaul's heart wasn't rejoicing.

"The fact that he works in intelligence already says a lot, no?" the voice on the other end of the line insisted.

Shaul scratched his chin through his beard. "It should tell us a lot, yes."

"But you're afraid it doesn't?"

"Sometimes such identity cards fall into the wrong hands, don't they? I see no reason why Israeli intelligence should want to kidnap my brother-in-law, sister-in-law, and a psychologist. I can't imagine a reason for that."

"And you *can* imagine a reason why other people would want to kidnap them?"

Shaul glanced over his shoulder, at the old man in the wheelchair, the old woman with Francois's notebook on her lap, and at Dr. Blau, who looked more like an absentminded professor than a talented diagnostician. Quietly he said, "I could make all sorts of guesses, but none of them are very logical. I have no idea, for instance, what connection my brother-in-law has to all this."

"Maybe there's no connection," Pinchas's father-in-law said. "Maybe he was simply in the wrong place at the wrong time…"

The man was tough, no question about that. But right now he was friendly and ready to help. Shaul decided to reveal a bit more: "There's a neighbor here who heard my brother-in-law on the phone with that Yair fellow a short time before he disappeared. Apparently, they all—"

"Just a minute," said the voice at the other end of the line. "Do you know your brother-in-law's phone number?"

"Yes, but it hasn't been answering since last night."

"That's a long time," Pinchas's father-in-law agreed. "But let's try, first of all, to check where he was last, before his cell signal was lost."

"Thank you," Shaul said slowly. "I'll send you the number."

"Excellent," the other man said. "But look. I was somehow able to fit the other request into the monthly fee I pay the guy. This is a different story. He charges according to the job. If you need this information urgently, it will cost you about fifty-five hundred shekels. He'll want it transferred to his account before transmitting the data."

"How do you do that?"

"I'll handle it for you. That is—for Pinchas. My daughter always said that you're a close friend of his. And in exchange..."

Here we go. . .

"In exchange, I want you to put pressure on him to come stay with us for at least a month—him, my daughter, and the babies, when they're discharged from the NICU. One favor in exchange for another."

Shaul's head was spinning. "I don't know what the expected time-table is," he said, "but logic says that the babies will probably spend more than a month in the hospital..."

"Then let him and my daughter come for two weeks right now. And another three with the babies. After all the years they've waited, they deserve to be happy. I don't want them to have to cope alone with the hardship of trying to raise triplets."

Hardship?

Until that moment, Shaul had never thought that anyone could see it that way.

"Raising triplets is a blessed challenge, though very complicated," he said diplomatically. "I'll try to talk to Pinchas. I'll even put pressure on him. But I can't promise anything."

"Are you an honest man? Can I depend on your word?"

"I'm an honest man, and you can depend on my word. I'll talk to Pinchas. I'll tell him how important this is to you. Of course, you'll have to meet him halfway in areas that are important to him. But we'll talk about that after we deal with the problem we're looking at right now."

"I'll have to be satisfied with that," Pinchas's father-in-law grumbled. "Just make sure to transfer the payment to me as soon as possible. I'm not in the business of giving out loans."

"No problem. I'll give you both their numbers—my brother-in-law's and sister-in-law's—and then I'll be in touch with you to get your bank account number information."

"Two phone numbers will cost double. I don't give discounts. But I agree with you. I wouldn't leave any blind corners."

Shaul took a deep breath. "All right," he said. "Thank you."

"And remember our agreement."

"Absolutely."

"Good. I'll get back to you as fast as I can."

"Wonderful."

Shaul removed his glasses and rubbed his forehead.

"What happened?" Blau asked.

"They're going to try to locate the last signal that was received from my brother-in-law's and sister-in-law's phones." Shaul felt worn out. "And then we'll try to see what we can do with that information."

"A clever kidnaper will get rid of the signal. He'll take the cellphone and make sure the last signal comes from a place as far away as possible from the place his victims are stashed," Blau said. "If you're paying already, ask for the string of signals starting from nine p.m. last night, downstairs, until he disappeared."

Shaul preferred not to think about how much this request would cost, but he nodded. "I'll take care of it."

He rubbed his forehead again. What he needed—if he couldn't get a few consecutive hours of sleep—was a brimming cup of caffeine.

"Listen, my son said something about Francois and secrets. Secrets that people are afraid to tell." Shaul strained to recall the details. "Secrets that must not be kept because they cause others to make mistakes. Something like that…"

"Is there a way you can reach him?" asked Blau, eyes narrowing. "This could be important."

"I'll call Pinchas's father-in-law to submit our request, and then I'll call the school," Shaul said. A thought occurred to him. "He said that the person Francois was troubled about had lied to his employer, and if they discovered the truth they would fire him," he said in a single breath, as though he were reciting the names of Haman's ten sons. "And the man I spoke to now says that Yair Neiman is an agent for one of Israel's intelligence units. He has more than one known forged identity."

---

The car had only suffered a few superficial scrapes. He merged it back into traffic without difficulty, fueled by gasoline fumes and a powerful fury.

He had done so much for Israel!

Yair gripped the wheel with rigid fingers, and the muscles of his foot on the pedal were tense.

He had saved, with absolute certainty, the lives of hundreds, if not thousands, of soldiers and tens of thousands of citizens. He deserved medals of valor and public recognition—recognition he would never receive. But he had known what he was signing up for when he'd joined the service.

But if he couldn't be shown honor—did he have to be treated with scorn?

Why had that fool Dreyfus thought there was a chance he'd let him go to the police and spill everything to them?

Yair had never talked to another soul about Mirage with such freedom. Even though many in the Mossad knew about him, when he'd spoken with Dr. Dreyfus he'd added details and explained procedures.

He'd revealed too much. Given away too much. And Francois had asked too many questions and listened too intently to the answers.

Then he'd asked again. And fallen silent. Waiting for him to speak.

That's what psychologists did. He'd always known that. But he hadn't known how supportive that silence could be. How encouraging. Promising you that everything could be fixed. That there was a way to deal with every problem.

But that had been an illusion. An illusion that Francois had sold him in exchange for good money.

When the moment of truth arrived, instead of helping him cope with the reality, instead of listening to him the way he was supposed to, he had begun to say all kinds of stressful things.

*He* was not to blame for what happened. The psychologist was the one who was in the wrong. Everything that had happened was his fault.

102

JARNAIL FINISHED HIS PRAYERS AT THE KOSEL, FEELING AS though a decade-old weight had rolled off his shoulders. The scorn, the humiliation, all the years of depression and pain that had passed since he'd tried to intervene in the corruption case and was ejected from the Indian diplomatic corps…all of it erased. Purified.

A dove flitted past, beating its wings heavily. He touched the stones one last time, kissed his fingers, and began walking backward, ignoring with an effort the vibration of the phone in his jacket pocket.

Only when he was far from those holy stones, and from the plaza that had been designated as a place to pray, did he put his hand in his pocket and return the call.

"Yes, Shaul?" he said, dragging himself back to the present world.

"We have new information." Shaul's voice was restrained. "We know who the kidnaper is. That is, we know the false name he is using, that he belongs to one of Israel's intelligence agencies, and that he suffers from delusions revolving around some friend named Mirage."

"Mirage. An illusionary vision."

"Yes. It's also a Jewish-Iranian name."

"Okay," Jarnail said. "What else do you know?"

"We know the last place there was a signal from my brother-in-law and his wife. Both of them in the same place."

"Where?"

"Here in Yerushalayim. In the neighborhood of Katamon. They gave me a location for Waze."

"Give it to me," Jarnail said. He paused a beat. "I'm writing it down."

"And you'll come?" Shaul asked, after he dictated the location.

"Of course." Jarnail lengthened his stride. "The minute I manage to grab a taxi."

"And your friends?"

Jarnail swallowed. "I was unsuccessful in obtaining their cooperation. I'm sorry."

This was a blow. Shaul absorbed it with difficulty. "Everything is from *Shamayim*, and it's all for the good," he said. "But maybe you should try again? Now that we have an address, and the picture is a little clearer?"

Jarnail flagged down a cab and got inside. "To Katamon," he told the driver. To Shaul, he replied, "After learning that the kidnaper belongs to Israeli intelligence? Not a chance, Shaul. Zero chance they'll cooperate. But pray hard. I hope we'll have heavenly assistance anyway. Don't worry."

"Yesterday, I had someone in here who was also afraid that a member of his family had been kidnaped," said the driver when Jarnail had hung up.

"Really?" Jarnail's brows rose. "There aren't many kidnapings in the State of Israel."

"True," the driver said, glancing at him in the rearview mirror. "Poor guy. He was so stressed. His brother-in-law had disappeared or something. Leaving children alone, without supervision. Afterward, I was upset with myself for not offering to help... A pity."

Jarnail gave him a long look. "You thought of helping him?" he asked.

"I have a friend of a friend who understands these kinds of things," he said. "A guy who knows everyone and can help when help is needed."

"Then let's go," Jarnail said. "Call him. The man you drove yesterday and me? We have ties to that family."

---

The discussion of "Benny's" situation was abruptly broken off at a sound from the entrance announcing Yair's return. The tall, handsome, smiling young man who had locked them in hours earlier had left behind a series of threats and warnings and then disappeared. The man who walked into the house was a different person. His shirt, which boasted a stain of something that looked like a soft drink, was untucked. His hair was messy, and his hand held a gun.

"It's your fault!" he told Francois hoarsely, his voice wavering between apology and anger. "*You* are to blame. You did this. It's all because of you. You didn't leave me a choice. Because of you, I'm going to suffer pangs of conscience for the rest of my life."

Francois took a deep breath, staring at the gun's black muzzle. "I'm in your hands, Yair," he said quietly. "But is it possible that you are in someone else's hands?"

"Whose hands?" The gun shook slightly.

"I suggest that we sit down, the three of us, and talk," Francois said in a firm voice. "After we're done talking, you can do what you want."

Yair's eyes darted around the room with a fighter's tension. "What do you mean?"

"I mean that the three of us should sit down. You, me, and the person in your head—Mirage. Bring two chairs, and the three of us will sit down and talk. I'm not only a psychologist. I'm also an expert in family counseling and arbitration. It would be a good idea to do this before we part ways. Is it okay with you if Mirage enters the room now?"

Yair's eyes went to Gadi and Shuli. "He can come in, but they have to go."

Home? Shuli's heart fluttered with hope. But the hope was short-lived.

"Let them go into the next room."

Leave Francois here alone?

"Yes," Francois responded to the question they hadn't voiced. "Go. That's an excellent idea. And you bring in chairs for the two of you, Yair. For you and Mirage."

This instruction was carried out. Yair used his leg to drag over the chairs that Gadi and Shuli had occupied and arranged them for himself and Mirage.

"So, tell me, Yair." Francois's voice was steady and rang with authority. "What is the state of your relationship with Mirage? Have you been telling Mirage the truth, or have you been hiding things from him?"

Yair was taken aback. "Why should I hide things?" he asked petulantly.

"It's clear to me that you've been hiding things from him," Francois said. "After all, you're not in touch with him constantly, and you do things that affect him and can have an impact on him. Yet you don't tell him about them. Could it be that you're not really such good friends?"

Yair shook his head. "He's my best friend. He's the only one who's there when times are hard." He swallowed. "And sometimes it's very hard."

"I agree." Francois nodded. "The two of you have a good bond. You've been together for many years. Still, there's something that's disturbing your relationship."

"Nothing is disturbing our relationship."

"Fact," Francois said softly. "Look how tense you are."

Yair chuckled nervously, and the gun trembled in his hand. "I'm tense because of you. Because you said he doesn't exist, that I'm sick, that I need to go to the police! Not because of him!"

Francois lifted his hands in a gesture of surrender. "Look, I don't have your abilities. When I can't see someone, I say he doesn't exist. For example, right now I don't see Mirage. He's sitting next to you, right?"

"Yes."

"But I don't see him. That's why I offered you the advice of a person who has a limitation." He smiled affectionately. "It doesn't bother me that you have Mirage. I'm glad you have such a good friend. What bothers me is that he's messing up your life. That you don't know what to do and what not to do, what is truth and what is a lie. Mirage is hurting you through the confusion he creates in your life. And since you can't get angry at him because he's your friend, and you can't get angry at your boss because people who work for the Mossad don't get angry at their bosses...you have no one to get angry at but me. It's all right. It's perfectly all right. That's part of a psychologist's job, to absorb the client's anger."

Silence filled the room, a silence that made Gadi and Shuli worry about what was taking place in there. Finally, they heard Francois's voice again.

"So what does Mirage have to say about all this?"

"He says"—Yair's voice was shaky and tense—"that he's helped the State of Israel a great deal. I would even say that most of the good things that have happened over the past fifteen years regarding Israel's operations in Iran have happened because of him. He gave our hesitant politicians a lot of strength and courage. He quietly helped them make decisions. He's a good person."

Francois nodded and took a sip of the cold coffee that Shuli had prepared for him earlier.

"So let's see how we can help you work as effectively as possible with your unseen Mirage and your very-much-seen boss," he said, resting the empty cup on the table. "Our goal is to reach a place where you can achieve what's best for you and be at least as successful as your father was. And that will happen when you succeed in working with Mirage in a way that won't make you angry or alarmed."

"Yes," said Yair. "That...sounds good. But you didn't talk that way before. What a pity."

"We need to reach a place where you won't become confused from living a double life and be able to do your work properly," Francois went on, ignoring Yair's comment. "That can spell the difference between what Mirage says and your own very proper thoughts, as an Israeli who knows the ins and outs of Iran as well as one possibly can. I think it may be that because you were so alone in your unique work, you dressed all your thoughts with someone else's figure and created a conversation that helped you move forward."

"You said it's a hallucination!" Yair shrilled.

"Yes," Francois admitted. "I said it's a hallucination, and I thought it was a problem. But now that I see you pointing your gun at me, I think that's an even bigger problem."

Yair looked at him and looked at the gun. He burst out laughing. "Yes," he said, still laughing. "You can definitely say that this is a bigger problem. For me, too. Not only for you."

# 103

LAUGHTER IS AMAZING. IT'S A HIDDEN MIRACLE THAT EVEN has the power to change the existing atmosphere between a kidnaper and his victim.

"Look," Francois said after a few minutes of shared laughter. "I'm a person who learns from his clients. That's why I changed my mind. I've never met a person like you, so I gave you advice better suited to other people. But you're different from the others, so you need advice geared specifically to you. What I think we need to do is find, together, a way that will help you come to terms with your own personal reality."

Yair ran his left hand over his face. "So you're saying that I don't have to tell anyone that Mirage is not exactly real?"

Francois shook his head. "I'm not going to make that decision for you, because you know yourself best. I'm interested in having you live a life of quality and meaning, of balance and contentment. And if Mirage is the means by which you can achieve that quality of life, it doesn't really matter if we call him an illusion or a cluster of thoughts… If it doesn't bother you that Mirage is 'not exactly real,' and if you can manage your life and control it, what difference does it make if this phenomenon is known by conservative medicine as a hallucination?"

"You said it would be a good idea for me to take medication."

Francois tried very hard not to look at the loaded gun. "If the hallucinations are dangerous, they're treated with medication. If not—they don't prescribe medication. It's not obligatory."

"Now you probably think that they're very dangerous." Yair sounded dejected.

"What I think is that we have to find out what *you* think. Do you think you can establish a bond with Mirage that you can control? Is the relationship between the two of you such that you can tell him, 'Don't bother me now'? The test of sanity is in the ability to control the imagination. The cluster of thoughts. Because sometimes the goal is so special and important that the reality changes."

Yair clenched his teeth and shook his head. "I don't understand exactly what you're trying to say," he said. "And Mirage says that you say a lot of nice words—but in actuality, at the moment of truth, they're worth nothing."

"And what do *you* think? Is he right?" Francois asked pleasantly. "Please answer me honestly."

<hr />

On the other side of the wall, Shuli and Gadi stood helpless.

"We have to do something," Shuli whispered. "He's trying to buy us some time, and we're just standing here like…" She couldn't think of an appropriate analogy.

"Tell me what to do and I'll do it," Gadi said. "Because I don't have a clue."

"Maybe you can surprise him from behind?" she asked. "And knock away his gun?"

Gadi wrinkled his nose. "And if the gun discharges a bullet while it's flying?"

"The question is, which is the greater danger," she whispered, starting to tear up. "Gadi, he could kill us. I saw it in his eyes. He could do it."

Gadi shrugged. "That still doesn't turn me into a person who can attack him and grab his gun, Shuli. Let's be logical, okay?"

She closed her eyes, lips whispering snatches of *Tehillim*. Then she opened them again and said, "We can't just wait for him to shoot us in the head."

"*Chas v'shalom.*" He sighed. "Shuli, I know that I'm the last person who would ordinarily be saying this, but here goes: Sometimes we're helpless and we have to leave it all in the hands of HaKadosh Baruch Hu. We have no way to help ourselves, but we don't have to fall apart, because He can help us."

He was really the last person who'd be saying that. Hesitantly, she smiled. "*Ein od milvado*," she said.

"Right," Gadi agreed. "That's the idea."

"'When Yisrael looks heavenward...'" Shuli seized on the song that her parents sang every *shalosh seudos*. Then she looked at her husband and said, "The roof! That's an idea!"

---

"What do I think?" Yair repeated. "I think that you've helped me in a lot of ways, including today."

"Thank you." Francois smiled. "But I asked what you think about what Mirage says. Is Mirage correct in saying that I'm talking nonsense?"

"I don't know." Yair's foot bobbed impatiently. "I don't know how I got into this mess. I don't understand how it happened. And it's making me very anxious."

Francois looked at him in distress and said, "Look, Yair, you don't have to be anxious. There aren't two views here, mine and Mirage's. We're all on your side. Mirage is on your side, and I'm on your side. It's just that our views about what's best for you are different. It can happen that two opinions can both have your best interests in mind.

"With two people who are both on your side, you should be happy. You don't need to feel tense or anxious. If you're tense, you can ask yourself and your advisers—in this case, Mirage and me—what to do. You are the one who gets to choose. You're in control of Mirage, whether he's an illusion or a cluster of thoughts. And, by the way, you're also in control of me. Your gun proves that."

"But you're against Mirage," Yair said.

"I'm not against Mirage. I'm for you." Francois had endless patience. "There's no need to become alarmed at the conflict. You don't have to be upset that your two advisers have different opinions. Mirage doesn't get to decide, and neither do I. The choice is yours. Only yours."

"You confused me," Yair complained. "You confused me, you caused me to suffer, you pushed me over the edge, and you caused me to kidnap you and get tangled up with the law. And now you're telling me not to be alarmed? *Now* you say that? You should have told me that before. Before everything!"

The address that Shaul had given Jarnail took him to a calm street in the Katamon neighborhood, a place of single-family homes surrounded by yards. "Every house here is worth seven, eight million shekels, easy," the driver said, half to himself and half to Jarnail. "A good place to live."

Not an especially logical location to keep kidnaping victims, Jarnail thought. He was certain that all they'd probably find here would be the broken fragments of cellphones that had been tossed from a moving vehicle and crushed beneath the wheels of passing cars.

But this was all they had at the moment, so this was what they must work with. Especially since, from the point of view of the police, the disappearances hadn't yet reached the stage of being worrisome.

"Are you sure this is where you need to go?" the driver asked. "There was no mistake in the address? Call your friend who gave it to you. Let him check again."

That was a good idea. But Shaul, who mentioned that he was on his way, repeated exactly the same numbers.

"I'll get out here," Jarnail told the driver. "Thanks for being the middleman." A few minutes earlier, the driver had provided the number of the friend of a friend who was sending some men over for support.

"You're welcome." The driver half-smiled. "Of course, if anyone asks, I wasn't involved."

"I don't know you," Jarnail promised. "It's all good."

He got out of the cab, straightened up, adjusted his cuffs, and looked around. What caught his attention was the glint of sunlight reflecting off a piece of glass set in the limbs of one of the trees facing him.

A camera?

He bent over to tie his shoelace, and when he straightened again, he sent another glance at the place where he'd seen the flash of reflected light. His guess was confirmed.

Security cameras aren't unusual. But the location of this one was unusual enough to make him curious. Unless an Israeli cabinet minister or a paranoid millionaire lived here, it was reasonable to assume that the person who'd put the camera there had a very good reason for protecting the entrance to his home. It hadn't occurred to him, apparently, that it would be that very security measure that would expose him…

Jarnail walked with a measured pace toward the tree with the camera, stopping directly underneath in a spot where, in his estimation, the camera wouldn't be able to capture more than the tips of his shoes. He took out his cellphone and activated one of the successful programs that had been inserted by the Indian intelligence service, one that he hadn't bothered to delete after leaving the diplomatic corps. Three presses, a security code, and now all he had to do was move the phone slowly and steadily to scan the area in front of him. The program diminished ambient noise and focused on signals emanating from hidden cameras. Seconds later, it provided Jarnail with a map highlighting the areas in which he would be exposed to watching eyes.

The net, it turned out, was well focused. The cameras covered the area from the street to one of the large iron gates. They also showed him clearly which of the structures to concentrate on.

He stood thoughtfully for a moment and then called back the person with whom he had spoken a few minutes earlier. The friend of a friend.

"I forgot one thing I need," Jarnail said. "Do you have a karaoke system? It needs to be a powerful one."

"Karaoke?" the other man asked. "I don't recognize a code like that."

Jarnail smiled. "It's not a code. It's exactly what it sounds like. I need a serious karaoke machine—a good microphone and powerful amplifiers."

"What for?" the man asked.

"To conduct a negotiation," Jarnail answered quietly. "This is a fortress, my friend. We don't have too many other options."

The other man said, "I'll get one." He paused, and then added, "You know what? I have an idea for you. I can make him think that he's surrounded by the police…"

104

FREIDA HAD A WHITE PORCELAIN TEA SET DECORATED WITH pink roses. It looked odd against the background of the apartment's modern design, and even odder in the context of the reality they were dealing with.

"You need to drink something before you leave," she said seriously. "It's starting to get late, and you haven't eaten anything today. Make a *berachah* and have a drink and some cookies."

It didn't seem right to be drinking tea from European teacups when people they knew and loved were being held captive. But Freida was adamant. "A person without sugar in his blood makes mistakes," she declared. "It's precisely because there are so many important things at stake that you have to eat. Besides, as Moishe always says, before you do something important, you have to have a cup of tea and say a *Shehakol* with *kavanah*."

This last argument was the decisive one, in Shaul's view. He reached out to lift his cup, recited the blessing slowly and with concentration, and then let the sweetness flow through him. "I put in a lot of sugar," he heard Freida say to him and the doctor at his side.

The sugar boost did seem to clarify his thoughts. "We need to go to the police," he said, opening his eyes.

Blau coughed as if the tea had turned solid and become stuck in his throat. "If you want a bunch of imbeciles who will take you in for three days of questioning, leaving Francois and your brother-in-law to die, go ahead. Call them," he invited. "I was also naïve once, but—"

Blau had tried to save lives, Shaul remembered, and in return the State had revoked his license to practice medicine. Life experience wasn't always a pleasant thing.

"You have to go by the book," Blau said mockingly. "Are you familiar with that expression? And if people die in the meantime, why should you care?"

"There are good policemen," Freida said. "My brother was a policeman. He died in 2002." She gazed at the two men in distress. "But if someone from the Mossad or the Shabak is involved in this, it's reasonable to guess that it really will take time for them to discover who the kidnaper is and whether he's working on his own or on a superior's instructions." She picked up the plate of cookies and extended her hand. "The cookies are excellent. My granddaughter made them. Take, take."

"We have proof that he's mentally unstable," Shaul insisted, gesturing at the pages. "I think that with all due respect to our efforts and the information we've come up with until this point, right now we need help from the police."

Blau sighed and crumbled a cookie between his fingers. "Shall I give you some statistics?" he said mildly. "What percentage of kidnaped people remained alive twelve hours after being taken? It's not a very reassuring number."

Twelve hours. Terror seized Shaul as he looked at the clock hanging on the wall facing him. Gadi had last been seen at ten p.m. It was now after nine-thirty.

"You've convinced me," he said. "Let's go. Now." He glanced at his cup of tea, decided that he hadn't had enough to be obligated to say a *berachah acharonah*, and stood up. "But I'm calling my wife on the way. She's with my brother-in-law's children now. I'll ask her to update the police with all the information we have."

"No problem." Blau nodded. "Just...give them Freida's number as the contact person."

"Gladly," the old woman said. "And don't worry. My memory, *baruch Hashem*, is excellent."

After covering a few more technical details, they parted from the elderly couple and went to the door. Moishe, seated in his wheelchair, said something.

"Just a minute," Freida gasped. "Just a minute..."

They stopped.

"Moishe says that good words are better than guns," she said breathlessly, walking as fast as she could toward the kitchen. "But still…" There was a clatter of utensils. "It's better if you have one." Another noise, and then she returned to the living room holding a blue velvet bag. "Moishe was a contractor, so in the year 2017, when terrorism spiked, he got a license for this gun," she said. "Take it and take care of it."

"This is not legal," Blau said, as though wondering if she was aware of that.

"It's not legal," she agreed. "But if Moishe says—"

Shaul turned toward the old man. "Thank you."

Moishe said something. This time, Shaul understood his meaning without Freida's translation. He was wishing them luck.

———————

"We're on our way," Shaul reported to Jarnail when they'd entered Dr. Blau's small car.

"I'm already here," Jarnail said with his usual calm. "This is a serious fortress. Plenty of security cameras. Wait a second…"

The call was cut off. Shaul looked at Blau, who was driving, and shrugged. "He's there. He said it's a fortress."

"I heard."

A muffled vibration interrupted them. "This time, it's *my* phone," Blau apologized. "Can you put it on speakerphone for me, please?"

"Yosef?" A dignified, authoritative voiced filled the car. "How are you?"

"I'm fine, Doctor," Blau said curtly. "What is it?"

"You're really angry at me," the doctor on the other end of the line said with a sigh of his own. "Simply because I'm part of the establishment, eh?"

"No, not just because of that. Mostly because you didn't speak up—"

"But, Yosef, you know I didn't do that because I never dreamed that someone would think seriously about dismissing you! I was certain that you would come away with nothing more than a slap on the wrist, and that—"

"Defending me wasn't worth the trouble," Blau finished. "What a pity."

"You're earning much more now," the other doctor pointed out. "Your livelihood hasn't suffered."

"But my heart has." Blau fell silent, and then added, "And not only mine. My children's, too."

"I know. And I'm sorry that things worked out this way. I think about you all the time. This very morning, Zahava Polsky, our head nurse, asked me for a favor for some baby from India that a *chareidi* couple adopted, and I told her that I'll only help her if she talks to Dr. Sigav and wins his support for you."

"He won't agree," Blau said. "A wasted favor."

"When Zahava Polsky asks for something, no one can refuse," the doctor said. "Including me. Look at me, calling you about this baby though it's very uncomfortable for me to ask you for help without offering anything in exchange…"

"Look, Dr. Silver—Adam—I'm busy right now," Blau said. "An urgent matter of life and death. But I'll get back to you later."

Shaul, who had been sitting beside him in silence, placed a hand on his arm. "My baby," he said soundlessly.

"What?" Blau was not as discreet. "Just a second, Doctor. What's that you're saying, Shaul?"

"It's my baby," Shaul whispered again. "Can you listen to him for a minute?"

Blau's pupils widened, and then he looked back at the road. "Actually, I'm driving right now," he said. "Do you want to give me some general information?"

He listened in silence to the secret medical language of which Shaul understood only a portion. He paused, and then said, "You've checked the carnitine, right? What about clostridium botulinum?"

Silence. "No. We haven't checked that. But the mother said the baby wasn't exposed to honey."

"Come on, can mothers be responsible for everything a crawling baby puts in her mouth?" Blau asked dismissively. "Besides, doesn't the baby go to a babysitter? And there are always the rare occurrences… They've found clostridium botulinum in baked potatoes, cheese with onions, garlic preserved in oil, or…" He stopped a moment. "Or even in soil. Ask them whether there's any construction going on nearby. Maybe that's the cause."

"That's a very rare infection." Dr. Silver was hesitant.

"Rare, but existent," Blau said. "I really have to go now."

"We'll look into it," Dr. Silver said. "And we'll be in touch. Also about your own matter. Don't worry."

"I won't," Blau said dryly. "Thank you."

A thick silence filled the little car when the call was over.

"I never imagined that Benny Sofer's father was a person who adopts abandoned babies from India," Blau finally said. "I pictured him completely differently. Someone with bulging eyes and a fiery spirit of vengeance. Not the calm, measured man sitting beside me right now."

Shaul sighed. "It's a long story," he said quietly. "And we weren't involved in the school's decision. At any stage. At the time, we were in—"

"In India," Blau finished.

"Yes. Exactly. Apart from that, I spoke with your son, and I know that he is presenting things very differently. And my connection with Francois was formed when I brought my son to him for therapy. After certain classmates made his life miserable for two years without anyone knowing."

"Yes?" Blau's light-gray eyes were as large as pools.

A level of trust had been forged between them, the result of two hours of work toward a mutual goal. Shaul nodded silently.

"I'm sorry," Dr. Blau said quietly. "I didn't know."

"I'm sorry, too. Very sorry," Shaul said. "The world is so complicated."

"Very complicated," Blau agreed.

The men were wrapped in silence during the remaining minutes of the drive, until they reached the location Pinchas's father-in-law had given them less than thirty minutes earlier.

---

It was natural for Shuli to search for a miracle. She had always been stubborn. Gadi decided to be patient.

"What do you want on the roof?" he asked. "Do you think he didn't secure the door leading up there the way they secured all the other exits in this house?"

"Let's try anyway," she whispered in response. "Let's try quietly, while Francois is keeping him busy here."

To try. To try in a place where they had no chance.

For some reason, Gadi remembered his final days at the *kollel*. He recalled how helpless he had felt when told, "Unfortunately, there won't be room for you for the next *zeman*." The despair that had engulfed him when he didn't succeed in finding another *kollel* willing to open its doors to him. And why was all this happening? Because of a complaint about the *rosh kollel's* slow pace in learning and a humorous imitation of some of his favorite sayings. He had been only twenty-two then. The mortification had been so intense!

Shuli hadn't wanted him to give up. She had even been ready to move to some remote town, where he could have a fresh start. But he hadn't agreed to be pushed into a place where he didn't stand a chance.

That situation, strangely, seemed to him to parallel the one that the two of them were facing now. Was this what they meant when they said that a man's whole life passes before his eyes during his last moments?

Gadi swallowed, surprised at the salty taste in his mouth.

"Okay," he said. "The roof, you said?"

"The roof," she confirmed.

He moved slowly, heavily. "How do you get up there?"

Shuli passed a hand over her eyes. "I have no idea. But there's an overhead storage area, and this is an old house. Maybe there's a way to go up through the storage area..."

Gadi's eyes sparkled when he heard what she said. The idea was better than Shuli realized.

"We can climb into the storage area and hide there," he said. "Come on. Now."

"You're angry at me because I called Mirage an illusion and caused you to become confused," Francois said. "I apologize for that, Yair. But I don't think I harmed you. This confusion allows you to make a decision. A fog can be uncomfortable, but it opens up new possibilities. Take a deep breath. Don't be afraid of the confusion. Know that you are strong, smart, and experienced enough to make decisions—as opposed to what Mirage may believe. This is your test. Are you sane or not? Understand?"

Yair looked at him. Then, slowly, he lowered his gun.

Francois's sigh of relief seemed to echo around the room. At least in his own ears.

"Tell you the truth?" Yair said, his voice a bit morose. "I was anxious about taking that information to the newspapers, you know? I was angry that the Mossad didn't believe Mirage's report that Iran is developing biological weapons that will target fruits and vegetables." He paused to breathe. "I knew that they would trust outside sources more. Some silly reporter from the *Daily Telegraph*, and not me, who spent the best twenty years of my life learning to read between the lines and pinpoint the atmosphere there."

"So you were the 'secret Iranian source' that the *Daily Telegraph* relied on?"

"Not me," Yair said. "Of course not. It was Mirage."

A smile threatened to steal onto Francois's lips when he suddenly understood that Yair had no trouble speaking Farsi with a perfect accent. But a smile in this situation could spell his end. It was swallowed almost at the moment it began to tremble on his lips.

"And what do you think now?" he asked dryly. "That is, what do you and Mirage think about the mess that's been created?"

Yair lifted the gun and rubbed its side unawares. "They took things too far. Everyone—the reporter, the Knesset... All these threats aren't good for the Iranian leadership. They could attack first. And that would be bad."

"And?"

"And I need to go tell them all, 'Hey, I fooled you. Mirage doesn't really exist.'" Yair's anger sparked again. "Those were your words, dear Mr. Dreyfus."

"Doctor," Francois corrected gently.

"Dr. Dreyfus," Yair amended. Acknowledging Dreyfus's title and authority calmed him down somewhat.

"And that idea, I see, is one that you consider very bad."

"Obviously," Yair snapped. "Do you want me to ruin my reputation? To tell them all that I'm crazy?"

"We concluded that you're not crazy," Francois reminded him. "That Mirage is a figment of your imagination, employed to process facts and utilize them."

"You'll come with me to explain that to them, eh?"

"If you wish," said the psychologist. "Gladly."

"I can't." Yair set down the gun again. "They can't know that I came to you. It's...against the rules. If I need help, I'm supposed to go to one of their psychologists. But it's all a game there. I can't trust anyone."

"I'm happy that you trust me."

Yair sighed. "You're here because I don't exactly trust you," he reminded the psychologist. "You said that you would have to go to the police."

"I opened up new avenues of thought for you."

Another sigh. "You opened a door to bad things," he said. "That wasn't your job."

"My job is to help you."

"And it would help me if my reputation were destroyed, after everything I've done for Israel?"

Yair's anger made his words emerge in a roar. But Francois spoke quietly. "You're saying that you understand that the situation has spiraled out of control, but you don't want to destroy your good name," he summarized. "Why don't you want to destroy your name?"

"Would anyone?" Yair shot back.

At that moment, there was a noise outside, and then a guttural voice said, "Yair. Yair Neiman. We know that you're there. We want to talk to you."

Yair stared blankly at Francois for a moment before reacting. "Raise your hands," he said in a hard voice. "Stand up."

Francois obeyed in silence. Yair cautiously moved until he was standing behind him with the gun touching the psychologist's shoulder. A wail of a siren from outside, and then the blue flicker of a patrol car, intensified the sense of unease in the room.

Yair was tired, Francois thought. He was tense. At the bursting point. They didn't have much time left to talk. Perhaps they had no time left at all. And Yair, he knew, was capable of making irrational decisions they would all regret.

"What, exactly, is the problem?" he asked, face to the window.

"I don't want to destroy my reputation," Yair said curtly. "I don't want this to be in the newspapers."

"The truth is more important. If you believe that, take it all the way to the end," Francois suggested.

"Which truth?" Yair was confused.

Silence. Francois wished he could turn around to read the other man's expression.

"I don't understand. Which truth are you talking about?" Yair demanded again.

"You did everything you did because of a certain truth, right?" Francois asked gently.

"Yes. I want them to attack Iran. It's time. Each passing day increases the danger."

"So go all the way with it. Go out and tell them that clearly. Without cloaking your words behind masks."

"Hah!" Yair pretended to laugh, but the laughter sounded false. "The fact that everyone will think I'm a liar, after everything I've invested in this country, will push them to attack Iran?"

"Which is preferable? For you to kill me, kill everyone, and then the police will break in and kill you, either accidentally or deliberately? And the media will report that the Mossad mistakenly recruited a madman. Is that better, do you think?"

"They won't kill me. I'll escape."

"Yair Neiman!" called the guttural voice. "We know you're there. We want to talk to you!"

"You won't be able to escape," Francois said quietly. "They're too good. They'll burst in here before you manage to escape. It could be completely different if you cooperate with them."

Yair breathed heavily.

"You want to pass on your information," Francois said. "You want to expose it to the nation. You want a secure avenue of retreat and a safe place for the rest of your life in a place where Israel has no extradition treaty. A place where you can enjoy the money they paid Mirage all these years..."

It was a wild guess, but it hit the bull's eye. For years, the Mossad had been putting hundreds of thousands of dollars into Mirage's pockets. Mirage, in return, had supplied them with a wealth of attractive information about the situation in Iran. And because a nonexistent person doesn't require an apartment, clothes, or food, nearly all of it—excluding gifts that Mirage had bought Yair over the course of time—was sitting in his bank account.

"You need to decide now," Francois urged. "Those men—we've got to assume they're from the Yamam, Israel's counterterrorism unit. You know how they operate, right? They don't wait long. It's part of their tactics, not to give the people inside much time to think. Decide now which is more important to you—your reputation, or your love for the State of Israel. And then act. Do the right thing."

105

Even before Waze informed them that they had reached their destination, he and Shaul realized that they were in the right place. Seven or eight cars were blocking the upscale street, and black-uniformed policemen had gathered around the tall figure of Jarnail.

"What's this?" Shaul asked.

"Your friend from the embassy must have called the police," Blau said. "We'll have to figure out what to tell them."

Shaul blinked. "Look at the symbol on their arms," he said quietly.

Yosef Blau automatically moved his glasses to the bridge of his nose, squinting. "I see a Magen David," he said.

"That's the problem," Shaul said. "The Israeli police wear a star, not a Magen David. And it has a wreath of leaves around it, not a circle."

"Really?" Blau took off his glasses and gave Shaul a long look.

"I don't know much about statistics, and no department chiefs call to consult with me," Shaul said with a smile, "but my instincts tell me that they're not policemen. And they made sure they can't be accused of impersonating police officers. But the kidnaper inside will see a serious array of power confronting him, not just three unprotected citizens."

"A bad idea," Blau stated. "The police make kidnapers nervous. The last thing we want is to make him jumpy."

Francois's arms were starting to hurt. "Yair," he asked delicately, "what does Mirage say about this? The two of you have a lot of experience with emergency situations, right?"

"He says that I can't wait for them to break into the house. That I have to continue the mission…" Yair's voice shook. "I can't let them arrest me, Francois. I'm really sorry…"

*Ribbono shel Olam.* Francois's knees buckled. *What else can I say? What else can I do? Give me words. Show me what I'm supposed to do.*

This prayer was his constant refrain in his treatment room, where words were capable of building or destroying a life. It rose up in him now as the second of the possibilities became more tangible than ever before. So close to being carried out.

"I believe you," he found himself saying. "The information that Mirage brought all these years helped our prime ministers immensely in the last few decades. It helped them arrive at difficult decisions. We must allow him to continue to live. So I have an idea. Let's switch clothes. I'll go out, to the people waiting out there, and you'll go up to the attic and hide until they all go away." He took a deep breath. "May I turn around, Yair? Do you agree with me that that's a good idea?"

"There's no attic here," Yair said. "And there's no reason for us to switch clothes. They don't know what I look like, right?"

"So, a storage loft," Francois said, arms still in the air. "I'm turning around, Yair."

The other man sighed. Dr. Dreyfus decided that this was answer enough.

"Go hide," he urged. "I'll go out to them and say that the last time you were here was several hours ago."

Yair looked at him, his eyes rimmed in black. "Why are you doing this?" he asked.

*Because I want to live,* Francois thought. Out loud, he said, "I believe that you're right. That you have a mission. You need to get out of here and carry it out. That's all."

"And you won't give me away?" Yair's breaths were labored.

"No. Why should I? Like I said, as a psychologist I can guarantee confidentiality."

"You said that there are certain cases—"

"That's not this case," Francois cut him off. "Run, Yair. Before they break in."

"So go outside," Yair said.

"Give me the gun."

Yair shook his head. "You don't need it. I do. But here are the keys—"

The keys.

Francois gasped when he saw the key ring. His hand shook as he accepted it.

"Thank you," he said. "May you merit doing a lot of good, Yair."

Yair looked at him for a moment. Then he nodded and, gun in hand, turned and left the kitchen.

He was free?

It wasn't likely that this was some sort of trap. Francois stumbled toward the door, put the key in the lock, and carefully turned it.

The door yielded easily, revealing the foyer he had entered so innocently less than twenty-four hours before to speak with a "very influential person"—something that had been easy to believe upon seeing the house's luxurious external appearance.

A moment before he stepped outside, he stopped.

Gadi! His wife!

Slowly, he turned back, toward the kitchen, which no longer held Yair. Toward the empty living room. His voice trembled oddly as he called, "Gadi? Gadi? Come!"

But Gadi didn't come.

A reasonable response. But considering the circumstances…

"Yair Neiman. Yair Neiman, we want to talk to you," the voice from outside repeated.

Francois took a deep breath. No, he was not going to abandon the two people who had come to rescue him, and who were now the hostages of an armed madman who would apologize in a pain-filled voice before putting a bullet in them.

"Gadi? Mrs. Phillips?" He retreated a step. "Gadi? Where are you? I made a deal with Yair…"

Yair had vanished somewhere in the house. And he had a gun. He had some influence with Yair. But the man wasn't that sane. What would he do if he encountered Gadi and Shuli in his feverish attempt to escape?

Shuli wept silently in the innermost portion of the storage loft. Gadi sat hunched up beside her, head between his knees, firmly gripping a small metal rod that would, with absolute certainty, slip right through his fingers if someone else tugged at it with any strength at all.

Why bother, then?

"Gadi, are you davening? Please daven."

Sure. Of course. That was the only thing they could do now. Besides saying *viduy*, maybe.

"I—"

"Daven. Make a resolution." She rubbed her nose. "Let go of the cynicism for a minute, okay?"

A sound came from below. The sound of chairs being dragged. The chairs that he had overturned earlier in a helpless attempt to cover their tracks. Yair was here.

*Ribbono shel Olam.* A wave of dizziness assailed Gadi, and the fingers clutching the metal rod were damp. *Ribbono shel Olam, I try to be a good person. To do what I'm supposed to do—*

Someone had grasped the handle from the outside.

Now everything depended on whether or not he could convince him that the storage loft was locked.

*But...*

Two fingers separated him from their kidnaper. A thumb and a forefinger, which barely managed to hold on to the little piece of metal.

*But maybe You expect me to be like Shaul—to do not only what I have to, but also what's right.*

He was crying.

He hadn't cried in years.

*So, okay, Ribbono shel Olam. Okay. Just save us, okay?*

Life was calling to Francois from the other side of the door. It was calling to him with all the usual, routine voices of everyday. In the sweetness of the birdcalls, in the noise of the cars. Inside, there was only silence. And the sound of a dragging chair.

His insides clenched, and acid filled his mouth.

He stumbled toward the front door and opened it wide. Then he stumbled back into the house.

"Yair?" he screamed. "Where are you? Come back!"

"Changed your mind?" Hair unkempt and gun in hand, Yair returned to the hallway.

"I thought..." Francois lost hold of his words for a moment, something that didn't happen to him often. "I thought that we need another moment—to get ready. Do you have a way to communicate with them? To tell them that you are prepared to negotiate? I want another minute. To think."

"You want them to burst in here and kill me," Yair accused.

"No, no." Francois couldn't bear the sight of the gun. "Absolutely not. I want to help you, Yair. I really do. You have a mission, and I want to help you do it right."

"Mirage says you're lying."

Mirage was smart.

"You want me to let your friends go with you."

Yes. That's right.

"I want us to negotiate!" he screeched. "I don't want you to turn into a fugitive. I want you to be able to leave. To go abroad." No. Those were not the right words. He realized that after he'd said them. He saw all his avenues of escape closing in the other man's eyes.

"Okay," Yair said, grabbing his arm. "Come on."

106

FOR ONE TERRIFYING MOMENT, FRANCOIS THOUGHT YAIR was going to drag him back into the house. A moment later, he discovered that he was being pulled toward the front door, now standing open, and from there to the courtyard. He was pulled to a halt by Yair's strong arm, which was tight around his shoulders and arm, while his other hand held the gun to Francois's temple.

"I'm prepared to conduct a negotiation with you," he told the people on the other side of the gate. "Whoever wants to talk to me can come in."

"No one is going in," Jarnail said quietly to the others. "I don't allow it."

He was the only one among them who had undergone any sort of training in how to respond in such situations, and they accepted his authority.

"Yair," he said, raising his voice, "how are you?"

"I'm fine, thank you."

In the silence that filled the street, his voice rang clearly.

"How is Dr. Dreyfus?" Jarnail asked. "And Mr. and Mrs. Phillips?"

"They're all right. And they will continue to be all right. If you don't do something stupid."

"We do not intend to do something stupid, Yair," Jarnail said. "We are here with good intentions."

Yair grinned, eyes scurrying hither and thither, scanning the group beyond the gates.

"Who are you?" he asked.

"Do you mean, which unit do we belong to?" Jarnail asked pleasantly.

"You..." Yair shook his head. "Are they real?" he asked Francois. "Or is this a hallucination, too?"

"They're real," Francois said.

"But..." Yair was stressed. "They don't look right."

They didn't look right. Jarnail, standing between a tall man with bristly hair in a police uniform, and a man wearing the garb of an ultra-Orthodox *chareidi* Jew with a rabbinical appearance, complimented Yair on his discernment. At this point, he wasn't sure what to do.

"What do you want, Yair?" he asked, deciding to avoid giving a direct answer to the man's question.

"I?" Yair took a deep breath. He wanted Israel to attack Iran. Now. No—preferably, yesterday. But he could not say that, despite the fact that he saw no media cameras in the vicinity.

"It's a long story," Francois said in his place. "And it's a bit problematic to shout it out like this, in the middle of the street."

"We can speak on the phone," Jarnail suggested. "Or communicate in writing. Whichever you prefer, Yair."

"He wants immunity," Francois said. "And the chance to leave Israel safely." Yair, at his side, nodded his head.

"Immunity for what?" The wheels in Jarnail's mind began to turn.

"It's a long story," Yair repeated hoarsely.

"It's a long story," Francois said, louder.

"Let him release Francois," Shaul said to Jarnail. "And Francois will give us the details."

Jarnail, to whom this idea hadn't occurred, nodded.

"If it's not feasible to relate the story out loud," he suggested, "and Francois already knows it—let him come to us and tell us everything."

Yair laughed. "And then you'll shoot me, right?"

"No," said Jarnail. "Word of honor."

"Is there any of that commodity left in the world—honor?" Yair asked. "Don't try to make a fool of me."

"Let him go back inside and release Francois after he's secured himself indoors," Shaul suggested. "Also, I don't know if it's a good idea to remind him that there are two other hostages..."

The notion appealed to Jarnail. Less than three minutes later, they saw Francois stumble through the garden toward the street on shaky legs.

"Francois, are you wearing explosives?" Jarnail called.

"No, no." Francois's legs could no longer carry him, and he sat down on the pavement. "It's all good."

"Are Gadi and his wife all right?" Shaul asked, approaching him ahead of the others.

"They were all right the last time I saw them. And Yair doesn't want to hurt anyone. He's...a good person."

"The Stockholm syndrome doesn't usually develop so quickly," Jarnail said with a warm smile. "Do you want to get into one of the cars? Get out of the heat? Have something to drink? To eat?"

"I need...a sweater." Francois was shivering. "It got cold all of a sudden."

"Geva!" The man with the bristly haircut roared. "Take this man to your car and turn on the heat."

Francois gazed at them from the sidewalk, helpless.

"Give me your hand," Shaul offered. "Come, I'll help you get up."

"We need to talk," the psychologist said, rising slowly and with an effort. "Yair—"

"We'll talk about everything," Shaul promised. "Jarnail, you're coming with us, right?"

"So what's the long story?" Blau asked, as the four of them walked toward Geva's car. "Let's save you trouble and tell you that we know that Yair works for Israeli intelligence and that he suffers from hallucinations."

"He has an imaginary friend," Francois said, still trembling, "He calls him Mirage, and he, so to speak, transmits to him secret information from Iran. And because he's a handler of agents with a great deal of experience, the Mossad believes whatever he hands over to them in Mirage's name."

"Oh, no," Jarnail said. "So the present security situation..."

"Isn't everyone saying that it's an illusion?" Francois chuckled. "Well, it is. That's the precise word, right out of the dictionary."

"How did he do that?" Blau rubbed his forehead. "Didn't they ask for documentation? It's bizarre!"

"He is very senior and very respected," Francois said. "He's also smart. I tend to believe that he actually met with somebody regularly, didn't record their conversations, and afterward convinced his superiors that this was his man in Iran." He shivered.

"We got to that in our last session. He blurted a few things, and I suddenly understood everything. I told him that he couldn't drag an entire country, and maybe the entire world, into a war. That he had to fix this. Go to his superiors. He became...very insistent."

"You scared him," Shaul said gently.

"I pushed him into a corner. I should have been wiser. Handled it myself. But I thought..." He shrugged. "I don't know what I thought. But I'm a simple citizen. Would anyone have believed me if I had called the police with a story like that?"

"Maybe they would have," Blau said. "Those fools believe everything."

"Yosef doesn't like the police," Shaul said with a smile. "He's allowed, no?"

"There were also the ethics involved and his emotional state." Francois's lips quivered. "Maybe I was arrogant? I thought I was handling it the right way."

"Let's move on," Jarnail said. "Not because this is not interesting, Francois. It's just that we have two other people inside..."

"I almost managed to get them out. But they must be hiding." Francois swallowed and couldn't help but shiver.

"What does Yair want?" Jarnail asked quietly. "What is his goal?"

"He needs an escape hatch," said Francois, trying to regain his equilibrium. "He knows that he did something wrong. But he doesn't want to admit his mistake. He needed to find a way to get away from the inferno without burning himself." He gave a twisted smile. "Which won't happen now that you people are here and know everything."

"We're not the police," said Jarnail. "I'm just a friend of Shaul's. And those"—he gestured with his head at the uniformed men—"are just costumes." He gave a short laugh. "I'm not even an Israeli. I'm a citizen of India. I'm here for Shaul and his friend."

They fell silent.

"First, I'll call my wife and tell her to cancel the police." Shaul pulled his phone out of his pocket. "It seems we don't really need the police here."

"What do we need?" Blau asked.

"A way to show that Mirage is illegitimate and his reports untrustworthy, without exposing Yair to blame."

Shaul returned to them, his expression tense. "I asked my wife to say that we found our missing people. I hope we won't regret this decision."

"We've been talking about what to do to calm Yair down, to make him stop being afraid that a war is about to break out because of him without exposing him as illegitimate or revealing his secret."

Shaul considered this. "Tell me," he said to Jarnail after a moment. "You've been in touch with many senior Israeli officials... Do you happen to have the personal phone number of, say, Ehud Barak? Or, better yet, someone who's still relevant?"

"I have all sorts of numbers," Jarnail said. "The problem is that when you lose your position in disgrace, people suddenly don't want to help you."

"On the contrary. You're not going to ask for help. You're going to give it. You're going to call him, or whoever it is, to do him a favor," Shaul said. "To whisper in his ear that you've heard they've also received intelligence from a person calling himself 'Mirage,' and you wanted, as a friend, and as a friend of the State of Israel, to let them know that your intelligence service has discovered that he's a liar."

Jarnail breathed deeply. "I'll be walking into deep mud," he said. "I could become completely besmirched."

"On the contrary," Shaul said again, and smiled. "Tell him that you want a favor in exchange. A call to his friends in India, the restoration of your good name, and even your return to diplomatic service."

Jarnail had to breathe deeply again—this time in astonishment. "You think it will work?" he asked. There was hope in his voice.

"I'll pray that it does," Shaul said, smiling. "Let's try it now."

# 107

J ARNAIL WEIGHED SHAUL'S SUGGESTION SERIOUSLY, AND then said, "I have an even better idea, Shaul. Do you have a way of reaching one of the *chareidi* Knesset members? I think it will be more believable if you're the one who heard the information from me first and are pressuring me to pass it on to the official authorities."

"I don't know anyone," Shaul said. "But Rabbi Schwab certainly does."

"And he'll give you the number?"

Shaul smiled. "I think so. Let's give it a try."

Their hearts beat more quickly than usual as Shaul waited for the connection to go through. When it did, they listened to Shaul calmly inquire after his former boss's health and well-being, answer a few questions, and then say, "I called because I urgently need the number of one of our Knesset members. Preferably one on the Foreign Affairs and Defense Committee."

Silence ensued for a moment. "No, I don't have any names. But I've come across some information that must be passed on to the higher-ups." Another silence. "Yes, I understand that you can't give me direct numbers. But this is an emergency situation. We're talking about sensitive security intelligence."

He was quiet, listening. "Fine," he said. "I'll wait. Tell him that it's urgent. Very, very urgent."

He ended the call and smiled apologetically at the others. "He didn't want to give me any numbers, but he'll try to pave the way for me. Maybe that's for the best. They'll pick up a call from him faster than from some anonymous caller."

"And until then?"

Shaul raised his brows. "Let's say that—" The phone in his hand vibrated. "An unknown number," he said, staring at the screen. "Apparently, there's no 'until then.'"

He took a step back, and another step to the side. Looking back at the men who were intently watching him, he said, "Hello, Rav Gewirtz. Thank you very much for getting back to me. Do you mind if we switch to Yiddish?"

Shaul's Yiddish was rusty from years of disuse. Still, by combining it with words in biblical Hebrew and some modern-day Ivrit, he managed to transmit his main point: He worked for an international firm that supplied irrigation systems to third-world countries, a firm that had recently won a large bid with the UN. He had a partner from India, the son of a government minister and son-in-law to one of the wealthiest men in that large country, who had worked in the Indian embassy in Israel for seven years. The man was now in Israel on business and wished to pass on important information to the heads of Israeli security. Information that could change the picture regarding the article recently printed in the *Daily Telegraph* about biological weapons allegedly in the hands of Iran.

Rabbi Gewirtz listened, asked a few questions that revealed the quickness of his mind, and then requested contact information for Shaul's partner. He thanked Shaul for calling and disconnected. Jarnail's phone rang a minute later, evidence that the MK was taking the matter seriously.

Jarnail was happy to take the call. It turned out that at the start of his diplomatic career, he had met Gewirtz at an event in the Israeli president's house. Jarnail had asked him several questions about inner ultra-Orthodox politics and amused Gewirtz with the wealth of his knowledge, after which the two men had exchanged a number of updates about mutual acquaintances. Jarnail dived straight into the matter at hand.

"I have some information for you," he said. "There is a person who calls himself Mirage who sells confidential information from Iran to all sorts of international agencies. It would be worthwhile to put out feelers about him in your Iranian division, because we've discovered recently that he is not trustworthy."

He fell silent, listening intently. "I prefer not to say who 'we' are," he said with a small smile. "But if I'm bringing you intelligence information, then…" Another silence. "I will repeat what I know. We have an eighty-nine percent probability that the person calling himself Mirage supplied the information to the *Daily Telegraph* reporter and that he was the reporter's only source. Apart from that, we also know—with nearly complete certainty—that this Mr. Mirage has also given your government false information."

A deep breath as he listened.

"I am a friend of Israel," Jarnail responded. "That is the reason. But if you benefit from this information, I will be glad to meet with you and request a small favor." Another silence. "I hope to be available at this number for the next few hours. Thank you."

He ended the call and nodded at Shaul, who was walking behind him, far from the parked car. "He'll get back to me," Jarnail said wearily. "I believe that I will succeed in undermining Mirage's legitimacy and good reputation. The next step is to convince Yair to leave the country. I'm sure a man like him has a slew of passports and escape plans."

"Why should he believe us?"

"First of all, because we'll get rid of the police." Jarnail nodded his head at the scattered vehicles. "And second, in case you hadn't noticed, Francois has an influence on him."

"Do you want Francois to go back inside and talk to him?"

"I don't know if we have any other choice."

"That's asking a great deal."

"I know." A sigh. "Let's take the first step and get these men out of here."

"No," Shaul said. "Let's do something else. Let's have Yair understand that everything that's happened here stays with us and that the police were never here at all."

"Good idea." Jarnail looked around. "But let's hurry. I'm surprised that no neighbors have come out of their houses yet to find out what all the commotion is about."

"Considering the socioeconomic status of the neighbors, they're probably all abroad," Shaul said with a trace of humor. "On vacation or business."

Jarnail responded with a tight smile of his own. "Meanwhile,

I've managed not to lie," he said. "I hope—" The phone in his hand vibrated. "Go deal with your idea," he said hastily. "I'll try to move things forward at this end."

---

He knew. His fine-tuned intuition hadn't failed him. The chief of staff alternately rubbed his hands together and shook his head.

"I served in this country before your tenure as chief of staff," the man from India told him over the phone. "I don't think we ever met." Then he named a number of important people, and the Israeli military commander-in-chief hastened to jot them down. "I'm sure you'll be able to receive positive information from them about me. A free India is the fruit of your war with the British, and I personally admire the *Tanach* and the Jewish people and am a great friend of your nation. Therefore, as I told MK Gewirtz, I have the privilege and also the obligation to share with you some information that could be very significant for Israel and prevent you from launching an unnecessary war." His voice carried a smile. "Or, if you don't view it as unnecessary, at least mitigate the prewar storm."

"Gewirtz told me something like that," the chief of staff said. "He said that one of our informants—"

"An informant named Mirage. I don't know if that's his real name or his handle. But we're talking about a veteran and successful informant who has passed on a great deal of information to your people over the years, much of which has been fabricated or distorted."

"Do you have proof?"

Jarnail sighed. "I can try to get it. But…it's complicated. For now, I think it's enough for you to know that we have near-total certainty that he is the only person behind the information in the *Daily Telegraph*, and he is also the one who provided your intelligence service with the same information. Try to put pressure on the *Daily Telegraph* and look through your files to review everything he's told you lately with a suspicious eye. I will try to get more information for you, but I can't promise anything."

"I appreciate this very much," the chief of staff said. "Is there a way to repay you?"

"I am doing this out of friendship," Jarnail said with a glance at Shaul. "I do not expect anything in return. But if my information ends up being of benefit to you, I will be glad to receive a small favor."

"I'll hold on to your phone number," the chief of staff promised. "After we get past this wave and I have a bit of time, I'll be very happy to meet with you and hear how we can return the favor."

"That would be wonderful." Jarnail smiled. "Good luck to us all."

# 108

"WE NEED YOUR HELP, DR. DREYFUS."
Shaul leaned toward the gray-haired man in the car and spoke in a low voice. "Do you have the strength to help us?"

"We do what we have to do," Francois said, his hands beginning to tremble again. "What do you need?"

"For you to talk to Yair on the megaphone. Tell him that we're getting close to coming up with a solution to the problem. But we need to speak with him directly and not through a megaphone."

"There's no cellphone reception in there. Not anywhere in the apartment. I tried everything."

"Let him go up to the roof."

Francois weighed this notion. "I can tell him that," he said hesitantly. "But he may be afraid that you have a sniper waiting across the street…"

"He trusts you," Blau reminded gently. "You did it once. You can do it again."

Francois inhaled deeply, his breath shaky. "I can try."

"*B'ezras Hashem*, you will also succeed."

One of the counterfeit police officers brought over a package of moist wipes, and Francois passed it over his face and neck. "Pray," he said.

His voice was a little hoarse as he accepted the megaphone. Shaul, standing nearby, saw the unnatural tremor in the muscles of his throat.

"Yair? This is Francois. There have been some positive developments, but we can't discuss it like this, shouting and disturbing half the street. Is there a way for you to call us? You have my cellphone number, correct?"

He took another deep breath. "Yair, if you can hear me but have no way to call me, open and shut the window shutter in the living room."

Not a shutter moved. Not a curtain stirred. The handsome villa, with its antiquated look, remained as calm and silent as if he hadn't spoken.

"Yair, can you hear me?" Francois repeated. "If you have no way to talk to me—"

A melody cut him off. His cellphone came to life.

"I do, but it takes time," Yair said. "Not everything in life is easy. That's what you always say, right?"

"Yes, yes. Exactly so," Francois agreed as his eyes searched for something to sit on. Not finding it, and with his legs incapable of holding him up, he sank onto the pavement. "Listen, Yair," he said. "First of all, I want to tell you something that will surprise you. The people out here are not the police. I can even send you proof…"

"Proof is good," Yair said slowly. "Why didn't they call the police?"

"Because Francois is an adult, and they saw no reason to worry about him before forty-eight hours had passed from the time he disappeared," Shaul whispered. "Tell him that he's on speakerphone."

"I'm putting you on speakerphone, Yair. There are people here who know more than I do and can give you more satisfactory answers," Francois said. "Is that all right with you?"

"No, it's not. Earlier, you said that it's impossible to speak about this out loud. Didn't you?"

Francois didn't want to argue or explain the difference. Better to give Yair a sense of victory right now.

"Then"—he motioned for Shaul to sit beside him on the pavement—"I'm letting this nice man named Shaul talk to you."

"Shalom, Yair," Shaul said.

"Shalom, Shaul," Yair said. The fact that his voice sounded completely normal slightly surprised Shaul.

"Listen, Yair," he said. "The police weren't interested in Francois's disappearance because forty-eight hours hadn't yet passed. So we worked alone. We brought a few…" He hesitated, choosing his words. "Fellows who usually get along without the police, and they wore fake uniforms in order to make a good impression. But the minute I give the word, they'll leave the area. They're interested only in the money we're giving them, not in you."

"Not true!" the bristly fellow hissed to Jarnail. "We came to help! Why is he saying that?"

"To calm Yair down so that he won't panic," Jarnail replied in a whisper.

The other man nodded his understanding with a faint, "Aha."

"If you have binoculars, maybe you can see through the window," Shaul said. "Their uniforms are counterfeit. Look at the emblem on the uniforms."

"Later," Yair said shortly. "What is your proposal?"

"You want to protect the State of Israel, right?" Shaul asked.

"Yes." Yair's voice was hesitant.

Shaul picked up on the hesitation. "We want to help you do that. We're trying to get a message to the prime minister, through the Indian embassy in Israel, that Mirage, despite his previous good work, made a mistake this time. And that maybe we don't have to go out to war right now."

Yair's sigh of relief came through. "The Indian embassy?" he asked suspiciously. "What's their connection with this?"

"We have friends there who can help," Shaul said. "Who are pre-pared to help. That's our solution to the first problem. The second problem is that you don't want to be around people who will start asking questions about Mirage. Right?"

"You want to keep him to yourself," Francois whispered.

Shaul repeated the words out loud.

"What's your solution?" Yair's voice was sharp.

"We'll book a flight for you and drive you to the airport," Shaul said. "That's the solution. What do you think?"

"Who says the police won't arrest me as soon as I walk into the terminal?"

There were several answers to this question. Shaul hesitated.

"You're not saying anything," Yair snapped.

"Look," Shaul said slowly. "I could tell you that I promised I won't give you away to the police, and I'm an honest man."

Yair laughed. "A liar could say the exact same thing."

Shaul laughed along with him. "But I really *am* an honest man," he said. "In any case, you're smarter than I am. What do you suggest?"

A breath. Then another. "You'll arrange the matter of Mirage through the Indian embassy?"

"Yes."

"And you'll make sure they explain to the prime minister that Iran should be attacked, but it doesn't have to be right now?"

"Whatever you say."

"Okay."

Silence.

"So what's the next step, Yair?"

"I..." A long silence. "I'll tell the couple here to go into one of the rooms, and I'll booby-trap the exit. Only after I reach my destination abroad will I give you the code to neutralize the explosives."

"Sounds reasonable," Shaul said, trying to keep his tone steady though his heart was pounding. "But what happens if you forget to give us the code? And you just disappear?"

"I won't forget."

"That's what you're saying now," Shaul said softly.

The sound of Yair's breathing was so loud that Shaul was afraid the man was on the point of a nervous breakdown that could endanger those still inside the house. Francois's whispered "Don't pressure him" alarmed Shaul.

"Okay, Yair," he said quickly. "Okay. Whatever you say. So...get ready, and we'll take you to the airport."

"You bought the ticket already?" Yair's voice was muffled.

"We'll buy it now," Shaul promised. "I'm passing you to a friend of mine who will arrange everything with you. Okay?"

"First I want to talk to Dr. Dreyfus."

"Fine. No problem at all. Here he is," Shaul said. But the psychologist shook his head, and Blau whispered, "Tell him that there's a possibility that he had a heart attack and we're taking him to the ER now."

"Really?" Yair sounded lost when he heard the news. "I...I hope nothing happens to him. I...I don't want anything to happen to him. It's just that..."

"He'll be all right," Shaul hastened to say. "And he'll be happy to hear that you succeeded in achieving your goals. I'm transferring you to someone who will help you choose a flight destination. Whichever one you want."

"Okay." Yair sounded weak. "Tell Francois that I wish him a speedy recovery."

"I'll tell him."

"Thank you."

The small phone changed hands again. As Blau helped Francois into his car, Jarnail conducted a long, technical discussion about flight times, which concluded with Yair choosing a flight to Crete that was due to lift off shortly, and from there two additional flights to Germany and England so that he could more easily shake off anyone who might be following him.

'Of course, you can decide not to use either one of them," Jarnail added with a trace of mischievousness, "and choose a third destination. We only ask that you send us the code to neutralize the bomb immediately after you land in Crete…"

"And if I don't?" Yair was tense.

Jarnail searched for an answer. "Maybe we won't take the trouble of sorting out the mess that Mirage created. And whatever happens afterward will be on your conscience."

"What if I don't have one?"

"You have a conscience. That's what Francois said. He admires you, you know."

"Really?"

"Yes. Absolutely. Despite everything. He thinks that you're an honest person, someone who can be trusted. A person with values."

Jarnail heaped on the compliments, hoping that the power of the praise would increase Yair's sense of indebtedness. "Come, finish making your arrangements and come out to us. We're waiting for you with a car and keys."

When the call was cut off without warning, he bit his lip. Depending on the conscience of a person who had already kidnaped three people and threatened to kill them didn't sound to him like a very smart idea.

But they were doing the best they could. They would have to be satisfied with that for the present, and hope they wouldn't have cause to later regret the choices they were making now.

## 109

WHEN THE CALL WITH YAIR ENDED AND JARNAIL DROPPED the hand that was holding his cellphone and looked around, he suddenly realized that he had a problem.

"You said a car and keys," said the guy with the hair brushed straight up. "Which car and keys were you talking about exactly?"

Jarnail passed a hand over his forehead. "Shaul came here in a car…"

"But the other guy, the doctor, is taking it to the hospital now," the other one said. "You don't expect me to give my car to some insane kidnaper, do you?"

Jarnail's shoulders slumped. "That would be a really big favor."

"Call the doctor, tell him to come back, and I'll tell one of the boys to take the Frenchman to the hospital," the bristly-haired man said generously.

But Blau wouldn't hear of it. "I don't want to waste time. He needs to reach the ER quickly."

"Maybe you should call him a taxi?" one of the young men asked. "Or…if you want, I have no problem with breaking into one of these cars around here…" At a look from his boss, he broke off.

"I don't want to call a taxi," Jarnail said. "I don't want to give him an opportunity to snatch someone else in an effort to protect himself. I want to calm him down and get him out of here. And to get the code to neutralize the bomb on the inner door." With a sigh, he added, "You know what? I'm not a Jew. But I want to become one. Partly because I've seen the way Jews are prepared to move out of their comfort zone to help others. You're all brothers, and you'll do anything to save someone else's life."

"That doesn't include giving up your car," Geva said. Then he sighed. "Look, pal. It's not that we're bad or anything. But our cars don't have locators. If he parks it in some hole, it will stay there until Mashiach comes."

"My brother-in-law, Gadi, has one," Shaul said, gesturing at Gadi's car, parked not far away. "Maybe he'll give this gentleman his keys?"

This was a very good idea. Jarnail looked over at Shaul gratefully before he picked up the megaphone. "Yair," he said, "if you want to feel secure, take Gadi's car keys. His car is here, and we can use it."

Silence.

"Looks like he's very busy inside," said the bristly-haired fellow. "I just don't understand one thing. Where does he have the money to buy a villa like this? This is a super-expensive neighborhood."

"I don't think it's his," Jarnail said.

He decided not to share all his thoughts with this man. Even what he already knew was too much.

———————

The megaphone came to life again from time to time. In the darkness of the storage loft, Gadi couldn't make out the words. He could only sense the vibration that the sounds made in the walls.

"Gadi," Shuli whispered. "Give me your phone for a minute, okay?"

"Don't you have yours?" He didn't want to release his grip on the metal stick for an instant, even though his holding on to it was foolish.

"My pocketbook is still downstairs," Shuli said. "Let me have your phone, okay?"

"What for?" he asked as the light from the device filled the cramped, dark space.

"My grandmother also lived in an old house," Shuli panted, "and there was an exit from the storage loft onto the roof..." She ran the phone's flashlight over the ceiling and sighed. "Apparently, this one doesn't have it."

"Maybe the phone will work here?" Gadi said. "Try, okay?"

"No. There's no reception."

He swallowed. "You were right," he said. "I shouldn't have felt so insulted by that *rosh kollel*."

"Rabbi Schwartz?"

"Yes."

"That was a long time ago." She was silent. "A lot has happened since then."

"But that was the beginning."

She sighed. "Yes. But we can't blame him for everything. Not everyone who's kicked out of *kollel* opens a company that's trading on the Stock Exchange today, right?"

"True," Gadi said. "Though I did have tremendous *siyatta d'Shmaya*."

"We should have given more *tzedakah*," she said.

"We tried."

"Shaul took too much on himself." Her voice was low. "He's still repaying debts because of your sisters."

Gadi was quiet.

"Gadi?"

"What?"

"Will you take their debts from him when we get out of here?"

"He has eleven children," Gadi said. "He's not working only because of those debts, as you know."

"Ricki's making a nice income." Shuli's cramped limbs were aching. "She's also willing to make do with little. But Shaul could have been a *talmid chacham*."

"And I couldn't?" He was insulted.

"You could have, too."

She was silent.

"Gadi?"

"What?"

"You remember, in the last will we drew up, we promised my brother payment if he would undertake to care for the children?" Her voice shook. "Why should you mind giving that money to Shaul while we're still alive?"

He swallowed. And swallowed again.

"You should have done it anyway," she pressed.

"You didn't want to either," he remembered suddenly.

"I know."

"So all of a sudden you want to because you're afraid—"

"Yes." Shuli's lips were dry, and her head was spinning. "Because

I'm very afraid. And because, in any case, there's a chance that our money will fall into other hands."

"You'll have four thousand shekels less each month," he warned. "That's a lot of money."

"I know. There are families who live on that amount," she whispered. "Promise me, Gadi. Okay?"

Using the couple's car was a good idea. A much better idea than his own car, which had probably been impounded by now. Yair scanned the living room with his eyes, searching for the car keys. They weren't there. It was probably with those two, who were hiding in the same storage loft where he'd wanted to hide.

He could go up there and take the keys from them.

Yes.

A good idea.

"Gadi?"

"What?"

"Promise."

"Forever? Every month? That's crazy."

"Until he's free of his debts."

Silence.

"Gadi." She was becoming hysterical. "We're going to die!"

"Don't scream!" he begged.

"I'm not screaming." She tried to control her voice. "Really, Gadi. You're not going back to *kollel*, right? What's the point of regretting something so far in the past? But helping your sisters today is something you *can* do."

Gadi was silent as he mulled it over. "All right," he relented. "I'll handle it for Shaul. Okay."

*Here they are,* said Mirage. *The keys. There, on the couch. Don't you see them between the cushions?*

Yair turned around.

*No, the small couch!*

Ah. There they were. Yes.

They were peeking out at him from between the sofa cushions. Yair picked them up.

He hadn't seen the keys earlier. He was certain of it. So that meant that Mirage *did* exist! Why had Francois said that he didn't?

He looked down into the dark eyes of the short man standing before him.

"Let's go," Mirage said. "Everything has become very complicated. The best thing is for us to get out of here."

"You also don't want there to be a war?" he asked weakly. "You urged me—"

"I did not. What are you talking about?" Mirage defended himself. "You were offended because they didn't listen to you this time. So I told you that they're fools who listen to all sorts of 'foreign sources' and not to people who are living and breathing on the ground itself. The rest was your idea. I just made the call for you, that's all."

They shouldn't fight. Mirage was the only one he had left.

Mirage and his money.

He must stay on good terms with him. Despite everything. But maybe...maybe the time had come to recognize that his friend also had his weak spots.

"Ready to go?" Mirage asked. "You have the other set of papers, right?"

Yes. He had two sets. Two passports, with two names. That morning, he had taken them out of his home safe. He knew there'd be trouble. He'd sensed it.

"Then let's get out of here."

# 110

"I'M READY TO GO." FROM THE CELLPHONE'S SPEAKERPHONE rose Yair's dry voice. "Warn the men you brought with you to hold their fire. I'm not giving you the neutralization code for the bomb until I arrive in Crete. And you won't be able to pry the information out of me by force. My trainers at the Mossad taught me well."

"We do not intend to do anything in opposition to our agreement," Jarnail was quick to respond, his voice as calm as a pond in summer. "There's no reason to worry."

There were plenty of reasons, Yair thought. But remaining here in the house and waiting for the Yamam, the civilian counter-terrorism unit, to come and kill him was an even worse idea. Especially since the Mossad, which owned this lovely villa and used it as a safe house for dignitaries who came to Israel on an unofficial visit, had probably already given them the plans for the house, including every entry and exit point.

A sudden chuckle rose up inside him.

He was losing it. Completely.

He didn't need them at all. He could leave through the back door and manage on his own. There were taxis in the world. Even buses. And they'd said that they hadn't reported him to the police. It didn't look as though they had enough men to surround the house.

Why bother with them at all?

What was he thinking?

"They wanted to help you," Mirage reminded him. "To give the right people the right information about the false information."

Right.

But they would apparently do that even if he suddenly vanished from sight.

He didn't need them.

The only thing he needed was to be calm and to sleep well. Something that hadn't happened since the story had broken in the *Daily Telegraph* and the whole situation blew up. Lack of sleep could drive even a sane person crazy.

---

"He's not coming out," Shaul said. "How long will we have to wait for him?"

"As long as he wants." Jarnail's lips were white. "I'm concerned about the serious way he spoke about the trap your brother-in-law and his wife are in."

"We should be glad that he's serious."

"If he calls to tell us how to neutralize the bomb—then, yes."

"Hashem will help."

"Yes."

Shaul's lips were whispering.

"You know so many chapters of *Tehillim* by heart?" one of the lads asked after about twenty minutes.

Shaul motioned for him to wait, finished his *kapitel*, and said, "I keep repeating the same ones over and over. If you guys want to help, I can say it out loud."

The bristly-haired fellow was approaching them. "There's an annoying neighbor who keeps insisting on knowing why we're here," he reported to Jarnail. "What do I do with him?"

"Tell him that we're about to leave. That everything is all right. There was a threat directed at his neighbor, but everything is under control and we're about to…" He searched for the right phrase. "Close up shop."

"Okay."

Time passed. Slowly.

"They stopped talking on the megaphone," Gadi said.

"Sometimes there are breaks in negotiations," she said. "Maybe they need time to give him what he's demanding."

"I can't feel my feet anymore," Gadi added a moment later.

She breathed deeply. "You don't really mean that, Gadi." She had guessed what was coming next.

"You stay here."

"You can't seriously mean that. You see that there's a negotiation going on. Why do you have to put yourself back in his hands?"

"Shuli, he was here. He knows that we're here. If he isn't coming, it's either because he doesn't want to or because he can't."

"Why wouldn't he be able to?"

The air in the storage loft was close and stifling. The question that had been troubling her for the past half-hour was how people had survived six years in all sorts of tiny bunkers without a steady supply of water and food.

"Maybe they shot him through the window?"

"If they shot him, they'd already have broken into the house."

"Maybe they don't know if they got him."

"We would have heard the shooting."

"This loft is pretty soundproof."

"Gadi, I don't want you to go. Isn't it foolish to expose yourself to that madman when the happy ending is so near? A minute before the last page?"

"You know the difference between foolishness and genius? Victory."

He opened the door and slowly straightened his legs. The pain of renewed circulation made him close his eyes. It was a few long minutes before he was ready to move on to the next stage.

———

"Rav Gewirtz called me. They want more details. They want to meet with me."

"You can go. It's important."

"I told them that I'm busy and that I don't have many more details to give them. Listen, I can't do anything until Yair comes out."

And he wasn't coming out.

"I'm calling Blau," said Shaul.

"What for?"

"To ask Francois what to do now."

But no one answered Blau's phone.

---

Four thousand shekels a month was a great deal. Even for him. Gadi, though generally not of a spiritual bent, sensed his good decision accompanying him as he left the hallway in his stockinged-feet, and looked right and left.

Nothing. The hallway was empty.

Downstairs? In the living room? The kitchen?

Their children sometimes sneaked into the living room when he wanted quiet, some time to himself, and thought that he didn't see them when they hid behind the wall and peeked at him before going quietly into the living room and taking the book or notebook they'd left behind.

He wasn't that foolhardy.

But Yair had never forbidden him to walk around the house. Besides, his intuition, growing stronger by the second, told him that the man was simply not here.

And the keys were stuck in the front door. As though waiting for him.

"Gadi?" Shuli was apparently quieter than he was. Her sudden whisper made him jump. "Could it be a trap?"

Gadi hesitated.

"It looks to me like a miracle," he whispered back. "But let me go out first.."

She put a hand over her mouth and glanced rapidly back. But no frightening shadow shot out of the kitchen.

"Good luck," she whispered.

Slowly, he walked to the door, turned the key in the lock, and opened the door into a darkened, empty foyer.

He stepped in. Slowly.

Pressed the alarm button. Searched for the right key.

Put the key in the keyhole. A delicate turn, and then a click that could mean only one thing. The door was unlocked.

He opened it and moved silently into a lush courtyard. Above, the sky was blue. He saw Shaul, waiting beyond the fence, a *Sefer Tehillim* in his hand.

"Should I come out?" Shuli whispered.

A lump in his throat prevented Gadi from answering immediately.

"Wait," he whispered. "I'm crossing the courtyard. You run after me if I make it in one piece."

"Good luck," she whispered from behind. But he was already running.

Now it was her turn.

She stood frozen. Why was everything suddenly black?

Slowly she grew limp and let her body fall into the void.

***

"You just fainted, Shuli." It was Gadi, and he was crying. "Everything's okay. An ambulance is on its way. You don't have to get up."

But she wanted to get up. She wanted to run from this place. The words emerged brokenly from her lips.

"There's no need," he insisted. "It looks like he's gone. He doesn't seem to be here."

"You checked?"

"There are guys here, and they're checking. But that's what it looks like. Do you think you can get up?"

If getting up meant getting out of here, she could.

"The children," she said, sitting up abruptly. "Did you call them?"

"Ricki's with them. Shaul updated her."

"Good." Her strength departed again, but she managed to rise to her feet. "Let's go," she said. "I want to get out of here."

"What about the ambulance?"

"Cancel it."

"Mr. Phillips?" A young man emerged from the house. "These are your keys, right?"

His car. A million and a half shekels on the road.

As he plucked the tossed keys from the air, the world suddenly seemed like a very strange place.

"Gadi?" It was Shaul.

"Shuli wants to go home. She wants us to cancel the ambulance."

"If she feels well, we can do that."

"So cancel it, okay?"

"Gladly."

"And Shaul?"

"What?"

"I have to apologize to you for a few things. I've been giving it a lot of thought."

Shaul understood. Gadi saw as much in his changing expression.

"I'll sit down with you later to crunch the numbers, okay? Right now, I'm going to take Shuli home. The children are waiting for us."

Shaul slowly nodded. "Thank you," he said. "But, Gadi?"

Gadi turned.

"Thank you, really. But I'm sure that you didn't think only about that, right? There are other things, smaller things..." His voice dropped, leaving the possibilities open. "Sometimes those things are just as important."

On another day, Gadi would have had a sharp retort. He would have been furious at his brother-in-law's insinuations.

But this was today, and Shaul was the only one in the world who had come here to help him. Today Gadi had quite a different reaction.

The fact that he was tearing up didn't matter at all. Not after Francois had succumbed to a panic attack and Shuli had fainted at the last minute.

"Thank you," he told Shaul, embracing him. "Thank you for everything."

---

### BABY'S LIFE SAVED THROUGH ALERTNESS OF MAZOR HOSPITAL MEDICAL STAFF

Through the cooperation of Mazor Hospital and the Institute for Biological Research in Israel, the life of an eight-month-old baby girl was saved when she was diagnosed with botulism. Botulism is caused by a rare and lethal toxin called *clostridium botulinum*, which acts to shut down the neurotransmitters in the nerves and can lead to paralysis and death.

The eight-month-old girl was hospitalized approximately two weeks ago suffering from unusual symptoms that did not fit with the usual array of childhood illnesses. Thanks to the alert doctors at Mazor, the suspicion arose that the disruption in the baby's nervous system, which could have led to paralysis of the spinal muscles and her breathing, was caused by the botulism toxin, which is very rarely found in Israel.

Botulism attacks the nervous system and the muscles and causes extreme weakness. The illness usually begins with a disruption in eye movement, weak crying, and a cessation of the sucking instinct and nursing. Within a matter of days, it can develop to the point where breathing stops and death ensues.

To diagnose this complex and scientifically challenging illness, the doctors on the hospital's pediatric ward, under the management of Dr. Adam Silver, were assisted by the staff of the Institute for Biological Research in Israel, a government facility that engages in research and development in a variety of areas for the purpose of protecting the citizens of Israel from chemical and biological threats.

Identifying this rare toxin was possible within about three hours because of the unique and cutting-edge techniques that the institute has developed, and close cooperation between the hospital staff, a group of specialists in the disease, and the international biology lab at the institute.

The baby was admitted to the hospital's NICU and treated with special antibodies, developed by the Institute for Biological Research in Israel, which binds to the toxin and prevents it from penetrating the neural network.

This week, the baby was pronounced out of danger. She was transferred to the pediatric ward and is expected to be released in the coming days.

Dr. Zahir Nassar, an expert in pediatric neurology in Mazor Hospital, explains: "The baby's diagnosis was rare. The symptoms with which she arrived at the hospital were consistent with several emergent neurological conditions, each of which has a different treatment regimen. The staff was immediately summoned to do a complete and encompassing study of the case. There is no question that the cooperation of the medical staff and the devoted assistance of the Institute for Biological Research saved the baby's life, both through the expert diagnosis and through the quality of the antibody treatment. Because of this rapid and dedicated treatment, the little girl's neurological function will be fully restored, without any trace of the adventure she has been through."

Dr. Nir Glick, a specialist in pediatric medicine at Mazor, adds: "Botulism is the name of a disease caused by a toxin manufactured by a bacterium belonging to the clostridium family, which has the ability to penetrate the body through different means, among them eating honey, soil, or other food that contains the bacterium. In a mature adult body, the bacterium is unable to thrive and develop. When it reaches a baby's intestines, however, it multiplies and manufactures the toxin, which can be lethal. Early diagnosis is critical for saving the child's life. I am happy that we had the privilege of taking part in the rapid and efficient treatment that has given this child a complete recovery."

# Epilogue

THERE ARE PEOPLE WHO HAVE GOOD TASTE.
Like Ahuvi's babysitter, Varda, who went to great lengths to be of assistance. The set tables looked as if they had emerged from the pages of a catalogue. But perhaps that wasn't so surprising, considering the sum that Shuli had budgeted for this *seudas hodaah*...

It was to be a joint feast of thanksgiving. For Ahuvi's recovery, and for the episode for which Gadi didn't want to make a separate *seudah*, because he "preferred not to have people talk about me. That's legitimate, right?"

"Ricki?"

"Yes?"

Ricki turned around, her face radiant, ready to answer yet another question about the precise placement of the flowers on the bar.

"I..." The babysitter hesitated. "I...I've been waiting to say this to you for a long time..."

"Yes?"

"That maybe...it was because of me. What happened to Ahuvi, I mean. Shortly before Ahuvi was hospitalized, my son had his *upsherin*. It's possible that Ahuvi may have been exposed to honey at my house. I mean, it's logical to think that that's what happened. I'm so sorry."

Silence rang in Ricki's ears. As if all the sounds of existence had ceased.

"But she's healthy," the babysitter's voice said, as if from a distance, beyond the dark mountains. "You...you forgive me, don't you?"

Anger suffused every cell in Ricki's body. Anger at reality. At the suffering they'd undergone because of this woman's neglect. And anger over the fact that for all this time, two full months, the woman had waited to make her apology.

The commotion at the door as Jarnail and his entire family walked in afforded her a wonderful opportunity to avoid the question.

But...no.

"Everything is from *Shamayim*," she conceded. "This is what HaKadosh Baruch Hu wanted to happen."

"And you forgive me?"

"Now that she's healthy? Yes, I can forgive you. I do forgive you."

"Thank you." The woman smiled. "That's how your sister said you'd react. She said that you truly believe in *hashgachah pratis*. It's not just lip service."

"Minna?"

"No, your other sister. Shuli."

"Ah. Thank you. Everything's all right. You don't have to worry."

Here was Minna. And Zahava. Minna had promised not to give away the secret of Ahuvi's antecedents. Though she wasn't at all stupid, Ricki had a feeling that she was going to have to make her repeat the promise out loud this evening. Just when all the most curious women in the neighborhood were standing nearby.

But the first thing she had to do was go over to Ruth, wife of Yirmiyahu (Jarnail), and give her a hug.

"You look so beautiful in that kerchief!" she said in English. "And it's so special that you brought the children. I am so happy!"

"Thank you," Ruth said shyly. "We also brought you a present. Something small..."

"You didn't have to do that."

"We did, we did." She took a small package from her stylish pocketbook. "Keep it safe, because it's valuable. There's also a letter inside that Yirmiyahu received from the Department of Justice today." Her eyes glowed. "The pressure by the Israeli government helped. They deleted his criminal record. Deleted it all. And they even offered him a post in our embassy in the United States. My father was so happy! If only Shaul was prepared to continue working in the firm with Yirmiyahu, everything would be perfect, wouldn't it?"

"Shaul loves Yirmiyahu. It's not because of him."

"It's because he wants to learn Torah," Ruth agreed. "I know. But at least part-time? A few hours?" She looked at Ricki and laughed. "It's okay, I didn't mean to pressure you. On the contrary—both Yirmiyahu and I very much admire his decision."

"It's a lot smaller than your decision."

"I'm not sure," Ruth said thoughtfully. "Sometimes I think that the distance between all steps is equal. Every person has an equally hard time lifting himself from his present step to the next one."

"Ima!" Miri tugged at Ricki's sleeve. "You're missing the pictures!"

"Rini's friend agreed to take family pictures," Ricki apologized, drawn away by the six-year-old to the studio corner that the young photographer had arranged in advance. She studied her family with a loving eye.

"You sit here, Ima." Miri led her mother to a chair in the center, beside Shaul.

"And hold the baby, please," the photographer instructed. "Let her sit up straight, if she can."

This wasn't easy. Ahuvi had once again become active and energetic. She had also recently learned how to give kisses. And she did so with an overwhelming amount of love and sweetness.

"Amazing girl," Ricki told her, "sit nicely for just a minute, okay? Do you want to give the nice lady a smile?"

Good-natured and curious, Ahuvi chose to cooperate. The photographer captured the moment from several angles.

"They came out beautifully," she said, regarding the photos with satisfaction. "But that's no trick. A beautiful family makes beautiful pictures."

"A talented photographer gives credit to her subjects," Ricki told her. "I heard that the pictures of the triplets were also wonderful."

"Ah, yes." The photographer blushed. "I never thanked you for the recommendation. They're so adorable! My friends in the photography course melted when they saw them."

"Dr. Dreyfus is here!" Benny exclaimed, interrupting their conversation. "Abba, come say hello to him."

"Well, everyone's here," Shuli said. "That is, nearly everyone. Let's hope Yair Neiman doesn't suddenly pop in."

Ricki fervently hoped not. It had been hard enough for her to invite the Blau family to this event. But there was no denying that if not for Dr. Blau's help they wouldn't be here today.

And if not for Ahuvi—she smiled at her baby, a lofty soul that had descended to the world in the most unexpected place—if not for Ahuvi, on whose behalf Shaul had been in the right place at the right time, Dr. Blau would most likely have lost his life, as a result of which neither Gadi, Shuli, nor Francois would be here today. And all this without even taking into account the war whose outcome no one could predict, and which, according to MK Gewirtz, had been prevented literally at the last minute.

But it wasn't just Ahuvi. Not if you thought about it down to its depths.

It was also her. And mostly Shaul. Who hadn't been afraid, at the right moment, to make the right decision.

One person. One moment. A whole world.

The equation could sometimes seem inexplicable. But that's the way it worked. Exactly like that.

---

"Abba, can I go with you to give the key back to the *gabbai*?"

"Of course," Shaul said, throwing an alert glance at his eighteen-year-old. "Did something happen, Rini?"

"That nurse, the one who made the hospital call Dr. Blau?"

"Yes?" They walked slowly down the dark, deserted street, moving from one circle of light to the next.

"She insisted on sitting between me and Aunt Minna. And she asked me all kinds of questions."

"Really?"

"She asked if I know the truth about Ahuvi. I couldn't tell her that I didn't." Rini was stressed. "And she asked me why you and Ima did it. I didn't know what to say."

"What *did* you say?" Shaul gripped the keys tightly in his fist.

"I told her that you and Ima thought it was the right thing to do." Rini smiled bashfully. "But she didn't believe me, Abba. She said there were other reasons. That people don't do things like that just because it's the right thing. She said there must be another secret here."

"Yes," Shaul said. "It's very hard to make a decision that will impact the next forty years just because it's the right thing. I agree with her. People who take a drastic step because of something like that end up falling apart later on. A person has a heart, not just a brain. He can't go on for years just because he's doing his duty."

Their destination was waiting on the other side of the street. Shaul stopped walking.

"Then why—" Rini began cautiously.

"It's not all about logic, Rini. It's also about the heart, which senses the existence of a Creator and knows that He is always with us holding our hand. And it's because of the ability to tell the difference between the illusions of this false world and the truth.

"So it's not only about an obligation. It's also about love. When the heart is in it, one can do anything."

# Acknowledgments

EVERY STORY IS A MIRACLE—AND NOT A HIDDEN ONE, EITHER. A story is a harrowing sea voyage between rocks of reality and islands of words, whose ending may be known without knowing how, when, or in what shape the story's heroes will arrive there. And the author, like those heroes, is rocked in the storm, holding tightly to the oars—sorry, the keyboard—and hoping for a miracle.

The story you have just participated in is one of those miracles. Story lines that linked together as if of their own volition. And, above all, details of reality that I didn't consider in advance and turned out, over the course of writing, to be wonderfully suited to the story. A miracle...

I am ever grateful to the Creator of the world for every one of these miracles and for the privilege He has given me to work in a field that I've always dreamed about. Apart from reading books, there is no more wonderful pastime than writing them!

My thanks to the members of my dear family for their support and company all through the journey. For the comments and the remarks. And, most of all, for the caring.

A special thank you to my father, Dr. Oz Martin, who contributed more to this book than to any of my other ones and guided Francois in coping with Yair Nava with wisdom and professionalism.

Thank you to my mother, for creating the concept for this volume—but certainly not only for that.

Thanks to my father-in-law and mother-in-law for their constant devotion and caring.

To the ArtScroll team, for another wonderful English-language book: Libby Lazewnik, whose translation flows so beautifully; Suri Brand, for her excellent editorial skills in a very complex plot; Eli Kroen for the striking cover; Tova Finkelman for the meticulous proof-reading, and Estie Dicker for the layout. Another thank you to my dear friends (including my sisters!) for providing a wonderful support net-work during moments of creative frustration and for joining whole-heartedly in moments of joy. To my children, who participate in the work of writing in so many ways, and above all—to you, the readers, for giving me the privilege of taking you on this journey.

*L'hitra'ot,* until next time…

Maya Kenan
Adar 5782